Problems in Human Assessment

McGraw-Hill Series in Psychology

BEACH, HEBB, MORGAN, AND NISSEN / *The Neuropsychology of Lashley*
VON BÉKÉSY / *Experiments in Hearing*
BERKOWITZ / *Aggression: A Social Psychological Analysis*
BERLYNE / *Conflict, Arousal, and Curiosity*
BLUM / *Psychoanalytic Theories of Personality*
BROWN / *The Motivation of Behavior*
BROWN AND GHISELLI / *Scientific Method in Psychology*
BUCKNER AND MCGRATH / *Vigilance: A Symposium*
COFER / *Verbal Learning and Verbal Behavior*
COFER AND MUSGRAVE / *Verbal Behavior and Learning: Problems and Processes*
CRAFTS, SCHNEIRLA, ROBINSON, AND GILBERT / *Recent Experiments in Psychology*
DAVITZ / *The Communication of Emotional Meaning*
DEESE AND HULSE / *The Psychology of Learning*
DOLLARD AND MILLER / *Personality and Psychotherapy*
ELLIS / *Handbook of Mental Deficiency*
EPSTEIN / *Varieties of Perceptual Learning*
FERGUSON / *Statistical Analysis in Psychology and Education*
FORGUS / *Perception: The Basic Process in Cognitive Development*
GHISELLI / *Theory of Psychological Measurement*

GHISELLI AND BROWN / *Personnel and Industrial Psychology*
GILMER / *Industrial Psychology*
GRAY / *Psychology Applied to Human Affairs*
GUILFORD / *Fundamental Statistics in Psychology and Education*
GUILFORD / *The Nature of Human Intelligence*
GUILFORD / *Personality*
GUILFORD / *Psychometric Methods*
GUION / *Personnel Testing*
HAIRE / *Psychology in Management*
HIRSCH / *Behavior-genetic Analysis*
HIRSH / *The Measurement of Hearing*
HURLOCK / *Adolescent Development*
HURLOCK / *Child Development*
HURLOCK / *Developmental Psychology*
JACKSON AND MESSICK / *Problems in Human Assessment*
KARN AND GILMER / *Readings in Industrial and Business Psychology*
KRECH AND CRUTCHFIELD / *Individual in Society*
LAZARUS / *Adjustment and Personality*
LAZARUS / *Psychological Stress and the Coping Process*
LEWIN / *A Dynamic Theory of Personality*
LEWIN / *Principles of Topological Psychology*
MAHER / *Principles of Psychopathology*
MARX AND HILLIX / *Systems and Theories in Psychology*

Problems in
Human Assessment

EDITED BY ~

Douglas N. Jackson
UNIVERSITY OF WESTERN ONTARIO

Samuel Messick
EDUCATIONAL TESTING SERVICE

McGraw-Hill Book Company
NEW YORK / ST. LOUIS / SAN FRANCISCO / TORONTO / LONDON / SYDNEY

We understand that it is not considered the privilege of editors to dedicate compilations of other people's writings. But we beg an indulgence to honor the memory of four distinguished contributors to the field of psychological assessment who are prominent in this volume:

Irving Lorge
Edward K. Strong
Lewis M. Terman
Louis Leon Thurstone

Preface

The assessment of individual differences is one of the oldest of the traditional areas of psychology. As such, it is widely represented in college curricula by instruction in psychological testing, as well as by a number of related course titles. Since assessment can be viewed both as a scientific discipline and as an area of applied psychology, this instruction has served two interrelated needs. On the one hand, many students wishing to make a career of the scientific study of human characteristics, whether in psychology, education, sociology, or some other behavioral science, have found that a basic understanding of the concepts and methods of assessment is of great value. On the other hand, large numbers of students are preparing themselves for professional careers in which they may be called upon to interpret psychological tests or to make a variety of assessment decisions. Such careers abound in psychology and education, particularly in industrial and clinical psychology, vocational rehabilitation, guidance, personnel administration, vocational and educational counseling, and any number of related disciplines. For many of these students, formal college course work in assessment will offer their first opportunity to become acquainted with the literature of psychological and educational measurement, and this acquaintance should be well grounded if it is to reach the depths required for their future professional commitments.

The research literature in the psychological-assessment area spans many professional journals and books. With increasing college enrollments and the consequent heavy demands placed upon library facilities, there is a practical limit to the opportunities for introducing the student directly to original sources. Since important educational functions may be served by an early introduction of the primary substance of a discipline (beyond that which is usually possible in a textbook), we felt that a focused selection of papers addressed to important contemporary issues would be useful in teaching assessment courses. This was one of the primary reasons that we undertook the editing of this volume.

Equally important, however, was our hope that the volume might serve as a source book for the established scientist and professional. By organizing a volume of broad scope, containing some classics and some representative research reports from the contemporary literature, we have attempted to provide a cross section of modern thought in assessment. We have not tried to shield the reader from controversial issues but rather have sought to air divergent points whenever they seemed to highlight important conceptual or research problems. The reader can thereby derive some benefit from appraising the issues firsthand and forming his own conclusions. It is thus our hope that the availability of a relatively large number of basic theoretical, methodological, and empirical reports on assessment in a single volume will serve as a convenient reference for the professional psychologist, administrator, or educator, as well as for the scholar.

Of course, we necessarily had to exercise considerable editorial discretion in making the selections. Since there were a great many more excellent articles than would fill the available space, the task of selection was particularly onerous. In some areas of intense research interest, this editorial decision was especially difficult to make because of our desire to sample broadly from the assessment literature. Thus, while it is our opinion that the volume contains some outstanding examples of contemporary research and thinking in assessment, it should also be noted that there are many other works that we would have liked to include.

A word about our choice of title. We chose to use the term "assessment" and not "measurement" in the title of this book to highlight a broadened approach to the appraisal of human differences. Assessment as a term denoting appraisal of persons was popularized by Henry Murray and his coworkers in the late thirties, partly with the intention of broadening the scope and meaning of the more limited and simplistic, criterion-oriented methodology that characterized the measurement area of that time. Today, however, the formal basis of measurement is part of a broader philosophy of science in which the nature of substantive constructs is taken into account in evaluating the adequacy of their measurement and the properties and correlates of the measures in turn help to determine the adequacy and generality of the constructs. Measurement theory has thus become intertwined with substantive theory, and measurement methodology has become an integral part and not just an adjunct of psychological science. Since we firmly believe that the same general principles hold both for psychological measurement in its formal sense and for the field and clinical evaluation procedures usually implied by the term "assessment," we decided to highlight the generality of these principles by using a single name for the domain of interest. In the choice between measurement and assessment, we decided to apply the latter, more general term to encompass both. Thus, it is quite appropriate and in our opinion desirable to include under the same covers articles on the fundamental nature of measurement and articles on projective testing, to survey at the same time techniques like factor analysis and the interview, and to report current thinking both on actuarial prediction and on what a clinician can do well. It is our hope, thereby, that measurement specialists may be challenged by the intricacies of assessment problems which are broader than those of univariate selection and that those who assess individual differences without clearly understanding the measurement basis for their inferences may benefit from the explicitness of test theory and other formally based measurement techniques.

A number of individuals have helped us substantially in the task of editing this volume. Katherine D. Baker made an important contribution in preparation of manuscripts and maintenance of records, as did Suzanne Lundquist. Sara B. Matlack and Ann King carefully supervised preparation of the index, and proofreading was skillfully carried out by Marie Davis and Frances Shaffer. During the year when editorial work was initiated, Jackson was a special research fellow of the National Institute of Mental Health at the Institute for the Study of Human Problems, Stanford University, and Messick was a fellow of the Center for Advanced Study in the Behavioral Sciences. We wish to thank the members of the staffs of these two institutions for generously providing facilities and assistance.

The various publishers who agreed to allow their copyrighted works to be reprinted deserve a note of thanks. We have acknowledged particular publishers and copyright sources on the first page of each selection. Our special thanks go to the American Psychological Association and to the publishers of *Educational and Psychological Measurement* and of *Psychological Reports* for permitting us to reprint works which constitute a major portion of this volume.

Douglas N. Jackson
Samuel Messick

Contents

Part 1

THE SCIENCE
OF ASSESSMENT

The process of assessment involves the appraisal of the level or magnitude of some attribute. Sometimes only the relative order of objects with respect to the attribute is appraised; sometimes the intervals or differences between objects are ordered or even equated; sometimes objects are assessed relative to a zero point, so that the ratio of one value to another becomes meaningful. To denote the order or magnitude of an object with respect to an attribute it has proved extremely useful to employ the real numbers as labels, since certain relations are defined among the real numbers that represent properties of order (i.e., $10 > 5 > 4 > 2$), equal intervals (i.e., $10 - 9 = 5 - 4$), and equal ratios (i.e., $^{10}\!/_6 = \frac{1}{2}$). Thus, the process of measurement has come to mean the assigning of numbers to objects (or to some property of the objects) in such a way that certain relations among the numbers correspond to certain relations among the objects.

Through this use of numbers, mathematics has become intimately associated with measurement theory, and mathematical models have come to provide the formal basis for various types and levels of measurement (see Chapter 3). In the first chapter of this part, Harold Gulliksen emphasizes that mathematics also plays a broad role in the general scientific enterprise. He discusses the scientific use of mathematics in the presentation of data, in the translation of psychological hypotheses from verbal to mathematical language, in the derivation of implications that can be tested experimentally, and in the evaluation of the agreement between theory and data. Concepts of assessment are critical in this sequence at several points but particularly at the stage of organizing the data. Furthermore, since the empirical establishment and evaluation of a measurement scale essentially involve these same steps, it would seem that a measurement theory does not differ in kind from a substantive theory but rather in referent. A substantive theory usually involves relations between two or more variables, each of which is assessed in terms of its own measurement theory. Thus, as we shall see in greater detail in Part 2, "The Logic of Assessment," the role of measurement is intricately involved in the process of science, so much so, for example, that some of its major concepts, such as construct validity, were derived from the philosophy of empirical science and not from mathematical models.

In the second chapter of this part, Lee J. Cronbach discusses two separate disciplines within scientific psychology: one experimental, which studies behavior in controlled situations as a function of experimental conditions; and the other correlational, which studies consistent individual differences. In his discussion of these two approaches, of their potential contributions to each other, and of the need for a united discipline, common problems of assessment, whether of the individual or of the present situation or of antecedent influences, become clear. As we shall see, one of the major problems of assessment is that of marshaling evidence, in the form of theoretically relevant empirical relations, to support the inference that an observed response consistency reflects a particular psychological construct. Although somewhat different empirical procedures are employed for this purpose in the two disciplines, this basic assessment problem is essentially the same in each, and in this sense assessment is a generic concern in scientific psychology.

Chapter 1

Mathematical Solutions
for Psychological Problems

HAROLD GULLIKSEN

The mathematical formulation of psychological theories as a guide to research, a major interest of mine for a number of years, traces back among American psychologists to L. L. Thurstone. A pioneer in this field, almost 30 years ago, he set up a psychological theory for learning, expressed it in mathematical form and found that the curves deduced from this theory gave reasonable fits to learning data. Since Thurstone [18], there has been an accelerated growth of interest in the subject.

In some discussions of the usefulness of mathematics in psychological work the question is raised: "Which is better, to develop mathematical formulations, or to

This article is reprinted from the *American Scientist*, 1959, with the permission of the author and the Society of Sigma Xi.

This article was prepared as a technical report in connection with research supported by Office of Naval Research contract Nonr 1858-(15) and National Science Foundation Grant G-642 to Princeton University and by the Educational Testing Service. This material was presented as an invited address at the meetings of the Eastern Psychological Association in Philadelphia on April 12, 1958.

perform experiments?" Some apparently regard these as mutually exclusive choices. Such an attitude seems to miss the central idea, which is that mathematics is one method—and sometimes an extremely effective method—for thinking about psychological research. Cronbach [3] has shown very clearly the close relationship between the experimental and the mathematical branches of psychology.

The psychologist who conducts his experiments in the laboratory as well as the psychologist whose observations are collected in a nonlaboratory situation would both *think* about the data collected and about its relation to some psychological hypotheses. It has been found very effective (though of course not essential) to do some of our scientific thinking in a mathematical idiom.

The function of mathematics is to give a clear statement of hypotheses, so that it is possible to make a more accurate determination of the extent to which psychological theory and experimental data agree. I hope in this presentation to show that the

3

mathematics is intimately concerned both with the formulation of psychological hypotheses and with the analysis of experimental data.

The general nature of the approach to be presented here has been indicated by many different writers on scientific method, see for example Hempel [7], and may be illustrated by Figure 1–1. We begin with verbally stated psychological assumptions. These are translated into mathematical language. The great advantage of such translation is that rigorous pathways of reasoning (known as theorems) have been worked out by mathematicians, so that the scientist by using these pathways may move surely and swiftly from a set of assumptions toward their various implications. A few of the theorems derived should be such that they can be subjected to experimental tests. That is to say, these equations which are testable involve two or more "observation terms"—concepts that can be measured experimentally. The agreement between these theorems and the experimental data is checked by statistics.

Particular attention should be drawn to the fact that statistics are not interpreted here in the usual manner. The usual application of statistics in psychology consists of testing a "null hypothesis" that the investigator hopes is false. For example, he tests the hypothesis that the experimental group is the *same* as the control group even though he has done his best to make them perform differently. Then a "significant" difference is obtained which shows that the data do *not* agree with the hypothesis tested. The experimenter is then pleased because he has shown that a hypothesis he didn't believe, isn't true. Having found a "significant difference," the more important next step should not be neglected. Namely, formulate a hypothesis that the scientist *does* believe and show that the data do *not differ significantly* from it. This is an indication that the newer hypothesis may be regarded as true. A definite scientific advance has been achieved. This viewpoint is illustrated in reference [6].

We are discussing here the *formulation* of the *theory* such that nonsignificant differences are pleasing to the investigator.

Many different investigators now are proceeding with the development of such theories explicitly formulated in mathematical terms. The survey of such work found in Bush, *et al.* [1], illustrates the widespread interest in and use of mathematics to aid in precise statement of psychological theories.

The great variety of developments and the various kinds of mathematics used—algebra, calculus, probability, set theory, matrix theory—may well tend to discourage a person who wishes to attempt mathematical theorizing in any given area. There are so many possibilities. It might be a simplification to indicate two approaches that have been found to be very useful in a number of different psychological problems. I refer to:

1. the use of matrix theory and in particular the concept of rank of a matrix, and
2. the multidimensional scaling methods.

In this discussion I shall consider only errorless data in describing the theory. Let us turn now to our first topic, matrix theory. We will consider the concept of a *matrix* and the concept of the *rank* of a matrix.

In terms of the outline in Figure 1–1, we

Figure 1–1 *Mathematical formulation of psychological theories.*

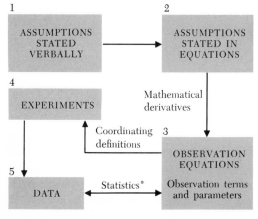

° Nonsignificant differences for a *correct* theory.

shall consider, first, the presentation of data, next, the translation of a psychological hypothesis from verbal to mathematical language, and finally, the problem of agreement of data with hypothesis.

PRESENTING DATA AS A MATRIX

Let us consider some of the very general characteristics of the basic data in the field of psychology. One possible description of psychology is that it deals with responses of organisms to stimuli. The job of the psychologist is to observe and study behavior.

Figure 1–2 illustrates this point, showing the differential response of an organism, O_1, to stimulus 1 and to stimulus 2. At the simplest observational level, the responses may be put into only two classes, designated by 1's and 0's. The response of organism 1 to stimulus 1 shown here may be designated R_{11}. In this case, $R_{11} = 1$. The response of organism 1 to stimulus 2 (R_{12}) is in the other response class, $R_{12} = 0$.

Figure 1–3 illustrates the response of another organism, organism 2, to the same two stimuli. The response of organism 2 to stimulus 1 is in the zero class, e.g., $R_{21} = 0$, while $R_{22} = 1$.

The responses of each of a number of organisms or observers to each of a set of stimuli constitute the basic data of a number of psychological experiments. Depend-

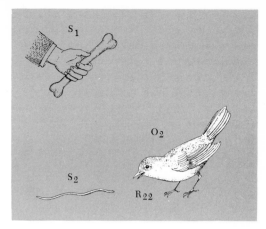

Figure 1–3   *Differential response to stimuli–II.*

ing upon the nature of the experimental records, we may have at one extreme the responses put into only two classes—positive and not positive (designated one and zero). At the other extreme, we may have each response put into one of a large number of classes. For example, the number of cc's of saliva secreted may be measured, and the response designated by this number. Reaction time may be measured in thousandths of a second, the entry for each response being this time measure.

Table 1–1 indicates this general form of psychological *data* for a great many psychological experiments. We have here a column for each stimulus, and a row for each subject, organism, or observer. The experimenter measures or classifies the response in some way, and enters in each cell of the table an appropriate number for the response of an organism (designated in

Figure 1–2   *Differential response to stimuli–I.*

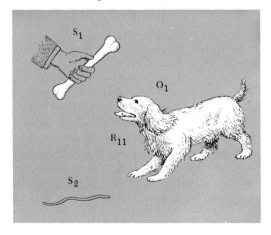

Table 1–1   Data Matrix for Typical Psychological Experiment

Organisms	Stimuli				
	S_1	S_2	$\ldots S_g \ldots$		S_K
O_1	R_{11}	R_{12}	$\ldots R_{1g} \ldots$		R_{1K}
O_2	R_{21}	R_{22}	$\ldots R_{2g} \ldots$		R_{2K}
$\vdots$					
O_i	R_{i1}	R_{i2}	$\ldots R_{ig} \ldots$		R_{iK}
$\vdots$			(R = Response)		
$\ldots R_{Ng} \ldots$		O_N		R_{N1} R_{N2}	R_{NK}

general by a subscript i) to a stimulus (designated in general by g). The response, as shown in Table 1–1 is designated in general by R_{ig}.

A matrix is any "rows-by-columns" arrangement (N by K) of a set of NK numbers. For example, if each of N persons takes K tests, the experimental results may be presented as a matrix of K columns (one for each test) and N rows (one for each person). The reported brightness of a set of lights may be represented in matrix form, as may judgments on pitch of a set of sounds, the saturation or hue of a set of colors, the excellence of a set of handwriting specimens, or the beauty of a set of pictures. These illustrations are from the area of psychophysics or psychological scaling.

We are attempting to answer questions such as "What are the important stimulus characteristics?" or perhaps "How sensitive is this individual to sounds, tones, colors, or pictures?"

The generality and flexibility of this matrix representation can be shown by another illustration. Each column could represent successive presentations of a learning situation (successive trials). The response or score of subject i on trial g (designated R_{ig}) could, at the simplest level, be 1 for a correct response and 0 for a response that was not correct. It might, in more detailed analysis, represent the score on each trial, such as the number correct or number incorrect, the reaction time, or the running time for a maze.

Thus we can see that the results of a very large variety of psychological experiments in diverse fields such as psychophysics, testing, or learning, can be presented as such a rectangular array of numbers. Such a set of numbers is called a *matrix*.

It should also be noted that one is not limited to using *stimuli* as column designators and persons as row designators. Any two-way arrangement (i.e., rows-by-columns) that suits the purposes of the experiment is appropriate. One very usual form is that in which the columns represent different tests, the rows represent the same tests, and the cell entry is the correlation of the row test with the column test. Another type of data matrix from psychophysics may be illustrated. Suppose a set of, say, six stimuli is presented in all possible pairs and the subject is asked to give a number representing the ratio of their strengths. For example, he may be asked to judge the relative brightness of two lights.

Here both the columns and the rows represent the stimuli involved; the judgment of the ratio of the stimulus at the top of the column to that at the side is entered in each cell [see reference 20].

The great advantage of regarding a set of data as a matrix lies in the fact that over the last 80 years mathematicians have developed numerous operations and theorems that apply to matrices. See, for example, [5]. It is not unreasonable to hope, and experience with matrix theory has borne out the hope, that if we utilize the vast accumulation of pathways of reasoning provided by the theorems of matrix algebra, we should be able to move much more swiftly and surely from the postulates or assumptions of a theory to the various deductions that follow from these assumptions, in particular to derive the observation equations that can be tested experimentally.

Here, then, we have a very promising relationship between matrix theory and psychology. A great many very general classes of psychological experiments give data that are presented very naturally in the matrix form.

MATRIX MULTIPLICATION

What does such a rectangular arrangement of numbers have to do with science? Just this, that science seeks to find the underlying simplicity in an apparent complexity of appearance. For example, the scores on 30 or 40 tests, according to many factor analyses, turn out to be represented as differentially weighted composites of only five or ten Primary Mental Abilities.

This type of theory regarding the rela-

Table 1–2   Illustrative Factor Analysis Matrices

test score matrix.

$$
\text{Tests}\;
\begin{array}{c}
a\\b\\c\\d
\end{array}
\overset{\text{Persons}}{
\begin{bmatrix}
v & w & x & y & z\\
4 & 6 & 1 & 3 & 5\\
16 & 4 & 2 & 18 & 6\\
12 & 8 & 2 & 12 & 8\\
16 & 14 & 3 & 15 & 13
\end{bmatrix}}
=
\text{Tests}\;
\begin{array}{c}
a\\b\\c\\d
\end{array}
\overset{\substack{\text{Factor}\\ \text{Weights}\\ \text{for Tests}}}{
\begin{bmatrix}
I & II\\
1 & 0\\
0 & 2\\
1 & 1\\
2 & 1
\end{bmatrix}}
\times
\overset{\text{Persons}}{
\begin{bmatrix}
v & w & x & y & z\\
4 & 6 & 1 & 3 & 5\\
8 & 2 & 1 & 9 & 3
\end{bmatrix}}
\begin{array}{c}
I\\II
\end{array}\text{Factors}
$$

Test Scores for Persons

$$
\begin{bmatrix}
a_1x_1+a_2x_2 & a_1y_1+a_2y_2 & a_1z_1+a_2z_2\\
b_1x_1+b_2x_2 & b_1y_1+b_2y_2 & b_1z_1+b_2z_2\\
c_1x_1+c_2x_2 & c_1y_1+c_2y_2 & c_1z_1+c_2z_2
\end{bmatrix}
=
\overset{\substack{\text{Factor}\\ \text{Weights}\\ \text{for}\\ \text{Tests}}}{
\begin{bmatrix}
a_1 & a_2\\
b_1 & b_2\\
c_1 & c_2
\end{bmatrix}}
\times
\overset{\substack{\text{Factor}\\ \text{Scores}\\ \text{for}\\ \text{Persons}}}{
\begin{bmatrix}
x_1 & y_1 & z_1\\
x_2 & y_2 & z_2
\end{bmatrix}}
$$

$$X \;=\; F \;\cdot\; P$$

tionship between abilities and test scores [see references 10 and 19] is illustrated in the upper half of Table 1–2. It shows the scores for five persons on each of two hypothetical factors, and the weight that each of these two factors has in each of four tests. The score on test *a* is the same as the score on factor 1. The score on test *b* is double the score on factor 2. Test *c* is the sum of the two factor scores, and test *d* is the score on factor 2, plus twice the score on factor 1. Each *row* of the "weights" matrix gives the weights for the *two* factors for *one* test. Note that the set of factor scores of the individuals is a 2×5 matrix and that the set of weights for each factor in each test is a 4×2 matrix. The 4×5 matrix of test scores is formed from the other two matrices. This matrix, which is computed in this way from products of terms in two other matrices, is called the *product* of these two matrices. It is obtained by what is termed *matrix multiplication.*

A generalization of this type of theory is shown in the lower half of Table 1–2. Here we have a psychological idea verbally stated—"test scores are linear combinations of factor scores." Designating each matrix by a letter, the operations shown are trans-lated into a mathematical statement $X = FP$.

MATRIX RANK

Now for a new concept—the *rank* of a matrix. What is known as the rank of the product matrix X cannot be larger than the smallest number of rows or columns in either of the factors. In this illustration, X is of rank two or less since F has two columns and P has two rows. Or, we may say that the rank of X is indicated by the number of terms added for each cell. Here we have two terms added for each cell (e.g., $a_1x_1 + a_2x_2$) the rank is two. If the second column of F and the second row of P had been unnecessary, then X would be of rank one; while if a third column of F and a third row of P were necessary, then X would be of rank three. This concept of rank of a matrix is a central concept in matrix theory.

For another illustration of the use of matrix theory in simplification of a set of data, let us return to the ratio scaling data that were mentioned a while ago.

Table 1–3 shows a hypothetical set of data. We have four stimuli designating the

Table 1–3   Matrices for Ratio Judgments

Ratio Judgments

$$
\begin{array}{c}
 \\
A \\
B \\
C \\
D
\end{array}
\begin{array}{cccc}
A & B & C & D \\
\left[\begin{array}{cccc}
a/a & b/a & c/a & d/a \\
a/b & b/b & c/b & d/b \\
a/c & b/c & c/c & d/c \\
a/d & b/d & c/d & d/d
\end{array}\right]
\end{array}
=
\left[\begin{array}{c}
1/a \\
1/b \\
1/c \\
1/d
\end{array}\right]
\times
\left[\begin{array}{cccc}
a & b & c & d
\end{array}\right]
$$

$$M \;=\; R \cdot S$$

rows and columns. Each cell entry is assumed to be the number at the top divided by the number at the side. This ratio is shown in the body of this matrix. However, division by a number may also be represented as multiplication by the reciprocal. Thus the data matrix which we might designate M is, according to the hypothesis, the product of the matrix R times S, the stimulus intensities times their reciprocals. Matrix M is thus of rank one.

Here again we have a verbally stated psychological hypothesis—"ratio judgments for two stimuli represent the subjective intensity of the first divided by the subjective intensity of the second"—translated into the mathematical statement $M = RS$, where S is the set of subjective intensity values for each stimulus, R is the set of reciprocals of these values, and M is the set of experimentally obtained judgments. As in the previous illustration, the left side of the equation M indicates the data; the right side indicates the theoretical simplification.

This use of matrices and matrix multiplication to state a psychological hypothesis, it may be noted, differs markedly from the preceding equation for a linear combination of test scores. In the case of the test scores one might have only one factor, or two as illustrated in Table 1–2, or three, four, or, frequently, more. In factor studies of test batteries, 10 to 15 factors are usually found. For the sensation ratio scaling procedure, the hypothesis as stated does not allow such leeway. R must consist of only one column, S must consist of only one row, and the product of corresponding elements must equal unity.

In both of these illustrations of a psychological idea translated into matrix language, it is important to note that the mathematics is not something extraneous which is attached after the experiment has been completed. The mathematical equations are a statement of the psychological ideas and change appropriately with each change in these ideas.

We see that the determination of rank of a matrix, provided the rank is small, is a device for expressing a large array of data in terms of a simpler set of (let us say) concepts. This is one of the goals of science —to explain a large array of data in terms of a smaller set of concepts. Matrices can be designed for that purpose and hence are valuable tools for simplification, in expressing many tests, for example, in terms of few factors, in reducing many items to only a few. In general, whenever the matrix is appropriate, the scientific interest is in simplification.

We now have a mathematical language in which to state the psychological theory. But what about experimental verification?

The beauty of matrix theory for our purposes, and a large part of its power, lies in the fact that given—and this is critical—given any matrix, there are standard methods for determining its rank.

There are high-speed computing programs for determining the *latent roots* of a matrix. The rank of the matrix is given by the number of non-zero latent roots. In this discussion we will simply use the term *latent roots* without further exposition.

Here, of course, we have our statistical questions entering. How large a root is non-zero, and how small should a number be

Table 1–4   Paired Comparison Data Matrix

	Handwriting Specimens—Proportions of Judgments								
	50a	50b	50c	70a	70b	70c	80a	80b	80c
50a		.52	.67	.95	.99	.98	.99	.97	.94
50b	.48		.60	.85	.95	.96	.98	.98	.95
50c	.33	.40		.76	.78	.92	.91	.86	.96
70a	.05	.15	.24		.76	.87	.95	.79	.78
70b	.01	.05	.22	.24		.74	.80	.52	.71
70c	.02	.04	.08	.13	.26		.59	.26	.56
80a	.01	.02	.09	.05	.20	.41		.15	.31
80b	.03	.02	.14	.21	.48	.74	.85		.61
80c	.06	.05	.04	.22	.29	.44	.69	.39	

to be regarded as essentially zero? In some studies, there is relatively little reasonable doubt. In others, we have only a reasonably small range of uncertainty.

We will consider in some detail the utility of matrix theory in three areas: (1) Psychophysics; (2) Linguistics; (3) Learning.

PSYCHOPHYSICS

An introduction to work in the area of psychophysics may be found in Torgerson [20]. We will give some concrete illustrations of the usefulness of matrix theory for some of the problems in this area.

Now let us consider some data from a study in psychophysics—a paired comparisons experiment on handwriting [6]. Nine samples of handwriting were selected from the Ayres handwriting scale. The 36 possible pairs of these nine specimens were presented. The judge was to indicate which was the better specimen in each pair. The results are shown in Table 1–4. Out of 100 judges, 52 judged specimen 50b to be better than 50a, while 48 judged 50a to be better than 50b, and correspondingly for the other entries. Symmetrical entries sum to unity.

Let us consider how these data may be used to test a theory—the law of comparative judgment—proposed by L. L. Thurstone. In developing this law three assumptions are made, which we may designate as *linearity, difference,* and *normality* assumptions.

1. Each stimulus in the set (as shown at the top left of Table 1–5) can be specified by a single number—designated a, b, etc.—which is the "scale value"

Table 1–5   Matrices and Latent Roots for the Law of Comparative Judgment

Thurstone's Law of Comparative Judgment	Latent Roots Handwriting
$D_{ab} = a\text{-}b$ $D_{cd} = c\text{-}d$	$+7.68i$
	$-7.68i$
	$+.94i$
	$-.94i$
	$+.47i$
	$-.47i$
	$+.18i$
	$-.18i$

a   b   c   d

x   x   x   x

$$
\begin{array}{c} a \\ b \\ c \\ d \end{array}
\begin{bmatrix} a\text{-}a & a\text{-}b & a\text{-}c & a\text{-}d \\ b\text{-}a & b\text{-}b & b\text{-}c & b\text{-}d \\ c\text{-}a & c\text{-}b & c\text{-}c & c\text{-}d \\ d\text{-}a & d\text{-}b & d\text{-}c & d\text{-}d \end{bmatrix}
=
\begin{bmatrix} a, & -1 \\ b, & -1 \\ c, & -1 \\ d, & -1 \end{bmatrix}
\times
\begin{bmatrix} 1 & 1 & 1 & 1 \\ a & b & c & d \end{bmatrix}
$$

$$X = D \cdot S$$

of that stimulus. This is the *linearity* assumption.

2. When presented with any pair of stimuli in a paired comparisons experiment, the subject's response is determined by the difference between the two stimuli. $D_{ab} = a - b; D_{cd} = c - d;$ etc. This set of differences, matrix X at the left of Table 1–5, is shown to be the product of two matrices. Since the first factor has two columns, and the second has two rows, matrix X is of rank 2. This is the *difference* assumption.

3. The proportion of judgments "*i* greater than *j*" is related to interstimulus differences by some distribution function. Thurstone suggested the Gaussian or normal distribution as a reasonable first guess. We may call this the *normality* assumption.

It is possible now to develop an observation equation which will simultaneously test the usability of these three assumptions. The proportions shown in Table 1–4 are transformed into normal deviates to obtain this matrix X, and its latent roots are obtained to see if it is of rank two.

It should be noted that, as is usually the case, all three assumptions, the *linearity*, *difference*, and *normality* assumptions, are necessary for this test. If the matrix is of rank two, then these three assumptions may be regarded as in agreement with the data. If the matrix is not rank two, then one or more of the assumptions should be altered— or the experiment may be inappropriate.

The latent roots are shown at the right of Table 1–5. If the theory fits perfectly, the six smallest roots are zero. The matrix of normal deviates is seen to be dominantly rank two, since there are two large roots $+7.68i$ and its conjugate $-7.68i$. There is, however, a small component, definitely not zero, which remains to be accounted for.

The matrix analysis has presented a problem. How can the theory be modified to give a closer fit to these data? Or, how can the experimental conditions be modified to make these roots smaller?

Another theoretical account of paired comparisons has been presented by Bradley and Terry and also by Luce [11] and others, based on linearity and ratio assumptions.

Each stimulus, say i and j, has a value (say v_i and v_j). The proportion of judgments $i > j$ is given by $p_{ij} = v_i/(v_i + v_j)$ as indicated in Table 1–6. If we try to make some matrix rank statement about the set of p_{ij}'s, nothing useful has been pointed

Table 1–6   Paired Comparisons Analyzed by Logistic

Luce Bradley-Terry Law	Handwriting Latent Roots of XX'
$p_{ij} = \dfrac{v_i}{v_i + v_j}$	
	28,848.88
$\dfrac{1}{p_{ij}} = \dfrac{v_i + v_j}{v_i} = 1 + \dfrac{v_j}{v_i}$	1,839.99
	411.91
	102.21
$x_{ij} = \dfrac{1}{p_{ij}} - 1 = \dfrac{v_j}{v_i}$	0.78
	0.01
	0.00
	0.00
	0.00

$$\begin{bmatrix} v_1/v_1 & v_2/v_1 & v_3/v_1 & v_4/v_1 \\ v_1/v_2 & v_2/v_2 & v_3/v_2 & v_4/v_2 \\ v_1/v_3 & v_2/v_3 & v_3/v_3 & v_4/v_3 \\ v_1/v_4 & v_2/v_4 & v_3/v_4 & v_4/v_4 \end{bmatrix} = \begin{bmatrix} 1/v_1 \\ 1/v_2 \\ 1/v_3 \\ 1/v_4 \end{bmatrix} \times \begin{bmatrix} v_1 & v_2 & v_3 & v_4 \end{bmatrix}$$

$$X = R \cdot V$$

out as yet. However, if we take the reciprocal of the proportions we have $1/p_{ij} = (v_i + v_j)/v_i = 1 + v_j/v_i$. This equation suggests defining a new quantity, say, x_{ij} $x_{ij} = 1/p_{ij} - 1 = v_j/v_i$. We now have a very simple expression and, according to the theory we are considering, the matrix X composed of elements x_{ij} is of rank *one*.

For the same handwriting data, the latent roots of the matrix XX' are shown at the right of Table 1–6. We see that the data are dominantly of rank one, but this theory also leaves something to be desired. How can we either modify the theory or alter the experimental conditions to get a closer agreement between theory and data?

This matrix X, it may be noted, will contain reciprocal elements such as x_{ij} and x_{ji} which may be equal respectively to 100 and 0.01. The problem of assessing deviations due to error in such a matrix may prove difficult. Possibly utilizing a new matrix composed of elements y_{ij} where $y_{ij} = \log x_{ij}$ would prove easier. If matrix X is of rank one, then Y will be of rank two but will have the advantage of being skew symmetric with equal errors for symmetric entries.

Stevens [17] has recently suggested a psychophysical law $y = ax^b$ where y is the psychological value, x is the physical value, and a and b are two constants. Here b is a characteristic of the particular type of stimuli used and a may perhaps be thought of as representing the sensitivity of the subject (see Table 1–7).

We may now state this law more precisely, letting g represent the subject and i the stimulus: $y_{gi} = a_g x_i^{b_i}$. The matrix

formulation here shows that this hypothesis implies that the y_{gi} matrix is of rank one, a point that can be tested with a good set of data.

LINGUISTICS

Now let us turn to an investigation in the field of linguistics. Cliff [2] working at Princeton has suggested the hypothesis that adverbs multiply adjectives. For example, if *very good* is twice as good as *good,* then *very bad* is twice as bad as *bad*. In general, the scale values of a set of such adverb-adjective combinations would be rank one. However, from a realistic viewpoint, there is no data matrix here. Our scaling methods give no origin, so some arbitrary and unknown constant must be added to each cell to take into account the arbitrary origin, giving the matrix shown in Table 1–8. Interestingly, it is of rank two, as is shown by expressing X as the product of the two matrices, C and S.

We have a clearly formulated theory of linguistic behavior that can be tested with scaling data. Now for the experiment.

A set of nine adverbs and 15 adjectives which might be used to describe people was selected. These constituted a 150-item successive intervals rating schedule as shown at the top of Table 1–9. This schedule was given to 130–210 students in each of three universities, Wayne, Dartmouth and Princeton.

We will consider only the 150 scale values for the stimuli. These 150 values are arranged in a 10 × 15 matrix. This is the

Table 1–7   Matrices for the Power Law

$$
\begin{array}{c}
\text{Psychophysical Law} \\
\text{(Stevens)} \\
y = ax^b
\end{array}
\qquad
\begin{array}{c}
\text{Interpretation I} \\
y_{gi} = a_g x_i^{b_i}
\end{array}
$$

$$
\begin{bmatrix}
y_{11} & y_{12} & y_{13} & y_{14} \\
y_{21} & y_{22} & y_{23} & y_{24} \\
y_{31} & y_{32} & y_{33} & y_{34} \\
y_{41} & y_{42} & y_{43} & y_{44} \\
y_{51} & y_{52} & y_{53} & y_{54}
\end{bmatrix}
=
\begin{bmatrix}
a_1 \\
a_2 \\
a_3 \\
a_4 \\
a_5
\end{bmatrix}
\times
\begin{bmatrix}
x_1^b & x_2^b & x_3^b & x_4^b
\end{bmatrix}
$$

Table 1–8 Matrices for the Adverb-Adjective Study

Linguistics Study (Cliff)

| Adverb-Adjective Scale Values (Unknown Additive Constant) | Adverb Values | Adjective Values |

$$\begin{bmatrix} av+k & aw+k & ax+k & ay+k \\ bv+k & bw+k & bx+k & by+k \\ cv+k & cw+k & cx+k & cy+k \\ dv+k & dw+k & dx+k & dy+k \\ ev+k & ew+k & ex+k & ey+k \end{bmatrix} = \begin{bmatrix} a & 1 \\ b & 1 \\ c & 1 \\ d & 1 \\ e & 1 \end{bmatrix} \times \begin{bmatrix} v & w & x & y \\ k & k & k & k \end{bmatrix}$$

$$X \quad = \quad C \quad \cdot \quad S$$

matrix X referred to in Table 1–8. In the lower part of Table 1–9 we see a 5×8 subset taken from the original 10 by 15 matrix. We can see that in general the results were as hypothesized. *Very bad* is lower, with a scale value of 6, than *bad*, with a scale value of 10. *Very good* (32) is higher than *good* (27). We ask, however, whether the original 10 by 15 matrix is a matrix of rank two? Let us look at the latent roots to see if two are non-zero and

the rest are zero. The roots of XX' are given at the bottom right of Table 1–9.

From this we see an amazing verification of Cliff's hypothesis [2]. One root of over 600, one of 10, and the other eight (all positive), all total to 0.5. The rank two hypothesis accounts for 99.92 per cent of the total sum of squares, 0.08 per cent being in the eight roots that will be ignored. Nor is this result a fluke, since the results at Princeton and at Dartmouth are

Table 1–9 Illustrative Scale Values from the Adverb-Adjective Study

	Most unfavorable ↓					Neutral ↓					Most favorable ↓
Slightly bad	□	□	□	□	□	□	□	□	□	□	□
Very good	□	□	□	□	□	□	□	□	□	□	□
Rather evil	□	□	□	□	□	□	□	□	□	□	□
Slightly good	□	□	□	□	□	□	□	□	□	□	□
Immoral	□	□	□	□	□	□	□	□	□	□	□

	Wicked	Evil	Bad	Ordinary	Average	Nice	Good	Admirable	Latent roots	
									(1)	654.46
Slightly	13	14	15	20	20	23	24	25	(2)	10.04
Rather	10	11	12	20	22	26	28	29	(3–10)	.51
Unmodified	6	6	10	21	22	26	27	30	Trace	665.01
Very	4	5	6	21	20	30	32	33	Per cent of trace	99.92
Extremely	1	1	5	19	21	34	34	36		

practically identical with those at Wayne.

The values for the nine adverbs are shown in Table 1–10. Again the actual numbers were found to be very similar from one group to the other, for both the adverbs and the adjectives. There is marked agreement, not only in the general principle of rank two, but in the detailed results. The zero point is also in the same place for each of the three sets of data.

LEARNING

A fascinating application of the concept of rank of a matrix has been developed by Ledyard Tucker in the field of learning. Innumerable learning experiments over the past 70 years have investigated various theories regarding the learning process. Is improvement with practice due to a law of recency, a law of frequency, or a law of effect? Does learning proceed by trial and error or by insight? Is the learning process characterized by continuity or discontinuity? In something like 95% of these experiments conclusions were drawn on the basis of averages—average over trials of the number of errors or time for each subject, for example, or an average over subjects for

each trial to obtain a learning curve that would be smoother than that for a single individual. Practically all learning experiments, designed to test any particular learning theory, have analyzed the data and interpreted the results on the assumption that the average learning curve for the group was a reasonable representation of the learning curve for each individual in the group as a means of testing learning theories. There has been no test of this basic assumption. Only rarely has it been explicitly recognized that such an assumption was implicit in the method of data analysis. In a few studies parameters have been developed and obtained for individual learning curves [e.g., 14, 18]. Tucker [21] has recently shown how it is possible to determine the extent to which the average learning curve correctly represents the process for each individual or conceals and distorts significant characteristics of the learning curves for the individuals studied.

Consider the subjects-by-trials matrix shown in Table 1–11, where each cell entry gives the score (number right, or errors, etc.) for each subject on each trial. The usual practice in analyzing learning curves is to average each column and use these averages as the learning curve for the

Table 1–10   Scale Values for Adjectives and for Adverbs

Wayne — N = 213

	c_i	1		s_j	K
			Evil	−1.25	2.08
Unmodified	1.00	.99	Wicked	−1.16	1.95
Slightly	.56	1.00	Contemptible	−.91	1.75
Somewhat	.69	1.00	Immoral	−1.18	1.94
Rather	.85	1.02	Disgusting	−.81	1.62
Pretty	.94	1.00	Bad	−1.02	2.03
Quite	1.04	.99	Inferior	−.81	2.01
Decidedly	1.22	1.00	Ordinary	−.08	2.08
Unusually	1.29	1.01	Average	−.04	2.12
Very	1.32	1.01	Nice	1.01	1.74
Extremely	1.59	1.00	Good	1.08	1.75
			Pleasant	1.00	1.84
			Charming	.80	2.14
			Admirable	.98	2.00
			Lovable	.84	2.17

Table 1–11   Learning Matrix

$$
\underset{\text{Persons}}{}
\begin{bmatrix}
a_1t_1 & a_1t_2 & a_1t_3 & \cdots & a_1t_6 \\
a_2t_1 & a_2t_2 & a_2t_3 & \cdots & a_2t_6 \\
a_3t_1 & a_3t_2 & a_3t_3 & \cdots & a_3t_6 \\
\vdots & \vdots & \vdots & & \vdots \\
a_kt_1 & a_kt_2 & a_kt_3 & \cdots & a_kt_6
\end{bmatrix}
=
\begin{bmatrix}
a_1 \\ a_2 \\ a_3 \\ \vdots \\ a_k
\end{bmatrix}
\times
\begin{bmatrix} t_1 & t_2 & t_3 \cdots t_6 \end{bmatrix}
$$

Trials   Weights   Theoretical Curve

$$
t_1\bar{a} \quad t_2\bar{a} \quad t_3\bar{a} \quad \cdots \quad t_6\bar{a}
$$

Average Curve

group. When does this procedure give a correct representation of the data, and when does it conceal important characteristics of the data?

Investigation shows that one condition under which the average learning curve could legitimately represent the group exists if the total matrix is of rank one. If one has, as in Table 1–11, a standard learning curve that appears with different weights in different subjects, then the average curve as shown at the bottom of Table 1–11 would be the original one multiplied by an average for the weights.

Further study shows another possibility. We may have the two-way analysis of variance situation, in which the cell entry is essentially equal to the row mean plus the column mean with negligible interaction. In this case X is of rank two and other restrictions apply also. Generalizing these two cases we may say that the average learning curve can be, in some reasonable sense, a correct representation of the individual learning curves if

$$r_{ig} = a_i t_g + b_i$$

where r_{ig} is the score of person i on trial g, t_g is the generalized learning curve for the set of data, a_i and b_i are parameters characterizing the individual. Rank one mentioned above is the special case in which b_i is zero. The special case of rank two which fits a two-way analysis of variance is obtained by letting a_i equal unity so that

$$r_{ig} = t_g + b_i$$

Skinner [16] has inveighed against "aver-aged" or "smoothed" learning curves. The method presented here, it will be noted, does not use such procedures but deals with the set of individual curves, one for each subject in the group.

Thus we find a result which is critical for all learning studies that report average learning curves. Such an average curve may be appropriate if the rank of the data matrix is one or if its rank is two. For any higher rank some aspects of the data which may be very important are concealed by the average curve. For example, if one has a mixed group of "late" and "early" learners, each following a simple S curve, as shown by the two solid lines in Figure 1–4, the average can give a very misleading idea of the course of learning, as shown by the broken average line in the figure. This point has been discussed in considerable detail by Merrell [12].

R. Allen Gardner conducted some probability learning experiments as a member of an Army research group at Fort Knox and has given Ledyard Tucker his data on several of these experiments. I shall present

Figure 1–4   *Illustration of spurious complexity of group curve.*

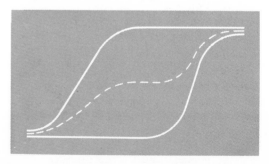

Tucker's analysis of two learning situations. In one experiment, the subjects were told to guess whether L or S would be shown on the next trial. For 12 subjects it was 70% L and 30% S, for another 12, 70% S and 30% L. The number of guesses for the dominant letter was recorded. For 420 presentations these were grouped into 21 "trials" with 20 presentations in each trial, so the score on a given trial for a given person R_{ij} was some number from zero to 20—the number of times he guessed the letter chosen as dominant by the experiment. Using 24 subjects and 21 trials gave, then, a 24 × 21 matrix for the data, say matrix R.

Does the average learning curve represent adequately each person in the group?

Let us look at the latent roots of $R'R$ to see if one or two are large and the others are essentially zero. At the top of Figure 1–5 is the graph of latent roots in order of size shown by X's. The largest is 92,780, the second largest 420, and so on slowly down to zero. Possibly a better idea is given by taking the successive differences as shown by the circles on the same graph. How big is the step from one root to the next larger? These are uniformly between 1 and 100 for the first 19 steps shown. The next step is 92,370. The largest root is clearly non-zero. The others seem relatively small and can perhaps be regarded as essentially zero, so the average learning curve represents each person in the group reasonably well if adjusted by a weight for that person.

The average curve is shown by the circles in the middle of the figure. The learning curve from factor analysis is shown by the X's. In order to make the two sets of data distinct the first and last points were displaced by a specified distance. To the extent that the same distance is maintained elsewhere, the two curves are the same.

In another experiment any one of four letters was presented, the proportions being 0.7, 0.1, 0.1, 0.1. A record was kept of the number of times the dominant letter was guessed in each set of 20 presentations.

Figure 1–5 *Analysis for probability learning data.*

LEARNING DATA (Gardner)

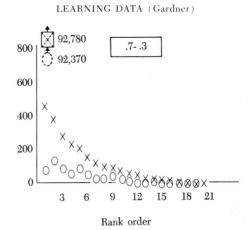

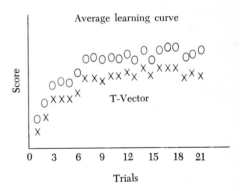

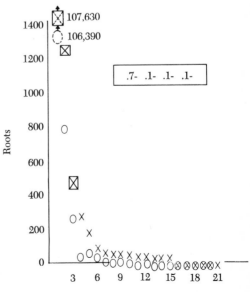

Again 24 subjects were each given 420 presentations, making a 24 × 21 matrix with a "number of guesses of dominant letter" score—a number from 0–20 in each cell. Is this matrix like the 0.7–0.3 one? Does the average curve represent the trend for each person in the group?

Let us look at the corresponding latent roots shown at the bottom of Figure 1–5 by the X's. The scale here is the same as for the other graph. Let us first look at the circles which represent successive differences. Again we have many in the 0–100 band. Not 19 as at the right, however—only 17. There is then a jump to 230, then to 770, and then to 106,390. Clearly one will lose relatively little (about $2\frac{1}{2}\%$) of the sum of squares by considering only the average learning curve. However, the second largest root of 1240 and even the third largest one of 470 may not be negligible as the other 18 apparently are.

Analyzing this as a three-factor system shows that we may regard the data as revealing three learning curves, a dominant one rising early and two lesser ones, one rising at about trial 5 and another at about trial 12. We may regard the data as composed of various weighted combinations of these three curves instead of only one. Using only one curve would lose about $2\frac{1}{2}\%$ of the sum of squares. Using three factors loses only 0.9%.

EXPERIMENTAL DESIGN

There is a very general and a very important consequence which becomes clear from matrix theory. The experimental design must take account of any hypothesis regarding rank, e.g., of the complexity of the field actually represented by the data. It is not possible to verify that the rank of a matrix is k, unless the *smaller* dimension of the data matrix is $2k$ to $4k$. To insure stability of results it is desirable that the larger dimension be $5k$ to $10k$. For a concrete illustration, if one is working with what may be a 10-factor system (rank 10)

then some 40 tests and 100 subjects should be used.

Sometimes investigators are tempted into believing that hundreds of observations on five subjects constitute a good experimental procedure. However, matrix theory demonstrates that five subjects are inadequate unless one has only a one-factor (rank one) system. Too few cases cannot be compensated for by taking 10 or even 100 times as many observations.

At the other extreme one finds studies which use only, say, five tests or five measures, where the investigator feels he has done a thorough study because he used several thousand subjects. Again, the same principle applies. Five tests are adequate for studying a one-factor system but not for two or more factors. Too few measures cannot be compensated for by taking even 100 times as many subjects.

This simple appreciation of the relationship between number of cases or number of measures (whichever is smaller) and the complexity of the field actually represented in the data is an important contribution of matrix theory to experimental design.

We have seen some illustrations from psychophysics, from linguistics, and from learning, where the data are naturally presented in matrix form, where psychological theories are readily translated into special types of matrices and matrix multiplication, and where the experimentally obtained data matrix must have a specified rank in order to agree with the theory. In each of these cases matrix theory has furnished a useful mathematical language for stating and testing a psychological theory.

MULTIDIMENSIONAL SCALING

I also wish to sketch briefly the multidimensional scaling procedures, since they have been found useful in a very great variety of problems. The growth of this field is presented in reference [20].

The unique characteristics of multidimensional scaling can best be seen by comparing and contrasting it first with linear scaling and second with factor analysis.

In comparing multidimensional scaling with the usual linear scaling, we note that the linear psychological scaling methods necessitate knowing the dimension to be scaled before the experiment can be started. For example, in paired comparisons or in successive intervals the subjects are asked to judge "which is *louder*?" "which is *redder*?" "which is *higher* in pitch?" etc. That is, it is necessary for the experimenter to know which dimensions he wishes to study and to be able to communicate the meaning of each of these different sorts of qualities, or dimensions, to the subjects.

In the multidimensional scaling methods, no matter what type of stimuli or what qualities are being investigated, the experimenter need communicate only one concept to the subjects, "more like." The basic question is "Is *A* more like *B* or more like *C*?" as illustrated in Figure 1–6. It is well to emphasize the extreme generality of this experimental technique. *A*, *B*, and *C* may be colors, odors, sounds, handwriting specimens, adjectives, or attitude statements. The same basic question also applies to relative similarities of personality, to relative friendliness of individuals in a group, and to many other situations. From this basic and uniform judgment of "relative similarity" the analytical method takes over

Figure 1–6 *Method of triads.*

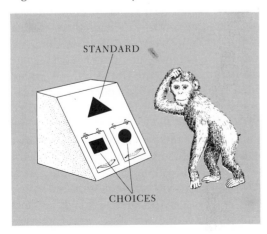

STANDARD

CHOICES

and determines the dimensionality needed to account for the set of judgments obtained.

Using multidimensional scaling we may investigate any given area by a method that does not depend on a preconceived set of ideas regarding the particular dimensions in that area. For example, the area of vision can be investigated using solely the judgment of "relative similarity" to see if dimensions corresponding to hue, saturation, and brightness occur. A beginning on such studies has been made by Helm, Mellinger, Messick and Torgerson [see reference 20]. The same holds for the area of audition. If investigated solely with the concept of relative similarity, will one find two, three, or more dimensions? Olfaction is another area in which multidimensional methods might make a similar contribution.

In more complex areas of interpersonal relations the multidimensional methods may be used to determine the complexity of the field. Anton Morton has one study under way in the area of "Friendships" and has tentative results from multidimensional scaling showing a four-dimensional structure. Some of these dimensions agree with certain unidimensional measures such as scholastic ability or athletic ability.

Personality could also be investigated with the concept of relative similarity of persons, to determine the perceived dimensionality of the field and then study the relationship of these dimensions to various single dimensions shown in personality tests.

To the extent to which this method can be used in an area, it is a very basic and powerful tool for determining the structure of perceived differences in a given area.

Multidimensional scaling methods may be contrasted with factor-analytic methods. In factor analysis one begins with measures of a group of individuals on a large number of different variables. Analysis results in a smaller number of dimensions than variables, which accounts for the interrelations of the variables. In multidimensional scaling one begins with a concept of relative similarity between various pairs of objects. ("Is *A* more like *B* than *C* is like *D*?" Or, for triads, "Is *A* more like *B* than *A* is like *C*?") Using *only* this *one* kind of measure, analysis yields the "similarity structure" of the set of objects employing one or three or ten, etc., dimensions to account for the total set of inter-object distances.

It is important to see how something which looks like a single dimension-similarity—namely, distance between two points—can be used to give many dimensions.

As a simple illustration, in Figure 1–7 the distances $D_{ij} = 1$, $D_{jk} = 4$, $D_{ik} = 5$ represent a linear series | | | | | |, while the distances $D_{ij} = 3$, $D_{jk} = 4$, $D_{ik} = 5$ cannot be represented as a linear series but must be represented as a two-dimensional set.

In general it has been proved by Young and Householder [see reference 20] that, given a set of interpoint distances, the dimensionality of that set of points can be determined. Form the matrix of squared interpoint distances $d_{ij}{}^2$ as shown at the right of Figure 1–7. Border it with a row and column of 1's and a zero in the diagonal as illustrated in the figure. The dimensionality of the set of points $(1,2, \ldots, i, j, \ldots$ etc.) is two less than the rank of the bordered matrix.

For a one-dimensional set of points the rank of the matrix is three. If the rank of

the matrix is five, for example, then the k points involved are representable in $5 - 2 = 3$ dimensions.

The first study using multidimensional scaling was by Marion Richardson [15] who verified the Munsell color system for a portion of the color pyramid. Richardson also supervised a study by Klingberg [8] in 1940 of the relative friendliness of the Great Powers. Klingberg found a three-dimensional structure for the United States, Great Britain, France, Italy, Germany, and Japan. The shorter the distance, the lower the judged probability of war between the two powers involved. Adding a seventh power—Russia—to the system introduced a fourth dimension.

Work in the multidimensional scaling area lapsed during World War II and was renewed again in 1950 by Torgerson at Princeton. When a set of red color papers from the Munsell series was scaled in this manner, having the subject judge only relative similarity without any mention of brightness or saturation, these two dimensions were present. Figure 1–8 shows the configuration Torgerson obtained at the bottom and the Munsell configuration at the top. The similarity of the two is clear. Dimension A is equivalent to value and dimension B is equivalent to chroma.

Messick [13] at Princeton used multidimensional scaling on a set of attitude statements, seven from a war scale, seven from a capital punishment scale, and seven from a scale of attitude toward criminals. Subjects were asked to judge the similarity of these statements. These three scales might be conceived as related in different ways. For example, one might have a one-dimensional structure for all three scales from a "pro-war, pro-capital punishment, and anti-corrective treatment of criminals" at one extreme to an "anti-war, anti-capital punishment, and pro-correction of criminals" at the other extreme. One might characterize this as a "humanitarian" dimension. Another possibility for perceiving the structure of these three scales would be one dimension for the war and capital punish-

Figure 1–7   *Multidimensional scaling.*

INTERPOINT DISTANCES AND
DIMENSIONALITY

	I	II
$D_{ij} =$	1	3
$D_{jk} =$	4	4
$D =$	5	5

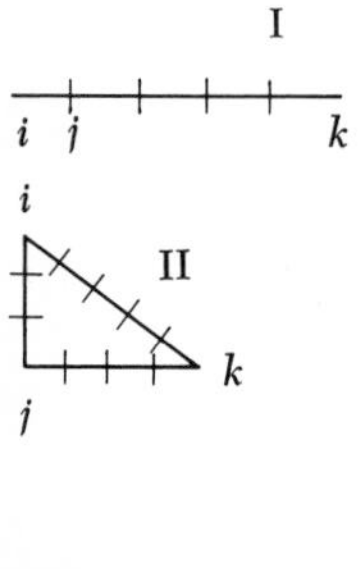

$$
\begin{array}{cccccc}
0 & D_{12}{}^2 & D_{13}{}^2 & \cdots & D_{1k}{}^2 & 1 \\
D_{21}{}^2 & 0 & D_{23}{}^2 & \cdots & D_{2k}{}^2 & 1 \\
D_{31}{}^2 & D_{32}{}^2 & 0 & \cdots & D_{3k}{}^2 & 1 \\
\vdots & \vdots & \vdots & & \vdots & \vdots \\
D_{k1}{}^2 & D_{k2}{}^2 & D_{k3}{}^2 & \cdots & 0 & 1 \\
1 & 1 & 1 & \cdots & 1 & 0
\end{array}
$$

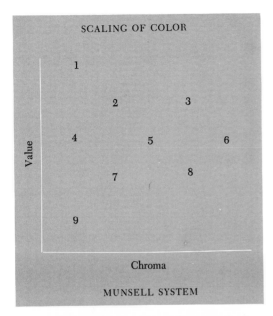

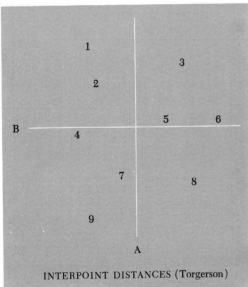

Figure 1–8 *Multidimensional scaling of color.*

as shown in Figure 1–9. Furthermore, the points numbered 1 to 7 are from the war scale and follow a nearly vertical line. The 14 lettered points are from the other two scales, the upper case letters representing statements from the capital punishment scale and the lower case letters representing statements from the attitude toward criminals scale. Again, this is not a fluke. Compare the results from seminary students with those from Air Force cadets as shown in Figure 1–9. The two lines intersect at about 70°. There are only subtle differences between the two groups of subjects.

These illustrations give some idea of the general applicability of multidimensional scaling to problems in psychophysics or in attitude measurement. Wherever it is possible to make consistent judgments of "relative similarity" of a set of psychological objects the multidimensional scaling methods can take over and determine the dimensionality of that set of objects, be they sounds, pictures, attitude statements, or personalities.

The multidimensional methods have wide applicability in many fields of psychology.

SUMMARY

I have attempted here to show the value of the mathematico-deductive approach to various psychological problems, and in particular to indicate the very general applicability of two techniques:

1. The usefulness of matrix algebra for expressing a large number of psychological theories and for comparing the theory (observation equations) with data.
2. The generality of multidimensional scaling as an approach to a variety of psychological problems.

In each case I have tried to stress the close tie between the mathematical statement and the psychological statement. For every

ment scales, indicating an attitude toward killing other persons, and a second dimension for the correction of criminals. A third possibility is for the three scales to be relatively independent of each other and to constitute three dimensions. The actual results of Messick's analysis showed none of these three, but a fourth possibility. The three scales fell into two well-defined lines

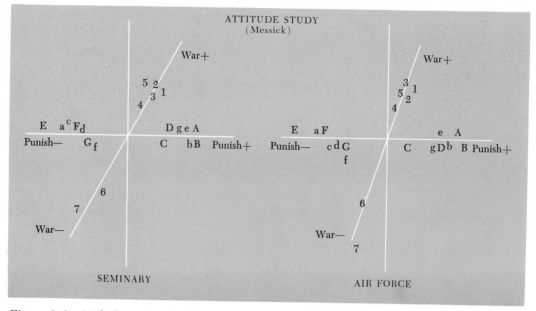

Figure 1–9   *Multidimensional scaling of attitude statements.*

variation in psychological assumptions there must be a matching variation in the mathematical equations.

When psychological theories are translated into mathematical equations the mathematician can give the psychologist powerful tools for deriving the implications of his assumptions and for testing their correspondence with data.

REFERENCES

1. BUSH, R. R., ABELSON, R. P., and HYMAN, R. *Mathematics for Psychologists: Examples and Problems.* New York: Social Science Research Council, 1956. (Prepared for the Committee on Mathematical Training of Social Scientists.)
2. CLIFF, NORMAN. Adverbs as multipliers. *Psychological Review,* 1959, *66,* 27–44.
3. CRONBACH, L. J. The two disciplines of scientific psychology. *The American Psychologist,* 1957, *12,* 671–684.
4. ECKART, CARL and YOUNG, GALE. The approximation of one matrix by another of lower rank. *Psychometrika,* 1936, *1,* 211–218.
5. FRAZER, R. A., DUNCAN, W. J., and COLLAR, A. R. *Elementary Matrices.* New York: Cambridge University Press, 1955.
6. GULLIKSEN, HAROLD and TUKEY, JOHN. Reliability for the law of comparative judgment. *Psychometrika,* 1958, *23,* 95–110.
7. HEMPEL, C. G. Fundamentals of Concept Formation in Empirical Science. In *International Encyclopedia of Unified Science,* Vol. 2, No. 7. Chicago: University of Chicago Press, 1952.
8. KLINGBERG, F. L. Studies in the measurement of relations between sovereign states. *Psychometrika,* 1941, *6,* 335–352.
9. LAZARSFELD, P. F. Mathematical thinking in the social sciences. Glencoe, Ill.: Free Press, 1954. 444 pp.
10. LORD, F. M. A Theory of Test Scores. *Psychometric Monographs,* 1952, No. 7.
11. LUCE, R. D. *Individual Choice Behavior: A Theoretical Analysis.* New York: John Wiley & Sons, Inc., 1959.
12. MERRELL, MARGARET. The relationship of individual growth to average growth. *Human Biology,* 1931, *3,* 37–70.
13. MESSICK, S. J. The perception of social attitudes. *Journal of Abnormal and Social Psychology,* 1956, *52,* 57–66.
14. RASHEVSKY, NICHOLAS. *Mathematical Biophysics.* Revised Edition. Chicago: University of Chicago Press, 1948. xxxiii + 669 pp.
15. RICHARDSON, M. W. Multidimensional psychophysics. *Psychological Bulletin,* 1938, *35,* 659–660.

16. SKINNER, B. F. Reinforcement today. *The American Psychologist*, 1958, *13*, 94–99.

17. STEVENS, S. S. On the psychophysical law. *Psychological Review*, 1957, *64*, 153–181.

18. THURSTONE, L. L. The learning function. *Journal of General Psychology*, 1930, *3*, 469–493.

19. THURSTONE, L. L. *Multiple Factor Analysis*. Chicago: University of Chicago Press, 1947 (pages 1–50 are an introduction to matrix theory).

20. TORGERSON, W. S. *Theory and Methods of Scaling*. New York: Wiley and Sons, 1958.

21. TUCKER, L. R. Determination of parameters of a functional relation by factor analysis. *Psychometrika*, 1958, *23*, 19–23.

Chapter 2

The Two Disciplines
of Scientific Psychology

LEE J. CRONBACH

No man can be acquainted with all of psychology today, as our convention program proves. The scene resembles that of a circus, but a circus grander and more bustling than any Barnum ever envisioned—a veritable week-long diet of excitement and pink lemonade. Three days of smartly paced performance are required just to display the new tricks the animal trainers have taught their charges. We admire the agile paper-readers swinging high above us in the theoretical blue, saved from disaster by only a few gossamer threads of fact, and we gasp as one symposiast thrusts his head bravely between another's sharp toothed jaws. This 18-ring display of energies and talents gives plentiful evidence that psychology is going places. But whither?

In the simpler days of psychology, the presidential address provided a summing-

This article is reprinted from the *American Psychologist*, 1958, with the permission of the author and the American Psychological Association.

This article was the Address of the President at the Sixty-fifth Annual Convention of the American Psychological Association, New York, New York, September 2, 1957.

up and a statement of destination. The President called the roll of the branches of psychology—praising the growth of some youngsters, tut-tutting patriarchally over the delinquent tendencies of others—and showed each to his proper place at the family table. My own title is reminiscent of those grand surveys, but the last speaker who could securely bring the whole of psychology within one perspective was Dashiell, with his 1938 address on "Rapprochements in Contemporary Psychology" [15]. My scope must be far more restricted.

I shall discuss the past and future place within psychology of two historic streams of method, thought, and affiliation which run through the last century of our science. One stream is *experimental psychology;* the other, *correlational psychology*. Dashiell optimistically forecast a confluence of these two streams, but that confluence is still in the making. Psychology continues to this day to be limited by the dedication of its investigators to one or the other method of inquiry rather than to scientific psychology as a whole.

A stream of thought is identified by many features: philosophical underpinnings, methods of inquiry, topical interests, and loci of application. The experimental and correlational streams have all these aspects, but I am concerned with them as disciplines within scientific psychology. The job of science is to ask questions of Nature. A discipline is a method of asking questions and of testing answers to determine whether they are sound. Scientific psychology is still young, and there is rapid turnover in our interests, our experimental apparatus and our tests, and our theoretical concepts. But our methods of inquiry have become increasingly stable, and it is these methods which qualify us as scientists rather than philosophers or artists.

THE SEPARATION OF THE DISCIPLINES

The experimental method—where the scientist changes conditions in order to observe their consequences—is much the more coherent of our two disciplines. Everyone knows what experimental psychology is and who the experimental psychologists are. Correlational psychology, though fully as old as experimentation, was slower to mature. It qualifies equally as a discipline, however, because it asks a distinctive type of question and has technical methods of examining whether the question has been properly put and the data properly interpreted.

In contrast to the Tight Little Island of the experimental discipline, correlational psychology is a sort of Holy Roman Empire whose citizens identify mainly with their own principalities. The discipline, the common service in which the principalities are united, is the study of correlations presented by Nature. While the experimenter is interested only in the variation he himself creates, the correlator finds his interest in the already existing variation between individuals, social groups, and species. By "correlational psychology" I do not refer to studies which rely on one statistical procedure. Factor analysis is correlational, to be sure, but so is the study of Ford and Beach [23] relating sexual behavior to differences along the phylogenetic scale and across the cultural spectrum.

The well-known virtue of the experimental method is that it brings situational variables under tight control. It thus permits rigorous tests of hypotheses and confident statements about causation. The correlational method, for its part, can study what man has not learned to control or can never hope to control. Nature has been experimenting since the beginning of time, with a boldness and complexity far beyond the resources of science. The correlator's mission is to observe and organize the data from Nature's experiments. As a minimum outcome, such correlations improve immediate decisions and guide experimentation. At the best, a Newton, a Lyell, or a Darwin can align the correlations into a substantial theory.

During our century of scientific psychology, the correlators have marched under many flags. In perhaps the first modern discussion of scientific method in psychology (1874), Wundt [54] showed how "experimental psychology" and "ethnic psychology" (i.e., cross-cultural correlations) supplement each other. In one of the most recent (1953), Bindra and Scheier [4] speak of the interplay of "experimental" and "psychometric" method. At the turn of the century, the brand names were "experimental" and "genetic" psychology, although experimenters were also beginning to contrast their "general psychology" with the "individual psychology" of Stern and Binet.

In 1913, Yerkes made the fundamental point that all the correlational psychologies are one. His name for this branch was "comparative psychology."

Although comparative psychology in its completeness necessarily deals with the materials of the psychology of infant, child, adult, whether the being be human or infra-human; of animal or plant [!]— of normal and abnormal individuals; of social groups and of civilizations, there is no reason why specialists in the use of the comparative method should not be so distinguished, and, if it seems necessary, labelled [55].

Even in advocating research on animals [56], Yerkes is emphatic in defining the goal as correlation across species. In France, *la psychologie comparée* continues to include all of differential psychology; but in America, as Beach [2] has lamented, comparative psychology degenerated into the experimental psychology of the white rat and thereby lost the power of the correlational discipline.

Except for the defection of animal psychologists, the correlational psychologists have remained loosely federated. Developmental psychologists, personality psychologists, and differential psychologists have been well acquainted both personally and intellectually. They study the same courses, they draw on the same literature, they join the same divisions of APA.

Experimental and correlational psychologists, however, grew far apart in their training and interests. It is now commonplace for a student to get his PhD in experimental psychology without graduate training in test theory or developmental psychology, and the student of correlational branches can avoid experimental psychology only a little less completely. The journals of one discipline have small influence on the journals of the other [14]. Boring even dares to say [5, p. 578] that there is a personality difference between the fields: the distinction being that correlational psychologists like people!

Certainly the scientific values of psychologists are sharply divided. Thorndike [9, 44] recently asked American psychologists to rate various historic personages by indicating, on a forced-choice questionnaire, which have made the greatest contributions to psychology. A factor analysis of the ratings shows two distinct factors (Figure 2–1). One bipolar factor (irrelevant to our present discussion) ranges from verbal to quantitative psychologists. The other factor has at one pole the laboratory experiment-

ers like Stevens, Dodge, and Ebbinghaus, and at the opposite pole those like Binet, May, and Goodenough who collect and correlate field data. A psychologist's esteem for the experimenters is correlated $-.80$ (-1.00, corrected for attenuation) with his esteem for scientists who use correlational methods.

There was no such schism in 1913 when Yerkes stated the program of correlational psychology. Genetic psychology and experimental psychology were hard at work on the same problems. Terman demonstrated in his 1923 presidential address [43] that the mental test was within the tradition of experimental, fundamental research in psychology, and had quotations to show that the contemporary experimentalists agreed with him. Wells and Goddard, in 1913, had been asked to lecture on mental tests within the Holy Temple itself, the Society of Experimental Psychologists. And, in 1910, the High Priest Titchener had said:

> Individual psychology is one of the chief witnesses to the value of experiment. It furnishes the key to many, otherwise inexplicable differences of result, and it promises to allay many of the outstanding controversies. . . . There can be no doubt that it will play a part of steadily increasing importance [46].

But when Terman spoke in 1923, the common front had already been fatally breached. Watson had announced that experimental treatment could make and unmake individual differences at will, thus stripping them of scientific importance. Thurstone had taken the first firm stride in the opposite direction:

> I suggest that we dethrone the stimulus. He is only nominally the ruler of psychology. The real ruler of the domain which psychology studies is the individual and his motives, desires, wants, ambitions, cravings, aspirations. The stimulus is merely the more or less accidental fact . . . [45, p. 364].

The personality, social, and child psychologists went one way; the perception and

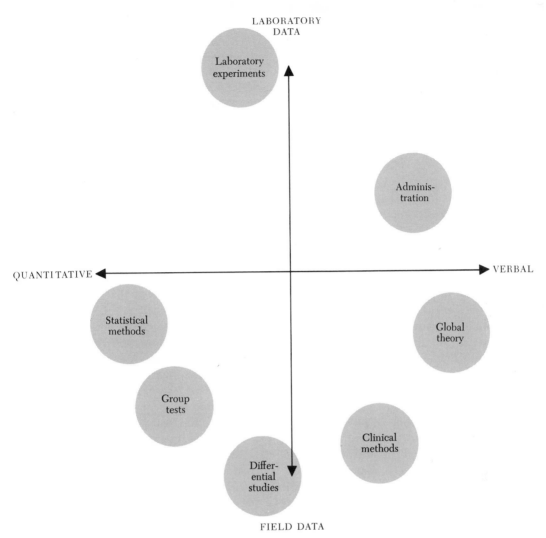

Figure 2–1 *Factors accounting for esteem of leaders in psychology by American psychologists (based on correlations presented by Thorndike [44], corrected for attenuation and refactored).*

learning psychologists went the other; and the country between turned into desert.

During the estrangement of correlational and experimental psychology, antagonism has been notably absent. Disparagement has been pretty well confined to playful remarks like Cattell's accusation that the experimental psychologist's "regard for the body of nature becomes that of the anatomist rather than that of the lover" [7, p. 152], or the experimentalist Bartlett's [1, p. 210] satire on the testers emerging from World War I, "chanting in unaccustomed harmony the words of the old jingle

'God has a plan for every man
And He has one for you.' "

Most correlationists have done a little experimenting in the narrow sense, and experimenters have contributed proudly to testing work under wartime necessity. But these are temporary sojourns in a foreign land. [For clear expressions of this attitude, see 5, pp. 570–578 and 52, p. 24.]

A true federation of the disciplines is required. Kept independent, they can give only wrong answers or no answers at all regarding certain important problems. It is shortsighted to argue for one science to discover the general laws of mind or behavior and for a separate enterprise concerned with individual minds, or for a one-way dependence of personality theory upon learning theory. Consider the physical sciences as a parallel. Physics for centuries was the study of general laws applying to all solids or all gases, whereas alchemy and chemistry studied the properties and reactions of individual substances. Chemistry was once only a descriptive catalogue of substances and analytic techniques. It became a systematic science when organized quantitative studies yielded principles to explain differences between substances and to predict the outcomes of reactions. In consequence, Mendeleev the chemist paved the way for Bohr the physicist, and Fermi's physics contributes to Lawrence's chemistry; the boundary between chemistry and physics has become almost invisible.

The tide of separation in psychology has already turned. The perceiver has reappeared in perceptual psychology. Tested intelligence and anxiety appear as independent variables in many of the current learning experiments. Factor analytic studies have gained a fresh vitality from crossbreeding with classical learning experiments [e.g., 18, 22]. Harlow, Hebb, Hess, and others are creating a truly experimental psychology of development. And students of personality have been designing subtle combinations of experimental and correlational method [see, for example, 29] which may ultimately prove to be our parallel to the emergence of physical chemistry.

CHARACTERIZATION OF THE DISCIPLINES

In the beginning, experimental psychology was a substitute for purely naturalistic observation of man-in-habitat. The experimenter placed man in an artificial, simplified environment and made quantitative observations of his performance. The initial problem was one of describing accurately what man felt, thought, or did in a defined situation. Standardization of tasks and conditions was required to get reproducible descriptions. All experimental procedures were tests, all tests were experiments. Kraepelin's continuous-work procedure served equally the general study of fatigue and the diagnosis of individuals. Reaction time was important equally to Wundt and to Cattell.

The distinctive characteristic of modern experimentation, the statistical comparison of treatments, appeared only around 1900 in such studies as that of Thorndike and Woodworth on transfer. The experimenter, following the path of Ebbinghaus, shifted from measurement of the average mind to measuring the effect of environmental change upon success in a task [51]. Inference replaced estimation: the mean and its probable error gave way to the critical ratio. The standardized conditions and the standardized instruments remained, but the focus shifted to the single manipulated variable, and later, following Fisher, to multivariate manipulation. The experiment thus came to be concerned with between-treatments variance. I use the word "treatment" in a general sense; educational and therapeutic treatments are but one type. Treatment differences are equally involved in comparing rats given different schedules of reinforcement, chicks who have worn different distorting lenses, or social groups arranged with different communication networks.

The second great development in American experimental psychology has been its concern with formal theory. At the turn of the century, theory ranged far ahead of experiment and made no demand that propositions be testable. Experiment, for its part, was willing to observe any phenomenon, whether or not the data bore on theoretical issues. Today, the majority of experimenters derive their hypotheses explicitly from theoretical premises and try to nail their results into a theoretical structure. This deductive style has its undeniable defects, but one can not question the net gains from the accompanying theoretical sophistication. Discussions of the logic of operationism, intervening variables, and mathematical models have sharpened both the formulation of hypotheses and the interpretation of results.

Individual differences have been an annoyance rather than a challenge to the experimenter. His goal is to control behavior, and variation within treatments is proof that he has not succeeded. Individual variation is cast into that outer darkness known as "error variance." For reasons both statistical and philosophical, error variance is to be reduced by any possible device. You turn to animals of a cheap and short-lived species, so that you can use subjects with controlled heredity and controlled experience. You select human subjects from a narrow subculture. You decorticate your subject by cutting neurons or by giving him an environment so meaningless that his unique responses disappear [cf. 25]. You increase the number of cases to obtain stable averages, or you reduce N to 1, as Skinner does. But whatever your device, your goal in the experimental tradition is to get those embarrassing differential variables out of sight.

The correlational psychologist is in love with just those variables the experimenter left home to forget. He regards individual and group variations as important effects of biological and social causes. All organisms adapt to their environments, but not equally well. His question is: what present characteristics of the organism determine its mode and degree of adaptation?

Just as individual variation is a source of embarrassment to the experimenter, so treatment variation attenuates the results of the correlator. His goal is to predict variation within a treatment. His experimental designs demand uniform treatment for every case contributing to a correlation, and treatment variance means only error variance to him.

Differential psychology, like experimen-
tal, began with a purely descriptive phase. Cattell at Hopkins, Galton at South Kensington, were simply asking how much people varied. They were, we might say, estimating the standard deviation while the general psychologists were estimating the central tendency.

The correlation coefficient, invented for the study of hereditary resemblance, transformed descriptive differential research into the study of mental organization. What began as a mere summary statistic quickly became the center of a whole theory of data analysis. Murphy's words, written in 1928, recall the excitement that attended this development:

> The relation between two variables has actually been found to be statable in other terms than those of experiment. . . . [Moreover,] Yule's method of "partial correlation" has made possible the mathematical "isolation" of variables which cannot be isolated experimentally. . . . [Despite the limitations of correlational methods,] what they have already yielded to psychology . . . is nevertheless of such major importance as to lead the writer to the opinion that the only twentieth-century discovery comparable in importance to the conditioned-response method is the method of partial correlations [35, p. 410].

Today's students who meet partial correlation only as a momentary digression from their main work in statistics may find this excitement hard to comprehend. But partial correlation is the starting place for all of factor analysis.

Factor analysis is rapidly being perfected into a rigorous method of clarifying multivariate relationships. Fisher made the experimentalist an expert puppeteer, able to keep untangled the strands to half-a-dozen independent variables. The correlational psychologist is a mere observer of a play where Nature pulls a thousand strings; but his multivariate methods make him equally an expert, an expert in figuring out where to look for the hidden strings.

His sophistication in data analysis has

not been matched by sophistication in theory. The correlational psychologist was led into temptation by his own success, losing himself first in practical prediction, then in a narcissistic program of studying his tests as an end in themselves. A naive operationism enthroned theory of test performance in the place of theory of mental processes. And premature enthusiasm[1] exalted a few measurements chosen almost by accident from the tester's stock as the ruling forces of the mental universe.

In former days, it was the experimentalist who wrote essay after anxious essay defining his discipline and differentiating it from competing ways of studying mind. No doubts plagued correlationists like Hall, Galton, and Cattell. They came in on the wave of evolutionary thought and were buoyed up by every successive crest of social progress or crisis. The demand for universal education, the development of a technical society, the appeals from the distraught twentieth-century parent, and finally the clinical movement assured the correlational psychologist of his great destiny. Contemporary experimentalists, however, voice with ever-increasing assurance their program and social function; and the fact that tonight you have a correlational psychologist discussing disciplinary identities implies that anxiety is now perched on *his* window ledge.

Indeed, I do speak out of concern for correlational psychology. Aptitude tests deserve their fine reputation; but, if practical, validated procedures are to be our point of pride, we must be dissatisfied with our progress since 1920. As the Executive Committee of Division 5 itself declared this year, none of our latter-day refinements or innovations has improved practical predictions by a noticeable amount. Correlational psychologists who found their self-esteem upon contributions to theory can point to monumental investigations such as the *Studies of Character* and *The Authoritarian*

Personality. Such work does throw strong light upon the human scene and brings important facts clearly into view. But theories to organize these facts are rarely offered and even more rarely solidified [30; 31, p. 55].

POTENTIAL CONTRIBUTIONS OF THE DISCIPLINES TO ONE ANOTHER

Perhaps it is inevitable that a powerful new method will become totally absorbing and crowd other thoughts from the minds of its followers. It took a generation of concentrated effort to move from Spearman's tetrad equation and Army Alpha to our present view of the ability domain. It took the full energies of other psychologists to move from S-R bonds to modern behavior theory. No doubt the tendency of correlationists to ignore experimental developments is explained by their absorption in the wonders and complexities of the phenomena their own work was revealing. And if experimentalists were to be accused of narrowminded concentration on one particular style and topic of research, the same comment would apply.

The spell these particular theories and methods cast upon us appears to have passed. We are free at last to look up from our own bedazzling treasure, to cast properly covetous glances upon the scientific wealth of our neighbor discipline. Trading has already been resumed, with benefit to both parties.

The introduction of construct validation into test theory [12] is a prime example. The history of this development, you may recall, was that the APA's Committee on Psychological Tests discovered that available test theory recognized no way of determining whether a proposed psychological interpretation of a test was sound. The only existing theory dealt with criterion validation and could not evaluate claims that a test measured certain psychological traits or states. Meehl, capitalizing on the methodological and philosophical progress

---

[1] This judgment is not mine alone; it is the clear consensus of the factor analysts themselves [see 28, pp. 321–325].

of the experimenters, met the testers' need by suggesting the idea of construct validity. A proposed test interpretation, he showed, is a claim that a test measures a construct, i.e., a claim that the test score can be linked to a theoretical network. This network, together with the claim, generates predictions about observations. The test interpretation is justified only if the observations come out as predicted. To decide how well a purported test of anxiety measures anxiety, construct validation is necessary; i.e., we must find out whether scores on the test behave in accordance with the theory that defines anxiety. This theory predicts differences in anxiety between certain groups, and traditional correlational methods can test those predictions. But the theory also predicts variation in anxiety, hence in the test score, as a function of experience or situations, and only an experimental approach can test those predictions.

This new theory of validity has several very broad consequences. It gives the tester a start toward the philosophical sophistication the experimenter has found so illuminating. It establishes the experimental method as a proper and necessary means of validating tests. And it re-establishes research on tests as a valuable and even indispensable way of extending psychological theory.

We may expect the test literature of the future to be far less saturated with correlations of tests with psychologically enigmatic criteria, and far richer in studies which define test variables by their responsiveness to practice at different ages, to drugs, to altered instructions, and to other experimentally manipulated variables. A pioneering venture in this direction is Fleishman's revealing work [21, 22] on changes in the factorial content of motor skills as a function of practice. These studies go far beyond a mere exploration of certain tests; as Ferguson has shown [19, 20], they force upon us a theory which treats abilities as a product of learning, and a theory of learning in which previously acquired abilities play a major role.

Perhaps the most valuable trading goods the correlator can offer in return is his multivariate conception of the world.

No experimenter would deny that situations and responses are multifaceted, but rarely are his procedures designed for a systematic multivariate analysis. The typical experimental design and the typical experimental law employ a single dependent variable. Even when more than one outcome is measured, the outcomes are analyzed and interpreted separately. No response measure, however, is an adequate measure of a psychological construct. Every score mixes general construct-relevant variance with variance specific to the particular measuring operation. It is all right for the agriculturist to consider size of crop as the fundamental variable being observed: that is the payoff for him. Our task, however, is to study changes in fundamental aspects of behavior, and these are evidenced only indirectly in any one measure of outcome.

The correlational psychologist discovered long ago that no observed criterion is truly valid and that simultaneous consideration of many criteria is needed for a satisfactory evaluation of performance. This same principle applies in experimentation. As Neal Miller says in a recent paper on experiments with drugs:

> Where there are relatively few facts it seems easy to account for them by a few simple generalizations. . . . As we begin to study the effects of a variety of drugs on a number of different behavioral measures, exceptions and complexities emerge. We are forced to reexamine and perhaps abandon common-sense categories of generalization according to convenient words existing in the English language. As new and more comprehensive patterns of results become available, however, new and more precise generalizations may emerge. We may be able to "carve nature better to the joint" and achieve the simplicity of a much more exact and powerful science [32, pp. 326–327].

Theoretical progress is obstructed when one restricts himself to a single measure of response [34]. Where there is only one dependent variable, it is pointless to introduce intervening variables or constructs. When there are many response variables, however, it is mandatory to subsume them under constructs, since otherwise we must have a separate set of laws for every measure of outcome. Dealing with multiple response variables is, as Miller says [33], precisely the problem with which the factor analysts have been concerned. Factor analysis, by substituting formal for intuitive methods, has been of great help in locating constructs with which to summarize observations about abilities. It is reasonable to expect that multivariate treatment of response measures would have comparable value in experimental psychology.

Experimenters very probably have even more to gain from treating *in*dependent variables as a continuous multivariate system. The manifold treatment categories in a Fisherian design are established a priori. In agriculture, the treatment dimensions the farmer can manipulate are obvious: fertilizer, water, species of seed, and so on. In a more basic science, we require genotypic constructs to describe situations, constructs like the physical scientist's temperature and pressure. The conditions the psychologist most easily manipulates—stimulus form, injunction to the subject, strength of electric shock—are not chosen because we intend to apply these specific conditions when we get around to "controlling behavior." They are used because these conditions, we hope, embody scientifically useful constructs.

The experimenter has no systematic way to classify and integrate results from different tasks or different reinforcers. As Ferguson remarks [20, p. 130; see also 19, p. 100]: "No satisfactory methodology has emerged for describing particular learning tasks, or indicating how one task differs from another, other than by a process of simple inspection." We depend wholly on the creative flair of the theorist to collate the experiments and to invent constructs which might describe particular situations,

reinforcements, or injunctions in terms of more fundamental variables. The multivariate techniques of psychometrics are suited for precisely this task of grouping complex events into homogeneous classes or organizing them along major dimensions. These methods are frankly heuristic, but they are systematically heuristic. They select variables with minimal redundancy, and they permit us to obtain maximum information from a minimum of experimental investment.

In suggesting that examining treatment conditions as a statistical universe is a possible way to advance experimental thinking, I am of course echoing the recommendations of Egon Brunswik [6, esp. pp. 39–58]. Brunswik criticized the Fisherian experimenter for his ad hoc selection of treatments and recommended that he apply the sampling principles of differential psychology in choosing stimuli and conditions. A sampling procedure such as Brunswik suggests will often be a forward step, but the important matter is not to establish laws which apply loosely to a random, unorganized collection of situations. The important matter is to discover the organization among the situations, so that we can describe situational differences as systematically as we do individual differences.

Research on stress presents a typical problem of organization. Multivariate psychophysiological data indicate that different taxing situations have different effects. At present, stressors can be described and classified only superficially, by inspection. A correlational or distance analysis of the data groups treatments which have similar effects and ultimately permits us to locate each treatment within a continuous multidimensional structure having constructs as reference axes. Data from a recent study by Wenger, Clemens, and Engel [50] may be used as an illustration. Figure 2–2 shows the means of standardized physiological scores under four different stress conditions: mental arithmetic, a letter association test, hyperventilation, and a cold pressor. The "profiles" for the four conditions are

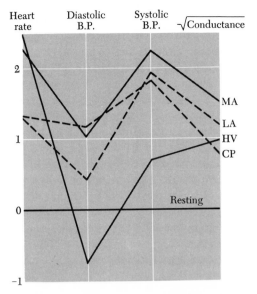

Figure 2–2 *Mean response to four stressors expressed in terms of resting standard scores [data from 50].*

very significantly different. I have made a distance analysis to examine the similarity between conditions, with the results diagrammed in Figure 2–3. There is a general factor among all the treatments, which distinguishes them from the resting state, and a notable group factor among three of them. According to these data, a mental test seems to induce the same physiological state as plunging one's foot into ice water!

Figure 2–3 *Multivariate diagram showing similarity between four stressors.*

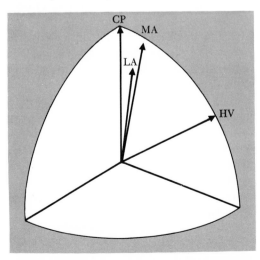

Much larger bodies of data are of course needed to map the treatment space properly. But the aptness of an attempt in this direction will be apparent to all who heard Selye's address to the APA last year. His argument [40] that all stressful situations lead to a similar syndrome of physiological changes is strongly reminiscent of Spearman's argument regarding a general factor linking intellectual responses. The disagreement between Selye and other students of stress clearly reduces to a quantitative question of the relative size of specific and nonspecific or general factors in the effects of typical stressors.

APPLIED PSYCHOLOGY DIVIDED AGAINST ITSELF

Let us leave for the moment questions of academic psychology and consider the schism as it appears in applied psychology. In applied psychology, the two disciplines are in active conflict; and unless they bring their efforts into harmony, they can hold each other to a standstill. The conflict is especially obvious at this moment in the challenge the young engineering psychology offers to traditional personnel psychology.

The program of applied experimental psychology is to modify treatments so as to obtain the highest average performance when all persons are treated alike—a search, that is, for "the one best way." The program of applied correlational psychology is to raise average performance by treating persons differently—different job assignments, different therapies, different disciplinary methods. The correlationist is utterly antagonistic to a doctrine of "the one best way," whether it be the heartless robot-making of Frederick Taylor or a doctrinaire permissiveness which tries to give identical encouragement to every individual. The ideal of the engineering psychologist, I am told, is to simplify jobs so that every individual in the working population will be able to perform them satisfactorily, i.e., so that differentiation of treatment will be unnecessary. This goal guides activities ranging from the sober to the bizarre: from E. L. Thorndike and Skinner, hunting the one best sequence of problems for teaching arithmetic, to Rudolf Flesch and his admirers, reducing *Paradise Lost* to a comic book. If the engineering psychologist succeeds: information rates will be so reduced that the most laggard of us can keep up, visual displays will be so enlarged that the most myopic can see them, automatic feedback will prevent the most accident-prone from spoiling the work or his fingers.

Obviously, with every inch of success the engineer has, the tester must retreat a mile. A slight reduction in information rate, accomplished once, reduces forever the validity and utility of a test of ability to process data. If, once the job is modified, the myopic worker can perform as well as the man with 20/20 vision, Snellen charts and orthoraters are out of business. Nor is the threat confined to the industrial scene. If tranquilizers make everybody happy, why bother to diagnose patients to determine which treatments they should have? And if televised lessons can simplify things so that every freshman will enjoy and understand quantum mechanics, we will need neither college aptitude tests nor final examinations.

It is not my intention to warn testers about looming unemployment. If test technology is not greatly improved, long before the applied experimentalists near their goals, testing deserves to disappear. My message is my belief that the conflicting principles of the tester and the experimenter can be fused into a new and integrated applied psychology.

To understand the present conflict in purposes, we must look again at historical antecedents. Pastore [36] argues with much justice that the testers and classifiers have been political conservatives, while those who try to find the best common treatment for all — particularly in education — have been the liberals. This essential conservatism of personnel psychology traces back to the days of Darwin and Spencer.

The theory of evolution inspired two antagonistic movements in social thought [10, 42]. Darwin and Herbert Spencer were real determinists. The survival of the fittest, as a law of Nature, guaranteed man's superiority and the ultimate triumph of the natural aristocrats among men. As Dewey put it, Spencer saw "a rapid transit system of evolution . . . carrying us automatically to the goal of perfect man in perfect society" [17, p. 66]. Men vary in their power of adaptation, and institutions, by demanding adaptation, serve as instruments of natural selection among men. The essence of freedom is seen as the freedom to compete for survival. To Spencer, to Galton, and to their successors down to the present day, the successful are those who have the greatest adjustive capacity. The psychologist's job, in this tradition, is to facilitate or anticipate natural selection. He seeks only to reduce its cruelty and wastage by predicting who will survive in schools and other institutions as they are. He takes the system for granted and tries to identify who will fit into it. His devices have a conservative influence because they identify persons who will succeed in the existing institution. By reducing failures, they remove a challenge which might otherwise force the institution to change [49].

The experimental scientist inherits an interpretation of evolution associated with the names of Ward, James, and Dewey. For them, man's progress rests on his intelligence; the great struggle for survival is a struggle against environment, not against competitors. Intelligent man must reshape his environment, not merely conform to it. This spirit, the very antithesis of Spencerian laissez-faire, bred today's experimental social science which accepts no institution and no tradition as sacred. The individual is seen as inherently self-directing and creative. One cannot hope to predict how he will meet his problems, and applied differential psychology is therefore pointless [39, p. 37].

Thus we come to have one psychology which accepts the institution, its treatment, and its criterion and finds men to fit the institution's needs. The other psychology takes man—generalized man—as given and challenges any institution which does not conform to the measure of this standard man.

A clearer view of evolution removes the paradox:

> The entire significance of the evolutionary method in biology and social history is that every distinct organ, structure, or formation, every grouping of cells or elements, has to be treated as an instrument of adjustment or adaptation to a particular environing situation. Its meaning, its character, its value, is known when, and only when, it is considered as an arrangement for meeting the conditions involved in some specific situation [16, p. 15].

We are not on the right track when we conceive of adjustment or adjustive capacity in the abstract. It is always a capacity to respond to a particular treatment. The organism which adapts well under one condition would not survive under another. If for each environment there is a best organism, for every organism there is a best environment. The job of applied psychology is to improve decisions about people. The greatest social benefit will come from applied psychology if we can find for each individual the treatment to which he can most easily adapt. This calls for the joint application of experimental and correlational methods.

INTERACTION OF TREATMENT AND INDIVIDUAL IN PRACTICAL DECISIONS

Goldine Gleser and the writer have recently published a theoretical analysis [11] which shows that neither the traditional predictive model of the correlator nor the traditional experimental comparison of mean differences is an adequate formulation of the decisions confronting the applied psychologist. Let me attempt to give a telescoped version of the central argument.

The decision maker has to determine

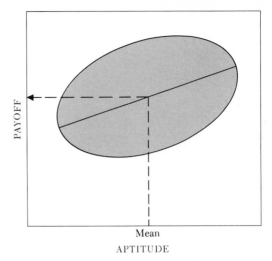

Figure 2–4   *Scatter diagram and payoff function showing outcome as a function of individual differences.*

what treatment shall be used for each individual or each group of individuals. Psychological data help a college, for example, select students to be trained as scientists. The aim of any decision maker is to maximize expected payoff. There is a payoff function relating outcome (e.g., achievement in science) to aptitude dimensions for any particular treatment. Figure 2–4 shows such a function for a single aptitude. Average payoff—if everyone receives the treatment—is indicated by the arrow. The experimentalist assumes a fixed population and hunts for the treatment with the highest average and the least variability. The correlationist assumes a fixed treatment and hunts for aptitudes which maximize the slope of the payoff function. In academic selection, he advises admission of students with high scores on a relevant aptitude and thus raises payoff for the institution (Figure 2–5).

Pure selection, however, almost never occurs. The college aptitude test may seem to be intended for a selection decision; and, insofar as the individual college is concerned only with those it accepts, the conventional validity coefficient does indicate the best test. But from a societal point of view, the rejects will also go on into other social institutions, and their profit from this treatment must be weighed in the balance

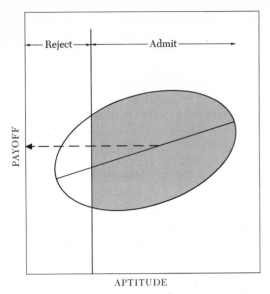

Figure 2–5   *Increase in payoff as a result of selection.*

along with the profit or social contribution from the ones who enter college. Every decision is really a choice between treatments. Predicting outcome has no social value unless the psychologist or the subject himself can use the information to make better choices of treatment. The prediction must help to determine a treatment for every individual.

Figure 2–6   *Payoff functions for two treatments.*

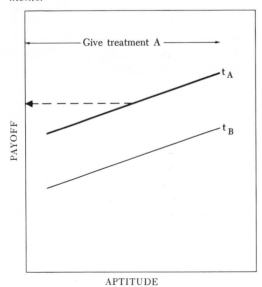

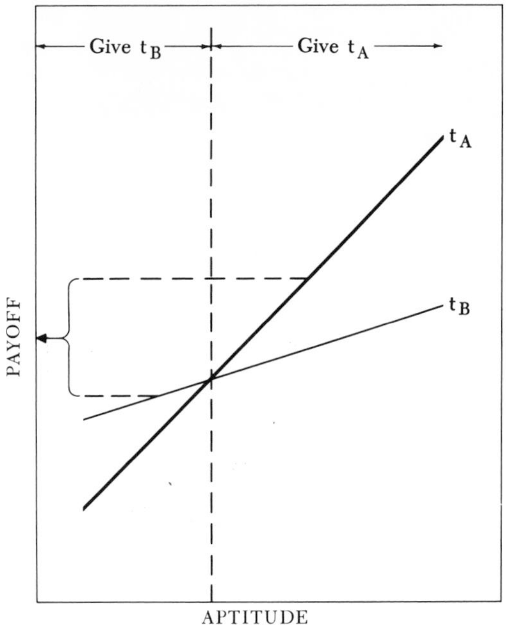

Figure 2–7   *Payoff functions for two treatments.*

Even when there are just two treatments, the payoff functions have many possible relationships. In Figure 2–6 we have a mean difference between treatments, and a valid predictor. The predictor—though valid—is useless. We should give everyone Treatment A. In Figure 2–7, on the other hand, we should divide the group and give different treatments. This gives greater payoff than either treatment used uniformly will give.

Assigning everyone to the treatment with the highest average, as the experimentalist tends to recommend, is rarely the best decision. In Figure 2–8, Treatment C has the best average, and we might assign everyone to it. The outcome is greater, however, if we assign some persons to each treatment. The psychologist making an experimental comparison arrives at the wrong conclusion if he ignores the aptitude variable and recommends C as a standard treatment.

Applied psychologists should deal with treatments and persons simultaneously. Treatments are characterized by many dimensions; so are persons. The two sets of

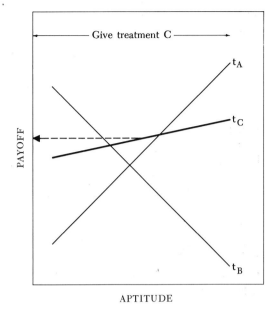

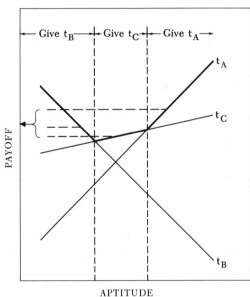

Figure 2–8 *Payoff functions for three treatments.*

dimensions together determine a payoff surface. For any practical problem, there is some best group of treatments to use and some best allocation of persons to treatments. We can expect some attributes of persons to have strong interactions with treatment variables. These attributes have far greater practical importance than the attributes which have little or no interaction. In dividing pupils between college preparatory and noncollege studies, for example, a general intelligence test is probably the wrong thing to use. This test, being general, predicts success in all subjects, therefore tends to have little interaction with treatment, and if so is not the best guide to differential treatment. We require a measure of aptitude which predicts who will learn better from one curriculum than from the other; but this aptitude remains to be discovered. Ultimately we should *design* treatments, not to fit the average person, but to fit groups of students with particular aptitude patterns. Conversely, we should seek out the aptitudes which correspond to (interact with) modifiable aspects of the treatment.

My argument rests on the assumption that such aptitude-treatment interactions exist. There is, scattered in the literature, a remarkable amount of evidence of significant, predictable differences in the way people learn. We have only limited success in predicting which of two *tasks* a person can perform better, when we allow enough training to compensate for differences in past attainment. But we do find that a person learns more easily from one *method* than another, that this best method differs from person to person, and that such between-treatments differences are correlated with tests of ability and personality. The studies showing interaction between personality and conditions of learning have burgeoned in the past few years, and the literature is much too voluminous to review in passing. Just one recent finding will serve in the way of specific illustration, a study done by Wolfgang Böhm at Vienna [38, pp. 58–59]. He showed his experimental groups a sound film about the adventures of a small boy and his toy elephant at the zoo. At each age level, a matched control group read a verbatim text of the sound track. The differences in average comprehension between the audiovisual and the text presentations were trivial. There was, however, a marked interaction. For some reason yet unexplained, a general mental test correlated only .30 with text learning, but it predicted film learning with an average correlation of .77.[2] The difference was consistent at all ages.

Such findings as this, when replicated and explained, will carry us into an educational psychology which measures readiness for different types of teaching and which invents teaching methods to fit different types of readiness. In general, unless one treatment is clearly best for everyone, treatments should be differentiated in such a way as to maximize their interaction with aptitude variables. Conversely, persons should be allocated on the basis of those aptitudes which have the greatest interaction with treatment variables. I believe we will find these aptitudes to be quite unlike our present aptitude measures chosen to predict differences *within* highly correlated treatments.

THE SHAPE OF A UNITED DISCIPLINE

It is not enough for each discipline to borrow from the other. Correlational psychology studies only variance among organisms; experimental psychology studies only variance among treatments. A united discipline will study both of these, but it will also be concerned with the otherwise neglected interactions between organismic and treatment variables [41]. Our job is to invent constructs and to form a network of laws which permits prediction. From observations we must infer a psychological description of the situation and of the present state of the organism. Our laws should permit us to predict, from this description, the behavior of organism-in-situation.

There was a time when experimental psychologists concerned themselves wholly with general, nonindividual constructs, and correlational psychologists sought laws wholly within developmental variables. More and more, nowadays, their investigations are coming to bear on the same targets. One psychologist measures ego in-

volvement by a personality test and compares the behavior of high- and low-scoring subjects. Another psychologist heightens ego involvement experimentally in one of two equated groups and studies the consequent differences in behavior. Both investigators can test the same theoretical propositions, and to the extent that their results agree they may regard both procedures as embodiments of the same construct.

Constructs originating in differential psychology are now being tied to experimental variables. As a result, the whole theoretical picture in such an area as human abilities is changing. Piaget [37] correlates reasoning processes with age and discovers a developmental sequence of schemata whose emergence permits operational thought; Harlow [24] begins actually to create similar schemata in monkeys by means of suitable training. It now becomes possible to pursue in the controllable monkey environment the questions raised by Piaget's unique combination of behavioral testing and interviewing, and ultimately to unite the psychology of intelligence with the psychology of learning.

Methodologies for a joint discipline have already been proposed. R. B. Cattell [8] has offered the most thorough discussion of how a correlationist might organize data about treatment and organism simultaneously. His factor analytic procedures are only one of many choices, however, which modern statistics offers. The experimenters, some of them, have likewise seen the necessity for a united discipline. In the very issue of *Psychological Review* where the much-too-famous distinction between *S-R* and *R-R* laws was introduced, Bergmann and Spence [3] declared that (at the present stage of psychological knowledge) the equation $R = f(S)$ must be expanded into

$$R = f(S, T, D, I)$$

The added variables are innate differences, motivation, and past experience—differential variables all. Hull [26, 27] sought general laws just as did Wundt, but he added

---

[2] Personal communication.

that organismic factors can and must be accounted for. He proposed to do this by changing the constants of his equations with each individual. This is a bold plan, but one which has not yet been implemented in even a limited way. It is of interest that both Hull [27, p. 116] and Tolman [47, p. 26] have stated specifically that for their purposes factor analytic methods seem to have little promise. Tucker, though, has at least drawn blueprints of a method for deriving Hull's own individual parameters by factor analysis [48]. Clearly, we have much to learn about the most suitable way to develop a united theory, but we have no lack of exciting possibilities.

The experimenter tends to keep his eye on *ultimate* theory. Woodworth once described psychological laws in terms of the *S-O-R* formula which specifically recognizes the individual. The revised version of his *Experimental Psychology* [53, p. 3], however, advocates an *S-A-R* formula, where *A* stands for "antecedent conditions." This formulation, which is generally congenial to experimenters, reduces the present state of the organism to an intervening variable (Figure 2–9). A theory of this type is in principle entirely adequate to explain, predict, and control the behavior of organisms; but, oddly enough, it is a theory which can account only for the behavior of organisms of the next generation, who have not yet been conceived. The psychologist turns to a different type of law (Figure 2–10) whenever he deals with a subject whose life history he has not controlled or

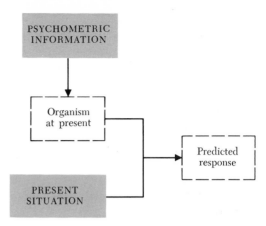

Figure 2–10 *Theoretical model for prediction from ahistoric data.*

observed in every detail. A theory which involves only laws of this type, while suitable for prediction, has very limited explanatory value. The theory psychology really requires is a redundant network like Figure 2–11. This network permits us to predict from the past experience or present characteristics of the organism, or a combination of the two, depending on what is known. Filling in such a network is clearly a task for the joint efforts of experimental and correlational psychology.

In both applied work and general scientific work, psychology requires combined, not parallel, labors from our two historic disciplines. In this common labor, they will

Figure 2–11 *Theoretical network to be developed by a united discipline.*

Figure 2–9 *Theoretical model for prediction from historic data.*

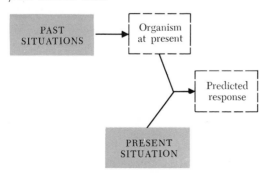

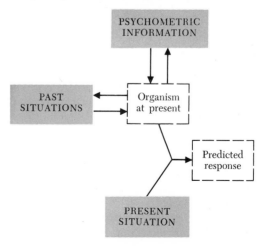

almost certainly become one, with a common theory, a common method, and common recommendations for social betterment. In the search for interactions we will invent new treatment dimensions and discover new dimensions of the organism. We will come to realize that organism and treatment are an inseparable pair and that no psychologist can dismiss one or the other as error variance.

Despite our specializations, every scientific psychologist must take the same scene into his field of vision. Clark Hull, three sentences before the end of his *Essentials of Behavior* [27, p. 116], voiced just this need. Because of delay in developing methodology, he said, individual differences have played little part in behavior theory, and "a sizeable segment of behavioral science remains practically untouched." This untouched segment contains the question we really want to put to Nature, and she will never answer until our two disciplines ask it in a single voice.

REFERENCES

1. BARTLETT, F. C. Fifty years of psychology. *Occup. Psychol.*, 1955, 29, 203–216.
2. BEACH, F. A. The snark was a boojum. *Amer. Psychologist*, 1950, 5, 115–124.
3. BERGMANN, G., & SPENCE, K. W. The logic of psychophysical measurement. *Psychol. Rev.*, 1944, 51, 1–24.
4. BINDRA, D., & SCHEIER, I. H. The relation between psychometric and experimental research in psychology. *Amer. Psychologist*, 1954, 9, 69–71.
5. BORING, E. G. *History of experimental psychology.* (2nd ed.) New York: Appleton-Century-Crofts, 1950.
6. BRUNSWIK, E. *Perception and the representative design of psychological experiments.* Berkeley: Univer. California Press, 1956.
7. CATTELL, J. McK. The biological problems of today: Psychology. *Science*, 1898, 7, 152–154.
8. CATTELL, R. B. *Factor analysis.* New York: Harper, 1952.
9. CLARK, K. E. *America's psychologists.* Washington, D.C.: APA, 1957.
10. CORWIN, E. S. The impact of the idea of evolution on the American political and constitutional tradition. In S. PERSONS (Ed.), *Evolutionary thought in America.* New Haven: Yale Univer. Press, 1950. Pp. 182–201.
11. CRONBACH, L. J., & GLESER, GOLDINE C. *Psychological tests and personnel decisions.* Urbana: Univer. Illinois Press, 1957.
12. CRONBACH, L. J., & MEEHL, P. E. Construct validity in psychological tests. *Psychol. Bull.*, 1955, 52, 281–302.
13. CRONBACH, L. J., & NEFF, W. D. Selection and training. In Com. on Undersea Warfare Panel on Psychology and Physiology, *Human Factors in Undersea Warfare.* Washington, D.C.: Nat. Res. Coun., 1949. Pp. 491–516.
14. DANIEL, R. S., & LOUTTIT, C. M. *Professional problems in psychology.* New York: Prentice-Hall, 1953.
15. DASHIELL, J. F. Some rapprochements in contemporary psychology. *Psychol. Bull.*, 1939, 36, 1–24.
16. DEWEY, J. *Studies in logical theory.* Chicago: Univer. Chicago Press, 1903.
17. DEWEY, J. *The influence of Darwin on philosophy and other essays.* New York: Holt, 1910.
18. EYSENCK, H. J. Reminiscence, drive, and personality theory. *J. abnorm. soc. Psychol.*, 1956, 53, 328–333.
19. FERGUSON, G. A. On learning and human ability. *Canad. J. Psychol.*, 1954, 8, 95–112.
20. FERGUSON, G. A. On transfer and human ability. *Canad. J. Psychol.*, 1956, 10, 121–131.
21. FLEISHMAN, E. A. Predicting advanced levels of proficiency in psychomotor skills. In *Proc. Sympos. on Human Engng.* Washington, D.C.: Nat. Acad. Sci., 1956. Pp. 142–151.
22. FLEISHMAN, E. A., & HEMPEL, W. E., JR. Changes in factor structure of a complex psychomotor test as a function of practice. *Psychometrika*, 1954, 19, 239–252.
23. FORD, C. S., & BEACH, F. A. *Patterns of sexual behavior.* New York: Harper, 1952.
24. HARLOW, H. F. The formation of learning sets. *Psychol. Rev.*, 1949, 56, 51–65.
25. HARLOW, H. F. Mice, men, monkeys, and motives. *Psychol. Rev.*, 1953, 60, 23–32.
26. HULL, C. L. The place of innate individ-

ual and species differences in a natural-science theory of behavior. *Psychol. Rev.*, 1945, *52*, 55–60.

27. HULL, C. L. *Essentials of behavior.* New Haven: Yale Univer. Press, 1951.

28. LAUGIER, H. (Ed.) *L'analyse factorielle et ses applications.* Paris: Centre National de la Recherche Scientifique, 1955.

29. LAZARUS, R. S., & BAKER, R. W. Personality and psychological stress—a theoretical and methodological framework. *Psychol. Newsletter,* 1956, *8,* 21–32.

30. McCANDLESS, B. R., & SPIKER, C. C. Experimental research in child psychology. *Child Develpm.,* 1956, *27,* 75–80.

31. McCLELLAND, D. C. Personality. In P. R. FARNSWORTH (Ed.) *Annu. Rev. Psychol., 1956.* Stanford: Annual Reviews, 1956. Pp. 39–62.

32. MILLER, N. E. Effects of drugs on motivation: The value of using a variety of measures. *Ann. N.Y. Acad. Sci.,* 1956, *65,* 318–333.

33. MILLER, N. E. Liberalization of basic S-R concepts: Extensions to conflict behavior and social learning. In S. KOCH (Ed.), *Psychology: A study of a science.* Vol. II. *General systematic formulations, learning, and special processes.* New York: McGraw-Hill, 1959, 196–293.

34. MILLER, N. E. Objective techniques for studying motivational effects of drugs on animals. In E. TRABUCCHI (Ed.), *Proc. Int. Sympos. on Psychotropic Drugs.* Amsterdam, Netherlands: Elsevier Publishing Co.

35. MURPHY, G. *An historical introduction to modern psychology.* (3rd ed.) New York: Harcourt, Brace, 1932.

36. PASTORE, N. *The nature-nurture controversy.* New York: Kings Crown Press, 1949.

37. PIAGET, J. *Psychology of intelligence.* M. PIERCY and D. E. BERLYNE (Trans.). London: Routledge and Kegan Paul, 1950.

38. ROHRACHER, H. Aus der wissenschaftlichen Arbeit des Psychologischen Institutes der Universität Wien. *Wiener Z. Phil., Psychol., Pädag.,* 1956, *6,* 1–66.

39. SCOON, R. The rise and impact of evolutionary ideas. In S. PERSONS (Ed.), *Evolutionary thought in America.* New Haven, Yale Univer. Press, 1950. Pp. 4–43.

40. SELYE, H. Stress and disease. *Science,* 1955, *122,* 625–631.

41. SHEN, E. The place of individual differences in experimentation. In Q. McNEMAR and M. A. MERRILL (Eds.), *Studies in personality.* New York: McGraw-Hill, 1942. Pp. 259–283.

42. SPENGLER, J. J. Evolutionism in American economics. In S. PERSONS (Ed.), *Evolutionary thought in America.* New Haven: Yale Univer. Press, 1950. Pp. 202–266.

43. TERMAN, L. M. The mental test as a psychological method. *Psychol. Rev.,* 1924, *31,* 93–117.

44. THORNDIKE, R. L. The psychological value systems of psychologists. *Amer. psychologist,* 1954, *9,* 787–790.

45. THURSTONE, L. L. The stimulus-response fallacy in psychology. *Psychol. Rev.,* 1923, *30,* 354–369.

46. TITCHENER, E. B. The past decade in experimental psychology. *Amer. J. Psychol.,* 1910, *21,* 404–421.

47. TOLMAN, E. C. The determinants of behavior at a choice point. *Psychol. Rev.,* 1938, *45,* 1–41.

48. TUCKER, L. R. Determination of parameters of a functional relation by factor analysis. *Research Bulletin* 55–10. Princeton, N.J.: Educational Testing Service, 1955.

49. TYLER, R. W. Can intelligence tests be used to predict educability? In K. EELLS et al., *Intelligence and cultural differences.* Chicago: Univer. Chicago Press, 1951. Pp. 39–47.

50. WENGER, M. A., CLEMENS, T. L., & ENGEL, B. T. Autonomic response patterns to four stimuli. Unpublished manuscript, 1957.

51. WOODWORTH, R. S. *Dynamic psychology.* New York: Holt, 1918.

52. WOODWORTH, R. S. *Experimental psychology.* New York: Holt, 1938.

53. WOODWORTH, R. S., & SCHLOSBERG, H. *Experimental psychology.* (2nd ed.). New York: Holt, 1954.

54. WUNDT, W. *Principles of physiological psychology.* Vol. 1. (5th ed.) E. B. TITCHENER (Trans.). New York: Macmillan, 1904.

55. YERKES, R. M. Comparative psychology: A question of definitions. *J. Phil. Psychol., and sci. Methods,* 1913, *10,* 580–582.

56. YERKES, R. M. The study of human behavior. *Science,* 1914, *29,* 625–633.

2 ~

THE LOGIC
OF ASSESSMENT

The period since 1950 has witnessed an increasing emphasis upon the logical foundation of assessment. New and fundamentally different conceptions of measurement, reliability, validity, and test theory have transformed the nature of psychological testing and its relation to psychological theory. What was primarily a "psychotechnology" (to borrow Loevinger's term) based largely upon *ad hoc* considerations of empirical validity, prediction, and the like has developed into an emerging science of assessment. While the applications of psychological tests continue to expand, systematic interest has more recently centered upon the use of test scores in the service of psychological theory. The use of tests to facilitate the *understanding* of psychological processes has thus displaced the *prediction* of criteria as a primary goal.

In the first chapter in this part, the late Irving Lorge probes deeply into the meaning of the term "to measure." Lorge carefully reviews interpretations of fundamental counting operations and the rules and logic whereby these operations may be considered isomorphic with latent psychological variables or constructs. As indicated in the Preface, we used the term "assessment" in the title of this book to imply a broader scope for the subject matter than that usually suggested by the restricted connotations of the term "measurement." We thus wished to encompass explicitly within the proper domain of human assessment several diverse forms of evaluation, including classification. But the evaluation of even the most informal kind of assessment, like the clinical interview, must depend upon some sort of counting operation. In a sense, then, informal classificatory procedures and other "broad-band" techniques may be considered to be processes that, at least in principle if not in fact, rest upon a formal model of measurement. It is in this sense that Lorge's essay on the fundamental nature of measurement is relevant and basic to a wide range of assessment problems.

In the next chapter, Cronbach and Meehl develop in some detail the concept of construct validity, a term introduced in the 1952 *Technical Recommendations for Psychological Tests and Diagnostic Techniques*. In contrast to the more familiar concepts of *content, concurrent*, and *predictive* validity, the process of construct validation links a particular test to a more general trait or theoretical construct, which itself may be embedded in a more comprehensive theoretical network. Rather than treating validity only in terms of one or more correlation coefficients with specific criterion measures, test validation in this framework becomes integrated with hypothesis testing and with the traditional means by which scientific theories are evaluated.

The next chapter, which consists of Jane Loevinger's classic monograph, argues not only that test and theory validation ought to go hand in hand but that tests, if they are to represent instruments of psychological theory, must be developed systematically in terms of that theory. The validation process implies a program of test development in which substantive theory plays a dominant role at every stage of the process, from definition of variables and item writing to evaluation of the test's structural properties and external validity. In this analysis, Loevinger shows little patience with approaches that allow test developers refuge in mechanical, *ad hoc* procedures like empirical item selection.

In an important explication of the validational problem, Campbell and Fiske next propose that the evaluation of validity requires a kind of triangulation using more than one trait and more than one method. This approach allows one to rule out irrelevant variance so as better to identify the convergence of valid variance. In a critique of the construct-validity conception in Chapter 7, Harold P. Bechtoldt maintains that the traditional wisdom of assessment should not be abandoned. In Chapter 8, Donald T. Campbell provides a set of practical recommendations for test standards, translating recent developments into concrete proposals for test evaluation. In the final chapter in Part 2, Rokeach and Bartley succinctly distinguish correlation from causality and discuss some pitfalls in leaping from observed response consistencies to psychological theorizing.

Chapter 3

The Fundamental Nature of Measurement

IRVING LORGE

COLLABORATORS: LEE J. CRONBACH
DOUGLAS E. SCATES / LEDYARD TUCKER

"Measure" is one of the thousand most common words in printed English. As is usual with words that have had a long history and wide currency, "measure" has many different meanings and applications. In a count of its occurrence in a sample of two and a half million words, "measure" occurred more than four hundred times and was used in forty different ways.

In a basic study of usage, the primary senses of "measure," as a noun, referred to all of these: the process of, the result of, the instrument for, and the units used in, measuring. Not only did "measure" mean the act or the process of determining the extent, duration, and dimensions of a thing, but it also meant the instrument by which the process is done; the units in which the instruments are graduated; and the results of the act itself. This single word does mean, then, the act of weighing, the balance in which weighing is done, or, again, the grams that are used to balance, and the

This article is reprinted from *Educational Measurement,* E. F. Lindquist (Ed.), 1951, with the permission of the American Council on Education.

numeral that expresses the result; it can mean the process of measuring, the ruler that is used, the inches in which it is graduated, and the number that gives the over-all length.

The word "measure," in addition, refers to less exact instruments, processes, and units. Among the forty meanings, it was used also to refer to any instrument used as a basis for comparison even when that comparison involved the processes of estimation or judgment. As used popularly, "measure" not only refers to procedures that have precision, but also to acts of objective estimation. "Measure" refers to the determination of the charge on the electron and also to the estimation of beauty; it refers to the determination of the weight of an automobile and also to the estimation of an individual's intelligence. "Measure" more frequently refers to acts of subjective estimate of amounts or degrees of proportion than it does to precise objective determination.

It is obvious, however, that "measure" involves even more than the lexicographer's detailed consideration of the different senses of the word. The confusion surrounding the word, may, indeed, be the consequent of assuming that the word must mean just one process, or one instrument, or one unit, or one result. When somebody uses the word correctly in one of its senses, he may still fail to communicate adequately what he intends. There are some people, unfortunately, who are even worse. They insist that the word "measure" means just what they "choose it to mean—neither more nor less."

If all scientists would agree to restrict "measurement" to a single meaning, then confusion would be minimized. Such unanimity is not an immediate prospect. Measures include the length of a table, the duration of a storm, the weight of a diamond, the resistance of an electric circuit, the achievement of a pupil, the visual response of a clam, or the expressed pain of a patient. Each of these different measures not only involves different objects but also different purposes. For instance, the length of the table may be needed to judge whether it will fit in a recess. The respective purposes for the other measures may be: making a record of the day's weather, setting a price upon a jewel, passing on the safety of a radio, evaluating the performance of a teacher, measuring the light threshold of an infrahuman organism, or selecting an anesthetic for an operation. A single sense among the variety of purposes and objects for the word "measure" is far from likely.

Most people expect that a measurement will be expressed by a quantity. In general, measurement involves the assignment of a class of numerals to a class of objects. Measurement, therefore, must consider three factors: first, it must deal with the classes of objects; second, it must deal with the classes of numerals; and third, it must deal with the rules for assigning numerals to objects. The choice of the word "numeral" in place of the more usual "number" is deliberate. For purposes of exposition, the word "numeral" refers to the symbols

1, 2, 3, . . . , whereas the word "number" refers to the meanings of the numerals. Numbers can refer to a person's social security registration, to his order in a line, to his weight on a scale. These meanings imply different relations among the numerals as symbols. Measurement is concerned with these relations.

The definition, further, refers to classes of objects. Each area of science deals with its own kind of subject matter. The physicist, for instance, deals with gases, liquids, and solids in terms of molecules, atoms, electrons, mesons, and charges. The psychologist, on the other hand, deals with behavior in terms of capacity, learning, and achievement. The subject matter or content of chemistry and of physics deals with classes of objects that are less variable than are the classes of objects studied by the biologists or the psychologist. The differences among classes of objects necessarily involve differences in the kinds of measurement of objects. The differences, moreover, are not only between the subject matter of psychology and of physics, but also between the kinds of workers in these diverse fields. In the last analysis, as Heraclitus announced, "man is the measure of all things." It is man who studies gases and solids, who studies behavior and culture. In this sense, measurement rests on the perceptual equipment of the observer. Fundamentally, *man* makes judgments of wider, longer, heavier, and stronger, or makes estimates of quicker, smarter, and happier. Very often man extends his range of observation by machines such as microscopes and balances, or by devices such as intelligence or achievement tests. The training of scientists, to a degree, affects the kinds of observation made and the kinds of instrument used; it affects, as well, the level of precision of his observations.

The subject matter, the conceptual organization, the nature of the instruments, and the training of the scientists interact to influence the nature of the observations made. Some observations can be made directly, for instance, the measurement of lengths can be made by juxtaposing two objects, or the measurement of weight by balancing two weights, or the measurement of time by contrasting two periods of time. Other observations, however, can only be estimated from their effects. In temperature, the variations in the height of a column of alcohol or of mercury are known to be related to variations in temperature. In scholastic achievement, the variations in the quality of the performance on tests are presumed to be related to variations in the amount, or even in the quality, of what is learned. The estimate of achievement in school, just as of temperature in a room, can be observed only by its effects.

Direct observation involves perceptions of the thing or of the property of the thing itself. Indirect observation involves inferences about the thing or its properties from its effects on other things or from its own performances. The inference about a property from its effects involves either an assumption about a relation between effect and property, or a demonstration about the relation between effect and property. In the case of temperature, an established relation has been discovered between thermal dynamics and the height of a mercury column. In achievement, however, the relationship between items of information acquired and behavior has not yet been fully demonstrated.

There are many kinds of observations that could be made about things or people. For instance, a piece of window glass reflects light, transmits light, affects the path of raindrops, gets warm, etc. An individual, on the other hand, remembers facts, pursues hobbies, develops skills, etc. So many are the effects upon things and upon persons that it is never possible to catalogue them all. To focus attention, the scientist, particularly, limits observation to a class of effects or to a class of direct observations. The distinction is between observing the thing for itself as opposed to observing it for inferences about the thing.

In scientific observations, whether direct or indirect, the conditions for observation are carefully specified in terms of time, place, and circumstance. In physics and chemistry, observations at sea level at 25° centigrade may differ markedly from observations of the same thing at 0° centigrade and in an airplane 3,500 feet above sea level. In psychology, the behavior of an individual at 2 A.M. at his desk in his own home may differ markedly from his behavior at 10 A.M. at his desk in his classroom. The statement about the observations, necessarily, must contain specification of condition.

What is to be observed is, however, crucial. No observation can be made unless man has arrived at some concept of it. For ages, man disregarded certain objects or their effects because he did not know of them or their behavior. He did not notice ultraviolet radiation, nor the fact that quartz reacted differently from glass to ultraviolet light. Nor did he notice electrical currents in the brain, or that some people can taste phenylthiocarbamide. What is observed depends upon man's conceptual equipment to translate sensory experiences into the notion of a property or of a characteristic. The notion of property involves the commonness of observations as sensed by the observer.

The concept of a *property* or *characteristic* of an object or of a person is crucial in measurement. Every object has as many apparent, and different, characteristics or properties as there are different ways one can conceive of it. Physical objects have properties such as height, weight, color, shape, function, etc. Humans have not only the properties of physical objects, but also such other characteristics as intelligence, health, age, education, and personality. In science the attempt is made to observe a single property, characteristic, aspect, or trait of the object at a time.

The property observed, therefore, is dependent upon man's ability to conceive of it and, then, of his ability to observe it. Frequently, in making attempts to observe a conceived-of characteristic, the conception of the characteristic undergoes significant change. The adequacy of observation is a primary antecedent to the adequacy of measurement.

Statements about a property are empirical since they depend upon what is experienced. Such statements are called existential since they communicate what is observable by the senses or by extensions (machines) of the senses. In science, different observers must agree about the observation. This implies social acceptance about the fact of the observed phenomenon. If only one observer and no one else could make the observation, there could be no demonstration of its wider acceptability. In general, science demands a "reproducibility" of observations. Whenever conditions and methods are identical, the observations should be identical unless the object underwent some changes during the observation or subsequent to it.

A property, therefore, should be rigorously defined. It is usual to specify the conditions under which the observation can be made. In the observation of the tensile strength of steel, the specification of the operations of preparing the sample, of fastening it in the instrument, and of the instrument itself, are necessary to the definition of the property of "tensile strength." Similarly, in the observation of the aptitude of students for graduate study, the specification of the operations for giving the test, of motivating the student, and of the intelligence scale itself, may be necessary to the definition of the property.

Judges try to make estimates of some given property or characteristic of an object with little or no regard for any of its other properties or characteristics, and with little or no attention to its surrounding environment. The length of a table may be estimated as longer than some present, or remembered, or thought-of standard of length without any attention to other characteristics of the table; the judgment is made without reference to its color, width, height, wood, style, shape, or other property. Psychometrists try to make estimates of the "intelligence" of an adult with little

or no consideration of his race, personality, or economic circumstance, and with little or no attention to his dress, the time of day, the furnishings in the room, and so on.

A property is some feature that is considered to be common to all objects of a given kind or class, but that need not be considered to be present in all objects whatsoever. From object to object in a given class, therefore, there will be some feature that is common to all the objects. It may be that the amount of this property will vary among the objects within the class, but regardless of other differences, there will be resemblance in the possession of amounts of the common property. Objects, of course, may have several properties in common. As already indicated, humans have properties of height, girth, and weight in common. Some judges may try to consider variations in these three characteristics independently; others may try to regard the combination of the three traits plus others under the *property name* of health. The property, thus, may be relatively simple and narrow, or it may be relatively complex and comprehensive. The property or trait, comprehensive or narrow, is attributed to the object by some person or persons.

The attribute, therefore, rests upon the direct or indirect perception of an observer. The ascription of a property to a class of objects, however, requires that differences in other characteristics be ignored, while the attention is given some main feature or quality. A property, broad or narrow, that can be seen, recognized, or classified only by a unique observer, however, cannot be considered a property capable of measurement or enumeration. In science, at least, there must be an agreement among expert observers that the property does exist, and such observers must agree in excess of chance upon whether a particular reaction does or does not demonstrate the property. (If different judges of the same incident cannot agree whether telepathy took place in the behavior they observed, no scientific analysis of the data is possible.) If judges perceive the same differences, then, the perceived differences may become the basis for classification and enumeration and, in some instances, measurement. The perception of resemblances and differences becomes the basis for measurement.

Empirical measurement depends upon the occurrence of a sense datum and its interpretation by an observer. Weight, even though measured by machine, nevertheless is ultimately related to the kinesthetic sensation of heavier and lighter. The machine—that is, scales—merely allows for a simple and relatively objective perception of the effects of weight. In this sense, the Geiger counter is a machine that enables the observer to perceive a specified class of effects by extending the range of human sensation. Other machines facilitate classification and comparison of objects by the control of systematic, chance, or erratic conditions, or by magnifying effects. These machines, therefore, allow more precise determinations of a particular class of effects. In the absence of instruments for extension of the senses, or in the absence of machines for the control of conditions, or in the absence of devices for the recording of more precise estimates, human observations are very liable to error. These sources of error include parallax, optical illusions, confusion of perceptions as in the size-weight illusion, biases, and sets. Instruments are a means for approximating more closely the property under observation. Instruments are steadily improved upon, so that the newer instruments make for closer and closer approximations to the measurement of a specific property. The object to be observed causes a variation in the instrument; the observer's sense impression leads to a recorded, objective, representation of the property.

But there is a limit to the closeness of approximation in the measurement of a property by an observer or by an instrument. In calorimetry it is well known that the temperature of the measuring device affects the temperature of the material under observation. In routine measurement, the observation is corrected by calculation for the influence of the instrument. In this sense, the instrument affects the measurement. In intelligence testing the examiner can affect the score of the candidate. In individual testing, encouragement or its lack influences the child's performance. At present, however, there is no way of estimating a suitable correction for the rapport between examiner and child. Much of the attention of the physical sciences is devoted to the reduction of the interaction of the instrument upon the characteristic under observation. In the field of psychology, the growing emphasis upon social psychology illustrates the recognition of the influences of many factors upon perception.

CLASSIFICATION AND ENUMERATION

Perhaps the simplest form of observation is to perceive that two objects are similar or dissimilar in their "response" to some situation. Eventually the observer notes that he is recognizing the same likeness or difference with respect to a great many object-pairs, and at this point he abstracts the similarity as a conceived property. He may then group objects which are similar in this respect into classes, using such dichotomies as short *vs.* not-short, heavy *vs.* not-heavy, or perhaps, intelligent *vs.* not-intelligent. The definition of the subclasses "intelligent" and "not-intelligent," or the subclasses "heavy" or "not-heavy," becomes the primary consideration for classification. The definition requires a specification of the basic distinguishing signs for judging inclusion within a class. Objects or persons then can be sorted into the class by a kind of "go," "no-go" criterion. Whenever observers can agree on the stigmata for class inclusion, then they can communicate to each other by using some class name to designate objects within the class. In this way, there may be agreement on the class "heavy objects," or "dull persons," or "basketball players."

All objects that "go" into the class are considered the same or equal under the convention that all other differences are disregarded; that is, all the objects that make a certain response are put together, even if other responses are not alike. Of course, within such a class as defined, further subclasses may be recognized on the basis of some characteristic common to the members of the subgroup but not to all the members of the class. Thus, the subclasses of "forwards" and "centers" may be found within the class "basketball players." If the definition is so clear and precise that observers can agree in placing certain persons into the class "basketball players," or certain basketball players into the subgroup "centers," these persons can be enumerated or counted. Class membership, therefore, rests upon an observer's acceptance of observable likenesses or resemblances so that each class member has the sign distinguishing it from all non-class members.

While enumeration assumes that the class is homogeneous, members of the class "basketball players" may differ among themselves in the quality of success as a basketball player. Certainly, coaches have to make judgments that some player or players are better (or worse) than others. The coach may define two mutually exclusive subclasses of good and poor players; he may even make three or four such classes. If, within the total class, the distinction of better or worse (stronger or weaker, heavier or lighter) is made, a comparison is intended. It is the comparison among objects that gives the first level of the relationship of subclasses to each other. The objective of scientific observation is to systematize a comparison so that existential statements about property and relationships within property can be structured in reference to the working conception of the property or trait or characteristic.

RANKING

Even after all objects have been placed into their respective subclasses, it may be possible to make a further existential statement indicating their relative order within the subclass. If coaches could agree upon the sorting, several consecutive subclasses of basketball players could be formed such as superior, average, and below average. As a matter of fact, always assuming the perceptual ability of the judge, there may be as many subclasses as there are players. In either case, the players would be ordered in terms of the property "success as a basketball player." In some instances objects may be ranked even though discrete subclasses cannot be distinguished. Although the hues of the solar spectrum, for example, can be ordered, they can be divided into the classes "reds," "yellows," etc., only by imposing arbitrary boundaries.

Observers can recognize differences in the relative amount of many properties. Shades of blue can be distinguished in the range from the pure hue to a nearly washed-out white; apples can be graded on the basis of discriminable marks; and the scholastic successes of children are judged by their teachers. It is not unusual for a teacher to rank one student ahead of another in scholastic success. As a matter of fact, some teachers can arrange the students in a class in a rank order, so that Robert stands ahead of Jane who stands ahead of Elizabeth.

Ranking may be based on a judgment of some observed property, as when contestants are arranged according to beauty. Sometimes the ranking is based on direct comparison, as may be the case in a ladder tournament where one determines the order of basketball teams by permitting them to play against each other, pair by pair. A good example of ranking based on direct comparison is the replacement series of metals. When zinc is dropped in a copper solution, copper plates out and the zinc dissolves. But copper will not replace zinc in a zinc solution. By successive experiments, it is found that a replacement order exists, beginning with gold, the easiest to replace: gold, mercury, copper, zinc, sodium. Such an order can be established without an understanding of the property

All that is necessary is to observe a hierarchical relation. For metals, a hierarchy exists, since sodium replaces all the metals listed before it, zinc replaces all those listed before it, and so on. Never is the order reversed, as it would be if copper could replace sodium. Sometimes comparison can be made but ranking cannot. If we observe a teen-ager order ice cream on many occasions, we may find that she consistently takes chocolate rather than banana, and that she takes banana rather than vanilla; but that when given the choice between chocolate and vanilla, she takes vanilla. Ranking is not possible unless objects possess the property under discussion (in this case, desirability) in increasing degree, so that one object has the property to a greater extent than any object below it in the series.

For instance, if problem-solving ability were considered to be a unidimensional property, individuals could be ordered according to the level of problem that each was able to solve. It would have to assume that the problems exist in a perfect order, and the individual could do all of the problems up to a certain one and none beyond it. Usually this requirement is not satisfied in educational and psychological measurement, which indicates that the property being investigated is a complex resultant of several simpler properties. Size is a property which does not permit perfect ordering. If size is defined by the operation, ability to pass through apertures of increasing area, some objects can pass through apertures of increasing area, some objects can pass through an aperture that apparently smaller objects cannot, because of differences in shape. We cannot arrange a miscellaneous collection of objects, and be sure that one object will pass through every aperture that an object nearer to the "large" end of the scale will pass through. Size, as a property, can be clarified by redefining it in terms of the unidimensional properties, such as length, breadth, and thickness.

The value of such observations of order is great. One of the earliest ordered observations involved the development of a method of communicating wind velocity. Lacking an instrument for measuring wind velocity, judgments were made about it. About thirty different subclasses were recognized from a calm up to a hurricane. Intermediate steps were gentle wind, breeze, and gale. For purposes of reporting, however, all wind velocities that experts called "calm" were symbolized by the numeral 1; all wind velocities called "gentle wind," numeral 2, and so on, up to numeral 30 for "hurricane." The numerals are labels in an arbitrary hierarchical order. As a matter of fact, numbers 6, 7, 8, . . . 35 or 4, 8, 13, 15, . . . 47 could have been used to label the subclasses from "calm" to "hurricane." From these statements, one cannot say that two hours of calm would move a ship as far as one hour of gentle wind.

Two objects may be one numeral apart, and, yet, that difference may be either very small or very large. Suppose a teacher were to rank the heights of the members of a class of thirty-three youngsters. It is reasonable to expect substantial reliability in such ranks. Pupils in ranks fifteen, sixteen, and seventeen, as measured on a stadiometer, would probably differ little in height, but pupils in ranks one and two and those in ranks thirty-two and thirty-three would differ much more in their measured heights. The numbers assigned to the rank orders give useful information about relative position, or direction of differences, but they do not allow inferences of absolute amount or of the difference or ratio between the amount of one object and the amount of another.

Ranks are not fixed. If thirty-two pupils were ranked in height, the set of numerals first, second, third, . . . could be put into one-to-one correspondence with Robert, Jane, Elizabeth, and so on, to John who is paired off, let us say, as thirty-second. If some independent observer arranged the thirty-two students in the same order, there would be a feeling of confidence about the number assigned to each pupil. There may be students, in existence, however, who possess amounts of the quality "height" that would require some of them to be placed ahead of Robert, or between Jane and Elizabeth. These new students would change the rank order and the sequence of numbers assigned. The ordinal numbers merely mean that 1 (for first) has a rank higher than 2 (for second) and that since 2 has a rank higher than 3, 1 must rank higher than 3.

Ordinal arrangement can be developed into a more complete observation if it is possible to assess how near to each other the objects are in the property in question. If several objects can be said to be equally spaced in terms of the degree to which they possess the property in question, the distance between any two of them may be taken as a linear unit of measurement. To describe the interval between two notes in a melody, the tone or step is a suitable unit. The difference between C and D is accepted to be exactly that between D and E. Any interval can be described in terms of the number of submultiples of the unit from one end to the other of it for example, C to G is three and a half steps or seven semitones. In the measurement, a distance between two sounds (an octave, a tone, a cycle) is chosen as a unit. The particular unit (though not the nature of the unit) is necessarily arbitrary, and is chosen for reasons of historical accident, convenience, or invariance (as in the use of the cadmium line in the spectrum as a measure of length). If one has a measuring device on which successive equal intervals are in some way "marked" or recorded, one may compare an object with the standard. The observer reads the number of units needed to "equal" the test object. The comparing and reading are visual in the case of length, but a device such as a pitch pipe can be used as a standard for tone, and the comparison is made by the appropriate operation of listening and comparing.

The particular unit chosen must have relation to the perceived property. In measuring income, the dollar is a suitable unit if the property under study is the money each person receives. In those terms, appropriate in an accounting office, the gap between $1,000 and $2,000 is the same as the gap between $5,000 and $6,000. But if the income is conceived in terms of goodness of living permitted, the count of dollars does not linearly represent the increase in reward. The increase from $1,000 to $2,000 may represent the change from penury and misery to the bare ability to obtain necessities; the increase from $5,000 to $6,000 may represent the change from a comfortable level to the beginnings of luxury, or it may represent the comfortable level with an opportunity to safeguard it with savings. No satisfactory unit for measuring income, conceived as reward, has been developed.

In some fields, an increased understanding of the relation of the perceived property to other important properties has led to increasingly satisfactory units. In estimating hearing, a primitive measure was the distance at which a child could hear a sound. In the watch test, a ticking watch was brought closer and closer to the child, until he could just hear it. This is a simple experimental device for arranging children in order, in terms of keenness of hearing. The score on the test (distance) could be taken as a scaled measurement only if observers agree that children who hear at 20 feet, 15 feet, and 10 feet, respectively, differ from each other by equal degrees of keenness. Another method that might be used is to produce varying sounds at standard distance. A primitive scientist might have dropped increasing weights on a drumhead, and noted the smallest weight that would produce a sound the child could hear. In modern times, these crude methods can be replaced with an electronic technique. The intensity of the stimulus might be measured by the pressure of the sound waves emitted by the resonator, the unit of pressure being the dyne, which is a unit abstracted from the falling of weights. Then hearing might be scored in terms of the number of dynes per square centimeter. Such a scale is not linear. If a sound of 20 dynes per square centimeter force is compared with another of 40 dynes, an observer asked to locate the sound halfway between the two in loudness will set the resonator not at 30 dynes, but at 28, the geometric mean. As the experiments of Weber and others show, the equal intervals of the hearing scale have a logarithmic, not a linear, relation to units of force. Similarly, it can be shown that since the force of the sound decreases proportionately as the *square* of the distance from the source, the distance measured in the watch test is not a linear measure of sound. From many studies of the nature of hearing, of what it means to say that one sound is twice as loud as another, has come a unit of measure known as the decibel. The decibel is a logarithmic function of the power of the sound; the sound that is 1 decibel louder than another is ten times as strong in terms of dynes, and a 2-decibel difference corresponds to a ratio of 100 to 1 in sound energy. The decibel is a unit on a scale having equal-*appearing* intervals, linear with relation to loudness as judged by observers. The establishment of equal-appearing intervals rests on the agreement of judges in setting the tone halfway between two standard tones.

The linearity of a scale, it should be noted, is linearity with relation to some judgment or some operation. The householder can use number of pounds as a unit in buying coal, because the weight is roughly in terms of B.T.U. per dollar. Although the ton is a useful unit, the buyer can judge value more accurately with a unit such as the B.T.U., which indicates the amount of *heat* he will purchase, rather than with a unit such as *tons* which indicates the amount of *coal* purchased.

Because measurement always deals with a property which has been previously perceived, and is to some degree familiar, there is a danger of believing that the "obvious" unit is in some way peculiarly right for measuring the property. There is a compatibility between the notions of the height of persons and the length of a measuring stick that makes the inch an appealing unit for measuring growth. In fact,

common sense rejects as absurd any suggestion that the footrule does not provide a scale of equal intervals for height. Yet height can be measured in years rather than inches! All that is required is the median height of six-year-olds, seven-year-olds, etc. Then, if we have a record of these data, we may compare a given child with the standards and report that he has seven-year-old height; or, perhaps even more precisely, that his "height age" is 7.2 years. The only justification for this seemingly roundabout and "unnatural" measuring scale is that in some studies one year of growth makes a unit for a scale of equal intervals, whereas the inch does not. An analogy is found in the measurement of the maturity of trees. Once, the largest, or thickest, tree of a species was thought to be oldest. Now, we rely on a count of the annular rings as a measure of age, even though the rings are unequally spaced on a footrule.

Very frequently, scientific observation is concerned with making statements about differences in amount. It is true that the observer using the scale for wind velocities can say that there is an observable difference between a calm and a gentle wind, or between a gale and a hurricane. The scientist, however, would like to state how much difference there is between adjacent or different velocities. To make such statements of difference, however, implies that juxtaposition, for example, putting two weights in the same pan of a balance, will yield a weight equivalent to their sum, or that putting two objects on top of one another will yield a height equal to their sum. Height is such a property. Neither a 36-inch child nor a 30-inch child can reach the jam jar on the top shelf; but their heights may be added, when one stands on the other's shoulders, so that they do reach the shelf. Psychological properties rarely permit addition. If Sarah knows 200 French words, and Jane knows 250, their total vocabulary may be only 320 words, since many words appear in both vocabularies. Two readers, each capable of reading at the third-grade level, cannot by combining read a book of sixth-grade difficulty. Very few of the properties with which education and psychology are concerned can be measured by additive scales. The physicist, on the other hand, is able to measure with the additive scales for length, time, mass, volume, electrical resistance, heat, and several other properties. Properties such as density and temperature, which are not themselves represented in additive scales, may be derived from, and measured by, combinations of properties for which there are additive scales.

In an operationally defined additive scale, one may make meaningful statements about the *amount* of a difference. The difference from 48° to 32° is accepted as equal to that from 16° to 32°, because the units of the temperature scale are equal by definition. But the difference cannot be interpreted as 16 times a unit of temperature, since there is no invariant unit of temperature permitting addition. On the other hand, chronology is a scale for which the additive principle holds. It is meaningful to say that two events occurred ten years apart, since the year is an additive unit, demarked by the earth's rotation about the sun. "One year later" is an additive statement, marking off the point in time one revolution beyond the base point, just as "one foot above his head" implies the addition of lengths. In the best-developed additive scales, it is operationally demonstrated that *units* of the property may be added.

Even additive scales fall short of complete measurement until an absolute zero is established so that the investigator can answer the question "How much?" Additive scales permit measurement of differences, but cannot report absolute magnitudes unless they can measure the difference between the object and a zero point. For example, the chronological scale permits comparisons of times, but the number "1902 A.D." does not state how much time elapsed prior to the designated event. The birth of Christ is an arbitrary zero, useful as a bench mark but meaningless as a number, since time did not begin at that instant. Because these numbers are not based on zero, multiplication and division of them is not meaningful. 2000 A.D. does not represent twice as late a point in time as 1000 A.D.; nor did the age of the earth double from year 1 to year 2. In order to make statements of absolute magnitude, a ratio scale is required.

The zero for a measure of a property is the amount that is conceived to represent "just not any of" the property. Zero illumination is total darkness. Absolute zero for intensity of sound is the point where movement of the air (or other conductive medium) ceases. Heat, on the other hand, had no absolute zero until relatively recently. Even when the temperature is 32° F. or 0° F., objects have not reached the point of no-heat-at-all. A ratio scale can be established when an additive property has a functional relation to a phenomenon which does have an absolute zero. When heat was related to thermal motion, and zero heat was equated to the cessation of thermal motion, the ratio scale for heat became a possibility. One object could justifiably be said to have twice as much heat energy as another. A scale may have an absolute zero and yet not permit measurement, if the additive property has not been proved. Absolute zero error in rifle marksmanship may be readily conceptualized in terms of zero deviation from the bull's-eye, but marksmanship itself has no scale of additive units for measuring accuracy.

The notion of absolute measurement was considered by Gauss around 1830. The acceptance of the concept has been slow. In physics, studies of the conservation and dissipation of energy lead to Thomson's absolute scale of temperature about 1848. The extension to electrical phenomena occurred around the same time. In physics, a hypothetically observable but nonexistent phenomenon (just not any distance between two points, just not any deflection of an inertia-free galvanometer) is related to the zero point of the interval scale. In some scales now used without a true zero, a zero may yet be defined. Conceivably, for example, measures of radioactivity might set the age of the earth closely enough that absolute times could be used for the earthly chronology (not for eternity). In the social and psychological fields, unfortunately, outside referents have not been conceptualized. It will perhaps not be possible to establish true zeros for behavioral properties such as prejudice or sociability. It is unlikely that a measure will be developed which permits the statement that child A is twice as good as child B in ability to solve problems. Nor can a handwriting sample of zero legibility be defined, since no matter how poor the sample, there is always the probability of a worse one.

Thus far, the emphasis of this chapter has been upon observations, and upon the human ability to classify observations. In essence, classification depends upon the human recognition and conceptualization of some uniformity among observations. The greater the exactness of the formulation of the concept of the characteristic of the property, the greater the abstractness of it. In this sense, the concept of a property involves an abstraction from the concrete, or perceived, observations.

The concept of a characteristic may be such that things, people, or events may be considered to have it or to lack it. At this level, objects, for instance, may be separated into two groups, the have's and the have-not's. The concept, however, may be one that recognizes differences in degree or in amount. The concept of a property that recognizes differences in degree has been called an *intensive magnitude*. An intensive magnitude represents the kind of property whose observations can be arranged in a recognizable order, but where two observations or events cannot be added. For instance, an observation of eighteen arithmetic examples for John and of twelve for Jane is not thirty for both. Another illustration of a property of intensive magnitude is E. L. Thorndike's achievement scale in drawing [6]. The plates of the drawings can be arranged in a recognizable order from best to worst performance, but the value of any two drawings cannot be considered equal to any third.

The property of weight, however, is such that objects can be arranged in a *definite* order, that there is a limit which means "just not any" weight, that the sum of any two would equal a third. Such a property has *extensive* magnitude. The distinction between intensive and extensive magnitude is given in the following table.

Intensive

1. Recognizable order
2. Indeterminate zero, i.e., zero is arbitrary or normative
3. Has some relation (not perfect) to an external criterion
4. The sum of two substances of different values *is not equal* to that of a substance with the value of the numerical sum of these values

Extensive

1. Definite order
2. Absolute zero, i.e., zero is "just not any of"
3. Has an invariant relation to an external criterion
4. The sum of two substances of different values *is equal* to a substance of the value equal to the numerical sum of these values

The concept of property distinguishes between extensive and intensive magnitudes.

An intensive magnitude refers to observations which can be placed in order and for which the order is transitive and asymmetrical. First, it must be clear that a class of objects B $(i = l$ to $n)$ have a common property. (I) If the objects have a common property, then either

$$B_i = B_j \quad \text{or}$$
$$B_i < B_j \quad \text{or}$$
$$B_j > B_i$$

This is the statement of asymmetry. And (II) if $B_i < B_j$, and $B_j < B_k$, then $B_i < B_k$. This is the statement of transitivity.

It must be noted that the equal sign of

(I) and the less sign of (II) refer to *observed* relationships. The statement of equality, moreover, is not necessary to the placement of all objects in an asymmetrical and transitive order. Campbell [1] has shown that in genealogy, the construct "=" does not exist. In such a situation "<" is read "is descended from." Yet the line of descent can be ordered in time.

The Mohr scale of hardness merely indicates that, in terms of the expressed relation of scratching as evidence of hardness, minerals can be placed in "scratch order." There is no evidence that the hardness of a diamond is any multiple of the hardness of any other minerals.

In order to express the concept "multiple," the property under observation must be capable of physical addition. Properties that can be physically added are called "extensive." It is necessary to demonstrate that in addition to the conditions of asymmetry and transitivity, the following conditions also apply:

III. if $B_i = B'_i$ and if $B_j = B'_j$,
then $B_i + B_j = B'_i + B'_j$

IV. if $B_i + B_j = B_k$, then $B_j + B_i = B_k$

V. if $B_i = B'_i$, $B_j = B'_j$, and $B_l = B'_l$, then
$(B_i + B_j) + B_l = B'_i + (B'_j + B'_l)$

VI. if $B_i < B_j$, then $B_i + B_k < B_j + B_k$
if $B_k \neq 0$

It must be understood that the property B is common to all objects B_i and the operations of addition and of combination correspond to the physical process as does the joining of two sticks together or the putting of two weights in the same pan.

Since measurement involves the assignment of numerals to properties, it is necessary to understand the formal conventions about numbers. The formal conventions among numbers are essentially arbitrary. Each number system represents a certain set of formal and logical relations among the symbols. Numerals may be nominal, ordinal, and cardinal. Nominal numbers are mere symbols for identification without further property. Ordinal numbers refer to the order of objects as first, second, and third. Cardinal numbers refer to enumeration of objects which can be counted regardless of order.

Just as words have a variety of meanings, so do the numerals. Much of the difficulty would be reduced if there were different symbols representing a nominal number, a rank order, an interval scale, or a ratio. There is little likelihood that four such sets of symbols will be developed. The scientist must be ever on his guard to recognize from context whether the 1, 2, . . . refer to nominal, order, count, or ratio.

The numeral assumes that all objects or events given the same designation, whether a name or a number, are equivalent with reference to the named property. Nominal scales merely name, by number, letter, or other symbols, all objects having the same property. Rank-order or ordinal scales assume that the objects or events have a common property and that the objects differ in the amount of that property. Essentially an ordinal scale is concerned with the arrangement of events into a hierarchy from least to most. Rank order scales have been used in the estimation of the velocity of winds, the hardness of minerals, the conduct of pupils, the taste of foods, and so forth. Interval scales employ some invariant referent, such as a degree in temperature (defined as 1/100 the difference between freezing and boiling of a specified substance), or one j.n.d. (just noticeable difference) in brightness. For an additive scale, the units must be operationally addible. In ratio scales, the lower end of the scale is anchored at the point corresponding to "just none" of the property being measured.

A numeral may be used as the name of a particular object, as the name of a particular set or subclass of objects, as the enumeration of all of the objects in a set, as a rank of an object in an ordered sequence, as the amount of some property. The number 428, for instance, can refer to a particular safe deposit box, or to all eight-inch files of model 42, or to the fact that

Table 3–1   A Classification of Scales of Measurement

Scale	Basic Empirical Operations	Mathematical Group-structure	Permissible Statistics (invariantive)	Typical Examples
Nominal	Determination of equality	Permutation group $x'=f(x)$ [$f(x)$ means any one-to-one substitution]	Number of cases Mode Contingency correlation	"Numbering" of football players Assignment of type or model numbers to classes
Ordinal	Determination of greater or less	Isotonic group $x'=f(x)$ [$f(x)$ means any monotonic increasing function]	Median Percentiles	Hardness of minerals Quality of leather, lumber, wool, etc. Pleasantness of odors
Interval	Determination of equality of intervals or differences	General linear group $x'=ax+b$	Mean Standard deviation Rank-order correlation Product-moment correlation	Temperature (Fahrenheit and centigrade) Calendar dates "Standard scores" on achievement tests (?)
Ratio	Determination of equality of ratios	Similarity group $x'=ax$	Coefficient of variation Logarithmic transformations	Length, weight, force, etc. Pitch scale (mels) Loudness scale (sones)

Measurement is the assignment of numerals to objects or events according to rule. The rules and the resulting kinds of scales are tabulated above. The basic operations needed to create a given scale are all those listed in the second column, down to and including the operation listed opposite the scale. The third column gives the mathematical transformations which leave the scale form invariant. Any numeral, x, on a scale can be replaced by another numeral x' where x' is the function of x listed in column 3. The fourth column lists, cumulatively downward, some of the statistics that show invariance under the transformations of column 3. (For further details, see S. S. Stevens [5].) (Reprinted by permission of S. S. Stevens, Harvard University.)

the shipping clerk had on hand just 428 hammers; it can also refer to a student's scholastic position in his graduating class, to the score a student reaches on an intelligence test, to the melting point of an alloy of zinc, to the length of a wall in inches, and to the weight of a hog in pounds.

When a numeral is used to tag a safe deposit vault, or to give a code number to a salesman, it serves no other purpose than that of identifying a specific object. When, however, it is used to designate all model 42 eight-inch files as 428, it recognizes the equivalence of each model 42 eight-inch file with every other. The number 428 is assigned to the specific deposit box or to the salesman or the files in an arbitrary and capricious manner. Some record of the in-

tended identification must be available for recognizing the reference.[1] The key is necessary to make the numbers intelligible in communication.

The fact that there are 428 objects classified as hammers, however, is a different kind of numeral. It is that number of the series of natural numbers, beginning with 1, that is paired off with the last member of the class of hammers. The convention adopted is that the sequence of natural numbers 1, 2, 3, . . . exists and that all

[1] In some instances, the numeral may be somewhat more meaningful. For example, Washington, D.C., may be assigned the number 226 because it is uniquely identified as that many miles south of New York City on the Pennsylvania Railroad.

objects of the class may be considered to have the property of hammerness or to lack that property. The class or set is defined by any property which each object considered must either have or lack. Enumeration is a specific operation by which the sequence of natural numbers is paired off with each unit of the class "hammers" until the supply of hammers is exhausted. The number that is assigned to the last hammer constitutes the count.

If the first natural number is paired with the first object, then, the natural number paired with the last object is the cardinal number representing the count. If the symbols refer to ordinal sequence, the numbers can have meaning only with reference to the set of ranks used. Any addition of new members to the class changes the interpretation of the ordered number. Pure rank as eighth means that if the pairing begins with first, then between first and eighth are six other ranks. The interpretation of eighth-in-a-sequence-of-eight and eighth-in-a-sequence-of-five-hundred obviously cannot be the same.

The numerals assigned to the temperature scale or the length scale, however, do not refer to discrete properties. They refer to continuous property. The numeral 1 can no longer be considered fixed and unvarying. The numeral 1 refers to an approximation such as $1 \pm a$ is the variation in reading the results of a juxtaposition of scale and object. As a matter of fact, unless the zero is established, the amounts can refer only to additions of units. When the zero

of the scale has been established, then ratios can be reported such as $A/B = K$.

Stevens [5] has made a succint classification of scales of measurement, see Table 3-1. His table shows the relationship between the formal concept of numbers (that is, scales) and the existential concept of property (that is, basic empirical operation) together with the mathematical group structure of the numbers, their permissible statistics, and typical examples. This table summarizes the relationship between number or symbol and property of observation.

REFERENCES

1. CAMPBELL, N. R. *An account of the principles of measurement and calculation.* London: Longmans, 1928.
2. FEIFEL, H. Qualitative differences in the vocabulary responses of normals and abnormals. *Genet. psychol. Monogr.,* 1949, *39,* 151–204.
3. JONES, H. E., and CONRAD, H. S. The growth and decline of intelligence: a study of a homogeneous group between the ages of ten and sixty. *Genet. psychol. Monogr.,* 1933, *13,* 223–298.
4. NORRIS, K. E. *The three r's and the adult worker.* Montreal: McGill University, 1940.
5. STEVENS, S. S. On the theory of scales of measurement. *Science,* 1946, *103,* 677–680.
6. THORNDIKE, E. L. The measurement of achievement in drawing. *Teachers College Record,* 1913, *14,* 345–382.
7. THORNDIKE, R. L. Growth of intelligence during adolescence. *J. genet. Psychol.,* 1948, *72,* 11–15.

Chapter 4

Construct Validity
in Psychological Tests

LEE J. CRONBACH / PAUL E. MEEHL

Validation of psychological tests has not yet been adequately conceptualized, as the APA Committee on Psychological Tests learned when it undertook (1950–54) to specify what qualities should be investigated before a test is published. In order to make coherent recommendations the Committee found it necessary to distinguish four types of validity, established by different types of research and requiring different interpretation. The chief innovation in the Committee's report was the term *construct validity*.[1] This idea was first formulated by a subcommittee (Meehl and R. C. Challman) studying how proposed

This article is reprinted from the *Psychological Bulletin,* 1955, with the permission of the authors and the American Psychological Association.

Paul E. Meehl worked on this problem in connection with his appointment to the Minnesota Center for Philosophy of Science. We are indebted to the other members of the Center (Herbert Feigl, Michael Scriven, Wilfrid Sellars) and to D. L. Thistlethwaite of the University of Illinois for their major contributions to our thinking and their suggestions for improving this paper.

[1] Referred to in a preliminary report [58] as *congruent validity.*

recommendations would apply to projective techniques, and later modified and clarified by the entire Committee (Bordin, Challman, Conrad, Humphreys, Super, and the present writers). The statements agreed upon by the Committee (and by committees of two other associations) were published in the *Technical Recommendations* [59]. The present interpretation of construct validity is not "official" and deals with some areas where the Committee would probably not be unanimous. The present writers are solely responsible for this attempt to explain the concept and elaborate its implications.

Identification of construct validity was not an isolated development. Writers on validity during the preceding decade had shown a great deal of dissatisfaction with conventional notions of validity, and introduced new terms and ideas, but the resulting aggregation of types of validity seems only to have stirred the muddy waters. Portions of the distinctions we shall discuss are implicit in Jenkins' paper, "Validity for what?" [33], Gulliksen's "Intrinsic validity" [27], Goodenough's distinction between tests as "signs" and "samples" [22], Cronbach's separation of "logical" and "empirical" validity [11], Guilford's "factorial validity" [25], and Mosier's papers on "face validity" and "validity generalization" [49, 50]. Helen Peak [52] comes close to an explicit statement of construct validity as we shall present it.

FOUR TYPES OF VALIDATION

The categories into which the *Recommendations* divide validity studies are: predictive validity, concurrent validity, content validity, and construct validity. The first two of these may be considered together as *criterion-oriented* validation procedures.

The pattern of a criterion-oriented study is familiar. The investigator is primarily interested in some criterion which he wishes to predict. He administers the test, obtains an independent criterion measure on the same subjects, and computes a correlation. If the criterion is obtained some time after the test is given, he is studying *predictive validity*. If the test score and criterion score are determined at essentially the same time, he is studying *concurrent validity*. Concurrent validity is studied when one test is proposed as a substitute for another (for example, when a multiple-choice form of spelling test is substituted for taking dictation), or a test is shown to correlate with some contemporary criterion (e.g., psychiatric diagnosis).

Content validity is established by showing that the test items are a sample of a universe in which the investigator is interested. Content validity is ordinarily to be established deductively, by defining a universe of items and sampling systematically within this universe to establish the test.

Construct validation is involved whenever a test is to be interpreted as a measure of some attribute or quality which is not "operationally defined." The problem faced by the investigator is, "What constructs account for variance in test performance?"

Construct validity calls for no new scientific approach. Much current research on tests of personality [9] is construct validation, usually without the benefit of a clear formulation of this process.

Construct validity is not to be identified solely by particular investigative procedures, but by the orientation of the investigator. Criterion-oriented validity, as Bechtoldt emphasizes [3, p. 1245], "involves the *acceptance* of a set of operations as an adequate definition of whatever is to be measured." When an investigator believes that no criterion available to him is fully valid, he perforce becomes interested in construct validity because this is the only way to avoid the "infinite frustration" of relating every criterion to some more ultimate standard [21]. In content validation, *acceptance* of the universe of content as defining the variable to be measured is essential. Construct validity must be investigated whenever no criterion or universe of content is accepted as entirely adequate to define the quality to be measured. Determining what psychological constructs account for test performance is desirable for almost any test. Thus, although the MMPI was originally established on the basis of empirical discrimination between patient groups and so-called normals (concurrent validity), continuing research has tried to provide a basis for describing the personality associated with each score pattern. Such interpretations permit the clinician to predict performance with respect to criteria which have not yet been employed in empirical validation studies [cf. 46, pp. 49–50, 110–111].

> We can distinguish among the four types of validity by noting that each involves a different emphasis on the criterion. In predictive or concurrent validity, the criterion behavior is of concern to the tester, and he may have no concern whatsoever with the type of behavior exhibited in the test. (An employer does not care if a worker can manipulate blocks, but the score on the block test may predict something he cares about.)

Content validity is studied when the tester *is* concerned with the type of behavior involved in the test performance. Indeed, if the test is a work sample, the behavior represented in the test may be an end in itself. Construct validity is ordinarily studied when the tester has no definite criterion measure of the quality with which he is concerned, and must use indirect measures. Here the trait or quality underlying the test is of central importance, rather than either the test behavior or the scores on the criteria [59, p. 14].

Construct validation is important at times for every sort of psychological test: aptitude, achievement, interests, and so on. Thurstone's statement is interesting in this connection:

> In the field of intelligence tests, it used to be common to define validity as the correlation between a test score and some outside criterion. We have reached a stage of sophistication where the test-criterion correlation is too coarse. It is obsolete. If we attempted to ascertain the validity of a test for the second space-factor, for example, we would have to get judges [to] make reliable judgments about people as to this factor. Ordinarily their [the available "judges"] ratings would be of no value as a criterion. Consequently, validity studies in the cognitive functions now depend on criteria of internal consistency . . . [60, p. 3].

Construct validity would be involved in answering such questions as: To what extent is this test of intelligence culture-free? Does this test of "interpretation of data" measure reading ability, quantitative reasoning, or response sets? How does a person with A in Strong Accountant, and B in Strong CPA, differ from a person who has these scores reversed?

Example of construct validation procedure. Suppose measure X correlates .50 with Y, the amount of palmar sweating induced when we tell a student that he has failed a Psychology I exam. Predictive validity of X for Y is adequately described by the coefficient, and a statement of the experimental and sampling conditions. If someone were to ask, "Isn't there perhaps another way to interpret this correlation?" or "What other kinds of evidence can you bring to support your interpretation?", we would hardly understand what he was asking because no interpretation has been made. These questions become relevant when the correlation is advanced as evidence that "test X measures anxiety proneness." Alternative interpretations are possible; e.g., perhaps the test measures "academic aspiration," in which case we will expect different results if we induce palmar sweating by economic threat. It is then reasonable to inquire about other *kinds* of evidence.

Add these facts from further studies: Test X correlates .45 with fraternity brothers' ratings on "tenseness." Test X correlates .55 with amount of intellectual inefficiency induced by painful electric shock, and .68 with the Taylor Anxiety scale. Mean X score decreases among four diagnosed groups in this order: anxiety state, reactive depression, "normal," and psychopathic personality. And palmar sweat under threat of failure in Psychology I correlates .60 with threat of failure in mathematics. Negative results eliminate competing explanations of the X score; thus, findings of negligible correlations between X and social class, vocational aim, and value-orientation make it fairly safe to reject the suggestion that X measures "academic aspiration." We can have substantial confidence that X does measure anxiety proneness if the current theory of anxiety can embrace the variates which yield positive correlations, and does not predict correlations where we found none.

KINDS OF CONSTRUCTS

At this point we should indicate summarily what we mean by a construct, recognizing that much of the remainder of the paper deals with this question. A construct is some postulated attribute of people, assumed to be reflected in test performance. In test validation the attribute about which we make statements in interpreting a test is a construct. We expect a person at any time to possess or not possess a qualitative attribute (amnesia) or structure, or to possess some degree of a quantitative attribute (cheerfulness). A construct has certain associated meanings carried in statements of this general character: Persons who possess this attribute will, in situation X, act in manner Y (with a stated probability). The logic of construct validation is invoked whether the construct is highly systematized or loose, used in ramified theory or a few simple propositions, used in absolute propositions or probability statements. We seek to specify how one is to defend a proposed interpretation of a test; *we are not recommending any one type of interpretation.*

The constructs in which tests are to be interpreted are certainly not likely to be physiological. Most often they will be traits such as "latent hostility" or "variable in mood," or descriptions in terms of an educational objective, as "ability to plan experiments." For the benefit of readers who may have been influenced by certain eisegeses of MacCorquodale and Meehl [40], let us here emphasize: Whether or not an interpretation of a test's properties or relations involves questions of construct validity is to be decided by examining the entire body of evidence offered, together with what is asserted about the test in the context of this evidence. Proposed identifications of constructs allegedly measured by the test with constructs of other sciences (e.g., genetics, neuroanatomy, biochemistry) make up only *one* class of construct-validity claims, and a rather minor one at present. Space does not permit full analysis of the relation of the present paper to the MacCorquodale-Meehl distinction between hypothetical constructs and intervening variables. The philosophy of science pertinent to the present paper is set forth later in the section entitled, "The nomological network."

THE RELATION OF CONSTRUCTS TO "CRITERIA"

CRITICAL VIEW OF THE CRITERION IMPLIED

An unquestionable criterion may be found in a practical operation, or may be established as a consequence of an operational definition. Typically, however, the psychologist is unwilling to use the directly operational approach because he is interested in building theory about a generalized construct. A theorist trying to relate behavior to "hunger" almost certainly invests that term with meanings other than the operation "elapsed-time-since-feeding." If he is concerned with hunger as a tissue need, he will not accept time lapse as *equivalent* to his construct because it fails to consider, among other things, energy expenditure of the animal.

In some situations the criterion is no more valid than the test. Suppose, for example, that we want to know if counting the dots on Bender-Gestalt figure five indicates "compulsive rigidity," and take psychiatric ratings on this trait as a criterion. Even a conventional report on the resulting correlation will say something about the extent and intensity of the psychiatrist's contacts and should describe his qualifications (e.g., diplomate status? analyzed?).

Why report these facts? Because data are needed to indicate whether the criterion is any good. "Compulsive rigidity" is not really intended to mean "social stimulus value to psychiatrists." The implied trait involves a range of behavior-dispositions which may be very imperfectly sampled by the psychiatrist. Suppose dot-counting does not occur in a particular patient and yet we find that the psychiatrist has rated him as "rigid." When questioned the psychiatrist tells us that the patient was a rather easy, free-wheeling sort; however, the patient *did* lean over to straighten out a skewed desk blotter, and this, viewed against certain other facts, tipped the scale in favor of a "rigid" rating. On the face of it, counting Bender dots may be just as good (or poor) a sample of the compulsive-rigidity domain as straightening desk blotters is.

Suppose, to extend our example, we have four tests on the "predictor" side, over against the psychiatrist's "criterion," and find generally positive correlations among the five variables. Surely it is artificial and arbitrary to impose the "test-should-predict-criterion" pattern on such data. The psychiatrist samples verbal content, expressive pattern, voice, posture, etc. The psychologist samples verbal content, perception, expressive pattern, etc. Our proper conclusion is that, from this evidence, the four tests and the psychiatrist all assess some common factor.

The asymmetry between the "test" and the so-designated "criterion" arises only because the terminology of predictive validity has become a commonplace in test analysis. In this study where a construct is the central concern, any distinction between the merit of the test and criterion variables would be justified only if it had already been shown that the psychiatrist's theory and operations were excellent measures of the attribute.

INADEQUACY OF VALIDATION IN TERMS OF SPECIFIC CRITERIA

The proposal to validate constructual interpretations of tests runs counter to suggestions of some others. Spiker and McCandless [57] favor an operational approach. Validation is replaced by compiling statements as to how strongly the test predicts other observed variables of interest. To avoid requiring that each new variable be investigated completely by itself, they allow two variables to collapse into one whenever the properties of the operationally defined measures are the same: "If a new test is demonstrated to predict the scores on an older, well-established test, then an evaluation of the predictive power of the older test may be used for the new one." But accurate inferences are possible only if the two tests correlate so highly that there is negligible reliable variance in either test, independent of the other. Where the correspondence is less close, one

must either retain all the separate variables operationally defined or embark on construct validation.

The practical user of tests must rely on constructs of some generality to make predictions about new situations. Test X could be used to predict palmar sweating in the face of failure without invoking any construct, but a counselor is more likely to be asked to forecast behavior in diverse or even unique situations for which the correlation of test X is unknown. Significant predictions rely on knowledge accumulated around the generalized construct of anxiety. The *Technical Recommendations* state:

> It is ordinarily necessary to evaluate construct validity by integrating evidence from many different sources. The problem of construct validation becomes especially acute in the clinical field since for many of the constructs dealt with it is not a question of finding an imperfect criterion but of finding any criterion at all. The psychologist interested in construct validity for clinical devices is concerned with making an estimate of a hypothetical internal process, factor, system, structure, or state and cannot expect to find a clear unitary behavioral criterion. An attempt to identify any one criterion measure or any composite as *the* criterion aimed at is, however, usually unwarranted [59, p. 14–15].

This appears to conflict with arguments for specific criteria prominent at places in the testing literature. Thus Anastasi [2] makes many statements of the latter character: "It is only as a measure of a specifically defined criterion that a test can be objectively validated at all. . . . To claim that a test measures anything over and above its criterion is pure speculation" (p. 67). Yet elsewhere this article supports construct validation. Tests can be profitably interpreted if we "know the relationships between the tested behavior . . . and other behavior samples, none of these behavior samples necessarily occupying the preeminent position of a criterion" (p. 75). Factor analysis with several partial criteria might be used to study whether a test measures a postulated "general learning ability." If the data demonstrate specificity of ability instead, such specificity is "useful in its own right in advancing our knowledge of behavior; it should not be construed as a weakness of the tests" (p. 75).

We depart from Anastasi at two points. She writes, "The validity of a psychological test should not be confused with an analysis of the factors which determine the behavior under consideration." We, however, regard such analysis as a most important type of validation. Second, she refers to "the will-o'-the-wisp of psychological processes which are distinct from performance" [2, p. 77]. While we agree that psychological processes are elusive, we are sympathetic to attempts to formulate and clarify constructs which are evidenced by performance but distinct from it. Surely an inductive inference based on a pattern of correlations cannot be dismissed as "pure speculation."

SPECIFIC CRITERIA USED TEMPORARILY: THE "BOOTSTRAPS" EFFECT

Even when a test is constructed on the basis of a specific criterion, it may ultimately be judged to have greater construct validity than the criterion. We start with a vague concept which we associate with certain observations. We then discover empirically that these observations covary with some other observation which possesses greater reliability or is more intimately correlated with relevant experimental changes than is the original measure, or both. For example, the notion of temperature arises because some objects feel hotter to the touch than others. The expansion of a mercury column does not have face validity as an index of hotness. But it turns out that (a) there is a statistical relation between expansion and sensed temperature; (b) observers employ the mercury method with good interobserver agreement; (c) the regularity of observed relations is increased by using the thermometer (e.g., melting points of samples of the same material vary

little on the thermometer; we obtain nearly linear relations between mercury measures and pressure of a gas). Finally, (d) a theoretical structure involving unobservable microevents—the kinetic theory—is worked out which explains the relation of mercury expansion to heat. This whole process of conceptual enrichment begins with what in retrospect we see as an extremely fallible "criterion"—the human temperature sense. That original criterion has now been relegated to a peripheral position. We have lifted ourselves by our bootstraps, but in a legitimate and fruitful way.

Similarly, the Binet scale was first valued because children's scores tended to agree with judgments by schoolteachers. If it had not shown this agreement, it would have been discarded along with reaction time and the other measures of ability previously tried. Teacher judgments once constituted the criterion against which the individual intelligence test was validated. But if today a child's IQ is 135 and three of his teachers complain about how stupid he is, we do not conclude that the test has failed. Quite to the contrary, if no error in test procedure can be argued, we treat the test score as a valid statement about an important quality, and define our task as that of finding out what other variables—personality, study skills, etc.—modify achievement or distort teacher judgment.

EXPERIMENTATION TO INVESTIGATE CONSTRUCT VALIDITY

VALIDATION PROCEDURES

We can use many methods in construct validation. Attention should particularly be drawn to Macfarlane's survey of these methods as they apply to projective devices [41].

Group differences. If our understanding of a construct leads us to expect two groups to differ on the test, this expectation may be tested directly. Thus Thurstone and Chave validated the Scale for Measuring

Attitude Toward the Church by showing score differences between church members and nonchurchgoers. Churchgoing is not *the* criterion of attitude, for the purpose of the test is to measure something other than the crude sociological fact of church attendance; on the other hand, failure to find a difference would have seriously challenged the test.

Only coarse correspondence between test and group designation is expected. Too great a correspondence between the two would indicate that the test is to some degree invalid, because members of the groups are expected to overlap on the test. Intelligence test items are selected initially on the basis of a correspondence to age, but an item that correlates .95 with age in an elementary school sample would surely be suspect.

Correlation matrices and factor analysis. If two tests are presumed to measure the same construct, a correlation between them is predicted. (An exception is noted where some second attribute has positive loading in the first test and negative loading in the second test; then a low correlation is expected. This is a testable interpretation provided an external measure of either the first or the second variable exists.) If the obtained correlation departs from the expectation, however, there is no way to know whether the fault lies in test A, test B, or the formulation of the construct. A matrix of intercorrelations often points out profitable ways of dividing the construct into more meaningful parts, factor analysis being a useful computational method in such studies.

Guilford [26] has discussed the place of factor analysis in construct validation. His statements may be extracted as follows: "The personnel psychologist wishes to know 'why his tests are valid.' He can place tests and practical criteria in a matrix and factor it to identify 'real dimensions of human personality.' A factorial description is exact and stable; it is economical in explanation; it leads to the creation of pure tests

which can be combined to predict complex behaviors." It is clear that factors here function as constructs. Eysenck, in his "criterion analysis" [18], goes farther than Guilford, and shows that factoring can be used explicitly to test hypotheses about constructs.

Factors may or may not be weighted with surplus meaning. Certainly when they are regarded as "real dimensions" a great deal of surplus meaning is implied, and the interpreter must shoulder a substantial burden of proof. The alternative view is to regard factors as defining a working reference frame, located in a convenient manner in the "space" defined by all behaviors of a given type. Which set of factors from a given matrix is "most useful" will depend partly on predilections, but in essence the best construct is the one around which we can build the greatest number of inferences, in the most direct fashion.

Studies of internal structure. For many constructs, evidence of homogeneity within the test is relevant in judging validity. If a trait such as *dominance* is hypothesized, and the items inquire about behaviors subsumed under this label, then the hypothesis appears to require that these items be generally intercorrelated. Even low correlations, if consistent, would support the argument that people may be fruitfully described in terms of a generalized tendency to dominate or not dominate. The general quality would have power to predict behavior in a variety of situations represented by the specific items. Item-test correlations and certain reliability formulas describe internal consistency.

It is unwise to list uninterpreted data of this sort under the heading "validity" in test manuals, as some authors have done. High internal consistency may *lower* validity. Only if the underlying theory of the trait being measured calls for high item intercorrelations do the correlations support construct validity. Negative item-test correlations may support construct validity, provided that the items with negative correlations are believed irrelevant to the postulated construct and serve as suppressor variables [31, p. 431–436; 44].

Study of distinctive subgroups of items within a test may set an upper limit to construct validity by showing that irrelevant elements influence scores. Thus a study of the PMA space tests shows that variance can be partially accounted for by a response set, tendency to mark many figures as similar [12]. An internal factor analysis of the PEA Interpretation of Data Test shows that in addition to measuring reasoning skills, the test score is strongly influenced by a tendency to say "probably true" rather than "certainly true," regardless of item content [17]. On the other hand, a study of item groupings in the DAT Mechanical Comprehension Test permitted rejection of the hypothesis that knowledge about specific topics such as gears made a substantial contribution to scores [13].

Studies of change over occasions. The stability of test scores ("retest reliability," Cattell's "N-technique") may be relevant to construct validation. Whether a high degree of stability is encouraging or discouraging for the proposed interpretation depends upon the theory defining the construct.

More powerful than the retest after uncontrolled intervening experiences is the retest with experimental intervention. If a transient influence swings test scores over a wide range, there are definite limits on the extent to which a test result can be interpreted as reflecting the typical behavior of the individual. These are examples of experiments which have indicated upper limits to test validity: studies of differences associated with the examiner in projective testing, of change of score under alternative directions ("tell the truth" vs. "make yourself look good to an employer"), and of coachability of mental tests. We may recall Gulliksen's distinction [27]: When the coaching is of a sort that improves the pupil's intellectual functioning in school,

the test which is affected by the coaching has validity as a measure of intellectual functioning; if the coaching improves test taking but not school performance, the test which responds to the coaching has poor validity as a measure of this construct.

Sometimes, where differences between individuals are difficult to assess by any means other than the test, the experimenter validates by determining whether the test can detect induced intra-individual differences. One might hypothesize that the Zeigarnik effect is a measure of ego involvement, i.e., that with ego involvement there is more recall of incomplete tasks. To support such an interpretation, the investigator will try to induce ego involvement on some task by appropriate directions and compare subjects' recall with their recall for tasks where there was a contrary induction. Sometimes the intervention is drastic. Porteus finds [53] that brain-operated patients show disruption of performance on his maze, but do not show impaired performance on conventional verbal tests and argues therefrom that his test is a better measure of planfulness.

Studies of process. One of the best ways of determining informally what accounts for variability on a test is the observation of the person's process of performance. If it is supposed, for example, that a test measures mathematical competence, and yet observation of students' errors shows that erroneous reading of the question is common, the implications of a low score are altered. Lucas in this way showed that the Navy Relative Movement Test, an aptitude test, actually involved two different abilities: spatial visualization and mathematical reasoning [39].

Mathematical analysis of scoring procedures may provide important negative evidence on construct validity. A recent analysis of "empathy" tests is perhaps worth citing [14]. "Empathy" has been operationally defined in many studies by the ability of a judge to predict what responses will be given on some questionnaire by a subject he has observed briefly. A mathematical argument has shown, however, that the scores depend on several attributes of the judge which enter into his perception of *any* individual, and that they therefore cannot be interpreted as evidence of his ability to interpret cues offered by particular others, or his intuition.

THE NUMERICAL ESTIMATE OF CONSTRUCT VALIDITY

There is an understandable tendency to seek a "construct validity coefficient." A numerical statement of the degree of construct validity would be a statement of the proportion of the test score variance that is attributable to the construct variable. This numerical estimate can sometimes be arrived at by a factor analysis, but since present methods of factor analysis are based on linear relations, more general methods will ultimately be needed to deal with many quantitative problems of construct validation.

Rarely will it be possible to estimate definite "construct saturations," because no factor corresponding closely to the construct will be available. One can only hope to set upper and lower bounds to the "loading." If "creativity" is defined as something independent of knowledge, then a correlation of .40 between a presumed test of creativity and a test of arithmetic knowledge would indicate that at least 16 per cent of the reliable test variance is irrelevant to creativity as defined. Laboratory performance on problems such as Maier's "hatrack" would scarcely be an ideal measure of creativity, but it would be somewhat relevant. If its correlation with the test is .60, this permits a tentative estimate of 36 per cent as a lower bound. (The estimate is tentative because the test might overlap with the irrelevant portion of the laboratory measure.) The saturation seems to lie between 36 and 84 per cent; a cumulation of studies would provide better limits.

It should be particularly noted that rejecting the null hypothesis does not finish the job of construct validation [35, p. 284]. The problem is not to conclude that the test "is valid" for measuring the construct variable. The task is to state as definitely as possible the degree of validity the test is presumed to have.

THE LOGIC OF CONSTRUCT VALIDATION

Construct validation takes place when an investigator believes that his instrument reflects a particular construct, to which are attached certain meanings. The proposed interpretation generates specific testable hypotheses, which are a means of confirming or disconfirming the claim. The philosophy of science which we believe does most justice to actual scientific practice will now be briefly and dogmatically set forth. Readers interested in further study of the philosophical underpinning are referred to the works by Braithwaite [6, especially Chapter III], Carnap [7; 8, pp. 56–69], Pap [51], Sellars [55, 56], Feigl [19, 20], Beck [4], Kneale [37, pp. 92–110], Hempel [29; 30, Sec. 7].

THE NOMOLOGICAL NETWORK

The fundamental principles are these:

1. Scientifically speaking, to "make clear what something *is*" means to set forth the laws in which it occurs. We shall refer to the interlocking system of laws which constitute a theory as a *nomological network*.
2. The laws in a nomological network may relate (*a*) observable properties or quantities to each other; or (*b*) theoretical constructs to observables; or (*c*) different theoretical constructs to one another. These "laws" may be statistical or deterministic.
3. A necessary condition for a construct to be scientifically admissible is that it occur in a nomological net, at least *some* of whose laws involve observables. Admissible constructs may be

remote from observation, i.e., a long derivation may intervene between the nomologicals which implicitly define the construct, and the (derived) nomologicals of type *a*. These latter propositions permit predictions about events. The construct is not "reduced" to the observations, but only combined with other constructs in the net to make predictions about observables.

4. "Learning more about" a theoretical construct is a matter of elaborating the nomological network in which it occurs, or of increasing the definiteness of the components. At least in the early history of a construct the network will be limited, and the construct will as yet have few connections.

5. An enrichment of the net such as adding a construct or a relation to theory is justified if it generates nomologicals that are confirmed by observation or if it reduces the number of nomologicals required to predict the same observations. When observations will not fit into the network as it stands, the scientist has a certain freedom in selecting where to modify the network. That is, there may be alternative constructs or ways of organizing the net which for the time being are equally defensible.

6. We can say that "operations" which are qualitatively very different "overlap" or "measure the same thing" if their positions in the nomological net tie them to the same construct variable. Our confidence in this identification depends upon the amount of inductive support we have for the regions of the net involved. It is not necessary that a direct observational comparison of the two operations be made—we may be content with an intranetwork proof indicating that the two operations yield estimates of the same network-defined quantity. Thus, physicists are content to speak of the

"temperature" of the sun and the "temperature" of a gas at room temperature even though the test operations are nonoverlapping because this identification makes theoretical sense.

With these statements of scientific methodology in mind, we return to the specific problem of construct validity as applied to psychological tests. The preceding guide rules should reassure the "toughminded," who fear that allowing construct validation opens the door to nonconfirmable test claims. *The answer is that unless the network makes contact with observations, and exhibits explicit, public steps of inference, construct validation cannot be claimed.* An admissible psychological construct must be behavior-relevant [59, p. 15]. For most tests intended to measure constructs, adequate criteria do not exist. This being the case, many such tests have been left unvalidated, or a finespun network of rationalizations has been offered as if it were validation. Rationalization is not construct validation. One who claims that his test reflects a construct cannot maintain his claim in the face of recurrent negative results because these results show that his construct is too loosely defined to yield verifiable inferences.

A rigorous (though perhaps probabilistic) chain of inference is required to establish a test as a measure of a construct. To validate a claim that a test measures a construct, a nomological net surrounding the concept must exist. When a construct is fairly new, there may be few specifiable associations by which to pin down the concept. As research proceeds, the construct sends out roots in many directions, which attach it to more and more facts or other constructs. Thus the electron has more accepted properties than the neutrino; *numerical ability* has more than *the second space factor.*

"Acceptance," which was critical in criterion-oriented and content validities, has now appeared in construct validity. Unless substantially the same nomological net is accepted by the several users of the construct, public validation is impossible. If A uses *aggressiveness* to mean overt assault on others, and B's usage includes repressed hostile reactions, evidence which convinces B that a test measures *aggressiveness* convinces A that the test does not. Hence, the investigator who proposes to establish a test as a measure of a construct must specify his network or theory sufficiently clearly that others can accept or reject it [cf. 41, p. 406]. A consumer of the test who rejects the author's theory cannot accept the author's validation. He must validate the test for himself, if he wishes to show that it represents the construct as *he* defines it.

Two general qualifications are in order with reference to the methodological principles 1–6 set forth at the beginning of this section. Both of them concern the amount of "theory," in any high-level sense of that word, which enters into a construct-defining network of laws or lawlike statements. We do not wish to convey the impression that one always has a very elaborate theoretical network, rich in hypothetical processes or entities.

Constructs as inductive summaries. In the early stages of development of a construct or even at more advanced stages when our orientation is thoroughly practical, little or no theory in the usual sense of the word need be involved. In the extreme case the hypothesized laws are formulated entirely in terms of descriptive (observational) dimensions although not all of the relevant observations have actually been made.

The hypothesized network "goes beyond the data" only in the limited sense that it purports to *characterize* the behavior facets which belong to an observable but as yet only partially sampled cluster; hence, it generates predictions about hitherto unsampled regions of the phenotypic space. Even though no unobservables or high-order theoretical constructs are introduced, an element of inductive extrapolation appears in the claim that a cluster including some elements not-yet-observed has been

identified. Since, as in any sorting or abstracting task involving a finite set of complex elements, several nonequivalent bases of categorization are available, the investigator may choose a hypothesis which generates erroneous predictions. The failure of a supposed, hitherto untried, member of the cluster to behave in the manner said to be characteristic of the group, or the finding that a nonmember of the postulated cluster does behave in this manner, may modify greatly our tentative construct.

For example, one might build an intelligence test on the basis of his background notions of "intellect," including vocabulary, arithmetic calculation, general information, similarities, two-point threshold, reaction time, and line bisection as subtests. The first four of these correlate, and he extracts a huge first factor. This becomes a second approximation of the intelligence construct, described by its pattern of loadings on the four tests. The other three tests have negligible loading on any common factor. On this evidence the investigator reinterprets intelligence as "manipulation of words." Subsequently it is discovered that test-stupid people are rated as unable to express their ideas, are easily taken in by fallacious arguments, and misread complex directions. These data support the "linguistic" definition of intelligence and the test's claim of validity *for* that construct. But then a block design test with pantomime instructions is found to be strongly saturated with the first factor. Immediately the purely "linguistic" interpretation of Factor I becomes suspect. This finding, taken together with our initial acceptance of the others as relevant to the background concept of intelligence, forces us to reinterpret the concept once again.

If we simply *list* the tests or traits which have been shown to be saturated with the "factor" or which belong to the cluster, no construct is employed. As soon as we even *summarize the properties* of this group of indicators—we are already making some guesses. Intensional characterization of a domain is hazardous since it selects (abstracts) properties and implies that new tests sharing those properties will behave as do the known tests in the cluster, and that tests not sharing them will not.

The difficulties in merely "characterizing the surface cluster" are strikingly exhibited by the use of certain special and extreme groups for purposes of construct validation. The P_d scale of MMPI was originally derived and cross-validated upon hospitalized patients diagnosed "Psychopathic personality, asocial and amoral type" [42]. Further research shows the scale to have a limited degree of predictive and concurrent validity for "delinquency" more broadly defined [5, 28]. Several studies show associations between P_d and very special "criterion" groups which it would be ludicrous to identify as "*the* criterion" in the traditional sense. If one lists these heterogeneous groups and tries to characterize them intensionally, he faces enormous conceptual difficulties. For example, a recent survey of hunting accidents in Minnesota showed that hunters who had "carelessly" shot someone were significantly elevated on P_d when compared with other hunters [48]. This is in line with one's theoretical expectations; when you ask MMPI "experts" to predict for such a group they invariably predict P_d or M_a or both. The finding seems therefore to lend some slight support to the construct validity of the P_d scale. But of course it would be nonsense to *define* the P_d component "operationally" in terms of, say, accident proneness. We might try to subsume the original phenotype and the hunting-accident proneness under some broader category, such as "Disposition to violate society's rules, whether legal, moral, or just *sensible*." But now we have ceased to have a neat operational criterion, and are using instead a rather vague and wide-range class. Besides, there is worse to come. We want the class specification to cover a group trend that (nondelinquent) high school students judged by their peer group as least "responsible" score over a full sigma higher on P_d than those judged most "responsible" [23, p. 75]. Most of the behaviors contributing to such sociometric

choices fall well within the range of socially permissible action; the proffered criterion specification is still too restrictive. Again, any clinician familiar with MMPI lore would predict an elevated P_d on a sample of (nondelinquent) professional actors. Chyatte's confirmation of this prediction [10] tends to support *both*: (*a*) the theory sketch of "what the P_d factor is, psychologically"; and (*b*) the claim of the P_d scale to construct validity for this hypothetical factor. Let the reader try his hand at writing a brief phenotypic criterion specification that will cover both trigger-happy hunters and Broadway actors! And if he should be ingenious enough to achieve this, does his definition also encompass Hovey's report that high P_d predicts the judgments "not shy" and "unafraid of mental patients" made upon nurses by their supervisors [32, p. 143]? And then we have Gough's report that *low* P_d is associated with ratings as "good-natured" [24, p. 40], and Roessell's data showing that high P_d is predictive of "dropping out of high school" [54]. The point is that all seven of these "criterion" dispositions would be readily guessed by any clinician having even superficial familiarity with MMPI interpretation; but to mediate these inferences explicitly requires quite a few hypotheses about dynamics, constituting an admittedly sketchy (but far from vacuous) network defining the genotype *psychopathic deviate*.

Vagueness of present psychological laws. This line of thought leads directly to our second important qualification upon the network schema. The idealized picture is one of a tidy set of postulates which jointly entail the desired theorems; since some of the theorems are coordinated to the observation base, the system constitutes an implicit definition of the theoretical primitives and gives them an indirect empirical meaning. In practice, of course, even the most advanced physical sciences only approximate this ideal. Questions of "categoricalness" and the like, such as logicians raise about pure calculi, are hardly even statable for empirical networks. (What, for example, would be the desiderata of a "well-formed formula" in molar behavior theory?) Psychology works with crude, half-explicit formulations. We do not worry about such advanced formal questions as "whether all molar-behavior statements are decidable by appeal to the postulates" because we know that no existing theoretical network suffices to predict even the *known* descriptive laws. Nevertheless, the sketch of a network is there; if it were not, we would not be saying *anything* intelligible about our constructs. We do not have the rigorous implicit definitions of formal calculi (which still, be it noted, usually permit of a multiplicity of interpretations). Yet the vague, avowedly incomplete network still gives the constructs whatever meaning they do have. When the network is very incomplete, having many strands missing entirely and some constructs tied in only by tenuous threads, then the "implicit definition" of these constructs is disturbingly loose; one might say that the meaning of the constructs is underdetermined. *Since the meaning of theoretical constructs is set forth by stating the laws in which they occur, our incomplete knowledge of the laws of nature produces a vagueness in our constructs* [see Hempel, 30; Kaplan, 34; Pap, 51]. We will be able to say "what anxiety is" when we know all of the laws involving it; meanwhile, since we are in the process of discovering these laws, we do not yet know precisely what anxiety is.

CONCLUSIONS REGARDING THE NETWORK AFTER EXPERIMENTATION

The proposition that x per cent of test variance is accounted for by the construct is inserted into the accepted network. The network then generates a testable prediction about the relation of the test scores to certain other variables, and the investigator gathers data. If prediction and result are in harmony, he can retain his belief that the test measures the construct. The construct is at best adopted, never demonstrated to be "correct."

We do not first "prove" the theory, and then validate the test, nor conversely. In any probable inductive type of inference from a pattern of observations, we examine the relation between the total network of theory and observations. The system involves propositions relating test to construct, construct to other constructs, and finally relating some of these constructs to observables. In ongoing research the chain of inference is very complicated. Kelly and Fiske [36, p. 124] give a complex diagram showing the numerous inferences required in validating a prediction from assessment techniques, where theories about the criterion situation are as integral a part of the prediction as are the test data. A predicted empirical relationship permits us to test all the propositions leading to that prediction. Traditionally the proposition claiming to interpret the test has been set apart as the hypothesis being tested, but actually the evidence is significant for all parts of the chain. If the prediction is not confirmed, any link in the chain may be wrong.

A theoretical network can be divided into subtheories used in making particular predictions. All the events successfully predicted through a subtheory are of course evidence in favor of that theory. Such a subtheory may be so well confirmed by voluminous and diverse evidence that we can reasonably view a particular experiment as relevant only to the test's validity. If the theory, combined with a proposed test interpretation, mispredicts in this case, it is the latter which must be abandoned. On the other hand, the accumulated evidence for a test's construct validity may be so strong that an instance of misprediction will force us to modify the subtheory employing the construct rather than deny the claim that the test measures the construct.

Most cases in psychology today lie somewhere between these extremes. Thus, suppose we fail to find a greater incidence of "homosexual signs" in the Rorschach records of paranoid patients. Which is more strongly disconfirmed—the Rorschach signs or the orthodox theory of paranoia? The negative finding shows the bridge between the two to be undependable, but this is all we can say. The bridge cannot be used unless one end is placed on solider ground. The investigator must decide which end it is best to relocate.

Numerous successful predictions dealing with phenotypically diverse "criteria" give greater weight to the claim of construct validity than do fewer predictions, or predictions involving very similar behaviors. In arriving at diverse predictions, the hypothesis of test validity is connected each time to a subnetwork largely independent of the portion previously used. Success of these derivations testifies to the inductive power of the test-validity statement, and renders it unlikely that an equally effective alternative can be offered.

IMPLICATIONS OF NEGATIVE EVIDENCE

The investigator whose prediction and data are discordant must make strategic decisions. His result can be interpreted in three ways:

1. The test does not measure the construct variable.
2. The theoretical network which generated the hypothesis is incorrect.
3. The experimental design failed to test the hypothesis properly. (Strictly speaking this may be analyzed as a special case of 2, but in practice the distinction is worth making.)

For further research. If a specific fault of procedure makes the third a reasonable possibility, his proper response is to perform an adequate study, meanwhile making no report. When faced with the other two alternatives, he may decide that his test does not measure the construct adequately. Following that decision, he will perhaps prepare and validate a new test. Any rescoring or new interpretative procedure for the original instrument, like a new test, requires validation *by means of a fresh body of data.*

The investigator may regard interpretation 2 as more likely to lead to eventual advances. It is legitimate for the investigator to call the network defining the construct into question, if he has confidence in the test. Should the investigator decide that some step in the network is unsound, he may be able to invent an alternative network. Perhaps he modifies the network by splitting a concept into two or more portions, e.g., by designating types of *anxiety,* or perhaps he specifies added conditions under which a generalization holds. When an investigator modifies the theory in such a manner, he is now required to *gather a fresh body of data* to test the altered hypotheses. This step should normally precede publication of the modified theory. If the new data are consistent with the modified network, he is free from the fear that his nomologicals were gerrymandered to fit the peculiarities of his first sample of observations. He can now trust his test to some extent, because his test results behave as predicted.

The choice among alternatives, like any strategic decision, is a gamble as to which course of action is the best investment of effort. Is it wise to modify the theory? That depends on how well the system is confirmed by prior data, and how well the modifications fit available observations. Is it worth while to modify the test in the hope that it will fit the construct? That depends on how much evidence there is—apart from this abortive experiment—to support the hope, and also on how much it is worth to the investigator's ego to salvage the test. The choice among alternatives is a matter of research planning.

For practical use of the test. The consumer can accept a test as a measure of a construct only when there is a strong positive fit between predictions and subsequent data. When the evidence from a proper investigation of a published test is essentially negative, it should be reported as a stop sign to discourage use of the test pending a reconciliation of test and construct, or final abandonment of the test. If the test has not been published, it should be restricted to research use until some degree of validity is established [1]. The consumer can await the results of the investigator's gamble with confidence that proper application of the scientific method will ultimately tell whether the test has value. Until the evidence is in, he has no justification for employing the test as a basis for terminal decisions. The test may serve, at best, only as a source of suggestions about individuals to be confirmed by other evidence [15, 47].

There are two perspectives in test validation. From the viewpoint of the psychological practitioner, the burden of proof is on the test. A test should not be used to measure a trait until its proponent establishes that predictions made from such measures are consistent with the best available theory of the trait. In the view of the test developer, however, both the test and the theory are under scrutiny. He is free to say *to himself privately*, "If my test disagrees with the theory, so much the worse for the theory." This way lies delusion, unless he continues his research using a better theory.

REPORTING OF POSITIVE RESULTS

The test developer who finds positive correspondence between his proposed interpretation and data is expected to report the basis for his validity claim. Defending a claim of construct validity is a major task, not to be satisfied by a discourse without data. The *Technical Recommendations* have little to say on reporting of construct validity. Indeed, the only detailed suggestions under that heading refer to correlations of the test with other measures, together with a cross reference to some other sections of the report. The two key principles, however, call for the most comprehensive type of reporting. The manual for any test "should report all available

information which will assist the user in determining what psychological attributes account for variance in test scores" [59, p. 27]. And, "The manual for a test which is used primarily to assess postulated attributes of the individual should outline the theory on which the test is based and organize whatever partial validity data there are to show in what way they support the theory" [59, p. 28]. It is recognized, by a classification as "very desirable" rather than "essential," that the latter recommendation goes beyond present practice of test authors.

The proper goals in reporting construct validation are to make clear (*a*) what interpretation is proposed, (*b*) how adequately the writer believes this interpretation is substantiated, and (*c*) what evidence and reasoning lead him to this belief. Without *a* the construct validity of the test is of no use to the consumer. Without *b* the consumer must carry the entire burden of evaluating the test research. Without *c* the consumer or reviewer is being asked to take *a* and *b* on faith. The test manual cannot always present an exhaustive statement on these points, but it should summarize and indicate where complete statements may be found.

To specify the interpretation, the writer must state what construct he has in mind, and what meaning he gives to that construct. For a construct which has a short history and has built up few connotations, it will be fairly easy to indicate the presumed properties of the construct, i.e., the nomologicals in which it appears. For a construct with a longer history, a summary of properties and references to previous theoretical discussions may be appropriate. It is especially critical to distinguish proposed interpretations from other meanings previously given the same construct. The validator faces no small task; he must somehow communicate a theory to his reader.

To evaluate his evidence calls for a statement like the conclusions from a program of research, noting what is well substantiated and what alternative interpretations have been considered and rejected. The writer must note what portions of his proposed interpretation are speculations, extrapolations, or conclusions from insufficient data. The author has an ethical responsibility to prevent unsubstantiated interpretations from appearing as truths. A claim is unsubstantiated unless the evidence for the claim is public, so that other scientists may review the evidence, criticize the conclusions, and offer alternative interpretations.

The report of evidence in a test manual must be as complete as any research report, except where adequate public reports can be cited. Reference to something "observed by the writer in many clinical cases" is worthless as evidence. Full case reports, on the other hand, may be a valuable source of evidence so long as these cases are representative and negative instances receive due attention. The report of evidence must be interpreted with reference to the theoretical network in such a manner that the reader sees why the author regards a particular correlation or experiment as confirming (or throwing doubt upon) the proposed interpretation. Evidence collected by others must be taken fairly into account.

VALIDATION OF A COMPLEX TEST "AS A WHOLE"

Special questions must be considered when we are investigating the validity of a test which is aimed to provide information about several constructs. In one sense, it is naive to inquire "Is this test valid?" One does not validate a test, but only a principle for making inferences. If a test yields many different types of inferences, some of them can be valid and others invalid (cf. Technical Recommendation C2: "The manual should report the validity of each type of inference for which a test is recommended"). From this point of view, every topic sentence in the typical book on Rorschach interpretation presents a hypothesis requiring validation, and one should validate inferences about each aspect of the

personality separately and in turn, just as he would want information on the validity (concurrent or predictive) for each scale of MMPI.

There is, however, another defensible point of view. If a test is purely empirical, based strictly on observed connections between response to an item and some criterion, then of course the validity of one scoring key for the test does not make validation for its other scoring keys any less necessary. But a test may be developed on the basis of a theory which in itself provides a linkage between the various keys and the various criteria. Thus, while Strong's Vocational Interest Blank is developed empirically, it also rests on a "theory" that a youth can be expected to be satisfied in an occupation if he has interests common to men now happy in the occupation. When Strong finds that those with high Engineering interests scores in college are preponderantly in engineering careers 19 years later, he has partly validated the proposed use of the Engineer score (predictive validity). Since the evidence is consistent with the theory on which all the test keys were built, this evidence alone increases the presumption that the *other* keys have predictive validity. How strong is this presumption? Not very, from the viewpoint of the traditional skepticism of science. Engineering interests may stabilize early, while interests in art or management or social work are still unstable. A claim cannot be made that the whole Strong approach is valid just because one score shows predictive validity. But if thirty interest scores were investigated longitudinally and all of them showed the type of validity predicted by Strong's theory, we would indeed be caviling to say that this evidence gives no confidence in the long-range validity of the thirty-first score.

Confidence in a theory is increased as more relevant evidence confirms it, but it is always possible that tomorrow's investigation will render the theory obsolete. The Technical Recommendations suggest a rule of reason, and ask for evidence for each *type* of inference for which a test is recommended. It is stated that no test developer can present predictive validities for all possible criteria; similarly, no developer can run all possible experimental tests of his proposed interpretation. But the recommendation is more subtle than advice that a lot of validation is better than a little.

Consider the Rorschach test. It is used for many inferences, made by means of nomological networks at several levels. At a low level are the simple unrationalized correspondences presumed to exist between certain signs and psychiatric diagnoses. Validating such a sign does nothing to substantiate Rorschach theory. For other Rorschach formulas an explicit a priori rationale exists (for instance, high *F%* interpreted as implying rigid control of impulses). Each time such a sign shows correspondence with criteria, its rationale is supported just a little. At a still higher level of abstraction, a considerable body of theory surrounds the general area of *outer control*, interlacing many different constructs. As evidence cumulates, one should be able to decide what specific inference-making chains within this system can be depended upon. One should also be able to conclude—or deny—that so much of the system has stood up under test that one has some confidence in even the untested lines in the network.

In addition to relatively delimited nomological networks surrounding *control* or *aspiration,* the Rorschach interpreter usually has an overriding theory of the test as a whole. This may be a psychoanalytic theory, a theory of perception and set, or a theory stated in terms of learned habit patterns. Whatever the theory of the interpreter, whenever he validates an inference from the system, he obtains some reason for added confidence in his overriding system. His total theory is not tested, however, by experiments dealing with only one limited set of constructs. The test developer must investigate far-separated, independent sections of the network. The more diversified the predictions the system is

required to make, the greater confidence we can have that only minor parts of the system will later prove faulty. Here we begin to glimpse a logic to defend the judgment that the test and its whole interpretative system is valid at some level of confidence.

There are enthusiasts who would conclude from the foregoing paragraphs that since there is some evidence of correct, diverse predictions made from the Rorschach, the test as a whole can now be accepted as validated. This conclusion overlooks the negative evidence. Just one finding contrary to expectation, based on sound research, is sufficient to wash a whole theoretical structure away. Perhaps the remains can be salvaged to form a new structure. But this structure now must be exposed to fresh risks, and sound negative evidence will destroy it in turn. There is sufficient negative evidence to prevent acceptance of the Rorschach and its accompanying interpretative structures as a whole. So long as any aspects of the overriding theory stated for the test have been disconfirmed, this structure must be rebuilt.

Talk of areas and structures may seem not to recognize those who would interpret the personality "globally." They may argue that a test is best validated in matching studies. Without going into detailed questions of matching methodology, we can ask whether such a study validates the nomological network "as a whole." The judge does employ some network in arriving at his conception of his subject, integrating specific inferences from specific data. Matching studies, if successful, demonstrate only that each judge's interpretative theory has some validity, that it is not completely a fantasy. Very high consistency between judges is required to show that they are using the same network, and very high success in matching is required to show that the network is dependable.

If inference is less than perfectly dependable, we must know which aspects of the interpretative network are least dependable and which are most dependable. Thus, even if one has considerable confidence in a test "as a whole" because of frequent successful inferences, one still returns as an ultimate aim to the request of the Technical Recommendation for separate evidence on the validity of each type of inference to be made.

RECAPITULATION

Construct validation was introduced in order to specify types of research required in developing tests for which the conventional views on validation are inappropriate. Personality tests, and some tests of ability, are interpreted in terms of attributes for which there is no adequate criterion. This paper indicates what sorts of evidence can substantiate such an interpretation, and how such evidence is to be interpreted. The following points made in the discussion are particularly significant.

1. A construct is defined implicitly by a network of associations or propositions in which it occurs. Constructs employed at different stages of research vary in definiteness.
2. Construct validation is possible only when some of the statements in the network lead to predicted relations among observables. While some observables may be regarded as "criteria," the construct validity of the criteria themselves is regarded as under investigation.
3. The network defining the construct, and the derivation leading to the predicted observation, must be reasonably explicit so that validating evidence may be properly interpreted.
4. Many types of evidence are relevant to construct validity, including content validity, interitem correlations, intertest correlations, test-"criterion" correlations, studies of stability over time, and stability under experimental intervention. High correlations and high stability may constitute either

favorable or unfavorable evidence for the proposed interpretation, depending on the theory surrounding the construct.

5. When a predicted relation fails to occur, the fault may lie in the proposed interpretation of the test or in the network. Altering the network so that it can cope with the new observations is, in effect, redefining the construct. Any such new interpretation of the test must be validated by a fresh body of data before being advanced publicly. Great care is required to avoid substituting a posteriori rationalizations for proper validation.
6. Construct validity cannot generally be expressed in the form of a single simple coefficient. The data often permit one to establish upper and lower bounds for the proportion of test variance which can be attributed to the construct. The integration of diverse data into a proper interpretation cannot be an entirely quantitative process.
7. Constructs may vary in nature from those very close to "pure description" (involving little more than extrapolation of relations among observation-variables) to highly theoretical constructs involving hypothesized entities and processes, or making identifications with constructs of other sciences.
8. The investigation of a test's construct validity is not essentially different from the general scientific procedures for developing and confirming theories.

Without in the least *advocating* construct validity as preferable to the other three kinds (concurrent, predictive, content), we do believe it imperative that psychologists make a place for it in their methodological thinking, so that its rationale, its scientific legitimacy, and its dangers may become explicit and familiar. This would be preferable to the widespread current tendency to engage in what actually amounts to construct validation research and use of constructs in practical testing, while talking an "operational" methodology which, if adopted, would force research into a mold it does not fit.

REFERENCES

1. AMERICAN PSYCHOLOGICAL ASSOCIATION. *Ethical standards of psychologists.* Washington, D.C.: American Psychological Association, Inc., 1953.
2. ANASTASI, ANNE. The concept of validity in the interpretation of test scores. *Educ. psychol. Measmt.*, 1950, **10**, 67–78.
3. BECHTOLDT, H. P. Selection. In S. S. Stevens (Ed.), *Handbook of experimental psychology.* New York: Wiley, 1951. Pp. 1237–1267.
4. BECK, L. W. Constructions and inferred entities. *Phil. Sci.*, 1950, **17**. Reprinted in H. Feigl and M. Brodbeck (Eds.), *Readings in the philosophy of science.* New York: Appleton-Century-Crofts, 1953. Pp. 368–381.
5. BLAIR, W. R. N. A comparative study of disciplinary offenders and non-offenders in the Canadian Army. *Canad. J. Psychol.*, 1950, **4**, 49–62.
6. BRAITHWAITE, R. B. *Scientific explanation.* Cambridge: Cambridge Univer. Press, 1953.
7. CARNAP, R. Empiricism, semantics, and ontology. *Rév. int. de Phil.*, 1950, II, 20–40. Reprinted in P. P. Wiener (Ed.), *Readings in philosophy of science,* New York: Scribner's, 1953. Pp. 509–521.
8. CARNAP, R. *Foundations of logic and mathematics. International encyclopedia of unified science,* I, No. 3. Pages 56–69 reprinted as "The interpretation of physics" in H. Feigl and M. Brodbeck (Eds.), *Readings in the philosophy of science.* New York: Appleton-Century-Crofts, 1953. Pp. 309–318.
9. CHILD, I. L. Personality. *Annu. Rev. Psychol.*, 1954, **5**, 149–171.
10. CHYATTE, C. Psychological characteristics of a group of professional actors. *Occupations,* 1949, **27**, 245–250.
11. CRONBACH, L. J. *Essentials of psychological testing.* New York: Harper, 1949.
12. CRONBACH, L. J. Further evidence on response sets and test design. *Educ. psychol. Measmt.,* 1950, **10**, 3–31.
13. CRONBACH, L. J. Coefficient alpha and the internal structure of tests. *Psychometrika,* 1951, **16**, 297–335.
14. CRONBACH, L. J. Processes affecting scores on "understanding of others" and "assumed similarity." *Psychol. Bull.,* 1955, **52**, 177–193.
15. CRONBACH, L. J. The counselor's problems from the perspective of communication theory. In Vivian H. Hewer (Ed.), *New perspectives in counseling.* Minneapolis: Univer. of Minnesota Press, 1955.
16. CURETON, E. E. Validity. In E. F. Lindquist (Ed.), *Educational measurement.* Washington, D.C.: American Council on Education, 1950. Pp. 621–695.
17. DAMRIN, DORA E. A comparative study of information derived from a diagnostic problem-solving test by logical and factorial methods of scoring. Unpublished doctor's dissertation, Univer. of Illinois, 1952.
18. EYSENCK, H. J. Criterion analysis—an application of the hypothetico-deductive method in factor analysis. *Psychol. Rev.,* 1950, **57**, 38–53.
19. FEIGL, H. Existential hypotheses. *Phil. Sci.,* 1950, **17**, 35–62.
20. FEIGL, H. Confirmability and confirmation. *Rév. int. de Phil.,* 1951, **5**, 1–12. Reprinted in P. P. Wiener (Ed.), *Readings in philosophy of science.* New York: Scribner's, 1953. Pp. 522–530.
21. GAYLORD, R. H. Conceptual consistency and criterion equivalence: a dual approach to criterion analysis. Unpublished manuscript (PRB Research Note No. 17). Copies obtainable from ASTIA-DSC, AD-21 440. Defense Documentation Center, Alexandria, Va.
22. GOODENOUGH, FLORENCE L. *Mental testing.* New York: Rinehart, 1950.
23. GOUGH, H. G., McCLOSKY, H., & MEEHL, P. E. A personality scale for social responsibility. *J. abnorm. soc. Psychol.,* 1952, **47**, 73–80.
24. GOUGH, H. G., McKEE, M. G., & YANDELL, R. J. Adjective check list analyses of a number of selected psychometric and assessment variables. Unpublished manuscript. Berkeley: IPAR, 1953.

25. GUILFORD, J. P. New standards for test evaluation. *Educ. psychol. Measmt,* 1946, **6,** 427–439.

26. GUILFORD, J. P. Factor analysis in a test-development program. *Psychol. Rev.,* 1948, **55,** 79–94.

27. GULLIKSEN, H. Intrinsic validity. *Amer. Psychologist,* 1950, **5,** 511–517.

28. HATHAWAY, S. R., & MONACHESI, E. D. *Analyzing and predicting juvenile delinquency with the MMPI.* Minneapolis: Univer. of Minnesota Press, 1953.

29. HEMPEL, C. G. Problems and changes in the empiricist criterion of meaning. *Rév. Int. de Phil.,* 1950, **4,** 41–63. Reprinted in L. Linsky, *Semantics and the philosophy of language.* Urbana: Univer. of Illinois Press, 1952. Pp. 163–185.

30. HEMPEL, C. G. *Fundamentals of concept formation in empirical science.* Chicago: Univer. of Chicago Press, 1952.

31. HORST, P. The prediction of personal adjustment. *Soc. Sci. Res. Council Bull.,* 1941, No. 48.

32. HOVEY, H. B. MMPI profiles and personality characteristics. *J. consult. Psychol.,* 1953, **17,** 142–146.

33. JENKINS, J. G. Validity for what? *J. consult. Psychol.,* 1946, **10,** 93–98.

34. KAPLAN, A. Definition and specification of meaning. *J. Phil.,* 1946, **43,** 281–288.

35. KELLY, E. L. Theory and techniques of assessment. *Annu. Rev. Psychol.,* 1954, **5,** 281–311.

36. KELLY, E. L., & FISKE, D. W. *The prediction of performance in clinical psychology.* Ann Arbor: Univer. of Michigan Press, 1951.

37. KNEALE, W. *Probability and induction.* Oxford: Clarendon Press, 1949. Pages 92–110 reprinted as "Induction, explanation and transcendent hypotheses" in H. Feigl and M. Brodbeck (Eds.), *Readings in the philosophy of science.* New York: Appleton-Century-Crofts, 1953. Pp. 353–367.

38. LINDQUIST, E. F. *Educational measurement.* Washington, D.C.: American Council on Education, 1950.

39. LUCAS, C. M. Analysis of the relative movement test by a method of individual interviews. *Bur. Naval Personnel Res. Rep.,* Contract Nonr-694 (00), NR 151–13. Princeton, N.J.: Educational Testing Service, March 1953.

40. MacCORQUODALE, K., & MEEHL, P. E. On a distinction between hypothetical constructs and intervening variables. *Psychol. Rev.,* 1948, **55,** 95–107.

41. MACFARLANE, JEAN W. Problems of validation inherent in projective methods. *Amer. J. Orthopsychiat.,* 1942, **12,** 405–410.

42. McKINLEY, J. C., & HATHAWAY, S. R. The MMPI: V. Hysteria, hypomania, and psychopathic deviate. *J. appl. Psychol.,* 1944, **28,** 153–174.

43. McKINLEY, J. C., HATHAWAY, S. R., & MEEHL, P. E. The MMPI: VI. The K scale. *J. consult. Psychol.,* 1948, **12,** 20–31.

44. MEEHL, P. E. A simple algebraic development of Horst's suppressor variables. *Amer. J. Psychol.,* 1945, **58,** 550–554.

45. MEEHL, P. E. An investigation of a general normality or control factor in personality testing. *Psychol. Monogr.,* 1945, **59,** No. 4 (Whole No. 274).

46. MEEHL, P. E. *Clinical vs. statistical prediction.* Minneapolis: Univer. of Minnesota Press, 1954.

47. MEEHL, P. E., & ROSEN, A. Antecedent probability and the efficiency of psychometric signs, patterns or cutting scores. *Psychol. Bull.,* 1955, **52,** 194–216.

48. *Minnesota Hunter Casualty Study.* St. Paul: Jacob Schmidt Brewing Company, 1954.

49. MOSIER, C. I. A critical examination of the concepts of face validity. *Educ. psychol. Measmt,* 1947, **7,** 191–205.

50. MOSIER, C. I. Problems and designs of cross-validation. *Educ. psychol. Measmt,* 1951, **11,** 5–12.

51. PAP, A. Reduction-sentences and open concepts. *Methodos,* 1953, **5,** 3–30.

52. PEAK, HELEN. Problems of objective observation. In L. Festinger and D. Katz (Eds.), *Research methods in the behavioral sciences.* New York: Dryden Press, 1953. Pp. 243–300.

53. PORTEUS, S. D. *The Porteus maze test and intelligence.* Palo Alto: Pacific Books, 1950.

54. ROESSEL, F. P. MMPI results for high school drop-outs and graduates. Unpublished doctor's dissertation, Univer. of Minnesota, 1954.

55. SELLARS, W. S. Concepts as involving laws and inconceivable without them. *Phil. Sci.,* 1948, **15,** 287–315.

56. SELLARS, W. S. Some reflections on lan-

guage games. *Phil. Sci.*, 1954, **21**, 204–228.

57. SPIKER, C. C., & McCANDLESS, B. R. The concept of intelligence and the philosophy of science. *Psychol. Rev.*, 1954, **61**, 255–267.

58. Technical recommendations for psychological tests and diagnostic techniques: preliminary proposal. *Amer. Psychologist,* 1952, **7**, 461–476.

59. Technical recommendations for psychological tests and diagnostic techniques. *Psychol. Bull. Supplement,* 1954, **51**, 2, Part 2, 1–38.

60. THURSTONE, L. L. The criterion problem in personality research. *Psychometric Lab. Rep.*, No. 78. Chicago: Univer. of Chicago, 1952.

Chapter 5

Objective Tests as Instruments of Psychological Theory

JANE LOEVINGER

The central concepts of classical test theory are reliability and validity. The concept of reliability was criticized from the beginning, and at present the most widely accepted view appears to be that what was formerly called reliability encompasses two independent components, homogeneity and stability. The notion of validity as correlation with an outside criterion appeared to be a simpler and less vulnerable concept than reliability, however difficult it was to obtain adequate criteria. The rather sudden appearance of the term "construct validity" indicates that the second concept of classical test theory is undergoing criticism and revision.

The purposes of the present monograph are:

(a) to celebrate the extension of the concept of validity as an indication that psychometrics is recognized as truly the handmaiden of psychology rather than merely of psychotechnology;

(b) to argue that, since predictive, concurrent, and content validities are all essentially *ad hoc*, construct validity is the whole of validity from a scientific point of view;

(c) to analyze the components of construct validity, in particular propos-

This work is reprinted from *Psychological Reports*, 1957, Monograph Supplement 9, with the permission of the author and Southern University Press.

This monograph was written in part while the author held the Margaret M. Justin Fellowship of the American Association of University Women. This investigation was also supported in part by a research grant, M-1213, from the National Institute of Mental Health, of the National Institutes of Health, Public Health Service.

The author owes more than an ordinary debt of gratitude for detailed criticism of early versions of the manuscript to Drs. Jack Block, Clyde Coombs, Lee Cronbach, Louis Guttman, Paul Meehl, Blanche Sweet, and Robert M. W. Travers. They have helped to increase areas of mutual agreement and sharpen points of disagreement. Permission to quote unpublished material has been granted by Drs. Block, Sweet, and Milton Whitcomb.

While this monograph was developed independently, it is a pleasure to record the priority of Jessor and Hammond [60] with respect to some of the ideas presented here, particularly that the concept of construct validity implies a program not only of test analysis but also of test construction.

ing "structural component" as name for a previously only partly recognized aspect; and

(d) to relate secular trends in test behavior to the validity problem.

The presentation of these and related topics as a single monograph has an overriding purpose: to develop a coherent view of psychometrics, a mutually implicative test theory and method of test construction. Many current lines of research in psychometrics are discussed, either as contributing to or as contrasting with the present system. It would be unjust, however, to read the monograph as a review of psychometric literature. No attempt is made to evaluate any contribution or any line of work *in toto*, nor is inclusive coverage of current literature sought. If the exposition appears to claim that only the present view is admissible, that is an artifact of the argument, not an expression of belief or intention.

EXTENSION OF THE CONCEPT OF VALIDITY

Because of the difficulties to which the classical concept of validity led, there have been many attempts to modify and redefine validity in recent years, culminating in recognition that the new concept is essentially different from classical validity and requires an identifying name.

The term *construct validity* was proposed by the APA Committee on Psychological Tests, which drew up the *Technical Recommendations for Psychological Tests and Diagnostic Techniques* [121]. The concept was suggested by a subcommittee composed of Meehl and Challman. It was expounded later by Cronbach and Meehl [20] in a paper which reviewed more fully the history of the concept. The circumstances which gave rise to these two contributions were somewhat restrictive. Obviously, the official *Technical Recommendations* were constrained to approve the best in current practice, and the paper by Cronbach and Meehl grew out of that

endeavor. The present monograph, being without official sanction or origin, is in position to take advantage of the work done by official committees and by Cronbach and Meehl but also to propose a more radical reformulation of the validity problem. This reformulation is not intended chiefly as criticism of the previous excellent contributions. The organization of the present monograph follows approximately that of Peak's chapter on objective tests [92], which Cronbach and Meehl also acknowledge as their closest predecessor. The province is large; specific overlap with Peak and with Cronbach and Meehl will therefore be avoided.

A. CRITIQUE OF CLASSICAL VALIDITY CONCEPT

Validity has often been defined as the extent to which a test measures what it is supposed to measure. This definition is too vague, too remote from actual measuring operations, to be useful; it is consistent with all the current meanings of validity. What will be referred to as the classical definition of validity is the one which by far predominates in psychometric literature, to wit, correlation with a criterion.

What the *Technical Recommendations* [121] call predictive and concurrent validities seems indistinguishable from what Peak [92] calls "blindly empirical validity" and is exactly the classical conception of validity in test theory. Surely no one will dispute the legitimacy of computing a validity coefficient for an existing test in reference to a situation where it is deemed a suitable predictive or discriminative device. The contention of the present monograph is that classical validity is not a suitable basic concept for test theory; it does not provide an adequate basis for test construction.

The classical definition of validity has been stated:

The validity of a test is the correlation of the test with some criterion. In this sense a test has a great many different "validities." For example, the ACE Psychological Examination has one validity for predicting grades in English and a different validity for predicting grades in Latin. It is also found in studying various validity coefficients for a given test that they vary from school to school, and from time to time. In other words, validity cannot be regarded as a fixed or a unitary characteristic of a test. As new uses for a test are contemplated, new validity coefficients must be determined; and, when use of a test is continued, the validity coefficients must be redetermined at intervals [43, p. 88].

The above quotation is the essence of the single paragraph devoted to the "Meaning of validity" in Gulliksen's text on test theory.

Meehl and Rosen [89], in a review of current uses of predictive and concurrent validity coefficients, have carried further the demonstration of the specificity of classical validity. They are particularly concerned with the case where the criterion to be predicted is a dichotomous one. In such prediction, or discrimination, there are two possible errors: one can select an individual who should not be selected or reject an individual who should not be rejected, meaning by selection and rejection no more than assignment to the two distinguished groups.

The dichotomous criterion is particularly important for test theory, for one of the commonest methods of test construction is to select those items which best distinguish two groups believed to differ with respect to the dimension to be measured. In this kind of empirical keying, the ability of an item to discriminate the two criterion groups is the chief or only basis for its inclusion in the test.

Three different cases of dichotomous criteria must be distinguished. A truly dichotomous criterion is one which is not reasonably conceived as two extremes of a continuum. Examples are not easy to find. One possibility is a series of patients all of whom complain of headaches; the problem is to separate those whose complaint is at least partly organic from those whose symptoms are entirely psychogenic. Again, of all patients discharged from a mental hospital, those readmitted and those not readmitted are substantially distinct groups.

A second case might be referred to as a dichotomized criterion. Here the problem is to predict which individuals fall above a given cutting score in an essentially continuous criterion. In studies done in a military setting, passing or failing a given course of study is often the criterion to be predicted. Presumably the course grades initially fall into a more or less continuous distribution. While passing or failing a course is in a way similar to being readmitted to a mental hospital or not, the cutting point between "pass" and "fail" seems less arbitrary, less subject to administrative whim, in the case of hospital readmission.

In a third case, and probably the most common one, an essentially continuous distribution is being measured and the test is expected ultimately to discriminate throughout its range. For item selection, however, only individuals at the two extremes of the distribution are used.

Consider the first case, a truly dichotomous criterion. Meehl and Rosen [89] have shown that validity measured in terms of false positives and false negatives is altered when nothing changes except the proportion of true positives and true negatives. The optimal cutting score depends on the proportions in the two groups, and for this reason they advocate that an inflexible cutting score not be set for any psychometric device. Merely changing the proportion in the two groups without any alteration in the nature of the individuals included should not affect item choice, however, when items are chosen according to their ability to discriminate the groups.

Consider now the second case, the dichotomized criterion. Any change in administrative conditions which leads to shifting the cutting point on the criterion will not only alter the validity of the total test and shift the optimal cutting score on the test; it will also change the composition of the criterion groups. Thus, discriminative powers of the items will be differentially affected. In general, some items will become more valid and some less. A test whose items are selected to be those with optimal validity one year will not have optimally valid items in later years if the cut between pass and fail has changed. Lord [76] and Cronbach and Warrington [21] have contributed papers on one relevant point, the dependence of the optimal item difficulty on the criterion cutting point.

In the third case, where only the extremes of the distribution are used to establish the validity of the items, considerations similar to those of the second case prevail. It has been demonstrated in a number of papers [71] that for the situation most usual in psychological testing, i.e., low item intercorrelations, optimal item difficulty is approximately at the median of the distribution. Where only the extremes of the distribution are used to test item validity, insufficient evidence in regard to item difficulty is obtained. It should be noted, too, that apart from the problem of item difficulty, knowledge of the ability of the item to discriminate the extremes of a distribution is not substitutable for knowledge of how accurately it discriminates near the median.

Now a serious test construction project is an arduous and expensive business. No one recommends attempting to construct and standardize tests except on the basis of large samples representative of some specifiable population. Major test construction is rarely if ever undertaken with the intention of putting a test to a single use. Meehl and Rosen [89] show, however, that even when the administrative or clinical setting remains unaltered in other respects, if the test is used in a slightly different manner, the validity is altered. They give as an example the use of a neuropsychiatric screening test by the Army. If a test is constructed to predict which inductees will later be given neuropsychiatric discharges, it is not thereby validated for selecting inductees. A test constructed to select those draftees for whom examination by a psychiatrist is desirable prior to induction is not thereby validated as a selection instrument for the draftees for whom psychiatrists have difficulty in making a decision to induct into the Army. Such changes in test utilization involve changes in the composition of criterion groups, even though the trait to be measured and the criterion cutting point remain the same. Not only the validity coefficient and the optimal cutting score but also item validities are affected by such changes. A scale selected to discriminate hysterics from normals would be quite different from a scale selected to discriminate hysterics from early schizophrenics.

In short, it is difficult to discover any circumstances under which the classical concept of validity is a suitable basis for test construction. Military situations where large numbers of men are processed in short periods of time offer the most promising possibility of an administrative setting stable enough to justify test construction on the basis of classical validity. But it is well known that administrative fiat can change radically a selection per cent without advance warning. Indeed, apart from any such argument as the foregoing, many tests devised in the military situation have been declared obsolete before they were completed.

Since expositions of test theory such as Gulliksen's [43] *Theory of Mental Tests* devote far more space to reliability than to validity, it may be charged that arguing against classical validity as the basic concept of test theory is to attack a straw man. But reliability as a central concept also leads to problems and contradictions, some of which the writer has called attention to previously [69, 71] and some of which will be discussed under Secular Trends in Tests Behavior, below. In consideration of such problems Brogden [5], among others, argued that validity rather than reliability is the central concept of test theory. In this respect it is interesting to contrast Gulliksen's text with the *Technical Recommendations;* where the former is devoted predominantly to reliability theory with validity given only minor emphasis, the more recent official publication devotes about three times the space to validity that it does to reliability.

Lord strongly defends the importance of specific validity, stating that the concept of over-all validity "is not basic to psychometrics. The discriminating power of the test for a specified decision problem regarding a specified examinee is the truly basic concept" [78, p. 509]. Lord's view will be seen to represent the opposite pole from that represented by the present monograph.

A strong proponent of the present view is Cattell, who has written:

> Particularized validation is not only devoid of proper scientific interest but deceptive in its promise of practical economy. . . . Its absurdity is most cogently argued by the demands of practical economy and efficiency alone; for a specific test for every occupation and life situation is its logical and impossible conclusion [11, pp. 549–550].

The writer believes that the most fruitful direction for the development of psychometric devices, and hence of psychometric theory, is toward measurement of traits which have real existence in some sense; that this orientation is antithetical to one which places first emphasis on prediction, decisions, or "utility;" that most decision-oriented psychometric studies would be more fruitfully formulated as trait-oriented studies; and that such legitimately pressing decisions as must inevitably be made will also best be served by a predominantly trait-oriented psychometrics.

An economist, Jacob Marschak, has stated the argument concisely:

> Theory provides us with solutions which are potentially useful for a large class of decisions. It is welcome because we cannot foresee which particular decisions we shall have to take. Our decisions may or may not be such as to leave certain properties of the system

unchanged. Hence, the more we know about its properties the better. If we merely want to know how long it takes to boil an egg, the best is to boil one or two without going into the chemistry of protein molecules. The need for chemistry is due to our want to do other and new things [82, p. 214].

The argument against classical criterion-oriented psychometrics is thus two-fold: it contributes no more to the science of psychology than rules for boiling an egg contribute to the science of chemistry. And the number of genuine egg-boiling decisions which clinicians and psychotechnologists face is small compared with the number of situations where a deeper knowledge of psychological theory would be helpful. This argument challenges Meehl's [88] plea for a good clinical cookbook and Cronbach's [18] advocacy of decision and utility theory.

B. CONSTRUCT VALIDITY: ELUCIDATION OF TERMS

As originally proposed, construct validity was one of four kinds of validity, the other three being content, predictive, and concurrent validities. Predictive and concurrent validities are, following the above argument, *ad hoc.* Content validity is established by the judgment of the investigator that the items are valid; it is thus also contingent upon a special, non-generalizable circumstance, to wit, the particular investigator. (But see the fuller discussion of content validity under Components of Construct Validity, A, below.) Since *ad hoc* arguments are scientifically of minor importance, if not actually inadmissable, what is left, construct validity, is the whole of the subject from a systematic, scientific point of view.

Thus, in place of the classification of validity proposed in the *Technical Recommendations,* it is here recommended that two basic contexts for defining validity be recognized, administrative and scientific. There are essentially two kinds of administrative validity, content and predictive-concurrent. There is only one kind of validity which exhibits the property of transposability or invariance under changes in administrative setting which is the touchstone of scientific usefulness: that is construct validity.

Neither the *Technical Recommendations* nor Cronbach and Meehl gave a formal definition of construct validity. In the former paper the term was introduced as follows: "Construct validity is evaluated by investigating what psychological qualities a test measures, i.e., by demonstrating that certain explanatory constructs account to some degree for performance on the test. . . . Essentially, in studies of construct validity we are validating the theory underlying the test" [121, p. 14].

Cronbach and Meehl's introduction of the term was: "*Construct validation* is involved whenever a test is to be interpreted as a measure of some attribute or quality which is not 'operationally defined.' The problem faced by the investigator is, 'What constructs account for variance in test performance?' " [20, p. 282].

The proponents of the term *construct validity* have, I believe, been misled by their philosophical sophistication into using a term less precise and less intuitively appealing than a naively realistic term would be, such as, perhaps, *essential validity.* There are indications of reification of *constructs* among some psychologists to mean general or central traits. Among psychologists who do not like constructs, they apparently stand for a non-preferred level of generalization. The term *trait* seems also to have acquired definite, albeit private, connotations for many psychologists. A useful distinction which MacCorquodale and Meehl [81] have made between intervening variables and hypothetical constructs, in terms of degree of abstraction from the data, was perhaps the jumping off point; but assigning to constructs a particular place in personality organization is a vast extrapolation from their thesis.

A dictionary [122] definition of construct is: "Something constructed; specif., *Psychol.*, an intellectual synthesis." In the present paper both *construct* and *trait* are used in their general or dictionary meanings. Connotations of depth, level, or locus are specifically disclaimed. Traits exist in people; constructs (here usually about traits) exist in the minds and magazines of psychologists. People have constructs too, but that is outside the present scope.

Construct connotes construction and artifice; yet what is at issue is validity with respect to exactly what the psychologist does not construct: the validity of the test as a measure of traits which exist prior to and independently of the psychologist's act of measuring. It is true that psychologists never know traits directly but only through the glass of their constructs, but the data to be judged are manifestations of traits, not manifestations of constructs. Cronbach and Meehl and their colleagues on the APA committee appear reluctant to assign reality to constructs or traits. Considering traits as real is, in the present view, a working stance and not a philosophical tenet.

That the distinction made here between traits and constructs is free of metaphysical implications is seen by comparing it to the familiar distinction between parameter and statistic. The parameter is what we aim to estimate; the corresponding statistic represents our current best estimate of it. Just so, the trait is what we aim to understand, and the corresponding construct represents our current best understanding of it. The distinction between trait and construct can be dispensed with no better than the distinction between parameter and statistic.

Thus, in conceptualizing the problem of validity I find myself far from the naively operational but actually *ad hoc* reasoning of traditional discussions of validity, but objecting to the confusion of constructs and traits which may be read into the term construct validity. With this understanding, the subject of the present monograph is construct validity.

Three elements are involved, the test, the traits measured, and what the tester says the test measures (construct, interpretation, theory). With three elements, two independent relationships can be specified. This can be done two quite different ways. The *Technical Recommendations* [121, p. 15] imply that the two questions subsumed under construct validity are: to what extent does the test measure whatever is specified by a given construct? And, to what extent does that construct embody a valid hypothesis? An alternative formulation of the two relationships is: to what extent does the test measure a trait that "really" exists? And, how well does the proposed interpretation correspond to what is measured by the test?

The former pair of questions divides construct validity into the validity of the test for the construct and the validity of the construct. Cronbach and Meehl, following Peak, state that what is at stake is usually both, that the evidence for the two kinds of validity is usually not separable, except where either the test or the construct has been established over a long period of time.

The latter pair of questions divides the topic into the intrinsic validity of the test and the validity of the interpretation, though for practical purposes validity usually would also cover validity of the interpretation. The superiority of the latter formulation lies in the fact that information under the two headings comes somewhat separately. (This discussion is not intended to imply that the actual process of test construction should follow such a separation.) The magnitude of the interrelationships of the items among themselves and the magnitude of the highest external correlations of the test score are evidence that something systematic is being measured. The content of the items, the nature of their interrelationships, and the nature of the outside variables showing varying degrees of interrelationship with the test score are relevant to proposed interpretations. The former set of relations may be thought of as giving psychometric meaning to the test, the latter as giving its psychological meaning.

Cronbach and Meehl are led by their adherence to the former pair of questions to state, "A consumer of the test who rejects the author's theory cannot accept the author's validation. He must validate the test for himself, if he wishes to show that it represents the construct as *he* defines it" [20, p. 291]. Do they mean that validational studies are communicable only among such coteries as are agreed on theoretical issues? Such a stand assigns a very minor role to tests as instruments for the development of theory.

Suppose I claim that I can measure "Strength of the tendency to repress the Oedipus complex." Any psychologist can reject the title of the test and therewith the interpretation, since both are based on what Cronbach and Meehl call a "nomological network" which extends beyond the test validation enterprise. But any evidence for the cohesion of the various items or for the predictive power of the test is public and not contingent on acceptance of psychoanalytic theory. Someone with a different theoretical outlook can reject the proffered interpretation, but he cannot reject at the same time whatever evidence there is of something to be interpreted.

From a practical view, whichever pair of questions is asked, both must be answered. A clinician gets no help from a highly valid test which he cannot interpret. Test theory must make provision for answering both questions. In the remainder of this paper validity will be taken to cover both the extent to which a test measures anything and the validity of its interpretation.

RELATION OF TEST BEHAVIOR TO THEORY

A. TEST RESPONSES AS SIGNS AND AS SAMPLES

Although the view of test behavior espoused here is somewhat different from that of Goodenough [37, Ch. 7], her terminology is useful in describing it. The present view is that responses to items are always and essentially both *signs* and *samples* of behavior. In referring to some test responses as signs, Goodenough meant that they represented and indicated the presence of traits and of other behavior which they did not resemble. In referring to test responses as samples, Goodenough was describing tests in which the items are essentially similar to the behavior which it is desired to predict. In a literal sense, the items of every test are both signs and samples. One would not give a test at all unless one could make inferences from test behavior to behavior outside the test situation. This representative quality is the whole reason for giving tests, as Goodenough implied [37, p. 102]. At the same time, test behavior is behavior and must be assumed to obey the same laws and be determined by the same factors as other behavior. In this sense, all test responses have the character of a sample of behavior.

In principle, every trait of a person is represented in each of his actions. Some kinds of actions are such insensitive indicators of certain traits as to be worthless as their signals. If an action is an extremely sensitive indicator of a trait, it may for short be called a manifestation of that trait. It seems reasonable to assume that manifestations of a trait in a test situation will share some of the properties of other manifestations of the same trait. The multiple reference of every action must not be forgotten. The many sources and many meanings of every response induce scepticism about the value of searching for rigorously structured, pure, unidimensional patterns.

One of the aims of psychological theory is to determine the structure of personality, to find the traits which determine behavior. Unfortunately for the simplicity and success of this enterprise, behavior in its everyday forms cannot be uniquely itemized and classified. There are no natural units for the study of behavior. The problem of discrete, unambiguously identifiable units of behavior can be solved by use of objective test items. Because tests are samples, what we know about behavior in general applies to test behavior. Because tests are signs, what we learn from tests can help structure and interpret knowledge of other, more amorphous behavior.

The problem then becomes one of finding items which are sensitive signs of those areas of behavior which are significant for practical and for theoretical purposes. This has proved somewhat easier with respect to abilities than with respect to personality. The present concern is therefore mainly with personality tests, but much of what is said could be applied with slight change to ability tests. What is required might be called a "psychology of objective test behavior." There is needed a theory, supported by data, of what kinds of traits or what levels of personality can be measured by different kinds of personality tests.

B. THE PROBLEM OF HOMOGENEITY

There is a bifurcation in test theory. If the aim of testing is to predict optimally a single criterion, then any item measuring aspects of behavior which are related to that criterion may be included in the test; such items may be independent of each other or even negatively correlated, at least theoretically. Homogeneity of test content is either ignored or deliberately eschewed. If, however, tests are conceived as instruments of psychological theory rather than as devices of psychotechnology, then one has to face the considerable problem of constructing tests which are homogeneous with respect to some trait. The present proposal is that the problem of test homogeneity be viewed in intimate relation with what is known of the complex causation of behavior, and of the fact that traits are manifest in a multiple, alternative, and at times dialectically opposed manner.

A number of attempts to meet the problem of homogeneity have been devised on the basis of a more or less strict logical or mathematical definition of homogeneity. The most important of these is Guttman's [44] scale analysis. A perfect scale is composed of a set of items such that if A has a higher rank than B, then A is as high as or higher than B on every item. Then for each total score there is just one configuration of item responses. Thus, knowing any individual's score on the test as a whole, one can reproduce each of his answers, a situation obviously different from the usual one in psychological testing. When consideration is restricted to dichotomous items and cumulative tests, that is, tests where each item is scored one or zero and the item scores are added to obtain the total score, a Guttman-type scale is identical with what Loevinger [69] called a perfectly homogeneous test. In this kind of test there is an order of the items such that each individual obtains a score of one on every item up to the one corresponding to his total score and zero on all subsequent items. Scale analysis has come into wide usage in sociology, but the sets of items which prove to be almost perfect scales are usually hardly more than several rephrasings of a single question. They have thus not provided new insights into psychological traits as yet.

Recently Coombs [13] has devised models for conceptualizing completely homogeneous tests. He has propounded a "theory of psychological scaling" which divides psychological tests into two types, which he denotes by Task A and Task B. Tests of ability and expressions of preferences between stimuli illustrate Task A. The judgment of which stimulus has more of some attribute illustrates Task B. In Task A each stimulus and each individual is assumed to have a "scale value"; whether the individual scores plus on an item (agrees, succeeds) depends on whether his scale value is greater than that of the item. The scale value of the individual is assumed to be the same regardless of the item. So far one may be led to suppose that the notion of "scale value" corresponds to such intuitive ideas as ability and trait. However, in Task B the individual is postulated to assume a scale value equal to that of the item as he proceeds from one item to another. Thus it appears that what Coombs calls "scale value" is an arbitrary construct, or set of constructs, which does not correspond closely to intuitive notions about traits.

An interesting feature of Coombs' system, but one which makes it more recondite, is that he emphasizes a formal similarity between the people taking the test and the items, which he refers to as stimuli. Corresponding to Task A is Dual Task A, and corresponding to Task B is Dual Task B. A test falls in the category of Dual Task A if each stimulus (item) classifies the individual as being above or below the item's scale value. A test falls in the category of Dual Task B if each item grades the several individuals with respect to each other on an attribute. In Dual Task B the item itself does not have a scale value. Thus an essay question permits sorting individuals with respect to some attribute, but the question itself does not have a scale value. A problem in arithmetic, however, has a scale value which, in effect, each person taking the test measures himself against (Dual Task A).

Hovland and Sherif [57, 96] have pointed out the inconsistency between Thurstone's method of constructing attitude tests by equal-appearing intervals (Task B) and recent findings concerning influence of personality traits on perception and judgment. They have added data showing the difficulty of isolating the two types of task. Both Edwards [26] and Peak [92] have pointed out that the work of Hovland and Sherif is difficult to integrate with Coombs' separation of Task A and Task B.

Workers in the field of personality measurement have recognized and struggled for years with the fact that self-reports concerning personality traits are subject to such massive systematic distortion as to make them virtually worthless as direct measurements of personality traits. One of the most promising methods for dealing with this problem lies precisely in the direction of straddling what Coombs calls Task A and Task B, stating preferences between stimuli and judging stimuli with respect to an attribute. Campbell [9] has provided an able review of such indirect attitude measures. His paradigm for the construction of disguised tests of attitudes is:

> . . . a plausible task, (a) which your respondents will all strive to do well, (b) which is sufficiently difficult or ambiguous to allow individual differences in response, and (c) which can be loaded with content relative to the attitude you seek to measure. Test the responses of individuals for persistent selectivity in performance, for correlated or non-random errors [9, pp. 33–34].

The Berkeley F-scale [2] is an example of a disguised test calling for pseudo-judgments (Task B) which in fact reflect prejudices (Task A). Examples of items are: "Most people don't realize how much our lives are controlled by plots hatched in secret places" [2, p. 257]; "The business man and the manufacturer are much more important to society than the artist and the professor" [2, p. 255]. Other items in the F-scale seem to be within the realm of Task A: "There is hardly anything lower than a person who does not feel a great love, gratitude, and respect for his parents" [2, p. 255]. The decision as to whether this item is purely Task A or contains an admixture of Task B is difficult. The distinction is essential to Coombs' theory of scaling, since in one case there is zero correlation between scale values of persons and items, in the other case the correlation is unity. Unfortunately, the scale values correspond to no measurable quantities; so no empirical test is available.

Coombs maintains (personal communication) that such data as those of Hovland and Sherif have no bearing on his distinction between Task A and Task B. His system is apparently so abstract that data have no bearing on his assumptions, and certainly intuition gives no clue as to their validity. One cannot help wondering how such a system can make enough contact with reality to contribute to solution of psychological problems. But Coombs aims, no less than does the present monograph, to integrate psychological and psychometric

considerations in his work. Faced with data which do not conform to a unidimensional model, Coombs [15, p. 5] points out that one can proceed to a stochastic (probabilistic) model which allows for error, or one can proceed to account for the data in terms of several dimensions. Coombs' recourse is to multidimensional analysis. But not many more than two or three variables can be handled at a time in this kind of analysis. Coombs has thus equipped us with a kind of analysis which can handle, say, 10 items all of which are completely determined by the same two or three component variables. But where are such items to be found, and how will we know that we have found them? Can we expect anything other than psychological trivialities to turn up in such form?

The problem of making inferences about a single trait from a set of responses all of which are multiply determined is a substantial one. Clinicians, in drawing inferences, are faced with a similar problem. They do not seek aspects of behavior which are determined by a single trait, for there are none. Nor do they seek to analyze all of the many causes of the behaviors they observe. To be confident that one's multidimensional analysis is complete, there must always be many more behaviors observed than there are component causes, and there is no way to insure obtaining any such situation. The clinician searches for a common theme or thread in behaviors which are superficially diverse. When an item of behavior is viewed as an indication of a trait, all other traits and influences which determine it operate as errors. If the observed behaviors are sufficiently diverse, the errors are uncorrelated and more or less cancel each other out.

This solution carries the implication that inferences about individuals will never be made with certainty but will always carry some probability of error. Since that probability of error can, in appropriate circumstances [72], be made arbitrarily small, the objection is not too serious. This solution is what Coombs and others call "actuarial measurement"; it stays within the main stream of psychometrics, beginning with Spearman.

C. OBSERVATION PRIOR TO MEASUREMENT

Considerations adduced so far have led to rejection of a single external criterion or of rigid or univocal inter-item relationships as the sole touchstone of psychological measurement. Both prediction and structure will recur later in the discussion as components of construct validity, but they cannot stand alone as guides to test construction, prediction because it changes with every slight change in circumstance, rigid structure because such relationships are not found in the most important areas of psychological measurement. Measurement in psychology is a complex process, requiring correspondingly complicated concepts. The theory of measurement being developed herein is germane only to a particular kind of data. It is necessary now to explain that limitation.

The term *objective test* is used in the present monograph in the sense of *structured tests viewed behavioristically*. Objective tests are distinguished on the one hand from projective tests and on the other from rating scales. The former distinction relates to item structure. Projective tests involve free response, as do most interviews, while objective tests, in the sense that the term is used here, require in principle that every individual choose one of the stated alternatives for each item. (Speed tests are usually objective, but they are almost as inconvenient statistically as projective tests and are arbitrarily excluded from the present discussion.) Rating scales usually refer to a different person than the one responding. Self-ratings, when the response is scored categorically, are not excluded here from objective tests. Attitude tests, interest tests, and self-rating questionnaires are alike considered objective tests, as are, of course, power tests of ability, since the responses on such tests are viewed here simply as behavior with

no automatic ascription of validity to the apparent content. As Campbell [9] has pointed out, in a review which advocates the use of structured disguised tests, the task of validating disguised measures is identical with that of validating apparently undisguised ones. In view of the well-known deviousness of human nature, the safest course appears to be to assume that all tests are disguised ones. In a direct or undisguised test it is after all only the motives of the investigator, not those of his *Ss*, which are undisguised. The present use of the term *objective tests* has coexisted for many years with a contrary usage which contrasts objective tests and questionnaires.

The requirement of objectivity imposes on us a behavioristic attitude towards the psychological meaning of test responses; equally it implies restrictions on the psychometric meaning of responses. Although many of the considerations of the present paper may apply more widely, the discussion will be directly concerned only with dichotomous items for reasons which are by no means arbitrary or trivial. Most of test theory, indeed, has been worked out for dichotomous items, but the justification, if any, has been chiefly statistical simplicity and convenience.

An alternative to dichotomous items is Likert-type items. For such items an extreme statement is presented together with a rating scale, often having between four and seven points. S may be required to check, for example, one of the following, "Strongly agree," "Agree," "Disagree," or "Strongly disagree." Very often arbitrary scores will be assigned to the alternatives, from 4 for "Strongly agree" to 1 for "Strongly disagree." The scores on the relevant items are then cumulated to form the total score. This procedure implicitly assumes that the difference between agreeing strongly and simply agreeing is the same as the difference between agreeing and disagreeing, an assumption which is neither reasonable nor in accord with what is known about the independence of intensity and direction of conviction. It has been found repeatedly that some individuals have a tendency to express or accept extreme opinions as such, regardless of the topic. This fact introduces a spurious correlation between items and between tests composed of Likert-type items.

Likert-type items have at times been defended on the grounds that the intensity component is valid variance for some purposes. But, in principle, all components of test variance must be valid for some purposes. The problem is that in life the various components of variance are confounded. The task of psychometrics is to isolate, to identify and, so far as possible, to measure separately the important components of variance. Likert-type items, or any other test techniques which deliberately confound various sources of variance, operate in the wrong direction.

McQuitty [83, 84] has at times handled three-choice items by treating each of the three responses to an item as if it were a separate item. In this case the assumption that the three alternatives lie on a single continuum is avoided, but other difficulties are introduced. For two such three-choice items there will be nine coefficients of correlation, some of them probably based on very small numbers of cases. Moreover, the nine coefficients will not be experimentally independent; choosing one of the three alternatives excludes the possibility of choosing one of the other two. Thus no two of the nine coefficients can be introduced into the same correlation matrix for analysis by usual methods.

In many tests responses are recorded in several categories but are scored dichotomously. This procedure appears to be the general rule in scale analysis [100, 107] where it leads to special difficulties which will be discussed under Components of Construct Validity, B, below. Where several different responses are given a single score, the subsequent analysis does not deal with responses as raw data but rather with what MacCorquodale and Meehl [81] have called an intervening variable. Indeed, what are called "raw scores" in traditional psychometrics are summaries of several responses rather than the original responses and therefore are intervening variables. (The exceptional case where to each score there corresponds just one configuration of responses is what Guttman calls a perfect scale.) Since intervening variables are not responses, they do not in general have the characteristics of individual manifestations of a trait. For example, two scores which relate to a single trait would ordinarily correlate more highly than two responses which manifest the same trait because scores are more reliable than single responses. The distinction between responses and scores is crucial to the present view. The basis of the psychometrics advocated here is analysis of responses prior to analysis of scores. Thus psychometrics remains imbedded in psychology.

Restriction of the present consideration to dichotomous items is not a commitment to the check-list form of personality test, where the individual simply checks those items he likes or agrees with. Coombs [14] refers to such items as "irrelative"; items which involve a choice among alternatives he refers to as "relative." Dichotomous items can also be relative; that is, an individual can be presented with a forced choice between a pair of alternatives. In this instance one of the alternatives, say, the first, can be thought of as chosen or not chosen. No information is lost and no spurious information is introduced in the dichotomous representation of such items.

When Likert-type items are scored as continua, each item is in effect considered a little measurement. With dichotomous items, however, it is possible to think of each item not as representing a measurement but merely as an observation. A certain bit of behavior, the positive alternative, is either present or absent. The individual either checked the first alternative response or he did not. Most expositions of psychometrics, it is true, discuss dichotomous items as imperfect representations of underlying traits which are conceived of as continuous and often as normally distributed.

The present paper will endeavor to show how a theory of measurement can be based on dichotomous items conceived as observations without introduction of any surplus meaning of measurement into the individual items.

In an early monograph on attitude measurement Thurstone [106] distinguished two types of tests, *increasing probability* and *maximum probability* tests. Thurstone's method of test construction by equal-appearing intervals led to a maximum probability type of tests; each item is assigned a scale value and an individual's score is some average of the scale values of the items on which he scores plus. Ordinary tests of ability are increasing probability tests. The two types of tests were often confused, as pointed out by Loevinger [70], who proposed the terms *cumulative* and *differential* for the types of test. Coombs [14] has generalized the distinction somewhat with the terms *monotone* and *non-monotone* items. A monotone item is one for which an increase in the amount of the underlying trait will never decrease the probability of answering plus on the item. Non-monotone items are not excluded from the present discussion. But Thurstone-type tests, which assign a scale value to items as a means of computing a score, have a surplus meaning of measurement attached to items, just as Likert-type items do. They are therefore excluded from the discussion. Some of the ways in which combinations of dichotomous items can generate actuarial measurement of traits are discussed under Components of Construct Validity, B, in connection with the structural component of validity.

The present monograph is, in summary, restricted to consideration of dichotomous items viewed as present-absent observations of behavior whose psychological referents must be established by evidence. The alternatives lead either to injecting psychological or psychometric surplus meaning into the observations or to combining several observations into a single intervening variable. In the former case objectivity is surrendered, whereas intervening variables

lose some of the character of samples of behavior.

D. THE PSYCHOLOGY OF OBJECTIVE TEST BEHAVIOR

Let us return to the psychology of objective test behavior. The naive assumption that the trait measured by a personality test item is always related in a simple, direct way to the apparent content of the item has long since been disproven. Content, of course, is not a negligible factor, but content mediates the traits brought into play by an item in a more subtle and indirect fashion than early workers (and some present ones?) believed. Interaction of type of item with area of content in the setting of the objective test situation must be reckoned with.

A model of this kind of theorizing is Schafer's essay [95] on psychoanalytic interpretation of Rorschach responses. One cannot be willing permanently to settle for pure theory without rigorous empirical checks, even though agreeing with Schafer that there are methodological difficulties in the verification of his hypotheses. Nevertheless, his book is a valuable example of how theory, in his case, psychoanalytic theory, can generate hypotheses about the relationship of various traits (drives, defenses, and adaptive qualities) to various aspects of test behavior.

Although less searching from a psychodynamic view than Schafer's book, an earlier paper by Lindzey [68] concerning the Thematic Apperception Test illustrates the integration of theory with data as well as the integration of psychometric with psychological considerations. Such a review of objective test behavior is needed. Undoubtedly many papers focused on other topics can be made to yield data for such a review.

Meehl's paper [85] on the dynamics of structured personality tests represents a noteworthy milestone. He contrasted two approaches to such tests. In the first S is asked about his behavior as a substitute for observing the behavior. Frequently associated with this approach is *a priori* construction of scoring keys, "requiring the assumption that the psychologist building the test has sufficient insight into the dynamics of verbal behavior and its relation to the inner core of personality that he is able to predict beforehand what certain sorts of people will say about themselves when asked certain sorts of questions" [85, p. 297]. The second approach "consists simply in the explicit denial that we accept a self-rating as a feeble surrogate for a behavior sample, and substitutes the assertion that a 'self-rating' constitutes an intrinsically interesting and significant bit of verbal behavior, the non-test correlates of which must be discovered by empirical means" [85, p. 297].

At the time Meehl was writing it was probably true that *a priori* scales and undisguised scales were almost identical; psychologists did not know enough about objective test behavior to guess in advance the nature of disguised verbal expressions. Accumulated experience of the past ten years would lead one to separate partially the question of whether items are disguised and whether their significance can be guessed in advance by an astute psychologist. Meehl's example of nonsomatic items in the *Hy* scale of the Minnesota Multiphasic Personality Inventory (MMPI) illustrates just this point. These items, he points out, all seem to say, "I am psychiatrically and socially well-adjusted." Since these items as a group are good indications of hysteria and hysteroid temperament, they are not valid if taken as direct representations of behavior. When viewed as indications of lack of insight, repression and dissociation, and the *belle indifference* of these patients, the items are seen to possess a theoretical relation to the syndrome which, empirically, they signify. Presumably today the meaning of such responses is more likely to be disguised from patients than from test constructors; but this statement is not to be taken as advocacy of *a priori* construction of scoring keys.

Meehl cites as examples of the empirical approach the MMPI and the Strong Inter-est Blank. While the Strong test was, indeed, constructed empirically, it has not been tied primarily to traits but to external predictions. A more important predecessor of the MMPI is the M-F test of Terman and Miles [101], which has been almost lost in limbo. Far more of contemporary personality measurement derives from their ingenious set of studies than is currently acknowledged. In particular, the principle that the possibility of measuring a trait accurately may depend on S not knowing what the investigator is measuring was dramatized, if not introduced, in their work. E. L. Kelly [62] participated in experimental demonstration of the principle. Campbell [9] cites some earlier but less impressive uses of disguised tests.

A few further references may clarify the purview of the psychology of objective test behavior. Meehl [85] observed that while ambiguity in wording and inaccuracy of memory are sources of error in the traditional view of self-ratings, for the MMPI they may be sources of discrimination. Elias [27] found evidence that ambiguously worded items served projective purposes better than explicitly worded ones. Dorris, Levinson, and Hanfmann [22] found some evidence that third person items are better measures of defended against or unrecognized personality tendencies than first person items. Owens [91] found that validity was raised markedly by changing the format of a test from that of choosing or not choosing each of 30 statements to that of forced choice between 27 pairs of more or less contrary statements. The second (paired choice) test included a number of items taken directly from the first test, and these were, in fact, the most valid items of the second test. Some, but not all, more recent studies have confirmed the advantage of forced choice items [34].

Let us suppose that we have made some progress in finding combinations of types of items and areas of content which are reasonably sensitive indicators of basic personality traits. Clearly, theory is needed to find such items. But how can theory in turn be enriched by them? Objective test items are uniquely accessible to study in their relations to each other, in the distribution of responses in the population, and in their relations to outside variables. Such data have much to offer in clarification and extension of psychological theory.

COMPONENTS OF CONSTRUCT VALIDITY

The APA Committee on Psychological Tests divided validity into four types, content validity, concurrent validity, predictive validity, and construct validity, with the implication that it is optional which kind of validity is proposed for a test [121]. With respect to construct validity, all of the other kinds of validity are possible supporting evidence, but again there is an implication of option. This analysis of validity was accepted by Cronbach and Meehl. The categories were not claimed to be logically coordinate; the fact that they are not is nonetheless disturbing.

The construct validity of a psychological test, that is, its validity as a measure of real traits, is in the present monograph conceived as having three aspects: the substantive component, structural component, and external component. These three aspects are mutually exclusive, exhaustive of the possible lines of evidence for construct validity, and mandatory. The substantive component is somewhat different from what was previously called content validity. The structural component includes, but is not exhausted by, such concepts as homogeneity and functional unity. The external component includes relation to non-test behavior, factorial pattern or relation to other tests, and absence of distortions. The predictive and concurrent validities of the previous papers are an alternative subdivision of the external component.

Thurstone [103, Ch. 14] proposed similar categories of evidence for the validity of factors. The suggestion that tests have internal and external validity has come from many sources, including Cattell [11, p. 545], Peak [92], and Guttman [47, p.

57]. Internal validity is here divided into substantive and structural components, again following many others.

The three aspects of validity are closely related to three stages in the test construction process: constitution of the pool of items, analysis of the internal structure of the pool of items and consequent selection of items to form a scoring key, and correlation of test scores with criteria and other variables. Any test composed of items contains an explicit or implied commitment with respect to each of these steps. Some items were considered for inclusion and some were not. Of those considered, some were included and some were not, often but not always on the basis of structural considerations; the nature of the scoring key, in any case, contains an implied commitment to a particular structure [92]. And a test cannot be presented seriously for clinical use unless something is known of its external correlations, possibly leading to modification in the test or in its interpretation. None of these steps in test construction is optional, and none is without consequence for the validity of the test in use.

A. SUBSTANTIVE COMPONENT

1. Use of content in item selection

There are many methods which have been used to select items to form a test. They can be classified according to whether the chief criterion is internal consistency, external validity, or reasonableness of content. Perhaps all major test construction projects have used a combination of criteria, but generally they have relied predominantly on a single one. The discussion in this section does not seek to evaluate these methods as a whole but simply to show how content is utilized in the several methods.

a. Content validity

According to the *Technical Recommendations*, "Content validity is evaluated by showing how well the content of the test samples the class of situations or subject matter about which conclusions are to be drawn" [121, p. 13]. Concern with content validity is appropriate when one wants to know how S will perform "in a given universe of situations of which the test situation constitutes a sample" [121, p. 13].

Clearly, tests of educational achievement have most often been constructed with a concept similar to content validity as their justification. Achievement tests, as such, are not within the scope of the present monograph; nothing said herein is intended as criticism of methods of constructing such tests. Guttman, however, has for some years advocated content validity in the context of tests as measures of traits.

Using the term *attribute* to mean item (implying, item as observation rather than as miniature measurement), Guttman states, "An attribute belongs to the universe by virtue of its content. The investigator indicates the content of interest by the title he chooses for the universe, and all attributes with that content belong in the universe" [44, p. 141].

Guttman's emphasis on the investigator's decision as to the nature of the universe and whether any particular items fall in it is the justification for the charge made previously under Extension of the Concept of Validity that the argument of content validity is *ad hoc*. To change the investigator would ordinarily be to change at least somewhat the definition of the universe and the delimitation of the items within it, as Goodenough [37, p. 104] pointed out. Studies by Ruth Tolman, Grayson, and Forer [31, 38] illustrate this point. Clearly, however, the *Technical Recommendations* and some other expositions of content validity seek to avoid this arbitrariness. The *Technical Recommendations* list as essential criteria for content validity:

> If a test performance is to be interpreted as a sample of performance in some universe of situations, the manual should indicate clearly what universe is represented and how adequate the sampling is. . . . The universe of content should be defined in terms of the sources

from which items were drawn, or the content criteria used to include and exclude items. . . . The method of sampling items within the universe should be described [121, p. 20].

The problem which arises is that the more one objectifies the nature of the universe from which the sample of items is to be drawn, the less likely is the universe to represent exactly the trait which the investigator wishes to measure. Moreover, for any given trait name, two investigators would not necessarily specify the same objective domain from which to draw a sample, nor the same method of sampling. Should a vocabulary test be drawn from an unabridged dictionary, an abridged dictionary, or a list of words in common use? And which one? One must either decide arbitrarily in favor of one such alternative and run the corresponding risk that another investigator might make a different decision, or one must demonstrate that the choice is inconsequential. To accomplish the latter requires a great deal of data and thus introjects strong considerations other than those of pure content.

A work sample test would seem to provide an optimal instance of content validity. Consider again, vocabulary. Certainly every word which can be defined correctly is a part of vocabulary. But Tucker [109] found that certain words had very low relation to the test as a whole, despite the fact that most words had a high relationship to vocabulary as a whole. The "poor" words had some common characteristics, but they could not have been identified in advance; they were not technical words. Apparently one will do a better job of measuring vocabulary as a whole, vocabulary as a trait, by omitting than by including the aberrant words. But to do so is to admit considerations other than content.

Both the authors of the *Technical Recommendations* and Guttman consider essential the evaluation of the internal consistency of the set of items considered to measure a given universe of content. Guttman envisages, and the *Technical Rec-*

ommendations do not exclude, possible elimination of a small percentage of items if they do not hold together with the rest of the test. Thus some utilization of empirical evidence is regularly expected even when the chief basis of test construction is content.

"The heart of the notion of content validity" [67, p. 299] is that the test items are samples of the trait-universe to which generalization will be made. In the great majority of psychological tests the behavior sampled is verbal and the trait to which generalization is made includes much nonverbal behavior. Thus content validity is not applicable to such tests. But the point can be pushed further. Test behavior is always utilized as a sign of non-test behavior, as emphasized previously under Relation of Test Behavior to Theory. The very fact that one set of behaviors occurs in a test situation and the other outside the test situation introduces an instrument error which is ignored by the concept of content validity. The psychodynamics of testing, "the psychology of objective test behavior," can never safely be omitted in drawing inferences from test behavior. The graduate student who performs most brilliantly on his qualifying examinations will not necessarily be the most brilliant professor, nor will the one who becomes amnesic on his examination necessarily be equally blank under less stressful circumstances. More strikingly, the person who is best able to respond in a test situation in a warm and friendly manner is not necessarily the warmest and most friendly person; it is quite conceivable that there are traits such that the capacity to simulate them indicates their absence rather than their presence.

There is a continuum of tests ranging from those whose content is most similar to the behavior it is desired to predict to those whose content least resembles the behavior to be predicted. The problem introduced here is the problem of the disguise of measurement. Considerations of content are most fruitful for theory, however, precisely in those cases where the test is most dis-

guised, where the content bears the least apparent relation to the trait. The term *substantive validity*, which will be defined presently, is introduced in the present monograph because of the conviction that considerations of content alone are not sufficient to establish validity even when the test content resembles the trait, and considerations of content cannot be excluded when the test content least resembles the trait.

b. Empirical keying

At the opposite extreme from tests justified solely in terms of reasonableness of content are those justified only in terms of empirical properties of items. The term empirical keying usually refers to selection of items according to their correlation with an external criterion, a method whose deficiencies have been explored previously under Relation of Test Behavior to Theory. It might as well refer also to selection of items according to a criterion of internal consistency, such as factor analysis. At this point in the discussion the distinction between external and internal empirical criteria will not be important. Examples of empirically keyed tests are the MMPI, which began with a collection of all personality test items of a certain type then in use, and biographical inventories, where even more heterogeneous items are included in the original test form. A particular key for such a test will often involve only a small proportion of the items.

In the case of many empirical keys which are used over a period of years, for example, those of the *Strong Vocational Interest Blank*, little or no attempt is ever made to examine the content for common themes in a given key. One suspects that some ultra-empiricists would consider such examination of content as immoral or unscientific. Yet an experimentalist is not considered more scientific if he collects data and walks away from it without seeking explanation of the behavioral dynamics which account for it. If theory is fully to profit from test construction as a part of psychology, every item included in a scoring key must be accounted for; a less strong case can be made for explaining the exclusion of items [cf. Jessor and Hammond, 60].

Even among the test constructors who are interested in examining the content of empirical keys, it would almost certainly be considered gross scientific impropriety to delete items because no reasonable connection could be found between them and the content chiefly indicated for the test. This attitude is the opposite of that indicated by the term content validity; yet the criteria for choosing one view rather than the other are not easily applied to a particular situation.

The dangers of pure empiricism must not be underestimated. There is always a probability that an item be included in a scoring key by chance; the probability can be reduced, at considerable cost, but it cannot be made zero. Quite apart from inclusion of items by chance, items may be included because of fortuitous but misleading correlation with the trait measured. Travers [108] has worked out a striking example of the dangers of pure empiricism in the absence of hypotheses.

There appears to be no convincing reason for ignoring content nor for considering content alone in determining the validity of a test or of individual items. The problem is to find a coherent set of operations permitting utilization of content together with empirical considerations.

2. The universe and the pool

The first step in test construction is constructing or (often) collecting a pool of items. Some decision, broad or narrow, is made as to content at that point. "I wish I were not so shy" was not considered for inclusion in the pool of items from which the Stanford-Binet was constructed; problems in long division were clearly inappropriate for inclusion in the MMPI. A test constructor must have some purpose in mind, and this purpose defines the universe of discourse or area of content from which he will choose items for the original pool.

The primary purpose may be to improve an external prediction, to measure a trait postulated by theory, or to investigate the structure of some aspects of behavior. (Whichever is the investigator's chief purpose, he is ultimately involved in all three enterprises if he wishes to relate his test to theory.)

An unfortunate confusion between the pool of items and the area of content has arisen in test theory [74]. This confusion is signalized by the term "universe of items." Papers on test theory often assume that items are chosen randomly [77] or simply independently and without regard to empirical properties [48] from a universe of items possessing a characteristic such as some form of homogeneity. In practice, tests are usually constructed by choosing the best items from the pool used in the test construction research. While the pool is chosen on an *a priori* basis, the choice of items from the pool is made according to the properties of the items revealed by empirical study.

The point to note is the difference between what actually takes place in constructing a test and the process implicitly assumed in test theories. Random selection from a "universe of items" does not describe selection of the pool of items or of the scoring key. So far as constitution of the pool is concerned, selection of a single item automatically excludes many others which differ only slightly from the chosen one. Thus several items are neither randomly nor independently selected. The term "universe of items," moreover, obscures the fact that between the presumably unlimited number of items representing a given content and the finite pool of items actually studied there intervenes an idiosyncratic, nonreproducible process, the process by which the given investigator or group of investigators constructs or selects items to represent that content. Although this process, the constitution of the pool of items, is a universal step in test construction, it has not been adequately recognized by test theory. But this step in test construction is crucial for the question of whether evidence for the validity of the test will also be evidence for the validity of a construct.

Cronbach and Meehl point out that in any characterization of a cluster of items

> . . . an element of inductive extrapolation appears in the claim that a cluster including some elements not-yet-observed has been identified. Since, as in any sorting or abstracting task involving a finite set of complex elements, several nonequivalent bases of categorization are available, the investigator may choose a hypothesis which generates erroneous predictions. The failure of a supposed, hitherto untried, member of the cluster to behave in the manner said to be characteristic of the group, or the finding that a nonmember of the postulated cluster does behave in this manner, may modify greatly our tentative construct [20, p. 292].

The reasoning of the above quotation is not, I believe, open to question. Guttman has made similar observations about the successive redefinition of "universes" according to whether predictions are verified. Logically, of course, predictions are indistinguishable from concurrent correlations. It follows directly from the above quotation that to characterize a cluster of items with any confidence requires a knowledge not only of a number of items included in the cluster but also of many items which fail to meet requirements for inclusion in the cluster. Indeed, the excluded items might reasonably be required to exceed greatly the items included. The present proposal is that this requirement be met not in a lengthy series of investigations, though verifying studies are always in order, but primarily in the very constitution of the pool of items from which the test is chosen.

The use of tests for the elucidation of constructs suggests the following principles, in descending order of generality:

At very least, the items in the pool should be drawn from an area of content defined more broadly than the trait expected to be measured.

When possible, the items of the pool should be chosen so as to sample all possible contents which might comprise the putative trait according to all known alternative theories of the trait. Thus the empirical data utilized for construction of the scoring key simultaneously test hypotheses about the underlying trait. This principle has been advocated and practiced by Thurstone [104] and Guilford [40, 42].

The proportion of items of different content is not specified by the previous principle, but may affect the outcome of factorial studies. A principle which suggests itself here is one (or perhaps a modification of one) proposed by Brunswik [7]: that *the various areas or sub-areas of content should be represented in proportion to their life-importance.* This suggestion is similar to one made by T. L. Kelley [61] and by Cattell [11, p. 215], who assumed that life-importance could be judged by dictionary representation.

A recent proposal by Guttman[1] seems to offer an alternative to representation of areas of content according to life-importance. Stephenson [99] earlier advocated a similar design for Q-sort items. Guttman proposes that what might be called the logical dimensionality of an area be predetermined by the investigator; e.g., a set of items may differ in form, content, complexity, and other dimensions. These dimensions correspond to Fisher's "factors" in analysis of variance designs. Guttman proposes to call them "facets" to avoid confusion with factor analysis. Each facet has a set of values; for example, the content possibilities might be words, numbers, and geometric figures, the forms multiple choice, true-false, and completion, and so on. The experimental design Guttman proposes is that each value of each facet be paired with each value of every other facet,

---

[1] Dr. Guttman has presented a number of papers on facet analysis which have not as yet been published. This discussion is based on a mimeographed paper by him, "What lies ahead for factor analysis?" issued from the Center for Advanced Study in the Behavioral Sciences, Stanford University, 1956.

as in an analysis of variance design. The intention apparently is to combine this experimental design with a new form of factor analysis which Guttman calls radex theory [50]. Until further details and examples are published, it is not possible to evaluate the proposal as a whole. The following comments are meant only to apply to facet analysis in present context, not in all the many applications which Guttman foresees for it.

Logical analysis of an area of content on some such basis as facet analysis, if supplementary to the principles proposed above, is valuable to insure complete coverage of the area and has been practiced by psychologists professionally engaged in test construction and analysis for many years. As an alternative principle to representation in terms of theories at stake or in terms of life-importance of sub-areas, it is not acceptable. Pairing every value of every facet with every value of other facets may at times be a highly artificial procedure. Some contents may adapt themselves far more readily to some forms than others. Moreover, important sub-areas of content may be missed by this design. For example, problems may involve words or numbers or words and numbers. It may make sense for several values of a single facet to be represented in a single item. This possibility violates the neat but artificial Fisherian design which Guttman proposes. Brunswik's [8] criticism of factorial design is particularly apposite to Guttman's facet analysis and Stephenson's similar proposal.

It should be noted that neither Stephenson nor Guttman uses facet analysis exclusively. The examples in the foregoing exposition are those of the writer and not of Stephenson or Guttman. The point is that these are simply elaborate and complicated examples of content validation, of *a priori* definition of constructs. Neither Guttman nor Stephenson advocates the objective delineation of constructs through observation of the variety of items included in and excluded from the cluster defining the construct in the manner envisaged in the present monograph.

3. *The concept of substantive validity*

The proposal of this monograph is that the pool of items be constituted on the basis of some broad area of content. The empirical relations among the items, and perhaps between items and criteria, serve as basis for selection of items from the pool to form a scoring key. If the pool has been properly constituted, the process of test construction also tests a family of hypotheses about the trait to be measured. The principles by which the pool of items is constituted have been discussed above; the next section will discuss some principles for the selection of items from the pool. The *substantive component* of validity is the extent to which the content of the items included in (and excluded from?) the test can be accounted for in terms of the trait believed to be measured and the context of measurement. Context includes psychological theory and, in particular, "the psychology of objective test behavior."

The program implied by content validation is inclusion of items in a test solely on the basis of theory; empirical keying implies inclusion of items in a test solely on the basis of data. The present program is that items be included in the original pool on the basis of a judgment of relevance to a broadly defined field. The final selection of items shall be made, however, on the basis of empirical findings. The substantive component of validity is the ability of theory to account for the resultant content; it cannot be determined unless the pool of items is broader in scope than the test.

B. STRUCTURAL COMPONENT

1. *The concept of structural validity*

The *structural component* of validity refers to the extent to which structural relations between test items parallel the structural relations of other manifestations of the trait being measured. This concept will seem novel to many psychologists, but undoubtedly others will find it congenial or even familiar. The concept of structural validity includes both the fidelity of the structural model to the structural characteristics of non-test manifestations of the trait and the degree of inter-item structure. Given fidelity of item structure, the more highly structured test may be said to have greater structural validity. Since previous discussions of structure have put more emphasis on degree of structure than fidelity of structure, the present paper will reverse the emphasis. Previous reviews of structural theory include chapters by Peak [92] and Coombs [14].

The concept of structural fidelity is based on the ideas developed previously under Relation of Test Behavior to Theory. By confining consideration to dichotomous items considered as observations rather than as miniature measurements, we have insured that the test responses can be considered legitimate samples of behavior. Since test behavior is a sample of behavior in general, it may be assumed to share the characteristics of other behaviors, in particular, the structural characteristics. If the analysis were based on scores rather than on the original item responses, those structural characteristics might well be obscured.

For any given trait it seems reasonable to assume that there is an upper limit to the intercorrelation of its manifestations, which might be called its characteristic intercorrelation. For example, two manifestations of numerical ability would be expected to be more closely related than, say, two manifestations of aggressiveness. Two manifestations of verbal facility would be more closely related than two manifestations of introversion. It is necessary to add, however, that the characteristic correlation is an upper limit and that the lower limit is always zero, as one proceeds from those actions most determined by the given trait to those least determined by it.

According to this line of thinking, the same characteristic value would define the upper limit of correlation of two non-test manifestations of a trait, of two items measuring that trait (ignoring distortions produced by the test situation, which would

raise the inter-item r), and of an item with a non-test manifestation. If this view proves correct, such inferences as can be drawn from test behavior will not be based on direct correspondence between individual items and particular behaviors outside the test situation, except in so far as both are related to a central trait. (Cf. Lazarsfeld's definition of a pure test: "All interrelationships between the items should be accounted for by the way in which each item alone is related to the latent continuum" [65, p. 367].) The injunction against interpretation of individual items is not, of course, a new one, but the present reason is somewhat different from the usual one. It is unfortunate, however, that the weakness of item responses as measures of extra-test behaviors led most psychometricians to concentrate on total scores almost to the exclusion of individual responses. The problem of the structural relations of responses was thereby obscured.

Sociologists have in recent years shown great preference for the structural model of Guttman-type scales. Studies by Riley, *et al.* [93], and some other users of Guttman scales appear to be predicated on the assumption that the most rigorously structured mathematical model is invariably the preferred one. This view is contrary to the view proposed here, that the outstanding virtue of a model is its fidelity to what is known about manifestations of the trait or type of trait involved.

The question arises, how can items be found which have at least apparently a closer or more rigorous relation to each other than is in fact characteristic of manifestations of the given trait? There is no unique coefficient of correlation for two dichotomous items. Some coefficients are prejudiced in favor of and some against items which differ in difficulty. In order to define uniquely the characteristic correlation of the manifestations of a given trait, further specifications must be made, such as "phi coefficient for two items each of which characterizes half the population." The Guttman-scalability of a set of items can be raised by choosing those items which are widely spaced in difficulty or its analog, rather than those items clustered near median difficulty. That, in fact, is how scales are usually produced [100]. The same thing is accomplished by selection of cutting points when multiple choice items are reduced to dichotomies in the Cornell technique of scale analysis [46]. Loevinger [71] has shown that while selecting items spaced in difficulty raises scalability, it lowers validity for tests whose characteristic item correlation is not high, which is most often the case. While the argument is statistical rather than empirical, there is extraordinarily little empirical evidence for raising validity by improving scalability, considering the amount of interest in scale analysis.

Guttman, indeed, does not sanction improvement of scalability by selection of items, at least as a general practice. He has argued[2] that such use of the scale model puts the investigator in the position of Spearman, who was criticized for arguing in favor of a single general factor on the basis of a set of tests "purified" by deleting those found to have "overlapping specifics." Thus Guttman favors use of scale analysis to determine the degree of scalability characteristic of what he calls "the universe," rather than production of an artificially precise measure of an intrinsically non-precise trait. In this respect Guttman's view is closer to that of the present monograph, which advocates fidelity to the structural characteristics of the trait, than to that of his own disciples. However, in dichotomizing multiple choice items so as to maximize scalability [46], Guttman is permitting a practice which he otherwise eschews, since this practice is equivalent to selection of items.

A Guttman-type scale exists when all responses of the Ss can be reproduced from knowledge of their total scores; this is the definition of a scale. Then in substituting scores for patterns of item responses, no information is lost. So bemused have sociologists been by the demonstrated virtues of true Guttman-type scales that other devices in addition to selection and dichotomization of items have been used for artificial production of scales. Stouffer, Borgatta, Hays, and Henry [100] have used "contrived items," each composed of several items; scalability is then sought for the contrived items rather than the original responses. Guttman [49] has proceeded in a different direction, assigning to each non-scale response pattern a corresponding scale pattern, by a method called "image analysis" or the "Israel Alpha technique for scale analysis." Neither method retains all the information in the original data, which was the virtue of a true scale, and neither method has been shown to maximize any desirable quality of a test. Stouffer's method is shown to be slightly better than older techniques of item selection based on scale analysis.

Occasionally recognized but much more often forgotten in the circles where scale analysis is practiced is the distinction between the discovery of structure in a set of items and the imposition of structure upon the items. If tests are to serve as instruments of theory, no consideration is more crucial. Guttman [44] early took a stand against empirical item selection altogether, since he believed the function of structural analysis to be discovery rather than creation of structure. Nonetheless, he has sanctioned many methods which, in effect, create structure.

Coombs has been far more perceptive with respect to this point [13, 14], repeatedly and in various contexts stressing the difference between a structure which may or may not appear in a set of items and a structure which the methods employed cannot fail to reveal. The model of a perfect scale was one which a set of items could or could not conform to; presumably in practice the conformity was never perfect. On the other hand, some kinds of

---

[2] Mimeographed paper, "A personal history of the development of scale analysis," issued from the Center for Advanced Study in the Behavioral Sciences, Stanford University, 1955.

image analysis cannot fail to produce a perfect scale. Thurstone's method of constructing attitude scales by equal-appearing intervals can hardly fail to produce a scale with equal-appearing intervals. Yet Thurstone's method need not and Guttman's analysis does not involve selection or rejection of items. The writer, in connection with published research [23], has systematically searched pools of as many as 50 items and failed to find any combination of items for which Kuder-Richardson Formula 20 revealed appreciable homogeneity, say, .4. Thus, the question of whether structure is imposed or discovered is different from whether item selection is permitted.

The present monograph proposes that items be selected from a large pool on the basis of empirical properties, in particular, that those items be selected which best conform to an appropriate structural model. The method should be such that items which conform to the model may or may not appear. Ordinarily the degree of structure of the resulting test should also be assessed.

Selection of items does raise a somewhat different problem, that of cross-validation. Tukey states: "In every field of science, and particularly in fields where data and analysis [are] complex, there are two different phases of quantitative analysis—exploration and confirmation—and almost always, when dealing with *complex* problems, these have to be carried out on *different* samples of data" [111, p. 66]. Thus if a given set of items is discovered to have structural coherence in one set of data, the hypothesis of structural coherence must be tested with a fresh set of data.

2. Some kinds of structure

What kinds of structure are known to exist among the manifestations of various traits? An exhaustive list of possible structures will not be attempted here; such lists quickly sink to a lifeless and pedantic level.

a. Quantitative models

The most obvious kind of structure is the one in which the number of manifestations is an index of the amount of the trait. Such a trait is appropriately measured by a cumulative test, that is, a test whose score is the number of items marked plus. This structure is the one which has been most adequately explored statistically. Different kinds of structure have the cumulative or additive character, the difference lying in the degree of relationship among the items.

When the degree of relationship among items is low or moderate, optimal construct validity is produced by selecting "median equivalent items," i.e., those items having highest intercorrelations and lying closest to 50% difficulty or its analog ("marginal frequency"). This is the model which has been most thoroughly exploited in psychological test theory and will here be called the classical quantitative model. The method of Loevinger, Gleser, and DuBois [75] for constructing homogeneous subtests from a large pool of items has been evolved explicitly for this type of data. Items are selected for their ability to maximize a coefficient equivalent to the Kuder-Richardson Formula 20, which is considered currently the best measure of test homogeneity [121].

When the intercorrelation of the items is very high, spacing the items in difficulty improves validity. What constitutes "high" depends on the number of items and other factors [71]. Guttman's scale model [44], which is similar to a model for a perfectly homogeneous test proposed by Loevinger [69], is appropriate for this case. Unfortunately Guttman does not publish the relationship between the computational techniques he recommends and the brilliant mathematical derivations from which they derive their prestige. This observation is conspicuously true of his coefficient of reproducibility, which has often been criticized. His recently proposed methods of image analysis are ostensibly based on image theory [48], but the intermediate steps in the reasoning are not available in accessible publications.

Guttman's scale model and Loevinger's

model of a homogeneous test are discussed more extensively by Peak [92], who criticizes them on grounds which appear to be similar to what is here called structural fidelity. Humphreys [58] and Carroll [10] have made similar criticisms.

Tucker [109] has recently worked out a model for cumulative tests intermediate between the classical quantitative type and the Guttman-scalable type. Most words in a long vocabulary list conformed to his model. The model may be described as follows: the items are assumed to be homogeneous in the sense that all correlation between them is accounted for by a single ability, as in Lazarsfeld's latent structure analysis. The scale of ability is so chosen that the regression of proportion passing the item on ability is described by approximately the same ogive for all items, except that the ogive varies parallel to the scale of ability. The shifting of the ogive for different items corresponds to changes in difficulty level. Items are dispersed in difficulty, like the Guttman scale and unlike the classical quantitative model, which concentrates difficulties near the 50% mark. The relation between an individual's total score and his score on any item is probabilistic rather than almost certain, as in Guttman scales. Perhaps Tucker's model represents the closest approach to Guttman scales which can be expected with psychological test materials.

Methodologically, working out a structural model in conjunction with a test construction problem which is intrinsically interesting appears highly desirable. Empty models, models which apply to no content, are thereby guarded against. Tucker's type of scalability may therefore be expected to find further use. For most purposes, however, and certainly where personality tests are the chief concern, it suffices to consider traits whose manifestations are not highly correlated.

b. Class models

When a clinician states that the meaning of a symptom, say, withdrawal from social situations, must be judged by the context in which it occurs, he implies a different structure from the cumulative one. Translation of this kind of clinical judgment into a structural model is not entirely obvious. One might translate it: of the several manifestations which characterize this trait, all, or perhaps all but one or two, must be present in order for one to say that the trait is present. The trait, then, is either present or absent. Its manifestations do not indicate amount, but if a sufficient number are present, signalize the presence of the trait. A smaller number have no significance in relation to the given trait. Clearcut clinical examples which follow this structure are not easy to find, whether because of the fluidity of present nosology or because clinicians are accustomed to thinking in more idiosyncratic terms. To take an example from medicine, fever and cough may indicate several diseases, fever and rash may also indicate several diseases, but fever, cough, and rash together strongly suggest a diagnosis of measles. There are other characteristic signs, particularly the history of onset, but some variation is observed. An example from test theory is Harrower-Erickson's [53] nine Rorschach signs. Presence of five or more is said to indicate neurosis. The example is not a perfect one, since the signs are all summaries rather than simple responses.

The foregoing pattern might be called a class pattern. It describes a class of people rather than a trait present to greater or less degree in all of us. Traits of the latter type, present in everyone to a degree, often follow the cumulative pattern described at the beginning of this section and might be expected to arise in relation to developmental experiences shared by all or by large segments of the population. Class patterns might be expected to be appropriate in relation to the problem of diagnosis. Historically, however, the patterns have not been used in that fashion. Hathaway and McKinley [54] used classification of patients into diagnostic categories as part of the original validational enterprise of the MMPI.

But the supposed traits defined by keys chosen for ability to discriminate diagnostic groups from normals were then treated as quantitative traits, as if they measured a characteristic more or less present in everyone. It may be true that various diagnostic groups represent extreme cases with respect to universal traits. Such a proposition requires proof, and the success of the original keys for the MMPI has not been such as to constitute such proof. According to French's [32] review, many of the personality traits found in factor analyses have been established either in normal populations or in pathological groups but not in both. (Construction of a model adequate to the complexities of clinical diagnosis will not be attempted here.)

Lazarsfeld's [65, 66] latent structure analysis is a general set of methods for handling data which do not conform to Guttman's scale model. In principle the methods are very general indeed; in practice the only methods which are well elaborated are those which account for a set of responses to items by assigning the individuals to (an arbitrary number of?) latent classes. Each latent class is homogeneous with respect to the trait presumed to be measured. The items are assumed to be pure measures of the trait, in the sense that all correlation between them is accounted for by that trait. Thus, within any latent class there is no correlation between items. In addition to the assumption about the number of latent classes, some assumption must be made about the form of the regression of items on latent classes. In general, both monotone and non-monotone items can be included (unlike most other methods), and the latent classes may or may not be assumed to be points on a single continuum. Observed frequencies of the various patterns of responses are then used to make inferences about the proportions of the population within the several latent classes. Those inferred proportions are utilized with the observed item frequencies to generate the expected frequencies of various response patterns. The expected frequencies are then compared with observed frequencies in order to test the goodness of fit of the inferred structure.

Hays and Borgatta [55] have shown that more than one assumed structure within the framework of latent class theory can generate data which agree reasonably well with a single set of observed data. This problem has been recognized by Lazarsfeld but has not been sufficiently investigated, at least in available work.

An investigation by Chiang [12], although not mentioning latent structure analysis, appears to be concerned with essentially the same mathematical problem. Chiang demonstrates that for four or five items the power of the test of any latent structure is poor unless the number of individuals is in the thousands. To have a reasonable chance of detecting the falsity of an assumed structure, even with about a thousand cases, eight items are needed. Most if not all published instances of latent structure analysis have utilized fewer than eight items; typically, four items are used.

In view of Chiang's work, or, to put the matter another way, in view of the many arbitrary assumptions which must be made to apply latent class analysis, there is some question how valuable a tool it will prove to be in terms of contribution to theory. Strangely enough, published illustrations of its use concern chiefly traits which are more easily conceptualized as quantitative than as categorical, such as soldiers' attitude towards the Army [64].

c. Dynamic models

Neither the cumulative models nor class models are adequate for dynamic traits. Psychoanalytic theory postulates, and some psychologists who reject other aspects of psychoanalysis also accept, that opposing tendencies may have a common motivational source. Peak [92] assumed that dynamic organization of traits could be demonstrated only by time changes. The view of the present monograph is that it should be possible to find structural traces of dynamic organization, though admittedly the crucial evidence is not yet in.

One dynamic structural possibility is that two particular manifestations of the same trait may be mutually exclusive or in a less extreme case, negatively correlated. Cattell [11, Ch. 5], who discussed this possibility at length, showed that the effect of this structure may be to attenuate a positive relation. Frenkel-Brunswik [33] found in a study of adolescents that ratings of overt behavior on "exuberance" and "irritability" correlated .30 and .42 with intuitive ratings of the drive for aggression by clinicians who knew the Ss well. The two behavioral ratings were negatively correlated ($r = -.52$) and the multiple correlation of drive for aggression with exuberance and irritability was .73. She cited these data as evidence for the principle of alternative manifestations of a drive [33, p. 302].

A somewhat different dynamic structure may be derived from the notion of neurotic conflict. The notion that conflict is characteristic of neurosis and self-consistency characteristic of normality has been the basis of a number of researches, including those of Zubin [120], Winthrop [116], and McQuitty [83]. Winthrop [116] defined consistency in terms of formal logic, thereby ignoring a distinction made earlier by Zubin [120], among others, between the logical and the psychological meaning of an item. It is thus not surprising that his chief empirical discovery was that normal college students responded to his test in a markedly illogical fashion.

Zubin [120] defined consistency in terms of empirically determined patterns of response, differentiating, however, patterns characteristic of normal from those of pathological groups. His normal group had on the average the most patterns altogether and the fewest abnormal patterns. The neurotic group had on the average fewest patterns altogether despite having the greatest number of abnormal patterns, exceeding in both respects the psychotic

and the organic groups of patients. Zubin's method, which consisted essentially of looking for all possible patterns of response, is unwieldy because of the large number of possible patterns with a reasonably large pool of items. He solved this problem by examining only a small fraction of the possibilities, clearly an unsatisfactory solution.

Several studies by McQuitty [83, 84] have also been concerned with measurement of "personality integration" and with testing various hypotheses about the relation of such integration to mental health. While considerable ingenuity in the invention of methodology was exercised, the methods are not comparable with those discussed in the present monograph.

An unpublished study has taken the same basic idea, that conflict is evidence of maladjustment or neurosis, and combined it with content considerations. Dr. Jack Block,[3] in investigating the postulated dimension of ego-control, found the most maladjusted individuals tended not to be those extreme in the direction of over-control or extreme in the direction of under-control. Rather, the psychologically most disturbed individuals appeared to be those who manifested, in some extreme, inconsistent, unintegrated fashion, both over- and under-control simultaneously. This pattern differs from the one of alternative manifestations, since there is no necessary contradiction between one particular manifestation of control and another particular one. The contradiction resides in the individuals, and the techniques for demonstrating the existence of the contradiction must be correspondingly different.

From a formal point of view the problem of "scatter" in measurement of abilities resembles the problem of dynamic structure. Two quite different kinds of scatter have been studied, intra-test and inter-test scatter. In the case of intra-test scatter, the

---

[3] Mimeographed report, "The development of a MMPI-based scale to measure ego-control," issued at the Institute for Personality Assessment and Research, University of California, 1953.

test items are all assumed to be equivalent in function and the dispersion of successes and failures along the scale of difficulty (or its analog) represents S's tendency to inconsistency. In the case of inter-test scatter, the functions called on by the several tests are not assumed to be identical. Many studies have attempted to show, with varying degrees of success, characteristic patterns of relatively high and low scores for different clinical syndromes [39, 59]. The Wechsler-Bellevue test has been most often studied in this regard, but other tests have also been used. Even when studying inter-test scatter there must be an assumption of community of function in the several subtests, else there would be no basis for establishing a general level and thus of measuring scatter. The general level is established by some aspect of S's performance, often by a test such as vocabulary which is presumably not easily subject to deterioration. The two types of scatter might be termed "pure scatter" (intra-functional) and "patterned scatter" (inter-functional). The possibility must be recognized that what appears to be pure scatter may in fact be an unrecognized pattern. Both types of scatter have theoretical implications, but patterned scatter can be expected to be more fruitful theoretically. There are many possible ways of measuring scatter; theoretical implications of the various coefficients have not been fully explored.

3. Pattern analysis and configural scoring

The topics of configural scoring and pattern analysis [35] have received attention in many quarters recently and must be related to the present discussion. All of these methods, with the notable exception of a recent exposition by Haggard [52], appear to be criterion-oriented; that is, they are methods of combining data so as to improve prediction of a single specified criterion. Cronbach and Gleser [19] have shown that measures of profile similarity in general are simple measures of linear distance in a space equal in dimensionality to the number of tests; such models assume linear or additive combination of tests. The term "configural scoring" has been used for non-linear combination of test and item scores [86, 56]. Methods such as Lykken's [80] actuarial pattern analysis and duMas' [24, 25] manifest structure analysis include both linear and non-linear models.

Meehl [86] introduces his discussion of configural scoring with a paradox: he displays an instance where each of two variables fails to predict the criterion but the two scored together have high validity. But here Meehl has introduced a paradox vaster than he apparently intended, and it is the paradox of all actuarial pattern analysis. The broader paradox is this: no item of information can ever be discarded as useless for any prediction. For even if it seems to have no correlation with the criterion, it may, when scored configurally with other items, yield valid prediction. There is no means for assigning any reasonable limit to the number of items which must be considered as possible predictors, nor to the possible combinations which must be examined. Shall we measure the universe and intercorrelate everything in it? Worse, there is no limit to the variety of relationships which must be explored.

In practice, suggestions of various kinds are made for limiting the scope of the search. Indeed, in view of the present access to electronic computing machines, the limiting consideration is not the examination of large numbers of combinations of data but the fractionation of the sample to the point that the number of cases for most patterns is too small to be useful. Collection of patterns which exceed the level of significance only by chance would also appear to be a problem where almost unlimited instances are available.

Lykken [80] proposes to collect criterion data for MMPI profiles by using 9 scales. If each scale is dichotomized, as he proposes, there are still 512 possible patterns. One wonders how Lykken is confident that the non-linear relationships which actuarial pattern analysis is to reveal do not occur within the dichotomized segment of a scale rather than between segments.

One difference between the approach of the present monograph and that of the various advocates of pattern analysis is that the latter do not separate clearly the steps of assembling a pool of items and of selecting the best items from the pool. Orientation of pattern analysis towards prediction of specific criteria rather than towards measurement of traits is another difference. Related to both of the foregoing points is the differing utilization of theory in pattern analysis and the present approach.

Tukey [111] has criticized a symposium on "Statistics for the clinician" for the paucity of theoretical considerations, the tendency of many psychologists to throw the whole problem of finding relationships into the lap of the statistician rather than providing hypotheses to guide the statistics. This approach has not been the pathway to advances in other fields, he indicates.

Tukey's point may be stated differently. We cannot cling to every bit of our data and still do scientific research, for every event is ultimately unique. For example, we agree to regard as identical all responses of "yes" to the question "Were you born in the United States?" regardless of the angle at which the pen met the paper, etc. Some generalization has already taken place when, say, all responses to a dichotomous item are classed in one of two categories. This classification is justified by our beliefs about the greater relevance of some aspects of response than others. Two different ways of saying yes are considered equivalent. This matter is discussed in greater detail by Meehl [87, Ch. 6].

For any considerable number of items to be manageable, there must again be a decision that certain groups or patterns of response are equivalent; in principle, this decision does no more violence to the data than the one already taken. It is at this point that I would apply Tukey's suggestion that we utilize theoretical (or at least

substantive) considerations. The choice of a structural or statistical model, here advocated to be based on psychological considerations, automatically reduces drastically the number of response patterns which are considered different. For example, with a cumulative model scoring plus on any three keyed items is equivalent to scoring plus on any other three keyed items. The net effect of ultra-empiricism is that data reduction, choice of intervening variables, takes place in the dark—"dichotomize every MMPI scale at the median"—instead of in the light of theory.

4. Use of structural models

In view of the relative novelty of the concept of structural validity, an exhaustive list of possible structural relations prevailing among the several manifestations of a single trait is not in order. The purpose of this section chiefly is to point out that psychological theories postulate a variety of such structures. The kinds of structure explored above have been classified as cumulative models, class models, and dynamic models. While cumulative models differentiate individuals with respect to degree and class models differentiate them with respect to kind, use of scatter in diagnosis implies that either the degree of structure (intra-functional scatter) or the nature of the structure (inter-functional scatter) is itself what differs among individuals.

Much of what has been called structural theory in contemporary psychometrics has not been included in the foregoing discussion. The reason lies in another terminological misfortune: at least two different kinds of structure are involved. That to which the present paper refers is the structure which subsists among the various manifestations of a trait. A name for this kind of analysis might be *score-structure analysis*.

Most of the work of Guttman and Coombs and in the field of factor analysis has been thought of as analysis of the components which contribute to the causation or formation of tests responses or scores. This kind of analysis may be called *component structure analysis*. (Lazarsfeld's latent structure analysis is similar to score-structure analysis.) While such analyses have been conceived in terms of components, the data have, of course, been the same as for score-structure analysis, and the formal models and their properties may prove to have application in a different manner than their originators intended. Guttman's [50] simplex theory, an aspect of radex theory, which is a kind of generalization of factor analysis, has been explicitly worked out both in terms of component analysis and of score-structure analysis.

To analyze the manner in which the component traits determine responses and scores is a more fundamental enterprise than simply studying which responses go together in some fashion. The former pursuit is beset with difficulties. The structural component of validity, as conceived herein, is not concerned in the first instance with the mediational pathway of the observed responses. Such mediational pathways are part of the "theory" which it is hoped that objective tests will illuminate. The manner of achieving that illumination is the subject matter of the present monograph and its predecessors [20, 92, 60]. Such mediational mechanisms as psychological theories have postulated are often far more complex than can be accommodated by present component models. Such mechanisms as condensation, displacement, isolation, and reaction formation elude not only additive models but also the more complex models of Coombs (compensatory, conjunctive, disjunctive) [15] and Guttman (simplex, circumplex, radex) [50, 51]. With further development of the theory of objective test behavior and further development of component models, the latter may better serve the former.

It seems unlikely, though, that the path from data to theory will be greatly illuminated by single mathematical coups, however brilliant. Multiple factor analysis has an enormous advantage over recently proposed models. The conditions for making inferences from data, as formulated, e.g., in a recent paper on simple structure by Tucker [110], are the outcome of mutual criticism of many workers over a long period of time and in connection with a wide variety of substantive problems. Work of Guttman, Lazarsfeld, and Coombs is accompanied by no such clear-cut rules for inference; indeed, escape clauses are frequent, such as, "Sampling errors will not be considered."

The reader is urged to keep the following questions in mind in utilizing or evaluating the use of structural models:

Does the chosen structure conform to what is known of non-test manifestations of the putative trait?

Is the degree of structure or degree of conformity to the model quantitatively evaluated?

Does the model impose structural characteristics on the data? To the extent this is true, no theoretical conclusions can be drawn from the structure.

Is the model used for selecting data? If so, degree of structure should be evaluated on a new sample not so used.

Are the parameters of structure (number of factors, number of classes, etc.) uniquely determined? To the extent that they are not, caution must be exercised in ascribing theoretical importance to the results.

Proponents of various structural models sometimes study narrow or even artificial kinds of data, then indicate with a wave of the hand that all other kinds of data will also be illuminated by the given model. Periodic reviews of structural theory should encourage wider and more discriminating use of available models. Nor will the light shine in only one direction. One can only deplore the presentation of psychometrics in terms of hypothetical monsters whose test answers are determined by the spinning of internal roulette wheels [66].

The surest beacon for psychometric theory is real involvement in the solution of psychological problems.

C. EXTERNAL COMPONENT

While the problems of substantive and structural criteria for the construct validity of a test were treated sketchily in the *Technical Recommendations* and by Cronbach and Meehl and have consequently been treated at length above, the problem of external criteria for validity was ably treated. Many aspects of the problem discussed recently will not be repeated or reviewed.

In discussing substantive and structural components concern has been with responses to individual items. While individual items may be studied in relation to external criteria, most of what comes under the heading of external validity concerns correlation with total score. The method of constructing a total score from the item pattern necessarily implies a commitment about the structure of the items, and thus about the structure of the trait measured. That is, in a cumulative test, where the total score is the number of items scored plus, an additive model is implied. The indiscriminate use of this model may account for some of the difficulties which psychologists encounter in attempting to measure dynamic traits. The total score, with its implied commitment as to structure, is not a datum of observation but is an intervening variable.

External validity may be subdivided in various ways. The *Technical Recommendations* use a temporal division, concurrent and predictive validities. This division appears to be almost arbitrary and inconsequential. But determining whether right now X is psychotic is different from predicting whether at some future time X will become psychotic. The terms *discriminative validity* and *predictive validity* convey the distinction.

Another division of external validity compares the relation to other test scores with the relation to non-test behavior and other non-test data. By relating the test scores to other tests, one can make indirect use of whatever is known of the validity of the other tests. Factorial pattern comes under this heading. Surely no test, however, is acceptable for clinical use unless it is in some way tied to a non-test criterion, whether that be behavior ratings, group differences, or whatever. The warning of the *Technical Recommendations* [121, p. 15] is cogent here: the test must show relevance to non-test behavior, but it need not be equivalent to non-test behavior.

Another subdivision of external criteria is into those which are predicted to show a positive (or negative) relation to the test score and those which are predicted to show no relation to the test score. The problem of variables which ought not to show relation to the given test score is that of distortions of measurement. Distortions are errors of measurement which are correlated with true scores or with other obtained scores rather than being random with respect to all other scores as classical test theory assumes. An example of a distortion is a response set [17]. A similar example is the IBM answer-sheet-marking factor found by Whitcomb and Travers (personal communication) to overshadow other effects which they wished to study. Facade can act as a distorting factor in studies which are intended to measure other personality traits; since it is found so ubiquitously, it should be studied more thoroughly in its own right. All of the factors responsible for secular trends in test responses, to be discussed under Secular Trends in Test Behavior, are also distortions, as are unfinished items in non-speed tests. Demonstration of negligible relationship with known sources of distortion is an essential, not an optional, step in test validation.

Cronbach and Meehl [20] discussed correction for distortions of measurement in terms of suppressor variables. Recently Brogden [6] has proposed a method of constructing forced choice items which makes use of the principle of the suppressor variable. The objection to suppressor variables is, of course, that they introduce another fallible score and thus another source of error variance. Loevinger [72] has proposed an alternative approach of selecting originally those items least weighted with distortions.

Eysenck [28, 29] has proposed a method, called "criterion analysis,"[4] which combines external validation and study of internal structure. Briefly, he introduces into a factor analytic study a measure which represents the criterion. The tests are factored by any of several methods, and the axes rotated so that one axis coincides with the criterion measure. His method is therefore an alternative to simple structure as a principle for rotation of axes. Sidestepping the technical problems, some of which are discussed by Lubin [79], the question arises how the method of criterion analysis relates to the two steps of ascertaining structural unities and subsequently analyzing external correlations. Is the same thing accomplished, something more, or something less?

One may note, first, that complete dependence on factor analysis restricts one to an additive structural model, but this is perhaps a minor point. In some examples of criterion analysis quoted by Eysenck there is clear evidence of significant distortion in the criterion. For example, groups which were intended to be matched except for the fact that one group was rated as neurotic and the other was a normal control turned out to be significantly different in age and intelligence. Rotation towards such an axis produces a melange of neuroticism, age, intelligence, and who knows what else. Eysenck fails to recognize that such flaws in criterion groups and corresponding distortions in criterion measures are the rule rather than the exception. In many problems control groups are almost

a contradiction in terms, or, as Rogers, et al. [94], found, somewhat destructive of the purpose of the study. Such difficulties in external criteria led to the extension and revision of the concept of validity in the direction of construct validity.

The regularity with which measures of motor control and speed turn out to be the most promising measures of neurosis in studies under Eysenck's direction induces the suspicion that age and/or general physical condition is the chief component of his "neurotic tendency" factor. In one major study [29, Ch. 4] a measure of intelligence was more highly correlated with the neurotic-normal criterion than any other measure except one questionnaire, a fact somewhat concealed by his *ad hoc* explanations. Neither criterion analysis nor any other computational gimmick takes the place of careful consideration of possible sources of distortion.

While Eysenck's method of criterion analysis seems to be a step backwards towards criterion-oriented validity, it does point to a weakness in attempts to establish the existence of traits by means of factor analysis alone. It seems reasonable to require that complete validation of any test include a demonstration of some non-zero relationship with a non-test variable. Cronbach and Meehl specified that validity must include some external relationships. They did not specify non-test variables, but the illustrations adduced in their paper appear to indicate sympathy with such a requirement.

In Section B of this chapter, choice of structural model was presented as an intuitive problem. Magnitude of external correlations may help to decide between alternative structures. In *Measurement and Prediction* [97] there is record of attempts to find scalable aspects of neurotic tendency. A clinician might have told the investigators that neurosis is far too variable in its manifestations to conform to a scale model, but apparently none did. There were several sets of items which proved to be scalable, but such items were extremely

---

[4] The term "criterion analysis" is sometimes used to cover a broad range of techniques, rather than just the one so designated by Eysenck. See, for example, Lafitte [63].

poor at differentiating neurotic from normal soldiers. The one subtest (psychosomatic complaints) which was more or less adequate at differentiating neurotics was not scalable but formed what Guttman calls a quasi scale. Very likely such items would best be handled by classical test methods, that is, a cumulative model assuming low intercorrelations between items. Even where the structure of the items is of central interest, external correlations provide the court of last appeal.

SECULAR TRENDS IN TEST BEHAVIOR

What has been presented in this paper so far may be called a *theory of the first test*. It presents in rough outline a complete theory for construction and evaluation of a test without reference to test-retest coefficients or parallel forms of tests. Part of the traditional theory of reliability, the part that deals with homogeneity, has been assimilated to the topic of the structural component of validity. The other part of reliability theory, the part that deals with stability of test scores, has been omitted and does not appear to be needed. One cannot, however, propose a test theory which bypasses the major part of traditional theory without serious presentation of reasons.

A. CIRCULARITY OF CLASSICAL RELIABILITY THEORY

Consider the statistical theory of reliability. On a previous occasion [69, Ch. 1] I have argued that reliability can be defined only in a circular manner. Gulliksen's [43] definitive summary of test theory, which has become available since the argument was first made, illustrates it well. Gulliksen derives the basic equations twice, first in terms of a definition of random error, then in terms of a definition of true score. Both derivations begin, of course, with the assumption or definition that the obtained score is the sum of true and error scores.

Under the heading, "Definition of random errors," the error score is defined as having a mean of zero, zero correlation with true score, and *"the correlation between errors on one test and those on another parallel test is zero"* [43, p. 7, italics in original]. Under the heading, "Definition of parallel tests in terms of true score and error variance," Gulliksen states, *"For two parallel tests, the errors of measurement are equal"* [43, p. 12, italics in original]. Thus parallel tests are needed as part of the definition of error scores, and errors are needed as part of the definition of parallel tests.

In the following chapter, derivations are in terms of true score. True score is defined as the limit of the average score on a number of parallel tests, as the number increases without limit. Parallel tests are defined as tests equal in observed means, standard deviations, and mutual intercorrelations [43, pp. 28–29]. Reliability is then defined as the correlation between parallel tests [43, p. 31, footnote]. Thus parallel tests are defined in terms of their correlation (reliability), and reliability is defined as the correlation between parallel tests. It is not surprising that a theory which begins with a circularity ends in paradox [71].

The basic difficulty in the theory of reliability can be stated other ways. The true score is defined as the limit of a series which may not in fact converge, or, if it does converge, is not approximated usefully by the first term in the series, which is the term whose meaning is at stake. Or, reliability is defined in terms of a set of operations, to wit, repeated testing with no effect of repetition, which cannot in the nature of things be performed.

To circumvent or ameliorate this basic contradiction various methods of estimating reliability have been employed. There has for a long time been some recognition and recently widespread recognition that estimates of reliability based on a single administration of a test are estimates of something completely different from what is estimated by a test-retest coefficient. That the same statistical theory of reliability should continue to be used for both kinds of coefficients is remarkable testimony to the obduracy of psychometricians. Correlation of parallel forms of tests combines some of the advantages and some of the disadvantages of test-retest and single-form reliabilities and, in addition, involves the circularity of parallel forms being defined in terms of the very correlation which they will then be used to estimate.

Gulliksen says of the parallel forms method of determining reliability: "Generally speaking, this method is best, provided that we can regulate the interval between the two tests and the activity of the subjects during that interval so that the influence of practice, fatigue, and other similar effects will be negligible" [43, pp. 214–215]. The question arises: for what kinds of psychological tests has it been established that influences of practice, fatigue, boredom, sophistication, and other temporary or cumulative influences have a negligible effect on the second test? It is probably true, as Gulliksen claims, that such effects on test behavior, which will here be called *secular trends*, can be detected in terms of change either in mean or in variance. But traditional test theory assumes that secular trends in test behavior do not exist, and most reliability coefficients are reported without reference to whether they have or have not occurred.

To belittle the advance which reliability theory represented over the earlier naive view of test scores would be both folly and impropriety. The recognition that the obtained test score was an imperfect estimate of something more fundamental was a tremendous step forward. The various coefficients for estimating reliability and the statistical theory of reliability arose in attempting to assay how well obtained scores succeeded in measuring the more fundamental or "true scores." The import of the preceding chapters of this monograph is that recent developments in test theory, particularly the concept of construct validity, enable us to conceptualize what

the obtained score is an estimate of and to evaluate how good an estimate it is without reference to a retest or a parallel test.

The basic assumption of reliability theory, which implies that secular trends do not exist, has been carried over into a number of recent contributions to psychometrics. Guttman [45] has written papers on estimation of test-retest reliability coefficients; however, the assumption that there is no effect from repeating a test does not appear to be incorporated into his theories of scale analysis, of image analysis, or into radex theory. Coombs and Lazarsfeld, however, have incorporated the classical assumption into their thinking more essentially. Lazarsfeld [66] uses the term "brainwashing" to help his readers conceptualize what is assumed to take place between test and retest. Anderson [3], however, has presented a computational technique for latent structure analysis which does not require estimation of item reliabilities.

B. THE PROBLEM OF SECULAR TRENDS

Consider this possibility. A test of ability given without forepractice proves to have high predictive validity, but test-retest correlation is low. Given with considerable forepractice the test-retest coefficient is high but the nature of the test has changed so that predictive validity is low. Here is another "attenuation paradox" [71], i.e., a set of experimental conditions under which raising reliability lowers validity, contrary to the relationship stated in the classical correction for attenuation. The example is by no means implausible. It was proposed by Thorndike [102] in 1919. It demonstrates the intimate relation between secular trends and the validity problem.

The necessity of conforming as far as possible to the assumptions of reliability theory has led to a neglect of and glossing over of the problem of secular trends in test behavior. There is every reason to suppose that in general they occur. The "theory of the first test" can ignore them. But in practical and also in research situations retests and parallel forms are often necessary. Second tests, whether retests or parallel forms, must be interpreted with respect to most or all of the factors bearing on first tests and also all of the factors influencing trends in test behavior as such. Thus coefficients of stability, when properly identified as to the conditions under which they were obtained, have an important place in test theory. They belong, however, to "theory of the second test." On occasion results from further testings will also be available, as in longitudinal studies.

One reason for the importance of the topic of secular trends is that such trends create artifacts, either spurious stability or spurious change, in research primarily directed toward study of stability and change in other traits. Thus the topic is intimately related to the subjects of trait consistency, developmental changes, intra-individual differences, and pathological and therapeutic processes.

A major conceptualization and review of the literature on intra-individual response variation has been made by Fiske and Rice [30]. They separate intra-individual response variation into three types. Type I consists of variation in response due to spontaneous change in the organism and is assumed not to depend on the order of presentation of stimuli. Type II includes variation which may be influenced by the order of presentation, but effects of fatigue, learning, and cyclic change are arbitrarily excluded. Type III includes changes where the stimulus situation changes, as in studies of rigidity, and is included to throw the previous types into perspective. Insofar as variation in response is spontaneous and not a function of order of presentation (Type I), the assumptions of traditional reliability theory would appear to be supported. Fiske and Rice, however, believe that such variability is lawful and has correlates, and that belief appears to be somewhat at variance with the traditional assumption of random error; the contradiction is not direct, for the traditional assumption is concerned with a quantity,

Fiske and Rice with its standard deviation. It is not clear how rigorous were the standards for deciding whether a given study exhibited Type I or Type II variation. (Indeed, the classification of a study, or even the existence of the defined types of variation, represents a complex inference. It would appear generally desirable for review articles to adopt less disputable categorizations of studies.)

Type II variation corresponds closely to what is here called secular trends. However, systematic factors such as fatigue and learning are not excluded from secular trends insofar as they produce distortion in measures of other traits. Despite the heroic proportions of the Fiske and Rice review, which had 233 references, important evidence for the existence of secular trends was omitted, such as evidence for rise in IQ with repeated testing, even when the tests are as much as a year apart.

Among early papers on systematic changes on retest for ability are those of Thorndike [102] and Adkins [1]; neither is mentioned by Fiske and Rice. Windle [115] has reviewed the literature on "Test-retest effect on personality questionnaires." He presents a table of 41 studies of retest of untreated groups; of those 41 studies only 4 are listed in the bibliography of Fiske and Rice's paper. The general trend of the studies reviewed by Windle is for retests on personality inventories to show improved adjustment.

Bayley [4] in a recent review has shown that increments in measured intelligence where the same individuals are retested exceed previous expectations, even when the retest occurs after a considerable time lapse. She acknowledges that practice effects probably account for some of the increment but lays greater stress on the possibility that intelligence continues to develop during maturity.

Recognition that systematic changes occur on retest has coexisted with classical reliability theory over a period of many years, with only rare recognition of the contradiction between fact and the assumptions of theory. Clearly there are questions here which need clarification by further evidence or by re-examination of existing data. The concept of secular trends in test behavior is needed to prevent dependence on traditional test-retest correlations from obscuring substantial problems, those of changes in means and variances.

C. IMPLICATIONS FOR CONSTRUCT VALIDITY

That there is no received method for dealing with secular trends is borne out by inspection of the *Technical Recommendations*. Secular trends are mentioned just once, in connection with stability of scores: "The manual should report changes in mean score as well as the correlation between the two sets of scores" [121, p. 232]. That requirement is considered essential, but there is no follow-up. What should be done in case there is a sizeable mean change from test to retest?

The common belief, explicit in Peak and not disavowed in the *Technical Recommendations* or Cronbach and Meehl, is that knowledge of stability contributes to our confidence in the construct validity of the test because we ordinarily are interested in traits which have some longevity; stability should not exceed, however, whatever stability might reasonably characterize the underlying trait. The traditional correction for attenuation is often interpreted as a precise statement of relation between stability and validity; however, it belongs to the part of psychometric theory which treats coefficients of homogeneity (such as split-half correlation) and coefficients of stability (such as test-retest correlation) as identical.

The supposed connection between test-retest (or parallel forms) stability and construct validity is, I submit, a *non sequitur*. The basis for the *non sequitur* is failure to recognize the fact that the first and the second tests may, and in general must be assumed to, bear different relations to the underlying trait, just by virtue of being first and second. This topic is another aspect of the "psychology of objective test behavior." In the case of projective tests, secular trends in test behavior are so conspicuous that the notion of test-retest stability often is not applied to them [16]. Yet secular trends of a less conspicuous sort are regularly found in other kinds of tests; the difference is one of degree.

Suppose a mean gain of 5 raw score points is found on retesting children with a certain test in a given age range. What procedure should the test user follow? Should he subtract five points from each second test and then refer to norms for the first test? The *Technical Recommendations* do not say. So doing would ignore any possible change in variance on retest. Separate norms for retests would seem more defensible. Failure to recommend separate norms for retests is perhaps the only serious criticism that can be made of the work of the APA Committee on Test Standards.

Perhaps, however, the implication of the *Technical Recommendations* is that if the change in mean score from test to retest is appreciable, the validity of the test is open to question. But if the correlation between test and retest is much less than unity, validity of test and retest may differ considerably.

Assume the validity of the first test is investigated first. Neither change in mean score nor low correlation between test and retest places any restriction on the validity of the first test. If the test-retest coefficient is very high, then the second test may be assumed to have similar validity to the first, provided care is taken to use retest norms. Since high correlation is consistent with sizeable changes in mean and standard deviation, referral of retests to first test norms may seriously impair the validity of resultant inferences.

Occurrence of an appreciable mean change does not in itself imply any decrement in test-retest correlation. Intuitively, however, one assumes that some factor must cause the mean change, and that this implies a factor influencing the retest which does not influence the original score. On this reasoning one would be surprised if a sizeable mean change would occur where test-retest correlation was near to unity. Such coefficients as are commonly found do not rule out the possibility of fairly large discrepancies between correlations of the two tests with external criteria and other variables.

In conclusion, neither the magnitude of the test-retest coefficient nor the magnitude of changes in mean and variance from test to retest has direct bearing on the construct validity of the first test. Norms for the first test can properly be used in the interpretation of retest scores only when the correlation between the two tests is very high and changes in mean and standard deviation are negligible. In other cases the retest is, from the point of view of construct validity, a new test, and must be validated and, especially, standardized accordingly.

ALTERNATIVE APPROACHES

The title of the present paper outlines a province that many psychologists will recognize as their own. The scope and length of this monograph and, to be candid, the cathexis of my own view preclude a thorough review here of alternative ways of organizing the field. At the same time it would be misleading not to acknowledge major predecessors. The reader will recognize that the intention of this chapter is clarification of the present contribution by contrast rather than a disinterested exposition and evaluation of alternatives.

A. OTHER KINDS OF DATA

Approaches utilizing rating scales and projective techniques have been excluded from consideration but it seems desirable to relate such techniques briefly to the discussion. Consider first rating scales. As they are ordinarily used, the trait rated is identical with the trait in which one is interested, and the problem of substantive validity cannot arise. Similarly, the question of structural validity cannot arise in the case of a single rating of a trait, since the rater is expected to weigh and evaluate all the manifestations of the trait before making his rating. Thus the sole criterion for this kind of rating is external validity.

Rating scales can be used in a manner formally similar to test items. Wittenborn [118] has utilized ratings of specific symptomatic behaviors in a factor analytic study. The resultant clusters have been examined for substantive and structural validity and do in fact appear to make psychiatric sense.

Suppose there were an objective test with 5000 items, and each S is instructed to answer "some" of them. The number of answers per S might range, say, from 5 to 500, and of course different Ss answering the same number would generally choose different items. The question of which items are interrelated can be asked with meaning. But unfortunately the problems of how many responses different Ss make and which questions they choose to answer, while themselves meaningful data, make it virtually impossible to study the relations of the items. The illustration is analogous to projective tests, except that in the latter the number of possible responses is far greater. The price paid for the richness of the response as a reflection of the mental processes of the S is the difficulty in comparing data from several Ss.

Any kind of score for a projective test, like a score for an objective test, is an intervening variable rather than an original datum. The response to an item is a datum, a single manifestation of personality or item of behavior. Structural validity refers to the structural relations of the original data and not of the intervening variables or scores. Evidence for the structure of the *items* is what establishes that a *scorable test* exists in the data. Thus the structural component of validity, as the term is used here, although not meaningless for projective tests, is difficult to establish. Wittenborn [117], again, has devised some approaches to the problem of the structural validity of certain Rorschach scoring categories. Whether he has satisfactorily solved the difficult methodological problems is not entirely clear. The substantive component of validity, although used in relation to objective tests as referring to items, appears to be meaningful when applied to interpretation of Rorschach scoring categories.

Schafer [95], on occasion, uses the sequence of responses in a Rorschach administration as a map of the personality dynamics of S. The rules for such inference are not at present sufficiently explicit so that group differences can be clearly predicted. Empirical verification of the rules is still not planned for. This kind of interpretation can be compared with the notion of structure as used in the present paper. The suggestion here is that there are populations with respect to which one has certain intuitions about the structural relations of the several manifestations of one trait. This structure should also obtain in the several items which comprise a test of that trait. The same two assumptions appear to be made by Schafer, but his technique skips the step of finding those items which best conform to the given structure and instead utilizes structural (sequential) differences as measures of trait differences. Any non-equivalence in the stimulus situation preceding the several responses must be taken into account intuitively.

Interpretation of response sequence may also be compared to the notion of secular trends in test behavior. Again there is an assumption of the equivalence of the several stimulus situations. Except for this instance, there are not many examples in psychological testing of constructive use of factors making for secular trends in test responses.

A recent study by Wittenborn, *et al.* [119] is of interest both because it utilizes data from interviews in a manner formally similar to objective test data and because Wittenborn has evolved a method superficially similar to that advocated in the present monograph. The differences between Wittenborn's method and that of the writer should sharpen the focus of the present argument. The purpose of Wittenborn's monograph is to demonstrate that interviews yield data from which scores can be obtained which are usable in the same manner as ordinary test scores. He speaks of standard "bits of information" derived from interview protocols. The phraseology suggests the notion of items as observations as opposed to miniature measurements, as developed under Relation of Test Behavior to Theory, Section C, above. Wittenborn, however, studies the interrelations of such items by means of tetrachoric correlation, a coefficient which assumes not only that each item is actually a measurement of an underlying continuum, but also that the continuum is normally distributed, the correlation between any two items is characterized by linear regression, and so on.

Further, Wittenborn searches for clusters among the items of information scored from the interviews. Unfortunately, he makes no use of statistical methods worked out for this problem, such as the method of Wherry and Winer [114] or that of Loevinger, Gleser, and DuBois [75]. The latter method, in particular, provides formal solutions for two problems: when to stop adding items to a cluster and when two clusters should be combined. Wittenborn does not appear to have satisfactory solutions to these problems. For example, he presents two separate clusters whose intercorrelation is .56 but whose self-correlation is in each case .44. Although the split-half correlation reported is less appropriate as an index of homogeneity than one based on the Kuder-Richardson Formula 20, they are probably not far apart in magnitude. These data strongly suggest that the between-cluster item intercorrelations exceed the within-cluster intercorrelations, which surely is contrary to the author's intention.

Finally, Wittenborn admits that content was taken into account along with coefficients in formation of clusters. Now if the intention of his monograph had been to provide scoring keys for clinical use, this procedure would be excusable at least as an interim measure. But the purpose of the monograph was to demonstrate that scorable clusters exist. For research purposes it seems imperative to separate the decisions which are guided by content from the decisions which are guided by numerical data. One method of doing so is outlined under Components of Construct Validity, above. Clusters are formed on the basis of data alone, without prejudice from content. Examination of content then serves as a check on the value and the interpretation of clusters or scoring keys thus derived.

B. OTHER KINDS OF ANALYSIS

The Berkeley studies on the authoritarian personality [2] exemplify the explicit utilization of theory in construction of objective test items. While the tests, F scale, E scale, and others, were modified as a result of empirical findings, it is not clear how much the test results yielded for theory in the Berkeley studies. Structural considerations were excluded in test construction. Likert-type items were used, introducing a spurious element into the intercorrelation of their several scales.

By far the chief instrument for using empirical relations of test behaviors to define constructs has been factor analysis. The many contributions of Thurstone are preeminent; perhaps in this country insufficient credit is given Spearman, Burt, and Thomson. Vernon [112], in summarizing factorial studies of ability, found support for the English predilection for hierarchical structure of mental abilities. More recently Guilford [41] has derived from a review of factorial studies a new picture of mental organization. Other investigators, too, have been concerned with the implications for psychology of the results of factor analysis.

There is, however, some question whether factor analytic studies have entirely lived up to optimistic advance notices of their contributions to psychological theory. Alternative structural theories have been presented with equally optimistic advance notices, have less clear rules for making theoretical inferences, and have as yet yielded less for theory.

Suppose, as in the Q-sort technique, an S is given 100 first person statements, which he is to sort into piles according to how closely they characterize him. Does the distribution he arrives at differ from the distribution his neighbor arrives at in content or in structure? Neither notion seems clearly to apply. It is difficult to see what substitutes in the Q-sort technique for the demonstration in other objective tests that structure does exist, which implies not only a common trait underlying several responses but also a community of meaning in the reading of single items and test instructions. Relatively little use is made of responses in Q-technique, however. What is usually used is again an intervening variable, namely, the correlation between pairs of distributions obtained under different circumstances. These correlations are themselves treated as data and related to other variables, so that a hierarchy of intervening variables is established [94]. Relationship between the hypothesis tested and the data observed has then become tenuous indeed.

Finally, the reader will recognize that the approach of this paper has been cross-sectional and probabilistic-functional in Brunswik's [8] sense, or confined to "R-technique," if we may disregard for the moment Cattell's wish to confine the term to factor analytic studies. What of the alternatives developed by Cattell [11], Stephenson [98], and Mowrer [90], to wit, P-, Q-, O-technique, and so on? These techniques substitute tests or occasions as the dimension of replication for the more usual replication of people; in place of correlating tests, people or occasions may be correlated. The "covariation chart" in terms of which the alternative techniques are developed is by itself, I believe, somewhat obstructive of progress. The feeling that it induces in some scientists, that any ways of collecting and collating data that are possible are also necessary, seems misguided. It is too much like the research plan of the mythical chemist: take substances from the storeroom in alphabetical order and place in the cyclotron. Where P-technique and Q-technique methods grow out of the nature of a problem investigated, they may well be the most appropriate methods, but that must be decided in specific context. As programs, their disadvantages seem to outweigh the advantages. The excessive time requirements of P-technique factor analysis will surely drive psychologists farther away from the generality of the population and into the company of special types of people. The basis for this conclusion is easily demonstrated by attempting to get the cooperation of various kinds of people for brief paper-and-pencil tests.

As the discussion of the structural component under Components of Construct Validity illustrates, the study of types and configurations is not the exclusive province of Q-technique, and the study of dynamic processes is not the exclusive province of P-technique. Many of the problems discussed above, such as the relation of secular trends to the validity problem, assume a different form in relation to alternative techniques.

Anyone who proposes a radical departure from traditional psychometric techniques must be prepared to assume the burden of proving the superiority of his methods to classical ones, for classical *methods* have clearly established their worth, at least in the field of ability measurement. But there is a lack of any coherent correspondence between classical psychometric theory and psychometric techniques; so pragmatic success does not support equally classical *theory*. The present monograph proposes a test theory which differs radically from the generally accepted one but advocates

methods which are not widely at variance with classical methods. Considerations adduced in this essay do not, however, justify dogmatic rejection of more radical innovations of technique.

A PSYCHOMETRICS

A. THEORY

In summary, historical and litigious passages may be neglected in order to review what has been presented as an outline for a psychometrics. The basic concept is that of the construct validity of the test, the degree to which it measures some trait which really exists in some sense. Construct validity can be established only by convergence of several lines of evidence. Evidence for construct validity can be broken down into evidence that the test measures something systematic and evidence for the particular interpretation of what it measures. The degree of internal structure of the items and the magnitude of external correlations are the former, or psychometric, evidence; the nature of the structure, content of the items, and nature of the external relations are the latter, or psychological, evidence.

Test behavior is in the first instance responses to items. Such responses are both signs and samples. Because they are samples of behavior in general, they must be subject to the same laws as behavior. Because they are signs, inferences may be drawn from the organization of test responses to the organization of other behavior. Thus psychometrics must draw from but can also contribute to psychological theory.

There are three criteria for the construct validity of a test, mutually exclusive, exhaustive, and mandatory. These criteria are that the substance or content of the items shall be consistent with the proposed interpretation, that the structural relations of the items shall be consistent with the structural relations of non-test manifestations of the same trait, and that the external correlations of the test score shall not all be zero and shall be consistent with predictions based on what is known of the postulated trait. Each item response is viewed as a bit of behavior rather than as a miniature measurement. Surplus meaning, psychological or psychometric, is avoided in interpreting item responses. In order for a test score to be useful, however, it must be demonstrated to have at once psychological and psychometric meaning, that is, the test score must be demonstrated to serve as a measure of some trait, subject, of course, to a margin of error.

The reasoning by which observations are parlayed into measurement may be summarized for the classical quantitative case. Several items which measure such a trait have greater probability of being answered in the positive direction, the greater the amount of the trait. A cluster of items measuring a common trait can be detected by the mutual intercorrelation of the items. The sum of several such items constitutes a score which tends to be greater, the greater the amount of the trait. The proportion of variance of the total score which is determined by the common trait can be large, even though for each item the proportion of variance determined by that trait is small. It is not assumed that the underlying trait or the observed scores are distributed according to the normal or indeed any other particular curve. That many observed distributions conform more or less to the normal curve may be a consequence of the fact that the scores are obtained by summing many items, each largely composed of error variance.

Full utilization of objective tests in clinical and in research settings depends on further development of a theory of test behavior and integration of that theory with the rest of psychology: what levels of personality, what impulses, defenses, and adaptive traits, are accessible to objective tests with different formal and content characteristics?

The foregoing considerations relate to theory of the first test. In order to interpret re-test or parallel form scores, there must also be available a theory of the second test, which requires study of secular trends in test behavior.[5]

B. METHOD

The program of test construction implied by the foregoing concepts may be summarized as follows:

1. The pool of items should be constituted so as to sample some area of content defined more broadly than the anticipated test. When feasible, all possible alternative constructs should determine the definition of the area of content. A wide and systematic sampling of the area of content, guided by the life-importance of sub-areas, is highly desirable.

2. The choice of the structural model for test construction should be based on what is known of the manifestations of the trait or type of trait measured in and outside of the test situation. Alternative structural models may be used with final selection based on empirical or theoretical criteria or a combination. The pool of items is administered to a normative sample and the best items are selected from the pool in conformity with the structural model chosen. Those items constitute the test or the scoring key. Degree of structure is ascertained by administering the test to a new sample.

[5] Dr. R. M. W. Travers has called my attention to his recent work showing the existence of secular trends within a single test administration for certain kinds of test materials and has raised the question of whether such tests are excluded from the discussion. The discovery of secular trends within a single test is not, of course, entirely new; similar observations have led to the virtual abandonment of the split-half method of computing test reliability. The external correlations of a test score are what they are regardless of trends within the several items which contribute to the score. There seems no reason, therefore, to exclude such tests from the discussion. A complete and rigorous treatment of score-structural theory, which has not been attempted in this monograph, certainly requires consideration of the problem Travers has raised, but the major points of the present discussion will not be affected.

3. The test score is then correlated with external (test and non-test) variables, both those that are expected to show relationship and those not expected to show relationship (sources of distortion).

The empirical findings of steps 2 and 3 are examined for concordance with alternative theories, or explanations, or constructs. The minimum criterion for acceptable validation is that the interpretation of the test scores be over-determined. If a separate principle or explanation must be invoked for each line of evidence, validation is not convincing.

The present view is a kind of operationism but certainly not the kind which states or implies that any set of operations defines a concept. Garner, Hake, and Eriksen [36] have suggested, in line with current versions of operationism in philosophy, that only *convergent* operations define a concept. The present paper is an attempt to make such a view explicit in relation to test construction.

C. APPLICATION

For a detailed example of the application of concepts similar to those developed in the present monograph, the reader is referred to a recent article by Jessor and Hammond [60]. They treat at length the use of the Taylor Anxiety Scale as an instrument of psychological theory.

A fragment of some research by Dr. Blanche Sweet and the writer will illustrate a number of points. A large number of items covering everyday problems of family life was collected and administered to a number of groups, particularly mothers of college students and girls of college age, many of whom were not, however, students.

Item 130 reads: "130a. After all the sacrifices parents make, teen-age children should be grateful to them. 130b. Teenagers cannot be expected to be grateful to their parents." *Ss* are required to choose one of the alternatives. A naive belief that behavior is directly translated into test response would lead one to expect that parents would tend to choose the former and adolescents the latter response. In fact, the trend is the other way, with the adolescent girls tending to choose the first alternative and the mothers tending to choose the second. The item belongs to a cluster whose predominant theme lies in the punitive versus permissive dimension. It is plausible that a group of young unmarried women would have a slightly more punitive and disciplinarian attitude than a matched group of mature women having had the experience of motherhood. A group of young women who had just enlisted in the Marine Corps were the most punitive group tested. A group of Vassar graduates, most of whom were also mothers, were the most permissive group tested.

The substance of the cluster makes sense, though many of the items obviously are not direct representations of observable behavior. A cumulative model seems adequate for the structure of this trait, that is, it seems reasonable to suppose that the wider the variety of situations in which the person chooses the more punitive alternative, the more punitive he is. Relationships with external variables, in this case group differences, are in concordance with the interpretation suggested by the content of the items.

Kinds of hypotheses that can be tested in such a course of test construction are:

(a) Those that concern organization of attitudes. Are individuals who are stern and punitive towards children equally rigorous in their demands on parents? Or, alternatively, are there "child-centered" and "parent-centered" people? Is authoritarianism a single trait? Or are there aspects of authoritarianism which vary more or less independently?

(b) Those that concern the relation of verbally expressed attitudes to personality structure. Granted that every single response reflects a variety of traits; do the clusters or themes among the items reflect consciously or unconsciously held attitudes? How superficial or fundamental in the defensive and adaptive structure are such attitudes?

(c) Those that concern the dynamics of trait formation. For example, if the finding that young inexperienced women tend to be more disciplinarian than more mature women is confirmed, other hypotheses will be suggested. Do individuals whose control of their own impulses is not firmly established tend to mistrust other people's capacity for reasonable impulse control, hence believe in more or less rigid patterns of discipline?

Evidence for the various kinds of hypotheses does not fit neatly into compartments. The hypotheses overlap, as does evidence for them. None of the three kinds of hypotheses has direct reference to nonverbal behavior. The validity of the test is conceived to lie neither in the degree of obvious or literal correspondence between observable behavior and expressed attitudes nor in the degree of predictability of particular behaviors on the basis of the test. The common error of classical psychometrics and naively operational experimental-theoretical psychology has been to assume that only behavior is worth predicting. Circumstances contrive to keep behavior largely unpredictable, however constant its propensities. The focus of our psychometrics, as of our psychology, should remain within the behaving person.

The example illustrates also a point closely related to a major point of Cronbach and Meehl's paper, that the process of test validation is virtually coterminous with the use of tests for substantive contributions to psychology. What has been presented as a method of test validation is also a method of testing some kinds of psychological hypotheses. Other hands can assay this method of theory testing in comparison with experimental alternatives.

SUMMARY

Logically, the kind of validity a test achieves is independent of the method of test construction. If one asks, however, how best to construct a test, the answer is that each kind of validity contains by implication a program of test construction. The programs implied by content validity and classical (predictive and concurrent) validity are not appropriate for major test construction projects. Only construct validity, which aims at measuring real traits, promises tests which will both draw from and contribute to psychology.

The lines of evidence which together establish the construct validity of a test refer to its content, its internal structure, and relation to outside variables. A single explanation or theory must encompass all evidence, for construct validation to be approximated.

Systematic factors affecting retests with the same or parallel form result in secular trends in test behavior. In general, secular trends must be assumed to exist; classical reliability theory assumes that they do not. A method of test construction based on construct validation can dispense with test-retest and parallel form reliability.

A psychometrics with construct validity as its central concept can be used as framework for viewing many recent contributions to psychometrics, some of which contribute to a construct-oriented psychometrics and others of which contrast with it.

REFERENCES

1. ADKINS, D. C. The effects of practice on intelligence test scores. *J. educ. Psychol.*, 1937, 28, 222–231.
2. ADORNO, T. W., FRENKEL-BRUNSWIK, E., LEVINSON, D. J., & SANFORD, R. N. *The authoritarian personality.* New York: Harper, 1950.
3. ANDERSON, T. W. On estimation of parameters in latent structure analysis. *Psychometrika*, 1954, 19, 1–10.
4. BAYLEY, N. On the growth of intelligence. *Amer. Psychologist*, 1955, 10, 805–818.
5. BROGDEN, H. E. Variation in test validity with variation in the distribution of item difficulties, number of items, and degree of their intercorrelation. *Psychometrika*, 1946, 11, 197–214.

6. BROGDEN, H. E. A rationale for minimizing distortion in personality questionnaire keys. *Psychometrika*, 1954, 19, 141–148.

7. BRUNSWIK, E. *Systematic and representative design of psychological experiments.* Berkeley: Univer. of Calif. Press, 1947.

8. BRUNSWIK, E. Representative design and probabilistic theory in a functional psychology. *Psychol. Rev.*, 1955, 62, 193–217.

9. CAMPBELL, D. T. The indirect assessment of social attitudes. *Psychol. Bull.*, 1950, 47, 15–38.

10. CARROLL, J. B. Criteria for the evaluation of achievement tests. In *Proceedings, 1950 Invitational Conference on Testing Problems.* Princeton: Educ. Testing Service, 1951. Pp. 95–99.

11. CATTELL, R. B. *Description and measurement of personality.* Yonkers-on-Hudson: World Book, 1946.

12. CHIANG, C. L. On the design of mass medical surveys. *Human Biol.*, 1951, 23, 242–271.

13. COOMBS, C. H. *A theory of psychological scaling.* Ann Arbor: Engineering Res. Inst., Univer. of Michigan, 1952.

14. COOMBS, C. H. Theory and methods of social measurement. In L. Festinger & D. Katz (Eds.), *Research methods in the behavioral sciences.* New York: Dryden, 1953. Pp. 471–535.

15. COOMBS, C. H., & KAO, R. C. *Nonmetric factor analysis.* Ann Arbor: Engineering Res. Inst., Univer. of Michigan, 1955.

16. CRONBACH, L. J. Statistical methods applied to Rorschach scores: a review. *Psychol. Bull.*, 1949, 46, 393–429.

17. CRONBACH, L. J. Further evidence on response sets and test design. *Educ. psychol. Measmt*, 1950, 10, 3–31.

18. CRONBACH, L. J. Report on a psychometric mission to Clinicia. *Psychometrika*, 1954, 19, 263–270.

19. CRONBACH, L. J., & GLESER, G. C. Assessing similarity between profiles. *Psychol. Bull.*, 1953, 50, 456–473.

20. CRONBACH, L. J., & MEEHL, P. E. Construct validity in psychological tests. *Psychol. Bull.*, 1955, 52, 281–302.

21. CRONBACH, L. J., & WARRINGTON, W. G. Efficiency of multiple-choice tests as a function of spread of item difficulties. *Psychometrika*, 1952, 17, 127–147.

22. DORRIS, R. J., LEVINSON, D. J., & HANF-MANN, E. Authoritarian personality studied by a new variation of the sentence completion technique. *J. abnorm. soc. Psychol.*, 1954, 49, 99–108.

23. DUBOIS, P. H., LOEVINGER, J., & GLESER, G. C. *The construction of homogeneous keys for a biographical inventory.* Res. Bull. 52–18, Air Training Command, Human Resources Research Center, 1952, Lackland Air Force Base.

24. DUMAS, F. M. *Manifest structure analysis.* Missoula: Montana State Univer. Press, 1955.

25. DUMAS, F. M., FROST, C. H., & RASHLEIGH, C. H. A manifest structure analysis of information files. *J. clin. Psychol.*, 1956, 12, 139–143.

26. EDWARDS, A., & COOMBS, C. H. A theory of psychological scaling. *Psychometrika*, 1954, 19, 89–91. (Review)

27. ELIAS, G. Self-evaluative questionnaires as projective measures of personality. *J. consult. Psychol.*, 1951, 15, 496–500.

28. EYSENCK, H. J. Criterion analysis—an application of the hypothetico-deductive method to factor analysis. *Psychol. Rev.*, 1950, 57, 38–53.

29. EYSENCK, H. J. *The scientific study of personality.* London: Routledge & K. Paul, 1952.

30. FISKE, D. W., & RICE, L. Intra-individual response variability. *Psychol. Bull.*, 1955, 52, 217–250.

31. FORER, B. R., & TOLMAN, R. S. Some characteristics of clinical judgment. *J. consult. Psychol.*, 1952, 16, 347–352.

32. FRENCH, J. W. *The description of personality measurements in terms of rotated factors.* Princeton: Educ. Testing Service, 1953.

33. FRENKEL-BRUNSWIK, E. Psychoanalysis and the unity of science. *Proc., Amer. Acad. Arts Sci.*, 1954, 80, 271–350.

34. FURST, E. J., & FRICKE, B. G. Development and applications of structured tests of personality. *Rev. educ. Res.*, 1956, 26, 26–55.

35. GAIER, E. L., & LEE, M. C. Pattern analysis: the configural approach to predictive measurement. *Psychol. Bull.*, 1953, 50, 140–148.

36. GARNER, W. R., HAKE, H. W., & ERIKSEN, C. W. Operationism and the concept of perception. *Psychol. Rev.*, 1956, 63, 149–159.

37. GOODENOUGH, F. L. *Mental testing*. New York: Rinehart, 1949.

38. GRAYSON, H. M., & TOLMAN, R. S. A semantic study of concepts of clinical psychologists and psychiatrists. *J. abnorm. soc. Psychol.*, 1950, 45, 216–231.

39. GUERTIN, W. H., FRANK, G. H., & RABIN, A. I. Research with the Wechsler-Bellevue Intelligence Scale: 1950–1955. *Psychol. Bull.*, 1956, 53, 235–257.

40. GUILFORD, J. P. Some lessons from aviation psychology. *Amer. Psychologist*, 1948, 3, 3–11.

41. GUILFORD, J. P. The structure of intellect. *Psychol. Bull.*, 1956, 53, 267–293.

42. GUILFORD, J. P., KETTNER, N. W., & CHRISTENSEN, P. R. The nature of the general reasoning factor. *Psychol. Rev.*, 1956, 63, 169–172.

43. GULLIKSEN, H. *Theory of mental tests*. New York: Wiley, 1950.

44. GUTTMAN, L. A basis for scaling qualitative data. *Amer. sociol. Rev.*, 1944, 9, 139–150.

45. GUTTMAN, L. A basis for analyzing test-retest reliability. *Psychometrika*, 1945, 10, 255–282.

46. GUTTMAN, L. The Cornell technique for scale and intensity analysis. *Educ. Psychol. Measmt*, 1947, 7, 247–280.

47. GUTTMAN, L. The problem of attitude and opinion measurement. In S. A. Stouffer, et al., *Measurement and prediction*. Princeton: Princeton Univer. Press, 1950. Pp. 46–59.

48. GUTTMAN, L. Image theory for the structure of quantitative variates. *Psychometrika*, 1953, 18, 277–296.

49. GUTTMAN, L. The Israel Alpha technique for scale analysis. In M. W. Riley, et al., *Sociological studies in scale analysis*. New Brunswick: Rutgers Univer. Press, 1954. Pp. 410–415.

50. GUTTMAN, L. A new approach to factor analysis: the radex. In P. F. Lazarsfeld (Ed.), *Mathematical thinking in the social sciences*. Glencoe, Ill.: Free Press, 1954. Pp. 258–348.

51. GUTTMAN, L. A generalized simplex for factor analysis. *Psychometrika*, 1955, 20, 173–192.

52. HAGGARD, E. A. *Intraclass correlation and the analysis of variance*. New York: Dryden, 1958.

53. HARROWER-ERICKSON, M. R. The value and limitations of the so-called "neurotic signs." *Rorschach Res. Exch.*, 1942, 6, 109–114.

54. HATHAWAY, S. R., & McKINLEY, J. D. A multiphasic personality schedule: I. Construction of the schedule. *J. Psychol.*, 1940, 10, 249–254.

55. HAYS, D. G., & BORGATTA, E. F. An empirical comparison of restricted and general latent distance analysis. *Psychometrika*, 1954, 19, 271–279.

56. HORST, P. Pattern analysis and configural scoring. *J. clin. Psychol.*, 1954, 10, 3–11.

57. HOVLAND, C. I., & SHERIF, M. Judgmental phenomena and scales of attitude measurement: item displacement in Thurstone scales. *J. abnorm. soc. Psychol.*, 1952, 47, 822–832.

58. HUMPHREYS, L. G. Individual differences. In C. P. Stone & D. W. Taylor (Eds.), *Annual review of psychology*. Stanford: Annual Reviews, 1952. Pp. 131–150.

59. HUNT, H. F. Testing for psychological deficit. In D. Brower & L. E. Abt (Eds.), *Progress in clinical psychology*. Vol. 1, Sec. 1. New York: Grune and Stratton, 1952. Pp. 91–107.

60. JESSOR, R., & HAMMOND, K. R. Construct validity and the Taylor anxiety scale. *Psychol. Bull.*, 1957, 54, 161–170.

61. KELLEY, T. L. The future psychology of mental traits. *Psychometrika*, 1940, 5, 1–15.

62. KELLY, E. L., MILES, C. C., & TERMAN, L. M. Ability to influence one's score on a typical pencil-and-paper test of personality. *Charact. & Pers.*, 1936, 4, 206–215.

63. LAFITTE, J. Spearman's form of criterion analysis. *Brit. J. stat. Psychol.*, 1954, 7, 57–60.

64. LAZARSFELD, P. F. The interpretation and computation of some latent structures. In S. A. Stouffer, et al., *Measurement and prediction*. Princeton: Princeton Univer. Press, 1950. Pp. 413–472.

65. LAZARSFELD, P. F. The logical and mathematical foundation of latent structure analysis. In S. A. Stouffer, et al., *Measurement and prediction*. Princeton: Princeton Univer. Press, 1950. Pp. 362–412.

66. LAZARSFELD, P. F. A conceptual introduction to latent structure analysis. In P. F. Lazarsfeld (Ed.), *Mathematical thinking in the social sciences*. Glencoe, Ill.: Free Press, 1954. Pp. 349–387.

67. LENNON, R. T. Assumptions underlying the use of content validity. *Educ. psychol. Measmt*, 1956, 16, 294–304.

68. LINDZEY, G. Thematic Apperception Test: interpretive assumptions and related empirical evidence. *Psychol. Bull.*, 1952, 49, 1–25.

69. LOEVINGER, J. A. A systematic approach to the construction and evaluation of tests of ability. *Psychol. Monogr.*, 1947, 61, No. 4 (Whole No. 285).

70. LOEVINGER, J. The technic of homogeneous tests compared with some aspects of "scale analysis" and factor analysis. *Psychol. Bull.*, 1948, 45, 507–529.

71. LOEVINGER, J. The attenuation paradox in test theory. *Psychol. Bull.*, 1954, 51, 493–504.

72. LOEVINGER, J. Effect of distortions of measurement on item selection. *Educ. psychol. Measmt*, 1954, 3, 441–448.

73. LOEVINGER, J. Some principles of personality measurement. *Educ. psychol. Measmt*, 1955, 15, 3–17.

74. LOEVINGER, J. The universe. *Amer. Psychologist*, 1955, 10, 399. (Abstract)

75. LOEVINGER, J., GLESER, G. C., & DuBois, P. H. Maximizing the discriminating power of a multiple-score test. *Psychometrika*, 1953, 18, 309–317.

76. LORD, F. M. The relation of the reliability of multiple-choice tests to the distribution of item difficulties. *Psychometrika*, 1952, 17, 181–194.

77. LORD, F. M. Sampling fluctuations resulting from the sampling of test items. *Psychometrika*, 1955, 20, 1–22.

78. LORD, F. M. Some perspectives on "The attenuation paradox in test theory." *Psychol. Bull.*, 1955, 52, 505–510.

79. LUBIN, A. A note on "criterion analysis." *Psychol., Rev.*, 1950, 57, 54–57.

80. LYKKEN, D. T. A method of actuarial pattern analysis. *Psychol. Bull.*, 1956, 53, 102–107.

81. MacCORQUODALE, K., & MEEHL, P. E. On a distinction between hypothetical constructs and intervening variables. *Psychol. Rev.*, 1948, 55, 95–107.

82. MARSCHAK, J. Probability in the social sciences. In P. F. Lazarsfeld (Ed.), *Mathematical thinking in the social sciences*. Glencoe, Ill.: Free Press, 1954. Pp. 166–215.

83. McQUITTY, L. L. A statistical method for studying personality integration. In O. H. Mowrer (Ed.), *Psychotherapy: theory and research*. New York: Ronald, 1953. Pp. 414–462.

84. McQUITTY, L. L. Theories and methods in some objective assessments of psychological well-being. *Psychol. Monogr.*, 1954, 68, No. 14 (Whole No. 385).

85. MEEHL, P. E. The dynamics of "structured" personality tests. *J. clin. Psychol.*, 1945, 1, 296–303.

86. MEEHL, P. E. Configural scoring. *J. consult. Psychol.*, 1950, 14, 165–171.

87. MEEHL, P. E. *Clinical vs. statistical prediction*. Minneapolis: Univer. of Minnesota Press, 1954.

88. MEEHL, P. E. Wanted—a good cookbook. *Amer. Psychologist*, 1956, 11, 263–272.

89. MEEHL, P. E., & ROSEN, A. Antecedent probability and the efficiency of psychometric signs, patterns, or cutting scores. *Psychol. Bull.*, 1955, 52, 194–216.

90. MOWRER, O. H. "Q technique"—description, history, and critique. In O. H. Mowrer (Ed.), *Psychotherapy: theory and research*. New York: Ronald, 1953. Pp. 316–375.

91. OWENS, W. A. Item form and "false-positive" response on a neurotic inventory. *J. clin. Psychol.*, 1947, 3, 264–269.

92. PEAK, H. Problems of objective observation. In L. Festinger & D. Katz (Eds.), *Research methods in the behavioral sciences*. New York: Dryden, 1953. Pp. 243–299.

93. RILEY, M. W., RILEY, J. W., JR., & TOBY, J. *Sociological studies in scale analysis*. New Brunswick: Rutgers Univer. Press, 1954.

94. ROGERS, C. R., & DYMOND, R. F. (Eds.) *Psychotherapy and personality change*. Chicago: Univer. of Chicago Press, 1954.

95. SCHAFER, R. *Psychoanalytic interpretation in Rorschach testing*. New York: Grune and Stratton, 1954.

96. SHERIF, M., & HOVLAND, C. I. Judgmental phenomena and scales of attitude measurement: placement of items with individual choice of number of categories. *J. abnorm. soc. Psychol.*, 1953, 48, 135–141.

97. STAR, S. A. The screening of psychoneurotics in the Army: technical development of tests. In S. A. Stouffer, *et al.*, *Measurement and prediction*. Princeton: Princeton Univer. Press, 1950. Pp. 486–548.

98. STEPHENSON, W. Some observations on Q technique. *Psychol. Bull.*, 1952, 49, 483–498.

99. STEPHENSON, W. *The study of behavior: Q-technique and its methodology.* Chicago: Univer. of Chicago Press, 1953.

100. STOUFFER, S. A., BORGATTA, E. F., HAYS, D. G., & HENRY, A. F. A technique for improving cumulative scales. *Publ. Opin. Quart.*, 1952, 16, 273–291.

101. TERMAN, L. M., & MILES, C. C. *Sex and personality.* New York: McGraw-Hill, 1936.

102. THORNDIKE, E. L. Tests of intelligence; reliability, significance, susceptibility to special training and adaptation to the general nature of the task. *Sch. & Soc.*, 1919, 9, 189–195.

103. THURSTONE, L. L. *Multiple factor analysis.* Chicago: Univer. of Chicago Press, 1947.

104. THURSTONE, L. L. Psychological implications of factor analysis. *Amer. Psychologist,* 1948, 3, 402–408.

105. THURSTONE, L. L. The criterion problem in personality research. *Educ. psychol. Measmt*, 1955, 15, 353–361.

106. THURSTONE, L. L., & CHAVE, E. J. *The measurement of attitude.* Chicago: Univer. of Chicago Press, 1929.

107. TOBY, J., & TOBY, M. L. A method of selecting dichotomous items by cross-tabulation. In M. W. Riley, *et al., Sociological studies in scale analysis.* New Brunswick: Rutgers Univer. Press, 1954. Pp. 339–355.

108. TRAVERS, R. M. W. Rational hypotheses in the construction of tests. *Educ. psychol. Measmt*, 1951, 11, 128–137.

109. TUCKER, L. R. Some experiments in developing a behaviorally determined scale of vocabulary. Paper read at Amer. Psychol. Ass., San Francisco, Sept., 1955.

110. TUCKER, L. R. The objective definition of simple structure in linear factor analysis. *Psychometrika*, 1955, 20, 209–225.

111. TUKEY, J. W. Discussion: symposium on statistics for the clinician. *J. clin. Psychol.*, 1950, 6, 61–74.

112. VERNON, P. E. *The structure of human abilities.* London: Methuen, 1950.

113. WECHSLER, D. *The measurement of adult intelligence.* (3rd Ed.) Baltimore: Williams and Wilkins, 1944.

114. WHERRY, R. J., & WINER, B. J. A method for factoring large numbers of items. *Psychometrika*, 1953, 18, 161–179.

115. WINDLE, C. Test-retest effect on personality questionnaires. *Educ. psychol. Measmt*, 1954, 14, 617–633.

116. WINTHROP, H. Semantic factors in the measurement of personality integration. *J. soc. Psychol.*, 1946, 24, 149–175.

117. WITTENBORN, J. R. Statistical tests of certain Rorschach assumptions: the internal consistency of scoring categories. *J. consult. Psychol.*, 1950, 14, 1–19.

118. WITTENBORN, J. R. Symptom patterns in a group of mental hospital patients. *J. consult. Psychol.*, 1951, 15, 290–302.

119. WITTENBORN, J. R., *et al.* A study of adoptive children. I. Interviews as a source of scores for children and their homes. *Psychol. Monogr.*, 1956, 70, No. 1. (Whole no. 408).

120. ZUBIN, J. The determination of response patterns in personality adjustment inventories. *J. educ. Psychol.*, 1937, 28, 401–413.

121. Technical recommendations for psychological tests and diagnostic techniques. *Psychol. Bull. Suppl.*, 1954, 51, Part 2, 1–38.

122. *Webster's new collegiate dictionary.* (2nd Ed.) Springfield, Mass.: Merriam, 1951.

3-75

Chapter 6

Convergent and Discriminant Validation by the Multitrait-Multimethod Matrix

DONALD T. CAMPBELL / DONALD W. FISKE

In the cumulative experience with measures of individual differences over the past 50 years, tests have been accepted as valid or discarded as invalid by research experiences of many sorts. The criteria suggested in this paper are all to be found in such cumulative evaluations, as well as in the recent discussions of validity. These criteria are clarified and implemented when considered jointly in the context of a multitrait-multimethod matrix. Aspects of the validational process receiving particular emphasis are these:

1. Validation is typically *convergent*, a

This article is reprinted from the *Psychological Bulletin,* 1959, with the permission of the authors and the American Psychological Association.

The new data analyses reported in this paper were supported by funds from the Graduate School of Northwestern University and by the Department of Psychology of the University of Chicago. The authors are also indebted to numerous colleagues for their thoughtful criticisms and encouragement of an earlier draft of this paper, especially Benjamin S. Bloom, R. Darrell Bock, Desmond S. Cartwright, Loren J. Chapman, Lee J. Cronbach, Carl P. Duncan, Lyle V. Jones, Joe Kamiya, Wilbur L. Layton, Jane Loevinger, Paul E. Meehl, Marshall H. Segall, Thornton B. Roby, Robert C. Tryon, Michael Wertheimer, and Robert F. Winch.

confirmation by independent measurement procedures. Independence of methods is a common denominator among the major types of validity (excepting content validity) insofar as they are to be distinguished from reliability.

2. For the justification of novel trait measures, for the validation of test interpretation, or for the establishment of construct validity, *discriminant* validation as well as convergent validation is required. Tests can be invalidated by too high correlations with other tests from which they were intended to differ.

3. Each test or task employed for measurement purposes is a *trait-method unit,* a union of a particular trait content with measurement procedures not specific to that content. The systematic variance among test scores can be due to responses to the measurement features as well as responses to the trait content.

4. In order to examine discriminant validity, and in order to estimate the relative contributions of trait and

method variance, *more than one trait* as well as *more than one method* must be employed in the validation process. In many instances it will be convenient to achieve this through a multitrait-multimethod matrix. Such a matrix presents all of the intercorrelations resulting when each of several traits is measured by each of several methods.

To illustrate the suggested validational process, a synthetic example is presented in Table 6–1. This illustration involves three different traits, each measured by three methods, generating nine separate variables. It will be convenient to have labels for various regions of the matrix, and such have been provided in Table 6–1. The reliabilities will be spoken of in terms of three *reliability diagonals,* one for each method. The reliabilities could also be designated as the monotrait-monomethod values. Adjacent to each reliability diagonal is the *heterotrait-monomethod* triangle. The reliability diagonal and the adjacent heterotrait-monomethod triangle make up a *monomethod block.* A *heteromethod block* is made up of a *validity* diagonal (which could also be designated as monotrait-

heteromethod values) and the two *heterotrait-heteromethod* triangles lying on each side of it. Note that these two heterotrait-heteromethod triangles are not identical.

In terms of this diagram, four aspects bear upon the question of validity. In the first place, the entries in the validity diagonal should be significantly different from zero and sufficiently large to encourage further examination of validity. This requirement is evidence of convergent validity. Second, a validity diagonal value should be higher than the values lying in its column and row in the heterotrait-heteromethod triangles. That is, a validity value for a variable should be higher than the correlations obtained between that variable and any other variable having neither trait nor method in common. This requirement may seem so minimal and so obvious as not to need stating, yet an inspection of the literature shows that it is frequently not met, and may not be met even when the validity coefficients are of substantial size. In Table 6–1, all of the validity values meet this requirement. A third common-sense desideratum is that a variable correlate higher with an independent effort to measure the same trait than with measures designed to get at different traits which hap-

Table 6–1 A Synthetic Multitrait-Multimethod Matrix

Traits	Method 1			Method 2			Method 3		
	A_1	B_1	C_1	A_2	B_2	C_2	A_3	B_3	C_3
Method 1 A_1	(.89)								
B_1	.51	(.89)							
C_1	.38	.37	(.76)						
Method 2 A_2	.57	.22	.09	(.93)					
B_2	.22	.57	.10	.68	(.94)				
C_2	.11	.11	.46	.59	.58	(.84)			
Method 3 A_3	.56	.22	.11	.67	.42	.33	(.94)		
B_3	.23	.58	.12	.43	.66	.34	.67	(.92)	
C_3	.11	.11	.45	.34	.32	.58	.58	.60	(.85)

The validity diagonals are the three sets of italicized values. The reliability diagonals are the three sets of values in parentheses. Each heterotrait-monomethod triangle is enclosed by a solid line. Each heterotrait-heteromethod triangle is enclosed by a broken line.

pen to employ the same method. For a given variable, this involves comparing its values in the validity diagonals with its values in the heterotrait-monomethod triangles. For variables A_1, B_1, and C_1, this requirement is met to some degree. For the other variables, A_2, A_3, etc., it is not met and this is probably typical of the usual case in individual differences research, as will be discussed in what follows. A fourth desideratum is that the same pattern of trait interrelationship be shown in all of the heterotrait triangles of both the monomethod and heteromethod blocks. The hypothetical data in Table 6–1 meet this requirement to a very marked degree, in spite of the different general levels of correlation involved in the several heterotrait triangles. The last three criteria provide evidence for discriminant validity.

Before examining the multitrait-multimethod matrices available in the literature, some explication and justification of this complex of requirements seems in order.

Convergence of independent methods: the distinction between reliability and validity. Both reliability and validity concepts require that agreement between measures be demonstrated. A common denominator which most validity concepts share in contradistinction to reliability is that this agreement represent the convergence of independent approaches. The concept of independence is indicated by such phrases as "external variable," "criterion performance," "behavioral criterion" [1, pp. 13–15] used in connection with concurrent and predictive validity. For construct validity it has been stated thus: "Numerous successful predictions dealing with phenotypically diverse 'criteria' give greater weight to the claim of construct validity than do . . . predictions involving very similar behavior" [9, p. 295]. The importance of independence recurs in most discussions of proof. For example, Ayer, discussing a historian's belief about a past event, says "if these sources are numerous and independent, and if they agree with one another, he will be

reasonably confident that their account of the matter is correct" [2, p. 39]. In discussing the manner in which abstract scientific concepts are tied to operations, Feigl speaks of their being "fixed" by "triangulation in logical space" [11, p. 401].

Independence is, of course, a matter of degree, and in this sense, reliability and validity can be seen as regions on a continuum. [Cf. 21, pp. 102–103.] Reliability is the agreement between two efforts to measure the same trait through maximally similar methods. Validity is represented in the agreement between two attempts to measure the same trait through maximally different methods. A split-half reliability is a little more like a validity coefficient than is an immediate test-retest reliability, for the items are not quite identical. A correlation between dissimilar subtests is probably a reliability measure, but is still closer to the region called validity.

Some evaluation of validity can take place even if the two methods are not entirely independent. In Table 6–1, for example, it is possible that Methods 1 and 2 are not entirely independent. If underlying Traits A and B are entirely independent, then the .10 minimum correlation in the heterotrait-heteromethod triangles may reflect method covariance. What if the overlap of method variance were higher? All correlations in the heteromethod block would then be elevated, including the validity diagonal. The heteromethod block involving Methods 2 and 3 in Table 6–1 illustrates this. The degree of elevation of the validity diagonal above the heterotrait-heteromethod triangles remains comparable and relative validity can still be evaluated. The interpretation of the validity diagonal in an absolute fashion requires the fortunate coincidence of both an independence of traits and an independence of methods, represented by zero values in the heterotrait-heteromethod triangles. But zero values could also occur through a combination of negative correlation between traits and positive correlation between methods, or the reverse. In practice, perhaps all that can be hoped for is evidence for relative validity, that is, for common variance specific to a trait, above and beyond shared method variance.

Discriminant validation. While the usual reason for the judgment of invalidity is low correlations in the validity diagonal [e.g., the Downey Will-Temperament Test, 18, p. 337ff] tests have also been invalidated because of too high correlations with other tests purporting to measure different things. The classic case of the social intelligence tests is a case in point [17, 20]. Such invalidation occurs when values in the heterotrait-heteromethod triangles are as high as those in the validity diagonal, or even where within a monomethod block, the heterotrait values are as high as the reliabilities. Loevinger, Gleser, and DuBois [15] have emphasized this requirement in the development of maximally discriminating subtests.

When a dimension of personality is hypothesized, when a construct is proposed, the proponent invariably has in mind distinctions between the new dimension and other constructs already in use. One cannot define without implying distinctions, and the verification of these distinctions is an important part of the validational process. In discussions of construct validity, it has been expressed in such terms as "from this point of view, a low correlation with athletic ability may be just as important and encouraging as a high correlation with reading comprehension" [1, p. 17].

The test as a trait-method unit. In any given psychological measuring device, there are certain features or stimuli introduced specifically to represent the trait that it is intended to measure. There are other features which are characteristic of the method being employed, features which could also be present in efforts to measure other quite different traits. The test, or rating scale, or other device, almost inevitably elicits systematic variance in response due to both groups of features. To the extent that ir-

relevant method variance contributes to the scores obtained, these scores are invalid.

This source of invalidity was first noted in the "halo effects" found in ratings [19]. Studies of individual differences among laboratory animals resulted in the recognition of "apparatus factors," usually more dominant than psychological process factors [22]. For paper-and-pencil tests, methods variance has been noted under such terms as "test-form factors" [24, 25] and "response sets" [7, 8, 16]. Cronbach has stated the point particularly clearly: "The assumption is generally made . . . that what the test measures is determined by the content of the items. Yet the final score . . . is a composite of effects resulting from the content of the item and effects resulting from the form of the item used" [7, p. 475]. "Response sets always lower the logical validity of a test. . . . Response sets interfere with inferences from test data" [7, p. 484].

While E. L. Thorndike [19] was willing to allege the presence of halo effects by comparing the high obtained correlations with common sense notions of what they ought to be (e.g., it was unreasonable that a teacher's intelligence and voice quality should correlate .63) and while much of the evidence of response set variance is of the same order, the clear-cut demonstration of the presence of method variance requires both several traits and several methods. Otherwise, high correlations between tests might be explained as due either to basic trait similarity or to shared method variance. In the multitrait-multimethod matrix, the presence of method variance is indicated by the difference in level of correlation between the parallel values of the monomethod block and the heteromethod blocks, assuming comparable reliabilities among all tests. Thus the contribution of method variance in Test A_1 of Table 6–1 is indicated by the elevation of $r_{A_1B_1}$ above $r_{A_1B_2}$, i.e., the difference between .51 and .22, etc.

The distinction between trait and method is of course relative to the test constructor's intent. What is an unwanted response set for one tester may be a trait for another who wishes to measure acquiescence, willingness to take an extreme stand, or tendency to attribute socially desirable attributes to oneself [7, 8, 10, 16]. . . .

Relation to construct validity. While the validational criteria presented are explicit or implicit in the discussions of construct validity [1, 9], this paper is primarily concerned with the adequacy of tests as measures of a construct rather than with the adequacy of a construct as determined by the confirmation of theoretically predicted associations with measures of other constructs. We believe that before one can test the relationships between a specific trait and other traits, one must have some confidence in one's measures of that trait. Such confidence can be supported by evidence of convergent and discriminant validation. Stated in different words, any conceptual formulation of trait will usually include implicitly the proposition that this trait is a response tendency which can be observed under more than one experimental condition and that this trait can be meaningfully differentiated from other traits. The testing of these two propositions must be prior to the testing of other propositions to prevent the acceptance of erroneous conclusions. For example, a conceptual framework might postulate a large correlation between Traits A and B and no correlation between Traits A and C. If the experimenter then measures A and B by one method (e.g., questionnaire) and C by another method (such as the measurement of overt behavior in a situation test), his findings may be consistent with his hypotheses solely as a function of method variance common to his measures of A and B but not to C.

The requirements of this paper are intended to be as appropriate to the relatively atheoretical efforts typical of the tests and measurements field as to more theoretical efforts. This emphasis on validational criteria appropriate to our present atheoretical level of test construction is not at all incompatible with a recognition of the desirability of increasing the extent to which all aspects of a test and the testing situation are determined by explicit theoretical considerations, as Jessor and Hammond have advocated [14].

Relation to operationalism. Underwood [23, p. 54] in his effective presentation of the operationalist point of view shows a realistic awareness of the amorphous type of theory with which most psychologists work. He contrasts a psychologist's "literary" conception with the latter's operational definition as represented by his test or other measuring instrument. He recognizes the importance of the literary definition in communicating and generating science. He cautions that the operational definition "may not at all measure the process he wishes to measure; it may measure something quite different" [23, p. 55]. He does not, however, indicate how one would know when one was thus mistaken.

The requirements of the present paper may be seen as an extension of the kind of operationalism Underwood has expressed. The test constructor is asked to generate from his literary conception or private construct not one operational embodiment, but two or more, each as different in research vehicle as possible. Furthermore, he is asked to make explicit the distinction between his new variable and other variables, distinctions which are almost certainly implied in his literary definition. In his very first validational efforts, before he ever rushes into print, he is asked to apply the several methods and several traits jointly. His literary definition, his conception, is now best represented in what his independent measures of the trait hold *distinctively* in common. The multitrait-multimethod matrix is, we believe, an important practical first step in avoiding "the danger . . . that the investigator will fall into the trap of thinking that because he went from an artistic or literary conception . . . to the construction of items for a scale to measure it, he has validated his artistic conception" [9, p. 55]. In contrast with the *single opera-*

tionalism now dominant in psychology, we are advocating a *multiple operationalism*, a *convergent operationalism* [12, 13], a *methodological triangulation* [4, 6], an *operational delineation* [5], a *convergent validation*.

Underwood's presentation and that of this paper as a whole imply moving from concept to operation, a sequence that is frequent in science, and perhaps typical. The same point can be made, however, in inspecting a transition from operation to construct. For any body of data taken from a single operation, there is a subinfinity of interpretations possible; a subinfinity of concepts, or combinations of concepts, that it could represent. Any single operation, as representative of concepts, is equivocal. In an analogous fashion, when we view the Ames distorted room from a fixed point and through a single eye, the data of the retinal pattern are equivocal, in that a subinfinity of hexahedrons could generate the same pattern. The addition of a second viewpoint, as through binocular parallax, greatly reduces this equivocality, greatly limits the constructs that could jointly account for both sets of data. In Garner's [12] study, the fractionation measures from a single method were equivocal—they could have been a function of the stimulus distance being fractionated, or they could have been a function of the comparison stimuli used in the judgment process. A multiple, convergent operationalism reduced this equivocality, showing the latter conceptualization to be the appropriate one, and revealing a preponderance of methods variance. Similarly for learning studies: in identifying constructs with the response data from animals in a specific operational setup there is equivocality which can operationally be reduced by introducing transposition tests, different operations so designed as to put to comparison the rival conceptualizations [5].

Garner's convergent operationalism and our insistence on more than one method for measuring each concept depart from Bridgman's early position that "if we have more than one set of operations, we have more than one concept, and strictly there should be a separate name to correspond to each different set of operations" [3, p. 10]. At the current stage of psychological progress, the crucial requirement is the demonstration of some convergence, not complete congruence, between two distinct sets of operations. With only one method, one has no way of distinguishing trait variance from unwanted method variance. When psychological measurement and conceptualization become better developed, it may well be appropriate to differentiate conceptually between Trait-Method Unit A_1 and Trait-Method Unit A_2, in which Trait A is measured by different methods. More likely, what we have called method variance will be specified theoretically in terms of a set of constructs. . . . It will then be recognized that measurement procedures usually involve several theoretical constructs in joint application. Using obtained measurements to estimate values for a single construct under this condition still requires comparison of complex measures varying in their trait composition, in something like a multitrait-multimethod matrix. Mill's joint method of similarities and differences still epitomizes much about the effective experimental clarification of concepts.

The evaluation of a multitrait-multimethod matrix. The evaluation of the correlation matrix formed by intercorrelating several trait-method units must take into consideration the many factors which are known to affect the magnitude of correlations. A value in the validity diagonal must be assessed in the light of the reliabilities of the two measures involved: e.g., a low reliability for Test A_2 might exaggerate the apparent method variance in Test A_1. Again, the whole approach assumes adequate sampling of individuals: the curtailment of the sample with respect to one or more traits will depress the reliability coefficients and intercorrelations involving these traits. While restrictions of range over all traits produces serious difficulties in the interpretation of a multitrait-multimethod matrix and should be avoided whenever possible, the presence of different degrees of restriction on different traits is the more serious hazard to meaningful interpretation.

Various statistical treatments for multi-trait-multimethod matrices might be developed. We have considered rough tests for the elevation of a value in the validity diagonal above the comparison values in its row and column. Correlations between the columns for variables measuring the same trait, variance analyses, and factor analyses have been proposed to us. However, the development of such statistical methods is beyond the scope of this paper. We believe that such summary statistics are neither necessary nor appropriate at this time. Psychologists today should be concerned not with evaluating tests as if the tests were fixed and definitive, but rather with developing better tests. We believe that a careful examination of a multitrait-multimethod matrix will indicate to the experimenter what his next steps should be: it will indicate which methods should be discarded or replaced, which concepts need sharper delineation, and which concepts are poorly measured because of excessive or confounding method variance. Validity judgments based on such a matrix must take into account the stage of development of the constructs, the postulated relationships among them, the level of technical refinement of the methods, the relative independence of the methods, and any pertinent characteristics of the sample of Ss. We are proposing that the validational process be viewed as an aspect of an ongoing program for improving measuring procedures and that the "validity coefficients" obtained at any one stage in the process be interpreted in terms of gains over preceding stages and as indicators of where further effort is needed.

The design of a multitrait-multimethod matrix. The several methods and traits included in a validational matrix should be selected with care. The several methods used to measure each trait should be appropriate to the trait as conceptualized. Although this view will reduce the range of suitable methods, it will rarely restrict the measurement to one operational procedure.

Wherever possible, the several methods in one matrix should be completely independent of each other: there should be no prior reason for believing that they share method variance. This requirement is necessary to permit the values in the hetero-method-heterotrait triangles to approach zero. If the nature of the traits rules out such independence of methods, efforts should be made to obtain as much diversity as possible in terms of data-sources and classification processes. Thus, the classes of stimuli *or* the background situations, the experimental contexts, should be different. Again, the persons providing the observations should have different roles *or* the procedures for scoring should be varied.

Plans for a validational matrix should take into account the difference between the interpretations regarding convergence and discrimination. It is sufficient to demonstrate convergence between two clearly distinct methods which show little overlap in the heterotrait-heteromethod triangles. While agreement between several methods is desirable, convergence between two is a satisfactory minimal requirement. Discriminative validation is not so easily achieved. Just as it is impossible to prove the null hypothesis, or that some object does not exist, so one can never establish that a trait, as measured, is differentiated from all other traits. One can only show that this measure of Trait A has little overlap with those measures of B and C, and no dependable generalization beyond B and C can be made. For example, social poise could probably be readily discriminated from aesthetic interests, but it should also be differentiated from leadership.

Insofar as the traits are related and are expected to correlate with each other, the monomethod correlations will be substantial and heteromethod correlations between traits will also be positive. For ease of interpretation, it may be best to include in the matrix at least two traits, and preferably two sets of traits, which are postulated to be independent of each other.

In closing, a word of caution is needed. Many multitrait-multimethod matrices will show no convergent validation: no relationship may be found between two methods of measuring a trait. In this common situation, the experimenter should examine the evidence in favor of several alternative propositions: (*a*) Neither method is adequate for measuring the trait; (*b*) One of the two methods does not really measure the trait. (When the evidence indicates that a method does not measure the postulated trait, it may prove to measure some other trait. High correlations in the hetero-trait-heteromethod triangles may provide hints to such possibilities.) (*c*) The trait is not a functional unity, the response tendencies involved being specific to the nontrait attributes of each test. The failure to demonstrate convergence may lead to conceptual developments rather than to the abandonment of a test.

SUMMARY

This paper advocates a validational process utilizing a matrix of intercorrelations among tests representing at least two traits, each measured by at least two methods. Measures of the same trait should correlate higher with each other than they do with measures of different traits involving separate methods. Ideally, these validity values should also be higher than the correlations among different traits measured by the same method. These desirable conditions, as a set, are rarely met. Method or apparatus factors make very large contributions to psychological measurements.

The notions of convergence between independent measures of the same trait and discrimination between measures of different traits are compared with previously published formulations, such as construct validity and convergent operationalism. Problems in the application of this validational process are considered.

ok
3-75

REFERENCES

1. AMERICAN PSYCHOLOGICAL ASSOCIATION. Technical recommendations for Psychological tests and diagnostic techniques. *Psychol. Bull., Suppl.,* 1954, 51, Part 2, 1–38.

2. AYER, A. J. *The problem of knowledge.* New York: St. Martin's Press, 1956.

3. BRIDGMAN, P. W. *The logic of modern physics.* New York: Macmillan, 1927.

4. CAMPBELL, D. T. *A study of leadership among submarine officers.* Columbus: Ohio State Univer. Res. Found., 1953.

5. CAMPBELL, D. T. Operational delineation of "what is learned" via the transposition experiment. *Psychol. Rev.,* 1954, 61, 167–174.

6. CAMPBELL, D. T. *Leadership and its effects upon the group.* Monogr. No. 83. Columbus: Ohio State Univer. Bur. Business Res., 1956.

7. CRONBACH, L. J. Response sets and test validity. *Educ. psychol. Measmt,* 1946, 6, 475–494.

8. CRONBACH, L. J. Further evidence on response sets and test design. *Educ. psychol. Measmt,* 1950, 10, 3–31.

9. CRONBACH, L. J., and MEEHL, P. E. Construct validity in psychological tests. *Psychol. Bull.,* 1955, 52, 281–302.

10. EDWARDS, A. L. *The social desirability variable in personality assessment and research.* New York: Dryden, 1957.

11. FEIGL, H. The mental and the physical. In H. Feigl, M. Scriven, and G. Maxwell (Eds.), *Minnesota studies in the philosophy of science.* Vol. II. *Concepts, theories and the mind-body problem.* Minneapolis: Univer. Minnesota Press, 1958.

12. GARNER, W. R. Context effects and the validity of loudness scales. *J. exp. Psychol.,* 1954, 48, 218–224.

13. GARNER, W. R., HAKE, H. W., and ERIKSEN, C. W. Operationism and the concept of perception. *Psychol. Rev.,* 1956, 63, 149–159.

14. JESSOR, R., and HAMMOND, K. R. Construct validity and the Taylor Anxiety Scale. *Psychol. Bull.*, 1957, 54, 161–170.

15. LOEVINGER, J., GLESER, G. C., and DuBOIS, P. H. Maximizing the discriminating power of a multiple-score test. *Psychometrika*, 1953, 18, 309–317.

16. LORGE, I. Gen-like: Halo or reality? *Psychol. Bull.*, 1937, 34, 545–546.

17. STRANG, R. Relation of social intelligence to certain other factors. *Sch. and Soc.*, 1930, 32, 268–272.

18. SYMONDS, P. M. *Diagnosing personality and conduct.* New York: Appleton-Century, 1931.

19. THORNDIKE, E. L. A constant error in psychological ratings. *J. appl. Psychol.*, 1920, 4, 25–29.

20. THORNDIKE, R. L. Factor analysis of social and abstract intelligence. *J. educ. Psychol.*, 1936, 27, 231–233.

21. THURSTONE, L. L. *The reliability and validity of tests.* Ann Arbor: Edwards, 1937.

22. TRYON, R. C. Individual differences. In F. A. Moss (Ed.), *Comparative Psychology.* (2nd ed.) New York: Prentice-Hall, 1942. Pp. 330–365.

23. UNDERWOOD, B. J. *Psychological research.* New York: Appleton-Century-Crofts, 1957.

24. VERNON, P. E. Educational ability and psychological factors. Address given to the Joint Education-Psychology Colloquium, Univer. of Illinois, March 29, 1957.

25. VERNON, P. E. *Educational testing and test-form factors.* Research Bulletin 58–3. Princeton: Educational Testing Service, 1958.

good example of applications of Construct validity

Chapter 7

Construct Validity: A Critique

HAROLD P. BECHTOLDT

In order to accomplish more effective communication between test publishers and test users, a series of "essential," "very desirable," and "desirable" characteristics of the content of test manuals was provided in 1954 by the APA Committee on Psychological Tests [1]. In the following year two members of the committee, L. J. Cronbach and P. E. Meehl [25], prepared an extended statement on the topic of construct validity, a term introduced in the *Technical Recommendations* to refer to one of the several distinctions noted in the use of the term validity. It should be emphasized that these distinctions refer only to ways of talking about tests and test performances and not to empirical questions. However, the conclusions, generalizations, or predictions arising from empirical investigations are involved since such statements influence both the design of subsequent experiments

This article is reprinted from the *American Psychologist*, 1959, with the permission of the author and the American Psychological Association.

The encouragement and constructive suggestions of my associates in the Department of Psychology and in the Child Welfare Research Station are gratefully acknowledged.

and the development of theoretical formulations. It is, therefore, appropriate to take note of the way psychologists speak about "construct validity."

Methods of protecting test consumers from a laissez-faire business philosophy are not being considered at the moment. While the *Technical Recommendations* are clearly restricted to commercial nonresearch devices, the concept of construct validity has been presented as of fundamental importance to many psychologists. It has been said that "Construct validation is important at times for every sort of psychological test: aptitude, achievement, interest, and so on. . . . Much current research on tests of personality is construct validation . . ." [25, pp. 282–283]. The article dealing with the elaboration of the notion of construct validity has been termed "one of the most important papers for the differential psychologist appearing during the span of this [1954–1956] review" [31, p. 81]. In further support of this position, we find another writer stating: "since predictive, and content validities are all essentially *ad hoc*, construct validity is the whole of validity

133

from a scientific point of view" [35, p. 636]. Still a fourth very favorable comment states: "Construct validity is an important new concept which has immediate implications for both psychometrician and experimentalist" [32, p. 161].

The primary concern of this paper is with the formulation of construct validity as presented in the several articles noted above. A major objective is to consider critically, but necessarily incompletely, the suggestion that psychologists make a place for the notion of construct validity in their methodological thinking. Some of the "dangers" associated with the concept will be discussed as well as the implication that an "operational methodology" is less appropriate for research involving test data, at least in practical testing[1] [25, p. 300].

Since this is a type of philosophical treatment by a psychologist who is not a philosopher, the philosophical orientation of this analysis must be made clear. The philosophical position taken here is that of one of the branches of logical positivism, sometimes termed logical empiricism, logical behaviorism, or neobehaviorism. Most psychologists are probably familiar with this philosophical point of view as presented by Bergmann [9, 10, 11, 12, 13, 14, 15], by Bergmann and Spence [16], and by Brodbeck [17, 18, 19], and from articles by psychologists such as Spence [40, 41, 42, 43] or Spiker and McCandless [45]. It must also be pointed out that this philosophical position differs, with respect to several central issues, from that taken by Cronbach and Meehl who have used the writings of Beck [8], Carnap [21], Feigl [26, 27], Hempel [30], Pap [38], and Sellars [39] among others in presenting their formulation of construct validity. The marshaling of references and appeal to authority, however, are of limited value in science and

perhaps even in the philosophy of science. The crucial question in science is the matter of empirical laws and the relations among them. The appraisal of a philosophical analysis of science would be in terms of the success achieved in the clarification of the knowledge and methods used by scientists.

Specifically, it is proposed to use the terms of one branch of logical positivism in analyzing what has been said and done about construct validity in terms of two questions:

1. How are tests and testing used in psychology?
2. What relation, if any, does the use of tests and testing have to the notion of construct validity?

TESTS AND TESTING

Although neither the *Technical Recommendations* nor subsequent elaborations specify a definition of the term "test," a statement from representatives of the APA to the Congress of the United States is available [2]. In a discussion of aptitudes and abilities, it is stated that "Psychological tests are nothing more than careful observations of actual performance under standard conditions." Testing, then, would refer to the process of obtaining these observations. The distinguishing phrase "careful observations of performance under standard conditions" will, therefore, be substituted for the possibly more emotionally toned words "psychological tests."

As given, this definition of tests is a very general one. The definition carries no implication as to the use to be made of the observations as would terms such as aptitude, diagnostic, or achievement. The statement further specifies nothing about the classification of content. No restrictions are stated as to method of responding nor of classifying responses as to any of their many conceivable properties such as presence or absence, rate, style or quality, per-

[1] Cronbach and Meehl explicitly state they are not advocating construct validation over other methods [25, p. 284, 300], but their treatment is somewhat inconsistent on this point. The other papers noted above are definitely favorable toward construct validity as the preferred concept.

sistence, intensity or amplitude, accuracy or relative probability of occurrence. Conceivably, the careful observations could be obtained with complete mechanical control of the stimuli, the time intervals, the feedback or reinforcements, and the recording of responses.

This definition of "psychological tests" states the basic preliminary point of this discussion. "Careful observations of performance under standard conditions" are used by psychologists everywhere: in the laboratory, in the clinic, in the schools, and in industry. There are no fundamental distinctions between "psychological test" observations per se and any other equally systematic controlled observations of performance used by psychologists.

The first question can, therefore, be phrased as: "How are careful observations of performance under standard conditions used in psychology?" The work of nearly all psychologists represents two distinctive ways in which observations of performance are used. Stated in the language of the logical behaviorists, these uses are, first, in the definition of psychological concepts of varying degree of abstractness and, second, in the statement of laws about concepts and of relations among such laws. The laws, or generalizations, are statements about how the referents of some concepts affect other concepts. Each such law in psychology regularly involves one concept referring to properties of behavior and one or more other concepts which may refer to features, past and/or present, of the organism's physical environment, to physiological states or events within their bodies, or to other concepts defined by experimentally independent observations of behavior [10, 11, 15, 18, 19, 42].

In the terminology of the philosophy of science being used, sets of these laws or generalizations relating defined concepts, if deductively connected, are called theories with some of the laws called the axioms, logically implying other laws, termed theorems. As a goal for psychology, the development of systems of deductively connected empirical laws is generally accepted, and the quantitative comprehensive theories of physics have been held up as prototypes of those for psychology. However, it is also generally agreed that in psychology we have no comprehensive theories as the term is used in physics—certainly no axiomatized system like that used in atomic physics, nor even a start in the development of the very general laws required for comprehensive theories [25, 42, 43].

An answer to the first question of how psychological tests are used in psychology has now been indicated. Psychological tests like any other "careful observations of performance" are used in the definition of concepts varying in abstractness; in the development of psychological laws, i.e., those concerned with the prediction of behavior and of changes in behavior; and in the development of limited sets of deductively interrelated empirical laws. It is contended that this formulation of how observations of performance are *currently* used, and will be used for some time, is inclusive, logically sound, experimentally useful, and sufficient.

CONSTRUCT VALIDITY AND TESTS

Consider now the second question which deals with the relation between the careful observations of performance obtained by the use of tests on the one hand and the formulation of construct validity on the other. From the viewpoint of logical positivism sketched in outline form above, what can be said about construct validity?

Although no explicit definition of construct validity is offered by any of the writers dealing with this topic, a number of statements are made from which one is to induce the class characteristics:

> Construct validation is involved whenever a test is to be interpreted as a measure of some attribute or quality which is not "operationally defined." The problem faced by the investigator is, "What constructs account for variance in test performance?" . . . Construct validity

is not to be identified solely by particular investigative procedures, but by the orientation of the investigator [25, p. 282].

Construct validity is ordinarily studied when the tester has no definite criterion measure of the quality with which he is concerned, and must use indirect measures. Here the trait or quality underlying the test is of central importance, rather than either the test behavior or the scores on the criteria [1, p. 14].

An answer to the second question will involve consideration, among others, of the above illustrative statements.

OPERATIONAL DEFINITIONS

Construct validation is introduced by Cronbach and Meehl as being involved whenever a test is to be interpreted as a measure of some attribute or quality which is not operationally defined, with considerable emphasis placed on the rejection of the necessity for operationally defined concepts or constructs. From the view here taken, there either are no cases to which construct validity would apply in an embryonic empirical science, excepting only the simple characters being named by "undefined descriptive terms" [15, p. 14]; or a different definition of "operationally defined" is used; or the discussion is not germane to an empirical science of psychology.

Can the discrepancy be a matter of the simple notion of an operational definition? An operational definition is simply a verbal statement of the *if-then* type specifying the observable conditions or rules of procedure under which the term is to be applied in the definition of descriptive or empirical concepts or variables [15, 17]. The only contributions made by operational definitions to an empirical science are those of clarity, objectivity, and precision or accuracy of statement; such definitions enable one to determine, and eventually eliminate, the "ignorance" and "error" represented in any "imperfect" formulation. Terms like hostility, aggression, psychopathic deviate, intelligence, and mechanical ability have some referents and some rules for their use. They are operationally defined in any empirical study, but the specification for their use may change with time. Without specification of rules, or changes therein, for using such defined terms, neither accurate communication nor precise experimentation is possible in any science.

The process of developing definitions for a concept is, in actual practice, neither simple nor unerring. Any creative investigator "breaking ground" will usually have one or more hunches or guesses about the way two or more things in which he is interested might influence one another. As long as the notion remains so personal, so private, and so imprecise that the referents of terms cannot be designated nor the necessary conditions considered as achieved, the guesses are outside the realm of empirical science. When, however, an investigator states explicitly a set of rules or conditions for the application of his terms, the statements are of scientific interest. The explicit statement constitutes an initial definition of the concept; but like any formulation, the initial one may well be useless, somewhat useful, or entirely satisfactory. Those definitions that are of limited usefulness will be re-examined in terms of the available empirical evidence. One common course of action taken in experimental psychology to increase the usefulness of a concept involves redefining the notion by a second, but different, explicit statement [44]. After several experimental studies have resulted in one or more changes of definition, one might say the early concepts were imprecise, incomplete, vague, or of limited usefulness. But, strictly speaking, each change of definition introduces a new concept. These definitions are *not* alternative definitions of the same concept.

The term "vague" so often applied to "imprecise" concepts requires further comment. Vague may refer to that which has not been defined, to the ambiguous, or to the "private" and "subjective." Or the term may refer to an incomplete explicit definition used in an early statement of a concept. These referents are not identical. Dissatisfaction expressed by investigators with an initial "rough," incomplete definition is a reaction against ignorance and error rather than against a strategy of investigation. To admit ignorance as a temporary state of science is one thing. To raise vagueness or lack of definition to the central status of a methodological principle is another. The "constructs" of construct validity appear to be "vague," open, and "not explicitly defined" as a matter of principle rather than as a matter of ignorance.

The statement that changes in the rules properly imply the use of a new word or a subscript to the old word has met with definite objection when applied to the area of intelligence tests [31, p. 88]. However, the fear that such practice prevents the gradual evolution of ideas is baseless; the logical empiricists recognize the gradual and continuous replacement by scientists of less useful concepts with more useful ones [9]. At each stage of development of a concept, however, the rules for the current usage of the term are to be stated.

In the *Technical Recommendations* [1, p. 15], it is stated with emphasis that "*behavior-relevance* in a construct is not logically the same as *behavior-equivalence*" and that psychological constructs need not be *equivalent* to any direct operational behavior measure. Since concepts and, for the moment, constructs may vary in degree of abstractness or length of the definitional chains, there may indeed be many steps between the undefined basic terms, possibly including direct or immediate observations of behavior, and highly abstract defined concepts.

The distinction between undefined and defined descriptive terms is technically based on the principle of (direct) acquaintance, undefined terms naming characters or properties with which the person is directly acquainted. All other descriptive terms are defined [15, p. 14–15]. The definition, i.e., the conditional features of the *if-then* statement, is reasonably simple for the case of the "response time" property of the eyelid

reflex, of a finger withdrawal, or of some vocalization. The definitional operations are somewhat different, perhaps more complex, but still expressed in terms of manifest behavior, when the W, $F+$, or d responses among others to each Rorschach card are evaluated. Meehl [37] has reported how Halbower used fairly complex and involved procedures to define a few objective personality descriptions in terms of the observed responses of patients to the MMPI. Other "response defined" and rather "abstract" concepts of interest to psychologists include most of the "psychological qualities" or "attributes" or traits presented in the discussions of construct validity [23, 25].

Since nearly all defined psychological concepts require very complicated definitional chains, the concepts are indeed not "behaviorally equivalent" if we restrict "behavior-equivalence," for example, to speed or accuracy of any one response. The concepts are, however, defined in terms of properties of observable behavior under specified conditions and in accordance with specified procedures. If the APA test committee were restricting the definition of terms to the "immediately, or almost immediately, observable" characters or properties of manifest behavior, its dissatisfaction with "operational definitions" would be understandable. This condition would imply a definition of "operationally defined" which is far more restrictive and limited than that recommended by the logical behaviorists [13]. However, if the advocates of construct validity are contending that explicit definitions of terms in empirical science are not essential, then the issue is basic; such disagreement is one that has both "philosophical" and scientific overtones.

CHARACTERISTICS OF CONSTRUCTS

Although the matter of requiring single explicit definitions of concepts or terms may, or may not, be a point of basic disagreement, an issue does seem to arise in connection with the term "construct." That the notion of "construct" is fundamental to the discussion of construct validity seems indicated [1, 25, 31, 32]. A construct is presented by Cronbach and Meehl as involving at least three characteristics. First, it is a *postulated attribute* assumed to be reflected in test performances; second, it has *predictive* properties; and third, the *meaning* of a construct is given by the laws in which it occurs with the result that clarity of knowledge of the construct is a positive function of the completeness of that set of laws, termed the nomological net.

Meaning. The third of these characteristics uses the term "meaning" which has at least two technical interpretations. On this point, disagreement among philosophers of science again will be found. The logical empiricists have distinguished between two technical usages of the term: one to refer to the operational definition or empirical referent of a concept, i.e., the "meaning" of a concept, and the second usage to refer to the usefulness or "significance" of a concept as indicated by the theoretical or empirical laws into which it enters [10, 15, 17]. The logical behaviorists say that a defined concept may be without significance, but significant concepts must be defined. From the logical behaviorists' point of view, the third characteristic above states that concepts vary in usefulness or significance with the greater significance associated with both the number and theoretical or empirical implications of the laws into which they enter.

The development and use of the Taylor Manifest Anxiety Scale (MAS) provides an example of the distinction between meaning and significance. The "meaning" of "manifest anxiety" is given by the procedures for presenting the selected verbal statements or items and for combining the weighted responses of each subject. The resulting score then defines (is the meaning of) the variable "manifest anxiety." Implicit in the defining procedures are such require-ments as: to be used with English-speaking adults having a United States cultural background, etc. The usefulness or significance of the MAS score depends on the relations of the MAS with other variables. Two kinds of relations involving the MAS scores have been investigated: one deals with certain drive properties of the MAS variable in experimental studies of simple learning phenomena, and the other involves the congruence of two or more response defined variables both including in the title the word "anxiety." Since both types of relations have been shown to be statistically significant in two or more studies, the MAS can be said to have some degree of usefulness or significance [43, 46, 47]. If no theoretical or empirical relation could be demonstrated between the MAS and any other variable, the MAS would be said to be well defined or meaningful but without significance.

Significance and validity. For a number of years one aspect of the "significance" of a variable has been fairly precisely expressed by the notion of "empirical validity." Empirical validity refers to the results of empirical tests of relations between a dependent variable of behavior and one or more independent or predictor measures. There will, of course, be as many indices of validity of a variable as there are dependent variables with which it can be paired [3, 4, 22]. A determination of the usefulness or empirical validity of the MAS as a predictor of some other variable also entitled "anxiety" and defined by psychiatric ratings or by responses to other sets of stimuli can be made. But such an appraisal is not an index of the significance of the MAS as a drive variable in Spence's [43] theory of performance in simple learning situations.

Yet, the "meaning" of the concept of manifest anxiety, according to the formulation of construct validity, is to be given by the laws into which it enters. Which of the many laws, or sets of laws, are to be used? All of them or only those related by a "theory," a theory some writer may prefer, for example, to the one initially formulated? In construct validity terms the concept may have no "meaning" or some "meaning," the appraisal depending on an arbitrary or even capricious selection of a "theory" and of the dependent variables with which the given variable or concept is paired. The logical empiricists would simply say the defined concept is related to some variables but not to others or that the concept enters into some laws but not others. The confusion resulting from the use of the single word "meaning" for both definition and significance seems unnecessary and undesirable.

Constructs and "the criterion." The meaning-significance confusion also occurs in the statements of the relation of constructs to "criteria." It is suggested [1, p. 14; 25, p. 282] that construct validity is to be investigated whenever no criterion or universe of content is accepted as entirely adequate to define the quality to be measured. A failure to separate the defining operations, including content restrictions, from the empirical matter of relations with other variables is evident. In accordance with the construct validity notion, a quality or variable can be defined, when a criterion is available, by the relation of the test to the criterion rather than by the operations of the test itself. But when no criterion is available, the quality is not defined; instead, the construct validity of the test is to be investigated. Three points need to be made with regard to the central position of the "criterion" in this decision making process. First, a criterion measure is a behavioral or response defined variable used as the dependent variable in an investigation. As a behavioral measure, some sequence of operations involving "careful observations of performance" is selected or developed at some (usually earlier) time as the conditional features of the definition. Second, the defining operations are in no way intrinsically different from those used to define any other behavioral variable such as one utilized, for example, as an independent variable. Third, if a variable is *accepted*

as the dependent variable, i.e., as the criterion, then indeed a status difference may be created which is reflected in several technical procedures such as the assignment of errors of prediction to the dependent variable and the weighting of the independent variables so as to minimize the errors of prediction. But in no other way is a criterion variable any different from any other test or response defined variable.

Differences among experimenters in the types of prediction they wish to make and in the problems of interest to them are reflected in the emphasis placed on the criterion. In situations where the experimenter is task oriented or problem oriented, as is the case in most applied studies and in "practical testing," the dependent variable would be *defined first* and perhaps given status by *naming* it "the criterion," whether intermediate or final. In such admittedly practical problems, the criterion-orientation seems entirely reasonable. The question asked is of the form: "What defined variables of any kind can be used to predict performance on the criterion?" Those variables that show significant relations with the criterion are said to be "valid" (useful) predictors. No claim to theoretical usefulness is involved; the demonstration of one or more stable empirical relations is both necessary and sufficient [4]. In other experimental situations in which the experimenter is interested in a variable per se or as a part of some theoretical formulation, i.e., when he can be said to be variable oriented, no special status is given to the dependent variable of behavior. In this second case the dependent variable, in fact, is usually selected or developed *after* the independent variable is defined. A "criterion" or behavioral measure will be selected in the second case so that the effect of the independent or experimental variable may be exhibited if the variable enters into the theory or nomological net as hypothesized. The term validity properly could also be applied to such cases in precisely the same sense as in the problem oriented situation. However, the experimental psychologists, who have long used this variable oriented approach and research procedure, have not found the naming of such relations necessary.

Prediction. The second characteristic of a construct appears at first glance to give no occasion for concern. Cronbach and Meehl state [25, p. 284]:

> A construct has certain associated meanings carried in statements of this general character: Persons who possess this attribute will, in situation X, act in manner Y (with a stated probability).

The "associated meanings" appear to include the class of "test interpretations," i.e., various predictions, as well as whatever "accounts for variance in test performance." The form of the statement is that of the common predictive model. Such statements are laws. The second characteristic asserts that constructs must enter into laws.

Now the notion of explanation in science is often presented, in part, in terms of such a predictive model. If the predictions are logically deduced from other laws and are sustained experimentally, the new observations are said to be "understandable," to be explained by the "axioms" or premises of the set [15]. However, many predictions in psychology are not deduced from a set of premises but are essentially statements of the reproducibility of previous empirical results. For such "predictions" as well as for "deduced" statements, an empirical test of the accuracy of the prediction regarding behavior Y requires only rules, operations, or procedures for determining, first, whether "manner Y" occurs; second, whether situation X is present; and, third, whether the persons with whom we are dealing have the attribute.

For these empirical checks, the concepts must be defined. Every example used by Cronbach and Meehl to elucidate how construct validation can be accomplished requires some definition of the attribute in behavioral terms. The well-known proce-

dures for evaluating changes in a dependent variable as a function of one or more independent variables are exemplified by their illustrations. In fact, the several recommended validation procedures of construct validity are those regularly used by research psychologists investigating hypotheses involving psychological concepts. It is, therefore, considered that, *in practice,* the second characteristic of lawful relations is empirically sound; nothing new or confusing is involved.

Postulated attributes. The first of the three characteristics of a construct, however, is considered as a serious source of confusion. The statement is that a construct is a postulated attribute assumed to be reflected in test performance. This notion also appears in such statements as: the trait or quality underlying the test is of central importance, rather than either the test behavior or the scores on the criteria [1, p. 14]; or "the" or the "real" trait is being "indirectly" or "not really" measured by the test performance [20, 35]. The "postulation" and "assumption" features of this characteristic are more accurately labeled hunches, guesses, or working hypotheses about relations among concepts, i.e., about laws or sets of laws termed theories. The third characteristic states that a hypothesis or even a theory about test behavior has been formulated.

As postulated attributes assumed to be reflected in test performance, many possible sets of words or symbols, often referred to as "theories" or "models" [19], may be generated by an ingenious, talented, and persistent writer. As literary or mathematical exercises, they may indeed be accurate, elegant, and internally consistent. The question, however, is the relevance of these formulations to behavior and to experimental investigation of the statements. If the constructs or psychological attributes are response defined, either by a simple or complicated series of *if-then* statements, and if the behaviors involved in these definitions are the performances under consideration, then the statements are not hypotheses about empirical relations but are definitions [15]. Essentially, such statements apply new names and/or transformations to old things. A "construct," in such cases, is a defined concept or variable, values of which are assigned to an individual on the basis of "careful observations of his performance under standard conditions." That "ability" is so defined has been noted by Lord who states:

> Since, in the final analysis, the only observable variables under consideration are the item responses, any operational definition of ability for present purposes must consist of a statement of a relationship between ability and item responses [36, p. 4].

Nearly all postulated constructs listed in the papers on construct validity are also of the defined type. It is here suggested that a considerable number, if not all, of the so-called theoretical formulations in psychology dealing with postulated attributes simply use complex definitional transformations of a person's performance as a substitute for an empirical theory. Such transformations indeed may prove to be useful in "practical" situations involving communications with clients and employers. The new names and related hunches (surplus meanings) also may reduce (or increase) the generation of false "working hypotheses," but the transformations as such are neither theories nor laws. The transformations provide only definitions of concepts.

The possibility of psychologists confusing tautologies with empirical or theoretical relations was recognized by the APA test committee [1] and by Cronbach and Meehl [25]. In several statements dealing with the nomological net, they insist upon "explicit public steps of inference," upon "contact with observations," and upon "accuracy of prediction" as the final test of a theory. It is also clear that both Cronbach and Meehl favor testing directly or indirectly the hypotheses of the network. However, more than earnest requests for logically correct deductions having some contact with empirical observations is necessary in extending the important but difficult process of building an empirical theory of behavior that will indicate how certain variables may account for variance in test performance. As shown below, the formulation of construct validity can be interpreted as making less of a contribution to the development of such a theory than does an empirically oriented methodology using explicit operational definitions of the variables.

VARIABLES AFFECTING BEHAVIOR

What can be said as to the variables affecting any given behavior, including test performance? It has been demonstrated empirically that behavior is influenced by the amount of formal or informal practice or training on similar materials or methods of response. Strong response tendencies and habits of acquiescence or of avoidance of painful or noxious stimuli would be expected to affect behavior in many given situations. Characteristics of the examiner, of the cultural setting, or of the physiological states of the organism may lead to temporary or persistent behaviors under specified conditions. Surely the formulation of the basic concepts assumed to be reflected in test performance must include reference to such conditions and to other concepts defined by various experimental manipulations or operations. Such empirical concepts are appropriate answers to the question: "What constructs account for variance in test performance?" [25, p. 282]. That response defined variables, such as traits, are emphasized in the papers on construct validity as examples of the basic explanatory concepts probably is a reflection of the lack of control and of knowledge of the experiential history of the subjects used in studies involving human behavior. This lack of knowledge and lack of control of the subjects makes the task of developing laws and theories difficult, but probably not impossible.

As practical devices for the prediction of behavior, traits are clearly useful. That they may also be introduced into theoretical formulations of behavior has been shown by Taylor, Spence, and their associates in terms of the Manifest Anxiety Scale [43, 46]. That the theoretical use of response defined variables is not widely understood is clear from several discussions dealing with the validity of the A scale [6, 31, 32, 34, 43]. The confusion attendant upon the notion of construct validity will be obvious to the readers of these papers.

TRAITS IN PSYCHOLOGICAL THEORIZING

The chief difficulty of the trait or response defined variable approach in the development of theoretical formulations is the fact that a given behavior can arise from many different combinations of experimental conditions. These different conditions involve different concepts and different sets of explanatory laws. Any one of dozens of so-called theories or sets of explanatory constructs can be postulated or assumed and be "correct" in terms of the agreement between prediction and observation. Cronbach [24] has recently added a valuable postscript to this point in a paper dealing with social-perception scores. He says:

> To interpret a score as a reflection of subtle interpersonal relations, or of covert attitudes about another person, may be to force complex meanings into a very simple phenomena (p. 353).

And then he adds:

> . . . if a behavior which looks like "projection" can arise out of many different processes, there is little point in trying to formulate hypotheses using the concept of "projection" (p. 375).

The point at issue is the development of a theory, or nomological net, using response defined variables which will have explanatory, predictive properties in specified situations. The theory would consist of a set of meaningful concepts and statements about how each given concept enters into specified laws. With such a theory, it is possible to determine whether a given concept, as defined, actually does enter into those laws. To the degree to which the predictions are sustained under the specified boundary conditions of the theory, the concept has significance and, apparently, "construct validity." Extending the hypotheses to include other concepts represents the process of "elaborating the nomological network" [25, p. 290]. Tests of the accuracy of the hypotheses will utilize, among others, the several experimental "validation" procedures of "construct validity." However, as a theory develops and achieves some limited successes, the number of inappropriate and irrelevant "tests" of stated hypotheses can be expected to grow also. Although labeled as "tests of the theory," such studies often represent unwarranted generalizations or improper extensions of the hypotheses or serious misconceptions about the concepts or the structure of the theory itself [43].

It must be emphasized that the private, inductive process involved in the invention of hypotheses, of ideas, or of concepts is not being questioned. There are neither rules nor deductive or inductive principles for the invention of fruitful hypotheses or the definition of significant concepts or the formulation of comprehensive theories. There are no logical reasons why some "theory" of behavior must a priori contain defined concepts expressing currently popular "common sense" notions or explanations. Nor are there any reasons to specify some test form or method of test (apparatus) construction as inherently useful or logically necessary in order for the test to be consistent with the procedures of construct validation or with the principles of logical behaviorism [for an opposing view, see 32, p. 162].

Neither is there any justification for proposing the techniques of empirical, or "classical," validity as the sole methods to be used in selecting test items. The "adequacy" of any technique as a basis for test construction is a matter of the usefulness of the resulting test for empirical or theoretical purposes [for a contrary view, see 35, p. 637]. However, it is generally recognized that tests developed by utilizing relations with a "criterion" have at least some empirical significance, although they may, or may not, enter into any set of theoretical relations.

What is being questioned is the tendency to consider as a part of a public empirical science hunches involving "vague," ill-defined variables and relations between such variables, these hunches being derived primarily from the observed performance. The extent to which this activity is common in so-called "theorizing" in psychology can perhaps be judged from the frequency with which one encounters "deductions" involving sufficient, but not necessary, conditions such as the following taken from Johnson [33]:

> If "Old Dog Tray" was run through a large and powerful sausage-grinder, he is dead; he is dead, therefore, he was sausaged (p. 723).

Amusing? But what about this one?

> If a person has an over-compensated inferiority complex, he blusters, is aggressive, domineering, and dogmatic; this man blusters, is aggressive, domineering and dogmatic; therefore, he has an inferiority complex.

The weaknesses and dangers of the postulational technique used *without* explicit definitions or empirical referents or "interpretations" for the premises can perhaps be even more clearly seen in the "valid" deduction and "contact with observations" implicit in this old syllogism: "Bread is made of stone, stone is good to eat; therefore, bread is good to eat." The conclusion is "true to fact," but the usual interpretations of the premises are not fulfilled.

Other instances of the postulation of ex-planatory constructs from behavior in a circular way are often found in discussions of mental abilities and of personality traits. Although frequent reference is made in the literature on construct validity to factor analysis, we find Thurstone quite clear on the point that an ability is *defined* by a specific test procedure and the method of scoring [48]. Each test defines a separate ability; several tests involving the "same content" but different methods of presenting the stimuli or of responding likewise define different abilities. Thurstone also clearly *names* the "reference or common abilities" as those used to express the scores on the remaining tests in terms of an assumed linear function. The factors, for all experimental purposes, are literally defined as composite scores on specified subsets of tests in such batteries as the Primary Mental Abilities Tests [49] or the Educational Testing Service Kit of Reference Tests [28].

It is well to note, in connection with statements about factors, that the "interpretation" of the common source of variance of a "factor" and the "identification" of a "factor" in two different sets of tests as the "same factor" are both statements of hypotheses. Some "empirical generalization" of response tendencies over a variety of stimulus or treatment conditions which can be experimentally varied is implicit in both of these formulations. And, as for any other hypotheses, empirical tests of the predictions are called for. Such tests require unambiguous definitions of the "factors." That the empirical results may not sustain such predictions or "hypotheses" is logically sound and empirically consistent with observations [5].

The danger of circularity of a formulation involving the notion of an "ability" or a "factor" as a concept can easily be eliminated; the "ability" variable can be defined in advance of an experiment through the use of observations experimentally independent of the behavior and hypothesis to be investigated. This "operational methodology" principle has been extended to some types of factor analysis investigations themselves with a restatement of the factor problem [7].

RELATION OF TESTS TO CONSTRUCT VALIDITY

An answer to the second question dealing with the relation between the use of tests and the notion of construct validity now can be stated. The relation is simply the linguistic one between any set of empirical observations on the one hand and any philosophy of science formulation on the other, and logically nothing more. The formulation of construct validity as a way of speaking is not restricted to, nor dependent upon, test concepts or performances; rather, the presentation is that of a general methodological viewpoint. For example, recent articles dealing, in part, with construct validity [20, 35] have mentioned the correspondence between the construct validity formulation and that of "convergent operationalism" advocated for the definition of properties or characteristics of perception [29]. The use of multiple and implicit, rather than single explicit, definitions of terms and the meaning-significance confusion indeed are common to the two notions.

There is, however, a historical accident or coincidence that may account for the identification of construct validity with the area of psychological tests. General dissatisfaction has been expressed from time to time with the usefulness of empirical and statistical concepts of tests and testing; such concepts have been considered inadequate for professional psychological testing activities. Statements of such views tend to create a climate favorable to the acceptance of a new formulation, like construct validity, which emphasizes the language and problems of the practicing counselor or clinician. And the inception and development of the methodological viewpoint of construct validity, in addition, represents a laudable attempt to introduce into clinical and counseling testing activities some integration and understanding of the kind represented by the term theory. That construct validity was the creation of psychologists "interested in and sympathetic to constructs evidenced by performance but distinct from it" is the historical accident.

CONCLUSION

A major objective of this paper has been to consider critically the suggestion that psychologists make a place for the notion of construct validity in their methodological thinking. This suggestion is rejected for the several reasons given above. The renaming of the process of building a theory of behavior by the new term "construct validity" contributes nothing to the understanding of the process nor to the usefulness of the concepts. The introduction into discussions of psychological theorizing of the aspects of construct validity discussed in some detail above creates, at best, unnecessary confusion and, at the worst, a nonempirical, nonscientific approach to the study of behavior.

A supplementary objective has been to consider also the relative merits of construct validity and of logical behaviorism plus an operational methodology for the development of psychology as a science. It is suggested here that the terminology of logical behaviorism and the techniques of an "operational methodology" are to be preferred for the formulation and investigation of an empirical, deductive theory of (test) behavior. The statement that an "'operational' methodology . . . would force research into a mold it does not fit" [25, p. 300] is rejected as not consistent with published evidence. Considerable space has been devoted to showing how an "operational methodology" can be used in psychological research to improve both the "understanding" and the "prediction" of behavior.

It is, therefore, recommended that the formulation of construct validity, as presented in the several papers noted in this critique, be eliminated from further consideration as a way of speaking about psychological concepts, laws, and theories.

REFERENCES

1. AMERICAN PSYCHOLOGICAL ASSOCIATION, Committee on Psychological Tests. *Technical recommendations for psychological tests and diagnostic techniques.* Washington, D.C.: APA, 1954.

2. AMERICAN PSYCHOLOGICAL ASSOCIATION. Report of testimony at a congressional hearing. *Amer. Psychologist,* 1958, **13,** 217–223.

3. ANASTASI, ANNE. The concept of validity in the interpretation of test scores. *Educ. psychol. Measmt.,* 1950, **10,** 67–78.

4. BECHTOLDT, H. P. Selection. In S. S. Stevens (Ed.), *Handbook of experimental psychology.* New York: Wiley, 1951. Pp. 1237–1267.

5. BECHTOLDT, H. P. Factor analysis of the Airman Classification Battery with civilian reference tests. *HRRC res. Bull.,* 1953, No. 53–59. (a)

6. BECHTOLDT, H. P. Response defined anxiety and MMPI variables. *Iowa Acad. Sci.,* 1953, **60,** 495–499. (b)

7. BECHTOLDT, H. P. Statistical tests of hypotheses in confirmatory factor analysis. *Amer. Psychologist,* 1958, **13,** 380. (Abstract)

8. BECK, L. W. Constructions and inferred entities. *Phil. Sci.,* 1950, **17.** (Reprinted: In H. Feigl & M. Brodbeck (Eds.), *Readings in the philosophy of science.* New York: Appleton-Century-Crofts, 1953. Pp. 368–381.)

9. BERGMANN, G. Outline of an empiricist philosophy of physics. *Amer. J. Physics,* 1943, **11.** (Reprinted: In H. Feigl & M. Brodbeck (Eds.), *Readings in the philosophy of science.* New York: Appleton-Century-Crofts, 1953. Pp. 262–287.)

10. BERGMANN, G. The logic of psychological concepts. *Phil. Sci.,* 1951, **18,** 93–110.

11. BERGMANN, G. Theoretical psychology. *Annu. Rev. Psychol.,* 1953, **4,** 435–458.

12. BERGMANN, G. Sense and nonsense in operationism. *Scient. Mon.,* 1954, **79,** 210–214. (Reprinted: In Ph. Frank (Ed.), *The validation of scientific theories.* Boston: Beacon, 1956. Pp. 41–52.)

13. BERGMANN, G. Psychoanalysis and the unity of science: Else Frenkel-Brunswik: A review. *J. Phil.,* 1955, **52,** 692–695.

14. BERGMANN, G. The contribution of John B. Watson. *Psychol. Rev.,* 1956, **63,** 265–276.

15. BERGMANN, G. *Philosophy of science.* Madison: Univer. Wisconsin Press, 1957.

16. BERGMANN, G., & SPENCE, K. W. Operationism and theory in psychology. *Psychol. Rev.,* 1941, **48,** 1–14.

17. BRODBECK, M. The philosophy of science and educational research. *Rev. educ. Res.,* 1957, **27,** 427–440.

18. BRODBECK, M. Methodological individualisms: Definition and reduction. *Phil. Sci.,* 1958, **25,** 1–22. (a)

19. BRODBECK, M. Models, meaning, and theories. In L. Gross (Ed.), *Symposium on sociological theory.* Evanston: Row Peterson, 1958. (b)

20. CAMPBELL, D. T., & FISKE, D. W. Convergent and discriminant validation by the multitrait-multimethod matrix. *Psychol. Bull.,* 1959, **56,** 81–105.

21. CARNAP, R. Foundations of logic and mathematics. In *International encyclopedia of unified science.* Vol. I, No. 3. Pp. 56–59. (Reprinted: The interpretation of physics. In H. Feigl & M. Brodbeck (Eds.), *Readings in the philosophy of science.* New York: Appleton-Century-Crofts, 1953. Pp. 309–318.)

22. CRONBACH, L. J. *Essentials of psychological testing.* New York: Harper, 1949.

23. CRONBACH, L. J. The two disciplines of scientific psychology. *Amer. Psychologist,* 1957, **12,** 671–684.

24. CRONBACH, L. J. Proposals leading to analytic treatment of social perception scores. In R. Tagiuri & L. Petrullo (Eds.), *Person perception and interpersonal behavior.* Stanford: Stanford Univer. Press, 1958. Pp. 353–379.

25. CRONBACH, L. J., & MEEHL, P. E. Construct validity in psychological tests. *Psychol. Bull.,* 1955, **52,** 281–302.

26. FEIGL, H. Existential hypotheses. *Phil. Sci.,* 1950, **17,** 35–62.

27. FEIGL, H. Confirmability and confirmation. *Rev. int. Phil.,* 1951, **5,** 1–12. (Reprinted: In P. P. Wiener (Ed.), *Readings in philosophy of science.* New York: Scribner, 1953. Pp. 522–530.

28. FRENCH, J. W. *Manual for kit of selected tests for reference aptitude and achievement factors.* Princeton: Educ. Testing Service, 1954.

29. GARNER, W. R., HAKE, H. H., & ERIKSEN, C. W. Operationism and the concept of perception. *Psychol. Rev.*, 1956, **63**, 149–159.

30. HEMPEL, C. G. *Fundamentals of concept formation in empirical science.* Chicago: Univer. Chicago Press, 1952.

31. JENKINS, J. J., & LYKKEN, D. T. Individual differences. *Annu. Rev. Psychol.*, 1957, **8**, 79–112.

32. JESSOR, R., & HAMMOND, K. R. Construct validity and the Taylor Anxiety Scale. *Psychol. Bull.*, 1957, **54**, 161–170.

33. JOHNSON, H. M. On verifying hypotheses by verifying their implicates. *Amer. J. Psychol.*, 1954, **67**, 723–727.

34. KAUSLER, D. J., & TRAPP, E. P. Methodological considerations in the construct validation of drive-oriented scales. *Psychol. Bull.*, 1959, **56**, 152–157.

35. LOEVINGER, JANE. Objective tests as instruments of psychological theory. *Psychol. Rep.*, 1957, **3**, 635–694.

36. LORD, F. A. Theory of test scores. *Psychometr. Monogr.*, 1952, No. 7.

37. MEEHL, P. E. Wanted: A good cookbook. *Amer. Psychologist*, 1956, **11**, 263–272.

38. PAP, A. Reduction-sentences and open concepts. *Methodos*, 1953, **5**, 3–30.

39. SELLARS, W. S. Concepts as involving laws and inconceivable without them. *Phil. Sci.*, 1948, **15**, 287–315.

40. SPENCE, K. W. The nature of theory construction in contemporary psychology. *Psychol. Rev.*, 1944, **51**, 47–68.

41. SPENCE, K. W. The postulates and methods of behaviorism. *Psychol. Rev.*, 1948, **55**, 67–78.

42. SPENCE, K. W. The empirical basis and theoretical structure of psychology. *Phil. Sci.*, 1957, **24**, 97–108.

43. SPENCE, K. W. A theory of emotionally based drive (*D*) and its relation to performance in simple learning situations. *Amer. Psychologist*, 1958, **13**, 131–141.

44. SPENCE, K. W., & ROSS, L. E. A methodological study of the form and latency of eyelid responses in conditioning. *J. exp. Psychol.*, 1959, **58**, 376–381.

45. SPIKER, C. C., & McCANDLESS, B. R. The concept of intelligence and the philosophy of science. *Psychol. Rev.*, 1954, **61**, 255–266.

46. TAYLOR, J. A. The relationship of anxiety to the conditioned eyelid response. *J. exp. Psychol.*, 1951, **41**, 81–92.

47. TAYLOR, J. A. A personality scale of manifest anxiety. *J. abnorm. soc. Psychol.*, 1953, **48**, 285–290.

48. THURSTONE, L. L., *Multiple-factor analysis.* Chicago: Univer. Chicago Press, 1947.

49. THURSTONE, L. L. & THURSTONE, T. G. *Primary mental abilities.* (Manual and tests) Chicago: Science Research Associates, 1950.

Chapter 8

Recommendations for APA Test Standards regarding Construct, Trait, or Discriminant Validity

DONALD T. CAMPBELL

The occasion for this paper is the publication by Harold Bechtoldt [2] of an eloquent attack on the category of construct validity. The philosophical problems upon which Bechtoldt takes issues with Cronbach and Meehl [12] are far removed from the practical business of designing, validating, and selling tests and are problems upon which competent philosophers are in disagreement. They are issues for which philosophy offers no orthodoxy upon which practitioners can depend and issues which make little or no difference to the prac-

This article is reprinted from the *American Psychologist*, 1960, with the permission of the author and the American Psychological Association.

This paper has been improved through extended comments on a previous draft made by H. P. Bechtoldt, L. J. Cronbach, D. W. Fiske, K. R. Hammond, and J. Loevinger, and the author wishes to express gratitude for their generous help. This is not to imply that any of them would completely agree with the paper in its present form.

ticing scientist, as Hochberg [21] has argued. In this situation, it would seem inappropriate if the eloquence of Bechtoldt's attack led to the removal of the category of construct validity from the next edition of *Technical Recommendations for Psychological Tests and Diagnostic Techniques* [1]. Instead, it is here argued that there should be a considerable strengthening of a set of precautionary requirements more easily classified under *construct* validity than under *concurrent* or *predictive* validity as presently described.

While not denying the presence of a serious philosophical disagreement nor its relevance to psychology, this paper will emphasize the common ground implicit in psychology's tradition of test validation efforts. The philosophical disagreement will remain, but it need not produce a lack of consensus about desirable evidence of test validity. Bechtoldt's argument is indeed

147

more against the role of construct validity in discussions of philosophy of science and psychological theory, rather than an objection to specific statements of desirable evidence of test validity contained under that rubric. He probably would not claim, for example, that the presentation of concurrent, predictive, and content validity in the *Technical Recommendations* is an exhaustive statement of the desirable evidence of test validity.

Test validity and test reliability are not concepts belonging to the philosophy of science. Instead they are concepts which have developed in the course of the mutual criticisms of test constructors and test users, concepts which relate to the implicit and explicit claims of test constructors and test salesmen. Had test designers from the beginning been so abstemious as to merely present copies of their tests and those of others and to report correlation coefficients between them for specified populations on specified dates under specified administrators and conditions of administration, then no validity problem, no validity requirements, would have ever been developed.

The actual situation has always been different and, for the published tests to which the *Technical Recommendations* addresses itself, seems likely to continue to be so. In the labels given tests, in statements of intent and descriptive material, many explicit and implicit claims are made. These claims amount to assertions of empirical laws between the test and other possible operations. Requirements for evidence as to reliability and validity are requirements that some of these laws be examined and confirmed. Our insistence on the importance of such evidence comes from our cumulative experience, in which test constructors and users have frequently been misled. Test constructors and users as we have known them have generally been prone to reifying and hypostatizing, prone to assume that their tests were tapping dispositional syndromes with other symptoms than those utilized in the test. The requirements of

validity demand that the implications of such hypostatizing be sampled and checked. Were the hypostatizing tendency to be effectively eradicated, such requirements would indeed become obsolete. If indeed the hypostatizations are unjustified, there is no better way of extinguishing them than attempting to verify them.[1] Validation procedures are just this.

CONSTRUCT OR TRAIT VALIDITY IN THE HISTORY OF TEST VALIDATION EFFORTS

Validation efforts have thus naturally been related to the intents and claims of the tests in question. In some instances, as occasionally for personnel selection tests, there have been quantitative or dichotomous institutional discriminations which it was economically advantageous to be able to predict. Where tests were offered as predictors of these practical decisions, evidences of the accuracy of prediction were the relevant validity data. Such validity efforts are subsumed in the *Technical Recommendations* under the terms *predictive* and *concurrent* validity. The latter is usually but an inexpensive and presumptive substitute for the former, and together they might be called *practical* validity. Note the asymmetry of the validational correlation of this type: because of the socially institutionalized and valued nature of the "criterion," it is taken as an immutable given, even when, as in college grades or factory production records, it might be known to have many imperfections or sources of invalidity in itself, if judged from a theoretical point of view. Beginning with James McKeen Cattell's efforts to predict college grades from reaction time measures, many psychological tests have been validated and invalidated by this process.

But *not all* psychological tests have been designed solely to predict performance against extant institutional decision situa-

[1] For a justification of validational requirements on psychological grounds, see Campbell [4], especially pp. 172–179.

tions. There are, in fact, relatively few settings which produce such criteria; and these are often so patently complex in the determinants of success as to be uninteresting to the scientist, who would rather measure purer, more single-factored traits for which society produces no correspondingly pure criteria. A good half of the validation efforts for personality tests since 1920 have been of this latter type and cannot be readily subsumed under practical validity. They fit best under construct validity as first described in the 1954 *Technical Recommendations*, even though construct validity was described there primarily as a possibility for the future. Subsequent presentations [12, 22] have tended to tie construct validity to tests developed and validated in the context of explicit theoretical structures or "nomological nets." Such developed theory was usually lacking and was not typically employed in these older validation efforts, even where, as for the numerous introversion-extroversion tests, a theoretical background may have been present.

It may be wise, therefore, to distinguish two types of construct validity. The first of these can appropriately be given the old-fashioned name *trait validity*. It is applicable at that level of development still typical of most test development efforts, in which "theory," if any, goes no farther than indicating a hypothetical syndrome, trait, or personality dimension. The second type could be called *nomological validity* and would represent the very important and novel emphasis of Cronbach and Meehl on the possibility of validating tests by using the scores from a test as interpretations of a certain term in a formal theoretical network and through this, to generate predictions which would be validating if confirmed when interpreted as still other operations and scores. When the Taylor Manifest Anxiety Scale is validated against psychiatrists' ratings [31, pp. 316–317], trait validation is being illustrated. Validated by generating the correct predictions of performance in learning situations, when test scores are interpreted as differences in D in the Hull-Spence learning theory [31, pp. 307–310], nomological validation is shown. The desirability of going still further in designing tests in detailed consideration of formal theory is an aspect of nomological validity advocated by Jessor and Hammond [22].

Among commercially published tests, nomological validity evidence is apt to be rare for some time to come, and it is therefore to trait validity criteria that this paper is primarily addressed. If one prefers to regard this as merely the old common sense notion of validity, and not needing any new label such as construct validity, this is acceptable. But the *Technical Recommendations* presentation of concurrent and predictive validity is not adequate to cover it. A number of distinctions between trait validity and practical validity can be noted. In trait validity, no a priori defining criterion is available as a perfect measure or defining operation against which to check the fallible test. Instead, the validator seeks out some independent way of getting at "the same" trait. Thus he may obtain specially designed ratings for the purpose. This independent measure has no status as *the* criterion for the trait, nor is it given any higher status for validity than is the test. Both are regarded as fallible measures, often with known imperfections, such as halo effects for the ratings and response sets for the test. Validation, when it occurs, is symmetrical and equalitarian. The presumptive validity of both measures is increased by agreement. Starting from a test, the validating measure is selected or devised on the joint criteria of independence of method and relevance to the trait.

The Downey Will-Temperament Tests, the moral knowledge tests, the introversion-extroversion tests, the social intelligence tests, the empathy tests: all have been invalidated without recourse to correlating test scores with *criterion* variables. They have instead been invalidated by cumulative evidence of the trait-validity sort. Inspecting the classic surveys of the validity of personality tests on a study by study basis shows more than half of the validational efforts cited by Symonds [29] and Vernon [34] to be of this type. An even half of the items in Ellis' [14] review are of this type. For personnel selection tests, the role of trait validation procedures would be much smaller, of course, but even here it is relevant. Trait validity is thus an important part of our cumulative experience in finding some tests worthless. It deserves to be represented among the precautionary standards attempting to prevent the needless publication and sale of worthless tests in the future.

Common to trait validity and practical validity is evidence of convergence or agreement between highly independent measures. Peculiar to trait validity considerations is the requirement of *discriminant* validity [5], the requirement that a test not correlate too highly with measures from which it is supposed to differ. Instances of invalidation by *high* correlation were already available when Symonds summarized the literature in 1931. He cites, for example, the moral knowledge tests. The interests of the 1920's had led to the development of such tests by several persons. These moral knowledge tests, it turned out, individually correlated more highly with intelligence tests than they did with each other and on this ground were abandoned. The case of the social intelligence tests [28, 33] is similar. Predictive or concurrent validity considerations would not have invalidated these tests, as they did indeed predict the practical criteria which a general intelligence test would predict, although perhaps not as well.

An ubiquitous class of cases in which high correlations have been invalidating are those instances of strong trait-irrelevant methods factors. These include the halo effects in ratings [20, 32], response sets [9, 10] and social desirability factors [13] in questionnaires, and stereotypes in interpersonal perception [11, 17]. Where feasible procedures are available to check on the strength of these trait-irrelevant methods factors in their contribution to reliable test variance, such procedures should certainly be tried before offering the test for general use.

SUGGESTED ADDITIONS TO THE RECOMMENDED EVIDENCES OF VALIDITY

Upon the basis of psychology's experience, more exhaustively assembled and discussed elsewhere (as in previous and subsequent references), the following additions to the *Technical Recommendations* in the category of construct validity are suggested:

1. *Correlation with intelligence tests.* A new test, no matter what its content, should be correlated with an intelligence test of as similar format as possible (e.g., a group intelligence test for a group personality test, etc.). If correlations are reported with independent trait-appropriate or criterion measures, it should be demonstrated that the new test correlates better with these measures than does the intelligence test.

This requirement is already somewhat recognized. Some test manuals for empathy and for personality traits report low correlations with intelligence as evidence favorable to validity. One major challenge to the validity of the F Scale, for example, is its high correlation with intelligence and the fact that its correlations with ethnocentrism, social class, conformity, and leadership are correlations previously demonstrated for test intelligence [e.g., 7].

2. *Correlations with social desirability.* A new test of the voluntary self-descriptive sort should be correlated with some measure of the very general response tendency of describing oneself in a favorable light no matter what the trait-specific content of the items. If correlations are reported with trait-appropriate or criterion measures, then it should be demonstrated that the new test predicts these measures better than does the general social desirability factor. In lieu of this, construction features designed to eliminate the social desirability factor should be specified, as in the forced choice pairing of items previously equated on

social desirability. Edwards [13] reviews the evidence necessitating this requirement.

3. *Correlations with measures of acquiescence and other response sets.* Tests of the voluntary self-description type employing responses with multiple levels of endorsement (e.g., L-D-I, A-a-?-d-D, etc.) should report correlations with external measures of acquiescence response set and other likely response sets. For check lists, the correlation with general frequency of checking items independent of content should be reported. It should be demonstrated that the tests predict trait-appropriate or criterion measures better than do the response set scores. In lieu of this, it should be demonstrated that the test construction and scoring procedures are such as to prevent response sets from being confounded with trait-specific content in the total score, as through the use of items worded in opposite directions in equal numbers, etc. Cronbach [9, 10] and others [e.g., 6] have illustrated the extent to which extant tests have in fact produced scores predominately a function of such trait-irrelevant sources of variance. (This is not to rule out the deliberate utilization of response-set variance, where the intent to do so is made explicit.)

4. *Self-description and stereotype keys for interpersonal perceptual accuracy tests.* Measures of empathy, interpersonal perception, social competence, and the like should compare the results of efforts to replicate the scores of particular social targets with the use of self-descriptions and stereotype scores as predictors; or such scores should be based upon competence in differentiating among social targets rather than upon the absolute discrepancy in predictions for a single social target. Gage, Leavitt, and Stone [17] and Cronbach [11] have described how misleading scores can be without such checks. Similarly, Q type correlations offered as validity data should be accompanied by control correlations based upon random matches, as in the manner of Corsini [8] and Silverman [26].

5. *Validity correlations higher than those for self-ratings.* Advocates of personality tests implicitly or explicitly claim that their scores are better measures (in some situations at least) than much quicker and more direct approaches such as simple self-ratings. While correlations with self-rating may in some circumstances be validating, it should also be demonstrated that the test scores predict independent trait-appropriate or criterion measures better than do self-ratings. The available evidence [as sampled, for example, by Campbell and Fiske, 5] shows that this may only rarely be the case.

6. *Multitrait-multimethod matrix.* The demonstration of discriminant validity and the examination of the strength of method factors require a validational setting containing not only two or more methods of measuring a given trait, but also the measurement of two or more traits. This requirement is implicit in several of the points above and has been present in the range of validational evidence used in our field from the beginning [e.g., Symonds, 29]. It is frequently convenient to examine such evidence through a multitrait-multimethod matrix. Particularly does this seem desirable where the test publisher offers a multiple-score test or a set of tests in a uniform battery. Achievement and ability tests need this fully as much as do personality tests. A detailed argument for this requirement is presented elsewhere [5].

DEMURRERS FROM SOME CONNOTATIONS OF CONSTRUCT VALIDITY

It is believed that the originators of the term "construct validity" would find in the above description of trait validity, including its discriminant aspects and the suggested additions, nothing incompatible with construct validity as they originally intended it. For this reason and for reasons of economy of conceptualization, it seems desirable to emphasize the essential identity. There may be, nonetheless, several points at which the connotations of the original presentation are at variance with the emphases of this paper and of the orientation toward validity represented by the multitrait-multimethod matrix. These connotations may very well have been inadvertent aspects of the illustrations used in the presentation rather than intended. In other cases they may be connotations elicited only in the minds of a few readers. A primary source has been informal conversations with hardheaded psychologists who have failed to see the need for the concept or who have felt that they disagreed with it. These demurrers are deliberately overstated here for purposes of expository clarity. As will be seen from the discussions subsumed under them, there are included some complaints which the present writer feels are totally unjustified, as well as others upon which the presentation of construct validity may be in need of clarification.

1. *Construct validity is new.* Through the use of hypothetical illustrations rather than classic instances, and through the references to formal theory, the connotation has been created that construct validity was offered as a new type of validation procedure. Actually it is as old as the concept of test validity itself, and it (or trait validity) is needed in any inventory of the useful procedures by which tests have been shown to be invalid in the past.

2. *Construct validity is only for tests developed in the context of formal theory.* While the illustrations of the *Technical Recommendations* presentation clearly contradict this, the term "construct," the reference to nomological nets, and the accompanying argument from disputed positions within the philosophy of science have furthered this impression. The heterogeneity of validational approaches encompassable within construct validity is indeed so great that its subdivision into trait and nomological validation might well improve accuracy of communication at the practical level.

3. *Construct validity confuses reliability and validity.* While this criticism is perhaps accurately applied to some of the precursors to the concept of construct validity, and to some published claims of construct validity, details of the formal presentations belie this. However, *Technical Recommen-*

dations is weak in making explicit the common denominator among all of the major validity notions, and their common difference from reliability. Reliability is agreement between measures maximally similar in method. The best examples of concurrent, predictive, and construct validity all represent agreement between highly different and independent measurement procedures. This essential common component in all validity is spelled out in more detail by Campbell and Fiske [5].

4. *Construct validity represents the abandonment of operationalism.* Like all of the pragmatist and positivist calls for observable evidence as opposed to untestable metaphysical speculation, construct validation is a kind of operationalism, as the term is generally used. Where verifying operations against which to check tests are not automatically available (as they are for predictive and concurrent validity), it calls for the generation of independent operations for this purpose. The only kind of operationalism with which it is in disagreement is the totally unpracticed kind referred to by Bridgman in his original presentation [3], as when he said: "if we have more than one set of operations we have more than one concept, and strictly there should be a separate name to correspond to each different set of operations" (p. 10). We may call this "exhaustive-definitional-operationalism" if it is taken as alleging that for every theoretical construct there is one perfect defining operation and that this operation exhaustively defines that theoretical construct.

Bridgman probably no longer holds to this extreme view, if he ever did. No theoretical psychologist who attempts to relate theory with data employs this exhaustive-definitional-operationalism. To take an illustration from the range of authorities Bechtoldt cites: it is clear, for example, that the Manifest Anxiety Scale [30] was *not* introduced as the exhaustive definition of the Hull-Spence theoretical construct D, but rather as a tentative operational representation of D, not excluding the representation of D by hours of food deprivation, etc. in other studies. In the initial presentation [30] it was considered an empirically meaningful question (rather than a matter of definition) to ask whether the MAS might not be representing $_sH_R$ instead of D. Spence [27] has clearly said that had the experiments using the MAS been negative, the other portions of the theory were sufficiently well confirmed "that we would have had no hesitancy about abandoning the A-Scale [MAS] as being related to D in our theorem." Further, MAS scores have never been assumed to be *solely* a function of D, but rather, some degree of impurity is conceded [e.g., 31, p. 303].

The general spirit of operationalism as endorsed by such varied persons as Margenau [24, pp. 232–242; 25], Feigl [15], and Frank [16] is certainly compatible with construct validity. Where the emphasis is upon test operations, distinguishing operations, operational verification, multiple operations [16], or convergent operations [18, 19], the compatibility is particularly clear.

5. *Construct validity makes possible pseudo-validation of invalid tests.* Many of us identified with structured measurement techniques and hardheaded validational procedures are still smarting from having lost to projective techniques in the late 1930's and early 1940's a battle that was never fought. As we see it, the structured personality tests provided in the form of scores specific predictions verifiable against other measures, such as ratings by psychologists and peers, performance in experimental situations, etc. The methodological commitments of the field made certain that these predictions be checked, resulting in a disappointing collection of validity data, disappointing not only because of numerous .00 correlations but also because .30s and .40s looked like failure against expectations in the .80s and .90s. This record of "failure" led to the wholesale supplanting of structured tests with projective tests without any *transition studies* utilizing both types in competitive prediction against the same independent meas-

ures. On their part, the projective tests were surrounded by an interpretive framework which evaded validation. The scientific evidence justifying the introduction of projectives was solely the evidence of the "failure" of the structured approaches and not in the least evidence of the superior validity of the projectives. This seemed a very unfair victory. Now belatedly projective tests are being checked in ways similar to those that invalidated the structured tests, and the evidence for projectives looks even worse. It would seem very undesirable if construct validity provided a rationalization for continued evasion of this evidence.

That construct validity could do so in some instances would be made possible by the joint application of several features. The presentation of construct validity emphasized the wide variety of validational evidence, without prescribing any particular type of evidence for all users. This makes possible a highly opportunistic selection of evidence and the editorial device of failing to mention the construct validity probes that were not confirmatory. When the multiplicity of possible evidences is combined with the small samples available in clinical studies, capitalizing on chance sampling variations from zero validity becomes a very real possibility. The multiplicity of extenuating circumstances known to the sensitive clinician in specific situations and for particular patients further dilutes the applicability of statistical tests. These possibilities should certainly be discouraged in any new edition of *Technical Recommendations* and, of course, are neither inherent in nor limited to construct validation procedures.

It is one of the valuable by-products of the rigid and "cookbook" character of the multitrait-multimethod matrix that it forces the investigator to specify in advance the correlations that will be validating if high, forces him to examine others which will be *in*validating if high, and provides a setting for examining the comparative validity of techniques. Likewise, where a detailed and explicit nomological net is employed in the validational procedure, such evasion of in-validation seems unlikely. It is also unlikely where the test constructor commits himself in advance to the most appropriate independent data series for validational purposes and then attempts to predict this both with his new test and with simple self-ratings (or other rival devices).

When the evasion of invalidation is being considered, it seems well to note the evasion made possible by the combination of plausible a priori considerations, "face validity," and the kind of operationalism which says "intelligence is what the Stanford Binet (1916 edition) measures." Contrasted with this, the approach of construct validation forces the test designer into checking out the implicit and explicit claims by which he convinces others that his test is worth buying and using.

6. *Construct validity encourages the reification of traits.* Bechtoldt has ridiculed the proponents of construct validity on this score. Such ridicule is telling because we have all been taught to avoid naive reification, and we hate to appear unsophisticated. Were it not for such reasons of vanity, the simplest answer would be that test constructors and buyers are in fact prone to such reification. Such reification implies laws which can and should be sample-checked in the validation process. There is no better cure for such reification than entering the trait or the test in a multitrait-multimethod matrix. Even for the more successful tests, this is a humbling experience, generating modesty and caution.

Reifying tendencies are not limited to the trait-reifying construct validators, however. Still more pernicious is the score-reifying which has accompanied the popular use of intelligence, achievement, and vocational interest tests, for example. We are all occasionally appalled at the literal interpretations and assumptions of immutable three-digit perfection with which some users regard these test scores. Even test constructors are on occasion childishly naive in assuming their test scores to measure perfectly what they intended when they wrote the items.

Often they use a pseudosophisticated operationalism to disguise this: what the test measures *is* the trait. Intent and achievement are slurred.

In such settings, one feels the need for a methodological perspective which emphasizes the imperfection inherent in scores: the variable effects of guessing, the biases in personality tests imposed by idiosyncracies in vocabulary, the impurities contributed by token compliance, the misreading of items, the clerical errors in answering, the response sets, the inevitable factorial complexity, and the like. A perspective which exhaustively defines constructs in terms of obtained test scores can only inconsistently or indirectly admit such imperfection. It is, however, an essential part of the critical-realist position that all measurement is, to some degree at least, imperfect; and this feature is one that strongly recommends it as describing the orientation of the scientist to scientific truth. Note that the critical-realist position is not entirely out of favor with sophisticated philosophers of science and might even claim a plurality of those in the logical positivist camp.

7. *Construct validity leads to a confusion of "significant correlation" with "identity."* There is in current psychological writing a frequent lapse into an implicit assumption of construct purity on the part of tests that have been found to be "valid" and an implicit assumption of complete intersubstitutibility on the part of different operations which have in one setting been found "significantly correlated." Too frequently there are inference sequences of this order: A correlates .50 with B, B correlates .50 with C, therefore A equals C—employed even when, with a little more work, the relation of A to C could be directly examined. Some users of the concept of construct validity have been guilty of this identification, but it is by no means limited to them, nor necessarily incurred as a result of their validity rationale. Some such thinking is involved whenever the implicit assumption is made that all of the correlates of a given

test involve the same sources of systematic variance from within the inherently complex test. As a matter of fact, the emphasis upon the presence of construct-irrelevant sources of variance in test scores should be a major deterrent to such lapses.[2]

---

[2] A further possible demurrer may be briefly discussed. Bechtoldt gives the following example [taken from Johnson, 23] of faulty inference presumably typical of construct validity discussions: "If a person has an over-compensated inferiority complex, he blusters, is aggressive, domineering, and dogmatic; this man blusters, is aggressive, domineering, and dogmatic; therefore, he has an inferiority complex." As a logical syllogism this is, of course, invalid, but inductive science is well recognized by philosophers since Hume to lack logical validity in this sense. Bechtoldt does not make explicit enough to the casual reader that this logical invalidity is present in *all* efforts to relate theory to observations. For example, the theoretical validity of the MAS takes essentially this form: increase in *D* in the Hull-Spence behavior theory predicts more rapid learning in Conditions A, B, and C, and slower learning in Conditions D, E, and F; high (vs. low) MAS scorers show more rapid learning in Conditions A, B, and C, and slower learning in Conditions D, E, and F; therefore MAS is (may be tentatively considered to be) a measure of *D*. All theories in science relate to observations in this *logically* unjustified manner and, concomitantly, are held tentatively. Note, however, that the "invalid" syllogism can rule out many theories, in that it sets up requirements which many theory-data sets do *not* meet. These are more stringent the more specific and numerous the implications of the theory. The scientific (as opposed to logical) validity of a theory becomes a matter of, first, the number and rigor of such tests to which the theory has been exposed and successfully survived and, second, the number of available rival theories which as efficiently subsume the same complex of data. Bechtoldt is, of course, correct in pointing out that many actual uses of the phrase "construct validity" in the literature have been in settings in which the stringency of the requirements are so weak and the number of available plausible rival hypotheses so numerous that the degree of confirmation of theory is trivial. But if his presentation connotes that this weakness is specific to construct validity, or to response-inferred constructs, this connotation is in serious error. The advocates of construct validity take second place to none in their insistence upon greater rigor in testing theory and in their demand for vigilance in seeking out data series which will distinguish between rival interpretations. Critical-realist aspirations in science lead directly to this emphasis, as opposed to a possible nominalist complacency which says that all you have anyway are operations and correlations and all efforts to interpret these are specious, superfluous, and extra-scientific.

REFERENCES

1. AMERICAN PSYCHOLOGICAL ASSOCIATION, Committee on Psychological Tests. *Technical recommendations for psychological tests and diagnostic techniques.* Washington, D.C.: APA, 1954. (Reprinted from: *Psychol. Bull., Suppl.,* 1954, **51**, 201–238.)

2. BECHTOLDT, H. P. Construct validity: A critique. *Amer. Psychologist,* 1959, **14**, 619–629.

3. BRIDGMAN, P. W. *The logic of modern physics.* New York: Macmillan, 1927.

4. CAMPBELL, D. T. Methodological suggestions from a comparative psychology of knowledge processes. *Inquiry,* 1959, **2**, 152–182.

5. CAMPBELL, D. T., & FISKE, D. W. Convergent and discriminant validation by the multitrait-multimethod matrix. *Psychol. Bull.,* 1959, **56**, 81–105.

6. CHAPMAN, L. J., & BOCK, R. D. Components of variance due to acquiescence and content in the F Scale measure of authoritarianism. *Psychol. Bull.,* 1958, **55**, 328–333.

7. CHRISTIE, R. Authoritarianism reexamined. In R. Christie & M. Jahoda (Eds.), *Studies in the scope and the method of the authoritarian personality.* Glencoe, Ill.: Free Press, 1954. Pp. 123–196.

8. CORSINI, R. J. Understanding and similarity in marriage. *J. abnorm. soc. Psychol.,* 1956, **52**, 327–332.

9. CRONBACH, L. J. Response sets and test validity. *Educ. psychol. Measmt.,* 1946, **6**, 475–494.

10. CRONBACH, L. J. Further evidence on response sets and test design. *Educ. psychol. Measmt.,* 1950, **10**, 3–31.

11. CRONBACH, L. J. Proposals leading to analytic treatment of social perception scores. In R. Tagiuri & L. Petrullo (Eds.), *Person perception and interpersonal behavior.* Stanford: Stanford Univer. Press, 1958. Pp. 353–379.

12. CRONBACH, J. L., & MEEHL, P. E. Construct validity in psychological tests. *Psychol. Bull.,* 1955, **52**, 281–302.

13. EDWARDS, A. L. *The social desirability variable in personality assessment and research.* New York: Dryden, 1957.

14. ELLIS, A. The validity of personality questionnaires. *Psychol. Bull.,* 1946, **43**, 385–440.

15. FEIGL, H. Operationism and scientific method. *Psychol. Rev.*, 1945, **52**, 250–259.

16. FRANK, P. Foundations of physics. In O. Neurath, R. Carnap, & C. Morris (Eds.), *International Encyclopedia of Unified Science.* Vol. II. Chicago: Univer. Chicago Press, 1946, 1955.

17. GAGE, N. L., LEAVITT, G. S., & STONE, G. C. The intermediary key in the analysis of interpersonal perception. *Psychol. Bull.*, 1956, **53**, 258–266.

18. GARNER, W. R. Context effects and the validity of loudness scales. *J. exp. Psychol.*, 1954, **48**, 218–224.

19. GARNER, W. R., HAKE, H. W., & ERIKSEN, C. W. Operationism and the concept of perception. *Psychol. Rev.*, 1956, **63**, 149–159.

20. GUILFORD, J. P. *Psychometric methods.* (Rev. ed.) New York: McGraw-Hill, 1954.

21. HOCHBERG, H. Intervening variables, hypothetical constructs and metaphysics. Paper read at American Association for the Advancement of Science, Chicago, December, 1959.

22. JESSOR, R., & HAMMOND, K. R. Construct validity and the Taylor Anxiety Scale. *Psychol. Bull.*, 1957, **54**, 161–170.

23. JOHNSON, H. M. On verifying hypotheses by verifying their implicates. *Amer. J. Psychol.*, 1954, **67**, 723–727.

24. MARGENAU, H. *The nature of physical reality.* New York: McGraw-Hill, 1950.

25. MARGENAU, H. On interpretations and misinterpretations of operationalism. *Scient. Mon.*, 1954, **79**, 209–210.

26. SILVERMAN, L. H. A *Q*-sort study of the validity of evaluations made from projective techniques. *Psychol. Monogr.*, 1959, **73**, (7, Whole No. 477).

27. SPENCE, K. W. A theory of emotionally based drive (*D*) and its relation to performance in simple learning situations. *Amer. Psychologist*, 1958, **13**, 131–141.

28. STRANG, R. Relation of social intelligence to certain other factors. *Sch. Soc.*, 1930, **32**, 268–272.

29. SYMONDS, P. M. *Diagnosing personality and conduct.* New York: Appleton-Century, 1931.

30. TAYLOR, J. A. The relationship of anxiety to the conditioned eyelid response. *J. exp. Psychol.*, 1951, **41**, 81–92.

31. TAYLOR, J. A. Drive theory and manifest anxiety. *Psychol. Bull.*, 1956, **53**, 303–320.

32. THORNDIKE, E. L. A constant error in psychological ratings. *J. appl. Psychol.*, 1920, **4**, 25–29.

33. THORNDIKE, R. L. Factor analysis of social and abstract intelligence. *J. educ. Psychol.*, 1936, **27**, 231–233.

34. VERNON, P. E. The assessment of psychological qualities by verbal methods. *Med. Res. Council Industr. Hlth. Bd. Rep.*, 1938, No. 83.

Chapter 9

Some Pitfalls in Psychological Theorizing

MILTON ROKEACH / S. HOWARD BARTLEY

The purpose of this paper is to draw attention to certain examples of confusing psychological statements. These could be classified as involving circularity, lack of parsimony, and indefinite regress. It is hoped that pointing to these examples will lead to their avoidance.

SOME EXAMPLES INVOLVING CIRCULARITY

We often invest words taken from our everyday language with theoretical or technical meaning. As a result, many of the ambiguities in our scientific language are the reflection of the confusion in everyday communication. In everyday language, much of the meaning of terms is gained from *context*. In scientific language, meaning of words should be established by *definition*. To the extent that one depends upon context rather than upon definition for

This article is reprinted from the *American Psychologist*, 1958, with the permission of the authors and the American Psychological Association.

meaning, the event referred to is necessarily vague, and often enough the word refers to both stimulus and response. This confusion arises because we do not have words in everyday language which distinguish physical events from the perceptions they evoke.

As conventionally employed, the word, light, for example, refers both to what one experiences and to the energy that elicits the experience. So do the following terms: flash, color, sound, odor, taste. Such adjectives as bright, dull, cold, warm, etc. likewise describe the stimulus as well as the resulting experience. We can point to similar examples in other areas of psychology. Frustration is a term that pertains to a state of the individual and also the conditions which induce the state. The same is true with threat, conflict, goal, task orientation, and configuration. No doubt the reader can think of other terms as well.

The most obvious way to eliminate such circularity is to employ different terms to denote physical events and the perceptions

157

evoked by such events. One of us, for example, uses the following scheme to avoid this type of circularity:

Terms for Physical Events	Terms for Perceptions Evoked
1. photic radiation	1. light
2. pulse (photic)	2. flash
3. acoustic stimulus	3. sound
4. olfactory stimulus	4. smell, odor, etc.

Admittedly this would be more difficult in the fields of social psychology and personality theory, but nevertheless there is the same need for it.

A second kind of circularity arises when part of the perceptual response pattern is made, in effect, explanatory to the rest of it. A case in point is the way we commonly use the term, cue. Cues, as commonly used, are actually features of the response pattern itself, rather than its explanation. Suppose it is asked why a triangle in a drawing is seen as in front of another. An explanation frequently given is that certain "cues" are responsible. When one asks what the "cues" are, one hears such replies as: "one triangle overlies the other" or "one is seen to be lower than the other on the page." It will be noted that the "cues" are part of what the observer sees, thus are part of the overall response itself. Thus, in the language just quoted, part of a perceptual response is made explanatory to the rest. Explanations must lie outside of the thing explained. In a similar vein, we often hear it said that the color of an object affects its size. Color, like size, is something perceived rather than something out there in the stimulus world.

We come now to the third example of circularity. In statements of the form, "x is a function of y," we have a tautology when y is merely a synonym of x. We have come across such propositions as the following: maladjustment is a function of ego-strength; rigidity is a function of intolerance of ambiguity; role behavior is a function of role expectation. Another example from social psychology is the attributing of attitudes to

one's frame of reference. It seems to us that these are tautological if the terms used are not independently defined and measured; and often they are not.

SOME EXAMPLES OF LACK OF PARSIMONY

One of the most disconcerting features of contemporary psychology is the unnecessary multiplication of concepts. For example, we believe the reader would be hard put to define and measure each of the following concepts so that the terms would be clearly discriminable from each other.

1. Anxiety, insecurity, threat, ego threat, achievement anxiety, ego orientation, ego strength
2. Frustration tolerance, tolerance of ambiguity, tolerance of instability
3. Compulsiveness-obsessiveness, intolerance of ambiguity, rigidity, perseveration, fixation, channelization, *Einstellung*, set
4. Fascistic personality, antidemocratic personality, authoritarian personality, authoritarian character, obsessive-compulsive personality, rigid personality, sado-masochistic personality

It seems to us that, before we invoke a new term, we are obligated to consider whether we are adding unnecessarily to an already unparsimonious state of affairs. If we cannot point to a real difference between the concept we propose to use and those used by others who preceded us, we should refrain from injecting it into the literature. The mere fact that one uses a new term implies that there *is* a difference, and it seems to us this carries with it the obligation to make the difference explicit. What is particularly unfortunate is the fact that failure to do so is often associated with a disregard for the work of others on essentially the same problem. Thus, a consequence of the unnecessary proliferation of concepts is a needless fragmentation of knowledge. A greater regard for parsimony would probably lead to unification rather than fragmentation of research findings.

AN EXAMPLE OF AN INDEFINITE REGRESS

Let us consider the way the phrase, to underlie, is employed in psychology. That which underlies is explanatory to, basic to, fundamental to, or causal to the behavior referred to. Perhaps those who use this word take its meaning to be self-evident, but we do not believe it is. We have never seen it defined. Because it is not defined, it is sometimes employed euphemistically to talk about cause and effect relations when there is no information about what is cause and what is effect.

In such research, speaking of one variable as underlying another is purely arbitrary. It reminds us of an equally arbitrary statement often seen in research of a correlational nature: "For purposes of this research, we shall consider x as the independent variable and y as the dependent variable." We suspect, therefore, that the word underlie is often superfluous in psychology. Consider the typical statement: "S's behavior is a function of underlying anxiety." The same statement without the adjective, underlying, seems to mean the same thing.

To make matters even more complicated, theorists, particularly those concerned with psychodynamics, invoke different levels of depth. To declare there are various depth levels is like saying that there are manifest (phenotypic) variables that are a function of latent (genotypic) variables which are, in turn, a function of yet more latent (more genotypic) variables. This would be appropriate if only there were operations that permitted such differentiations. But it is extremely difficult to specify such operations.

Each season brings with it a fresh crop of underlying variables that are supposedly more underlying than the crop of the previous season. This state of affairs, along with the fact that it is difficult to find operations which permit differentiation of one depth level from another, provides the ingredients for an indefinite regress. There is no telling when rock bottom is reached. Having no way to pin down depth, the indefinite regress is potentially a circular procedure as well—if you will, a circular indefinite regress.

Part 3

THE METHODOLOGY
OF ASSESSMENT

Methodology provides the basic framework for the development of assessment devices, the bone upon which the muscle of test content is shaped. The form that a test finally takes—its quality and appropriateness for designated purposes—depends not only upon carefully selected content but also upon the adequacy of methods used in its development as well. Thus, a necessary precondition for a sound program of test development or assessment is an awareness of methodological alternatives. But knowledge of alternatives is not enough. It is necessary to apply such knowledge by selecting an appropriate alternative at each stage of the assessment task. Making well-informed decisions about methodology is like choosing a route on a road map: it is difficult to do properly without knowing where you are going, and if it is done improperly, you may never reach your destination. Since even the choice between a superhighway and a dirt road depends upon where you are going, we not only must consider the nature and power of alternative methods but must evaluate them relative to particular assessment objectives.

The methodology of assessment spans a broad area, encompassing such diverse topics as item selection, the use of sound judgment in evaluating a test for a particular purpose, and technical considerations in the estimation of reliability or in the measurement of growth or change. One assessment problem may require merely the routine application of a well-known reliability formula, while another may demand considerable innovation in the solution of a unique problem. It is fortunate, however, that assessment problems are rarely entirely unique. Others have also had to communicate about test properties, to estimate reliability, or to appraise test structure. There has evolved a series of well-accepted practices and standards for evaluating test properties, many of which are based upon well-founded mathematical rationales. By applying this accumulated knowledge about methodology appropriately, one can improve considerably the chances of making a correct assessment decision or of choosing a beneficial assessment strategy.

In the introductory selection of Part 3, "Hiawatha Designs an Experiment," M. G. Kendall gives lighthearted poetic expression to a serious assessment aim. In the meter of Longfellow, Kendall expresses allegorically the importance of accuracy in measurement. Whether inaccuracy results in lost arrows or in unstable test scores, its consequences are usually not readily remedied by even the most heroic attempts at statistical wizardry.

In the appraisal of a test or diagnostic technique, accuracy of measurement is but one of several standards applied. Many such standards have been developed informally over the years, reflecting the accumulated experience of assessment specialists in evaluating a vast number of diverse tests. These initially informal standards have been codified in a formal set of principles of good test practice. These comprise the second selection in this section, the "Standards for Educational and Psychological Tests and Manuals," prepared by a joint committee of the American Psychological Association, the American Educational Research Association, and the National Council on Measurement in Education. Of course, before one can evaluate a test, it is necessary to have certain information at hand upon which to base a judgment. The "Standards" outlines the kinds of information that should be included in the technical manual published with the test. These standards provide valuable guidelines both for test publishers and for consumers. For the publisher this selection provides an objective professional standard for tests and test manuals as an alternative to the standards of the marketplace. For the informed test consumer these recommendations represent the best single listing of the kinds of data and information essential for appraising a published psychological test.

There are a multitude of potential bases for classifying assessment techniques. Donald T. Campbell in Chapter 12 offers a useful typology, especially for attitude and personality assessment. Campbell fully recognizes the implications of the varying motives of the assessee to deceive himself and others. He notes how the aim of more valid estimation may be served by a kind of flanking operation in which the assessment task avoids the arousal of test-taking defensiveness by approaching the evaluation of the trait indirectly or obliquely. Campbell's typology is thus far more than static classification; it points the way to the development of novel assessment procedures based upon relatively neglected types of assessment strategies.

Lee J. Cronbach (Chapter 13) contrasts the differing cultural and philosophical orientations of clinical and measurement psychology. Cronbach argues eloquently for cultural pluralism, maintaining that through exchanges of information and research problems each area may prosper. In particular, he admonishes measurement psychologists to be on the alert for possible research problems arising from their consultation with clinical psychologists and to avoid rigidity in the insistence that a particular empirical problem be unrealistically simplified to fit an existing measurement model. He provides, on the basis of his theoretical work with Gleser, an excellent example of the need for a liberalizing of classical test theory so as to take into account decision problems frequently encountered in practice, such as those of multiple classification.

The subpart "The Evaluation of Measurement Properties" takes up the general question of the test as a measuring instrument. Robert L. Thorndike discusses the rationale and procedures used to select items to produce a test having certain optimal properties, such as high reliability or high validity. He describes a variety of useful and economical procedures for conducting routine item analyses. The increasing availability of modern high-speed computers has greatly expanded opportunities for using item-analysis techniques that combine rigor with flexibility.

In a second contribution to this section, Robert L. Thorndike (in collaboration with a distinguished committee) thoroughly reviews a traditional cornerstone of assessment methodology, the concept of reliability. Proceeding from a consideration of the logical foundations of the concept of measurement error, he demonstrates the close correspondence between statistical procedures and the purposes they are designed to serve. Then, rather than permitting statistical procedures per se to dictate the choice of an experimental plan, Thorndike subordinates these considerations to the more fundamental ones of estimating different sources of reliability, relating these in turn to the purposes of the investigator. The choice among statistical procedures thus depends upon their alternative sensitivity in reflecting particular sources of unreliability. Thorndike next presents a set of concrete recommendations for the interpretation of reliability estimates, introducing the important concept of *true score*. He illustrates the crucial link between experimental problems, like the effect of test speededness, and measurement problems involved in reliability estimation. Finally, he reminds the reader that precision is a necessary but not a sufficient prerequisite for the fundamental goal of validity. Though extremely valuable, precision is best conceived as one of several crucial steps in an assessment program.

While the concept of reliability has found its primary application in the area of psychological testing, the closely allied concept of reproducibility—the degree to which a person's individual item responses may be derived or reproduced from his total score—has been applied particularly to attitude scaling. White and Saltz in Chapter 16 review alternative interpretations of the reproducibility concept. They give particular attention to the important work of Guttman and Loevinger, who have developed methods for estimating test and item homogeneity. An important feature of the White and Saltz presentation is their attempt to integrate this work with parallel developments in test theory and reliability estimation.

One important application of psychological and educational tests is to the measurement of change, whether this is viewed as maturation of intellectual ability, as the result of specific learning experience, or as the consequence of some experimental treatment. Frederic M. Lord (Chapter 17) approaches this problem with the powerful tools of test theory. The question of change over occasions would seem to be a simple one. Why not simply subtract the first score from the second one? Lord's analysis points to the possible errors in such an approach. Observed test scores are a combination of a hypothetical true score and errors of measurement. Thus a person who takes the same test on two occasions will likely obtain a different score even in the absence of any experimental treatment or intellectual growth. Such a change would be due to fluctuations of the error component rather than to systematic differences in the true score reflecting the trait being measured. This raises a problem in the measurement of change, because considerable care is required to disentangle that portion of the observed change score due to psychologically meaningful change from that portion due to errors of measurement. A further complication in studying change, as Lord has shown, is that the variability of errors of measurement depends upon the true score. For example, a person with a very high score on a test is more likely to obtain a somewhat lower score on a parallel form of the test administered immediately after the first one. But it would probably be incorrect to conclude that the person had shown a decrement in the attribute being measured. More likely, the score obtained on the first test would have been an over-estimate of his true score. Lord recommends a set of procedures useful in estimating "real" or true-score gain that takes into account these and other problems. The mathematical rationale makes explicit the assumptions involved in the procedures recommended by Lord, as well as the assumptions in alternative procedures recommended by others.

Sechrest and Jackson in Chapter 18 consider the nature of deviation as it may be expressed in test responses. They are not referring here to the kind of error that may be introduced by random fluctuations in test scores but rather to a systematic tendency for an assessee to structure his responses in a manner consistently different from that of other people. Taking as a point of departure the interesting and provocative work of Irwin A. Berg and his associates, Sechrest and Jackson scrutinize the variety of ways in which a person might be considered generally deviant. They evaluate a number of psychological processes hypothesized to underlie consistent deviation in test responses and discuss various measurement problems inherent in the identification of deviant response tendencies.

In the subpart "The Analysis of Structure," a group of distinguished authors examine one of the important recurring issues in assessment: the determination of dimensions of interrelation among measures as a basis for evaluating both the nature of the measures and the nature of the traits being assessed. Louis L. Thurstone, who had a profound influence on the development of multiple-factor analysis, defines in Chapter 19 the essential goal of factor analysis as he saw it. Thurstone's view is that scientific discovery and explanation ultimately require the identification of primary or elementary processes. The factor problem is thus considered one of identifying the primary, invariant traits and abilites that serve to determine individual performance. In Chapter 20, Hans J. Eysenck distinguishes between different applications of factor analysis, particularly emphasizing the distinction between the *exploration* of uncharted areas of psychology and the *evaluation and verification of hypotheses.*

In Chapter 21, Raymond B. Cattell illustrates how the analysis of structure in correlations between tests may be generalized. Cattell points out that it is possible to analyze the structure not only between tests correlated over persons but also between tests correlated over occasions, between persons correlated over tests, etc. Cattell has essentially considered the three data modes of *tests, persons,* and *occasions* and has generated factor-analytic research designs that represent the various combinations of these modes taken in pairs. Recently, Ledyard R Tucker has developed a rationale with powerful analytical tools for the joint analysis of all three modes, i.e., of data obtained from the administration of several tests to several persons on more than one occasion.

In Chapter 22, Tucker discusses a technical problem of great importance in factor analysis: the criteria for developing rotational procedures. The problem is that mathematical methods used to derive the dimensions or factors underlying a set of correlation coefficients produce reference axes that are usually not in an ideal location from the viewpoint of psychological meaningfulness. Thurstone pointed to the necessity of graphically transforming or rotating the reference axes to positions in which only a few tests would have high loadings on each factor, thereby permitting simpler factor interpretations. Such rotation was said to yield a simple structure. Factors so derived were observed to be more invariant from one study to the next. But such a method, depending as it does upon the skill and judgment of the experimenter, was subject to criticism on the grounds that it was subjective and possibly arbitrary. Tucker's criteria objectify the notion of simple structure and exemplify a critical stage in the development of wholly analytical rotation procedures; once objective standards have been specified, the precision of numerical methods and the speed of the large computers may be substituted for the fallibility of human judgment.

Factor analysis is a powerful tool, one which is extremely useful in the solution of a wide variety of problems. But there are certain assumptions and preconditions regarding the nature of the data which must be met before the method may be meaningfully applied. Unfortunately not all investigators who have sought answers to research problems with factor analysis have had their data in a proper form. Thus, erroneous, misleading, or meaningless results may emerge. In Chapter 23, J. P. Guilford surveys many of the more frequent mis-applications of factor analysis. His careful review should be studied by all who plan to use factor analysis to aid in the interpretation of psychological data.

Factors may take on a variety of interpretations, from mere summary descriptions of particular data on the one hand to theoretical constructs on the other. Joseph R. Royce in the final chapter in Part 3 argues cogently for the interpretation of factors as the elements of theory. Basing his descriptions of constructs upon Margenau's analysis, Royce illustrates how the usual first-order common factors may be interpreted as *epistemic* or data-oriented constructs. Such factors derive most of their meaning from their links with observations. Higher-order factors can be interpreted, according to Royce, as *constitutive* or more strictly theoretical constructs, which derive their meaning from their links with other constructs, rather than being strictly observable. It is one important goal of psychological science to develop laws that explain relations between constructs and between observations and theoretical constructs. Factor analysis can contribute to this quest by aiding in the identification and definition of empirically meaningful theoretical constructs: the important elements of theory which, although not directly observable themselves, have empirical consequences that might be reflected, for example, in the intercorrelations among the observed measures.

Chapter **10** ~

Hiawatha Designs an Experiment

MAURICE G. KENDALL

1. Hiawatha, mighty hunter,
   He could shoot ten arrows upwards
   Shoot them with such strength and
       swiftness
   That the last had left the bowstring
   Ere the first to earth descended.
   This was commonly regarded
   As a feat of skill and cunning.

2. One or two sarcastic spirits
   Pointed out to him, however,
   That it might be much more useful
   If he sometimes hit the target.
   Why not shoot a little straighter
   And employ a smaller sample?

3. Hiawatha, who at college
   Majored in applied statistics,
   Consequently felt entitled
   To instruct his fellow men on
   Any subject whatsoever,
   Waxed exceedingly indignant
   Talked about the law of error,
   Talked about truncated normals,
   Talked of loss of information,
   Talked about his lack of bias,
   Pointed out that in the long run
   Independent observations
   Even though they missed the target

Had an average point of impact
Very near the spot he aimed at
(With the possible exception
Of a set of measure zero).

4. This, they said, was rather doubtful.
   Anyway, it didn't matter
   What resulted in the long run;
   Either he must hit the target
   Much more often than at present
   Or himself would have to pay for
   All the arrows that he wasted.

5. Hiawatha, in a temper,
   Quoted parts of R. A. Fisher
   Quoted Yates and quoted Finney
   Quoted yards of Oscar Kempthorne
   Quoted reams of Cox and Cochran
   Quoted Anderson and Bancroft
   Practically *in extenso*
   Trying to impress upon them
   That what actually mattered
   Was to estimate the error.

6. One or two of them admitted
   Such a thing might have its uses.
   Still, they said, he might do better
   If he shot a little straighter.

7. Hiawatha, to convince them,
   Organized a shooting contest
   Laid out in the proper manner
   By experimental methods
   Recommended in the textbooks

This poem is reprinted from the *American Statistician*, 1959, with the permission of the author and the American Statistical Association.

(Mainly used for tasting tea, but
Sometimes used in other cases)
Randomized his shooting order
In factorial arrangements
Used the theory of Galois
Fields of ideal polynomials,
Got a nicely balanced layout
And successfully confounded
Second-order interactions.

8. All the other tribal marksmen
Ignorant, benighted creatures,
Of experimental set-ups
Spent their time of preparation
Putting in a lot of practice
Merely shooting at a target.

9. Thus it happened in the contest
That their scores were most impressive
With one notable exception
This (I hate to have to say it)
Was the score of Hiawatha,
Who, as usual, shot his arrows
Shot them with great strength and
     swiftness
Managing to be unbiased
Not, however, with his salvo
Managing to hit the target.

10. There, they said to Hiawatha
That is what we all expected.

11. Hiawatha, nothing daunted,
Called for pen and called for paper
Did analyses of variance
Finally produced the figures
Showing, beyond peradventure,
Everybody else was biased

And the variance components
Did not differ from each other
Or from Hiawatha's.
(This last point, one should acknowledge
Might have been much more convincing
If he hadn't been compelled to
Estimate his own component
From experimental plots in
Which the values all were missing.
Still, they didn't understand it
So they couldn't raise objections.
This is what so often happens
With analyses of variance.)

12. All the same, his fellow tribesmen
Ignorant, benighted heathens,
Took away his bow and arrows,
Said that though my Hiawatha
Was a brilliant statistician
He was useless as a bowman.
As for variance components,
Several of the more outspoken
Made primeval observations
Hurtful to the finer feelings
Even of a statistician.

13. In a corner of the forest
Dwells alone my Hiawatha
Permanently cogitating
On the normal law of error,
Wondering in idle moments
Whether an increased precision
Might perhaps be rather better,
Even at the risk of bias,
If thereby one, now and then, could
Register upon the target.

Chapter 11

Standards for Educational and

Psychological Tests and Manuals

DEVELOPMENT AND SCOPE OF THE STANDARDS

Psychological and educational tests are used in arriving at decisions which may

This material is reprinted with the permission of the copyright holder, the American Psychological Association.

Standards for Educational and Psychological Tests and Manuals has been approved by the governing bodies of the American Psychological Association (APA), the American Educational Research Association (AERA), and the National Council on Measurement in Education (NCME). The current statement constitutes a revision of two documents: (*a*) *Technical Recommendations for Psychological Tests and Diagnostic Techniques* which was prepared by a committee of the APA and published in March 1954 by this organization, and (*b*) *Technical Recommendations for Achievement Tests* which was put together by two committees of the AERA and the National Council on Measurements Used in Education (now known as the National Council on Measurement in Education—NCME) and issued under a January 1955, copyright by the National Education Association. An APA committee and a combined AERA-NCME committee were consolidated in late 1963 into one truly joint APA-AERA-NCME committee of eight members that worked as one body in the formulation of the present technical standards. The committee members were: John W. French, Cochairman, Committee on Test Standards, APA, William B. Michael, Cochairman, Committee on Test Standards, AERA-NCME, Oscar K. Buros, Herbert S. Conrad, Lee J. Cronbach, Max D. Engelhart, J. Raymond Gerberich, and Willard G. Warrington.

have great influence on the ultimate welfare of the persons tested, on educational points of view and practices, and on development and utilization of human resources. Test users, therefore, need to apply high standards of professional judgment in selecting and interpreting tests, and test producers are under obligation to produce tests which can be of the greatest possible service. The test producer, in particular, has the task of providing sufficient information about each test so that the users will know what reliance can safely be placed on it.

Professional workers agree that test manuals and associated aids to test users should be made complete, comprehensive, and unambiguous, and for this reason there have always been informal "test standards." Publishers and authors of tests have adopted standards for themselves, and standards have been proposed in textbooks and other publications. Through application of these standards, the best tests have attained a high degree of quality and usefulness.

Until 1954, however, there was no statement representing a consensus concerning what information is most helpful to the test consumer. In the absence of such a guide, it was inevitable that some tests did appear with less adequate supporting information than did others of the same type, and that facts about a test which some users regarded as indispensable had not been reported because they seemed to the test producer to be relatively unimportant or, perhaps, too revealing of a weakness in the test. The first report was the outcome of an attempt to survey the possible types of information that test producers might make available, to indicate roughly the relative importance of each type of information, and to make recommendations regarding test preparation and publication.

This second report brings the first ones up to date and takes account of 12 years of progress and of the helpful criticisms of many test publishers and users. Questionnaires and letters of inquiry were sent to professional and research workers in the area of educational and psychological measurement, and several open committee meetings and invitational conferences were held. The current report contains many of the suggestions made by scores of interested people—test authors, test publishers, research workers, college teachers of measurement, and public school personnel including counselors, administrators, curriculum coordinators, and teachers. The particular biases of the committee members are obviously present, although a conscientious effort was made to take a position, in use of technical vocabulary and statistical methodology, in harmony with the practices of the majority of research and professional personnel in the field of testing.

In 1966 as well as in 1954, issuing specifications for tests could indeed discourage the development of new types of tests. So many different sorts of tests are needed in present educational and psychological practice that limiting the kind or the specifications would not be sound procedure. Appropriate standardization of tests and manuals, however, need not interfere with innovation. One purpose of the revised recommendations presented here is to assist test producers in bringing out a wide variety of tests that will be suitable for all the different purposes for which tests should be used, and to make those tests as valuable as possible.

INFORMATION STANDARDS AS A GUIDE TO PRODUCERS AND USERS OF TESTS

As in the two previous sets of recommendations *the essential* principle underlying this document is that a test manual should carry information sufficient to enable any qualified user to make sound judgments regarding the usefulness and interpretation of the test. This goal means that certain research is required prior to release of a test for general use by psychologists or school personnel. The results should be reported or summarized in the manual, and the manual should help the reader to interpret these results.

A manual is to be judged not merely by its literal truthfulness, but by the impression it leaves with the reader. If the typical professional user is likely to obtain an inaccurate impression of the test from the manual, the manual is poorly written. Ideally, manuals would be tested in the field by comparing the conclusions of a group of typical readers with the judgment of measurement specialists regarding the test. In the absence of such trials, the standards proposed are intended to apply to the spirit and tone of the manual as well as to its literal statements.

A manual must often communicate information to many different groups. Many tests are used by classroom teachers or psychometrists with very limited training in testing. These users will not follow technical discussion or understand detailed statistical information. At the other extreme of the group of readers, the available information about any test should be sufficiently complete for specialists in the area to judge the technical adequacy of the test. Sometimes the more technical information can be presented in a supplementary handbook, but it is most important that there be made available to the person concerned with the test a sound basis for whatever judgments his duties require.

Although it is not appropriate to call for a particular level of validity and reliability, or otherwise to specify the nature of the test, it *is* appropriate to ask that the manual give the information necessary for the user to decide whether the accuracy, relevance, or standardization of the test makes it suitable for his purposes. *These standards of test description and reporting exist without a statement of minimum statistical specifications.*

The aim of the present standards is partly to make the requirements as to information accompanying published tests explicit and conveniently available. In arriving at those requirements, it has been necessary to judge what is presently the reasonable degree of compromise between pressures of cost and time, on the one hand, and the ideal, on the other. The test producer ordinarily spends large sums of money in developing and standardizing a test. Insofar as these recommendations indicate the kind of information that would be most valuable to the people who use tests, test authors and publishers can allocate their funds to gathering and reporting those data. The completion of predictive validity studies related to job criteria, for example, is essential before a vocational interest inventory can be used practically, but they are only a desirable addition for a values inventory and irrelevant for an inventory designed to diagnose mental disorders. These standards, therefore, represent an attempt to state what type of studies should be completed before a test is ready for release to the profession for operational use. They are already reached by many of the better tests.

TESTS TO WHICH THE STANDARDS APPLY

These recommended standards cover not only tests as narrowly defined, but also most *published* devices for diagnosis, prognosis, and evaluation. The standards apply to interest inventories, personality inventories, projective instruments and related clinical techniques, tests of aptitude or ability, and achievement tests—especially those in an educational setting. The same general types of information are needed for all these varieties of tests. General recommendations have been prepared with all these techniques and instruments in mind. Since each type of test presents certain special requirements, additional comments have been made to indicate specific applications of the standards to particular tests or techniques. Many principles of specific importance in measurement of achievement have been cited.

Tests can be arranged according to degree of development. The highest degree of development is needed for tests distributed for use in practical situations where the user is unlikely to carry out validity studies for himself. Such a user must assume that the test does measure what it is presumed to measure on the basis of its title and manual. For instance, if a clerical aptitude measure is used in vocational guidance under the assumption that this will predict success in office jobs, there is very little possibility that the counselor could himself determine the validity of the test for the wide range of office jobs to which his clients might go.

At the other extreme of the continuum are tests in the very beginning stages of their development. At this point, perhaps the investigator is not sure whether his test is measuring any useful variable. Sometimes, because the theory for interpreting the test is undeveloped, the author can restrict use of the test to situations where he himself knows the persons who will use the test, can personally caution them as to its limitations, and can use the research from these trials as a way of improving the test or the information about it.

Between these tests which are so to speak embryonic and the tests which are released for practical application without local validity studies, are tests released for somewhat restricted use. There are many tests which have been examined sufficiently to indicate that they will probably be useful tools for psychologists, but which are released with the expectation that the user will verify suggested clinical interpretations by studying the subsequent behavior of persons in treatment. Examples are certain tests of spatial ability, and some inventories measuring such traits as introversion.

The present standards apply to devices which are distributed for use as a basis for practical judgments rather than solely for research. Most tests which are made available for use in schools, clinics, and industry are of this practical nature. Tests released for operational use should be prepared with the greatest care. They should be released to the general user only after their developer has gathered information which will permit the users to know for what purpose the test can be trusted. These statements regarding recommended information apply with especial force to tests distributed to users who have only that information which is provided in the test manual and other accessories. In the preparation of the standards, no attention was paid to tests which are privately distributed and circulated only to specially trained users. The standards also do not apply to tests presented in journal articles, unless the articles are intended to fulfill the functions of a manual.

A brief discussion of problems of projective techniques is needed here because of the opinion occasionally voiced that these devices are so unlike other testing procedures that they cannot be judged according to the same standards. Even though the data from projective tests are more often qualitative than quantitative, these devices should be accompanied by appropriate evidence on validity, reliability, and standards of scoring and interpretation. A projective test author need not identify his test's validity by correlating it with any simple criterion. But if he goes so far as to

make any generalization about what "most people see" or what "schizophrenics rarely do," he is making an out-and-out statistical claim and should be held to the usual rules for supporting it. Obviously, when quantitative information is asked for in the standards, it is expected to apply where a quantitative kind of claim has been made. If a projective test makes no such claim, a quantitative standard would not be meaningful for it.

On the other hand, clinicians sometimes forget that the words "more," "usual," "typical," and the like are *quantity* words. Any textual discourse containing such words, or any verbal statement describing a correspondence between test performance and personality structure is making a quantitative claim. The only difference between such a verbal statement and a statistical table is the relative exactness of the latter. For this reason, many of the standards apply to aspects of projective instruments for which verbal rather than numerical interpretations are suggested.

THREE LEVELS OF STANDARDS

Manuals can never give all the information that might be desirable, because of economic limitations. At the same time, restricting this statement of recommendations solely to essential or indispensable information might tend to discourage reporting of additional information. To avoid curtailment of the presentation of information in test manuals, recommendations are grouped in three levels: ESSENTIAL, VERY DESIRABLE, and DESIRABLE. Each proposed requirement is judged in the light of its importance and the feasibility of attaining it.

The statements listed as ESSENTIAL are intended to represent the consensus of present-day thinking concerning what is normally required for operational use of a test. Any test presents some unique problems, and it is undesirable that standards should bind the producer of a novel test to an inappropriate procedure or form of reporting. The ESSENTIAL standards indicate what information will be needed for most tests in their usual applications. When a test producer fails to satisfy this need, he should do so only as a considered judgment. In any single test, there may be some ESSENTIAL standards which do not apply.

If some type of ESSENTIAL information is not available on a given test, it is important to help the reader recognize that the research on the test is incomplete in this respect. A test manual can satisfy all the ESSENTIAL standards by clear statements of what research has been done and by avoidance of misleading statements. It will not be necessary to perform much additional research to satisfy the standards, but only to discuss the test so that the reader fully understands what is known (and unknown) about it.

The category VERY DESIRABLE is used to draw attention to types of information which contribute greatly to the user's understanding of the test. They have not been listed as ESSENTIAL for various reasons. For example, if it is very difficult to acquire information (e.g., long-term follow-up), such information cannot always be expected to accompany the test. However, the information is still very desirable, since many users wish it, but it is not classed as ESSENTIAL so long as its usefulness is debated.

The category DESIRABLE includes information which would be helpful, but less so than the ESSENTIAL and VERY DESIRABLE information. Test users welcome any information of this type the producer offers.

When a test is widely used, the producer has a greater responsibility for investigating it thoroughly and providing more extensive reports than when the test is limited or restricted in its use. The large sale of such tests makes such research financially possible. Therefore, the producer of a popular test can add more of the VERY DESIRABLE and DESIRABLE information in subsequent editions of the manual. For tests having limited sale, it is unreasonable to expect that as much of these two categories of information will be furnished. In making such facts available, the producer performs a service beyond the level that can reasonably be anticipated for most tests at this time.

CAUTIONS TO BE EXERCISED IN USE OF STANDARDS

Almost any test can be useful for some functions and in some situations, but even the best test can have damaging consequences if used inappropriately. Therefore, primary responsibility for improvement of testing rests on the shoulders of test users. These standards should serve to extend the professional training of these users so that they will make better use of the information about tests and the tests themselves. The standards draw attention to recent developments in thinking about tests and test analysis. The report should serve as a reminder regarding features to be considered in choosing tests for a particular program.

It is not inconceivable that many test makers and test publishers could fulfill to a highly adequate degree most of the standards presented and still produce a test that would be virtually worthless from the standpoint of fulfilling its intended or stated objectives. In the instance of educational achievement tests such a risk can be great. Thus one might have access to a carefully standardized achievement test for which both estimates of reliability and comprehensiveness of norms would be judged quite satisfactory; yet the test might fail almost completely to duplicate or to reflect basic instructional objectives or specific outcomes of the teaching-learning process. Too frequently in educational measurement attention is restricted to criterion-related validity. Efforts should also be directed toward both the careful construction of tests around the content and process objectives furnished by a two-way grid and the use of the judgment of curricular specialists concerning what is highly valid in reflecting the desired outcomes of instruction.

Professional thinking about tests is much influenced by test reviews, textbooks on testing, and courses in measurement. These standards may be helpful in improving such aids, for instance, by suggesting features especially significant to examine in a test review. The standards can be a teaching aid in measurement courses. It is important to note that publication of superior information about tests by no means guarantees that tests will be used well. The continual improvement of courses which prepare test users and of leadership in all institutions using tests is a responsibility in which everyone must share.

THE STANDARDS

A. DISSEMINATION OF INFORMATION

The test user needs information to help him select the test that is most adequate for a given purpose, and most of that information must come from the test producer. The practices of authors and publishers in furnishing information have varied. With some tests, the user is offered directions for administering and scoring the test, norms of uncertain origin, and virtually nothing more. In contrast, other tests have manuals that furnish extensive information on their development, their validity and reliability, the bases for their norms, the kinds of interpretations that are appropriate, and the uses for which the tests can best be employed.

A1. When a test is published for operational use, it should be accompanied by a manual (or other published and readily available information) that makes every reasonable effort to follow the recommendations in this report. ESSENTIAL

A1.1. If certain information needed to support interpretations suggested in the manual cannot be presented at the time the manual is published, the manual should satisfy the intent of standard A1 by pointing out the absence and importance of this information. ESSENTIAL

A1.2. Where the information is to extensive to be fully reported in the manual the ESSENTIAL information should be summarized and accompanied by references to other existing sources of information, such as technical supplements, articles, or books. VERY DESIRABLE

A1.21. When information about the test is provided by the author or publisher in a separate publication, that publication should meet the same standards of accuracy and freedom from misleading impressions as apply to the manual. ESSENTIAL

A1.22. Promotional material for a test should be accurate and complete and should not give the reader false impressions. ESSENTIAL

A2. The test and its manual should be revised at appropriate intervals. While no universal rule can be given, it would appear proper in most circumstances for the publisher to withdraw a test from the market, if the manual is 15 or more years old and no revision can be obtained. (See also C6.71.)

A2.1. Competent studies of the test following its publication, whether the results are favorable or unfavorable to the test, should be taken into account in revised editions of the manual or its supplementary reports. Pertinent studies by investigators other than the test authors and publishers should be included. VERY DESIRABLE

A2.2. When new information obtained by the test author or others indicates significant facts and recommendations presented in the manual to be incorrect, a revised manual should be issued promptly. ESSENTIAL

A2.3. When the test is revised or a new form is issued, the manual should be suitably revised to take changes in the test into account. ESSENTIAL

A2.31. If a short form of the test is prepared by reducing the number of items or organizing a portion of the test into a separate form, new evidence should be obtained and reported for that shorter test. ESSENTIAL

A2.32. When a short form is prepared from a test, the manual should present evidence that the items in the short form represent the items in the long form or measure the same characteristics as the long form. VERY DESIRABLE

A2.4. When a test is issued in revised form the new copyright date should be indicated on both the test and the manual. The nature and extent of the revision and the comparability of data between the old test and the revised test should be explicitly stated. Dates should be given for the collection of new data and the establishment of new norms. ESSENTIAL

B. INTERPRETATION

Responsibility for making inferences as to the meaning and legitimate uses of test results in a particular setting rests with the user, but in making such judgments he is dependent upon the available information about the test.

The manual cannot fully prepare the user for interpretation of any test. He will sometimes have to make judgments that have not been substantiated by the published evidence. Thus the vocational counselor cannot expect to have regression equations available for each job about which he makes tentative predictions from test scores. The clinician must bring general data and theory into his interpretation of data from a personality inventory, because research on no instrument is complete. The degree to which the manual can be expected to prepare the user for accurate interpretation and effective use of the test varies with the type of test and the purpose for which it is used.

B1. The test, the manual, record forms, and other accompanying material should assist users to make correct interpretations of the test results. ESSENTIAL

B1.1. Names given to published tests, and to scores within tests, should be chosen to minimize the risk of misinterpretation by test purchasers and subjects. ESSENTIAL

B1.11. Devices for identifying interests and personality traits through self-report should be entitled "inventories," "questionnaires," or "checklists," rather than "tests." VERY DESIRABLE

B1.2. The manual should draw the user's attention to data that need to be taken into special account in the interpretation of test scores. VERY DESIRABLE

B1.3. When case studies are used in the manual to illustrate interpretations of test scores, the examples presented should include some relatively complicated cases where interpretation is somewhat ambiguous. VERY DESIRABLE

B1.4. If any systematic error resulting from testing conditions, regional factors, and other things, is likely to enter the test score, the manual should warn the user about it and discuss its probable size and direction. ESSENTIAL

B1.5. The manual should draw attention to, and warn against, any serious error of interpretation that is known to be frequent. ESSENTIAL

B2. The test manual should state implicitly the purposes and applications for which the test is recommended. ESSENTIAL

B2.1. If a test is intended for research use only, and is not distributed for operational use, that fact should be prominently stated in the accompanying materials. ESSENTIAL

B3. The test manual should indicate the qualifications required to administer the test and to interpret it properly. ESSENTIAL

The following categorization of tests has been found useful by the American Psychological Association:

Level A. Tests or aids that can adequately be administered, scored, and interpreted with the aid of the manual and a general orientation to the kind of institution or organization in which one is working (e.g., achievement or proficiency tests).

Level B. Tests or aids that require some technical knowledge of test construction and use, and of supporting psychological and educational fields such as statistics, individual differences, psychology of adjustment, personnel psychology, and guidance (e.g., aptitude tests, adjustment inventories applicable to normal populations).

Level C. Tests and aids that require substantial understanding of testing and supporting psychological fields, together with supervised experience in the use of these devices (e.g., projective tests, individual mental tests).

The manual might identify a test according to one of the foregoing levels, or might employ some form of statement more suitable for that test.

B3.1. The manual should not imply that the test is "self-interpreting," or that it may be interpreted by a person lacking proper training. ESSENTIAL

B3.2. Where a test is recommended for a variety of purposes or types of inference, the manual should indicate the amount of training required for each use. ESSENTIAL

B3.3. The manual should draw the user's attention to the kind of references with which he should become familiar before attempting to interpret the test results. The references might be to books or articles dealing with related psychological theory or with the particular test in question. VERY DESIRABLE

B4. Statements in the manual reporting relationships are by implication quantitative and should be stated as precisely as the data permit. If data to support such statements have not been collected, that fact should be made clear. ESSENTIAL

B4.1. When the term "significant" is employed, the manual should make clear whether statistical or practical significance is meant, and what practical significance the statistically significant reliable differences have. ESSENTIAL

B4.2. When the statistical significance of a relationship is reported, the statistical report should be in a form that makes clear the sensitivity or power of the significance test. ESSENTIAL

B4.3. The manual should clearly differentiate between an interpretation (*a*) that is applicable only to average tendencies in a group, and (*b*) that is applicable to an individual within the group. ESSENTIAL

B4.4. The manual should state clearly what interpretations are intended for each subscore as well as for the total test. ESSENTIAL (See also C1.2.)

C. VALIDITY

Validity information indicates the degree to which the test is capable of achieving certain aims. Tests are used for several types of judgment, and for each type of judgment, a different type of investigation is required to establish validity. For purposes of describing the uses for three kinds of validity coefficients, we may distinguish three of the rather numerous aims of testing:

1. *The test user wishes to determine how an individual performs at present in a universe of situations that the test situation is claimed to represent.* For example, most achievement tests used in schools measure the student's performance on a sample of questions intended to represent a certain phase of educational achievement or certain educational objectives.

2. *The test user wishes to forecast an individual's future standing or to estimate an individual's present standing on some variable of particular significance that is different from the test.* For example, an academic aptitude test may forecast grades, or a brief adjustment inventory may estimate what the outcome would be of a careful psychological examination.

3. *The test user wishes to infer the degree to which the individual possesses some hypothetical trait or quality (construct) presumed to be reflected in the test performance.* For example, he wants to know whether the individual stands high on some proposed abstract trait such as "intelligence" or "creativity" that cannot be observed directly. This may be done to learn something about the individual, or it may be done to study the test itself, to study its relationship to other tests, or to develop psychological theory.

Different types of tests are often used for each of the different aims, but this is not always the case. There is much overlap in types of tests and in the purposes for which they are used. Thus, a vocabulary test might be used (*a*) simply as a measure of present vocabulary, the universe being all the words in the language, (*b*) as a screening device to discriminate present or potential schizophrenics from organics, or (*c*) as a means of making inferences about "intellectual capacity."

To determine how suitable a test is for each of these uses, it is necessary to gather the appropriate sort of validity information. The kind of information to be gathered depends on the aim or aims of testing rather than on the type of test. The three aspects of validity corresponding to the three aims of testing may be named content validity, criterion-related validity, and construct validity.

Content validity is demonstrated by showing how well the content of the test samples the class situations or subject matter about which conclusions are to be drawn. Content validity is especially important for achievement and proficiency measures and for measures of adjustment or social behavior based on observation in selected situations. The manual should justify the claim that the test content represents the assumed universe of tasks, conditions, or processes. A useful way of looking at this universe of tasks or items is to consider it to comprise a *definition* of the achievement to be measured by the test. In the case of an educational achievement test, the content of the test may be regarded as a definition of (or a sampling from a population of) one or more educational objectives. The aptitudes, skills, and knowledges required of the student for successful test performance must be precisely the types of aptitudes, skills, and knowledges that the school wishes to develop in the students and to evaluate in terms of test scores. Thus evaluating the content validity of a test for a particular purpose is the same as subjectively recognizing the adequacy of a definition. This process is actually quite similar to the subjective evaluation of the criterion itself. Unless, however, the aim of an achievement test is specifically to forecast or substitute for some criterion, its correlation with a criterion is *not* a useful evaluation of the test.

Criterion-related validity is demonstrated by comparing the test scores with one or more external variables considered to provide a direct measure of the characteristic or behavior in question. This comparison may take the form of an expectancy table or, most commonly, a correlation relating the test score to a criterion measure. Predictive uses of tests include long-range forecasts of one or more measures of academic achievement, prediction of vocational success, and prediction of reaction to therapy. For such predictive uses the criterion data are collected concurrently with the test; for example, when one wishes to know whether a testing procedure can take the place of more elaborate procedures for diagnosing personality disorders. A test that is related to one or more concurrent criteria will not necessarily predict status on the same criterion at some later date.

Whether the criterion data should be collected concurrently with the testing or at a later time depends on whether the test is recommended for prediction or for assessment of present status.

Construct validity is evaluated by investigating what qualities a test measures, that is, by determining the degree to which certain explanatory concepts or constructs account for performance on the test. To examine construct validity requires a combination of logical and empirical attack. Essentially, studies of construct validity check on the theory underlying the test. The procedure involves three steps. First, the investigator inquires: From this theory, what hypotheses may we make regarding the behavior of persons with high and low scores? Second, he gathers data to test these hypotheses. Third, in light of the evidence, he makes an inference as to whether the theory is adequate to explain the data collected. If the theory fails to account for the data, he should revise the test interpretation, reformulate the theory, or reject the theory altogether. Fresh evidence would be required to demonstrate construct validity for the revised interpretation.

A simple procedure for investigating what a test measures is to correlate it with other tests. We would expect a valid test of numerical reasoning, for example, to correlate more highly with other numerical tests than with clerical perception tests. Another procedure is experimental. If it is hypothesized, for example, that form perception on a certain projective test indicates probable ability to function well under emotional stress, this inference may be checked by placing individuals in an experimental situation producing emotional stress and observing whether their behavior corresponds to the hypothesis.

Construct validity is ordinarily studied when the tester wishes to increase his understanding of the psychological qualities being measured by the test. A validity coefficient relating test to criterion, unless it is established in the context of some theory, yields no information about *why* the correlation is high or low, or about how one might improve the measurement. Construct validity is relevant when the tester accepts no existing measure as a definitive criterion of the quality with which he is concerned (e.g., in measuring a postulated drive such as need for achievement), or when a test will be used in so many diverse decisions that no single criterion applies (e.g., in identifying the ability of Peace Corps trainees to adapt to new cultures). Here the traits or qualities underlying test performance are of central importance. It must be remembered, however, that, without a study of criterion-related validity, a test developed for diagnosis or prediction can be regarded only as experimental.

These three aspects of validity are only conceptually independent, and only rarely is just one of them important in a particular situation. A complete study of a test would normally involve information about all types of validity. A first step in the preparation of a predictive (*criterion-related*) instrument may be to consider what *constructs* are likely to provide a basis for selecting or devising an effective test. Sampling from a *content* universe may also be an early step in producing a test whose use for *prediction* is the ultimate concern. Even after satisfactory *prediction* has been established, information regarding *construct* validity may make the test more useful; it may, for example, provide a basis for identifying situations other than the validating situation where the test is appropriate as a predictor. To analyze *construct* validity, all the knowledge regarding validity would be brought to bear.

The three concepts of validity are pertinent to all kinds of tests. It is the intended use of the test rather than its nature that determines what kind of evidence is required.

Intelligence or scholastic aptitude tests most often use criterion-related validity to show how well they are able to predict academic success in school or college, but the nature of the aptitudes measured is often judged from the content of the items,

and the place of the aptitude within the array of human abilities is deduced from correlations with other tests.

For achievement tests, content validity is usually of first importance. For example, a testing agency has a group of subject-matter specialists devise and select test items that they judge to cover the topics and mental processes relevant to the field represented by the test. Similarly, a teacher judges whether the final test in his course covers the kinds of situations about which he has been trying to teach his students certain principles or understandings. The teacher also judges content when he uses a published test, but he can appropriately investigate criterion-related validity by correlating this test with tests he has prepared or with other direct measures of his chief instructional objectives. When the same published achievement test is used for admissions testing, it may reasonably be checked against a later criterion of performance. In any theoretical discussion of what is being measured by the achievement test, a consideration of construct validity is required. Whether the score on a science achievement test, for example, reflects reading ability to a significant degree, and whether it measures understanding of scientific method rather than mere recall of facts are both questions about construct validity.

Development of a personality inventory will usually start with the assembly of items covering content the developer considers meaningful. Such inventories are then likely to be interpreted with the aid of theory; any such interpretation calls for evidence of construct validity. In addition, a personality inventory must have criterion-related validity, if, for example, it is to be used in screening military recruits who may be maladjusted.

Interest measures are usually intended to predict vocational or educational criteria, but many of them are also characterized by logical content and constructs. This makes it more likely that they can provide at least a rough prediction for the very many occupations and activities that exist and for which specific evidence of criterion-related validity has not been obtained.

For projective techniques, construct validity is the most important, although criterion-related validity using criteria collected either concurrently with the testing or afterwards may be pertinent if the instruments are to be used in making diagnostic classifications.

C1. The manual should report the validity of the test for each type of inference for which it is recommended. If its validity for some suggested interpretation has not been investigated, that fact should be made clear. ESSENTIAL

C1.1. Statements in the manual about validity should refer to the validity of particular interpretations or of particular types of decision. ESSENTIAL

C1.2. Wherever interpretation of subscores, score differences, or profiles is suggested, the evidence in the manual justifying such interpretation should be made explicit. ESSENTIAL (Also see B4.4.)

C1.21. If the manual for an inventory suggests that the user consider responses to separate items as a basis for personality assessment, it should either present evidence supporting this use or call attention to the absence of such data. The manual should warn the reader that inferences based on responses to single items are subject to extreme error, hence should be used only to direct further inquiry, as, perhaps, in a counseling interview. ESSENTIAL

C2. Item-test correlations should not be presented in the manual as evidence of criterion-related validity, and they should be referred to as item-discrimination indices, not as item-validity coefficients. ESSENTIAL

Content validity

C3. If a test performance is to be interpreted as a sample of performance or a definition of performance in some universe of situations, the manual should indicate clearly what universe is represented and how adequate is the sampling. ESSENTIAL

C3.1. When experts have been asked to judge whether items are an appropriate sample of a universe or are correctly scored, the manual should describe the relevant professional experience and qualifications of the experts and the directions under which they made their judgments. VERY DESIRABLE

C3.11. When the items are selected by experts, the extent of agreement among independent judgments should be reported. DESIRABLE

C3.2. In achievement tests of educational outcomes, the manual should report the classification system used for selecting items. DESIRABLE

C3.21. Where an achievement test has been prepared according to a two-way topic-by-process outline, that outline should be presented in the manual, with a list of the items identified with each cell of the outline. VERY DESIRABLE

C3.3. Conclusions in the manual based on logical analysis of content should be carefully distinguished from those based on empirical findings. ESSENTIAL

C3.4. Any statement in the manual of the relation of items to a course of study (or other source of content) should mention the date when the course of study was prepared. ESSENTIAL

Criterion-related validity

C4. All measures of criteria should be described completely and accurately. The manual should comment on the adequacy of the criterion. Whenever feasible, it should draw attention to significant aspects of performance that the criterion measure does not reflect and to irrelevant factors that are likely to affect it. ESSENTIAL

C4.1. The manual should report the validity of the test for each criterion about which a recommendation is made. If validity for some recommended interpretation has not been tested, that fact should be made clear. ESSENTIAL

C4.2. For any type of prediction the manual should report test-criterion correlations for a variety of institutions or situations. Where validity studies have been confined to a limited range of situations, the manual should remind the reader of the risks involved in generalizing to other types of situations. ESSENTIAL

C4.3. Since the criterion measure is a sample of possible criterion data, the agreement of that sample with other similar samples that might have been used as measures of the criterion should be reported. If evidence on this question cannot be given, the author should make this clear and should discuss the probable extent of agreement of the sample with other samples as judged from indirect evidence. VERY DESIRABLE

C4.31. If validity coefficients are corrected for errors of measurement *in the criterion*, the computation of the reliability coefficient of the criterion should be explained, and both corrected and uncorrected coefficients should be reported in the manual. ESSENTIAL

C4.32. For users who are technically oriented, breakdown of test variance into the following sources is appropriate: variance relevant to the criterion, variance explained as form-to-form or trial-to-trial inconsistency, and a reliable-irrelevant remainder. VERY DESIRABLE

C4.4. The time elapsing between the test administration and the collection of criterion data should be reported in the manual. If the criterion data are collected over a period of time, beginning and ending data should be included. ESSENTIAL

C4.41. If a test is recommended for long-term predictions, but comparisons with concurrent criteria only are presented, the manual should emphasize that the validity of predictions is undetermined. ESSENTIAL

C4.5. The criterion score should be determined independently of test scores. The manual should describe any precautions taken to avoid contamination of the criterion or should warn the reader of possible contamination. ESSENTIAL

C4.6. When the validity of a test is appraised by its agreement with psychiatric diagnoses, the diagnostic terms or categories should be defined specifically and clearly described. VERY DESIRABLE

C4.61. When the validity of a test is appraised by its agreement with psychiatric judgment, the training, experience, and professional status of the psychologist(s) or psychiatrist(s) should be stated, and the nature and extent of his contacts with the patients should be reported. VERY DESIRABLE

C4.7. When the validity of a test for predicting occupational performance is reported, the manual should describe the duties of the workers as well as give their job titles. VERY DESIRABLE

C4.71. Where a wide range of duties is subsumed under a given occupational label, the test user should be warned against assuming that only one pattern of interests or abilities is compatible with the occupation. VERY DESIRABLE

C4.72. The amount and kind of any schooling or job training received by the subjects between the time of testing and the time of criterion collection should be stated. VERY DESIRABLE

C4.8. When the validity of a test for predicting grades in a course is reported, the reader of the manual should be given a reasonably clear understanding regarding the types of performance required in the course, the nature of instructional method, and the way in which performance is measured. If the test was administered after the course was started, this fact should be specified. ESSENTIAL

C4.9. Local collection of evidence on criterion-related validity is frequently more useful than published data. In such cases the manual should suggest appropriate emphasis on local validity studies, giving advice on how to conduct the studies and how to set up usable expectancy tables or other means for interpreting the results of the studies. VERY DESIRABLE

Criterion-related validity sample

C5. The sample employed in a validity study and the conditions under which testing is done should be consistent with the recommendations made in the manual. They should be described sufficiently for the user to judge whether the reported validity is pertinent to his situation. ESSENTIAL

C5.1. Basic statistics that should be reported in the manual for the validation sample are measures of central tendency and variability. ESSENTIAL

C5.11. If the test scores that are analyzed have a distribution markedly different from the distribution of the group with whom the test is ordinarily to be used, correlations or other measures of discrimination in the group to whom the test is likely to be given should be estimated. In reporting such estimates, the manual should cite the original coefficient, the distribution characteristics used in making the new estimate, and the statistical procedure. ESSENTIAL

C5.2. The validity sample should be described in the manual in terms of those variables known to be related to the quality tested, such as age, sex, socioeconomic status, and level of education. Any selective factor determining the composition of the sample should be indicated. ESSENTIAL

C5.3. If the validity sample is made up of records accumulated haphazardly or voluntarily submitted by test users, this fact should be stated in the manual, and the test user should be warned that the group is not a systematic or random sample of any specifiable population. Probable selective factors and their presumed influence on test variables should be stated. ESSENTIAL

C5.4. The validity of a test should be determined on subjects who are at the age or in the same educational or vocational situation as the persons for whom the test is recommended in practice. Any deviation from this requirement should be described in the manual. ESSENTIAL

C5.41. If an ability test is to be used for educational or occupational selection, its validity should be established using subjects who are actual candidates and who are therefore motivated to perform well. If the subjects used in a validity study did not believe that their test scores would be used in making decisions about them, this fact should be made clear. VERY DESIRABLE

C5.5. If the validity of the test is likely to be different for subsamples that can be identified when the test is given, the manual should report the results for each subsample separately or should report that no differences were found. VERY DESIRABLE

C5.6. In collecting data for a validity study, the person who administers, scores, or interprets the test should have only that information about the examinees that is ordinarily expected to be available in practical use of the test. If there is any possible contamination associated with prior favorable or unfavorable knowledge about the examinees, the manual should discuss its effect on the outcome of the study. ESSENTIAL

Criterion-related validity analysis

C6. Any statistical analysis of criterion-related validity should be reported in the manual in a form from which the reader can determine what confidence is to be placed in judgments or predictions regarding the individual. ESSENTIAL

C6.1. Statistical procedures that are well known and readily interpreted should be preferred in the manual for reporting validity. Any uncommon statistical techniques should be explained, and references to descriptions of them should be given. ESSENTIAL

C6.11. A report in the manual or elsewhere concerning the criterion-related validity of tests should ordinarily include: (*a*) one or more correlation coefficients of a familiar type, (*b*) descriptions of the efficiency with which the test separates criterion groups, (*c*) expectancy tables, or (*d*) charts that graphically illustrate the relationship between test and criterion. ESSENTIAL

C6.12. If a test is suggested for the differential diagnosis of patients, the manual should include evidence of the test's ability to place individuals in diagnostic groups rather than merely to separate diagnosed abnormal cases from the normal population. ESSENTIAL

C6.2. An overall validity coefficient should be supplemented with a report regarding the regression slope and intercept and the standard error of estimate at different points along the score range. VERY DESIRABLE

C6.3. When information other than the test scores is known to have an appreciable degree of criterion-related validity and is ordinarily available to the prospective test user, the manual should report the validity of the other information and the resulting multiple correlation when the new test information is combined with it. ESSENTIAL

C6.31. If the validity of a test is demonstrated by comparing groups that differ on the criterion, the manual should report whether and by how much the groups differ on other available variables that are relevant. VERY DESIRABLE

C6.4. When a scoring key or the selection of items is based on a tryout sample, the manual should report validity coefficients based on one or more separate cross-validation samples, rather than on the tryout sample or on a larger group of which the tryout sample is a part. ESSENTIAL

C6.5. If the manual recommends certain regression weights for combining scores on the test or for combining the test with other variables, the validity of the composite should be based on a cross-validation sample. VERY DESIRABLE

C6.6. Whenever it is proposed that decisions be based on a complex nonlinear combination of scores, it should be shown that this combination has greater validity than some simpler linear combination. VERY DESIRABLE

C6.7. To ensure the continued correct interpretation of scores, the validity of the suggested interpretations should be rechecked periodically and the results reported in subsequent editions of the manual. VERY DESIRABLE

C6.71. If the validity of a suggested test interpretation has not been checked within 15 or 20 years, the test should be withdrawn from general sale and distributed, if at all, only to persons who will conduct their own validity studies. DESIRABLE (See A2.)

Construct validity

C7. If the author proposes to interpret the test as a measure of a theoretical variable (ability, trait, or attitude), the proposed interpretation should be fully stated. The interpretation of the theoretical construct should be distinguished from interpretations arising under other theories. ESSENTIAL

C7.1. The manual should indicate the extent to which the proposed interpretation has been substantiated and should summarize investigations of the hypotheses derived from the theory. ESSENTIAL

C7.11. Each study investigating a theoretical inference regarding the test should be summarized in a way that covers both the operational procedures of the study and the implications of the results for the theory. VERY DESIRABLE

C7.12. The manual should report correlations between the test and other relevant tests for which the interpretation is relatively clear. VERY DESIRABLE

C7.13. The manual should report the correlations of the test with other available measures of the same attributes that have been generally accepted. VERY DESIRABLE

C7.2. The manual should report evidence on the extent to which constructs other than those proposed by the author account for variance in scores on the test. VERY DESIRABLE

C7.21. The manual for any specialized test or inventory used in educational selection and guidance should report its correlation with a well-established measure of verbal and quantitative ability in an appropriately representative population. VERY DESIRABLE

C7.22. Whenever a test has been included in factorial studies that indicate the proportion of the test variance attributable to widely known reference factors, such information should be presented in the manual. VERY DESIRABLE

C7.23. For any personality measure, evidence should be presented on the extent to which scores are susceptible to an attempt by the examinee to present a false or unduly favorable picture of himself. VERY DESIRABLE (See C5.41.)

C7.24. If a personality questionnaire calls for "yes-no" or "agree-disagree" responses, the manual should report evidence on the degree to which the scores reflect a set to acquiesce. DESIRABLE

C7.25. If a test given with a time limit is to be interpreted as measuring a hypothetical psychological attribute not specifically related to speed, evidence should be present in the manual concerning the effect of speed on the test scores and on their correlation with other variables. ESSENTIAL

C7.26. Where a low correlation or small difference between groups is advanced as evidence *against* some counterinterpretation, the manual should report the confidence interval for the parameter. The manual should also correct for or discuss any errors of measurement that may have lowered the apparent relationship. DESIRABLE

D. RELIABILITY

Reliability refers to the accuracy (consistency and stability) of measurement by a test. Any direct measurement of such consistency obviously calls for a comparison between at least two measurements. (Whereas "accuracy" is a general expression, the terms "consistency" and "stability" are needed to describe, respectively, form-associated and time-associated reliability.) The two measurements may be obtained by *retesting* an individual with the identical test. Aside from practical limitations, retesting is not a theoretically desirable method of determining a reliability coefficient if, as usual, the items that constitute the test are only one of many sets (actual or hypothetical) that might equally well have been used to measure the particular ability or trait. Thus, there is ordinarily no reason to suppose that *one* set of (say) 50 vocabulary items is especially superior (or inferior) to another comparable (equivalent) set of 50. In this case it appears desirable to determine not only the degree of response variation by the subject from one occasion to the next (as is accomplished by the retest method), but also the extent of sampling fluctuation involved in selecting a given set of 50 items. These two objectives are accomplished most commonly by correlating scores on the original set of 50 items with scores by the same subjects on an independent but similar set of 50 items—an "alternate form" of the original 50. If the effect of content-sampling *alone* is sought (without the effects of response variability by the subject), or if it is not practical to undertake testing on two different occasions, a test of 100 items may be administered. Then the test may be divided into two sets of 50 odd-numbered items and 50 even-numbered items; the correlation between scores on the odd and the even sets is a "split-half" or "odd-even" correlation, from which a reliability (consistency) coefficient for the entire test of 100 items may be estimated by the Spearman-Brown formula (involving certain generally reasonable assumptions). Essentially the same type of estimated reliability coefficient may be obtained from item-analysis data through use of the Kuder-Richardson formulas (which involve various assumptions, some more reasonable and exact than others). It should be noted that despite the possible heterogeneity of content, the odd-even correlation between the sets of items may be quite high if the items are easy and if the test is administered with a short time limit. Such odd-even correlations are in a sense spurious, since they merely reflect the expected correlation between two sets of scores each of which is a measure of rate of work. (See D5.2.)

From the preceding discussion, it is clear that *different methods of determining the reliability coefficient take account of different sources of error.* Thus, from one testing to the other, the retest method is affected not only by response variability of the subjects but also by differences in administration (most likely if different persons administer the test on the two occasions). Reliability coefficients based on the single administration of a test ignore response variability and the particular administrative conditions: their effects on scores simply do not appear as errors of measurement. Hence, "reliability coefficient" is a generic term referring to various types of evidence; each type of evidence suggests a different meaning. It is essential that *the method used to derive any reliability coefficient should be clearly described.*

As a generic term reliability refers to many types of evidence, each of which describes the agreement or consistency to be expected among similar observations. Each type of evidence takes into account certain kinds of errors or inconsistencies and not others. The operation of measurement may be viewed as a sample of behavior; in a typical aptitude or achievement test the person is observed on a particular date as he responds to a particular set of questions or stimuli, and his responses are recorded and scored by a particular tester or system. The occasion is a sample from the period of time within which the same general inquiry would be pertinent; some sampling error is involved in selecting any one date of observation. The items that constitute the test are only one of many sets (actual or hypothetical) that might have been used to measure the same ability or trait. The choices of a particular test apparatus, test administrator, observer, or scorer, are also sampling operations. Each such act of sampling has some influence on the test score. It is valuable for the test user to know how much a particular score would be likely to change if any one of these conditions of measurement were altered.

There are various components that may contribute to inconsistency among observations: (*a*) response variation by the subject (due to changes in physiological efficiency, or in such psychological factors as motivation, effort, or mood): these may be especially important in inventories of personality; (*b*) variations in test content or the test situation (in "situational tests" which include interacting persons as part of the situation, this source of variation can be relatively large); (*c*) variations in administration (either through variations in physical factors, such as temperature, noise, or apparatus functioning, or in psychological factors, such as variation in the technique or skill of different test administrators or raters); and (*d*) variations in the process of observation. In addition to these errors of observation, scoring-error variance in test scores reflects variation in the process of scoring responses as well as mistakes in recording, transferring, or reading of scores.

The estimation of clearly labeled components of error variance is the most informative outcome of a reliability study, both for the test developer wishing to improve the reliability of his instrument and for the user desiring to interpret test scores with maximum understanding. The analysis of error variance calls for the use of an appropriate *experimental* design. There are many different multivariate designs that can be used in reliability studies; the choice of design for studying the particular test is to be determined by its intended interpretation and by the practical limitations upon experimentation. In general, where more information can be obtained at little increase in cost, the test developer should obtain and report that information.

Although estimation of clearly labeled components of error variance is the most informative outcome of a reliability study, this approach is not yet prominent in reports on tests. In the more familiar reliability study the investigator obtains two measures and correlates them, or derives a correlation coefficient by applying one of several formulas to part or item scores within a test. Such a correlation is often interpreted as a ratio of "true variance" to "true variance plus error variance." Many different coefficients, each involving its own definition of "true" and "error" variance, may be derived from a multivariate reliability experiment with the presence of controls for such factors as those of content, time, and mode of administration. Hence, any single correlation is subject to considerable misinterpretation unless the investigator makes clear just what sampling errors are considered to be error in the particular coefficient he reports. The correlation between two test forms presented on different days has a different significance from an internal-consistency coefficient, for example, because the latter allocates day-to-day fluctuations in a person's efficiency to the true rather than to the error portion of the score variance.

In the present set of *Standards,* the terminology by which the 1954 *Technical Recommendations* classified coefficients into several types (e.g., coefficient of equivalence) has been discarded. Such a terminological system breaks down as more adequate statistical analyses are applied and methods are more adequately described. Hence it is recommended that test authors work out suitable phrases to convey the meaning of whatever coefficients they report; as an example, the expression, "the stability of measurements by different test forms as determined over a 7-day interval," although lengthy, will be reasonably free from ambiguity.

General principles

D1. The test manual should report evidence of reliability that permits the reader to judge whether scores are sufficiently dependable for the recommended uses of the test. If any of the necessary evidence has not been collected, the absence of such information should be noted. ESSENTIAL

D1.1. The test manual should furnish, in so far as feasible, a quantitative analysis of the total inconsistency of measurement into its major identifiable components; viz., fluctuations or inconsistency in responses of the subject; inconsistency or heterogeneity within the sample of test content (such as the stimulus items, questions, and situations); inconsistencies in administration of the test; inconsistency among scorers, raters, or units of apparatus; and mechanical errors of scoring. VERY DESIRABLE

D1.2. A measure of reliability or errors of measurement should be reported in the test manual even when a test is recommended solely for empirical prediction of criteria. VERY DESIRABLE

D1.3. The standards for reliability should apply to every score, subscore, or combination of scores (such as a sum, difference, or quotient) which is recommended by the test manual (either explicitly or implicitly) for other than merely tentative or pilot use. ESSENTIAL

D1.4. For instruments that yield a profile having a low reliability of differences between scores, the manual should explicitly caution the user against casual interpretation of differences between scores, except as a source of tentative information requiring external verification. ESSENTIAL

D1.5. The manual should state the minimum difference between two scores ordinarily required for statistical significance. VERY DESIRABLE

D2. In the test manual reports on reliability or error of measurement, procedures, and samples should be described sufficiently to permit a user to judge to what extent the evidence is applicable to the person and problems with which he is concerned. ESSENTIAL

D2.1. The reliability of a school intelligence or achievement test should generally be estimated separately for each of many classes at each of several grade levels within each of several school systems. The mean and standard deviation for each sample should be reported in the test manual, along with its reliability coefficients. VERY DESIRABLE

D2.2. The reliability sample should be described in the test manual in terms of any selective factors related to the variable being measured. ESSENTIAL

D2.21. Demographic information, such as distributions of the subjects with respect to age, sex, socioeconomic level, intellectual level, employment status or history, and minority group membership should be given in the test manual. DESIRABLE

D2.3. If reliability coefficients are corrected for range, both the uncorrected and the corrected coefficients should be reported in the test manual, together with the standard deviation of the group actually tested and the standard deviation assumed for the corrected sample. ESSENTIAL

D2.4. When a test is recommended or ordinarily employed to make discriminations within various particular categories of persons, the reliability and error of measurement within that category should be independently investigated and reported in the test manual. ESSENTIAL

D2.41. When reported in the test manual, a reliability analysis for an intelligence or achievement test intended to effect usable differentiation within a single school grade should be based on children within the given grade only, not on a multigrade sample with a wider range of ability. ESSENTIAL

D2.42. The test manual should report whether the error of measurement varies at different score levels. If there is significant change in the error of measurement from level to level, this fact should be reported. VERY DESIRABLE

D3. Reports of reliability studies should ordinarily be expressed in the test manual in terms of variances for error components (or their square roots) or standard errors of measurement, or product-moment reliability coefficients. ESSENTIAL

D3.1. The manual should make clear that measures of reliability do not demonstrate the criterion-related validity of the test. ESSENTIAL

Comparability of forms

D4. If two forms of a test are published, both forms being intended for possible use with the same subjects, the means and variances of the two forms should be reported in the test manual along with the coefficient of correlation between the two sets of scores. If necessary evidence is not provided, the test manual should warn the reader against assuming comparability. ESSENTIAL

D4.1. Whenever feasible, the test manual should present a summary of item statistics for each form, such as a frequency distribution of item difficulties and of indices of item discrimination. DESIRABLE

D4.2. Whenever the content of the items can be described meaningfully, it is advisable that a comparative analysis of the forms be presented in the test manual to show how similar they are. VERY DESIRABLE

D4.3. Whenever two sets of performances on a test are correlated to determine comparability and stability, the interval of time between the testings should be specified in the test manual. ESSENTIAL

D4.4. To show comparability over the range of scores, the test manual should present a table showing what raw scores on the two forms occupy the same percentile positions in the population. The data may be obtained from appropriately stratified samples adequately large in relation to the reported size of the standard deviation (stratified on sex and other salient variables). If one sample receives each form, care must be taken to control differential practice and fatigue effects through use of an appropriate design of test administration. DESIRABLE

Internal consistency

D5. If the test manual suggests that a score is a measure of a generalized, homogeneous trait, evidence of internal consistency should be reported. ESSENTIAL

D5.1. Estimates of internal consistency should be determined by the split-half methods or methods of the Kuder-Richardson type, if these can properly be used on the data under examination. Any other measure of internal consistency which the author wishes to report in addition should be carefully explained in the test manual. ESSENTIAL

D5.2. Whenever reliability coefficients based upon internal analysis are reported, the test manual should present evidence that speed of work has a negligible influence on scores. ESSENTIAL

D5.3. When a test consists of separately scored parts or sections, the correlation between the parts or sections should be reported in the test manual along with relevant means and standard deviations. DESIRABLE

D5.31. If the test manual reports the correlation between a subtest and a total score, it should be pointed out that part of this correlation is artificial. VERY DESIRABLE

D5.4. If several questions within a test are experimentally linked so that the reaction to one question influences the reaction to another, the entire group of questions should be treated preferably as an "item" when data arising from application of the split-half or appropriate analysis-of-variance methods are reported in the test manual. ESSENTIAL

D5.5. If a test can be divided into sets of items of different content, and if it is desired to estimate its correlation with another test of similarly distributed content, the internal analysis reported in the test manual should be determined by procedures designed for such tests. VERY DESIRABLE

Comparisons over time

D6. The test manual should indicate to what extent test scores are stable, that is, how nearly constant the scores are likely to be if a test is repeated after time has lapsed. The manual should also describe the effect of any such variation on the usefulness of the test. The time interval to be considered depends on the nature of the test and on what interpretation of the test scores is recommended. ESSENTIAL

D6.1. In any report in the test manual concerning the determination of the stability of scores by repeated testing, alternate forms of the test should have been used to minimize recall of specific answers, especially if the time interval is not long enough to assure forgetting. VERY DESIRABLE

D6.11. Every time the correlation between scores on two halves of a given form or on two alternate forms of a test is reported in the test manual, the split-half coefficient, Spearman-Brown index, or a Kuder-Richardson Formula 20 estimate of consistency should be cited for the given form or for each alternate form along with a coefficient reflecting stability of the scores on each form from one administration to a subsequent administration. VERY DESIRABLE

D6.2. The report in a test manual of a study of consistency over time should state what period of time elapsed between tests and should give the mean and standard deviation of scores at each testing, as well as the correlation. ESSENTIAL

D6.3. If test scores are likely to be retained in a person's record to be consulted as new questions about him arise, the test manual should indicate the length of time following the test during which the score may continue to be used effectively for the recommended purposes. The manual should report evidence regarding the extent to which scores change within and subsequent to this interval. VERY DESIRABLE

D6.31. In reporting on stability, the test

manual should describe the relevant experience or education of the group between testings. ESSENTIAL

E. ADMINISTRATION AND SCORING

E1. The directions for administration should be presented in the test manual with sufficient clarity and emphasis that the test user can duplicate, and will be encouraged to duplicate, the administrative conditions under which the norms and the data on reliability and validity were obtained. ESSENTIAL

E1.1. The directions published in the test manual should be complete enough that persons tested will understand the task in the way the author intended. ESSENTIAL

E1.12. The directions to the examinee in the test manual should clearly point out critical matters, such as instructions on guessing, time limits, and procedures for marking answer sheets. VERY DESIRABLE

E1.2. If expansion or elaboration of instructions described in the test manual is permitted, the conditions under which they may be done should be clearly stated either in the form of general rules or in terms of giving numerous examples, or both. VERY DESIRABLE

E1.21. If in rare instances the examiner is allowed freedom and judgment in elaborating instructions or giving examples, empirical data should be presented in the test manual regarding the effect of variation in examiner procedures upon scores. If empirical data on the effect of variation in examiner procedures are not available, this fact should be stated explicitly, and the user should be warned that the effects of such variations are unknown. DESIRABLE

E2. The procedures for scoring the test should be presented in the test manual with a maximum of detail and clarity so as to reduce the likelihood of scoring error. ESSENTIAL

E2.1. The test manual should furnish scoring instructions which maximize the accuracy of scoring an objective test by outlining a procedure for checking the obtained scores for computational or clerical errors. VERY DESIRABLE

E2.2. Where subjective processes enter into the scoring of a test, evidence on the degree of agreement between independent scorings under operational conditions should be presented in the test manual. If such evidence is not provided, the manual should draw attention to

scoring variations as a possible significant source of errors of measurement. VERY DESIRABLE

E2.21. The bases for scoring and the procedures for training the scorers should be presented in the test manual in sufficient detail to permit other scorers to reach the degree of agreement reported in studies of scorer agreement given in the manual. VERY DESIRABLE

E2.22. If persons having various degrees of supervised training are expected to score the test, studies of the interscorer agreement at each skill level should be presented in the test manual. DESIRABLE

E2.3. If the test is designed to use more than one method for the examinee's recording his responses, such as hand-scored answer sheets, machine-scored answer sheets, or entering of responses in the test booklet, the test manual should report data on the degree to which results from these methods are interchangeable. ESSENTIAL

E2.4. If an unusual or complicated scoring system is used, the test manual should indicate the approximate amount of time required to score the test. DESIRABLE

E2.5. The test manual should recommend that "correction for guessing" formulas or multiple-regression analysis should usually be used with multiple-choice and true-false items unless: (a) there is either no time limit, or a generous time limit *and* a warning is given by the proctor near the end concerning the amount of time remaining; and (b) instructions are unequivocal to mark every item, including *pure guesses.* ESSENTIAL

E2.51. When the test manual indicates that the "correlation for guessing" formula is to be used, examinees should be instructed to make the best choice that they can on items the answers of which they do not know, and to skip an item *only* if an answer would be a *pure guess.* ESSENTIAL

F. SCALES AND NORMS

F1. Scales used for reporting scores should be so carefully described in the test manual as to increase the likelihood of accurate interpretation and the understanding of both the test interpreter and the subject. ESSENTIAL

F1.1. Standard scores should in general be used in preference to other derived scores. The system of standard scores should be consistent with the purposes for which the test is intended, and should be described in detail in the test manual. The reasons for choosing that scale in preference to other scales should also be made clear in the manual. VERY DESIRABLE

F1.2. Whenever it is suggested in the test manual that percentile scores are to be plotted on a profile sheet, the profile sheet should be based on the normal probability scale or some other appropriate nonlinear transformation. VERY DESIRABLE

F1.3. If grade norms are provided, tables for converting scores to standard scores or percentile ranks within each grade should also be provided in the test manual. DESIRABLE

F2. If scales are revised, new forms added, or other changes made, the revised test manual should provide tables of equivalence between the new and the old forms. This provision is particularly important in cases where data are recorded on cumulative records. ESSENTIAL

F3. Local norms are more important for many uses of tests than are published norms. In such cases the test manual should suggest appropriate emphasis on local norms and describe methods for their calculation. VERY DESIRABLE

F4. Except where the primary use of a test is to compare individuals with their own local group, norms should be published in the test manual at the time of release of the test for operational use. ESSENTIAL

F4.1. Even though a test is used primarily with local norms, the test manual should give some norms to aid the interpreter who lacks local norms. DESIRABLE

F5. Norms should be reported in the test manual in terms of standard scores or percentile ranks which reflect the distribution of scores in an appropriate reference group or groups. ESSENTIAL

F5.1. Measures of central tendency and variability of each distribution should be given in the test manual. ESSENTIAL

F5.2. In addition to norms, tables showing what expectation a person with a test score has of attaining or exceeding some relevant criterion score should be given in the test manual whenever possible. Conversion tables translating test scores into proficiency levels should be given whenever possible. Conversion tables translating test scores into proficiency levels should be given when proficiency can be de-scribed on a meaningful absolute scale. DESIRABLE

F6. Norms presented in the test manual should refer to defined and clearly described populations. These populations should be the groups to whom users of the test will ordinarily wish to compare the persons tested. ESSENTIAL

F6.1. The test manual should report the method of sampling from the population of examinees and should discuss any probable bias in this sampling procedure. ESSENTIAL

F6.11. Norms reported in any test manual should be based on a well-planned sample rather than on data collected primarily on the basis of availability. ESSENTIAL

F6.12. In the instance of achievement tests the adequacy of the normative sample described in the test manual should be judged primarily in terms of the number of schools as well as the number of cases, provided, of course, that the number of students in each school is large enough to reflect the performance associated with certain levels on the stratifying variables. ESSENTIAL

F6.2. The description of the norm group should be sufficiently complete in the test manual that the user can judge whether his sample data fall within the population data represented by the norm group. The description should include number of cases, classified by such relevant variables as age, sex, and educational status. If cluster sampling is employed, the description of the norm group should state the number of separate groups tested. ESSENTIAL

F6.3. The number of cases on which the norms are based should be reported in the test manual. If cluster sampling is employed, the number and description of the separate groups included in the sample should be cited. ESSENTIAL

F6.31. If the sample on which norms are based is small or otherwise undependable, the user should be cautioned explicitly in the test manual regarding the possible magnitude of errors arising in interpretation of scores. ESSENTIAL

F6.4. The test manual should report whether scores vary for groups differing on age, sex, amount of training, and other equally important variables. ESSENTIAL

F6.5. Norms on subtests or groups of test items should be reported in the test manual only if data on the validity and reliability of such subtests or groups of items are also indicated. ESSENTIAL

F6.6. Some profile sheets record, side by side, scores from tests so standardized that for different scores the person is compared to different norm groups. The test manual should recommend profiles of this type for use only when tests are intended to assess or to predict the person's standing in different situations or when he competes with the different groups.

Whenever such mixed scales are compared, the fact that the norm groups differ (or may differ) should be made clear on the profile sheet. VERY DESIRABLE

F6.7. The conditions under which normative data were obtained should be reported in the test manual. The conditions of testing, including the circumstances under which the subjects took the test, and their levels of motivation, should be reported. ESSENTIAL

Chapter 12

A Typology of Tests, Projective and Otherwise

DONALD T. CAMPBELL

To judge from the pages of many psychological journals, the projective test movement is here to stay. But the rubric *projective,* once useful in mobilizing a reaction against older diagnostic procedures, has been stretched to include such a heterogeneous variety of measures that its denotational value has become attenuated. In a paper on indirect attitude measurement [5], the present writer proposed a typology of test formats which has turned out to be one of the most cited features of that paper. Since that typology is now deemed to be inadequate, and since the denotational problem still remains, this second effort is offered. From an initial focus on personality tests comes three dichotomies, which generate eight test types. Five of these types contain tests commonly re-garded as "projective," and only two are unrelated to personality measurement.

THE THREE DICHOTOMIES

1. *Voluntary vs. objective.* In the *voluntary* test the respondent[1] is given to understand that any answer is acceptable, and that there is no external criterion of correctness against which his answers will be evaluated. He is encouraged in idiosyncrasy and self description.

The test assignment may state "this is *not* a test of your ability," or "there are *no* right

---

[1] The term *respondent* is borrowed from social psychology to refer to the person from whom data is collected, and whose personality is being examined. The term *subject,* or S, as commonly used in experimental psychology reports is felt to be connotatively inappropriate. More clinically oriented terms, such as *patient* or *client,* are too specialized to designate the full range of respondents employed in personality research.

This article is reprinted from the *Journal of Consulting Psychology,* 1957, with the permission of the author and the American Psychological Association.

or wrong answers" or "answer in terms of how *you* really feel." In contrast, in an *objective* test the subject is told, either explicitly or implicitly, that there is a correct answer external to himself, for which he should search in selecting his answer. The concepts of "accuracy" and "error" are in the subject's mind. Phenomenologically he is describing the external, objective world, although in so doing he is inevitably reflecting his idiosyncratic view of that world, and can be unselfconsciously "projecting" in an important meaning of that word, as will be illustrated more fully in the discussion of test types 5 and 6 below.[2]

2. *Indirect vs. direct.* In the *direct* test, the respondent's understanding of the purpose of the test and the psychologist's understanding are in agreement. Were the respondent to read the psychologist's report of the test results, none of the topics introduced would surprise him. This is obviously so in an achievement test given at the end of a course. It is equally true for the typical public opinion poll. It is probably so for the usual diagnostic interview. It is so for many interest tests and adjustment inventories.

In the *indirect* test, the psychologist interprets the responses in terms of dimensions and categories different from those held in mind by the respondent while

answering. If a person tells stories to pictures under the belief that his thematic creativity is being measured, and the psychologist then interprets the products as depth projections, the test is *indirect*. If a person expresses his likes and dislikes about a series of drawings, and is as a result classified as an oral-pessimist, the test is *indirect*. If a respondent believes he is participating in a general survey of the public's opinion on a variety of harmless issues, and gets scored, however invalidly, as a paranoid proto-fascist, the test is *indirect*. In general, whenever responses are taken as symptoms, rather than as literal information, the test is *indirect*.

Characteristic of the *indirect* test is a *façade*. By this is meant a false assignment to the respondent which distracts him from recognizing the test's true purpose and which provides him with a plausible reason for cooperating. Initially the TAT had such a façade: "This is a test of your creative imagination." The objective test façade is used in an important class of indirect tests of social attitudes, in which the respondent tries to show his knowledge of current events and is scored for the bias he shows in the directionality of his errors [5, 14]. The expression of aesthetic taste, participation in public opinion surveys, judgments of moral right and wrong, and judgments of logical consistency all have been used as façades in indirect tests of personality, interests, or social attitudes.

The potential ethical problems arising from the application of personality and attitude tests in administrative situations [e.g., 21] would seem to center around this one dimension of indirection.

3. *Free-response vs. structured.* This dichotomy is already well established in the classification of personality and attitude assessment procedures. Typically, the projective tests have been open-ended, free, unstructured, and have had the virtue of allowing the respondent to project his own organization upon the material.

The *free-response* format has the advantage of not suggesting answers or alter-

[2] The distinction here made partially overlaps the discussion by Rosenzweig [18] on levels of response to projective tests. His category *subjective* clearly belongs with the *voluntary* class as here defined, emphasizing the subject's self-conscious focus on describing himself. In his *projective* category, the respondent looks away from himself at some "ego-neutral" object, as in the phenomenologically *objective* orientation of this paper. His category called *objective* is not the same as the present usage, but refers to the psychologist's orientation, and includes a behavior-sampling approach not relevant to the present discussion. The distinction is also related to Cattell's discussion of varieties of projective tests [8]. When he classifies certain approaches as a variety of objective tests employing misperception, his usage is in agreement with that of the present writer. This agreement is limited, however, and on many points the analyses differ, as when Cattell places the TAT and the Tautophone in the same subtype. In the present analysis, the TAT is *voluntary*, and the Tautophone the most classic example of the *objective* assignment among projective personality measures.

natives to the respondent, of not limiting the range of alternatives available, nor of artificially expanding it through the suggestions provided in the prepared alternatives. In the multiple-choice Rorschach the respondent can see images pointed out to him by the prepared alternatives which he would never have noticed on his own. The *structured* format was typical of the personality and attitude measurement devices of the first flowering of such tests in the period from 1920 to 1935, and hence provides the tradition against which both the projective test movement and modern survey research techniques were revolting [e.g., 11]. But even this dimension is not uniquely associated with projective tests, as the two earliest papers in English using the concept of projection in a testing setting [15, 7] used structured response formats.

THE EIGHT TEST TYPES

1. *Voluntary, indirect, free-response.* These are the classic projective techniques, including free association, the Rorschach, the Thematic Apperception Test, doll play, drawing, and such projective questions as, "What do you admire most in people?" or "What is the most embarrassing thing you can think of?" It is in this category that most inventiveness has been shown, and the present paper makes no effort to cite even a fraction of the appropriate studies.[3]

2. *Voluntary, indirect, structured.* In this category would be found the multiple-choice Rorschach and multiple-choice association tests. In addition, indirect questionnaires would fall in this cell, such as the *F* scale measure of authoritarian personality trends [1]. Where Osgood's semantic differential [16] is used to measure indirectly

---

[3] No effort has been made to provide bibliographical references for the well-known projective tests. Such references are available in a number of sources [e.g., 2]. Where, in the effort to supply adequate illustrations of each category, a less well-known test is cited, representative bibliographical references are provided.

attitudes toward parents, and other important figures, it belongs in this category, as would a Q-sort approach [10] to unconscious identification, for example. Humor tests and annoyance inventories used for indirect diagnostic purposes also belong here. The Barron-Welsh art preference test [3] is another good example of this category. The Blacky test [4] contains both free-response and structured features, and in part belongs here.

3. *Voluntary, direct, free-response.* This category is epitomized by sentence-completion tests, essay-type questionnaires, the autobiographical assignment frequently given in personality research, and the open-ended interview in public opinion surveys. Of these the sentence completion tests, at least, are commonly regarded as projective, but are classified here in the belief that rarely is the respondent unaware that he has been revealing his own attitudes.

4. *Voluntary, direct, structured.* This category would include the classic quantitative efforts to measure adjustment, personality, interests, and attitudes, including the Woodworth inventory, the Thurstone and Likert attitude tests, the Strong and Kuder interest inventories, the Bernreuter, the MMPI, the many biographical inventories, and many others. When these are scored with an empirical key, or are presented in a forced-choice format, the respondent may be in the dark about the psychologist's interpretation of a particular response. But even in these instances, the topics and dimensions of interpretation used by the psychologist are still congruent with the purposes of the test as understood by the respondent. Since in general most test constructors tend to introduce some efforts at disguise, were too strict an interpretation placed upon this dimension, the category of direct tests would be very small indeed.

5. *Objective, indirect, free-response.* These are projective tests using the objective test façade, focusing the respondent's attention on the external world but allowing an unstructured response situation. The

oldest and most used of the projective tests in this category is the "Verbal Summator" or "Tautophone" [13, 19]. A recording of indistinct vowel sounds is presented with some such instructions as "This is a recording of a man talking. He is not speaking very plainly, but if you listen carefully you will be able to tell what he is saying. I'll play it over and over again, so that you can get it, but be sure to tell me as soon as you have an idea of what he is saying." Subjects almost unanimously accept the facade and produce intelligible verbal content which they are totally unaware comes from themselves. It should be noted that there are also several auditory apperception or auditory association methods which should not be confused with the Tautophone and which belong clearly in category 1.

Sherriffs' Intuition Questionnaire [20] is another excellent example of this category. His instructions read "Give a probable explanation for the behavior indicated in each of the following excerpts from life histories taken from a random sample of the population. Include the motivation underlying the behavior and the origins of the motivation." This technique has seen very successful application by French [12] in the measurement of achievement and affiliation motives. Day's [9] task of asking respondents to explain a sample of day dreams is similar.

Rechtschaffen and Mednick's Autokinetic Word Technique [17] belongs here. In the autokinetic illusion, a single dot of light in an otherwise totally dark room appears to move. They presented a random series of exposure periods and told the respondents that words were being written by the point of light, which they were to report. All of their respondents "saw" words, and when told about the nature of the experiment were shocked to learn that they had themselves fabricated the content.

The assignment to judge the character of persons presented in photographs can be presented as an objective task. Common statements in psychology texts as to the impossibility of making valid judgments of

this kind may create a problem, although with a properly prepared set of materials [e.g., 6] the phenomenological validity of the task is great enough so that even college students will accept it as a legitimate objective task.

6. *Objective, indirect, structured.* For many of the test formats of type 5, structured forms could be prepared. The trait judgments from the photographs assignment has been used in both *free-response* and *structured* forms [e.g., 6], and indeed used a structured response in its first application by Murray [15]. The much used *error-choice* approach to attitude measurement [14] is another typical example of this category.

7. *Objective, direct, free-response;* and

8. *Objective, direct, structured.* The three dichotomies which have generated the above six types of personality test, produce these two remaining categories. These turn out to be the typical tests of ability or achievement, in free-response and in structured form, the latter category being characteristic of almost all standardized tests in these areas.

SUMMARY

From a consideration of differences among personality measurement approaches, three dichotomies or dimensions of distinction have been drawn. The joint application of these generates eight test types. Of these, six are appropriate to the field of personality measurement. These are:

1. Voluntary, Indirect, Free-Response.
2. Voluntary, Indirect, Structured.
3. Voluntary, Direct, Free-Response.
4. Voluntary, Direct, Structured.
5. Objective, Indirect, Free-Response.
6. Objective, Indirect, Structured.

Examples are provided for all six types. While category 1 contains the most typical projective tests, tests called projective are found in all except category 4. Categories 5 and 6 are the least developed but should be given particular attention, as they can involve the unselfconscious projection of personality content upon the phenomenologically objective environment.

REFERENCES

1. ADORNO, T. W., *et al. The authoritarian personality.* New York: Harper, 1950.
2. ANDERSON, H. H., & ANDERSON, GLADYS L. *An introduction to projective techniques.* New York: Prentice-Hall, 1951.
3. BARRON, F., & WELSH, G. S. Artistic perception as a factor in personality types: Its measurement by a figure-preference test. *J. Psychol.,* 1952, **33,** 199–203.
4. BLUM, G. S., & HUNT, H. F. The validity of the Blacky Pictures. *Psychol. Bull.,* 1952, **49,** 238–250.
5. CAMPBELL, D. T. The indirect assessment of social attitudes. *Psychol. Bull.,* 1950, **47,** 15–38.
6. CAMPBELL, D. T., & BURWEN, L. S. Trait judgments from photographs as a projective device. *J. clin. Psychol.,* 1956, **12,** 215–221.
7. CATTELL, R. B. *A guide to mental testing.* London: Univer. of London Press, 1933.
8. CATTELL, R. B. Principles of design in "projective" or misperception tests of personality. In H. H. Anderson & Gladys L. Anderson (Eds.), *An introduction to projective techniques.* New York: Prentice-Hall, 1951.
9. DAY, DOROTHY. Dream interpretation as a projective technique. *J. consult. Psychol.,* 1949, **13,** 416–420.
10. FIEDLER, F. E. A method of objective quantification of certain counter-transference attitudes. *J. clin. Psychol.,* 1951, **7,** 101–107.
11. FRANK, L. K. Projective methods for the study of personality. *J. Psychol.,* 1939, **8,** 389–413.
12. FRENCH, E. G. Some characteristics of achievement motivation. *J. exp. Psychol.,* 1955, **50,** 232–236.
13. GRINGS, W. W. The verbal summator technique and abnormal mental states. *J. abnorm. soc. Psychol.,* 1942, **37,** 529–545.
14. HAMMOND, K. R. Measuring attitudes by error-choice; an indirect method. *J. abnorm. soc. Psychol.,* 1948, **43,** 38–48.
15. MURRAY, H. A. The effect of fear upon estimates of the maliciousness of other personalities. *J. soc. Psychol.,* 1933, **4,** 310–339.
16. OSGOOD, C. E. The nature and measurement of meaning. *Psychol. Bull.,* 1952, **49,** 197–237.
17. RECHTSCHAFFEN, A., & MEDNICK, S. A. The autokinetic word technique. *J. abnorm. soc. Psychol.,* 1955, **51,** 346.
18. ROSENZWEIG, S. Levels of behavior in psychodiagnosis with special reference to the Picture-Frustration study. *Amer. J. Orthopsychiat.,* 1950, **20,** 63–72.
19. SHAKOW, D., & ROSENZWEIG, S. The use of the Tautophone as an auditory apperceptive test for the study of personality. *Charact. & Pers.,* 1940, **8,** 216–266.
20. SHERRIFFS, A. C. The "intuition questionnaire": A new projective test. *J. abnorm. soc. Psychol.,* 1948, **43,** 326–337.
21. WESCHLER, I. R. Problems in the use of indirect methods of attitude measurements. *Publ. Opin. Quart.,* 1951, **15,** 133–138.

Chapter 13

Report on a Psychometric Mission to Clinicia

LEE J. CRONBACH

Of necessity, members of the Psychometric Society devote their attention primarily to the domestic problems of psychometrics. We must think also, however, of our foreign relations, for Psychometrikans serve chiefly through their contribution to other psychologists. I wish to discuss particularly our relations with a growing power located at a great distance around the psychological world from us, namely, Clinicia.

The recent opening of Clinicia to science offers us a great challenge. For while the natives of Clinicia are busy and happy, they are regrettably unchastened by the stern and moral truths on which *our* civilization is built. To remedy this, some of us are already serving as missionaries, informing Clinicians about the Psychometric way of life. This is a report on our experiences.

Clinicia differs much from our own land of Psychometrika. One of my colleagues, a member of Anthropologists Anonymous, has kindly prepared comparable descriptions of both cultures to help us view them with equal objectivity. He writes:

This article is reprinted from *Psychometrika*, 1954, with the permission of the author and the Psychometric Society. It was given as the Presidential Address of the Psychometric Society, September 5, 1954.

Psychometrika is a small nation, but possesses technical secrets which give it vast power. A small task force of Psychometrikans, armed with devices which seem primitive today, conquered the United States Army in 1916; and the young braves of the following generation overcame the U. S. Air Force in the 1940's with a new and awesome weapon called the *stanine*. In times of peace, Psychometrika is a hive of productivity, noted chiefly for its output of incisive scientific instruments, incomprehensible mathematical formulas, and unfavorable book reviews.

The culture of Psychometrika is strikingly conservative and formalized, with a tremendous emphasis on standardization. In the Orthodox temples of Psychometrika, the youth are told daily that they should never use a test which is not completely standardized. Few Psychometrikans, however, allow this belief to interfere with the sale of tests they manufacture.

For all its interest in norms and standards, the Society is not totally restrictive of individuality. Deviations from the norm are indeed given much consideration, provided they are *standard* deviations.

Religion has no place in Psychometric

culture, and members are taught to suspect all forms of faith. The nearest to a religious belief is the Psychometrikan's loyalty to the so-called *Law of Parsimony*. Performing the ritual gyrations prescribed by this law, the Psychometrikan undergoes a mystical experience in which various deities appear before his eyes and name themselves to him. These deities, or *Factors* as they are called in the native language, are very numerous. Since "Factor Analysis" is a highly personal experience, each Psychometrikan has his own assemblage of *Factors*, different from that of his neighbors. This is one reason why faith in the *Factors* is slight.

In a culture which profits from technical achievements, anthropologists expect to find a strong taboo against communication, intended to guard technical secrets from the outer world. In Psychometrika this is indeed the case. New discoveries are shared only within the inner aristocracy who can read the peculiar private code in which high-caste Psychometrikans communicate. The origin of this secret language has aroused considerable speculation, since the alphabet shows traces of the language of ancient Greece. According to legend, the language was created by Pythagoras himself. His manuscript supposedly was preserved for 2000 years, before a typesetter was found brave enough to commence publication of *Psychometrika*.

In contrast to the forbidding coasts of Psychometrika, the shores of Clinicia are an alluring tropical paradise. Only its borders have been penetrated, for the rich yield of these shoreline plantations is sufficient to support in comfort the vast population of Clinicians.

Climate is of fundamental importance to Clinicia's prosperity and its ideology. Each native believes himself personally responsible for the climate; little Clinicians are taught special rituals they must perform to keep their climate warm. One climate-maintaining ritual is built chiefly around the repetition of the phrase, *Uh-huh*. This phrase is believed to have magical therapeutic effects when given the proper inflection.

Clinicians have a highly developed verbal culture, and a richness of vocabulary unsuspected by the tourist who thinks the Clinical language consists only of *Uh-huh* and its variations. Whereas Psychometrika has roots in Greek culture, many founders of Clinicia came from Vienna and have imbued its institutions with the cheerful air of a *Mittleuropeanischer Kaffeeklatsch*.

Clinicians are markedly sociable. Strong taboos are imposed against disagreements or other barriers to sociality. As a consequence, Clinicia has developed a language of great poetic beauty and obscurity. In this obscure language, a Clinician can speak for hours on uncertain matters without fear of contradiction.

Strains on the individual are eliminated in Clinicia. The taboo against disputation bolsters self-esteem by guaranteeing that all judgments the Clinician makes will be validated by others. And Clinical activities provide opportunities for pleasant companionship—if you like people. These inventions provide a fine culture, from the point of view of mental health—so fine, indeed, that the anthropologists who visit become permanent residents, and thereafter talk as obscurely as the natives.

The views of this anthropologist are not necessarily my own. I am sure we Psychometrikans are not secretive, nor lacking in faith. It is just because we believe in our system that we undertake, in one manner or another, the missionary's role.

The missionary to Clinicia has a difficult task, because historic conflicts cause many Clinicians to regard us as unsympathetic and even hostile. No Psychometrikan can hear without a thrill of pride our motto: *If anything exists, it can be measured*. This is an optimistic creed, and not chauvinistic as slogans go. But some among us flaunt the more brazen slogan: *If something cannot be measured, it does not exist!* Some Psychometrikans cannot resist an opportunity for a quarrel, or a chance to prove intellectual superiority by picking off an easy target. According to Greenwood [3], the arrogance of Karl Pearson set back the use of statistics in medical fields for a long while. We keep such antagonism alive; only a very few years ago, an entire Presidential address before a measurement society was devoted to destructive criticism of a major Clinical research effort.

Antagonism begins because Psychometrikans believe that Clinicians are impatient with rigorous reasoning. This is true. Wisely or unwisely, the Clinician is trying to solve practical problems for which the present science of psychology is grossly inadequate. Because research gains ground so slowly, some practitioners do ignore research and substitute testimonials for evidence. The Clinician going about his daily business, however, is not the person with whom Psychometrikans should communicate.

There exists a substantial class of Clinical research workers with intelligence, imagination, and respect for truth, who have influence on practicing Clinicians. Clinical researchers feel too much the urgent need for results, and try to establish short-cut solutions instead of concentrating on less spectacular fundamentals. Moreover, Clinical research is done in a setting which encourages wishful interpretation of results, excessive a posteriori speculation, special pleading, and an undeniable general soft-headedness. The Clinical worker relies too little on rationales and too much on diffuse exploration of too many variables with too few subjects. Granting all these criticisms, it is still true that the Clinical researcher wants to establish his findings solidly, and he wants to improve his research methodology. Many Clinical investigators have already been converted to our beliefs, and where their understanding is primitive, they want to learn more.

We often fail to give the help the Clinician is ready for. Particularly this occurs when the measurement specialist gives too little attention to the Clinical problem and dashes off a procedure to be followed for answering a *different* question from the one asked. Clinicia is a seller's market for any methodological nostrum: factor analysis, Q-technique, discriminant function, or some other. Just say that your method deals with patterns of scores, or with the total personality, and you will be mobbed by would-be users. However, while it is easy

to seduce the Clinician, you cannot hold his affections unless your glamorous proposals lead to satisfying consummations. If the Clinician feeds his data into your process, and then can only puzzle over ground-up fragments that come out, he learns not to ask your help again.

The methodologist must make sure he understands the Clinician's question before suggesting techniques. This is not easy, especially because the Clinician often asks an unanswerable question. He wants to study the "pattern" of performance, without specifying just which data and relations constitute a pattern. I had an opportunity recently to ask a group of clinical investigators just what they meant by "studying the configuration of the data." I got six consecutive answers, and each answer was different. One person wanted to study ratios of scores; one wanted a best linear composite to predict a criterion; one wanted to examine the interpretations of a test protocol by an expert diagnostician; and so on. If faced by ambiguous, inadequately thought-out questions, what is the Psychometrikan to say? One thing he cannot say: "Here is the meaning your question should have—and I happen to have in my knapsack just the remedy for that problem." Rather, the Psychometrikan must proceed, question by question, to help the Clinician define *his* idea.

Psychometrikans are in a peculiarly good position to help the Clinician just because we take quite different views of the world. The Psychometrikan views the world as one of simple relationships. Wherever he looks he perceives linear regressions, unit weights, and orthogonal variables. On the other hand the Clinician's first premise is that nature is complicated, too complicated to be caught in a simple net. No scientific generalization can take enough things into account to satisfy the Clinician.

Neither philosophy is more correct than the other. The Clinician's passion for complexity is almost certainly a valid way to conceive of the universe. The Psychometrikan's passion for reduction is a practical compromise, to simplify problems enough so that scientific methods can come to grips with them.

This conflict of philosophies is an old one. In the late Middle Ages, there was a great battle between two schools of philosophic thought. One school of thought, identified particularly with William of Ockam, thought that metaphysical reasoning was trapped in the lush overgrowth of Scholastic philosophy. Ockam's followers hacked indiscriminately at this growth with the famous "Razor" of Parsimony. The principal sufferers from the Ockamite attacks were followers of Duns Scotus, who had freely invented constructs and ingenious distinctions to explain circumstances. But Ockam attacked constructs and complexities, with a logic that devastated Scholasticism [6]. Into the ensuing vacancy marched inductive science, with Newton and Leibnitz carrying the flag of Parsimony.

Today's Clinician joins the Scholastic in saying, "There are more things in heaven and earth, Horatio, than are dreamt of in thy philosophy." Are we intolerant if, as scientists and therefore inheritors of Ockam, we scorn this view? The Ockamite says we should ignore those things not absolutely necessary to explain observations. Why prate, says he, of non-linear regressions or configurational relationships where no one has proved them? Wait, he counsels, until they force themselves on our attention. His opponent argues that we should look for these relations because in a complex world it would be remarkable if such relations were absent [5]. Admittedly, it takes vast amounts of data to establish such complex relations with confidence. But should we turn our backs upon the possibility?

Modern statistics has shown that Ockam's position is arbitrary. In testing a hypothesis, we run two kinds of risk: of accepting the hypothesis when it is untrue, of rejecting it when it is true. Ockam, with his advice never to reject the null hypothesis *praeter necessitatem,* said in effect that he was willing to risk any amount of error of the second kind, provided he could set an infinitesimal *P*-value on the risk of error of the first kind. The choice of risks is not a matter of absolute principle, as Ockam implied. It is a matter of research strategy in a particular situation [2]. The problem is one of balancing the risk of overlooking fresh trails against the risk of chasing phantoms. Clinicians are conditioned to fear the first of these errors; Psychometrikans abhor the second. These opposing biases can between them set a good scientific course.

When the Psychometrikan contributes to Clinical progress, he is rewarded by pride in the power of his methods and concepts. But commerce with a foreign land cannot be long sustained unless it is a two-way commerce. Clinicia has an exportable surplus of one commodity, namely, measurement and research problems. Fortunately, these problems make the best of raw material for research in psychometrics. Working with Clinicians we often learn that our present measurement theories are inadequate or incorrect in some basic particular.

Repeatedly a serious attempt to state a Clinician's problem in psychometric terms has shown that his thinking is defensible even though it violates our beliefs. Clinical conclusions frequently are incorrect. But when a practicing psychologist believes in a conclusion which conflicts with accepted generalizations in psychometrics, we need to look for built-in limitations in *our* theoretical model which may make it inconsistent with reality. The usual outcome of such scrutiny is neither to accept nor reject the practitioner's conclusion as it stands, but rather to restate it precisely and establish the conditions under which it holds.

Our restatement of Ockam's problem has already illustrated how more comprehensive models improve thinking. Work with utility theory under our current ONR contract provides further instances and illustrates how psychometric results can grow out of clinical perplexities.

In industrial, clinical, and educational testing, grossly unreliable scores or differences between scores are used as bases for decision. Psychometric doctrine condemns this practice. It cannot be dismissed outright, however, because there are too many instances where critical and able testers find it profitable. No skilled Binet tester, for instance, would ignore bizarre answers on single items or signs of undue dependence on examiner approval, although these indicators are unreliable. If careful Clinical testers use indicators which our theory condemns, could our theory be wrong?

An answer was first suggested by Shannon's information theory. That theory points out that a communication device—and a test is one—can be evaluated in terms of bandwidth and fidelity. Hitherto, only fidelity, i.e. accuracy, has concerned psychometrics. Bandwidth refers to the number of messages a channel carries, or the number of questions a message can answer. Both bandwidth and fidelity are desirable. According to Shannon, we increase one at the expense of the other. A homogeneous, Guttman-type test yields high precision, but covers little ground. The interview, the essay-test, and the projective test are wideband devices: great breadth, little precision. Applying a decision-theory or utility model to such concepts has permitted rigorous analysis of a large number of problems. (This work has been performed under contract N6ori-07146 with the Office of Naval Research.)

Should indicators of low validity be used as a basis for decisions? Restate that in these terms: If you have a fixed testing time, would it be better to use many short tests covering different dimensions, or one accurate test? To answer this question, our theory requires that you specify the mathematical nature of the decision process. To arrive at one illustrative result, let us specify that a counselor is going to make a large number of decisions about a high-school student: decisions about courses, about remedial help, about disciplinary treatment, etc. Each is a Yes-No decision. Test questions bearing on each decision are available. Detailed assumptions are required.

Specifically, we assume that the utility of assigning a person to any treatment is linearly related to his score on some criterion scale, that this criterion and the test have a normal bivariate distribution, and

that the proportion of persons assigned to a treatment is the same for each decision. For fixed length of test, tests have uniform reliability, uniform validity against their own criterion, and zero validity against others. The treatment under consideration is specified before the test is introduced; this procedure is to be distinguished from adaptive treatment assumptions, where the treatment is modified according to the adequacy of the test as a basis for classification. The problem can be solved for any alternative assumptions if these are unacceptable.

Figure 13–1 shows the change in validity as a test is lengthened. [Values assumed for validity and reliability of the unit test ($k = 1$) are .10 and .30, respectively.] In the decision problem assumed, utility is proportional to validity [cf. 1]. If our total testing time is used for one test ten units long, the gain from the test is shown at point a. Here we have good information for one decision, but the others are made on a chance basis. If two 5-unit tests bearing on two decisions are used, each one contributes the utility shown at $k = 5$ on the scale (b). Hence if n equal tests are given, such that their combined length is ten units long, the utility of the combined tests follows the upper curve in Figure 13–2. If this represented the true situation, we would find it profitable to give a separate test for each decision no matter how short the test is.

But cost must be considered. Assume an initial cost c_0 of setting up a test, giving instructions, etc. Beyond that, assume that the cost of giving a test increases by c_1 for each unit increase in length. Then the straight line in Figure 13–2 shows the

Figure 13–1 *Change in validity as test is lengthened (After [4]).*

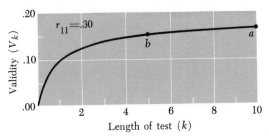

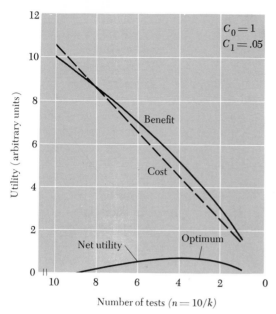

$$C_0 = 1$$
$$C_1 = .05$$

Figure 13–2　*Combined utility of tests of fixed total length.*

number of variables the counselor in our problem should attempt to measure.

We have established in principle that there is an optimal bandwidth, for any c_0 and v_1/r_{11}. The lower c_0 is, the greater the optimum bandwidth. It is worth sacrificing fidelity to attain this bandwidth. This evidence tends to justify the Clinician's reliance on the interview, for example. An interview gives fallible answers, but it compensates by increased bandwidth. Our results also post the warning that it is unwise to cover too many questions too hastily. Bandwidth can be too wide. With our general formulation, we can ask in any given decision problem exactly *how far* one should sacrifice fidelity. We end, not by condemning the procedure of the practical psychologists, but only by specifying its limits. We can accept his general aim and indicate how he can best attain it.

Permit me, in closing, to spell out the obvious moral: Psychometric missions to Clinicia must continue. We should, as friends of psychology, offer every contribution we can to improvement in Clinical research and practice. But the far more commanding reason for working with Clinicia is that we gain thereby a deeper mastery of those arts for which the Psychometric Society stands.

assumed cost of n equal tests of fixed total length. By subtracting cost from the top curve, we have the lower curve showing *net* utility from each set of tests. Figure 13–3 is similar, with a lower cost. There is a best value of n which represents the

Figure 13–3　*Combined utility of tests of fixed total length.*

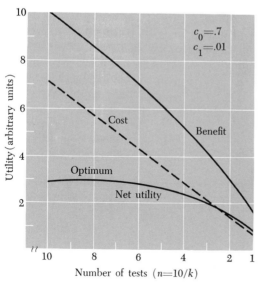

$$c_0 = .7$$
$$c_1 = .01$$

REFERENCES

1. BROGDEN, H. E. On the interpretation of the correlation coefficient as a measure of predictive efficiency. *J. educ. Psychol.*, 1946, **37**, 65–76.
2. FESTINGER, L. Book review of McNemar, *Psychological Statistics, Psychometrika*, 1950, **15**, 209–213.
3. GREENWOOD, M. The statistician and medical research. *Brit. med. J.*, 1948, **2**, 467–468.
4. GULLIKSEN, H. Theory of mental tests. New York: Wiley, 1950.
5. THORBURN, W. M. The myth of Ockam's Razor. *Mind*, 1918, **27** ns, 345–353.
6. de WULF, M. History of medieval philosophy, Vol. II. New York: Longmans, Green, 1926.

Chapter *14* ~

The Analysis and Selection of Test Items

ROBERT L. THORNDIKE

FACTORS IN ITEM EVALUATION

The effectiveness of a test depends on the characteristics of the items which compose it. In both its reliability and its validity a test score is the resultant of the validities, reliabilities, and intercorrelations of its component items. In order to produce the most effective test, therefore, we must study each one of the pool of items from which the test is to be assembled. The choice of items for the final form of a test is based in part on the detailed specifications for the content of the final test which were prepared as a part of the process of planning the test. It is based in part on certain statistical characteristics of each item. There are two statistical aspects of the individual item with which we shall be concerned. The first is the difficulty level of the item for the group being studied. The second is the degree to which the item differentiates those who are high from those who are low

This article is reprinted from Dr. Thorndike's book *Personnel Selection*, 1949, with the permission of the author and John Wiley & Sons, Inc.

on some standard. This standard may sometimes be performance on the complete pool of items, in which case we are concerned with the internal consistency of the items. The standard may sometimes be an external criterion of job performance, in which case we are concerned with the validity of each individual item.

ITEM DIFFICULTY

Let us consider first the role of difficulty as a factor in item selection. If an item is to be useful in distinguishing between those who are high and those who are low on a certain trait, it is apparent that the item must not be so easy as to be passed by every member of the group nor so difficult as to be failed by every member. In neither of these extreme cases does the item make *any* contribution to the discrimination which the test is to make between different individuals. Within these two extremes, the difficulty of a test item is still a significant factor in evaluating the item. In general a single item will make the largest number of discriminations between pairs of individuals if it is at a difficulty level such that it is passed by 50 per cent of the group.

Taking a single item, we can visualize the number of discriminations which it makes in the following way. An item which is given to 100 subjects and passed by one discriminates between that one and any one of the remaining 99, and thus makes 99 discriminations. An item which is passed by 10 and failed by 90 discriminates between each one of the group of 10 and each one of the group of 90. If we took the individuals by pairs, there would be 10 × 90 = 900 combinations in which that item discriminated between the two members of a pair. An item which was passed by 50 individuals of the group of 100 and failed by the remaining 50 would discriminate each member of the first 50 from each member of the remaining 50. There would then be 50 × 50 = 2500 combinations in which the item would discriminate between the members of a pair of individuals chosen from the total group of 100. Figure 14–1 shows the relationship between difficulty level, expressed as percentage succeeding with the item, and number of discriminations made by the item.

Clearly, the item that is passed by approximately one-half the individuals makes discriminations between many more pairs of individuals than the item that is passed by a very small or a very large percentage of the total group. Differences in difficulty do not affect the frequency of discrimina-

Figure 14–1 *Number of discriminations as a function of item difficulty.*

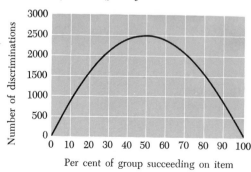

Per cent of group succeeding on item

tion so much in the middle difficulty ranges (from 25 to 75 per cent success, let us say), but they become increasingly critical as the extreme values are approached.

Both theoretical and empirical studies indicate that a test discriminates most reliably among the members of a group being tested when the average difficulty level of the items in the test is such that approximately 50 per cent of the group succeed with an item. The exact distribution of item difficulties that will be most effective in any given case involves also a consideration of the relationship among the items. In proportion as the correlation between each item and each other item is high, a test will require a relatively wide scatter of item difficulties around the average level of 50 per cent difficulty. In proportion as the correlation between separate items is low, the most advantageous scatter of item difficulties may be expected to be small. . . .

ITEM DISCRIMINATION

We turn now to a consideration of the ability to discriminate high-scoring individuals as an item characteristic. As was indicated, this discrimination may be in terms of total score on the test, or it may be in terms of some external criterion score of job performance. In some cases one type of analysis will be appropriate, in some cases the other. There may be some cases in which both seem reasonable. To clarify the situations that call for analysis of the relationship of item to total test score (internal consistency analysis) and the situations that call for analysis of the relationship of item to an external criterion (item validation), let us consider two types of testing instrument.

In the first type of testing instrument, the items in a given test blank are included in a single score purely from considerations of convenience and not because of an essential unity in the items themselves. This type of instrument is perhaps best illustrated by the biographical data blank, in which a great variety of questions are asked about the individual's past history. Certain personality questionnaires and interest inventories also fall into this class. As these instruments are tried out in preliminary form, they include a wide range of items which have only a superficial relationship to one another. They are held together not by any basic functional relationship, but rather by the superficial fact that all the items refer to facts of personal history, statements about likes and dislikes, or statements of individual feelings or behavior. They may have very little unity in terms of what the individual items purport to measure. Convenience and a certain superficial resemblance in the form of the items make it desirable to include them within a single test blank. There is no reason however to think of the items as representing a single unified aspect of the individual's development.

In such a situation, it is very appropriate to inquire into the validity of each single item. Each item is in a very real sense a little test all by itself. Each item must necessarily be judged on its own merit as far as validity is concerned. There is no determinable a priori basis for scoring the items and combining them into a score. The only basis for arriving at a selection of items or a scoring of items is in terms of the empirical validity of each item. In this type of test, therefore, it is entirely appropriate to determine the effectiveness of each item (and of each possible response to it) in discriminating with respect to some outside criterion of success on the job. An item response is valid in so far as the individuals who choose that response are more successful on the job, or more frequently successful, than those who do not choose that response to that item.

Where the separate test items represent such a heterogeneous assortment of materials, there is no a priori reason for expecting correlation among the separate items and consequently no justification for analyzing the relationship of a single item to a score based on the whole pool of items. As a matter of fact, as we noted, there is no

basis for arriving a priori at a pooled score for a set of items, and consequently there is no meaningful score against which the internal consistency of the test items could be checked. In this case, then, there is no point in carrying out an internal consistency item analysis.

Let us consider, in sharp contrast with the type of test blank just described, a test which has been developed for the purpose of measuring a limited and specific segment of ability. This might, for example, be a test of the extent of general vocabulary. In such a test, each item purports to help assess some single unified aspect of ability. Furthermore by the nature of the test, expert opinion is able to identify in advance the "right" answer for each item. It is possible to score the items in the test without reference to an external standard. If a hundred such items have been prepared, the scoring key for the total test can be developed a priori without reference to any empirical results. In this case it is appropriate to ask to what extent a particular test item measures the same function in the individuals tested as is measured by the test as a whole. This is possible because (1) a total test score can be obtained and (2) such a score will be meaningful because it was the purpose of the test-maker that each item contribute to the measurement of a single homogeneous function.

When the items in a test are completely homogeneous in that each item measures exactly the same factors or aspects of individual ability in the same combination, correlation of the separate items with an external criterion of success loses its meaning. In so far as the single items measure exactly the same combination of abilities, they necessarily differ in validity only as one item is more reliable than another. That is, their correlations with an external criterion depend only on their reliabilities. When the items are truly homogeneous, a difference in item reliability is directly reflected in differences in correlation with total test score. In this case, all the relevant information about the item is provided by its internal consistency item analysis, and any further analysis of individual items against an external criterion is futile.

The two examples described in the previous paragraphs represent extremes. At the one extreme, we had a testing instrument in which each component item could be thought of as a separate little test by itself, having no intrinsic relationship to the other items and necessarily being validated on its own merits. At the other extreme we pictured a test composed of items all of which were homogeneous measures of exactly the same functions in an individual. In the first test only item validation makes sense as a procedure for analyzing single items. In the second only internal consistency analysis provides an appropriate measure for evaluating single items. In actual practice the situation may not be so clearcut. Many tests may have a degree of both homogeneity and heterogeneity. It may be possible to score the items a priori and to arrive at a total score, and yet the functions measured by the items may have enough diversity so that validation of the single items is appropriate. It is significant to note, however, that, as validation of the single items becomes more meaningful, internal consistency analysis becomes less meaningful, and the more appropriate internal consistency analysis is, the less we may expect item validation to contribute.

PROCEDURES FOR CALCULATING ITEM INDICES

INDICES OF ITEM DIFFICULTY

An indication of the difficulty level of an item is given by the percentage of individuals in a given population who can answer the question or solve the problem. The smaller the percentage succeeding on the item, the more difficult the item, and vice versa. This type of index has been criticized on the grounds that infrequency of answering may sometimes be a function of the obscure and esoteric nature of the

information called for by the item rather than any fundamental intellectual complexity of the concept or process required. Thus, there is no more fundamental intellectual difficulty in knowing that a wombat is an animal than in knowing that a dog is. However, knowledge of the meaning of wombat is certainly very much rarer than knowledge of the meaning of dog. "Difficulty" in this instance does not represent complexity of concept but rather rarity of the concept in common experience. Recognizing this limitation, we may still accept the percentage of those knowing the answer to an item as a useful operational measure of its difficulty.

The raw percentage succeeding on an item gives a crude difficulty index. However, that percentage suffers from two limitations. In the first place, some of those who got the correct answer on the item may have done so by chance, that is, by guessing or by some other procedure which did not involve knowledge of the required information or working through of the problem. In the second place, it is only for a rectangular distribution of ability that percentage of success provides a linear scale of difficulty. If we consider the ability measured by the test as having approximately a normal distribution, equal differences in percentage of success will generally not correspond to equal steps in the scale of difficulty. We shall now consider the adjustments and transformations which may be applied to take care of these problems.

First, let us consider the problem of correcting difficulty indices for chance success. Our effort here is to get an estimate of the percentage of individuals in the group who arrived at the right answer through correct knowledge or correct reasoning and to rule out those who got the answer by guesswork. Any correction for guessing involves something of an approximation. The usual allowance is based upon two assumptions. In the first place, it is assumed that an individual who selects an incorrect answer to a test item does so on the basis of absence of information or understanding rather than on the basis of misinformation or misunderstanding. In the second place, it is assumed that for a person who does not know the correct answer all the response options on an item are equally attractive. If we accept these assumptions, we shall expect a certain percentage of those who do not *know* the right answer to select that answer by chance. This percentage will be the average of the percentages choosing each of the wrong answers. We subtract this percentage from the raw percentage of success on the item to arrive at our estimate of the percentage actually knowing the answer to the item.

The correction which we have just described is given in algebraic form by the formula

$$P_c = \frac{R = [W/(n-1)]}{R + W + O} \qquad (1)$$

in which P_c = the percentage actually knowing the answer to the item

 R = the number giving the right answer

 W = the number giving a wrong answer

 O = the number choosing to omit the item

 n = the number of response alternatives for the item

Of the above concepts, the only one that is likely to present any ambiguity is the number choosing to omit the item. An omitted item is one that was read by the examinee and then omitted by choice. In a speeded test there may be some confusion between items that were omitted by choice of the examinee because he did not know the answer to them and items that the examinee did not have time to attempt. A practical basis for differentiating between the two is to assume that all items up to and including the last one for which an answer was marked were attempted and that the first unanswered item after the last answered one was also attempted. We then assume that starting with the second item after the last one answered the remaining

items were not tried. If, for example, on a 100-item test the last item for which an answer was marked was the 84th, all unmarked items up to and including No. 85 would be counted as omissions, and Nos. 86–100 would be counted as not attempted.

It should be noted that the formula in the preceding paragraph depends on the two assumptions stated above. The two assumptions will rarely be exactly satisfied. Deviation from the assumed conditions will have opposite and somewhat compensatory effects in the two cases. If one or more of the misleads for an item are quite implausible and unattractive, the number of effective response alternatives for that item is reduced. This means that the probability of obtaining the right answer by guessing is increased since the guess is between, say, three instead of five alternatives. In this case, the formula would tend to undercorrect for the possibility of guessing the right answer. On the other hand, individuals often arrive at a wrong answer not as a result of ignorance and blind guessing but through wrong information or wrong mental processes. If all the individuals who gave wrong answers gave them for genuine reasons, guessing would not enter into the picture. In this case, all those who gave the right answer must also have given it because of correct information and correct mental operations. No correction for chance would then be indicated, and our formula would be over-correcting. In practice we do not know to what extent these two compensatory factors are operating, so that the corrected value for the percentage succeeding on an item is only an estimate of the percentage in the group who really knew the answer or solved the problem.

Though the corrected value for the percentage knowing an item is only an approximation and is limited by the underlying assumptions which we have discussed, it may usually be expected to give a truer picture than the raw value. It is of value particularly for comparing the difficulties of items which either (1) differ sharply in the frequency with which examinees omit the item or (2) differ in the number of the misleads. Raw percentages of correct response cannot meaningfully be compared in these cases.

The inequality of units which results from using percentage of success as an index of item difficulty can be overcome if we are willing to make some assumption as to the shape of the distribution of the trait being tested in the group to whom the tests were administered. The usual assumption is that the trait is normally distributed. If that assumption is made, the percentages can be translated into scale values on the base line of the normal curve. Thus, 50 per cent success corresponds to a scale value of 0.00, 75 per cent success to a scale value of −0.67, 25 per cent success to a scale value of +0.67, and so forth. With this type of scaling, it is possible to compare the difficulty of items which have been tried out on different groups, provided that there is some way to determine the difference in mean and standard deviation of ability in the two groups.

INDICES OF ITEM DISCRIMINATION

Many indices have been proposed to show the degree to which an item is effective in discriminating between those of high and low ability on either total test score or some outside criterion. Any attempt to list and discuss all the proposed types of statistical manipulation would be futile. In this section, therefore, a selection is made of those procedures which appear to have special advantages either because of extreme simplicity and ease of computation or because of the effectiveness with which they fit into the pattern of standard statistics for analyzing and combining test scores.

When we are carrying out an item analysis we encounter two major types of situation. In one, we are relating performance on the item to some type of continuous measure. This continuous variable is often score on the total test of which the

item is a component, but the continuous measure may be some type of external criterion. The second situation is one in which we are relating performance on the item to some dichotomy, either an arbitrary dichotomy into which the continuous variable of total test score has been thrown or a dichotomy on some criterion variable. The procedures which are available to us in these two situations are somewhat different and need to be considered separately. We will turn our attention first to the comparison of item performance with score on some continuous variable.

Item analysis against a continuous score. When the variable against which an item is being analyzed is available to us as a continuously distributed score, there are several approaches for dealing with it. The most elegant procedure is to retain and use the continuously distributed score. However, as we shall see, the computational procedures involved in this case become quite laborious. The second alternative is to set some arbitrary dividing point on the scale of scores and throw the continuous variable into an arbitrary dichotomy. That is, we can split the group into the top half and the bottom half, for example, in terms of the continuous score variable. A third alternative is to compare two relatively extreme groups with regard to the continuous variable. That is, we may take a fraction from the top of the group and a fraction from the bottom of the group, rejecting a fraction from the middle, and compare performance on the single test item for those two extreme groups.

We shall first consider procedures for evaluating items when the continuous variable is retained as a quantitative score. When we wish to determine the relationship of each item to a continuously distributed score, the procedures available to us are the biserial correlation coefficient and the point biserial correlation coefficient. In the present case, performance on the item constitutes the dichotomy. Either the individual gave a particular response to the item or he did not. Total test score constitutes the continuum. We wish to establish the degree of relationship between the single item and the total score. We may use either the biserial correlation coefficient or the point biserial, depending on whether we wish to consider the dichotomy on the item as real or as artificial.

If we think of success or failure on the item as representative of some continuous underlying ability and of the split into those who succeed and those who fail as an arbitrary splitting of individuals with regard to this underlying quality, the particular location of the split depending on the difficulty of the particular item, then it seems reasonable to use a biserial correlation coefficient. That is, item success or failure is thought of as the symptom of some basic underlying variable. Interest is considered to be centered primarily in the underlying ability of which the item is only a symptom. The biserial correlation coefficient has one feature that is particularly worthy of consideration in this connection. The value which it takes does not depend on the proportion in the passing and in the failing group. This means that the index of item validity or discrimination is separated entirely from the matter of item difficulty. The two facts about the item can be separately determined, and in evaluating the item separate account can be taken of each.

The point biserial correlation differs from the biserial in the nature of the assumptions which it makes and in the effect which item difficulty has on the resulting values. The point biserial assumes in effect that those who pass and those who fail on a test item are two categorically distinct groups. It assumes that the groups can be distinguished but that within each group all the members are to be thought of as alike. The use of point biserial correlations in item analysis has the practical effect that the resulting indices are in part a function of item difficulty. Point biserial correlations tend to become smaller, other things being equal, as the proportion succeeding on the item departs from 50 per cent. In general

neither of these characteristics of the point biserial recommend it for item analysis. The assumption that passers and failers on an item are categorically distinct groups is not a very reasonable one.[1] Certainly both those who pass and those who fail represent a range of ability with regard to the underlying function which the item to some degree measures. The confusion of item validity with item difficulty also appears generally undesirable. It seems much more defensible to obtain separate information on the validity or discriminating quality and on the difficulty of an item and then to combine those two facts explicitly and rationally rather than to use a single index which combines them in unspecified proportions. . . .

Item analysis against dichotomized groups. In all the other item analysis procedures discussed here the continuous nature of the variable against which the item is being compared is sacrificed in the interest of ease of computation. Two groups are specified, representing a higher and a lower group with respect to the continuous variable. In the procedures which we shall consider first, these two groups include between them all the cases. That is, some dividing line is arbitrarily set up for this continuous score; those falling above the dividing line constitute one group and those falling below the dividing line constitute the other. The usual and simplest procedure is to choose the dividing line so that the total group is split into two halves. Essentially the same procedures apply when the dichotomy is already established in the data, i.e., when the criterion is a dichotomy.

Where a group has been split in this manner, there are several possible approaches to item evaluation. One is extremely simple and serves quite adequately the needs of many makers of informal tests

[1] For a few items of the biographical data type the assumption of categorical differences seems appropriate. Items referring to sex, marital status, race, etc., are examples.

and many analysts interested only in some help in the editorial improvement and refinement of their tests. This simple procedure is merely to compute the percentage succeeding on the item in the upper group on total test score and the percentage succeeding on the item in the lower group on total test score. A crude evaluation of the item may be obtained from these two percentages. As a procedure for weeding out the most unsatisfactory items, this technique is reasonably satisfactory. It has the advantage of great simplicity and a minimum of computation. All that is required is to separate the answer sheets of the subjects tested into two piles in terms of total score and to tally the number of correct responses, incorrect responses, omissions, and items not tried for each item within each fraction. Either the raw percentage of correct responses, or the percentage corrected for chance successes may be computed from these figures. The corrected percentages are obtained by applying formula 1 to the count for each fraction of the group.

If further refinement is desired in the treatment of the percentages of success and failure on each item for the two fractions which comprise the complete group, it is possible to compute either a tetrachoric correlation or a phi coefficient from these percentages. We have a fourfold table based on the categories of success and failure on the item and high or low on total score. The percentages in each of the four cells of this table provide the basis for computing either the tetrachoric correlation or the phi coefficient. Which of the two we decide to use depends on the type of assumption made with regard to the continuity of the underlying distributions in the two variables. If we assume that they are continuous and normally distributed, the tetrachoric correlation is appropriate. If we assume that they represent discrete categories, the phi coefficient is chosen. The tetrachoric correlation is unaffected by item difficulty, whereas the phi coefficient, like the point biserial correlation, reflects the difficulty level of the particular item.

ITEM ANALYSIS WITH EXTREME GROUPS

If we decide to translate our continuous scores into the two categories of a higher and a lower group, we immediately introduce the possibility of analyzing only two extreme groups, dropping out those in the middle. If the relationship of item score to test score is linear, so that the percentage of success on the item increases steadily as total score increases, taking groups from the extremes will sharpen the differences which we observe in a single item. An item will clearly make a sharper distinction between the top tenth and the bottom tenth of the total population than it will between the top half and the bottom half. However, this increasing sharpness of discrimination is more or less balanced by the loss of information which results from including only some of the available individuals. Though an item would discriminate more sharply between the top 10 and the bottom 10 of 1000 individuals than it would between the top and bottom 500, we may anticipate that a comparison of different items based on the top and bottom 10 of 1000 would be less dependable than the comparison based on the top and bottom 500. Is there an optimum point at which the ideal balance of sharpness of discrimination combined with stability in the resulting values is obtained? Kelley [4] has shown that the ratio of the obtained difference to its standard error is a maximum when the top group and bottom group each includes approximately 27 per cent of the total population tested. That is, given that we are going to sacrifice the quantitative nature of our test scores, we can get the most accurate arrangement of items in order from most to least discriminating if we base our item analysis on only the top and bottom 27 per cent of the total group. Using either a larger or smaller percentage than this results in a loss in the accuracy with which the items can be ranked from most to least discriminating. This appears to be one case in which we can both have our cake and eat it too. We can reject the middle 46 per cent of cases, reducing the clerical labor of tallying almost by half, and at the same time increase the precision of our results. In general, then, any program of item analysis which proposes to sacrifice the quantitative nature of a continuous test score in order to gain economy in computation should also exclude the middle 46 per cent of the group. The result will be both a substantial additional economy in tabulation and some increase in the precision of the results. Our next concern is to consider procedures for dealing with item statistics based on the top and bottom 27 per cent of the total group.

The first step in any evaluation of test items by comparing the top with the bottom 27 per cent of the total group tested is to determine the percentage of cases succeeding with the item in the top group and the percentage of cases succeeding with the item in the bottom group. The procedure of correcting for chance success is the same as it was when the results for all individuals were analyzed. Formula 1 is also used, and it usually is desirable to make the correction if there are many omissions by the group taking the test.

The most satisfactory item validity index based on the upper and lower 27 per cent is the estimate of the coefficient of correlation between item and test obtainable from tables prepared by Flanagan [2]. These tables are based on the assumption that the variables underlying both item success and test score have a continuous normal distribution. Utilizing tables of the normal bivariate frequency distribution, Flanagan calculated correlation coefficients corresponding to the possible percentages of success in the upper and lower groups. These correlation coefficients are estimates of the product-moment correlation between the two underlying continuous normally distributed variables.

Flanagan's table . . . makes it extremely simple to compute item validity coefficients from the percentages of success in the upper and lower 27 per cent. By entering the table in the appropriate row and column, the correlation may be read directly. . . .

ITEM ANALYSIS AGAINST A CRITERION AVAILABLE ONLY AS A DICHOTOMY

The procedures for calculating the item indices discussed so far were developed with reference to a variable which yields continuous scores. It is sometimes necessary to relate item success to a dichotomous criterion of job performance. This situation arises when we are studying the validities of items with respect to some such criterion as graduation versus elimination in training. The statistical procedures available to us are essentially the same as those that we can apply to a continuous score when the continuous score has been forced into a dichotomy. We have discussed these in a previous section. The only difference is that in the present case the percentages falling in the "success" and "failure" categories are predetermined by the criterion dichotomy. These percentages will, of course, usually not be 50–50, and the computation of tetrachoric correlations or phi coefficients will have to take account of the percentage values.

USE OF ITEM VALIDITIES

When the items in a test are more or less heterogeneous, so that different items may be expected to measure somewhat different combinations of abilities, it becomes appropriate to determine the validity of each separate item. Each item is analyzed with respect to an external criterion of job success, and the correlation of the item with the criterion is determined. Assuming that we now have a validity coefficient for each item, how shall we use that information to best advantage?

As soon as the validity is determined for each item, we are in effect treating each item as a separate test. It is as if we had validity coefficients for a very large number of very brief tests. Our problem is to combine those very brief tests in such a way that the composite will have the highest possible correlation with our criterion. The factors which make an item desirable for inclusion in a test are the same as those which make a test desirable for inclusion in a test battery, that is, validity and uniqueness. An item (or a test) will be esteemed as a valuable addition to the other items (or tests) in proportion to (1) its high validity and (2) its low correlation with the other items (or tests). The virtue of high validity in the single items is directly apparent. The importance of low intercorrelations is equally great, though less obvious. An item will add to the validity of an existing pool if it covers aspects of individual performance *not already covered* by that pool of items. This uniqueness is represented statistically by low correlation with other items. . . .

If we abandon the complete analysis of item validities and item intercorrelations as an impractical procedure for determining item weights, we are thrown back on some approximation procedure which will be simpler but still reasonably accurate. Our problem is to select from a pool of n items some group of k items, where $k \leq n$, which will, when each item is given the same weight, give a score which has the maximum correlation with the criterion. We shall consider three possible ways of proceeding.

The simplest approach is to ignore item intercorrelations entirely. The choice of the items to be weighted is then based exclusively on the validity of the single items. Some standard of validity is chosen. Any item is weighted if its validity is as great as or greater than the specified standard. If items are found that have validity coefficients numerically as large as the standard

but with negative sign, those items may be given negative weight if negative weights are permitted in the test under consideration. For some types of tests, such as biographical data questionnaires, it will be appropriate to analyze each response option for each item separately, and to key any response option which has a validity coefficient whose absolute size without regard to sign comes up to the specified minimum. Take, for example, the following item:

At what age did you first go out with girls?
A. 14 years old or earlier.
B. 15 or 16 years old.
C. 17 or 18 years old.
D. 19 years old or older.
E. Have never gone out with girls.

It might be found that options A and B had positive validities which came up to the specified standard, option C had substantially zero validity, and options D and E had negative validity up to the standard. The scoring of this item would give a plus credit to individuals who chose either response A or B, no credit on response C, and a negative credit for responses D or E.

If item intercorrelations are ignored, the only problem to be faced in item selection is that of setting the standard for including items. The problem is to select a level of item validity which will yield the maximum validity in the composite score. The addition of certain items with unit weights may add nothing to the validity of the test score, even though the validity of the items is positive. This may be illustrated by a hypothetical example. Suppose we have 5 items with validities of 0.25, 0.20, 0.15, 0.10, and 0.05, respectively. Let us see what validity we would obtain from a test composed of 1, 2, 3, 4, and finally all 5 of these items when the correlation of each item with each other is assumed to be first 0.50, then 0.20, and finally 0.00. Using the standard formula for the correlation of sums, we arrive at the figures shown in the table. An examination of Table 14–1 shows that the maximum validity for the total score is

Table 14–1 Validity of Composite Score from Five Items of Different Validities

Items Included	Size of Item Intercorrelations		
	.50	.20	.00
1	.250	.250	.250
1 & 2	.260	.290	.318
1, 2, & 3	.245	.293	.346
1, 2, 3, & 4	.222	.277	.350
1, 2, 3, 4, & 5	.194	.250	.335

obtained when 2, 3, and 4 items, respectively, are included in the test score for the three illustrations chosen. In each case, inclusion of the least valid item or items results in a lower validity for the total score. Inclusion of the least valid items adds an amount of non-valid variance which outweighs any increase in the valid variance resulting from their inclusion in the test.

The problem is to select the group of items that will yield a score having maximum validity as applied to a new sample of cases. This involves, in addition to the problem of determining the critical value of item validity which gives maximum validity in the specific sample studied, a consideration of the regression of item validity coefficients from that sample to new samples.

Since the item intercorrelations are unknown and have an undetermined effect on the validity of the composite score, no analytical solution of this problem is possible. A sequence of operations for selecting a group of items to be retained and weighted is outlined in the following paragraphs.

1. When the validity coefficients for the separate items or item responses have been computed, the validities should be examined to determine whether the complete set might reasonably have arisen by chance. Because of the unknown correlation between items and especially between item responses, a rigorous test of this point probably will not be possible. However, if the distribution of item validities corresponds closely to what might be expected as a result of sampling fluctuations from a popu-

lation in which all the validities were zero, any further detailed analysis devoted to selecting certain items for weighting is almost certain to be futile.

2. Given that the distribution of validities seems not to be attributable to chance, several scoring keys can be set up, setting different levels of validity as the minimum for an item to be weighted. Thus, four keys might be tried, the first weighting all items with a validity of ±0.15 or over, the second all with a validity of ±0.12 or over, the third all with validity of ±0.10 or over, and the fourth all with validity of ±0.08 or over.

3. The papers can then be scored with each of the keys described above. The score resulting from each of the keys can be correlated with the criterion, and it can be determined empirically which key gives the score with the highest validity.

4. In choosing the key to be recommended for use on new samples, consideration must be given to the regression which will occur as we move to a new group of individuals. If the scoring key is composed almost exclusively of items whose validity is of the same sign (all plus or all minus), it is desirable to use a key that sets a standard of validity somewhat lower than that which yields maximum test validity for the specific sample analyzed. The tendency of items to regress toward the group average makes the items with highest validity relatively less outstanding in the new sample, and maximum validity can be achieved by weighting a somewhat larger group of items. However, if the scoring key includes both positively and negatively weighted items in somewhat comparable numbers, the standard of validity which gives the key with maximum validity for the sample studied may be expected to give the key which will also be most valid for new samples. Regression of item validities takes place in this case also, but since the average of all item validities is approximately zero and regression takes place toward that value, the proportional size of the validities for different groups of items will be maintained.

The second general attack upon the problem of selecting items to be weighted in scoring key takes account of item intercorrelations through a series of approximations. The general procedure is to set up an initial key for the tests by keying a rather small pool of the most valid items. A score is obtained for each individual, based on this key. The validity of these scores is determined. Then the correlation of each item with this score is obtained. That is, the score on the new key is used as the continuous variable for the item analysis.[2] We then have for each item (1) its correlation with the criterion and (2) its correlation with the initial pool of weighted items. We also know the validity of the score based on the initial pool of items. Given these values, we can compute for each item its *partial correlation* with the criterion when score on the initially chosen pool of items is held constant. This tells us what additional contribution each item would make to the validity of the initial pool. The analysis for each of the items already in the pool tells how much that item would add to the rest of the items in the pool.

We can now choose a second pool of items to be scored, selecting those with the largest partial correlations. This selection takes account not only of the validity of the single items, but also of their correlation with the initial pool of scored items. It consequently comes closer to being the best set of items. The whole process can now be repeated, if desired, scoring the

tests on the second pool of items, correlating each item with this second pool score, and determining the contribution which each item makes to this second pool. It has been reported, on the basis of a procedure resembling this one, that the pool of items stabilizes quite promptly, and that further approximations after the first or second contribute very little to the validity of the resulting key.[3]

In this procedure, the problem of how rigorous a standard to set for item inclusion remains. If the test is such that only positive weights are to be considered, a standard procedure would be to include at each approximation all items whose partial correlations with the criterion were positive, when correlation with the previous key was held constant, no matter how small they were. This appears to be an unduly liberal procedure, however, and probably would not yield a final key with the maximum validity. If both positively and negatively weighted items are to be included, the sign of the partial correlation cannot serve as a guide to item inclusion, and the absolute magnitude of the partial must be used instead. The problem becomes one of determining at what size of partial correlation the additional valid variance covered by the item balances the additional nonvalid variance which is introduced by adding the item with unit weight. As in the previous method, several keys may be prepared, each based on a different standard of size of partial correlation, and the resulting validities may be compared empirically. This is a laborious undertaking but is probably the only defensible one unless some rational basis can be established for the choice of cutting value.

A third alternate procedure for approximating the best set of items starts with the total set of available items, rather than a small pool of the most valid, and prunes off the useless ones.[4] Initially, the validity of

---

[2] For items that were included in the original pool, the correlation should be corrected for the spurious element introduced by including the item itself in the composite. This is accomplished by the formula

$$r = \frac{r_{it}\sigma_t - \sigma_i}{\sqrt{\sigma_i{}^2 + \sigma_t{}^2 - 2\sigma_i\sigma_t r_{it}}}$$

where r_{it} = the correlation of the item and the total score
σ_t = the standard deviation of the total score
σ_i = the standard deviation of the individual item

[3] This method is a variation of one proposed by Flanagan [1].
[4] This approach is a variant of one proposed by Horst [3].

each item is determined. A scoring key is prepared for the complete test. For tests of knowledge or ability, this key may be prepared a priori. For measures of interest, adjustment, personal history, and the like, it is prepared on the basis of the item validities. The key may be limited to positive weights, and probably would be in tests of ability, or it may include both positive and negative weighting of items. Once the key has been prepared, each test paper is scored with it. Correlations of each item with total score on the test are now obtained. The correlation of total score with criterion is also required.

Given the above data, we may proceed to calculate the partial correlation of each item with the criterion when score on the total test is held constant. (The total test usually includes a large enough number of items so that the inclusion of each item in the total score with which it is being correlated will hardly have an appreciable effect.) A reduced test may then be prepared by eliminating those items with the least promising partial correlations. If negative weights are being used, these will be the items for which the *absolute* size of the partial correlations is least. If only positive weights are being used, all items with negative partial correlations will be the first to be eliminated.

The elimination of items may well proceed in two or even more stages. That is, as a first approximation the most unpromising items are eliminated. The reduced test is then scored for each individual. The validity of the reduced score is determined, and the correlation of each item with the reduced score is computed. Partial correlations with the criterion, holding total score on the reduced test constant, provide the basis for further pruning out of the least effective items. This stepwise procedure is more exact than a single elimination of items because the total score used for the second pruning will correspond more closely to the score on the final refined test. The correlations on the basis of which certain items are rejected will correspond more closely to the correlations with the final effective test.

Once again, we face the problem of how many items to screen out of the original item pool. In some cases the decision may be dictated by the desired length of the final test. Administrative considerations may dictate the inclusion of the best 75, or 100, or 150 items. The partial correlations in this and the previous method then serve to identify those items. When no such consideration exists, a feasible procedure is to decrease the size of the total pool of items by successive steps. With each successive pruning, the correlation of total score with criterion score may be determined. When this correlation commences to decrease, it is time to stop further reductions in the pool of items. Because of regression effects, we may anticipate that, for continued use in new samples, maximum validity will be obtained from a pool of items somewhat larger than that yielding maximum validity in the specific sample analyzed.

The procedures just discussed for item selection on the basis of item validities represent rather substantial undertakings, in terms of the amount of computation which is involved. They can probably be justified only when the item validities are based on a large group and when it is anticipated that the test items will be extensively used, so that the investment of a good deal of time is justified to arrive at the best selection from among them. These procedures have probably never been given an adequate empirical trial, so that it is not possible to estimate how much improvement in validity the more refined procedures may be expected to add to rough, intuitive procedures of item selection.

USE OF INTERNAL CONSISTENCY DATA

In tests made up of a more or less homogeneous group of items, in which each item purports to tap the same psychological functions as the others, it is appropriate to examine the internal consistency of the individual items. We determine the correlation of each item with the total score based on the whole set of items. This type of analysis, which can be carried out as soon as a preliminary form of the test has been administered to an experimental group, provides information of value both for the selection of test items and for the editorial revision of items. We must now consider the use of internal consistency data in these two ways.

The logic of using internal consistency data for item selection is somewhat more complex than the logic of using item validities for this same purpose. The internal consistency of single items is related to the homogeneity of the total test. The higher the internal consistencies are, the more homogeneous will be the test. But how high a degree of homogeneity is desirable in a test? In the case of validity, this question does not arise, since validity is the ultimate goal in test construction. The more valid the total score in the test, the better satisfied we will be. However, homogeneity in a test is not an end in itself. It is a means to attaining validity in the test score, to attaining validity in a battery of tests, or to attaining a degree of analytical clarity in the interpretation of the score on the test.

An item that shows a very low correlation with total score on a test is either very unreliable or measures functions quite different from those measured by the rest of the items in the test. In either case, items showing very low correlations with the test as a whole, and particularly those showing negative correlations, are probably undesirable items. They should either be rejected completely or else revised and tried out again. If we are interested in developing a test which will yield a single score with some unity of meaning, a score to which a single name can reasonably be applied, the items at the low end of the scale for internal consistency are clearly the least desirable. Is the reverse true? Are items with highest internal consistency generally the most desirable?

The item showing high internal consistency *must* have a substantial degree of reliability. This will be an attractive feature of such an item. It must also have a large amount of overlapping of the functions covered by the other items in the test. Up to a point this is good, since the test is supposed to have a substantial amount of unity and coherence. However, a test is also supposed to have a certain amount of breadth and scope, and should cover in a representative fashion the scope with which it deals. Exclusive preoccupation with item internal consistency may lead to an undue narrowing of the scope of the test.

Suppose that a preliminary form has been prepared for a survey test of knowledge of physical science. Let us assume that of the 200 items in this test 80 deal with physics, 80 deal with chemistry, 20 deal with geology, and 20 deal with astronomy. Given any specialization of knowledge, we may expect greater correlation between items within the same field than from one field to another. Because of their predominance in the total score, we may expect the physics and chemistry items to show higher item-test correlations. It is entirely possible that if we select from the total pool the 100 items with highest internal consistency we shall limit the final test exclusively to physics and chemistry items. This represents a narrowing of range of content which may be quite inappropriate to the original purpose of the test. Internal consistency data must be used with discretion within the framework of the original outline and specifications for a test. They cannot override the outline, and they do not provide a substitute for a definite content outline for the test.

The selection of items on the basis of internal consistency contributes to the reliability and the homogeneity of the resulting test score. Empirical evidence supports our previous discussion in indicating that this information is most effective in the negative sense. That is, internal consistency data are more useful as a means for the discovery and elimination of the usually rather small percentage of unsatisfactory items than as a means of selecting a small fraction of items that can be identified as *the best*. Empirical studies show that tests made up of items with intermediate internal consistency values have very nearly the same reliability as tests made up of items with the highest internal consistency. It is only when items in the lower ranges of internal consistency are used that reliability of the resulting test suffers.

Our discussion in previous paragraphs suggests that there may sometimes be a question as to what should be used as the total score, against which the single items should be analyzed. In the illustration of the physical science survey test, we might inquire whether we should be interested in the correlation between an astronomy item and score on the total of all the items of all types or the total of all astronomy items. The problem is that of deciding how broad a range of content and function should really be thought of as homogeneous. Logically, we are usually on stronger ground when the total score represents a single narrowly defined type of test material. Items may then be correlated with subtest totals, where the subtests are composed of a single item type. Homogeneity is a matter of degree, after all, and there is no entirely clear-cut definition of what constitutes a single unified test.

Internal consistency data should be used in item selection first of all to screen out the definitely unsatisfactory test items. Beyond that point, the data should be used, in connection with item difficulty data and with the outline of specifications for the test, to select the more promising items in each specified segment of content or function measured. In addition, internal consistency item analysis data provide a most valuable source of information to the item writer in revising and improving the items which he has written. For this purpose, data are needed with regard to each of the response options on an item. The analysis should show the percentage choosing each option separately for the upper and lower fraction (usually 27 per cent) of the group

on the basis of total score. These data may be used in revising and rewriting the item. Such rewriting and revision may be worth while not merely to salvage poor items but also to improve details of items which are in general satisfactory.

Consider the following item for a test of chemical information:

If copper and zinc are melted down together and the molten mixture is allowed to cool, the product will be

   A. An alloy.
   B. An amalgam.
   C. A new chemical compound.
   D. A salt.
   E. Monel metal.

Suppose that analysis of the upper and lower 27 per cent of a group completing a course in high-school chemistry gives the following results:

	Per Cent Choosing	
Choice	Top 27%	Bottom 27%
Option A	79	53
Option B	12	8
Option C	5	18
Option D	0	1
Option E	3	15
Omitted	1	5

A study of these results shows that option D was attracting almost no choices from anyone in either group. This suggests that option D may well be replaced by a more attractive mislead, if one can be thought of. The test editor would rack his brain for a more plausible wrong answer to substitute for D. Option B is attractive, but it attracts the wrong people. It draws more choices from the upper than from the lower group. It looks as though the word "amalgam" is meaningless to many in the lower group, whereas those in the upper group have enough of an idea of its meaning to confuse it with "alloy." By its nearness in meaning to the correct answer, this mislead lowers the discrimination of the item in the group studied. The test editor would consider finding a different option to take the place of option B.

In general, a study of the percentages choosing each response option will reveal two types of inadequacies, as illustrated in the preceding example. Some response options are non-functioning, i.e., they are not attracting any choices from either group. Some misleads fail to discriminate or discriminate in the reverse direction, i.e., they are chosen as often or more often by the upper as by the lower group. Each of these provides a cue to the test editor for revision of the item. This revision often takes the form of replacing the deficient misleads. It may also sometimes result in rewording of the stem of the test item.

REFERENCES

1. FLANAGAN, J. C. A short method for selecting the best combination of test items for a particular purpose. *Psychol. Bull.,* 33, 1936, 603–604.

2. FLANAGAN, J. C. General considerations in the selection of test items and a short method of estimating the product-moment coefficient from the data at the tails of the distribution. *J. educ. Psychol.,* 30, 1939, 674–680.

3. HORST, A. P. Item selection by means of a maximizing function. *Psychometrika,* 1, 1936, 229–244.

4. KELLEY, T. L. The selection of upper and lower groups for the validation of test items. *J. educ. Psychol.,* 30, 1939, 17–24.

Chapter 15

Reliability

ROBERT L. THORNDIKE

COLLABORATORS: LEE J. CRONBACH / EDWARD E. CURETON
TRUMAN L. KELLEY / ALBERT K. KURTZ
MARION W. RICHARDSON / L. L. THURSTONE

Whenever we measure anything, whether in the physical, the biological, or the social sciences, that measurement contains a certain amount of chance error. The amount of chance error may be large or it may be small, but it is universally present to some extent. Two sets of measurements of the same features of the same individuals will never *exactly* duplicate each other. In some cases the discrepancies between two sets of measurements may be expressed in miles and in other cases in millionths of a millimeter, but if the unit is fine enough in relation to the accuracy of the measurements, discrepancies will always appear. The fact that repeated sets of measurements never exactly duplicate one another is what is meant by "unreliability." However, at the same time, repeated measurements of a series of objects or individuals will ordinarily show *some* consistency. The block of wood which was the heaviest the

This paper was reprinted from *Educational Measurement.* F. Lindquist, (Ed.), 1951, with permission of the author and the American Council on Education.

first time the set of blocks was weighed will tend to be among the heaviest blocks the second time, and consistency will be the rule among all the blocks of the set. The same, to a degree, will be the case for the weights of the boys in a classroom, or for their performance upon a test of reading comprehension. This tendency toward consistency from one set of measurements to another is the reverse of the fact of variation which we have just considered, and will be designated "reliability."

The consistency of a set of measurements may be approached from two rather different viewpoints. In the first, one is concerned with the actual magnitude of errors of measurement, expressed in the same units in which individual scores are expressed. One thinks of a series of repeated measurements of some characteristic of a particular object, and of the distribution of scores which would result from this repeated measurement. Thus, if a chemical analysis were carried out on successive samples from a batch of steel in order to determine the percentage of carbon in the steel, the percentage would vary somewhat from sample to sample. If the analysis were repeated 100 times, there would result 100 estimates of the true percentage. These estimates would fall into a frequency distribution, for which measures of central tendency and variability could be computed. The variability of the values in the frequency distribution of repeated measurements, typically expressed as the standard deviation of the distribution, provides a statement of the actual size of the errors of measurement. This statistic is called the "standard error of measurement."

A similar series of repeated measurements could be obtained for anatomical measures such as height or weight. Theoretically, such a series could also be obtained for measurements of reading comprehension, number facility, or any other behavior function. In practice, however, a series of repetitions of the *same* measurement is almost certain to be impossible in the case of human behavior because the individual does not remain the same under the impact of repeated measurements. In educational and psychological testing, the standard error of measurement must always be estimated indirectly by other methods.

A second approach to consistency in measurement may be made in terms of the consistency with which the individual maintains his position in the total group on repetition of a measurement procedure. If two equivalent measures are obtained for each individual within a group, a more or less direct index of the consistency of the measurements is available in the correlation between the two sets of scores. This may be called the "reliability coefficient." For many purposes, the reliability coefficient lends itself to direct and simple interpretation, since it gives directly the proportion of the variance (s^2) of any test score distribution that may be attributed to systematic differences between individuals and not to chance errors. The virtues of the two approaches to the concept of reliability will be compared later in the chapter.

It should already be clear from the discussion that wherever there is reliability in a set of measurements there is also some degree of unreliability. The two are cut from the same pie, being always present together, the one becoming more as the other becomes less. That is, in one situation the consistency of the measurements from one repetition to another may be very marked and the variations quite minor. This would tend to be the case in simple measurements of the common physical properties of a group of objects. In another situation, the consistency may be almost vanishingly small, so there is practically no relationship between an individual's or object's standing in the group upon one set of measurements and the standing upon another. Theoretically, either consistency or inconsistency may be thought of as approaching zero as a limit, but in practice both are usually present to some degree in any measurement procedure.

The degree of reliability of a set of measurements is a very important consideration, both in the practical day-to-day use of tests and in research projects of various kinds. Some consideration will be given to the importance of reliability, and of data concerning reliability of a particular measuring instrument, in each of these two contexts.

In practical work in measurement and evaluation, we obtain a score for an individual upon some test in order to arrive at some judgment about him, and usually to take some practical action with regard to him. For example, a boy is given a reading test to determine whether he is making satisfactory progress or whether he needs special attention and possibly remedial work. Sometime later he may take a series of achievement examinations so that a college may decide whether he is to be admitted to pursue a course of studies there. Still later, he may be given an interest inventory in order to provide some suggestion as to whether he should be encouraged to specialize in law, medicine, engineering, or some other field. In selecting a test to be used for a practical testing project, and in interpreting the test results, the educator or guidance worker is concerned about the accuracy of the instrument. Other things being equal (in particular, validity) he will always choose the most reliable test from among those available, the one which will provide the most precise estimate of the quality being studied. In interpreting the results from administration of a test, it is always desirable to know how much the obtained score is likely to vary from a true evaluation of the individual's ability to perform on the type of test which has been used.

Clearly, any degree of unreliability in the score resulting from the application of a measuring device is distressing to the educator, guidance worker, industrial personnel officer, or other individual who must use that score as a basis for a practical decision. Unreliability introduces a question mark after the score, and means that any judgment based upon it must be tentative. The lower the reliability of the score, the more tentative the judgment or decision must be, until in the extreme case, as the reliability approaches zero, the score provides absolutely no basis at all for any judgment or decision. The question of the relevancy of the score to the action judgment, though crucial, is a different question and one which falls outside the scope of this chapter. The point which is being made here is that as the reliability of a score decreases, the low reliability makes tentative *any* judgment which is based on that score, and that as the reliability approaches zero, basing *any* judgment on it becomes impossible. The problem of interpretation of scores at different levels of reliability will be discussed more fully later in the chapter.

Reliability becomes of critical importance in research studies at a number of points. In any study of prediction and in any study of improvement resulting from training, *some* degree of reliability in the measure of the criterion being predicted or in the ability being trained is imperative if one is to achieve any prediction on the one hand

or any evidence of improvement on the other. One can make no worth-while prediction of a completely unreliable criterion, and one can produce no improvement in a measure of performance which depends entirely upon chance factors. The accuracy of prediction which it is possible to achieve or the amount of improvement in performance which can be shown is limited by the reliability of the measure through which the performance is manifested. Data on reliability of both test and criterion are necessary if the research worker is to be able to interpret the extent to which the imperfect correlation between test and criterion is due to lack of overlapping in function and the extent to which it is due to lack of precision in both measures.

In the analytical study of the relationships among groups of tests information concerning reliability is again crucial. Only with that information available is it possible to determine the extent to which lack of correlation among tests arises because the measures cover unrelated aspects of behavior and the extent to which lack of correlation is due to a lack of consistency within each one of the separate measures.

LOGICAL CONSIDERATIONS IN EVALUATING RELIABILITY

The evaluation of the reliability of a measuring instrument involves two types of operations, one experimental and the other statistical. On the one hand, it is necessary to apply the instrument to a defined group of cases following a specified experimental design and under specified experimental conditions. On the other, the scores resulting from such administration must be analyzed by appropriate procedures to yield a statistical value which will represent the reliability characteristics of the test. These two aspects are to some extent independent, in that the same essential statistical procedures may be applied to data gathered in quite a variety of ways.

Traditionally, in discussions of reliability

determination, the lion's share of the discussion has been devoted to the statistical techniques involved. It is the conviction of the author that much more attention than has usually been accorded it needs to be given to the experimental aspect. The experimental procedures are very closely bound up with the logical aspects of the problem, so that one must first make an analysis of what is to be accomplished by and what purposes are served by a measure of reliability. The experimental operations must be planned with these purposes in view and evaluated in the light of them. For that reason, the next sections of this chapter are devoted to an analysis of the logical and experimental aspects of reliability. Consideration of statistical procedures follows discussion of the various experimental procedures, a given procedure being discussed in connection with the experimental procedure with which it has the closest connection.

RELIABILITY AND ANALYSIS OF VARIANCE

Whenever a measuring device is applied to a group of individuals and a score is obtained for each individual in the group, the resulting distribution of scores will spread out over an appreciable range of score values. The variation in any set of scores arises from a number of different factors. Consider measurements of weights of each of the children in a particular school classroom. These differ due to variations in the age of the children, their sex, their parentage, the nourishment which they have received during the years of their life, whether they have been sick recently, whether or not they took a drink of water just before coming to be weighed, the exact angle from which the nurse happened to be looking at the scales, and a host of other factors, minor and major, fugitive and lasting.

The variation in a set of scores arises in part because of systematic differences among the individuals in the group with respect to the quality being measured. In part it arises from unpredictable inaccuracies in the measurement of the separate individuals. Thus, in the example above, variations among children with respect to how large a breakfast they had eaten, how much clothing they had on, how recently they had taken a drink, the angle from which the nurse read the scales, and the like, could be thought of as variable inaccuracies or errors of measurement for different children. These variations would account for some part, though possibly a small one, of the variations in weight recorded from the different children in the class. The evaluation of the reliability of any measure reduces to a determination of how much of the variation in the set of scores is due to systematic differences among the individuals in the group and how much to inaccuracies in measurement of the particular individuals.

There are a number of different statistics which have been developed as summary values to describe the variability in a set of scores. These include the range, interquartile range, average deviation, standard deviation, and variance. For the purposes of the present discussion, the most useful statistic for describing the variability of a set of scores seems to be the variance (σ^2)[1] or the square of the standard deviation. The particular advantage of the variance, for the present discussion, is that it can be broken down into the separate parts which combine additively to give the total. Thus, if the variance of weight in pounds of pupils in a class were 150, this might break up into a variance of 125 permanently associated with the individuals and a variance of 25 associated with the accidents of that particular set of measurements. These parts add together to make up the total variance of 150 for the set of scores. Whenever a number of independent factors combine to produce a score, it is possible to make an analysis of variance into fractions which are associated with particular factors, and

[1] In symbolism for representing the variance of a distribution, σ^2 will be used to represent the theoretical population value, while s^2 will designate the value obtained from a specific limited sample.

these fractions will sum up to give the total variance.[2] That is,

$$\sigma^2 = \sigma_a^2 + \sigma_b^2 + \ldots + \sigma_k^2$$

where σ^2 is the total variance of the distribution of scores and $\sigma_a^2, \sigma_b^2, \ldots, \sigma_k^2$ are the parts of the variance associated with factors $a, b, \ldots, k$ respectively. Thus, the variance in weight of pupils in our classroom might be broken down into variance associated with age, variance associated with sex, variance associated with family, and other variances associated with every other definable stable characteristic of the individuals in the group. There will also be variance which is associated only with the one particular set of measurements, that is, which will not be reproduced another time. This may be designated *"error"* variance. The existence of this error variance corresponds to the fact of unreliability, and its amount relative to the total of all variance is a measure of the degree of unreliability.

It is well to pause briefly at this point and see with just what general type of error we are concerned here when we talk of error variance. Not every type of error, not every discrepancy from the value which an omniscient recording angel would register for the specimen in question qualifies as a part of the error variance. Suppose we were weighing children on scales which were adjusted incorrectly in such a way that on the average each child was given a weight two pounds above his "true" weight. This adjustment error is uniform and systematic and results in a "constant error." As described, it actually does not contribute to variance at all, though it does make every observation incorrect. In our present discussion, we are not concerned with such constant errors, disastrous though they may be to scientific precision. Again, suppose that the scales on which we were weighing children were in error in such a way they credited each child with two pounds for each pound he weighed in excess of 50 pounds. This would not be a

constant error, but it would be systematic, that is, it is statable in definite terms and predictable for any child. This is still not the type of error with which we are concerned in discussions of reliability. The type of errors which we have in mind when we speak of "chance errors of measurement" are errors which are essentially unpredictable from anything we may know about the individual or his previous performance. These errors may be defined as follows:

$$\Sigma\, e_1 x_1 = \Sigma\, e_2 x_2 = \Sigma\, e_1 e_2 = 0$$

where e_1 and e_2 refer to error on two forms of a test, and x_1 and x_2 each refer to "true score"[3] on the corresponding form. What we are saying is that the type of error in which we are concerned is error which is unrelated to the individual's true score or to his error on another form of the test.

Let us designate the variance of true scores of a group on a trait by σ_∞^2 and the variance of errors of measurement by σ_e^2. If the magnitude of the error of measurement is unrelated to the magnitude of the true score, we have,

$$\sigma^2 = \sigma_\infty^2 + \sigma_e^2$$

That is, the variance of the obtained scores equals the sum of the variance in true scores and the variance arising from errors of measurement. It is also possible to relate these fractions of variance to the reliability coefficient which was discussed earlier in the chapter. We have

$$r_{11} = \frac{\sigma_\infty^2}{\sigma^2} \tag{1}$$

and

$$r_{11} = 1 - \frac{\sigma_e^2}{\sigma^2} \tag{2}$$

That is, the numerical value of the reli-

---

[2] When factors are not independent, it becomes necessary to analyze covariances as well as variances.

[3] We shall repeatedly have occasion to use the expression "true score" throughout this chapter. The term is convenient but a little misleading. As we speak of it, true score is not the ultimate fact in the book of the recording angel. Rather, it is *the score resulting from all determinable systematic factors*, including any systematic biasing factors which may produce systematic incorrectness in the scores. This larger expression should be understood whenever the term "true score" is used.

ability coefficient of a test corresponds exactly to the proportion of the variance in test scores which is due to true differences between individuals in the quality being evaluated by the test. A test is unreliable in proportion as it has error variance.

It becomes clear that the basic problem in determining the reliability of a testing procedure becomes that of *defining* what shall be thought of as true variance between individuals and what shall be thought of as error variance. When this definition has been reached, the next step is to devise those series of experimental and statistical operations which will provide the best estimates of the defined fractions of variance. The next section will deal, therefore, with the analysis of types and sources of variance in test scores. After this analysis, various experimental operations which have been proposed to provide data for estimating reliability will be considered, each set of operations being evaluated in terms of the logical analysis.

SOURCES OF VARIANCE IN TEST SCORES

As noted above, variance in a set of scores from any test or measuring device arises from a great variety of specific sources. However, these may profitably be grouped, for purposes of discussion, into a few major categories. A classification of sources of variance is presented in Table 15–1.[4] The categories given here probably do not exhaust the possible range of categories. Certainly, many more subcategories could be listed under most of the major headings, and those which are presented should be thought of as illustrative rather than exhaustive. A consideration of each of the categories will provide the basis for a decision as to which fractions of variance should be thought of as true, systematic variance in the quality or qualities being measured and which should be thought of as error variance.

Variance within a set of scores arises first

[4] A similar analysis, differing in detail, has been formulated by Cronbach [2].

Table 15–1   Possible Sources of Variance in Score on a Particular Test

I. *Lasting and general characteristics of the individual*
  A. Level of ability on one or more general traits, which operate in a number of tests
  B. General skills and techniques of taking tests
  C. General ability to comprehend instructions

II. *Lasting but specific characteristics of the individual*
  A. Specific to the test as a whole (and to parallel forms of it)
    1. Individual level of ability on traits required in this test but not in others
    2. Knowledges and skills specific to particular forms of test items
  B. Specific to particular test items
    1. The "chance" element determining whether the individual does or does not know a particular fact. (Sampling variance in a finite number of items, not the probability of his guessing the answer.)

III. *Temporary but general characteristics of the individual*
  (Factors affecting performance on many or all tests at a particular time)
  A. Health
  B. Fatigue
  C. Motivation
  D. Emotional strain
  E. General test-wiseness (partly lasting)
  F. Understanding of mechanics of testing
  G. External conditions of heat, light, ventilation, etc.

IV. *Temporary and specific characteristics of the individual*
  A. Specific to a test as a whole
    1. Comprehension of the specific test task (insofar as this is distinct from I B)
    2. Specific tricks or techniques of dealing with the particular test materials (insofar as distinct from II A 2)
    3. Level of practice on the specific skills involved (especially in psychomotor tests)
    4. Momentary "set" for a particular test

B. Specific to particular test items
   1. Fluctuations and idiosyncrasies of human memory
   2. Unpredictable fluctuations in attention or accuracy, superimposed upon the general level of performance characteristic of the individual

V. *Systematic or chance factors affecting the administration of the test or the appraisal of test performance*
   A. Conditions of testing—adherence to time limits, freedom from distractions, clarity of instructions, etc.
   B. Unreliability or bias in subjective rating of traits or performances

VI. *Variance not otherwise accounted for (chance)*
   A. "Luck" in selection of answers by "guessing"

---

of all because different individuals possess different amounts of certain general and persistent traits (category I of Table 15–1). Thus, in a series of intellectual tests some type of ability to reason deductively might be a general quality which entered into a number of the tests and which, for each of the tests, accounted for part of the individual differences in performance. Or several arithmetic tests might have a common factor of facility with numbers. Verbal comprehension is likely to enter into a wide range of tests requiring reading. Almost any test performance will depend in part upon general abilities which are also involved in a number of other types of test performance. The type of variance which is now under discussion represents a persistent, lasting characteristic of each individual, causing stable individual differences in test performance. Since it arises from a persisting feature of each individual, this variance is clearly systematic variance and should be so treated in any sequence of operations set up to provide an estimate of reliability.

Two rather special types of persisting general factors deserve some particular mention. These are the general ability to comprehend instructions and what we may speak of as "test-wiseness." These factors

are mentioned because they are likely to enter into any test score, whether we want them to or not. That is, performance on many types of tests is likely to be in some measure a function of the individual's ability to understand what he is supposed to do on the test. Particularly as the test situation is novel or the instructions complex, this factor is likely to enter in. At the same time, test score is likely to be in some measure a function of the extent to which the individual is at home with tests and has a certain amount of sagacity with regard to tricks of taking them. Freedom from emotional tension, shrewdness with regard to when to guess, and a keen eye for secondary and extraneous cues are likely to be useful in a wide range of tests, particularly those which are not well constructed. The presence of variance in score due to variation in comprehension of instructions and in test-wiseness is usually undesirable from the point of view of the purposes of the test in question. It usually represents systematic invalid variance serving systematically to reduce the validity of the test. However, these factors must be recognized. They present a challenge to the author of the test, who will try to minimize them, except where their presence is specifically desired, by providing the clearest possible instructions and a minimum of secondary cues. These factors present a problem of validity rather than one of reliability; as far as our present analysis is concerned, they represent a general, lasting quality of the individual and must be treated as such.

In addition to variance which is common to a range of tests, each test will have some variance which arises from persistent characteristics of the individuals being studied but which is specific to the particular area being tested (category II). That is, there is some variance which will be present in spelling tests, for example, but not in tests of any other performance. There are, of course, degrees of specificity of knowledge or skill, so that further narrowing down may take place even within a given field.

In addition to variance which characterizes the field of performance, such as spelling or numerical computation, there may be variance associated with the specific form and manner of testing. In the case of spelling this might relate to oral presentation as in a spelling bee, writing words from dictation, or recognition of errors in words presented in a printed test. A numerical operations test might be presented in free-response or multiple-choice form, and variance might be associated with that feature. Finally, in any test there is likely to be variance associated with the particular sample of test items. There will be a certain amount of variation in specific bits of knowledge or skill, so that even the individual who has high over-all ability in the area in question will lack certain specific items of knowledge or skill and the individual low in general performance will succeed on isolated items not known by his generally more proficient fellow. The sampling of items—words to be comprehended, formulas to be known, generalizations to be applied, and the like—will be a source of variation in the resulting test scores. Given two tests made up of samples independently chosen in the same way from the same universe of items, individuals will fail to receive identical scores on the two tests because of variation in the particular items which each individual happens to have the skill or information to answer.

At this point we begin to encounter some difficulty in the logical determination of what shall be allocated to systematic variance and what to error variance. Variance specific to the area covered by the test (category II A 1) is certainly systematic variance, and any operation for determining reliability should be so planned that this type of variance is treated as systematic. The problems arise in connection with variance associated with the particular test format and with the particular sampling of test items. The question is one of finding the most useful definition. How broadly shall we define what we are measuring? Shall we define it in terms of an area of content only? In terms of an area of content and form of test? In terms of an area of content, form of test, and particular set of test items?

The first definition above leads to experimental procedures which appear to come closer to evaluating test validity than test reliability. That is, if format is considered a source of error variance, we are led to correlate tests with different types of items and manner of presentation. We are then beginning to inquire whether the test is consistent with other measures rather than whether that particular test measures consistently. The third definition appears so narrow as to have little practical meaning in most cases. We are rarely interested in performance on a limited set of test items for their own sake. We are almost always interested in test performance as an indication of ability to perform on the whole universe of items of which the test represents a limited sample. The variance due to the sample of items is, therefore, in an entirely true sense part of the error of measurement. In conclusion, then, it seems that the most meaningful definition of reliability will allocate to systematic variance that variation arising from the specific abilities required in the area being studied (category II A 1) and that arising from knowledges and skills specific to the particular form of the test (category II A 2), but will allocate to error variance that variation in performance arising from the particular sampling of test items (category II B).

The above discussion brings home one very important point. There is no single, universal, and absolute reliability coefficient for a test. Determination of reliability is as much a logical as a statistical problem. The appropriate allocation of variance from different sources calls for practical judgment of what use is to be made of the resulting statistical value. This point will become increasingly apparent as the discussion continues.

A third group of factors making for variation in test scores are certain general but temporary characteristics of the individual or of the testing situation. These include such factors as state of health, amount of sleep the previous night, presence or absence of worries or other distracting influences, and a host of other internal factors which may have bearing upon the efficiency of the individual's work. Different test performances will be susceptible to these factors in varying degrees, but all will probably be influenced by them in some measure. The factors vary both in their permanence and their generality. Some may change from day to day, some from hour to hour. There may even be very short time fluctuations in efficiency which represent a change from minute to minute. In general, however, we may think of these factors as ones which characterize an individual at a particular testing session but not at another session.

Here, again, a problem arises as to what allocation is to be made of variance of this type. Once again, the problem becomes that of determining the type of consistency which it seems significant to measure. Is it important to determine how consistent a measure we have of the individual as he exists at a particular moment? Or is it important to determine how consistent his performance is from day to day and week to week? For some purposes the former may be the significant information, for some purposes the latter. If our interest lies in studying the intercorrelations among a battery of tests which have been given at one time, the appropriate measure of reliability for use in conjunction with those correlations would seem to be a measure of consistency at that moment in time. However, if the test results are to be used for predicting something about the individual at some later date or evaluating the result of training over some extended period, the more meaningful definition of reliability would appear to be that phrased in terms of consistency over a period of time. There are other specific purposes for which tests might be used, and in each case it will be necessary to decide whether it is more

meaningful for the temporary characteristics of the individual (category III) to be thought of as a source of systematic variance or as a source of error variance.

Our general discussion so far has provided no indication as to whether this or any other *possible* source of variance does in fact yield practically significant amounts of variance. That is, we have not shown whether or not it makes any *practical* difference what we do with variance in the above category. That cannot be a matter of general theoretical discussion, but must be a matter of specific empirical evidence in each case. The answer will probably vary widely in different areas of measurement. We might guess, for example, that in a simple power test of vocabulary less of the variance would be accounted for by temporary characteristics of the individual, than in a test of mood or feeling tone, for which substantial day-to-day swings might be expected.

A further group of factors making for variation in test performance is made up of certain relatively temporary and specific factors. In this category are included influences which tend to be more limited both in time and in scope than those discussed in the immediately preceding paragraphs. Certain of these factors characterize performance on a test as a whole. If the test is novel and the instructions difficult, individuals may vary in the extent to which they "catch on" to the nature of the task. In part this will probably represent general ability to understand instructions (category I B), but in part it may represent temporary or "chance" variations superimposed on that general ability. Again, a test may call for certain specific tricks or techniques of which the individual does or does not "get the hang." Furthermore, performance on many tests, particularly measures of complex coordination or skill, is susceptible to considerable improvement through practice. A temporary feature of some importance may be the individual's practice level at the moment of testing. Finally, there are certain factors which, for the lack of any better term, we may group together under the heading of "mental-set" at the time of taking the test. Was the subject emphasizing speed or accuracy if it was a speeded test? To what cues was he particularly alert if it was a perceptual task? What was his momentary mood if it was an attitude or interest questionnaire?

The factors grouped in this category (IV A) are the ones whose presence and significance in any given case are probably most open to question. In many types of simple and standard tests they can perhaps be ignored. However, in novel types of tests, highly speeded tests, measures into which introspective interpretation enters heavily, and perhaps other types, the possibility of encountering variance from such sources as have just been discussed must be given serious consideration. The rationale for allocation of this type of variance would appear to follow much the same lines as that for variance attributable to general temporary conditions (category III) discussed previously.

In addition to factors specific to a particular test and date of testing, there may be even more specific and temporary factors. These are factors which are specific to an item or a few items and a minute or a few minutes of time. These factors appear as short-time fluctuations of memory or attention, momentary blockings of performance, cyclic variations in effort, and a variety of other fluctuations superimposed upon the general level of performance. These factors (category IV B), insofar as they affect score, introduce variable and unpredictable error into the score, and the treatment of the resulting variance should always be such that it is allocated to error variance.

For some situations we must recognize sources of variance not only in the subject being tested but in the conditions of giving and appraising the test. On the one hand factors of timing of a test, test instructions, amount of noise and distraction, and the

like may vary from person to person or subgroup to subgroup. One can see that this type of variation is especially likely to arise in the case of tests which are individually administered by a number of examiners, tests which are closely timed, or tests which have very complex instructions. On the other hand, variance may be introduced in appraising the test performance or other behavior which is to yield a score. This is true in proportion as the appraisal depends on the judgment of another human being. In essay examinations, rating scales of all sorts, projective tests, or in fact anything which calls for interpretation or evaluation by an observer or scorer, variance due to the scorer will enter in. There will be variance associated with different scorers, variance associated with changes in the scorer from time to time, and variance representing unpredictable scorer inconsistency. These types of variance (category V) become important only in certain particular measurement situations; but wherever they occur they constitute error variance, and procedures should be planned to identify them and treat them as error.

Finally, we must introduce the concept of "chance" to take care of variance not otherwise accounted for. We can never find antecedent factors which will account for all the variance in a set of test scores. Some variance arises from guessing at answers, some from other obscure variable influences which we cannot define or specify. The variance of this type (category VI) is error variance in its purest form, and the operations which define reliability must allocate it to that category.

PROCEDURE FOR ESTIMATING RELIABILITY

The evaluation of the reliability of a measuring instrument requires a determination of the consistency of repeated measurements of the same object or group of objects. In the physical sciences many repetitions of a measurement of a single object or phenomenon may provide a reasonable method for estimating the precision of the measurement procedure. In dealing with human behavior, however, the individual is likely to be changed as a result of the operation of measurement, and it usually is necessary to limit sharply the number of times a single individual is measured. In practice, therefore, all procedures of reliability estimation generally useful to psychology and education are based upon getting a small number of measurements, typically only two, for each individual in a representative group. Stability of results is achieved by increasing the number of individuals measured rather than the number of measurements of each. These measurements provide sets of scores, again usually two for each individual, for analysis. The usual analysis has consisted of computation of the coefficient of correlation between the two sets of scores, yielding an estimate of average consistency for the group.

We have defined the reliability coefficient of a test as the ratio of the variance of true scores to the variance of obtained scores (made up of true measure and error). Where two equivalent forms of a test are available, it can be shown that this reliability coefficient is in fact the correlation between the two forms. Equivalent forms in this situation are defined as tests which overlap completely in their true score variance, and for which the proportion of true score to total variance is the same.

We must now determine how equivalent measures may be set up, so that the correlation between them may be obtained, and how the true variance of a set of scores may be estimated so that its ratio to the total variance may be calculated. These are, in fact, one and the same problem. Equivalent tests will be defined as tests which have identical true variance, but no overlap in error variance. Or the reverse, the true variance of a set of test scores will be defined as that which is common to that test and an equivalent test. We must next consider what actual testing operations will correspond satisfactorily to the logical requirements for equivalent tests. These logical requirements have been considered in the previous section, in connection with the desired allocation of different fractions of variance.

A number of different testing and statistical procedures have been proposed to provide the necessary coefficient of correlation between equivalent measures. Many of these represent efforts to develop short-cuts to the preparation and administration of two separate tests built to the same set of specifications, and therefore assumed to be equivalent. Others have been defended as preferable procedures. We shall consider the major sets of experimental and statistical procedures in turn, describing each and evaluating each in terms of its treatment of different categories of variance. The major procedures are:

1. Administration of two equivalent tests and correlation of the resulting scores.
2. Repeated administration of the same test form or testing procedure and correlation of the resulting scores.
3. Subdivision of a single test into two presumably equivalent groups of items, each scored separately, and correlation of the resulting two scores.
4. Analysis of the variance among individual items, and determination of the error variance therefrom.

A section will be devoted to each of the above procedures in turn, describing various subprocedures and discussing the problems which arise with each.

1. RELIABILITY DEFINED BY EQUIVALENT TEST FORMS

Since the formal definition of reliability has been phrased in terms of the correlation between two equivalent sets of measures, it seems obvious that the procedure for reliability determination which makes use of two equivalent tests will measure up to our logical requirements. This is in fact true, provided we can establish satisfactory procedures for preparing truly equivalent tests. This is a problem in the logic and practice of test construction. In preparing equivalent test forms, there is danger, on the one hand, that the two tests will vary so much in content and format that each will have some specific variance (category II A) distinct from the other, in which case the correlation between the two will underestimate the reliability. There is the reverse danger that the two forms may overlap to such an extent in specific details of content that variance due to specific sampling of content (category II B) may be common to the two tests. In that case, this variance will be treated as systematic rather than chance variance, and the obtained correlation will overestimate the reliability.

The best guarantee of equivalence for two test forms would seem to be that a complete and detailed set of specifications for the test be prepared in advance of any final test construction. The set of specifications should indicate item types, difficulty level of items, procedures and standards for item selection and refinement, and distribution of items with regard to the content to be covered, specified in as much detail as seems feasible. If each test form is then built to conform to the outline, while at the same time care is taken to avoid identity or detailed overlapping of content, the two resulting test forms should be truly equivalent. That is, each test must be built to the specifications, but within the limits set by complete specifications each test should present a random sampling of items. In terms of the practical operations of test construction, it will often be efficient to assemble two equivalent test forms from a single pool of items which have been given preliminary tryout. Within the total test if the test is homogeneous in the character of its content, or within parallel homogeneous sections of a heterogeneous test, items from the pool should be assigned to the two forms in such a way as to give the

same distribution of item difficulties and the same distribution of item-test correlations in each form.[5]

Two tests constructed in the above way will treat as systematic variance that variance in categories I and II A of Table 15–1. They will treat as error variance that in categories II B, IV B, and VI. The allocation of variance in categories III and IV A will depend upon the time interval between the administration of the two forms. If they are given in immediate sequence, this last variance will be treated as systematic variance; if some time intervenes between the testings, this variance will be allocated to error. For most uses of the resulting statistic, it will probably be more meaningful to let some time elapse between the two testings, thus treating temporary day-to-day fluctuations as errors of measurement. The question arises as to how long an interval should elapse. For most purposes, the answer to this lies in the thought that it is day-to-day fluctuations which we wish to allocate to error. An interval of a few weeks would usually appear sufficient. With longer intervals the problem of genuine growth and change in the individual is encountered, and the coefficient may be lowered because of these changes. Of course, for some purposes we may be interested in consistency of performance over an extended period of time, but consistency of this type represents a rather different concept of reliability.

In most of the usual types of tests of ability or achievement, preparing equivalent forms should not present undue diffi-

[5] If homogeneity is assumed for the materials in a test (or subtest), some check upon the degree to which equivalence has been achieved may be obtained by examining item correlations within and between the two test forms. On the average, these should be equal. An estimate of the extent to which this is the case might be obtained by subdividing each of the forms into two halves, by some such procedure as taking alternate items, and getting all the correlations among the resulting four scores. If we find approximately that

$$r_{12}r_{34} = r_{13}r_{24} = r_{14}r_{23}$$

this evidence supports the equivalence of the two tests.

culty. There are some situations, however, in which equivalence will be very difficult to achieve. This is true when either (a) the test task is essentially unique or (b) a single exposure to the test changes the individual to such an extent that he is really a different individual at the second exposure. The former case may occasionally arise in connection with unusual problem-type tasks. The second case is the more common source of difficulty. In any task which is sufficiently novel so that the experience of being tested adds a significant increment to the individual's practice with the task, he is a somewhat different individual at the time of a subsequent test. In novel tasks, or in tasks which present essentially a learning situation, the changes may be quite marked. The problem of defining reliability for such a changing function is a very difficult one, and no completely satisfactory solution seems available.

2. RELIABILITY DEFINED BY REPETITION OF IDENTICAL TEST FORM

In some cases, obtaining two equivalent measures will reduce to repetition of identically the same measuring instrument, the only difference being the time at which it is administered and perhaps the person by whom it is administered. That is, two equivalent measures of weight could be obtained by weighing the members of the group being studied on the same scales at two times ten days apart. The same situation would hold for almost any physiological or anatomical measurement. In these cases, we do not encounter the problem of sampling items from a larger universe of behavior, and so distinct equivalent test forms are neither meaningful nor possible. Equivalence in this case means identity of measuring instrument and procedure.

There are also certain behavioral measures in which the situation of sampling from a large universe of items does not arise. This is the case in simple repetitive tasks of motor speed and skill or of perceptual judgment. Thus, in a test of simple

reaction time, in which a measurement of the individual is obtained by timing repeatedly his simple reaction to some stimulus, the test task is so defined that no varied sampling from a more extensive universe of behavior is involved. Here, again, repetition of the same test provides the meaningful definition of "equivalent measures." The same would tend to be true of the type of perceptual judgment which is involved in the simple psychophysical experiment, as with judgments of brightness, length, weight, and so forth. In all these cases, repetition of the test appears to provide an acceptable procedure for reliability determination.

In most measures of intellect, temperament, or achievement, however, repetition of the same test form and correlation of the two sets of scores is less defensible as an operation for determining reliability. In these cases, a particular test consists of a limited sample from a much larger universe of possible items. The test score has practical significance insofar as it is representative of the individual's ability to respond to all of the tasks in the universe which it undertakes to sample. Reliability is a matter of the adequacy of the sampling of items as well as the consistency of behavior by each individual. In other words, in this case sampling of items (category II B) is an appreciable source of variance. Practical usefulness for the result dictates that this variance be treated as error variance in determining the reliability of the test. Repeating the same test form holds the sampling of items constant so that this factor is treated as systematic rather than error variance. Reliability coefficients calculated from a repetition of the same test may be expected to be higher than those based upon parallel, equivalent forms to the extent that this variance associated with sampling of items is a factor.

A second possible difficulty with repetition of the same test, which may or may not be important in any given case, is actual memory of particular items and of the previous response to them. Insofar as this memory is effective in leading the individual to repeat the same response he made the time before, the results on two test administrations tend to be abnormally alike. The same answers may be repeated not because the individual is consistent in his behavior, and arrives at the same conclusion in the same way, but because he happens to have a memory of his previous response. In effect, some of the variance associated with momentary memories and chance choices (categories IV B and V) becomes common to the two testings and is treated as systematic variance. Memory of previous responses is likely to be a factor in proportion as (a) the test is short, (b) the test items are distinctive and memorable, and (c) the interval between testings is short.

Another element that should be considered in deciding whether a repeated test is comparable to the original test is the attitude of the person tested. Especially where a test is quite long, as is the case with some interest and personality inventories, for example, repetition may be tedious for the subject, and he may therefore give more haphazard responses. This would, of course, operate to lower the correlation between the two testings. If a test score is likely to be greatly affected by motivation, as when the test requires very rapid or very concentrated work, it is especially important that the subject should feel that both testings will have equal significance for him. If one were to retest a group of men who had been accepted for pilot training, for example, and correlate these scores with scores earned during the initial classification period, before the men were sure of being accepted, the changed motivational conditions might well reduce the correlation and yield an underestimate of reliability. This matter of changed attitude and motivation could also affect a retest with an equivalent form of the test, but is probably likely to be most acute when the same test form is repeated.

In summary, for those types of tests in which sampling of items and memory of previous responses are not an issue and for which reasonable comparability of motivation seems likely, a second application of the same test at a later date and correlation of the two sets of scores provides an adequate set of operations for reliability estimation. In the many other cases, however, in which the factors of sampling and memory are significant sources of variance, repetition of the same test form will yield an estimate of reliability which tends to be systematically too high. In these latter cases the procedure is to be avoided. The correlation will also be unrepresentative, and probably too low, if the attitude of the subject changes from one testing to the other.

3. RELIABILITY DEFINED BY SUBDIVISION OF SINGLE TOTAL TEST

The preparation and administration of two equivalent test forms, though quite satisfactory as a procedure for estimating reliability, presents certain practical difficulties. These center around the problems of the time and labor involved both in the construction and the administration of two complete test forms. If only a single form of a test is needed for the research or practical use to which the test is to be put, it often seems unduly burdensome to prepare two separate tests merely in order to obtain an estimate of reliability. Furthermore, when a test is developed and administered as part of a research project, time for the administration of an equivalent form of the test is often not conveniently available. In the interests of economy it becomes desirable to set up procedures for extracting an estimate of reliability from a single administration of a single test. One group of such procedures subdivides the total test artificially into two half-length tests and correlates the scores on those. This correlation gives the reliability, not of the full test, but of one only half as long. The reliability of the full test must be estimated by the use of formula (3) or (4), on page 231. The second group of procedures is based essentially upon the analysis of variance among single test items. The procedures for sub-dividing the test will be considered in this section, and the next section will be devoted to procedures based upon analysis of the single items.

Manner of assembling part scores. If a test is composed of $2n$ separate items or parts, there are $(2n)!/[2\,(n)!(n)!]$ ways in which two subtests, each composed of n items, can be assembled from it. Certain procedures have been proposed for selection from among these possible alternatives, either on logical grounds or on grounds of convenience. The more usual procedures include: (a) selecting sets of items for the two half-tests which appear equivalent in content and difficulty, (b) putting alternate items or trials in each half-test, (c) putting alternate groups of items or trials in each half-test, (d) using the first half of the items or trials as one half-test and the second half as the other.

We must consider the specific merits of these different procedures, together with questions as to the logical acceptability of split-test procedures in general. Before entering into these considerations, however, it will be appropriate to indicate how we may obtain an estimate of the reliability of the *whole* test from the correlations between two *half-tests*.

Reliability of total test from part-test correlations. It can readily be shown that the correlation between the sum of two sets of scores, x_1 and x_2, and the sum of two other sets of scores, x_3 and x_4, is given by the formula

$$r_{(x_1+x_2)(x_3+x_4)} =$$
$$\frac{r_{13}\sigma_1\sigma_3 + r_{14}\sigma_1\sigma_4 + r_{23}\sigma_2\sigma_3 + r_{24}\sigma_2\sigma_4}{\sqrt{\sigma_1^2 + \sigma_2^2 + 2r_{12}\sigma_1\sigma_2}\sqrt{\sigma_3^2 + \sigma_4^2 + 2r_{34}\sigma_3\sigma_4}}$$

Let x_1 and x_2 represent scores on two halves of one form of a test and x_3 and x_4 represent scores on two halves of another equivalent form of the test. If we now assume that all terms of the type $r_{ij}\sigma_i\sigma_j$ are equal, so that any one of them can be represented by $r_{12}\sigma_1\sigma_2$, and that the standard deviations of

the two full-length tests are equal, we get

$$r_{(1+2)} = \frac{4r_{12}\sigma_1\sigma_2}{\sigma_1^2 + \sigma_2^2 + 2\sigma_1\sigma_2 r_{12}} \quad (3)$$

where $r_{(1+2)}$ is the reliability of the full-length test made up of 1 and 2. If it is assumed further that $\sigma_1 = \sigma_2$, this expression simplifies to

$$r_{(1+2)} = \frac{2r_{12}}{1 + r_{12}} \quad (4)$$

This is the familiar Spearman-Brown formula, originally presented by Spearman [13] in 1910, for estimating the reliability of a measure from the score on a smaller segment of behavior.

When the standard deviations of the two half-length tests are actually equal, formulas (3) and (4) will give identical results. When the two standard deviations are not actually equal, formula (4) will give a higher value as the estimate of $r_{(1+2)}$. This higher value may, in fact, be the better estimate, since the assumption that the terms $r_{ij}\sigma_i\sigma_j$ are equal may not be a very defensible one if the σ's are not equal. In practice, differences between the results by the two formulas are likely to be small.

A number of expressions have been developed which are algebraic equivalents of (3), but which are based on different ones of an interrelated set of values. A number of equivalent forms of formula (3) are presented in Table 15–2. This table indicates the values which are required by each formula, the formula itself, and the source for the formula.

Formula (4) may be generalized to any increase in the length of the test, and it then becomes

$$r_{nn} = \frac{nr_{11}}{1 + (n-1)r_{11}} \quad (5)$$

where r_{nn} is the reliability of a test n times the length of the test from which the observed correlation, r_{11}, was obtained.

The assumptions which were made in arriving at formula (5) should be noted. They were equality of the standard deviations of the part scores and equality of the

Table 15–2   Equivalent Formulas for Estimating
Reliability from Half-length Tests

Entering Statistics	Formula	Source
$r_{12} \, \sigma_1 \, \sigma_2$	$\dfrac{4\sigma_1 \, \sigma_2 \, r_{12}}{\sigma_1{}^2 + \sigma_2{}^2 + 2\sigma_1 \, \sigma_2 \, r_{12}}$	Flanagan in [12]
$\sigma_1 \, \sigma_2 \, \sigma_t$	$2\left[1 - \dfrac{\sigma_1{}^2 + \sigma_2{}^2}{\sigma_t{}^2} \right]$	Guttman [4]
$\sigma_1 \, \sigma_t \, r_{1t}$	$\dfrac{4(\sigma_1 \, \sigma_t \, r_{1t} - \sigma_1{}^2)}{\sigma_t{}^2}$	Mosier [10]
$\sigma_{(1-2)} \, \sigma_t$	$1 - \dfrac{\sigma_{(1-2)}{}^2}{\sigma_t{}^2}$	Rulon [12]
$\sigma_1 \, \sigma_{(1-2)} \, r_{1(1-2)}$	$\dfrac{4(\sigma_1{}^2 - \sigma_1 \, \sigma_{(1-2)} \, r_{1(1-2)})}{4\sigma_1{}^2 + \sigma_{(1-2)}{}^2 - 4\sigma_1 \, \sigma_{(1-2)} \, r_{1(1-2)}}$	Cronbach*

* This form of presentation, together with the last formula, was suggested in a personal communication by Lee Cronbach.

part score intercorrelations. These conditions will be satisfied in those cases in which (a) the part scores are equivalent, in the sense described on page 228 (that is, the specifications for each part are the same in terms of content, number of items, distribution of item difficulties, and distribution of item internal consistency measures), and (b) the nature of the function measured by later items or trials of a lengthened test is not changed as a result of the experience with earlier items or trials. However, Kelley [8] has indicated that formula (5) is not sensitive to differences in variability between the fractions of the test or even to differences in the level of reliability of the sections of the test. The value given by the formula is a close approximation to the actual correlation of longer tests even when the standard deviations and reliabilities of the unit-length tests show appreciable variation. The more serious limitations lie in the manner in which the experimental procedures allocate certain fractions of the variance. These points will be discussed presently.

General evaluation of reliability estimation from part scores. In general, estimating reliability from two parts of the same total test differs from reliability estimation from

the administration of two separate tests in two respects: (a) the two parts are not separately timed, and (b) the performances on the two parts are necessarily adjacent or even intermingled in time. A question may be raised as to the comparability of the two part scores, but the same issue arises with regard to any two test scores, whether they stem from artificial subdivisions of the same total test or from separate and distinct test forms.

The use of a single common time limit for a test becomes of critical importance whenever the test is in some degree a speed test. This can be seen most clearly by considering a pure speed test, in which each individual could do each item if he were given enough time and in which individuals differ only in the number of items which they can do within the limited amount of time available. In this case it is completely impossible to extract two meaningful scores from a test with a single time limit. The score which an individual makes upon a group of items will depend solely upon where the items are placed in the test. If the two part scores are made up one of the odd-numbered and the other of the even-numbered items, each individual will *necessarily* have practically identical scores on the two halves, because opportunity to attempt items has been systematically equated for the two half-scores. On the other hand, if one half-score is made up of the first half of the items on the test and the other of the second half, scores on the two halves cannot possibly be compared meaningfully because the individual can score on the second part only insofar as he has already completed and got a perfect score on the first part.

In practice, no test is an absolutely pure speed test of the sort which we have imagined in the previous paragraph. However, there are a good many tests which involve speed to some extent. Insofar as speed, as distinct from "power," or level of performance with unlimited time, is a factor in the test performances of a group of individuals, the results from split-test procedures for determining reliability will lack meaning. The amount of distortion of the results will be a function of the extent to which individual differences in score depend upon individual differences in speed of performance. In general, split-test estimates for speeded tests are misleadingly high. This fact has not always been appreciated by test authors and publishers, and in interpreting published reliability data the reader must watch out for this misuse of the split-test method.

The second limitation upon split-test reliabilities is the lack of time interval between the two performances. The two performances are not only adjacent in time, but in most cases even intermingled. This means that the day-to-day fluctuations in conditions (category III) and even the minute-to-minute variance in performance (category IV) are equated for both part scores and tend to be allocated to systematic rather than error variance. This means that split-test reliabilities, even of wholly unspeeded tests, may be expected to be in error on the high side, and insofar as variance of the above types is substantial we may expect a substantial overestimation of the effective reliability of the test.

We shall now turn our attention to the various possible ways of subdividing a test,

and consider the specific limitations and advantages of each.

Selection of half-tests equated for content and difficulty. Since the total test was presumably constructed to conform to certain specifications (as to content, difficulty, and the like), it is only reasonable that each of the half-tests should conform to these same specifications. The best guarantee of equivalence in the two half-tests would seem to be that the items for each be specifically chosen so as to be equivalent. In other words, the same procedures which were described on page 228 as appropriate in the construction of the two equivalent forms can be applied to the problem of subdividing the items within a single form. Items should be selected for each half-test so as to make it conform to the specifications for the total test, but within these limits chance should determine which items go in which half of the test.

This would appear to be the most defensible procedure for obtaining two half-scores from a test. Its disadvantages are chiefly practical ones, in that it requires work, and also ideally some data about the individual items, to obtain effective equivalence. It may also involve some sacrifice of convenience in scoring the tests.

A compromise between the equivalent-forms and split-test procedures should be noted, at this point, which appears to gain many of the advantages of both procedures. This is to prepare only the amount of testing material which is to be used in the final testing operation, but to arrange it in two equivalent and separately timed halves. If convenience requires it, the two half-length tests can be administered in immediate succession, but with separate time limits. Except that the two scores are obtained from segments of behavior which are immediately adjacent in time, this procedure is the counterpart of testing with separate comparable forms, yet only enough test materials for a single test need be prepared. In other cases, the two half-length tests can be given on different days. If that preliminary tryout of the test materials which should be expected of any good testing instrument is carried out, preparation of suitably equivalent half-tests should not be difficult. This permits the determination of an equivalent-forms reliability without the labor incident to constructing two full-length tests. The separate timings of the halves will permit studies of reliability for research purposes. The sum of the two half-test scores will, of course, provide a total score for the test. If the test is to be widely used for other than research purposes, in the edition which is prepared for general use, it may be desirable and will usually be quite practical to merge the two halves into the more usual test with single timing. This procedure is strongly recommended to research workers.

Alternate items as a basis for splitting test. A procedure which has been widely adopted for splitting a test to yield two half-scores is that of treating the odd-numbered items as one half-test and the even-numbered items as the other. This procedure has simplicity and objectivity as considerations to recommend it. It also appears to be related to the frequent practice of grouping together in a test form items of similar structure and of graduating the difficulty of the items from easy to hard. If the items within the test are arranged in this systematic fashion, the odd-even procedure provides a simple way of approximating equivalence in the two half-scores. If there are several successive items on the same topic or of the same type, this procedure will automatically divide them evenly between the two half-tests. If the items progress in difficulty, approximate equivalence of the half-tests in difficulty level is guaranteed. However, this makes very definite assumptions, which may not be warranted in a given case, as to the manner in which the test items are arranged in the full test.

The odd-even items split provides, at best, only a rough-and-ready approximation to equivalence in the two half-tests. It is particularly in the case of this procedure that certain other issues are raised, which we may well discuss now. If, either because of very close similarity of content or because of moment-to-moment fluctuations in efficiency, performance on successive items tends to be more alike than upon items widely separated in the test, we may find that the error of measurement in successive items is not independent but correlated. That is, variance in categories II B and IV B of Table 15–1 which should be treated as error variance may be common to successive items. By systematically allocating successive items to the two half-scores, this variance becomes common to the two and is treated as systematic variance. The odd-even procedure is pre-eminently the one which makes short-time fluctuations in individual performance operate to give an appearance of reliability rather than the reverse.

Alternate groups of items as basis for splitting test. In some cases, several items may be unduly closely related in content. Examples of this would be a group of reading comprehension items all based on the same passage, a group of items all referring to the same chart or table, or a group of mechanical comprehension items all referring to a single diagram. Another example is a test consisting of a number of matching exercises, each of which consists of a homogeneous group of items. A group of items such as any of these may well seem to share specific content (category II B). In that case it will be preferable to put all the items in a single group into one half-score, and base the two half-scores on alternate groups of items. This procedure reduces one of the objections to the odd-even items procedure. Insofar as there is any difference between the two, this procedure may be expected to give a somewhat more conservative and a more appropriate estimate of reliability than odd vs. even items.

First vs. second half as basis for splitting test. In order to avoid the possibility of correlated errors of measurement arising from relatively short-time fluctuations in performance, the procedure has sometimes been adopted of correlating score on the first half of a test with score on the second half. This introduces obvious difficulties whenever the test is not quite homogeneous in content or when items become harder as the test proceeds. If there is a systematic shift in content or function from the beginning to the end of the test, the first and last half are clearly not equivalent. In the ordinary test of aptitude or achievement, this procedure would seem likely to give a less satisfactory approximation to equivalence in the two half-scores than would the odd-even items procedure.

Even when the formal content of a test is homogeneous from beginning to end, as in the case of a series of trials in some complex motor task, the function may change qualitatively for the individual subject. That is, with continued practice the individual may find that the demands and character of the task change. What was initially a problem in discovering correct responses and procedures may, with practice, have changed to a task in developing maximum speed and precision of motor control. Thus, even identity of the external definition and formal requirements of the task cannot guarantee equivalence of the task as faced by the subject. On the one hand, this raises some question as to the interpretation of first vs. second half procedures (or of retest procedures) for evaluating reliability. At the same time it makes these procedures very interesting for comparison with an odd-even split-half determination. The amount that the first vs. second half measure is lower than that from odd vs. even items provides some indication of the extent to which either (a) momentary fluctuations worked to inflate the odd-even coefficient or (b) a progressive change in function with practice worked to lower the first vs. second half values. No simple way of discriminating between these two effects appears available for the traditional single test period. When the data

consist of a series of trials of a learning problem, introduction of a considerable time interval between trials would appear to minimize the first factor.[6]

4. ANALYSIS OF VARIANCE AMONG ITEMS

Any procedure for subdividing a total test into a particular two halves must be chosen somewhat arbitrarily from among the very large number of possible ways of making that subdivision. With that in mind, several workers have developed procedures to make use of all the information about consistency of performance from item to item within the test and thus provide a unique estimate of internal consistency. The procedures and basic formulas which are discussed here were first presented by Kuder and Richardson [9]. The derivation of the most generally useful formula (Kuder-Richardson formula #20) has subsequently been carried out on the basis of less restrictive assumptions by Jackson and Ferguson [7], and has been related directly to the approach through analysis of variance by Hoyt [6].

This general approach yields a type of reliability estimate analogous to those obtained from subdividing a test and has many of the same characteristics and limitations. *In particular*, these procedures are not applicable to a test which involves the element of speed and is administered with a single time limit. The assumption is implicit in the method that the individual has attempted each item. Item character-

[6] A technique has been suggested by Cureton for estimating the reliability for a learning function or performance which shows change with practice at a particular moment in its life history. If a series of trials are given, the correlations may be obtained between each possible pair of trials. If all correlations separated by a fixed number of trials are separately averaged (that is, the average of adjacent trials, those separated by one intervening trial, those separated by two, and so forth), a function may be plotted showing the relationship of average correlation to trial separation. This will generally be found to drop as the separation between the trials increases. By extrapolating backward to zero separation, one gets an estimate of the reliability (on the average) for a single trial.

istics, such as item difficulty, item variance, and item intercorrelations, become quite meaningless when any appreciable percentage of the group has not had time to read and attempt the item. For example, if omits are treated as wrongs, item intercorrelations toward the end of a speeded test become grossly inflated by the common group of subjects who never attempted the items. If individuals having omits are not included in the population from which item intercorrelations are computed, there is no uniform population upon which statistical analyses can be based. In other words, the same difficulties with speeded tests which were met in the case of a split test are again encountered in those procedures which analyze consistency of performance on single items. Consistency of performance cannot be evaluated unless the subject had an opportunity to perform.

Again, analysis of the consistency between items or trials of a test provides an estimate of consistency at a specific time. The temporary factors which were grouped in categories III and IV A of Table 15–1 remain relatively constant for each individual during a single test period, and are, therefore, considered as systematic rather than error variance. No estimate of the day-to-day consistency of the individual is possible with those procedures.

The most generally useful of the formulas for estimating reliability from the relationship of total test variance to item variance is Kuder-Richardson formula #20. This formula is

$$r_{tt} = \frac{n}{n-1} \left\{ \frac{s_t^2 - \sum_{i=1}^{n} p_i q_i}{s_t^2} \right\} \qquad (6)$$

where r_{tt} = reliability of the total test
n = number of items in the test
s_t^2 = variance of the total test
p_i = proportion passing item i
$q_i = 1 - p_i$

Perhaps the most general derivation of this formula is that by Jackson and Ferguson [7]. They define a pair of equivalent tests, T and T', as tests for each of which the variance is equal, for each of which the average item covariance is equal, and for which the average covariance of items within a test is equal to the average covariance of items of one test with items of the other. That is

$$s_t^2 = s_{t'}^2$$

and

$$\overline{r_{ij} s_i s_j} = \overline{r_{i'j'} s_{i'} s_{j'}} = \overline{r_{ij'} s_i s_{j'}}$$

If this definition is accepted, formula (6) can be derived quite simply. We must examine this definition, therefore, to see what is implied by it, so that the uses and limitations of the formula may be clarified.

The first implication in the above definition is homogeneity of content. The average $\overline{r_{ij'} s_i s_{j'}}$ includes terms of the type $r_{ii'} s_i s_i$, that is, covariance of pairs of matched items from the two parallel tests. Within the single form of the test, of course, these matched pairs do not appear. If the average within-test covariance is to be as great as the average between-test covariance, it must be accepted that the average covariance of these pairs of matched items is no greater than the average covariance of other item pairs. In proportion as heterogeneity appears in the test from item to item or from one group of items to another, Kuder-Richardson formula #20 will provide an underestimate of the correlation between equivalent forms. Since the terms in the above average which are based on matched item pairs are only n out of a total of n^2 terms, and since the difference in average covariance between matched and unmatched terms will often not be very great, the underestimation can be expected to be rather small in magnitude.

A second implication of this derivation of Kuder-Richardson formula #20 is that the test be essentially a power test. If there is a speed factor such that individuals fail to answer an appreciable number of items, a common factor is generated among the items of a single form of the test such that the average covariance among items within a test is raised above the average covariance between items on different forms of the test. That is, there will then be a substantial pool of individuals who necessarily have failed both items of a pair because they have not had time to attempt either of the items. On parallel forms of a test, where the testing operations are experimentally independent, different persons may have failed to complete the items, and so the covariance between a pair of items may be less. Therefore, on a speeded test an estimate of consistency based on a single testing will be too high. No general statement can be made as to the magnitude of this effect, but in measures in which individual differences are almost entirely a matter of speed, the overestimation may be substantial. This is the same spurious source of reliability which we have previously noted in the case of split-half reliability estimates.

A third implication, or perhaps limitation of the derivation of this formula is that changes in the individual from one time to another are not considered as a source of variation. If they are a significant source, then obviously the average covariance between items within a single test form, all of which are administered to the individual at the same time, will be higher than the average covariance between items on different forms given at different times. In proportion as this variance over time increases, the Kuder-Richardson formula #20 will overestimate the reliability obtained from separate testings. It provides an estimate of precision in appraising the performance of an individual at a particular point in time.

In summary, the factors which serve to distort the reliability estimates from Kuder-Richardson formula #20, and the nature of their effects, are as follows:

1. *Heterogeneity of item content* operates to lower the value obtained by the Kuder-Richardson formula, but probably produces rather a small distortion in most cases.
2. *The speed factor* operates to raise the value obtained with the Kuder-Richardson formula, whenever there are unattempted items, by an amount which is unknown but probably becomes quite substantial in highly speeded tests.
3. *Diurnal variation* which is not represented in the Kuder-Richardson estimate (or any other based on a single administration), has the result that the values obtained are likely to be high by an unknown amount as estimates of consistency over a period of time.

It would appear, therefore, that this formula is most serviceable in estimating the consistency of performance on a relatively homogeneous power test when interest is focused on consistency of performance at a particular point in time.

In addition to the original development by Kuder and Richardson [9] and one by Jackson and Ferguson [7], this same essential formula has also been derived by Guttman and by Hoyt. Guttman [4] derived this expression as one of a series of expressions to provide minimum estimates of reliability, but his estimates are minimum only if one considerably restricts the types of error variance in which one is interested.[7] We have seen above how under certain very important circumstances the Kuder-Richardson formula may become an overestimate.

Hoyt [6] attacked directly the problem of estimating test reliability from consistency of individual performance upon the

[7] Guttman has developed a series of expressions which purport to represent "lower bounds" for the reliability coefficient. One of these expressions has been represented in Table 15–2 and one is identical with Kuder-Richardson formula #20.

These expressions are based on a single test administration, and purport to be minimum estimates of what the correlation would be between two administrations of the test. In interpreting Guttman's formulas, however, it is essential to note the manner in which he defines reliability. Guttman explicitly eliminates from the sources of error with which he is concerned both (a) diurnal variation and (b) variation due to the sampling of items. It is only for a type of reliability which refers to performance on a particular set of items at a particular moment in time that his formulas provide "lower bounds."

items of a test by analysis of variance techniques. He assumed that the score of an individual on a test may be divided into four independent (mutually uncorrelated) components, as follows: (1) a component common to all individuals and to all items; (2) a component associated with the item; (3) a component associated with the individual; (4) an error component that is independent of 1, 2, and 3. It is assumed further that the error component of each item is normally distributed, that the variance of the error component is the same for each item, and that the error components for any two distinct items are uncorrelated. When these conditions are met, it is possible to analyze the variance in test scores into the variance contributed by each of the last three components. (The first component is a constant for all items and all individuals, and hence is not a source of variance.) Reliability may be estimated from the expression

Reliability =

$$1 - \frac{\text{Error variance}}{\text{Variance among individuals}} \quad (7)$$

If data are available for a total of N students on each of n items, the situation may be illustrated as follows:

Student	Items 1	2	3 · · · n	Scores
1				t_1
2				t_2
3				t_3
.				.
.				.
.				.
N				t_N
Totals	p_1	p_2	$p_3 \dots p_n$	$\sum_{i=1}^{n} p_i = \sum_{i=1}^{N} t_i$

In the above table, the t's represent scores of individual students, while the p's represent numbers of correct responses on the particular items of the test. The sum of squares "among students" is

$$\frac{1}{n} \sum_{i=1}^{N} t_i^2 - \frac{\left(\sum_{i=1}^{N} t_i \right)^2}{nN} \quad (8)$$

and the variance among students is this quantity divided by N minus 1. The sum of squares "among items" is

$$\frac{1}{N} \sum_{i=1}^{n} p_i^2 - \frac{\left(\sum_{i=1}^{n} p_i \right)^2}{nN} \quad (9)$$

and the variance among items is this quantity divided by n minus 1. The total sum of squares is

$$\frac{\left(\sum_{i=1}^{N} t_i \right) \left(nN - \sum_{i=1}^{N} t_i \right)}{nN} \quad (10)$$

that is, the number of correct responses times the number of incorrect responses divided by the total number of responses. The residual or error sum of squares is the total sum of squares minus that attributable to the two systematic factors of individual and item. The error variance is the error sum of squares divided by $(n - 1)(N - 1)$.

It has been indicated that the result obtained by Hoyt's procedure is identical with that from Kuder-Richardson formula #20, so nothing new is added so far as analysis of items of a test is concerned. The analysis of variance approach, however, appears useful for obtaining reliability estimates from items or trials which are scored with a range of scores, and not merely as "passed" or "failed." Thus, where several trials of a psychomotor test had been given, it would be possible to analyze the variance in performance into a portion of variance associated with trials, a portion associated with individuals, and a residual or error variance.[8] A quite general formula, applicable wherever a number of observations

---

[8] This type of analysis has been elaborated further by Alexander [1] with a consideration of problems of identifying and eliminating trend effects.

have been made upon each individual or specimen has recently been presented by Horst [5]. This formula is applicable to the case when the number of observations differs from one specimen to another, and so is quite general in character. Horst shows that it reduces to the Spearman-Brown or to the Kuder-Richardson formulas under specific conditions. Horst's formula is

$$r = 1 - \frac{\dfrac{\sum \dfrac{\sigma_i{}^2}{n_i - 1}}{N}}{\sigma_M{}^2} \qquad (11)$$

where N = the number of persons

n_i = the number of measures for person i

σ_i = the standard deviation of these measures for person i, and

σ_M = the standard deviation of the means for N persons

There may be some occasions upon which investigators will wish to use Kuder-Richardson formula #21. This is a simplification of formula #20, arrived at by assuming that all the items are of the same difficulty. The formula then becomes

$$r_{tt} = \frac{n}{n-1} \frac{\sigma_t{}^2 - n\overline{p}\,\overline{q}}{\sigma_t{}^2} \qquad (12)$$

In this formula $\overline{p} = M_t/n$ and $\overline{q} = 1 - \overline{p}$. Thus, the only values which are required in this formula are the number of items, the mean, and the standard deviation for the total test. When the item difficulties are not actually equal, the value yielded by this formula will be lower, and sometimes substantially lower, than that resulting from K-R #20. However, in a number of cases of fairly long power tests, the differences between the two formulas have been found [11] not to be greater than .05.

In the Kuder-Richardson formulas, it has been assumed that total score on the test is simply the unweighted sum of the number of correct responses. If items are weighted differentially, if wrong responses are weighted, and particularly if failures to respond are treated differently from wrong responses, the formulas become somewhat more complex. Dressel [3] has presented a generalized form of formula (6) above, suitable for use when weights are applied differentially to items and to rights, wrongs, and omits. Changing notation somewhat, we let

p_i = proportion of correct responses

$q_i = 1 - p_i$

p_i' = proportion of wrong responses

$q_i' = 1 - p_i'$

a_i = weight applied to correct response on item i

b_i = weight applied to wrong response on item i

Assuming that omitted items are not weighted, we get

$$r_{tt} = \frac{n}{n-1}\left[1 - \frac{\sum\limits_1^n a_i{}^2 p_i q_i + \sum\limits_1^n b_i{}^2 p_i' q_i' - 2\sum\limits_1^n a_i b_i p_i p_i'}{\sigma_t{}^2} \right] \qquad (13)$$

This formula is equivalent to formula (6) in that case in which rights and wrongs are variably and differently weighted and omits are unweighted. However, these omits are those which the individual has presumably attempted, but elected to omit. This formula is no more acceptable than the others for tests which, because of their speed element, include many nonattempted items.

At this point it is perhaps appropriate to compare explicitly the measures of consistency which are obtained by correlating scores on equivalent forms of a test, by whatever experimental operations these have been obtained, with those based on analysis of the items in a single test. The difference in what is accomplished in these two approaches is sufficiently great so that some writers have objected to any use of the term "reliability" for the latter type, insisting that it be spoken of as "internal consistency." The basic difference is found in the relationship of *homogeneity* of the functions measured to the two types of indices of consistency of performance.

In the case of the Kuder-Richardson formulas and derivatives thereof, homogeneity of function measured is the basic assumption. Each item in the test is considered to measure the same factor or the same weighted combination of factors as every other. Variation in the factors measured from item to item results in a lower index of consistency, since this difference in factors measured lowers the correlation between items in just the same way that error variance does. A necessary condition for obtaining a high consistency index in this case is, therefore, substantial correlation of each item with every other, that is, a substantial factor common to all.

In an estimate of consistency obtained by correlating equivalent test forms, by contrast, it is theoretically possible to get perfect consistency from test to test even though no item within a single test form has *any* correlation with any other item in that test. Thus, if one test, X, is made up of items x_1, x_2, x_3, and a parallel form, Y, of the test is made up of items y_1, y_2, and y_3, and if x_1 correlates perfectly with y_1, x_2 with y_2, and x_3 with y_3, then the two tests will have a perfect correlation with one another even if the correlations between x_1, x_2, and x_3 are all zero. The illustration has intentionally been made extreme and unrealistic to dramatize the point that in terms of consistency of performance from one testing to another, a very mixed and heterogeneous measure may yield a very stable score. This type of stability is not represented in the Kuder-Richardson internal-consistency analyses.

REFERENCES

1. ALEXANDER, H. W. The estimation of reliability when several trials are available. *Psychometrika*, 1947, 12, 79–100.
2. CRONBACH, L. Test reliability: Its meaning and determination. *Psychometrika*, 1947, 12, 1–16.
3. DRESSEL, P. L. Some remarks on the Kuder-Richardson reliability coefficient. *Psychometrika*, 1940, 5, 305–310.
4. GUTTMAN, L. A basis for analysing test-retest reliability. *Psychometrika*, 1945, 10, 255–282.
5. HORST, A. P. A generalized expression for the reliability of measures. *Psychometrika*, 1949, 14, 21–32.
6. HOYT, C. Test reliability obtained by analysis of variance. *Psychometrika*, 1941, 6, 153–160.
7. JACKSON, R. W. B., & FERGUSON, G. A. Studies on the reliability of tests. University of Toronto, Department of Education, Research Bulletin, No. 12, 1941. 132pp.
8. KELLEY, T. L. Note on the reliability of a test. *J. educ. Psychol.*, 1924, 15, 193–204.
9. KUDER, G. F., & RICHARDSON, M. W. The theory of estimation of test reliability. *Psychometrika*, 1937, 2, 151–160.
10. MOSIER, C. I. A short cut in the estimation of the split-halves coefficient. *Educ. psychol. Measmt*, 1941, 1, 407–408.
11. RICHARDSON, M. W., & KUDER, G. F. The calculation of test reliability coefficients based on the method of rational equivalence. *J. educ. Psychol.*, 1939, 30, 681–687.
12. RULON, P. J. A graph for estimating reliability in one range knowing it in another. *J. educ. Psychol.*, 1930, 21, 140–142.
13. SPEARMAN, C. Coefficient of correlation calculated from faulty data. *Brit. J. Psychol.*, 1910, 3, 271–295.

Chapter 16

The Measurement of Reproducibility

BENJAMIN W. WHITE / ELI SALTZ

Much of our knowledge of human behavior is based upon data obtained through the administration of multiple-choice tests to groups of subjects. Such instruments are used in many ways: selection, attitude measurement, ability measurement, and clinical diagnosis, to name only a few. Particularly since the publication of Guttman's model for measuring a test's reproducibility [7], there has been increasing concern over one aspect of the responses of groups of subjects to groups of items—the extent to which the patterns of subjects' responses can be predicted from their total scores. While these considerations have been of great interest to social and clinical psychologists, they have also proved pertinent to constructors of ability tests. It is the purpose of this article (*a*) to examine some of the techniques which have been devised to assess a test's "reproducibility," "homogeneity," or internal consistency, (*b*) to evaluate these techniques against certain criteria, and (*c*) to suggest possible logical

This article is reprinted from *Psychological Bulletin*, 1957, with the permission of the authors and the American Psychological Association.

relationships of these techniques to the concept of reliability.

In the ensuing discussion the word *test* will be used to describe any technique whereby two or more subjects respond to two or more stimuli in such a way that the responses of all subjects to each item can be dichotomized. It is assumed that every subject responds to every such item. It is further assumed that the experimenter assigns a value of unity to all responses on one side of the dichotomy and a value of zero to the rest. A "total score" for a subject is computed by adding the weights assigned to his responses thus dichotomized. With this system, a subject's total score is the number of responses he has made which fall into the unity-weighted class.

Often such scores are presumed to yield an ordering of the subjects on some hypothetical linear continuum, ability, or trait. For some time social scientists have been aware that this process of assigning a simple order to people on the basis of their responses to a number of test items is a legitimate representation of their test be-

241

havior only when their responses possess certain characteristics. There are many ways of stating this, but for the purposes of this discussion, it will be most convenient to use the following: a total score, computed by counting the number of test responses which have been classified in one of two ways, will yield a perfect mapping of the entire pattern of responses of all subjects when, and only when, the inter-item covariances are maximal.

For purposes of illustration, consider a six-item test. On such a test, total scores can take seven possible values from 0 to 6. When interitem covariance is maximal, there is only one way in which a subject can make any given total score. Naturally he can make a total score of 0 only by "failing" all six items, and a score of 6 only by "passing" all six items. He can make a score of 1 only by passing the easiest item. By "easiest" is meant the item which was passed by more subjects than any other. Similarly he can make a score of 2 only by passing the two easiest items. In other words, given the information that the interitem covariances are maximal, the order of difficulty of the items, and a subject's total score, one can tell exactly which items the subject got wrong and right. On such a test there are only seven ways in which people respond to the items, and each of these corresponds with one of the seven possible total scores.

At the other extreme, consider a six-item test whose items are independent, i.e., exhibit zero covariances. Such a test could yield 2^6 or 64 different response patterns. There would be 15 different ways in which a person could get a total score of 2, for example. In this situation, given knowledge of the total score, the order of difficulty of the items, and the fact of zero covariance between items, one would not be able to reconstruct a subject's pattern of responses to the test, unless the total score happened to be 0 or 6. Representation of the test behavior of the subjects with the conventional total score would result in a considerable loss of information.

Various indices have been developed

which will permit the tester to ascertain the degree to which the total scores of a given test yield a complete mapping of the responses of all subjects to all the items (reproducibility). These indices differ not only in their computational formulas, but in their underlying assumptions, though all start with the same primary data: the dichotomized responses of a group of subjects to a group of test items. Four criteria are suggested against which each index may be evaluated.

1. *Does it yield a theoretical maximum value which is the same for any test?*
2. *Does it yield a theoretical minimum value which is the same for any test?*
3. *Does it permit evaluation of the null hypothesis that the obtained reproducibility index is not significantly different from chance?*
4. *Does it permit evaluation of each item in the test as well as of the test as a whole?*

The rationales for these criteria are reasonably straightforward. If maximum or minimum possible values differ from test to test, it is difficult to evaluate one test against another. For example, two tests having reproducibility quotients of .90 are differently evaluated when it is discovered that the minimum theoretical reproducibility of one is .60, and of the other .90. If the quotient does not have a known sampling distribution, there is the possibility that the obtained quotient does not differ significantly from chance. And finally, if the items cannot be evaluated, it is difficult to improve reproducibility by omission or inclusion of specific items.

In the light of these criteria, we propose to discuss several techniques which have been devised to yield an index of reproducibility. In order to demonstrate the computations involved in each technique, we shall use the responses of ten subjects to a six-item test, illustrated in Table 16–1.

In this matrix the rows represent subjects and the columns test items. The marginal entries at the bottom of the matrix indicate the number of subjects who "passed" a

Table 16–1 Responses of Ten Subjects to a Six-Item Test Where Rows and Columns Are Unordered

Subject	Item 1	2	3	4	5	6	Total Score
A	0	0	0	1	0	0	1
B	1	0	1	1	1	1	5
C	0	0	1	0	0	0	1
D	1	1	1	0	1	1	5
E	1	0	1	1	1	0	4
F	0	0	1	0	1	0	2
G	0	1	1	0	0	0	2
H	1	0	1	0	1	0	3
I	1	0	1	0	1	1	4
J	1	0	0	1	1	0	3
Item difficulty	6	2	8	4	7	3	

Table 16–2 Responses of Ten Subjects to a Six-Item Test Where Rows and Columns Are Ordered

Subject	Item 2	6	4	1	5	3	Total Score
D	1	1	0	1	1	1	5
E	0	1	1	1	1	1	5
B	0	0	1	1	1	1	4
I	0	1	0	1	1	1	4
H	0	0	0	1	1	1	3
J	0	0	1	1	1	0	3
G	1	0	0	0	0	1	2
F	0	0	0	0	1	1	2
C	0	0	0	0	0	1	1
A	0	0	1	0	0	0	1
Item difficulty	2	3	4	6	7	8	

given item, and the marginals in the last column of the matrix represent the number of items each subject "passed."

GUTTMAN'S REPRODUCIBILITY

Guttman [7] originated the term reproducibility. The term means essentially the degree to which one can reproduce a subject's entire response pattern from a knowledge of his total score and the order of difficulty of the items. Originally Guttman's technique of obtaining the index of reproducibility involved mechanical operations on a matrix of N subjects and K test items similar to Table 16–1. A device, the scalogram board, permits interchange of rows and columns of this matrix in a particular manner so that the unity entries are maximally concentrated above the main diagonal of the matrix. Such rearrangement of the response matrix in Table 16–1 is shown in Table 16–2.

It should be noted that if there are any ties in total score or in the number of subjects passing items, the arrangement of the matrix may not be unique. In this example the order of the columns is unique since there are no ties in the number of subjects passing items, but the order of rows is not, since there are two subjects at each total score level. In such cases further permuta-

tions of rows and columns are made until errors are minimized. The index of reproducibility is a function of the number of errors, i.e., unity entries which are below the diagonal and zero entries which are above it. This diagonal is not necessarily exactly coincident with the main diagonal, and Guttman has several rules to be followed in its determination. Since Guttman's original procedure is unwieldy, we shall in this illustration use a procedure developed by Jackson [10] for arriving at cutting points for each item. For all practical purposes, Jackson's R_t quotient is identical with Guttman's.[1] Jackson's method is illustrated in Table 16–3.

This is the same matrix shown in Table 16–2, except that the unity and zero entries under each item have been placed in separate columns. In order to draw cutting points, one simply draws a line across each column at the place where the number of zero entries above the line and the number of unit entries below the line (errors) are minimized. These cutting points are seen as descending steps in the table. In the first column there is one entry of unity which

[1] It should be noted that many people have suggested modifications in the calculations of Guttman's R_t [3, 6, 11, 17, 18]. These refinements of procedure are, by and large, identical in their logical properties with Guttman's quotient, and were so intended by their authors. Consequently no space is given to them in this article.

Table 16–3   Jackson's Method of Computing Reproducibility (R), Minimum Reproducibility (MR), and Plus Percentage Ratio (PPR) *

	Item											
	2		6		4		1		5		3	
Subject	+	−	+	−	+	−	+	−	+	−	+	−
D	1		1			(0)	1		1		1	
E		0	1		1		1		1		1	
B		0		0	1		1		1		1	
I		0	(1)		0		1		1		1	
H		0		0	0		1		1		1	
J		0		0	0	(1)	1		1			(0)
G	(1)			0		0		0		(0)	1	
F		0		0		0		0	1		1	
C		0		0		0		0		0	1	
A		0		0	0	(1)		0		0		0
# right (P)	2		3		4		6		7		8	
# wrong (Q)		8		7		6		4		3		2
Errors	1		1		3		0		1		1	
R_i	.90		.90		.70		1.00		.90		.90	
MR_i	.80		.70		.60		.60		.70		.80	
PP_i	.10		.20		.10		.40		.20		.10	
PPR_i	.50		.67		.25		1.00		.67		.50	

* Rights are listed under +. Wrongs are listed under −. Total errors = 7; $R_t = 88\%$; $MR_t = 70\%$; $PP_t = 18\%$; $PPR_t = .61$.

falls below the cutting line and this has been put in parentheses. If the cutting line had been drawn directly below this unity entry, the five zero entries above it would be counted as errors and put in parentheses. In this illustration there is a unique cutting point for five of the six items, i.e., a line which yields an absolute minimum number of errors. In Item 5, however, the line could be either where it is drawn, or two rows higher. Either solution yields one error. The lower one was chosen because it yielded an additional cutting point for the scale,[2] whereas the higher cutting point would have been identical for that of Item 1.

[2] In Jackson's method, the cutting points are used to determine minimum number of errors. Once the minimum number of errors has been determined the exact locations of the cutting points no longer enter into the computation of reproducibility. Consequently, for Jackson's method it doesn't

After the cutting points have been assigned, the errors in each column are counted. From these it is possible to compute the reproducibility for each item (R_i)

matter which of the two cutting points is used for Item 5, since both result in one error. However, Guttman's original procedure made use of the specific cutting point used. Guttman assigned the cutting points to the row marginals (the total scores) and then rescored every S on the basis of the cutting points. All Ss below the lowest cutting point would be scored as having failed all the items. In Table 16–3, for example, Item 3 has the lowest cutting point; subject A is below this cutting point and so he would be rescored as having failed all the items. All Ss between the first and second cutting points would be rescored as having passed one item, and so forth. The Guttman reproducibility index indicates the percentage of actual reproducibility as compared with the maximum reproducibility obtained by these rescoring processes. Therefore, if two items are given the same cutting point, the number of different classes or "cutting point scores" will be decreased—that is, the number of discriminations made by the scale is diminished.

by dividing the number of errors (E) by the number of subjects (N) and subtracting the quotient from 1.

$$R_i = 1 - \frac{E}{N} \tag{1}$$

The reproducibility for the entire test (R_t) may be computed by summing the errors for all items

$$\left(\sum_{i=1}^{k} E \right)$$

dividing this by the number of subjects (n) times the number of items (k), and subtracting the quotient from 1.

$$R_t = 1 - \frac{\sum\limits_{i=1}^{k} E}{NK} \tag{2}$$

For this example, the reproducibility of the test is 88.3 per cent, somewhat below the 90 per cent figure which Guttman uses as one criterion of scalability.

The Guttman index of reproducibility meets our first criterion in that it has an absolute maximum of 100 per cent for any test with more than one item, and our fourth criterion in that one can compute the index for each item as well as for the test as a whole. However, it suffers a serious shortcoming in having no unique minimal value. As Jackson [10] and others [1, 2, 13, 14] have pointed out, the index of reproducibility is drastically affected by the difficulty levels of the items in a test. The reason for this is that the difficulty of an item (percentage of persons passing) places a limit on the likelihood of an error: passing a difficult item, and failing an easy one. The reproducibility figure can approach its absolute lower limit of 50 per cent only when all the items have a difficulty level of 50 per cent, a trivial case in which 100 per cent reproducibility could be obtained only if one-half the subjects passed all the items while the other half failed all the items. With even slight departures from this strict condition, the lower limit of the reproducibility index

rises sharply. In our illustrative example minimum reproducibility is 70 per cent. This fact makes it exceedingly difficult to evaluate an obtained index of reproducibility. With short scales and wide spread in item difficulties, Guttman's figure of 90 per cent may on occasion be very little higher than the minimum reproducibility of the scale.

JACKSON'S PLUS PERCENTAGE RATIO (PPR)

In order to circumvent this drawback of Guttman's reproducibility index, Jackson [10] has developed another statistic which he calls the Plus Percentage Ratio (PPR). Unlike the Guttman index, PPR has the same absolute minimum for all tests. Referring again to Table 16–3, note the minimum reproducibility figures in the row labelled MR_i. Here the minimum reproducibility figure for each item (MR_i) is obtained by dividing the number of subjects who got a given item right (# right), or wrong (# wrong), whichever figure is the larger, by the number of subjects (N).

$$MR_i = \frac{\begin{array}{c}\text{\# rights or \# wrongs}\\\text{(whichever is larger)}\end{array}}{N} \tag{3}$$

The minimum reproducibility for the entire test (MR_t) is computed by taking for each item the number of rights

$$\left(\sum_{i=1}^{k} \text{\# rights} \right)$$

or the number of wrongs

$$\left(\sum_{i=1}^{k} \text{\# wrongs} \right)$$

whichever number is larger, summing the numbers so obtained over all items and dividing this sum by the product of the number of items (K) and the number of subjects (N).

$$MR_t = \frac{\sum\limits_{i=1}^{k} \begin{array}{c}\text{\# rights, or \# wrongs}\\\text{(whichever is larger)}\end{array}}{KN} \tag{4}$$

In the next to the last row of Table 16–3, the "Plus %$_i$" (PP_i) figures are listed. Here the differences between the obtained reproducibility and the minimum reproducibility ($R_i - MR_i$) for each item are entered. These figures indicate how much better obtained reproducibility is than the minimum for that item. In the last row, the "Plus % Ratios" (PPR_i) are entered for each item. These figures may be obtained by dividing the Plus % figure for a given item by one minus the minimum reproducibility (MR_i) for that item.

$$PPR_i = \frac{R_i - MR_i}{1 - MR_i} \tag{5}$$

The Plus Percentage Ratio for the total test (PPR_t) is similarly computed by dividing the difference between R_t and MR_t by one minus MR_t.

$$PPR_t = \frac{R_t - MR_t}{1 - MR_t} \tag{6}$$

The Plus % Ratio has a distinct advantage over the index of reproducibility in that it has both an absolute maximum of one and an absolute minimum of zero for any test of more than one item. For the test illustrated here the PPR_t is .61. As Jackson points out, testers should be prepared for the fact that this index will almost inevitably be lower than the Guttman index of reproducibility, often considerably lower. The index has not often been used on well-known tests, so it is difficult to say what an acceptable level should be. Jackson tentatively suggests 70 per cent. It remains to be seen whether this figure is a reasonable one in mental testing or attitude scaling. The PPR in any event has much to recommend it since it circumvents one of the most serious criticisms which has been leveled at Guttman's reproducibility index.

LOEVINGER'S INDEX OF HOMOGENEITY (H)

HOMOGENEITY OF A TEST (H_t)

A rather different approach to the measurement of the reproducibility of mental tests has been put forth by Loevinger, who uses the following as a definition of homogeneity [13, p. 29].

The definitions of perfectly homogeneous and perfectly heterogeneous tests can be restated in terms of probability. In a perfectly homogeneous test, when the items are arranged in the order of increasing difficulty, if any item is known to be passed, the probability is unity of passing all previous items. In a perfectly heterogeneous test, the probability of an individual passing a given item A is the same whether or not he is known already to have passed another item B.

It can be seen that this definition comes quite close to the Guttman notion of reproducibility, and in fact the perfectly reproducible and the perfectly homogeneous test are identical.

With the test items arranged in order of increasing difficulty, Loevinger computes the quantity S by finding, for *all pairs of items*, the proportion of subjects who have passed both items (P_{ij}). From this is subtracted the theoretical proportion who would have passed both items had they been independent ($P_i P_j$). These differences are summed over the $k(k-1)$ pairs of items (i.e., each item is paired with every other item in the test).

$$S = \sum_{i=1}^{k-1} \sum_{j=i+1}^{k} P_{ij} - P_i P_j \tag{7}$$

For a test made up of completely independent items, S would have a value of zero. S does not have an upper limit of unity when the test is perfectly homogeneous. The upper limit is fixed by the proportion of subjects passing the more difficult item in each pair (P_j).

$$S_{max} = \sum_{i=1}^{k-1} \sum_{j=i+1}^{k} P_j - P_i P_j \tag{8}$$

The homogeneity of a test (H_t) is then given by the ratio of these two quantities

$$H_t = \frac{S}{S_{max}} \tag{9}$$

This procedure is exactly analogous to that used by Jackson in computing the Plus Percentage Ratio. This can be seen more easily if Loevinger's equation is rewritten as follows:

$$H_t = \frac{S}{S_{max}}$$

$$= \frac{\sum\limits_{i=1}^{k-1} \sum\limits_{j=i+1}^{k} (1 - P_{\hat{\imath}j}) - (1 - P_{\hat{\imath}}P_j)}{\sum\limits_{i=1}^{k-1} \sum\limits_{j=i+1}^{k} 1 - (1 - P_{\hat{\imath}}P_j)} \quad (10)$$

The first term in the parentheses of the numerator $(1 - P_{\hat{\imath}j})$ indicates the proportion of subjects passing a harder item *and* failing an easier one subtracted from unity. This is very like the reproducibility coefficient which is given by the proportion of errors subtracted from unity. The second term in the numerator $(1 - P_{\hat{\imath}}P_j)$ is the product of the proportion of subjects passing the harder item and the proportion failing the easy item, this product then subtracted from unity. The quantity $(1 - P_{\hat{\imath}}P_j)$ is analogous to Jackson's minimum reproducibility. The denominator is seen to be the difference between unity (perfect reproducibility) and minimum reproducibility. The two methods differ only in the procedure for counting errors. Loevinger's technique involves the equivalent of an examination of all pairs of items $i \neq j$ and counting every occasion upon which the harder item is passed and the easier item failed. In the illustrative example, such a tabulation yields a total of 13 errors, whereas Jackson's error count is 7. This is the reason that Loevinger's H_t will usually be lower than Jackson's PPR_t. The former is .23, and the latter .61. In Jackson's system for counting errors, a deviant response is counted only once no matter where it occurs in the response pattern. For example, if items are arranged in order of decreasing difficulty, a response pattern of $(1, 0, 0, 0)$ would be credited with one error, while in Loevinger's system, since the passed item was the hardest of the four, there would be

three errors. The two methods also have somewhat different ways of computing minimum reproducibility, Jackson's yielding a figure of .70, and Loevinger's .72.

Loevinger points out that her formula for H_t is equivalent to

$$H = \frac{\sigma_x{}^2 - \sigma_{het}^2}{\sigma_{hom}^2 - \sigma_{het}^2} \quad (11)$$

where all the variances refer to total raw scores. The first term in the numerator $(\sigma_x{}^2)$ is the variance of the obtained scores, the second numerator term (σ_{het}^2) is the variance of the total scores which would be obtained from items of the same difficulty which were completely independent, and the first term in the denominator (σ_{hom}^2) is the variance in total scores which would be obtained if the same items were perfectly correlated. The raw score variance of a test made up entirely of independent items is the familiar

$$\sum_{i=1}^{k} pq$$

or the sum of the item variances. The raw score variance of a test made up wholly of perfectly correlated items is given by

$$\sigma_{hom}^2 = \sum_{i=1}^{k} P_i Q_i$$

$$+ 2 \sum_{i=1}^{k-1} \sum_{j=i+1}^{k} P_j - P_i P_j \quad (12)$$

The first term on the right of this equation is the item variance employed above, and the second term is two times a sum which is seen to be identical to S_{max}.

This relationship is interesting since it shows that total score variance increases with reproducibility, being at a minimum when the item covariances are zero, and reaching an upper limit when item covariances are maximal.

Both Loevinger's H_t and Jackson's PPR have the advantage of being uninfluenced by the distribution of item difficulties which makes them preferable to the Guttman reproducibility index when it is given without further information. The procedures are objective and can be reduced to routine computations. When "errors" occur mainly on item pairs which are close together in difficulty level, the two procedures should yield practically identical indices, but if there are "errors" which occur in item pairs which are widely different in difficulty level, Loevinger's H_t will be lower than Jackson's PPR_t. Loevinger's technique has the aesthetic advantage of making full use of the information contained in the response matrix, but the practical drawback of being tedious to compute when the number of items is large since $k(k-1)$ cross breaks have to be made to compute the P_{ij}s. However, Jackson's method is also laborious since it requires an initial posting of the entire response matrix.

The sampling distribution of H_t is unknown, and Loevinger advises that it should not be used as an estimate of homogeneity unless the sample of subjects exceeds 100.

HOMOGENEITY OF AN ITEM WITH A TEST (H_{it})

Loevinger's H_t yields an index for the test as a whole, but does not provide an index of the homogeneity of each item with the test. For this purpose, she suggests another index, (H_{it}), the logic of which is the same as that employed in H_t. In a perfectly homogeneous test, subjects passing a given item should have higher total scores than those failing the item. The starting point is a formula developed by Long [15].

Long's Index =
$$1 - \frac{2 \sum \text{"passes" below "fails"}}{PQ} \quad (13)$$

In 13, the numerator is two times the number of subjects passing a given item who have total scores lower than those of subjects who failed the same item, and the denominator is the product of the number of passes on the item (P) and the number of fails (Q). Loevinger points out that difficulties arise when two subjects have identical total scores, one of whom has failed the item and the other has passed it. There is also the question of whether the response to the item should in this computation be included in the total score. In order to circumvent these difficulties with Long's index, Loevinger proposes the modification

$$H_{it} = 1 - \frac{2 \sum \text{"passes" below or tied with "fails"}}{PQ - \sum \text{"passes" one above "fails"}} \quad (14)$$

It is clear that this index can take values from minus to plus unity, but it is not clear that a zero value is obtained when there is no relation between an item and the total test. The sampling properties of the index are unknown and will have to be investigated to establish the value to be expected for a chance relation. The obtained H_{it} values for the illustrative test may be seen in the last column of Table 16–6.

GREEN'S SUMMARY STATISTICS METHOD (I)

Green [4, 5] has recently developed a method for computing an index of consistency for a test (I) which has all the advantages of Jackson's PPR, and Loevinger's H_t, plus greater ease of computation. Like Jackson's PPR, I is given by

$$I = \frac{Rep - Rep_{ind}}{1.00 - Rep_{ind}} \quad (15)$$

where Rep is the obtained reproducibility of the test, Rep_{ind} is the reproducibility which would be obtained with the same set of item difficulties and complete independence between items, and 1.00 is perfect reproducibility.

Green's method of computing errors is the same as that employed in 10 above, except that the summation is not over all pairs of items, $i \neq j$, but only over those item pairs whose members are adjacent in difficulty level. Green's reproducibility is given by

$$Rep = 1 - \frac{1}{NK} \sum_{i=1}^{k-1} n_{\hat{i},i+1}$$

$$- \frac{1}{NK} \sum_{i=2}^{k-2} n_{\overline{i-1},\hat{i},i+1,i+2} \qquad (16)$$

where N is the number of subjects, K the number of items. Items are ranked in order of difficulty, the most difficult item receiving rank k, and the easiest item rank 1. The quantity $n_{i,i+1}$ is the number of subjects who both fail the ith item and pass the next most difficult item $(i+1)$. There will be $k-1$ such item pairs. The last quantity, $n_{i-1,i,i+1,i+2}$ is the number of subjects who have failed both item $i-1$ and i and passed both item $i+1$ and $i+2$. There will be $k-3$ such terms in this summation.

The reproducibility that would be expected if the items had their observed difficulties, but were mutually independent is given by

$$Rep_{ind} = 1 - \frac{1}{N^2K} \sum_{i=1}^{k-1} n_{\hat{i}}n_{i+1}$$

$$- \frac{1}{N^4K} \sum_{i=2}^{k-2} n_{\hat{i}}n_{i+1}n_{i+2}n_{\overline{i-1}} \qquad (17)$$

These values for Rep and Rep_{ind} are then put in 15 to obtain I, which will be unity for a perfectly reproducible test and zero for a test whose items are completely independent. Green suggests that I should be .50 for a test before its items can be considered scalable. Since this method makes only a partial count of the "errors" in a response matrix, it produces a slight overestimate of reproducibility. In one empirical investigation [5] it was found that the average discrepancy between Green's reproducibility and the exact reproducibility of ten scales was .002.

Following a suggestion of Guttman [7], Green furnishes an approximation to the standard error of Rep.

$$\sigma_{Rep} \approx \sqrt{\frac{(1-Rep)(Rep)}{NK}} \qquad (18)$$

With this standard error it is possible to ascertain whether an obtained Rep is significantly larger than Rep_{ind}. Green warns, however, that when such a test yields borderline significance, one should be cautious in interpretation since both Rep and σ_{Rep} are approximations. A high significance level does not necessarily indicate that the items are homogeneous, merely that the item intercorrelations are significantly greater than zero.

For the illustrative test, the computation of Rep, Rep_{ind}, and I are shown in Table 16–4.

The obtained Rep is .917, as compared with Jackson's .88, and .78 by Formula 10.

Table 16–4   Green's Method of Computing Reproducibility (Rep), Chance Reproducibility (Rep_{ind}), and Index of Consistency (I)

Subjects	Items 2	6	4	1	5	3	Total Scores
D	1	1	0	1	1	1	5
E	0	1	1	1	1	1	5
B	0	0	1	1	1	1	4
I	0	1	0	1	1	1	4
H	0	0	0	1	1	1	3
J	0	0	1	1	1	0	3
G	1	0	0	0	0	1	2
F	0	0	0	0	1	1	2
C	0	0	0	0	0	1	1
A	0	0	1	0	0	0	1
Rank order of difficulty	6	5	4	3	2	1	
n_i		2	3	4	6	7	8
$n_{\hat{i}}$		8	7	6	4	3	2
$n_{\hat{i},i+1}$			1	2	1	0	1
$n_{\hat{i-1},i,i+1,i+2}$				0	0	0	

$$Rep = 1 - \frac{1}{(10)(6)} (1+0+1+2+1)$$

$$- \frac{1}{(10)(6)} (0+0+0) = .917$$

$$Rep_{ind} = \frac{1}{(10^2)(6)} (7 \cdot 2 + 6 \cdot 3 + 4 \cdot 4 + 3 \cdot 6 + 2 \cdot 7)$$

$$- \frac{1}{10^4(6)} (4 \cdot 6 \cdot 3 \cdot 2 + 3 \cdot 4 \cdot 4 \cdot 3 + 2 \cdot 3 \cdot 6 \cdot 4)$$

$$= .860$$

$$I = \frac{Rep - Rep_{ind}}{1.00 - Rep_{ind}} = \frac{.916 - .860}{1.000 - .860} = .407$$

The index of consistency (I) is seen to be .41, as compared with Jackson's *PPR* of .61, and Loevinger's H_t of .23.

THE PHI COEFFICIENT (ϕ_{it})[3]

A measure of item reproducibility can be derived from the phi coefficient. This measure has the advantages of an absolute maximum of 1.00, an absolute minimum of 0.00, a known sampling distribution, and direct relationship to conventional test construction procedure.

The logic behind the procedure is simple. Take as an example an item which 30 per cent of the subjects pass and 70 per cent fail. If the item is perfectly reproducible in a perfectly reproducible test, the 30 per cent of the subjects with the highest total scores should all pass the item; the 70 per cent with the lowest total scores should all fail the item. Subjects can easily be ranked on total score and this distribution cut in the same ratio as the pass-fail ratio on any particular item being evaluated. It is then simple to determine the number of persons high on total score who pass the item, the number of high persons who fail the item, the number of low persons who fail the item and who pass the item. The data may be put in a fourfold table as in Table 16–5.

Obviously, one has only to determine the marginal sums (which are determined by the pass-fail ratio of the item) and one of

Table 16–5   Item-total Score Phi Coefficient (ϕ_{it})

		Total Score*		
		Low	High	Total
Item Score	Pass item i	A	B	$A+B$
	Fail item i	C	D	$C+D$
	Total	$A+C$	$B+D$	N

* Total score distribution is broken so that number of subjects in low group is equal to number failing item i: $(C + D = A + C)$.

[3] The writers find that Cronbach [1, p. 324] has anticipated them in this suggested manner of estimating reproducibility.

the cell frequencies, since the rest can be computed by subtraction from the marginals.

Splitting subjects on the basis of total score in the same ratio as the pass-fail split on an item may produce a problem if several subjects are tied for total score across the cutting points. The tied subjects should be randomly distributed between the high and low groups so that the total scores are split in the same ratio as the pass-fail ratio. Take as a simple example the case in which 100 subjects have answered a questionnaire in such a manner that the pass-fail ratio on a particular item is 30/70. To evaluate this item, the subjects must be split on total score so that the highest 30 per cent constitute one group and the lowest 70 per cent constitute the second group. If three persons are tied for rank 30 in total score, two will be arbitrarily considered ranks 29 and 30 respectively, and will be placed in the high group. The third person will be assigned rank 31, and, despite the fact that his score is the same as that of two subjects in the high group, he will be placed in the low group. If the total number of subjects is reasonably large, and if the number of subjects having the *critical tied score* is not a large percentage of the total number of subjects, this will not distort the resulting phi.

Since the marginals for the total score have been determined in a manner that forces them to be equal for the marginal for the particular item the usual phi formula can be simplified to

$$\phi_{it} = \frac{BC - AD}{(A + B)(C + D)} \tag{19}$$

where the quantities A, B, C, and D correspond to cell entries in Table 16–5 above.

The null hypothesis for such a phi coefficient is, in every case, that the obtained phi is not significantly greater than zero. This can be tested by a chi square or a Fisher exact test on the fourfold table.

If the investigator desires to "purify" his test, he must choose a cutting point and select all the items with phi coefficients above this cutting point to constitute his reproducible scale. New total scores can then be computed on the basis of the selected items, and phi coefficients recalculated to give an estimate of the reproducibility of the new scale. The coefficients for some of the items not included in the new total score may be so high that these items can be included in the scale, while those for some of the included items may drop to a level which makes it advisable to exclude them.

Unlike some indices of reproducibility, this index is not affected by extremes of item difficulty. This is true because phi is not an index of the frequency in one cell, but is determined by the intercorrelation between cells. The method has a disadvantage, a purely aesthetic one, but one that may prejudice some workers against it; the phi coefficients so obtained are not likely to yield many values in the .80's or .90's. The phi coefficients computed for the items in the illustrative test are shown in Table 16–6, where they may be compared with those computed by Jackson's PPR_i and Loevinger's H_{it}.

Though this method of computing a phi coefficient between a test item and the total score has the advantages of a known sampling distribution, absolute maximum and minimum values, and freedom from restrictive distribution assumptions, it does not furnish an index for the test as a whole. It is possible however to derive one by an averaging of the obtained phi coefficients. Such an approach is shown in Formula 20, which Cronbach says is analogous to Guttman's formula for reproducibility.

$$R = \frac{1}{K} \sum_{i=1}^{k} 1 - 2p_i q_i (1 - \phi_{it}) \qquad (20)$$

Cronbach explains [1, p. 324]:

The correlation of any two-choice item with a total score on a test may be expressed as a phi coefficient, and this is common in conventional item analysis. Guttman dichotomizes the test scores at a cutting point selected by inspection of the data. We will get similar results if we dichotomize scores at that point which cuts off the same proportion of cases as pass the item under study. [Our ϕ_{it} will be less in some cases than it would be if determined by Guttman's inspection procedure.] Simple substitution in Guttman's definition . . . leads to [Formula 20 above] where the approximation is introduced by the difference in ways of dichotomizing. The actual R obtained by Guttman will be larger than that from [this formula].

In our example the value turns out to be .80 as compared with the reproducibility figure of .88.

This composite index for the entire test will have a maximum value of 1.00 and a chance value of

$$\frac{1}{K} \sum 1 - 2p_i q_i$$

which approaches .50 as the average item difficulty approaches 50 per cent. The sampling distribution of this statistic, to our knowledge, is not known.

DISCUSSION

This concludes the exposition of the major methods which have been put forward to give an index of the reproducibility of tests. Of those which yield indices for the test as a whole, several meet serious objections which have been leveled at Guttman's scalogram analysis. The techniques of Jackson, Loevinger, and Green are all objective, and result in measures which are not affected by the distribution of item difficulties. All have the same underlying ra-

Table 16–6   Item-total Score Phi Coefficients for Illustrative Six-item Test

Item	ϕ_{it}	PPR_i	H_{it}
1	1.000	1.000	1.000
2	.375	.500	.714
3	.375	.500	.333
4	.167	.250	.619
5	.524	.667	.867
6	.524	.667	.889

tionale, but differ slightly in the way in which "errors" are counted. Loevinger's H_t is the most conservative of the three since all possible errors are counted; Jackson's PPR_t is the least conservative, and Green's I will usually fall between the two. The principal and not inconsiderable advantage of Green's technique is ease of computation, an important factor when the number of subjects and test items is large. Green's technique is the only one discussed that gives an estimate of significance for the reproducibility of the entire test.

Of the methods for computing the homogeneity of an item with the total test, the phi coefficient seems the most desirable because computation is easy and because the significance level of the obtained statistic can be determined exactly. Almost any of the commonly used item-analysis statistics—point biserial, biserial, or Flanagan correlation coefficient—may of course be interpreted as an index of item reproducibility, since in a reproducible test any person passing a given item will pass more other items than a person failing that item. They differ from the phi coefficient mainly in the number of assumptions they impose upon the data. Those employing conventional item-analysis statistics have been quite willing to assume an interval scale and a distribution function, usually normal, while those working within the framework of the concept of reproducibility have in general foresworn the unit of measurement and have thus confined themselves to distribution-free statistics.

All the reproducibility indices rest upon the same assumption that in a reproducible or homogeneous test, one can reproduce the entire response pattern of passes and fails, given the total number of items correct, and the item difficulties. All the methods employ the same data in the response matrix. All agree that in the response matrix of the perfectly reproducible test there will be no instances in which a subject passes an item more difficult than one he has failed. This is equivalent to saying either that all interitem covariances are maximal, or that

the variance in total scores is maximal. Conversely, the test with lowest reproducibility will exhibit zero interitem covariances, and minimal variance in total scores.

REPRODUCIBILITY AND FACTOR ANALYSIS

It is obvious that the phi coefficient method of determining the homogeneity of an item with total test is very similar to the procedure in classical test construction for "purifying" a test.

A common procedure for evaluating an item in conventional test construction is to compare the number of subjects passing the item among the 27 per cent of the sample making the highest total scores as opposed to the 27 per cent making the lowest total scores. A "good" item is one that discriminates between these highs and lows. Consequently, the items which would be chosen as producing the most reproducible scale in the phi procedure for obtaining reproducibility would also be selected as the most discriminating in conventional test statistics. This point is important when considering the relationship between reproducibility and factor analysis.

Several authors have been concerned with the question of the relationship between reproducibility and factor analysis. Loevinger [14] has stated that factor analysis and reproducibility are unrelated. Humphreys [9] appears to agree with Loevinger on this point and attacks reproducibility for not being as satisfactory a tool for research as factor analysis. He feels that reproducibility will lead to a confusing multiplicity of tests, while a factor analytic approach will not. Humphreys uses the hypothetical case of the problems involved in constructing a mechanical information test. The criterion of reproducibility, he fears, would require the construction of separate tests for the cross saw, the brace and bit, the pipe wrench, etc. On the other hand, all these tests would probably appear on a single common factor that would be orthogonal to other factors.

The writers disagree with both Loevinger and Humphreys, feeling that reproducibility and factor analysis are closely related. This relationship can be made obvious by consideration of the Wherry-Gaylord iterative analysis [19]. This is a method for discovering homogeneous groupings of items in a test. It involves correlating each item with the total score. Items with the highest correlations are selected and the test rescored on the basis of these items. All the items are then correlated with the new total scores. This procedure is continued until a stable group of items is extracted. These items constitute a single factor. The remaining items can be rescored and additional factors extracted. The first factor removed would be the general factor. As can be seen, the phi method of obtaining reproducibility corresponds very closely to the Wherry-Gaylord extraction of the general factor. The principal differences are that the Wherry-Gaylord does not require that the finally selected items have a range of item difficulties, and does not cut total scores at the same ratio as the item-difficulty levels. Evidence reported by Wherry, Campbell, and Perloff [20] suggests that the Wherry-Gaylord general factor will correspond to the general factor obtainable in a Thurstone multiple factor analysis. The present writers found similar evidence in an analysis of a morale scale. After the morale scale had been subjected to a Thurstone multiple factor analysis, it was administered to a new group of subjects and subjected to a phi reproducibility scaling. The resulting scale was almost identical in item content with the Thurstone general factor.

While it appears to be true that a highly reproducible scale will tend to measure a single factor (since the phi analysis will isolate the general factor in the test items), not all single factor tests will be highly reproducible scales. This is because a reproducible scale must have a range of difficulty levels if all persons are not to be forced into two categories: either all items passed or all items failed. The following example points up the reason this is true. If all items were at the 50-per-cent difficulty level, and if the test were perfectly reproducible, the 50 per cent of the subjects with the highest total scores would score correct on all items; the 50 per cent of the subjects with the lowest total scores would score incorrect on all items. This restriction is not necessary for all single-factor tests. Single-factor tests can have all items at the same difficulty level and still have a wide range of total scores due to the almost inevitable presence of error variance in the items. Reproducibility is impossible in such a case. Despite this lack of reproducibility, the single-factor test might be quite adequate since, if two persons score high on a single-factor test it is because they are high in the factor, and the differential patterns of their responses must be irrelevant for prediction since the differential patterns must be a result of error variance and do not represent stable patterns. If the differential patterns were differentially predictive, the test could not be a single-factor test. In those situations, therefore, where it is desirable to have all items at the same difficulty level, reproducibility is usually not a useful approach. The exception to this rule is the case in which a single discrimination is desired—e.g., pass vs. fail. In this case all items should have pass per cents which are proportional to the pass per cent desired for the whole test [16].

In many practical test-construction situations, where the logic of the situation is not incompatible with reproducibility, it appears to the writers that obtaining a general-factor test through phi reproducibility is simpler than through a Thurstone multiple-factor analysis. In addition to the relative ease of computation, the set of items so obtained should form not only a single-factor test, but also a reproducible scale.

REPRODUCIBILITY AND RELIABILITY

It is obvious that the techniques for computing so-called reliability coefficients from a single test administration employ exactly the same data which have been used to compute the indices of reproducibility described above. Cronbach [1] has already pointed out the intimate relation of Guttman's reproducibility to the Kuder-Richardson Formula 20, which he has rechristened *alpha*. The key term in *alpha* is the ratio of two variances, $\Sigma pq / \sigma_x^2$. As Loevinger points out [13, p. 31] Σpq gives the raw score variance which would be obtained from a test whose items were completely independent, (σ_{het}^2); and σ_x^2 is the obtained raw score variance. Loevinger's Formula 11 has these same quantities in it, plus a third representing the raw-score variance of a test whose items were perfectly correlated. It should be noted that the lower limit of *alpha* is always zero, but the upper limit is dependent upon the distribution of item difficulties. The obtained *alpha* for our illustrative test is .47, and the upper limit of *alpha* for this set of item difficulties is .88.

In order to make *alpha* independent of the distribution of item difficulties, Horst [8] has developed a formula which turns out to be identical with Loevinger's 11, except for a correction term composed of the ratio of the maximal to obtained score variance. Since this ratio has a lower limit of 1.00, figures obtained by Horst's method will necessarily be larger than Loevinger's except in the perfect case. The Horst formula for the reliability coefficient corrected for dispersion of item difficulties is given below

$$r_{tt} = \frac{\sigma_x^2 - \sum pq \left(\frac{\sigma_{max}^2}{\sigma_x^2} \right)}{\sigma_{max}^2 - \sum pq} \qquad (21)$$

The striking similarity of the Loevinger Formula 11 and the Horst Formula 21 cause one to suspect that the difference between single-trial reliability and homogeneity or reproducibility is more apparent than real.

The critical difference between the "reproducibility" and the "reliability" camps of test construction is seen most clearly in the ways they interpret their indices. When a test shows perfect reproducibility, it will also show perfect reliability by any of the formulas described so far. In order for this unlikely event to occur, several conditions must be met: all the items must be homogeneous in content, all subjects must be similarly constituted in the trait, attitude, or ability being tapped; and this trait, attitude, or ability must remain stable during the testing period. *Any* departure from these conditions will cause *any* of these measures to fall, and there is no way to tell on the basis of the response matrix alone what is amiss. An astute dropping of rows or columns from the matrix (subjects and/or items) will, of course, make things look better. In any event, a low figure indicates that considerable information will be lost in attempting to order subjects on a single linear continuum on the basis of their total scores. It is here that techniques such as Lazarsfeld's latent structure analysis [12] may be used to determine the minimal number of dimensions (classes) needed to account for the information contained in a response matrix. With this technique, a subject, instead of being given a total score, is assigned a probability of belonging in each of several classes. No unidimensionality is assumed, so there is no question of item or subject elimination to force unidimensionality, a procedure routinely employed by those addicted to Guttman scaling and classical test construction. When any such item-elimination procedure is used in test construction, a reliability or reproducibility figure computed on the final sample of items cannot be evaluated until the new version of the test has been administered to another sample of subjects. A low reproducibility figure is generally taken as an indication of item heterogeneity in a test, while a low reliability figure of the Kuder-Richardson variety is usually seen as an indication of the presence of considerable error variance. In the absence of other information, either interpretation is equally plausible, or suspect, since, as was pointed out above, the indices employ the same information from the response matrix.

ITEMS AND SUBJECTS

There is no reason why the techniques of computing reproducibility or single trial reliability cannot be reversed to yield coefficients about the homogeneity of subjects, instead of test items. It is surprising that this has not been done more often, especially in the area of attitude measurement. Lack of reproducibility in a response matrix is just as likely to be due to heterogeneity in the population tested, as to heterogeneity in the test items. For most of the indices described above, computation of subject homogeneity would merely involve switching row and column marginals in the formulas. Such a technique would seem to be a promising one for the identification of deviants.

WHY REPRODUCIBILITY OR SINGLE-TRIAL RELIABILITY?

Having come this far, it is high time we asked why a test with high reproducibility or single-trial reliability is a good thing. Social scientists are all too prone to assume that it is, and to think no further about it. As Cronbach [1] has pointed out, reproducibility is in a sense a measure of the redundancy in a test. For many purposes, this is undesirable. Whenever test results are used to predict a dichotomous criterion such as hire–not hire, pass–fail, butcher–candlestickmaker, psychotic–normal — in short to classify subjects—it can be argued that the last thing in the world a test should have is high internal consistency. The real need is a set of items highly related to the criterion but not to each other. This is, of course, a restatement of the multiple-correlation approach to prediction. Ideally each item would represent a different pure factor. In such a situation, interest lies not in ordering subjects on some linear hypothetical trait, attitude, or ability continuum, but in an efficient dichotomization of the subjects or an ordering on the basis of the probability of membership in a class.

To the extent that the test items are redundant, valuable testing time is wasted. It is a mistake to think such a test is "measuring" something, in the usual sense of that word. That a test can differentiate between neurotics and normals is no indication that "neuroticism" is a trait on which people can be ordered in some simple fashion. Much confusion in clinical literature is based on this fallacy. Unless the instrument exhibits high homogeneity-reproducibility – single-trial reliability, there is no reason to assume that the score on the test can yield an ordering of the subjects on some unidimensional continuum which can be given a label.

It is the person doing "basic" research who is apt to be more interested in ordering subjects on a unidimensional continuum. For him, the question of the internal consistency of his multiple-item test or questionnaire is of immediate concern. He may start with the unshakable conviction that the trait he has in mind *is* unidimensional, in which case he will engage in an often lengthy process of test construction, weeding out items until he achieves an instrument with internal consistency at a satisfactorily high level. This type of worker usually longs for an infinite population of items and subjects. When this longing is fulfilled, or even approximated, he can usually come up with a selection of items which, when administered to an appropriate population, will yield a response matrix of the desired internal consistency. He may even regard this achievement as support for his initial assumption about the unidimensionality of the trait, though the logic of such a conclusion is somewhat less than perfect, considering the amount of information thrown away in order to make things come out so neatly.

On the other hand, he may begin with a more modest aim: to find out, for a given set of items, the minimum number of parameters needed to account for the obtained responses of subjects to these items. If he finds that the response matrix shows high reproducibility or high single-trial reliability, he is apt to be pleased because life is so simple; but if he does not find his data so neatly arranged, he is likely to resign himself to fairly laborious procedures in order to find out the dimensionality of the data he has collected rather than to attribute any departure from unidimensionality to error variance.

The important point is that all the techniques mentioned here, whether they are regarded as indices of reproducibility, homogeneity, or single-trial reliability, are based upon the same raw data in the response matrix; and all are more or less interchangeable with a little algebraic manipulation, though, as we have seen, they yield different numbers. How the number is interpreted depends not upon which one of these formulas is employed, since they are all basically equivalent, but upon what assumptions are made. One can assume that the items are homogeneous and that the subjects are similarly constituted in the trait being measured, in which case one uses the index as a measure of intraindividual trait stability. On the other hand, one can assume trait stability and subject homogeneity, in which case the index is said to reflect the homogeneity of the items. As was mentioned above, one may equally well assume trait stability and item homogeneity and employ the index as a measure of the homogeneity of the subjects. Any pair of assumptions appears to be about as plausible as any other. The important point is that from a single response matrix there is no way of telling what assumptions are reasonable. An obtained index, be it Jackson's PPR_t, Loevinger's H_t, Green's I, Cronbach's *alpha*, or Horst's r_{tt}, will be less than 1.00 when any or all of these conditions are not met. The plausibility of the assumptions can be ascertained only by recourse to further data, and the kind of data required will be different for testing each assumption. An estimate of intraindividual trait stability, for example, demands retesting the same subjects with the same items, but such retest data will be of little value in arriving at estimates of subject or item heterogeneity.

The one thing these indices of reproducibility or single-trial reliability will reflect without equivocation is the amount of information thrown away by representing the subject's performance on the test by a total score based on the number of items passed. They indicate, in other words, how adequately a unidimensional model fits the obtained data.

Proponents of homogeneity or reproducibility have been criticized because their criteria for a "good" test are unrealistically strict. It is true that perfect reproducibility will occur when, and only when: (*a*) the factors determining subjects' responses to the test do not change during the testing period, (*b*) the factors determining subjects' responses to the test are the same for all subjects, and (*c*) all the items in the test are identical in the factors determining the responses they elicit. It is also true that perfect single-trial reliability will be obtained only under the same circumstances. These are stringent conditions, and they are seldom, if ever, met. Human beings are just not that simple, but the fault is hardly Guttman's. There is nothing wrong in continuing to assume that many human abilities, attitudes, and traits are unidimensional continua, but we should be fully aware that this is at best a useful first approximation, and that an appreciable proportion of the information in our raw data will thereby be sacrificed on the altar of error variance.

REFERENCES

1. CRONBACH, L. J. Coefficient alpha and the internal structure of tests. *Psychometrika,* 1951, **16**, 297–334.
2. FESTINGER, L. The treatment of qualitative data by "scale analysis." *Psychol. Bull.,* 1947, **44**, 146–161.
3. FORD, R. N. A rapid scoring procedure for scaling attitude questions. *Publ. Opin. Quart.,* 1950, **14**, 507–532.
4. GREEN, B. F. Attitude measurement. In

G. Lindzey (Ed.), *Handbook of social psychology.* Cambridge: Addison-Wesley, 1954.

5. GREEN, B. F. A method of scalogram analysis using summary statistics. *Psychometrika,* 1956, **21,** 79–88.

6. GUTTMAN, L. The Cornell technique for scale and intensity analysis. *Educ. psychol. Measmt,* 1947, **7,** 247–279.

7. GUTTMAN, L. The basis for scalogram analysis. In S. A. Stouffer et al., *Measurement and prediction.* Princeton: Princeton Univer. Press, 1950.

8. HORST, P. Correcting the Kuder-Richardson reliability for dispersion of item difficulties. *Psychol. Bull.,* 1953, **50,** 371–374.

9. HUMPHREYS, L. G. Test homogeneity and its measurement. *Amer. Psychologist,* 1949, **4,** 245. (Abstract)

10. JACKSON, J. M. A simple and more rigorous technique for scale analysis. In *A manual of scale analysis.* Part II. Montreal: McGill Univer., 1949. (Mimeographed.)

11. KAHN, L. H., & BODINE, A. J. Guttman scale analysis by means of IBM equipment. *Educ. psychol. Measmt,* 1951, **11,** 298–314.

12. LAZARSFELD, P. F. The logic and mathematical foundation of latent structure analysis. In S. A. Stouffer et al., *Measurement and prediction.* Princeton. Princeton Univer. Press, 1950.

13. LOEVINGER, JANE. A systematic approach to the construction and evaluation of tests of ability. *Psychol. Monogr.,* 1947, **61,** No. 4 (Whole No. 285).

14. LOEVINGER, JANE. The technic of homogeneous tests compared with some aspects of "scale analysis" and factor analysis. *Psychol. Bull.,* 1948, **45,** 507–529.

15. LONG, J. A. Improved overlapping methods for determining the validities of test items. *J. exp. Educ.,* 1934, **2,** 264–268.

16. LORD, F. M. Some perspectives on "the attenuation paradox in test theory." *Psychol. Bull.,* 1955, **52,** 505–510.

17. MARDER, E. Linear segments: a technique for scalogram analysis. *Publ. Opin. Quart.,* 1952, **16,** 417–431.

18. NOLAND, E. W. Worker attitude and industrial absenteeism: a statistical appraisal. *Amer. sociol. Rev.,* 1945, **10,** 503–510.

19. WHERRY, R. J., & GAYLORD, R. H. The concept of test and item reliability in relation to factor pattern. *Psychometrika,* 1943, **8,** 247–269.

20. WHERRY, R. J., CAMPBELL, J. T., & PERLOFF, R. An empirical verification of the Wherry-Gaylord iterative factor analysis procedure. *Psychometrika,* 1951, **16,** 67–74.

Chapter 17

Further Problems in the Measurement of Growth

FREDERIC M. LORD

The attempt to measure gains or growth by means of psychological tests encounters a number of rather basic, sometimes controversial, measurement problems. The present paper attempts a survey and discussion of several of these. A problem already treated in a previous article [4] will be briefly summarized first in order to facilitate a discussion of its relation to other problems in the area.

ESTIMATING THE GAIN OF EACH INDIVIDUAL

Suppose that at the beginning of a course in hygiene the weight of student a is w_{1a}, and at the end of the course his weight is w_{2a}. The gain, $w_{2a} - w_{1a}$, is a commonly used measure whose interpretation is not open to question.

This article is reprinted from *Educational and Psychological Measurement*, 1958, with the permission of the author and the copyright holder, G. Frederic Kuder.

Suppose now that instead of measuring the student's weight, we attempt to measure his spelling ability. A pretest, t_1, is administered to each student at the beginning of the school year and a parallel post-test, t_2, at the end of the year. The resulting scatterplot might be the same as that obtained for weight. One is tempted to compute the gain $g_a = t_{2a} - t_{1a}$, and to conclude that those students with positive values of g_a can spell more words correctly at the end than at the beginning of the year. This is of course the usual procedure.

Suppose, however, to take an extreme example, that there is experimental evidence showing that the actually-obtained scatterplot is exactly the same as the plot that would have been found if the two parallel forms of the test had been administered simultaneously. Since score differences between two parallel tests are, by definition, caused by errors of measurement, the changes resulting after a year of course work, under this supposition, are the same as those produced by errors of measurement. The only possible conclusion is that each student's true score has remained the same, and that the various observed gains are entirely due to errors of measurement.

This situation calls attention to a fact that deserves more emphasis: we are interested in observed test scores only insofar as they allow us to make inferences about true scores. If we hire the ten applicants having the highest observed scores on a civil service examination, we do so not because we want to hire applicants with high *observed* scores, but because we want to hire applicants with high *true* scores and we infer that high true scores are likely to accompany high observed scores.

In the present situation we are interested in the observed scores only insofar as they enable us to make inferences about the examinee's true gain, which is defined as the difference between his true scores on the pretest and on the post-test: $\gamma_a = \tau_{2a} - \tau_{1a}$, where τ represents true score. At this point it should be clear that the observed gain provides an accurate estimate of the true gain *only* when the initial and final measurements are perfectly reliable. Whenever we are dealing with unreliable measures, such as test scores, special statistical procedures that take into account the degree of unreliability of the test must be used in order to obtain satisfactory estimates of true gain. It may be stated here without proof that the estimated true gain, which is of course the *estimated difference* between true scores, is *not* the same as the *difference* between *estimated* true scores.

Since the only information available about each examinee is his pretest score and his post-test score, it seems reasonable to try to estimate his true gain by means of a multiple regression equation, using these two observed scores as predictors. Practical formulas and methods for computing purposes have been given in a previous article [4]. It is to be noted that for a number of pupils the estimated true gain

may be positive even though the actually observed gain is negative.[1]

CORRELATING GAIN WITH OTHER VARIABLES

Attempts to correlate various variables with gain have led to considerable controversy, particularly in the field of personality testing. There seem to be quite a variety of ways in which the use of gain may involve either statistical or logical difficulties. Suppose it is desired to know the correlation between initial standing and gain for some specified group of students. If the variable in question is reliably measured, as is the case with physical weight, then the research worker can compute and interpret

[1] The development in [4] may be generalized in various ways—for example, to the case where there are three or more testings, or to the case where pretest and post-test do not have the same standard error of measurement. The latter generalization was presented by Quinn McNemar in an article "On Growth Measurement" in the Spring 1958 issue of this journal. The practical worker will use McNemar's formulas in preference to those in [4] whenever separate reliability determinations are available for pretest and post-test. If the standard errors of measurement for the two tests are considerably different, however, he should be especially wary lest the cause of this difference be such that either (a) the relationship between observed scores and true gain is seriously curvilinear, (b) the pretest and post-test have metrics with different units of measurement, or (c) the pretest and post-test are not measuring the same psychological dimension.

When he states that equation 29 in [4] is in error because it is not the same as his equation 4, Professor McNemar apparently overlooks the fact that the former equation is described as giving "the standard error of an estimated gain," whereas the latter gives the standard error of estimate of the *true* gain. He is quite right, however, in objecting to the statement in [4] regarding multiple testings. If three testings have been held, the estimated gain of any pupil from the first to the second testing, plus his estimated gain from the second to the third testing, will in general exactly equal his estimated gain from the first to the third testing only if the scores for all three testings are used as predictors in the regression equation for estimating the gain between any pair of them. Since all three scores are available, it is both appropriate and profitable to use them in this way; the statement in [4], however, incorrectly indicated that the additive property of estimated gains holds when each estimate of gain is derived from two testings only.

the correlation without hesitation. In the case of test scores, which are not perfectly reliable, the situation illustrates very nicely the sort of problem that arises from the unreliability of measuring instruments and the consequent need for thinking in terms of true scores rather than in terms of observed scores.

If the research worker correlates pretest score with observed gain, he is correlating t_1 with the quantity $t_2 - t_1$. Now it is known that t_1 contains an error of measurement, say, e_1. (There is also an error of measurement, e_2, in t_2; but this error may be ignored for the present.) If e_1 appears in t_1 with a positive sign, then, of necessity, it appears in the quantity $t_2 - t_1$ with a negative sign; if e_1 appears in t_1 with a negative sign, then it appears in the quantity $t_2 - t_1$ with a positive sign. Thus there tends to be a spurious negative correlation between pretest and observed gain. This fact was first pointed out by Sir Godfrey Thomson in 1924. His article contains the necessary formulas for eliminating the spurious effect and estimating the correlation between initial standing and true gain [6, 7].

In the usual situation where it is desired to correlate gain with some measure other than initial or final score, there is ordinarily no spurious effect; and the desired correlation may be computed by very familiar methods. Consider, first, the simple product-moment correlation between any predictor variable, c, and observed gain. This correlation, $r_{cg} = r_{c(t_2-t_1)}$, can be interpreted in straightforward fashion as just what it is— the correlation between the variable c and the observed gain. Since the variable g is likely to be much less reliably measured than most ordinary test-score variables, it may be desirable to correct the correlation for attenuation. The corrected correlation is $r_{c\gamma} = r_{cg}/\sqrt{r_{gg}}$, where r_{gg} is the reliability of the observed gain. This reliability is readily computed from the pretest and post-test reliabilities and from the correlation between pretest and post-test by standard formulas.

It is implicit in the use of the word gain that the initial and final measures are expressed in the same metric. In the case where the variable under consideration is the student's weight in pounds, there seems to be little question that the initial and final measures are expressed on the same scale. In the case of test scores, this may not be so obvious. Even though the pretest and post-test consist of the same test questions and are physically identical, it is quite possible to maintain that the student has changed drastically during the course of instruction and that, even though we eliminate practice effect from consideration, the test no longer measures the same thing when given after instruction as it did before instruction. If this is asserted, then the pretest and post-test are measuring different dimensions and no amount of statistical manipulation will produce a measure of gain or of growth.

Suppose, for example, that at the beginning of the instruction we have measured the students' ability in arithmetic and at the end of the instruction we have measured the students' ability in algebra; and suppose that we want to know the relation between effectiveness of training in algebra and some third variable. A common but fallacious procedure, which still causes much controversy and which has cast a pall of doubt over the whole use of gains, is to correlate the third variable with the difference between the *standardized* algebra score and the standardized arithmetic score.

Now, the difference between standardized score on algebra and standardized score on arithmetic is a statistical artifact with various undesirable properties. If we are trying to measure the effect of training in algebra, we are not really interested in any such statistical artifact. There may be situations where we are actually interested in such difference scores even though the two tests do not measure the same dimension, but for most problems we must abandon the difference score and resort to partial correlation techniques. We must compute the partial correlation between the third variable, c, and the post-test, t_2, with the pretest, t_1, held constant. It will simplify matters to consider the case of normally distributed variables. In this case, this partial correlation, denoted by $r_{ct_2.t_1}$, is equal to the ordinary correlation between c and post-test in any group of people having a constant pretest score.

What is the relationship of this partial correlation coefficient to the correlation between c and observed gain? Or to the correlation between c and true gain? One difference is that the use of "gain" by definition supposes that pretest and post-test have the same metric, whereas no such assumption is necessary with the use of partial correlation.

The presence of errors of measurement seriously complicates matters here. *The sign of the partial correlation coefficient may actually change from negative to positive or from positive to negative when errors of measurement are removed.* Thus all correlations under discussion should be corrected for attenuation.

For purposes of the present discussion, however, a comparison of the two correlation coefficients can be made most clearly by considering only perfectly reliable measures, such as physical weight measured in pounds. What, then, is the relation between $r_{cw_2.w_1}$ and $r_{c(w_2-w_1)}$? The results of this comparison may seem paradoxical; so the development will bear close watching.

The general relationship between these two correlations is too complicated to be of help here. Instead, let us ask what can be inferred about the partial correlation in the special situation where the correlation of the third variable with gain is zero.

We are going to be concerned only with the sign of the partial correlation and not with its magnitude. Thus we can simplify matters by working with the part correlation $r_{c(w_2.w_1)}$ instead of the partial correlation $r_{cw_2.w_1}$ since these two always have the same sign. The part correlation is by definition [2] equal to the correlation between an ordinary variable and a residual. In this case, $r_{c(w_2.w_1)} = r_{c[(w_2-\overline{w_2})-b(w_1-\overline{w_1})]}$, where $\overline{w_1}$ and $\overline{w_2}$ are the mean values for the group and b is the ordinary regression coefficient for predicting w_2 from w_1. The quantity in brackets is a residual; that is, it

is the deviation of w_2 from the regression line used to predict it from w_1. Since adding or subtracting a constant to all the values of a variable will not alter its correlation with some other variable, the means in the foregoing equations may be omitted, leaving the simpler result $r_{c(w_2.w_1)} = r_{c(w_2-bw_1)}$. Note that w_2 and w_1 have not been assumed to be expressed in terms of standard scores, since such an assumption would destroy the meaning of the difference $w_2 - w_1$ as the gain in weight.

Since we are concerned only with the sign of the partial or part correlation, we can replace each correlation coefficient by the corresponding covariance. Consider $s_{cw_2.w_1} = s_{c(w_2.w_1)} = s_{c(w_2-bw_1)}$. The partial correlation will have the same sign as this last covariance, which is readily rewritten as $s_{c(w_2-bw_1)} = s_{cw_2} - bs_{cw_1}$.

This last expression is to be compared with the covariance between variable c and gain: $s_{c(w_2-w_1)} = s_{cw_2} - s_{cw_1}$. It is clear that the two covariances differ because of the coefficient b. Now $b = s_{w_2}r_{w_1w_2}/s_{w_1}$, by the usual formula for a regression coefficient, where s_{w_1} and s_{w_2} are standard deviations. Since the correlation $r_{w_1w_2}$ will be less than 1, b will also be less than 1 as long as the standard deviation of the w's for the group does not increase sharply between the initial and final measurements.

The two covariances being compared differ by the quantity $(1 - b)s_{cw_1}$. Assuming that b is less than 1, as will usually be the case, we have the following result: *If the correlation between c and gain in weight is zero, then the partial correlation $r_{cw_2.w_1}$ will always have the same sign as the correlation between c and w_1.* For example, under the conditions stated, any third variable that has a positive correlation with initial weight will also have a positive partial correlation with final weight when initial weight is held constant.

Manning and DuBois [5] studied the relationship of various predictors to gain in performance as measured by parallel forms of an achievement test. They found that observed gain, $t_2 - t_1$, had almost zero correlation with each of their predictors and that residual gain, $t_2 - bt_1$, had significant positive correlation with each of their predictors. This latter result is what must be expected according to the foregoing algebra.

The fact that predictors correlate more highly with residual gain than they do with observed gain does not mean that residual gain is a better measure of gain than is observed gain. To return to physical weight, the difference $w_2 - w_1$ *is* the gain in weight; the residual $w_2 - bw_1$ is *not* the gain in weight, except of course in the unusual case when b is equal to 1. The fact that various predictors correlate more highly with the residual than they do with gain is a result of the correlation of the predictor with initial standing. The predictors would presumably correlate still more highly with the average of initial and final standing, but this fact does not make this average a good measure of gain.

At this point it would be natural, but incorrect, to conclude that the partial correlation coefficient under discussion can have no important place in a study of growth. To complete the paradox, it now remains to show that, although this partial correlation does not represent the correlation between the predictor and gain for the group of individuals measured, nevertheless this partial correlation coefficient is for most purposes a preferable measure of the relationship between predictor and gain.

Again assuming multivariate normality, we can state that in any group of individuals each of whom has the same weight initially, the correlation between predictor and final weight is equal to the partial correlation $r_{cw_2.w_1}$. In other words, this partial correlation is the correlation between c and w_2 for any group of individuals having a fixed w_1. It is also true that when w_1 is fixed, the gain, $w_2 - w_1$, is perfectly correlated with w_2. Thus

$$r_{cw_2.w_1} = r_{cw_2}, \text{ when } w_1 \text{ is fixed}$$

also

$$r_{cw_2.w_1} = r_{c(w_2-w_1)}, \text{ when } w_1 \text{ is fixed}$$

Consider now the following dilemma. We have a group of individuals in which predictor and observed gain are uncorrelated so that $r_{c(w_2-w_1)} = 0$ *for the total group*. We have already found that if the predictor is positively correlated with w_1, then we may expect the partial correlation to be positive; hence, *when w_1 is fixed, $r_{c(w_2-w_1)} > 0$*. In a word, the predictor is uncorrelated with gain in the total group but the predictor is positively correlated with gain in every subgroup obtained by sectioning the total group on initial weight. The mere existence of such a situation is confusing enough.

Now suppose the predictor, c, represents the amount of vitamins added to the diet between the initial and final weighing of the students. We are anxious to increase the weight of the students and we wish to know whether adding vitamins to their diet will achieve this result. We discover that the amount of vitamins eaten is uncorrelated with gain in weight for the *total* group but that it is positively correlated with gain in weight for every subgroup of the total group. What do we conclude as to the value of the use of vitamins? And why? The resolution of this dilemma follows a familiar line of reasoning. Professor DuBois, for example, resolved it some time ago [2, 3, 5]. Suppose that a controlled experiment was made with infants all of whom had the same weight at birth; and suppose it were found that the amount of vitamins eaten was correlated with gain in weight for either sex studied separately, but that there was no correlation when the two sexes were combined into a single group. In such a case, the results of interest are clearly those obtained when sex is held constant—in such a study one avoids combining heterogeneous groups whenever possible. The conclusion suggested by the data would be that the addition of vitamins to the diet *does* tend to produce a gain in weight, even though amount of vitamins given is uncorrelated with gain in weight in the total group.

Just as it is important to hold sex constant in such an experiment, so also is it important to hold initial weight constant.

All the subjects could be separated into subgroups according to initial weight and each subgroup studied separately; it is usually more convenient, however, to achieve this result by the use of partial correlation techniques.

The conclusion is that when one wishes to study the effect of some outside variable on gain in weight, or on gain in test score, the ordinary correlation between the outside variable and gain is *not* the coefficient of primary interest. For reasons that arise from the logic of the problem rather than from any purely statistical considerations, the decisive coefficient is the partial correlation between the third variable and final status, with initial status held constant. Partial correlation techniques seem to have been neglected in many cases where they are required.

DO GOOD STUDENTS GAIN MORE THAN POOR STUDENTS?

Table 17–1 is presented to illustrate a somewhat different type of problem. The data (borrowed from [1]) represent an attempt to evaluate the results of training in a certain course in each of six different colleges. The students in each college are separated into five groups according to their score on the pretest. The figures in the body of the table are the mean observed gain for each subgroup of students, as shown by a retesting at the end of the school year. It is clear that the higher the initial score, the less the observed gain. There are at least four possible explanations of the results:

1. The good students are actually learning less than the poor students. For example, the teachers may be devoting all their attention to the poor students, with the stated result.

2. The result is simply a manifestation of the well-known phenomenon of regression towards the mean.

3. The results are simply the effect of errors of measurement. Those students who score high initially are, more often than not, lucky in the sense that the error of measurement in their score happened to be positive. Since those students who are lucky on the first test administration will have no more than average luck on the second test administration, their average score will necessarily decline.

4. The scale of measurement of the test is compressed at the upper end, so that actually a gain of one or two points for the initially high scoring students represents as much real gain, in some sense, as a gain of five or six points occurring in a lower portion of the score scale. Such a compression of the scale is bound to exist, for example, whenever some students score near the ceiling of the pretest,

Table 17–1   Mean Gains for Students on Test of Science Reasoning and Understanding, Classified according to Pretest Standing*

College	Initially Low Group	Initially Low-middle Group	Initially Middle Group	Initially High-middle Group	Initially High Group
A	11.08	6.74	4.19	3.33	0.89
B	4.86	5.83	−0.10	2.82	−0.07
C	5.94	6.20	3.75	2.67	0.43
D	10.28	6.44	5.62	4.34	1.31
E	4.19	2.63	−0.57	−1.09	−2.04
F	7.05	6.76	4.54	2.69	0.29
Average	6.26	5.16	2.93	2.04	0.31

* Data taken from Dressel, P. L. and Mayhew, L. B. *General Education: Exploration in Evaluation*, American Council on Education, 1954.

so that it is physically impossible for them to show any sizable gain on the post-test.

Let us take these possible explanations up one at a time. The first explanation is not expressed in sufficiently accurate language for it to be capable of either confirmation or rejection. There is no way of knowing exactly what would be meant by a statement that this initially good student has learned as much during the year as this initially poor student. Furthermore, there seems to be no unique and generally satisfactory way to assign a clear meaning to such a statement. Lacking a definition of what is meant by "equality" of gain, it is of course impossible to assign a meaning to a statement of inequality.

It is worth pointing out that although it may be impossible to find a unique definition for equality of gain when the two individuals being compared start at very different points on the score scale of the test, it is quite possible to define equality of gain when the two individuals start at exactly the same point on the score scale.

Next, consider the second possible explanation. Is the observed poor performance of the initially high scoring students simply the result of regression towards the mean? Let us eliminate the effect of errors of measurement from the discussion by supposing that the gains in the table represent accurately measured physical weight rather than test score. It is clear that if the second weighing of each student had occurred immediately after the first, at the beginning of the year, there would have been no gains, no losses, and no regression towards the mean. All gains and losses found when the students are weighed at the end of the year can therefore be attributed to something that happened in the elapsed interval of time. Since the gains and losses are attributable to events occurring during the year, they are real and are not attributable to any statistical phenomenon. The conclusion is that when errors of measurement are eliminated from the picture, regression toward the mean is not an explanation at all. It is merely a description of the nature of

the scatterplot. The reasons for the so-called regression are to be found in real life and not in statistical theory.

When errors of measurement are present, on the other hand, they do produce a situation that is usefully described as regression toward the mean. The student who is exceptionally lucky on the initial testing will not in general be exceptionally lucky on the second testing. This effect tends to produce a decline in the scores of the initially high scoring students.

One procedure for determining whether the observed results could be attributed solely to errors of measurement would be to estimate the true gain of each individual by means of the method of reference [4]. In accordance with this method, a scatterplot could be prepared from the data summarized in Table 17–1 and oblique straight lines drawn to show the estimated true gain for each student. It should then be clear whether or not the true gains of the initially high scoring students tend to be numerically higher or lower than those of the initially low scoring students.

There is, however, a much simpler and more obvious procedure which involves fewer assumptions and which will yield the same conclusions when the assumptions are met. On the one hand, prepare the scatterplot showing the relationship between pretest and post-test. On the other hand, obtain experimentally a representation of what the scatterplot would be like if the two tests were administered simultaneously at the beginning of the school year. Superimpose these two scatterplots. Any difference between the two scatterplots is attributable to the teaching or to other events occurring during the year. If there is no difference, then the observed changes during the year can be attributed entirely to errors of measurement.

ARE NUMERICALLY EQUAL GAINS REALLY EQUAL?

The foregoing procedure should provide an answer to the questions asked insofar as this is possible within the limits imposed by the nature of the score scale. As already mentioned, if some of the students obtain a virtually perfect score on the pretest, it is obviously impossible for them to show appreciable gain when they take the post-test. This is an extreme illustration of the well-known fact that the test-score scale does not ordinarily provide units of measurements that are clearly equal in different parts of the scale. This fact introduces serious difficulties into any study of growth—difficulties that I have largely ignored up to this point.

The most damaging objection to the test-score scale is that equal scores do not necessarily mean equal ability. If people having the same score cannot be said to have equal ability, then we cannot be sure that a person having a high score has more ability than a person having a low score. This objection can be raised to the observed-score scale on any test, but in many cases only because each test score involves an error of measurement. If the test is a homogeneous test in the factorial sense, then the true score scale will not suffer from this kind of difficulty, which can thus be avoided by thinking in terms of *true* scores and working with estimated true scores; or, what is simpler in some cases, working with ordinary observed scores and thinking of them as estimates of true scores.

In the case of tests that are not factorially pure, there may be no practical way out of this difficulty. There is a theoretical way out however—simply to split the test into factorially pure subtests and treat each one separately.

Let us limit the discussion to factorially pure tests. Equal true scores now represent equal ability in the trait measured, and an examinee with a high true score is surely to be ranked above an examinee with a lower true score. Observed scores are used to provide inferences regarding true scores. Any problems arising from the fallibility of these inferences can be handled by an application of the theory of statistical inference provided some mathematical model is available for the relationship between true score and observed score.

Let us now see where the objections raised to the test-score scale leave us with respect to the various problems discussed earlier. To take a favorable example, suppose that the tests under consideration are measures of spelling ability and that each consists of a representative sample of words drawn from the unabridged Webster's Dictionary. Suppose all the words in the dictionary have been stratified according to subject matter, difficulty, discriminating power, and so forth. Each test is then a stratified random sample of all the words in the dictionary. In such a situation, the true score on the test has a clear meaning: it represents the number of words in the dictionary that the examinee would spell correctly if these could somehow be administered to him without undue fatigue, practice effect, etc.

If we are using a 100-item spelling test and if the estimated true gain of a student during the course of the school year is found to be five points on this test, this means very simply that we estimate that at the end of the school year he can spell correctly five per cent more of the words in the Webster's Dictionary than he could at the beginning of the school year. Such a statement seems to have a clear practical meaning upon which practical educational decisions may be based. If a student's estimated true gain is negative, it is inferred that during the year he has forgotten how to spell more words than he has learned; the educational decision based on this inference may be quite different from that in the preceding case.

Thus one is on fairly sure ground when a single student is considered by himself. Trouble arises as soon as the gains of two students having different pretest scores are to be compared. If one student has an estimated true gain of five points and another student has an estimated true gain of two points we can, to be sure, infer that the first student has learned how to spell more words than the second during the year. Unless the two students started at the same point in the score scale, however, it cannot be concluded that the first student has really *learned* more than the second, except in some very arbitrary sense. If the two students started at different ability levels, the words learned by the first student may have been short, easy words compared with those learned by the second student. (There can be no such difference between students starting at the same ability level, as long as the pretest and posttest items are all homogeneous factorially; since if such a difference occurred, except for some isolated pair of students, it would automatically introduce an additional common factor among the test items.)

Whenever we correlate gains with some third variable, we are treating *numerically* equal gains at different parts of the score scale as if they were really equal. The use of partial correlations in no way avoids this difficulty.

Faced with this type of difficulty, the experimenter should build his test in such a way that he is willing to treat numerically equal gains in different parts of the score scale as if they were at least approximately equal. This is to a considerable extent an arbitrary decision on his part. However, to make an admittedly arbitrary decision is better than to forego all comparisons of growth between different parts of the score scale. The difficulties with the score scales do not prevent us from measuring growth; they merely require us to specify the scale of measurement in terms of which our conclusions are valid.

This is not a good situation, but it will have to do until we find some reason for choosing one of the available scales as more convenient than all the others. When (and if) such a reason is found, then everyone should be willing to agree that the units of this scale shall be equal by definition.

REFERENCES

1. Dressel, P. L., & Mayhew, L. B. *General education: exploration in evaluation.* American Council on Education, 1954.
2. DuBois, P. H. *Multivariate correlational analysis.* New York: Harper & Bros., 1957.
3. DuBois, P. H., & Manning, W. H. Methods of research in technical training. Technical Report No. 3, ONR Contract No. Nonr–816(02). St. Louis: Washington Univer., 1957.
4. Lord, F. M. The measurement of growth. *Educ. psychol. Measmt,* 1956, 16, 421–437.
5. Manning, W. H., & DuBois, P. H. Gain in proficiency as a criterion in test validation. Technical Report No. 4, ONR Contract No. Nonr–816(02). St. Louis: Washington Univer., 1957.
6. Thomson, G. H. A formula to correct for the effect of errors of measurement on the correlation of initial values with gains. *J. exp. Psychol.,* 1924, 7, 321–324.
7. Zieve, L. Note on the correlation of initial scores with gains. *J. educ. Psychol.,* 1940, 31, 391–394.

Chapter 18

Deviant Response Tendencies: Their Measurement and Interpretation

LEE SECHREST / DOUGLAS N. JACKSON

In recent years a wide variety of systematic biases in the response tendencies of individuals have been identified. Few of these, however, are of greater potential theoretical or practical importance than the one described by Berg [5], accounted for in terms of his "deviation hypothesis," and further elaborated in a number of research studies [1, 2, 6, 7, 8, 9, 21, 30].

The initial statement of the deviation hypothesis was: "Deviant response patterns tend to be general; hence those deviant behavior patterns which are significant for abnormality and thus regarded as symptoms are associated with other deviant response patterns which are in noncritical areas of behavior and which are not regarded as symptoms of personality aberration" [5, p. 62].

It is our purpose to attempt a clarification and explication of the measurement and interpretation of deviant response tendencies. We have gained the impression from a study of published reports and from our own research on deviant response tendencies that certain conceptions in this area, not necessarily attributable to Berg, permit a variety of interpretations, some of which are, in our view, mutually exclusive or otherwise untenable. Here as elsewhere in personality assessment, measurement procedures are intimately related to questions of interpretation; alternative indices of deviant tendencies may result in very different scores for particular individuals, and hence will have varying theoretical implications. By explicitly delineating alternative interpretations and measurement operations, we hope to provide a sounder basis for an appraisal of the conditions under which various interpretations of the deviation hypothesis are and are not supported by empirical observations. In this venture we shall discuss first the *generality assumption,* and then take up the question of alternative conceptual and measurement definitions of deviant response tendencies.

This article was reprinted from *Educational and Psychological Measurement,* 1963, with permission of the authors and the copyright holder, G. Frederic Kuder.

267

THE GENERALITY OF DEVIATION

It has been suggested [7] that psychotics, lawyers, cardiac patients, transvestites, young normal children, character disorders, the obese, the feebleminded, psychoneurotics and persons suffering from constipation, among others, represent deviant groups which might be expected to manifest their particular propensities toward deviation not only in a modality relevant to their particular symptoms and to items with relevant content, but also in response to one or more of the following: preference for abstract drawings, food aversion questionnaires, stimuli for conditioned responses, autokinetic and spiral aftereffect situations, vocabulary test items, figure drawings, musical sounds, and olfactory stimuli. Berg [7, p. 95] has stated: "Indeed, any content which produces deviant response patterns will serve, judging from the available evidence. . . . Accordingly, for personality and similar tests, a particular item content is unimportant."

We would like to examine the generality assumption of the deviation hypothesis and what would appear to be its corollary, the alleged unimportance of item content. If it is proposed that deviant response tendencies are wholly general, that is, that an individual who is deviant on any one measure is likely to be deviant on all other measures, the deviation hypothesis has some rather overwhelming implications. One is naturally suspicious of such universal rules in psychology, having learned through hard experience that psychological processes are usually more complicated than the initial optimistic attempts at explanation would suggest [cf. 16]. On the other hand, it might be objected that what is actually being proposed is only that deviations in critical areas, for example, psychopathological symptoms, are likely to be associated with deviations in certain noncritical areas. Nevertheless, if one supposes that some general factor of deviation tendencies accounts for the association between deviations in critical and noncritical areas, then deviations in noncritical areas might be expected to be associated, if all variables, critical and noncritical, shared a mutual relation to a common factor of general deviation. The alternative, of course, is a limitation on the deviation hypothesis, a restatement in a probably more accurate but unfortunately less interesting form; namely, "Deviant response tendencies are sometimes associated." If so stated, the task of the researcher then becomes one of determining the limiting conditions under which the deviation hypothesis might be said to hold. The specific ways in which people are deviant then become of central importance in appraising the generality of the deviation hypothesis. If specific deviant responses to particular personality items show significant discriminant validity for identifying certain psychopathological symptoms, then it is reasonable to inquire into the properties, even the content, of these particular differentiating items.

There is, of course, the danger of lapsing into triviality in proposing that deviant response tendencies are less than completely general. Probably there are few, if any, persons who are not deviant in some manner or other, and it would necessitate little courage to stipulate that persons who were deviant in one way would be found to be deviant in some other way. At the least one must answer, if not in *all* other ways, then in what other ways.

It might naturally occur to one that deviant response tendencies should be associated even in noncritical areas. If deviation tendencies are general in the sense that persons tend to perform in a deviant manner in a variety of situations, it would be useful to appraise the extent to which normal subjects showed deviant behavior over varying classes of responses. It should be noted that the generality assumption would not necessarily require that correlations be found between independent measures of deviant responding, although the correlational model is conceptually simpler and thus, perhaps, preferable. Relationships between various deviation measures might be considered lawful if subjects deviant in one direction on one measure were deviant in any direction on a second measure. For example, if there were a relationship between deviant height and deviant intelligence, it might be found that deviantly tall subjects were either brighter *or* duller than normally tall subjects and that similar findings obtained for the deviantly diminutive. Obviously in such a case the height-intelligence correlation might well be zero.

In an empirical evaluation of the generality of deviant response tendencies, the authors [32] followed both a correlational and a nondirectional approach to the analysis of deviant responding. Very little evidence appeared in the data in support of the generality of "noncritical" deviant responses in normal subjects.

Of course, such a finding of broad generality would indeed be surprising. A generality hypothesis in one of its simplest forms—that deviation is assumed to be unidirectional and associated across diverse measures—would require all variables to be correlated in some degree. Numerous unpublished doctoral dissertations disconfirm such a naïve and somewhat absurd one-dimensional formulation. It should be noted that Berg (personal communication, 1960) explicitly disavows this interpretation of the deviation hypothesis.

In the light of the paucity of evidence that deviant response tendencies are broadly general, and especially in the light of the compelling logical reasons that they cannot all be correlated, we might examine the alternative, that is, that those individuals who are deviant on *one* measure, or in *one* way, will be deviant in *some* other way. We have already pointed out that there is the danger of triviality in such a statement, but triviality may be avoided if we are clear in a specification of the limitations we are imposing on the deviation hypothesis. We also believe, however, that when we begin to examine the logical status of a limited deviation hypothesis, there are considerations, some already mentioned above, which seem definitely to

contradict the statement that "particular stimulus content is unimportant for measuring behaviors in terms of the Deviation Hypothesis" [7]. For it becomes apparent that it is not true that just any old content will suffice, not even content which yields deviant responses. Undoubtedly there are ways, for example, in which schizophrenics might *not* differ from normals, e.g., in cigarette preferences, even though there are many cigarette preferences which are deviant. Once we begin to specify that not all deviant response measures are equally good, content becomes compellingly important.

As a matter of fact, writers in the area of the deviation hypothesis never really seem to have gone beyond the statement that deviant response tendencies are general in denoting the Deviation Hypothesis. Research efforts have never really proposed or attempted to demonstrate generality of deviant response tendencies *within* groups. Research on the deviation hypothesis has centered on the study of various "criterion" groups which may be supposed to be deviant in some "critical" way. Such criterion groups are contrasted most frequently with normal groups, but occasionally with each other, for evidence of deviation and non-critical modes. It has never been made clear, however, just what constitutes a "critical" deviation. *Why* is it assumed that lawyers, cardiac patients, young normal children, and sufferers from constipation are critically deviant? What would *not* constitute, then, a critical deviation, and who would not be the unproud possessor of one?

RESPONSE STYLES AND DEVIATION

One line of interpretation of deviant responses favored by Berg [cf. 7, 8] is to note first that there are certain modal response preferences to personality questionnaires and other devices in the general population from which certain defined criterion groups may be found to depart to a significant degree. The emphasis here is not upon a deviant response to a particular category of content, e.g., a schizophrenic responding "true" to the item, "I hear voices when there is no one around," but rather upon some systematic pattern of responding which differentiates normal subjects from the deviant criterion group. These consistent tendencies, variously termed "response sets" [14, 15]; "biased responses" [2, 3, 4, 5, 8]; "response style" [23, 25, 27] or "stylistic variance" [36], have been proposed as serving as the basis upon which criterion groups may be differentiated from normal groups, even when the item content is not "critical," i.e., when there is no *a priori* basis for interpreting the content as relevant to the considerations upon which the criterion group was chosen.

Thus, it has been proposed by Barnes [3, 4] that neurotics respond deviantly "false" and psychotics respond deviantly "true" to MMPI items. This finding was interpreted by Jackson and Messick [23, 24, 25, 26] and Wiggins [36] as indicating that in personality questionnaires acquiescence may be differentially elicited at varying levels of item desirability within various criterion groups, since it is known that response probability is a function of item desirability [cf. 18].

If this were as far as the argument went, i.e., that there are certain noncontent determinants of responses which might have validity for certain purposes, there would be little room for disagreement, for the evidence already accumulated is impressive, and the research of Berg and his students has substantially contributed to this literature. However, there is a tendency to go considerably beyond this point. Not only are we told that content is unimportant [7], but furthermore that, because young, normal children and schizophrenics had a similar pattern of deviant responses on the *Perceptual Reaction Test* (PRT) [10] when contrasted with normal adults [21], the results were considered to support the notion that "schizophrenic responses are characterized by immaturity" [8, p. 352].

We shall not dwell on the question of by what rule of logic one may conclude that when A and B differ in some particular respect from C, but not from each other, they are necessarily alike in other aspects as well, or the question of why it is not concluded by similar logic that young, normal children are schizophrenic. Rather, the point to be emphasized is that, because in most structured inventories the number of response alternatives is severely restricted (the PRT has only four alternatives), any deviant pattern is likely to be correlated with any other. To take a more extreme example for illustrative purposes, if there are only two response alternatives for an item, and one is keyed "normal," then for a set of such items all "deviation" keys keyed for every item must be perfectly correlated. The "generality" of deviation under such conditions would be spurious, or, at best, indeterminate.

It is for precisely this reason that Jackson and Messick [25] have proposed, with evidence, that in cases in which response alternatives are markedly limited, and where massive response style effects are revealed, as in the MMPI, the opportunities for valid differential diagnoses on the basis of test scores are severely restricted, even though the test may distinguish pathological groups generally from normals. Barnes' [2] finding that pathological groups can be distinguished from normals with a seven-minute PRT about as well as with the much longer MMPI is important evidence bearing on this point, but it need not necessarily be taken as evidence for the alleged "generality" of deviation, except perhaps insofar as pathological groups may generally show a higher rate of random responding (cf. below). One approach to this dilemma, one followed out of necessity by Strong [33] in the area of vocational interests after finding that professional groups appeared similar to one another when contrasted with "men in general," and attempted with some success by Barnes [2] with psychiatric patients, is to contrast the responses of different "deviant" criterion groups, in an attempt to find discriminating items and keys. Unfortunately, in the quest for evidence bearing on the "generality" of deviation, the favored procedure has called for contrasting various deviant groups with normals rather than the more sensitive differential approach. For most purposes of assessment, the latter approach will yield more useful and interpretable information.

DEFINITION OF DEVIATION

We believe that the idea of deviation or of being deviant might be considered and applied in quite a number of different ways, not all of which are equally important and not all of which are entirely compatible with each other. We would like to consider a bit more extensively the nature or definition of the deviant response itself, or perhaps we should say the nature of deviant responses, for, as we hope to show, there are a variety of ways in which persons may contrive to be deviant on a single test or assessment device. For that matter, the determinants of the same deviant response are very likely different for different persons.

We want to describe six definitions of sources of deviation. These are: (a) *absolute deviation;* (b) *relative deviation;* (c) *statistical infrequency;* (d) *extremeness of traits;* (e) *unique structuring of traits;* and (f) *randomness of response.*

ABSOLUTE AND RELATIVE DEVIATIONS

First of all, Berg has stated, ". . . we have defined a deviant response as one which differs from the modal response or from a criterion group response" [7]. There are, in that statement, two definitions of deviation. The first, which we prefer to call *relative deviation,* makes use of the responses which are atypical in the group being studied. That is, the modal responses are identified, and all other responses are termed deviant. The second, which we shall call *absolute deviation,* requires the identification of some group which may on *a priori* grounds

be termed deviant. Those noncritical responses which differentiate the *a priori* deviant group from a comparable normal group may be used to develop a deviant response key. Barnes [2] has developed a key on the PRT based on an absolute definition of deviation. Barnes' key, the Delta scale, was devised to distinguish hospitalized psychiatric patients from normal subjects. Sechrest and Jackson [32] followed the relative keying procedure and developed a key based on the modal and deviant responses of college and nursing students. The relative deviation key yields scores which, for college students, correlate .70 with Delta scores based on absolute deviation tendencies. Since, in that sample, neither the Deviation nor the Delta key had Kuder-Richardson Formula 21 reliabilities in excess of .70, the obtained correlation would seem to indicate some substantial similarity between the two methods of developing keys. Apparently those responses which are unusual in a normal population are, for the most part, those which are typical of pathological groups. And, of necessity, those responses which distinguish pathological groups from normals must be infrequent since by definition the criterion group will always be the smaller one. Thus, in practice, relative and absolute deviation keys are certain to be correlated. Nonetheless, the correlation need not be unity, even when corrected for attenuation, for the criterion group will probably not be characterized by all the responses which are infrequent in the normal group.

There are some rather evident connotational differences between a definition of deviation couched in terms of discrepancy from some modal response pattern on the one hand and a definition in terms of similarity to some deviant group on the other. In the case of similarity to some deviant group as the defining property, there is at least the implicit assumption of "critical" similarity for groups which are alike in noncritical ways. Hesterly and Berg [21], for example, report that young normal children differ from normal adults but do not differ from adult schizophrenics, with the stated conclusion that young normal children and adult schizophrenics are alike in their "immaturity." On the other hand, to define deviation in terms of departure from the modal or typical pattern is to imply that to be deviant is to deviate from some particular group and that whether one is deviant at a given time depends on the context within which one is being evaluated. An Eskimo is a deviant in Chicago but not in the Yukon. A schizophrenic is deviant among us—but is he in a psychiatric hospital? We want to make it clear that we are not necessarily endorsing nor deprecating either definition of deviation. We simply believe that they are different and that the difference should be recognized.

STATISTICAL INFREQUENCY AS DEVIATION

There is another way in which the idea of deviation is employed, particularly with respect to the measurement operations involved, if not necessarily in connotative meaning. Very often, it appears, the term deviant is applied to the statistically infrequent event or object without respect to the larger context in which it appears. We believe that the criterion of statistical infrequency is being invoked when, for example, various occupational groups are spoken of as deviant "criterion" groups and comparisons are made between such deviant groups as lawyers, engineers, or physicians and "people in general" (normals?). Now it is only in the purely statistical and artificial sense of infrequency that any occupational group could be considered deviant. There is no single occupational group that contains anything like a majority, or even a substantial minority, of the workers who constitute "people in general." Everyone is deviant in his occupation when contrasted with "people in general"—steamfitters, plumbers, chemists, bookkeepers, taxi drivers, even psychologists. Used in such a way, that is, to describe as deviant

the members of any occupational group, or the members of any other class of objects solely on the basis of the fact that there are not many of them, the deviation hypothesis is divested of much of its meaning and becomes little more than an affirmation of individual differences. Deviation makes sense only when the number of possible classes is limited and when, we might add, the discrepancies in frequency are marked. As an instance of the latter point, we would be reluctant to call men in our society deviant because they are outnumbered by women.

EXTREMENESS OF CHARACTERISTICS AS DEVIATIONS

The term deviant is also applied to those persons who appear at the extreme of some dimension, e.g., intelligence or height, although the exact rules for application are not clear. There are two somewhat different conceptions of the deviant which are consistent with a rather ancient argument in psychology. There is, first, a frequent use of the term deviant to describe a group of individuals who depart in a single, uniform direction from an undifferentiated mass of "normal" or nondeviant subjects. Thus, for example, typical practice is to identify persons as anxious and nonanxious, pathological and nonpathological, feebleminded and normal, etc. Viewed in such a manner, deviation may be looked upon as a unipolar trait with some degree of rarity in the population, and the distribution of deviation scores should be markedly skewed with a mode of 0, that is, no deviation.

However, there is also the possibility that deviation could be considered a bipolar trait yielding a normal distribution with the mode at a point separating those subjects who deviate in either direction. We might, then, want to identify the anxious, the average and the nonanxious persons with both the anxious and nonanxious being deviant in the population. Or, we could consider both tall and short persons deviant, the nondeviants representing those persons of medium degree of height.

Now presumably for either the Delta or the Deviation key the subject who obtains a high score, that is, who answers many items in the deviant direction is deviant. And he should be deviant in other ways. However, even a deviation scale has two ends, and subjects may score low as well as high on such a scale. For example, in their sample of nursing students Sechrest and Jackson [32] found that the mean and median of the distribution of Deviation scores were almost identical and the scores ranged from just a little better than two and one half standard deviations below the mean to about the same range above the mean. What of those persons who scored well below the mean on the Deviation key? They might appropriately be described as being deviantly nondeviant. (Wiggins [37] has suggested the term "hypercommunality" to refer to this type of responding.) They adhered to the modal responses *more consistently* than did other subjects. There were a number of lines of evidence which pointed to the probable accuracy of the conclusion that low scoring subjects are deviant and in certain of the same ways as high scoring subjects. To take but one example, both high and low scoring subjects received more nominations on the sociometric type variables "most pleasant" and "least pleasant." High scorers were not consistently seen as either more pleasant or less pleasant than low scorers. Both were simply named more often than middle scorers. This finding was consistent across a variety of different traits. Thus, subjects scoring either deviantly high or deviantly low were more salient in their group. There were, however, some instances in which both the high and low scoring deviants were deviant on other measures, but in opposite directions. For example, a verbal intelligence measure indicated that, as compared with a middle scoring group on the Deviation measure, the high scorers were lower in intelligence and the low scorers were

higher in intelligence. Since we may just as well consider as deviant those who depart from the typical in one direction as another, deviant scorers on any particular measure do not in the sources of their deviation constitute a homogeneous group. We would conclude that it is appropriate to consider deviation as having more than a unidirectional interpretation.

UNIQUE STRUCTURING OF TRAITS AS DEVIATION

There is still another way in which persons may be deviant or in which deviant response tendencies may arise. Generally we are bound in our thinking, concerning the relationships between traits of characteristics of persons, to the conception of uniform relationships in the samples with which we deal. Those persons who do not conform to our models or our ideas are simply relegated to the anonymous ranks of error if they are considered at all. Yet, such persons may represent alternatives to our usual conceptions of the universe of "average people." Consider the correlation scatterplot given in Figure 18–1. We usually assume that the relationship between two measures of intelligence is positive. And in this case the relationship between ACE Q and L scores is positive. The correlation is .46. However, note that it is not positive for all of the subjects. For those represented by the small circles in the plot, the relationship could certainly not be considered to be positive and significant. In one sense at least, or in the sense that they lower the correlation, they are deviant. One possibility is that for these subjects there is some unique structuring of abilities that is not found among most persons.

From the standpoint of traditional test theory, it might be argued that by inferring the existence of unique structuring of traits, one ignores the possibility that such deviation is merely error of measurement. Such an argument appears compelling—save for one thing. Utilizing data previously re-

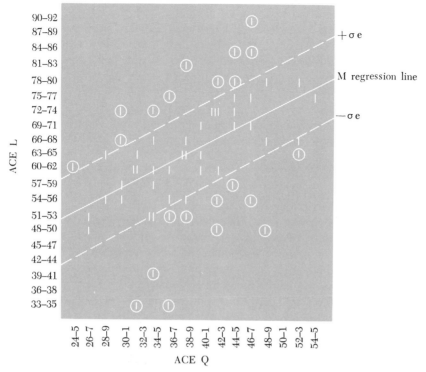

Figure 18–1   *Correlation scatterplot for ACE Q and L scores illustrating correlational "outliers."*

ported [31], we have plotted the correlations between three distinctly separate pairs of variables[1] and have identified those persons whose locations on the plots fall outside lines drawn parallel to and one standard error from the mean regression line for the regression of the one variable on the other (e.g., see Figure 18–1). In a sample of 60 nursing students a total of 35 were correlational "outliers" on one or more of the correlation plots. The remaining 25 were, then, consistent performers who would produce very high correlations. Their other interesting characteristic was that they scored significantly lower on the PRT-Deviation Key than did those subjects who were keeping the correlations low. The mean PRT-D score for the consistent group

was 17.28 and for the "outlier" group 20.66 ($t = 2.50$; $p < .02$). This finding has been supported, though at a lower level of significance (.10 $< p <$ .20), for three correlations involving different variables in a group of 123 college students.

This problem of uniqueness in the structuring of traits or abilities should be afforded increased attention in psychometric methodology. While for many purposes it would be more realistic to base generalizations from factor analytic results upon consistent but unique organizations of traits in homogeneous subsets of subjects, most research workers concerned with the factor analysis of correlations between test scores assume that for each test the score of each person is the weighted sum of his factor scores, the weights being constant for each test, and the factor scores bearing the same interpretation for all people [28, p. 522]. Other than the factor analysis of correlations between persons prior to separate analyses of tests—a method used extremely

---

[1] The three pairs of variables and the correlations between them were: ACE-L score vs. ACE-Q score, .46; MMPI Pd scale vs. Reputational unpredictability, .37; Reputational social intelligence vs. Reputational pleasantness, .59. Choice of variables upon which to calculate regressed scores was accomplished by toss of a coin.

infrequently, possibly because it is not widely understood—or, alternatively, the *a priori* selection of subsets of subjects thought to share certain unique clusterings of traits, there is not a factor analytic method available to take into account analytically possible lack of homogeneity of the structure of characteristics in different people. Because a factor analysis of correlations between people cannot take into account the influence of moderator variables or other curvilinear effects, and *a priori* clustering is cumbersome, imprecise, and requires more information than is usually available, a method for categorizing subjects homogeneous with regard to their constellation of traits is urgently needed. An approach to this problem recently outlined by Tucker [34] promises its eventual solution. Application of a line of reasoning similar to that described above to individual differences in multidimensional scaling [35] has been found to be quite useful [26].

RANDOM RESPONDING AND DEVIATION

We would like to offer one additional and tentative hypothesis about the nature of deviant responses. There are obviously any number of determinants of a score which constitutes the total number of deviant or atypical responses that an individual makes on a given task or during a particular period of time. One of these may be sheer carelessness in responding. Parenthetically, let it be said that we are not denying that carelessness may in and of itself be an interesting response. Nevertheless, it may be pointed out that, if a subject responds randomly or carelessly to a set of items, it is inevitable that he will make an unusual number of deviant responses just as a "pair of dice" will show markedly deviant personality "scores" [13]. This, of course, provided the entire rationale for the F scale of the MMPI. Therefore, to the extent that carelessness contributes to higher deviation scores, or, to put it another way, to the extent that higher deviation

scores are correlated with careless responding, we would expect higher than average deviation scores to be less reliable than lower scores. From a population of 183 college students and nursing students [32], the 45 who scored highest on the Deviation key and the 45 who scored lowest were selected as representing the extremes of the distribution and separate odd-even reliabilities were computed for both groups. While we are somewhat embarrassed to offer as evidence a corrected reliability of $-.10$ for the high group and $.30$ for the low group, it is clear that the two reliabilities differ in a way which is consistent with the hypothesis that deviant responses may be careless responses. One additional bit of data bearing on the carelessness hypothesis stems from the analysis of the Deviation scores of subjects who are correlation "outliers," i.e., whose performance is predicted poorly by regression scores. The possible relationship between deviation as carelessness and as a unique structuring of traits is evident. To the extent that performances are careless and unreliable, correlations between any two sets of variables will be attenuated. Perhaps then, deviant response tendencies may be, in part, a reflection of the rate of random responding for a subject.

SUMMARY AND CONCLUSIONS

A critical analysis and review of issues raised by studies bearing on Berg's deviation hypothesis was undertaken with the aim of explicating certain issues relevant to the hypothesis: *viz.*, assumptions implicit in the deviation hypothesis, the problem of generality, response styles and deviation, definitions of deviation, and problems of measurement and interpretation.

Very early in our attempts to understand the deviation hypothesis, we concluded that without further clarification and definition of concepts such as "deviant response patterns" and "general" in the statement "Deviant response patterns are general . . ." [5], and of the corresponding measurement operations of the concepts, the hypothesis was altogether too broad and lacking in clarity to permit differential prediction. Further elaborations of the hypothesis, some of which are not attributable to Berg, reveal complexities, inconsistencies, and several problems worthy of systematic study.

Our conclusions are stated in the following ten propositions.

1. Deviant response patterns are less than completely general in the sense that they are all associated in the general population.

2. The expectation that criterion groups will differ in some respects from the general population on certain behavioral measures reflects a general affirmation of faith in the psychology of individual differences, and it should not be considered as an hypothesis confirmable in the usual specific sense [11, 19].

3. If it is admitted that deviant response tendencies are less than completely general, then it is appropriate to inquire into the properties of items or measures differentiating deviant subgroups. The content of items or scales may be one important relevant property determining differential responses.

4. Response patterns of criterion groups which deviate from normals may appear similar due to imposed restriction of available alternatives on structured questionnaires, rather than necessarily being due to underlying identities in psychological processes. Such data are not necessarily interpretable as evidence supporting the generality of deviant response patterns.

5. Where interest is focused upon unique psychopathological processes, contrasting responses of particular deviant groups will yield more useful information concerning differential processes than will contrasting deviant groups from normal subjects, particularly in cases in which response alternatives are limited and massive response styles effects predominate.

6. Deviant response tendencies may often be better understood in terms of particular relatively uncorrelated response styles, such as tendencies to acquiesce and respond desirably, operating in a given assessment device, than in terms of "general deviation."

7. There are a variety of separate measurement definitions of deviant response tendencies having very different implications for theory and assessment. Deviant response tendencies may be considered in terms of: (a) absolute, or (b) relative deviation; (c) statistical infrequency; (d) extremeness of traits; (e) unique structuring of traits; and (f) randomness of responding. Deviation measures based upon each of these definitions should receive systematic study.

8. Serious problems in the measurement of deviant response tendencies arise out of the application of global indices of deviation. Measures should be constructed and studied yielding information regarding: (a) the direction of deviation; (b) the atypically nondeviant performance; (c) multidimensionality due to consistent individual differences in deviant responses to different classes and types of content, item formats, item wording and style, and other response determinants [16, 22].

9. Gain in precision of measurement of deviant response tendencies will result from an analysis of optimal item splits [12, 17, 20, 29], taking into account and balancing the gain from using extreme "right-wrong" proportions in identifying deviant responses with the loss of information about the total group inherent in such extreme item splits.

10. Berg and his colleagues have per-

formed a valuable service in emphasizing the importance of studying deviant response patterns. However, the study of such patterns should be increased in scope and complexity to take into account the many ways in which different people may be deviant, the role of different classes of content in eliciting deviant responses, and particular types of noncritical deviations unique to a given psychopathological group, among other things. New analytical methods for treating data are required to do justice to the complexity of deviant response patterns.

REFERENCES

1. ADAMS, H. E., & BERG, I. A. Schizophrenia and deviant response sets produced by auditory and visual test content. *J. Psychol.*, 1961, 51, 393–398.
2. BARNES, E. H. The relationship of biased test responses to psychopathology. *J. abnorm. soc. Psychol.*, 1955, 51, 286–290.
3. BARNES, E. H. Factors, response bias, and the MMPI. *J. consult. Psychol.*, 1956, 20, 419–421.
4. BARNES, E. H. Response bias and the MMPI. *J. consult. Psychol.*, 1956, 20, 371–374.
5. BERG, I. A. Response bias and personality: The deviation hypothesis. *J. Psychol.*, 1955, 40, 60–71.
6. BERG, I. A. Deviant responses and deviant people: The formulation of the deviation hypothesis. *J. counsel. Psychol.*, 1957, 4, 154–161.
7. BERG, I. A. The unimportance of test item content. In B. M. Bass and I. A. Berg (Eds.), *Objective approaches to personality assessment.* New York: D. Van Nostrand, 1959.
8. BERG, I. A. Measuring deviant behavior by means of deviant response sets. In I. A. Berg and B. M. Bass (Eds.), *Conformity and deviation.* New York: Harper, 1961.
9. BERG, I. A., & COLLIER, J. S. Personality and group differences in extreme response sets. *Educ. psychol. Measmt*, 1953, 13, 164–169.
10. BERG, I. A., HUNT, W. A., & BARNES, E. H. *The perceptual reaction test.* Evanston, Ill., 1949.
11. BOLLES, R., & MESSICK, S. Statistical utility in experimental inference. *Psychol. Rep.*, 1958, 4, 223–227.
12. BROGDEN, H. E. Variation in test validity with variation in the distribution of item difficulties, number of items, and degree of their correlations. *Psychometrika*, 1946, 11, 197–214.
13. BURNHAM, P. S., & CRAWFORD, A. B. The vocational interests and personality test scores of a pair of dice. *J. educ. Psychol.*, 1935, 26, 508–512.
14. CRONBACH, L. J. Response set and test validity. *Educ. psychol. Measmt*, 1946, 6, 475–494.
15. CRONBACH, L. J. Further evidence on response sets and test designs. *Educ. psychol. Measmt*, 1950, 10, 3–31.
16. CRONBACH, L. J. Proposals leading to analytic treatment of social perception scores. In R. Tagiuri and L. Petrullo (Eds.), *Person perception and interpersonal behavior.* Stanford: Stanford Univer. Press, 1958. Pp. 352–379.
17. CRONBACH, L. J., & WARRINGTON, W. G. Efficiency of multiple-choice tests as a function of spread of item difficulties. *Psychometrika*, 1952, 17, 127–147.
18. EDWARDS, A. L. *The social desirability variable in personality assessment and research.* New York: Dryden Press, 1957.
19. FEIGL, H. Confirmability and confirmation. *Review of international philosophy*, 1951, 5, 268–279. Reprinted in P. P. Wiener, *Readings in the philosophy of science.* New York: C. Scribner's Sons, 1953. Pp. 522–530.
20. GULLIKSEN, H. The relation of item difficulty and interitem correlation to test variance and reliability. *Psychometrika*, 1945, 10, 79–91.
21. HESTERLY, S. O., & BERG, I. A. Deviant responses as indicators of immaturity and schizophrenia. *J. consult. Psychol.*, 1958, 22, 389–393.
22. JACKSON, D. N. The measurement of perceived personality trait relationships. In N. Washburn (Ed.), *Values, decisions, and groups.* New York: Pergamon Press, 1962.

23. JACKSON, D. N., & MESSICK, S. Content and style in personality assessment. *Psychol. Bull.*, 1958, 55, 243–252.

24. JACKSON, D. N., & MESSICK, S. Acquiescence and desirability as response determinants on the MMPI. *Educ. psychol. Measmt*, 1961, 21, 771–792.

25. JACKSON, D. N., & MESSICK, S. Response styles and the assessment of psychopathology. In S. Messick and J. Ross (Eds.), *Measurement in personality and cognition.* New York: Wiley, 1962.

26. JACKSON, D. N., & MESSICK, S. Individual differences in social perception. *Brit. J. soc. clin. Psychol.*, 1962.

27. JACKSON, D. N., & MESSICK, S. Response styles on the MMPI: Comparison of clinical and normal samples. *J. abnorm. soc. Psychol.*, 1962, 65, 285–299.

28. LOEVINGER, JANE. The technic of homogeneous tests compared with some aspects of "scale analysis" and factor analysis. *Psychol. Bull.*, 1948, 45, 507–529.

29. LORD, F. M. The relation of the reliability of multiple-choice tests to the distribution of item difficulties. *Psychometrika*, 1952, 17, 181–194.

30. ROITZSCH, J. C., & BERG, I. A. Deviant responses as indicators of immaturity and neuroticism. *J. clin. Psychol.*, 1959, 15, 417–419.

31. SECHREST, L., & JACKSON, D. N. Social intelligence and accuracy of interpersonal predictions. *J. Pers.*, 1961, 29, 167–182.

32. SECHREST, L., & JACKSON, D. N. The generality of deviant response tendencies. *J. consult. Psychol.*, 1962, 26, 395–401.

33. STRONG, E. K., JR. *Manual for Vocational Interest Blank for Men.* Stanford: Stanford Univer. Press, 1935.

34. TUCKER, L. R. Implications of factor analysis of three-way matrices for measurement of change. In C. W. Harris (Ed.), *Problems in measuring change.* Madison: Univer. Wisconsin Press, 1963, pp. 122–138. *Psychometrika*, 1963, 28, 333–368.

35. TUCKER, L. R., & MESSICK, S. Individual differences in multidimensional scaling. Research Memorandum 60-15. Princeton, N.J.: Educational Testing Service, 1960.

36. WIGGINS, J. S. Definitions of social desirability and acquiescence in personality inventories. In S. Messick and J. Ross (Eds.), *Measurement in personality and cognition.* New York: Wiley, 1962.

37. WIGGINS, J. S. Strategic, method, and stylistic variance in the MMPI. *Psychol. Bull.*, 1962, 59, 224–242.

Chapter *19* ~

The Factor Problem

LOUIS L. THURSTONE

ON THE NATURE OF SCIENCE

Factor analysis is concerned with methods of discovering and identifying significant categories in psychology and in other sciences. It is therefore of interest to consider some phases of science in general that bear on the problem of finding a methodology for a psychological science.

It is the faith of all science that an unlimited number of phenomena can be comprehended in terms of a limited number of concepts or ideal constructs. Without this faith no science could ever have any motivation. To deny this faith is to affirm the primary chaos of nature and the consequent futility of scientific effort. The constructs in terms of which natural phenomena are comprehended are man-made inventions. To discover a scientific law is merely to discover that a man-made scheme serves to unify, and thereby to simplify, comprehension of a certain class of natural phenomena. A scientific law is not to be thought of as having an independent existence which some scientist is fortunate to stumble upon. A scientific law is not a part of nature. It is only a way of comprehending nature.

A simple example is the concept "force." No one has ever seen a force. Only the movement of objects is seen. The faith of science is that some schematic representation is possible by which complexities of movement can be conceptually unified into an order. The error of a literal interpretation of a force vector as the pictorial representation of a corresponding physical entity is seen in the resolution of forces. If a particle moves with uniform acceleration in a certain direction, it is, of course, possible to describe the movement by one force, or by two, or by three or more coplanar forces. This resolution of a movement into several simultaneous and superimposed movements is frequently done in order that a convenient and habitual reference frame may be retained. While the ideal constructs of science do not imply physical reality, they do not deny the possibility of some degree

This article is reprinted from *Multiple-factor Analysis*, 1947, with the permission of Mrs. Thelma G. Thurstone and the University of Chicago Press.

279

of correspondence with physical reality. But this is a philosophical problem that is quite outside the domain of science.

Consider, as another example, Coulomb's inverse-square law of electrical attraction. A postulated force is expressed as a function of the linear separation of the charges. Now, if the charges were to be personified, they would probably be much surprised that their actions were being described in terms of their linear separations. No one assumes that there is a string between the charges, but Coulomb's law implies that the length of such a string is to be used in our simplified scheme of comprehending the postulated charges. It is more likely that the whole space surrounding the charges is involved in the phenomena of attraction and that Coulomb's law is a fortunate short cut for representing approximately a part of the phenomena that are called "charges" and "attractions." It is not unlikely that all these entities will eventually vanish as such and become only aspects of an order more involved than Coulomb's law implies but not so chaotic as to individualize completely every moment of nature.

A science of psychology will deal with the activities of people as its central theme. A large class of human activity is that which differentiates individuals as regards their overt accomplishments. Just as it is convenient to postulate physical forces in describing the movements of physical objects, so it is also natural to postulate abilities and their absence as primary causes of the successful completion of a task by some individuals and of the failure of other individuals in the same task.

The criterion by which a new ideal construct in science is accepted or rejected is the degree to which it facilitates the comprehension of a class of phenomena which can be thought of as examples of a single construct rather than as individualized events. It is in this sense that the chief object of science is to minimize mental effort. But in order that this reduction may be accepted as science, it must be demon-strated, either explicitly or by implication, that the number of degrees of freedom of the construct is smaller than the number of degrees of freedom of the phenomena that the reduction is expected to subsume. Consider, as an example, any situation in which a rational equation is proposed as the law governing the relation between two variables. If three observations have been made and if the proposed equation has three independent parameters, then the number of degrees of freedom of the phenomena is the same as the number of degrees of freedom of the equation, and hence the formulation remains undemonstrated. If, on the other hand, one hundred experimentally independent observations are subsumed by a rational equation with three parameters, then the demonstration can be of scientific interest. The convincingness of a hypothesis can be gauged inversely by the ratio of its number of degrees of freedom to that of the phenomena which it has demonstrably covered. It is in the nature of science that no scientific law can ever be proved to be right. It can only be shown to be plausible. The laws of science are not immutable. They are only human efforts toward parsimony in the comprehension of nature.

If abilities are to be postulated as primary causes of individual differences in overt accomplishment, then the widely different achievements of individuals must be demonstrable functions of a limited number of reference abilities. This implies that individuals will be described in terms of a limited number of faculties. This is contrary to the erroneous contention that, since every person is different from every other person in the world, people must not be classified and labeled.

Each generalization in the scientific description of nature results in a loss in the extent to which the ideal constructs of science match the individual events of experience. This is illustrated by simple experiments with a pendulum, in which the mass, the period, and the locus of the center of gravity with reference to a fulcrum are involved in the ideal construct that leads to experimental verification. But the construct matches only incompletely the corresponding experimental situation. The construct says nothing about the rusty setscrew and other extraneous detail. From the viewpoint of immediate experience, scientific description is necessarily incomplete. The scientist always finds his constructs immersed in the irrelevancies of experience. It seems appropriate to acknowledge this characteristic of science, in view of the fact that it is a rather common notion that the scientific description of a person is not valid unless the so-called "total situation" has been engulfed. A study of people does not become scientific because it attempts to be complete, nor is it invalid because it is restricted. The scientific description of a person will be as incomplete from the viewpoint of common sense as the description of other objects in scientific context.

The development of scientific analysis in a new class of phenomena usually meets with resistance. The faith of science that nature can be comprehended in terms of an order acknowledges no limitation whatever as regards classes of phenomena. But scientists are not free from prejudice against the extension of their faith to realms not habitually comprehended in the scientific order. Examples of this resistance are numerous. It is not infrequent for a competent physical scientist to declare his belief that the phenomena of living objects are, at least in some subtle way, beyond the reach of rigorous scientific order.

One of the forms in which this resistance appears is the assertion that, since a scientific construct does not cover all enumerable details of a class of phenomena, it is therefore to be judged inapplicable. Since the analysis of cell growth by mathematical and physical principles does not cover everything that is known about cells, the biologist judges the analysis to be inapplicable. Since no mathematical analysis that can be conceived would cover all the

subtle mysteries of personality, this realm is frequently judged to be outside the domain of rigorous science. But physical scientists accept rigorous scientific analyses about physical events that leave fully as much beyond the scientific constructs. Every explosion in the world has been different from every other explosion, and no physicist can write equations to cover all the detail of any explosive event. It is certain that no two thunderstorms have been exactly alike, and yet the constructs of physics are applied in comprehending thunder and lightning, without any demand that the detail of the landscape be covered by the same scientific constructs.

The attitudes of people on a controversial social issue have been appraised by allocating each person to a point on a linear continuum as regards his favorable or his unfavorable affect toward the psychological object. Some social scientists have objected because two individuals may have the same attitude score toward, say, pacifism, and yet be totally different in their backgrounds and in the causes of their similar social views. If such critics were consistent, they would object also to the statement that two men have identical incomes, for one of them earns while the other one steals. They should also object to the statement that two men are of the same height. The comparison should be held invalid because one of the men is fat and the other is thin. This is again the resistance against invading with the generalizing and simplifying constructs of science a realm which is habitually comprehended only in terms of innumerable and individualized detail. Every scientific construct limits itself to specified variables without any pretense of covering those aspects of a class of phenomena about which it has said nothing. As regards this characteristic of science, there is no difference between the scientific study of physical events and the scientific study of biological and psychological events. What is not generally understood, even by many scientists, is that no scientific law is ever intended to represent any event pictorially. The law is only an abstraction from the experimental situation. No experiment is ever completely repeated.

There is an unlimited number of ways in which nature can be comprehended in terms of fundamental scientific concepts. One of the simplest ways in which a class of phenomena can be comprehended in terms of a limited number of concepts is probably that in which a linear attribute of an event is expressed as a linear function of primary causes. Even when the relations are preferably non-linear and mathematically involved, it is frequently possible to use the simple linear forms as first approximations. A well-known example of this type of relation is that in which the chroma of a spectral color is expressed as a linear function of two arbitrarily chosen primaries. If two spectral colors are chosen arbitrarily for use as primaries, it is possible to express any intermediate color as a linear function of the two arbitrarily chosen primaries. The coefficients of the two terms of this linear function represent the angular sizes of the two sectors into which a color rotator is divided. When the rotator is spun, the intermediate color is seen. But here, as elsewhere in science, although the chroma of the resulting color is expressed in terms of the linear function of the arbitrary primaries, it does not follow that the saturation and the gray-values are expressed by the same law. There is still debate about which colors are to be considered primary. This question can be settled only by discovering that a certain set of primaries gives the most parsimonious comprehension of some phase of color vision. A parallel in the delineation of human traits is their description, in first approximation, as linear functions of a limited number of reference traits. The final choice of a set of primary reference traits or faculties must be made in terms of the discovery that a particular set of reference traits renders most parsimonious our comprehension of a great variety of human traits.

THE PURPOSE OF FACTOR ANALYSIS

A factor problem starts with the hope or conviction that a certain domain is not so chaotic as it looks. The range of phenomena that is represented in any factor analysis will be referred to as its *domain*. If a particular investigation is limited to measurements in visual perception, it is likely that auditory effects will be outside of its domain. The factorial methods were developed primarily for the purpose of identifying the principal dimensions or categories of mentality; but the methods are general, so that they have been found useful for other psychological problems and in other sciences as well. Factor analysis can be regarded as a general scientific method, although originally developed for the solution of psychological problems. Some of the principles can be illustrated to best advantage in terms of simple mechanical or geometrical examples; and these will be used occasionally, especially when it is desired to illustrate a logical principle without involving the distractions of controversial or nebulous subject matter.

The factorial methods were developed for the study of individual differences among people, but the individual differences may be regarded as an avenue of approach to the study of the processes which underlie these differences. If a process is invariant in all its characteristics in an experimental population of individuals, then there exist no individual differences as regards such a process, and it cannot be investigated by factorial means.

Thus, if we select an experimental population of individuals who are all equally good or equally bad in some form of visual perception, then we cannot expect to identify or differentiate such processes by factorial methods. It is only to the extent that the individuals of an experimental population exhibit individual differences in a process and its effects that these effects can become accessible to investigation by factorial methods.

When a particular domain is to be investigated by means of individual differences, one can proceed in one of two ways. One can invent a hypothesis regarding the processes that underlie the individual differences, and one can then set up a factorial experiment, or a more direct laboratory experiment, to test the hypothesis. If no promising hypothesis is available, one can represent the domain as adequately as possible in terms of a set of measurements or numerical indices and proceed with a factorial experiment. The analysis might reveal an underlying order which would be of great assistance in formulating the scientific concepts covering the particular domain. In the first case we start with a hypothesis that determines the nature of the measurements that enter into the factorial analysis. In the second case we start with no hypothesis, but we proceed, instead, with a set of measurements or indices that cover the domain, hoping to discover in the factorial analysis the nature of the underlying order. It is this latter application of the factorial methods that is sometimes referred to as an attempt to lift ourselves by our own boot straps, because the underlying order in a domain can be discovered without first postulating it in the form of a hypothesis. This is probably the characteristic of factor analysis that gives it some interest as a general scientific method.

Factor analysis is not restricted by assumptions regarding the nature of the factors, whether they be physiological or social, elemental or complex, correlated or uncorrelated. For example, some of the factors may turn out to be defined by endocrinological effects. Others may be defined in biochemical or biophysical parameters of the body fluids or of the central nervous system. Other factors may be defined by neurological or vascular relations in some anatomical locus; still other factors may involve parameters in the dynamics of the autonomic nervous system; still others may be defined in terms of experience and schooling. Factor analysis assumes that a variety of phenomena within a domain are related and that they are determined, at least in part, by a relatively small number of functional unities or factors. The factors may be called by different names, such as "causes," "faculties," "parameters," "functional unities," "abilities," or "independent measurements." The name for a factor depends on the context, on one's philosophical preferences and manner of speech, and on how much one already knows about the domain to be investigated. The factors in psychological investigations are not ordinarily to be thought of as elemental things which are present or absent, like heads or tails in the tossing of coins.

The exploratory nature of factor analysis is often not understood. Factor analysis has its principal usefulness at the border line of science. It is naturally superseded by rational formulations in terms of the science involved. Factor analysis is useful, especially in those domains where basic and fruitful concepts are essentially lacking and where crucial experiments have been difficult to conceive. The new methods have a humble role. They enable us to make only the crudest first map of a new domain. But if we have scientific intuition and sufficient ingenuity, the rough factorial map of a new domain will enable us to proceed beyond the exploratory factorial stage to the more direct forms of psychological experimentation in the laboratory.

In a domain where fundamental and fruitful concepts are already well formulated and tested, it would be absurd to use the factorial methods except for didactic purposes to illustrate factorial logic. In such situations there are available more direct methods of investigating rival hypotheses. In the relatively young sciences and in the new domains of the older sciences, the factorial experiments will be useful. It seems quite likely that the new methods will be applied with profit in the field of meteorology, but it is not likely that they will ever be used in classical mechanics.

In factorial investigations of mentality

we proceed on the assumption that mind is structured somehow, that mind is not a patternless mosaic of an infinite number of elements without functional groupings. The extreme, opposite view would be to hold that mind has no structure at all. *In the interpretation of mind we assume that mental phenomena can be identified in terms of distinguishable functions, which do not all participate equally in everything that mind does.* It is these functional unities that we are looking for with the aid of factorial methods. It is our scientific faith that such distinguishable mental functions can be identified and that they will be verified in different types of experimental study. No assumption is made about the nature of these functions, whether they are native or acquired or whether they have a cortical locus.

In order to illustrate the method, let us consider a set of gymnastic stunts that might be given to a group of several hundred boys of comparable age. A factor analysis starts with a table of intercorrelations of the variables. If there were twenty different stunts, we should have a square 20×20 table showing the correlation of every performance with every other performance. Our question now is to determine whether these relations can be comprehended in terms of some underlying order, which is simpler than the whole table of several hundred experimentally determined coefficients of correlation. Let us suppose that some of the stunts require principally strength of the right arm, that others require principally a good sense of balance, that still others require speed of bodily movement. Several tests that require good sense of balance might not require arm strength, while those which require a strong arm might require very little bodily balance. We might then find that the correlations can be comprehended in terms of a small number of functional unities, such as sense of balance, arm strength, or speed of bodily movement. Each of the gymnastic tests might require one or several of these

functional unities; but it is not likely that every test will require every one of the functional unities that are represented by the whole set of gymnastic tests. A factorial analysis would reveal these functional unities, and we would say that each of them is a primary factor in the battery of tests. Now, if we should take any one of these functional unities, such as sense of balance, and represent it in a new set of twenty tests of great variety which all required bodily balance, we might find that there are really several primary factors involved in this domain. For example, there might conceivably be a separate balancing factor for each of the semicircular canals, or there might be some other breakdown of the balancing factors that would be revealed in an extensive study of balancing tests.[1] A new set of more refined primary factors might be found within the domain of bodily balance. This process might continue with the factorial investigation of more and more restricted domains, as long as the functional unities continued to be difficult to conceive in direct experimentation. Eventually, the factorial methods, which are essentially exploratory, would yield to the reformulation of a problem in terms of the fundamental rational constructs of the science involved. It is not unlikely that factorial analyses will point the way in the work of inventing significant and fundamental scientific concepts.

Let us consider, next, an example in the sensory and perceptual fields. Let us start with a set of twenty perceptual tests involving several of the modalities. Some of the tests might require visual acuity; others would require keen discrimination of rhythm; still others might require speed of perception. Each of the perceptual tests might involve one or more of these functional unities; but few would require all these functions. Some of the tests, for example, might not depend on visual acuity.

---

[1] Several such factors might appear in the place of specific variance and uninterpreted common-factor variance in the earlier studies.

In this simple case we should not be surprised to find factorially the primary functional unities that are obvious at the start.

If we turn to the more central functions that are involved in the intellectual and temperamental differences among people, it seems reasonable to suppose that here also we may expect to find functional unities that will some day be as obvious as the sensory and perceptual unities are obvious to us now.

Our work in the factorial study of the human mind rests on the assumption that mind represents a dynamical system which can eventually be understood in terms of a finite number of parameters. We have assumed, further, that all these parameters, or groups of parameters, are not involved in the individual differences of every kind of mental task. Just as we take it for granted that the individual differences in visual acuity are not involved in pitch discrimination, so we assume that in intellectual tasks some mental or cortical functions are not involved in every task. This is the principle of "simple structure" or "simple configuration" in the underlying order for any given set of attributes.

Observation and educational experience lend plausibility to the conception that the mental abilities are determined by a great multiplicity of causes or determiners and that these determiners are more or less structured or linked in groups. This multiplicity of determiners can be thought of as a field of elements in which all are not equally closely linked. Some elements may be quite independent in their actions, while others may be rather closely associated. The factors are probably functional groupings, and it would be a distortion to assume that they must be elemental. We know precious little about the determiners of human talent and temperament, and we should not impose upon our thinking an unnecessarily rigid causal frame.

If we grant that men are not all equal in intellectual endowment and in temperament and if we have the faith that this domain can be investigated as science, then we must make the plausible and inevitable assumption that individual differences among men can be conceived in terms of a finite number of traits, parameters, or factors. Some of the factors may be found to be anatomically determined; others will be physiological; while others will be defined, at first, in experiential, educational, and social terms. As scientists, we must believe that a set of categories can be found for the understanding of mentality, which have, by their simplicity, a prior claim on our conceptual formulations.

FACTOR ANALYSIS AND EMPIRICAL PREDICTION

Factor analysis involves a number of well-known statistical procedures, and it is only natural for the student to begin his study of factor theory with a statistical point of view. In some respects this point of view is legitimate and useful, but there are some fundamental differences between the objectives of factor analysis and the customary objectives in statistical work that might as well be made explicit at the start. Some of the controversial questions in factor theory have their source in misunderstandings about the objectives for which factor theory was developed.

Many statistical problems take a form in which a certain number of indices are available for each member of a statistical population, and it is desired to predict some new index in terms of the known or given indices for each member of the population. A familiar example in psychological work is the prediction of student scholarship in terms of indices that are available at the time of college entrance. Prediction problems of this type are resolved by writing a regression equation, in which the dependent variable which is to be predicted is expressed as a linear function of the independent variables. The weight given to each independent variable is called its "regression coefficient," and the weights are so determined as to minimize the sum of the squares of the residual errors. The multiple correlation coefficient is the correlation between the predicted values of the dependent variable and the actually observed values. When the residual errors are small, the multiple correlation is high. Factor analysis differs from these statistical problems in that there is no distinction between independent and dependent variables. In factor analysis one does not select some one variable which is to be predicted or determined by the other variables. All the variables in factor analysis are treated alike in this sense. Whenever the investigator pivots his attention on one of the given variables which is central in importance and which is to be predicted by a set of independent variables, he is not talking about a factor problem. He is then talking about a customary statistical problem, involving a regression equation and multiple correlation. If he looks upon the whole set of variables as representing a domain that is to be explored and if his object is to discover whether there is some underlying order among these variables, then he is talking about a factor problem. Of course, it is possible to treat the same set of data successively by the two points of view. In the first case we are concerned about the prediction of one of the variables from the others, while in the second case we try to discover some underlying order in the whole system of traits.

It might be noted, in passing, that the distinction between independent and dependent variables is not intrinsic in the phenomena themselves. The differentiation between independent and dependent variables reflects only the attitude or purpose of the investigator. What is an independent variable for one investigator can be a dependent one for another investigator working with the same data. Sometimes an author reveals his bias unwittingly in the way he plots diagrams. What he plots as a base line is likely to be his independent variable. What he plots as ordinates is likely to be his dependent variable. In this way we may show that a depression is caused by unemployment or that unemployment is caused by a depression.

In the factor problem as well as in the statistical prediction problem, one is concerned about residuals and how to minimize them. This is practically universal in problems that involve observational data. In the statistical prediction problem, one's attention is centered on the one variable which is to be predicted and on how to minimize the residual errors in that prediction. In the factor problem, one is concerned about how to account for the observed correlations among all the variables in terms of the smallest number of factors and with the smallest possible residual errors. Here we have the practical problem that, as we postulate more and more factors to account for the observed correlations, the residuals get smaller and smaller. Hence, every factor problem must deal with the practical question of determining when the addition of a new factor causes only a negligible reduction in the residuals. The mathematical theory of this problem has not yet been adequately solved, but there have been developed practical methods of dealing with it. There seems to be some question as to whether the nature of the problem is such that a rigorous solution exists; but that is for later discussion.

There are problems in which the distinction between multiple correlation and factor theory is not sharply drawn, and we shall describe one example here. If a set of twenty independent variables is to be used for the prediction of a certain criterion, one's first impulse might be to write a regression equation of twenty terms in which each of the twenty given variables is weighted so as to give the best possible prediction of the dependent variable. In many situations such a solution would give regression coefficients which are so grossly in error that their absurdity can be seen by inspection. This result happens if the supposedly independent variables are not linearly independent. If the intercorrelations of those twenty variables can be accounted for in terms of, say, six factors, then we should be justified in using only six terms in the regression equation. Any additional terms in that equation would be likely to give absurd results, since they would imply that we rely on more factors than are really present in the supposedly independent variables. The intercorrelations of the twenty variables might then be analyzed factorially in order to determine six groups, each of which would give an average or composite. These six composites could then be weighted in a regression equation of six terms for as many independent variables. Such a problem is, however, only a prediction problem, and the prediction might be accomplished as well by different groupings of the twenty given variables or indices. In the more fundamental factorial problem the object is to discover whether the variables can be made to exhibit some underlying order that may throw light on the processes that produce the individual differences shown in all the variables.

In statistical prediction, the independent variables are given, and the problem is to predict some one dependent variable. The weights that are given to the independent variables do not ordinarily have any direct physical interpretation, because they depend on the number of given variables, their dispersions, and their correlations among themselves and with the variable that is to be predicted. The weights or regression coefficients are ordinarily treated merely as numerical coefficients which happen to maximize the multiple correlation. Their use is justified, not because of the meaning that can be attributed to their numerical values, but rather to the mere fact that a prediction can be made with the minimum residual.

In factor analysis, all the given variables are treated as co-ordinate as regards independence or dependence. The object of a factor problem is to account for the tests, or their intercorrelations, in terms of a small number of derived variables, the smallest possible number that is consistent with acceptable residual errors. The weights that are given to these derived variables are given more direct physical interpretation than is usually the case with regression coefficients. The derived variables are of scientific interest only in so far as they represent processes or parameters that involve the fundamental concepts of the science involved. Whereas the statistical prediction problem demands merely that a good prediction shall be made, the factorial problem demands that there shall be a meaningful interpretation of the small number of derived variables in terms of which the whole set of given variables can be comprehended.

Since it is the derived variables, or factors, that are the objective of a factorial analysis, one might regard them as dependent variables. This interpretation would agree with the usual meaning of the terms "independent" and "dependent," if the factors had previously been isolated and if we had started out to determine which tests constitute the best appraisal of a given factor. Such a problem would be similar to the familiar problem in test construction when the object is to determine the relative validities of several tests for a given criterion. In the exploratory type of problem for which the factorial methods were developed, the object is to discover the underlying order in a system of variables and to identify their nature. In this use of the factorial methods there is no distinction between independent and dependent variables.

Chapter 20

The Logical Basis of Factor Analysis

HANS J. EYSENCK

Few methods of statistical analysis have encountered as much resistance among both statisticians and psychologists as has factor analysis. In addition to this critical attitude towards factor analysis as a whole, there is an internecine quarrel amongst practitioners which has split the whole field into schools, factions, and individual snipers. Is this turmoil due to any inherent flaws in the method, or is it due to some confusion about aims and techniques? It will be the burden of this paper to show that the latter possibility is the more likely cause, and to attempt the construction of a rational scheme into which all the existing methods of analysis can be fitted. The stress is throughout on the *logic* as opposed to the *mathematics* of factor analysis; disputes about the latter are much less fundamental and much more easily settled than discussions about the former.

In assigning a place to factor analysis in the general field of statistics, we may with advantage follow Kendall [12, p. 60], who

This article is reprinted from the *American Psychologist*, 1953, with the permission of the author and the American Psychological Association.

draws a distinction between analysis of *dependence* and analysis of *interdependence*.

In the latter we are interested in how a group of variates are related among themselves, no one being marked out by the conditions of the problem as of greater prior importance than the others, whereas in the analysis of dependence we are interested in how a certain specified group (the dependent variates) depend on the others. The distinction is perhaps seen at its simplest in the bivariate case: correlation between two variates is a matter of interdependence, and is a symmetrical relationship between them; the regression of one on the other is a matter of dependence and is not a symmetrical relationship—the regression of x on y is not the same as the regression of y on x.

The position of factor analysis in the group of techniques using analysis of interdependence is shown in the accompanying figure quoted from Kendall [12, p. 61].

I have said: "*The* position of factor analysis," but the use of this clause suggests erroneously that there is one technique, one method, and one aim underlying the quite variegated activities of factor analysts. In

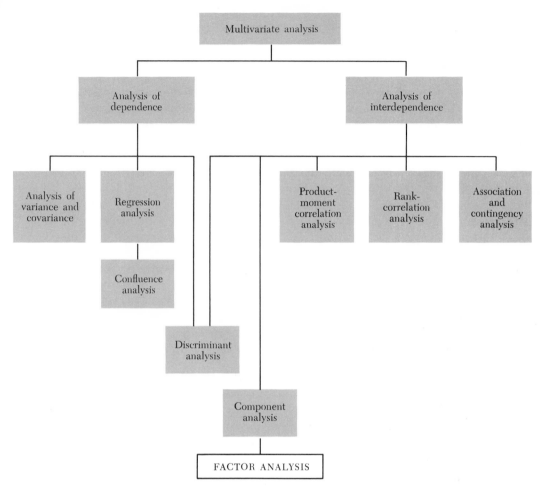

actual fact, there are three main aims which factor analysts try to achieve, three main views regarding the nature of factors which are closely related to these aims, and a large variety of methods of extraction and techniques of rotation. If we would understand these many different approaches, we must start with a statement of the questions which factor analysis is trying to answer. This is particularly important because of the tendency of many critics to reject the factorial answer to a certain question, not because the answer is inadequate, but because the question is misunderstood.

This point is well made, in quite another connection, by the philosopher Collingwood, who writes:

> You cannot tell whether a proposition is "true" or "false" until you know what question it was intended to answer . . . a proposition which in fact is "true" can always be thought "false" by any one who takes the trouble to excogitate a question to which it would have been the wrong answer, and convinces himself that this was the question it was meant to answer. And a proposition which in fact is significant can always be thought meaningless by any one who convinces himself that it was intended as an answer to a question which, if it had really been intended to answer it, it would not have answered at all, either rightly or wrongly [5, p. 30].

The three aims of factor analysis are the same three aims which give rise to other branches of statistics. As Kelley [13, p. 22] puts it: "The first function of statistics is to be purely descriptive, and its second function is to enable analysis in harmony with hypothesis, and its third function to suggest by the force of its virgin data analyses not earlier thought of." Kelley makes clearer his second and third points by adding: "We may say that there are two occasions for resort to statistical procedures, the one dominated by a desire to prove a hypothesis, and the other by a desire to invent one" [13, p. 12]. We may exemplify this threefold use of statistics by reference to an example. We find that in a given population there exists a correlation of .6 between height and weight; this fact serves to *describe* this population in just the same way that the mean height or the mean weight would be descriptive constants characterizing this population. We find that in a given population there exists a correlation of .2 between height and intelligence; this is also descriptive of this population, of course, but it may in addition suggest a hypothesis to us—the hypothesis, for instance, that favorable environmental circumstances are conducive to greater bodily height and to better performance on intelligence tests. This hypothesis may suggest to us that intelligence should also be correlated with weight (deduction 1), and that greater educational homogeneity within the group over which the correlation between height and intelligence is being run should reduce that correlation (deduction 2). We therefore calculate further correlations to prove or disprove our hypothesis—disprove in this case, because both deductions are falsified by the facts—thus using statistics to carry out "analysis in harmony with hypothesis."

Most psychologists and statisticians are aware, either explicitly or more frequently implicitly, of these three uses of statistics; it is in their application to factor analysis that problems of communication arise. I shall therefore discuss the use of factor analysis at these three levels in some detail, giving a formal definition of the term "factor" appropriate to each level.

Factors as descriptive statistics. Whatever else may be the function of a factor, it is always descriptive of a given sample or population. It is small wonder, therefore, that many definitions of factor analysis stress this point to the exclusion of any other. Thus Holzinger and Harman [11, p. 1] write: "Factor analysis is a branch of statistical theory concerned with the resolution of a set of descriptive variables in terms of a small number of categories or factors. . . . The chief aim is . . . to attain scientific parsimony or economy of description." Similarly Kelley [15, p. 120]: "[Factor analysis] represents a simple straightforward problem of description in several dimensions of a definite group functioning in definite manners." We may thus arrive at the following definition: *A factor is a condensed statement of (linear) relationships obtaining between a set of variables which can be used mathematically to stand for these variables.*

There is no implication in factors so defined of any psychological meaning, of any causal implications, or of any hypotheses, either suggested or proved. Few psychologists have found this view of factor analysis very attractive, and examples of its use are few and far between. Probably the best known is the work of Adams and Fowler [1] and of Kelley [14] on vocational interests. Correlating 35 interests on 800 men, they extracted five factors which accounted for all the significant covariation. These factors were not rotated or in any way interpreted, but were simply given meaningless names based on the initial letters of some of the interests having high loadings on each factor. Thus factor "NEVCOM" contrasts nature-loving, religious, and salesmanship with power, mechanical, spatial, orderliness, verbal, and musical interests. The fact that psychologically these factors make no sense would not be a correct criticism of the analysis which was intended to be purely descriptive; descriptively these nonsense factors are as good as any other set. The obvious convenience of having five factors instead of 35 variables in a regression equation, for instance, is undoubted, and may furnish justification for this very limited type of analysis. (We would of course lose whatever contributions specific factors might have made, possibly a very serious loss indeed.)

Factors suggesting a hypothesis. A factor, however it may have been obtained, may suggest a hypothesis to the investigator. In so far as it does that, the factor ceases to be merely descriptive and becomes part of theoretical psychology. We may give a formal definition of factor analysis from this point of view and say: A *factor is a condensed statement of (linear) relationships obtaining between a set of variables, suggestive of hitherto undiscovered causal relationships.*

As an example of this type of approach, contrasting with Kelley's analysis mentioned above, we may cite Thurstone's [23] analysis of the intercorrelations between 18 of Strong's interest scales. Thurstone emerged with four factors, labelled interest in science, interest in language, interest in people, and interest in business. Later work, summarized elsewhere [9], has on the whole confirmed Thurstone's analysis, and there is little doubt that the hypothesis suggested to him by the analysis has psychological meaning, and fits into psychological theory, while Kelley's analysis does neither. In other words, Thurstone's work adds to the merely descriptive function a psychological hypothesis which appears reasonable on a priori grounds, and which can be checked and submitted to experimental verification or disproof.

It may be argued that hypotheses can be generated in other ways than by factor analysis. That of course is undeniable, and there is no guarantee that factorial hypotheses will be superior to hypotheses arrived at by simple observation, by theoretical analysis, or even by *Schreibtischexperiment.* As an example of a hypothesis thus derived, we may quote Spranger's [20] purely theoretical analysis of interest patterns into the theoretical, economic, aesthetic, social, political, and religious. A factorial investigation of this hypothesis by Lurie [16]

gave rise to four factors: social, theoretical, religious, and what he calls Philistine, i.e., combining the economic and political interests, and opposing them to the aesthetic interests. This investigation thus gives results in line both with Thurstone's and with Spranger's hypotheses, but as Lurie's work is essentially an example of factor analysis supporting or disproving a hypothesis, no more will be said about it.

While it must be admitted that hypotheses may be formed in a variety of ways, the factorial method has one definite advantage. It provides *ab initio* data relevant to the formation of such hypotheses, and it rules out a large number of possible hypotheses which might otherwise have been entertained. Something similar, of course, is done when hypotheses are based on a simple observational study; indeed, it will be argued later on that much observational and clinical work is essentially similar to factor analysis in principle, though inferior to it because of its lower degree of rigor and accuracy. In a well-studied field, there are probably enough well-documented observations to make hypothesis-formation easy; in a relatively new field, the help of factor-analytic methods may be very important in accelerating the formation of reasonable, worthwhile hypotheses, and in discarding poor ones.

Factors supporting or disproving a hypothesis. It is obvious that factor analysis cannot be used as a formal part of the hypothetico-deductive process in relation to just any type of hypothesis. The great majority of psychological hypotheses require some form of analysis of dependence, and thus rule out the factor-analytic approach. But there are a number of hypotheses, particularly those concerned with structure and organization, which require factor-analytic methods, and which are difficult at the moment to disprove or support by non-factorial methods. All type- and trait-hypotheses, for example, fall into this category, as I have tried to show elsewhere [6, 9], and even Freudian theories have shown themselves amenable to the factorial method of proof [10].

Our definition of a factor as supporting or disproving a hypothesis follows directly from these considerations. We may say that *a factor is a condensed statement of (linear) relations obtaining between a set of variables which is in agreement with prediction based on theoretical analysis.*

Such predictions may be of varying degrees of exactitude. We may predict merely that certain items or tests will be found to have positive projections on a factor, while other items or tests will have negative projections; this is the most elementary level of prediction. Much more refined prediction is possible in relatively well-studied fields. Thurstone would probably be able to specify with considerable precision the position of a newly constructed test in the cognitive multi-factor space, or to construct a new test to specification, i.e., to lie at a particular place in the multi-factor space. The writer has been able to write social-attitude items to specification within a defined two-factor space with negligible errors. Many other examples of relatively precise predictions could be given; the majority of cases, however, would undoubtedly be at a much lower level of precision.

Frequently psychologists fail to state the exact nature of their hypotheses, and discuss their findings as if they had selected their tests at random, without any kind of hypothesis in mind. Occasionally such blind empiricism does seem to lie at the back of factorial work; factor analysis is sometimes used as a last resort to try and rescue worthless data accumulated at random from the fate such data so richly deserve. It need hardly be said that such use of factor analysis is valueless, but the fact that it occurs should not be used as an argument against the method as such; similar faulty use may be the fate of all statistical methods. It is probably safe to say that in the great majority of cases items and tests are included in a factor analysis on the basis of fairly specific hypotheses which are seldom

verbalized in the write-up of the experiment because (*a*) lengthy discussions would be required, which most editors would refuse to print, and (*b*) results are already available to show which hypotheses have been verified, so that there seems little point in discussing those which have been disproved.

It will have been noticed that in passing from the purely descriptive use, there has been a definite change in the implication of the term *factor*. For Kelley, there is no causal reference implied in a factor; for Spearman, Thurstone, and those who follow their methodology there quite clearly is such a reference. This causal implication characterizes not only the interpretation of factors as suggestive of a hypothesis, but also the next level of factors as proving a hypothesis, and since from the psychological point of view this causal implication is precisely what lends interest and value to factor analysis, it may be opportune here to give a definition of a factor which brings out this element. We may therefore offer the following definition: *A factor is a hypothetical causal influence underlying and determining the observed relationships between a set of variables.*

This definition serves a useful function in drawing attention to the close link between the hypothesis-generating and the hypothesis-proving functions of factor analysis, as opposed to the purely descriptive. It will often be found that in one and the same investigation there will be factors which support a hypothesis and factors which generate one. Elsewhere [6] a factor analysis has been reported of a large matrix of neuroticism tests designed to test a hypothesis regarding this particular factor. The analysis did indeed confirm the hypothesis; it also gave rise, however, to another factor which suggested that pencil-and-paper, verbal-type tests are separated in a clear-cut fashion from nonverbal, objective-behavior tests. Such a verbal-nonverbal factor, well known in the cognitive field, suggests various hypotheses which require testing; thus we find in the same analysis confirmation of one hypothesis, and suggestions for further hypotheses. This mutual stimulation between proof and suggestion might indeed be regarded as a prominent feature of factor-analytic work, and may recommend the method to those used to this interplay among hypothetico-deductive lines in other sciences.

While this interplay of proof and suggestion is valuable and important, it has often led to interpretations highly vulnerable to criticism. As has been pointed out elsewhere [7], it has been one of the worst abuses of factor analysis that practitioners have often carried out an analysis *suggesting* a hypothesis, and have then gone on to argue that their analysis has *proved* this hypothesis. The distinction is fundamental, and much of the criticism often made of factor analysis is ultimately referable to this failure to be clear about the status of the factors isolated.

We have discussed so far the *aims* of factor analysis; we must now turn to the *nature* of the factors isolated. A factor may be regarded as a purely statistical concept, an "artifact" if you like, akin to an average, a variance, or an epsilon. This view of the nature of a factor clearly corresponds with the descriptive aim as outlined above. As such, the concept is clear and does not require further discussion.

Secondly, a factor may be regarded as a principle of classification. This is the view of Burt [3], who likens factors to lines of longitude and latitude. According to this view, factor analysis first removes whatever is common to all the tests or items correlated, and then proceeds by means of a series of bipolar factors to disclose the principal ways of classifying the material under discussion. This is done without rotation of axes, it being assumed apparently that the principles of classification would remain invariant under change of tests or items correlated. This assumption is almost certainly mistaken in the majority of cases, but does not seem to be an indispensable part of this view of the nature of factors.

The third way of looking at factors is to regard them "as if" they were causal agencies. This view is implied in the definition given of the term "factor" a little while ago; it is given clear expression by Thurstone [22, p. 54], who writes: "One of the simplest ways in which a class of phenomena can be comprehended in terms of a limited number of concepts is probably that in which a linear attribute of an event is expressed as a linear function of primary causes." Spearman's [19, p. 75] view is similar: ". . . if meaningful as opposed to statistical, a factor is taken to be one of the circumstances, facts, or influences which produce a result."

There are two main criticisms of this view. Some writers hold the view that even if such causes could be identified in mental life, factor analysis could still not be relied upon to identify and isolate them. Thus Kelley, continuing the quotation in which he defined factors as being purely descriptive, says: ". . . he who assumes to read more remote verities into the factorial outcome is certainly doomed to disappointment" [13, p. 22]. Burt [3, p. 231] objects to the use of causal terms on philosophical grounds; he admits, however, that in certain cases "the language of causation is not only convenient, it is almost unavoidable, if we are to remain comprehensible." His main objection appears to be not to the language of causation as such, but rather to the reification of factors.

It is at this point that we encounter the central problem in our quest for the logical basis of factor analysis. It is here, also, that most critics have claimed to find the most vulnerable spot in the armour of factor analysts. If a given factorial solution is "purely arbitrary," just one of an innumerable number of possible solutions, and if it carries no causal implications, then it appears to many critics to differ fundamentally from other types of mathematical solutions, and to give rise to concepts much more insecurely based than those in other sciences.

This type of criticism appears to be

based on a profound misunderstanding of the nature of scientific laws and concepts. As Thurstone [22, p. 51] points out:

> . . . the constructs in terms of which natural phenomena are comprehended are man-made inventions. To discover a scientific law is merely to discover that a man-made scheme serves to unify, and thereby to simplify, comprehension of a certain class of natural phenomena. A scientific law is not to be thought of as having an independent existence. . . . A scientific law is not a part of nature. It is only a way of comprehending nature.

In a sense, therefore, the concepts and laws to which factor analysis gives rise are "statistical artifacts"; they are so in the same way that all other scientific concepts and laws are "artifacts." Spearman's g (general intelligence) is a statistical artifact to precisely the same extent, and for the same reasons, that Newton's g (gravitational force) was a mathematical artifact. Neither has any actual existence, in the sense that a falling stone or an individual who is acting intelligently can be said to exist; both concepts are abstractions which serve to unify and simplify a complex class of phenomena, and both had to be discarded or amended when new facts showed them to be incapable of accounting for all the phenomena. It does not appear reasonable to criticize factor analysis for showing features which are characteristic of all science.

Nor is the alleged "subjectivity" of factor analysis absent in universally accepted forms of dimensional analysis in physics. The physicist Bridgman [2, p. 1] points out that "there is nothing absolute about dimensions—they may be anything consistent with a set of definitions which agree with experimental fact." And Scott-Blair [18] has given an example of alternative dimensional analyses of the phenomena of heat. We may, therefore, dismiss this criticism also as applying to all science equally, rather than just to factor analysis. All science, in a sense, is an "artifact" and "subjective"; the important point is that this artificiality and subjectivity are closely circumscribed by the need always to remain in accord with the facts science sets out to unify and simplify. Those who have had experience in trying to formulate a hypothesis, whether factorial or otherwise, which would account for a large number of different phenomena will not usually be worried about having to choose one of a very large number of such theories; they will be thankful indeed if even one theory can be found which is not decisively contradicted by several indisputable facts. Psychologists sometimes tend to overcome this difficulty by disregarding those facts not in accord with their particular theory; there is little in the history of science that would encourage such a policy of neglect.

Granted that the most usual objections to factor analysis and the "causal" status of factors are invalid and based on an imperfect understanding of scientific methodology as a whole, our argument cannot be based entirely on disproof of criticism; it would seem desirable to argue more directly from positive evidence. There are four such proofs. The first proof relates to conditions where the causal relations are relatively well understood, and where we can compare the results of factor analysis with independent knowledge of the conditions responsible for the results. An excellent proof of this nature is supplied by the outstanding work of Wenger [24] on the "autonomic imbalance" factor. Following Eppinger and Hess, whose theory of "sympatheticotonia" postulated a predominance in certain subjects of sympathetic innervation, Wenger gave a battery of tests involving measures of the effects of autonomic innervation to various groups of subjects, including children and normal and neurotic adults, and carried out a Thurstone-type factor analysis of the resulting intercorrelations. Simple structure revealed in each of several analyses a clearly marked factor of "autonomic imbalance," having high saturations in the predicted direction on the predicted variables. Here we have an intelligible "cause" underlying the observed correlations, and the coincidence of factor saturations with theoretically predicted pattern is surely too striking to be ascribed entirely to chance. It may be noted incidentally that until taken up by factor analysts the Eppinger-Hess theory lay dormant, except for theoretical discussion, for some thirty years, because no other statistical-experimental procedure lent itself to the investigation of this type of hypothesis.

The second type of proof relates to the simultaneous change of scores on all the tests defining a factor when the hypothetical physiological basis of that factor is experimentally altered. As an example we may quote the work of Petrie [17] on the after-effects of lobotomy in neurotic subjects. Basing her work on the hypothesis that patients after operation showed changes on the factors of neuroticism and extraversion-introversion along the lines of *decreasing* amount of neuroticism and *increasing* amount of extraversion, she administered before operation two sets of six tests defining these two factors respectively, and predicted the direction in which change would take place. In all cases tests carried out after operation verified the prediction; in other words, all the tests defining the factor of neuroticism showed changes in the direction of lessened neuroticism, and all the tests defining extraversion showed changes in the direction of increased extraversion. This dynamic proof for the functional unity and biological reality of the factors in question is particularly impressive because of the paucity of statistically significant changes on personality tests previously reported in the literature.

The third method of proof is based on the following argument. It is possible to calculate an approximate index of hereditary determination, such as Holzinger's h^2, for any test which has been applied to a sufficiently large sample of identical and fraternal twins. It is difficult to see how a factor, which is merely a linear combination of test scores, can have a higher h^2 than any of the constituent tests, unless this factor is based on some very definite, underlying biological reality or function which is itself inherited. There is at least one study [6] in which it has been shown that the factor of neuroticism has a higher h^2 (.810) than any of the constituent tests which are combined to give that factor score; the highest individual test h^2 was .701. It seems difficult to dismiss as "subjective" and as a "statistical artifact" a factor having such very definite and obvious relation to biological reality.

The last method of proof suggested here is more indirect than the others, but logically equally important. Factor analysis is often considered to be a complete innovation, something different from, and possibly even contrary to, the usual methods of scientific investigation. It is the burden of this paper to point out that quite on the contrary methods logically identical with factor analysis, though mathematically less exact and rigorous, have been used from the very dawn of science to deal with the type of problem involved in the study of "interdependence." In doing so, they have led on to hypotheses regarding "causes" and to analyses of "dependence" which have greatly clarified the field, and which would have been impossible without the preceding "factorial" investigations. As this point is crucial to my argument, I shall give two examples of what I have in mind.

Let us take first of all the concept of disease. If we take a particular disease, such as tuberculosis, we know now that it is caused by an identifiable "cause," namely the tubercle bacillus, acting on a human body which may vary from case to case in its resistant properties. This particular disease, however, was known and isolated long before the "cause," the bacillus, was discovered; indeed, unless the disease had already been known as a unitary entity it is difficult to see how its "cause" could have been discovered. How, then, was the disease identified? It was identified essentially in factorial terms, i.e., by the fact that certain physical symptoms—loss of weight, breathing difficulties, high temperature, coughing-up of blood, etc.—tended to go together (intercorrelate) in a certain manner as a "syndrome." No symptom by itself is decisive (none is factorially pure), but the syndrome (factor) suggests one underlying cause which gives rise to the various symptoms, and which may sometime be identified. In a similar way, we identify mental diseases in what is essentially a factorial manner, i.e., in terms of the observed intercorrelation of various symptoms; anyone reading Kraepelin or Bleuler will be able to follow this process in its clearest and most obvious manner. In the mental field we have not yet discovered the underlying cause of the various patterns we observe; until we do we have to rest content, as we had to in the case of physical medicine before the advent of Pasteur, with syndromes (factors). All that factor analysis does is to make explicit and rigorous what the clinician does in any case, often implicitly and without full understanding of his methodology. Both the clinician and the factor analyst may be mistaken, and group together what does not in fact (causally) belong together; medical history indicates a number of errors as well as a remarkable number of successes in this preliminary method of grouping together symptoms in terms of underlying "diseases." It seems reasonable to assume that greater rigor and awareness of the pitfalls involved may decrease the number of errors; there is no way of guaranteeing complete success. The point to stress is that this "factorial" stage is an indispensable preliminary to the "causal" stage; our factor or syndrome tells us what symptoms go together in such a way that we can with some hope of success go on to look for a single underlying cause.

My second example relates to the field of taxonomy in flora [21] and fauna [4]. Until the advent of Darwin and the theory of evolution, the only way of telling "what goes with what" in the plant and animal kingdoms was by means of morphology, i.e., by noting degrees of similarity of a large number of outwardly observable characteristics. Thus, specimens agreeing on a large percentage of such characteristics (correlating highly together) were considered to be closely related; specimens

agreeing on a small percentage of characteristics only (correlating together at a low level) were considered to be only remotely related. By means of an implicit and nonrigorous factor analysis of these similarities or correlations the whole elaborate system of 19th century systematics was built up. The theory of evolution made it possible to check the resulting taxonomic picture with its implied causal influences against the directly observable causal development shown by Darwinian research. The remarkable result was that in its main outline the picture required very little change; there were many details which had to be modified, but by and large morphology had been an extremely accurate guide to causal relations [4, 20]. So here also we find that subsequent causal "analysis of dependence" verifies in considerable detail the results of "analysis of interdependence" carried out along essentially factorial lines. And again, the advances made by Darwin would not have been possible without the spade work of the "systematists" and their implicit factorial approach.[1]

It may seem fanciful to regard these time-honored methods of analysis as similar in essence to modern factor analysis; yet it would be difficult to deny the essential identity between past and present as long as we consider the logical basis of the procedures involved. It is widely recognized

[1] It might be pointed out that factorial logic plays a part even in such apparently remote fields as in the definition of a metal. A metal is electropositive, forms metallic crystals, its halides generally form ionic aggregates and are nonvolatile, but give conducting solutions in water, and its oxides are usually basic. There are, however, exceptions to these rules. Thus $SnCl_4$ is a volatile liquid; ZnO and Al_2O_3 are amphoteric, and some higher oxides such as CrO_3 are acid. Graphite, arsenic, and tellurium, on the other hand, exhibit metallic properties, while counted among the nonmetals. The concept "metal," therefore, rests on the intercorrelation of the various indices enumerated; these correlations are far from perfect, and the only reason for using the term "metal" is the logical implication of a fundamental common feature which unites all metals in a group, and sets them off in comparison with the other elements. This may be an unusual way of looking at chemical concepts, but the logical similarity of derivation is too striking to be passed over.

that the correlation coefficient is merely the statistical expression of what Mill called the "method of concomitant variation," and Mill's fifth canon—"Whatever phenomenon varies in any manner, whenever another phenomenon varies in some particular manner, is either a cause or an effect of that phenomenon, or is connected with it through some fact of causation"—certainly preceded in time the statistical superstructure erected on this logical foundation. It is difficult, therefore, to see why a similar process of growth from logical implication and nonrigorous use to statistical elaboration and explicit formulation should not have taken place with respect to factor analysis.

We may conclude, then, that there is both direct and indirect evidence that factorial procedures may lead to genuine causal determinants. It would not be reasonable to say that such a happy outcome would inevitably attend the application of factor analysis; under certain circumstances it may be predicted with confidence that no causal hypotheses will be suggested or proved by factorial methods. In part the outcome of a factorial investigation is determined, of course, by such imponderable factors as the sagacity of the investigator, his skill in framing hypotheses and constructing tests, and his desire to use factor analysis as a hypothetico-deductive tool, rather than as a purely descriptive method. But in part there is no doubt that the actual method of analysis itself will determine the outcome.

At the purely descriptive level, there is little to choose between the methods of analysis advocated by Hotelling, Tryon, Thurstone, or Kelley; the slight advantages of "principal components" are offset by the greater ease of computation of "centroids," and so forth. It is when we come to the problem of rotation that the crucial step occurs. It is clear that we cannot expect a factor to be related in any direct manner to a hypothetical cause unless the factor is unique and invariant in its derivation. Unrotated factors of any kind are usually neither unique nor invariant. This problem is disregarded by writers like Kelley and Burt because the aim for which they use factor analysis is not that of isolating causal determinants. It would appear, however, that Burt at least is not justified in regarding unrotated factors as giving rise to stable "principles of classification" any more than they give rise to causal determinants; they may occasionally bear a superficial resemblance to such more stable factors but logically a Burtian solution is at the same level of pure *ad hoc*, elementary description as is Kelley's.

If we wish, then, to obtain factors which are not ruled out *ab initio* from fitting into a general descriptive-causal scheme because of lack of uniqueness and invariance, rotation becomes necessary. Here the only scheme which deserves serious consideration is Thurstone's suggestion of rotation into "simple structure," with its attendant concepts of "oblique factors" and "second-order factors." I have on occasion been somewhat critical of Thurstone's earlier work, and it is only right to say here that his recent amplification and development of the more rigid framework of "Vectors of the Mind," together with experimentation of my own, have led me to a reversal of this attitude, into almost complete agreement with Thurstone's latest position. Logically, his method of rotation and experimentation generally amount to this. If we can treat our test domain as if its communality were due to a small number of isolable causes, then our best way of isolating and measuring these causes is by purification, i.e., by selection of tests whose variance is due, not to all these causes at once, but only to one or at most two. This should give us clear-cut differentiation and separation of factors; at the same time, the fact that such selection is practicable provides an impressive proof for the usefulness of the original assumption. Logically this argument seems faultless; mathematically, the scheme has not been worked out to perfection, but there seems to be no difficulty in principle.

In certain practical situations, the full Thurstonian procedure may not be practicable for various reasons, and when we have available an external criterion which embodies a certain hypothesis which we are interested in testing, the method of "criterion analysis" which I have described elsewhere [8] may serve as a substitute. This method appears particularly apposite in personality research outside the cognitive field, for reasons which also have been given elsewhere.

We must now pull together what of necessity has been a somewhat rambling discussion of a large number of related points. This summary can best be put as a series of numbered propositions; these are not meant to be taken as definitive in any sense, but they may serve to give some orientation to the very discursive criticisms of factor analysis which appear from time to time in the literature, and which are almost wholly concerned with the logic, rather than with the mathematics, of factor analysis.

1. Factor analysis is a mathematical procedure which resolves a set of descriptive variables into a smaller number of categories, components, or factors. These factors themselves, in the first instance, may be regarded as having a purely descriptive function.

2. Under certain circumstances, factors may be regarded as hypothetical causal influences underlying and determining the observed relationships between a set of variables. It is only when regarded in this light that they have interest and significance for psychology.

3. The logical justification for inferring a causal factor from observed correlations is identical with the general scientific justification for inferring causes from effects; more specifically, there is formal identity between factorial procedures in psychology and taxonomic and nosological work in

other sciences (medical, botany, zoology).

4. The term "cause," in this context, is a concept which aids in the simplification and unification of natural phenomena; like all scientific concepts it is abstract and consequently an "artifact." A scientific concept is not a part of nature; it is rather a way of comprehending nature.

5. Factors, and the causal determinants which they suggest, are "subjective" in the same sense that physical dimensions are "subjective"; they "may be anything consistent with a set of definitions which agree with experimental facts." Their value and importance arises from the objective reference given them by this agreement "with experimental fact."

6. Criticism of factor analysis as a whole, or of one method of analysis by a writer favoring another method, is often vitiated by (a) lack of historical perspective, (b) lack of scientific sophistication, (c) lack of understanding of the particular problem which the factor analyst is trying to solve. It is usually easy for the critic to invent a problem which the analyst did not try to answer, but to which his answer would have been wrong or nonsensical. This is not a useful form of criticism.

7. The factorial method, no more than any other, cannot guarantee the correctness of the causal hypotheses suggested by it. Historical evidence reviewed suggests, however, that it is more successful than any alternate method, and that the hypotheses generated by it have proved remarkably accurate when direct experimental test became possible.

8. As indicated above, much nosological work in medicine and psychiatry is essentially of a factorial kind, although lacking the rigor and explicitness of factor analysis. It seems likely

that a more formal use of these recent mathematical developments will improve more intuitive "clinical" types of analysis.

9. Methods of statistical analysis, and particularly questions of rotation, are dependent on one's views of the aims of factor analysis, and of the nature of factors; implications of causality require rotation into simple structure, while purely descriptive aims are satisfied equally by nonrotated factors.

10. In the present stage of development of psychology, factor analysis is an indispensable method of taxonomic and nosological research. Knowledge of its historical roots, its logical basis, as well as its statistical methodology, should form part of the training of every psychologist who wishes to understand the standard scientific method of defining concepts in personality research.

REFERENCES

1. ADAMS, J. K., & FOWLER, H. M. *Report on the reliability of two forms of an activity preference blank.* Washington, D.C.: U.S. Dept. Commerce, 1946.
2. BRIDGMAN, P. W. *Dimensional analysis.* New Haven: Yale Univer. Press, 1931.
3. BURT, C. *The factors of the mind.* London: Univer. of London Press, 1940.
4. CARTER, G. S. *Animal evolution. A study of recent views of its causes.* London: Sedgewick & Jackson, 1951.
5. COLLINGWOOD, R. G. *An autobiography.* London: Penguin Books, 1939.
6. EYSENCK, H. J. *The scientific study of personality.* London: Routledge & Kegan Paul, 1952.
7. EYSENCK, H. J. The uses and abuses of factor analysis. *Appl. Statist.,* 1952, **1**, 45–49.
8. EYSENCK, H. J. Criterion analysis—an application of the hypothetico-deductive method to factor analysis. *Psychol. Rev.,* 1950, **57**, 38–53.
9. EYSENCK, H. J. *The structure of human personality.* London: Methuen, 1953.
10. GOLDMAN-EISLER, F. The problem of orality and of its origin in early childhood. *J. ment. Sci.,* 1951, **97**, 765–781.
11. HOLZINGER, K. J., & HARMAN, H. H. *Factor analysis: a synthesis of factorial methods.* Chicago: Univer. of Chicago Press, 1941.
12. KENDALL, M. G. Factor analysis. *J. Roy. stat. Soc.,* 1950, **12**, 60–73.
13. KELLEY, T. L. *Fundamentals of statistics.* Cambridge: Harvard Univer. Press, 1947.
14. KELLEY, T. L. Report of an activity-preference test for the classification of service personnel: *OSRD Report.* No. 4484, 1944.
15. KELLEY, T. L. Comment on Wilson and Worcester's "Note on Factor Analysis." *Psychometrika,* 1940, **5**, 117–120.
16. LURIE, W. A. A study of Spranger's value-types by the method of factor analysis. *J. soc. Psychol.,* 1951, **8**, 17–37.
17. PETRIE, A. *Personality and the frontal lobes.* London: Routledge & Kegan Paul, 1952.
18. SCOTT-BLAIR, G. W. *Measurement of mind and matter.* London: Dobson, 1950.
19. SPEARMAN, C. *The abilities of man.* London: Macmillan, 1927.
20. SPRANGER, E. *Types of men.* Halle: Niemeyer, 1928.
21. SWINGLE, D. B. *A textbook of systematic botany.* New York: McGraw-Hill, 1946.
22. THURSTONE, L. L. *Multiple-factor analysis. A development and expansion of the vectors of the mind.* Chicago: Univer. Chicago Press, 1947.
23. THURSTONE, L. L. A multiple factor study of vocational interests. *Personnel J.,* 1932, **10**, 198–205.
24. WENGER, M. A. Studies of autonomic balance in Army Air Forces personnel. *Comp. Psychol. Monogr.,* 1948, **19**, No. 4, 1–111.

Chapter 21

The Three Basic Factor
Analytic Research Designs—
Their Interrelations and Derivatives

RAYMOND B. CATTELL

Factor analysis began with the correlation of tests measured on populations of persons, but other arrangements have since been stumbled upon, or deliberately thought out for special purposes, from time to time. In 1946 the present writer formulated the *covariation* chart [4], which integrated in a single conception the accumulation of existing usages and revealed certain new, logically-possible designs of factor analysis.

The purpose of this review of current practice is to call attention to some possible misconceptions and show new directions of practical usefulness. The first effect of the examination of logical possibilities in the covariation chart was to provoke a realization that up to the time of that analysis only a small corner of the universe of effective factor-analytic designs had become actively inhabited by researchers. The "chart" thus proffered powerful new covariation tools, especially in relation to the multi-

This article is reprinted from the *Psychological Bulletin*, 1952, with the permission of the author and the American Psychological Association.

variate problems of clinical psychology, sociology, and physiology, which, except for a few recent examples in P and Q techniques, still need illustration. It is proposed here to develop those theorems into more explicit practical corollaries for experimental work and to investigate the true interrelations and precise limitations of the various techniques. For in some recent approaches, e.g., the use of Q technique by Stephenson [12], it would seem that there is some loss of perspective on methodological relationships.

BASIC REFERENTS IN COVARIATION INVESTIGATIONS

All scientific method deals with observations of covariation, but factor analysis covers that half of the methodological realm which has to do with simultaneous variation in many variables, not the univariate variation of so-called "controlled" classical experiment [6]. In either region a single act of measurement has five essential referents or signatures, as follows:

1. A defined set of *circumstances,* time, place, etc., in which the attribute (reaction, trait, operation) is observed. In psychology this is the "stimulus situation."
2. The *attribute* itself, which is defined by an operation of observing or measuring certain things. In psychology this is the "response."
3. An *object,* usually in psychology an organism, to which the attribute is referred.
4. If the observation is to be quantified there is reference also to a *scale* or unit by which the measurement is to be rendered numerical.
5. An *observer,* or, in behavioral data, a set of observers capable of mutually confirmatory evidence.

Although these are exhaustive of the essential signatures for an act of measurement, each of the five is susceptible to some subdivision into subparameters. For example, the stimulus situation has many dimensions besides those of time and place required to define it, and therefore to define the measurement. However, we do not normally expressly define all of these, but merely give sufficient direction to fix and reproduce relevant *circumstances or conditions.* It is unfortunate for clarity that the term "test" is often regarded as defining both stimulus situation and response, whereas it defines wholly only the response measured. The definition of stimulus situation or occasion must be regarded as an additional referent, in which the test material is only a part. For example, an intelligence test still needs definition of the stimulus conditions in which it is given.

For the great majority of psychological experiments in which factor analysis is used we can reduce the essential referents from five to three, namely: circumstances, persons, and attributes, wherein the attribute is an operation of measurement which includes reference to that part of the stimulus situation [1] which remains fixed, and the circumstance (or "occasion") referent is

restricted to whatever in the situation varies from occasion to occasion. This reduction to three referents is convenient for initial presentation of the main issues, but we shall include all five later.

If these three primary definers of a psychological observation are arranged as three distinct series (geometrically as axes) we get the covariation chart, as shown in Figure 21–1, within which all possibilities of correlation for factor analytic work should be contained (except for the special extensions of the two remaining parameters).

Thus the commonest correlation is on a series of persons, each measured on two attributes, and representable in the chart by two parallel lines, as shown in the channel labelled "*R* technique," starting from two attributes ("tests") j_5 and j_7. Incidentally, it should be kept in mind that mathematically speaking these axes are not continuous or ordered but represent discrete series, i.e., populations of individual reference points (tests, persons, occasions) having any order in which the sampling happens to present them.

Any pair of parallel lines drawn within the parallelepiped of the covariation chart will represent a possible correlation, for it will indicate measurements of one character, made in two different forms upon a series belonging to a single class. Thus in addition to the correlation of tests j_5 and j_7 for a series of people, as just illustrated for the classical *R* technique, we can draw a channel to the left (Figure 21–1) which represents a correlation of j_5 and j_7 upon a series of occasions $k_o \cdot \cdot \cdot k_n$, for one person i_o.

Or again, we can take two occasions, as shown at k_2 and k_4 and correlate the series of people $i_o \cdot \cdot \cdot i_n$ on a test j_o, as labelled *T* technique. This, incidentally, is a reliability coefficient, and a whole matrix of such pairs of occasions could be factorized to find "factors in occasions (circumstances)" producing similar behavior on a test. Channels drawn in any one *plane* amount to correlatable series in which the same thing is held constant. For the present

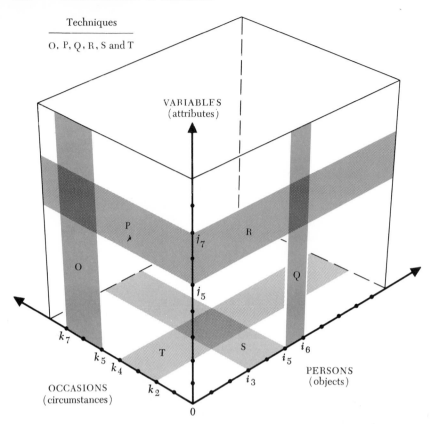

Figure 21-1   *The covariation chart.*

we propose to refer only to rectangular series drawn parallel to an edge, omitting the special problems of "staggered" (lead and lag) correlations, etc.

THE UTILITIES OF THE BASIC DESIGNS

It may help to fix the above six designs in mind, for the purpose of further abstract reasoning about them, if we expand briefly on the special scientific utilities of each.

1. *R technique,* factoring attributes on populations of persons, is the daily bread of the psychometrist and needs no description. Its factors are *common traits,* applicable to measuring individual differences of persons and having a meaning rooted in the behavioral relations of *a whole population and its environment.* If simple structure is applied, to give natural, functional, and not merely mathematical factors, the factors will tend to be invariant in loading pattern,

differing from sample to sample principally in slight changes of obliquity of the factors [13].

2. *P technique,* correlating attributes within one person, is, by contrast, the agent for discovering *unique traits* and particularly for that unravelling of connections of dynamic traits and symptoms for which the clinician has hitherto had nothing more positive than free association [9, 10]. It is an ideal method for determining, along with other dynamic structures, the structure of the self sentiment, as shown in two recent studies [9, 11]. In two other studies it has shown a potency unequalled by any other method but fully controlled physiological experiment for revealing the connections of interest in psychosomatics [10, 14]. Its value in sociology, economics, and social psychology has been shown in two studies factorizing longitudinal series for single communities or nations, thus introducing a more positive and precise calculus in relation to historical influences and trends [7,

THE THREE BASIC FACTOR ANALYTIC RESEARCH DESIGNS

8]. By this method both the factor structure and the quantification of the factors are unique to the individual social or animal organism, the scaling thus having to be ipsative [3], whereas in R technique the scaling is normative and the uniqueness of the individual is only a uniqueness of pattern in *common* dimensions.

For the above reasons the factors obtained by P technique have no *necessary* mathematical relation to those obtained by R technique. The half dozen pioneer studies so far published suggest, however, that a *scientific* relation will exist in that the structural patterns of the individual unique factors will tend to scatter about the loading pattern of the corresponding R technique common factor. The R and P factors may also differ in total variance contribution. For example the surgency-desurgency factor of elation-depression seems to stand higher in factors of intra-individual variance than in inter-individual variance [5, 9, 10, 14].

3. *Q technique* has its chief use as a classificatory device for finding the subpopulations in a nonhomogeneous population (like Lazarsfeld's "latent structure analysis" or latent subgroup analysis), and for the special purpose of quantifying the extent to which an individual may be regarded as belonging to certain species and subspecies. Whether this can be considered a process of defining types depends upon the meaning one assigns to the term "type."[1] In social psychology it has value in picking out roles, i.e., common patterns of social response shown by many persons; but this can be dealt with also by S technique described below. Strictly, Q technique is a factor analytic design and as such should proceed *beyond* the mere examination of a matrix for "type" *clusters* to the further derivation of abstract *factors*. If it does this it may have the additional utility of providing a new, independent avenue to discovering the universal factors of R technique, and an avenue which may be more convenient than R technique in some special circumstances. This transposability of R and Q technique results is denied by Stephenson, though Sir Cyril Burt claims to have demonstrated it [2] and some statisticians agree with this demonstration.

4. *O technique* is perhaps the more important of the two *occasion-correlating* techniques. It tests one person on a whole series of tests for two occasions (k_5 and k_7 in Figure 21–1) and determines the similarity of the total person (or, at least, as much of him as is included in the series of tests) on two occasions. The most obvious use for the factorization of a matrix from such pairings of occasions is for investigating multiple personality [4, p. 99] and the change of the self-structure under psychotherapy. The nature of the factors has to be inferred from the attribute pattern for those occasions which are most highly loaded in the given factor. This approach also lends itself to analysis of stimulus situations, for the nature of the circumstances in each occasion can be manipulated, or at least recorded, and the factors among occasions will thus show how situations group themselves in regard to their effects on the total personality. Some alleged instances of Q technique are really O technique, and would be more correctly evaluated if this were explicitly recognized.

5. *T technique* may be remembered by the mnemonic that it is *test-retest* factorization. Like O technique it correlates occasions, but it does so, as the covariation chart above shows, by repeating the same test for a matrix of different occasions on a population of persons. It is thus a factorization of reliability coefficients, but naturally the significance of the design would hinge

---

[1] I have suggested elsewhere [3] that "type" is being used for four distinguishable concepts: (*a*) continuous types, e.g., a tall and a short type of man, where a whole factor pattern varies in level of elements continuously from extreme to extreme; (*b*) discontinuous types, e.g., man and pigmy, where the pattern is essentially the same as in continuous types but the measurements are bimodal or discontinuous; (*c*) continuous species types, where the pattern itself differs, but in a continuous way, e.g., businessmen and artists; and (*d*) discontinuous species types, e.g., dogs and ducks, where the pattern is distinct and discontinuous as to distribution in nature. Some uses of Q technique to find types slur these differences.

upon recording the particular *circumstances* of each occasion of re-administration, as in *O* technique. The factors among such defined occasions would again be factors in the general stimulus situation as judged by effects on the population. But they would differ from *O* technique in being factors with respect to some single response, e.g., an opinion poll on a definite issue, instead of to a sample of the responses of the total personality, and in applying to a population instead of a single person. Because of this analysis of circumstances according to the effects they produce on the distribution of response with a population, *T* technique might be called a "social climate" thermometer and is likely to find its most valuable application in quantifying phases of business cycles and in getting more historical meaning out of opinion polls than the present poverty of statistical methods permits.

6. *S technique* may be remembered by the mnemonic that its principal immediate use is to detect and define *social roles*. It correlates two persons on their reactions to a single stimulus (test) on a series of occasions. (A role is defined as a pattern of responses to different occasions which is modal among individual patterns, i.e., it is a cluster or factor among people in responses to social occasions.) The loading of a person in the factor would show the extent to which he is successfully assuming the role. *S* technique also has promise in determining the internal structure of a group or institution; for example, by correlating the responses of members of a family over many occasions on their response to a single issue it would indicate the functional subgroups within the family. Because of this capacity to reveal the degree to which individuals belong to groups characterized by homogeneity of functioning in regard to a series of historical events, *S* technique is *par excellence* the method for social psychology.

REFERENCES

1. BURT, C. L. Correlations between persons. *Brit. J. Psychol.*, 1937, **28**, 59–96.
2. BURT, C. L. A comparison of factor analysis and analysis of variance. *Brit. J. Psychol.*, Statist. Sect. 1947, **1**, 3–26.
3. CATTELL, R. B. Psychological measurement: Normative, ipsative, interactive. *Psychol. Rev.*, 1944, **51**, 292–303.
4. CATTELL, R. B. *The description and measurement of personality.* New York: World Book Co., 1946.
5. CATTELL, R. B. *Personality: A systematic theoretical and factual study.* New York: McGraw-Hill, 1950.
6. CATTELL, R. B. *Factor analysis: An introduction and manual for the psychologist and social scientist.* New York: Harper, 1952.
7. CATTELL, R. B. The psychological dimensions of social progress in Britain, determined by *P*-technique, 1835–1935. *Hum. Relat.*, in press.
8. CATTELL, R. B., & ADELSON, M. The dimensions of social change in the U.S.A. as determined by *P*-technique. *Soc. Forces*, 1951, **30**, 190–201.
9. CATTELL, R. B., CATTELL, A. K. S., & RHYMER, R. M. *P*-technique demonstrated in determining psychophysiological source traits in a normal individual. *Psychometrika*, 1947, **12**, 267–288.
10. CATTELL, R. B., & LUBORSKY, L. *P*-technique demonstrated as a new clinical method for determining personality and symptom structure. *J. gen. Psychol.*, 1950, **42**, 3–24.
11. CROSS, PATRICIA. Comparison of *P*- and *R*-technique determinations of ergic structure in common attitudes. Unpublished M.A. thesis, Univer. of Illinois, 1951.
12. STEPHENSON, W. The foundations of psychometry: Four factor systems. *Psychometrika*, 1936, **1**, 195–209.
13. THURSTONE, L. L. The effects of selection in factor analysis. *Psychometrika*, 1945, **10**, 165–198.
14. WILLIAMS, H. V. M. A *P*-technique study of personality factors in the psychosomatic areas. Unpublished Ph.D. dissertation, Univer. of Illinois, 1949.

Chapter 22

The Objective Definition of Simple Structure in Linear Factor Analysis

LEDYARD R TUCKER

The principle of simple structure, proposed by Thurstone as a solution to the problem of indeterminacy of position of axes in the factorial structure, has received wide support and use in factor analysis. There have been, however, a variety of criticisms including (1) a skepticism regarding whether this principle of simplicity did, in reality, adequately parallel nature, and (2) a feeling of disturbance at the subjectivity involved both in theory and in application. The first problem, that of the validity of the simple structure concept, may be settled only by experimental studies. It is the pur-

This article is reprinted from *Psychometrika,* 1955, with the permission of the author and the Psychometric Society.

This research was jointly supported by Princeton University, the Office of Naval Research under contract N6onr-270-20, and the National Science Foundation under grant NSF G-642. The author is especially indebted to Harold Gulliksen for his many exceedingly helpful comments and suggestions made during the course of this development. A debt of gratitude is also owed to Mrs. Gertrude Diederich, who performed many intricate calculations in the experiments on computing procedures. The author further wishes to express his appreciation to Frederic M. Lord and David R. Saunders, who read the manuscript and made a number of very useful suggestions.

pose of this paper to assist in solving the second problem, that of subjectivity, by attempting to develop a more objective and operational view of the simple structure concept.

Two major concepts of the nature of factors are used to justify the principle of simple structure. Thurstone's views might best be summarized by the following quotations: "In the interpretation of mind we assume that mental phenomena can be identified in terms of distinguishable functions, which do not all participate equally in everything that mind does. . . . No assumption is made about the nature of these functions, whether they are native or acquired or whether they have a cortical locus" [3, p. 57]. "Just as we take for granted that the individual differences in visual acuity are not involved in pitch discrimination, so we assume that in intellectual tasks some mental or cortical functions are not involved in every task. This is the principle of 'simple structure' or 'simple configuration' in the underlying order for any given set of attributes" [3, p. 58]. Cattell [1] expresses a similar view. In contrast to the foregoing, Holzinger and Harman

[2] express a variant view that factor analysis, as a branch of statistical analysis, conveys information in the original data with an aim of parsimony which should not be construed as a search for fundamental categories. Similarly, Vernon [4] takes a position that ". . . it should be clear that a factor is a construct which accounts for the objectively determined correlations between tests, in contrast to a faculty which is a hypothetical mental power" [4, p. 8]. Others have taken views on either of these two sides, with still others sticking to some middle ground. Since each of these views can be interpreted as yielding support for the desirability of simple structure, we believe that the definitions to follow could be derived from either view and will not distinguish between them. Some such view is necessary, however, as an initial step toward acceptance of the simple structure concept.

RELATION BETWEEN DESIGN OF FACTOR ANALYSIS STUDIES AND SIMPLE STRUCTURE

The factorial study of human behavior might best be conceived as a program of studies rather than in terms of isolated, separate studies. Each study should build upon the knowledge gained from previous studies and add further to the verified fund of knowledge. Early studies in some domain, or class of behavior, will be more exploratory in nature and be made with less perfected batteries of measures. As knowledge increases concerning the interrelations of the various behaviors in such a domain, it should be possible to construct more satisfactory batteries for factorial analysis. Confirmatory studies should aid in firmly establishing the factorial structure.

In exploratory studies a fully determined simple structure solution should not be expected and rotation of axes will probably be continued on subjective bases. There may well be an attempt to maximize the number of small, insignificant factor load-

ings; but some attention may also be given to interpretive possibilities. While some assistance may be obtained from analytic procedures, it seems inevitable that the rotation of axes for exploratory studies will remain an art. This paper does not attempt to present a method for rotation of axes to simple structure in exploratory studies. Rather, in contrast, the definitions and procedure to follow are to be conceived as applying primarily to the more perfected factorial studies.

A major premise of the present argument is that the objective definition of a simple structure is dependent on both an adequate study design and on objective analytic criteria. Not all factorial studies may possess a simple structure, only those studies involving an appropriate battery of measures made on an appropriate sample of individuals. Some requirements set forth by the analytic criteria may be met only in the study design. It is desirable, however, that there be a maximum of freedom in the design of factorial studies so as to fit as many situations as possible. For example, an experimenter should be in a position to test objectively hypotheses concerning the relations of complex measures to factorially simpler ones. Thus, it is desirable that the analytic criteria permit complex variables and not limit the study design to factorially pure measures. The factorial simple structure needs to be unambiguously present, however, in the data. This is a function of the study design.

REQUIREMENTS FOR OBJECTIVE DEFINITION OF SIMPLE STRUCTURE

Following is a proposed list of requirements for satisfactory objective criteria for simple structure. These requirements should be interpreted as applying to individual studies since invariance of factorial results over various changes in the population of individuals sampled and in the battery of measures is a matter for experimental verification. It will be noted, however, that small variations of factor loadings and projections from ideal values are permitted. These small variations from ideal might result either from random sampling error peculiar to the sample of individuals measured or from errors of approximation in the basic factorial model.

A second point to be noted is that a choice is made as to kind of projection employed relating test vectors to factors. In the case of correlated factors, orthogonal projections of test vectors on normals to hyperplanes are used. These orthogonal projections for a particular factor depend upon location of only the hyperplane for that factor and upon the test vectors. They are independent of the locations of all other hyperplanes. A further reason for this choice as to type of projection is that the square of this type of projection can be interpreted to represent the independent contribution of the factor to the variance of the variable.

a. *Basic requirements*
  1. Emphasis is placed on a maximum concentration of vectors along hyperplanes, that is, on a maximum number of zero projections on normals to the hyperplanes, allowance being made for small variations in observed projections.
  2. The vectors interpreted as being in each hyperplane span a space of $(r - 1)$ dimensions, allowance being made for small variations in observed projections, where r is the number of dimensions in the common-factor space.
  3. Exactly as many simple structure factors are obtained as there are dimensions in the common-factor space.
b. *Types of freedom explicitly permitted*
  4. Oblique factors are permitted.
  5. A minority of highly complex measures whose vectors have projections on several, up to all, factors is permitted in the battery being analyzed.
c. *Operational requirements*
  6. The choice as to which projections

are to be interpreted as zero is made on objective grounds.
  7. An objectively determined best fit to the data is involved.
  8. The best fit is unbiased in the limiting sense that when the variance of projections interpreted as zero is small, the mean of these projections is near zero.
  9. Statistical tests exist which indicate the plausibility of accepting any particular solution as a simple structure.
  10. An automatic computational procedure is available for use with any particular study.

The first three, or basic, requirements relate as much to the study design as to the objective criteria for simple structure. Each factorial study for which there is to be an objectively defined simple structure should be so designed that the configuration of vectors satisfies these requirements. For the objective analytical criteria, on the other hand, these basic requirements form the essential framework. The first requirement parallels the concept of simple structure. The second requirement is necessary for the hyperplanes to be determinate. Consider, for example, a group of vectors for one hyperplane such that there was a two-dimensional space into which they only had small projections that could be interpreted as zero. The normal to the hyperplane could be located anywhere in this space and satisfy the first requirement. The location of the hyperplane would not be unique. In order for the location of the hyperplane to be definite it is necessary for the vectors in this hyperplane to have small projections into only one dimension, that of the normal to the hyperplane. The third requirement pertains most directly to the study design in the sense that there must be as many hyperplanes of vectors that satisfy the first two requirements as there are dimensions in the common-factor space. The study design should be such that the number of common factors extracted should be quite definite. When the third requirement is met by the study design, it is necessary, but probably not difficult, for the objective criteria to meet it also.

The types of freedom explicitly permitted in requirements four and five were selected because they touch on controversial, or possibly controversial, points. Factorial practice has been divided on the point of oblique versus orthogonal factors. It is the opinion of the author that in the present context maximum liberty should be permitted. Whenever it seems advisable, a restriction could be inserted to the effect that only orthogonal factors were permitted. This could be a function of the study being analyzed or of the opinion of the analyst. The case for complex measures has been previously mentioned in this article. It is desirable for experimenters to be able to check in an objective fashion on hypotheses related to complex variables. Allowance for measures that have loadings on all factors is at variance with Thurstone's requirement [3, p. 335] that each row of the factorial matrix have at least one zero loading. In the opinion of the author this becomes an unnecessary restriction in case the basic requirements previously listed are met.

The last five, or operational, requirements relate to desirable aspects of objective criteria for simple structure. Requirement six could be met by the establishment of a range of projections, centering on zero, to be interpreted as negligible or zero projections. The limits for this range could be considered as generalized constants to be defined by the analyst on a priori grounds.

A best fit of the data in some statistical sense as per requirement seven is certainly desirable. That this best fit should be unbiased, as per requirement eight, is also desirable. It is this requirement, however, that is likely to differentiate between an ideal objective criterion and various approximate ones. Requirements nine and ten are quite crucial, but at the same time may be the most difficult to satisfy. The statistical test of requirement nine is necessary for scientific acceptability, but it may be the last point to be solved for objective criteria for simple structure. The automatic computing procedures should be as economical as possible. It may be, however, that the computations for an ideal objective criterion will be so complex and extensive that such a criterion will be applied only to a few critical studies. Approximate criteria that involve simple computations might be adequate in many cases and would be highly desirable. Developments in high-speed computers, however, may influence the relative economies of the criteria.

REFERENCES

1. CATTELL, R. B. Factor analysis. New York: Harper, 1952.
2. HOLZINGER, K. J., & HARMAN, H. H. Factor analysis. Chicago: Univer. Chicago Press, 1941.
3. THURSTONE, L. L. Multiple-factor analysis. Chicago: Univer. Chicago Press, 1947.
4. VERNON, P. E. The structure of human abilities. London: Methuen and Co., Ltd., 1950. (New York: Wiley.)

Chapter 23

When Not to Factor Analyze

J. P. GUILFORD

The apparent increase in the utilization of factor-analytical methods is undoubtedly gratifying to all those who have championed those methods. Their application to research in clinical psychology as well as to research in what has traditionally been known as experimental psychology speaks well for their versatility.

It seems desirable, however, to interject some words of caution, in view of the number of misuses of factor analysis that are appearing from time to time in published articles. Many a report that includes an account of a factor analysis is faulty because of failure to take certain precautions to assure an adequate solution by that approach.

In some instances there have been poor choices of experimental variables or of populations, or of both. Sometimes it seems as if the investigator, feeling the urge to factor analyze, applies the method to his next investigation in which intercorrelations are conveniently available. Too many experimental variables have been analyzed

just because they are conveniently at hand. More specifically, scores from such sources as the *Strong Vocational Interest Blank*, the *Kuder Preference Record*, Bernreuter's *Personality Inventory*, the *Minnesota Multiphasic Personality Inventory*, and the Guilford-Martin personality inventories are inappropriate experimental variables to use under most conditions of analysis. Why these variables are inappropriate will be explained in what follows.

If any research tool is to give meaningful results, it must be applied in the right place and in the proper manner. Writers on factorial methods have expressed warnings from time to time concerning requirements and limitations for the use of those methods. The most common misuses of those methods, however, cannot be entirely excused on the grounds of unfamiliarity with the literature on factor-analysis techniques. Many of the misuses and abuses could have been avoided if the investigators had observed the ordinary good rules of experimental controls and of population sampling.

The use of a complicated statistical procedure like factor analysis does not permit one to forget about the usual safeguards

This article is reprinted from the *Psychological Bulletin*, 1952, with the permission of the author and the American Psychological Association.

that should surround scientific observations. Statistical operations do not compensate for carelessness in making observations. Rather, they presuppose careful observations. They then serve as an important aid in seeing order in the observations and in making sense of that order. Under inappropriate conditions of observation, data may appear to have an order that is misleading if not fictitious. There is no statistical magic that will give a good ordered view of nature when the data do not permit.

The discussion here will not attempt to include all the errors and pitfalls that have occurred in connection with factor analyses. In the first place, the context is limited to those factorial methods in which rotation of reference axes is an important feature. It is assumed that some rotational procedure is usually necessary to achieve an order in data that has a parallel in psychological concepts. In other words, the bias is in favor of the principle that rotations of reference axes are generally needed to yield a meaningful reference frame. It is also assumed that the order underlying a number of experimental variables is substantially simpler than the data from which it was extracted. In others words, the number of common factors is definitely less than the number of experimental variables. When the term "factor" is used hereafter, the idea of "common factor" is implied.

SOME COMMON FAULTS IN FACTOR ANALYSIS

1. *Too many factors are often extracted for the number of experimental variables.* Too many factors for the number of experimental variables are likely to preclude a good rotational solution. Thurstone has repeatedly emphasized that in a rotational solution the position of each reference axis must be overdetermined [8]. A good rule is to have at least three variables for every factor expected. If there has been good preparatory planning of the study, one can predict the probable number of factors and

whether the variables are well distributed among the factors. A paucity of variables is not only a handicap in making rotations but also in the interpretation of factors. It requires several tests all substantially loaded with a factor to indicate the generality of the factor and to define it satisfactorily.

2. *Too many experimental variables are factorially complex.* Rotations and interpretations would be much simplified if each variable were of complexity one; that is, if it measured only one common factor to any appreciable extent. This is an ideal that we achieve in test construction only once in many attempts. There is little excuse for taking almost any variable that is handy. Such variables, where there has been no effort to restrict them, are very likely to measure two or more common factors. With appropriate planning and careful test construction we can do much to reduce the complexity of tests in preparation for an analysis. The effort will pay off in terms of facilitated rotations and interpretations. It may make the difference between success and failure in achieving a solution that is acceptable.

3. *Sometimes a common factor fails to come out because it is substantially represented in only one experimental variable.* For a common factor to emerge in a particular set of experimental variables, more than one variable must have substantial variance in that factor.[1] It is otherwise left as specific variance so far as that particular analysis is concerned. This is ordinarily not a serious matter. It may merely mean that an opportunity has been missed to find a certain factor that is actually present.

But this is sometimes not the whole story. If this factor should be represented in minor amounts in some other variables, this common-factor variance may be extracted. But there is likely to be trouble in making rotations. If the rotating is done entirely blindly (without regard to known land-

---

[1] This assumes the usual practice of using communalities in the diagonal cells of the correlation matrix.

marks of psychological meaning) such a factor is frequently lost. Its variance may be divided several ways.

A recent example of this occurred in analyzing a battery of reasoning tests. A test of numerical operations had been put in the battery to assure the segregation of the number-factor variance expected in some of the reasoning tests. The number factor is so well established and a numerical-operations test is such a unique measure of it, that any solution not preserving this factor would be very suspect. Only the insistence of an axis through the numerical-operations test preserved the factor. This undoubtedly led to a clearer picture with respect to the reasoning factors.

This same fault comes out in a similar manner in connection with the analysis of scores from some personality inventories. Where some of the scores are fairly unique for single factors, those factors either do not come out in the analysis, or if weakly represented in other scores the rotational solution tends to break up their variances. This is particularly true when fewer common factors are extracted than actually are present in the scores.

4. *Not enough factors are extracted.* Experience has shown that it pays to extract a liberal number of factors. Most criteria for deciding how many factors to extract are not sufficiently liberal. No harm appears to be done in extracting too many factors. If more than the proper number of factors are extracted, the rotations will lead to the rejection of one or more of them as "residual" factors. The presence of one or two extra factors often helps to clear up the general picture of the structure for the factors that are of genuine significance.

Some investigators seem to fear that the last factors extracted are entirely a matter of error variance. It is as if they believe that up to a certain point in the extractions all variance extracted is common-factor variance and after that all variance extracted is error variance. The fact that the late-extracted variance helps to clear up the structure in rotations and to improve psy-chological meaningfulness of the factors is some evidence that true variance may be extracted late as well as early. There seems to be no good reason for rejecting the idea that error variance is also extracted early as well as late.

From this discussion it would seem to follow that the best criterion of when to cease extracting factors is the size of the larger factor loadings. As long as they are large enough to contribute something to other factors in rotation or to be built up into something psychologically meaningful they probably should have been extracted.

5. *Correlation coefficients used in analysis are often spurious.* Thurstone has often emphasized the point that the correlations used in factor analysis should be between variables that are linearly independent [8]. This means that there should be no reason for covariation except that due to common factors.

There are a number of situations in psychological investigations in which specific and error variances actually contribute to intercorrelations where they should not be permitted to do so. One common situation is in connection with personality inventories in which the same items are scored with weights for more than one trait variable. This is especially true of the Bernreuter *Personality Inventory,* the *Strong Vocational Interest Blank,* and the Guilford *Inventory of Factors STDCR.* It is true to some extent of the *Guilford-Martin Inventory of Factors GAMIN.* For every item that is weighted in two scores there is a contribution to the obtained correlation between those scores. Insofar as the item measures factors in common to the two scores this is legitimate. But the item's contribution to any total score also includes some specific and error variance. The specific and error variances thus contribute to the intercorrelations of items.

Let us assume that two scores were designed to measure two factors that are actually orthogonal or independent. But in the two scoring keys there are a number of items weighted similarly. There would consequently be a positive correlation, perhaps a substantial one, between scores in these two variables. A negative correlation could also be brought about between scores for two independent factors if the weights were in the opposite direction when items were scored for both factors. The positive and negative intercorrelations among scores on the *Strong Vocational Interest Blank* are largely influenced by these positive and negative correlations of weights. To what extent the intercorrelations of multi-scored inventories represent actual degrees of relationship of the variables the test author intended to measure and to what extent they represent these incidental communities of specific and error variances is unknown.

The writer is often asked why some of the scores on his inventories intercorrelate so strongly when the scores were designed to measure factors. This question confuses two different things: on the one hand the factors, and on the other hand the scores which were designed to measure those factors. Factors and their corresponding scores are logically and operationally distinct variables.

There are several reasons for the correlation of factor scores. One is the fact of intercorrelations of the factors themselves. It is very probable that some of the temperament and interest factors are actually interrelated. It is the writer's belief that at the present time we are not in a very good position to determine the extent of those intercorrelations satisfactorily. Just as there are adventitious conditions that distort the intercorrelations of experimental variables, there are also incidental disturbing conditions that give the appearance of intercorrelations of factors in an oblique solution in a factor analysis.

In addition to the genuine intercorrelations of factors themselves, there is the overlap of specific and error variances mentioned above contributing to the correlations among the scores of the factors. There is also the fact that items themselves are factorially complex. The items designed to measure factor A, on the whole, may be frequently involved with factor B and items designed to measure factor B may be involved with factor A. The factors A and B might be orthogonal but under the present level of skills in item writing it may be difficult to effect a separation in the items written to measure either factor. Even though no items were weighted for both factors in scoring, both scores would carry variance in both factors. The solution may be in the use of suppression variables [6]. We should have to make some assumption about the actual factor intercorrelations, however, to assure by this method a degree of interrelation of scores consistent with interrelation of factors.

If a set of scores for factors were properly slanted so that each score measures one factor and one only, the intercorrelations of those scores would represent the intercorrelations of the factors. The factor analysis of these intercorrelations would give the second-order factors. When the intercorrelations of factor scores are distorted by all the sources of error that have just been described, however, it can be seen that an analysis will yield results that are difficult to interpret, at best.

6. *Correlations of ipsative scores are sometimes used in an analysis.* The term "ipsative measurement" was emphasized by Cattell [2]. Ipsative measurements can best be defined by contrast to the more common "normative measurements." In normative measurements there is a scale for every *trait* and a population of individuals is distributed about the mean of that population. In ipsative measurements, there is a scale for every *individual* and a population of an individual's trait scores is distributed about that individual's mean. Normative scores are used to indicate inter-individual differences in a trait. Ipsative scores are used to indicate intra-individual differences in a number of traits. We compare individuals with respect to a trait by using normative scores. We compare trait quantities within an individual by using ipsative scores.

For the usual factor analysis (R-technique) in which the experimental variables are individual differences, normative scores are properly used. We correlate scores over a population of individuals. When the factor analysis is by the Q-technique, in which individuals are intercorrelated, we should use ipsative scores. The scores are then correlated over a population of traits or qualities. It is improper to use normative scores in a Q-technique analysis and to use ipsative scores in an R-technique analysis. Unfortunately, both of these mistakes are sometimes made.

One of the best examples of ipsative measurements in common practice is found in the scores from the *Kuder Preference Record*. Though these scores are not entirely ipsative, they partake strongly of the properties of ipsative measurements. The reason for this lies in the forced-choice type of item used. Where interest variables are pitted against one another rather systematically for preferential judgments, the result is that a high preference for any one interest to that extent means low preferences for other interests. It is consequently impossible for an individual to score very high in all, or nearly all, of the Kuder interest variables, as should be possible in normative scoring.

The typical profile of an individual on the Kuder inventory is distinguished by the unusual number of extreme scaled scores, high and low. This is approved by the counselor, who wants to high-light differences among the interest traits. But it represents a kind of measurement that is not suited to intercorrelations of the usual kinds where normative measurements are needed. The correlations of the Kuder scores with each other and with outside variables are of questionable meaning to the extent that they are ipsative in nature. The effect on the intercorrelations of the Kuder scores is that about two-thirds of them are negative [5, p. 615].

The scores on the Strong interest inventory have some of the ipsative quality about them, in view of the preferential items in some parts of that inventory. The effects of these parts are superimposed upon the effects of correlations of weights already mentioned.

Scores based upon the complete paired-comparison presentation of items are even more completely ipsative. The means of all individuals in the trait scores involved are equated, which would not be true in normative measurements. Such scores would be appropriate for analysis by the Q-technique, if the score sample were sufficiently large, but not by the ordinary R-technique.

7. *A pair of factors is very much confined to the same experimental variables.* This is not a very common circumstance, but one for which one should be on the alert. If factors A and B are commonly measurable by the same tests, so that in the battery being analyzed no test having variance in the one factor is free of variance in the other, factors A and B may be difficult to separate. This is especially true where an insufficient number of factors has been extracted. Sometimes one can detect the fact that two well-known factors have thus "telescoped" into one. But how often this happens with factors that are new or unknown is hard to say. The difficulty can be forestalled to some extent by care in the selection and the construction of tests to be analyzed.

8. *The population on which the analysis is based is heterogeneous.* Although no tests of statistical significance are usually made in connection with a factor analysis, the common sampling problems have a bearing upon the success of the analysis. Too often, samples are taken from populations that happen to be most available. What is worse, different populations are thrown together without questioning what effect this may have upon the intercorrelations.

Although a number of studies have shown that the same factors may be found in the same tests when analyzed in somewhat different populations (e.g., white vs. Negro, male vs. female) with somewhat similar factor loadings [3, 6], the combining of populations is a different matter. If there are notable differences between means in both of two variables, there is a correlation between the means of those two variables. Correlations between means influence correlations of scores when such populations are thrown together.

One should not pool the data derived from different populations for the purpose of computing intercorrelations, then, unless he can show that differences in population means on the experimental variables are insignificant or unless he makes allowances for any "between-means" correlations. One procedure would be to compute the correlation matrix for each population separately. If the corresponding coefficients are similar they may be averaged to obtain a single matrix for analysis. The chief external conditions on which homogeneity should ordinarily be achieved are the familiar ones of age, sex, and education, wherever it is suspected that any of the experimental variables are related to those conditions.

9. *Not enough attention is given to requirements for correlation coefficients.* A factor analysis ordinarily begins with correlation coefficients. The results of the analysis can be no better than the data with which the analysis begins. Even elementary statistical textbooks mention the conditions needed in order that the correlation in a sample shall be a good estimate of the correlation in the population. Yet, it is apparent that many who analyze pay little attention to the question of whether those conditions are satisfied. At least, in their reports very little is said about the satisfaction of those conditions.

The least that the investigator can do is to examine the form of the frequency distribution of each variable that is correlated. The distributions should not be markedly skewed, truncated, or multi-modal. Any of these departures from unimodal, complete, and symmetrical distributions can endanger proper estimates of population correlations. The departures would probably have to be severe enough as to be obvious by inspection in order to justify concern. In other words, it would not require statistical tests of such departures to tell whether one should do something about them. If all distributions are fairly unimodal and symmetrical, the chances are that regressions are rectilinear and that homoscedasticity would prevail in the bivariate plots.

One cannot depend upon standard psychological tests to yield the regular forms of distributions just specified for computing Pearson product-moment r's. Distributions vary as a test is administered to different populations. The form of distribution for new and untried tests, particularly, is likely to be irregular unless pains have been taken by pre-testing to assure regular distributions.

The remedies for irregular distributions, should they occur, are common knowledge. Skewed distributions can be normalized to some standard scale, provided the raw-score scale has considerable range. They cannot be satisfactorily normalized if there are too few raw-score categories or if there is truncation. For a distribution with undue numbers of cases in end categories there is only one very convenient remedy—to dichotomize the distribution.

Dichotomizing a distribution means the computing of biserial r's with other variables that are not dichotomized. Since biserial r's are fairly good estimates of Pearson r's, they may be mixed with the Pearson r's for the analysis. Some investigators hesitate to dichotomize a distribution for computing a biserial r when the sample distribution is skewed or truncated, in view of the assumption of normality that is made about the dichotomized variable. The assumption of normality underlying the computation of a biserial r is that the *population* distribution is normally distributed. The population distribution can be normal even though the sample distribution is not, due to a faulty measuring scale. If there is no decisive information to the contrary, the population distribution on a psychological variable may often be assumed to be normal.

If more than one distribution is dichotomized, the coefficient to use is the tetrachoric r for a pair of such distributions. If the sample is fairly large (at least approximately 400) it would be convenient and defensible to dichotomize all the distributions. Whatever dichotomizing is done should divide distributions as near the medians as possible, in order to minimize the standard errors of the coefficients. Dichotomizing distributions near the medians has another virtue in connection with factor analysis. It tends to equate difficulty levels of the tests. It has been suggested that comparable difficulty levels should be achieved in order to avoid distortions in correlation coefficients [1].

10. *Difficulty levels of tests often vary substantially.* It is well known that variations in difficulty level of tests relative to the ability level of the population affect the form of distributions of scores. Inappropriate difficulty level is followed by skewing, and skewing, as was pointed out above, is followed by distortions in correlation coefficients. Certain remedies for skewing were pointed out above, but they are only corrections after the fact. Scaling and dichotomizing in order to eliminate the effects of skewing appear to take care of the biases due to inappropriate difficulty levels, but they may not do so completely.

If we dichotomize a seriously skewed distribution for a very difficult test, have we effected the same kind of division of the sample as we would have done with an easier test? We do not know. We do know that a symmetrical distribution makes better use of the available range of scores. If we have a relatively short test of 20 to 25 items, for example, and if the distribution is skewed, the range of utilized score categories becomes very much restricted. With a symmetrical distribution there is opportunity for a larger range and a finer scaling.

It follows that we should attempt to avoid skewed distributions from the start. This can be achieved by good test construction and by selecting tests with optimal adjustment of difficulty level to the status

of the population. If we assure regular distributions, we may then compute the more reliable Pearson r's and avoid the recourse to scaling and dichotomizing or other remedial measures.

HOW THE FAULTS APPLY TO STANDARD TESTS

It was stated earlier that the scores from certain personality inventories are not suitable variables for use in factor-analysis investigations. The reasons are now much more easily presented in terms of the principles just discussed.

The scores on the *Strong Vocational Interest Blank* are not good variables for analysis because they entail the faults numbered 1, 2, 5, and 6. Covering the scope of vocational interests (also some temperament qualities that are latent in the scores) as they do, the scores may be no more numerous than the factors involved. Most of the scores are probably factorially complex, since the distinguishing qualities of a vocational group are numerous. No attempt was made to seek score categories that are functionally unique. The intercorrelations of the scores are quite generally influenced by the multi-scoring technique which contributes identical specific and error variances to two or more scores. The use of some forced-choice items introduces some ipsative properties into the scores, though this feature is probably of relatively small importance in the Strong inventory.

The *Kuder Preference Record* scores are not suitable variables for factor analysis by the usual R-technique because of faults 1, 3, and 6. Among the limited number of Kuder scores there may be more factors than scores. It is possible that one or more of the Kuder scores actually approach univocality for primary interests. If so, within the context of the Kuder score variables, these scores would yield no common factors in an analysis. If other variables were brought into the picture those factors might emerge. The strong ipsative property of the Kuder scores, however, renders their use for intercorrelations among themselves and with other variables so questionable as to preclude attempts at analysis by the R-technique.

The analysis of the Guilford-Martin inventory scores by themselves in the search for first-order factors is of little use because of faults 1, 3, and 5. From previous factorial analyses of single items the indications are that there are 13 distinct factors involved. For the most part, each factor is strongly represented in only one score. For the *Inventory of Factors STDCR,* there are seriously biased scores due to multiple scoring of items. This is a minor feature of the *Inventory for Factors GAMIN.* In studies which include other variables in which any of these 13 factors are expected, it would be well to use the appropriate scores from these inventories as reference variables. Even then, it has been the policy of the writer not to include some combinations of these scores in the same analysis but to determine the correlation of a new factor with these scores after the analysis has been completed. Another procedure has been to break up the items scored for any one factor into two or three groups, each more homogeneous in appearance than the total list, and to include the part scores in the analysis. The multiple scoring of items is avoided in this procedure.

Analysis of Bernreuter's *Personality Inventory* and of the *Minnesota Multiphasic Personality Inventory,* with total scores as variables, is precluded by reason of faults 1, 2, and 5. Neither are these same scores helpful in connection with analyses of other scores because of their probable complexity and their unknown factorial compositions.

Applications of factor analysis to scores from the Rorschach instrument also encounter to a marked degree some of the difficulties mentioned here, as well as others that have not been mentioned. Many of the customary Rorschach scores are linearly dependent and distributions are usually irregular.

AVOIDING FAULTY STEPS IN FACTOR ANALYSIS

Ways of avoiding the faults discussed above are fairly obvious. Some of them have been mentioned in discussing the faults. It is perhaps of more value to stress good principles of "hygiene" for factor analysis than to dwell upon errors.

Requirements for effective factorial investigations have been mentioned more than once in the literature [4]. Of all the general policies that might be mentioned, the one that seems to be in need of emphasizing most is that considerable careful planning should precede an analysis. It is in the designing of the particular study and later in the interpreting of factors that the psychologist can really show his skill as a psychological investigator. He should enjoy those aspects of his investigation most. What happens between the planning and interpretation stages can be carried out by laboratory assistants and clerks. If the genuinely psychological aspects of the investigation are not conducted with thoughtfulness and care, no amount of computational activity will make up for those deficiencies.

Briefly, a factorial study should begin with a decision as to the scope of the domain to be investigated. If one does not wish to run the risk of being involved with an unwieldy list of experimental variables, he will find it wise to select a rather limited domain for a single analysis. A domain that is not likely to involve more than 15 factors or 50 experimental variables is good policy. It is not necessary to analyze for all common factors simultaneously. The structures of the factors from limited studies can be made to fit together to complete the larger picture. There is also much to be gained from repeating analyses with variations and with combinations of domains.

The initial planning should emphasize the formation of hypotheses as to what factors are likely to be found in the selected domain and as to the probable properties of such factors. There should be no hesitation to indulge in this type of activity. Perhaps some of the more rigorously inclined investigators have avoided this approach because they have seen some of their less rigorous colleagues "dream up" hypothetical traits to accept them as established fact. Explicit hypothesis formation is something of which psychologists have done too little in their planning of research. It should make for more substantial progress for the factor analyst to begin an investigation by asking "May I assume the existence of factor X?" or "Does factor Y have these properties, or these, or these?" With properly designed experimental variables, the answer from the analysis should be of the form, "Yes, you may," or "No, you may not assume the existence of factor X"; "Factor Y is more like this than it is like that." Some investigators may be afraid of the cliché "You get out of a factor analysis exactly what you put into it." The experienced analyst only wishes that he could come closer to achieving this status of omniscience and control!

Tests especially constructed for a particular study are likely to give much clearer answers to the hypotheses than are tests already available, except where there is previous knowledge of factors in those tests. It is important for each test to be as homogeneous functionally as we can make it. It is desirable to select items for internal consistency. The usual item-analysis procedures will not assure the construction of a one-factor test. The scale-analysis methods of Guttman might be helpful in achieving one-factor tests. The cumbersomeness of the procedure makes the cost rather prohibitive, however, and the end result may be a score that measures something entirely too specific. The best practical recourse is to the psychologist's skill in defining a hypothesized factor, in writing items, and in editing them. Ordinary item-analysis procedures will be of material help in assuring a large proportion of true variance in the scores.

In the selection of experimental variables, it is important to take into account all variances in already known factors. If one cannot exclude all common variances in known factors that he wants to leave out of the picture, it becomes necessary to put in the battery a good measure or two for each such factor. This not only identifies the factor but also segregates its variance so that it does not muddy the waters with respect to the rest of the factor structure.

With these general suggestions, most of which are not new, in mind, and with observance of the suggestions expressed or implied in connection with the various faults discussed in this paper, the one who would factor analyze will be on the road to an effective use of a very useful research tool.

REFERENCES

1. CARROLL, J. B. The effect of difficulty and chance success on correlations between items or between tests. *Psychometrika,* 1945, **10,** 1–19.
2. CATTELL, R. B. Psychological measurement: ipsative, normative, and interactive. *Psychol. Rev.,* 1944, **51,** 292–303.
3. DUDEK, F. J. The dependence of factorial composition of aptitude tests upon population differences among pilot trainees. *Educ. psychol. Measmt,* 1948, **8,** 613–633; 1949, **9,** 95–104.
4. GUILFORD, J. P. Creativity. *Amer. Psychol.,* 1950, **5,** 444–454.
5. GUILFORD, J. P., & LACEY, J. I. (Eds.). *Printed classification tests.* Army Air Forces Aviation Psychology Research Program Report No. 5. Washington, D.C.: Government Printing Office, 1947.
6. GUILFORD, J. P., & MICHAEL, W. B. Approaches to univocal factor scores. *Psychometrika,* 1948, **13,** 1–22.
7. MICHAEL, W. B. Factor analysis of tests and criteria: A comparative study of two AAF pilot populations. *Psychol. Monogr.,* 1949, **63** (3), Whole No. 298.
8. THURSTONE, L. L. *Multiple factor analysis.* Chicago: Univ. of Chicago Press, 1947.

Chapter 24

Factors as Theoretical Constructs

JOSEPH R. ROYCE

The relevance of the theory and methodology of factor analysis to the empirical-theoretical concerns of general psychology has not been clearly perceived. Primarily because of historical precedent and the complexity of the domain of psychology, there has been a bifurcation between what Cronbach [5] has referred to as the two sciences of psychology—the correlational approach and the experimental approach. Methodologically this split is a reflection of multivariate as opposed to bivariate problem solving. The fact that these two modes of attack need not remain divergent is evident by the extensive degree to which one multivariate approach, the analysis of variance design, has been utilized by both experimentalists and correlationists during the past two decades. This development reflects the fact that the analysis of variance methodology is essentially a link between the classical single variable design and the multivariable factor analytic design. It is a link in the sense that it is logically closer to the single variable design, involving essentially only an extension of the single variable experiment to the effect of several conditions on the same dependent variable. In both experimental designs, the investigator is working with dependent and independent variables which are known. But variance analysis is also concerned with simultaneously determining the effect of many independent variables on one dependent variable. Hence, it is a bridge to factor analysis, in the sense that it puts the stress on analyzing many variables at one time. An important difference between the single variable design and analysis of variance, on the one hand, and factor analysis, on the other, is that factor analysis is concerned with the simultaneous identification of several *unknowns*. Furthermore, factor analysis per se is *not* concerned with dependent or independent variables.

Over a decade ago the writer attempted a synthesis of the multivariate and bivariate designs in an effort to help clarify the situation [16]. The recent emergence of a new society[1] and its publications,[2] dedi-

This paper was reprinted from the *American Psychologist*, 1963, with permission of the author and the American Psychological Association.

[1] The Society of Multivariate Experimental Psychology.

[2] Plans are in progress for the publication of a *Journal of Multivariate Psychology* and a *Handbook of Multivariate Experimental Psychology.*

cated to bridging the gap between the two sciences, is strongly indicative of a forth-coming rapprochement. This paper is offered in the spirit of this rapprochement, with focus on the theoretical rather than the methodological aspects of the problem.

This paper is essentially concerned with one question: What is a factor? Factors have been defined as dimensions, determinants, functional unities, parameters, and taxonomic categories. In terms of their theoretical significance they have been referred to as convenient classificatory conceptualizations [2], as real [24], and as artifactors [14]. Factors have also been described as general, group, specific, and bipolar. Factor analysis has been both overplayed and underplayed. It has been overplayed in the sense that it has been applied to inappropriate problems, and it has also been misapplied to appropriate problems. It has been underplayed in the sense that certain critics have claimed it has nothing to contribute to the advancement of psychology.

Without getting bogged down in the many methodological problems which require solution (e.g., the problem of a unique mathematical solution in arriving at simple structure, the problem of the unknown communalities, the problem of when to stop factoring, the necessity for determining standard errors for factor loadings, etc.), and without getting into the question of how to interpret the factors which empirically emerge (all of the above are soluble in principle, and present procedures work in practice, in spite of methodological shortcomings), let us move into the more important issues of contemporary theoretical psychology as they relate to the factors of factor analysis. Let us enter into this with the understanding that we are thinking of a factor as a determinant of covariation, which means that we have made the assumption that factor analysis is capable of uncovering invariant factors, factors which are demonstrably repeatable despite variations in initial factoring, populations sampled, measurements, and, in some cases, even species. In short, by a factor we shall mean a true variable, a process or determinant which accounts for covariation in a specified domain of observation.

THEORETICAL CONCEPTUALIZING IN CONTEMPORARY PSYCHOLOGY

The contemporary paradigm for theoretical analysis is Woodworth's [27] S-O-R (stimulus-organism-response) extension of the behavioristic S-R formulation. Although neobehaviorists such as Skinner [19, 20] continue to focus on S-R relationships, other investigators focus on S, O, R, S-O, O-R, and S-O-R combinations. Spence [21, 22], for example, speaks of S-S laws, R-R laws, and S-R laws, and Brunswik [4] outlines the S-O conceptual focus of Gestalt psychology and psychophysics, among others. Within this framework, the variable to be observed is traditionally referred to as the dependent variable, and the variable which is experimentally manipulated is referred to as the independent variable. While the dependent variable is usually an R variable, and the independent variable is usually an S variable, it is important to note that any class of variable (i.e., S, O, or R) can either be dependent or independent, depending on the purpose of the investigator.

Theorizing within the scientific enterprise is fraught with semantic confusion and epistemological argument concerning the knowledge giving qualities of empiricism and rationalism. Logical positivism and operationism, originating out of problems which arose in the physical sciences, were bound to have an important impact on the theoretical language of psychology. Thus, an important element in the matrix of contemporary theoretical psychology is the requirement that psychological concepts be operationally defined [3], and further, that such concepts be closely tied to observables [23].

A perennial dimension of discourse within scientific theory is that of description-explanation. The question is properly raised concerning the extent to which a given theoretical concept is merely descriptive or more pervasively explanatory. In general, empiricists tend to offer descriptive concepts which stay close to the data, whereas rationalists tend to go beyond the data in search of all-encompassing explanatory concepts. This is a continual debate in all the sciences, including contemporary psychology. It is perhaps most obvious in the contrast between the descriptive concepts of Skinner [20] and the (over?-) reaching for explanatory concepts which is evident in psychoanalysis [12].

The impulse to involve explanatory concepts lies behind the efforts of all theorists, including those with a behavioristic orientation. The behaviorist is typically operationistic, however. Thus, two impulses, the operational on the one hand and the explanatory on the other, tend to run counter to one another, thereby setting up an apparently unresolvable tension. Tolman [25] and Hull [8] tried to work their way out of this impasse by introducing the intervening variable, an operationally defined concept which is not necessarily directly observable, but which is anchored at either the S input or the R output of the S-O-R sequence.

MacCorquodale and Meehl [10] indicated that some of these inferred concepts seemed to have more surplus meaning than others, and that it would be necessary to make a distinction between such theoretical constructs. They proposed that we refer to the surplus meaning concepts as hypothetical constructs, and that we restrict the usage of the term intervening variables for those terms which lie closer to the empirical data. Since these inferred constructs lie essentially between S and R (i.e., within O) in the S-O-R paradigm, Rozeboom [18] has suggested that we refer to all such constructs, whether hypothetical or intervening, as mediation variables.

THEORETICAL CHARACTERISTICS OF FACTORS

How are factors embedded within the matrix of contemporary theoretical psychology? My exposition of this begins with Margenau's [11] thinking (see Figure 24–1) on the C plane and the P plane, and Feigl's [7, pp. 17–22] concept of the nomological net. Margenau refers to the empirical component of science as the P or perceptual plane and the theoretical component as the C plane. The C plane structure of science must, at more than one point, be anchored, or epistemically correlated [13], with the P plane. According to some theorists those concepts which are closest to the data, indicated in parallel lines in Figure 24–1, are the most operational. Those which are farther removed are less operational. Margenau makes the point that mature scientific theory cannot exist without such nonoperational concepts. He also makes it clear that mature theory implies a very

Figure 24–1 *Schematic diagram showing the theoretical structure of a highly formalized science. (The circles are constructs, labeled C. The lightface lines represent formal connections, and the boldface lines show the linkage of constructs to observable data in the P plane. All C constructs are multiply connected, i.e., they involve at least two arms, either connecting with other constructs or with observables in the P plane. C' and C'' constructs suffer from formal weakness, reflecting only one connection. C' is a peninsular construct—or no connection. C'' is an insular construct—with the remaining constructs in the conceptual field. Adapted from Margenau [11, Chaps. 5 and 6].)*

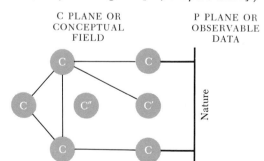

C PLANE OR CONCEPTUAL FIELD

P PLANE OR OBSERVABLE DATA

tight logical network (either verbally or mathematically, preferably mathematically); without this formal network it would be impossible to maintain the necessary empirical-logical links. It is only because of its powerful deductive mathematics that physics can sometimes get by with minimal points of empirical contact. Unfortunately the situation in less well-developed sciences, such as psychology and the social sciences, is not as tightly knit as in physics. In the nonphysical sciences there are a large number of constructs of the C′ and C″ type, that is, constructs which show relatively few formal connections to other constructs in the nomological net. The situation in these fields is more accurately depicted in Figure 24–2. This figure is the same as Figure 24–1 except for the preponderance of C′ and C″ constructs and the dotted connecting lines. The C′ constructs on the right are connected to the P plane, but none of them has a solid line connection to other constructs in the nomological net. The C″ constructs on the left are multiply (i.e., two or more arms) connected in the C plane, but none of them (in and of themselves) has a firm formal linkage to the P plane. Such an isolated set of theoretical constructs is described by Margenau as an island universe, consistent in itself but not empirically verifiable. Unless a convincing set of formal connections can be found which is capable of eventually making sufficient contact with the P plane, such nomological nets or theoretical structures must be cast aside as useless fictions. The dotted lines in Figure 24–2 indicate that the connections between constructs in the nonphysical sciences are verbal and relatively loose, or even nonexistent. This formal weakness results in varying degrees of separation between the observables of empirical data, on the one hand, and the inferred constructs of a theoretical structure, on the other hand. This lack of a sufficient number of convincing formal multiple connections in the C plane, combined with weakness of epistemic correlation (between the theoretical or rational and the observable or empirical, i.e., the preponderance of C′ constructs to the right of Figure 24–2 rather than more C constructs), suggests that less well-developed sciences, such as psychology, need to stay closer to the P plane until they can provide tight formal nets in the C plane. This point is crucially brought out by an analysis of Constructs C_1 and C_2 in Figure 24–2. Construct C_1 provides the key to the possibility of bringing the island universe to the left of it into scientific reality because of its multiple connections to the P plane on the right, and its linkage to the C″ set of constructs via Construct C_2 on the left. A shift of one or two of the remaining center connections from dotted line to solid line (i.e., the case of C_3, or either of the C′ constructs) would represent a significant increase in the probability of accepting the total theoretical structure, and obviously the greater the number of multiple connections on the right side of the C plane, the more we would be able to confirm and extend the nomological net. Finally, if all the dotted line connections were changed to solid line connections the C″ constructs would all become C constructs, and we should have

Figure 24–2   *Illustration of a typical structure in the social and behavioral sciences. (Adapted from Torgerson [26, p. 5]; Margenau [11, Chaps. 5 and 6].)*

C PLANE   P PLANE

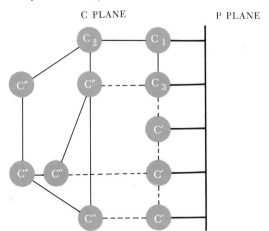

a nomological net comparable to that depicted in Figure 24–1.

Where do factors fit in the nomological net? In terms of the S-O-R paradigm, factors emerge inductively out of a situation involving a standard stimulus input with a variable (covariation) response output. In other words, factors are O variables intermediate between S and R variables. We infer functional unities which are determinants of the covarying response pattern. These mediating variables may be either intervening variables or hypothetical constructs, depending on their depth of penetration into the nomological net.

A diagram similar to Figure 24–1 is useful as a description of the relationships between first-order and higher-order factors. It is indicated here as Figure 24–3. First-order factors, such as the Primary Mental Abilities, emerge from an analysis of the raw data (i.e., the R matrix). In general, second-order factors emerge from an analysis of the first-order factors; third-order factors emerge from an analysis of the second-order factors; etc. We must stipulate the qualification "in general," however, because it is occasionally possible for a higher-order factor to emerge from a first-order analysis.[3] If we now superimpose Figure 24–3 on Figure 24–1 we have Figure 24–4, which represents an analysis of factors in terms of the Margenau-Feigl nomological net. From Figure 24–4 it is obvious that most first-order factors, which lie closest to the data, are intervening variables. Higher-order factors, which are based on the first- or second-order constructs, are hypothetical constructs. Note that Factor X is purposely placed between the first- and second-order. This factor represents the occasional higher-order factor

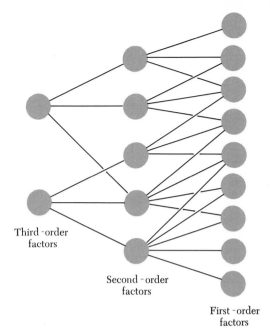

Third-order factors

Second-order factors

First-order factors

Figure 24–3   *Diagram showing the relationships between first-order and higher-order factors.*

which can be identified from the primary data.

It is also important to note that all links between consructs are solid line links, indicating the tight formal net required for concepts which are relatively far removed

Figure 24–4   *Superimposition of Figure 24–3 on Figure 24–1 in order to show the location of factors in the nomological net.*

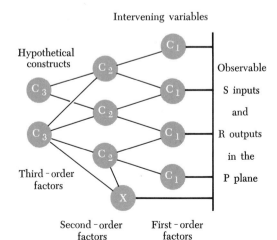

C PLANE   P PLANE

Intervening variables

Hypothetical constructs

Third-order factors

Second-order factors   First-order factors

Observable

S inputs

and

R outputs

in the

P plane

---

[3] General factors, such as reasoning, could emerge from a first-order analysis of a battery of intelligence tests, or it might emerge from a second-order analysis of factors which share this same reasoning factor. Thurstone felt that Spearman's g was one of several general factors which would probably emerge in the second-order domain. It now begins to look as if the Spearman g kind of factor will likely occur at the third-order or higher level.

from the raw data. This point raises the issue of factors as descriptive versus explanatory concepts. It would seem obvious that this continuum would run from right to left in Figure 24-4, with the descriptive factors at the P plane end of the diagram, and the more explanatory factors lying deeper and deeper within the nomological net. The presumption is that a relatively few hypothetical constructs at the third- or fourth-order level would eventually acount for those concepts which lie to the right of it. While Figure 24-4 represents a formally tight network of the type required for mathematico-deductive theorizing it must be pointed out that the factorial theoretical structure is accomplished via the logic of matrix algebra rather than by the usual mathematical equations. In short, I am saying that this nomological net reflects a tight structure of concepts, each of which is algebraically (i.e., via matrix algebra) related to the others, but that subsequent complex equations defining the functional relationships between said concepts remain to be worked out. In other words, at this juncture we must remind ourselves that factor analysis is a method for identifying important variables, but it does not, in and of itself, provide rational equations for linking said concepts.

This point should provide clarification for the statement that factor analysis per se does not deal with dependent and independent variables. Rather, it simply identifies those variables which are likely to be useful in evolving a theoretical scheme—in other words, it deals with neutral or what might be termed nondependent variables. Such neutral variables can subsequently be studied in the usual classical single variable manner in an attempt to determine empirical and rational equations. In other words, factors can subsequently serve as either dependent or independent variables. In the former case we are dealing with the S-O portion of the S-O-R paradigm where the factors within O are dependent upon, or are a function of, the stimulus conditions. An example might be one of the memory

factors (O factor) as a function of meaningfulness of the material to be learned (S input). In the second case we are dealing with the O-R portion of the S-O-R paradigm where the factors within O serve as predictors or independent variables in terms of a specified response. An example would be memory (O factor) as a predictor of pilot success (R output). The question of whether the memory factor is a dependent or independent variable is clearly a function of the purpose of the investigation.

The final issue to be discussed revolves around the question of the extent to which factors are operationally defined. I suggest that they are *all* operationally defined, because in every case they emerge inductively as a function of several specifiable variables. The operations which are implied for a second- or third-order factor are as clearly specifiable as are those for first-order factors. The complication comes out of the fact that higher-order factors are further removed from the original observations. In other words, the higher-order operations are clear, but the empirical basis for higher-order factors is weaker. But empirical weakness is the price we pay for evolving those higher-order hypothetical constructs which take on stronger explanatory power. As long as such concepts are logically linked to lower-order concepts, which are in turn empirically anchored to the P plane, we can fruitfully sacrifice the loss of empiricism in higher-order constructs. The history of science demonstrates that such developments are, in fact, in the natural course of events as a science matures, and we should, therefore, encourage rather than discourage the identification of such tightly linked hypothetical constructs.

Since the focal point of factors of behavior is within the organism (in the S-O-R paradigm), and since those hypothetical constructs which penetrate deep within the nomological net carry the potential of broad explanatory powers, and since the deepest portion of the theoretical structure of organismic variables obviously carries us inside the skin of the organism, the writer sees the theoretical-experimental extension of factor analysis into the domain of comparative-physiological psychology as being of the greatest importance for the advancement of factor analysis, beyond the level of mathematical elegance, into the realm of fruitful knowledge concerning the complex, multivariate mechanisms of behavior [15, 17].[4]

SUMMARY AND CONCLUSIONS

There has been a bivariate-multivariate methodological bifurcation within psychology which shows signs of being alleviated. Now that the methodological issue shows promise of being resolved, it is important

[4] A further work by the author, "Factorial Studies in Comparative-Physiological Psychology," is in preparation.

Since the origins of factor analysis are historically rooted in psychometric theory, and since its substantive contributions are best known in intelligence and aptitude testing, it is desirable that we point explicitly to certain recent contributions in psychometric theory which are consistent with the exposition presented here. The writer is thinking of the concept of construct validity, first expressed by the APA Committee on Psychological Tests [1], and later developed more fully by Cronbach and Meehl [6], and Loevinger [9]. This concept was proposed as one of four kinds of validity, the other three being content, predictive, and concurrent validities. In the APA [1] publication, construct validity is defined as "investigating what psychological qualities a test measures, i.e., by demonstrating that certain explanatory constructs account to some degree for performance on the test. . . . Essentially, in studies of construct validity we are validating the theory underlying the test" [p. 14]. Similarly, Cronbach and Meehl [6] state that construct validity implies a "postulated attribute of people, assumed to be reflected in test performance" [p. 282]. Thus, it would appear that theoretical constructs can manifest themselves in test data, which are standardized samples of behavior, as well as in the data of the laboratory, the clinic, and the field. The suggestion here is that factorial validity is one kind of construct validity, since such internal consistency reveals what a given test measures.

Whether we are interested in factor analysis in such experimental domains as comparative-physiological psychology, perception, or learning, or in the more traditional psychometric domains, the point is that factors are concerned with the identification of theoretical constructs, inferred functional unities, which are the determinants of the observed matrix of covariation.

that we look at the corresponding bifurcation which remains in terms of theroetical structure.

The essential question this paper seeks to answer is: What is a factor? The answer to this question must relate itself to contemporary issues within theoretical psychology. The answer which emerges is cast in terms of Margenau's C and P planes and Feigl's nomological net. A factor is seen as a variable, process, or determinant which accounts for covariation in a specified domain of observation. Within the standard paradigm of S-O-R, the conceptual focus of factor analysis is on O variables. When the postfactorial focus is on S-O relationships, factors can best be seen as dependent variables. When the postfactorial focus is on O-R relationships, factors can best be seen as predictors or independent variables. Thus, factors are seen as variables which mediate between S inputs and R outputs. This means they can be seen as either intervening variables or hypothetical constructs, depending on how deeply they penetrate the nomological net.

First-order factors, being close to the observable data, are seen as intervening, descriptive variables. They do an excellent job of summarizing masses of confusedly interrelated observations. Higher-order factors, which are farther from the data, are seen as hypothetical constructs. They carry the potential of providing broad and penetrating explanations on the basis of a relatively small number of constructs.

Factors, as such, do not provide the empirical and rational equations which link theoretical constructs. Factor analysis can only identify those constructs which can eventually be related by mathematical equations. All factors are operationally defined, however, in spite of the fact that higher-order factors become empirically weaker as they move away from the P plane. The movement away from empirical anchorage toward rational confirmation is to be expected, however, as theoretical structure becomes more capable of encompassing broader domains of knowledge.

REFERENCES

1. AMERICAN PSYCHOLOGICAL ASSOCIATION. Technical recommendations for psychological tests and diagnostic techniques. *Psychol. Bull. monogr. Suppl.*, 1954, 51 (2, Part 2).

2. ANASTASI, ANNE. Faculties versus factors: A reply to Professor Thurstone. *Psychol. Bull.*, 1938, 35, 391–395.

3. BORING, E. G., BRIDGMAN, P. W., FEIGL, H., ISRAEL, H., PRATT, C. C., & SKINNER, B. F. Symposium on operationalism. *Psychol. Rev.*, 1945, 52, 241–294.

4. BRUNSWIK, E. The conceptual focus of some psychological systems. *J. unified Sci.*, 1939, 8, 36–50.

5. CRONBACH, L. The two disciplines of scientific psychology. *Amer. Psychologist*, 1957, 12, 671–684.

6. CRONBACH, L., & MEEHL, P. E. Construct validity in psychological tests. *Psychol. Bull.*, 1955, 52, 281–302.

7. FEIGL, H., & SCRIVEN, M. (Eds.) *The foundations of science and the concepts of psychology and psychoanalysis.* Minneapolis: Univer. Minnesota Press, 1956.

8. HULL, C. L. *Principles of behavior.* New York: Appleton-Century, 1943.

9. LOEVINGER, JANE. Objective tests as instruments of psychological theory. *Psychol. Rep.*, 1957, 3, 635–694. (Monogr. Suppl. No. 9.)

10. MacCORQUODALE, K., & MEEHL, P. E. On the distinction between hypothetical constructs and intervening variables. *Psychol. Rev.*, 1948, 55, 95–109.

11. MARGENAU, H. *The nature of physical reality.* New York: McGraw-Hill, 1950.

12. MUNROE, RUTH L. *Schools of psychoanalytic thought.* New York: Dryden Press, 1955.

13. NORTHROP, F. S. C. *The logic of the sciences and the humanities.* New York: Macmillan, 1947.

14. ROBERTS, A. W. H. Artifactor-analysis: Some theoretical background and practical demonstrations. *J. Nat. Inst. Personnel Res., Johannesburg*, 1959, 7, 168–188.

15. ROYCE, J. R. The factorial analysis of animal behavior. *Psychol. Bull.*, 1950, 47, 235–239.

16. ROYCE, J. R. A synthesis of experimental designs in program research. *J. gen. Psychol.*, 1950, 43, 295–303.

17. ROYCE, J. R. Factor theory and genetics. *Educ. psychol. Measmt*, 1957, 17, 361–376.

18. ROZEBOOM, W. W. Mediation variables in scientific theory. *Psychol. Rev.*, 1956, 63, 249–264.

19. SKINNER, B. F. *The behavior of organisms: An experimental analysis.* New York: Appleton-Century, 1938.

20. SKINNER, B. F. Are theories of learning necessary? *Psychol. Rev.*, 1950, 57, 193–216.

21. SPENCE, K. W. The nature of theory construction in contemporary psychology. *Psychol. Rev.*, 1944, 51, 47–68.

22. SPENCE, K. W. Theoretical interpretations of learning. In S. S. Stevens (Ed.), *Handbook of experimental psychology.* New York: Wiley, 1951.

23. STEVENS, S. S. Psychology and the science of science. *Psychol. Bull.*, 1939, 36, 221–263.

24. THURSTONE, L. L. *Multiple-factor analysis.* Chicago: Univer. Chicago Press, 1947.

25. TOLMAN, E. C. *Purposive behavior in animals and men.* New York: Century, 1932.

26. TORGERSON, W. S. *Theory and methods of scaling.* New York: Wiley, 1958.

27. WOODWORTH, R. S., & SCHLOSBERG, H. *Experimental psychology.* (Rev. ed.) New York: Holt, 1954.

4 ~

ASSESSMENT
FOR SELECTION

Oone of the most important applications of psychological testing is in personnel selection, whether in school and college, the military, government, or industry. A considerable body of knowledge has developed around the problems of selection, including such diverse topics as decision making, the uses and abuses of test scores, and methods for detecting faking.

In the first selection of Part 4, C. Northcote Parkinson trenchantly but humorously describes some selection procedures in which decisions do not depend upon test scores. It is tempting to dismiss Parkinson's analysis as pure humor and entertainment, but the editors believe that important truths lurk here.

In Chapter 26, J. P. Guilford distills from his World War II experience with the United States Army Air Force selection program—one of the largest selection problems ever faced—many important observations about psychological testing, some of which question traditional dogmas of selection.

Chapter 27 presents a model selection study in which Newman, Howell, and Cliff demonstrate how a work sample may be incorporated into a selection battery as an intermediate criterion. Assessment techniques are then evaluated in terms of their concurrent validity, as evidenced by their correlation with the work sample. Such a procedure permits realistic estimation of validity over the entire range of applicants, rather than over the more restricted range of successful applicants.

In Chapter 28, Norman Frederiksen points out that we should evaluate the criterion measures in selection studies as well as the predictors to ensure that the ultimate selection goals are being served. Validity studies may produce misleading results if the criterion measure of success is inadequate and only partially captures the intrinsic quality of the desired objectives.

In Chapter 29, David R. Saunders explicates the nature of moderator variables. These are variables that are not themselves related to a criterion but that affect the magnitude of the relation between some other variable and the criterion. Readers who are interested in surveying moderator effects in a variety of selection situations are referred to a series of articles by Ghiselli[1] on this topic.

Lee Sechrest, in a paper on incremental validity (Chapter 30), develops the idea that for purposes of practical prediction a significant relationship is not enough. In addition, questions of cost and of improvement over traditional procedures must be evaluated. In these observations Sechrest was anticipated by others, including Meehl[2] (who as far as we know first proposed the term "incremental validity").

In Chapter 31, Edward E. Cureton introduces an element of mystery in portraying one type of bad test practice—the misapplication and improper evaluation of the results of empirical item selection—that leads him to exclaim, "Validity, Reliability, and Baloney."

The problem of faking has plagued those who have attempted to apply personality-measuring devices to situations like selection, in which the assessee might be rewarded for creating an unrealistically favorable impression. Warren T. Norman ingeniously demonstrates in Chapter 32 how variance due to faking may be markedly reduced. Through application of analytic procedures on item statistics derived from questionnaires given under normal and "fake good" experimental sets, he shows that it is possible to build personality scales that are not especially distorted by faking, at least for the criterion chosen.

In a far-reaching analysis of prediction, Meehl and Rosen (Chapter 33) establish the importance of taking into account known probabilities of particular outcomes. The authors provide a mathematical basis for understanding many empirical facts of prediction, such as the observation that rare events, like suicide, are extremely difficult to predict with accuracy exceeding chance. They show how predictive success is intimately associated with base rates for various alternatives, as well as with validity. A strong implication to be drawn from the Meehl and Rosen thesis is that in some cases predictive validity may not have any specific referent apart from antecedent probability. This article should be studied by all who aspire to predict.

---

[1] Ghiselli, E. E. The prediction of predictability. *Educ. Psychol. Measmt*, 1960, **10**, 3–8.

[2] Meehl, P. E. Some ruminations on the validation of clinical procedures. *Canad. J. Psychol.*, 1959, **13**, 102–134.

Chapter 25

The Short List or
Principles of Selection

C. NORTHCOTE PARKINSON

A problem constantly before the modern administration, whether in government or business, is that of personnel selection. The inexorable working of Parkinson's Law ensures that appointments have constantly to be made and the question is always how to choose the right candidate from all who present themselves. In ascertaining the principles upon which the choice should be made, we may properly consider, under separate heads, the methods used in the past and the methods used at the present day.

Past methods, not entirely disused, fall into two main categories, the British and the Chinese. Both deserve careful consideration, if only for the reason that they were obviously more successful than any method now considered fashionable. The British method (old pattern) depended upon an interview in which the candidate had to establish his identity. He would be confronted by elderly gentlemen seated round a mahogany table who would presently ask him his name. Let us suppose that

This article is reprinted from *Parkinson's Law*, 1957, with the permission of Houghton Mifflin Company and John Murray Ltd.

the candidate replied, "John Seymour." One of the gentlemen would then say, "Any relation of the Duke of Somerset?" To this the candidate would say, quite possibly, "No, sir." Then another gentleman would say, "Perhaps you are related, in that case, to the Bishop of Watminster?" If he said "No, sir" again, a third would ask in despair, "To whom then are you related?" In the event of the candidate's saying, "Well, my father is a fishmonger in Cheapside," the interview was virtually over. The members of the Board would exchange significant glances, one would press a bell and another tell the footman, "Throw this person out." One name could be crossed off the list without further discussion. Supposing the next candidate was Henry Molyneux and a nephew of the Earl of Sefton, his chances remained fair up to the moment when George Howard arrived and proved to be a grandson of the Duke of Norfolk. The Board encountered no serious difficulty until they had to compare the claims of the third son of a baronet with the second but illegitimate son of a viscount. Even then they could refer to a Book of Precedence.

329

So their choice was made and often with the best results.

The Admiralty version of this British method (old pattern) was different only in its more restricted scope. The Board of Admirals were unimpressed by titled relatives as such. What they sought to establish was a service connection. The ideal candidate would reply to the second question, "Yes, Admiral Parker is my uncle. My father is Captain Foley, my grandfather Commodore Foley. My mother's father was Admiral Hardy. Commander Hardy is my uncle. My eldest brother is a Lieutenant in the Royal Marines, my next brother is a cadet at Dartmouth and my younger brother wears a sailor suit." "Ah!" the senior Admiral would say. "And what made you think of joining the Navy?" The answer to this question, however, would scarcely matter, the clerk present having already noted the candidate as acceptable. Given a choice between two candidates, both equally acceptable by birth, a member of the Board would ask suddenly, "What was the number of the taxi you came in?" The candidate who said "I came by bus" was then thrown out. The candidate who said, truthfully, "I don't know," was rejected, and the candidate who said "Number 2351" (lying) was promptly admitted to the service as a boy with initiative. This method often produced excellent results.

The British method (new pattern) was evolved in the late nineteenth century as something more suitable for a democratic country. The Selection Committee would ask briskly, "What school were you at?" and would be told Harrow, Haileybury, or, Rugby, as the case might be. "What games do you play?" would be the next and invariable question. A promising candidate would reply, "I have played tennis for England, cricket for Yorkshire, rugby for the Harlequins, and fives for Winchester." The next question would then be "Do you play polo?"—just to prevent the candidate's thinking too highly of himself. Even without playing polo, however, he was evidently worth serious consideration. Little time, by contrast, was wasted on the man who admitted to having been educated at Wiggleworth. "Where?" the chairman would ask in astonishment, and "Where's that?" after the name had been repeated. "Oh, in *Lancashire!*" he would say at last. Just for a matter of form, some member might ask, "What games do you play?" But the reply "Table tennis for Wigan, cycling for Blackpool, and snooker for Wiggleworth" would finally delete his name from the list. There might even be some muttered comment upon people who deliberately wasted the committee's time. Here again was a method which produced good results.

The Chinese method (old pattern) was at one time so extensively copied by other nations that few people realize its Chinese origin. This is the method of Competitive Written Examination. In China under the Ming Dynasty the more promising students used to sit for the provincial examination, held every third year. It lasted three sessions of three days each. During the first session the candidate wrote three essays and composed a poem of eight couplets. During the second session he wrote five essays on a classical theme. During the third, he wrote five essays on the art of government. The successful candidates (perhaps two per cent) then sat for their final examination at the imperial capital. It lasted only one session, the candidate writing one essay on a current political problem. Of those who were successful the majority were admitted to the civil service, the man with the highest marks being destined for the highest office. The system worked fairly well.

The Chinese system was studied by Europeans between 1815 and 1830 and adopted by the English East India Company in 1832. The effectiveness of this method was investigated by a committee in 1854, with Macaulay as chairman. The result was that the system of competitive examination was introduced into the British Civil Service in 1855. An essential feature of the Chinese examinations had been their literary character. The test was in a knowledge of the classics, in an ability to write elegantly (both prose and verse) and in the stamina necessary to complete the course. All these features were faithfully incorporated in the Trevelyan-Northcote Report, and thereafter in the system it did so much to create. It was assumed that classical learning and literary ability would fit any candidate for any administrative post. It was assumed (no doubt rightly) that a scientific education would fit a candidate for nothing—except, possibly, science. It was known, finally, that it is virtually impossible to find an order of merit among people who have been examined in different subjects. Since it is impracticable to decide whether one man is better in geology than another man in physics, it is at least convenient to be able to rule them both out as useless. When all candidates alike have to write Greek or Latin verse, it is relatively easy to decide which verse is the best. Men thus selected on their classical performance were then sent forth to govern India. Those with lower marks were retained to govern England. Those with still lower marks were rejected altogether or sent to the colonies. While it would be totally wrong to describe this system as a failure, no one could claim for it the success that had attended the systems hitherto in use. There was no guarantee, to begin with, that the man with the highest marks might not turn out to be off his head; as was sometimes found to be the case. Then again the writing of Greek verse might prove to be the sole accomplishment that some candidates had or would ever have. On occasion, a successful applicant may even have been impersonated at the examination by someone else, subsequently proving unable to write Greek verse when the occasion arose. Selection by competitive examination was never therefore more than a moderate success.

Whatever the faults, however, of the competitive written examination, it certainly produced better results than any method that has been attempted since. Modern methods center upon the intelligence test and the psychological interview. The defect in the intelligence test is that high marks are gained by those who subsequently prove to be practically illiterate. So much time has been spent in studying the art of being tested that the candidate

has rarely had time for anything else. The psychological interview has developed today into what is known as ordeal by house party. The candidates spend a pleasant weekend under expert observation. As one of them trips over the doormat and says "Bother!" examiners lurking in the background whip out their notebooks and jot down, "Poor physical coordination" and "Lacks self-control." There is no need to describe this method in detail, but its results are all about us and are obviously deplorable. The persons who satisfy this type of examiner are usually of a cautious and suspicious temperament, pedantic and smug, saying little and doing nothing. It is quite common, when appointments are made by this method, for one man to be chosen from five hundred applicants, only to be sacked a few weeks later as useless even beyond the standards of his department. Of the various methods of selection so far tried, the latest is unquestionably the worst.

What method should be used in the future? A clue to a possible line of investigation is to be found in one little-publicized aspect of contemporary selective technique. So rarely does the occasion arise for appointing a Chinese translator to the Foreign Office or State Department that the method

Used by permission of Robert C. Osborn.

used is little known. The post is advertised and the applications go, let us suppose, to a committee of five. Three are civil servants and two are Chinese scholars of great eminence. Heaped on the table before this committee are 483 forms of application, with testimonials attached. All the applicants are Chinese and all without exception have a first degree from Peking or Amoy and a Doctorate of Philosophy from Cornell or Johns Hopkins. The majority of the candidates have at one time held ministerial office in Formosa. Some have attached their photographs. Others have (perhaps wisely) refrained from doing so. The chairman turns to the leading Chinese expert and says, "Perhaps Dr. Wu can tell us which of these candidates should be put on the short list." Dr. Wu smiles enigmatically and points to the heap. "None of them any good," he says briefly. "But how—I mean, why not?" asks the chairman, surprised. "Because no good scholar would ever apply. He would fear to lose face if he were not chosen." "So what do we do now?" asks the chairman. "I think," says Dr. Wu, "we might persuade Dr. Lim to take this post. What do you think, Dr. Lee?" "Yes, I think he might," says Lee, "but we couldn't approach him ourselves of course. We could ask Dr. Tan whether he thinks Dr. Lim would be interested." "I don't know Dr. Tan," says Wu, "but I know his friend Dr. Wong." By then the chairman is too muddled to know who is to be approached by whom. But the great thing is that all the applications are thrown into the wastepaper basket, only one candidate being considered, and he a man who did not apply.

We do not advise the universal adoption of the modern Chinese method but we draw from it the useful conclusion that the failure of other methods is mainly due to there being too many candidates. There are, admittedly, some initial steps by which the total may be reduced. The formula "Reject everyone over 50 or under 20 plus everyone called Murphy" is now universally used, and its application will somewhat reduce the list. The names remaining will still,

however, be too numerous. To choose between three hundred people, all well qualified and highly recommended, is not really possible. We are driven therefore to conclude that the mistake lies in the original advertisement. It has attracted too many applications. The disadvantage of this is so little realized that people devise advertisements in terms which will inevitably attract thousands. A post of responsibility is announced as vacant, the previous occupant being now in the Senate or the House of Lords. The salary is large, the pension generous, the duties nominal, the privileges immense, the perquisites valuable, free residence provided with official car and unlimited facilities for travel. Candidates should apply, promptly but carefully, enclosing copies (not originals) of not more than three recent testimonials. What is the result? A deluge of applications, many from lunatics and as many again from retired army majors with a gift (as they always claim) for handling men. There is nothing to do except burn the lot and start thinking all over again. It would have saved time and trouble to do some thinking in the first place.

Only a little thought is needed to convince us that the perfect advertisement would attract only one reply and that from the right man. Let us begin with an extreme example.

Wanted—Acrobat capable of crossing a slack wire 200 feet above raging furnace. Twice nightly, three times on Saturday. Salary offered £25 (or $70 U.S.) per week. No pension and no compensation in the event of injury. Apply in person at Wildcat Circus between the hours of 9 A.M. and 10 A.M.

The wording of this may not be perfect but the *aim* should be so to balance the inducement in salary against the possible risks involved that only a single applicant will appear. It is needless to ask for details of qualifications and experience. No one unskilled on the slack wire would find the offer attractive. It is needless to insist that candidates should be physically fit, sober, and free from fits of dizziness. They know that. It is just as needless to stipulate that those nervous of heights need not apply. They won't. The skill of the advertiser consists in adjusting the salary to the danger. An offer of £1000 (or $3000 U.S.) per week might produce a dozen applicants. An offer of £15 (or $35 U.S.) might produce none. Somewhere between those two figures lies the exact sum to specify, the minimum figure to attract anyone actually capable of doing the job. If there is more than one applicant, the figure has been placed a trifle too high.

Let us now take, for comparison, a less extreme example.

Wanted—An archaeologist with high academic qualifications willing to spend fifteen years in excavating the Inca tombs at Helsdump on the Alligator River. Knighthood or equivalent honor guaranteed. Pension payable but never yet claimed. Salary of £2000 (or $6000 U.S.) per year. Apply in triplicate to the Director of the Grubbenburow Institute, Sickdale, Ill., U.S.A.

Here the advantages and drawbacks are neatly balanced. There is no need to insist that candidates must be patient, tough, intrepid, and single. The terms of the advertisement have eliminated all who are not. It is unnecessary to require that candidates must be mad on excavating tombs. Mad is just what they will certainly be. Having thus reduced the possible applicants to a maximum of about three, the terms of the advertisement place the salary just too low to attract two of them and the promised honor *just* high enough to interest the third. We may suppose that, in this case, the offer of a K.C.M.G. would have produced two applications, the offer of an O.B.E., none. The result is a single candidate. He is off his head but that does not matter. He is the man we want.

It may be thought that the world offers comparatively few opportunities to appoint slack-wire acrobats and tomb excavators, and that the problem is more often to find candidates for less exotic appointments.

This is true, but the same principles can be applied. Their application demands, however—as is evident—a greater degree of skill. Let us suppose that the post to be filled is that of Prime Minister. The modern tendency is to trust in various methods of election, with results that are almost invariably disastrous. Were we to turn, instead, to the fairy stories we learned in childhood, we should realize that at the period to which these stories relate far more satisfactory methods were in use. When the king had to choose a man to marry his eldest or only daughter and so inherit the kingdom, he normally planned some obstacle course from which only the right candidate would emerge with credit; and from which indeed (in many instances) only the right candidate would emerge at all. For imposing such a test the kings of that rather vaguely defined period were well provided with both personnel and equipment. Their establishment included magicians, demons, fairies, vampires, werewolves, giants, and dwarfs. Their territories were supplied with magic mountains, rivers of fire, hidden treasures, and enchanted forests. It might be urged that modern governments are in this respect less fortunate. This, however, is by no means certain. An administrator able to command the services of psychologists, psychiatrists, alienists, statisticians, and efficiency experts is not perhaps in a worse (or better) position than one relying upon hideous crones and fairy godmothers. An administration equipped with movie cameras, television apparatus, radio networks, and X-ray machines would not appear to be in a worse (or better) position than one employing magic wands, crystal balls, wishing wells, and cloaks of invisibility. Their means of assessment would seem, at any rate, to be strictly comparable. All that is required is to translate the technique of the fairy story into a form applicable to the modern world. In this, as we shall see, there is no essential difficulty.

The first step in the process is to decide on the qualities a Prime Minister ought to have. These need not be the same in all circumstances, but they need to be listed and agreed upon. Let us suppose that the qualities deemed essential are (1) Energy, (2) Courage, (3) Patriotism, (4) Experience, (5) Popularity, and (6) Eloquence. Now, it will be observed that all these are general qualities which all possible applicants would believe themselves to possess. The field could readily, of course, be narrowed by stipulating (4) Experience *of lion-taming*, or (6) Eloquence *in Mandarin*. But that is not the way in which we want to narrow the field. We do not want to stipulate a quality in a special form; rather, each quality in an exceptional degree. In other words, the successful candidate must be the most energetic, courageous, patriotic, experienced, popular, and eloquent man in the country. Only one man can answer to that description and his is the only application we want. The terms of the appointment must thus be phrased so as to exclude everyone else. We should therefore word the advertisement in some such way as follows:

Wanted—Prime Minister of Ruritania. Hours of work: 4 A.M. to 11:59 P.M. Candidates must be prepared to fight three rounds with the current heavyweight champion (regulation gloves to be worn). Candidates will die for their country, by painless means, on reaching the age of retirement (65). They will have to pass an examination in parliamentary procedure and will be liquidated should they fail to obtain 95% marks. They will also be liquidated if they fail to gain 75% votes in a popularity poll held under the Gallup Rules. They will finally be invited to try their eloquence on a Baptist Congress, the object being to induce those present to rock and roll. Those who fail will be liquidated. All candidates should present themselves at the Sporting Club (side entrance) at 11:15 A.M. on the morning of September 19. Gloves will be provided, but they should bring their own rubber-soled shoes, singlet, and shorts.

Observe that this advertisement saves all trouble about application forms, testimonials, photographs, references, and short lists. If the advertisement has been correctly worded, there will be only one applicant, and he can take office immediately— well, almost immediately. But what if there is no applicant? That is proof that the advertisement needs rewording. We have evidently asked for something more than exists. So the same advertisement (which is, after all, quite economical in space) can be inserted again with some slight adjustment. The pass mark in the examination can be reduced to 85 per cent with 65 per cent of the votes required in the popularity poll, and only two rounds against the heavyweight. Conditions can be successively relaxed, indeed, until an applicant appears.

Suppose, however, that two or even three candidates present themselves. We shall know that we have been insufficiently scientific. It may be that the pass mark in the examination has been too abruptly lowered—it should have been 87 per cent, perhaps, with 66 per cent in the popularity poll. Whatever the cause, the damage has been done. Two, or possibly three, candidates are in the waiting room. We have a choice to make and cannot waste all the morning on it. One policy would be to start the ordeal and eliminate the candidates who emerge with least credit. There is, nevertheless, a quicker way. Let us assume that all three candidates have all the qualities already defined as essential. The only thing we need do is add one further quality and apply the simplest test of all. To do this, we ask the nearest young lady (receptionist or stenographer, as the case may be), "Which would you prefer?" She will promptly point out one of the candidates and so finish the matter. It has been objected that this procedure is the same thing as tossing a coin or otherwise letting chance decide. There is, in fact, no element of chance. It is merely the last-minute insistence on one other quality, one not so far taken into account: the quality of sex appeal.

26 ~

Some Lessons
from Aviation Psychology

J. P. GUILFORD

I propose to pass on to you some reflections upon experiences encountered during some four years of contact with psychological services in the Army Air Forces during the recent emergency, together with some impressions and conclusions. This choice is made with the belief that the comments are worth reporting and that there is something in them that may be of interest to those in various fields of psychology.

There will be no attempt to make a systematic coverage of the many types of services rendered or of implications for all types of psychological knowledge and techniques. Emphasis will be placed upon those aspects that came more directly within personal observation and those that are likely to be of general interest. The basic facts upon which the impressions and conclusions are based will soon appear in rather complete form in the Army Air Forces Aviation Psy-

This article is reprinted from the *American Psychologist,* 1949, with the permission of the author and the American Psychological Association. It was originally the presidential address read before the Western Psychological Association at San Diego State College, June 19, 1947.

chology Research Reports [4]. In what follows, more general conclusions will come first and more specific findings later. The selection of items mentioned reflects largely my limitation to procedures of selection and classification of personnel and of their training. The program was much more extensive than that, including clinical and rehabilitation services, investigations of equipment and its use, and evaluation of personnel after training and combat. I claim no personal ownership for any of the findings that will be reported here. They are the product of a large cooperative undertaking in which many individuals took part. There is not sufficient time to provide as complete background for each statement as I would like, or to add certain qualifications in some places. If any generalization seems improbable or unfair, as stated, I refer you to the complete reports for a more direct and complete account.

My first general observation is that during World War II the profession of psychology came of age. It is now recognized as having a distinct place among the profes-

335

sions and as having a number of unique services to offer. At the beginning of the war this was not apparent. On the one hand, many of our own number, myself included, realized that while we had made substantial progress since World War I, there were many pressing military problems for which we had no immediate answers. On the other hand, the great majority of those in command in the armed services were uninformed as to the nature of psychology and were often tolerantly skeptical. Like many of our undergraduate students, some of them could hardly even spell the word. It was fortunate that those in command were generally favorable to the idea of research in general and that they were ready to include psychologists among their research agents. It is fortunate, I felt many times, that, being pressed with the many human problems encountered in converting an untrained civilian population into a highly intricate and technical fighting force in a short time, those in command turned to the institutions of higher learning for aid. A strong indication of the truth of my first observation is the continued and enlarged demand for psychological personnel by the federal government, particularly by its branch, the Veterans Administration.

If one entered the armed services with some reservations as to the readiness of psychologists to be of use, those reservations were soon modified. It was evident on many an occasion that a very little psychology often went a very long way. Very often, a simple, isolated fact or principle, perhaps learned in beginning psychology, was the key to the solution of an important problem. Let no one maintain that remembering facts and principles is unimportant, for again and again the individual who had the pertinent information at hand without reference to books or notes was at a distinct advantage. Libraries, and even textbooks, were usually rather remote from military installations and combat zones, and time did not permit their utilization, sometimes, even when they were accessible.

As examples of how some very elemen-tary psychological knowledge made an important difference when applied to military problems, I will cite some experiences from the training of flexible gunners. The flexible gunner was the man who operated a machine gun in a bombing plane. He had one of the most complex firing problems ever known. It was little wonder that during the first part of the war his record in shooting down enemy planes was very disappointing. The task of such a gunner was relatively new. In the attempt to improve his training, a great many training devices and procedures were tried. When psychologists first came on the scene, it was immediately apparent to them that certain changes would mean a considerable improvement and that prevailing evaluations of training results left much to be desired. Millions of dollars were being spent upon expensive training devices, with almost no knowledge of whether they yielded anything in the way of learning.

One basic fact of learning is that the learner makes most rapid progress when he is aware of his errors, their nature, and amount, and the greatest benefit of this awareness comes when it follows immediately after the execution of the act. Considerable effort was therefore devoted to the invention and perfection of devices that would inform the learner of his hits and errors immediately, especially in the last state of his training, in air-to-air firing; that is, firing at a simulated attacking plane. One device informed him by means of flashes of light and the other by sounds in headphones when shots were on the target. This is only one example of the many training situations in which this very important principle of learning should be applied.

Another universal learning problem was that of transfer. This problem was ever present in the use of synthetic trainers, of which there were many. The same question arose in connection with the use of any particular training device or procedure; would things learned in practice with it prepare the learner to master more quickly his combat operations or his training at later stages? For example, skeet shooting had been adopted as a part of the preliminary training of a flexible gunner. At a meeting of training officers, it is reported, the procedure was defended on the ground that "You have to learn to walk before you can learn to run." This cliché seemed to settle the matter and little question was raised as to the effectiveness of skeet shooting as a step in the general training program. The possibility of *no* transfer effects, and even of *negative* effects, seemed not to have caused much concern. Later, psychologists aimed research at determining whether there was or was not improvement with each training procedure and to what extent it showed positive transfer effects in later performances of different kinds.

Once it became realized that the psychologist had something to offer, he was invited to take an active part in various kinds of undertakings. Because of his unusually liberal acquaintance with research techniques, he was in a strategic position to assume the leadership in comprehensive research programs that went beyond purely psychological problems. In headquarters and in policy-making conferences, he was frequently invited to participate and many types of questions were brought to him. For example, there were questions of morale. What could be done to meet the slump in motivation sometimes evident in flying personnel who had recently received their wings as graduates of flying schools in the Training Command but who must continue in a strenuous period of operational training? What could be done to improve the attitude of bombardiers and navigators who had returned from combat duty to be assigned to instructor training? What proportion of the graduates from flying training should be commissioned as second lieutenants and what proportion as flight officers? There were problems of personnel planning. How many candidates for flying training should be inducted each month in order to graduate the desired numbers in each assignment a number of months hence to man the planes that would

be ready for them? What should be the qualifying scores on selection and classification tests? Should women who are given pilot training be selected on the same basis as men? How can personnel returning from combat be best utilized? These were some of the questions on which counsel of the psychologists was sought.

One of the most important factors in making secure the position of the aviation psychologist in the AAF was the fact that he could show results in tangible terms. Care was taken from the beginning to keep full records and to validate procedures wherever possible. In this connection, it was quickly learned that generals do not want to see critical ratios, chi squares, or coefficients of correlation. There are many ways, preferably graphic or pictorial, in which the person who does not speak or read the language of statistics can be informed. With a little informal education he can also be led to make proper evaluations. It is strongly recommended that psychologists in general and those who serve agencies in particular make some effort to keep themselves and their clients informed as to the effectiveness of their efforts and to inform clients in a manner that they understand. There is no better way to assure continued acceptance or to assure oneself of one's own foundations.

One general conclusion that was brought home to us by repeated experience is that we should have greater respect for low correlations. Tradition had taught us that unless coefficients of correlation are substantial, for example .40 or above, there is too little relationship to bother with. We must face the fact, unpleasant though it may be, that in human behavior, complex as it is, low intercorrelations of utilizable variables is the general rule and not the exception. Highly valid predictions must ordinarily be based upon multiple indicators. Although each may add a trifle to the total variance of the thing predicted, by summation the aggregate prediction can mean a very substantial degree of correlation. Predictions based upon relationships represented by correlations that are very small, even between .10 and .20, may be practically useful when the conditions are right, and when large numbers of individuals are involved. If we are to place dependence upon low correlations, however, it must be remembered that very large samples are required to establish the fact of any correlation at all or to establish its size for weighting purposes.

One finding that was somewhat disconcerting is that the traditional psychological categories were so lacking in adequacy for a comprehensive and thoroughgoing survey of human resources. This held true for the typical job-analysis categories which are aimed toward a listing of distinct and irreducible psychological functions and traits, as well as for concepts from the experimental laboratory. The two sources are of course not independent; there are many categories common to both. At the beginning of the AAF psychological program, a list of 20 abilities and other traits was adopted as a basis upon which to construct selection and classification tests. Very few of these categories, though they were useful in suggesting test ideas, held up as descriptive of genuine variables in individual differences. In their stead, there emerged a list of about 27 concepts which seemed needed to take care of the obtained results, which were mainly in the form of test intercorrelations and validity coefficients. The two lists came close to agreement at some points, but there were many startling discrepancies.

The 27 categories were derived by the procedure of factor analysis. Of all approaches to test development and to the exploration of human resources, factor analysis seems to offer the most illuminating and fruitful results. Intercorrelations of tests and of tests with practical criteria became quite intelligible in terms of common factors. Both tests and criteria could be accurately and meaningfully described in relation to the same dependable categories. I have elaborated upon the many advantages of the factorial approach in a

forthcoming article [1] and so will not go into details on this point here. I wish merely to say that as a result of a factorial survey of AAF tests and criteria, a basis was laid not only for further material improvement in methods of selecting aircrew trainees but also for considerable new progress in vocational psychology in general. It is my firm conviction that the factorial categories and factorial theory and methods give us the stable foundation that vocational psychology needs.

The finding of 27 factors clearly indicates that the number of common traits needed to describe individuals is much greater than has been supposed. Only possibly two of these are not regarded as abilities, and the list does not include many abilities reported elsewhere. It was estimated that 20 of the 27 factors were involved to an appreciable degree in the pilot-training criterion. Incidentally, this shows just how complex a practical criterion may be. It is estimated that these 20 factors account for only about 70 per cent of the predictable variance in the pilot-training criterion. Not more than 80 per cent of the pilot-training criterion was predictable, the remaining portion being composed of error variance. How much of the unpredicted but predictable variance can be attributed to additional abilities and how much to temperamental or interest factors cannot be said.

It *can* be said, however, that the testing for pilot classification, like most testing practices, did not make the best use of the available testing time. In about eight hours of testing time, some 20 tests were administered but they covered less than half of the factors that should have been taken into account for maximal prediction. Twenty tests, at the rate of one factor per test, could take care of 20 factors, with a validity, it was estimated, of .72. Instead, the 20 tests covered eight factors with a validity of about .60.

Some specific findings concerning factors may be of interest. I will cite only certain results that were verified, some repeatedly, and that relate more directly to prewar results.[1] While it is believed that these findings do advance the understanding of human personality considerably, on most points it cannot be said that the final paragraph of the final chapter has been written. The method of analysis used was Thurstone's centroid extraction procedure followed by rotation of reference axes so as to minimize negative loadings and maximize the number of zero loadings.

First, to report a negative finding, there was no good evidence of a Spearman g factor or of any single group factor that could appropriately be called general intelligence. There were indications of intercorrelations among some of the factors and hence the possibility of second-order factors in which some investigators find support for a g factor. It is my belief, however, that under present conditions, with so few pure tests for any factors, we are not in a position to say definitely very much concerning the correlations among factors. The fact that a g factor did not emerge is not proof that it does not exist. We could, however, account for the facts very well without it.

Some of the better-known common factors reappeared in almost every analysis— verbal comprehension, numerical facility, and perceptual speed. There is nothing new to report in connection with these abilities except that it was found that a general-vocabulary test is the purest and strongest measure of the verbal factor.

One finding that promises to rank as a real discovery is that the space factor previously reported from several sources is not an irreducible variable. In the tests that have previously defined it, there is often a separate and distinct ability to visualize and probably a second type of space factor in some of them. The more common space factor seems best definable as the awareness of spatial relations or arrangements; a spatial orientation in which reference to the human body is important. It is involved in machine operations for it accounted for about 10 per cent of the pilot training cri-

[1] More complete but brief reports of the AAF factorial findings can be found elsewhere [2, 3].

terion and for as much as 20 per cent of the operation of gadgets in some psychomotor tests. The second space factor is ill defined at present. The visualization factor must be defined as a dynamic function, since it is most prevalent in tasks involving movements of machinery, transformations of objects, and changes in position.

A somewhat systematic survey was made of memory tests, with the result that three, and perhaps four, distinct memory factors were revealed. Thurstone's rote-memory factor was verified, although it would seem that the term "paired-associates" memory is a more exact description of it. Carlson's visual-memory factor was also verified. This factor might be regarded as a static form of visualization ability as contrasted with the dynamic visualization described above. It is a photographic or reproductive memory for visually observed material. A third memory factor may prove to be merely a specific or very narrow group factor, since it was restricted to tests requiring memorizing of pictures paired with names. There is indirect evidence for a fourth memory factor for which the hypothesis is offered that it is memory for content. It seems to be common to tests with complicated directions the after-effects of which are tested later in terms of performance of tasks as directed. It may also be evident in terms of recognition of verbal details not in verbatim form.

The area of reasoning abilities was not very much clarified by the AAF results. Evidence for three, and perhaps four, distinct factors was found. The findings do not fit very well the distinction between inductive and deductive reasoning which has been a philosophical tradition of long standing and which Thurstone adopted following his analyses. It would seem to me that hypotheses more in line with a psychological analysis of problem solving are more promising. There is a factor that became known as "general reasoning" because of its more common appearance in many kinds of reasoning tests. It was rarely entirely absent from them. I am inclined to the hypothesis that this factor is the ability to diagnose a problem; to understand its nature; to see what its requirements are. Another factor was unique to tests of practical judgment and similar tests and so was given the title of "judgment." It seems to be the ability to weigh several alternatives and to reach a wise decision. These two factors would seem to represent the first and last steps of problem solving. In order to fill the gap between these two, one might expect a factor defined as the ability to think of possible solutions rapidly. Such a factor was not found, but tests that should bring it out if it exists were being constructed and administered for analysis near the end of the war.

Two other reasoning factors (designated as reasoning because they appeared in reasoning tests) seem to involve kinds of operations by which an examinee could solve certain types of problems. One seemed to involve reasoning by analogy. One hypothesis concerning the other factor is that sequential reasoning is involved; solution must come in a step-by-step sequence, one step being dependent upon another. It can be seen that we still do not know very much about the psychology of reasoning. I do not believe that we shall know much about it until a number of factor-analysis studies have been focused upon this area.

In the field of psychomotor testing, some new light was thrown upon psychomotor factors and perhaps a new factor was uncovered. A factor identified as psychomotor coordination was found to be quite general. It was found in tests requiring small-muscle adjustments (finger-dexterity tests) as well as in tests requiring large-muscle adjustments (movements of arms, torso, and legs). A second factor was tentatively called "psychomotor precision," since it was involved in tests requiring rather accurate movements under speed conditions. A third factor was tentatively called "psychomotor speed," since it was found in tests in which sheer speed of marking an answer sheet was the salient common element. It is prob-

ably identifiable with the factor found before the war in tests of making tally marks and tests of other simple repetitive movements. The relation of this factor to simple reaction-time tests is problematical. As for reaction-time tests in general, we found that when they are complicated—for example, a test of discrimination reaction time or choice reaction time—a number of factors unexpectedly enter into the scores; for example, perceptual speed, spatial relations, and even the number factor.

It is probable that the AAF experiences have written the final chapter regarding the area popularly known as mechanical aptitude. A great many kinds of mechanical tests were analyzed—mechanical knowledge, mechanical comprehension, mechanical principles, mechanical functions (and malfunctions), and mechanical movements; also other tests not ordinarily designated as mechanical in their titles but often included in mechanical-aptitude batteries—surface development, block counting, pursuit, paper form board, and the like. Repeated results show that the only thing unique to tests of an obviously mechanical nature is a factor that can be definitely labeled as mechanical information or mechanical experience. Mechanical-knowledge tests are the best and purest measures of it. Mechanical aptitude in the popular sense is not a genuine unity at all, but a composite. Other factors that are common to tests that are predictive of success in mechanical training or mechanical occupations are now fairly well known abilities that are confined neither to mechanical tests nor to mechanical jobs. Depending upon the type of test and the type of mechanical job, it can be said with some confidence that among these additional factors are visualization, spatial relations, perceptual speed, and in some, a factor of length estimation. It is time that vocational counselors and others think of jobs and tasks in terms of patterns of underlying factors, each factor with an appropriate weight. Each mechanical task or occupation has its own unique pattern of demands upon human resources. The only excuse for using a term such as "mechanical aptitude" is that it serves as a very broad generalization covering loosely collected activities having only one thing in common; that they have something to do with machines or gadgets.

A similar situation exists with regard to the popular concept of clerical aptitude. Clerks are office workers and for practical convenience are included under a single category. Psychologically, the category is rather loose and is composed of heterogenerous elements. Each type of clerk, and even each particular assignment within a type, may call for a distinct pattern of abilities and traits. It is time we extricated ourselves from these as well as other semantic traps.

Thus far, I have spoken of findings with regard to abilities. The AAF program was not by any means confined to research on abilities. My emphasis upon them is partly due to the fact that I am best acquainted with that aspect of the program and partly due to the relatively greater progress along these lines. The usual greater difficulty encountered in attempting to assess temperamental and dynamic traits was also evident in the AAF. Most of the results along these lines were negative, but since most of the known procedures were given a serious trial in the selection of personnel, it is worth while to report the general outcome. There were a few promising leads. Psychologists who studied intensively the pilot in training and after combat were convinced of the importance of temperamental and dynamic traits for successful performance of duty on the one hand and for avoidance of maladjustments, operational fatigue, psychoneuroses, and psychoses on the other.

Almost all of the conclusions that I have to report are based upon procedures applied at the time of classification of trainees and follow-up studies limited to pilot trainees through their first stage of flying training. It was recognized that the most satisfactory method for validating the procedures would have been to follow personnel entirely through training and combat.

Under the prevailing circumstances this was impossible. On the other hand, psychological observers were convinced that primary pilot training was a sufficient ordeal to provide experimental evidence that could be generalized beyond that stage. The criterion of adjustment that is implied in what follows was the dichotomy of graduation versus elimination in primary pilot training. The greatest proportion of eliminees (who made up 10 to 60 per cent of each class) were failed for deficiency in learning to fly. Very small proportions were eliminated by reason of fear of flying or by their own request or for physical reasons. These categories were, as we found, highly intermixed and almost equally predictable by means of tests.

Certain published tests were used on experimental groups and validated against the pass-fail criterion. These tests included interest inventories, personality inventories, Rorschach and thematic apperception tests. As a general policy, it was planned that each validation sample should include at least one thousand trainees. In some of the studies there were departures from this standard, as will be noted.

Neither the Kuder Preference Record nor the Strong Vocational Interest Blank yielded any evidence of validity that was statistically significant. Validation of single items in the Strong test failed to provide any collection of items that could be keyed successfully for the prediction of pilot graduation in new groups of students. Other evidence showed that there was a real possibility of selection on the basis of interest, because a factor of pilot interest was isolated and could be identified. It was measurable by means of information tests and also by a score based upon biographical data. The hypothesis of Flanagan, that interest can be measured by means of information tests, was thus supported. Such a score may be very complex factorially, however, and its dominant variance may even be in another factor, frequently verbal. If information tests are to be used extensively to measure interests, steps should be taken, where necessary, to suppress the excess factor variance that they carry.

A number of the published personality inventories were given an experimental trial with pilot students, including the Bernreuter, Humm-Wadsworth, Adams-Lepley, Minnesota Multiphasic, and the Guilford-Martin inventories. Of these, three exhibited small but statistically significant validities for some scores. On the Humm-Wadsworth test, the hysteroid and epileptoid scores showed coefficients in the neighborhood of .20, based upon a sample of about 200. In both instances, a high, that is, abnormal, score correlated negatively with graduation. The Guilford-Martin Personnel Inventory showed coefficients ranging from .13 to .19 on the three scores, on a sample of more than 1000. In all traits, a good score correlated positively with graduation. The Inventory of Factors STDCR showed validity coefficients of .12 for the trait scores of cycloid and depression, on a sample of nearly 1200, a good score indicating graduation.

In spite of the demonstration of genuine, practical (pilot) validities for some scores on personality inventories, I should hesitate to recommend the use of this kind of instrument for selection to preferential appointments in the armed services or in other public agencies. Scores may be valid in spite of whatever biases the examinee is *able* to introduce and *may* introduce into his score, and yet the fact that examinees and others can maintain that scores are wilfully biased is a restraining consideration. Their use by a private agency I should say is a responsibility of that particular agency. It is the responsibility of the psychologist who recommends the use of *any* test to inform the user concerning the limitations and risks involved.

It was regarded as very important that the Rorschach test should be given full opportunity to show what it had to offer in a personnel-selection setting. It was recognized that neither time nor personnel requirements for the routine administration and use of this test were consistent with the mass testing required. The numbers of candidates tested per day ranged from 100 to 500 in a single examining unit. Yet the test was administered experimentally to several hundred students individually according to the prescribed procedures by members of the Rorschach Institute who were serving in one of the psychological units. Two methods of group administration were also tried, the Harrower-Erickson and our own version.

The results were almost entirely negative. From the individual administration of the test, neither the 25 indicators taken separately or collectively nor the intuitive prediction of the examiner based upon the data he had from the administration of the test gave significant indications of validity against the pass-fail criterion. There were two samples, one of nearly 300 and the other of nearly 200. The Harrower-Erickson group-administration form also gave no evidence of being valid for pilot selection. The AAF group-administration form when scored for the number of most popular responses showed a coefficient of +.24, based upon a sample of more than 600 students. This type of score is not only more objective than the traditional Rorschach scores but also departs considerably from the principles of the test and its use.

Another interesting result on the Rorschach test might be mentioned. Its use in the individual, customary form in convalescent hospitals has been reported [4]. In three groups (totaling approximately 150) of hospital patients diagnosed as psychoneurotic, most of them of the anxiety type, the mean scores obtained were not significantly different from the means obtained on a much larger sample of aviation students who were just going into training. The fact that it failed to discriminate anxiety cases and psychoneurotics as a group from presumably normal individuals of about the same age and the same sex is noteworthy, to say the least.

The thematic apperception test was not administered in the strictly Murray manner, but was given to students in groups of 28. Each student wrote out his stories. The "scoring" and interpretation, however, were conducted in the customary manner. Neither separate "scores" nor predictions based upon intuitions resulting from test data correlated significantly with the pass-fail criterion. A number of variations of the projective method were tried and the results were much the same, with one exception. This exception was a sentence-completion test which was developed and experimentally tried in a convalescent hospital. Its scores discriminated very well between psychoneurotics and normals, but the scoring was not cleared of a large subjective contribution.

A group of procedures that were used experimentally in pilot selection involved observations of the student under quasi-standardized situations and ratings made by the observer with respect to several traits. Some observations were made while the student was taking the routine psychomotor classification tests. Others were made while the student was resting with three other students between psychomotor tests. Others were made while students were jointly solving a problem (the Wiggly Block test). Still others were made while students were taking a psychomotor test that involved a stressful situation. Except for the last-mentioned situation, ratings of traits and predictions of pass-fail alike failed to correlate significantly with the pilot criterion. In the case of the stress situation, prediction based upon observations and the objective score on the psychomotor test were about equally valid (with a coefficient of about .25) but it is not certain how much the prediction depended upon the observed goodness of performance in the psychomotor test. They intercorrelated to the extent of about .60.

Quite generally, it was found that intuitive judgments and predictions based upon them were quite inferior to objective scores in terms of correlation with training criteria. The clinical summarizations of data in terms of single predictions of pass or fail

(more exactly, a graded prediction on a nine-point scale) were obtained in a number of ways. Some were based upon the results from a single test, e.g., Adams-Lepley, Humm-Wadsworth, or Rorschach. Some were based upon a personal interview of an hour's duration. Some were from observations of behavior and still others encompassed several of these different sources of information. None of these proved to be valid for the particular purpose intended. Furthermore, the intuitive predictions derived from different sources of information intercorrelated so low as to tolerate the hypothesis of zero relationships in many instances. Assuming that the conditions were favorable for giving psychological intuitive powers their proper opportunities, the conclusions seem obvious. There appears to be no scientifically demonstrated procedure based upon subjective judgment that approached in predictive value the use of objective test scores in the selection of pilot trainees. There is also no indication that data can be better integrated to make a composite prediction of success by a subjective, global look at the individual than they can be by the usual statistical summative procedures which have stood the test of time and experience. There are necessary places for psychological intuitions, but they should not replace objective test results and should be resorted to only after objective procedures have taken us as far as they can.

The physiological procedures utilized particularly by Wenger in connection with his assessment of autonomic dominance were given extensive attention. His hypothesis of an autonomic factor was upheld in an aviation-student population and its relationships to psychoneurosis, to combat fatigue, and to several traits of temperament as indicated by personality inventories were shown. It would seem that Wenger has gone a long way toward establishing physiological syndromes that may be associated with nervous and glandular properties as well as with temperamental qualities. His results suggest that medical examination of military personnel might well pay some attention to *composites* of measurement as well as to single variables.

Of a number of *performance* tests of temperamental traits that were tried, very few were promising. Tests that succeeded in frightening the examinee seemed to be even more frightening to the psychologists and to the air surgeons who held the final responsibility for our work. As reported earlier, a complicated stress-situation test showed acceptable pilot validity. Whether this validity could be attributed to temperamental variables or to other factors, perhaps psychomotor, was never determined. Another test, of muscular tension while in the act of handwriting, showed some promise.

One more technique is worthy of mention. This is the use of biographical data for vocational predictions. Utilized before the war by insurance agencies and by the Civil Aeronautics Administration research agencies, biographical information, it was found by both the Army and the Navy, could be scored effectively for the selection of pilots. The AAF also found it effective in the selection of navigators. The validity coefficients were usually between .25 and .40. The utility of such a test cannot be denied, and it is recommended for general use where quick results are desired and where the necessary research can be put into its development. It has certain limitations, however, that are worth pointing out. First, it is susceptible to the same kinds of biases as questionnaires and interest tests. The AAF Biographical Data Blank was administered to a senior high-school group with the instruction for the examinees to respond to items in a manner that would assure a score favorable to success in pilot training. On the average, they were able to modify their scores in the intended direction to a significant degree. Results seemed to show that under the usual testing conditions prevailing in the AAF, however, what little bias did occur did not affect the validity of the scores. Second, such a test has to be developed

specifically for each selective purpose, requiring a very large sample for item validation as well as the usual sample for score validation. Experience in the AAF tends to show that biographical-data tests measure recognizable factors, factors which may be measurable by other types of tests, e.g., mechanical experience and mathematical experience. This suggests that one should try to determine those factors as early as possible and develop more unique tests for them.

In closing, I would like to make one or two additional general comments by way of extracting further implications. I am definitely optimistic about the recognition that our science and our profession have earned and continue to enjoy. I am most anxious that this recognition should endure and that it should grow, for so many of the world's persistent problems depend upon the proper utilization of psychological knowledge and procedures. We psychologists occupy a key position, for in a world that has grown so small and in a world society that has become so interdependent, the problems of human relations are most important and their solution is paramount. We have won considerable confidence in our preparedness to solve certain types of human problems. In order to maintain that confidence we shall have to continue to demonstrate competence. In order to cope with the larger human problems successfully, we shall have to demonstrate increased competence. All of this leads to the same conclusion. We must see to it that the psychologists whom we train are fully prepared not merely to fulfil the requirements as we have recently found them but to do even better than that. During this unique period with its pressure for more trained psychologists, the market is definitely in our favor. It is such as to attract able students in large numbers in our direction. Let us recognize the fact that it requires a high level of ability and of stability to be a good psychologist and to be an effective public leader. Let us remember that of all scientists the psychologist must have the broadest educational base and the most varied and intensive drilling in logical, technical, and observational procedures. Psychologists will achieve positions of leadership and will remain in those positions by reason of sound preparation for them. If, as I have said before, psychology has arrived, this achievement is a vantage point at which even greater things are expected of us and which carries the challenge to be prepared to make good on new promises. Whether we go forward from there or stop where we are is up to us.

REFERENCES

1. GUILFORD, J. P. Factor analysis in a test-development program. *Psychol. Rev.*, 1948, **55**, 79–94.
2. GUILFORD, J. P. The discovery of aptitude and achievement variables. *Science*, 1947, **106**, 279–282.
3. GUILFORD, J. P., AND ZIMMERMAN, W. S. Some AAF findings concerning aptitude factors. *Occupations*, 1947, **26**, 154–159.
4. *Army Air Forces Aviation Psychology Research Reports*. Washington, D.C.: Government Printing Office, 1947. (See particularly Reports No. 5, 7, 11, and 15.)

Chapter 27

The Analysis and Prediction of a Practical Examination in Dentistry

SIDNEY H. NEWMAN / MARGARET A. HOWELL
NORMAN CLIFF

This paper reports the relationship between a practical examination and other methods used in the selection of dentists where the practical examination is viewed as a criterion of professional performance. Since 1950, a number of reports concerned with the prediction of success in dental school, such as those by Weiss [10] and Peterson [6], have appeared in the literature, as well as an analysis of the critical requirements in dentistry [9]. To the author's knowledge, however, the present study is the first report on a standardized, quantitatively-scored practical examination used in assessing dental competence.

Dentists applying for Regular Corps commissions in the United States Public Health Service are selected by the following methods, which were developed as a part of the Officer Selection and Evaluation Program [4]:

(1) *Practical examination.* Working in a Service dental clinic, each applicant makes

an Oral Diagnosis (performing a complete oral diagnosis and recommending therapy), performs an Amalgam Restoration (preparing and filling a cavity), and prepares an Inlay Restoration (constructing a gold inlay in a synthetic model tooth). Two Service Dental Officers, constituting a Local Board at the examining center, independently rate the applicant's performance in Oral Diagnosis and Amalgam Restoration by means of a specially-devised observation rating schedule, which contains scales for evaluating major components of the work and subscales for evaluating specific aspects of each component. A similar rating procedure is employed by a Central Board in Washington, D.C., which is composed of three Dental Officers who, independently and without knowledge of the identity of the applicant, rate the quality of the Inlay Restoration.

(2) *Professional examinations.* The applicants are given four objective three-hour professional examinations covering various areas of dental competence·and knowledge. These examinations consist of multiple-

This article is reprinted from *Educational and Psychological Measurement*, 1959, with the permission of the authors and the copyright holder, G. Frederic Kuder.

choice five-alternative items specially constructed to measure professional judgment and reasoning as well as factual knowledge. The construction of such professional examinations has been discussed by Newman [5].

(3) *Interview board.* A Board of three officers at the local examining center assesses the candidate's personal qualifications, using special Board interview procedures and rating methods.

(4) *File evaluation board.* The applicant's training, experience and work record are evaluated in Washington by a Board of three officers who follow carefully developed procedures in rating the contents of the applicant's file.

Scores derived from the methods described are combined in a final score which determines the applicant's standing in relation to other applicants. A physical examination is also required.

Four aptitude tests are administered experimentally: Verbal (analogies and opposites), Spatial (block rotation), Quantitative (arithmetic reasoning), and Mathematics (inferring simple functional relations). Scores from these tests are not included in an applicant's final selection score.

Of the various measures obtained, the Practical Examination is of particular interest since it is rare that a practical examination can be included as a part of a selection battery for professional personnel. For one reason, in many professions the diversity of the professional problems encountered is such that the work cannot be adequately sampled within a reasonable time. Also, in many situations a practical examination may not be a feasible selection method because of its administrative difficulties and expense.

For the purpose of investigating the degree to which other more widely applicable selection methods reflect professional abilities, the Practical Examination, as a sample of the clinical work of a dentist, can be viewed as a criterion. Treated as a criterion, the Practical Examination, when included in a selection battery, has the advantage of being available on all applicants so that validity coefficients are not affected by the restriction in range usually occurring in validation research on selected employee populations.

PROBLEMS

Two questions were raised: (a) How valid are written professional examinations, aptitude tests, Interviews, and File Evaluations when the Practical Examination is used as the criterion of professional performance? (b) What common factors are present in the Practical Examination and other assessment methods?

SAMPLE

Dentists applying for appointment in the Regular Corps at the Assistant (equivalent of Navy Lieutenant j.g.) and Senior Assistant (equivalent of Navy Lieutenant) grades, examined during 1954 through 1957, were included in the study. There were 100 applicants at the Assistant grade, and 58 at the Senior Assistant grade.

METHODS

SCORING

Each of the written tests, the professional examinations and the aptitude tests, provides a score based on the number of correct responses.

The File Evaluation and the Interview are scored by averaging over-all General Fitness for the Service ratings assigned independently by each of the three officers constituting a Board. Similarly, the Local Board portion of the Practical Examination is scored by averaging the ratings assigned on each part by the officers who observe and independently evaluate the applicant's work.

The Central Board, which evaluated the Inlay Restoration portion of the Practical Examination, tends to be composed of the same Board members each year. The distribution of the scores given by the most experienced member of the Board, who evaluated all of the applicants during the period covered by the study, was used as a basis for equating the means and variances of the ratings given by the various Board members [3, p. 274]. The adjusted ratings given by members of the Central Board on each rating scale were then averaged. The inter-rater reliabilities of the Local and Central Board scores have been found to be .90 or higher.

STATISTICAL ANALYSIS

(1) *Multiple correlations.* All possible intercorrelations were computed among the Interview, File Evaluation, four written professional examinations, the four aptitude tests, and eight major scales in the Practical examination (see Table 27–2).

The correlation of each of the selection methods with the total Practical Examination was obtained by use of a formula for the correlation between one measure and a weighted sum of other measures [7, p. 188]. In computing the correlations, the parts of the Practical were weighted as they are in actual use with the six major scales of the Local Board constituting 80 per cent of the total score, and the two major scales of the Central Board constituting 20 per cent. The weights for each of the scales may be seen in Table 27–2.

With the total Practical as a criterion, multiple correlations were computed in each of the applicant groups by the Wherry-Doolittle method of test selection [2]. In the multiple correlational work, the Interview was eliminated from the predictor battery; there was a possibility that its validity coefficient was spuriously high because some of the officers who interviewed an applicant at the local examining center also rated his performance in the Practical Examination.

The beta weights obtained in each applicant group were applied to the data for the other group in a type of cross-validation to determine the extent to which a single set of weights might be applicable for both groups, although the two grades of applicants cannot be considered samples from a common population.

(2) *Factor analysis.* The correlational matrix for the Assistant grade group of applicants was factor analyzed by Thurstone's Centroid Method [8]. Orthogonal rotations were made until simple structure appeared to be closely approximated. For the factor analytic work, ten representative subscales were added to the eight major scales of the Practical Examination for better definition of possible factors associated with parts of the Practical (see Table 27–2). Because of the small number of cases in the Senior Assistant grade, a factor analysis was not performed on this group.

RESULTS AND INTERPRETATION

VALIDITY

Validity coefficients for the various predictor selection methods are presented in Table 27–1. (To conserve space, intercorrelations among the predictors are not shown, but are available upon request.)[1] It may be seen that all of the selection methods *in actual use* produced significant validity coefficients. In the Senior Assistant, but not the Assistant grade, the Verbal and Spatial sections of the experimentally administered aptitude tests also yielded significant validity coefficients.

It may be noted that consistently higher validities were found for the Senior Assistant grade. This is difficult to explain; however, most of the Assistant grade applicants have just completed dental school, while the Senior Assistant applicants have had a

[1] The correlation matrices have been deposited as Document number 5999 with the ADI Auxiliary Publications Project, Photoduplication Service, Library of Congress, Washington 25, D.C.

Table 27–1   Validity of Predictors against Practical Examination Criterion

Predictors	Assistant Grade (N = 100)		Senior Assistant Grade (N = 58)	
	Validity	Beta Wt.	Validity	Beta Wt.
Interview‡	.64*		.86*	
File Evaluation	.59*	.53	.66*	.48
Verbal aptitude	.06		.28†	
Spatial aptitude	.14		.42*	.11
Quantitative aptitude	−.01		.23	
Mathematics aptitude	.12		.13	
Oral Medicine and Surgery	.34*	.20	.61*	
Basic Dental Sciences	.26*		.57*	.24
Operative and Prosthetic Dentistry	.32*		.43*	
Peridontia, Roentgenology, Pedodontia, Dental Public Health	.34*		.53*	
R		.62*		.71*
$\overline{R}$		.62*		.70*
R		.59*§		.70*¶

* Significant at .01 level
† Significant at .05 level
‡ Interview excluded from the predictor battery in the computation of multiple correlations
§ R based on beta weights obtained on Senior Assistant grade
¶ R based on beta weights obtained on Assistant grade

minimum of three years of professional experience beyond dental school. Since practically all of the experience differential is in clinical dentistry, it may make the Practical Examination a better criterion for the Senior Assistant applicants. That is, differences in clinical ability predictable by the selection methods may become more pronounced with clinical experience.

In both applicant grades, the highest validity occurred on the Interview, but as mentioned earlier, this correlation may be spuriously increased by the overlap in membership of the Interview and Local Practical Boards. The Interview and File Evaluation, which are independent measures, were highly correlated in both applicant grades (Assistant: $r=.61$; Senior Assistant: $r=.73$), and the File Evaluation was highly correlated with the Practical (Assistant: $r=.59$; Senior Assistant: $r=.66$). This suggests that an Interview conducted by a Board independent of the Practical would have yielded appreciable validities, though perhaps lower ones than shown in Table 27–1.

Multiple correlations based on the selec-tion battery for each grade and beta weights of the tests selected by the Wherry-Doolittle method are also presented in Table 27–1. With the Interview eliminated from the predictor battery, multiple corre-lations, not corrected for shrinkage, were .62 and .71 in the Assistant and Senior Assistant grades, respectively, establishing the high validity of the battery of pre-dictors. Both multiples were significant at the one per cent level. In both grades, the first selected predictor, and the one having the largest beta weight, was the File Evalu-ation, and the second selected predictor was a written professional examination. For the Assistant grade, this was the examina-tion in Oral Medicine and Surgery, and for the Senior Assistant grade, the one in the Basic Dental Sciences. It may be observed, however, that in both grades, Oral Medi-cine and Surgery was the professional examination having the highest validity. In the Senior Assistant grade, a third predictor was selected, the Spatial Relations aptitude test.

The beta weights obtained in one appli-cant grade applied to the validity data of the other grade resulted in multiple correlations of comparable size to the original ones. In the Assistant grade, this type of cross-validation multiple was .59, and in the Senior Assistant grade, .70; both multiples were significant at the one per cent level. These findings emphasize the consistency of the multiple validity coefficients.

Since the Wherry-Doolittle method of test selection does not provide a test of the significance of each successive increment to the squared multiple correlation, the F ratio was used for this purpose [1]. In each applicant group, the multiple correlation was significantly increased at the five per cent level by the addition of the selected professional examination. In the Senior Assistant grade, although the Spatial aptitude test was a selected predictor, it did not significantly increase prediction of the Practical Examination criterion.

From the predictors selected, it would appear that an evaluation of training and experience by means of the carefully developed, standardized File Evaluation Board procedure used here is highly predictive of dental skill, but that a more objective measure of dental knowledge, a professional examination, significantly increases the accuracy of this prediction. Spatial aptitude may become important in determining quality of work as the dentist becomes more experienced in clinical dentistry and professional training becomes further removed in time.

FACTORS

Table 27–2 presents the centroid and rotated factor matrices for the Assistant grade applicants. The correlation matrix on which the factor analysis was based is available upon request (footnote 1).

From the rotated loadings in Table 27–2, Factor I appears to be an objective test factor on which the professional examinations have the highest loadings. The professional examination in the Basic Dental Sciences, with a loading of .76, perhaps best represents this factor, although all of the professional examinations have high loadings of .66 or higher. The aptitude tests with the highest loadings (in the .50's) are the Verbal and Quantitative aptitude tests. The Mathematics aptitude test had a relatively low loading of .21 on Factor I, while the Spatial aptitude test had a loading of .41.

Factor II seems to be a general professional ability factor common to the Practical Examination and the other methods actually used in the selection of Dental Officers. The aptitude tests had insignificant negative loadings on this factor. Loadings of the Interview, the File Evaluation, and the parts of the Practical Examination were generally in the .50's or .60's on Factor II, while the loadings of the written professional examinations were only somewhat lower, ranging from .39 to .55. From the similarity of the loadings of all measures relating to professional skills and knowledges, it would appear that professional competence is to some extent general, influencing performance regardless of the mode of measurement.

The other three factors observed are primarily related to specific parts of the Practical Examination; their size may be inflated somewhat by a halo effect in the Board ratings.

Factor III is defined almost exclusively by the eight scales relating to Amalgam Restoration, all of which had loadings of about .50. Three other measures had loadings greater than .20 on this factor: Candidate-Patient Relations (Oral Diagnosis), Verbal aptitude, and Quantitative aptitude. The loadings of these three variables are not easily interpreted, and perhaps need not be in view of their size. However, while it is difficult to see how these particular aptitude tests relate to amalgam restoration, the loading of the Candidate-Patient Relations (Oral Diagnosis) scale is not unreasonable since this scale may be expected to correlate with the similar one from the Amalgam Restoration.

Factor IV is clearly a factor representing the Central Board's evaluation of the Inlay

Table 27-2 Centroid and Rotated Factor Matrices for Assistant Grade, N = 100 (Decimal points omitted)

Wt.*		Centroid Factor Loadings					Rotated Factor Loadings					
		I	II	III	IV	V	I	II	III	IV	V	h²
	Amalgam Restoration											
	Cavity Preparation—Outline form	74	22	37	18	−19	−02	48	64	03	42	81
	—Retention form	75	24	31	13	−15	−03	51	55	06	42	75
16	—Best judgment	81	26	33	14	−13	−03	55	58	08	47	86
	Finished Restoration—Anatomy	77	23	23	−07	−24	−01	68	45	−03	32	76
	—Occlusion	80	16	32	04	−24	06	61	56	−02	38	83
16	—Best judgment	81	28	28	03	−21	−05	65	54	01	39	86
04	Candidate-Patient Relations	72	28	35	06	−11	−08	52	50	−01	46	75
04	Habits of Work	77	33	30	10	−11	−11	55	53	07	46	82
	Oral Diagnosis											
	Adequacy of final dental diagnosis	74	21	26	−28	29	−00	57	03	02	70	82
	Adequacy of recommended treatment	74	17	21	−35	28	04	61	−03	01	67	82
08	Candidate-Patient Relations	72	25	32	−12	15	−05	51	23	01	63	71
32	Best Judgment	72	12	32	−33	25	08	56	03	−08	69	80
	Inlay Restoration											
	Cavity Preparation—Outline form	65	21	−64	16	09	−02	58	01	76	−01	90
	—Resistance form	66	20	−64	13	10	−02	59	−01	75	01	91
10	—Best judgment	66	20	−65	12	11	−02	60	−03	75	02	93
	Finished Restoration—Margins	66	09	−63	17	14	09	54	−02	77	03	89
	—Anatomy	65	10	−67	16	05	08	58	01	76	−06	91
10	—Best judgment	59	19	−55	25	08	−03	47	09	73	01	76
	Interview	63	15	11	−26	−11	03	63	15	−06	29	51
	File Evaluation	62	09	08	−24	−03	08	59	09	−01	31	46
	Verbal aptitude	22	−55	13	28	09	59	−15	21	13	15	45
	Spatial aptitude	22	−36	09	15	13	41	−05	11	12	18	23
	Quantitative aptitude	14	−52	12	32	07	54	−21	23	13	09	41
	Mathematics aptitude	15	−17	18	23	29	21	−18	11	15	34	22
	Oral Medicine and Surgery	56	−59	−18	−31	−18	72	55	−06	−01	−04	82
	Basic Dental Sciences	49	−66	−13	−26	−14	76	43	−06	−03	−03	77
	Operative and Prosthetic Dentistry	52	−60	−10	−16	−08	72	39	01	05	05	67
	Peridontia, Roentgenology, Pedodontia, Dental Public Health	54	−54	−11	−24	−16	66	48	−00	−01	01	67

* Weights used in computing the total Practical Examination score; these are relevant to the multiple correlations, but not to the factor analysis.

Restoration (preparing a gold inlay in a model tooth). All the scales completed by the Central Board had loadings in the .70's on this factor and no other variable had a loading greater than .15. A considerable proportion of the variance of the Inlay Restoration ratings is thus clearly independent of all other parts of the selection process.

Factor V appears to be a general Local Board factor, representing what is common to all of the scales completed by the Local Board. As such, it might be called the Clinical Effectiveness factor. It may be noted that the scales of the Oral Diagnosis best define this factor, having loadings in the .60's or .70's. That Factor V is not simply a result of the halo effect may be noted from the loadings of about .30 for three variables other than those in the Practical Examination. These are the Interview, the File Evaluation, and the Mathematics aptitude test. The Interview may actually correlate for spurious reasons, but the File Evaluation is experimentally independent of the Practical. The File Evaluation is loaded on two factors, II and V, in common with the Practical, so that this evaluation of training and experience predicts quality of dental performance to a considerable extent. The appreciable loading of the Mathematics aptitude test on Factor V is somewhat surprising, especially since it accounts for most of the communality of this variable. It may be that the intellectual qualities this test reflects, a logical approach to problems and some ingenuity in their solution, actually are relevant to performance, especially when it is noted that the diagnostic part of the Practical is that which had the highest loading on this factor.

The reader may note that all four of the aptitude tests had small positive loadings on each of the last three factors related to specific parts of the Practical, but low negative loadings on the general factor, Factor II. It was not found to be possible to rotate the factors to concentrate these loadings on a single factor without destroying the simplicity of factor structure for the Practical.

SIGNIFICANCE OF THE STUDY

It is felt that the results of this study, as the first report on a dental Practical Examination, may be of particular interest to others engaged in the selection of dentists, as well as to dental administrators, dental professors, and occupational analysts. The study may also have special relevance to the development of standardized practical or technic examinations for those involved in the evaluation of the clinical work of dental students or dentists.

As a criterion, the Practical Examination perhaps represents a reasonable sampling of the kinds of professional skills a dentist may be expected to exhibit. In a particular dental specialty, of course, other skills may be relevant. While the Practical may be an adequate work sample, it must be remembered that personality characteristics and other aspects of professional performance may be represented in an "ultimate" criterion to a greater extent than they are in the Practical.

Generalization to other professional groups may not be entirely justified, but the results of this study are suggestive of the usefulness of objective professional examinations and formalized, quantitative evaluations of training and experience in predicting professional competence. In situations where practical examinations are not feasible as a part of the selection battery, this study suggests that other methods of assessment and evaluation such as the ones used here may be fairly satisfactory substitutes in that they may be expected to be quite highly correlated with performance on a practical examination.

REFERENCES

1. Dwyer, P. S. The relative efficiency and economy of various test selection methods.

Psychological Research Section. Report No. 957, Adjutant General's Office, 1952.

2. GARRETT, H. E. *Statistics in psychology and education.* New York: Longmans, Green, & Co., Inc., 1947.

3. GUILFORD, J. P. *Psychometric methods.* New York: McGraw-Hill, 1936.

4. NEWMAN, S. H. The officer selection and evaluation program of the U.S. Public Health Service. *Amer. J. Publ. Hlth,* 1951, 41, 1395–1402.

5. NEWMAN, S. H. Professional examinations for Public Health Service officers. *Publ. Hlth Rep.,* 1952, 67, 917–922.

6. PETERSON, S. Validation of professional aptitude batteries: Test for dentistry. *Proceedings of the 1950 Conference on Testing Problems,* Educational Testing Service, 1951, 35–45.

7. THORNDIKE, R. L. *Personnel selection.* New York: Wiley & Sons, 1949.

8. THURSTONE, L. L. *Multiple-factor analysis.* Chicago: Univer. Chicago Press, 1947.

9. WAGNER, R. F. Critical requirements for dentists. *J. appl. Psychol.,* 1950, 34, 190–192.

10. WEISS, I. Prediction of academic success in dental school. *J. appl. Psychol.,* 1952, 34, 11–14.

Chapter 28

The Evaluation of
Personal and Social Qualities

NORMAN FREDERIKSEN

In considering what might be important in evaluating the personal and social qualities of a college candidate, the first question would seem to be: What qualities lead the college to look with favor on a candidate? More or less official statements on the subject are available in the college catalogues and some of them note particular social and personal qualities which are described as giving the candidate an advantage in being admitted.

Summarizing a large number of such statements might yield the following composite picture of the student sought by admissions officers in American colleges and universities: he is of good character and has a good personality (whatever that is); he is socially well-adjusted and mature, active in extracurricular activities, well-rounded, responsible, serious, and strongly motivated to succeed in college; and he possesses certain qualities of leadership.

Speech presented in 1953 to the Colloquium on College Admissions. It is reprinted from *College Admissions*, 1954, with permission of the author and the publisher, the College Entrance Examination Board.

OBJECTIVES OF THE COLLEGE

This list of characteristics isn't too bad; perhaps I should accept it and proceed to describe the latest highly technical and scientific ways of selecting students to fit our composite picture. But being somewhat compulsive, I would prefer to look farther. Let us find out what the colleges claim they are trying to do, what their basic objectives are, in order to see if these personal and social qualities really appear to be necessary to carry out those aims. It is possible, after all, that the reason for insisting on good character and social maturity is merely to reduce the case load in the office of the dean of men.

Here are some things college catalogues say about the objectives of the institutions. Consider what each statement implies regarding the personal and social qualities required in a student in order for the objective to be realized.

Some of the objectives are frankly and clearly vocational. Prairie View A and M ". . . endeavors to bring the students' training into closer relationship with life's occupations." Simmons ". . . combines liberal education with vocational preparation."

Other colleges, and not necessarily those with strong church connections, emphasize the moral virtues. Marymount ". . . aims to develop Christian women of a strong moral character, radiating a Christ-like personality . . . women who will be an uplifting influence in their homes, in their church and community, and model citizens of their state and country." Princeton, besides developing mental proficiency, says that "moral proficiency must be cultivated as well." It also seeks ". . . to communicate to our students the sense of duty that made our forebears strong." Haverford stresses ". . . the importance of sound ethical judgment based upon clear perception of individual and social aims."

A number of institutions stress heavily the development of individuals who will be valuable to society. Swarthmore, for example, says its purpose is ". . . to make its students more valuable human beings and more useful members of society." Reed has two aims: ". . . to offer students an opportunity to gain understanding of their environment and . . . to prepare them for intelligent action as individuals within society." Newcomb College of Tulane says, "In all cases, a prime objective is preparation for intelligent citizenship in a democracy."

Acquisition of knowledge, of course, is not neglected. Here is just one quotation from the Middlebury catalogue: "The curriculum is organized to provide students with a comprehensive and balanced knowledge of the sciences and arts, language and literature, history and philosophy, social, political, and economic institutions."

Macalester College stresses preparation for living in a slightly different sense. It seeks to be a place ". . . where intellectual horizons are widened and [students] find a reason for living and a source of joy in living." It desires to ". . . make life a joyous experience for the individual and a source of strength for society."

I would like to end these catalogue quotations with one that I find particularly interesting. It is from the Sarah Lawrence catalogue:

> Most educators believe that some common goals should be set for all students in college. These goals are sometimes stated in terms of subject matter. . . . They are sometimes stated in terms of the intellectual, moral, aesthetic and personal qualities the college seeks to develop. Certainly all students need to learn how to find information, to organize it, think about it, and make judgments about what they discover; they need to understand political and social institutions, and how these have developed; they need to understand physical and psychological forces operating in individual and social behavior; they need to understand art as a way of giving form to life.
>
> It is equally important, however, to recognize individual differences among students, differences in their life experience, their intellectual development, their personal qualities and particular abilities, and in their life goals. Educational planning is often compelled to ignore these individual differences, and often they are not taken into account in formulating educational goals. Recognition of individual differences is one of the main elements in our planning.

This explicit recognition of individual differences is an idea that I want to come back to later.

Have you considered the implications of these statements of objectives with regard to the specific personal and social qualities to be sought in college students? Let me summarize the objectives and then talk a bit about such implications.

The broad objectives which appear to be mentioned most often include the following:

1. Acquisition of information.
2. Development of ability to think critically.
3. Development of concern for social problems and value to the community and society.

4. Development of Christian faith, moral values, and ethical judgment.

While I do not claim to have made a scientific survey of a random sample of the population of college catalogues, nevertheless I believe that further study of official statements would bear out the thesis that the four types of aims I have just mentioned are very prominent in the minds of the authors of the catalogues. Let us for the time being ignore the host of more specific objectives which are listed, such as development of communication, preparation for family life, and appreciation of beauty. What is implied by our four main objectives with regard to selection of students on personal and social qualities?

Let us take *acquisition of information* first. What kind of student is best able to acquire information? I would say in all seriousness that you should select students who are unsocial, compulsive, shy, docile, and plodding, and whose interests center exclusively on scholarship, in order to best accomplish this objective.

How about *development of ability to think critically?* The implications of this one for personal and social qualities are harder to spot. We know only a little about the relationship of personality characteristics to thinking ability. We know of course that in certain psychotic conditions critical thinking is grossly impaired, as in paranoia. We also know that attitudes and prejudices similarly interfere with clear thinking of normal people in areas related to the prejudices. For example, syllogisms stated in terms like "A is greater than B" may be solved correctly; but when terms like "Republican" and "Communist" are substituted for the A's and B's, the answers may tend to be more closely related to one's prejudices than to the logical solution. We have some evidence that the errors in thinking due to prejudice can be reduced somewhat by training in contrast to what can be accomplished in treating paranoia. I suppose the implication for student selection is that paranoids should be excluded. In all seriousness, I don't believe we know enough

about personality today to justify excluding many others, from the standpoint of achieving the objective of teaching critical thinking.

How about *development of concern for social problems and value to the community and society?* Young people, of course, differ considerably in their interest in social problems. It should be possible to select those who are most sensitive to such problems for admission to college. But there are a couple of considerations which might give us pause. First, by selecting those with outstanding interest in social problems, we might possibly tend to eliminate those with primary interest and ability in some other area, such as mathematics, music, or science. Are we to *insist* that our artists and scientists be social-minded? An interest in social problems is certainly to be desired in our scientists, but are we to deny potential scientists an opportunity to be trained because they seem to lack an interest in society?

A second reason for hesitating about demanding an interest in social problems on the part of admittees is that those already possessing the characteristic don't need the training. We commonly welcome into our mathematics classes those who do not possess the skills being taught in the course. Certainly we require aptitude for learning mathematics which may be demonstrated by mastery of more elementary material, but we do not require achievement beyond a level suitable for beginners. Frankly, I do not know how to apply this analogy to selection on the basis of social interest. I do not know how to assess aptitude for acquiring concern for social problems and value to society.

Finally, we have the objective which deals with *development of Christian faith, moral values, and ethical judgment.* What has been said about social values applies about as well in this area. Insisting on possession of these characteristics might result in elimination of otherwise well-qualified people in other fields. Selection of students who already possess high moral values and good ethical judgment may mean that the students we select don't need our training in this respect. I will grant, however, that from the standpoint of preserving the peace we don't want to go too far down the scale of immorality in admitting students.

The reader may by now be thinking that this approach to the problem of what personal and social qualities are desired has not been particularly productive. The only positive suggestions have been that paranoids should not be admitted and that unsocial and compulsive people should be admitted. Undoubtedly I would be justified in adding to the list a quality variously referred to as drive, seriousness of purpose, or motivation, a characteristic which would seem to be appropriate to any of our objectives.

REQUIREMENTS VS. OBJECTIVES

I would now like to go back to my summary of what qualities the catalogues say are desired in their students. In the composite picture of the student being sought by admissions officers, he is of good character and has a good personality; he is socially well-adjusted and mature, active in extracurricular activities, well-rounded, responsible, serious, and strongly motivated to succeed in college; and he possesses qualities of leadership.

We now have side by side two summaries, one of what personal and social qualities the catalogues say the college is looking for and the other my interpretation of the qualities implied by the major stated objectives of the colleges. The only item common to the two lists is the one about being serious in purpose and strongly motivated. If we wish to equate the two statements about requiring good personality and eliminating psychotics, then there are two points of agreement. Unless my analysis of the situation is incorrect, there is very little justification for requiring most of the characteristics listed except, as suggested, to decrease the work load of the discipline committee or possibly to ensure that the

alumni will have a minimum of characters whom they would be embarrassed to claim as fellow graduates.

Let us now consider the negative as well as the positive aspect of the selection method implied by the list of personal and social characteristics desired by admissions officers. Is it right and proper to deny the opportunity to study at a particular college, or possibly *any* college, to a boy because he is shy and poorly adjusted socially; or because he has *not* participated in high school band, athletics, publications, or chemistry club; or because he is nervous and insecure; or because he has not been elected class president or captain of the football team, or given other evidence of "leadership"? Admittedly, the undesirable extremes of some of the traits such as morality should result in disqualification, but the denial of the opportunity to study in college because of most of these characteristics seems somewhat drastic to me. I realize that in practice admission is not denied to many people who are shy, nervous, and unsociable, but if I assume that the catalogue statements really reflect the honest intent of the admissions officer, then it must be concluded that these people got in either because the admissions office made mistakes or because there were not enough honest-to-goodness desirables to fill the quota.

EMPIRICAL EVALUATION METHODS

There is another way to approach this problem of what personal and social qualities are to be sought in college students. This is a method which has an honorable history in college admission work and which is continuing to bear fruit in numerous educational, military, and industrial applications. It is a method which is firmly grounded in empirical observation. I refer to the statistical methods of validation which have borne such fruit as the College Board Scholastic Aptitude Test.

According to this method, all that is necessary is to develop tests of those personal and social qualities which would appear to be promising, administer these tests to students during freshman week, and then, after the students have completed a substantial portion of their college work, study the relationship between each test and various measures of success. It isn't necessary that the tests be highly refined and reliable at the start, so long as they really do tap some important aspects of personality. Then, if any of the tests prove to have some correlation with any of the criteria of success, work can be continued by improving the tests, identifying more basic variables which account for the correlation, or undertaking whatever line of development suggests itself. Eventually one would thus hope to establish valid measures of qualities known to be important and to learn precisely how they should be used, taking due account of the magnitude of the errors in prediction.

Such studies have, of course, been done. In most such studies a measure of success in college, such as freshman average grade, has been employed. The results have almost always been disappointing. There have been some results which tend to substantiate a statement I made previously—that you should admit people who are unsocial, docile, and compulsive. The trouble, of course, is that freshman average grade is not a satisfactory criterion of success in college, if we really take account of more than the first of our four important objectives— the one about acquiring knowledge or information.

The point that validity studies may lead to misleading results if the criterion of success is inadequate may be illustrated by an example from a military application.[1] During World War II it was necessary to assign military personnel with the utmost care in order to avoid wasting manpower and to insure that the various military tasks were handled competently. One study was concerned with assignment of recruits to schools for Gunner's Mates in the Navy.

[1] Norman Frederiksen, *Statistical Study of the Achievement Testing Program in Gunner's Mates Schools* (NAVPERS 18079, June, 1948).

Correlations were computed between scores on each of the tests in the Navy classification test battery and grades in Gunner's Mate school. The tests included the General Classification Test and tests of reading comprehension, arithmetical reasoning, clerical aptitude, mechanical aptitude, and mechanical knowledge. The results clearly indicated that the best test for selecting Gunner's Mate school students was the test of reading comprehension.

It would have been simple to accept these findings, develop a prediction formula for use by classification officers, and go ahead with the assignments. However, it seemed a little peculiar to select Gunner's Mates on the basis of reading. It appeared that while the reading test was satisfactory for predicting grades the way they *were*, it might not be satisfactory for predicting grades the way they *should* be.

The duties of men in this specialty involve the operation, repair, and adjustment of naval guns, which require the disassembly and assembly of complicated and sometimes heavy equipment. In the schools, the curriculum covered small arms, 30 cal. machine guns, 20 mm. and 40 mm. anti-aircraft guns, and the 5 in. 38 cal. dual purpose gun. A little investigation revealed that the instruction was largely based on manuals and the grading was based on written examinations. It was said that in the early days of the war the instructors would let the students look at but not touch the guns because of a naval regulation forbidding unqualified personnel to handle equipment. The instructional methods were gradually changed, chairs were moved out of classrooms and tables and gun mounts were moved in, and the written examinations were replaced by performance tests. These new performance tests required such tasks as analyzing a casualty and repairing it, adjusting headspace or the oil buffer of a 30 cal. Browning machine gun, and replacing the inner cocking lever of the breech block of a 40 mm. gun. When validity studies were then made, results were more reasonable. The validity coefficients for the reading test went down and the validity coefficients for the mechanical aptitude and mechanical knowledge tests went up. It now became possible to use the empirical findings to good advantage in the selection of Gunner's Mate trainees. The tests now predicted grades as they *should* be, according to the best judgment available.

Let me describe one other example which I think illustrates the point that adequate criteria are necessary if validity studies are to be useful in telling us what characteristics have value in a selection situation. The purpose of a study being carried out by the Educational Testing Service is to determine the relative validity of various types of aptitude test items for predicting school grades at the ninth and twelfth grade levels. Some of the item types were intended to measure verbal ability and others to measure quantitative ability. The general results, at least according to my interpretation, were that verbal test items getting at straight, unimaginative knowledge, such as vocabulary items, were better than items getting at more creative and complex cognitive skills, such as reading comprehension items. Similarly, in the quantitative area, test items measuring simple computational ability were better predictors of grades than items getting at more imaginative and creative abilities such as arithmetical reasoning items.

I have argued with some of my colleagues that we should not necessarily follow the results of these validity studies in choosing item types for a new test of scholastic aptitude. The "clerical" type of items may be best for predicting grades the way they *are* but not for predicting grades the way they *should* be. It is comparatively easy for a teacher to note differences among pupils in accuracy of clerical detail, but much harder to evaluate differences in other more complex qualities which are presumably nurtured by the school. The result is that in many schools grades tend merely to reflect differences among pupils in willingness to sit down and painstakingly

copy, label, check, memorize, and recall. It is for somewhat similar reasons that I earlier stated that the personal qualities needed for mastery of information are compulsiveness and docility.

DETERMINATION OF CRITERIA

We see, then, that using validity studies as a basis for learning what personal and social qualities are important for success in college is not a simple straightforward matter. Nevertheless, it is a method which I recommend. I now propose to state how I would go about it.

In view of what has been said, it seems obvious that the first thing to do is to improve the criteria of success in college against which the selection measures are to be evaluated. This is a job which obviously the admissions officer cannot do by himself. Neither can anyone else do it by himself; the task would certainly require cooperation from a very large number of people at a university, and before that cooperation can be obtained it will be necessary to develop mutual understanding between faculty members, administration, and research workers. The task would require strong support from many members of the university from the president down.

The first job would be to go to work on the statements of objectives. I don't know who wrote the statements quoted above, but I doubt if the faculty had much to do with them. And the faculty is entrusted with the job of seeing that the objectives of the university are fulfilled. I wonder how many have even read the objectives of their institutions? The question should be seriously raised as to whether these statements are intended to be of promotional value primarily, or whether they are intended to serve as guides to be followed by the faculty in carrying out its daily work.

I suggest that the way to begin would be to ask every responsible member of the university staff to state in behavioral terms just how he would expect a student to be *different* as a consequence of the teaching, advising, coaching, or deaning performed. One would have to strive continually to get away from the use of clichés and adjectives and get into the use of *verbs*. It would be comparatively easy in some areas. The mathematics instructor might merely say, "I expect the student to be able to solve problems like this," and exhibit his final examination. And, providing the final examination is well conceived and based on serious thought as to what he is trying to accomplish in his course, this is the best possible way to answer the question. It is best because it is a method of communication which is unambiguous and is, in fact, ready to apply in measuring student progress.

Not all instructors would have it as easy as the mathematics instructor. The sociologist might believe that among other things he is teaching students to be more sensitive to social problems. It would be up to him to try to translate this into description of behavior that could be observed and evaluated. Mind you, I don't expect that everything would be reduced to multiple choice examinations in this process. Perhaps observation of the amount of volunteer work done for social service organizations by the student would be one of the evaluation methods the sociologist would use.

The people at a high administrative level who are responsible for objectives of the institution as a whole would perhaps have the hardest time. Perhaps, when faced with the problem of making specific what is meant by some highly abstract generalization, they would find that it is basically meaningless and drop it from consideration. It is conceivable that after mature consideration it might be decided that developing moral fiber is primarily the function of the home and church and should not be prominently mentioned as an objective of the college. Or more possibly, in the process of formulating descriptions of specific behaviors which exemplify and define the generalization, the concept itself might become clarified in such a way that it would become possible actually to do something

about it, whereas previously it had existed only as a reverent hope. A part of this whole process would be the critical examination of these objectives, throwing out some and reinforcing others, until the whole of the statements represented adequately the job the university was trying to do.

APPLICATION OF CRITERIA

The next step is to translate these behavior descriptions into evaluation methods. In some cases no translation would be needed, as in the case where the mathematics instructor says, "Here is an examination which defines the skills I expect my students to have as a consequence of taking my course." In other cases imaginative ways would have to be invented for measuring the extent to which the desired modes of behavior are exhibited. When this phase of work is completed, the instruments for evaluating outcomes can actually be applied to students, along with experimental selection tests, and we are now in a position to solve our problem of what personal and social qualities are needed on the basis of correlations with various criterion measures. The method will be successful to the extent that the procedure of defining objectives in terms of evaluation methods is successfully accomplished, and to the extent that selection measures of important social and personal qualities can be developed.

In the analysis of the data it would be important to keep separate various homogeneous groups of students in order to make it possible to discover, if it is so, that the characteristics desired in some students are different from those desired in others. The qualities desired in engineers may be different from those desired in musicians, for example.

This would involve a lot of work. But I seriously propose that it should be done. The beneficial effects to the university would not be limited to the admissions officer. The values coming from the introduction of methods of evaluation or quality control in industry are well known. I believe that there would be an immediate and dramatic improvement in the effectiveness with which the functions of the university are carried out.

THE FIRST STEP

I would like to end with a positive suggestion. A small start can be made by any admissions officer at his own institution. Discussions can be started with various deans and faculty members for the purpose of getting more precise ideas as to what skills and abilities are taught in each area and what characteristics are valued in students. I happen to know some faculty members who would say, "Don't send me the campus leader." Such discussions might help to stimulate further thinking and clarification of course and departmental objectives and might help give the admissions officer a better picture of the ideal student. The picture in engineering might be different from that in journalism or agriculture or liberal arts. This beginning might provide the impetus for a more thoroughgoing examination by the college of its objectives and evaluation methods. Every large study must have a small start.

Having these different pictures of the ideal student, then, should lead to increasing recognition of individual differences in candidates. The logical outcome of such a point of view is an approach to college admissions which is something like that of counseling. Instead of raising the same question each time, "Does this candidate fit our stereotype of the college man?" we begin to ask, "Will it be good for *this* student, with *his* abilities and interests and deficiencies, to come to my college to try to carry out his plans for a life and a career?" The recognition of individual differences among students—differences in mental endowment, in life experience, in personal qualities, and in special interests and abilities—should be a central concept in educational planning generally and in college admissions particularly. The individual characteristics of a student which make desirable *for him* a certain educational program are largely unknown at present. Carrying through a serious effort to develop adequate criteria against which to evaluate selection methods would, I believe, enable us to perform the functions involved in college admissions in a manner which would be of considerable benefit to students and colleges alike.

Chapter 29

Moderator Variables in Prediction

DAVID R. SAUNDERS

There are many examples of situations in which the predictive validity of some psychological measure varies systematically in accord with some other independent psychological variable. Thus, the multiple correlation coefficient for prediction of freshman college grades tends to be higher for women than for men [1]. The regression line for veterans tends to be different from that for non-veterans [3]. The prediction of freshman engineering grades from appropriate scales of the *Strong Interest Test* is lower for groups thought to be compulsive than for groups thought to be non-compulsive [4].

Analysis of covariance provides a statistical method for studying situations in which the degree or mode of predictability is thought to vary as a function of membership in one or another of designated groups, which are presumed to be distinct and homogeneous. On the other hand, the "moderated multiple regression" provides a simple generalization to the case in which the basic parameter is not membership in some group, but score on some continuous

This article is reprinted from *Educational and Psychological Measurement*, 1956, with the permission of the author and the copyright holder, G. Frederic Kuder.

variable. The "compulsiveness" of the third example cited above ought to be one illustration of such a continuous variable. The amount of prediction obtainable from the *Strong Engineer Scale Score* should vary continuously with the score on compulsiveness, and should not jump from one value to another at some arbitrary level of compulsiveness as required by the analysis of covariance. Evidence that this is indeed the case will be given below.

Other situations in which continuous variables can be conceived as moderating the predictive power of other variables might be the following: (a) Degree of "insight" may determine the degree of relationship between self-reports of personality and more objectively determined scores on the same traits. (b) Amount of "desire to make a good impression" may determine the relative efficacy of free-response and forced-choice types of personality inventory [6]. (c) Degree of "natural enthusiasm or ability to discover new interest" may determine the validity of interest measures for a variety of situations, even when "compulsiveness" is held constant. (d) Degree of "emotional stability" may determine the effectiveness of academic ability measures in predicting academic success. The class of situations in which the "moderated multiple regression" might be profitably studied can be made quite large [for further examples see 5], and can be seen to include a number of situations of potential practical significance.

I. MATHEMATICAL BASIS OF MODERATED REGRESSION

In the ordinary linear regression, the following equation is assumed to be capable of describing the experimental data when suitable values are assigned to the constants:

$$y = \bar{y} + \sum_i a_i x_i \qquad (1)$$

Suppose we now substitute for each of the parameters, a_i, in equation 1 a linear function of a second group of predictors ("compulsiveness," "insight," "enthusiasm," etc.), z_j, which are supposed to moderate the influence of the original predictors of the criterion variable. The z_j are, by definition, called moderator variables. The equation takes the following form:

$$y = \bar{y} + \sum_i \left(\sum_j b_{ji} z_j \right) x_i \qquad (2)$$

and this may be reduced to the following simpler general expression:

$$y = \bar{y} + \sum_i a_i x_i + \sum_j b_j z_j + \sum_{i,j} c_{ij} x_i z_j \qquad (3)$$

(The a's, b's, and c's are new constants in equation 3.) The result of this derivation is the equation of the moderated multiple regression. It will be observed that this equation has several properties which make it convenient to work with: (a) Routine procedures for fitting the equation to experimental data are already known [2; 7, p. 41]. Actually, once the appropriate product-variables, $x_i z_j$, have been computed from the original data, any conventional multiple correlation and regression method may be used to fit equation 3. (b) No square terms and no terms higher than the quadratic are called for. (c) Only certain multiplicative terms are specified as being of interest, namely, those involving one of the x's and one of the z's. (d) The form is invariant under linear changes in the scale of measurement of any of the predictors, despite the presence of the multiplicative terms. (e) In any given situation, linear changes in the scales of measurement can be chosen so that all the a's and b's of equation 3 become zero, and the prediction equation reduced to the form:

$$y = k + \sum_{ij} c_{ij} x_i z_j \qquad (4)$$

(f) The geometrical representation of the results is easily visualized, as shown in Figure 29–1 for a single x and z.

It is apparent from Figure 29–1 that this model might also be called the "ruled sur-

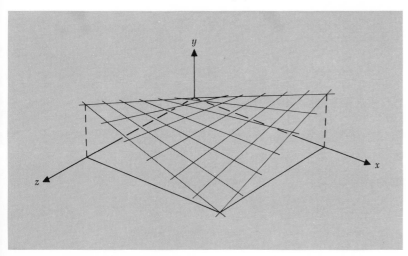

face regression"—any line in the regression surface that is parallel to the xy or the yz plane is a straight line, although lines not parallel to one of these planes will be parabolic. This property corresponds to the mathematical property of the surface that, if all the predictors but one are held constant, the residual regression line is an ordinary linear one, and the entire regression surface can be generated by regular motions of a straight line. On the other hand, this regression model does have certain disadvantages that might be overcome by employing a still more general quadratic regression—one which would include the other cross-product terms and the square terms. The principal difficulty with the present surface is its dependence upon constancy of units of measurement within any single scale or score, but this difficulty is shared with ordinary linear regression, and would not be completely solved by using a general quadratic model; the addition of the large number of additional constants to be fitted to data might more than offset the advantages.

II. SOME EXAMPLES OF MODERATED REGRESSION

This section provides illustrations of actual situations in which the ruled surface apparently provides a better representation of the data than an ordinary regression, whether with or without division of the sample into subgroups.

EXAMPLE 1

The data are for 153 engineering freshmen at Princeton University who completed the *Strong Interest Blank* on a voluntary basis at various times. The *Accountant Scale* of the Strong is used as a measure of "compulsiveness," while the *Engineer Scale* is used as a predictor of grade point average. Considering the entire group with the ordinary regression model, a correlation of .102 is obtained. (This value taken alone is "significant" at about the 10 per cent level, using a one-tailed test versus the null hypothesis.) The regression line is the heavy solid line in Figure 29–2.

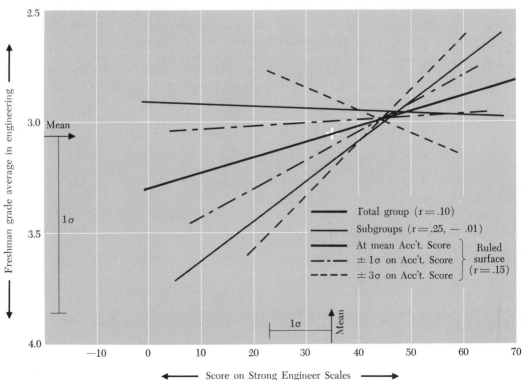

When the total group is divided into two approximately equal-sized subgroups, by splitting it near the median score on the *Accountant Scale*, two new correlation values are obtained within these groups. Within the "compulsive" subgroup the correlation is −.01, and within the non-compulsive subgroup it is .25. (Assuming that the direction of the difference in these correlations was predicted correctly, the difference is "significant" at about the 10 per cent level.) The regression lines associated with each of these groups are the fine solid lines in Figure 29–2.

When the total group is now reconsidered as a whole using the moderated regression model, a multiple correlation of .153 is obtained. This is higher than the average correlation found within the two subgroups, which was already higher than the correlation found in the total group with the linear regression model. On the other hand, the multiple correlation using the moderated model cannot be said to be "significantly" better than the multiple correlation using the linear model and the

same two predictors (*Engineering Scale* and *Accountant Scale*), unless one is willing to use the 15 per cent level of confidence.

This example was chosen for its face validity and must be regarded as illustrating the general form of relationship that can be portrayed with the moderated regression model. It is not indicative of the strength with which such relationships have been found to hold in other instances.

EXAMPLE 2

The data are for the same 153 engineering students as were employed in the first example, and the data presented are the same. The difference is that in this instance the *Mathematics-Science Teacher Scale* is used in place of the *Engineer Scale*. The various values of the correlations are shown on Figure 29–3. In this case it can be said that the contribution of the moderated model beyond that of the ordinary linear model is significant at the 5 per cent level. Also, the general level of the correlational

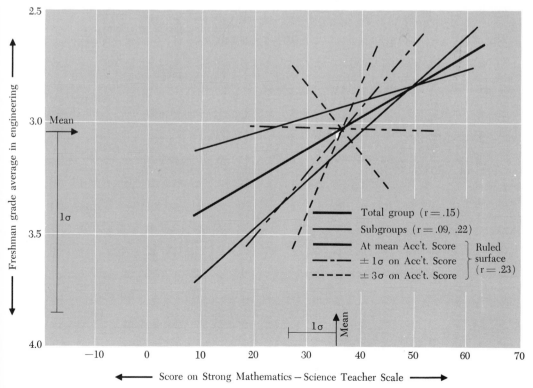

values obtained is somewhat higher, though still not so high as to call for immediate application.

Altogether, ten different scales from the *Strong Interest Test* were used in the role that has been taken by the *Engineer* and *Mathematics-Science Teacher Scales* in these two examples. The pertinent numerical results are summarized in Table 29–1.

In the first column of this table the significance of the original over-all correlations has been evaluated by a two-tailed *t*-test. In the case of scales having name validity for the criterion (average grades in engineering) a one-tailed test is more reasonable to use, and it is on this basis that the remaining two scales are shown.

Frederiksen's previous analysis [4] is summarized in the next group of columns. Column r_I shows the correlations in a "compulsive" subgroup, while column r_{II} shows the correlations in the complementary "noncompulsive" subgroup. As reported earlier, nine out of ten of these pairs of correlations have the higher absolute value for the "noncompulsive" subgroup. Five out of the ten differences are significant at the 10 per cent level or better, applying a one-tailed test.

The remaining group of columns is presented to permit an evaluation of a moderated regression as a means of representing the same data without resorting to subgrouping. R_{linear} is the ordinary multiple correlation obtained by including the Accountant score as a second predictor with the one listed at the left. Significant increases[1] in the multiple are found on three rows—for banker, psychologist, and mortician, the former being most highly significant. In these situations the *Accountant Scale* is operating as an ordinary "suppressor" variable, as would be expected from its observed correlation with the three scales. $R_{moderated}$ is obtained by adding the appropriate product score to the predictor battery of R_{linear}. The further increase in the multiple is significant in 5 out of 10 tries, three of these being at the 5 per cent level, and four of these being among the five cases for which significant differences were found for the subgroups analysis. In these instances the *Accountant Scale* is

[1] These increases were tested by taking

$$t = \sqrt{\frac{151\,(R^2 - t^2)}{1 - r^2}}$$

for 151 degrees of freedom, and converting to probability as in a two-tailed *t*-test.

Table 29–1   Correlations with Freshman Engineering Grades (Princeton)*

Predictor Scale N = 153	Original Correlation r	Subgroups Based on Accountant Score			Multiple Correlations Adding Accountant Score	
		r_I	r_{II}	Δr	R_{linear}	$R_{moderated}$
Psychologist	.311†	.36	.42	.06	.385†	.391
Mortician	−.289†	−.20	−.47	.27§	.343‡	.362§
Real Estate Salesman	−.233†	−.11	−.37	.26§	.248	.282‡
Chemist	.201‡	.10	.37	.27§	.228	.262‡
Banker	−.187‡	−.25	−.29	.04	.276†	.278
Mathematics-Science Teacher	.153§	.09	.21	.12	.163	.227‡
Mathematician	.152§	.14	.27	.13	.199	.217
Minister	.152§	.30	.08	−.22	.194	.194
Physicist	.129	.03	.30	.27§	.174	.214§
Engineer	.102	−.01	.25	.26§	.128	.153
Accountant	.082				(.082)	

* See text for statements of the hypotheses tested.
† Significant at or beyond the 1% level.
‡ Significant at or beyond the 5% level.
§ Significant at or beyond the 10% level.

operating as a "moderator" variable. Since the direction of this moderation was predicted from the original hypothesis about compulsiveness and predictability of interest scores, a suitable one-tailed test[2] was applied to evaluate the contribution of the product terms in the regression. Actually, the sign of the product term's beta weight is as predicted in all ten of the ten examples. The results using the *Mathematics-Science Teacher Scale* show the most significant moderator effect, with *Real Estate Salesman* and *Chemist* next.

We may note that the unique contribution of the ruled surface occurs where the subgroup analysis showed the largest expected differences in predictability. This makes it likely that the ruled surface actually does capitalize on the same properties of the data, as should be the case according to the theory. We may also note that it does so more efficiently and effectively than the subgroups analysis; the sample is treated as a whole, yet the multiple is always higher than the average *r* found in the subgroups—most markedly so in the cases for which the extra contribution of the product term is significant.

It is well-known that the various scores

of the Strong are mutually dependent, since they represent merely different weightings of the same 400 item responses. For this reason it is virtually impossible to provide an over-all significance statement for the ten trials of the *Accountant Scale* as a moderator variable. However, the general implication of these results was regarded as encouraging, and the decision was made to seek cross-validation of as many of the results as was conveniently possible.

REFERENCES

1. ABELSON, R. P. Sex differences in predictability of college grades. *Educ. psychol. Measmt*, 1952, 12, 638–644.
2. COURT, A. T. Measuring joint causation. *J. Amer. Statist. Assoc.*, 1930, 25, 245–254.
3. FREDERIKSEN, N., & SCHRADER, W. B. *Adjustment to college: A study of 10,000 veteran and non-veteran students in sixteen American colleges.* Princeton, N.J.: Educational Testing Service, 1950.
4. FREDERIKSEN, N., & MELVILLE, S. D. Differential predictability in the use of test scores. *Educ. psychol. Measmt*, 1954, 14, 647–656.
5. GAYLORD, R. H., & CARROLL, J. B. A general approach to the problem of the population control variable. *Amer. Psychologist*, 1948, 3, 310. (Abstract)
6. GORDON, L. V. Validities of the forced choice and questionnaire methods of personality measurement. *J. appl. Psychol.*, 1951, 35, 407–412.
7. RIDER, P. R. *An introduction to modern statistical methods.* New York: John Wiley & Sons, 1939.

---

[2] These increases were tested by taking

$$t = \sqrt{\frac{150(R_m{}^2 - R_l{}^2)}{1 - R_l{}^2}}$$

for 150 degrees of freedom, and converting to probability as in a one-tailed *t*-test. *t* is positive if the beta weights for the predictor and product variables have *un*like signs—negative if like.

Chapter 30

Incremental Validity

LEE SECHREST

The 1954 APA publication *Technical Recommendations for Psychological Tests and Diagnostic Techniques* [2] established minimum standards to be met in the production and promotion of psychometric instruments. Since that time there have appeared a considerable number of articles elaborating or extending the considerations involved in developing tests [e.g., 10, 12, 15, 7, 4, 6]. In one of the most recent developments, Campbell and Fiske [7] have suggested that a crucial distinction is to be made between convergent and discriminant validity. It is necessary to demonstrate not only that a measure covaries with certain other connotatively similar variables, but that its covariance with other connotatively dissimilar variables is limited.

Campbell [6] has suggested several possible additions to recommend validity indicators, all of which focus on the problem of *discriminant* validity, i.e., the demonstration that a test construct is not completely or even largely redundant with other better established or more parsimonious constructs. He has suggested, for example, that correlations with intelligence, social desirability and self-ratings should be reported since these variables are likely to be conceptually and theoretically simpler than most of our constructs. If a new test proves to be reducible to an intelligence or social desirability measure, its *raison d'être* probably vanishes.

It is the purpose of this note to suggest an additional validity construct and evidence which should be presented in the basic publications concerning *any test which is intended for applied, predictive use.*

This article is reprinted from *Educational and Psychological Measurement*, 1963, with the permission of the author and the copyright holder, G. Frederic Kuder.

The writer wishes to thank Donald T. Campbell and Douglas N. Jackson for helpful suggestions on an earlier version of this manuscript.

INCREMENTAL VALIDITY

Almost without exception evidence which is presented to support the validity of a psychological test is presented in the form of some improvement over results which would be expected by chance. However, in *clinical* situations, at least, tests are rarely, if ever, used in a manner consistent with the chance model. Almost always Rorschachs are interpreted after interviews, reading of case reports, conferences and the like. The meaning of a report that some Rorschach variable will predict better than chance becomes obscure under those circumstances. It seems clear that validity must be claimed for a test in terms of some *increment* in predictive efficiency over the information otherwise easily and cheaply available.

Cronbach and Gleser [9, pp. 30–32] and, as they point out, Conrad [8], have both discussed the problem of the base against which the predictive power of a test is to be evaluated. Cronbach and Gleser declare, "Tests should be judged on the basis of their contribution over and above the best strategy available, making use of prior information" [9, p. 31]. They do indicate that tests may be valuable in spite of low correlations if they tap characteristics either unobservable or difficult to observe by other means. Shaffer [16, p. 76] also suggested, "One can . . . study the degree to which the clinician is valid with and without the aid of a certain technique, and thereby assess the value of the test indirectly." We are not so sure that such an assessment is completely indirect.

In light of the above argument it is proposed that the publications adduced as evidence for the utility of a test in a clinical situation—and probably for most other uses —should include evidence that the test will *add to* or *increase* the validity of predictions made on the basis of data which are usually available. At a minimum it would seem that a test should have demonstrated incremental validity beyond that of brief case histories, simple biographical information and brief interviews. A strong case can also be made to demand that a test contribute beyond the level of simpler, e.g., paper and pencil, tests. As a matter of fact, Campbell's recommendation that new tests

be correlated with self-ratings is quite akin to some aspects of incremental validity.

ADEQUATE STATISTICAL EVIDENCE

When a test is added to a battery, the usual way to express its contribution is either by a partial correlation or by an increment to a zero order or multiple correlation. There is, perhaps, one objection to the partial or multiple correlation as a demonstration of incremental validity. That is, the increase, even if significant, is of somewhat undetermined origin and obscures the exact nature of the increment achieved.

Consider the matrix of correlations:

	1	2	0
1		60	40
2			40
0			

in which 1 and 2 are predictors of criterion 0. The multiple $R_{12.0} = .45$ and the partial $r_{20.1} = .22$. Both values might be considered to represent improvements over the zero order correlations. And yet, without knowing the reliabilities of 1 and 2, we will be unable to discern whether 2 contributes to the prediction of 0 because it represents a theoretical variable distinct from 1 or whether 2 has only the same, and informationally redundant, effect of increasing the length and, hence, the reliability of Test 1. It will often be important to know whether an increment results from a Spearman-Brown prophecy operation or from some contribution of theoretical importance. Kelley [13] suggested quite a number of years ago that when correlations between intelligence and achievement measures are properly treated the two measures prove to be almost completely overlapping. Thus, in his view, the two kinds of measures only combine to form a longer and more reliable measure of a single variable.

One solution to the problem might be the correction of inter-test correlations for attenuation. If the reliabilities are so low that the corrected correlation approaches unity, no increment to R nor a significant partial correlation will ensue. In the above example, given reliabilities for 1 and 2 of only .60, the correlation between them would become unity, the multiple would be .40, and the partial r .00. On the other hand, if both variables had reliability coefficients of .90, the correction for attenuation would have little effect on either R or partial correlation.[1]

EXEMPLARY INSTANCES OF INCREMENTAL VALIDITY RESEARCH

Demonstrations of incremental validity are not common in research literature except in prediction of academic performance. Unfortunately, where they occur the data often are discouraging. Winch and More [19] used a multiple correlation technique in an attempt to determine the increment produced by TAT protocols over a semi-structured interview and case history material. Their results provide no basis for concluding that the TAT contributes anything beyond what is given by interviews or case histories. Sines [17] discovered that the Rorschach apparently did yield better than chance predictions, but it seemingly not only did not add to other information obtained from interviews and a biographical data sheet, but it actually produced a net *decrement* in predictive accuracy. This in spite of *better than chance* "validity." Kostlan [14] found that judges made better than chance inferences about patients' behavior from only "minimal data" (age, occupation, education, marital status and source of referral). When test results were used to make the same judgments, only the social history yielded more accurate inferences than those made from simple biographical facts.

In the general area of prediction of academic success, data are widely available

[1] It is to be noted that correction for attenuation of the validity values is *not* suggested and should not be done.

indicating the increment over previous grades afforded by predictions based on psychometric data. Even in predicting academic performance, however, it is not always clear that the use of test data accomplishes anything beyond increasing the reliability of the ability measure based on grades. If treated as suggested above, it might be possible to determine whether a test contributes anything beyond maximizing the reliability of the general ability measure afforded by grades. Ford [11] has presented data concerning the prediction of grades in nursing school making use of, among other measures, the Cooperative General Science Test (CGST) and high school point average (HSPA). The correlation matrix between these variables is:

	CGST	HSPA	Grades
1. CGST		.33	.57
2. HSPA			.51
0. Grades			

The multiple correlation $R_{12.0}$ is .66 and the partial $r_{10.2}$ is .50. The split-half reliability of the CGST has been reported to be .88. While no reliability estimate for HSPA is known to the writer, several researchers have reported reliabilities for college grades [3, 5, 18]. If we take the median value of the three reported values of .78, .80, and .90 as a likely estimate for HSPA and then correct the r_{12} for attenuation, the .33 becomes .40. The multiple correlation then drops only to .65 and the partial correlation only to .46. It is obvious that for the prediction of grades in nursing courses the use of the Cooperative General Science Test results in an *increment* in validity over high school grades and that the increment may be regarded as more than a contribution to reliable measurement of a single factor.

SUMMARY

It is proposed that in addition to demonstrating the *convergent* and *discriminant* validity of tests intended for use in clinical situations, evidence should be produced for *incremental* validity. It must be demonstrable that the addition of a test will produce better predictions than are made on the basis of information other than the test ordinarily available. Reference to published research indicates that situations may well occur in which, in spite of better than chance validity, tests may not contribute to, or may even detract from, predictions made on the basis of biographical and interview information. It is further suggested that, when correlations for a given test are entered into a multiple correlation or partial correlation, the inter-predictor correlations be corrected for attenuation to determine whether an increase in the multiple or partial correlations is to be attributed to a mere increase in reliability of measurement of the predictor variable.

REFERENCES

1. American Council on Education, The Cooperative Test Service. A booklet on norms. New York, 1938.

2. American Psychological Association, Committee on Psychological Tests. *Technical recommendations for psychological tests and diagnostic techniques.* Washington, D.C.: APA, 1954. (Reprinted from *Psychol. Bull. Suppl.,* 1954, 51, 619–629.)

3. Anderson, Scarvia B. Estimating grade reliability. *J. appl. Psychol.,* 1959, 37, 461–464.

4. Bechtoldt, H. P. Construct validity: a critique. *Amer. Psychologist,* 1959, 14, 619–629.

5. Bendig, A. W. The reliability of letter grades. *Educ. psychol. Measmt,* 1953, 13, 311–321.

6. Campbell, D. T. Recommendations for APA test standards regarding construct, trait, or discriminant validity. *Amer. Psychologist,* 1960, 15, 546–553.

7. Campbell, D. T., & Fiske, D. W. Convergent and discriminant validation by the multitrait-multimethod matrix. *Psychol. Bull.,* 1959, 61, 81–105.

8. Conrad, H. Information which should be provided by test publishers and testing agencies on the validity and use of their tests. In *Proceedings, 1949, Invitational conference on testing problems.* Princeton, N.J.: Educational Testing Service, 1950, 63–68.

9. Cronbach, L. J., & Gleser, Goldine C. *Psychological tests and personnel decisions.* Urbana: Univer. Illinois Press, 1957.

10. Cronbach, L. J., & Meehl, P. E. Construct validity in psychological tests. *Psychol. Bull.,* 1955, 52, 281–302.

11. Ford, A. H. Prediction of academic success in three schools of nursing. *J. appl. Psychol.,* 1950, 34, 186–189.

12. Jessor, R., & Hammond, K. R. Construct validity and the Taylor Anxiety Scale. *Psychol. Bull.,* 1957, 54, 161–170.

13. Kelley, T. L. *Interpretation of educational measurements.* New York: World Book Co., 1927.

14. Kostlan, A. A method for the empirical study of psychodiagnosis. *J. consult. Psychol.,* 1954, 18, 83–88.

15. Loevinger, Jane. Objective tests as instruments of psychological theory. *Psychol. Rep.,* 1957, 3, 635–694. Monogr. Suppl. 9.

16. Shaffer, L. Information which should be provided by test publishers and testing agencies on the validity and use of their tests. Personality tests. In *Proceedings, 1949, Invitational conference on testing problems.* Princeton, N.J.: Educational Testing Service, 1950.

17. Sines, L. K. The relative contribution of four kinds of data to accuracy in personality assessment. *J. consult. Psychol.,* 1959, 23, 483–492.

18. Wallace, W. L. The prediction of grades in specific college courses. *J. educ. Res.,* 1951, 44, 587–595.

19. Winch, R. F., & More, D. M. Does TAT add information to interviews? Statistical analysis of the increments. *J. clin. Psychol.,* 1956, 12, 316–321.

Chapter 31

Validity, Reliability, and Baloney

EDWARD E. CURETON

It is a generally accepted principle that if a test has demonstrated validity for some given purpose, considerations of reliability are secondary. The statistical literature also informs us that a validity coefficient cannot exceed the square root of the reliability coefficient of either the predictor or the criterion. This paper describes the construction and validation of a new test which seems to call in question these accepted principles. Since the technique of validation is the crucial point, I shall discuss the validation procedures before describing the test in detail.

Briefly, the test uses a new type of projective technique which appears to reveal controllable variations in psychokinetic force as applied in certain particular situations. In the present study the criterion is college scholarship, as given by the usual grade-point average. The subjects were 29 senior and graduate students in a course in Psychological Measurements. These students took Forms Q and R of the *Coopera-*

This article is reprinted from *Educational and Psychological Measurement*, 1950, with the permission of the author and the copyright holder, G. Frederic Kuder.

tive Vocabulary Test, Form R being administered about two weeks after Form Q. The correlation between grade-point average and the combined score on both forms of this test was .23. The reliability of the test, estimated by the Spearman-Brown formula from the correlation between the two forms, was .90.

The experimental form of the new test, which I have termed the "B–Projective Psychokinesis Test," or Test B, was also applied to the group. This experimental form contained 85 items, and there was a reaction to every item for every student. The items called for unequivocal "plus" or "minus" reactions, but in advance of data there is no way to tell which reaction to a given item may be valid for any particular purpose. In this respect Test B is much like many well-known interest and personality inventories. Since there were no intermediate reactions, all scoring was based on the "plus" reactions alone.

I first obtained the mean grade-point average of all the students whose reaction to each item was "plus." Instead of using the usual technique of biserial correlation, however, I used an item-validity index based on the significance of the difference between the mean grade-point average of the whole group, and the mean grade-point average of those who gave the "plus" reaction to any particular item. This is a straightforward case of sampling from a finite universe. The mean and standard deviation of the grade-point averages of the entire group of 29 are the known parameters. The null hypothesis to be tested is the hypothesis that the subgroup giving the "plus" reaction to any item is a random sample from this population. The mean number giving the "plus" reaction to any item was 14.6. I therefore computed the standard error of the mean for independent samples of 14.6 drawn from a universe of 29, with replacement. If the mean grade-point average of those giving the "plus" reaction to any particular item was more than one standard error *above* the mean of the whole 69, the item was retained with a scoring weight of *plus one*. If it was more than one standard error *below* this general mean, the item was retained with a scoring weight of *minus one*.

By this procedure, 9 positively weighted items and 15 negatively weighted items were obtained. A scoring key for all 24 selected items was prepared, and the "plus" reactions for the 29 students were scored with this key. The correlations between the 29 scores on the revised Test B and the grade-point averages was found to be .82. In comparison with the Vocabulary Test, which correlated only .23 with the same criterion, Test B appears to possess considerable promise as a predictor of college scholarship. However, the authors of many interest and personality tests, who have used essentially similar validation techniques, have warned us to interpret high validity coefficients with caution when they are derived from the same data used in making the item analysis.

The correlation between Test B and the Vocabulary Test was .31, which is .08 higher than the correlation between the Vocabulary Test and the grade-point averages. On the other hand, the reliability of Test B, by the Kuder-Richardson Formula 20, was −.06. Hence it would appear that the accepted principles previously mentioned are called in question rather severely by the findings of this study. The difficulty may be explained, however, by a consideration of the structure of the B–Projective Psychokinesis Test.

The items of Test B consisted of 85 metal-rimmed labelling tags. Each tag bore an item number, from 1 to 85, on one side only. To derive a score for any given student, I first put the 85 tags in a cocktail shaker and shook them up thoroughly. Then I looked at the student's grade-point average. If it was B or above, I projected into the cocktail shaker a wish that the student should receive a high "plus" reaction score. If his grade-point average was below B, I projected a wish that he should receive a low score. Then I threw the tags on the table. To obtain the student's score, I counted as "plus" reactions all the tags which lit with the numbered side up. The derivation of the term "B–Projective Psychokinesis Test" should now be obvious.

The moral of this story, I think, is clear. When a validity coefficient is computed from the same data used in making an item analysis, this coefficient cannot be interpreted uncritically. And, contrary to many statements in the literature, it cannot be interpreted "with caution" either. There is one clear interpretation for all such validity coefficients. This interpretation is—

"Baloney!"

Chapter 32

Personality Measurement, Faking, and Detection: An Assessment Method for Use in Personnel Selection

WARREN T. NORMAN

Despite the plethora of devices and procedures currently available in the area of personality assessment, few, if any, appear to be suitable for use in personnel selection contexts. Without even raising the critical questions of demonstrable relevance and measurement precision, many have to be excluded on a simple cost basis. Elaborate situational performance tests, highly instrumented (so-called "objective") laboratory techniques, and the vast majority of projective and intensive diagnostic interviewing procedures are simply too expensive even to be considered for routine use in most personnel screening and selection settings.[1]

This article is reprinted from the *Journal of Applied Psychology*, 1963, with the permission of the author and the American Psychological Association.

Material included in this report stems in part from a project sponsored by the Personnel Laboratory, Aeronautical Systems Division, Air Force Systems Command, Lackland Air Force Base, Texas.

[1] Where questions of cost have been waived temporarily for the sake of research [e.g., Kelly & Fiske, 15; and the studies reviewed by Cronbach, 8, and by Loevinger, 16], the data obtained hardly warrant any prolonged grief by the personnel psychologist deprived of these techniques.

Self-report personality questionnaires, inventories, and check lists, while not usually precluded by considerations of cost alone, nonetheless do present problems of their own. As Dunnette, McCartney, Carlson, and Kirchner [9] have recently pointed out, research evidence has been accumulating for a number of years which indicates that for even the most carefully constructed devices of this sort—i.e., those using the most sensitive formats for stimulus presentation, and the most sophisticated methods of scoring key development so far suggested—the effects of attempted faking and "slanting" of responses are pronounced. A detailed analysis of this problem and a review of some of the more pertinent arguments and research findings which may eventually bear on its resolution have been presented elsewhere [21]. To put it briefly, there is little evidence to date to support any of the following as a *sufficient* means of solving or circumventing the problem of faking or response dissimulation on personality inventories and questionnaires: forced-choice sets of stimuli matched either on endorsement frequency or on rated "desirability";

auxiliary correction or suppressor scales; pseudoability or maximal performance tasks; empirical (i.e., contrasted groups) key construction methods, whether to content-relevant or irrelevant stimuli; or response set and stylistic response tendency measures.

This is not to say that these techniques are generally useless nor that there is no evidence or reasonable argument to support one or more of them in preference to alternative methods for certain purposes. Each of them does in fact represent an interesting and, in some cases, an ingenious effort to deal with the problem of faking or some related issue. The position is taken here, however, that the best that can be said at the present time for any of these approaches taken singly or for any combination of them thus far suggested is that the degree and generality of their effectiveness in dealing with the problems of response contamination and faking in the area of personality assessment is yet to be demonstrated. For some there are sufficient data and theoretical arguments already available to warrant a somewhat stronger statement.

One way to circumvent (rather than to solve) the problem of faking or slanting of inventory responses is well known and has been widely employed. By the judicious use of rating procedures with knowledgeable but disinterested informants, useful data on the personality attributes of the ratees can often be obtained. But for the psychologist concerned with personnel selection, this suggestion presents as many problems as it avoids. For example, although the problem of faked responses may not be so salient in this case as when the subject is also the respondent, still there are probably not many instances in which informants who are sufficiently "knowledgeable" are also "disinterested." And what about the broad class of other response sets (e.g., centrality versus extremity tendencies, inclusiveness versus exclusiveness, etc.), well known for their confounding effects when not all subjects are rated by the same informant or when multiple informants assess, but disagree on, the status of a given subject? The

list of problems could be lengthened considerably but there is no need; the reviews by Cronbach [5, 6] and by Guilford [13, Ch. 11] summarize nicely most of the critical problems of this sort. And of even greater importance, they offer numerous suggestions, based on an extensive body of research findings, by which the effects of many of these contaminants can be eliminated or effectively minimized.[2]

But even assuming that the major sources of contamination in ratings can, in principle, be effectively suppressed to yield valid and reliable assessments, it is likely that the costs and procedural complexities required to obtain such data would make this approach unfeasible also in the great majority of personnel screening and selection situations.

The research presented below grew out of just such a situation. In the attempt to provide a means for measuring a previously established set of relevant personality attributes, derived from ratings, within the scope of feasibility for a particular selection setting, a method of scoring key construction for self-report inventories was discovered. It is suggested that this method may have considerable generality and utility for other selection contexts because of the way in which it handles the problem of intentional faking or distortion of self-report inventory responses.

CRITERION VARIABLES

In a series of peer nomination rating studies using the scales from Cattell's condensed personality sphere set with groups of normal male subjects, Tupes and Christal [25, 26] have demonstrated the existence and relative orthogonality of five personality

[2] It is interesting to observe for how long a time and to what extent attention has been focused on the problems of response contamination in the area of rating procedures and how well formulated the remedial or prophylactic principles are in that domain compared to the recency of comparable research on self-report inventories and the relative chaos that is so apparent in this area at present.

factors. These findings have been replicated on other samples using modified data collection and analysis methods by Wherry, Stander, and Hopkins [27] and by Norman [22]. The populations on which these results are based ranged from United States Air Force officer candidates through college undergraduates to applicants for graduate school training programs in clinical psychology. In addition, Tupes [24] has demonstrated predictive validities for these factors against military officer effectiveness criteria. Table 32–1 lists the names that have been given to these factors and abbreviated labels for the 20 scales that have been found to load most highly on these factors in prior studies.

The remarkable stability of this five-factor structure, the implications this provides for the development of an adequate taxonomy for personality and results of the

use of these scales as predictors for a limited number of other performance criteria have been reviewed elsewhere [22]. For purposes of the present discussion, these rating factors are taken as a set of intermediate criteria for use in the development of self-report inventory measures of these variables and against which such measures are to be "validated."

PREDICTOR INSTRUMENTS AND THE INITIAL RATIONALE FOR KEY CONSTRUCTION

Despite the reservations listed earlier relative to the use of self-report inventory methods for personality assessment in selection contexts, the available research data, especially those based on forced-choice response formats, did seem to indicate that this approach held some promise of success

Table 32–1 Abbreviated Descriptions of the Peer Nomination Criterion Rating Scales and Their Factor Designations

Factor Name*	Number	Abbreviated Scale Labels†	
		Pole A	Pole B
I. Extroversion or Surgency	1	Talkative–Silent	
	2	Frank, Open–Secretive	
	3	Adventurous–Cautious	
	4	Sociable–Reclusive	
II. Agreeableness	5	Goodnatured–Irritable	
	6	Not Jealous–Jealous	
	7	Mild, Gentle–Headstrong	
	8	Cooperative–Negativistic	
III. Conscientiousness	9	Fussy, Tidy–Careless	
	10	Responsible–Undependable	
	11	Scrupulous–Unscrupulous	
	12	Persevering–Quitting, Fickle	
IV. Emotional Stability	13	Poised–Nervous, Tense	
	14	Calm–Anxious	
	15	Composed–Excitable	
	16	Not Hypochondriacal–Hypochondriacal	
V. Culture	17	Artistically Sensitive–Artistically Insensitive	
	18	Intellectual–Unreflective, Narrow	
	19	Polished, Refined–Crude, Boorish	
	20	Imaginative–Simple, Direct	

* Pole A.
† For the actual scale labels employed in data collection, see Cattell [3].
SOURCE: Based on original findings by Tupes and Christal [25].

in this effort. The early work by Jurgensen [14] had employed endorsement rate (or "preference index") as a basis for matching stimuli to construct forced-choice items. The later findings by Berkshire [1] clearly indicated, however, that this had been an unfortunate choice. Thus the susceptibility to faking of the Jurgensen Classification Inventory reported in the interim by Longstaff and Jurgensen [17] and the later but unfortunately similar experience of Maher [18] could plausibly both be laid to this cause, at least in part.

Berkshire's results did indicate, however, that somewhat more effective matching could be achieved if rated "job importance" of the stimuli were used instead as a matching index. In addition, Edwards [10, 11] had also argued in favor of a rated stimulus characteristic (in this case "social desirability") as a basis for constructing well-matched, forced-choice items. However, a review of the literature indicated that the use of *average* importance or desirability ratings as a basis for matching stimuli was probably not a fully adequate criterion for several reasons.

First, it is seldom possible to find stimulus pairs with exactly the same mean ratings. Edwards, who acknowledged this difficulty and settled for a .5 scale unit mean difference (on a 9-point scale) to pair A and B stems for his Personal Preference Schedule items, subsequently found a correlation of about .40 between endorsement frequencies for the A response and the A-B rated social desirability difference values over all items in his test. A more stringent mean "equivalence" criterion could, of course, always be required and, on the basis of the above result, certainly would seem to be warranted. But it still seemed doubtful that other findings of the fakability of the EPPS such as those by Borislow [2], by Corah, Feldman, Cohen, Gruen, Meadow, and Ringwall [4], or even those by Edwards, Wright, and Lunneborg [12] could be attributed wholly to just the looseness of the mean desirability criterion used in constructing this inventory.

A second point is therefore worth noting, i.e., that the use of *mean* ratings as a sole criterion for matching stimuli ignores other possibly relevant parameters of the rating distributions. Unless the variances of the ratings are both near zero—a criterion suggested by Maher [18] but one seldom attainable with such data—it is possible that the variances could be appreciably different or, even if not, that the correlation between the ratings of the two stimuli could be quite low. If either of these situations should obtain, then clearly for at least some of the respondents the two stimuli would be different as regards their importance or desirability parameters for them. The findings by Rosen [23], Borislow [2], and Messick [19] would in fact all seem to indicate that the general social desirability stereotype may well be the composite of a rather disparate set of "personal desirability" stereotypes held by different members of a population. The high correlations obtained by Edwards *between average* desirability scale values from pairs of samples from different populations in no sense precludes the possibility of such *intrasample* heterogeneity of opinion. However, this problem could, in principle at least, also be surmounted by requiring either nearly zero variances or, alternatively, nearly equal variances plus a high positive correlation in order for two stimuli to be paired.

Still a third aspect of this approach is somewhat more troublesome to dispose of, however. I refer here to the point that all of the criteria for matching so far discussed are based on parameters of the distributions of ratings from single-stimulus presentations whereas the final test format requires the respondent to make forced-choice discriminations between pairs of stimuli. This constitutes a major problem for two reasons. First, it is well known that much finer discriminations can be made between stimuli when they are presented together in pair comparisons than when they are presented one at a time. Thus, two items which are indistinguishable in desirability when presented and rated singly may be quite clearly differentiable in desirability when placed together in a pair comparison. Secondly, the use of single-stimulus rating data as a basis for constructing forced-choice items assumes that the desirability parameters of individual stimuli are not affected by being placed in different contexts. This is tantamount to saying, in effect, that it makes no difference what the content of the stimulus is with which a given other stimulus is paired as long as they both have the same single-stimulus desirability parameters. On the face of it this seems improbable. There exists, in fact, a considerable body of research data in the areas of sensory psychophysics and attitude scaling indicating that perceived attributes of stimuli are markedly affected by variations in the context or background in which they are presented. Unfortunately, these findings are neither sufficiently specific nor extensive enough to permit one to predict the direction and magnitude of the mutual influence any pair of personality descriptive items will have on each other when placed together in a forced-choice format.

Thus it would appear that if one were bent on constructing forced-choice items that were highly resistant to dissimulation tendencies, the most defensible approach on the basis of our present knowledge would be to construct a large number of such items but to retain for scoring only those which remain indistinguishable to respondents in terms of desirability, after they have been put in forced-choice form. By using single-stimulus rating parameters to pair the stimuli it would seem plausible that one could probably maximize the number of well-matched binary items eventually obtained. But one would need to subject all binary items initially formed to a final scaling analysis in order to identify those particular items that could confidently be used for scoring key construction. Only those items (a) for which the percentage of endorsement for a given response alternative under both straight, self-report conditions and under instructions to fake or dissimulate were constant (and

near 50% as well?) and (b) for which the percentage of respondents changing their responses under the two conditions were minimal could be considered well controlled for the contaminant according to this rationale.

On the basis of the considerations and findings outlined above, three forced-choice self-report inventories were developed. For the first of these an initial pool of 342 trait descriptive adjectives was compiled and each was then sorted into one or another of the peer rating criterion factor categories independently by each of three judges. The 193 items for which there was high interjudge agreement as to factor-pole relevance were compiled into booklet form for purposes of collecting desirability ratings for each term. Each adjective was then rated by a sample of male college students as to the degree of desirability that each felt would be implied by a self-endorsement to that characteristic by a person wishing to be admitted to the United States Air Force Officer Candidate School (OCS) program.[3] Means and variances of the desirability ratings for each adjective were then computed. Binary forced-choice items were formed by matching terms representing two different factors (based on staff judgments of their content) as closely as possible on these two distribution parameters. In all, 200 binary items were formed; some adjectives being used in more than one forced-choice item. These items were then arranged in a roughly systematic, alternating fashion, typed in booklet form, and the resulting instrument was named the Descriptive Adjective Inventory (DAI).

In the development of DAI, no effort was made to obtain or use information concerning the correlations between ratings of the separate adjectives in forming the forced-choice binary items. However, in constructing two other inventory forms which employ self-report statements instead of single word predicates, this criterion was also utilized to the degree permitted by the data.

[3] This particular stereotype was chosen for our purposes because of our current research support.

These two inventories, called the Forced-Choice Self-Report Inventory, Forms A and B (or FCSRI-A and FCSRI-B) contain 192 and 199 binary forced-choice items, respectively. No individual statement appears more than once in these two instruments. A more complete description of the development of these devices has been presented elsewhere [20]. Sample items from DAI and FCSRI forms are shown in Table 32–2.

In constructing items and initial scoring keys for DAI and FCSRI forms, we relied for item "validities" on our judgments of content relevance of the stimuli. These a priori keys were later replaced on DAI by preliminary empirical keys based on a small sample of men from whom both criterion ratings and test performances under straight self-report instructions had been obtained. The principal index used for selecting item categories for each of these preliminary empirical keys was a simple percentage difference in response between median split "highs" and "lows" on each criterion variable. Another sample had taken DAI under both self-report and attempted faking instructions and the percentage of endorsement or "popularity" indices for the items under these two conditions were also referred to when selecting items for these preliminary empirical scales.

The endeavor was to choose only those items for keying which had sizable discrimination indices against the rating criteria and minimal shifts in popularity under the two response conditions. We should have liked also to have had evidence that the validities of the items were maintained under the faked condition. But since criterion data were not available on the latter sample, and fake-take test protocols had not

been collected from the former, no analysis pertinent to this question was possible.

VALIDATION OF THE PRELIMINARY EMPIRICAL KEYS FOR DAI AND WHY THE ABOVE METHOD OF KEY CONSTRUCTION IS UNFEASIBLE

The major validation study was carried out at the University of Michigan during the academic year, 1960–61. During the fall semester, 215 men were recruited from fraternity houses on campus and were administered the peer nomination criterion rating scales, DAI, and the two forms of the FCSRI together with a large number of other devices. The total testing time per subject was approximately 15 hours. The DAI and FCSRI forms (plus two other instruments not specifically dealt with in this report) were given twice—first under straight self-report instructions to be as "honest and accurate" in describing oneself as possible, and about 2 weeks later under instructions to respond in the "most desirable manner possible to gain admission to United States Air Force OCS." Arrangements were made to pay each subject upon completion of the battery at the rate of $1.00 per hour to insure his cooperation and participation throughout all phases of the testing program.

Criterion rating groups of 6–16 men each were formed within each fraternity in such a way as to maximize interrater familiarity and minimize status differences owing to academic class standing. The DAI and FCSRI forms were filled out individually by each subject at his convenience according to each set of instructions during a

Table 32–2   Sample Items from the DAI and the FCSRI-A and FCSRI-B

DAI	FCSRI
A. Tactful	A. People consider me somewhat of an intellectual.
B. Thorough	B. I am delightful and pleasing to others.
A. Nervous	A. I like my friends to feel sorry for me when I am sick.
B. Preoccupied	B. I feel like a stranger with people.

2-week period immediately following receipt of the forms.

During the spring semester, 241 men living in university residence halls completed the same test battery under the same arrangements, bringing the total number of participants in the study to 456.

The ratings and test performances from the 215 fraternity men in the fall semester sample were scored and correlations between the criterion ratings and all preliminary keys for tests in the battery were computed. The results of this analysis for the preliminary empirical keys of DAI (described in the last section) were particularly enlightening. The validities against the criterion ratings for these keys under the straight-take condition were all statistically significant and moderate to low in magnitude (i.e., .40, .25, .40, .24, and .16 for Criterion Variables I–V, respectively). However, the validities for these same keys dropped uniformly to near zero under the faking condition. What is more, the correlations between the straight and fake administration scores on these keys also were nearly equal to zero. Finally, the mean profiles under the two conditions were not congruent (nor even parallel) as is clearly indicated in Figure 32–1. In this figure the mean profile for the five keys under the

straight-take condition is plotted as a horizontal line and the points on the mean profile for the fake-take condition are plotted as deviations in multiples of the standard errors of the straight-take means.

From Figure 32–1 and the criterion validities described above, it is apparent that for these preliminary keys, one does not have either control of distortions due to faking nor validities which are maintained under both conditions. In fact, the rank order of means under the fake condition is precisely what it should be to gain entrance to OCS if one takes the findings by Tupes [24] at face value! The fact that the deviations in Figure 32–1 are negative for Factors V, II, and IV is probably attributable wholly to the partially ipsatized character of these keys and the strong preference for Factor III responses under the faking condition.

Additional light is shed on the problem and a potentially satisfactory solution is suggested, however, if one examines another set of findings from these data.

Upon completion of the testing of the spring semester residence hall sample the 51 rating subgroups from both semesters were divided into a pair of double cross-validation samples (hereafter referred to as A and B) for use in all final test development and data analysis. The groups were assigned to the two samples so as to meet the following criteria as closely as possible. (a) There should be equal numbers of fraternity and residence hall subjects in each sample. (b) There should be equal numbers of freshmen, sophomores, juniors, and seniors or graduate students in each sample. (c) The criterion rating factor structures in each sample should be the same. The extent to which Criteria a and b were met is indicated in Table 32–3.

It can be seen from the marginal totals of Table 32–3 that the two samples are extremely well-matched on class standing and on type of residence. In addition the total numbers for the two samples are exactly equal. Even the differences in frequency within the class by type of resi-

Figure 32–1 *Comparisons between the mean profiles of scores on the preliminary empirical keys of the DAI under fake-take and straight-take conditions. (Based on 215 fraternity men in the sample. Values in parentheses are means.)*

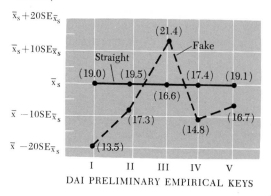

I   II   III   IV   V
DAI PRELIMINARY EMPIRICAL KEYS

Table 32–3   Composition of the Double Cross-validation Samples A and B

	Freshmen		Sophomores		Juniors		Seniors and Graduates		Totals	
	A	B	A	B	A	B	A	B	A	B
Fraternities	3	0	51	42	42	45	11	21	107	108
Residence halls	67	70	29	34	13	10	12	6	121	120
Total	70	70	80	76	55	55	23	27	228	228

dence cells are generally small. The data relevant to Criterion c are discussed elsewhere [22]. Suffice it to say here that the factor structures for these two samples were extremely well matched and that Criterion c was met handily.

Responses to all items on DAI, FCSRI-A, and FCSRI-B by each subject under both straight-take and fake-take conditions were punched into IBM cards for item analysis. Each of the double cross-validation samples was then divided into trichotomous criterion classes on each criterion variable with approximately 30% of the sample in the extreme classes and the remaining cases in the middle group. The overall popularity indices and the five matrices of percentage-difference discrimination indices among the trichotomous groups on each criterion variable were then computed separately for each sample for each of the two testing conditions for each test.

A preliminary examination of these data for DAI indicated that for the 200 items in this test: (a) the discrimination indices for the straight and fake conditions on each factor in each of the cross-validation samples were correlated approximately zero; (b) the correlations between the popularity indices under straight and fake conditions were .24 and .23 in Samples A and B, respectively; (c) the correlations between the discrimination indices under the *fake* condition between Sample A and Sample B were essentially zero for all five factors; *but* that (d) the correlations between the discrimination indices under the *straight* (self-report) condition between the two samples were moderately high; furthermore, (e) the correlations of the popularity

indices between the two samples were .97 for the straight condition and .98 for the fake condition!

Because of Findings a and b it was apparent that not enough (if any) items could be found which would permit the construction of keys whose validities would be maintained irrespective of the set assumed by the respondent. Findings c and d implied that the source of the difficulty lay in the fact that the large number of changes in response made between the two conditions were unrelated to criterion factor status. In addition, note that the straight by fake discrimination index correlations— Finding a—were zero and *not* negative. Thus, it was not likely that configural response patterns would be any more fruitful as a source of useful data than were the simpler response categories.

PROPOSED NEW METHOD FOR CONSTRUCTING EMPIRICAL PERSONALITY SCALES WHICH ARE WELL CONTROLLED FOR DISSIMULATION TENDENCIES

Findings d and e above, however, did suggest a method for constructing empirically valid scoring keys for forced-choice personality inventories which would possess a rather high degree of control over the effects of attempted faking. What is more, this method should in general yield satisfactory keys *whether the stimuli in the forced-choice items are well matched on the faking stereotype or not*. In fact, we shall see that it is even a considerable advantage if there are sizable shifts in the response proportions under the two conditions—especially if the percentages of response under the straight-take condition are close to 50%!

Based on the data cited above, it was clear that if one could depend on the respondents to follow directions and give honest and accurate responses, Finding *d* implied that cross-validatable keys could be developed. Finding *e* implied that the proportion of persons responding to each item in a given direction was extremely stable over different samples of persons under each of the two conditions taken separately. Thus, the *difference in popularity* of a response between the two conditions also would be a stable property of the items.

Now, to construct a scoring key for one of the criterion variables, suppose one were to initially select all the items on the test whose straight-take discrimination indices for the criterion factor were greater than some fixed amount, as he would do to build an ordinary empirical key. The actual number of items selected, however, should exceed the number of items wanted in the final key, the amount of the excess depending upon the number that will have to be discarded in the next step of the procedure. All items chosen, of course, should have statistically significant discrimination indices. The converse is probably not true, however, since, as will become apparent, one will want to maximize the number of items in the final key with straight-take popularity indices in the middle range where standard errors are larger.

Next, suppose one were to construct a distribution of these items on a continuum which runs from large negative differences in popularities through zero difference to large positive differences. The items which have a shift in popularity on the fake-take "away from" the keyed response (based on the straight-take data) will be plotted on one side of the zero point and those with shifts "toward" the keyed response on the other. Now if, as will generally be the case, the number of items on one side of the zero point is less than the number on the other, include all (or most) of the items from the less numerous set. Then begin to select additional items from the more numerous set, taking those with the largest discrimination indices first, *until the sum of the popularity-shift magnitudes on one side of the axis equals the sum on the other side.* All items with zero shifts might be added to the final key or not as desired. Scoring keys constructed in this manner will be hereafter referred to in this paper as Set III keys.

The first effect of this method, of course, is to give a key on which the mean test score under the straight-take condition will equal that under the faking condition. This is so because the mean of the test score distribution (under each condition) is equal to the sum of the item popularities (under that condition), which have been equated by the procedures described in the last paragraph. Since these popularity indices under each of the two conditions (and consequently the differences between them to a slightly lesser degree) were found to be extremely stable over different samples of persons—Finding *e* above—very little disparity should exist between the means of the scores under the two conditions even for a cross-validation sample. As a result, the straight- and fake-take mean profiles across such a set of scales should be congruent and the problem encountered with the preliminary empirical scales for DAI, illustrated in Figure 32–1, accordingly should be solved. Since shifts in mean scores under different response conditions are likely to be a serious source of mistakes in selecting personnel, it is important to balance carefully the items whose popularity shifts are in the keyed direction against those for which popularity shifts are in the opposite direction—even though one thereby eliminates from the key some otherwise valid items.

A second desirable effect of this method will usually occur automatically (but could be maximized easily for any given set of data). Since a percentage difference discrimination index of item validity was proposed this is likely to result in a preponderance of items in the final key with straight-take popularity indices in the middle range.[4] But if such items also have large fake-take shifts (in either direction), then *they will tend to have extreme fake-take popularities and correspondingly smaller item variances and interitem co-variances under the fake condition.* This means that the variance of the test scores on such a key under the fake-take condition will be smaller than that obtained under the straight-take condition. If in addition one elicits under the fake-take instructions inconsistent response sets across the items of the key, this should further lower the interitem covariances and further reduce the variance in test scores under this condition. The hypothesized effects of these item selection procedures are diagrammed in Figure 32–2.

Thus, if one is primarily concerned with selecting persons who are extreme on the variable, the chances of his getting persons who have scored high or low on such a measure by attempting to fake is relatively small. The *degree* to which faking is controlled in this way, of course, will be a function of the difference in variances and the size of the selection ratio.

The second effect of the proposed item selection procedure is, of course, the reason behind the seemingly paradoxical statement made earlier; namely, that in order to get both good control on the contaminant and valid measures of the criteria, one *wants* items in the pool for which large shifts in response frequencies occur under at-

tempted faking. This statement now should be qualified, however, to pertain to those items which have initial straight-take popularities in the middle range and have criterion validities of sufficient magnitude to be useful for inclusion in a scoring key.

These two qualifications suggest still one additional procedure that can be employed to achieve further control over the problem of faking. But here we want exactly the opposite pair of item characteristics to the two just described. If one can find an appreciable number of items which display large shifts in popularity under the two conditions but which have *extreme popularities* under self-report conditions and *near-zero validities* for all criterion variables, then the item is tailor-made for inclusion in a "detection" scale for identifying dissimulated test protocols. To build such a scale one simply keys for such items the responses which are infrequent under the straight-take condition. Scores on such a scale then indicate a performance on the test more or less similar to the modal faked performance, and if sufficiently high may constitute a basis for rejecting out of hand the test performance (and perhaps the respondent as well).

If the separation of straight and faked performances on such a detection scale is large and/or the selection ratio is high (hopefully, both), and if this scale is uncorrelated with the criteria and the measures of them, then its use can lower considerably the probability of selecting a "faker" without raising the probability of

---

[4] A percentage difference between median-split criterion highs and lows can attain its maximum value (100%) only when the overall popularity index is 50%—i.e., when all highs endorse the item and all lows do not. For popularities approaching either zero or 100%, the maximum percentage difference discrimination index attainable becomes progressively smaller. It is, of course, equal to zero at the popularity extremes whether the criterion groups are formed by a median split or by some other partition such as the approximate 30-40-30 percentages used here. A *t* ratio or probability associated with such a significance test statistic, if used as a validity index (as it has by some), would lead to the selection of more items with extreme popularities since the standard error of the percentage difference becomes smaller as item popularities become more extreme.

Figure 32–2 *Distributions of test scores for persons faking and those responding under straight self-report instructions for a hypothetical key of the sort described in the text.*

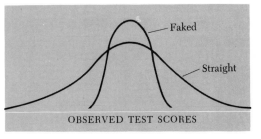

OBSERVED TEST SCORES

discarding valid highs on the content measures. But if one has to use all applicants, then elevated detection scores are troublesome since one then has prima facie evidence that the content scales he wishes to use are in all probability invalid for such a subject.

The arguments and evidence for constructing and using suppressor or correction scales to "adjust" content measures for the influence of response contaminants—usually test taking defensiveness or something similar—will not be discussed here. Suffice it to say that as long as the primary predictor is accounting for less than half the criterion variance—a situation universally true in personality assessment today and likely to persist for some time—one is well advised to attack the unexplained criterion variance rather than attempt to suppress invalid test variance. Statistically, a suppressor scale has to be a *very* effective suppressor—better than any currently available or likely to be constructed soon—to effect any appreciable improvement over an only moderately valid primary predictor.

It is interesting to note again that in the construction and use of detection scales, just as in the development of the Set III type criterion predictor measures proposed above, the success of the attempt depends, at least in part, upon having items in the inventory which *do* show marked shifts in frequency of endorsement under the two administrative conditions. In the next section evidence will be presented that indicates that these methods of scale construction can be used effectively to construct valid measures of personality characteristics while simultaneously controlling for the influence of faking tendencies.

RESULTS OF THE DOUBLE CROSS-VALIDATION ANALYSES OF THE SET III KEYS AND DETECTION SCALES FOR DAI, FCSRI-A, AND FCSRI-B

Set III scoring keys were developed according to the procedure described above for each of the five criterion variables on each of the three tests. This was done separately on each of the double cross-validation Samples A and B, thus yielding two keys for each criterion factor on each test. The 15 keys based on each sample were then used to score both the straight- and fake-take test performances by persons in the other (cross-validation) sample.

The extent to which the two desired faking-control properties of these keys were met is indicated in Figure 32–3 and in Table 32–4. In Figure 32–3 the distributions of Sample B scores on Sample A Set III keys for DAI are plotted. The medians of the two distributions for each scale are never more than two raw score points apart

Figure 32–3   *Distributions of persons in Sample B on the Set III Sample A keys for the DAI under straight self-report (solid line) and faking (dashed line) conditions.*

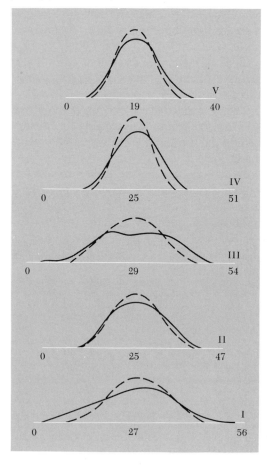

Table 32–4 Psychometric Characteristics of the Set III Keys for the DAI, FCSRI-A, and FCSRI-B and the Set III Summation Keys Developed on Samples A and B as Estimated from the Respective Cross-validation Data*

| | | Sample A Keys—Sample B Data | | | | | | | | Sample B Keys—Sample A Data | | | | | | | |
| | | | Means | | Standard Deviations | | Straight Reliability | Validities† | | | Means | | Standard Deviations | | Straight Reliability | Validities† | |
Test	Key	Number of Items	S	F	S	F	K-R 20	C_1	C_2	Number of Items	S	F	S	F	K-R 20	C_1	C_2
DAI	I	56	26.5	27.4	9.56	7.00	.87	.38	.46	52	25.2	24.2	7.59	4.98	.81	.45	.51
	II	47	25.4	24.7	6.53	5.41	.77	.36	.39	56	29.4	29.7	9.57	6.96	.88	.26	.29
	III	54	29.2	28.2	9.02	6.72	.86	.41	.41	53	27.3	28.7	8.26	5.54	.83	.42	.49
	IV	51	24.7	24.3	5.17	3.79	.58	.32	.40	54	27.3	27.3	6.00	4.52	.68	.25	.33
	V	40	19.2	18.8	4.94	4.16	.64	.33	.39	52	26.4	26.5	5.70	4.97	.65	.30	.31
FCSRI-A	I	55	28.7	29.4	8.20	6.25	.83	.41	.48	55	28.4	28.1	7.22	5.29	.77	.51	.52
	II	56	26.4	26.2	5.58	5.21	.60	.41	.39	53	25.0	25.5	7.32	5.06	.78	.28	.36
	III	54	26.4	25.5	6.66	5.57	.73	.47	.48	57	27.6	28.0	7.94	5.16	.81	.39	.48
	IV	49	25.3	26.2	5.16	3.91	.59	.28	.39	55	28.0	27.7	5.59	4.41	.60	.21	.26
	V	54	25.1	25.6	5.01	4.16	.50	.31	.34	49	23.7	23.9	5.99	4.64	.70	.30	.36
FCSRI-B	I	54	28.4	29.3	7.42	5.28	.79	.38	.44	51	26.7	26.2	6.47	4.72	.73	.45	.44
	II	54	25.4	25.1	5.46	4.80	.59	.22	.25	51	25.4	26.3	6.20	4.74	.70	.14	.22
	III	50	25.4	25.1	6.88	5.18	.77	.45	.45	53	26.6	27.3	6.91	4.95	.76	.39	.49
	IV	55	26.8	27.4	4.91	4.18	.49	.20	.34	50	25.8	25.4	5.35	4.71	.60	.14	.25
	V	52	25.4	26.3	4.55	4.21	.41	.26	.32	50	27.4	27.4	5.05	4.44	.56	.24	.27
Summation	I	165	83.6	86.1	22.99	15.57	.93	.43	.51	158	80.4	78.6	19.08	11.77	.91	.53	.55
	II	157	77.3	75.9	14.78	12.45	.84	.40	.42	160	79.9	81.6	21.01	13.93	.92	.26	.32
	III	158	81.0	78.5	20.45	14.28	.92	.49	.49	163	81.6	84.1	21.01	11.89	.92	.44	.54
	IV	155	76.9	77.8	12.45	8.73	.78	.33	.46	159	81.2	80.4	14.59	9.98	.83	.23	.32
	V	146	69.9	70.6	11.84	9.41	.76	.37	.43	151	77.3	78.0	14.16	10.58	.83	.33	.37

* N = 228 in each sample.
† Criterion C_1 = factor score from the peer nomination ratings obtained by simple summation of the scores obtained on the four salient scales for each factor. Criterion C_2 = C_1 minus the elevation component of the individual's factor score profile.

385

and in each case the range of the straight-take scores exceeds that for the fake-takes on both ends of the continuum. From Table 32–4 it can be seen that the means on all 15 Sample A keys for these subjects under the two conditions in no instance differ by more than one raw score point and in every case the standard deviations are greater under the straight-take condition. In the right half of Table 32–4 in the corresponding columns of means and standard deviations for the Sample B Set III keys estimated from Sample A data, essentially similar results may be found. In short, the method proposed does yield scoring keys for which mean profiles across the scales are, for all practical purposes, congruent and for which the straight self-report performances are more variable than those obtained under attempts to fake a desirable test protocol.

In this latter regard, the differences in variability are not so large as one might wish. It is clear from the distributions presented in Figure 32–3 that for any but the most extreme cut scores, sizable proportions of fakers would be obtained. There are, however, several reasons why this does not constitute a serious deterrent to the use of these scales for personnel selection purposes.

First, and perhaps of only limited relevance, is the fact that separation between the scores under the two conditions is better at the low end of Scale I and at the high end of Scales II through V. This relative skewing of the straight-take scores, apparent in the results for DAI plotted in Figure 32–3, is exactly the pattern desired in our present situation where persons to be selected should possess high scores on Variables II–V and low scores for Factor I [24]. Why the distributions display this pattern of relative skewing is not entirely clear at the present time, but presumably it is a function of the distributions of discrimination indices and/or popularities for items chosen from the two sides of the popularity shift continua.

A second, and more general reason for satisfaction with the relative magnitude of the variances is that the effect is apparently cumulative across additional measures, at least for some of the variables. That is, if one simply adds scores on Factor I scales for the three tests under each condition and plots these summation scores, the intersection of the two curves is *relatively* closer to the mean. For example, for Factor I scores on DAI, the two curves cross at a score of about 18. The proportion of straight-take scores less than 18 is .19, and the proportion of fake-takes in this same region is .08. For the summation score distributions on this variable the curves cross at a raw score of 68 and the corresponding proportions which score less than this value are .28 and .09, respectively. The differences in means and standard deviations for the summation score distributions are given at the bottom of Table 32–4.

The final and most poignant reason for unconcern about unwittingly getting fakers in the selection subsample is the effectiveness with which a faked answer sheet can be detected. In Figure 32–4, the Detection Scale for DAI based on Sample A item analysis data has been applied to the two kinds of answer sheets for persons in Sample B. The separation is remarkably good. The false positive and false negative rates are each about 9% using the intersection point based on the original validation sample as a cut score.

Happily, one can even improve on this by using the summation of the detection scales across the three tests. In Table 32–5, the means, standard deviations, and K-R 20

Figure 32–4   Distributions of persons in Sample B on the Sample A Detection Key for the DAI under straight self-report and faking conditions.

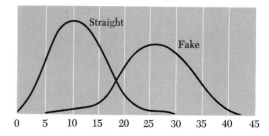

Table 32–5   Psychometric Characteristics of the Detection Keys for the DAI, FCSRI-A, and FCSRI-B and the Summation Detection Keys Developed on Samples A and B as Estimated from the Respective Cross-validation Data*

Detection Key for Test	Num- ber of Items	Means		Standard Deviations		Reliabili- ties K-R 20	
		S†	F‡	S	F	S	F
Sample A Keys–Sample B Data							
DAI	45	11.7	27.0	5.16	6.67	.70	.79
FCSRI-A	36	11.0	24.0	4.28	4.08	.61	.74
FCSRI-B	40	14.1	26.3	4.23	5.41	.53	.73
Summation	121	36.9	77.2	10.71	14.71	.79	.89
Sample B Keys–Sample A Data							
		S	F	S	F	S	F
DAI	47	12.9	28.2	5.75	6.87	.74	.79
FCSRI-A	39	12.0	24.7	4.54	5.34	.62	.73
FCSRI-B	41	14.5	27.2	4.11	5.30	.48	.71
Summation	127	39.3	80.2	11.86	14.84	.82	.88

* $N = 228$ in each sample.
† S = straight, self-report administration.
‡ F = attempted-fake administration.

reliabilities (all cross-validation sample estimates) for the detection scales on each instrument and for the Summation Detection Scales are presented. The means for straight and faked scores on each test run about 2.5 to 3 *raw score* sigma units apart and for the Summation Scales the separation is almost four times the standard deviation of the straight-take summation scores. The false positive and false negative rates for these Summation Keys are about 6%. Clearly if one can identify so large a proportion of faked answer sheets, he need not worry very much about getting such persons in his selection sample, even if such a person should happen to have a score on the content variable in the acceptable region.

Two additional features of the data in Table 32–5 are of interest before we return to the Set III content scale results. First, the standard deviations under straight-take are less than under the faking condition

and secondly, the reliabilities under the faking condition are uniformly higher than under the self-report condition. Both of these effects are desirable. The first means that straight-take scores are not only lower but more tightly clustered about their mean value than are the faked scores. The second implies that for precisely those scores one wants to "interpret" (i.e., the faked ones) the reliabilities or interpretabilities [cf. 7] are higher—in the case of the Summation Detection Scales, quite high.

It is of some importance to note that correlations between these detection scales with both the criterion factor scores and the Set III content scales are low. For the Sample A detection keys the highest value with any of the criterion ratings is a .16 between the Factor III and the DAI Detection Scale. For the detection scales on the separate tests versus their respective Set III keys the highest values are −.17 (DAI, V), −.24 (FCSRI-A, II), and −.34 (FCSRI-B,

II). For the Summation Detection Scale against the summation content scales the largest is a −.34 against Summation Scale II. It is also interesting to observe that the detection scales are rather uniformly negatively correlated with straight-take test scores on Variables II and III whereas they are correlated essentially zero with the criterion ratings on these factors. Thus, positive weighting of the detection scale (reverse suppressor situation) could conceivably improve prediction of the criterion ratings. But, for reasons briefly noted earlier, the improvement would likely not be very large.

And finally, the median correlation among the pairs of separate Sample A Detection Scales under the straight-take condition is .41 whereas under the faking condition the median of the three correlations is .61. This supports the data in Table 32–5, where we noted that the internal consistency reliabilities (K-R 20s) were higher for the faked data.

Reference to the last three columns in each half of Table 32–4 provides an indication of the reliabilities and validities for the Set III keys. It can be seen that the K-R 20s for the separate scales are reasonably high for Scales I, II, and III for each inventory, generally lower for Scales IV and V. For the Summation Scales, the reliabilities are really quite respectable, and for Variables I and III (and perhaps II, also), compare favorably with the best of available ability measures.

The validities in the first of the two columns (Criterion C_1) are correlations against the peer nomination rating factor scores; those in the other column (Criterion C_2) are the relationships against the rating factors with the elevation component of each individual's criterion score profile removed. That is, in this latter case, the validities are against criteria for which each subject has the same average profile across the criteria. Since, in general, elevated scores are "good" on these factors in terms of a general social desirability stereotype, the elevation component in the criterion ratings

for a subject is a rough measure of his "esteem" or "eminence" or "likability" or some such general evaluative attribute as perceived by his peers. If one is not so much concerned about this kind of general characteristic as about the "pattern" of attributes on the set of factors and the ability of one's tests to predict such differential traits, then the values in the C_2 column are more pertinent. They are also almost uniformly higher.

Unfortunately, it is the C_1 criteria we set out to measure since it was for these rating variables that Tupes [24] demonstrated predictive validity against his overall performance criterion. However, even the C_1 validities for the scales on the separate inventories are all positive, all statistically significant, and only 6 of the 30 coefficients are less than .25. While these magnitudes are not high by absolute standards, they compare favorably with those for other personality inventories when independent, non-self-report criteria are used. In addition, since the selection program for which these measures are intended typically selects only about 10% of the applicants, these scales can probably be used with some guarded confidence. The validities in the lower part of Table 32–4 for the longer summation scales are somewhat better against both criteria as one might expect.

In constructing the Set III keys, we were more concerned with maximizing validities of these scales against the criterion ratings and in controlling against susceptibility to faking than we were in the relationships among scales. Consequently, we permitted the keying of a given item on more than one scale if the discrimination indices warranted it. The effect of this, of course, is to give us spurious interscale correlations due to correlated item error components. As a consequence, it will be well, for the present at least, to avoid trying to interpret relationships among our inventory scales in substantive psychological terms. Nor should they, in their present form, be used in factor analyses or other theoretically oriented multivariate studies.

Finally, it should be pointed out that the scores on the Set III keys under the fake-take condition correlate appreciably with *nothing* (except, possibly, other fake-take scores). The highest correlation of one of these scales under this condition with any criterion variable in either sample (a total of 300 coefficients) is a .20 (between C_2 Factor III and the FCSRI-A Sample A key for Variable IV, sic!). The correlations between the same keys applied under the two conditions are all less than .27. The corresponding-variable Set III keys across the three tests do intercorrelate to a moderate degree under the fake-take condition. This latter is another reflection of a certain stability or consistency of the faking stereotypes of the persons in our samples previously noted in the intertest detection scale correlations.

Thus, it should be clear that if a person assumes a faking attitude comparable to the modal stereotype displayed by our subjects, psychological interpretations of his personality attributes on the basis of his Set III key scores on these tests is a fool's enterprise. Fakers of this sort, however, should be very easy to identify from their detection scale scores.

SUMMARY, DISCUSSION, AND SOME IMPLICATIONS OF THESE FINDINGS

The results presented in the last section indicate that if one constructs self-report inventory measures of personality characteristics by the method proposed in this paper using content-relevant stimuli and binary forced-choice item formats, then the following results can be achieved on cross-validation data:

1. Validities against peer nomination, rating criteria which are in the moderate range and which are slightly, but uniformly higher for criteria from which profile elevations have been removed.
2. Internal consistency estimates of reliability (K-R 20) which are moderate to high for the individual scales. For the longer summation scales these are uniformly over .75 and in the case of two (or possibly three) of the five variables, greater than .90.
3. Very tight control over the problem of faking as reflected in: (*a*) mean profiles across the scales which are congruent under straight self-report conditions and under instructions to attempt to fake; (*b*) variances for the faked answer sheets which are smaller than for the straight-take performances; and (*c*) detection scales which, for a single inventory key, identify about 91% of the fakers at a cost of misclassifying only about 9% of the nonfakers. With the longer Summation Detection Scales the false positive and false negative rates drop to about 6%.

With regard to this latter point, it is conceivable that little, if any, further improvement can be made in the detection of faked answer sheets. In the case of the false positives (i.e., those who get high detection scale scores under the straight-take conditions), it is just possible that they actually are like the modal faking stereotype in their personality make-up. It is also possible, of course, that for whatever reasons, these persons assumed a faking attitude under the initial straight self-report instructions. In the case of the false negatives (i.e., those with low detection scale scores under the faking condition), it could be either that they have markedly disparate notions of what constitutes a desirable set of test responses, that they misunderstood the instructions, or that they assumed that the best way to "fake one's way into OCS" was to be as "honest and accurate as possible." Whatever the case, a cursory inspection of the detection scale scores for these two kinds of cases reveals that, in most instances, the scores under the two conditions for such persons are highly similar. No follow-up of these cases by interview or other means was attempted, but this might have proved to be most interesting and quite feasible had we only anticipated how few cases we were going to miss with our detection scales.

By way of general evaluation of these findings it is clear that inventory measures constructed in the manner here proposed can be used with considerable confidence for personnel selection where one is interested in assessments of status on these criterion dimensions—at least in situations where the selection ratios are fairly small. In any event, the probabilities of mistaking intentional fakers as "honest and accurate" self-reporters are very low and, if all three inventories are used, all but negligible.

A word of caution is in order, however. A preliminary study based on a small sample of Peace Corps trainees who were asked to fake a different desirability stereotype (admission to Peace Corps volunteer status) after first taking DAI and FCSRI-A under standard straight-take instructions, yielded mean profiles on the original (Sample A) Set III keys which under the two conditions were markedly noncongruent. Nor did the original detection scales described above separate very adequately the straight-take from the faked performances by these subjects. Inspection of these data revealed that the straight-take mean profile on the Set III keys was only slightly different than that obtained from the subjects in the original cross-validation sample. But there were marked disparities between the profiles from these two groups based on their respective faked performances. Clearly the modal stereotype of what was seen as desirable by college males in order to gain admission to a military officer training school was quite different (and in ways that are not very surprising) from what was viewed as desirable by Peace Corps trainees in order to be accepted as a volunteer in that organization.

One implication of these findings is (unfortunately) quite clear. Control over faking of the sort achieved by Set III keys and detection scales, constructed for use in one setting with one class of respondents, may not generalize very widely. Just what the limits of generalizability attainable may be is as yet not fully known. But it does seem to be highly improbable that it will be possible to construct and standardize a single set of general purpose keys which can be used effectively in all settings for all classes of respondents. It may even prove to be necessary to build special purpose keys for each new context where they are desired. This is not a very happy prospect, but it is one that we may have to learn to live with all the same.

REFERENCES

1. BERKSHIRE, J. R. Comparisons of five forced-choice indices. *Educ. psychol. Measmt*, 1958, **18**, 553–561.
2. BORISLOW, B. The Edwards Personal Preference Schedule (EPPS) and fakability. *J. appl. Psychol.*, 1958, **42**, 22–27.
3. CATTELL, R. B. Confirmation and clarification of primary personality factors. *Psychometrika*, 1947, **12**, 197–220.
4. CORAH, N. L., FELDMAN, M. J., COHEN, I. S., GRUEN, W., MEADOW, A., & RINGWALL, E. A. Social desirability as a variable in the Edwards Personal Preference Schedule. *J. consult. Psychol.*, 1958, **22**, 70–72.
5. CRONBACH, L. J. Response sets and test validity. *Educ. psychol. Measmt*, 1946, **6**, 475–494.
6. CRONBACH, L. J. Further evidence on response sets and test design. *Educ. psychol. Measmt*, 1950, **10**, 3–31.
7. CRONBACH, L. J. Coefficient alpha and the internal structure of tests. *Psychometrika*, 1951, **16**, 297–334.
8. CRONBACH, L. J. Assessment of individual differences. In P. R. Farnsworth (Ed.), *Annu. Rev. Psychol.*, 1956, **7**, 173–196.
9. DUNNETTE, M. D., McCARTNEY, J., CARLSON, H. C., & KIRCHNER, W. K. A study of faking behavior on a forced-choice self-description checklist. *Personnel Psychol.*, 1962, **15**, 13–24.
10. EDWARDS, A. L. *Manual for the Edwards Personal Preference Schedule.* New York: Psychological Corporation, 1954.
11. EDWARDS, A. L. *The social desirability*

variable in personality assessment and research. New York: Dryden Press, 1957.

12. EDWARDS, A. L., WRIGHT, C. E., & LUNNEBORG, C. E. A note on "Social desirability as a variable in the Edwards Personal Preference Schedule." *J. consult. Psychol.*, 1959, **23**, 558.

13. GUILFORD, J. P. *Psychometric methods.* (2nd ed.) New York: McGraw-Hill, 1954.

14. JURGENSEN, C. E. Report on the "Classification Inventory," a personality test for industrial use. *J. appl. Psychol.*, 1944, **28**, 445–460.

15. KELLY, E. L., & FISKE, D. W. *The prediction of performance in clinical psychology.* Ann Arbor: Univer. Michigan Press, 1951.

16. LOEVINGER, J. Theory and techniques of assessment. In P. R. Farnsworth (Ed.), *Annu. Rev. Psychol.*, 1959, **10**, 287–316.

17. LONGSTAFF, H. P., & JURGENSEN, C. E. Fakability of the Jurgensen Classification Inventory. *J. appl. Psychol.*, 1953, **37**, 86–89.

18. MAHER, H. Studies of transparency in forced-choice scales: I. Evidence of transparency. *J. appl. Psychol.*, 1959, **43**, 275–278.

19. MESSICK, S. Dimension of social desirability. *J. consult. Psychol.*, 1960, **24**, 279–287.

20. NORMAN, W. T. Development of self-report tests to measure personality factors identified from peer nominations. *USAF ASD tech. Note*, 1961, No. 61-44.

21. NORMAN, W. T. Problems of response contamination in personality assessment. *USAF ASD tech. Note*, 1961, No. 61-43.

22. NORMAN, W. T. Toward an adequate taxonomy of personality attributes: Replicated factor structure in peer nomination personality ratings. *J. abnorm. soc. Psychol.*, 1963, **66**, 574–583.

23. ROSEN, E. Self-appraisal, personal desirability, and perceived social desirability of personality traits. *J. abnorm. soc. Psychol.*, 1956, **52**, 151–158.

24. TUPES, E. C. Relationships between behavior trait ratings by peers and later officer performance of USAF Officer Candidate School graduates. *USAF PTRC tech. Note*, 1957, No. 57-125.

25. TUPES, E. C., & CHRISTAL, R. E. Stability of personality trait rating factors obtained under diverse conditions. *USAF WADC tech. Note*, 1958, No. 58-61.

26. TUPES, E. C., & CHRISTAL, R. E. Recurrent personality factors based on trait ratings. *USAF ASD tech. Rep.*, 1961, No. 61-97.

27. WHERRY, R. J., STANDER, N. E., & HOPKINS, J. J. Behavior trait ratings by peers and references. *USAF WADC tech. Rep.*, 1959, No. 59-360.

Chapter 33

Antecedent Probability and the Efficiency of Psychometric Signs, Patterns, or Cutting Scores

PAUL E. MEEHL / ALBERT ROSEN

In clinical practice, psychologists frequently participate in the making of vital decisions concerning the classification, treatment, prognosis, and disposition of individuals. In their attempts to increase the number of correct classifications and predictions, psychologists have developed and applied many psychometric devices, such as patterns of test responses as well as cutting scores for scales, indices, and sign lists. Since diagnostic and prognostic statements can often be made with a high degree of accuracy purely on the basis of actuarial or experience tables (referred to hereinafter as *base rates*), a psychometric device, to be efficient), must make possible a greater number of correct decisions than could be made in terms of the base rates alone.

The efficiency of the great majority of psychometric devices reported in the clinical psychology literature is difficult or impossible to evaluate for the following reasons:

a. Base rates are virtually never reported. It is, therefore, difficult to determine whether or not a given device results in a greater number of correct decisions than would be possible solely on the basis of the rates from previous experience. When, however, the base rates can be estimated, the reported claims of efficiency of psychometric instruments are often seen to be without foundation.

b. In most reports, the distribution data provided are insufficient for the evaluation of the probable efficiency of the device in other settings where the base rates are markedly different. Moreover, the samples are almost always too small for the determination of optimal cutting lines for various decisions.

c. Most psychometric devices are re-

This article was reprinted from the *Psychological Bulletin*, 1955, with permission of the author and the American Psychological Association.

ported without cross-validation data. If a psychometric instrument is applied solely to the criterion groups from which it was developed, its reported validity and efficiency are likely to be spuriously high, especially if the criterion groups are small.

d. There is often a lack of clarity concerning the type of population in which a psychometric device can be effectively applied.

e. Results are frequently reported only in terms of significance tests for differences between groups rather than in terms of the number of correct decisions for individuals within the groups.

The purposes of this paper are to examine current methodology in studies of predictive and concurrent validity [1], and to present some methods for the evaluation of the efficiency of psychometric devices as well as for the improvement in the interpretations made from such devices. Actual studies reported in the literature will be used for illustration wherever possible. It should be emphasized that these particular illustrative studies of common practices were chosen simply because they contained more complete data than are commonly reported, and were available in fairly recent publications.

IMPORTANCE OF BASE RATES

Danielson and Clark [4] have reported on the construction and application of a personality inventory which was devised for use in military induction stations as an aid in detecting those men who would not complete basic training because of psychiatric disability or AWOL recidivism. One serious defect in their article is that it reports cutting lines which have not been cross validated. Danielson and Clark state that inductees were administered the Fort Ord Inventory within two days after induction into the Army, and that all of these men

were allowed to undergo basic training regardless of their test scores.

Two samples (among others) of these inductees were selected for the study of predictive validity: (a) A group of 415 men who had made a good adjustment (Good Adjustment Group), and (b) a group of 89 men who were unable to complete basic training and who were sufficiently disturbed to warrant a recommendation for discharge by a psychiatrist (Poor Adjustment Group). The authors state that "the most important task of a test designed to screen out misfits is the detection of the [latter] group" [4, p. 139]. The authors found that their most effective scale for this differentiation picked up, at a given cutting point, 55% of the Poor Adjustment Group (valid positives) and 19% of the Good Adjustment Group (false positives). The overlap between these two groups would undoubtedly have been greater if the cutting line had been cross validated on a random sample from the *entire population* of inductees, but for the purposes of the present discussion, let us assume that the results were obtained from cross-validation groups. There is no mention of the percentage of all inductees who fall into the Poor Adjustment Group, but a rough estimate will be adequate for the present discussion. Suppose that in their population of soldiers, as many as 5% make a poor adjustment and 95% make a good adjustment. The results for 10,000 cases would be as depicted in Table 33–1.

Table 33–1 Number of Inductees in the Poor Adjustment and Good Adjustment Groups Detected by a Screening Inventory (55% valid positives; 19% false positives)

Predicted Adjustment	Actual Adjustment				Total Predicted
	Poor		Good		
	No.	%	No.	%	
Poor	275	55	1,805	19	2,080
Good	225	45	7,695	81	7,920
Total actual	500	100	9,500	100	10,000

EFFICIENCY IN DETECTING
POOR ADJUSTMENT CASES

The efficiency of the scale can be evaluated in several ways. From the data in Table 33–1 it can be seen that if the cutting line given by the authors were used at Fort Ord, the scale could not be used directly to "screen out misfits." If all those predicted by the scale to make a poor adjustment were screened out, the number of false positives would be extremely high. Among the 10,000 potential inductees, 2080 would be predicted to make a poor adjustment. Of these 2080, only 275, or 13%, would actually make a poor adjustment, whereas the decisions for 1805 men, or 87% of those screened out, would be incorrect.

EFFICIENCY IN PREDICTION FOR ALL CASES

If a prediction were made for every man on the basis of the cutting line given for the test, 275 + 7695, or 7970, out of 10,000 decisions would be correct. Without the test, however, every man would be predicted to make a good adjustment, and 9500 of the predictions would be correct. Thus, use of the test has yielded a drop from 95% to 79.7% in the total number of correct decisions.

EFFICIENCY IN DETECTING GOOD
ADJUSTMENT CASES

There is one kind of decision in which the Inventory can improve on the base rates, however. If only those men are accepted who are predicted by the Inventory to make a good adjustment, 7920 will be selected, and the outcome of 7695 of the 7920, or 97%, will be predicted correctly. This is a 2% increase in hits among predictions of "success." The decision as to whether or not the scale improves on the base rates sufficiently to warrant its use will depend on the cost of administering the testing program, the administrative feasibility of rejecting 21% of the men who

passed the psychiatric screening, the cost to the Army of training the 225 maladaptive recruits, and the intangible human costs involved in psychiatric breakdown.

POPULATIONS TO WHICH
THE SCALE IS APPLIED

In the evaluation of the efficiency of any psychometric instrument, careful consideration must be given to the types of populations to which the device is to be applied. Danielson and Clark have stated that "since the final decision as to disposition is made by the psychiatrist, the test should be classified as a screening adjunct" [4, p. 138]. This statement needs clarification, however, for the efficiency of the scale can vary markedly according to the different ways in which it might be used as an adjunct.

It will be noted that the test was administered to men who were already in the Army, and not to men being examined for induction. The reported validation data apply, therefore, specifically to the population of *recent inductees*. The results might have been somewhat different if the population tested consisted of *potential inductees*. For the sake of illustration, however, let us assume that there is no difference in the test results of the two populations.

An induction station psychiatrist can use the scale cutting score in one or more of the following ways, i.e., he can apply the scale results to a variety of populations. (*a*) The psychiatrist's final decision to accept or reject a potential inductee may be based on both the test score and his usual interview procedure. The population to which the test scores are applied is, therefore, *potential inductees interviewed by the usual procedures for whom no decision was made.* (*b*) He may evaluate the potential inductee according to his usual procedures, and then consult the test score *only if* the tentative decision is to reject. That is, a decision to accept is final. The population to which the test scores are applied is *potential inductees tentatively rejected by the usual interview procedures.* (*c*) An alternative procedure is for the psychiatrist to consult the test score only if the tentative decision is to accept, the population being *potential inductees tentatively accepted by the usual interview procedures.* The decision to reject is final. (*d*) Probably the commonest proposal for the use of tests as screening adjuncts is that the more skilled and costly psychiatric evaluation should be made only upon the test positives, i.e., inductees classified by the test as good risks are not interviewed, or are subjected only to a very short and superficial interview. Here the population is *all potential inductees,* the test being used to make either a *final* decision to "accept" or a decision to "examine."

Among these different procedures, how is the psychiatrist to achieve maximum effectiveness in using the test as an adjunct? There is no answer to this question from the available data, but it can be stated definitely that the data reported by Danielson and Clark apply only to the third procedure described above. The test results are based on a selected group of men *accepted* for induction and not on a random sample of potential inductees. If the scale is used in any other way than the third procedure mentioned above, the results may be considerably inferior to those reported, and, thus, to the use of the base rates without the test.[1]

The principles discussed thus far, although illustrated by a single study, can be generalized to any study of predictive or concurrent validity. It can be seen that many considerations are involved in determining the efficiency of a scale at a given cutting score, especially the base rates of the subclasses within the population to which the psychometric device is to be applied. In a subsequent portion of this paper, methods will be presented for determining cutting points for maximizing the

efficiency of the different types of decisions which are made with psychometric devices.

Another study will be utilized to illustrate the importance of an explicit statement of the base rates of population subgroups to be tested with a given device. Employing an interesting configural approach, Thiesen [18] discovered five Rorschach patterns, each of which differentiated well between 60 schizophrenic adult patients and a sample of 157 gainfully employed adults. The best differentiator, considering individual patterns or number of patterns, was Pattern A, which was found in 20% of the patients' records and in only .6% of the records of normals. Thiesen concludes that if these patterns stand the test of cross validation, they might have "clinical usefulness" in early detection of a schizophrenic process or as an aid to determining the gravity of an initial psychotic episode [18, p. 369]. If by "clinical usefulness" is meant efficiency in a clinic or hospital for the diagnosis of schizophrenia, it is necessary to demonstrate that the patterns differentiate a higher percentage of schizophrenic patients from *other diagnostic groups* than could be correctly classified without any test at all, i.e., solely on the basis of the rates of various diagnoses in any given hospital. If a test is to be used in differential diagnosis among psychiatric patients, evidence of its efficiency for this function cannot be established solely on the basis of discrimination of diagnostic groups from normals. If by "clinical usefulness" Thiesen means that his data indicate that the patterns might be used to detect an early schizophrenic process among nonhospitalized gainfully employed adults, he would do better to discard his patterns and use the base rates, as can be seen from the following data.

Taulbee and Sisson [17] cross validated Thiesen's patterns on schizophrenic patient and normal samples, and found that Pattern A was the best discriminator. Among patients, 8.1% demonstrated this pattern and among normals, none had this pattern.

---

[1] Goodman [8] has discussed this same problem with reference to the supplementary use of an index for the prediction of parole violation.

Table 33–2   Number of Persons Classified as Schizophrenic and Normal by a Test Pattern among a Population of Gainfully Employed Adults (8.1% valid positives; 0.0% false positives)

| Classification by Test | Criterion Classification | | | | Total Classified by Test |
| | Schizophrenia | | Normal | | |
	No.	%	No.	%	
Schizophrenia	7	8.1	0	0	7
Normal	78	91.9	9,915	100	9,993
Total in class	85	100	9,915	100	10,000

There are approximately 60 million gainfully employed adults in this country, and it has been estimated that the rate of schizophrenia in the general population is approximately .85% [2, p. 558]. The results for Pattern A among a population of 10,000 gainfully employed adults would be as shown in Table 33–2. In order to detect 7 schizophrenics, it would be necessary to test 10,000 individuals.

In the Neurology service of a hospital a psychometric scale is used which is designed to differentiate between patients with psychogenic and organic low back pain [9]. At a given cutting point, this scale was found to classify each group with approximately 70% effectiveness upon cross validation, i.e., 70% of cases with no organic findings scored above an optimal cutting score, and 70% of surgically verified organic cases scored below this line. Assume that 90% of all patients in the Neurology service with a primary complaint of low back pain are in fact "organic." Without any scale at all the psychologist can say every case is organic, and be right 90% of the time. With the scale the results would be as shown in Section A of Table 33–3. Of 10 psychogenic cases, 7 score above the line; of 90 organic cases, 63 score below the cutting line. If every case above the line is called psychogenic, only 7 of 34 will be classified correctly or about 21%. Nobody wants to be right only one out of five times in this type of situation, so that it is obvious that it would be imprudent to call a patient psychogenic on the basis of this scale. Radi-

cally different results occur in prediction for cases below the cutting line. Of 66 cases 63, or 95%, are correctly classified as organic. Now the psychologist has increased his diagnostic hits from 90 to 95% on the condition that he labels only cases falling below the line, and ignores the 34% scoring above the line.

In actual practice, the psychologist may not, and most likely will not, test every low back pain case. Probably those referred for testing will be a select group, i.e., those who the neurologist believes are psychogenic because neurological findings are minimal or absent. This fact changes the population from "all patients in Neurology with a primary complaint of low back pain," to "all patients in Neurology with a

Table 33–3   Number of Patients Classified as Psychogenic and Organic on a Low Back Pain Scale Which Classifies Correctly 70% of Psychogenic and Organic Cases

| Classification by Scale | Actual Diagnosis | | Total Classified by Scale |
	Psychogenic	Organic	
A. Base Rates in Population Tested: 90% Organic; 10% Psychogenic			
Psychogenic	7	27	34
Organic	3	63	66
Total diagnosed	10	90	100
B. Base Rates in Population Tested: 90% Psychogenic; 10% Organic			
Psychogenic	63	3	66
Organic	27	7	34
Total diagnosed	90	10	100

primary complaint of low back pain *who are referred for testing.*" Suppose that a study of past diagnoses indicated that of patients with minimal or absent findings, 90% were diagnosed as psychogenic and 10% as organic. Section B of Table 33–3 gives an entirely different picture of the effectiveness of the low back pain scale, and new limitations on interpretation are necessary. Now the scale correctly classifies 95% of all cases above the line as psychogenic (63 of 66), and is correct in only 21% of all cases below the line (7 of 34). In this practical situation the psychologist would be wise to refrain from interpreting a low score.

From the above illustrations it can be seen that the psychologist in interpreting a test and in evaluating its effectiveness must be very much aware of the population and its subclasses and the base rates of the behavior or event with which he is dealing at any given time.

It may be objected that no clinician relies on just one scale but would diagnose on the basis of a configuration of impressions from several tests, clinical data and history. We must, therefore, emphasize that the preceding single-scale examples were presented for simplicity only, but that the main point is not dependent upon this "atomism." *Any complex configurational procedure in any number of variables, psychometric or otherwise, eventuates in a decision.* Those decisions have a certain objective success rate in criterion case identification; and for present purposes we simply treat the decision function, whatever its components and complexity may be, as a single variable. It should be remembered that the literature does not present us with cross-validated methods having hit rates much above those we have chosen as examples, regardless of how complex or configural the methods used. So that even if the clinician approximates an extremely complex configural function "in his head" before classifying the patient, for purposes of the present problem this complex function is treated as the scale. In connection with the more general

"philosophy" of clinical decision making see Bross [3] and Meehl [12].

APPLICATIONS OF BAYES' THEOREM

Many readers will recognize the preceding numerical examples as essentially involving a principle of elementary probability theory, the so-called "Bayes' Theorem." While it has come in for some opprobrium on account of its connection with certain pre-Fisherian fallacies in statistical inference, as an algebraic statement the theorem has, of course, nothing intrinsically wrong with it and it does apply in the present case. One form of it may be stated as follows:

If there are k antecedent conditions under which an event of a given kind may occur, these conditions having the antecedent probabilities $P_1, P_2, \ldots, P_k$ of being realized, and the probability of the event upon each of them is $p_1, p_2, p_3, \ldots, p_k$; then, given that the event is observed to occur, the probability that it arose on the basis of a specified one, say j, of the antecedent conditions is given by

$$P_{j(0)} = \frac{P_j p_j}{\sum\limits_{i=1}^{k} P_i p_i}$$

The usual illustration is the case of drawing marbles from an urn. Suppose we have two urns, and the urn-selection procedure is such that the probability of our choosing the first urn is $\frac{1}{10}$ and the second $\frac{9}{10}$. Assume that 70% of the marbles in the first urn are black, and 40% of those in the second urn are black. I now (blindfolded) "choose" an urn and then, from it, I choose a marble. The marble turns out to be black. What is the probability that I drew from the first urn?

$$P_1 = .10 \qquad P_2 = .90$$
$$p_1 = .70 \qquad p_2 = .40$$

Then

$$P_{1(b)} = \frac{(.10)(.70)}{(.10)(.70)+(.90)(.40)} = .163$$

If I make a practice of inferring under such circumstances that an observed black marble arose from the first urn, I shall be correct in such judgments, in the long run, only 16.3% of the time. Note, however, that the "test item" or "sign" *black marble* is correctly "scored" in favor of Urn No. 1, since there is a 30% difference in black marble rate between it and Urn No. 2. But this considerable disparity in symptom rate is overcome by the very low base rate ("antecedent probability of choosing from the first urn"), so that inference to first-urn origin of black marbles will actually be wrong some 84 times in 100. In the clinical analogue, the urns are identified with the subpopulations of patients to be discriminated (their antecedent probabilities being equated to their base rates in the population to be examined), and the black marbles are test results of a certain ("positive") kind. The proportion of black marbles in one urn is the valid positive rate, and in the other is the false positive rate. Inspection and suitable manipulations of the formula for the common two-category case, viz.,

$$P_{(0)} = \frac{Pp_1}{Pp_1 + Qp_2}$$

$P_{d(0)} =$ Probability that an individual is diseased, given that his observed test score is positive

$P =$ Base rate of actual positives in the population examined

$P + Q = 1$

$p_1 =$ Proportion of diseased identified by test ("valid positive" rate)

$q_1 = 1 - p_1$

$p_2 =$ Proportion of nondiseased misidentified by test as being diseased ("false positive" rate)

$q_2 = 1 - p_2$

yield several useful statements. Note that in what follows we are operating entirely with exact population parameter values; i.e., sampling errors are not responsible for the dangers and restrictions set forth. See Table 33–4.

1. In order for a positive diagnostic assertion to be "more likely true than false," the ratio of the positive to the negative base rates in the examined population must exceed the ratio of the false positive rate to the valid positive rate. That is,

$$\frac{P}{Q} > \frac{p_2}{p_1}$$

If this condition is not met, the attribution of pathology on the basis of the test is more probably in error than correct, *even though the sign being used is valid* (i.e., $p_1 \neq p_2$).

Example: If a certain cutting score identifies 80% of patients with organic brain damage (high scores being indicative of damage) but is also exceeded by 15% of the nondamaged sent for evaluation, in order for the psychometric decision "brain damage present" to be more often true than false, the ratio of actually brain-damaged to nondamaged cases among all seen for testing must be at least one to five (.19).

Piotrowski has recommended that the presence of 5 or more Rorschach signs among 10 "organic" signs is an efficient indicator of brain damage. Dorken and Kral [5], in cross validating Piotrowski's index, found that 63% of organics and 30% of a mixed, nonorganic, psychiatric patient group had Rorschachs with 5 or more signs. Thus, our estimate of $p_2/p_1 = .30/.63 = .48$, and in order for the decision "brain damage present" to be correct more than one-half the time, the proportion of positives (P) in a given population must equal or exceed .33 (i.e., $P/Q > .33/.67$). Since few clinical populations requiring this clinical decision would have such a high rate of brain damage, especially among psychiatric patients, the particular cutting score advocated by Piotrowski will produce an excessive number of false positives, and the positive diagnosis will be more often wrong than right. Inasmuch as the base rates for any given behavior or pathology differ from one clinical setting to another, *an inflexible cutting score should not be advocated for any psychometric device*. This statement applies

Table 33–4 Definition of Symbols*

Diagnosis from Test	Actual Diagnosis	
	Positive	Negative
Positive	p_1 Valid positive rate (proportion of positives called positive)	p_2 False positive rate (proportion of negatives called positive)
Negative	q_1 False negative rate (proportion of positives called negative)	q_2 Valid negative rate (proportion of negatives called negative)
Total with actual diagnosis	$p_1 + q_1 = 1.0$ (Total negatives)	$p_2 + q_2 = 1.0$ (Total positives)

* For simplicity, the term "diagnosis" is used to denote the classification of any kind of pathology, behavior, or event being studied, or to denote "outcome" if a test is used for prediction. Since horizontal addition (e.g., $p_1 + p_2$) is meaningless in ignorance of the base rates, there is no symbol or marginal total for these sums. *All values are parameter values.*

generally—thus, to indices recommended for such diverse purposes as the classification or detection of deterioration, specific symptoms, "traits," neuroticism, sexual aberration, dissimulation, suicide risk, and the like. When P is small, it may be advisable to explore the possibility of dealing with a restricted population within which the base rate of the attribute being tested is higher. This approach is discussed in an article by Rosen [14] on the detection of suicidal patients in which it is suggested that an attempt might be made to apply an index to subpopulations with higher suicide rates.

2. If the base rates are equal, the probability of a positive diagnosis being correct is the ratio of valid positive rate to the sum of valid and false positive rates. That is,

$$P_{d(o)} = \frac{p_1}{p_1 + p_2} \quad \text{if} \quad P = Q = \tfrac{1}{2}$$

Example: If our population is evenly divided between neurotic and psychotic patients the condition for being "probably right" in diagnosing psychosis by a certain method is simply that the psychotics exhibit the pattern in question more frequently than the neurotics. This is the intuitively

obvious special case; it is often misgeneralized to justify use of the test in those cases where base-rate asymmetry ($P \neq Q$) counteracts the ($p_1 - p_2$) discrepancy, leading to the paradoxical consequence that *deciding on the basis of more information can actually worsen the chances of a correct decision.* The apparent absurdity of such an idea has often misled psychologists into behaving as though the establishment of "validity" or "discrimination," i.e., that $p_1 \neq p_2$, indicates that a procedure should be used in decision making.

Example: A certain test is used to select those who will continue in outpatient psychotherapy (positives). It correctly identifies 75% of these good cases but the same cutting score picks up 40% of the poor risks who subsequently terminate against advice. Suppose that in the past experience of the clinic 50% of the patients terminated therapy prematurely. Correct selection of patients can be made with the given cutting score on the test 65% of the time, since $p_1/(p_1 + p_2) = .75/(.75 + .40) = .65$. It can be seen that the efficiency of the test would be exaggerated if the base rate for continuation in therapy were actually .70, but the efficiency were evaluated solely on the basis of a research study containing equal groups of continuers and non-continuers, i.e., if it were assumed that $P = .50$.

3. In order for the hits in the entire population which is under consideration to be increased by use of the test, the base rate of the more numerous class (called here positive) must be less than the ratio of the valid negative rate to the sum of valid negative and false negative rates. That is, unless

$$P < \frac{q_2}{q_1 + q_2}$$

the making of decisions on the basis of the test will have an adverse effect. An alternative expression is that $(P/Q) < (q_2/q_1)$ when $P > Q$, i.e., the ratio of the larger to the smaller class must be less than the ratio of the valid negative rate to the false negative rate. When $P < Q$, the conditions for the test to improve upon the base rates are:

$$Q < \frac{p_1}{p_1 + p_2}$$

and

$$\frac{Q}{P} < \frac{p_1}{p_2}$$

Rotter, Rafferty, and Lotsof [15] have reported the scores on a sentence completion test for a group of 33 "maladjusted" and 33 "adjusted" girls. They report that the use of a specified cutting score (not cross validated) will result in the correct classification of 85% of the maladjusted girls and the incorrect classification of only 15% of the adjusted girls. It is impossible to evaluate adequately the efficiency of the test unless one knows the base rates of maladjustment (P) and adjustment (Q) for the population of high school girls, although there would be general agreement that $Q > P$. Since $p_1/(p_1 + p_2) = .85/(.85 + .15) = .85$, the over-all hits in diagnosis with the test will not improve on classification based solely on the base rates unless the proportion of adjusted girls is less than .85. Because the reported effectiveness of

the test is spuriously high, the proportion of adjusted girls would no doubt have to be considerably less than .85. Unless there is good reason to believe that the base rates are similar from one setting to another, it is impossible to determine the efficiency of a test such as Rotter's when the criterion is based on ratings unless one replicates his research, including the criterion ratings, with a representative sample of each new population.

4. In altering a sign, improving a scale, or shifting a cutting score, the increment in valid positives per increment in valid positive *rate* is proportional to the positive base rate; and analogously, the increment in valid negatives per increment in valid negative *rate* is proportional to the negative base rate. That is, if we alter a sign the net improvement in over-all hit rate is

$$H'_T - H_T = \Delta p_1 P + \Delta q_2 Q$$

where H_T = original proportion of hits (over-all) and H'_T = new proportion of hits (over-all).

5. A corollary of this is that altering a sign or shifting a cut will improve our decision making if, and only if, the ratio of *improvement* Δp_1 in valid positive rate to *worsening* Δp_2 in false negative rate exceeds the ratio of actual negatives to positives in the population.

$$\frac{\Delta p_1}{\Delta p_2} > \frac{Q}{P}$$

Example: Suppose we improve the intrinsic validity of a certain "schizophrenic index" so that it now detects 20% more schizophrenics than it formerly did, at the expense of only a 5% increase in the false positive rate. This surely looks encouraging. We are, however, working with an outpatient clientele only 1/10th of whom are actually schizophrenic. Then, since

$$\Delta p_1 = .20 \qquad P = .10$$
$$\Delta p_2 = .05 \qquad Q = .90$$

applying the formula we see that

$$\frac{.20}{.05} \not> \frac{.90}{.10}$$

i.e., the required inequality does not hold, and the routine use of this "improved" index will result in an increase in the proportion of erroneous diagnostic decisions.

In the case of any pair of unimodal distributions, this corresponds to the principle that the optimal cut lies at the intersection of the two distribution envelopes [11, pp. 271–272].

MANIPULATION OF CUTTING LINES FOR DIFFERENT DECISIONS

For any given psychometric device, no one cutting line is maximally efficient for clinical settings in which the base rates of the criterion groups in the population are different. Furthermore, different cutting lines may be necessary for various decisions within the same population. In this section, methods are presented for manipulating the cutting line of any instrument in order to maximize the efficiency of a device in the making of several kinds of decisions. Reference should be made to the scheme presented in Table 33–5 for understanding of the discussion which follows. This scheme and the methods for manipulating cutting lines are derived from Duncan, Ohlin, Reiss, and Stanton [6].

A study in the prediction of juvenile delinquency by Glueck and Glueck [7] will be used for illustration. Scores on a prediction index for 451 delinquents and 439 nondelinquents [7, p. 261] are listed in Table 33–6. If the Gluecks' index is to be used in a population with a given juvenile delinquency rate, cutting lines can be established to maximize the efficiency of the index for several decisions. In the following illustration, a delinquency rate of .20 will be used. From the data in Table 33–6, optimal cutting lines will be determined for maximizing the proportion of correct predictions, or hits, for all cases (H_T), and for maximizing the proportion of hits (H_P) among those called delinquent (positives) by the index.

In the first three columns of Table 33–6, "f" denotes the number of delinquents scoring in each class interval, "cf" represents the cumulative frequency of delinquents scoring above each class interval (e.g., 265 score above 299), and p_1 represents the proportion of the total group of 451 delinquents scoring above each class interval. Columns 4, 5, and 6 present the same kind of data for the 439 nondelinquents.

MAXIMIZING THE NUMBER OF CORRECT PREDICTIONS OR CLASSIFICATIONS FOR ALL CASES

The proportion of correct predictions or classifications (H_T) for any given cutting

Table 33–5   Symbols to Be Used in Evaluating the Efficiency of a Psychometric Device in Classification or Prediction*

Diagnosis from Test	Actual Diagnosis		Total Diagnosed from Test
	Positive	Negative	
Positive	NPp_1 (Number of valid positives)	NQp_2 (Number of false positives)	$NPp_1 + NQp_2$ (Number of test positives)
Negative	NPq_1 (Number of false negatives)	NQq_2 (Number of valid negatives)	$NPq_1 + NQq_2$ (Number of test negatives)
Total with actual diagnosis	NP (Number of actual positives)	NQ (Number of actual negatives)	N (Total number of cases)

* For simplicity, the term "diagnosis" is used to denote the classification of any kind of pathology, behavior, or event studied, or to denote "outcome" if a test is used for prediction. "Number" means *absolute frequency*, not *rate* or *probability*.

Table 33–6   Prediction Index Scores for Juvenile Delinquents and Nondelinquents and Other Statistics for Determining Optimal Cutting Lines for Certain Decisions in a Population with a Delinquency Rate of .20*

Prediction Index Score	Delinquents			Nondelinquents			$1-p_2$	$.2p_1$	$.8p_2$	$.8q_2$	$Pp_1 + Qq_2$	$Pp_1 + Qp_2$	$\dfrac{Pp_1}{R_P}$
		cf 451			cf 439								
	(1)	(2)	(3)	(4)	(5)	(6)	(7)	(8)	(9)	(10)	(11)	(12)	(13)
	f	cf	p_1	f	cf	p_2	q_2	Pp_1	Qp_2	Qq_2	H_T	R_P	H_P
400+	51	51	.1131	1	1	.0023	.9977	.0226	.0018	.7982	.821	.024	.926
350–399	73	124	.2749	8	9	.0205	.9795	.0550	.0164	.7836	.839	.071	.770
300–349	141	265	.5876	23	32	.0729	.9271	.1175	.0583	.7417	.859	.176	.668
250–299	122	387	.8581	70	102	.2323	.7677	.1716	.1858	.6142	.786	.357	.480
200–249	40	427	.9468	68	170	.3872	.6128	.1894	.3098	.4902	.680	.499	.379
150–199	19	446	.9889	102	272	.6196	.3804	.1978	.4957	.3043	.502	.694	.285
<150	5	451	1.0000	167	439	1.0000	.0000	.2000	.8000	.0000	.200	1.000	.200

* Frequencies in columns 1 and 4 are from Glueck and Glueck [7, p. 261].

line is given by the formula, $H_T = Pp_1 + Qq_2$. Thus, in column 11 of Table 33–6, labelled H_T, it can be seen that the best cutting line for this decision would be between 299 and 300, for 85.9% of all predictions would be correct if those above the line were predicted to become delinquent and all those below the line nondelinquent. Any other cutting line would result in a smaller proportion of correct predictions, and, in fact, any cutting line set lower than this point would make the index inferior to the use of the base rates, for if all cases were predicted to be nondelinquent, the total proportion of hits would be .80.

MAXIMIZING THE NUMBER OF CORRECT PREDICTIONS OR CLASSIFICATIONS FOR POSITIVES

The primary use of a prediction device may be for *selection* of (*a*) students who will succeed in a training program, (*b*) applicants who will succeed in a certain job, (*c*) patients who will benefit from a certain type of therapy, etc. In the present illustration, the index would most likely be used for detection of those who are likely to become delinquents. Thus, the aim might be to maximize the number of hits only within the group predicted by the index to

become delinquents (predicted positives = $NPp_1 + NQp_2$). The proportion of correct predictions for this group by the use of different cutting lines is given in column 13, labelled H_P. Thus, if a cutting line is set between 399 and 400, one will be correct over 92 times in 100 if predictions are made *only* for persons scoring above the cutting line. The formula for determining the efficiency of the test when only positive predictions are made is $H_P = Pp_1/(Pp_1 + Qp_2)$.

One has to pay a price for achieving a very high level of accuracy with the index. Since the problem is to select potential delinquents so that some sort of therapy can be attempted, the proportion of this selected group in the total sample may be considered as a selection ratio. The selection ratio for positives is $R_P = Pp_1 + Qp_2$, that is, predictions are made only for those above the cutting line. The selection ratio for each possible cutting line is shown in column 12 of Table 33–6 labelled R_P. It can be seen that to obtain maximum accuracy in selection of delinquents (92.6%), predictions can be made for only 2.4% of the population. For other cutting lines, the accuracy of selection and the corresponding selection ratios are given in Table 33–6. The worker applying the index must use his own judgment in deciding upon the level of accuracy and the selection ratio desired.

MAXIMIZING THE NUMBER OF CORRECT PREDICTIONS OR CLASSIFICATIONS FOR NEGATIVES

In some selection problems, the goal is the selection of negatives rather than positives. Then, the proportion of hits among all predicted negative for any given cutting line is $H_N = Qq_2/(Qq_2 + Pq_1)$, and the selection ratio for negatives is $R_N = Pq_1 + Qq_2$.

In all of the above manipulations of cutting lines, it is essential that there be a large number of cases. Otherwise, the percentages about any given cutting line would be so unstable that very dissimilar results would be obtained on new samples. For most studies in clinical psychology, therefore, it would be necessary to establish cutting lines according to the decisions and methods discussed above, and then to cross validate a specific cutting line on new samples.

The amount of shrinkage to be expected in the cross validation of cutting lines cannot be determined until a thorough mathematical and statistical study of the subject is made. It may be found that when criterion distributions are approximately normal and large, cutting lines should be established in terms of the normal probability table rather than on the basis of the observed p and q values found in the samples. In a later section dealing with the selection ratio we shall see that it is sometimes the best procedure to select all individuals falling above a certain cutting line and to select the others needed to reach the selection ratio by choosing at random below the line; or in other cases to establish several different cuts defining *ranges* within which one or the opposite decision should be made.

DECISIONS BASED ON SCORE INTERVALS RATHER THAN CUTTING LINES

The Gluecks' data can be used to illustrate another approach to psychometric classification and prediction when scores for large samples are available with a relatively large number of cases in each score interval. In Table 33–7 are listed frequencies of delinquents and nondelinquents for prediction index score intervals. The frequencies for delinquents are the same as those in Table 33–6, whereas those for nondelinquents have been corrected for a base rate of .20 by multiplying each frequency in column 4 of Table 33–6[2] by

$$4.11 = \frac{(.80)}{(.20)} \frac{(451)}{(439)}$$

[2] The Gluecks' Tables XX–2, 3, 4, 5 [7, pp. 261–262] and their interpretations therefrom are apt to be misleading because of their exclusive consideration of approximately equal base rates of delinquency and nondelinquency. Reiss [13], in his review of the Gluecks' study, has also discussed their use of an unrepresentative rate of delinquency.

Table 33–7   Percentage of Delinquents (D) and Nondelinquents (ND) in Each Prediction Index Score Interval in a Population in Which the Delinquency Rate Is .20*

Prediction Index Score Interval	No. of D	No. of ND	Total of D and ND	% of D in Score Interval	% of ND in Score Interval	% of D and ND in Score Interval
400+	51	4	55	92.7	7.3	100
350–399	73	33	106	68.9	31.1	100
300–349	141	95	236	59.7	40.3	100
250–299	122	288	410	29.8	70.2	100
200–249	40	279	319	12.5	87.5	100
150–199	19	419	438	4.3	95.7	100
<150	5	686	691	.7	99.3	100
Total	451	1804	2255			

* Modification of Table XX–2, p. 261, from Glueck and Glueck [7].

Table 33–7 indicates the proportion of delinquents and nondelinquents among all juveniles who fall within a given score interval when the base rate of delinquency is .20. It can be predicted that of those scoring 400 or more, 92.7% will become delinquent, of those scoring between 350 and 399, 68.9% will be delinquent, etc. Likewise, of those scoring between 200 and 249, it can be predicted that 87.5% will not become delinquent. Since 80% of predictions will be correct without the index if all cases are called nondelinquent, one would not predict nondelinquency with the index in score intervals over 249. Likewise, it would be best not to predict delinquency for individuals in the intervals under 250 because 20% of predictions will be correct if the base rate is used.

It should be emphasized that there are different ways of quantifying one's clinical errors, and they will, of course, not all give the same evaluation when applied in a given setting. "Per cent valid positives" ($=p_1$) is rarely if ever meaningful without the correlated "per cent false positives" ($=p_2$), and clinicians are accustomed to the idea that we pay for an increase in the first by an increase in the second, whenever the increase is achieved not by an improvement in the test's intrinsic validity but by a shifting of the cutting score. But the two quantities p_1 and p_2 do not define our overall hit frequency, which depends also upon the base rates P and Q. The three quantities p_1, p_2, and P do, however, contain all the information needed to evaluate the test with respect to any given sign or cutting score that yields these values. Although p_1, p_2, and P contain the relevant information, other forms of it may be of greater importance. No two of these numbers, for example, answer the obvious question most commonly asked (or vaguely implied) by psychiatrists when an inference is made from a sign, viz., "How sure can you be on the basis of that sign?" The answer to this eminently practical query involves a probability different from any of the above, namely, the *inverse* probability given by Bayes' formula:

$$H_P = \frac{Pp_1}{Pp_1 + Qp_2}$$

Even a small improvement in the hit frequency to $H'_T = Pp_1 + Qq_2$ over the $H_T = P$ attainable without the test may be adjudged as worth while when the increment ΔH_T is multiplied by the N examined in the course of one year and is thus seen to involve a dozen lives or a dozen curable schizophrenics. On the other hand, the simple fact that an actual *shrinkage* in total hit rate may occur seems to be unappreciated or tacitly ignored by a good deal of clinical practice. One must keep constantly in mind that numerous diagnostic, prognostic, and dynamic statements can be made about almost all neurotic patients (e.g., "depressed," "inadequate ability to relate," "sexual difficulties") or about very few patients (e.g., "dangerous," "will act out in therapy," "suicidal," "will blow up into a schizophrenia"). A psychologist who uses a test sign that even cross validates at $p_1 = q_2 = 80\%$ to determine whether "depression" is present or absent, working in a clinical population where practically everyone is fairly depressed except a few psychopaths and old-fashioned hysterics, is kidding himself, the psychiatrist, and whoever foots the bill.

"SUCCESSIVE-HURDLES" APPROACH

Tests having low efficiency, or having moderate efficiency but applied to populations having very unbalanced base rates ($P < Q$), are sometimes defended by adopting a "crude initial screening" frame of reference, and arguing that certain other procedures (whether tests or not) can be applied to the subset identified by the screener ("successive hurdles"). There is no question that in some circumstances (e.g., military induction, or industrial selection with a large labor market) this is a thoroughly defensible position. However, as a general rule one should examine this type of justification critically, with the preceding considerations in mind. Suppose we have a test which distinguishes brain-tumor from non–brain-tumor patients with 75% accuracy and no differential bias ($p_1 = q_2 = .75$). Under such circumstances the test hit rate H_T is .75 regardless of the base rate. If we use the test in making our judgments, we are correct in our diagnoses 75 times in 100. But suppose only one patient in 10 actually has a brain tumor; we will drop our over-all "success" from 90% (attainable by diagnosing "No tumor" in all cases) to 75%. We do, however, identify 3 out of 4 of the real brain tumors, and in such a case it seems worth the price. The "price" has two aspects to it: We take time to give the test, and, having given it, we call many "tumorous" who are not. Thus, suppose that in the course of a year we see 1000 patients. Of these, 900 are non-tumor, and we erroneously call 225 of these "tumor." To pick up (100) (.75) = 75 of the tumors, *all* 100 of whom would have been called tumor-free using the base rates alone, we are willing to mislabel 3 times this many as tumorous who are actually not. Putting it another way, whenever we say "tumor" on the basis of the test, the chances are 3 to 1 that we are mistaken. When we "rule out" tumor by the test, we are correct 96% of the time, an improvement of only 6% in the confidence attachable to a negative finding over the confidence yielded by the base rates.[3]

Now, picking up the successive-hurdles argument, suppose a major decision (e.g., exploratory surgery) is allowed to rest upon a second test which is infallible but for practically insuperable reasons of staff, time, etc., cannot be routinely given. We administer Test 2 only to "positives" on (screening) Test 1. By this tactic we eliminate all 225 false positives left by Test 1, and we verify the 75 valid positives screened in by Test 1. The 25 tumors that slipped through as false negatives on Test 1

are, of course, not picked up by Test 2 either, because it is not applied to them. Our total hit frequency is now 97.5%, since the only cases ultimately misclassified out of our 1000 seen are these 25 tumors which escaped through the initial sieve Test 1. We are still running only 7½% above the base rate. We have had to give our short-and-easy test to 1000 individuals and our cumbersome, expensive test to 300 individuals, 225 of whom turn out to be free of tumor. But we have located 75 patients with tumor who would not otherwise have been found.

Such examples suggest that, except in "life-or-death" matters, the successive-screenings argument merely tends to soften the blow of Bayes' Rule in cases where the base rates are very far from symmetry. Also, if Test 2 is not assumed to be infallible but only highly effective, say 90% accurate both ways, results start looking unimpressive again. Our net false positive rate rises from zero to 22 cases miscalled "tumor," and we operate 67 of the actual tumors instead of 75. The total hit frequency drops to 94.5%, only 4½% above that yielded by a blind guessing of the modal class.

THE SELECTION RATIO

Straightforward application of the preceding principles presupposes that the clinical decision maker is free to adopt a policy solely on the basis of maximizing hit frequency. Sometimes there are external constraints such as staff time, administrative policy, or social obligation which further complicate matters. It may then be impossible to make all decisions in accordance with the base rates, and the task given to the test is that of selecting a subset of cases which are decided in the direction opposite to the base rates but will still contain fewer erroneous decisions than would ever be yielded by opposing the base rates without the test. If 80% of patients referred to a Mental Hygiene Clinic are recoverable with intensive psychotherapy, we would do bet-

---

[3] Improvements are expressed throughout this article as *absolute* increments in percentage of hits, because: (*a*) This avoids the complete arbitrariness involved in choosing between original hit rate and miss rate as starting denominator; and (*b*) for the clinician, the person is the most meaningful unit of gain, rather than a proportion *of* a proportion (especially when the reference proportion is very small).

ter to treat everybody than to utilize a test yielding 75% correct predictions. But suppose that available staff time is limited so that we *can* treat only half the referrals. The Bayes-type injunction to "follow the base rates when they are better than the test" becomes pragmatically meaningless, for it directs us to make decisions which we cannot implement. The imposition of an *externally* imposed selection ratio, not determined on the basis of any maximizing or minimizing policy but by nonstatistical considerations, renders the test worth while.

Prior to imposition of any arbitrary selection ratio, the fourfold table for 100 referrals might be as shown in Table 33–8. If the aim were simply to minimize total errors, we would predict "good" for each case and be right 80 times in 100. Using the test, we would be right only 75 times in 100. But suppose a selection ratio of .5 is externally imposed. We are then forced to predict "poor" for half the cases, even though this "prediction" is, in any given case, likely to be wrong. (More precisely, we handle this subset *as if* we predicted "poor," by refusing to treat.) So we now select our 50 to-be-treated cases from among those 65 who fall in the "test-good" array, having a frequency of $^{60}/_{65} = 92.3\%$ hits among those selected. This is better than the 80% we could expect (among those selected) by choosing half the total referrals at random. Of course we pay for this, by making many "false negative" decisions; but these are necessitated, whether we use the test or not, by the fact that the selection ratio was determined without regard for hit maximization but by external considerations. Without the test, our false

negative rate q_1 is 50% (i.e., 40 of the 80 "good" cases will be called "poor"); the test reduces the false negative rate to 42.5% ($= {}^{34}/_{80}$), since 15 cases from above the cutting line must be selected at random for inclusion in the not-to-be-treated group below the cutting line [i.e., $20 + ({}^{60}/_{65})15 = 34$]. Stated in terms of correct decisions, without the test 40 out of 50 selected for therapy will have a good therapeutic outcome; with the test, 46 in 50 will be successes.

Reports of studies in which formulas are developed from psychometrics for the prediction of patients' continuance in psychotherapy have neglected to consider the relationship of the selection ratio to the specific population to which the prediction formula is to be applied. In each study the population has consisted of individuals who were *accepted for therapy* by the usual methods employed at an outpatient clinic, and the prediction formula has been evaluated *only* for such patients. It is implied by these studies that the formula would have the same efficiency if it were used for the *selection* of "continuers" from all those *applying* for therapy. Unless the formula is tested on a random sample of applicants who are allowed to enter therapy without regard to their test scores, its efficiency for selection purposes is unknown. The reported efficiency of the prediction formula in the above studies pertains only to its use in a population of patients who have already been selected for therapy. There is little likelihood that the formula can be used in any practical way for further selection of patients unless the clinic's therapists are carrying a far greater load than they plan to carry in the future.

The use of the term "selection" (as contrasted with "prediction" or "placement") ought not to blind us to the important differences between industrial selection and its clinical analogue. The incidence of false negatives—of potential employees screened out by the test who would actually have made good on the job if hired—is of little concern to management except as it costs

Table 33–8   Actual and Test-Predicted Therapeutic Outcome

Test Pre-diction	Therapeutic Outcome		
	Good	Poor	Total
Good	60	5	65
Poor	20	15	35
Total	80	20	100

money to give tests. Hence the industrial psychologist may choose to express his aim in terms of minimizing the false positives, i.e., of seeing to it that the job success *among those hired* is as large a rate as possible. When we make a clinical decision to treat or not to treat, we are withholding something from people who have a claim upon us in a sense that is much stronger than the "right to work" gives a job applicant any claim upon a particular company. So, even though we speak of a "selection ratio" in clinical work, it must be remembered that those cases *not selected* are patients about whom a certain kind of important negative decision is being made.

For any *given* selection ratio, maximizing total hits is always equivalent to maximizing the hit rate for either type of decision (or minimizing the errors of either, or both, kinds), since cases shifted from one cell of the table have to be exactly compensated for. If *m* "good" cases that were correctly classified by one decision method are incorrectly classified by another, maintenance of the selection ratio entails that *m* cases correctly called "poor" are also miscalled "good" by the new method. Hence an externally imposed selection ratio eliminates the often troublesome value questions about the relative seriousness of the two kinds of errors, since they are unavoidably increased or decreased at exactly the same rate.

If the test yields a score or a continuously varying index of some kind, the values of p_1 and p_2 are not fixed, as they may be with "patterns" or "signs." Changes in the selection ratio, R, will then suggest shifting the cutting scores or regions on the basis of the relations obtaining among R, P, and the p_1, p_2 combinations yielded by various cuts. It is worth special comment that, in the case of continuous distributions, the optimum procedure is *not* always to move the cut until the total area truncated $= NR$, selecting all above that cut and rejecting all those below. Whether this "obvious" rule is wise or not depends upon the distribution characteristics. We have found it easy to

construct pairs of distributions such that the test is "discriminating" throughout, in the sense that the associated cumulative frequencies q_1 and q_2 maintain the same direction of their inequality everywhere in the range

$$\left(\text{i.e., } \frac{1}{N_2} \int_{-\infty}^{x_i} f_2(x)dx \right.$$
$$\left. > \frac{1}{N_1} \int_{-\infty}^{x_i} f_1(x)dx \text{ for all } x_i \right)$$

yet in which the hit frequency given by a single cut at R is inferior to that given by first selecting with a cut which yields $N_c < NR$, and then picking up the remaining $(NR - N_c)$ cases at random below the cut. Other more complex situations may arise in which different types of decisions should be made in different regions, actually reversing the policy as we move along the test continuum. Such numerical examples as we have constructed utilize continuous, unimodal distributions, and involve differences in variability, skewness, and kurtosis not greater than those which arise fairly often in clinical practice. Of course the utilization of any very complicated pattern of regions requires more stable distribution frequencies than are obtainable from the sample sizes ordinarily available to clinicians.

It is instructive to contemplate some of the moral and administrative issues involved in the practical application of the preceding ideas. It is our impression that a good deal of clinical research is of the "So—what?" variety, not because of defects in experimental design such as inadequate cross validation but because it is hard to see just what are the useful changes in decision making which could reasonably be expected to follow. Suppose, for example, it is shown that "duration of psychotherapy" is 70% predictable from a certain test. Are we prepared to propose that those patients whose test scores fall in a certain range should not receive treatment? If not, then is it of any real advantage therapeutically to "keep in mind" that the patient has 7 out of 10 chances of staying longer than

15 hours, and 3 out of 10 chances of staying less than that? We are not trying to poke fun at research, since presumably almost any lawful relationship stands a chance of being valuable to our total scientific comprehension some day. But many clinical papers are ostensibly inspired by practical aims, and can be given theoretical interpretation or fitted into any larger framework only with great difficulty if at all. It seems appropriate to urge that such "practical"-oriented investigations should be really *practical*, enabling us to see how our clinical decisions could rationally be modified in the light of the findings. It is doubtful how much of current work could be justified in these terms.

Regardless of whether the test validity is capable of improving on the base rates, there are some prediction problems which have practical import only because of limitations in personnel. What other justification is there for the great emphasis in clinical research on "prognosis," "treatability," or "stayability"? The very formulation of the predictive task as "maximizing the number of hits" already presupposes that we intend *not* to treat some cases; since if we treat all comers, the ascertainment of a bad prognosis score has no practical effect other than to discourage the therapist (and thus hinder therapy?). If intensive psychotherapy could be offered to all veterans who are willing to accept referral to a VA Mental Hygiene Clinic, would it be licit to refuse those who had the poorest outlook? Presumably not. It is interesting to contrast the emphasis on prognosis in clinical psychology with that in, say, cancer surgery, where the treatment *of choice* may still have a very low probability of "success," but is nevertheless carried out on the basis of that low probability. Nor does this attitude seem unreasonable, since no patient would refuse the best available treatment on the ground that even it was only 10% effective. Suppose a therapist, in the course of earning his living, spends 200 hours a year on nonimprovers by following a decision policy that also results in his

unexpected success with one 30-year-old "poor bet." If this client thereby gains $16 \times 365 \times 40 = 233,600$ hours averaging 50% less anxiety during the rest of his natural life, it was presumably worth the price.

These considerations suggest that, with the expansion of professional facilities in the behavior field, the prediction problem will be less like that of industrial *selection* and more like that of *placement*. "To treat or not to treat" or "How treatable" or "How long to treat" would be replaced by "What *kind* of treatment?" But as soon as the problem is formulated in this way, the external selection ratio is usually no longer imposed. Only if we are deciding between such alternatives as classical analysis and, say, 50-hour interpretative therapy would such personnel limitations as can be expected in future years impose an arbitrary R. But if the decision is between such alternatives as short-term interpretative therapy, Rogerian therapy, Thorne's directive therapy, hypnotic retraining, and the method of tasks [10, 16, 19], we could "follow the base rates" by treating every patient with the method known to have the highest success frequency among patients "similar" to him. The criteria of similarity (class membership) will presumably be multiple, both phenotypic and genotypic, and will have been chosen because of their empirically demonstrated prognostic relevance rather than by guesswork, as is current practice. Such an idealized situation also presupposes that the selection and training of psychotherapists will have become socially realistic so that therapeutic personnel skilled in the various methods will be available in some reasonable proportion to the incidence with which each method is the treatment of choice.

How close are we to the upper limit of the predictive validity of personality tests, such as was reached remarkably early in the development of academic aptitude tests? If the now-familiar ⅔ to ¾ proportions of hits against even-split criterion dichotomies are already approaching that upper limit, we may well discover that for many decision problems the search for tests that will significantly better the base rates is a rather unrewarding enterprise. When the criterion is a more circumscribed trait or symptom ("depressed," "affiliative," "sadistic" and the like), the difficulty of improving upon the base rates is combined with the doubtfulness about how valuable it is to have such information with 75% confidence anyhow. But this involves larger issues beyond the scope of the present paper.

AVAILABILITY OF INFORMATION ON BASE RATES

The obvious difficulty we face in practical utilization of the preceding formulas arises from the fact that actual quantitative knowledge of the base rates is usually lacking. But this difficulty must not lead to a dismissal of our considerations as clinically irrelevant. In the case of many clinical decisions, chiefly those involving such phenotypic criteria as overt symptoms, formal diagnosis, subsequent hospitalization, persistence in therapy, vocational or marital adjustment, and the numerous "surface" personality traits which clinicians try to assess, *the chief reason for our ignorance of the base rates is nothing more subtle than our failure to compute them.* The file data available in most installations having a fairly stable source of clientele would yield values sufficiently accurate to permit minimum and maximum estimates which might be sufficient to decide for or against use of a proposed sign. It is our opinion that this rather mundane taxonomic task is of much greater importance than has been realized, and we hope that the present paper will impel workers to more systematic efforts along these lines.

Even in the case of more subtle, complex, and genotypic inferences, the situation is far from hopeless. Take the case of some such dynamic attribution as "strong latent dependency, which will be anxiety-arousing as therapy proceeds." If this is so difficult to discern *even during intensive therapy* that a therapist's rating on it has too little reliability for use as a criterion, it is hard to see just what is the value of guessing it from psychometrics. If a skilled therapist cannot discriminate the personality characteristic after considerable contact with the patient, it is at least debatable whether the characteristic makes any practical difference. On the other hand, if it can be reliably judged by therapists, the determination of approximate base rates again involves nothing more complex than systematic recording of these judgments and subsequent tabulation. Finally, "clinical experience" and "common sense" must be invoked when there is nothing better to be had. Surely if the q_1/q_2 ratio for a test sign claiming validity for "difficulty in accepting inner drives" shows from the formula that the base rate must not exceed .65 to justify use of the sign, we can be fairly confident in discarding it for use with *any* psychiatric population! Such a "backward" use of the formula to obtain a maximum useful value of P, in conjunction with the most tolerant common-sense estimates of P from daily experience, will often suffice to answer the question. If one is really in complete ignorance of the limits within which P lies, then obviously no rational judgment as to the probable efficiency of the sign can be made.

ESTIMATION VERSUS SIGNIFICANCE

A further implication of the foregoing thinking is that the exactness of certain small sample statistics, or the relative freedom of certain nonparametric methods from distribution assumptions, has to be stated with care lest it mislead clinicians into an unjustified confidence. When an investigator concludes that a sign, item, cutting score, or pattern has "validity" on the basis of small sample methods, he has rendered a certain very broad null hypothesis unplausible. To decide, however, whether this "validity" warrants clinicians in using the test is (as every statistician would insist) a further and more complex question. To answer this question, we require more than knowledge that $p_1 \neq p_2$. We need in addition to know, with respect to each decision for which the sign is being proposed, whether the appropriate inequality involving p_1, p_2, and P is fulfilled. More than this, since we will usually be extrapolating to a somewhat different clinical population, we need to know whether altered base rates P' and Q' will falsify these inequalities. To do this demands *estimates* of the test parameters p_1 and p_2, the setting up of confidence belts for their difference $p_1 - p_2$ rather than the mere proof of their non-identity. Finally, if the sign is a cutting score, we will want to consider shifting it so as to *maintain* optimal hit frequency with new base rates. The effect upon p_1 and p_2 of a contemplated movement of a critical score or band requires a knowledge of distribution form such as only a large sample can give.

As is true in all practical applications of statistical inference, nonmathematical considerations enter into the use of the numerical patterns that exist among P, p_1, p_2, and R. But "pragmatic" judgments initially require a separation of the several probabilities involved, some of which may be much more important than others in terms of the human values associated with them. In some settings, over-all hit rate is all that we care about. In others, a redistribution of the hits and misses even without much total improvement may concern us. In still others, the proportions p_1 and q_2 are of primary interest; and, finally, in some instances the confrontation of a certain increment in the absolute frequency (NPp_1) of one group identified will outweigh all other considerations.

Lest our conclusions seem unduly pessimistic, what constructive suggestions can we offer? We have already mentioned the following: (*a*) Searching for subpopulations with different base rates; (*b*) successive-hurdles testing; (*c*) the fact that even a very small *percentage* of improvement may be worth achieving in certain

crucial decisions; (*d*) the need for systematic collection of base-rate data so that our several equations can be applied. To these we may add two further "constructive" comments. First, test research attention should be largely concentrated upon behaviors having base rates nearer a 50-50 split, since it is for these that it is easiest to improve on a base-rate decision policy by use of a test having moderate validity. There are, after all, a large number of clinically important traits which do not occur "almost always" or "very rarely." Test research might be slanted more toward them; the current popularity of Q-sort approaches should facilitate the growth of such an emphasis, by directing attention to items having a reasonable "spread" in the clinical population. Exceptions to such a research policy will arise, in those rare domains where the pragmatic consequences of the alternative decisions justify focusing attention almost wholly on maximizing Pp_1, with relative neglect of Qp_2. Secondly, we think the injunction "quit wasting time on noncontributory psychometrics" is really constructive. When the clinical psychologist sees the near futility of predicting rare or near-universal events and traits from test validities incapable of improving upon the base rates, his clinical time is freed for more economically defensible activities, such as research which will improve the parameters p_1 and p_2; and for *treating* patients rather than uttering low-confidence prophecies or truisms about them [in this connection see 12, pp. vii, 7, 127–128]. It has not been our intention to be dogmatic about "what is worth finding out, how often." We do suggest that the clinical use of patterns, cutting scores, and signs, or research efforts devoted to the discovery of such, should always be evaluated in the light of the simple algebraic fact discovered in 1763 by Mr. Bayes.

SUMMARY

1. The practical value of a psychometric sign, pattern, or cutting score depends jointly upon its intrinsic

validity (in the usual sense of its discriminating power) and the distribution of the criterion variable (base rates) in the clinical population. Almost all contemporary research reporting neglects the base-rate factor and hence makes evaluation of test usefulness difficult or impossible.

2. In some circumstances, notably when the base rates of the criterion classification deviate greatly from a 50 per cent split, use of a test sign having slight or moderate validity will result in an *increase* of erroneous clinical decisions.

3. Even if the test's parameters are precisely known, so that ordinary cross-validation shrinkage is not a problem, application of a sign within a population having these same test parameters but a different base rate may result in a marked change in the proportion of correct decisions. For this reason validation studies should present trustworthy information respecting the criterion distribution in addition to such test parameters as false positive and false negative rates.

4. Establishment of "validity" by exact small sample statistics, since it does not yield accurate information about the test parameters (a problem of estimation rather than significance), does not permit trustworthy judgments as to test usefulness in a new population with different or unknown base rates.

5. Formulas are presented for determining limits upon relations among (a) the base rates, (b) false negative rate, and (c) false positive rate which must obtain if use of the test sign is to improve clinical decision making.

6. If, however, external constraints (e.g., available staff time) render it administratively unfeasible to decide all cases in accordance with the base rates, a test sign may be worth applying even if following the base rates *would* maximize the total correct decisions, were such a policy possible.

7. Trustworthy information as to the base rates of various patient characteristics can readily be obtained by file research, and test development should (other things being equal) be concentrated on those characteristics having base rates nearer .50 rather than close to .00 or 1.00.

8. The basic rationale is that of Bayes' Theorem concerning the calculation of so-called "inverse probability."

REFERENCES

1. AMERICAN PSYCHOLOGICAL ASSOCIATION, AMERICAN EDUCATIONAL RESEARCH ASSOCIATION, AND NATIONAL COUNCIL ON MEASUREMENTS USED IN EDUCATION, JOINT COMMITTEE. Technical recommendations for psychological tests and diagnostic techniques. *Psychol. Bull.*, 1954, **51**, 201–238.

2. ANASTASI, ANNE, & FOLEY, J. P. *Differential psychology.* (Rev. Ed.) New York: Macmillan, 1949.

3. BROSS, I. D. J. *Design for decision.* New York: Macmillan, 1953.

4. DANIELSON, J. R., & CLARK, J. H. A personality inventory for induction screening. *J. clin. Psychol.*, 1954, **10**, 137–143.

5. DORKEN, H., & KRAL, A. The psychological differentiation of organic brain lesions and their localization by means of the Rorschach test. *Amer. J. Psychiat.*, 1952, **108**, 764–770.

6. DUNCAN, O. D., OHLIN, L. E., REISS, A J., & STANTON, H. R. Formal devices for making selection decisions. *Amer. J. Sociol.*, 1953, **58**, 573–584.

7. GLUECK, S., & GLUECK, ELEANOR. *Unraveling juvenile delinquency.* Cambridge, Mass.: Harvard Univer. Press, 1950.

8. GOODMAN, L. A. The use and validity of a prediction instrument. I. A reformulation of the use of a prediction instrument. *Amer. J. Sociol.*, 1953, **58**, 503–509.

9. HANVIK, L. J. Some psychological dimensions of low back pain. Unpublished doctor's thesis, Univer. of Minnesota, 1949.

10. HERZBERG, A. *Active psychotherapy.* New York: Grune & Stratton, 1945.

11. HORST, P. (Ed.) The prediction of personal adjustment. *Soc. Sci. Res. Coun. Bull.*, 1941, No. 48, 1–156.

12. MEEHL, P. E. *Clinical versus statistical prediction.* Minneapolis: Univer. of Minnesota Press, 1954.

13. REISS, A. J. Unraveling juvenile delinquency. II. An appraisal of the research methods. *Amer. J. Sociol.,* 1951, **57,** 115–120.

14. ROSEN, A. Detection of suicidal patients: an example of some limitations in the prediction of infrequent events. *J. consult. Psychol.,* 1954, **18,** 397–403.

15. ROTTER, J. B., RAFFERTY, J. E., & LOTSOF, A. B. The validity of the Rotter Incomplete Sentences Blank: high school form. *J. consult. Psychol.,* 1954, **18,** 105–111.

16. SALTER, A. *Conditioned reflex therapy.* New York: Creative Age Press, 1950.

17. TAULBEE, E. S., & SISSON, B. D. Rorschach pattern analysis in schizophrenia: a cross-validation study. *J. clin. Psychol.,* 1954, **10,** 80–82.

18. THIESEN, J. W. A pattern analysis of structural characteristics of the Rorschach test in schizophrenia. *J. consult. Psychol.,* 1952, **16,** 365–370.

19. WOLPE, J. Objective psychotherapy of the neuroses. *S. African Med. J.,* 1952, **26,** 825–829.

5 ~

ASSESSMENT OF
INTELLECTUAL ABILITIES

The history of the measurement of intelligence provides an excellent example of the continuing interplay between theoretical and practical considerations in the refinement of assessment techniques: Empirical evaluations of rudimentary measures or behavioral consistencies lead to a crystallization of the theoretical construct, in this case of what is meant by "intelligence," which in turn guides the subsequent development of specific measures; the properties and correlates of these measures then frequently present new evidence that requires certain elaborations or revisions of the theoretical conception, and so the cycle begins anew.

Shortly before the turn of the century, in the wake of Francis Galton's pioneering studies of individual variation and covariation, James McKeen Cattell undertook to administer to large groups of college students a variety of "mental tests" of sensory discrimination and other simple processes, such as reaction time, judgment of time intervals, perception of pitch, judgment of weights, and recall of letter series.[1] Unfortunately these tests proved to be poorly related both to each other and to practical criteria of intellectual functioning, such as educational achievement. In 1904, however, Charles Spearman argued that the poor intercorrelations among such tests of sensory discrimination were primarily due to the unreliability of the separate measures. When errors of measurement were taken into account, he found that substantial common variance was indeed shared by sensory tests and, furthermore, that this common sensory facility was almost perfectly correlated with the common element in estimates of intelligence obtained from school grades and teachers' ratings. Evidence for this single general intellectual function was derived from a consistent pattern of correlated achievements in such diverse fields as classics, French, English, mathematics, pitch discrimination, and music. On the basis of these findings, Spearman formulated a two-factor theory of ability which held that performance on any mental test was due to a general ability (labeled g) brought to bear on all tests and a specific ability (labeled s) unique to each particular test. Although the general ability operates in all test performances, it is not equally influential on all tests; mental tests differ in the extent to which they correlate with g, i.e., in the relative weights with which g and the particular s determine performance. One practical corollary of this model is what Spearman called "the theorem of the indifference of the indicator," which held that for purposes of assessing the amount of general intelligence possessed by a person any test is as good as any other, as long as its correlation with g is equally high.[2]

At about the same time in France, Alfred Binet had been challenged by a practical problem in public education to develop methods for diagnosing subnormal levels of intelligence. His innovations led to the construction of a scale of general intelligence that has dominated the conceptualization and measurement of this variable ever since. Binet did not choose, as Spearman might have, to rely upon any single test that might serve as well as any other test to estimate intelligence. Instead, he utilized numerous short varied subtests of different processes in a deliberate attempt to obtain a many-sided, heterogeneous coverage of the broad arena in which intelligence might manifest itself. Nor did he choose, as Galton and Cattell might have, to use measures of sensory discrimination. Instead, he emphasized more complex mental processes such as comprehension and reasoning: "To judge well, to comprehend well, to reason well, these are the essential activities of intelligence."[3] Binet tried out his subtests on large samples of children to obtain norms for different ages. Arranging the

[1] Cattell, J. McK. Mental tests and measurements. *Mind*, 1890, **15**, 373–381; Cattell, J. McK., & Farrand, L. Physical and mental measurements of the students of Columbia University. *Psychol. Rev.*, 1896, **3**, 618–648.

[2] Spearman, C. "General intelligence," objectively determined and measured. *Amer. J. Psychol.*, 1904, **15**, 201–292; Spearman, C. The theory of two factors. *Psychol. Rev.*, 1914, **21**, 101–115; Spearman, C. *The abilities of man*. New York: Macmillan, 1927.

[3] Binet, A., & Simon, T. *The development of intelligence in children*. Baltimore: Williams & Wilkins, 1916.

subtests in order of increasing difficulty and grouping them according to the age at which most children in the normative sample passed them, he was able to gauge the intellectual level of a child in terms of "mental age," i.e., the age of children in the norm group who were able to pass the highest level of item consistently passed by that child. The difference between the child's mental age and his chronological age indicated the degree of his retardation or superiority. Binet's scale was quickly revised for use in the United States by Lewis Terman, and the resulting "Stanford Revision" provided a standard against which other suggested measures of general intelligence—verbal or nonverbal, group-administered or individual, brief or intensive—were evaluated for years to come. Terman, following an earlier suggestion by Wilhelm Stern, decided to reckon intellectual status not in terms of the difference between mental age and chronological age but in terms of their ratio, which is the widely adopted and celebrated convention known as the IQ.[4]

The repeated success in a wide variety of applications of the Binet scale and other intelligence tests that followed gives persuasive testimony to the practical utility of the concept of general intelligence. Nonetheless, soon after the initial work of Spearman and Binet, evidence began to accumulate challenging the notion that a single underlying factor of general ability could account for the interrelations among all mental tests. Groups of tests were found that intercorrelated much more highly among themselves than they did with other tests. Three verbal tests, for example, might exhibit an average intercorrelation of 0.7, as might three quantitative tests, but the correlations between the two groups of tests would tend to average much lower, say about 0.3. Performances on these tests could not, therefore, be completely accounted for by a single general ability and six specific abilities. Additional, intermediate-level factors were required to take into account common processes shared by the tests within a particular group but not shared with tests in other groups. These factors, called group factors, are not as broad as g (they do not operate in all tests) nor as narrow as s (they are not limited to a single test); rather, they operate in sets of similar tests. A methodology called multiple-factor analysis was developed, primarily by L. L. Thurstone, to discover how many group factors were necessary to account for test intercorrelations and to determine weights that would indicate how much of the variance of each test was associated with each group factor.[5]

A half-dozen or so group factors were quickly delineated, some of

[4] Terman, L. *The measurement of intelligence.* Boston: Houghton Mifflin, 1916; Terman, L., & Merrill, M. A. *Measuring intelligence.* Boston: Houghton Mifflin, 1937.

[5] Thurstone, L. L. *The vectors of the mind.* Chicago: Univer. of Chicago Press, 1935; Thurstone, L. L. *Multiple-factor analysis.* Univer. of Chicago Press, 1947. Also of importance in the development of this technique were, Kelley, T. L. *Crossroads in the mind of man.* Stanford: Stanford Univ. Press, 1928; Thomson, G. H. *Factorial analysis of human ability.* Boston: Houghton Mifflin, 1939; and Burt, C. L. *The factors of the mind.* New York: Macmillan, 1941.

which were recognized by Spearman in his later writing. Continued application of multiple-factor analysis over the years has uncovered several more factors, and the number is still increasing. Among the first to be discovered were some that Thurstone called "primary mental abilities," factors which formed the basis for his multiple-factor representation of intelligence. Since none of these factors seemed pervasive enough to call "general ability," intelligence came to be thought of as a conglomeration of several important, independently varying abilities. After considerable controversy, there emerged the possibility of a rapprochement between the general-factor and the multiple-factor theories of intelligence in terms of what were called "second-order factors." Since the vast majority of mental tests tended to correlate positively with each other, the resulting group factors also tended to correlate positively with each other. Thus, the methods of multiple-factor analysis could be applied to the intercorrelations among the group (or first-order) factors to uncover second-order factors. Although a single general factor could not account for the intercorrelations among the tests, perhaps a single general factor would be found to account for the intercorrelations among the factors. If so, Spearman's g could be considered a general second-order factor that operates via the correlated first-order factors to determine test performance. In most of the subsequent analyses of intercorrelations among first-order factors, however, more than one second-order factor was obtained. Since these second-order factors are broader than those at the first order, Thurstone suggested that one of them, perhaps the inductive factor, might correspond to Spearman's g. To be sure, it was not as broad as Spearman had claimed, but it was important and influential nevertheless.[6]

The discovery of several primary mental abilities gradually had an impact upon the methods used for measuring intelligence. Psychologists began to describe intellectual status in terms of a profile of scores on several abilities rather than by a single index such as IQ. Edward L. Thorndike was one of the first to emphasize the relative heterogeneity of specific intellectual processes; he constructed an intelligence test known as CAVD that separately assessed skill in completions, arithmetic, vocabulary, and understanding directions and discourse.[7] David Wechsler, in his intelligence scales for adults and children, attempted to assess general intelligence as the composite of several separately measured intellectual functions, some involving verbal skills and some, performance skills. For each of the distinct functions, he provided a variety of graded subtests and separate norms, so that a profile of scores as well as a verbal IQ, a performance IQ, and a general IQ could be obtained.[8]

---

[6] Thurstone, L. L. Primary mental abilities. *Psychometr. Monogrs.*, 1938, No. 1; Thurstone, L. L. Psychological implications of factor analysis. *Amer. Psychol.*, 1948, 3, 402–408.

[7] Thorndike, E. L., Bregman, E. O., Cobb, M. V., & Woodyard, E. *The measurement of intelligence.* New York: Teachers Coll., Columbia Univer., Bureau of Publications, 1926.

[8] Wechsler, D. *The measurement of adult intelligence.* Baltimore: Williams & Wilkins, 1939.

In spite of this tendency to capitalize in practice upon both the differential information of specific abilities and the convergent information of general ability, we are still left at this point with an unhappy choice at the theoretical level between a theory of general intelligence that is inadequate to account for observed data and a theory of multiple abilities that offers an unorganized collection of miscellaneous skills increasing in number every year. Indeed, the proliferation of specific abilities has proceeded to such an extent that it is difficult to conceive of measuring all of them to evaluate an individual's intellectual status. In the pursuit of a coherent theory of intellectual functioning, then, it soon became clear that some mode of organizing the separate abilities would have to be found that would both take into account the varying amounts of interrelationship they display and provide a framework to guide individual assessment. One such organization suggested by British psychologists—particularly Cyril Burt and Philip E. Vernon—is a hierarchical arrangement of factors. For example, we have seen that not one but several second-order factors were required to account for the intercorrelations among the many first-order factors. We now consider the possibility of factor-analyzing the intercorrelations among the second-order factors to obtain third-order factors and so on until we are confronted at some higher order with a single factor, which might then be interpreted as Spearman's g. Burt and Vernon both favored a hierarchical structure for the various factors that placed g at the pinnacle and two major group factors immediately below. For Burt, these two broad group factors reflect logical thinking and aesthetic appreciation, both of which are thought to require the apprehension of abstract relations. For Vernon, the two major group factors derive from his attempts to integrate the results of several factor studies, wherein he observes that once the influence of g is removed, tests tend to fall into two main clusters —the verbal-numerical-educational type and the practical-mechanical-spatial-physical type. Below these broad group factors in the hierarchy would be found several minor group factors, and lower down still the various specific factors. The hierarchy organizes these factors very much like a tree, with the major group factors representing limbs stemming from the trunk of general intelligence, the minor group factors representing branches on the limbs, and the specific factors twigs on the branches.[9]

Although the details would certainly change as additional evidence accrues, this type of hierarchical model constitutes one important theory about the nature of intelligence. Another major theory about the structure of intellect is presented by J. P. Guilford in the first article of Part 5. Guilford organizes the various primary mental abilities not into a tree but into a three-dimensional grid or box. One dimension of the grid classifies abilities into five major groups accord-

---

[9] Burt, C. The structure of the mind: a review of the results of factor analysis. *Brit. J. Educ. Psychol.*, 1949, **19**, 100–111, 176–199; Vernon, P. E. *The structure of human abilities*. New York: Wiley, 1950.

ing to the kind of process or operation performed (cognition, memory, divergent thinking, convergent thinking, and evaluation); the second dimension of the grid classifies abilities into four categories according to the kind of content involved (figural, symbolic, semantic, and behavioral); and the third dimension classifies abilities into six categories according to the kind of product entailed by the application of a certain operation to a certain type of content (units, classes, relations, systems, transformations, and implications). These three dimensions of categorization generate 120 cells, each of which theoretically represents a separate ability identified by a particular kind of operation, content, and product. Only about fifty of these hypothesized factors are now known, but the properties of the empty cells are specified, so that the model also serves as a guide for future investigations of intellectual differences. Guilford's classification system thus provides an important bonus—it offers a prescription for test construction in as yet unexplored areas of intellectual functioning. Another noteworthy feature of this model is that it highlights a relatively new distinction in cognitive functioning—one that has been systematically investigated primarily in Guilford's own laboratory— namely, the properties of fluency, flexibility, and originality that characterize what Guilford has called "divergent thinking." These properties take us beyond the confines of accuracy and correctness, the *sine qua non* of intelligence, into the realm of creativity.

In the second article in Part 5, Guilford, Kettner, and Christensen illustrate the manner in which programmatic factor-analytic research, by the systematic appraisal of plausible rival hypotheses, can gradually resolve the meaning of an ability factor, in this case of the general reasoning factor.

Next, Louis Guttman briefly summarizes the views of Spearman, Thurstone, and Guilford on the nature of intellectual functioning and points out that the kind of three-dimensional categorization that Guilford offered is a special case of what he calls a "facet design." Guttman outlines the rudiments of a "facet analysis," pointing out the possibility that standard factor analyses of tests from all the cells in Guilford's grid might not only uncover the expected specific abilities stemming from the three-way interaction of operation, content, and product, but also more general factors as well (such as facility in cognizing semantic content regardless of type of product or facility in divergent thinking regardless of both kind of content and type of product).

In Chapter 37, Lloyd G. Humphreys appraises the advantages of the hierarchical model for organizing human abilities and illustrates techniques of factoring hierarchical data using a hypothetical logical hierarchy of mechanical information tests. He points out that for certain types of psychological data, as when several methods are used to measure each of several traits, complications might arise in the hierarchical formulation, since it may no longer be possible to trace a particular lower-order "twig" factor back to the main trunk along a single path. Humphreys turns next to a consideration of facet theory, which he finds particularly useful as a way of thinking about psychological tests and as a guide for test development. He recommends the construction of homogeneous tests by exercising "control of heterogeneity"; i.e., in the measurement of a particular element of a facet, homogeneity would be achieved by adding together as many elements on other facets as possible, so that not only is the common variance associated with the element in question increased but, equally important, the variance associated with any other element is minimized.

In Chapter 38, George M. Guthrie investigates the factorial structure of intellect in a non-Western culture to see if abilities frequently identified in the West would appear in comparable form and to see if cultural and educational differences influence the nature of memory and reasoning skills. When Guthrie administered a battery of standard ability tests in English to a large sample of bilingual Philippine women, along with some parallel versions in the Philippine dialect, Tagalog, several factors emerged that are clear replications of well-known primary abilities, including verbal comprehension, rote memory, visualization, motor speed, perceptual speed, ideational fluency, and numerical factors. Separate verbal factors were obtained for proficiency in English and Tagalog vocabulary, but facility in ideational fluency appeared to cut across both languages.

In the next selection (Chapter 39), Lewis M. Terman reviews his monumental longitudinal studies of gifted children. Undertaken in 1921, these studies of 1,500 California school children having Stanford-Binet IQs of 140 or higher are continued by follow-up investigations throughout the lives of the subjects. This research program has contributed immensely to our understanding of intellectual excellence and has served to bury such prevalent myths as the notion that child prodigies are abnormal or that they typically burn themselves out before achieving adult success. Indeed, just the opposite was found. The gifted children were superior to unselected children not only in tested intelligence but also in physique, health, social adjustment moral character, and school achievement as well. A thirty-year follow-up study has indicated that on the average this general superiority has been maintained and that the subjects have achieved remarkable success both in college and in their subsequent careers. These studies impresively demonstrate the value of general intelligence tests for predicting a wide variety of fields. Terman is quick to point out, however, that such tests do not enable one to predict differentially the direction the achievement will take. He grants that interests and specific abilities were very likely instrumental in the choice of a career and that measures of these characteristics might improve predictions and contribute to vocational guidance, but he insists "that to achieve greatly in almost any field, the special talents have to be backed up by a lot of Spearman's g."

The notion of giftedness has been expanded in recent years to embrace other varieties of excellence than those assessed by standard tests of general intelligence. In particular, a distinction has been championed by Guilford and others between the concept of intelligence and the concept of creativity.[10] Intelligence refers to the correctness and adaptiveness of response, and creativity refers to the fluency, flexibility, and originality of response. The personal and educational import of this distinction has recently been investigated by Jacob W. Getzels and Philip W. Jackson in a controversial study of highly intelligent and highly creative adolescents.[11] In Chapter 40, they review briefly the procedures and major findings of that study and present evidence suggesting that the two groups of intelligent and creative students also differ in their family environments. This raises intriguing possibilities about the origin and development of differences in mode of cognition.

In the final chapter of Part 5, Donald W. MacKinnon attempts to discover personal qualities that are predisposing toward creativity by comparing the performance of groups of creative and noncreative architects on a wide variety of assessment tasks. Although he found no differences between the two in general intelligence, the groups did differ significantly on many dimensions of personality, interests, and values. This investigation applies assessment techniques characteristic of the study of personality to the task of understanding the nature of one kind of giftedness or creative excellence. It is one example of several recent attempts to study cognitive consistencies within the framework of personality organization,[12] and as such it not only helps to increase our perspective about cognitive functioning but it provides a fitting introduction to the concerns of the next section on the "Assessment of Personality."

[10] Guilford, J. P. Creativity. *Amer. Psychol.*, 1950, **5**, 444–454. See also, Jackson, P. W., & Messick, S. The person, the product, and the response: conceptual problems in the assessment of creativity. *J. Pers.*, 1965, **33**, 309–329.

[11] Getzels, J. W., & Jackson, P. W. *Creativity and intelligence: explorations with gifted students.* New York: Wiley, 1962. See also, Wallach, M. A. & Kogan, N. *Modes of thinking in young children: a study of the creativity-intelligence distinction.* New York: Holt, Rinehart & Winston, 1965.

[12] Such as, Witkin, H. A., Lewis, H. B., Hertzman, M., Machover, K., Meissner, P. B. & Wapner S. *Personality through perception.* New York: Harper & Row, 1954; Witkin, H. A., Dyk, R. B., Faterson, H. F., Goodenough, D. R., & Karp, S. A. *Psychological differentiation,* New York: Wiley, 1962; Gardner, R. W., Holzman, P. S., Klein, G. S., Linton, H. B., & Spence, D. Cognitive control: a study of individual consistencies in cognitive behavior., *Psychol. Issues*, 1959, **1**, No. 4; and Gardner, R. W., Jackson, D. N., & Messick, S., Personality organization in cognitive controls and intellectual abilities. *Psychol. Issues*, 1960, **2**, No. 8.

Chapter 34

Three Faces of Intellect

J. P. GUILFORD

My subject is in the area of human intelligence, in connection with which the names of Terman and Stanford have become known the world over. The Stanford Revision of the Binet intelligence scale has been the standard against which all other instruments for the measurement of intelligence have been compared. The term IQ or intelligence quotient has become a household word in this country. This is illustrated by two brief stories.

A few years ago, one of my neighbors came home from a PTA meeting, remarking: "That Mrs. So-And-So, thinks she knows so much. She kept talking about the 'intelligence *quota*' of the children; 'intelligence *quota*'; imagine. Why, everybody knows that IQ stands for 'intelligence quiz.'"

This article is reprinted from the *American Psychologist*, 1959, with the permission of the author and the American Psychological Association.

The article was originally the Walter V. Bingham Memorial Lecture given at Stanford University on April 13, 1959.

The other story comes from a little comic strip in a Los Angeles morning newspaper, called "Junior Grade." In the first picture a little boy meets a little girl, both apparently about the first-grade level. The little girl remarks, "I have a high IQ." The little boy, puzzled, said, "You have a what?" The little girl repeated, "I have a high IQ," then went on her way. The little boy, looking thoughtful, said, "And she looks like such a nice little girl, too."

It is my purpose to speak about the analysis of this thing called human intelligence into its components. I do not believe that either Binet or Terman, if they were still with us, would object to the idea of a searching and detailed study of intelligence, aimed toward a better understanding of its nature. Preceding the development of his intelligence scale, Binet had done much research on different kinds of thinking activities and apparently recognized that intelligence has a number of aspects. It is to the lasting credit of both Binet and Terman that they introduced such a great variety of tasks into their intelligence scales.

Two related events of very recent history make it imperative that we learn all we can regarding the nature of intelligence. I am referring to the advent of the artificial satellites and planets and to the crisis in education that has arisen in part as a consequence. The preservation of our way of life and our future security depend upon our most important national resources: our intellectual abilities and, more particularly, our creative abilities. It is time, then, that we learn all we can about those resources.

Our knowledge of the components of human intelligence has come about mostly within the last 25 years. The major sources of this information in this country have been L. L. Thurstone and his associates, the wartime research of psychologists in the United States Air Forces, and more recently the Aptitudes Project[1] at the University of Southern California, now in its tenth year of research on cognitive and thinking abilities. The results from the Aptitudes Project that have gained perhaps the most attention have pertained to creative-thinking abilities. These are mostly novel findings. But to me, the most significant outcome has been the development of a unified theory of human intellect, which organizes the known, unique or primary intellectual abilities into a single system called the "structure of intellect." It is to this system that I shall devote the major part of my remarks, with very brief mentions of some of the implications for the psychology of thinking and problem solving, for vocational testing, and for education.

The discovery of the components of intelligence has been by means of the experimental application of the method of factor analysis. It is not necessary for you to know anything about the theory or method of factor analysis in order to follow the discussion of the components. I should like to say, however, that factor analysis has no

connection with or resemblance to psychoanalysis. A positive statement would be more helpful, so I will say that each intellectual component or factor is a unique ability that is needed to do well in a certain class of tasks or tests. As a general principle we find that certain individuals do well in the tests of a certain class, but they may do poorly in the tests of another class. We conclude that a factor has certain properties from the features that the tests of a class have in common. I shall give you very soon a number of examples of tests, each representing a factor.

THE STRUCTURE OF INTELLECT

Although each factor is sufficiently distinct to be detected by factor analysis, in very recent years its has become apparent that the factors themselves can be classified because they resemble one another in certain ways. One basis of classification is according to the basic kind of process or operation performed. This kind of classification gives us five major groups of intellectual abilities: factors of cognition, memory, convergent thinking, divergent thinking, and evaluation.

Cognition means discovery or rediscovery or recognition. Memory means retention of what is cognized. Two kinds of productive-thinking operations generate new information from known information and remembered information. In divergent-thinking operations we think in different directions, sometimes searching, sometimes seeking variety. In convergent thinking the information leads to one right answer or to a recognized best or conventional answer. In evaluation we reach decisions as to goodness, correctness, suitability, or adequacy of what we know, what we remember, and what we produce in productive thinking.

A second way of classifying the intellectual factors is according to the kind of material or content involved. The factors known thus far involve three kinds of material or content: the content may be figural, symbolic, or semantic. Figural content is

[1] Under Contract N6onr-23810 with the Office of Naval Research (Personnel and Training Branch).

concrete material such as is perceived through the senses. It does not represent anything except itself. Visual material has properties such as size, form, color, location, or texture. Things we hear or feel provide other examples of figural material. Symbolic content is composed of letters, digits, and other conventional signs, usually organized in general systems, such as the alphabet or the number system. Semantic content is in the form of verbal meanings or ideas, for which no examples are necessary.

When a certain operation is applied to a certain kind of content, as many as six general kinds of products may be involved. There is enough evidence available to suggest that, regardless of the combinations of operations and content, the same six kinds of products may be found associated. The six kinds of products are: units, classes, relations, systems, transformations, and implications. So far as we have determined from factor analysis, these are the only fundamental kinds of products that we can know. As such, they may serve as basic classes into which one might fit all kinds of information psychologically.

The three kinds of classifications of the factors of intellect can be represented by means of a single solid model, shown in Figure 34–1. In this model, which we call the "structure of intellect," each dimension represents one of the modes of variation of the factors.[2] Along one dimension are found the various kinds of operations, along a second one are the various kinds of products, and along the third are various kinds of content. Along the dimension of content a fourth category has been added, its kind of content being designated as "behavioral." This category has been added on a purely theoretical basis to represent the general area sometimes called "social intelligence." More will be said about this section of the model later.

In order to provide a better basis for

understanding the model and a better basis for accepting it as a picture of human intellect, I shall do some exploring of it with you systematically, giving some examples of tests. Each cell in the model calls for a certain kind of ability that can be described in terms of operation, content, and product, for each cell is at the intersection of a unique combination of kinds of operation, content, and product. A test for that ability would have the same three properties. In our exploration of the model, we shall take one vertical layer at a time, beginning with the front face. The first layer provides us with a matrix of 18 cells (if we ignore the behavioral column for which there are as yet no known factors) each of which should contain a cognitive ability.

THE COGNITIVE ABILITIES

We know at present the unique abilities that fit logically into 15 of the 18 cells for cognitive abilities. Each row presents a triad of similar abilities, having a single kind of product in common. The factors of the first row are concerned with the knowing of units. A good test of the ability to cognize figural units is the Street Gestalt Completion Test. In this test, the recognition of familiar pictured objects in silhouette form is made difficult for testing purposes by blocking out parts of those objects. There is another factor that is known to involve the perception of auditory figures—in the form of melodies, rhythms, and speech sounds—and still another factor involving kinesthetic forms. The presence of three factors in one cell (they are conceivably distinct abilities, although this has not been tested) suggests that more generally, in the figural column, at least, we should expect to find more than one ability. A fourth dimension pertaining to variations in sense modality may thus apply in connection with figural content. The model could be extended in this manner if the facts call for such an extension.

The ability to cognize symbolic units is measured by tests like the following:

[2] For an earlier presentation of the concept, see Guilford [2].

OPERATIONS

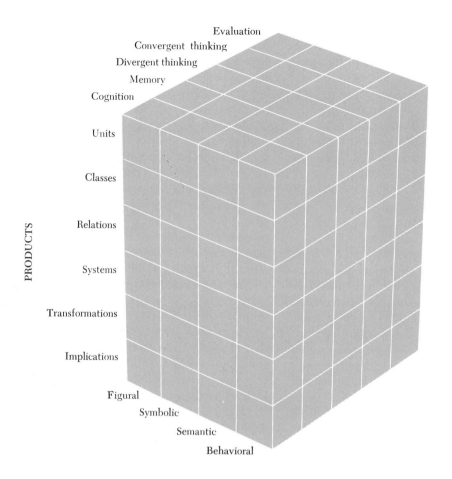

CONTENTS

Figure 34–1   *A cubical model representing the structure of intellect.*

Put vowels in the following blanks to make real words:

P__W__R

M__RV__L

C__RT__N

Rearrange the letters to make real words:

R A C I H

T V O E S

K L C C O

The first of these two tests is called Disemvoweled Words, and the second Scrambled Words.

The ability to cognize semantic units is the well-known factor of verbal compre-

hension, which is best measured by means of a vocabulary test, with items such as:

GRAVITY   means   _____

CIRCUS   means   _____

VIRTUE   means   _____

From the comparison of these two factors it is obvious that recognizing familiar words as letter structures and knowing what words mean depend upon quite different abilities.

For testing the abilities to know classes of units, we may present the following kinds of items, one with symbolic content and one with semantic content:

Which letter group does not belong?

XECM PVAA QXIN VTRO

Which object does not belong?

clam   tree   oven   rose

A figural test is constructed in a completely parallel form, presenting in each item four figures, three of which have a property in common and the fourth lacking that property.

The three abilities to see relationships are also readily measured by a common kind of test, differing only in terms of content. The well-known analogies test is applicable, two items in symbolic and semantic form being:

JIRE : KIRE : : FORA :

poetry : prose : : dance :

KORE KORA LIRE GORA GIRE

music walk sing talk jump

Such tests usually involve more than the ability to cognize relations, but we are not concerned with this problem at this point.

The three factors for cognizing systems do not at present appear in tests so closely resembling one another as in the case of the examples just given. There is nevertheless an underlying common core of logical similarity. Ordinary space tests, such as Thurstone's Flags, Figures, and Cards or Part V (Spatial Orientation) of the Guilford-Zimmerman Aptitude Survey (GZAS), serve in the figural column. The system involved is an order or arrangement of objects in space. A system that uses symbolic elements is illustrated by the Letter Triangle Test, a sample item of which is:

```
         d   —
       b   e   —
     a   c   f   ?
```

What letter belongs at the place of the question mark?

The ability to understand a semantic system has been known for some time as the factor called general reasoning. One of its most faithful indicators is a test composed of arithmetic-reasoning items. That the phase of understanding only is important for measuring this ability is shown by the fact that such a test works even if the examinee is not asked to give a complete solution; he need only show that he structures the problem properly. For example, an item from the test Necessary Arithmetical Operations simply asks what operations are needed to solve the problem:

A city lot 48 feet wide and 149 feet deep costs $79,432. What is the cost per square foot?	A. add and multiply B. multiply and divide C. subtract and divide D. add and subtract E. divide and add

Placing the factor of general reasoning in this cell of the structure of intellect gives us some new conceptions of its nature. It should be a broad ability to grasp all kinds of systems that are conceived in terms of verbal concepts, not restricted to the understanding of problems of an arithmetical type.

Transformations are changes of various kinds, including modifications in arrangement, organization, or meaning. In the figural column for the transformations row, we find the factor known as visualization. Common measuring instruments for this factor are the surface-development tests, and an example of a different kind is Part VI (Spatial Visualization) of the GZAS. A test of the ability to make transformations of meaning, for the factor in the semantic column, is called Similarities. The examinee is asked to state several ways in which two objects, such as an apple and an orange, are alike. Only by shifting the meanings of both is the examinee able to give many responses to such an item.

In the set of abilities having to do with the cognition of implications, we find that the individual goes beyond the information given, but not to the extent of what might be called drawing conclusions. We may say that he extrapolates. From the given information he expects or foresees certain consequences, for example. The two factors found in this row of the cognition matrix were first called "foresight" factors. Foresight in connection with figural material can be tested by means of paper-and-pencil mazes. Foresight in connection with ideas, those pertaining to events, for example, is indicated by a test such as Pertinent Questions:

> In planning to open a new hamburger stand in a certain community, what four questions should be considered in deciding upon its location?

The more questions the examinee asks in response to a list of such problems, the more he evidently foresees contingencies.

THE MEMORY ABILITIES

The area of memory abilities has been explored less than some of the other areas of operation, and only seven of the potential cells of the memory matrix have known factors in them. These cells are restricted to three rows: for units, relations, and systems. The first cell in the memory matrix is now occupied by two factors, parallel to two in the corresponding cognition matrix: visual memory and auditory memory. Memory for series of letters or numbers, as in memory span tests, conforms to the conception of memory for symbolic units. Memory for the ideas in a paragraph conforms to the conception of memory for semantic units.

The formation of associations between units, such as visual forms, syllables, and meaningful words, as in the method of paired associates, would seem to represent three abilities to remember relationships involving three kinds of content. We know of two such abilities, for the symbolic and semantic columns. The memory for known systems is represented by two abilities very recently discovered [1]. Remembering the arrangement of objects in space is the nature of an ability in the figural column, and remembering a sequence of events is the nature of a corresponding ability in the semantic column. The differentiation be-

tween these two abilities implies that a person may be able to say where he saw an object on a page, but he might not be able to say on which of several pages he saw it after leafing through several pages that included the right one. Considering the blank rows in the memory matrix, we should expect to find abilities also to remember classes, transformations, and implications, as well as units, relations, and systems.

THE DIVERGENT-THINKING ABILITIES

The unique feature of divergent production is that a *variety* of responses is produced. The product is not completely determined by the given information. This is not to say that divergent thinking does not come into play in the total process of reaching a unique conclusion, for it comes into play wherever there is trial-and-error thinking.

The well-known ability of word fluency is tested by asking the examinee to list words satisfying a specified letter requirement, such as words beginning with the letter "s" or words ending in "-tion." This ability is now regarded as a facility in divergent production of symbolic units. The parallel semantic ability has been known as ideational fluency. A typical test item calls for listing objects that are round and edible. Winston Churchill must have possessed this ability to a high degree. Clement Attlee is reported to have said about him recently that, no matter what problem came up, Churchill always seemed to have about ten ideas. The trouble was, Attlee continued, he did not know which was the good one. The last comment implies some weakness in one or more of the evaluative abilities.

The divergent production of class ideas is believed to be the unique feature of a factor called "spontaneous flexibility." A typical test instructs the examinee to list all the uses he can think of for a common brick, and he is given eight minutes. If his responses are: build a house, build a barn, build a garage, build a school, build a church, build a chimney, build a walk, and build a barbecue, he would earn a fairly high score for ideational fluency but a very low score for spontaneous flexibility, because all these uses fall into the same class. If another person said: make a door stop, make a paper weight, throw it at a dog, make a bookcase, drown a cat, drive a nail, make a red powder, and use for baseball bases, he would also receive a high score for flexibility. He has gone frequently from one class to another.

A current study of unknown but predicted divergent-production abilities includes testing whether there are also figural and symbolic abilities to produce multiple classes. An experimental figural test presents a number of figures that can be classified in groups of three in various ways, each figure being usable in more than one class. An experimental symbolic test presents a few numbers that are also to be classified in multiple ways.

A unique ability involving relations is called "associational fluency." It calls for the production of a variety of things related in a specified way to a given thing. For example, the examinee is asked to list words meaning about the same as "good" or to list words meaning about the opposite of "hard." In these instances the response produced is to complete a relationship, and semantic content is involved. Some of our present experimental tests call for the production of varieties of relations, as such, and involve figural and symbolic content also. For example, given four small digits, in how many ways can they be related in order to produce a sum of eight?

One factor pertaining to the production of systems is known as expressional fluency. The rapid formation of phrases or sentences is the essence of certain tests of this factor. For example, given the initial letters:

W_____ c_____ e_____ n_____

with different sentences to be produced, the examinee might write "We can eat nuts" or "Whence came Eve Newton?" In interpreting the factor, we regard the sentence as a symbolic system. By analogy, a figural system would be some kind of organization of lines and other elements, and a semantic system would be in the form of a verbally stated problem or perhaps something as complex as a theory.

In the row of the divergent-production matrix devoted to transformations, we find some very interesting factors. The one called "adaptive flexibility" is now recognized as belonging in the figural column. A faithful test of it has been Match Problems. This is based upon the common game that uses squares, the sides of which are formed by match sticks. The examinee is told to take away a given number of matches to leave a stated number of squares with nothing left over. Nothing is said about the sizes of the squares to be left. If the examinee imposes upon himself the restriction that the squares that he leaves must be of the same size, he will fail in his attempts to do items like that in Figure 34–2. Other odd kinds of solutions are introduced in other items, such as overlapping squares and squares within squares, and so on. In another variation of Match Problems the examinee is told to produce two or more solutions for each problem.

A factor that has been called "originality" is now recognized as adaptive flexibility with semantic material, where there must be a shifting of meanings. The examinee must produce the shifts or changes in meaning and so come up with novel, unusual, clever, or farfetched ideas. The Plot Titles Test presents a short story, the examinee being told to list as many appropriate titles as he can to head the story. One story is about a missionary who has been captured by cannibals in Africa. He is in the pot and about to be boiled when a princess of the tribe obtains a promise for his release if he will become her mate. He refuses and is boiled to death.

In scoring the test, we separate the re-

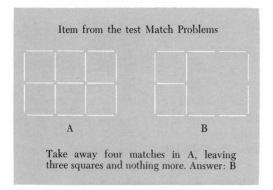

Item from the test Match Problems

A   B

Take away four matches in A, leaving
three squares and nothing more. Answer: B

FIGURE 34–2   *A sample item from the test
Match Problems. The problem in this item
is to take away four matches and leave
three squares. The solution is given.*

sponses into two categories, clever and non-clever. Examples of nonclever responses are: African Death, Defeat of a Princess, Eaten by Savages, The Princess, The African Missionary, In Darkest Africa, and Boiled by Savages. These titles are appropriate but commonplace. The number of such responses serves as a score for ideational fluency. Examples of clever responses are: Pot's Plot, Potluck Dinner, Stewed Parson, Goil or Boil, A Mate Worse Than Death, He Left a Dish for a Pot, Chaste in Haste, and A Hot Price for Freedom. The number of clever responses given by an examinee is his score for originality, or the divergent production of semantic transformations.

Another test of originality presents a very novel task so that any acceptable response is unusual for the individual. In the Symbol Production Test the examinee is to produce a simple symbol to stand for a noun or a verb in each short sentence, in other words to invent something like pictographic symbols. Still another test of originality asks for writing the "punch lines" for cartoons, a task that almost automatically challenges the examinee to be clever. Thus, quite a variety of tests offer approaches to the measurement of originality, including one or two others that I have not mentioned.

Abilities to produce a variety of implications are assessed by tests calling for elab-

oration of given information. A figural test of this type provides the examinee with a line or two, to which he is to add other lines to produce an object. The more lines he adds, the greater his score. A semantic test gives the examinee the outlines of a plan to which he is to respond by stating all the details he can think of to make the plan work. A new test we are trying out in the symbolic area presents two simple equations such as $B - C = D$ and $z = A + D$. The examinee is to make as many other equations as he can from this information.

THE CONVERGENT-PRODUCTION ABILITIES

Of the 18 convergent-production abilities expected in the three content columns, 12 are now recognized. In the first row, pertaining to units, we have an ability to name figural properties (forms or colors) and an ability to name abstractions (classes, relations, and so on). It may be that the ability in common to the speed of naming forms and the speed of naming colors is not appropriately placed in the convergent-thinking matrix. One might expect that the thing to be produced in a test of the convergent production of figural units would be in the form of figures rather than words. A better test of such an ability might somehow specify the need for one particular object, the examinee to furnish the object.

A test for the convergent production of classes (Word Grouping) presents a list of 12 words that are to be classified in four, and only four, meaningful groups, no word to appear in more than one group. A parallel test (Figure Concepts Test) presents 20 pictured real objects that are to be grouped in meaningful classes of two or more each.

Convergent production having to do with relationships is represented by three known factors, all involving the "eduction of correlates," as Spearman called it. The given information includes one unit and a stated relation, the examinee to supply the other unit. Analogies tests that call for completion rather than a choice between alternative answers emphasize this kind of ability. With symbolic content such an item might read:

pots   stop   bard   drab   rats ___?___

A semantic item that measures eduction of correlates is:

The absence of sound is _____.

Incidentally, the latter item is from a vocabulary-completion test, and its relation to the factor of ability to produce correlates indicates how, by change of form, a vocabulary test may indicate an ability other than that for which vocabulary tests are usually intended, namely, the factor of verbal comprehension.

Only one factor for convergent production of systems is known, and it is in the semantic column. It is measured by a class of tests that may be called ordering tests. The examinee may be presented with a number of events that ordinarily have a best or most logical order, the events being presented in scrambled order. The presentation may be pictorial, as in the Picture Arrangement Test, or verbal. The pictures may be taken from a cartoon strip. The verbally presented events may be in the form of the various steps needed to plant a new lawn. There are undoubtedly other kinds of systems than temporal order that could be utilized for testing abilities in this row of the convergent-production matrix.

In the way of producing transformations of a unique variety, we have three recognized factors, known as redefinition abilities. In each case, redefinition involves the changing of functions or uses of parts of one unit and giving them new functions or uses in some new unit. For testing the ability of figural redefinition, a task based upon the Gottschaldt figures is suitable. Figure 34–3 shows the kind of item for such a test. In recognizing the simpler figure within the structure of a more complex figure, certain lines must take on new roles.

In terms of symbolic material, the following sample items will illustrate how groups of letters in given words must be readapted to use in other words. In the test Camou-

flaged Words, each sentence contains the name of a sport or game:

I did not know that he was ailing.
To beat the Hun, tin goes a long way.

For the factor of semantic redefinition, the Gestalt Transformation Test may be used. A sample item reads:

From which object could you most likely make a needle?
  A. a cabbage
  B. a splice
  C. a steak
  D. a paper box
  E. a fish

The convergent production of implications means the drawing of fully determined conclusions from given information. The well-known factor of numerical facility belongs in the symbolic column. For the parallel ability in the figural column, we have a test known as Form Reasoning, in which rigorously defined operations with figures are used. For the parallel ability in the semantic column, the factor sometimes

Figure 34–3 *Sample items from a test Hidden Figures, based upon the Gottschaldt figures. Which of the simpler figures is concealed within each of the two more complex figures?*

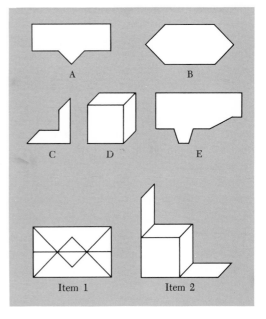

Item 1   Item 2

called "deduction" probably qualifies. Items of the following type are sometimes used.

> Charles is younger than Robert
> Charles is older than Frank
> Who is older: Robert or Frank?

EVALUATIVE ABILITIES

The evaluative area has had the least investigation of all the operational categories. In fact, only one systematic analytical study has been devoted to this area. Only eight evaluative abilities are recognized as fitting into the evaluation matrix. But at least five rows have one or more factors each, and also three of the usual columns or content categories. In each case, evaluation involves reaching decisions as to the accuracy, goodness, suitability, or workability of information. In each row, for the particular kind of product of that row, some kind of criterion or standard of judgment is involved.

In the first row, for the evaluation of units, the important decision to be made pertains to the identity of a unit. Is this unit identical with that one? In the figural column we find the factor long known as "perceptual speed." Tests of this factor invariably call for decisions of identity, for example, Part IV (Perceptual Speed) of the GZAS or Thurstone's Identical Forms. I think it has been generally wrongly thought that the ability involved is that of cognition of visual forms. But we have seen that another factor is a more suitable candidate for this definition and for being in the very first cell of the cognitive matrix. It is parallel to this evaluative ability but does not require the judgment of identity as one of its properties.

In the symbolic column is an ability to judge identity of symbolic units, in the form of series of letters or numbers or of names of individuals.

Are members of the following pairs identical or not?

825170493_____825176493
dkeltvmpa_____dkeltvmpa
C. S. Meyerson_____C. E. Meyerson

Such items are common in tests of clerical aptitude.

There should be a parallel ability to decide whether two ideas are identical or different. Is the idea expressed in this sentence the same as the idea expressed in that one? Do these two proverbs express essentially the same idea? Such tests exist and will be used to test the hypothesis that such an ability can be demonstrated.

No evaluative abilities pertaining to classes have as yet been recognized. The abilities having to do with evaluation where relations are concerned must meet the criterion of logical consistency. Syllogistic-type tests involving letter symbols indicate a different ability than the same type of test involving verbal statements. In the figural column we might expect that tests incorporating geometric reasoning or proof would indicate a parallel ability to sense the soundness of conclusions regarding figural relationships.

The evaluation of systems seems to be concerned with the internal consistency of those systems, so far as we can tell from the knowledge of one such factor. The factor has been called "experiential evaluation," and its representative test presents items like that in Figure 34–4 asking "What is wrong with this picture?" The things wrong are often internal inconsistencies.

A semantic ability for evaluating transformations is thought to be that known for some time as "judgment." In typical judgment tests, the examinee is asked to tell which of five solutions to a practical problem is most adequate or wise. The solutions frequently involve improvisations, in other words, adaptations of familiar objects to unusual uses. In this way the items present redefinitions to be evaluated.

A factor known first as "sensitivity to problems" has become recognized as an evaluative ability having to do with implications. One test of the factor, the Apparatus Test, asks for two needed improvements with respect to each of several common devices, such as the telephone or the toaster. The Social Institutions Test, a measure of the same factor, asks what things are wrong with each of several institutions, such as tipping or national elections. We may say that defects or deficiencies are implications of an evaluative kind. Another interpretation would be that seeing defects and deficiencies are evaluations of implications to the effect that the various aspects of something are all right.[3]

SOME IMPLICATIONS OF THE STRUCTURE OF INTELLECT

FOR PSYCHOLOGICAL THEORY

Although factor analysis as generally employed is best designed to investigate ways in which individuals differ from one another, in other words, to discover traits, the results also tell us much about how individuals are alike. Consequently, information regarding the factors and their interrelationships gives us understanding of functioning individuals. The five kinds of intellectual abilities in terms of operations may be said to represent five ways of functioning. The kinds of intellectual abilities

[3] For further details concerning the intellectual factors, illustrative tests, and the place of the factors in the structure of intellect, see Guilford [3].

distinguished according to varieties of products suggest a classification of basic forms of information or knowledge. The kind of organism suggested by this way of looking at intellect is that of an agency for dealing with information of various kinds in various ways. The concepts provided by the distinctions among the intellectual abilities and by their classifications may be very useful in our future investigations of learning, memory, problem solving, invention, and decision making, by whatever method we choose to approach those problems.

FOR VOCATIONAL TESTING

With about 50 intellectual factors already known, we may say that there are at least 50 ways of being intelligent. It has been facetiously suggested that there seem to be a great many more ways of being stupid, unfortunately. The structure of intellect is a theoretical model that predicts as many as 120 distinct abilities, if every cell of the model contains a factor. Already we know that two cells contain two or more factors each, and there probably are actually other cells of this type. Since the model was first conceived, 12 factors predicted by it have found places in it. There is consequently hope of filling many of the other vacancies, and we may eventually end up with more than 120 abilities.

The major implication for the assessment of intelligence is that to know an individ-

Figure 34–4 *A sample item from the test Unusual Details. What two things are wrong with this picture?*

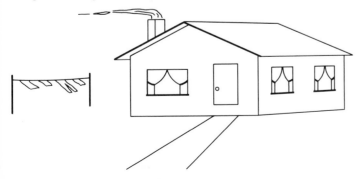

ual's intellectual resources thoroughly we shall need a surprisingly large number of scores. It is expected that many of the factors are intercorrelated, so there is some possibility that by appropriate sampling we shall be able to cover the important abilities with a more limited number of tests. At any rate, a multiple-score approach to the assessment of intelligence is definitely indicated in connection with future vocational operations.

Considering the kinds of abilities classified as to content, we may speak roughly of four kinds of intelligence. The abilities involving the use of figural information may be regarded as "concrete" intelligence. The people who depend most upon these abilities deal with concrete things and their properties. Among these people are mechanics, operators of machines, engineers (in some aspects of their work), artists, and musicians.

In the abilities pertaining to symbolic and semantic content, we have two kinds of "abstract" intelligence. Symbolic abilities should be important in learning to recognize words, to spell, and to operate with numbers. Language and mathematics should depend very much upon them, except that in mathematics some aspects, such as geometry, have strong figural involvement. Semantic intelligence is important for understanding things in terms of verbal concepts and hence is important in all courses where the learning of facts and ideas is essential.

In the hypothesized behavioral column of the structure of intellect, which may be roughly described as "social" intelligence, we have some of the most interesting possibilities. Understanding the behavior of others and of ourselves is largely nonverbal in character. The theory suggests as many as 30 abilities in this area, some having to do with understanding, some with productive thinking about behavior, and some with the evaluation of behavior. The theory also suggests that information regarding behavior is also in the form of the six kinds of products that apply elsewhere in the structure of intellect, including units, relations,

systems, and so on. The abilities in the area of social intelligence, whatever they prove to be, will possess considerable importance in connection with all those individuals who deal most with other people: teachers, law officials, social workers, therapists, politicians, statesmen, and leaders of other kinds.

FOR EDUCATION

The implications for education are numerous, and I have time just to mention a very few. The most fundamental implication is that we might well undergo transformations with respect to our conception of the learner and of the process of learning. Under the prevailing conception, the learner is a kind of stimulus-response device, much on the order of a vending machine. You put in a coin, and something comes out. The machine learns what reaction to put out when a certain coin is put in. If, instead, we think of the learner as an agent for dealing with information, where information is defined very broadly, we have something more analogous to an electronic computor. We feed a computor information; it stores that information; it uses that information for generating new information, either by way of divergent or convergent thinking; and it evaluates its own results. Advantages that a human learner has over a computor include the step of seeking and discovering new information from sources outside itself and the step of programming itself. Perhaps even these steps will be added to computors, if this has not already been done in some cases.

At any rate, this conception of the learner leads us to the idea that learning is discovery of information, not merely the formation of associations, particularly associations in the form of stimulus-response connections. I am aware of the fact that my proposal is rank heresy. But if we are to make significant progress in our understanding of human learning and particularly our understanding of the so-called higher mental processes of thinking, problem solving, and creative thinking, some drastic modifications are due in our theory.

The idea that education is a matter of training the mind or of training the intellect has been rather unpopular, wherever the prevailing psychological doctrines have been followed. In theory, at least, the emphasis has been upon the learning of rather specific habits or skills. If we take our cue from factor theory, however, we recognize that most learning probably has both specific and general aspects or components. The general aspects may be along the lines of the factors of intellect. This is not to say that the individual's status in each factor is entirely determined by learning. We do not know to what extent each factor is determined by heredity and to what extent by learning. The best position for educators to take is that possibly every intellectual factor can be developed in individuals at least to some extent by learning.

If education has the general objective of developing the intellects of students, it can be suggested that each intellectual factor provides a particular goal at which to aim. Defined by a certain combination of content, operation, and product, each goal ability then calls for certain kinds of practice in order to achieve improvement in it. This implies choice of curriculum and the choice or invention of teaching methods that will most likely accomplish the desired results.

Considering the very great variety of abilities revealed by the factorial exploration of intellect, we are in a better position to ask whether any general intellectual skills are now being neglected in education and whether appropriate balances are being observed. It is often observed these days that we have fallen down in the way of producing resourceful, creative graduates. How true this is, in comparison with other times, I do not know. Perhaps the deficit is noticed because the demands for inventiveness are so much greater at this time. At any rate, realization that the more conspicuously creative abilities appear to be concentrated in the divergent-thinking category, and also to some extent in the transformation category, we now ask whether we have been giving these skills appropriate exercise. It is probable that we need a better balance of training in the divergent-thinking area as compared with training in convergent thinking and in critical thinking or evaluation.

The structure of intellect as I have presented it to you may or may not stand the test of time. Even if the general form persists, there are likely to be some modifications. Possibly some different kind of model will be invented. Be that as it may, the fact of a multiplicity of intellectual abilities seems well established.

There are many individuals who long for the good old days of simplicity, when we got along with one unanalyzed intelligence. Simplicity certainly has its appeal. But human nature is exceedingly complex, and we may as well face that fact. The rapidly moving events of the world in which we live have forced upon us the need for knowing human intelligence thoroughly. Humanity's peaceful pursuit of happiness depends upon our control of nature and of our own behavior; and this, in turn, depends upon understanding ourselves, including our intellectual resources.

REFERENCES

1. Christal, R. E. Factor analytic study of visual memory. *Psychol. Monogr.*, 1958, **72**, No. 13 (Whole No. 466).
2. Guilford, J. P. The structure of intellect. *Psychol. Bull.*, 1956, **53**, 267–293.
3. Guilford, J. P. *Personality*. New York: McGraw-Hill, 1959.

Chapter 35

The Nature of the General Reasoning Factor

J. P. GUILFORD / NORMAN W. KETTNER /
PAUL R. CHRISTENSEN

In the report on primary mental abilities found in his first large factor analysis, Thurstone listed a factor whose unique property he thought to be an ability to reason under restrictive conditions [11]. Its largest loading was in a test of arithmetic reasoning. The same factor was not subsequently identified as such in his later analyses.

In the AAF Aviation Psychology Program research during World War II, a factor that was found repeatedly as a consistent feature of arithmetic-reasoning tests was called *general reasoning* [7]. Because of the unusual variety of tests found related to the factor, no clear definition of it was achieved. It was concluded that the ability is a kind of "general-purpose ability" or "trouble-shooting ability," which seems to come into play in a difficult test or one that contains some very difficult items.

A hypothesis concerning this factor that

This article is reprinted from *Psychological Review*, 1956, with the permission of the authors and the American Psychological Association.

would be appealing to some is that it is synonymous with general intelligence. Finding it in a large variety of tests would be one support for this idea. The fact that an arithmetic-reasoning test is a popular component of many intelligence tests would be another. Against the hypothesis, however, is a very stubborn fact. Analysis shows that many types of intelligence tests are not related to the factor; for some types, correlations are near zero.

No one has seriously maintained that the factor is the only ability to reason, for a number of reasoning factors have been found. Our own results show that there are as many as five that can be called reasoning factors.

At the beginning of the project studies of aptitudes at the University of Southern California, we favored the hypothesis that *general reasoning* has something significant to do with problem solving. Although not all problems are cast in arithmetical form, and there are indeed a great variety of problems, we tended to follow traditional thinking to the effect that underlying the solving of problems in general there is a common psychological core—that we can speak of problem solving in a generic sense. We have to admit that we do not know much about the nature of this phenomenon, but *general reasoning* might be one of the common elements.

Our first analysis of reasoning abilities began with five alternative hypotheses regarding the nature of *general reasoning* [2]. The factor might be:

1. A general ability to manipulate symbols. This would make the ability perhaps as broad as thinking itself, thus going beyond problem solving.

2. A general ability to solve problems. This narrows the conception to a more reasonable level.

3. An ability to define problems. This concentrates attention on the first steps of problem solving, and stops short of the actual solving activities.

4. An ability to test hypotheses. Hypothesis testing occurs during the defining of a problem and also at later stages.

5. An ability to organize a sequence of related steps. An arithmetic-reasoning problem that is at all complex requires a sequence of numerical operations to solve it. We know that the actual numerical operations depend upon the factor of *numerical facility*. An arithmetic-reasoning test is commonly loaded on both this and the *general-reasoning* factor.

Our first two factor analyses [2, 5] eliminated the first hypothesis, in agreement with previous analyses. Not all tests involving symbols are loaded on it. Furthermore, we found a new ability to manipulate symbols on a restricted scale. That is, it was confined characteristically to tests whose items approach equation form.

A recent analysis of planning abilities [4] has shown a factor that could be called "ordering ability," which in a way takes care of Hypothesis 5, for the factor is separate and distinct from *general reasoning*.

Results have more and more pointed to the elimination of Hypothesis 2, that the factor is a general problem-solving ability. There are too many tests involving problems in which the factor is absent. This is especially true where the test material is composed of figures rather than words and/or numbers. We have come to the view that a common, unique, *psychological* core for all problem solving does not exist [3]. Problems are simply too varied, and each type seems to call upon its own pattern of abilities—perceptual abilities as well as thinking abilities.

As we have gone from one analysis to another, our preferred hypothesis concerning the factor has undergone changes, without reaching a final resolution. The interpretation that was favored after each successive analysis can be briefly stated:

6. Effectiveness of trial-and-error manipulation of symbols in the solving of problems of certain kinds [2]. This gives much attention to the fact that problems that are so difficult as to involve the examinee in somewhat random attempts are the best material for measurement of the factor.

7. Ability to consider a number of conditions in defining or understanding a problem [5].

8. Ability to size up a test (or problem) situation to see what is demanded by it [12].

9. Ability to structure a problem [8].

10. Ability to find and maintain a problem structure when considerations are complex [4].

Examination of these suggestions shows that the original Hypothesis 3, that the factor is an ability to define problems, is very persistent. We also see that two new ideas have entered the picture. One emphasizes a possible trial-and-error aspect and the other emphasizes the complexity of the task. The latter idea suggests a span concept. Individuals may differ with respect to the level of complexity they can handle in thinking. The complexity may be calibrated ideally in terms of the number of elements, relations, or variables that the problem entails.

A very recent analysis [6], which was

concentrated on this factor, attempted to reach some decision among the three alternatives; that the factor is an ability (a) to understand or define a problem, (b) to think effectively by trial and error, and (c) to handle a complex set of elements, relations, or variables.

Tests designed to measure ability to understand problems concentrated on the first stages of solving arithmetic-reasoning problems. Given a question, what facts are or are not essential to finding an answer? Given a problem, what arithmetical operations are essential? Tests emphasizing trial and error presented problems in which trying one thing after another would be a natural mode of attacking the task. Tests emphasizing complexity either required the handling of many elements in every item or increased the number progressively throughout the test. It will have to be admitted that experimental separation of these features between sets of tests was not completely achieved.

The results throw considerable doubt on the trial-and-error hypothesis but do not eliminate it from all future consideration. The three tests especially designed to emphasize trial and error were not loaded on the factor.

One of the four tests designed to emphasize complexity had a relatively high loading on the factor, in fact the highest for any test in this analysis. This test is known as Ship Destination. In each item the problem is to tell how many miles a ship is from a port on a simple map. New conditions that modify the effective distance are added as the test progresses—wind direction, current direction, initial heading, and strength of wind and of current. In a sense, the test belongs in the category with arithmetic reasoning. Structuring the problem would still be important.

Two of the three tests designed to emphasize definition of problems had substantial loadings on the factor. The third had shown some relationship to the factor in two earlier analyses. It had been revised in the meantime, however, with an effort to slant the test toward some other factor. Perhaps this effort had succeeded too well.

Thus, we are forced back upon the hypothesis having to do with understanding problems. Just what kind of understanding is important and what kinds of problems, in addition to those of the arithmetic-reasoning type, are still to be determined.

During the course of our investigations, other hypotheses have been suggested from other sources. In his monograph on aptitude factors, French calls the factor "deduction" [1]. There are one or two other reasoning factors that have greater claim to this name and that have come out in analyses, distinct from *general reasoning*. This hypothesis is thus easily eliminated.

More recently Lucas and French [10] have suggested that the factor is the ability to do quantitative or mathematical reasoning. Under this hypothesis, it would be difficult to explain why the factor is consistently loaded in tests that present problems of a nonmathematical and nonquantitative type (such as reading comprehension) and in which it is difficult to see how numbers and mathematical thinking would help. We also have evidence from our project research that there is sometimes little or no relation of *general reasoning* to criteria of achievement in college mathematics [9]. We must therefore also reject this hypothesis.

In conclusion, we may say that it has been much easier to decide what *general reasoning* is not than to say what it is. We have given reasons for believing that it is not general intelligence, though it is undoubtedly one of the important intellectual abilities; it is not a broad ability to manipulate symbols, but there seems to be a narrow ability of this sort; it is not a generic ability to solve problems, though it undoubtedly plays a role in solving problems of certain types; it is not an ability to order a sequence of steps, but there is an ordering ability, which may be of some importance in planning; it is not an ability to use trial and error in problem solving; and it is not a general idea span, though the span concept may be found to apply in some limited way yet to be determined.

By elimination and by consistent indications of a positive nature, the best we can say is that *general reasoning* has something to do with comprehending or structuring problems of certain kinds in preparation for solving them. The range of problems that are pertinent is still to be determined. Whether this ability extends beyond problem solving is also to be determined. It may be a general ability to formulate complex conceptions of many kinds.

REFERENCES

1. FRENCH, J. W. The description of aptitude and achievement tests in terms of rotated factors. *Psychometr. Monogr.*, 1951, No. 5.
2. GREEN, R. F., GUILFORD, J. P., CHRISTENSEN, P. R., & COMREY, A. L. A factor-analytic study of reasoning abilities. *Psychometrika*, 1953, **18**, 135–160.
3. GUILFORD, J. P. Factors in problem solving. *ARTC Instructors J.*, 1954, **4**, 197–204.
4. GUILFORD, J. P., BERGER, R. M., & CHRISTENSEN, P. R. A factor-analytic study of planning, II. Administration of tests and analysis of results. *Psychol. Lab. Rep.*, Los Angeles: Univer. of Southern Calif., 1955, No. 12.
5. GUILFORD, J. P., GREEN, R. F., CHRISTENSEN, P. R., HERTZKA, A. F., & KETTNER, N. W. A factor-analytic study of Navy reasoning tests with the Air Force Classification Battery. *Educ. psychol. Measmt*, 1954, **14**, 301–325.
6. GUILFORD, J. P., KETTNER, N. W., & CHRISTENSEN, P. R. A factor-analytic investigation of the factor called general reasoning. *Psychol. Lab. Rep.* Los Angeles: Univer. of Southern Calif., 1955, No. 14.
7. GUILFORD, J. P., & LACEY, J. I. (Eds.) *Printed classification tests.* Washington, D.C.: Government Printing Office, 1947. (*AAF Aviat. Psychol. Program Res. Rep.*, No. 5.)
8. HERTZKA, A. F., GUILFORD, J. P., CHRISTENSEN, P. R., & BERGER, R. M. A factor-analytic study of evaluative abilities, *Educ. psychol. Measmt*, 1954, **14**, 581–597.
9. HILLS, J. R. The relationship between certain factor-analyzed abilities and success in college mathematics. *Psychol. Lab. Rep.*, Los Angeles: Univer. of Southern Calif., 1955, No. 15.
10. LUCAS, C. M., & FRENCH, J. W. *The factorial composition of the relative movement test.* Princeton: Educational Testing Service, 1953.
11. THURSTONE, L. L. Primary mental abilities. *Psychometr. Monogr.*, 1938, No. 1.
12. WILSON, R. C., GUILFORD, J. P., CHRISTENSEN, P. R., & LEWIS, D. J. A factor-analytic study of creative-thinking abilities. *Psychometrika*, 1954, **19**, 297–311.

Chapter 36

A Psychological Design for
a Theory of Mental Abilities

LOUIS GUTTMAN

The recent departure from our midst of two of the giants of factor analysis, Godfrey Thompson and Louis Thurstone, makes it appropriate for a symposium on the future of factor analysis to be held at this time. It is difficult to realize that already ten years have passed since Charles Spearman was taken also from us.

The theme for my present remarks comes from three of the papers given in July, 1955, at the International Colloquium on Factor Analysis, held in Paris. In these three papers, there appears to be such a strong convergence of thinking as to suggest the hypothesis that here is a direction in which the future of factor analysis may lie. Two of these papers were by outstanding disciples of Spearman and Thurstone, respectively: A. H. El-Koussy and J. P. Guilford. A paper of my own is the third of the trio. (Although not privileged to

This article is reprinted from *Educational and Psychological Measurement,* 1958, with the permission of the author and the copyright holder. The original title was "What lies ahead for factor analysis."

study personally with either Spearman or Thurstone, I consider myself a disciple of both.)

Stated briefly, the convergence has been toward *a psychological design for a theory of mental abilities.* The design is not unlike that which R. A. Fisher has called "factorial" in his design of experiments. Extension of Fisher's concepts to the case of common-factor analysis (where the word "factor" has a different meaning from that in Fisher's context) poses new problems of statistical inference, but it also shows *an immediate and unambiguous interpretation of Thurstone's concept of simple structure.* It also shows how Spearman's "g" may be associated with the idea of simple structure. In short, the new concept of design may help resolve some outstanding controversies. It also leads to new consequences of great importance to psychological theory and practice.

El-Koussy arrived at a design by studying a particular class of abilities concerned with physical space. Guilford arrived at essentially the same formal concept—but differing in psychological details of the facets—by trying to reorganize psychologically the empirical results of many studies which employed Thurstone's concept of simple structure. I myself arrived at the design idea for the problem of factor analysis as a special case of general meta-theoretical considerations for substantive analysis of multivariate problems met with in the behavioral sciences.

Both Spearman and Thurstone had always insisted that one must conceptualize—in substantive terms—what is being studied before one proceeds to design tests, gather data, and go through elaborate statistical analyses. Neither, however, succeeded in giving rules for designing such concepts; and hence each developed algebraic techniques of analysis of empirical data which need not be direct consequences of the psychological theories behind the data.

It is a tribute to Thurstone's profound intuition that he arrived at the concept of simple structure from general considerations which did not stem from a strict notion of design. With our present hindsight, we can now see that using only intuition was the hard way of achieving this, and that a clear definition of design yields the concept as a simple consequence. Similarly, the ingenious (but laborious and controversial) rotational devices for seeking factor reference axes can now be seen to be tackling things the hard way—but perhaps in the only way possible if there is no clear design—while a straightforward, unambiguous algebra can now be developed as a direct consequence of a given psychological design. In the future, we should be able to get more psychological information and fruitful interpretation with much less work.

Before going into details of this recent convergence and their implications, it may be helpful to discuss the history behind it. In particular, it may be helpful to think that Spearman was really two different personalities and that Thurstone also represented two different personalities. Each man was a psychologist interested in psychological theories of mental abilities, but each man was also concerned with more abstract statistical and algebraic theory. In each man, there was something of a split in personality because his algebra did not necessarily match his psychological theories. It might be hypothesized that such imperfect matching caused each to become highly involved in a particular kind of algebra and to devote his best efforts to a defense of it.

In an address before the American Psychological Association, Thurstone stated: "In the psychometric laboratory at Chicago we spend more time in designing the experimental tests for a factor study than on all of the computational work, including the correlations, the factoring, and the analysis of the structure. If we have several hypotheses about postulated factors, we design and invent new tests which may be crucially differentiating between the several hypotheses. This is entirely a psychological job with no computing. It calls for as much psychological insight as we can gather among students and instructors. . . . I mention this aspect of factorial work in the hope of counteracting the rather general impression that factor analysis is all concerned with algebra and statistics. These should be our servants in the investigation of psychological ideas. If we have no psychological ideas, we are not likely to discover anything interesting because even if the factorial results are clear and clean, the interpretation must be as subjective as in any other scientific work" [12, especially p. 277].

Thurstone suggested no guide[1] for theory construction beyond gathering insights from "students and instructors." Earlier, Spearman gave some instructions for what was required: ". . . nothing less than a general survey of the entire range of possible

---

[1] I have been in the same boat with respect to the problem of defining a universe of content for attitude. The notion of facet design in the present paper was actually first used for the problem of attitude research, and has helped solve the analogous problem there.

operations of knowing. To execute this gigantic task, there appears to be only one effective means. It consists in an appeal to the complete system of ultimate laws that govern all cognition" [7, p. 162]. Spearman goes on to describe "qualitative laws" for this purpose, as we shall remark again later. If we interpret his "laws" to mean "facets of design"—then the present convergence is toward what Spearman had also aimed.

It is true that, in his earlier work, Thurstone did concern himself with a substantive theory of mental ability, which he published in a book which seems virtually unknown today [8]. I myself have not read it as yet (but I plan to soon) and would not be surprised if no one else in this audience has. This was before his development of multiple factor analysis.

Thurstone again emphasized the need for psychological theory, as distinct from algebraic manipulations, in the preface to his monograph, *The Reliability and Validity of Tests:* " . . . the correlational methods have probably stifled scientific imagination as often as they have been of service. As tools in their proper place they are useful but as the central theme of mental measurement they are rather sterile. . . . In this country the reliability formulae have become a sort of fetish rather than a tool. It is almost as though 'busy-work' becomes science as soon as it can be made to sprout correlation coefficients. . . . What is needed in experimental psychology more than anything else is to formulate problems and investigations so as to reveal functional relations which should be rationalized whenever possible. This will advance psychology toward scientific respectability with more certainty than correlation coefficients, elaborate instrumentation, and discussion about points of view and the meaning of words" [9, Preface].

Then came Thurstone's work on multiple factor analysis. This was, of course, originally motivated by psychological considerations. He was vitally interested in the problem of the psychology of mental abilities,

and he gave his first textbook on the subject the title, *Vectors of Mind* [10]. Actually, virtually no psychology is discussed in this textbook. Instead, emphasis is laid on two distinct, abstract principles of *parsimony* for the analysis of multivariate data.

THURSTONE'S THREE ABSTRACT PRINCIPLES OF PARSIMONY

The first principle seems to derive historically as a generalization of Spearman's "g." While it is not true that Spearman hypothesized that mental abilities were intercorrelated *only* because of a single general factor, nevertheless he did devote a major portion of his discussions to the problem of the existence of such a general factor in addition to other general and group factors. Thurstone restated the Spearman hypothesis by discussing various kinds of general or group factors simultaneously. Thurstone made the explicit hypothesis that mental abilities could have their intercorrelations explained by a *relatively small number* of common-factors. The first principle of parsimony introduced by Thurstone, then, is that the number of common-factors should be relatively small compared to the large number of possible mental abilities or tests.

Since the first principle could lead only to the determination of a common-factor space, and since Thurstone conceived of factors as being reference axes in such a space, Thurstone recognized that some structural considerations would be desirable apart from mere counting of number of common-factors. To this end he introduced his celebrated principle of *simple structure*, which hypothesizes that not all common-factors should be involved in all abilities.

It is interesting that Thurstone did not derive these two principles from especially psychological considerations, but rather from general considerations as to what parsimony might mean in science. There is nothing in these principles which he believed peculiar to psychology. To emphasize this, in the second edition of his textbook he took the word "Mind" out of the title, and called the revision: "Multiple-Factor Analysis" [11]. His two principles are presented as general procedures for studying correlation matrices, and no discussion is made of psychological problems *per se*. A third principle is added, again from general considerations of parsimony, of "second-order factors."

It is this second Thurstone who emphasized abstract computational techniques rather than substantive psychological theory, who seems to have been followed mostly by his direct and indirect students. Given a correlation matrix without any substantive characterization of the rows and columns, such students will attempt a "blind" factor analysis of the table. Some, to be sure, do have some sort of substantive theory to begin with; but, nevertheless, they tend to rely on the statistical analysis to formalize the theory for them. Instead of asking: "To what kind of algebra does my theory lead?," they tend to ask: "To what psychological theory does my preconceived algebra lead?"

DIFFICULTIES WITH THE PARSIMONY PRINCIPLES

All three of Thurstone's principles lead to vexing problems from a purely mathematical or statistical point of view, and have led to a great deal of controversy on these grounds alone. One feature that does not seem to have been remarked on extensively has been their possible mutual incompatibility. In some cases it is possible to achieve small rank but without simple structure; and in other cases simple structure can be achieved, but at the expense of large rank. Which is preferable? These two principles arose historically at two different stages of Thurstone's work, and it appears a critical

examination of their interrelation has not been adequately made. This would also tend to indicate lack of a really general and consistent theory of parsimony.

A certain algebraic frailty has attended all work in factor analysis—whether on a theoretical or computational level—in which the communality concept is involved. In principle, the concept is sound and fundamental. But its full algebraic consequences and implications were revealed only most recently [6]. In particular, it has been shown [6] how use of second-order factors, in Thurstone's sense, may be quite illusory in the quest for parsimony because of certain problems of identifiability or determinacy of factor scores associated with use of communalities. There can be a direct contradiction between this third principle and Thurstone's first principle.

EMPIRICAL EVIDENCE AGAINST A SMALL NUMBER OF COMMON-FACTORS FOR MENTAL ABILITIES

As for the empirical truth of the hypothesis of a small number of common-factors for mental abilities, evidence constantly being accumulated by factor analysts throughout the world—notably among them Thurstone's students—now seems conclusive against it. The growth of the literature on factor analysis in psychology has been accompanied by an ever lengthening list of different common-factors.

Concern about this steady expansion led R. B. Cattell to initiate work with a committee of the American Psychological Association "to produce a universal indexing of discovered factors that will reduce chaos in this field" [1]. In a proposal submitted to the Paris colloquium, Cattell in essence suggested some kind of decimal system for listing common-factors as they become reported, in order that investigators will not duplicate the effort of others and can go on to discover even more common-factors.

John W. French [3] also has prepared a

collection of common-factors. Guilford's work, to which we refer in more detail shortly, is a result of his own concern with this problem. It was in the course of preparing "a new and complete list of the intellectual factors as we know them" [4] that Guilford has now been led to suggest a *psychology* of mental abilities. This psychology stresses structural features, and implicitly discards the notion of small rank as an initial point of departure.

It is a remarkable fact that textbooks in psychology do not discuss the overwhelming empirical evidence against the hypothesis of a small number of common-factors for mental abilities. Thurstone himself was, of course, aware of what was happening. This in part may have led him to his concept of "second-order factors," as an attempt to achieve parsimony despite the empirical failure of the first principle.

In the type of design of mental abilities toward which we seem to be converging, it is true that first, second, and higher-order factors may be discussed; and indeed they appear "naturally." But here "order" will mean order of *interaction* (in the sense of R. A. Fisher) between the facets of the design.

SPEARMAN'S PSYCHOLOGY

Upon re-reading his *Abilities of Man* with our present hindsight, it appears that Spearman's psychology was far superior to his algebra, and indeed there is no necessary connection between the two. Let us review the highlights of this book from our present point of view.

One of the opening chapters describes the "oligarchic doctrine of mental abilities, with the criticism that it leads to an endlessly growing list of faculties. Spearman points out that the oligarchic doctrine cannot necessarily be charged with ambiguity, "for the faculties are often furnished with definitions that appear to be tolerable enough" [7, p. 35]. In summarizing the literature on mental abilities over the cen-

turies, Spearman points out that Plato distinguished between two kinds of abilities: sense and intellect. Later, some writers added memory, and others added imagination or invention. Before the fall of the Roman Empire, speech and attention were frequently introduced to the list. And lastly, movement. "Any further increase in the number of faculties beyond these seven has, in general, only been attained by subdividing some or other of these. The Sense readily built up into as many different mental powers as there are different sense organs. The Intellect . . . was analyzed into the three stages of conception, judgment, and reasoning. The Memory was split into reproductive and reconstructive. The Imagination fell into active and passive" [7, p. 29].

Skipping to more recent times, "finally we arrive at those current faculties which do not obviously derive from the ancient seven, but instead indicate more or less originality. As instances may be quoted the following: 'censorship'; 'foresight'; 'keenness in noticing resemblance'; the power to 'break up a complex and properly evaluate and relate its parts'; the ability to 're-arrange a bit of mental content in a new and prescribed way.' Characteristic of all these is that in them the already noticed lack of system reached its highest degree. . . . Despite their being novel, no attempt is made to demonstrate, or even to discuss, their psychological foundation and significance. Their very authors do not consistently emphasize them from one writing to another. Small wonder, then, that in general nobody else takes any notice of them" [7, p. 34].

To install order in this chaos, Spearman proposed his own system which he summarizes as follows. ". . . all knowing originates in three fundamental laws with corresponding processes—the awareness of one's own experience, the education of relations and that of correlates. Each of these, again, admits of subclassification in an exhaustive manner, so that no considerable field of cognition need be overlooked. For such further subdivision, the most useful concepts have been (*a*) the different classes of relations that are cognizable, (*b*) the different kinds of fundaments that enter into these relations, and (*c*) the varying kinds and degrees of complexity in which such relations and fundaments can be conjoined.

". . . Besides these three qualitative laws, employment has also been made of the five quantitative ones. These latter, as much as the former, have served to map out the entire domain of ability and thus render the whole of it amenable to systematic investigation. These five laws are respectively those of Span, Retentivity (two kinds, inertia and disposition), Fatigue, Conation, and Primordial Potencies (including such influences as those of age, sex, heredity, and health)" [7, pp. 410–411].

This overview that Spearman himself has given of his system clearly shows a complex design for mental abilities. Spearman laments in several places that tests have not been constructed to cover many areas specified by such an overall design. But supposing one did have a complete battery of tests covering every aspect of the design. How should one go about analyzing the resulting data statistically?

R. A. Fisher has taught us how statistical analyses should flow from the design of the observations. But this kind of thinking, and the modern know-how for handling multivariate distributions, were largely lacking when Spearman began his great pioneering work. Spearman obviously—and explicitly—did not believe that intercorrelations amongst such a labyrinth of data could be accounted for by but a single general factor. While he did intend his "g" to play some general role in this configuration, it is not clear statistically what this was to be. From a rigorous point of view, it is impossible to formalize Spearman's problem of "g" in such a vast context without first formalizing the entire context. Since Spearman did not do the latter job, which would virtually require anticipating some of the most important achievements in modern

statistics, it is not to be wondered that the specialized algebra he did use was so misunderstood in the context of his general theory. It does not arise directly from his general theory, and has no clear relation to it from an algebraic or statistical point of view.

EL-KOUSSY'S PSYCHOLOGY

For some twenty-five years, El-Koussy has been studying the problem of space abilities. His paper at the Paris colloquium describes various results of numerical factor analyses of space ability tests and discusses problems of interpretation. El-Koussy concludes with the following consideration: "This aspect of content will probably bring in another suggestion. Every test could somehow be thought of as having at least three main aspects—the *content*, the *form*, and the *function*. The content may mean numbers, words, pictures, figures, symbols, solids, actual things, situation or time. The form may mean the form in which the test items are presented; i.e., classification, order opposites, analogies, . . . etc. The function may mean deduction, induction, memory, visualization, manipulations. . . . The evidence of factors appears sometimes in one aspect and sometimes in another. If tests are constructed to embrace all such aspects we may possibly know more about the relative importance of content and function.

"Space is a content having varied species but visualization, manipulation, thinking, etc., are functions. We want to determine the width and the implications of space as a factor irrespective of the mental functions and we also seek to know the width of the function as a factor irrespective of the content" [2].

El-Koussy points out the possible relation of such a design to Cyril Burt's concept of hierarchical levels of factors. The close similarity to Spearman's explicitly psychological concepts is also certainly evident. Again we may ask what the proper statistical analysis should be for the correlations between tests of a battery constructed according to such a scheme. A specific clue is given in El-Koussy's concluding paragraph cited above. This sounds as if one is interested in disentangling the separate contributions of elements of a facet from the interaction of facets, using "interaction" in the sense of R. A. Fisher.

GUILFORD'S PSYCHOLOGY

The ever-growing number of common-factors being "discovered" or "isolated" by various investigators led Guilford ". . . to prepare a new and complete list of the intellectual factors as we know them. Although I had been aware of the fact that there were some logical similarities and parallels among some of the factors, I was somewhat surprised at the extent to which the systematic features could be carried" [4]. Guilford focused on the forty or so factors of ability which were "isolated" by Thurstonian methods of rotation of axes to simple structure, positive manifold, and psychological meaning. But he set himself the new job of trying to find *structure for the psychological meaning.* By purely conceptual analysis, he arrived at the following design of meaning.

For brevity, let us schematize Guilford's results even more than he has done.

He finds it possible to distinguish between five kinds of *intellect:* memory, cognition, convergent thinking, divergent thinking, and evaluation. Each of these intellectual abilities can be used on each of three types of *content:* figural, structural, and conceptual. All told, then, there are 5×3, or 15 possible combinations of intellect and content. Each of these fifteen combinations can be broken down further into six varieties by another facet; namely, type of *thing:* fundaments (names), classes, relations, patterns or systems, problems, and implications.

Guilford does not actually have all six

types of things crosscut the fifteen intellect-content pairs. But let us assume that they—or some similar facet—will do the trick. We shall then have 15×6, or 90 possible combinations of one element from each of the three facets: intellect, content, and thing.

If such a three-faceted scheme should fulfill Spearman's requirements of "nothing less than a general survey of the entire range of possible operations of knowing," then we must conclude that all intellectual abilities can be accounted for by 90 common-factors. (Guilford actually believes that fewer than ninety common-factors may be required for this task.)

There is, of course, room for a great deal of controversy as to the adequacy of details in Guilford's facets and as to the completeness of the system. However, if future discussions should be directed largely to these problems, of *detail* and *completeness,* they will confirm our hypothesis as to the future path of factor analysis for mental abilities. The convergence that we are emphasizing is on the *notion of design,* and this should not be obscured by unsolved problems about detail or completeness of a given design.

CARTESIAN PRODUCTS AND THEIR FACETS

Designs such as El-Koussy's and Guilford's are called *Cartesian products of sets* by mathematicians. Thus, in Guilford's case, if I is the set of intellectual abilities (with five elements), if C is the set of three types of content, and if T is the set of six types of things, then by the Cartesian product ICT is meant the set of ordered triples, say of the form ict, where i is an element of I, c is an element of C, and t is an element of T. Each set in a Cartesian product is what Fisher calls a "factor" for his design of experiments, and an element of such a "factor" is what he calls "level of a factor." Since this use of the word "factor" is radically different from that of Spearman and Thurstone, we have proposed that the word *facet* be used instead of Fisher's [5]. A facet is nothing but a set involved in a Cartesian product. I, C, and T are the three facets of the Cartesian product ICT.

Following Spearman, should we regard "qualitative laws" or a facet design as being a set of instructions for a test constructor as to what kinds of items he should make up for tests, then Guilford's ICT design provides instructions for ninety varieties of tests.

An empirical study would consist of administering these ninety tests to a population, say P, of people. Furthermore, real numbers or scores would be assigned to the people for each test. The design of the entire experiment would then be

$$PICT \longrightarrow \text{real scores.}$$

What is the appropriate statistical analysis for this design of an experiment? Our problem is rather different from the ordinary one in R. A. Fisher's system in that we do not have any *a priori* uniform scales of measurement for "yield." The means and standard deviations of each of the ninety tests are in general arbitrary. Hence, in addition to the usual problems of the Fisher type, we have the problem of establishing comparable units of measurement before one can do an analysis of variance. In any event, our job would be to explain why a person got the score he did on a particular test in terms of the three facets of the test design.

Let s_{pict} be the observed score of person p on a test of design ict, where i, c, and t are elements of I, C, and T respectively. For example, if i = cognition, c = structural, and t = relations, then test ict is a test of cognition of structural relations. Since the standard deviations of the test scores are arbitrary, we shall have to seek weights w_{ict} so as to define "ideal" scores, say x_{pict}, where

$$x_{pict} = w_{ict} s_{pict} \qquad (1)$$

and such that an analysis of variance of the x_{pict} will be the best possible.

Following — but modifying — Fisher, we can try to "explain" x_{pict} in terms of *lower-order scores* for the members of P, say x_{pic}, x_{pit}, x_{pct}, x_{pi}, x_{pc}, x_{pt}, and x_p:

$$x_{pict} = x_{pic} + x_{pit} + x_{pct} + x_{pi} + x_{pc} \\ + x_{pt} + x_p + u_{pict} \qquad (2)$$

where u_{pict} is the score of subject p on the *unique* factor of test ict. All scores on the right of (2) except for u_{pict} are on common-factors in the Spearman-Thurstone sense. To avoid redundancy in the analysis of variance—and thereby satisfying Fisher's orthogonality condition—these common-factor scores can always (and without loss of generality) be adjusted to satisfy

$$\Sigma_c x_{pic} = \Sigma_i x_{pic} = \Sigma_t x_{pit} = \Sigma_i x_{pit} = \Sigma_c x_{pct} \\ = \Sigma_t x_{pct} = \Sigma_i x_{pi} = \Sigma_c x_{pc} = \Sigma_t x_{pt} = 0 \qquad (3)$$

Notice that (3) says nothing about summations over p, and this is where we part company with Fisher. The common-factors may be oblique or orthogonal to each other over p, the nature of the correlations being an automatic but empirical outcome of the analysis of the particular data.

RELATION TO SIMPLE STRUCTURE

Adherents to Thurstone's simple structure concept will be pleased to see this concept explicitly illustrated by (2). Each test does not involve all possible common-factors, but at most only seven! While there are 90 possible tests from Guilford's three-facet design, there are 78 possible common-factors of the type in the right of (2) $[(5 \times 3) + (5 \times 6) + (3 \times 6) + 5 + 3 + 6 + 1]$, but at most seven of the latter can contribute to the variance of any particular test.

Having 78 common-factors for 90 tests is a gross violation of Thurstone's first principle of parsimony, but having only 7 common-factors (out of a possible 78) per test is certainly a highly satisfying way of conforming to his second principle.

RELATION TO SPEARMAN'S "g"

One of the new kinds of statistical problems involved in the general theory of facet analysis is how to solve simultaneously for the weights w_{ict} in (1) and the common-factor scores and unique-factor scores in (2). This class of problems will be discussed on some other occasion. This is one of the new paths of statistical theory for factor analysis as well as for other kinds of multivariate problems.

The variances of the common-factor scores in (2) are in general unequal (which is one reason why "loadings" do not appear explicitly). Should the variance of a particular score happen to equal zero, the associated facet element, or combination of elements, does not contribute to the observed test scores.

We now come a full circle back to Spearman by looking at the last common-factor score, of lowest order in (2), namely x_p. If one wishes, one could interpret this to be Spearman's "g." It is associated with none of the three facets but is rather an average over all of them. What the magnitude of the variance of x_p is for the given population is an empirical problem. Should the variance vanish empirically, this would imply that there are no differential scores on "general intelligence" for the population. The relative size of the variance of x_p compared with the variances of the other common-factor scores will show the relative importance of "general intelligence" in performance on tests of mental abilities.

REFERENCES

1. CATTELL, R. B. A communication. *International Colloquium on Factor Analysis.* Paris, 1955.
2. EL-KOUSSY, A. H. Trends of research in space abilities. *International Colloquium on Factor Analysis.* Paris, 1955.
3. FRENCH, J. W. The description of aptitude and achievement tests in terms of rotated factors. *Psychometr. Monogr.,* No. 5, 1951.
4. GUILFORD, J. P. The structure of human intellect. (Paper presented to the National Academy of Sciences.) Pasadena, Calif., 1955.
5. GUTTMAN, L. An outline of some new methodology for social research. *Publ. Opin. Quart.,* 1954–55, **18**, 395–404.
6. GUTTMAN, L. The determinacy of factor score matrices with implications for five other basic problems of common-factor theory. *Brit. J. Statist. Psychol.,* 1955, **8**, 65–81.
7. SPEARMAN, C. *The abilities of man.* New York: Macmillan, 1927.
8. THURSTONE, L. L. *The nature of intelligence.* London: International Library of Psychology and Philosophy, 1924.
9. THURSTONE, L. L. *The reliability and validity of tests.* Ann Arbor, Mich.: Edwards Bros., 1931.
10. THURSTONE, L. L. *Vectors of mind.* Chicago: Univer. Chicago Press, 1936.
11. THURSTONE, L. L. *Multiple-factor analysis.* Chicago: Univer. Chicago Press, 1947.
12. THURSTONE, L. L. Psychological implications of factor analysis. *Amer. Psychologist,* 1948, **3**, 402–408. In Marx, M. H. *Psychological theory.* New York: Macmillan, 1951.

Chapter *37* ~

The Organization
of Human Abilities

LLOYD G. HUMPHREYS

I have been disturbed for several years at two related tendencies in the work on human abilities. One is the proliferation of factors as more and more experimental test batteries have been intercorrelated and factored. For example, Guilford [5] now recognizes more factors than Thurstone [11] had tests. The other is the continuing tendency to think of factors as basic or primary, no matter how specific, or narrow, or artificial the test behavior may be that determines the factor. This criticism, by the way, is not directed solely at those who search for genetic mechanisms underlying

This article is reprinted from the *American Psychologist,* 1962, with the permission of the author and the American Psychological Association.

The article was the presidential address for Division 5 of the American Psychological Association, delivered in New York City, September, 1961. The work was supported by Grant M 2509 of the National Institute of Mental Health. Grateful acknowledgment is also made to John Schmid, Jr., who first called the author's attention to the hierarchical model and with whom he spent many hours discussing alternative factorial solutions, and to Louis Guttman, whose visit to the University of Illinois in 1959 stimulated his thinking about facet theory.

factors. It is directed equally at those who look primarily for general laws of learning or at those middle-of-the-roaders who would look for laws of human development jointly dependent on nature and nurture. Just because a number of scores have been intercorrelated, the correlations factored, and some interpretable factors obtained is no adequate basis for concluding that these are the primary factors, that these are the factors for which measuring devices should be constructed, that these are the factors which should henceforth be used in practice or in further research. In other words, to paraphrase Gertrude Stein, I object to the conclusion that a factor is a factor is a factor.

These twin difficulties have become even more pressing with the development and wide use of high speed digital computers, and particularly with the increasing use of programs with those computers that objectively rotate the initially computed factors to "simple structure." The result can be empiricism at its blindest. Except for the decision as to the number of factors to rotate, which is a very important subjective

447

component in the procedure, factor analyses can now be ground out without having the basic data seen by human eye or touched by human hand.

Now I must admit that these criticisms of empiricism and objectivity come haltingly to my lips. My own orientation is highly empirical, but I can still detect misdirected empiricism. May I also remind you that I have been characterizing factor analysis for several years as a useful tool in hypothesis formation rather than as a method of hypothesis testing [9]. Our ability to make probability statements concerning the outcomes of experiments, either for decision making or for estimation purposes, lies at the very heart of the scientific method. Factor analysis simply does not qualify on this score. Let us, therefore, use it for what it can do; and since it is an aid in hypothesis formation, let us not neglect other aspects of hypothesis formation. In particular, when we factor, we need a model of the nature of individual differences. The factor analytic techniques do not automatically provide such a model. It must be provided by the investigator.

I start with the assumption, which I think is by now well supported, that test behavior can almost endlessly be made more specific, that factors can almost endlessly be fractionated or splintered. When two tests differ in only the slightest aspect so that by definition they are not parallel forms, but are almost as highly correlated as parallel forms, we have by present standards the definition of the ultimate primary factor. In order to construct systematically nonparallel tests that differ only in the slightest aspect, each must be made highly homogeneous. Following this pattern will lead to the collection of a very large number of tests, each of which might be scalable in the original Guttman [6] meaning of that term. For each there would be a near parallel form. Such tests would define many factors, probably many more than Guilford [5] is suggesting, but they would not be, in my book, candidates for the designation "primary."

HIERARCHICAL MODEL

One model that appealed to me several years ago as a way out of this morass, and one still applicable to a great deal of psychological data, is the hierarchical model in a single order that British writers, for example [see 12], have discussed for many years and for which Schmid and Leiman [10] and Wherry [13] have supplied computational solutions. Schmid and Leiman have also pointed out the algebraic identity between their hierarchical model and factoring in accordance with the simple structure model in several orders.

Vernon's structure has been supported by numerous British studies. Lack of support on this side of the Atlantic is due solely to the fact that American psychologists have been using a different model. At the top of Vernon's hierarchy is g, though Vernon interprets his factors in accordance with Thomson's theories rather than Spearman's. Below the major group factors are minor group factors. One is known as the verbal-numerical-educational factor and the other as the practical-mechanical-spatial-physical factor. The probable appearance of other factors at this level in the hierarchy is discussed, but such factors are not well known. Below the major group factors are minor group factors and below those the specific factors. The factor splintering that has taken place in recent test construction history, however, may introduce still further levels in the hierarchy between major and specific factors. Thus Vernon recognizes the need for factoring in at least three orders, since there are at least three levels of his hierarchy beyond specific factors, if the intercorrelations of ability measures are to be adequately described psychologically.

As compared to factoring in several orders, my preference for a hierarchy within a single order is based on rather simple grounds: it is easier to misinterpret factors in several orders. Most people assume that first-order factors are the primary ones just because they are first to appear. Second-order factors are rather mysterious because they are defined, not by tests, but by first-order factors. Third-order factors are completely incomprehensible. Thus Guilford [4], in his revision of the *Psychometric Methods,* concluded: "The writer reserves judgment with respect to the psychological validity of factors higher than the first-order ones." In contrast, the hierarchy of factors in a single order places the primary emphasis on the broadest factors (those in the highest order) and all factors are defined by the original test variables. First-order factors are typically placed where they belong, far down in the hierarchy with small loadings on a small number of variables. Their lack of generality in the test battery is indicative of their general psychological unimportance.

A LOGICAL HIERARCHY OF MECHANICAL INFORMATION

A hypothetical hierarchy from the field of mechanical information can be used to illustrate these points. I offer no apology for offering a "cooked-up" example. Principles can be seen more readily in this way.

I shall assume that there are four discriminable levels of specificity of tests of mechanical information. These are as follows: (*a*) information about specific tools, e.g., the cross-cut saw or the socket wrench; (*b*) information about groups of tools having a common function, e.g., saws or wrenches; (*c*) information about areas of mechanical interest, e.g., carpentry or automotive; (*d*) general mechanical information, sampling from several areas such as carpentry, automotive, metal working, and plumbing.

If certain reasonable assumptions are made concerning the interrelationships of items and tests in this hierarchy, the logical hierarchy will become evident empirically. These assumptions follow: (*a*) Intercorrelations of items within a Level 1 test will be higher than correlations between items in different Level 1 tests, i.e., their homogeneity coefficients are higher than their intercorrelations. (*b*) Correlations between Level 1 tests involving the same group of tools will be higher than those involving different groups, which will be higher in turn than those involving different areas. (*c*) Correlations between groups of tools will be higher for those involving the same area than for those involving different areas. (*d*) Correlations between areas of mechanical interest will be higher than those involving any one area of such interest and other factor measures, such as verbal comprehension or spatial visualization.

This four-stage hierarchy of mechanical information tests will generate three different levels of factors. Intercorrelations of Level 1 tests will produce tool group factors. Similarly, intercorrelations of Level 2 tests will produce area factors, and intercorrelations of Level 3 tests will produce the general mechanical information factor. Note that if we were to extract factors from item intercorrelations a fourth and most specific level of factor would result, namely, tool factors.

FACTORING HIERARCHICAL DATA

As an example of the consequence of the assumptions concerning this hierarchy of tests, a factor analysis model is presented. The first row of Table 37–1 contains arbitrary factor loadings, but so selected as to reflect the assumptions made, of a Level 1 test. The second and third row values were

Table 37–1   Factor Analysis Model for the Mechanical Information Area

Type of Test	General Mechanical Information	Area of Mechanical Interest	Tool Group
Level 1	.4000	.4500	.5000
Level 2	.4645	.5225	.5806
Level 3	.5721	.6435	.2439*
Level 4	.8418	.1894†	.0718‡

 * Indicates the loading which would be obtained on each of three factors of this type.
  † Indicates the loading which would be obtained on each of five factors of this type.
   ‡ Indicates the loading which would be obtained on each of 15 factors of this type.

computed from the first row by assuming that all Level 1 tests have comparable loadings and that each test at the more general level is the sum of three tests at the preceding level. For the fourth row five separate area tests were assumed.

The illustration thus uses 45 Level 1, 15 Level 2, and 5 Level 3 tests. The orthogonal factor model includes 15 tool-group factors, 5 area factors, and 1 general factor. We will examine the consequences of factor analyzing the 45 Level 1 tests.

The correlational matrix in this example would define only 15 factors, since there are no independent measures of anything but tool-group factors. Objective orthogonal rotations would neglect six important factors. The theoretical structure could be reproduced in orthogonal rotations only by extracting six additional factors (or adding six dimensions with zero loadings) and by rotating to meaningful positions. If 21 centroid factors were used in rotations, factors could not be treated as if they were all equally important; one could not simply try to approximate simple structure and achieve the desired result. The factor analyst instead would have to have a theoretical model in mind toward which his rotations would be directed.

If we use oblique axes, and obtain factors in all orders, we do not need to be as arbitrary. The 15 first-order factors would define 5 second-order factors and the latter would in turn define a general factor in the third order. If we had decided to start our analysis from items rather than from homogeneous tests, all of these factors would have been pushed back one order with a set of 45 tool factors being found in the first order. The original structure, in other words, is preserved in the full oblique solution.

It should be particularly noted, however, that fully meaningful psychological description is not obtained with oblique axes until factors at all orders have been exhausted. The factor analyst who uses oblique solutions and stops with the first order is not better off than the one who uses objective orthogonal rotations. The oblique solution in such a case can be distinctly less meaningful, on the other hand, than one obtained by subjective orthogonal rotations, i.e., by rotations directed toward a meaningful model.

PROBLEM OF SAMPLING OF TESTS

The solution, as in all cooked-up examples, is nice and neat. All of us recognize the difficulties that would be introduced by sampling errors alone. There is another sort of error, not generally recognized, that also makes the rotation and interpretation of factors difficult. Either by design or by accident, more tests are constructed in one area than another. Also, the more intensively an area is tilled, the more likely one will find a hierarchy of tests of varying degrees of specificity. Thus one fluency factor is divided into multiple fluency factors as a result of intensive test construction [3] and so on. Cattell [2] seems to have been more aware of this problem than anyone else, but he does not have a solution to it. Cattell writes in terms of density of sampling of tests from a given population, but does not arrive at independent definitions of a population of tests and *density* of sampling from that population.

To follow along this line, let us suppose that our test constructor is more interested in and has more knowledge about carpentry and automotive mechanics than about other areas of mechanical information. Thus he constructs several, let us say nine, Level 1 tests in each of those areas with each set of nine tests covering three tool groups. He covers three other areas less intensively, not going beyond Level 2 in his test construction, and provides three such tests in each area to define possible factors.

This matrix of 27 variables generates nine factors in the first order, though the a priori orthogonal model which is an extension of Table 1 requires 12 factors. An objective rotation of orthogonal factors is obviously faulty; so we shall proceed to the oblique

Table 37–2   Primary Pattern—First Order

Variables*	Factors								
	I	II	III	IV	V	VI	VII	VIII	IX
1–3	6990	0000	0000	0000	0000	0000	0000	0000	0000
4–6	0000	6990	0000	0000	0000	0000	0000	0000	0000
7–9	0000	0000	6990	0000	0000	0000	0000	0000	0000
10–12	0000	0000	0000	7824	0000	0000	0000	0000	0000
13–15	0000	0000	0000	0000	7824	0000	0000	0000	0000
16–18	0000	0000	0000	0000	0000	7824	0000	0000	0000
19–21	0000	0000	0000	0000	0000	0000	7824	0000	0000
22–24	0000	0000	0000	0000	0000	0000	0000	7824	0000
25–27	0000	0000	0000	0000	0000	0000	0000	0000	7824

* Variables with identical factor patterns are grouped together for economy in presentation. Three variables of each type were assumed since three would ordinarily be necessary in order to determine communalities and define factors. The first nine variables represent tool groups in this example; the remainder are Level 1, or tool information, variables.

solution. In this discussion, a first-order factor will refer to the computations made from the data of the example; reference to the a priori model will be in terms of tool-group factors, area factors, etc. The one-to-one correspondence between the model and factor orders observed in the first example does not hold in this case. Thus in Table 37–2 six first-order factors are tool-group factors and three are area factors; i.e., factors that were restricted to different orders in our first example now appear in the same order. Intercorrelations of these factors are shown in Table 37–3. When this matrix is factored, two of the three factors in the second order are seen to be area factors. The third is part of the general mechanical information factor. The one factor in the third order will pick up the rest of the general factor. The second-order factors,

their intercorrelations, and the third-order factor appear in Table 37–4.

In this example, which can be considered typical of many actual cases, even the oblique solution is messy. There are 13 factors in all orders when the model requires only 12. Two of the 13 overlap in interpretation though they are in different orders. Different levels of factors appear in the same order. Without knowledge of the structure which produced these results, it would be difficult to make adequate interpretation of the findings as they stand.

HIERARCHICAL TRANSFORMATION

In order to interpret factors in several orders, it is useful to transform, by the procedure described by Schmid and Leiman [10], the oblique factors in all orders to a

Table 37–3   Intercorrelations of First-order Factors

	I	II	III	IV	V	VI	VII	VIII	IX
I		4415	4415	3398	3398	3398	3398	3398	3398
II			4415	3398	3398	3398	3398	3398	3398
III				3398	3398	3398	3398	3398	3398
IV					5921	5921	2614	2614	2614
V						5921	2614	2614	2614
VI							2614	2614	2614
VII								5921	5921
VIII									5921
IX									

Table 37-4   Primary Pattern—Second and Third Orders

First-order Variables	Second-order Factors			Intercorrelations of Second-order Factors			
	X	XI	XII		X	XI	XII
I	6645	0000	0000	X		6646	6646
II	6645	0000	0000	XI			4415
III	6645	0000	0000	XII			
IV	0000	7695	0000				
V	0000	7695	0000	Second-order Variables	Third-order Factor XIII		
VI	0000	7695	0000				
VII	0000	0000	7695	X	1.0000		
VIII	0000	0000	7695	XI	.6645		
IX	0000	0000	7695	XII	.6645		

single orthogonal factor matrix with the number of factors equal to the sum of the factors in all orders. A matrix of this type is presented in Table 37–5. In the present example, if communalities for the third factor had not been accurately estimated, a further rotation would have been necessary after the transformation in order to collapse the two general factors into one. The choice of factors to rotate, however, would have been subjective; with accurate communalities the transformation automatically collapses the factors in question into a single factor. With this final orthogonal matrix there are no difficulties in trying to interpret factors in two or three orders—all factors are in the same order, all variables have a factor loading on each factor, and comparisons of loadings of different variables can readily be made.

The characteristics of the final transformed factor matrix can be likened to the growth of a tree. A main trunk, or trunks, branches into several limbs. These in turn branch into smaller limbs until, with a final branching, the twigs farthest from the trunk are reached. Each twig can be traced back to the main trunk along a single continuous path. This model is reproduced in Figure 37–1.

One might ask at this point whether factor measures are desired for the factors at all levels of the hierarchy. One possibility, of course, is to use nothing but "twig" tests since all the information contained in tests at other levels is available in the most specific. This course of action is not recommended for the obvious reason that there would simply be too many for the user to manage, or for the psychometri-

Table 37-5   Final Orthogonal Factor Matrix in Hierarchical Order

Variables	Factors												
	I	II*	III	IV	V	VI	VII	VIII	IX	X	XI	XII	XIII
1–3	4645	0000	0000	0000	5224	0000	0000	0000	0000	0000	0000	0000	0000
4–6	4645	0000	0000	0000	0000	5224	0000	0000	0000	0000	0000	0000	0000
7–9	4645	0000	0000	0000	0000	0000	5224	0000	0000	0000	0000	0000	0000
10–12	3997	0000	4495	0000	0000	0000	0000	4997	0000	0000	0000	0000	0000
13–15	3997	0000	4495	0000	0000	0000	0000	0000	4997	0000	0000	0000	0000
16–18	3997	0000	4495	0000	0000	0000	0000	0000	0000	4997	0000	0000	0000
19–21	3997	0000	0000	4495	0000	0000	0000	0000	0000	0000	4997	0000	0000
22–24	3997	0000	0000	4495	0000	0000	0000	0000	0000	0000	0000	4997	0000
25–27	3997	0000	0000	4495	0000	0000	0000	0000	0000	0000	0000	0000	4997

* This column represents the second-order general mechanical information factor which was merged with the third-order general factor by the transformation.

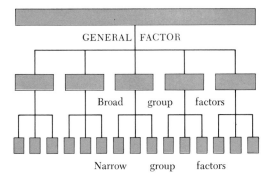

GENERAL | FACTOR

Broad   group   factors

Narrow   group   factors

Figure 37–1   *A three-stage hierarchy.*

cian to obtain adequate data on. The recommended procedure is to construct the broadest possible test, to move back toward the "trunk" as far as possible, without sacrifice of differential validity for the prediction problem at hand. Thus we can form the following guide lines for the present example: When mechanical tests are used in an aptitude battery, it is probable that the general mechanical information test is sufficiently specific. For assessing current skills for placement purposes, the area test would be necessary. In a shop training course, an examination over a small unit might be at the group level.

One might also ask how the use of the orthogonal transformation is related to the principle of parsimony which is frequently considered a primary aim of factor analysis. The direct answer is that psychological meaning is considered primary; parsimony is secondary. The most parsimonious solution with respect to number of dimensions is the unrotated use of the principal components which account for some given percentage of the total variance. A second answer is that matrices of oblique factors and their intercorrelations are no more parsimonious than the orthogonal matrix presented here when additional factors simply reflect those intercorrelations. As a matter of fact, the oblique solution may duplicate information in successive orders which results in the loss of dimensions in the orthogonal solution. In this sense the orthogonal transformation may result in a more parsi-

monious solution than the complete oblique procedure.

LIMITATION OF THE MODEL

Up until a year or so ago the preceding argument seemed very convincing, but unfortunately the hierarchical model is not sufficiently general. Consider, for example, the multitrait, multimethod matrix of Campbell and Fiske [1]. With traits along one dimension and with methods along another, as many tests are defined as the product of traits and methods. If one gets a single score, representing all methods, for each trait, a hierarchy of tests is obtained and the model seems adequate. But note that we get single scores for each trait only because we are usually interested in traits rather than in methods. It is also possible to add along the other dimension, obtaining a single score for each method, and obtain a second hierarchy. Twigs, to use the tree analogy, can no longer be traced back to a main trunk along a single path. Figure 37–2 illustrates this difficulty. Factoring of items would produce in the first order the tests of the trait-by-method matrix. Second-order factors would be both trait and method factors. The Schmid-Leiman transformation could still be used, but the resulting matrix of factor loadings would be quite complex. Even greater complexity is found if there are more than two dimensions whose prod-

Figure 37–2   *A two-facet example.*

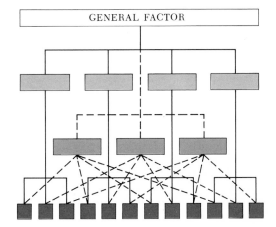

GENERAL FACTOR

uct determines the test domain. With three dimensions, in place of two routes from twigs to trunk, there are six such routes. It becomes difficult if not impossible to define all of the factors in the second and higher orders that are logically present, and the hierarchical model breaks down.

FACET THEORY

I have moved on, therefore, to what I infer Guttman [8] means by facet theory. Whether he will recognize what I have to say about facets and elements is questionable, but he must be credited with the original stimulation. Perhaps, prior to Guttman, some credit must also be given Thomson and Edward Thorndike because there is more than a superficial resemblance to their thinking. The contrast with the thinking of Spearman and Thurstone is also just as marked.

DEFINITIONS OF FACETS AND TESTS

Facets and the elements of facets are defined logically. Neither should be confused with factors. A facet is a logical dimension and its elements are the presence or absence of logically defined parts of that dimension. They must be manipulatable by the test constructor. They are not even very psychological as defined. Thus item content might be considered a facet and words, numbers, figures, and photographs would be its elements. A facet and its elements do not necessarily extend to all kinds of psychological tests. There is no necessity to strive for all-embracing categories. They may be restricted to a single domain such as achievement tests. A pragmatic test is applied to their definition, but this test does not refer to the behavior of examinees. They should be useful to the test constructor; they do not need to make a behavioral difference in all populations, or even in a single existing population. In general, they should be selected so that they are poten-

tially able to make a difference in behavior, but whether they do may depend upon finding the right people who have the right genetic or environmental background. Thus they may or may not define factors.

Facet theory *is* used to define tests. The product of all elements of all facets defines a hypothetical universe of tests and makes possible the extension of content validity standards to the aptitude area. Many combinations result in completely feasible tests; other combinations may be difficult if not impossible to construct. (I mentioned earlier that a given facet does not necessarily extend to all kinds of tests.) This universe of tests is composed of highly homogeneous tests, though a homogeneous test is not a measure of a single element. Quite the contrary. The most homogeneous test contains a single element from each applicable facet. Tests of single elements are quite heterogeneous by either common sense or statistical standards since all other dimensions must be collapsed in order to obtain behavioral reactions to the single element. The best analogy here is to a complex factorially designed analysis of variance problem possibly with incomplete blocks. This is illustrated by Figure 37–3, for a three-facet situation. In order to meas-

Figure 37–3   *Three facets creating 96 simple combinations of elements.*

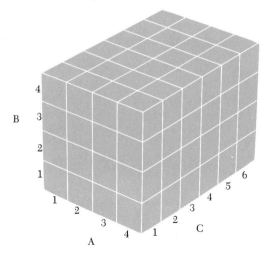

ure main effects one adds across all other dimensions. There are also interactions of various orders that are determined by the number of other dimensions over which one adds. Thus the facets and their elements not only determine a large number of quite homogeneous tests, but by collapsing one or more facets into a single score, by adding across dimensions, other broader tests are created.

For the example of Figure 37–3 a test of a general factor results by obtaining a single score for items from all (or a random sample of) the 96 cells. A series of quite broad tests results by collapsing, in succession, pairs of dimensions. Thus one can construct four tests of the A facet, by collapsing B and C, then four of the B, by adding across A and C, and finally six of the C, by adding across A and B. These broad tests are followed by narrower ones obtained by collapsing only a single dimension at a time. Thus there are 16 A B tests, 24 A C tests, and 24 B C tests. The narrowest tests are those determined by the 96 independent combinations of $4 \times 4 \times 6$ elements of the three facets.

RELATIONSHIPS TO SIMPLE STRUCTURE AND HOMOGENEITY

Consider the factoring of the set of tests, of all levels of homogeneity, systematically defined by facet theory. It is my prediction that simple structure would disappear. The beautiful examples of simple structure found with ability tests are by this reasoning the result of our test construction practices. Simple structure among human abilities reflects our ideas of what goes with what in a test. When I say that we get out only what we put in to the factor analysis, I realize that I am essentially repeating a favorite expression of Thurstone, but I also believe that my emphasis is different. I expect to find the tests constructed in accordance with these notions scattered throughout the factor space, with the exception that a positive manifold will still be found as long as negative item weights are not used, with a density depending largely on how systematically we vary the elements from test to test. The scatter will not be random, however; some elements, e.g., numbers, will produce more clustering than others will. It also follows that the simplex and circumplex patterns [7] among test intercorrelations will typically be more descriptive than factor patterns of the nature of human behavior in response to test questions when we deal with tests constructed systematically in accordance with facet theory. This, however, is a long story which I do not have time to follow up in this paper.

From the facet point of view there are no "pure" tests. One obtains better and better measures of an element by adding together as many elements on other facets as possible. Common variance associated with the element is increased while variance associated with other elements is decreased but cannot be reduced to zero by control of heterogeneity.

Facet theory thus gives one a new look at the concept of test homogeneity and the need for homogeneity. The implication for practice in test construction is deliberately to make the test as heterogeneous as possible within the limits of the definition of what you are trying to measure. This is what I meant in the preceding paragraph as "control of heterogeneity." An example of this point of view in practice might be the construction of a reasoning test. A good many tests are labeled reasoning, but one discovers in a particular example that the items are figures and only the analogies format is used. There are at least two facets of importance in reasoning: item content and item format. We can distinguish, as a minimum, the use of numbers, words, figures, and photographs as elements in the item content facet and the use of analogies, series, and classification as elements in the format facet. This 4×3 classification gives us 12 item types. All 12 should be used in the reasoning test, not just one. The only limitation on following this principle in this complete fashion is that of writing a feasible set of directions for the examinee. The deliberate introduction of maximum heterogeneity within the limits set by the definition of the test will result in a test with higher predictive validities than those with which we are familiar. Parenthetically, construct validity is not necessarily adversely affected by the lack of so-called purity. In my terms it would also be increased.

I have purposely neglected up to this point empirical studies of correlations among item types because I wished to stress the a priori analysis of facets and their elements. Correlational studies of what goes with what are, however, still useful and necessary. It may make little sense to construct all of the broad tests made possible by the facet approach, let alone many of the narrower ones, and part of the decision as to whether it makes sense is to determine whether the parts belong together empirically. Parts that don't belong together for one population at one point in time, however, may belong together in a different population or at a different point in time. Population differences may of course be either genetically or environmentally determined. Statistical analysis is important, but not controlling.

NATURE-NURTURE PROBLEM

One cannot talk about abilities for any length of time without turning to the subject of their origin. In this case we ask about the causes for differential behavior to the elements of facets. Facet theory basically has nothing to say about this question other than to recognize the opportunity for a lot of learning. Why should the switch from the analogies to the classification format make a difference in behavior? Or from the analogies to the series? I find it difficult to believe that some people are "born" to do series problems while others are born to do analogies. In general one would expect a specific learned component in every measure of each of the various element combinations. It is also possible, however, that good measures of functions likely to be genetically determined can be obtained by collapsing enough dimensions and adding together measures of enough specific element combinations. A general intelligence test constructed in accordance with this formulation would undoubtedly only partially resemble the Stanford-Binet or the Wechsler. I am certain that the "standard" intelligence test contains much too much verbal material, but a particular combination of nonverbal materials is even farther from the answer. The largest genetic contribution will probably be found in the very broadest, most heterogeneous tests.

SUMMARY

I have called attention to two unfortunate tendencies in recent work on human abilities: the proliferation of factors and the tendency to think of only the first-order factors as the primary ones. An alternative model is to place factors in hierarchical order as advocated by the British psychometricians, especially Vernon. The application of the hierarchical model to a logical hierarchy of possible tests of mechanical information is presented, some hypothetical correlations are factored in several orders, and the Schmid-Leiman transformation is used to convert the factors back into a single orthogonal matrix manifesting the hierarchical principle. The test constructor and user is free to select, for measurement purposes, factors at any level in the hierarchy that suit his needs, though it will in general be found that broad tests high in the hierarchy are most useful. The narrow, relatively specific factors that appear in the first order are placed in the hierarchy in the relatively unimportant position that their size and generality warrant.

In certain kinds of psychological data the hierarchical model breaks down. This is illustrated with respect to the multitrait-multimethod matrix of Campbell and Fiske.

As a more general way of thinking about psychological tests, facet theory of Guttman is suggested. Facet analysis would enable one to define a population of tests. It also clarifies and helps restate the need for homogeneity in a test. If a test is required for a selected element of a given facet, its homogeneity with respect to that definition is achieved only by striving for maximum heterogeneity along other facets. Controlled heterogeneity is the goal of test construction rather than maximum homogeneity in the statistical sense.

It would be nice to end this discussion with a listing of the facets and their elements that can be used in the construction of tests of human abilities. I have not spent the time on this problem that would be necessary to do an adequate job. It is also possible that my facets and elements would not be useful to another test constructor. Fortunately, Guilford has done a great deal of truly creative thinking about the structure of human intellect which can be adapted to the facet approach. Of course, he has been talking about factors rather than facets. As a consequence his definitions are frequently too psychological, and the elements are not as readily manipulatable by the test constructor as they should be, but a good many ideas suitable for the task outlined can be found in his papers. One does have to read them from the facet point of view, always keeping in mind the main idea that we do not want separate test scores for the elements, but that knowledge of the elements is necessary in order to make wise decisions about the kinds of items that should be included in a given test score to be used for a given purpose.

REFERENCES

1. CAMPBELL, D. T., & FISKE, D. W. Convergent and discriminant validation by the multitrait-multimethod matrix. *Psychol. Bull.*, 1959, **56**, 81–105.
2. CATTELL, R. B. *Factor analysis: An introduction and manual for the psychologist and social scientist.* New York: Harper, 1952.
3. FRUCHTER, B. The nature of verbal fluency. *Educ. psychol. Measmt*, 1948, **8**, 35–47.
4. GUILFORD, J. P. *Psychometric methods.* (2nd ed.) New York: McGraw-Hill, 1954.
5. GUILFORD, J. P. The structure of intellect. *Psychol. Bull.*, 1956, **53**, 267–293.
6. GUTTMAN, L. A basis for scaling qualitative data. *Amer. sociol. Rev.*, 1944, **9**, 139–150.
7. GUTTMAN, L. A new approach to factor analysis: The radex. In P. F. Lazarsfeld (Ed.), *Mathematical thinking in the social sciences.* Glencoe, Ill.: Free Press, 1954. Pp. 258–348.
8. GUTTMAN, L. An outline of some new methodology for social research. Paper read at World Association for Public Opinion Research and American Association for Public Opinion Research, Asbury Park, New Jersey, 1954.
9. HUMPHREYS, L. G. Individual differences. *Annu. Rev. Psychol.*, 1952, **3**, 131–150.
10. SCHMID, J., & LEIMAN, J. The development of hierarchical factor solutions. *Psychometrika*, 1957, **22**, 53–61.
11. THURSTONE, L. L. *Primary mental abilities.* Chicago: Univer. Chicago Press, 1938.
12. VERNON, P. E. *The structure of human abilities.* New York: Wiley, 1950.
13. WHERRY, R. J. Hierarchical solution without rotation. *Psychometrika*, 1959, **24**, 45–51.

Chapter 38

The Structure of Abilities
in a Non-Western Culture

GEORGE M. GUTHRIE

Our knowledge of the factorial structure of ability is based almost exclusively on data gathered from English speaking subjects. The degree to which factors found and confirmed in one culture will be found also in markedly different cultures remains unknown. Klineberg [11] has summarized the evidence that cultural factors make it virtually impossible to evaluate levels of ability across different cultures. For this reason, the conclusion of Porteus and Babcock [14] that marked differences in intelligence exist between different races has been questioned. The effect of environmental influences has been demonstrated within our own society, where subtle cultural factors appear to be responsible for some of the

This article is reprinted from the *Journal of Educational Psychology*, 1963, with the permission of the author and the American Psychological Association.

These data were collected during a Fulbright appointment at the Philippine Normal College, Manila. The author wishes to acknowledge the help of E. C. Ramirez, President, and his staff. He also wishes to acknowledge the helpful advice of J. W. French, S. Vandenberg, and D. R. Saunders.

differences between means found on different social groups. But the organization of abilities is another matter, and evidence is needed on the degree to which factorial structure remains constant across widely different cultures.

Among the factors that could produce differences in the factorial structure of abilities are the linguistic system, genetics, environmental demands, and the mode of life of the subjects. Whorf [23, pp. 78–83] made rather dramatic speculations about the manner in which different linguistic systems may mold a person's way of thinking. In order to evaluate the differences he postulates, we would have to study subjects whose linguistic system is considerably removed from our own, preferably some system outside of Indo-European languages. The Whorfian hypothesis, intriguing as it is, has been difficult to reduce to verifiable implications. With respect to hereditary influences, Vernon [21] insists that genetics may account for 75% of the variance in the level of ability, but he does not consider evidence on the role of genetic factors in the structure of abilities. If hereditary factors influence the level, it is possible that they also influence the correlations between samples of various abilities. Environmental demands lead to differing levels of development of abilities but whether specific demands can lead to specialized factors remains uncertain. For instance, do members of a society which leans strongly on authority and tradition develop reasoning abilities which are organized differently? Finally, the pattern of relationships between people may lead to subtle skills of interpersonal perception or memory. In some areas a different language must be used in speaking to a superior than in speaking to a subordinate. Does there emerge in such a society a set of correlated performances related to these role shifts? In short, we know that our tests are to some degree culture bound, but we do not know how general are our factors.

Since language differences are so obvious, nonverbal tests have often been used in the expectation that these would provide adequate measures which would be relatively free of cultural factors. The reports of Jahoda [9] and Scott [17], however, indicate that, in going to another culture, it is not enough simply to substitute nonverbal for verbal tests. We do not know what we are substituting because there are few reports of factored batteries on other than English speaking subjects.

Nadel [13, p. 195], reviewing the application of psychological tests in anthropological work, concluded,

We must admit the existence of different types of intelligence, and of the varied roles which different societies assign to them; we must also take them into account in constructing our tests of intelligence. . . . We should not so much be examining and measuring degrees of intelligence as analyzing different types and qualities of intelligence.

Eighteen years later Vernon [22] observed,

We must recognize that intelligence itself is a different entity in each group.

. . . Western civilization values highly symbolic reasoning . . . another group's intellect might be most fully extended in a very different field of activity say religious rituals, hunting or farming. It would be necessary then to devise tests within this field, and by means of factor analysis to arrive at the structure or makeup of the Highest Common Factor or g in the group's abilities. But if cultures were not too dissimilar, tests might be found which had good g loadings in both.

Biesheuvel [2], who has also had experience testing non-Western groups, after surveying factors that could influence test scores, suggested that by means of factor analysis "it should be possible to discover not only the basic constitutents of intelligence in any given case, but also its cultural and genetic determinants." This may be too much to hope for. He has developed his thesis with special reference to the study of African ability [3, 4].

Some of the questions about the generality of primary mental abilities may be answered by administering batteries of tests in English and in some non-Indo-European language to bilingual subjects. Vandenberg [20] has conducted such a study with Chinese students studying at American universities. He found five factors: spatial, verbal, number, memory, and perceptual speed which closely approximated those of Thurstone. In addition he found an ambiguous reasoning factor and a separate Chinese vocabulary test factor. He concluded that

. . . cultural influences play a role in the process leading to the formation of abilities underlying some of the factors, but that at least several potentialities exist in the adult human neurophysiological organization that are independent of one another and, to some extent, independent of the particular kind of cultural, linguistic, and educational background of the subjects tested.

Since the research to be reported was done in the Philippines it should be pointed out that, in addition to the work of Porteus, others who have used ability tests in the south Pacific area include Carreon [5], Dunlap [7], and Mann [12]. Each used tests in English, verbal and nonverbal; the closest approach to factor analysis was Dunlap's use of tetrad difference equations. A more detailed examination of the pattern of correlations between various tests should answer the question whether we can assume the same ability dimensions in another society.

This study is concerned with the structure of abilities in a non-Western population. The purpose is to determine the degree to which the primary mental abilities found in American samples will also appear in subjects with a different genetic, cultural, and linguistic background.

The Philippines present an unusual opportunity to clarify some of the issues on the generality of factors and the role of cultural and biological determinants in the differentiation of abilities. The population is of the Malayan race. They speak a number of Malayo-Polynesian dialects in their homes. Their environmental demands have been quite different. Their family system and patterns of interpersonal relationships depart in many ways from those of the west. At the same time, for the past 50 years they have had English as a language of instruction in the schools. Here, then, is a bilingual population to whom can be administered a standard battery of tests which has been used in American studies. While the level of performance should not be directly compared, the pattern of correlations can be examined to determine the degree to which intellectual activities group in the same manner that they do in this country. From this we may infer how primary are the primary mental abilities.

Several questions influenced the selection of tests. Would the frequently identified abilities emerge again? Would the verbal factor, which accounts for so much variance in American studies, appear as prominently in the Philippines with its less developed education emphasis? Is memory structured in the same way in the Philippines where,

with less reliance on writing, memory functions are more emphasized? In view of the perplexity Americans have sometimes experienced with Philippine reasoning processes, are reasoning factors organized there as they are in societies where people appear to reason in more familiar ways? Finally, what is the effect of giving a parallel test in a Philippine dialect?

METHOD

SUBJECTS

The subjects were women college students in education in their junior year. All were between the ages of 19 and 22. English had been the language of instruction throughout their entire school experience. More than three-quarters of the group came from the provinces of the Tagalog speaking regions near Manila on the island of Luzon. None listed English, Spanish, or Chinese as the language spoken in her home. About two-thirds listed Tagalog as her home language while the remainder listed other Philippine dialects, such as Ilocano, Bicolano, or Cebuano, all members of the Malayo-Polynesian language family. This means that all subjects were bilingual, speaking at least English and Tagalog. Many spoke several other Philippine dialects as well. Nearly all subjects appeared to revert to Tagalog or another dialect outside of the classroom. The subjects, therefore, had been raised in a Philippine language environment and had learned English in their school experience. They could take tests in either English or Tagalog.

Of some 350 subjects who were asked to participate in this study, 314 completed all of the tests. The tests were administered in groups as large as 75 in four 2-hour sessions, spaced over several weeks. The author and several Philippine proctors were present at all sessions. In order to insure familiarity with the tasks, somewhat longer explanations and practice sessions were given. All instructions were in English.

DEVELOPMENT OF THE TEST BATTERY

The battery of tests which was finally selected is shown in the order in which it was administered. The factor on which each test may load is suggested. Most of the tests were drawn from French's [8] kit. Additional tests were prepared in Tagalog, the Manila area dialect, to measure the verbal factor and ideational and verbal fluency. Tests were selected which had proven to be satisfactory measures of the verbal, numerical, spatial, and visualization factors. There were also tests of motor and of perceptual speed; of inductive, deductive, and general reasoning; and of both rote and meaningful memory. Memory functions were given special attention, with the selection of tests based on the work of Kelley [10].

Other considerations influenced the selection of tests. Since there appears to be a good deal of emphasis upon memorizing in Philippine education and less on problem solving, tests of memory functions were included with both meaningful and rote material, and with visual and auditory presentations. An index of academic achievement was included. Reasoning processes was another area of special interest. In order to control the influence of perceptual and motor speed appropriate tests were included. Similarly, fluency could spuriously raise correlations if not accounted for.

TESTS

1. Anagrams in Tagalog—Make Tagalog words from an 11-letter Tagalog word. Word fluency.
2. Topics in Tagalog—Write in Tagalog ideas about a given topic. The test topic is given in Tagalog. Ideational fluency.
3. Thing categories in Tagalog—List things in Tagalog that could have a certain characteristic. Ideational fluency.
4. Suffixes in Tagalog—List words in Tagalog ending with a given set of letters. Word fluency.
5. Following directions—Given a 5×5 matrix of letters, find which letter is indicated by increasingly complex directions. Verbal and induction. [Detroit Advanced Intelligence Test, 1.]
6. Analogies—Verbal. [Carnegie Mental Abilities Test.]
7. Number Series I—Pick out the number in a row of seven numbers which does not belong. Induction. [Detroit Advanced Intelligence Test.]
8. Disarranged Sentences—Sentences of from 5 to 12 words are presented with the word order scrambled. The subject is to indicate whether the sentence is true, false, or incomplete. Verbal and several other factors. [Carnegie Mental Ability Tests, 6.]
9. Anagrams—Make words from a 12-letter English word. Word fluency [19].
10. Number Series II—Select which of five alternative pairs of numbers will continue a series of numbers for which an introductory series of from four to seven have been presented. Induction. [Carnegie Mental Ability Tests.]
11. First and last letters in Tagalog— Words in Tagalog which begin and end with certain given letters. Word fluency.
12. Letter series—Fill in the next letter in a given series. Induction [19].
13. High Numbers—Draw a circle around each one- or two-digit number which is higher than the number on either the right or the left. Space, perceptual speed [19].
14. Spelling—Select the correctly spelled alternative from five. Word fluency, verbal [1].
15. Vocabulary—Select the word that means the same from four alternatives. Verbal [8].
16. Word Squares—Fill in the missing word in a matrix of words from a list of words. Words are selected to fulfill relationship suggested in the rows and columns. Deduction [8].
17. Same or Opposite—Draw a circle

around a word which means the same as or the opposite of the first word in a row of five words. Verbal [19].

18. Thing categories—Name as many things as possible that fall in a given category. Ideational fluency [8].

19. Writing LACK—Write this word as rapidly as possible for a given period. Speed [8].

20. Suffixes—Give as many words as possible that end in a given suffix. Word fluency [8].

21. Writing Digits—Write the Numbers 1–9 as rapidly as possible. Speed [8].

22. Mathematics Aptitude Test—Solve a series of arithmetic problems and select the right answer among five alternatives. General reasoning [8].

23. Division—Series of division problems with a one-digit divisor. Numerical [8].

24. Letter Groups—Select which four-letter group does not belong in four sets presented. Induction [8].

25. Writing x—Write x over a series of dots. Speed [8].

26. Digit Symbol—Write the same symbol under a digit as is found under that digit in a key at the top of the page. Memory. [Follows style of Wechsler.]

27. Reasoning—Draw a conclusion from two given sentences by filling in a missing word. Deduction [8].

28. Addition—Add up to three two-digit numbers. Numerical [8].

29. First Digit Cancellation—Mark out those instances in a row where the first digit of the row appears. Speed of discrimination [8].

30. Subtraction and Multiplication—Alternate rows of subtraction and multiplication problems. Numerical [8].

31. Verbal Classification—Categorize each of six words in one of two lists of four words each. Verbal [18].

32. Identical Forms—Select one of five forms which is identical with the first form in the row. Perceptual [18].

33. Paper Form Board—Mark an outlined

figure to show exact fit of a group of solid black pieces. Visualization [8].

34. Picture-Number Memory—Memorize the two-digit number that goes with each of 21 simple pictures. Memory [8].

35. Punched Holes—Mark the holes on a piece of paper if the hole had been punched with the paper folded a number of times. Visualization [8].

36. Figure Recognition—Pick out of a group of 60 pictures those 20 which were seen before. Memory [18].

37. Tagalog–non-Tagalog—The subject indicated whether or not Tagalog was the language spoken in her home.

38. Grade-Point Average. The subject's grade-point average during her junior year in college.

39. Completion—Fill in word to complete sentence with first letter of the word given. Verbal [18].

40. First Names—Recall first name when presented last name of 20 persons' names. Memory [8].

41. Word-Number Memory—Recall two-digits numbers paired with noun. Memory [18].

42. Digit Span—Digits presented orally in groups of three to nine, immediate recall. Memory.

43. Manila Story Recall—A three-paragraph story was presented orally. Recall as many ideas as possible. Meaningful memory [after 10].

44. Flags—Indicate whether same face of flag is shown on pairs of flags. Spatial [18].

45. Number Code—Learn a new number system on base 20 instead of 10. Numerical [18].

46. Tagalog Vocabulary—Select synonym for each word from four alternatives. Verbal. [Prepared especially for this research.]

47. Topics—Write as many ideas as possible about a suggested topic. Ideational fluency [8].

48. First and Last Letters—Write as many

words as possible beginning and ending with prescribed letters. Word fluency [8].

49. Number-Number Memory—Recall second number when presented first number of a pair. Memory [18].

50. Paragraph Recall—Fill in missing words in a paragraph that had been presented orally. Meaningful Memory [19].

In the testing sessions it was found that the subjects tended to give up rather quickly if the items became difficult, but they always completed the test even though they guessed after the first few items. Rarely were items omitted. The Cubes test and the False Premises test, with a two-alternative format, could not be used because the results clustered symmetrically around chance. There was little difficulty with subjects helping each other, but it was difficult to keep them from turning ahead to new tests before the instruction was given. The subjects experienced greatest difficulty understanding tests of spatial abilities. The reasons for this are not too clear, but others report the same difficulty with other subjects in this part of the world. In summary, the subjects were cooperative, but they tended to answer all items, reverting to guessing rather than sustaining effort.

RESULTS

ANALYSIS OF DATA

Product-moment correlations were computed between the scores of the tests and the matrix was first analyzed using the principal components solution with unities in the diagonal. Fourteen factors were extracted and rotated using Kaiser's varimax solution. The results are shown in Tables A–C.[1]

Subsequently the data were analyzed using a derived estimate of communalities

[1] Tables A–F have been deposited with the American Documentation Institute.

in the diagonal [15], and 22 factors extracted by the principal components method were rotated using both the varimax and ratiomax [16] solutions. The solutions are presented in Tables D–F (see Footnote 1). The extraction of such a large number of factors had the effect of dividing several factors found when only 14 were extracted. The ratiomax solution distributed the variance over the factors more evenly so that later factors accounted for more of the variance and accordingly were somewhat more readily interpreted. The results of the ratiomax solution are presented listing all tests with loadings of at least .25 on each factor.

INTERPRETATION

Of the 22 factors, 16 appear to be interpretable. The other 6 have only one high loading and, at this point, remain ambiguous. The factors are presented listing all tests with loading above .25.

Factor I	Numerical Facility	Loading
30	Subtraction and Multiplication	.77
23	Division	.72
28	Addition	.65
7	Number Series I	.27
45	Number Code	.26

This is a frequently found factor which is quite sharply delineated in this population. The simple arithmetic operations appear in a factor separate from other factors which also involve the manipulation of numbers.

Factor II	Verbal Comprehension	Loading
15	Vocabulary	.68
17	Same or Opposite	.66
39	Completion	.43
38	Grade-Point Average	.35
14	Spelling	.28
8	Disarranged Sentences	.26

This factor is specific to content presented in English. The Grade-Point Average loads higher on this factor than on any other factor. Even though facility in English is lower in this group, the verbal factor is sharply separated from reasoning and fluency factors which also involve words.

Factor III	Associative (Rote) Memory	Loading
34	Picture-Number Memory	.72
41	Word-Number Memory	.69
40	First Names	.39
49	Number-Number Memory	.35

All of the high loadings on this factor involve the association of material that does not have any particular meaningful relationship.

Factor IV	Visualization	Loading
33	Paper Form Board	.73
35	Punched Holes	.66
16	Word Squares	.25

The two visualization tests are followed by a reasoning test with a low loading. These two factors are often closely related. The differentiation of spatial ability and visualization which has been somewhat uncertain, appears here since the Flags test does not load their factor.

Factor V	A Factor Specific to Anagrams	Loading
9	Anagrams	.68
6	Analogies	.64
1	Anagrams in Tagalog	.26

When fewer factors were extracted, these three tests appeared in the word fluency factor with high loadings. It would appear that this should be considered a word fluency factor specific to anagrams regardless of the language of the test.

Factor VI	Motor Speed	Loading
25	Writing x	.63
19	Writing LACK	.60
21	Writing Digits	.36

This is clearly a motor speed factor on which some of the fluency tests have very low loadings.

Factor VII	Tagalog–Non-Tagalog	Loading
1	Anagrams in Tagalog	.74
37	Tagalog–non-Tagalog	.61
46	Tagalog Vocabulary	.26
2	Topics in Tagalog	.26

The factor is specific to the dialect background of the subjects. The vocabulary test in Tagalog loads this factor and not the general verbal factor. It is relatively specific to vocabulary and shows only a low loading of one of the fluency tests in Tagalog which were included in the battery.

Factor VIII	Ideational Fluency	Loading
47	Topics	.79
2	Topics in Tagalog	.36
18	Thing Categories	.30
3	Thing Categories in Tagalog	.28

This factor shows rather clearly that ideational fluency is not specific to the language system in which the subject is asked to work.

Factor IX	Inductive Reasoning	Loading
12	Letter Groups	.59
16	Letter Series	.50
24	Word Squares	.29

This factor was separated from a larger factor which included the visualization tests when the more extended factor extraction was carried out. In each of the tests the subject has to work out the pattern that is offered and then supply or select the item that completes or continues the pattern.

Factor X	Reasoning with Number Patterns	Loading
5	Following Directions	.61
7	Number Series I	.56
10	Number Series II	.36

This factor is somewhat obscure. It appears to involve problem solving operations with a number content.

Factor XI	Spelling	Loading
14	Spelling	.51
39	Completion	.42
20	Suffixes	.37
9	Anagrams	.26

This factor appeared with the larger verbal factor when fewer factors were extracted. The four tests involve working with the letters of a word and involve a minimum of meaning. It is interesting to note but difficult to interpret that this factor is separate from both the verbal and fluency factors. It is probably a function of the specific experiences of this population where spelling of English is strongly emphasized in schools.

Factor XII		Loading
45	Number Code	.65
6	Analogies	.31
38	Grade-Point Average	.30
43	Manila Story Recall	.25

In this population of subjects the Number Code test does not load highly the number factor as it did for Thurstone [18]. However both Number Code and Analogies loaded Thurstone's unnamed Factor 11. It would appear that this is a reasoning factor of some sort. There may be an element of understanding the task involved since many subjects had trouble with the instructions for the Number Code test.

Factor XIII	Word Fluency	Loading
4	Suffixes in Tagalog	.61
3	Thing Categories in Tagalog	.39
20	Suffixes	.34

This is a rather poorly defined word fluency factor. The First and Last Letters test in English appears in Factor XIV with a number of memory tests, while the parallel test in Tagalog shows its highest loading on Factor XVII, an unidentified factor with a good many fluency tests.

Factor XIV		Loading
48	First and Last Letters	.59
49	Number-Number Memory	.48
40	First Names	.27
41	Word-Number Memory	.25

This factor has one fluency and three memory tests. It would appear to involve an ability to recall according to certain rules. For reasons that are not at all clear

the First and Last Letters test, ordinarily thought a measure of word fluency, does not load fluency factors for this population. It may be an expression of their memorizing approach to the learning of English.

Factor XV	Facility with Digits	Loading
26	Digit Symbol	.69
21	Writing Digits	.47
22	Mathematics Aptitude Test	.26

This factor is restricted to material involving digits and appears to represent some facility or confidence in handling them. It may be a product of the methods used in teaching mathematics.

Factor XVI	Deductive Reasoning	Loading
10	Number Series II	.48
31	Verbal Classification	.42
50	Paragraph Recall	.41
27	Reasoning	.29
8	Disarranged Sentences	.28

These tests, insofar as they have a common element, appear to involve a deductive reasoning process. There is an element in each of these tests of evaluating the plausibility of alternative solutions or getting a sense of the abstraction involved in the problem.

Factor XVII		Loading
11	First and Last Letters in Tagalog	.58
2	Topics in Tagalog	.31
18	Thing Categories	.29
13	High Numbers	.27
20	Suffixes	.25

As was the case in the First and Last Letters test in English, the parallel test in Tagalog does not load highly the Word Fluency factor. Four of the five tests on this factor have been found to measure either Word or Ideational Fluency. It would appear that these two fluency factors may not be so sharply differentiated in this population.

Factor XVIII	Perceptual Speed	Loading
29	First Digit Cancellation	.60
32	Identical Forms	.41

This factor has been found in many studies.

Factor XIX		Loading
44	Flags	.53
20	Suffixes	.26
27	Reasoning	.26

With the elimination of the Cubes test, there was only one test in the battery designed to measure spatial ability. For this reason, a good space factor cannot be expected.

Factor XX	Span Memory	Loading
40	First Names	.59
42	Digit Span	.37

This factor is concerned with memory span. Notice that Paragraph Recall or meaningful memory does not load this factor. Other rote memory tests show loadings which approach .25.

Factor XXI		Loading
36	Figure Recognition	.61
50	Paragraph Recall	.35

Figure Recognition is the only visual recall test in the battery. A visual memory factor might have appeared if more tests which required the recall of visually presented material had been included.

Factor XXII		Loading
22	Mathematics Aptitude Test	.58
2	Topics in Tagalog	.29

As it stands, no interpretation of this factor is offered. Interpretation might have been possible if more general reasoning tests had been included. It should be noted that the Mathematics Aptitude Test does not load numerical or other reasoning factors with this group.

DISCUSSION

There is rather clear evidence that certain factors have emerged in this population which are clearly replications of earlier factors. These include numerical, verbal, rote memory, visualization, motor speed, perceptual speed, and ideational fluency. The cross-cultural status of reasoning factors is obscure. Our Factors IX, X, XII, and XVI are probably reasoning factors but they are not readily matched with results on American subjects. In order to clarify the differences in reasoning, if such exist, it would be necessary to include tests in Tagalog as well as English. The interesting point is that reasoning processes do show at least four factors when tests are given in English to these subjects, who for the most part do not habitually think in English.

The emergence of separate vocabulary factors in English and Tagalog parallels the findings of Vandenberg [20]. This is in contrast to the ideational fluency and anagrams factors which include tests in both languages. In view of this central role of the verbal factor in academic progress this finding may have considerable implications for educational exchanges.

Factors XI and XV appear to be products of the Philippine educational system. Spelling of English words is a more specific skill which can be separated from verbal facility. No spelling test was offered in Tagalog since Tagalog is written phonetically in western script. Similarly, facility with digits is differentiated from numerical ability. This is possibly a product of the method by which mathematics was taught to these subjects.

Memory tests were included because it has been said that Philippine education emphasizes memory at the expense of understanding. Four factors emerged: III, XIV, XX, and XXI, which are in whole or part memory factors. Rote memory appears clearly as Factor III, but meaningful memory tests appear on verbal, fluency, and reasoning factors and do not themselves define a factor. Factors XX and XXI are not very convincing instances of span or visual memory factors. Since the Grade-Point Average does not load any of the memory factors, there is little evidence in these results of the prevalence of memory activities said by some to so characterize Philippine education and oriental education generally. It may be that the lower facility in English of these subjects inhibits their spontaneity in that language and so gives rise to the frequent observation that these students rely heavily on memorizing. Parallel tests in Tagalog would possibly clarify some of these issues.

The Word Fluency tests in English and Tagalog do not appear on the same factor. There is much less evidence for a common word fluency factor across languages than for the ideational fluency factor. The First and Last Letters test in English may be more a measure of memory for this group. The same test in Tagalog appears with the heaviest loading on Factor XVII, a factor which is difficult to interpret. We are led to conclude that word fluency as measured by the tests in this battery is a very tenuously defined factor.

From these results we may generalize that the most frequently identified ability factors can be identified in this population. There are, however, verbal factors specific to the language in which the test is given. Other factors emerge which are possibly the product of instructional methods. These factors, obtained on tests given in English, tend to be more specific reflecting the fact that English is not the native language of the subjects and, with lower facility, less generalization of ability has taken place. Finally, all subjects were women. There is little systematic evidence whether the sex of subjects makes a difference in such a study as this. However, the possibility remains that results with male subjects or both sexes would not be the same.

In the same way that cross-culture studies of personality have shed much light on the modifiability of personality, and have offered opportunities to observe different effects on development of different environmental influences, cross-culture studies of the structure of abilities should clarify the role of environmental factors in the structure and development of abilities.

Bilingual populations afford an unusual opportunity for this kind of investigation since they can be given equivalent forms in two languages. Reasoning and memory activities represent especially fruitful areas for further investigation. Much remains to be done, however, to determine how equivalent tests are in dissimilar languages and how much a society influences the subject's definition of the testing situation itself.

REFERENCES

1. BAKER, H. J. *Detroit Advanced Intelligence Test.* Bloomington, Ill.: Public School Publishing, 1925.
2. BIESHEUVEL, S. Psychological tests and their application to non-European peoples. In G. B. Jeffrey (Ed.), *The year book of education.* London: Evans, 1949. Pp. 87–117.
3. BIESHEUVEL, S. The study of African ability: I. Intellectual potential of Africans. *Afr. Stud.,* 1952, **11,** 45–58.
4. BIESHEUVEL, S. The study of African ability: II. A survey of some research problems. *Afr. Stud.,* 1952, **11,** 105–117.
5. CARREON, M. L. *Philippine studies in mental measurement.* Yonkers-on-Hudson, New York: World Book, 1926.
6. CLEETON, G. U. *Carnegie Mental Ability Tests: Form A.* New York: Houghton Mifflin, 1932.
7. DUNLAP, J. W. Race differences in the organization of numerical and verbal abilities. *Arch. Psychol., N. Y.,* 1931. No. 124.
8. FRENCH, J. W. *Kit of selected tests for reference aptitude and achievement factors.* Princeton: Educational Testing Service, 1954.
9. JAHODA, G. Assessment of abstract behavior in a non-Western culture. *J. abnorm. soc. Psychol.,* 1956, **53,** 237–243.
10. KELLEY, H. P. *A factor analysis of memory ability.* Princeton: Princeton University, 1954.
11. KLINEBERG, O. *Race differences.* New York: Harper, 1935.
12. MANN, C. W. A test of general ability in Fiji. *J. genet. Psychol.,* 1939, **54,** 435–454.
13. NADEL, S. F. The application of intelligence tests in the anthropological field. In

F. C. Bartlett (Ed.), *The study of society, methods and problems*. New York: Macmillan, 1939. Pp. 184–198.

14. PORTEUS, S. D., & BABCOCK, M. E. *Temperament and race*. Boston: Gorham, 1926.

15. SAUNDERS, D. R. *The contribution of communality estimation to the achievement of factorial invariance*. (Res. Bull. No. 60–5) Princeton: Educational Testing Service, 1960.

16. SAUNDERS, D. R. Integrating the implementation of quartimax, varimax, oblimax and related rotational procedures. *Psychol. Rep.*, 1962, **10**, 241–242.

17. SCOTT, G. C. Measuring Sudanese intelligence. *Brit. J. educ. Psychol.*, 1950, **20**, 43–54.

18. THURSTONE, L. L. Primary mental abilities. *Psychometr. Monogr.*, 1938, No. 1.

19. THURSTONE, L. L., & THURSTONE, T. F. Factorial studies of intelligence. *Psychometr. Monogr.*, 1941, No. 2.

20. VANDENBERG, S. G. The primary mental abilities of Chinese students. *Ann. N.Y. Acad. Sci.*, 1959, **79**, 257–304.

21. VERNON, P. E. Recent investigations of intelligence and its measurement. *Eugen. Rev.*, 1951, **43**, 125–137.

22. VERNON, P. E. Use of intelligence tests in population studies. *Eugen. Quart.*, 1954, **1**, 221–224.

23. WHORF, B. L. *Language, thought and reality*. New York: Wiley, 1956.

Chapter 39

The Discovery and Encouragement
of Exceptional Talent

LEWIS M. TERMAN

I have often been asked how I happened to become interested in mental tests and gifted children. My first introduction to the scientific problems posed by intellectual differences occurred well over a half-century ago when I was a senior in psychology at Indiana University and was asked to prepare two reports for a seminar, one on mental deficiency and one on genius. Up to that time, despite the fact that I had graduated from a normal college as a Bachelor of Pedagogy and had taught school for five years, I had never so much as heard of a mental test. The reading for those two reports opened up a new world to me, the world of Galton, Binet, and their contemporaries. The following year my MA thesis on leadership among children [10] was based in part on tests used by Binet in his studies of suggestibility.

This article is reprinted from the *American Psychologist*, 1954, with the permission of the American Psychological Association. The article was originally the first Walter V. Bingham Memorial Lecture given at University of California at Berkeley, on March 25, 1954.

Then I entered Clark University, where I spent considerable time during the first year in reading on mental tests and precocious children. Child prodigies, I soon learned, were at that time in bad repute because of the prevailing belief that they were usually psychotic or otherwise abnormal and almost sure to burn themselves out quickly or to develop postadolescent stupidity. "Early ripe, early rot" was a slogan frequently encountered. By the time I reached my last graduate year, I decided to find out for myself how precocious children differ from the mentally backward, and accordingly chose as my doctoral dissertation an experimental study of the intellectual processes of fourteen boys, seven of them picked as the brightest and seven as the dullest in a large city school [11]. These subjects I put through a great variety of intelligence tests, some of them borrowed from Binet and others, many of them new. The tests were given individually and required a total of 40 or 50 hours for each subject. The experiment contributed little or nothing to science, but it contributed a lot to my

469

future thinking. Besides "selling" me completely on the value of mental tests as a research method, it offered an ideal escape from the kinds of laboratory work which I disliked and in which I was more than ordinarily inept. (Edward Thorndike confessed to me once that *his* lack of mechanical skill was partly responsible for turning *him* to mental tests and to the kinds of experiments on learning that required no apparatus.)

However, it was not until I got to Stanford in 1910 that I was able to pick up with mental tests where I had left off at Clark University. By that time Binet's 1905 and 1908 scales had been published, and the first thing I undertook at Stanford was a tentative revision of his 1908 scale. This, after further revisions, was published in 1916. The standardization of the scale was based on tests of a thousand children whose IQ's ranged from 60 to 145. The contrast in intellectual performance between the dullest and the brightest of a given age so intensified my earlier interest in the gifted that I decided to launch an ambitious study of such children at the earliest opportunity.

My dream was realized in the spring of 1921 when I obtained a generous grant from the Commonwealth Fund of New York City for the purpose of locating a thousand subjects of IQ 140 or higher. More than that number were selected by Stanford-Binet tests from the kindergarten through the eighth grade, and a group mental test given in 95 high schools provided nearly 400 additional subjects. The latter, plus those I had located before 1921, brought the number close to 1,500. The average IQ was approximately 150, and 80 were 170 or higher [13].

The twofold purpose of the project was, first of all, to find what traits characterize children of high IQ, and secondly, to follow them for as many years as possible to see what kind of adults they might become. This meant that it was necessary to select a group representative of high-testing children in general. With the help of four field assistants, we canvassed a school population of nearly a quarter-million in the urban and semi-urban areas of California. Two careful checks on the methods used showed that not more than 10 or 12 per cent of the children who could have qualified for the group in the schools canvassed were missed. A sample of close to 90 per cent insured that whatever traits were typical of these children would be typical of high-testing children in any comparable school population.

Time does not permit me to describe the physical measurements, medical examinations, achievement tests, character and interest tests, or the trait ratings and other supplementary information obtained from parents and teachers. Nor can I here describe the comparative data we obtained for control groups of unselected children. The more important results, however, can be stated briefly: children of IQ 140 or higher are, in general, appreciably superior to unselected children in physique, health, and social adjustment; markedly superior in moral attitudes as measured either by character tests or by trait ratings; and vastly superior in their mastery of school subjects as shown by a three-hour battery of achievement tests. In fact, the typical child of the group had mastered the school subjects to a point about two grades beyond the one in which he was enrolled, some of them three or four grades beyond. Moreover, his ability as evidenced by achievement in the different school subjects is so general as to refute completely the traditional belief that gifted children are usually one-sided. I take some pride in the fact that not one of the major conclusions we drew in the early 1920's regarding the traits that are typical of gifted children has been overthrown in the three decades since then.

Results of thirty years' follow-up of these subjects by field studies in 1927–28, 1939–40, and 1951–52, and by mail follow-up at other dates, show that the incidence of mortality, ill health, insanity, and alcoholism is in each case below that for the generality of corresponding age, that the great majority are still well adjusted socially, and that the delinquency rate is but a fraction of what it is in the general population. Two forms of our difficult Concept Mastery Test, devised especially to reach into the stratosphere of adult intelligence, have been administered to all members of the group who could be visited by the field assistants, including some 950 tested in 1939–40 and more than 1,000 in 1951–52. On both tests they scored on the average about as far above the generality of adults as they had scored above the generality of children when we selected them. Moreover, as Dr. Bayley and Mrs. Oden have shown, in the twelve-year interval between the two tests, 90 per cent increased their intellectual stature as measured by this test. "Early ripe, early rot" simply does not hold for these subjects. So far, no one has developed postadolescent stupidity!

As for schooling, close to 90 per cent entered college and 70 per cent graduated. Of those graduating, 30 per cent were awarded honors and about two-thirds remained for graduate work. The educational record would have been still better but for the fact that a majority reached college age during the great depression. In their undergraduate years 40 per cent of the men and 20 per cent of the women earned half or more of their college expenses, and the total of undergraduate and graduate expenses earned amounted to $670,000, not counting stipends from scholarships and fellowships, which amounted to $350,000.

The cooperation of the subjects is indicated by the fact that we have been able to keep track of more than 98 per cent of the original group, thanks to the rapport fostered by the incomparable field and office assistants I have had from the beginning of the study to the present. I dislike to think how differently things could have gone with helpers even a little less competent.

The achievement of the group to midlife is best illustrated by the case histories of the 800 men, since only a minority of the women have gone out for professional careers [15]. By 1950, when the men had an average age of 40 years, they had published 67 books (including 46 in the fields of science, arts, and the humanities, and 21 books of fiction). They had published more than 1,400 scientific, technical, and professional articles; over 200 short stories, novelettes, and plays; and 236 miscellaneous articles on a great variety of subjects. They had also authored more than 150 patents. The figures on publications do not include the hundreds of publications by journalists that classify as news stories, editorials, or newspaper columns; nor do they include the hundreds if not thousands of radio and TV scripts.

The 800 men include 78 who have taken a PhD degree or its equivalent, 48 with a medical degree, 85 with a law degree, 74 who are teaching or have taught in a four-year college or university, 51 who have done basic research in the physical sciences or engineering, and 104 who are engineers but have done only applied research or none. Of the scientists, 47 are listed in the 1949 edition of *American Men of Science*. Nearly all of these numbers are from 10 to 20 or 30 times as large as would be found for 800 men of corresponding age picked at random in the general population, and are sufficient answer to those who belittle the significance of IQ differences.

The follow-up of these gifted subjects has proved beyond question that tests of "general intelligence," given as early as six, eight, or ten years, tell a great deal about the ability to achieve either presently or 30 years hence. Such tests do not, however, enable us to predict what direction the achievement will take, and least of all do they tell us what personality factors or what accidents of fortune will affect the fruition of exceptional ability. Granting that both interest patterns and special aptitudes play important roles in the making of a gifted scientist, mathematician, mechanic, artist, poet, or musical composer, I am convinced that to achieve greatly in almost any field, the special talents have to be backed up by a lot of Spearman's g, by which is meant the kind of general intelligence that requires ability to form many sharply defined concepts, to manipulate them, and to perceive subtle relationships between them; in other words, the ability to engage in abstract thinking.

The study by Catharine Cox of the childhood traits of historical geniuses gives additional evidence regarding the role of general intelligence in exceptional achievement. That study was part of our original plan to investigate superior ability by two methods of approach: (a) by identifying and following living gifted subjects from childhood onward; and (b) by proceeding in the opposite direction and tracing the mature genius back to his childhood promise. With a second grant from the Commonwealth Fund, the latter approach got under way only a year later than the former and resulted in the magnum opus by Cox entitled *The Early Mental Traits of Three Hundred Geniuses* [1]. Her subjects represented an unbiased selection from the top 510 in Cattell's objectively compiled list of the 1,000 most eminent men of history. Cox and two able assistants then scanned some 3,000 biographies in search of information that would throw light on the early mental development of these subjects. The information thus obtained filled more than 6,000 typed pages. Next, three psychologists familiar with mental age norms read the documentary evidence on all the subjects and estimated for each the IQ that presumably would be necessary to account for the intellectual behavior recorded for given chronological ages. Average of the three IQ estimates was used as the index of intelligence. In fact two IQ's were estimated for each subject, one based on the evidence to age 17, and the other on evidence to the mid-twenties. The recorded evidence on development to age 17 varied from very little to an amount that yielded about as valid an IQ as a good intelligence test would give. Examples of the latter are Goethe, John Stuart Mill, and Francis Galton. It was the documentary information on Galton, which I summarized and

published in 1917 [12], that decided me to prepare plans for the kind of study that was carried out by Cox. The average of estimated IQ's for her 300 geniuses was 155, with many going as high as 175 and several as high as 200. Estimates below 120 occurred only when there was little biographical evidence about the early years.

It is easy to scoff at these post-mortem IQ's, but as one of the three psychologists who examined the evidence and made the IQ ratings, I think the author's main conclusion is fully warranted; namely, that "the genius who achieves highest eminence is one whom intelligence tests would have identified as gifted in childhood."

Special attention was given the geniuses who had sometime or other been labeled as backward in childhood, and in every one of these cases the facts clearly contradicted the legend. One of them was Oliver Goldsmith, of whom his childhood teacher is said to have said "Never was so dull a boy." The fact is that little Oliver was writing clever verse at 7 years and at 8 was reading Ovid and Horace. Another was Sir Walter Scott, who at 7 not only read widely in poetry but was using correctly in his written prose such words as "melancholy" and "exotic." Other alleged childhood dullards included a number who disliked the usual diet of Latin and Greek but had a natural talent for science. Among these were the celebrated German chemist Justus von Liebig, the great English anatomist John Hunter, and the naturalist Alexander von Humboldt, whose name is scattered so widely over the maps of the world.

In the cases just cited one notes a tendency for the direction of later achievement to be foreshadowed by the interests and preoccupations of childhood. I have tried to determine how frequently this was true of the 100 subjects in Cox's group whose childhood was best documented. Very marked foreshadowing was noted in the case of more than half of the group, none at all in less than a fourth. Macaulay, for example, began his career as historian at the age of 6 with what he called a

"Compendium of Universal History," filling a quire of paper before he lost interest in the project. Ben Franklin before the age of 17 had displayed nearly all the traits that characterized him in middle life: scientific curiosity, religious heterodoxy, wit and buffoonery, political and business shrewdness, and ability to write. At 11 Pascal was so interested in mathematics that his father thought it best to deprive him of books on this subject until he had first mastered Latin and Greek. Pascal secretly proceeded to construct a geometry of his own and covered the ground as far as the 32nd proposition of Euclid. His father then relented. At 14 Leibnitz was writing on logic and philosophy and composing what he called "An Alphabet of Human Thought." He relates that at this age he took a walk one afternoon to consider whether he should accept the "doctrine of substantial forms."

Similar foreshadowing is disclosed by the case histories of my gifted subjects. A recent study of the scientists and non-scientists among our 800 gifted men [15] showed many highly significant differences between the early interests and social attitudes of those who became physical scientists and those who majored in the social sciences, law, or the humanities. Those in medical or biological sciences usually rated on such variables somewhere between the physical scientists and the nonscientists.

What I especially want to emphasize, however, is that both the evidence on early mental development of historical geniuses and that obtained by follow-up of gifted subjects selected in childhood by mental tests point to the conclusion that capacity to achieve far beyond the average can be detected early in life by a well-constructed ability test that is heavily weighted with the g factor. It remains to be seen how much the prediction of future achievement can be made more specific as to field by getting, in addition, measures of ability factors that are largely independent of g. It would seem that a 20-year follow-up of the thousands of school children who have been given Thurstone's test of seven "primary mental abilities" would help to provide the answer. At present the factor analysts don't agree on how many "primary" mental abilities there are, nor exactly on what they are. The experts in this field are divided into two schools. The British school, represented by Thomson, Vernon, and Burt, usually stop with the identification of at most three or four group factors in addition to g, while some representing the American school feed the scores of 40 or 50 kinds of tests into a hopper and manage to extract from them what they believe to be a dozen or fifteen separate factors. Members of the British school are as a rule very skeptical about the realities underlying the minor group factors. There are also American psychologists, highly skilled in psychometrics, who share this skepticism. It is to be hoped that further research will give us more information than we now have about the predictive value of the group factors. Until such information is available, the scores on group factors can contribute little to vocational guidance beyond what a good test of general intelligence will provide.

I have always stressed the importance of *early* discovery of exceptional abilities. Its importance is now highlighted by the facts Harvey Lehman has disclosed in his monumental studies of the relation between age and creative achievement [8]. The striking thing about his age curves is how early in life the period of maximum creativity is reached. In nearly all fields of science, the best work is done between ages 25 and 35, and rarely later than 40. The peak productivity for works of lesser merit is usually reached 5 to 10 years later; this is true in some twenty fields of science, in philosophy, in most kinds of musical composition, in art, and in literature of many varieties. The lesson for us from Lehman's statistics is that the youth of high achievement potential should be well trained for his life work before too many of his most creative years have been passed.

This raises the issue of educational acceleration for the gifted. It seems that the schools are more opposed to acceleration now than they were thirty years ago. The lockstep seems to have become more and more the fashion, notwithstanding the fact that practically everyone who has investigated the subject is against it. Of my gifted group, 29 per cent managed to graduate from high school before the age of 16½ years (62 of these before 15½), but I doubt if so many would be allowed to do so now. The other 71 per cent graduated between 16½ and 18½. We have compared the accelerated with the nonaccelerated on numerous case-history variables. The two groups differed very little in childhood IQ, their health records are equally good, and as adults they are equally well adjusted socially. More of the accelerates graduated from college, and on the average nearly a year and a half earlier than the nonaccelerates; they averaged higher in college grades and more often remained for graduate work. Moreover, the accelerates on the average married .7 of a year earlier, have a trifle lower divorce rate, and score just a little higher on a test of marital happiness [14]. So far as college records of accelerates and nonaccelerates are concerned, our data closely parallel those obtained by the late Noel Keys [3] at the University of California and those by Pressey [9] and his associates at Ohio State University.

The Ford Fund for the Advancement of Education has awarded annually since 1951 some 400 college scholarships to gifted students who are not over 16½ years old, are a year or even two years short of high school graduation, but show good evidence of ability to do college work. Three quarters of them are between 15½ and 16½ at the time of college entrance. A dozen colleges and universities accept these students and are keeping close track of their success. A summary of their records for the first year shows that they not only get higher grades than their classmates, who average about two years older, but that they are also equally well adjusted socially and participate in as many extracurricular activities [17]. The main problem the boys have is in

finding girls to date who are not too old for them! Some of them have started a campaign to remedy the situation by urging that more of these scholarships be awarded to girls.

The facts I have given do not mean that all gifted children should be rushed through school just as rapidly as possible. If that were done, a majority with IQ of 140 could graduate from high school before the age of 15. I do believe, however, that such children should be promoted rapidly enough to permit college entrance by the age of 17 at latest, and that a majority would be better off to enter at 16. The exceptionally bright student who is kept with his age group finds little to challenge his intelligence and all too often develops habits of laziness that later wreck his college career. I could give you some choice examples of this in my gifted group. In the case of a college student who is preparing for a profession in science, medicine, law, or any field of advanced scholarship, graduation at 20 instead of the usual 22 means two years added to his professional career; or the two years saved could be used for additional training beyond the doctorate, if that were deemed preferable.

Learned and Wood [7] have shown by objective achievement tests in some 40 Pennsylvania colleges how little correlation there is between the student's knowledge and the number of months or years of his college attendance. They found some beginning sophomores who had acquired more knowledge than some seniors near their graduation. They found similarly low correlations between the number of course units a student had in a given field and the amount he knew in that field. Some with only one year of Latin had learned more than others with three years. And, believe it or not, they even found boys just graduating from high school who had more knowledge of science than some college seniors who had majored in science and were about to begin teaching science in high schools! The sensible thing to do, it seems, would be to quit crediting the individual high school or the individual college and begin crediting the individual student. That, essentially, is what the Ford Fund scholarships are intended to encourage.

Instruments that permit the identification of gifted subjects are available in great variety and at nearly all levels from the primary grades to the graduate schools in universities. My rough guess is that at the present time tests of achievement in the school subjects are being given in this country to children below high school at a rate of perhaps ten or twelve million a year, and to high school students another million or two. In addition, perhaps two million tests of intelligence are given annually in the elementary and high schools. The testing of college students began in a small way only 30 years ago; now almost every college in the country requires applicants for admission to take some kind of aptitude test. This is usually a test of general aptitude, but subject-matter tests and tests of special aptitudes are sometimes given to supplement the tests of general aptitude.

The testing movement has also spread rapidly in other countries, especially in Britain and the Commonwealth countries. Godfrey Thomson devised what is now called the Moray House test of intelligence in 1921 to aid in selecting the more gifted 11-year-olds in the primary schools for the privilege of free secondary education. This test has been revised and is given annually to about a half million scholarship candidates. The Moray House tests now include tests of English, arithmetic, and history. In 1932 the Scottish Council for Research in Education [18] arranged to give the Moray House test of intelligence (a group test) to all the 90,000 children in Scotland who were born in 1921, and actually tested some 87,000 of them. The Stanford-Binet tests have been translated and adapted for use in nearly all the countries of Europe and in several countries of Asia and Latin America. Behind the Iron Curtain, however, mental tests are now banned.

I have discussed only tests of intelligence and of school achievement. There is time to mention only a few of the many kinds of personality tests that have been developed during the last thirty-five years: personality inventories, projective techniques by the dozen, attitude scales by the hundred, interest tests, tests of psychotic and predelinquent tendencies, tests of leadership, marital aptitude, masculinity-femininity, et cetera. The current output of research on personality tests probably equals or exceeds that on intelligence and achievement tests, and is even more exciting.

Along with the increasing use of tests, and perhaps largely as a result of it, there is a growing interest, both here and abroad, in improving educational methods for the gifted. Acceleration of a year or two or three, however desirable, is but a fraction of what is needed to keep the gifted child or youth working at his intellectual best. The method most often advocated is curriculum enrichment for the gifted without segregating them from the ordinary class. Under ideal conditions enrichment can accomplish much, but in these days of crowded schools, when so many teachers are overworked, underpaid, and inadequately trained, curriculum enrichment for a few gifted in a large mixed class cannot begin to solve the problem. The best survey of thought and action in this field of education is the book entitled *The Gifted Child,* written by many authors and published in 1951 [16]. In planning for and sponsoring this book, The American Association for Gifted Children has rendered a great service to education.

But however efficient our tests may be in discovering exceptional talents, and whatever the schools may do to foster those discovered, it is the prevailing *Zeitgeist* that will decide, by the rewards it gives or withholds, what talents will come to flower. In Western Europe of the Middle Ages, the favored talents were those that served the Church by providing its priests, the architects of its cathedrals, and the painters of religious themes. A few centuries later the same countries had a renaissance that included science and literature as well as the arts. Although presumably there are as many potential composers of great music as there ever were, and as many potentially great artists as in the days of Leonardo da Vinci and Michaelangelo, I am reliably informed that in this country today it is almost impossible for a composer of *serious* music to earn his living except by teaching, and that the situation is much the same, though somewhat less critical, with respect to artists.

The talents most favored by the current *Zeitgeist* are those that can contribute to science and technology. If intelligence and achievement tests don't discover the potential scientist, there is a good chance that the annual Science Talent Search will, though not until the high school years. Since Westinghouse inaugurated in 1942 this annual search for the high school seniors most likely to become creative scientists, nearly 4,000 boys and girls have been picked for honors by Science Service out of the many thousands who have competed. As a result, "Science Clubs of America" now number 15,000 with a third of a million members—a twentyfold increase in a dozen years [2]. As our need for more and better scientists is real and urgent, one can rejoice at what the talent search and the science clubs are accomplishing. One may regret, however, that the spirit of the times is not equally favorable to the discovery and encouragement of potential poets, prose writers, artists, statesmen, and social leaders.

But in addition to the over-all climates that reflect the *Zeitgeist*, there are localized climates that favor or hinder the encouragement of given talents in particular colleges and universities. I have in mind especially two recent investigations of the differences among colleges in the later achievement of their graduates. One by Knapp and Goodrich [4] dealt with the undergraduate origin of 18,000 scientists who got the bachelor's degree between 1924 and 1934 and were listed in the 1944 edition of *American Men of Science*. The list of 18,000 was composed chiefly of men who

had taken a PhD degree, but included a few without a PhD who were starred scientists. The IBM cards for these men were then sorted according to the college from which they obtained the bachelor's degree, and an index of productivity was computed for each college in terms of the proportion of its male graduates who were in the list of 18,000. Some of the results were surprising, not to say sensational. The institutions that were most productive of future scientists between 1924 and 1934 were not the great universities, but the small liberal arts colleges. Reed College topped the list with an index of 132 per thousand male graduates. The California Institute of Technology was second with an index of 70. Kalamazoo College was third with 66, Earlham fourth with 57, and Oberlin fifth with 56. Only a half-dozen of the great universities were in the top fifty with a productivity index of 25 or more.

The second study referred to was by Knapp and Greenbaum [5], who rated educational institutions according to the proportion of their graduates who received certain awards at the graduate level in the six-year period from 1946 to 1951. Three kinds of awards were considered: a PhD degree, a graduate scholarship or fellowship paying at least $400 a year, or a prize at the graduate level won in open competition. The roster of awardees they compiled included 7,000 students who had graduated from 377 colleges and universities. This study differs from the former in three respects: (*a*) it deals with recent graduates, who had not had time to become distinguished but who could be regarded as good bets for the future; (*b*) these good bets were classified according to whether the major field was science, social science, or the humanities; and (*c*) data were obtained for both sexes, though what I shall report here relates only to men. In this study the great universities make a better showing than in the other, but still only a dozen of them are in the top fifty institutions in the production of men who are good bets. In the top ten, the University of Chicago is third, Princeton is eighth, and Harvard is tenth; the other seven in order of rank are Swarthmore 1, Reed 2, Oberlin 4, Haverford 5, California Institute of Technology 6, Carleton 7, and Antioch 9. When the schools were listed separately for production of men who were good bets in science, social science, and the humanities, there were eight that rated in the top twenty on all three lists. These were Swarthmore, Reed, Chicago, Harvard, Oberlin, Antioch, Carleton, and Princeton.

The causes of these differences are not entirely clear. Scores on aptitude tests show that the intelligence of students in a given institution is by no means the sole factor, though it is an important one. Other important factors are the quality of the school's intellectual climate, the proportion of able and inspiring teachers on its faculty, and the amount of conscious effort that is made not only to discover but also to motivate the most highly gifted. The influence of motivation can hardly be exaggerated.

In this address I have twice alluded to the fact that achievement in school is influenced by many things other than the sum total of intellectual abilities. The same is true of success in life. In closing I will tell you briefly about an attempt we made a dozen years ago to identify some of the nonintellectual factors that have influenced life success among the men in my gifted group. Three judges, working independently, examined the records (to 1940) of the 730 men who were then 25 years old or older, and rated each on life success. The criterion of "success" was the extent to which a subject had made use of his superior intellectual ability, little weight being given to earned income. The 150 men rated highest for success and the 150 rated lowest were then compared on some 200 items of information obtained from childhood onward [14]. How did the two groups differ?

During the elementary school years, the A's and C's (as we call them) were almost equally successful. The average grades were about the same, and average scores on achievement tests were only a trifle higher for the A's. Early in high school the groups began to draw apart in scholarship, and by the end of high school, the slump of the C's was quite marked. The slump could not be blamed on extracurricular activities, for these were almost twice as common among the A's. Nor was much of it due to difference in intelligence. Although the A's tested on the average a little higher than the C's both in 1922 and 1940, the average score made by the C's in 1940 was high enough to permit brilliant college work, in fact was equaled by only 15 per cent of our highly selected Stanford students. Of the A's, 97 per cent entered college and 90 per cent graduated; of the C's, 68 per cent entered but only 37 per cent graduated. Of those who graduated, 52 per cent of the A's but only 14 per cent of the C's graduated with honors. The A's were also more accelerated in school; on the average they were six months younger on completing the eighth grade, 10 months younger at high school graduation, and 15 months younger at graduation from college.

The differences between the educational histories of the A's and C's reflect to some degree the differences in their family backgrounds. Half of the A fathers but only 15 per cent of the C fathers were college graduates, and twice as many of A siblings as of C siblings graduated. The estimated number of books in the A homes was nearly 50 per cent greater than in the C homes. As of 1928, when the average age of the subjects was about 16 years, more than twice as many of the C parents as of A parents had been divorced.

Interesting differences between the groups were found in the childhood data on emotional stability, social adjustments, and various traits of personality. Of the 25 traits on which each child was rated by parent and teacher in 1922 (18 years before the A and C groups were made up), the only trait on which the C's averaged as high as the A's was general health. The superiority of the A's was especially marked in four volitional traits: prudence, self-confidence, perseverance, and desire to excel. The A's also rated significantly higher in 1922 on leadership, popularity, and sensitiveness to approval or disapproval. By 1940 the difference between the groups in social adjustment and all-round mental stability had greatly increased and showed itself in many ways. By that time four-fifths of the A's had married, but only two-thirds of the C's, and the divorce rate for those who had married was twice as high for the C's as for the A's. Moreover, the A's made better marriages; their wives on the average came from better homes, were better educated, and scored higher on intelligence tests.

But the most spectacular differences between the two groups came from three sets of ratings, made in 1940, on a dozen personality traits. Each man rated himself on all the traits, was rated on them by his wife if he had a wife, and by a parent if a parent was still living. Although the three sets of ratings were made independently, they agreed unanimously on the four traits in which the A and C groups differed most widely. These were "persistence in the accomplishment of ends," "integration toward goals, as contrasted with drifting," "self-confidence," and "freedom from inferiority feelings." For each trait three critical ratios were computed showing, respectively, the reliability of the A-C differences in average of self-ratings, ratings by wives, and ratings by parents. The average of the three critical ratios was 5.5 for perseverance, 5.6 for integration toward goals, 3.7 for self-confidence, and 3.1 for freedom from inferiority feelings. These closely parallel the traits that Cox found to be especially characteristic of the 100 leading geniuses in her group whom she rated on many aspects of personality; their three outstanding traits she defined as "persistence of motive and effort," "confidence in their abilities," and "strength or force of character."

There was one trait on which only the parents of our A and C men were asked to rate them; that trait was designated "common sense." As judged by parents, the A's are again reliably superior, the A-C difference in average rating having a critical ratio of 3.9. We are still wondering what self-ratings by the subjects and ratings of them by their wives on common sense would have shown if we had been impudent enough to ask for them!

Everything considered, there is nothing in which our A and C groups present a greater contrast than in drive to achieve and in all-round mental and social adjustment. Our data do not support the theory of Lange-Eichbaum [6] that great achievement usually stems from emotional tensions that border on the abnormal. In our gifted group, success is associated with stability rather than instability, with absence rather than with presence of disturbing conflicts—in short with well-balanced temperament and with freedom from excessive frustrations. The Lange-Eichbaum theory may explain a Hitler, but hardly a Churchill; the junior senator from Wisconsin, possibly, but not a Jefferson or a Washington.

At any rate, we have seen that intellect and achievement are far from perfectly correlated. To identify the internal and external factors that help or hinder the fruition of exceptional talent, and to measure the extent of their influences, are surely among the major problems of our time. These problems are not new; their existence has been recognized by countless men from Plato to Francis Galton. What is new is the general awareness of them caused by the manpower shortage of scientists, engineers, moral leaders, statesmen, scholars, and teachers that the country must have if it is to survive in a threatened world. These problems are now being investigated on a scale never before approached, and by a new generation of workers in several related fields. Within a couple of decades vastly more should be known than we know today about our resources of potential genius, the environmental circumstances that favor its expression, the emotional compulsions that give it dynamic quality, and the personality distortions that can make it dangerous.

REFERENCES

1. Cox, CATHARINE C. *The early mental traits of three hundred geniuses.* Vol. II of *Genetic studies of genius,* Terman, L. M. (Ed.) Stanford: Stanford Univer. Press, 1926.

2. DAVIS, W. Communicating science. *J. atomic Scientists,* 1953, 337–340.

3. KEYS, N. The underage student in high school and college. *Univer. Calif. Publ. Educ.,* 1938, **7,** 145–272.

4. KNAPP, R. H., & GOODRICH, H. B. *Origins of American scientists.* Chicago: Univer. of Chicago Press, 1952.

5. KNAPP, R. H., & GREENBAUM, J. J. *The younger American scholar: his collegiate origins.* Chicago: Univer. of Chicago Press, 1953.

6. LANGE-EICHBAUM, W. *The problem of genius.* New York: Macmillan, 1932.

7. LEARNED, W. S., & WOOD, B. D. The student and his knowledge. *Carnegie Found. Adv. Teaching Bull.,* 1938, No. 29.

8. LEHMAN, H. C. *Age and achievement.* Princeton: Princeton Univer. Press, 1953.

9. PRESSEY, S. L. *Educational acceleration: appraisals and basic problems.* Columbus: Ohio State Univer. Press, 1949.

10. TERMAN, L. M. A preliminary study in the psychology and pedagogy of leadership. *Pedag. Sem.,* 1904, **11,** 413–451.

11. TERMAN, L. M. Genius and stupidity: a study of some of the intellectual processes of seven "bright" and seven "dull" boys. *Pedag. Sem.,* 1906, **13,** 307–373.

12. TERMAN, L. M. The intelligence quotient of Francis Galton in childhood. *Amer. J. Psychol.,* 1917, **28,** 209–215.

13. TERMAN, L. M. (Ed.), *et al. Mental and physical traits of a thousand gifted children.* Vol. I of *Genetic studies of genius,* Terman, L. M. (Ed.) Stanford: Stanford Univer. Press, 1925.

14. TERMAN, L. M., & ODEN, M. H. *The gifted child grows up.* Vol. IV of *Genetic studies of genius,* Terman, L. M. (Ed.) Stanford: Stanford Univer. Press, 1947.

15. TERMAN, L. M. Scientists and nonscientists in a group of 800 gifted men. *Psychol. Monogr.,* 1954, **68,** No. 7, (Whole No. 378).

16. WITTY, P. (Ed.) *The gifted child.* Boston: Heath, 1951.

17. *Bridging the gap between school and college.* New York: The Fund for the Advancement of Education, 1953.

18. *The intelligence of Scottish children.* Scottish Council for Research in Education. London: Univer. of London Press, 1933.

Chapter 40

A Study of the Sources of Highly Intelligent and of Highly Creative Adolescents

JACOB W. GETZELS / PHILIP W. JACKSON

From the time Binet first constructed his intelligence test with the resulting ubiquitous IQ metric to the present, the problem of intellectual ability and giftedness has remained largely a psychological issue. The important question has been a psychometric one: how can we obtain a precise measure of the general ability called intelligence or of a group of factors comprising so-called mental capacity? When sociologists have attempted to deal with differential cognitive functioning and giftedness, their efforts have most frequently been restricted to relating social class or ethnic variables to *amount* of mental ability as represented by the aforementioned IQ.

As we have had occasion to remark elsewhere [1], involved in the IQ conception of intellectual functioning are several types of confusion, if not outright error. First, there is the limitation of the single metric itself, which not only restricts our perspective of the more general phenomenon, but places on the one concept a greater theoretical and predictive burden than it was intended to carry. Second, within the universe of intellectual functioning we have behaved as if the intelligence test represented an adequate sampling of *all* functions—the "gifted child," for example, has become synonymous with the "child with a high IQ." Third, we have so emphasized the measuring of different *amounts* of intellectual ability that we have neglected the understanding of different *kinds* of intellectual ability.

Despite its longevity there is nothing inevitable about the use of the IQ in defining intellectual ability and potential giftedness. Indeed, it may be argued that in many ways this metric is only an historical accident—a consequence of the fact that early inquiries in the field of intellectual functioning had as their social context the classroom and as their criterion academic progress. If the initial context of inquiry into mental ability had not been the classroom,

This article is reprinted from the *American Sociological Review,* 1961, with the permission of the authors and the American Sociological Association. The research was supported by a grant from the U.S. Office of Education.

other qualities defining intellectual functioning might have been identified just as the qualities measured by the IQ apparently were in the classroom. Indeed, even without shifting the context of inquiry from the classroom, if only the original criterion of learning had been changed, the qualities defining intellectual functioning and giftedness might also have been changed. For example, if we recognized that learning involves the production of novelty as well as the remembrance of course-content, then measures of creativity as well as the IQ might become appropriate defining characteristics of mental ability and giftedness. It is, of course, a commonplace to recognize people who seem to be highly "intelligent" (as measured by the IQ) but apparently not "creative" (whatever that seems to mean in any particular case), and people who are "creative" but not necessarily "intelligent" (at least as measured by the conventional IQ).

The research project from which we are drawing our present report was directed toward the following three related tasks:

1. To identify two groups of subjects differing significantly in *kind* of intellectual functioning—in this case, "intelligence" and "creativity."
2. To examine the personal-social behavioral concomitants of the two kinds of intellectual functioning—for example, would the groups also differ in levels of achievement, patterns of interpersonal relations, types of career aspirations, etc.?
3. To study in some depth the family environment of the two groups.

DIFFERENTIATING COGNITIVE STYLE: SUBJECTS, METHODS, FINDINGS

The methods and findings with respect to the first two tasks have already been reported in detail elsewhere [2, 3, 4] and will be presented here only insofar as is necessary to clarify the issues and findings with respect to the third task—determining the

relationship between type of intellectual functioning and family environment—which is the focus of this report.

The experimental groups were drawn from 449 adolescents comprising the total population of a Midwestern private secondary school[1] on the basis of performance on the following instruments:

1. *Standard IQ tests, most usually the Binet itself.*
2. *Five Creativity measures, taken or adapted from Guilford and Cattell, or constructed especially for the study, as follows:*
   a. Word Association. The subject was asked to give as many definitions as possible to fairly common stimulus-words, e.g., "bolt," "bark," "sack." His score depended on the absolute number of definitions and the number of different categories into which his definitions could be put.
   b. Uses for Things. The subject was required to give as many uses as he could for objects customarily having a single stereotyped function, e.g., "brick," "paperclip." His score depended on the number and originality of the uses he mentioned.
   c. Hidden Shapes. The subject was required to find a given geometric form hidden in more complex geometric forms or patterns.
   d. Fables. The subject was required to provide a "moralistic," a "humorous," and a "sad" ending to each of four fables in which the last line was missing. His score depended on the number, appropriateness, and originality of the endings.
   e. Make-up Problems. The subject was presented with four complex paragraphs, each containing a number of numerical statements, e.g., "the costs in building a house." He was re-

---

[1] The children in this school come in large measure from families who are in the employ of an urban university, or from families who, although not employed by the university, prefer to reside in or near the university community, and to send their children to its school because of its presumed excellence. The children are much above average in ability, the mean IQ of the total school being 132, with a standard deviation of 15.1.

quired to make up as many mathematical problems as he could that might be solved with the information given. His score depended upon the number, appropriateness, and originality of the problems.

What most of these verbal and numerical tests had in common was that the score depended not on a single pre-determined correct response as is frequently the case of the common intelligence test, but on the number, novelty, and variety of responses.

On the basis of the IQ measure and a summated score on the creativity measures, the two experimental groups were formed as follows:

1. The High Creativity Group. These were subjects at the top 20 per cent on the creativity measures when compared with same-sex age peers, but *below* the top 20 per cent in IQ. Their mean IQ was 127, with a range from 108 to 138. N = 26 (15 boys, 11 girls).

2. The High Intelligence Group. These were subjects in the top 20 per cent in IQ when compared with same-sex age peers, but *below* the top 20 per cent on the creativity measures. Their mean IQ was 150, with a range from 139 to 179. N = 28 (17 boys, 11 girls).[2]

Having thus identified two groups differing (at least by test score) in style of intellectual functioning—in effect, the objective of the first research task—we were ready to turn to our second task, which may now be put in the form of a direct question: What is the nature of the performance of the

---

[2] The initial samples of highly creative and highly intelligent subjects were larger than the final experimental groups. Because of the goals of the overall project, students who were also especially outstanding in qualities such as psychological health or morality were the subjects of independent study. In a sense, the present experimental groups may be said to represent relatively "pure" types since they do not include adolescents gifted as well in a number of these other characteristics. There were also students who were at once both "highly intelligent" and "highly creative." These too are not included in the present study.

groups on the following personal-social variables: school achievement, perception by teachers, production of fantasies, and choice of adult career? The findings were quite straightforward:

1. SCHOOL ACHIEVEMENT

Although there is a 23 point difference in average IQ between the high IQ's and the high Creatives, the school achievement of the two groups as measured by standardized achievement tests was *equally superior* to the population from which they were drawn.

2. PERCEPTION BY TEACHERS

The teachers were asked to rate all students in the school on the degree they enjoyed having them in class. The high IQ student was rated as more desirable than the average student, the high Creative was not.

3. FANTASY PRODUCTION

Six Thematic Apperception Test–type pictures were shown, and the subjects were required to write four-minute stories to each of the pictures. The stories of the two groups were found to be strikingly different, the Creative making significantly greater use of *stimulus-free themes, unexpected endings, humor,* and *playfulness.*

4. CAREER ASPIRATION

The two groups were asked to indicate their career aspirations and occupational choices. When these were analyzed into "conventional" (e.g., doctor, lawyer, engineer) and "unconventional" (e.g., adventurer, inventor, writer) categories, it was found that 16 per cent of the high IQ's and 62 per cent of the high Creatives had made "unconventional" career choices.

In short, two conclusions seemed clear from studying the children themselves: First, they could be differentiated by kind of preferred intellectual functioning, i.e., into high IQ and high Creativity groups. Second, when they were so differentiated, the two groups were equally superior in achievement to the population from which they were drawn, and they themselves differed significantly in a number of personal-social variables, including perception by teachers, fantasy production, and choice of career.

FAMILY ENVIRONMENT AND COGNITIVE STYLE: METHODS, SUBJECTS, FINDINGS

The central issue of the present report is: Do the two groups also vary systematically in the nature of their family environment? Accordingly, family inventories and 2–3 hour interviews were obtained from approximately 80 per cent of the mothers of the two groups. The analysis of these data may be discussed with respect to each of the following family variables:

1. Education and occupation of the parents.
2. Age of the parents.
3. Mother's recollection of her own family situation when she was her child's age.
4. Reading interests in the family, at least as represented by the number and type of magazines taken.
5. Parental satisfaction and dissatisfaction with the child and his school.
6. Parental satisfaction and dissatisfaction with their own child-rearing practices.
7. Mother's description of the kinds of friends preferred for her child.

1. EDUCATION AND OCCUPATION OF PARENTS

Educational data were available for the parents of 24 of the 28 high IQ's and for 24 of the 26 high Creatives. When these data were analyzed by simply dichotomizing college graduates versus others, the result obtained could be summarized as in Table 40–1.

Table 40–1   Number of College Graduates among Fathers and Mothers of the Two Experimental Groups

| | Number of College Graduates | | | |
	IQ (n=24)	Creative (n=24)	χ^2	p*
Father	21	15	4.0	.05
Mother	16	12	1.37	N.S.

* Because of the exploratory nature of this phase of the research many of the comparisons presented here were derived from the obtained data. Therefore, the probability values attached to the chi-squares in this and the following Tables must be viewed with caution.

The data were also dichotomized by parents having at least some graduate training as against those having no graduate training. The results of this analysis are given in Table 40–2.

Whichever analysis is undertaken, it seems that the parents of the high IQ child tend to have higher educational status than the parents of the high Creativity child. But what is perhaps more noteworthy is the greater specialized training of both the mother and the father of the high IQ's. The essential difference is probably not so much in the general level of cultivation, which is very high for both groups when compared to the general population, but in the significantly greater specialization of training or, if one will, "professionalization of education" of the high IQ group.

In this connection, the occupational data are relevant. The data for fathers are presented in Table 40–3, and for mothers in Table 40–4.

It appears that we are dealing not only with two different types of children but with two different types of parents. As

Table 40–2   Number of Parents Having Some Graduate Training

| | Having Graduate Training | | | |
	IQ (n=24)	Creative (n=24)	χ^2	p
Father	19	13	3.38	.10
Mother	13	5	5.69	.02

Table 40–3   Occupational Status of the Fathers of the Two Experimental Groups

Occupational Status	IQ (n=24)	Creative (n=24)	χ^2	p
University teaching, research, editing	15	7		
			6.15	.02
Business	4	11		
Medicine, law	5	6		

might be anticipated from the data on educational status, a greater proportion of the high IQ fathers than of the high Creativity fathers are found in the academic or educational occupations. But it is note-worthy that despite their greater profes-sional training, a greater proportion of the mothers of the high IQ children than of the high Creativity children are exclusively housewives, and do not hold other full- or part-time jobs. It would seem that the mothers of the high IQ subjects have more time to devote to their children than do the mothers of the high Creative subjects. In this connection, it will be shown from other sources of data that the high IQ mothers are in fact likely to be more vigilant about the "correct" upbringing of their children than the high Creativity mothers.

2. AGE OF PARENTS

The mean age is almost exactly the same for the two groups of mothers, and al-though the age of the fathers tended to be slightly greater for the high IQ group than for the high Creativity group, it was not significantly so. The significant and striking difference between the two groups was in

Table 40–4   Occupational Status of the Mothers of the Two Experimental Groups

Occupational Status	IQ (n=24)	Creative (n=24)	χ^2	p
Housewife only	18	11		
			4.27	.05
Full or part-time employment	6	13		

the discrepancy or congruence between the age of the father and mother. If the data are dichotomized as one year or less age difference and two years or more age dif-ference, the results may be summarized as in Table 40–5.

We may only conjecture at this time about the reasons for the age discrepancies or similarities between the parents of the present sample, and about the effects of these age factors on the family environ-ment. But two reasons for a number of the discrepancies seem relevant: waiting to fin-ish advanced academic training before risk-ing marital responsibilities, and waiting to be satisfactorily "settled" to maintain a family in the "right" style. Both reasons suggest an apparently greater insecurity among the high IQ parents than among the high Creativity parents, a suggestion that is also supported by subsequent interview data.

3. MOTHER'S MEMORIES OF OWN HOME

The relevant interview question was: How would you describe the home you lived in as a child? The responses were long and detailed—the mothers seemed to enjoy relating their own real or imagined childhood experiences to their children's present situation. Here, for example, is a fairly typical response by one of the IQ mothers:[3]

Table 40–5   Age Difference between Parents for the Two Experimental Groups

Age Difference between Parents	IQ (n=24)	Creative (n=24)	χ^2	p
0–1 year	4	13		
			7.38	.01
2 or more years	20	11		

[3] Here and throughout the paper the mothers' statements are taken from notes recorded during the interview. At the time these interviews were made the parents of five other experimental groups were also being studied. The interviewers did not know into which of the seven groups any mother belonged. The present quotations have been al-tered in irrelevant details to maintain anonymity.

It was as typically Midwestern middle class American as one could find. Neither rich nor poor. . . . The family belonged to important people in town. Father was the principal of the school, active in church and in the literary group. His was a large family, and there were many homes we could go to. Father died when I was thirteen. Mother began teaching school. We thought more about money. Then I worked while in college. I have some doubt about that—traumatic insecurity, especially financially. So abnormally thrifty ever since—keeping magazines. . . .I hope children won't miss these highlights of our life even if disasters. . . .

The problem of quantifying this kind of material is of course formidable, and many differences that one "feels" as one reads the complete sets of interviews "wash out" as one attempts to categorize. Nonetheless, certain categorical differences may be noted. For example, seven of the 22 IQ mothers for whom interview material is available say specifically of their home that it was "middle class," and only one of the 18 Creative mothers for whom interview material is available says this. Eight of the 22 IQ mothers describe their family in rather global-emotional terms; 12 of the 18 Creative mothers seem to do this. That is, the IQ mothers tend to be more "stereotypic" in their descriptions (they tend to put themselves in "classes"); the Creative mothers attempt rather more rounded descriptions.

But the chief categorical difference—and a very relevant one—lies in their reference to the financial status of their home and childhood. As the data in Table 40–6 show, the high IQ parents tend not only to mention finances significantly more often than the high Creativity parents, but to emphasize financial hardship more often. Whatever else these responses imply about the different remembrance of things past and areas of latent concern, they do tend to support the suggestion of greater insecurity among the parents of the high IQ children than among the parents of the high Creativity children.

Table 40–6 Mention of Financial Status and of Poverty in Descriptions of Own Home Life by Mothers of the Two Experimental Groups

	IQ (n=22)	Creative (n=18)	χ^2	p
Mention of finances	16	7	4.64	.05
Emphasis on poverty, financial hardship	9	1	4.84*	.05

* Yates correction applied.

4. READING INTERESTS IN THE HOME

It is almost impossible to obtain an exact measure of the reading habits of a family. Nonetheless, an attempt toward a partial assessment was made by asking the following interview questions: What magazines and newspapers do you subscribe to or buy regularly? What magazines do you read just once in a while?

Professional or scholarly journals, which would have increased the count for the high IQ parents, were omitted in the analysis. Despite this, there was a difference in the number of magazines coming into the homes of the high IQ and high Creativity subjects, a difference that is quite illuminating.

The 22 high IQ families reported reading "regularly" a total of 125 magazines, and "sometimes" 54 magazines. The 18 high Creative families reported reading "regularly" a total of 107 magazines, and "sometimes" 30 magazines. The respective means were 8.14 for the high IQ's and 5.94 for the high Creatives. If the families are divided into those mentioning six or fewer and those mentioning seven or more magazines, the relationship portrayed in Table 40–7 is observed.

Table 40–7 Number of Magazines "Taken" or Read in Homes of the Two Experimental Groups

Number of Magazines	IQ (n=22)	Creative (n=18)	χ^2	p
6 or fewer	7	12		
			4.34	.05
7 or more	15	6		

There seem to be significant quantitative differences between the two groups. There are also some noteworthy qualitative trends in the data. For example, 21 of the 22 high IQ mothers report taking or reading 50 "Mass Media Magazines" (*Time, Life, Newsweek, Reader's Digest*). This is about 28 per cent of their total. Sixteen of the 18 high Creative mothers report taking or reading 27 "Mass Media Magazines," which is about 19 per cent of their total. Conversely, five of the 22 high IQ mothers mention seven "Magazines of Liberal Political Comment" (*Reporter, Nation, New Republic*)—about 3 per cent of the total— but seven of the 18 high Creative mothers mention ten magazines in this category, i.e., about 7 per cent of their total. Perhaps the most noteworthy difference is in the number of children's magazines (*Boys Life, Junior Natural History Magazine,* etc.) mentioned by the two groups. Ten of the 22 high IQ mothers mention 17 such magazines, three of the 18 high Creativity mothers mention five such magazines.

5. PARENTAL SATISFACTION AND DISSATISFACTION WITH THE CHILD AND WITH HIS SCHOOL

A crucial issue in the present study of family environment and giftedness is the reaction of the parent to any unusual qualities in the child and the type of education the child is getting. Two interview questions are relevant here:

a. During your child's earliest years in school, did the teachers call to your attention or did you yourself notice anything unusual about him and school?

b. As far as the present school is concerned, what are the things you like best about the education your child is getting? Is there anything about your child's education at this school that you are not satisfied with?

The replies to both questions are quite consistent and informative. They will be discussed in turn.

a. Although the high IQ and the high Creativity parents report the same number of total observations and the same number of favorable and unfavorable qualities in their children as seen by *teachers,* the high IQ parents report both a greater number of total observations (59 against 31) and a greater number of unfavorable qualities as seen by *themselves.* When the latter data are dichotomized into "not more than one unfavorable quality" and "more than one unfavorable quality," the result is the relationship presented in Table 40–8.

What is noteworthy in these data is the greater "vigilance" and "critical" or at least "less accepting" attitude of the high IQ mothers—they both observe *more* about their children and they observe a greater number of *objectionable* qualities. It is as if they were on the look-out for things to improve about their children. (In this connection, the greater number of children's magazines the high IQ parents take is perhaps relevant.)

b. The same "vigilance" and critical attitude is seen in their attitudes toward the school their children are attending. Here again the high IQ parents report a greater number of total observations (138 against 95), and a significantly greater number of dissatisfactions, as shown in Table 40–9.

6. PARENTAL SATISFACTION WITH THEIR CHILD-REARING PRACTICES

Despite the apparent greater misgiving and uncertainty of the high IQ mother toward her child and toward the school, she expresses fewer misgivings and uncertainties than does the high Creative mother

Table 40–8 Number of Unfavorable Qualities Observed in Their Children by Mothers of the Two Groups

Number of Unfavorable Qualities Observed	IQ (n=23)	Creative (n=19)	χ^2	p
Not more than one	13	17	5.53	.02
More than one	10	2		

Table 40–9   Number of Unfavorable School Qualities Observed by Mothers of the Two Experimental Groups

Number of Un-favorable School Qualities Observed	IQ (n=23)	Creative (n=19)	χ²	p
Not more than one	7	12		
			4.5	.05
More than one	16	7		

Table 40–10   Mothers' Satisfaction and Dissatisfaction with Their Own Child Training Practices

Opinion of Own Child Training Practice	IQ (n=23)	Creative (n=19)	χ²	p
Satisfied	17	8		
			4.37	.05
Dissatisfied	6	11		

regarding her own child training practices. It is almost as if she were critical of others but "smug" about herself. The relevant interview question was: As you look back on the ways you have tried to make your child responsible to you as far as bed-time, playing outside, leaving the house, homework and so forth were concerned, would you say you were too lenient, not lenient enough, or what? The results are presented in Table 40–10.

7. KINDS OF FRIENDS PREFERRED FOR THEIR CHILDREN

There is one final set of data that rounds out the differences between the family environment of the high IQ and the high Creativity families, at least as represented by the mothers' attitudes. The interview question was: What qualities do you like to see in your child's friends?

Again, the high IQ mothers had somewhat more to say. But the striking finding was the difference in what they said. When the qualities mentioned are divided into two categories, the one relating to "external" characteristics (e.g., "good family,"

"good manners," "studious"), the other to "internal" characteristics (e.g., "sense of values," "interest in something," "openness—not secretive"), the result is the relationship summarized in Table 40–11.

Several sample responses may give some greater substance to these tabular differences. Here, for example, are two high IQ mothers describing the qualities they would like to see in their child's friends: (a) "Sunday school children, religious, go to church every Sunday, of parents whose standards are ours. Honest, sincere, clean-minded and clean-mouthed. Studious." (b) "Right between the eyes—aware of my own inadequacies. Intelligence is certainly foremost—admit to my snobbism. Kind of cultural background, not money. A level of family. What I don't like—wild kid who doesn't know how to behave in a house—dirty talk—I've put up with it—a certain amount is acceptable—outside can use up energies. Neither extroverted nor introverted." Here are two high Creativity mothers describing the qualities they would like to see in their child's friends: (a) "Like what I want to see in E . . . [her child]—it's the same thing. Valid sense of values—what a person is

Table 40–11   Characteristics Preferred for Children's Friends by Mothers of the Two Groups

Characteristics	IQ (n=23) X*	IQ (n=23) S	Creative (n=19) X*	Creative (n=19) S	t	p
External—Specific, e.g., good family, manners, studious	2.48	1.20	1.58	1.07	2.56	.02
Internal—General, e.g. sense of values, interests, openness	.91	1.12	1.79	1.47	2.13	.05

* These means refer to the average number of characteristics mentioned.

rather than what he appears to be. Satisfaction in creative constructive activity. Balance and maturity in interpersonal relations. Interest and enthusiasm for learning and reaching out beyond it to greater-understanding." (b) "Openness—not secretive that old folks won't understand. Interest in something to do—not bored expression. Temperate in manners and habits. Frankness and honesty. Interest in living." It is here in the projections of desirable traits for their children's friends that we may perhaps see the most honest aspirations for their own children. As the high Creative mother says, "It's the same thing." And it is here, as we have seen, that we again find some very striking differences indeed.

DISCUSSION AND SUMMARY

It is clear that the intellectual functioning of adolescents can be differentiated not only into quantitative categories of high and low IQ but also into qualitative categories among which are "high IQ without concomitantly high Creativity" and "high Creativity without concomitantly high IQ." The intellectual functioning represented by these two categories bears resemblance to Guilford's factors of "convergent" and "divergent" thinking [5]. When adolescents representing these qualitative categories are identified it is found that they also differ on a number of significant personal-social variables. For example, although both are equally superior to the average student in school achievement, they are perceived differently by teachers, they differ in the nature of their fantasy productions, and they aspire to different career goals.

With respect to these initial findings, and before a study of the family environments was undertaken, we suggested that,

> . . . the essence of the performance of our Creative adolescents lay in their ability to produce new forms, to risk conjoining elements that are customarily thought

of as independent and dissimilar, to go off in new directions. The creative adolescent possesses the ability to free himself from the usual, to "diverge" from the customary. He seemed to enjoy the risk and uncertainty of the unknown. In contrast, the high IQ adolescent seemed to possess to a high degree the ability and the need to focus on the usual, to be channelled and controlled in the direction of the right answer—the customary. He appeared to shy away from the risk and the uncertainty of the unknown and to seek out the safety and security of the known [see 2, p. 56].

In an attempt to relate the differences in intellectual behavior to a broader psycho-social context we found fruitful Maslow's formulations of Defense and Growth [see 3, p. 122]. He writes:

> Every human being has both sets of forces within him. One set clings to safety and defensiveness out of fear, tending to regress, hanging on to the past . . . afraid to take chances, afraid to jeopardize what he already has, afraid of independence, freedom, separation. The other set of forces impels him forward toward wholeness of self and uniqueness of self, toward full functioning of all his capacities, toward confidence in the face of the external world at the same time that he can accept his deepest, real, unconscious Self. . . . This basic dilemma or conflict between the defensive forces and the growth trends I conceive to be existential, imbedded in the deepest nature of the human being, now and forever into the future. . . . Therefore we can consider the process of healthy growth to be a never-ending series of free choice situations, confronting each individual at every point throughout his life, in which he must choose between the delights of safety and growth, dependence and independence. . . . Safety has both anxieties and delights; growth has both anxieties and delights [6].

In these terms, the high IQ adolescent may be seen as preferring the anxieties and delights of "safety," the high Creativity adolescent the anxieties and delights of "growth."

We would maintain that the intellectual differences between these groups and the underlying psycho-social orientations have their source not only in the immediate school experience but in the family environment in which the adolescents grew up. The family environment of these students, at least as portrayed by the mothers' interviews, is consonant with the psycho-social formulations applied to the groups. The parents of the high IQ student tend to recall greater financial difficulties during their own childhood and hence, at least by inference, may be said to have experienced in the past, and perhaps the present, greater real or imagined personal insecurity than is true for the parents of the highly creative students. The high IQ parents seem to be more "vigilant" with respect to their children's behavior and their manifest academic performance. As compared with the parents of the highly creative adolescents, the parents of the high IQ students tend at once to be more critical of both their children and the school; it is as if their standards were always just one step ahead of attainment. Nor is their vigilance limited to concern for their child's educational progress. They appear equally concerned with the desirable qualities possessed by their children's friends. The qualities they would like to see in their children's friends, which may in a sense be conceived as projections of the qualities they would like to see in their own children, focus upon such immediately visible virtues as cleanliness, good manners, studiousness. In contrast, the parents of the creative adolescents focus upon less visible qualities such as the child's openness to experience, his values, and his interests and enthusiasms.

When these differences in the parents' attitudes and aspirations are combined with differences in educational specialization, the age discrepancy between father and mother, and the kind of reading material available in the home, the over-all impression of the high IQ family is one in which individual divergence is limited and risks minimized, the over-all impression of the high Creative family is one in which individual divergence is permitted and risks are accepted. In this sense, the concepts of Defense and Growth which were used to distinguish the high IQ adolescent and the high Creative adolescent, seem also useful in distinguishing between their family environment.

CONCLUSION

Several concluding comments seem in order, particularly since the type of data presented here lends itself rather easily to misinterpretation and overgeneralization. First, in describing the high IQ and the high Creativity adolescents, we do not intend to give the impression of the one as representing "good guys" and the other "bad guys." The distinction we are making is analytic, not evaluative. Both convergent and divergent thinking are valuable in their separate ways. Second, in discussing the greater "vigilance" of the parents of the high IQ group, we do not intend to give support to the current unfortunate dichotomy between "bad" authoritarianism and "good" permissiveness. The issue is not all-or-none, either-or, but appropriate emphasis. Third, in adducing evidence for the greater "specialized education" and "bookishness" of the parents of the high IQ children as against the parents of the high Creativity children, we do not intend to suggest that the presence of books or specialized knowledge in the family leads inevitably to high IQ, the absence to high Creativity. It is not the presence of books or specialized knowledge but their use and meaning that make the difference. Finally, we should like to point out that at least as much by the issues raised as by the nature of the preliminary findings we have presented, the question of how types of cognition are shaped by types of family environment is a fruitful area for sociological examination.

REFERENCES

1. GETZELS, J. W., & JACKSON, P. W. The meaning of giftedness: an examination of an expanding concept. *Phi Delta Kappan,* 1959, 40, 75–78.
2. GETZELS, J. W., & JACKSON, P. W. The highly intelligent and the highly creative adolescent: a summary of some research findings. In C. W. Taylor (Ed.), *Research conference on the identification of creative scientific talent.* Salt Lake City: University of Utah Press, 1959, 46–57.
3. GETZELS, J. W., & JACKSON, P. W. Occupational choice and cognitive functioning: career aspirations of highly intelligent and of highly creative adolescents. *Journal of Abnormal and Social Psychology,* 1960, 61, 119–123.
4. GETZELS, J. W., & JACKSON, P. W. The study of giftedness: a multidimensional approach. In Co-operative Research Monograph No. 2 of the U.S. Office of Education, *The gifted student.* Washington, D.C.: U.S. Office of Education, 1960, 1–18.
5. GUILFORD, J. P. *A revised structure of intellect.* Reports from the Psychological Laboratory, No. 19. Los Angeles: University of Southern California, 1957.
6. MASLOW, A. H. Defense and growth. *Merrill-Palmer Quarterly,* 1956, 3, 37–38.

Chapter 41

The Nature and
Nurture of Creative Talent

DONALD W. MACKINNON

Whatever light I shall be able to shed on the nature and nurture of creative talent comes in the main from findings of researches carried on during the last six years in the Institute of Personality Assessment and Research on the Berkeley campus of the University of California, and supported in large part by the Carnegie Corporation of New York.

In undertaking such a study one of our first tasks was to decide what we would consider creativity to be. This was necessary, first, because creativity has been so variously described and defined, and second, because only when we had come to agreement as to how we would conceive creativity would we be in a position to know what kinds of persons we would want to study.

We came easily to agreement that true

This article is reprinted from the *American Psychologist*, 1962, with the permission of the author and the American Psychological Association. It was given as the Walter Van Dyke Bingham Lecture at Yale University, New Haven, Connecticut, April 11, 1962.

creativeness fulfills at least three conditions. It involves a response or an idea that is novel or at the very least statistically infrequent. But novelty or originality of thought or action, while a necessary aspect of creativity, is not sufficient. If a response is to lay claim to being a part of the creative process, it must to some extent be adaptive to, or of, reality. It must serve to solve a problem, fit a situation, or accomplish some recognizable goal. And, thirdly, true creativeness involves a sustaining of the original insight, an evaluation and elaboration of it, a developing of it to the full.

Creativity, from this point of view, is a process extended in time and characterized by originality, adaptiveness, and realization. It may be brief, as in a musical improvisation, or it may involve a considerable span of years, as was required for Darwin's creation of the theory of evolution.

The acceptance of such a conception of creativity had two important consequences for our researches. It meant that we would not seek to study creativity while it was still potential but only after it had been realized and had found expression in clearly identifiable creative products—buildings designed by architects, mathematical proofs developed by mathematicians, and the published writings of poets and novelists. Our conception of creativity forced us further to reject as indicators or criteria of creativeness the performance of individuals on so-called tests of creativity. While tests of this sort, that require that the subject think, for example, of unusual uses for common objects and the consequences of unusual events, may indeed measure the infrequency or originality of a subject's ideas in response to specific test items, they fail to reveal the extent to which the subject faced with real life problems is likely to come up with solutions that are novel and adaptive and which he will be motivated to apply in all of their ramifications.

Having thus determined that we would limit our researches to the study of persons who had already demonstrated a high level of creative work, we were still confronted with the problem of deciding from which fields of creative endeavor we would seek to recruit our subjects.

The fields which we finally sampled were those of creative writing, architecture, mathematics, industrial research, physical science, and engineering.

If one considers these activities in relation to the distinction often made between artistic and scientific creativity, it may be noted that we have sampled both of these domains as well as overlapping domains of creative striving which require that the practitioner be at one and the same time both artist and scientist.

Artistic creativity, represented in our studies by the work of poets, novelists, and essayists, results in products that are clearly expressions of the creator's inner states, his needs, perceptions, motivations, and the like. In this type of creativity, the creator externalizes something of himself into the public field.

In scientific creativity, the creative product is unrelated to the creator as a person, who in his creative work acts largely as a mediator between externally defined needs and goals. In this kind of creativeness, the creator, represented in our studies by industrial researchers, physical scientists, and engineers, simply operates on some aspect of his environment in such a manner as to produce a novel and appropriate product, but he adds little of himself or of his style as a person to the resultant.

Domains of creative striving in which the practitioner must be both artist and scientist were represented in our researches by mathematicians and architects. Mathematicians contribute to science, yet in a very real sense their important creative efforts are as much as anything else personal cosmologies in which they express themselves as does the artist in his creations. So, too, in architecture, creative products are both an expression of the architect and thus a very personal product, and at the same time an impersonal meeting of the demands of an external problem.

If in reporting the findings of our researches I draw most heavily upon data obtained from our study of architects [10], it is for two reasons. First, it is the study for which, in collaboration with Wallace B. Hall, I have assumed primary responsibility. Second, it is in architects, of all our samples, that we can expect to find what is most generally characteristic of creative persons. Architecture, as a field of creative endeavor, requires that the successful practitioner be both artist and scientist—artist in that his designs must fulfill the demands of "Delight," and scientist in that they must meet the demands of "Firmnesse" and "Commodity," to use the words of Sir Henry Wotton [18]. But surely, one can hardly think that the requirements of effective architecture are limited to these three demands. The successful and effective architect must, with the skill of a juggler, combine, reconcile, and exercise the diverse skills of businessman, lawyer, artist, engineer, and advertising man, as well as those of author and journalist, psychiatrist, educator, and psychologist. In what other profession can one expect better to observe the multifarious expressions of creativity?

It should be clear that any attempt to discover the distinguishing traits of creative persons can succeed only in so far as some group of qualified experts can agree upon who are the more and who are the less creative workers in a given field of endeavor. In our study of architects we began by asking a panel of experts—five professors of architecture, each working independently—to nominate the 40 most creative architects in the United States. All told they supplied us with 86 names instead of the 40 they would have mentioned had there been perfect agreement among them. While 13 of the 86 architects were nominated by all five panel members, and 9 nominated by four, 11 by three, and 13 by two, 40 were individual nominations each proposed by a single panel member.

The agreement among experts is not perfect, yet far greater than one might have expected. Later we asked 11 editors of the major American architectural journals, *Architectural Forum, Architectural Record,* the *Journal of the American Institute of Architects,* and *Progressive Architecture,* to rate the creativity of the 64 of the nominated architects whom we invited to participate in the study. Still later we asked the 40 nominated creative architects who actually' accepted our invitation to be studied to rate the creativity of the invited 64 architects, themselves included. Since the editors' ratings of the creativity of the architects correlated +.88 with the architects' own ratings, it is clear that under certain conditions and for certain groups it is possible to obtain remarkable agreement about the relative creativeness of individual members of a profession and thus meet the first requirement for an effective study of creative persons.

A second requirement for the successful establishment of the traits of creative individuals is their willingness to make themselves available for study. Our hope was to win the cooperation of each person whom we invited to participate in the research, but as I have already indicated in

the case of the architects, to obtain 40 acceptances, 64 invitations had to be sent out.

The invitation to this group, as to all the creative groups which we have studied, was to come to Berkeley for a·weekend of intensive study in the Institute of Personality Assessment and Research. There, in groups of ten, they have been studied by the variety of means which constitute the assessment method—by problem solving experiments; by tests designed to discover what a person does not know or is unable or unwilling to reveal about himself; by tests and questionnaires that permit a person to manifest various aspects of his personality and to express his attitudes, interests, and values; by searching interviews that cover the life history and reveal the present structure of the person; and by specially contrived social situations of a stressful character which call for the subject's best behavior in a socially defined role.

The response of creative persons to the invitation to reveal themselves under such trying circumstances has varied considerably. At the one extreme there have been those who replied in anger at what they perceived to be the audacity of psychologists in presuming to study so ineffable and mysterious a thing as the creative process and so sensitive a thing as a creative person. At the other extreme were those who replied courteously and warmheartedly, welcoming the invitation to be studied, and manifesting even an eagerness to contribute to a better understanding of the creative person and the creative process.

Here we were face to face with a problem that plagues us in all our researches: Are those who are willing to be assessed different in important ways from those who refuse? With respect to psychological traits and characteristics we can never know. But with respect to differences in creativeness, if any, between the 40 who accepted and the 24 who declined our invitation, we know that the two groups are indistinguishable. When the nominating panel's ratings of creativity were converted to standard scores and the means for the 24 versus the 40 were compared, they were found to be identical. When the editors' ratings were similarly converted to standard scores, the mean for the nonassessed group was slightly higher (51.9) than for the assessed sample (48.7), but the difference is not statistically significant.

Certainly we cannot claim to have assessed the 40 most creative architects in the country, or the most creative of any of the groups we have studied; but it is clear that we have studied a highly creative group of architects indistinguishable in their creativity from the group of 24 who declined to be studied, and so with the other groups too.

A third requirement for the successful determination of the traits of highly creative persons in any field of endeavor is that the profession be widely sampled beyond those nominated as most creative, for the distinguishing characteristics of the restricted sample might well have nothing to do with their creativeness. Instead they might be traits characterizing all members of the profession whether creative or not, distinguishing the professional group as a whole but in no sense limited or peculiar to its highly creative members. In the case of the architects, to use them once again as an example, two additional samples were recruited for study, both of which matched the highly creative sample (whom I shall now call Architects I) with respect to age and geographic location of practice. The first supplementary sample (Architects II) had had at least two years of work experience and association with one of the originally nominated creative architects. The second additional sample (Architects III) was composed of architects who had never worked with any of the nominated creatives.

By selecting three samples in this manner, we hoped to tap a range of talent sufficiently wide to be fairly representative of the profession as a whole; and we appear to have succeeded. The mean rating of creativity for each of the three groups—the ratings having been made on a nine-point scale by six groups of architects and experts on architecture—was for Architects I, 5.46; for Architects II, 4.25; and for Architects III, 3.54, the differences in mean ratings between each group being statistically highly significant.

So much for method and research design. I turn now to a discussion of the nature of creative talent as it has been revealed to us in our researches.

Persons who are highly creative are inclined to have a good opinion of themselves, as evidenced by the large number of favorable adjectives which they use in self-description and by the relatively high scores they earn on a scale which measures basic acceptance of the self. Indeed, there is here a paradox, for in addition to their favorable self-perceptions the very basic self-acceptance of the more creative persons often permits them to speak more frankly and thus more critically and in unusual ways about themselves. It is clear, too, that the self-images of the more creative differ from the self-images of the less creative. For example, Architects I, in contrast to Architects II and III, more often describe themselves as inventive, determined, independent, individualistic, enthusiastic, and industrious. In striking contrast Architects II and III more often than Architects I describe themselves as responsible, sincere, reliable, dependable, clear thinking, tolerant, and understanding. In short, where creative architects more often stress their inventiveness, independence, and individuality, their enthusiasm, determination, and industry, less creative members of the profession are impressed by their virtue and good character and by their rationality and sympathetic concern for others.

The discrepancies between their descriptions of themselves as they are and as they would ideally be are remarkably alike for all architects regardless of their level of creativeness. All three groups reveal themselves as desiring more personal attractiveness, self-confidence, maturity, and intellectual competence, a higher level of energy, and better social relations. As for differences, however, Architects I would ideally be more sensitive, while both Architects II and III wish for opposites if not incompatibles; they would ideally be more original but at the same time more self-controlled and disciplined.

As for the relation between intelligence and creativity, save for the mathematicians, where there is a low positive correlation between intelligence and the level of creativeness, we have found within our creative samples essentially zero relationship between the two variables, and this is not due to a narrow restriction in range of intelligence. Among creative architects who have a mean score of 113 on the Terman Concept Mastery Test [16], individual scores range widely from 39 to 179, yet scores on this measure of intelligence correlate −.08 with rated creativity. Over the whole range of intelligence and creativity there is, of course, a positive relationship between the two variables. No feeble-minded subjects have shown up in any of our creative groups. It is clear, however, that above a certain required minimum level of intelligence which varies from field to field and in some instances may be surprisingly low, being more intelligent does not guarantee a corresponding increase in creativeness. It just is not true that the more intelligent person is necessarily the more creative one.

In view of the often asserted close association of genius with insanity it is also of some interest to inquire into the psychological health of our creative subjects. To this end we can look at their profiles on the Minnesota Multiphasic Personality Inventory (MMPI) [7], a test originally developed to measure tendencies toward the major psychiatric disturbances that man is heir to: depression, hysteria, paranoia, schizophrenia, and the like. On the eight scales which measure the strength of these dispositions in the person, our creative subjects earn scores which, on the average, are some 5 to 10 points above the general population's average score of 50. It must be noted, however, that elevated scores of this degree on these scales do not have the same meaning for the personality functioning of persons who, like our subjects, are getting along well in their personal lives and professional careers, that they have for hospitalized patients. The manner in which creative subjects describe themselves on this test as well as in the life history psychiatric interview is less suggestive of psychopathology than it is of good intellect, complexity and richness of personality, general lack of defensiveness, and candor in self-description—in other words, an openness to experience and especially to experience of one's inner life. It must also be noted, however, that in the self-reports and in the MMPI profiles of many of our creative subjects, one can find rather clear evidence of psychopathology, but also evidence of adequate control mechanisms, as the success with which they live their productive and creative lives testifies.

However, the most striking aspect of the MMPI profiles of all our male creative groups is an extremely high peak on the *Mf* (femininity) scale. This tendency for creative males to score relatively high on femininity is also demonstrated on the Fe (femininity) scale of the California Psychological Inventory (CPI) [5] and on the masculinity-femininity scale of the Strong Vocational Interest Blank [15]. Scores on the latter scale (where high score indicates more masculinity) correlate −.49 with rated creativity.

The evidence is clear: The more creative a person is the more he reveals an openness to his own feelings and emotions, a sensitive intellect and understanding self-awareness, and wide-ranging interests including many which in the American culture are thought of as feminine. In the realm of sexual identification and interests, our creative subjects appear to give more expression to the feminine side of their nature than do less creative persons. In the language of the Swiss psychologist, Carl G. Jung [9], creative persons are not so completely identified with their masculine *persona* roles as to blind themselves to or to deny expression to the more feminine traits of the *anima.* For some, to be sure, the balance between masculine and feminine traits, interests, and identification, is a precarious one, and for several of our subjects it would appear that their presently achieved reconciliation of these opposites of their nature has been barely effected and only after considerable psychic stress and turmoil.

The perceptiveness of the creative and his openness to richness and complexity of experience is strikingly revealed on the Barron-Welsh Art Scale of the Welsh Figure Preference Test [17], which presents to the subject a set of 62 abstract line drawings which range from simple and symmetrical figures to complex and asymmetrical ones. In the original study [2] which standardized this scale, some 80 painters from New York, San Francisco, New Orleans, Chicago, and Minneapolis showed a marked preference for the complex and asymmetrical, or, as they often referred to them, the vital and dynamic figures. A contrasting sample of nonartists revealed a marked preference for the simple and symmetrical drawings.

All creative groups we have studied have shown a clear preference for the complex and asymmetrical, and in general the more creative a person is the stronger is this preference. Similarly, in our several samples, scores on an Institute scale which measures the preference for perceptual complexity are significantly correlated with creativity. In the sample of architects the correlation is +.48.

Presented with a large selection of one-inch squares of varicolored posterboard and asked to construct within a 30-minute period a pleasing, completely filled-in 8″ × 10″ mosaic [6], some subjects select the fewest colors possible (one used only one color, all white) while others seek to make order out of the largest possible number, using all of the 22 available colors. And, again citing results from the architects, there is a significant though low positive correlation of +.38 between the number of colors a subject chooses and his creativity as rated by the experts.

If one considers for a moment the meaning of these preferences on the art scale, on the mosaic test, and on the scale that measures preference for perceptual complexity, it is clear that creative persons are especially disposed to admit complexity and even disorder into their perceptions without being made anxious by the resulting chaos. It is not so much that they like disorder per se, but that they prefer the richness of the disordered to the stark barrenness of the simple. They appear to be challenged by disordered multiplicity which arouses in them a strong need which in them is serviced by a superior capacity to achieve the most difficult and far-reaching ordering of the richness they are willing to experience.

The creative person's openness to experience is further revealed on the Myers-Briggs Type Indicator [11], a test based largely upon Carl G. Jung's [8] theory of psychological functions and types.

Employing the language of the test, though in doing so I oversimplify both it and the theory upon which it is based, one might say that whenever a person uses his mind for any purpose, he performs either an act of perception (he becomes aware of something) or an act of judgment (he comes to a conclusion about something). And most persons tend to show a rather consistent preference for and greater pleasure in one or the other of these, preferring either to perceive or to judge, though every one both perceives and judges.

An habitual preference for the judging attitude may lead to some prejudging and at the very least to the living of a life that is orderly, controlled, and carefully planned. A preference for the perceptive attitude results in a life that is more open to experience both from within and from without, and characterized by flexibility and spontaneity. A judging type places more emphasis upon the control and regulation of experience, while a perceptive type is inclined to be more open and receptive to all experience.

The majority of our creative writers, mathematicians, and architects are perceptive types. Only among research scientists do we find the majority to be judging types, and even in this group it is interesting to note that there is a positive correlation (+.25) between a scientist's preference for perception and his rated creativity as a scientific researcher. For architects, preference for perception correlates +.41 with rated creativity.

The second preference measured by the Type Indicator is for one of two types of perception: sense perception or sensation, which is a direct becoming aware of things by way of the senses versus intuitive perception or intuition, which is an indirect perception of the deeper meanings and possibilities inherent in things and situations. Again, everyone senses and intuits, but preliminary norms for the test suggest that in the United States three out of four persons show a preference for sense perception, concentrating upon immediate sensory experience and centering their attention upon existing facts. The one out of every four who shows a preference for intuitive perception, on the other hand, looks expectantly for a bridge or link between that which is given and present and that which is not yet thought of, focusing habitually upon possibilities.

One would expect creative persons not to be bound to the stimulus and the object but to be ever alert to the as-yet-not-realized. And that is precisely the way they show themselves to be on the Type Indicator. In contrast to an estimated 25% of the general population who are intuitive, 90% of the creative writers, 92% of the mathematicians, 93% of the research scientists, and 100% of the architects are intuitive as measured by this test.

In judging or evaluating experience, according to the underlying Jungian theory of the test, one makes use of thought or of feeling; thinking being a logical process aimed at an impersonal fact-weighing analysis, while feeling is a process of appreciation and evaluation of things that gives them a personal and subjective value. A preference for thinking or for feeling appears to be less related to one's creativity

as such than to the type of materials or concepts with which one deals. Of our creative groups, writers prefer feeling, mathematicians, research scientists, and engineers prefer thinking, while architects split fifty-fifty in their preference for one or the other of the two functions.

The final preference in Jungian typology and on the test is the well-known one between introversion and extraversion. Approximately two-thirds of all our creative groups score as introverts, though there is no evidence that introverts as such are more creative than extraverts.

Turning to preferences among interests and values, one would expect the highly creative to be rather different from less creative people, and there is clear evidence that they are.

On the Strong Vocational Interest Blank, which measures the similarity of a person's expressed interests with the known interests of individuals successful in a number of occupations and professions, all of our creative subjects have shown, with only slight variation from group to group, interests similar to those of the psychologist, author-journalist, lawyer, architect, artist, and musician, and interests unlike those of the purchasing agent, office man, banker, farmer, carpenter, veterinarian, and interestingly enough, too, policeman and mortician. Leaving aside any consideration of the specific interests thus revealed we may focus our attention on the inferences that may be drawn from this pattern of scores which suggest that creative persons are relatively uninterested in small details, or in facts for their own sake, and more concerned with their meanings and implications, possessed of considerable cognitive flexibility, verbally skillful, interested in communicating with others and accurate in so doing, intellectually curious, and relatively disinterested in policing either their own impulses and images or those of others.

On the Allport-Vernon-Lindzey Study of Values [1], a test designed to measure in the individual the relative strength of the six values of men as these values have been conceptualized and described by the German psychologist and educator, Eduard Spranger [14], namely, the theoretical, economic, esthetic, social, political, and religious values, all of our creative groups have as their highest values the theoretical and the esthetic.

For creative research scientists the theoretical value is the highest, closely followed by the esthetic. For creative architects the highest value is the esthetic, with the theoretical value almost as high. For creative mathematicians, the two values are both high and approximately equally strong.

If, as the authors of the test believe, there is some incompatibility and conflict between the theoretical value with its cognitive and rational concern with truth and the esthetic value with its emotional concern with form and beauty, it would appear that the creative person has the capacity to tolerate the tension that strong opposing values create in him, and in his creative striving he effects some reconciliation of them. For the truly creative person it is not sufficient that problems be solved, there is the further demand that the solutions be elegant. He seeks both truth and beauty.

A summary description of the creative person—especially of the creative architect— as he reveals himself in his profile on the California Psychological Inventory [5] reads as follows:

He is dominant (Do scale); possessed of those qualities and attributes which underlie and lead to the achievement of social status (Cs); poised, spontaneous, and self-confident in personal and social interaction (Sp); though not of an especially sociable or participative temperament (low Sy); intelligent, outspoken, sharp-witted, demanding, aggressive, and self-centered; persuasive and verbally fluent, self-confident and self-assured (Sa); and relatively uninhibited in expressing his worries and complaints (low Wb).

He is relatively free from conventional restraints and inhibitions (low So and Sc), not preoccupied with the impression which he makes on others and thus perhaps capable of great independence and autonomy (low Gi), and relatively ready to recognize and admit self-views that are unusual and unconventional (low Cm).

He is strongly motivated to achieve in situations in which independence in thought and action are called for (Ai). But, unlike his less creative colleagues, he is less inclined to strive for achievement in settings where conforming behavior is expected or required (Ac). In efficiency and steadiness of intellectual effort (Ie), however, he does not differ from his fellow workers.

Finally, he is definitely more psychologically minded (Py), more flexible (Fx), and possessed of more femininity of interests (Fe) than architects in general.

There is one last finding that I wish to present, one that was foreshadowed by a discovery of Dr. Bingham in one of his attempts to study creativity. The subject of his study was Amy Lowell, a close friend of his and Mrs. Bingham's, with whom he discussed at length the birth and growth of her poems, seeking insight into the creative processes of her mind. He also administered to her a word association test and "found that she gave a higher proportion of unique responses than those of any one outside a mental institution" [3, p. 11]. We, too, administered a word association test to our subjects and found the unusualness of mental associations one of the best predictors of creativity, and especially so when associations given by no more than 1% to 10% of the population, using the Minnesota norms [13], are weighted more heavily than those given by less than 1% of the population. Among architects, for example, this weighted score is for Architects I, 204; Architects II, 128; and Architects III, 114; while for the total sample this measure of unusualness of mental associations correlates +.50 with rated creativity.

And Dr. Bingham, like us, found that there are certain hazards in attempting to study a creative poet. His searchings were rewarded by a poem Amy Lowell later wrote which was first entitled "To the

Impudent Psychologist" and published posthumously with the title "To a Gentleman who wanted to see the first drafts of my poems in the interest of psychological research into the workings of the creative mind." We, I must confess, were treated somewhat less kindly by one of our poets, who, after assessment, published an article entitled "My Head Gets Tooken Apart" [12].

Having described the overall design of our studies, and having presented a selection of our findings which reveal at least some aspects of the nature of creative talent, I turn now, but with considerably less confidence, to the question as to how we can early identify and best encourage the development of creative potential. Our findings concerning the characteristics of highly creative persons are by now reasonably well established, but their implications for the nurture of creative talent are far from clear.

It is one thing to discover the distinguishing characteristics of mature, creative, productive individuals. It is quite another matter to conclude that the traits of creative persons observed several years after school and college characterized these same individuals when they were students. Nor can we be certain that finding these same traits in youngsters today will identify those with creative potential. Only empirical, longitudinal research, which we do not yet have, can settle such issues. Considering, however, the nature of the traits which discriminate creative adults from their noncreative peers, I would venture to guess that most students with creative potential have personality structures congruent with, though possibly less sharply delineated than, those of mature creatives.

Our problem is further complicated by the fact that though our creative subjects have told us about their experiences at home, in school, and in college, and about the forces and persons and situations which, as they see it, nurtured their creativeness, these are, after all, self-reports subject to the misperceptions and self-deceptions of all self-reports. Even if we were to assume

that their testimony is essentially accurate we would still have no assurance that the conditions in the home, in school, and society, the qualities of interpersonal relations between instructor and student, and the aspects of the teaching-learning process which would appear to have contributed to creative development a generation ago would facilitate rather than inhibit creativity if these same factors were created in today's quite different world and far different educational climate.

In reporting upon events and situations in the life histories of our subjects which appear to have fostered their creative potential and independent spirit, I shall again restrict myself to architects. One finds in their histories a number of circumstances which, in the early years, could well have provided an opportunity as well as the necessity for developing the secure sense of personal autonomy and zestful commitment to their profession which so markedly characterize them.

What appears most often to have characterized the parents of these future creative architects was an extraordinary respect for the child and confidence in his ability to do what was appropriate. Thus they did not hesitate to grant him rather unusual freedom in exploring his universe and in making decisions for himself—and this early as well as late. The expectation of the parent that the child would act independently but reasonably and responsibly appears to have contributed immensely to the latter's sense of personal autonomy which was to develop to such a marked degree.

The obverse side of this was that there was often a lack of intense closeness with one or both of the parents. Most often this appeared in relation to the father rather than to the mother, but often it characterized the relationship with both parents. There were not strong emotional ties of either a positive or a negative sort between parent and child, but neither was there the type of relationship that fosters overdependency nor the type that results in severe rejection. Thus, if there was a certain distance in the relationship between child and parent, it had a liberating effect so far as the child was concerned. If he lacked something of the emotional closeness which some children experience with their parents, he was also spared that type of psychological exploitation that is so frequently seen in the life histories of clinical patients.

Closely related to this factor of some distance between parent and child were ambiguities in identification with the parents. In place of the more usual clear identification with one parent, there was a tendency for the architects to have identified either with both parents or with neither. It was not that the child's early milieu was a deprived one so far as models for identification and the promotion of ego ideals were concerned. It was rather that the larger familial sphere presented the child with a plentiful supply of diverse and effective models—in addition to the mother and father, grandfathers, uncles, and others who occupied prominent and responsible positions within their community—with whom important identifications could be made. Whatever the emotional interaction between father and son, whether distant, harmonious, or turbulent, the father presented a model of effective and resourceful behavior in an exceptionally demanding career. What is perhaps more significant, though, is the high incidence of distinctly autonomous mothers among families of the creative architects, who led active lives with interests and sometimes careers of their own apart from their husbands'.

Still other factors which would appear to have contributed to the development of the marked personal autonomy of our subjects were the types of discipline and religious training which they received, which suggest that within the family there existed clear standards of conduct and ideas as to what was right and wrong but at the same time an expectation if not requirement of active exploration and internalization of a framework of personal conduct. Discipline was almost always consistent and predictable. In most cases there were rules, family standards, and parental injunctions which were known explicitly by the children and seldom infringed. In nearly half the cases, corporal punishment was not employed and in only a few instances was the punishment harsh or cruel.

As for religious practices, the families of the creative architects showed considerable diversity, but what was most widely emphasized was the development of personal ethical codes rather than formal religious practices. For one-third of the families formal religion was important for one parent or for both, but in two-thirds of the families formal religion was either unimportant or practiced only perfunctorily. For the majority of the families, in which emphasis was placed upon the development of one's own ethical code, it is of interest to inquire into the values that were most stressed. They were most often values related to integrity (e.g., forthrightness, honesty, respect for others), quality (e.g., pride, diligence, joy in work, development of talent), intellectual and cultural endeavor, success and ambition, and being respectable and doing the right thing.

The families of the more creative architects tended to move more frequently, whether within a single community, or from community to community, or even from country to country. This, combined with the fact that the more creative architects as youngsters were given very much more freedom to roam and to explore widely, provided for them an enrichment of experience both cultural and personal which their less creative peers did not have.

But the frequent moving appears also to have resulted frequently in some estrangement of the family from its immediate neighborhood. And it is of interest that in almost every case in which the architect reported that his family differed in its behavior and values from those in the neighborhood, the family was different in showing greater cultural, artistic, and intellectual interests and pursuits.

To what extent this sort of cultural dislocation contributed to the frequently reported experiences of aloneness, shyness, isolation, and solitariness during childhood and adolescence, with little or no dating during adolescence, or to what extent these experiences stemmed from a natural introversion of interests and unusual sensitivity, we cannot say. They were doubtless mutually reinforcing factors in stimulating the young architect's awareness of his own inner life and his growing interest in his artistic skills and his ideational, imaginal, and symbolic processes.

Almost without exception, the creative architects manifested very early considerable interest and skill in drawing and painting. And also, with almost no exception, one or both of the parents were of artistic temperament and considerable skill. Often it was the mother who in the architect's early years fostered his artistic potentialities by her example as well as by her instruction. It is especially interesting to note, however, that while the visual and artistic abilities and interests of the child were encouraged and rewarded, these interests and abilities were, by and large, allowed to develop at their own speed, and this pace varied considerably among the architects. There was not an anxious concern on the part of the parents about the skills and abilities of the child. What is perhaps most significant was the widespread definite lack of strong pressures from the parents toward a particular career. And this was true both for pressures away from architecture as well as for pressures toward architecture by parents who were themselves architects.

The several aspects of the life history which I have described were first noted by Kenneth Craik in the protocols for the highly creative Architects I. Subsequently, in reading the protocols for Architects II and III as well as Architects I, a credit of one point for the presence of each of the factors was assigned and the total for each person taken as a score. The correlation of these life history scores with rated creativity of the architects is +.36, significant beyond the .005 level of confidence.

And now I turn finally to a consideration of the implications of the nature of creative

talent for the nurturing of it in school and college through the processes of education.

Our findings concerning the relations of intelligence to creativity suggest that we may have overestimated in our educational system the role of intelligence in creative achievement. If our expectation is that a child of a given intelligence will not respond creatively to a task which confronts him, and especially if we make this expectation known to the child, the probability that he will respond creatively is very much reduced. And later on, such a child, now grown older, may find doors closed to him so that he is definitely excluded from certain domains of learning. There is increasing reason to believe that in selecting students for special training of their talent we may have overweighted the role of intelligence either by setting the cutting point for selection on the intellective dimension too high or by assuming that regardless of other factors the student with the higher IQ is the more promising one and should consequently be chosen. Our data suggest, rather, that if a person has the minimum of intelligence required for mastery of a field of knowledge, whether he performs creatively or banally in that field will be crucially determined by nonintellective factors. We would do well then to pay more attention in the future than we have in the past to the nurturing of those nonintellective traits which in our studies have been shown to be intimately associated with creative talent.

There is the openness of the creative person to experience both from within and from without which suggests that whether we be parent or teacher we should use caution in setting limits upon what those whom we are nurturing experience and express.

Discipline and self-control are necessary. They must be learned if one is ever to be truly creative, but it is important that they not be overlearned. Furthermore, there is a time and place for their learning, and having been learned they should be used flexibly, not rigidly or compulsively.

If we consider this specifically with reference to the attitudes of perceiving and judging, everyone must judge as well as perceive. It is not a matter of using one to the exclusion of the other, but a question of how each is used and which is preferred. The danger for one's creative potential is not the judging or evaluating of one's experience but that one prejudges, thus excluding from perception large areas of experience. The danger in all parental instruction, as in all academic instruction, is that new ideas and new possibilities of action are criticized too soon and too often. Training in criticism is obviously important and so widely recognized that I need not plead its case. Rather I would urge that, if we wish to nurture creative potential, and equal emphasis be placed on perceptiveness, discussing with our students as well as with our children, at least upon occasion, the most fantastic of ideas and possibilities. It is the duty of parents to communicate and of professors to profess what they judge to be true, but it is no less their duty by example to encourage in their children and in their students an openness to all ideas and especially to those which most challenge and threaten their own judgments.

The creative person, as we have seen, is not only open to experience, but intuitive about it. We can train students to be accurate in their perceptions, and this, too, is a characteristic of the creative. But can we train them to be intuitive, and if so how?

I would suggest that rote learning, learning of facts for their own sake, repeated drill of material, too much emphasis upon facts unrelated to other facts, and excessive concern with memorizing, can all strengthen and reinforce sense perception. On the other hand, emphasis upon the transfer of training from one subject to another, the searching for common principles in terms of which facts from quite different domains of knowledge can be related, the stressing of analogies, and similes, and metaphors, a seeking for symbolic equivalents of experience in the widest possible number of sensory and imaginal modalities, exercises in imaginative play, training in retreating

from the facts in order to see them in larger perspective and in relation to more aspects of the larger context thus achieved—these and still other emphases in learning would, I believe, strengthen the disposition to intuitive perception as well as intuitive thinking.

If the widest possible relationships among facts are to be established, if the structure of knowledge [4] is to be grasped, it is necessary that the student have a large body of facts which he has learned as well as a large array of reasoning skills which he has mastered. You will see, then, that what I am proposing is not that in teaching one disdain acute and accurate sense perception, but that one use it to build upon, leading the student always to an intuitive understanding of that which he experiences.

The independence of thought and action which our subjects reveal in the assessment setting appears to have long characterized them. It was already manifest in high school, though, according to their reports, tending to increase in college and thereafter.

In college our creative architects earned about a B average. In work and courses which caught their interest they could turn in an A performance, but in courses that failed to strike their imagination, they were quite willing to do no work at all. In general, their attitude in college appears to have been one of profound skepticism. They were unwilling to accept anything on the mere say-so of their instructors. Nothing was to be accepted on faith or because it had behind it the voice of authority. Such matters might be accepted, but only after the student on his own had demonstrated their validity to himself. In a sense, they were rebellious, but they did not run counter to the standards out of sheer rebelliousness. Rather, they were spirited in their disagreement and one gets the impression that they learned most from those who were not easy with them. But clearly many of them were not easy to take. One of the most rebellious, but, as it turned out, one of the most creative, was advised by the dean of his school to quit because he had no talent; and another, having been failed in his design dissertation which attacked the stylism of the faculty, took his degree in the art department.

These and other data should remind all of us who teach that creative students will not always be to our liking. This will be due not only to their independence in situations in which nonconformity may be seriously disruptive of the work of others, but because, as we have seen, more than most they will be experiencing large quantities of tension produced in them by the richness of their experience and the strong opposites of their nature. In struggling to reconcile these opposites and in striving to achieve creative solutions to the difficult problems which they have set themselves they will often show that psychic turbulence which is so characteristic of the creative person. If, however, we can only recognize the sources of their disturbance, which often enough will result in behavior disturbing to us, we may be in a better position to support and encourage them in their creative striving.

REFERENCES

1. ALLPORT, G. W., VERNON, P. E., & LINDZEY, G. *Study of values: Manual of directions.* (Rev. ed.) Boston: Houghton Mifflin, 1951.
2. BARRON, F., & WELSH, G. S. Artistic perception as a possible factor in personality style: Its measurement by a figure preference test. *J. Psychol.*, 1952, 33, 199–203.
3. BINGHAM, MILLICENT TODD. Beyond psychology. In, *Homo sapiens auduboniensis: A tribute to Walter Van Dyke Bingham.* New York: National Audubon Society, 1953. Pp. 5–29.
4. BRUNER, J. S. *The process of education.* Cambridge, Mass.: Harvard Univer. Press, 1960.
5. GOUGH, H. G. *California Psychological Inventory manual.* Palo Alto, Calif.: Consulting Psychologists Press, 1957.
6. HALL, W. B. The development of a technique for assessing aesthetic predispositions and its application to a sample of professional research scientists. Paper read at Western Psychological Association, Monterey, California, April, 1958.
7. HATHAWAY, S. R., & McKINLEY, J. C. *Minnesota Multiphasic Personality Inventory.* New York: Psychological Corporation, 1945.
8. JUNG, C. G. *Psychological types.* New York: Harcourt, Brace, 1923.
9. JUNG, C. G. *Two essays on analytical psychology.* New York: Meridian, 1956.
10. MacKINNON, D. W. The personality correlates of creativity: A study of American architects. In G. S. Nielsen (Ed.), *Proceedings of the XIV International Congress of Applied Psychology, Copenhagen, 1961.* Vol. 2. Copenhagen: Munksgaard, 1962. Pp. 11–39.
11. MYERS, ISABEL B. *Some findings with regard to type and manual for Myers-Briggs Type Indicator, Form E.* Swarthmore, Pa.: Author, 1958.
12. REXROTH, K. My head gets tooken apart. In, *Bird in the bush: Obvious essays.* New York: New Directions Paperbook, 1959. Pp. 65–74.
13. RUSSELL, W. A., & JENKINS, J. J. The complete Minnesota norms for responses to 100 words from the Kent-Rosanoff Word Association Test. Technical Report No. 11, 1954, University of Minnesota, Contract N8 onr-66216, Office of Naval Research.
14. SPRANGER, E. *Types of men.* (Trans. by Paul J. W. Pigors) Halle (Saale), Germany: Max Niemeyer, 1928.
15. STRONG, E. K., JR. *Manual for Strong Vocational Interest Blanks for Men and Women, Revised Blanks (Form M and W).* Palo Alto, Calif.: Consulting Psychologists Press, 1959.
16. TERMAN, L. M. *Concept Mastery Test, Form T manual.* New York: Psychological Corporation, 1956.
17. WELSH, G. S. *Welsh Figure Preference Test: Preliminary manual.* Palo Alto, Calif.: Consulting Psychologists Press, 1959.
18. WOTTON, HENRY. *The elements of architecture.* London: John Bill, 1624.

Part *6* ~

ASSESSMENT OF PERSONALITY

The assessment of personality is perhaps the most challenging and difficult of any of the areas surveyed in this book. In the measurement of abilities the person being tested is ordinarily motivated to achieve his maximum performance. The tester and the examinee usually agree implicitly about the purposes of the testing—the examinee seeks to produce an optimal score so that he may be favorably considered or selected for some position, while the tester seeks to obtain an optimal score for each examinee as the best estimate of that person's true ability. In personality assessment, on the other hand, the person being assessed may be told that there are no right or wrong answers, that he should respond truthfully, and that he should report his sense impressions accurately; but for various reasons he may be consciously or unconsciously motivated to respond on the basis of other considerations. He may, for example, attempt to cover up undesirable characteristics in the interest of presenting himself in a favorable light. Or, alternatively, he may be oriented toward overemphasizing his complaints or faults to win sympathy, or for some other purpose. Perhaps, because he is confronted with an ambiguous situation and feels a reluctance to commit himself in the face of uncertainty, he refuses to place himself wholeheartedly within the instructional set provided by the test and therefore answers randomly or irrelevantly. In short, in personality assessment it is dangerous to assume that the assessee is fully motivated to provide a truthful, accurate self-portrayal. In most cases, even if he were so motivated, he would probably lack the ability to describe himself accurately. Like all of us, he undoubtedly falls back upon mechanisms of self-deception that heighten his accomplishments and diminish his faults in his own eyes. Thus, frankness of response and accuracy of self-description do not necessarily go hand in hand.

Yet, in spite of these enormous difficulties, personality assessment has made great strides. Considerable ingenuity has been displayed by several investigators in discovering ways to circumvent the respondent's defenses and even to make positive use of these defenses in certain assessment strategies. As many of the selections in Part 6 will illustrate, each of several areas within personality assessment has offered ingenious solutions to problems unique to that area. To highlight some of the problems and solutions in particular areas that have had a general impact upon progress in personality assessment, we have divided the selections of Part 6 into five subsections which encompass some of the major approaches to measurement in this field: (1) "Structured Personality Assessment," (2) "Clinical Inference and the Problem of Objectivity," (3) "Cognitive Approaches to Personality Assessment," (4) "Assessment in Social Contexts," and (5) "Assessment of Interests."

STRUCTURED PERSONALITY ASSESSMENT

The publication of the Minnesota Multiphasic Personality Inventory (MMPI) in the 1940s, likes its predecessor the "Strong Vocational Interest Blank in the area of interest measurement, represented an important milestone in the evolution of structured personality assessment. Up to that time, most questionnaires had been developed not on the basis of the actual responses of particular people to the items, but rather on the basis of the author's judgment that certain questions reflected a specified personality characteristic. Thus, a series of statements would be collected that were all thought to deal with some trait, such as sociability, and it was presumed that a respondent would answer these questions in terms of the degree to which he saw himself as possessing the trait. Such questionnaires were properly criticized for their relative transparency, their dependence upon the truthfulness of the respondent, their tacit assumption that each respondent interpreted the statements in the same way, and their dependence upon the good judgment of the test constructor. The development of the MMPI represented a radical departure from such traditional procedures in that the scores were derived not from an a priori judgment of how different people in theory should respond, but from an empirical analysis of how actual criterion groups did in fact respond. Paul E. Meehl, in the initial chapter of Part 6, carefully explicates the distinction between the traditional approach to personality assessment and that which is embodied in the method of empirical item selection. Meehl points out that it is not necessary to assume that structured personality-questionnaire items have precisely the same meaning for all respondents. On the contrary, he suggests that differences in interpretation of key words may well have a kind of "projective" value that helps to differentiate criterion groups. Meehl shows how a test constructor may proceed to develop scales that will separate criterion groups empirically even when he lacks a clear conceptual appreciation of the bases for the differentiation. Albert Rosen, in the following chapter on "Differentiation of Diagnostic Groups of Individual MMPI Scales," applies an extension of these principles to demonstrate the degree to which differing patterns of empirically derived MMPI-scale scores can separate three different psychopathological syndromes. It is important to note here that Rosen uses patterns of scores, rather than single scores, to distinguish different pathological groups. This is an approach favored by many who use psychological tests clinically.

A cookbook often serves the function of organizing and preserving the tested recipes of the best chefs so that these recipes may be routinely consulted by less experienced cooks as the occasion warrants. In "Wanted—A Good Cookbook" (Chapter 44), Paul E. Meehl suggests that an important analogy can be drawn between cookbooks for preparing and combining food for dinner and actuarial tables for organizing and combining test data to develop useful clinical characterizations of patients. The value of a cookbook is that it largely eliminates the cost of trial and error by incorporating previous experience into its rules. Similarly, one important value of an actuarial table for making clinical interpretations is that once it has been established it obviates the use of costly professional time. Meehl provides evidence for another important potential advantage of the actuarial table over the professional clinician in preparing diagnostic reports—it is generally more accurate. By selecting only variables that have been identified as relevant to a given interpretation in the past, and by weighting these variables appropriately, the actuarial table has the advantage of greater consistency over the human brain. However, the clinician has certain other skills that cannot easily be duplicated (see Meehl, Chapter 48).

If the application of psychological tests to human problems is to result in accurate interpretation and prediction, certain requirements should be met by test scores. In particular, greater accuracy will result if they are relatively free from systematic sources of bias. For example, if items on one scale are all keyed true and items on another are all keyed false, the two scales might be found to correlate negatively with each other, even though the traits purportedly represented by the scales are similar. This might come about by the operation of a general tendency on the part of the respondents to answer consistently "true" or consistently "false" to these items. Such a predisposition to respond in a particular way has been called a "response set," and if its operation is relatively enduring over time and displays some degree of generality beyond a particular test performance, it has been called a "response style." This latter term was introduced to emphasize the possibility that such consistencies in the manner of response might reflect stable personality characteristics. Although in general these personal modes of responding represent sources of error to be avoided in the measurement of specific traits, under other circumstances their operation might be profitably enhanced and capitalized upon for the assessment of stylistic aspects of personality.[1] In Chapter 45 on "Response Styles and the Assessment of Psychopathology," Douglas N. Jackson and Samuel Messick draw conceptual and measurement distinctions between response consistency attributable to content and that which is attributable to response style and response set. They report on the results of a series of factor-analytic investigations into the role of response styles on the MMPI. Their analyses highlight the extent to which such general propensities as the tendency to agree with many heterogeneous items or the tendency to respond desirably complicate the interpretation of dimensions of psychopathology and interfere with refined differential diagnosis. Such analyses, it is hoped, will contribute to a firmer foundation for developing new assessment devices that are relatively free from such effects.

CLINICAL INFERENCE AND THE PROBLEM OF OBJECTIVITY

There are many occasions in clinical practice, as well as in other assessment situations and in research, when information is obtained from a variety of sources and integrated by a human judge into a set of descriptive statements or predictions about behavior. This is a difficult task to do well. It places great demands upon the judgmental processes of the clinician. It requires first of all a sufficient range of clinical experiences upon which to base inferences. It requires that the clinician be able to sort out the relevant from the irrelevant, that he be sensitive to diverse manifestations of modes of thought and response, that he weight each appropriately, and that he organize them accurately into a meaningful relation. Finally, it requires that the clinician have available a suitable repertory of descriptive dimensions of personality with which to communicate his interpretations.

In Chapter 46, Roy Schafer presents a set of six criteria for judging the adequacy of interpretations. By applying these, he cogently distinguishes between legitimate and illegitimate inferences from projective test data. With admirable caution, he suggests that clinical interpretation, however "brilliant," must be supported by a broadly based sampling of observation. The carefully selected examples provide the reader with an opportunity to appraise the usefulness and power of Schafer's chosen theoretical vehicle for interpreting projective test reports, namely, psychoanalytic theory. Perhaps the most

---

[1] Jackson, D. N., & Messick, S. Content and style in personality assessment. *Psychol. Bull.*, 1958, **55**, 243–252.

important distinction between Schafer's application of this approach and that of some other diagnosticians is his attention to the pitfalls of speculating about the origins of a patient's observed modes of thought, as well as his attention to both the need for sufficient support and the requirements for identifying an observable form which the interpreted trend will take.

In Chapter 47, Gardner Lindzey makes explicit some of the implicit assumptions that form a foundation for the clinical use of the Thematic Apperception Test. He provides an exhaustive, critical examination of the logical assumptions and steps necessary in a chain of reasoning that attempts to link a set of stories told in response to a series of pictures to an assessee's needs or thought processes. By discussing these assumptions in the context of empirical research evidence, Lindzey identifies not only areas in which a clinician may move with confidence, but also those in which further research is needed. It is hoped that this sort of logical analysis of a particular projective device will serve as an example in the future for those who wish to develop new projective tests.

Paul E. Meehl, in Chapter 48, seeks an answer to a disturbing professional question—"What Can the Clinician Do Well?" Some psychologists interpreted Meehl's earlier review of studies bearing on the relative accuracy and efficiency of clinical versus statistical prediction as an attack upon the wisdom of applying any form of human judgment to assessment problems.[2] Here, the author is careful to emphasize that there certainly are important occasions when human judgment may be most appropriately utilized. But it should be used selectively, not wasted on routine problems for which actuarial procedures are more accurate and far less expensive. Meehl's emphasis, then, is that the clinical psychologist should make the fullest use of his uniquely human capabilities by reserving them for the unusual assessment situation and for psychotherapy and research, while seeking mechanical solutions for all those recurring problems for which a mechanical solution is feasible.

In Chapter 49, Charles E. Osgood and Zella Luria undertake a task that is both hazardous and replete with fascinating possibilities—a blind analysis of a case of multiple personality. They begin with the hypothesis that certain types of psychopathology may be viewed as disorders of conceptualization, in which the meaning of key concepts and their relationships to the self are misconstrued or idiosyncratically interpreted. Using the semantic differential, a technique for quantitatively evaluating the connotative meaning implicit in concepts, the authors proceed to characterize three personalities residing in a single person by contrasting certain critical meaning relationships as they hold for each personality separately. The high quality and overall accuracy of this blind analysis stem in part, of course, from the sensitivity and skill of the authors, but the results also testify to the cogency of the basic hypothesis and the power of the assessment strategy. This work provides an excellent example of the in-

---

[2] Meehl, P. E. *Clinical vs. statistical prediction.* Minneapolis, Minn.: Univer. of Minnesota Press, 1954.

sights that one can derive from the application of disciplined clinical inference to configural data.

Projective tests have several features intended to increase the likelihood that a subject will produce self-revealing data. Their unstructured form is appropriate for eliciting idiosyncratic responses, their ambiguity provides a degree of disguise, and the variety of response-eliciting elements within each stimulus complex provides ample opportunity for each subject to respond in his own idiom. While granting that these qualities constitute an advantage from the clinical point of view, Wayne H. Holtzman (Chapter 50) also notes that they may be inconsistent with many of the requirements of psychometric theory and with many assumptions implicit in the normative comparison of one individual's scores with those of others. Holtzman carefully reviews the logical and measurement problems involved in developing objective scoring procedures for projective tests and evaluates various strategies for overcoming these difficulties. He then introduces the reader to the Holtzman Inkblot Technique— a projective test explicitly devised to combine the best of the clinical and psychometric worlds. Holtzman shows how it is possible to incorporate into a projective-test format procedures that yield high parallel form and inter-judge reliability. The procedures for developing the Holtzman Inkblot Technique outlined in Chapter 50 represent a model for projective-test development in an era concerned with construct validity and not just predictive utility.

There have been many research approaches to the study of personality. Some have emphasized precision in measurement and concern for operational definitions and objectivity, while others have placed their faith in human judgment, broad theorizing, and intuitively based inferential processes. These approaches have occasionally come into conflict, with one side or the other arguing that its particular strategy was superior. On both sides there is sometimes criticism or even derogation of those efforts that do not employ the favored methods. In Chapter 51, Silvan S. Tomkins broadly appraises these alternative research strategies from the vantage point of both the philosophy of science and the psychology of personality. He eloquently maintains that there is little ground for proponents of either approach to feel smug or overconfident, for at one time or another both kinds of strategists have contributed much. Tomkins then goes on to suggest that this controversy is one more example of a conflict in ideologies that has permeated the history of knowledge for centuries—that preferences for these alternative research strategies have their origins in the more primitive beliefs of the scientist about the nature and value of man.

COGNITIVE APPROACHES TO PERSONALITY ASSESSMENT

There is a wealth of anecdotal, as well as scientific, evidence supporting the notion that the thoughts and perceptions of an individual bear his unique stamp. As Gardner Murphy has put it, each man observes the world through his own rose-colored glasses. The psychologist interested in assessing personality by means of cognition hopes that in addition to truly unique properties that distinguish a single individual there are also shared regularities in modes of thinking, perceiving, and remembering that can serve to differentiate among individuals. Through an appraisal of such consistent individual differences and their correlates, it is hoped that general explanatory constructs can be generated and tested. We will next consider the work of a number of investigators who have sought such regularities, often with gratifying results.

Louis L. Thurstone (Chapter 52) was one of the first psychologists to appreciate the scientific leverage that would be gained by assessing personality characteristics in terms of simple perceptual and cognitive judgments. In the Introduction to *A Factorial Study of Perception*, Thurstone succinctly identifies the major premise underlying such efforts: The attitudes or styles spontaneously adopted in coming to grips with perceptual and judgmental tasks will reveal basic variables of personality. These variables need not be the same as those derived from other methods of inquiry (such as the self-description of needs or the direct observation of people in social situations), for they reflect manifestations of personality in a different, more purely cognitive arena. This is not to say, however, that their operation is necessarily limited, for their influence and correlates may potentially extend to all areas of human functioning that are touched by cognition. The variables themselves, for example, might reflect the characteristic styles in which individuals scan and organize their perceptual environments, articulate and categorize stimuli, analyze problems, and remember past events. Their operation in particular instances, however, might be found to have a substantial impact upon such diverse functions as the control and expression of impulses, the mode of organizing effects and motives, the choice of pathological symptoms and defense mechanisms, and the ways in which people come to grips with social reality.[3] Although Thurstone's own efforts in this area were, like most beginnings, frankly exploratory, he laid an empirical foundation for others to build on. He developed and refined many perceptual and cognitive tests that are still in use today, and he uncovered several dimensions of perceptual consistency, particularly one called "flexibility of closure," that exemplify the fruitfulness of the approach.

Another major figure in this field is Herman A. Witkin, who began several years ago to study the characteristic ways in which people orient themselves in space, with particular reference to their adjustment to the upright. Witkin was concerned with the degree to which individuals used gravitational information from bodily cues as opposed to visual information from the stimulus field in orienting their own body (or some other object) to an upright position. He devel-

[3] See, Klein, G. S. Cognitive control and motivation. In G. Lindzey (Ed.), *Assessment of human motives*. New York: Holt, Rinehart & Winston, 1958; Gardner, R. W., Holzman, P. S., Klein, G. S., Linton, H. B., & Spence, D. Cognitive control: a study of individual consistencies in cognitive behavior. *Psychol. Issues*, 1959, **1**, No. 4; Witkin, H. A., Dyk, R. B., Faterson, H. F., Goodenough, D. R., & Karp, S. A. *Psychological differentiation*, New York: Wiley, 1962; and Shapiro, D. *Neurotic styles*. New York: Basic Books, 1965.

oped a number of original devices for studying this question, such as a tilted room in which the subject, seated in a tilted chair, is asked to adjust his body to the true upright. If he tilts his body far in the direction of the tilted room in order to make himself "straight," he is considered to be comparatively "field dependent." If, on the other hand, he manages to come close to the true upright, he is resisting the influence of the visual field and is comparatively "field independent." Witkin and his coworkers found marked stability within individuals, but enormous variation among individuals, in their relative reliance upon gravitational and visual cues in resolving this conflict. In Chapter 53, "The Perception of the Upright," Witkin traces the evolution of these studies, which range from an early emphasis upon stimulus and situational determinants of perception to those evaluating the central role played by the personality of the perceiver. Witkin's research is noteworthy for the great variety of phenomena investigated and for the scope of its theoretical orientation. Studies have been undertaken, for example, to explore the range of situations affected by individual consistencies in perceptual field dependence; to ascertain its correlates with measures of personality, intellectual functioning, and social influence; to appraise sex differences and developmental trends; and to clarify its role in psychopathology and alcoholic addiction. These studies have done much to reveal the manner in which seemingly prosaic perceptual phenomena have their roots in the nature of the perceiver and can thus be fully understood only in terms of a theory of perception that is cognizant of personality functioning.

In Chapter 54, Frank Barron demonstrates the manner in which a personality variable, in this case a dimension of "complexity-simplicity," may be educed from observed response consistencies. It had been noted that certain subjects in responding to the Barron-Welsh Art Judgment Test reliably preferred simple, symmetrical drawings, while others consistently preferred complex, asymmetrical ones. When Barron correlated measures of this bipolar dimension of preference with a variety of other scores, a coherent pattern emerged that enabled him to characterize subjects displaying extreme preferences for complexity or simplicity in more general terms. The nature and consistency of this pattern (or "correlational composite") formed the basis for an inductive leap, whereby the original empirical dimension of *preference* for complexity was generalized to a broader *personality variable* of complexity-simplicity. This study provides a good example of the "inductive correlational approach" to the investigation of personality, which typically proceeds by defining a personality disposition in terms of a single measure and then broadly surveying the diverse correlates of this score from a variety of sources. It is often regarded as a useful strategy when relatively little is known about a construct and when a more hypothetico-deductive approach cannot be easily employed.

In Chapter 55, James Bieri and Edward Blacker investigate a rather different conception of complexity, namely, the general complexity or degree of differentiation of a person's cognitive system. Since such overall "cognitive complexity" should manifest itself in a wide variety of settings, Bieri and Blacker sought to demonstrate this generality by intercorrelating indexes of complexity from two diverse stimulus realms: (1) complexity assessed by variability in the determinants used in responding to inkblots and (2) by the number of different constructs employed in describing other people. The significant correlations obtained not only support the generality of their construct but also serve to illustrate the relevance of cognitive variables both to personality and to social perception.

ASSESSMENT IN SOCIAL CONTEXTS

The importance of personality consistencies is perhaps most dramatically revealed by the behavioral differences displayed by individuals acting in social contexts. Personality-assessment specialists, in building upon this observation, have indeed found that judgments of personality made in structured or natural social situations serve as both an excellent primary source of information about personality and as realistic intermediate criteria for validating assessment devices based upon other kinds of information. The variety of social contexts in which useful data may be sought about personality is very large, as is the number of ingenious methods developed for appraising particular constructs of personality within these social settings. The two methods to be described next represent broad-band procedures in the sense that they do not pinpoint a particular personality variable, but rather have the potential for yielding information on a number of traits.

The first of these methods stems from assessment studies conducted during World War II in the selection and training of espionage agents. Building upon his earlier work at the Harvard Psychological Clinic, Henry A. Murray assembled a distinguished group of psychologists to participate with him in developing the basic rationale and procedures for the Living-in Assessment Program of the U.S. Office of Strategic Services (OSS). In such a program, assessees spend twenty-four hours a day for several days living in a house with several assessors. During this period, they eat, sleep, work, and play in a context of total assessment. They are asked to participate in a number of activities, some of which, like the stress interview described here, impose serious role-taking demands in situations chosen to exemplify criterion tasks. Other activities, even those that take the form of apparently lighthearted skits, also serve serious assessment aims in that they may reveal traits like flexibility and poise. In Chapter 56, Donald W. MacKinnon, a former member of the OSS staff, describes the stress interview, a contrived situation carefully designed to simulate its real-life counterpart. The approach used here views personality as more than a collection of static traits susceptible to passive attempts at assessment. It is not enough to ascertain the degree to which a particular trait is possessed under standard or optimal conditions—in addition one must determine the extent to which it will operate under different circumstances. It would seem to follow, then, that for purposes of predicting real-life performance a trait should be assessed under conditions that reveal its dynamic interaction with situational demands. From this standpoint, the assessments task becomes one of eliciting the relevant behavior with the appropriate situational manipulation. Thus, variables like emotional stability and security are appraised not only in situations of optimal comfort and support but also in situations where a deliberate, often devious attempt is alternately made to provoke or to disarm the candidate.

In Chapter 57, Bernard M. Bass summarizes results obtained with a different kind of structured social context for eliciting behavior relevant to personality traits. The "leaderless group discussion" was developed several decades ago by the German General Staff to appraise leadership potential. Typically, a group of subjects is seated around a table and assigned the task of resolving some general sort of question. The group might be asked, for example, to indicate the names of the five greatest men who ever lived. Subjects are given no instructions on how to proceed, but merely told how much time they have to complete the assignment. An observer watches inconspicuously and later rates the behavior of each participant on the dimensions considered important. Bass reviews the broad spectrum of situations that have been found to relate to judgments of performance in leaderless group discussions. An additional research study by Juola[4] has uncovered an important correlate (and possible contaminant) of such judgments: The sheer amount of time a given individual spends talking in the situation has a highly significant effect upon how he is rated. Thus, traits denoting leadership ability, for example, are ordinarily ascribed to persons who talk a great deal in the leaderless group discussion. There is an urgent need for further research to evaluate the extent to which alternative instructions or modifications in the experimental situation would yield information relevant to other determinants of judgment.

ASSESSMENT OF INTERESTS

One of the most successful applications of psychological tests to individual decision making has been in the area of interest measurement. Over four decades ago, the late Edward K. Strong undertook a task that was to occupy him for the remainder of his life. In the face of considerable skepticism, with virtually no financial support but with great tenacity and faith in the psychology of individual differences, Strong identified empirically the interest patterns of a large number of skilled, professional, and managerial groups, as revealed by responses to the four hundred items comprising the Strong Vocational Interest Blank (SVIB). These interest patterns have been found to be predictive of who will enter a particular occupation, who will continue to pursue it, and who will drop out. The enormous success of

---

[4] Juola, A. E. Leaderless group discussion ratings: what do they measure? *Educ. psychol. Measmt*, 1957, **17**, 499–509.

this approach is attested to by the extremely widespread use of the SVIB. In Chapter 58, Strong applies his inquiring mind to the intricate problem of specifying the nature of occupational satisfactions and how they differ from interests. Satisfaction is usually considered to be a pleasant, quiescent feeling of contentment at having arrived at some goal. Strong suggests, however, that a more important concept from the point of view of predicting future behavior is the notion of *anticipated* satisfaction, which accompanies progress toward a goal. Rather than measuring satisfaction at a given moment, he proposes instead that we measure motivation and inquire what an employee wants, what he expects to get, and how likely he thinks it is that he'll get it. These three components would then form the basis for an index of satisfaction: The higher the perceived likelihood of success, the greater should be the anticipated satisfaction, but the difference between aspiration and expectation should also contribute a degree of dissatisfaction. Strong notes that measuring satisfactions in this way is similar in some respects to measuring interests, but that the two also differ. Interests are associated with particular activities, whereas satisfactions, being intrinsically goal-oriented, implicate any appropriately instrumental activity that is available.

The Strong Vocational Interest Blank has evolved into a highly useful counseling instrument in the hands of the experienced psychologist. A number of rules of inference have been developed over the years regarding the use of interest patterns for helping a particular counselee make a more rational vocational decision. In Chapter 59, John G. Darley and Theda Hagenah illustrate with varied case materials some of the typical counseling problems encountered in practice. While building their rationale primarily around the SVIB, they also provide considerable wisdom concerning the more general use of test scores in individual counseling. Throughout the discussion the authors stress the importance of conducting counseling sessions in a manner that is meaningful to the counselee—for example, by striving for a problem orientation rather than a test orientation and by avoiding the premature introduction of test scores into the counseling process. After presenting illuminating case studies, Darley and Hagenah argue convincingly for the viewpoint that interest measurement belongs squarely in the domain of personality assessment, although much further research is required to identify the many links between interest patterns and personal needs and to unravel their mutual interactions in development.

The final article in this section (Chapter 60) is by another distinguished contributor to the field of interest measurement, G. Frederic Kuder, whose own interest inventory, the *Kuder Preference Record,* is the major competitor of the SVIB. From his wealth of experience, both in the practical substance of interest measurement and in the psychometrics of test construction, Kuder surveys anticipated development in interest and personality inventories. He discusses a variety of alternative strategies for maximizing the chances for correct decision making and for minimizing the effects of faking and other forms of distortion.

Chapter *42* ~

The Dynamics of "Structured" Personality Tests

PAUL E. MEEHL

In a recent article in the *Journal of Clinical Psychology* [3], Lt. Max L. Hutt of the Adjutant General's School has given an interesting discussion of the use of projective methods in the army medical installations. This article was part of a series describing the work of clinical psychologists in the military services, with which the present writer is familiar only indirectly. The utility of any instrument in the military situation can, of course, be most competently assessed by those in contact with clinical material in that situation, and the present paper is in no sense to be construed as an "answer" to or an attempted refutation of Hutt's remarks. Nevertheless, there are some incidental observations contained in his article which warrant further critical consideration, particularly those having to do with the theory and dynamics of "structured" personality tests. It is with these latter observations rather than the main burden of Hutt's article that this paper is concerned.

Hutt defines "structured personality tests"

This article is reprinted from the *Journal of Clinical Psychology* with the permission of the author and the copyright holder.

as those in which the test material consists of conventional, culturally crystallized questions to which the subject must respond in one of a very few fixed ways. With this definition we have no quarrel, and it has the advantage of not applying the unfortunate phrase "self-rating questionnaire" to the whole class of question-answer devices. But immediately following this definition, Hutt goes on to say that "it is assumed that each of the test questions will have the same meaning to all subjects who take the examination. The subject has no opportunity of organizing in his own unique manner his response to the questions."

These statements will bear further examination. The statement that personality tests assume that each question has the same meaning to all subjects is continuously appearing in most sources of late, and such an impression is conveyed by many discussions even when they do not explicitly make this assertion. It should be emphasized very strongly, therefore, that while this perhaps has been the case with the majority of question-answer personality tests, it is not by any means part of their

517

essential nature. The traditional approach to verbal question-answer personality tests has been, to be sure, to view them as self-ratings; and it is in a sense always a self-rating that you obtain when you ask a subject about himself, whether you inquire about his feelings, his health, his attitudes, or his relations to others.

However, once a "self-rating" has been obtained, it can be looked upon in two rather different ways. The first, and by far the commonest approach, is to accept a self-rating as a second best source of information when the direct observation of a segment of behavior is inaccessible for practical or other reasons. This view in effect forces a self-rating or self-description to act as surrogate for a behavior-sample. Thus we want to know whether a man is shy, and one criterion is his readiness to blush. We cannot conveniently drop him into a social situation to observe whether he blushes, so we do the next best (and often much worse) thing and simply ask him, "Do you blush easily?" We assume that if he does in fact blush easily, he will realize that fact about himself, which is often a gratuitous assumption; and secondly, we hope that having recognized it, he will be willing to tell us so.

Associated with this approach to structured personality tests is the construction of items and their assembling into scales upon an *a priori basis*, requiring the assumption that the psychologist building the test has sufficient insight into the dynamics of verbal behavior and its relation to the inner core of personality that he is able to predict beforehand what certain sorts of people will say about themselves when asked certain sorts of questions. The fallacious character of this procedure has been sufficiently shown by the empirical results of the Minnesota Multiphasic Personality Inventory alone, and will be discussed at greater length below. It is suggested tentatively that the relative uselessness of most structured personality tests is due more to *a priori* item construction than to the fact of their being structured.

The second approach to verbal self-ratings is rarer among test makers. It consists simply in the explicit denial that we accept a self-rating as a feeble surrogate for a behavior sample, and substitutes the assertion that a "self-rating" constitutes an intrinsically interesting and significant bit of verbal behavior, the non-test correlates of which must be discovered by empirical means. Not only is this approach free from the restriction that the subject must be able to describe his own behavior accurately, but a careful study of structured personality tests built on this basis shows that such a restriction would falsify the actual relationships that hold between what a man says and what he *is*.

Since this view of question-answer items is the rarer one at the present time, it is desirable at this point to elucidate by a number of examples. For this purpose one might consider the Strong Vocational Interest Blank, the Humm-Wadsworth Temperament Scales, the Minnesota Multiphasic Personality Inventory, or any structured personality measuring device in which the selection of items was done on a thoroughly empirical basis using carefully selected criterion groups. In the extensive and confident use of the Strong Vocational Interest Blank, this more sophisticated view of the significance of responses to structured personality test items has been taken as a matter of course for years. The possibility of conscious as well as unconscious "fudging" has been considered and experimentally investigated by Strong and others, but the differences in possible interpretation or *meaning* of items have been more or less ignored—as well they should be. One is asked to indicate, for example, whether he likes, dislikes, or is indifferent to "conservative people." The possibilities for differential interpretation of a word like *conservative* are of course tremendous, but nobody has worried about that problem in the case of the Strong. Almost certainly the strength of verbs like "like" and "dislike" is variably interpreted throughout the whole blank. For the present purpose the Multiphasic (referred to hereinafter as MMPI) will be employed because the present writer is most familiar with it.

One of the items on the MMPI scale for detecting psychopathic personality (Pd) is "My parents and family find more fault with me than they should." If we look upon this as a rating in which the *fact* indicated by an affirmative response is crucial, we immediately begin to wonder whether the testee can objectively evaluate how much other people's parents find fault with them, whether his own parents are warranted in finding as much fault with him as they do, whether this particular subject will interpret the phrase "finding fault" in the way we intend or in the way most normal persons interpret it, and so on. The present view is that this is simply an unprofitable way to examine a question-answer personality test item. To begin with, the empirical finding is that individuals whose past history and momentary clinical picture is that of a typical psychopathic personality tend to say "Yes" to this much more often than people in general do. Now in point of fact, they probably should say "No" because the parents of psychopaths are sorely tried and probably do not find fault with their incorrigible offspring any more than the latter deserve. An allied item is "I have been quite independent and free from family rule" which psychopaths tend to answer *false*—almost certainly opposite to what is actually the case for the great majority of them. Again, "Much of the time I feel I have done something wrong or evil." Anyone who deals clinically with psychopaths comes to doubt seriously whether they could possibly interpret this item in the way the rest of us do (*cf. Cleckley's* [1] "semantic dementia"), but they *say* that about themselves nonetheless. Numerous other examples such as "Someone has it in for me" and "I am sure I get a raw deal from life" appear on the same scale and are significant because psychopaths tend to *say* certain things about themselves, rather than because we take these statements at face value.

Consider the MMPI scale for detecting tendencies to hypochondriasis. A hypochondriac says that he has headaches often, that he is not in as good health as his friends are, and that he cannot understand what he reads as well as he used to. Suppose that he has a headache on an average of once every month, as does a certain "normal" person. The hypochondriac says he often has headaches, the other person says he does not. They both have headaches once a month, and hence they must either interpret the word "often" differently in that question, or else have unequal recall of their headaches. According to the traditional view, this ambiguity in the word "often" and the inaccuracy of human memory constitute sources of error; for the authors of MMPI they may actually constitute sources of discrimination.

We might mention as beautiful illustrations of this kind of relation, the non-somatic items in the hysteria scale of MMPI [2]. These items have a statistical homogeneity and the common property by face inspection that they indicate the person to be possessed of unusually good social and psychiatric adjustment. They are among the most potent items for the detection of hysterics and hysteroid temperaments, but they reflect the systematic distortion of the hysteric's conception of himself, and would have to be considered invalid if taken as surrogates for the direct observation of behavior.

As a last example one might mention some findings of the writer, to be published shortly, in which "normal" persons having rather abnormal MMPI profiles are differentiated from clearly "abnormal" persons with equally deviant profiles by a tendency to give statistically rare as well as psychiatrically "maladjusted" responses to certain other items. Thus a person who says that he is afraid of fire, that windstorms terrify him, that people often disappoint him, stands a better chance of being normal in his non-test behavior than a person who does not admit to these things. The discrimination of this set of items for various criterion groups, the intercorrelations with other scales, and the content of the items indicate strongly that they detect some verbal-semantic distortion in the interpretation and response to the other MMPI items which enters into the spurious elevation of scores achieved by certain "normals." Recent unpublished research on more subtle "lie" scales of MMPI indicates that unconscious self-deception is inversely related to the kind of verbal distortion just indicated.

In summary, a serious and detailed study of the MMPI items and their interrelations both with one another and non-test behavior cannot fail to convince one of the necessity for this second kind of approach to question-answer personality tests. That the majority of the questions seem by inspection to require self-ratings has been a source of theoretical misunderstanding, since the stimulus situation seems to request a self-rating, whereas *the scoring does not assume a valid self-rating to have been given*. It is difficult to give any psychologically meaningful interpretation of some of the empirical findings on MMPI unless the more sophisticated view is maintained.

It is for this reason that the possible differences in interpretation do not cause us any *a priori* concern in the use of this instrument. Whether any structured personality test turns out to be valid and useful must be decided on pragmatic grounds, but the possibility of diverse interpretations of a single item is not a good *theoretical* reason for predicting failure of the scales. There is a "projective" element involved in interpreting and responding to these verbal stimuli which must be recognized, in spite of the fact that the test situation is very rigidly structured as regards the ultimate response possibilities permitted. The objection that all persons do not interpret structured test items in the same way is not fatal, just as it would not be fatal to point out that "ink blots do not look the same to everyone."

It has not been sufficiently recognized by critics of structured personality tests that

what a man says about himself may be a highly significant fact about him even though we do not entertain with any confidence the hypothesis that what he says would agree with what complete knowledge of him would lead others to say of him. It is rather strange that this point is so often completely passed by, when clinical psychologists quickly learn to take just that attitude in a diagnostic or therapeutic interview. The complex defense mechanisms of projection, rationalization, reaction-formation, etc., appear dynamically to the interviewer as soon as he begins to take what the client *says* as itself motivated by other needs than those of giving an accurate verbal report. There is no good *a priori* reason for denying the possibility of similar processes in the highly structured "interview" which is the question-answer personality test. The summarized experience of the clinician results (one hopes, at least) in his being able to discriminate verbal responses admissible as accurate self-descriptions from those which reflect other psychodynamisms but are not on that account any the less significant. The test analogue to this experience consists of the summarized statistics on response frequencies, at least among those personality tests which have been constructed empirically (MMPI, Strong, Rorschach, etc.).

Once this has been taken for granted we are prepared to admit powerful items to personality scales regardless of whether the rationale of their appearance can be made clear at present. We do not have the confidence of the traditional personality test maker that the relation between the behavior dynamics of a subject and the tendency to respond verbally in a certain way must be psychologically obvious. Thus it puzzles us but does not disconcert us when this relation cannot be elucidated, the science of behavior being in the stage that it is. That "I sometimes tease animals" (answered *false*) should occur in a scale measuring symptomatic depression is theoretically mysterious, just as the tendency of certain schizophrenic patients to accept "position" as a determinant in responding to the Rorschach may be theoretically mysterious. Whether such a relation obtains can be very readily discovered empirically, and the wherefore of it may be left aside for the moment as a theoretical question. Verbal responses which do not apparently have any *self*-reference at all, but in their form seem to request an objective judgment about social phenomena or ethical values, may be equally diagnostic. So, again, one is not disturbed to find items such as "I think most people would lie to get ahead" (answered *false*) and "It takes a lot of argument to convince most people of the truth" (answered *false*) appearing on the hysteria scale of MMPI.

The frequently alleged "superficiality" of structured personality tests becomes less evident on such a basis also. Some of these items can be rationalized in terms of fairly deep-seated trends of the personality, although it is admittedly difficult to establish that any given depth interpretation is the correct one. To take one example, the items on the MMPI scale for hysteria which were referred to above as indicating extraordinarily good social and emotional adjustment can hardly be seen as valid self-descriptions. However, if the core trend of such items is summarily characterized as "I am psychiatrically and socially well adjusted," it is not hard to fit such a trend into what we know of the basic personality structure of the hysteric. The well known *belle indifférence* of these patients, the great lack of insight, the facility of repression and dissociation, the "impunitiveness" of their reactions to frustration, the tendency of such patients to show an elevated "lie" score on MMPI may all be seen as facets of this underlying structure. It would be interesting to see experimentally whether to the three elements of Rosenzweig's "triadic hypothesis" (impunitiveness, repression, hypnotizability) one might add a fourth correlate—the chief non-somatic component of the MMPI hysteria scale.

Whether "depth" is plumbed by a structured personality test to a lesser extent than by one which is unstructured is difficult to determine, once the present view of the nature of structured tests is understood. That the "deepest" layers of personality are not verbal might be admitted without any implication that they cannot therefore make themselves known to us via verbal behavior. Psychoanalysis, usually considered the "deepest" kind of psychotherapy, makes use of the dependency of verbal behavior upon underlying variables which are not themselves verbalized.

The most important area of behavior considered in the making of psychiatric diagnosis is still the form and content of the *speech* of the individual. I do not mean to advance these considerations as validations of any structured personality tests, but merely as reasons for not accepting the theoretical objection sometimes offered in criticizing them. Of course, structured personality tests may be employed in a purely diagnostic, categorizing fashion, without the use of any dynamic interpretations of the relationship among scales or the patterning of a profile. For certain practical purposes this is quite permissible, just as one may devote himself to the statistical validation of various "signs" on the Rorschach test, with no attempt to make qualitative or really dynamic personological inferences from the findings. The tradition in the case of structured personality tests is probably weighted on the side of non-dynamic thinking; and in the case of some structured tests, there is a considerable amount of experience and clinical subtlety required to extract the maximum of information. The present writer has heard discussions in case conferences at the University of Minnesota Hospital which make as "dynamic" use of MMPI patterns as one could reasonably make of any kind of test data without an excessive amount of illegitimate reification. The clinical use of the Strong Vocational Interest Blank is another example.

In discussing the "depth" of interpretation possible with tests of various kinds, it should at least be pointed out that the problem of validating personality tests, whether structured or unstructured, becomes more difficult in proportion as the interpretations increase in "depth." For example, the validation of the "sign" differentials on the Rorschach is relatively easier to carry out than that of the deeper interpretations concerning the basic personality structure. This does not imply that there is necessarily less validity in the latter class of inferences, but simply stresses the difficulty of designing experiments to test validity. A very major part of this difficulty hinges upon the lack of satisfactory external criteria, a situation which exists also in the case of more dynamic interpretations of structured personality tests. One is willing to accept a staff diagnosis of psychasthenia in selecting cases against which to validate the Pt scale of MMPI or the F% as a compulsive-obsessive sign on the Rorschach. But when the test results indicate repressed homosexuality or latent anxiety or lack of deep insight into the self, we may have strong suspicions that the instrument is fully as competent as the psychiatric staff. Unfortunately this latter assumption is very difficult to justify without appearing to be inordinately biased in favor of our test. Until this problem is better solved than at present, many of the "depth" interpretations of both structured and unstructured tests will be little more than an expression of personal opinion.

There is one advantage of unstructured personality tests which cannot easily be claimed for the structured variety, namely, the fact that falsehood is difficult. While it is true for many of the MMPI items, for example, that even a psychologist cannot predict on which scales they will appear nor in what direction certain sorts of abnormals will tend to answer them, still the relative accessibility of defensive answering would seem to be greater than is possible in responding to a set of inkblots. Research is still in progress on more subtle "lie" scales of MMPI and we have every reason to feel encouraged on the present findings. Nevertheless the very existence of a definite problem in this case and not in the case of the Rorschach gives the latter an advantage in this respect. When we pass to a more structured method, such as the T. A. T., the problem reappears. The writer has found, for example, a number of patients who simply were not fooled by the "intelligence-test" set given in the directions for the T. A. T., as was indicated quite clearly by self-references and defensive remarks, especially on the second day. Of course such a patient is still under pressure to produce material and therefore his unwillingness to reveal himself is limited in its power over the projections finally given.

In conclusion, the writer is in hearty agreement with Lieutenant Hutt that unstructured personality tests are of great value, and that the final test of the adequacy of any technique is its utility in clinical work. Published evidence of the validity of both structured and unstructured personality tests as they had to be modified for convenient military use does not enable one to draw any very definite conclusions or comparisons at the present time. There is assuredly no reason for us to place structured and unstructured types of instruments in battle order against one another, although it is admitted that when time is limited they come inevitably into a very real clinical "competition" for use. The present article has been aimed simply at the clarification of certain rather prevalent misconceptions as to the nature and the theory of at least one important structured personality test, in order that erroneous theoretical considerations may not be thrown into the balance in deciding the outcome of such clinical competition.

REFERENCES

1. CLECKLEY, H. *The Mask of Sanity*. St. Louis: Mosby, 1941.
2. McKINLEY, J. C., and HATHAWAY, S. R. The Minnesota Multiphasic Personality Inventory: V. Hysteria, hypomania, and psychopathic deviate. *J. appl. Psychol.*, 1944, 28, 153–174.
3. HUTT, MAX L. The use of projective methods of personality measurement in army medical installations. *J. clin. Psychol.*, 1945, 1, 134–140.

43~

Differentiation of Diagnostic Groups of Individual MMPI Scales

ALBERT ROSEN

A multiscaled instrument such as the MMPI is generally interpreted in terms of configurations of scale patterns and elevations. Information concerning the concurrent validity of individual scales can nevertheless be of considerable value. Besides indicating the degree of differentiation possible between diagnostic groups by means of individual scales, such information can also contribute to the enrichment of configural kinds of interpretations in the psychiatric setting. Of even broader significance is the fact that data on individual scale discrimination can add to our total comprehension of the meanings inherent in a specific scale and therefore are apt to suggest other significant relationships and inferences.

Although the present study was part of a larger project and not planned as a replication, the findings are of special interest be-

This article is reprinted from the *Journal of Consulting Psychology*, 1958, with the permission of the author and the American Psychological Association. The investigator is indebted to Leonard I. Schneider for suggestions leading to improved organization and clarity of the report.

cause of another report that virtually no differentiation between psychiatric groups is possible using individual MMPI scales. Rubin [6, 7] has reported that the MMPI cannot significantly differentiate between diagnostic groups in a VA psychiatric hospital. He selected at random 93 MMPI records of patients, the total group consisting of 8 chronic alcoholics without psychosis, 24 psychopaths, 33 schizophrenics, and 28 psychoneurotics. Using the analysis of variance method, he found that only one clinical scale, Sc, differentiated in some manner between the four diagnostic groups. This paper presents additional data on the discriminating power of the individual MMPI scales, as well as some possible explanations of Rubin's negative results.

PROCEDURE

Five groups from the psychiatry service of the Minneapolis VA Hospital were chosen which were composed of 307 patients diagnosed according to the Veterans Administration psychiatric nomenclature as follows: (a) anxiety reaction (anxiety state)—83 cases; (b) conversion reaction (conversion hysteria)—49 cases; (c) depressive reaction (neurotic depression)—36 cases; (d) somatization reaction (psychophysiological reaction, psychosomatic reaction, organ neurosis)—39 cases; and (e) schizophrenic reaction, paranoid type—100 cases.

The few published studies providing objective data for the evaluation of diagnostic reliability have emphasized that there is a high degree of inconsistency in psychiatric diagnosis [2, 3, 5]. If diagnostic unreliability does prevail, psychological research based upon a diagnostic criterion is apt to be of limited value, for patients classified within any one diagnostic group will be quite heterogeneous, and there will be considerable overlapping between groups.

Because of the importance to the present study of obtaining homogeneous diagnostic groups, only so-called "pure" cases were selected for each sample. Thus, a case was excluded if there was evidence that the patient had been given (a) two different diagnoses upon successive admissions, or (b) a diagnosis containing a statement of overlapping trends, as for example, "anxiety reaction with paranoid and schizoid trends." There was, however, one exception to this rule. Inasmuch as a large number of anxiety reaction cases suffer from depression, it was not feasible to exclude cases of "anxiety reaction with depression."

The procedure in selecting patients for the five diagnostic groups was as follows:

1. From a file listing the final diagnoses of all patients who had been tested, the names were selected of "pure" cases who had been diagnosed in one of the five categories listed above.[1]
2. For the purpose of increasing the homogeneity of each diagnostic group, there were included in the

[1] An exception was the group of patients diagnosed paranoid schizophrenia. Because of their abundance, 100 cases were selected from those most recently discharged.

study only male, white veterans who had been tested within 15 days after admission and who had not received insulin or electroshock therapy prior to the administration of the MMPI. The median number of days between admission and MMPI administration for each of the five final samples was between 3 and 4.

3. The MMPI records of the patients selected were obtained from their test folders, and a few additional cases were removed on the basis of extremely high L, F, K, and ? scores. In the final samples, the median number of ? items for each of the five diagnostic groups was 2–4, Q_3 was 6–14, and only 15 records contained more than 30 ? items.

RESULTS

The following procedure was used to test the significance of the differences in means of each MMPI scale for the five diagnostic groups:

1. The Bartlett test [4, p. 97] was applied and heterogeneity of variances ($p \leq .05$) of the five groups was found for six of the scales: F, K, Pd + .4K, Pa, Sc + 1K, and Si.
2. For each of these six scales, critical ratios were calculated for the 10 possible differences between means.
3. For each of the other seven scales with homogeneous variances, an analysis of variance test was made.

The mean scores of the diagnostic groups for each MMPI scale are shown in Figure 43–1 and listed in Table 43–1. These T scores are rounded numbers because all calculations were made with raw score means and variances. The F ratio is also recorded in Table 43–1 for the seven scales for which this statistic was computed. Since the curves for the Depression and Anxiety groups and for the Somatization and Conversion groups are almost identical, the

Table 43–1   Mean *T* Scores of Five Diagnostic Groups on Each MMPI Scale

MMPI Scale	Paranoid Schizophrenia (N = 100)	Depression (N = 36)	Anxiety (N = 83)	Somatization (N = 39)	Conversion (N = 49)	F Ratio
			Diagnostic Groups			
L	50	47	48	52	50	2.78°
F	70	58	58	54	54	
K	51	50	51	56	54	
Hs + .5K	71	71	73	79	76	2.33
D	81	88	81	71	70	8.94†
Hy	70	71	72	72	73	<1.00
Pd + .4K	74	64	63	59	59	
Mf	64	60	57	55	53	11.87†
Pa	72	62	60	57	55	
Pt + 1K	81	77	76	66	62	16.16†
Sc + 1K	87	67	67	62	60	
Ma + .2K	63	54	55	56	58	6.65†
Si	64	62	61	53	51	

° Significant at .05 level.
† Significant at .001 level.

median profiles for only three groups are shown in Figure 43–1 in order to avoid a confusion of lines. On seven of the scales there is an orderly hierarchy of mean scores, with the Paranoid Schizophrenia group being highest, and the Depression, Anxiety, Somatization, and Conversion groups following in order. These seven scales are F, Pd + .4K, Mf, Pa, Pt + 1K, Sc + 1K, and Si. On the D scale, this order

Figure 43–1   *Mean T scores for three diagnostic groups on each MMPI scale.*

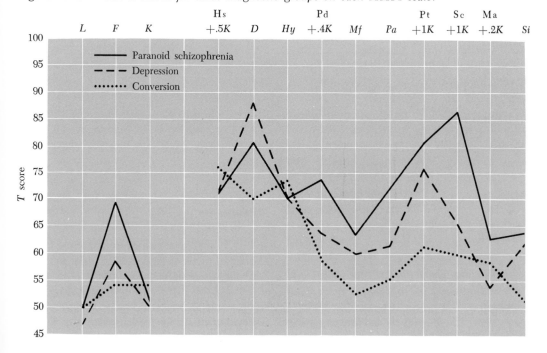

for the five groups is the same except for a reversal of the Depression and Paranoid Schizophrenia groups. In the profiles of the Somatization and Conversion groups, the $Hs + .5K$, D, and Hy scores are most elevated with D slightly lower than the other two. This is the so-called "V profile," frequently noted for individual cases diagnosed as conversion or somatization reaction.

Among the 130 possible differences in mean scale scores for the five diagnostic groups, 61 are significant at or beyond the .05 level, as listed in Table 43–2. Eleven such differences would be expected by chance if the statistical tests were independent [8]. Of these 61 differences, 17 are significant at the .05 level, 8 at the .01 level, 5 at the .001 level, and 31 at or beyond the .0001 level. The Anxiety and Depression groups are significantly different from each other only on the D scale, and the Somatization and Conversion groups are similar on every scale. If the Anxiety and Depres-

sion groups are combined, and the Somatization and Conversion groups are also treated as one group, each of these two groups is effectively differentiated from the other and from the Paranoid Schizophrenia group. Cross-validation of this finding is necessary, however, for the combining of groups was done after inspection of the data. Neither the $Hs + .5K$ nor the Hy scale differentiates the Somatization or Conversion groups from the other three groups.

DISCUSSION

The positive findings of the present study contrast sharply with the almost complete lack of MMPI differentiation between Rubin's diagnostic groups. Three possible explanations of the divergent results will be discussed as follows: (a) High $?$ scores in Rubin's records; (b) criterion contamination in the present study; and (c) criterion unreliability in Rubin's groups.

Table 43–2   Diagnostic Groups Significantly Different in Mean Scores on Each MMPI Scale*

	Diagnostic Groups				
MMPI Scale	Paranoid Schizophrenia ($N = 100$)	Depression ($N = 36$)	Anxiety ($N = 83$)	Somatization ($N = 39$)	Conversion ($N = 49$)
Mean score of above groups higher than score of—					
L	A D			A D	
F	D A S C				
K				P A D	
$Hs + .5K$					
D	S C	P A S C	S C		
Hy					
$Pd + .4K$	D A S C	C	C		
Mf	A S C	S C	C		
Pa	D A S C	S C	C		
$Pt + 1K$	A S C	S C	S C		
$Sc + 1K$	D A S C		C		
$Ma + .2K$	A D C S				D
Si	S C	S C	S C		

* Each capital letter in the body of the table denotes a diagnostic group as follows: P—Paranoid Schizophrenia; D—Depression; A—Anxiety; S—Somatization; C—Conversion. The table may be read as follows: There are 61 significant differences ($p \leq .05$) between the five diagnostic groups on the various scales. For example, on the L scale, there are four significant differences; the Paranoid Schizophrenia group scores higher than the Anxiety and Depression groups and the Somatization group has a higher mean score than the Anxiety and Depression groups.

HIGH ? SCORES

Rubin [7] reported that 9 of the 93 MMPI records in his study contained more than 100 unanswered items. The writer has seen the complete distribution of ? T scores[2] for the 93 records, and found that 34, or 37% of the records, contain more than 30 unanswered items. Of these 34, 16 have 31–50 such items, 7 have 51–90, 5 have 91–110, and 6 have more than 130 ? items.

Rubin also indicated that 21% of his records of psychotics had more than 100 unanswered items, whereas only 7% of the neurotics' records and none of the records of psychopaths had more than 100 ? items. Moreover, the mean ? scores of Rubin's psychotic, neurotic, and psychopathic groups are also in this descending order. The effect of a large number of unanswered items in any record is to reduce sharply the scores on the MMPI scales. If the number of unanswered items is highest for a group of psychotic patients, next highest for neurotics and still lower for psychopaths, the scores of the MMPI scales of the psychotic and neurotic groups might be reduced to the extent that these two groups could not be distinguished from each other or from the psychopathic group. This phenomenon has apparently occurred in Rubin's study, and could account in large part for his negative results.[3, 4]

CONTAMINATION OF THE CRITERION

The psychiatrists who made the final diagnoses of the cases included in this

[2] The distribution of ? scores was obtained through the courtesy of Paul E. Meehl.

[3] Aaronson and Welsh [1] have also discussed the possible effects of extremely high ? scores in Rubin's study.

[4] As a result of the misleading and indeterminable effect of high ? scores, it has been the practice at the Minneapolis VA Hospital for the past six years to discourage patients from making *any* ? responses. The Cannot Say cards have been removed from MMPI boxes to implement this practice, so that few records contain any unanswered items. The statistics reported here were computed in 1952.

study had access to the psychologists' interpretations of the MMPI records. It should be noted, however, that the MMPI interpretations were made in terms of the scale configurations, and therefore should have had minimal effect on the differentiating power of any individual scale. A further mitigating feature is that the psychiatrists claimed they were influenced by the MMPI interpretations primarily in the diagnosis of "borderline" cases. Nevertheless, the criterion contamination, although unavoidable, presents a serious limitation on the evaluation of the results because its effects cannot be precisely measured. Replication of this investigation in a clinical setting where MMPI results do not contribute to final diagnosis would be desirable.

DIAGNOSTIC UNRELIABILITY

In studies in which a diagnostic criterion is used, divergent results may often partly be attributed to the nonhomogeneity of diagnostic categories and to the resultant inconsistency of diagnoses. Any investigation based on highly unreliable criteria is doomed to negative or inconclusive outcomes. Rubin did not mention any attempt at diagnostic purification, and, in fact, the category of alcoholism, which Aaronson and Welsh [1] have indicated, generally overlaps considerably with the psychopathic and neurotic categories.

The null hypotheses which were tested in Rubin's study and in the present investigation can now be restated in order to evaluate further the divergent results and to emphasize the kinds of decisions which might be made in future research into the differentiability of diagnostic groups by means of the individual MMPI scales.

Rubin's null hypothesis may be formulated as follows: Individual MMPI scales do not differentiate the broad categories of neurosis, psychosis, psychopathic personality, and alcoholism without psychosis if the patients are selected without regard to diagnostic purity and to the number of unanswered items in their MMPI records. It is a contribution to our knowledge of the effectiveness of the MMPI to learn that Rubin's null hypothesis cannot be rejected when the MMPI is used in the manner which he employed. It remained to be determined, however, how effective the MMPI is in differentiating diagnostic groups when the size of the P scores is controlled and a reasonable degree of homogeneity is present in the criterion groups.

The null hypothesis tested in the present investigation may be stated as follows: Individual MMPI scales do not differentiate between groups of patients diagnosed in the categories of paranoid schizophrenia, neurotic depressive reaction, anxiety reaction, conversion reaction, and somatization reaction if (a) "pure" diagnostic groups of patients are selected (with the exception that cases of anxiety reaction with depression are included), (b) the number of P items in the MMPI records is kept to a minimum, and (c) an unmeasurable amount of criterion contamination occurs. It was found that the null hypothesis could be substantially rejected except for the comparison of the Depression and Anxiety groups, exclusive of the D scale, and likewise in the comparison of the Conversion and Somatization groups. If, however, the Depression and Anxiety groups are treated as one class, and the Conversion and Somatization groups are combined, each of these two groups is effectively differentiated from the other and from the Paranoid Schizophrenia group.

SUMMARY

A major purpose of this paper was to report an investigation into the effectiveness of the individual MMPI scales in diagnostic group differentiation. A correlated aim was to test the generality of the findings of Rubin who reported that only one MMPI scale differentiated in any manner between four diagnostic groups: psychotics, neurotics, psychopaths, and alcoholics without psychosis.

A total of 307 patients was selected who had been diagnosed in five categories: paranoid schizophrenia, neurotic depressive reaction, anxiety reaction, somatization reaction, and conversion hysteria. An attempt was made to select for each diagnostic category only "pure" cases without overlapping diagnostic trends whose MMPI records contained a minimum of unanswered items. Of 130 possible differences in means for 13 cases, 61 were significant at or beyond the .05 level. The positive findings of the present study, therefore, contrasted sharply with the results obtained by Rubin. Three possible explanations of the divergent results discussed were: large numbers of unanswered MMPI items and diagnostic overlapping in Rubin's groups and criterion contamination in the present study.

REFERENCES

1. AARONSON, B. S., & WELSH, G. S. The MMPI as diagnostic differentiator: A reply to Rubin. *J. consult. Psychol.*, 1950, **14,** 324–326.
2. ASH, P. The reliability of psychiatric diagnoses. *J. abnorm. soc. Psychol.*, 1949, **44,** 272–276.
3. BOISEN, A. T. Types of dementia praecox— A study in psychiatric classification. *Psychiatry*, 1938, **1,** 233–236.
4. EDWARDS, A. L. *Experimental design in psychological research.* New York: Rinehart, 1950.
5. MEHLMAN, B. The reliability of psychiatric diagnoses. *J. abnorm. soc. Psychol.*, 1952, **47,** 577–578.
6. RUBIN, H. The MMPI as a diagnostic aid in a veterans hospital. *J. consult. Psychol.*, 1948, **12,** 251–254.
7. RUBIN, H. A note on "reply to Rubin." *J. consult. Psychol.*, 1950, **14,** 327–328.
8. SAKODA, J. M., COHEN, B. H., & BEALL, G. Test of significance for a series of statistical tests. *Psychol. Bull.*, 1954, **51,** 172–175.

Chapter 44

Wanted—A Good Cookbook

PAUL E. MEEHL

Once upon a time there was a young fellow who, as we say, was "vocationally maladjusted." He wasn't sure just what the trouble was, but he knew that he wasn't happy in his work. So, being a denizen of an urban, sophisticated, psychologically oriented culture, he concluded that what he needed was some professional guidance. He went to the counseling bureau of a large midwestern university (according to some versions of the tale, it was located on the banks of a great river), and there he was interviewed by a world-famous vocational psychologist. When the psychologist explained that it would first be necessary to take a 14-hour battery of tests, the young man hesitated a little; after all, he was still employed at his job and 14 hours seemed like quite a lot of time. "Oh, well," said the great psychologist reassuringly, "don't

This article is reprinted from the *American Psychologist*, 1956, with the permission of the author and the American Psychological Association. It was originally the Presidential Address to the Midwestern Psychological Association, Chicago, April 29, 1955.

worry about *that*. If you're too busy, you can arrange to have my assistant take these tests *for* you. I don't care who takes them, just so long as they come out in quantitative form."

Lest I, a Minnesotan, do too great violence to your expectations by telling this story on the dust-bowl empiricism with which we Minnesotans are traditionally associated, let me now tell you a true story having the opposite animus. Back in the days when we were teaching assistants, my colleague MacCorquodale was grading a young lady's elementary laboratory report on an experiment which involved a correlation problem. At the end of an otherwise flawless report, this particular bobbysoxer had written: "The correlation was seventy-five, with a standard error of ten, which is significant. However, I do not think these variables are related." MacCorquodale wrote a large red "FAIL" and added a note: "Dear Miss Fisbee: The correlation coefficient was devised expressly to relieve you of all responsibility for deciding whether these two variables are related."

If you find one of these anecdotes quite funny, and the other one rather stupid (I don't care which), you are probably suffering from a slight case of bias. Although I have not done a factor analysis with these two stories in the matrix, my clinical judgment tells me that a person's spontaneous reactions to them reflect his position in the perennial conflict between the tough-minded and the tender-minded, between those for whom the proper prefix to the word "analysis" is "factor" and those for whom it is "psycho," between the groups that Lord Russell once characterized as the "simple-minded" and the "muddle-headed." In a recent book [10], I have explored one major facet of this conflict, namely the controversy over the relative merits of clinical and statistical methods of *prediction*. Theoretical considerations, together with introspections as to my own mental activities as a psychotherapist, led me to conclude that the clinician has certain unique, practically unduplicable powers, by virtue of being himself an organism like his client, but that the domain of straight *prediction* would not be a favorable locus for displaying these powers. Survey of a score of empirical investigations in which the actual predictive efficiency of the two methods could be compared, gave strong confirmation to this latter theoretical expectation. After reading these studies, it almost looks as if the first rule to follow in trying to predict the subsequent course of a student's or patient's behavior is carefully to avoid talking to him, and that the second rule is to avoid thinking about him!

Statisticians (and rat men) with castrative intent toward clinicians should beware of any temptation to overextend these findings to a generalization that "clinicians don't actually add anything." Apart from the clinician's therapeutic efforts—the power of which is a separate issue and also a matter of current dispute—a glance at a sample of clinical diagnostic documents, such as routine psychological reports submitted in a VA installation, shows that a kind of mixed predictive-descriptive state-ment predominates which is different from the type of gross prediction considered in the aforementioned survey. (I hesitate to propose a basic distinction here, having learned that proposing a distinction between two classes of concepts is a sure road to infamy.) Nevertheless, I suggest that we distinguish between: (*a*) the clinician's predictions of such gross, outcome-type, "administrative" dimensions as recovery from psychosis, survival in a training program, persistence in therapy, and the like; and (*b*) a rather more detailed and ambitious enterprise roughly characterizable as "describing the person." It might be thought that *a* always presupposes *b*, but a moment's reflection shows this to be false; since there are empirical prediction systems in which the sole property ascribed to the person *is* the disposition to a predicted gross outcome. A very considerable fraction of the typical clinical psychologist's time seems to be spent in giving tests or semi-tests, the intention being to come out with some kind of characterization of the individual. In part this characterization is "phenotypic," attributing such behavior-dispositions as "hostile," "relates poorly," "loss in efficiency," "manifest anxiety," or "depression"; in part it is "genotypic," inferring as the causes of the phenotype certain inner events, states, or structures, e.g., "latent n Aggression," "oral-dependent attitudes," "severe castration anxiety," and the like. While the phenotypic-genotypic question is itself deserving of careful methodological analysis, in what follows I shall use the term "personality description" to cover both phenotypic and genotypic inferences, i.e., statements of all degrees of internality or theoreticalness. I shall also assume, while recognizing that at least one group of psychologists has made an impressive case to the contrary, that the description of a person is a worthwhile stage in the total clinical process. Granted, then, that we wish to use tests as a means to securing a description of the person, how shall we go about it? Here we sit, with our Rorschach and Multiphasic results spread out before us.

From this mess of data we have to emerge with a characterization of the person from whose behavior these profiles are a highly abstracted, much-reduced distillation. How to proceed?

Some of you are no doubt wondering, "What is the fellow talking about? You look at the profiles, you call to mind what the various test dimensions mean for dynamics, you reflect on other patients you have seen with similar patterns, you think of the research literature; then you combine these considerations to make inferences. Where's the problem?" The problem is, *whether or not this is the most efficient way to do it.* We ordinarily do it this way; in fact, the practice is so universal that most clinicians find it shocking, if not somehow sinful, to imagine any other. We feed in the test data and let that rusty digital computer in our heads go to work until a paragraph of personality description emerges. It requires no systematic study, although some quantitative data have begun to appear in the literature [2, 3, 6, 7, 8, 9], to realize that there is a considerable element of vagueness, hit-or-miss, and personal judgment involved in this approach. Because explicit rules are largely lacking, and hence the clinician's personal experience, skill, and creative artistry play so great a role, I shall refer to this time-honored procedure for generating personality descriptions from tests as the *rule-of-thumb* method.

I wish now to contrast this rule-of-thumb method with what I shall call the *cookbook method.* In the cookbook method, any given configuration (holists please note—I said "configuration," not "sum"!) of psychometric data is associated with each facet (or configuration) of a personality description, and the closeness of this association is explicitly indicated by a number. This number need not be a correlation coefficient—its form will depend upon what is most appropriate to the circumstances. It may be a correlation, or merely an ordinary probability of attribution, or (as in the empirical study I shall report upon later) an average Q-sort placement. Whatever its form, the essential point is that the transition from psychometric pattern to personality description is an automatic, mechanical, "clerical" kind of task, proceeding by the use of explicit rules set forth in the cookbook. I am quite aware that the mere prospect of such a method will horrify some of you; in my weaker moments it horrifies me. All I can say is that many clinicians are also horrified by the cookbook method as applied in the crude prediction situation; whereas the studies reported to date indicate this horror to be quite groundless [10, Chap. 8]. As Fred Skinner once said, some men are less curious about nature than about the accuracy of their guesses [15, p. 44]. Our responsibility to our patients and to the taxpayer obliges us to decide between the rule-of-thumb and the cookbook methods on the basis of their empirically demonstrated efficiency, rather than upon which one is more exciting, more "dynamic," more like what psychiatrists do, or more harmonious with the clinical psychologist's self concept.

Let us sneak up the clinician's avoidance gradient gradually to prevent the negative therapeutic reaction. Consider a particular complex attribute, say, "strong dependency with reaction-formation." Under what conditions should we take time to give a test of moderate validity as a basis for inferring the presence or absence of this complex attribute? Putting it negatively, it appears to me pretty obvious that there are two circumstances under which we should *not* spend much skilled time on testing even with a moderately valid test, because we stand to lose if we let the test finding influence our judgments. First, when the attribute is found in almost all our patients; and second, when it is found in almost none of our patients. (A third situation, which I shall not consider here, is one in which the attribute makes no practical difference anyhow.) A disturbingly large fraction of the assertions made in routine psychometric reports or uttered by psychologists in staff conferences fall in one of these classes.

It is not difficult to show that when a

given personality attribute is almost always or almost never present in a specified clinical population, rather severe demands are made upon the test's validity if it is to contribute in a practical way to our clinical decision-making. A few simple manipulations of Bayes' Rule for calculating inverse probability lead to rather surprising, and depressing, results. Let me run through some of these briefly. In what follows,

P = Incidence of a certain personality characteristic in a specified clinical population. ($Q = 1 - P, P > Q$)

p_1 = Proportion of "valid positives," i.e., incidence of positive test finding among cases who actually have the characteristic. ($q_1 = 1 - p_1$)

p_2 = Proportion of "false positives," i.e., incidence of positive test findings among cases who actually lack the characteristic. ($q_2 = 1 - p_2$)

1. When is a positive assertion (attribution of the characteristic) on the basis of a positive test finding more likely to be correct than incorrect?

$$\frac{P}{Q} > \frac{p_2}{p_1}$$

Example: A test correctly identifies 80 per cent of brain-damaged patients at the expense of only 15 per cent false positives, in a neuropsychiatric population where one-tenth of all patients are damaged. The decision "brain damage present" on the basis of a positive test finding is more likely to be false than true, since the inequality is unsatisfied.

2. When does the use of a test improve over-all decision making?

$$P < \frac{q_2}{q_1 + q_2}$$

If $P < Q$ this has the form $Q < p_1/(p_1 + p_2)$.

Example: A test sign identifies 85 per cent of "psychotics" at the expense of only 15 per cent of false positives among the "non-psychotic." It is desired to make a decision on each case, and both kinds of errors are

serious.[1] Only 10 per cent of the population seen in the given setting are psychotic. Hence, the use of the test yields more erroneous classifications than would proceeding without the test.

3. When does improving a sign, strengthening a scale, or shifting a cut improve decision making?

$$\frac{\Delta p_1}{\Delta p_2} > \frac{Q}{P}$$

Example: We improve the intrinsic validity of a "schizophrenic index" so that it now detects 20 per cent more schizophrenics than it formerly did, at the expense of only a 5 per cent rise in the false positive rate. This surely looks encouraging. However, we work with an outpatient clientele only one-tenth of whom are actually schizophrenic. Since these values violate the inequality, "improvement" of the index will result in an increase in the proportion of erroneous diagnoses. N.B.—*Sampling errors are not involved in the above.* The values are assumed to be parameter values, and the test sign is valid (i.e., $p_1 > p_2$ in the population).

Further inequalities and a more detailed drawing out of their pragmatic implications can be found in a recent paper by Albert Rosen and myself [12]. The moral to be drawn from these considerations, which even we clinicians can follow because they involve only high-school algebra, is that a great deal of skilled psychological effort is probably being wasted in going through complex, skill-demanding, time-consuming test procedures of moderate or low validity, in order to arrive at conclusions about the patient which could often be made with

[1] Inequalities (2) and (3) are conditions for improvement if there is no reason to see one kind of error as worse than the other. In trait attribution this is usually true; in prognostic and diagnostic decisions it may or may not be. If one is willing to say how many errors of one kind he is prepared to tolerate in order to avoid one of the other kind, these inequalities can be readily corrected by inserting this ratio. A more general development can be found in an unpublished paper by Ward Edwards.

high confidence without the test, and which in other cases ought not to be made (because they still tend to be wrong) even with the test indications positive. Probably most surprising is the finding that there are certain quantitative relations between the base rates and test validity parameters such that the use of a "valid" test will produce a net rise in the frequency of clinical mistakes. The first task of a good clinical cookbook would be to make explicit quantitative use of the inverse probability formulas in constructing efficient "rules of attribution" when test data are to be used in describing the personalities of patients found in various clinical populations. For example, I know of an out-patient clinic which has treated, by a variety of psychotherapies, in the course of the past eight years, approximately 5000 patients, not one of whom has committed suicide. If the clinical psychologists in this clinic have been spending much of their time scoring suicide keys on the Multiphasic or counting suicide indicators in Rorschach content, either these test indicators are close to infallible (which is absurd), or else the base rate is so close to zero that the expenditure of skilled time is of doubtful value. Suicide is an extreme case, of course [14]; but the point so dramatically reflected there is valid, with suitable quantitative modifications, over a wider range of base rates. To take some examples from the high end of the base-rate continuum, it is not very illuminating to say of a known psychiatric patient that he has difficulty in accepting his drives, experiences some trouble in relating emotionally to others, and may have problems with his sexuality! Many psychometric reports bear a disconcerting resemblance to what my colleague Donald G. Paterson calls "personality description after the manner of P. T. Barnum" [13]. I suggest—and I am quite serious—that we adopt the phrase *Barnum effect* to stigmatize those pseudosuccessful clinical procedures in which personality descriptions from tests are made to fit the patient largely or wholly by virtue of their triviality; and in which

any nontrivial, but perhaps erroneous, inferences are hidden in a context of assertions or denials which carry high confidence simply because of the population base rates, regardless of the test's validity. I think this fallacy is at least as important and frequent as others for which we have familiar labels (halo effect, leniency error, contamination, etc.). One of the best ways to increase the general sensitivity to such fallacies is to give them a name. We ought to make our clinical students as acutely aware of the Barnum effect as they are of the dangers of countertransference or the standard error of r.

The preceding mathematical considerations, while they should serve as a check upon some widespread contemporary forms of tea-leaf reading, are unfortunately not very "positive" by way of writing a good cookbook. "Almost anything needs a little salt for flavor" or "It is rarely appropriate to put ketchup on the dessert" would be sound advice but largely negative and not very helpful to an average cook. I wish now to describe briefly a piece of empirical research, reported in a thesis just completed at Minnesota by Charles C. Halbower [4], which takes the cookbook method 100 per cent seriously; and which seems to show, at least in one clinical context, what can be done in a more constructive way by means of a cookbook of even moderate trustworthiness.[2] By some geographical coincidence, the psychometric device used in this research was a structured test consisting of a set of 550 items, commonly known as MMPI. Let me emphasize that the MMPI is not here being compared with anything else, and that the research does not aim to investigate Multiphasic validity (although the general order of magnitude of the obtained correlations does give some incidental information in that respect). What Dr. Halbower asked was this: given a Multiphasic profile, how does one arrive at a personality description from it? Using the

[2] I am indebted to Dr. Halbower for permission to present this summary of his thesis data in advance of his own more complete publication.

rule-of-thumb method, a clinician familiar with MMPI interpretation looks at the profile, thinks awhile, and proceeds to describe the patient he imagines would have produced such a pattern. Using the cookbook method, we don't need a clinician; instead, a $230-per-month clerk-typist in the outer office simply reads the numbers on the profile, enters the cookbook, locates the page on which is found some kind of "modal description" for patients with such a profile, and this description is then taken as the best available approximation to the patient. We know, of course, that every patient is unique—absolutely, unqualifiedly unique. Therefore, the application of a cookbook description will inevitably make errors, some of them perhaps serious ones. If we knew *which* facets of the cookbook sketch needed modification as applied to the present unique patient, we would, of course, depart from the cookbook at these points; but we don't know this. If we start monkeying with the cookbook recipe in the hope of avoiding or reducing these errors, we will in all likelihood improve on the cookbook in some respects but, unfortunately, will worsen our approximation in others. Given a finite body of information, such as the 13 two-digit numbers of a Multiphasic profile, there is obviously *in fact* (whether we have yet succeeded in *finding* it or not) a "most probable" value for any personality facet, and also for any configuration of facets, however complex or "patterned" [10, pp. 131–134]. It is easy to prove that a method of characterization which departs from consistent adherence to this "best guess" stands to lose. Keep in mind, then, that the raw data from which a personality description was to be inferred consisted of an MMPI profile. In other words, the Halbower study was essentially a comparison of the rule-of-thumb versus the cookbook method where each method was, however, functioning upon the same information—an MMPI. We are in effect contrasting the validity of two methods of "reading" Multiphasics.

In order to standardize the domain to be covered, and to yield a reasonably sensitive quantification of the goodness of description, Dr. Halbower utilized Q sorts. From a variety of sources he constructed a Q pool of 154 items, the majority being phenotypic or intermediate and a minority being genotypic. Since these items were intended for clinically expert sorters employing an "external" frame of reference, many of them were in technical language. Some sample items from his pool are: "Reacts against his dependency needs with hostility"; "manifests reality distortions"; "takes a dominant, ascendant role in interactions with others"; "is rebellious toward authority figures, rules, and other constraints"; "is counteractive in the face of frustration"; "gets appreciable secondary gain from his symptoms"; "is experiencing pain"; "is naive"; "is impunitive"; "utilizes intellectualization as a defense mechanism"; "shows evidence of latent hostility"; "manifests inappropriate affect." The first step was to construct a cookbook based upon these 154 items as the ingredients; the recipes were to be in the form of directions as to the optimal Q-sort placement of each item.

How many distinguishable recipes will the cookbook contain? If we had infallible criterion Q sorts on millions of cases, there would be as many recipes as there are possible MMPI profiles. Since we don't have this ideal situation, and never will, we have to compromise by introducing coarser grouping. Fortunately, we know that the validity of our test is poor enough so that this coarseness will not result in the sacrifice of much, if any, information. How coarsely we group, i.e., how different two Multiphasic curves have to be before we refuse to call them "similar" enough to be coordinated with the same recipe, is a very complicated matter involving both theoretical and practical considerations. Operating within the limits of a doctoral dissertation, Halbower confined his study to four profile "types." These curve types were specified by the first two digits of the Hathaway code plus certain additional requirements based upon clinical experience. The four

MMPI codes used were those beginning 123', 13', 27', and 87' [5]. The first three of these codes are the most frequently occurring in the Minneapolis VA Mental Hygiene Clinic population, and the fourth code, which is actually fifth in frequency of occurrence, was chosen in order to have a quasi-psychotic type in the study. It is worth noting that these four codes constitute 58 per cent of all MMPI curves seen in the given population; so that Halbower's gross recipe categories already cover the majority of such outpatients. The nature of the further stipulations, refining the curve criteria within each two-digit code class, is illustrated by the following specifications for code 13', the "hysteroid valley" or "conversion V" type:

1. Hs and $Hy \geq 70$.
2. $D < (Hs$ and $Hy)$ by at least one sigma.
3. K or $L > P$ and F.
4. $F \leq 65$.
5. Scales 4,5,6,7,8,9,0 all ≤ 70.

For each of these MMPI curve types, the names of nine patients were then randomly chosen from the list of those meeting the curve specifications. If the patient was still in therapy, his therapist was asked to do a Q sort (11 steps, normal distribution) on him. The MMPI had been withheld from these therapists. If the patient had been terminated, a clinician (other than Halbower) did a Q sort based upon study of the case folder, including therapist's notes and any available psychometrics (except, of course, the Multiphasic). This yields Q sorts for nine patients of a given curve type. These nine sorts were then pairwise intercorrelated, and by inspection of the resulting 36 coefficients, a subset of five patients was chosen as most representative of the curve type. The Q sorts on these five "representative" patients were then averaged, and this average Q sort was taken as the cookbook recipe to be used in describing future cases having the given MMPI curve. Thus, this modal, crystallized, "distilled-essence" personality description was obtained by

eliminating patients with atypical sortings and pooling sortings on the more typical, hoping to reduce both errors of patient sampling and of clinical judgment. This rather complicated sequence of procedures may be summarized thus:

Deriving cookbook recipe for a specified curve type, such as the "conversion V" above:

1. Sample of N = nine patients currently or recently in therapy and meeting the MMPI specifications for conversion V curve.
2. 154-item Q sort done on each patient by therapist or from therapist notes and case folder. (These sorts MMPI-uncontaminated.)
3. Pairwise Q correlations of these nine patients yields 36 intercorrelations.
4. Selection of subset N' = five "modal" patients from this matrix by inspectional cluster method.
5. Mean of Q sorts on these five "core" patients is the cookbook recipe for the MMPI curve type in question.

Having constructed one recipe, he started all over again with a random sample of nine patients whose Multiphasics met the second curve-type specifications, and carried out these cluster-and-pooling processes upon them. This was done for each of the four curve types which were to compose the cookbook. If you have reservations about any of the steps in constructing this miniature cookbook, let me remind you that this is all preliminary, i.e., *it is the means of arriving at the cookbook recipe.* The proof of the pudding will be in the eating, and any poor choices of tactics or patients up to this point should merely make the cookbook less trustworthy than it would otherwise be.

Having thus written a miniature cookbook consisting of only four recipes, Halbower then proceeded to cook some dishes to see how they would taste. For cross validation he chose at random four new Mental Hygiene Clinic patients meeting the four curve specifications and who had been seen in therapy for a minimum of ten hours. With an eye to validity generalization to a somewhat different clinical population, with different base rates, he also chose four patients who were being seen as inpatients at the Minneapolis VA Hospital. None of the therapists involved had knowledge of the patients' Multiphasics. For purposes of his study, Halbower took the therapist's Q sort, based upon all of the case folder data (minus MMPI) plus his therapeutic contacts, as the best available criterion; although this "criterion" is acceptable only in the sense of construct validity [1]. An estimate of its absolute level of trustworthiness is not important since it is being used as the common reference basis for a comparison of two methods of test reading.

Given the eight criterion therapist Q sorts (2 patients for each MMPI curve type), the task of the cookbook is to predict these descriptions. Thus, for each of the two patients having MMPI code 123', we simply assign the Q-sort recipe found in the cookbook as the best available description. How accurate this description is can be estimated (in the sense of construct validity) by Q-correlating it with the criterion therapist's description. These eight "validity" coefficients varied from .36 to .88 with a median of .69. As would be expected, the hospital inpatients yielded the lower correlations. The Mental Hygiene Clinic cases, for whom the cookbook was really intended, gave validities of .68, .69, .84, and .88 (see Table 44–1).

How does the rule-of-thumb method show up in competition with the cookbook? Here we run into the problem of differences in clinical skill, so Halbower had each MMPI profile read blind by more than one clinician. The task was to interpret the profile by doing a Q sort. From two to five clinicians thus "read" each of the eight individual profiles, and the resulting 25 sorts were Q-correlated with the appropriate therapist criterion sorts. These validity coefficients run from .29 to .63 with a median of .46. The clinicians were all Minnesota trained and varied in their experience with MMPI from less than a year (first-year VA trainees) through all training levels to PhD staff psychologists with six years' experience. The more experienced clinicians had probably seen over two thousand MMPI profiles in relation to varying amounts of other clinical data, including intensive psychotherapy. Yet not one of the 25 rule-of-thumb readings was as valid as the cookbook reading. Of the 25 comparisons which can be made between the validity of a single clinician's rule-of-thumb reading and that of the corresponding cookbook reading of the same patient's profile, 18 are significant in favor of the cookbook at the .01 level of confidence and 4 at the .05 level. The remaining 3 are also in favor of the cookbook but not significantly so.

Confining our attention to the more appropriate outpatient population, for (and upon) which the cookbook was developed, the mean r (estimated through z transformation) is .78 for the cookbook method, as contrasted with a mean (for 17 rule-of-thumb descriptions) of only .48, a difference of 30 points of correlation, which in this region amounts to a difference of 38 per cent in the validly predicted variance! The cookbook seems to be superior to the rule-of-thumb not merely in the sense of statistical significance but by an amount which is of very practical importance. It is also remarkable that even when the cookbook recipes are applied to patients from a quite different kind of population, their validity still excels that of rule-of-thumb MMPI readers who are in daily clinical contact with that other population. The improvement in valid variance in the hospital sample averages 19 per cent (see item 6 in Table 44–1).

A shrewd critic may be thinking, "Perhaps this is because all kinds of psychiatric patients are more or less alike, and the cookbook has simply taken advantage of this rather trivial fact." In answer to this objection, let me say first that to the extent the cookbook's superiority did arise from its actuarially determined tendency to "follow the base rates," that would be a per-

Table 44–1   Validation of the Four Cookbook Descriptions on New Cases, and Comparative Validities of the Cookbook MMPI Readings and Rule-of-Thumb Readings by Clinicians

1. Four patients currently in therapy Q-described by the therapist (10 hours or more therapy plus case folder minus MMPI). This is taken as best available criterion description of each patient.
2. MMPI cookbook recipe Q-correlated with this criterion description.
3. For each patient, 4 or 5 clinicians "read" his MMPI in usual rule-of-thumb way, doing Q sorts.
4. These rule-of-thumb Q sorts also Q-correlated with criterion description.
5. Cross-validation results in outpatient sample.

Validities	MMPI Curve Type			
	Code 123'	Code 27'	Code 13'	Code 87'
Cookbook	.88	.69	.84	.68
Rule-of-thumb (mean)	.75	.50	.50	.58

Range (4–5 readers) .55 to .63   .29 to .54   .37 to .52   .34 to .58
Mean of 4 cookbook validities, through $z_r = .78$
Mean of 17 rule-of-thumb validities, through $z_r = .48$
Cookbook's superiority in validly predicted variance = 38%

6. Validity generalization to inpatient (psychiatric hospital) sample with different base rates; hence, an "unfair" test of cookbook.

Validities	MMPI Curve Type			
	Code 123'	Code 27'	Code 13'	Code 87'
Cookbook	.63	.64	.36	.70
Rule-of-thumb (2 readers)	.37, .49	.29, .42	.30, .30	.50, 50.

Mean of 4 cookbook validities, through $z_r = .60$
Mean of 8 rule-of-thumb validities, through $z_r = .41$
Cookbook's superiority in validly predicted variance = 19%

fectly sound application of the inverse probability considerations I at first advanced. For example, most psychiatric patients are in some degree depressed. Let us suppose the mean Q-sort placement given by therapists to the item "depressed" is seven. "Hysteroid" patients, who characteristically exhibit the so-called "conversion V" on their MMPI profiles (Halbower's cookbook code 13), are less depressed than most neurotics. The clinician, seeing such a conversion valley on the Multiphasic, takes this relation into account by attributing "lack of depression" to the patient. But maybe he overinterprets, giving undue weight to the psychometric finding and understressing the base rate. So his rule-of-thumb placement is far down at the nondepressed end, say at position three. The cookbook, on the other hand, "knows" (actuarially) that the mean Q placement for the item "depressed" is at five in patients with such profiles—lower than the over-all mean seven but not displaced as much in the conversion subgroup as the clinician thinks. If patients are so homogeneous with respect to a certain characteristic that the psychometrics ought not to influence greatly our attribution or placement in defiance of the over-all actuarial trend, then the clinician's tendency to be unduly influenced is a source of erroneous clinical decisions and a valid argument in favor of the cookbook.

However, if this were the chief explanation of Halbower's findings, the obvious conclusion would be merely that MMPI was not differentiating, since any test-induced departure from a description of the "average patient" would tend to be more wrong than right. Our original question would then be rephrased, "What is the comparative efficiency of the cookbook and the rule-of-thumb method *when each is applied to psychometric information having some degree of intrinsic validity?*" Time permits me only brief mention of the several lines of evidence in Halbower's study which eliminate the Barnum effect as an explanation. First of all, Halbower had selected his 154 items from a much larger initial Q pool by a preliminary study of therapist sortings on a heterogeneous sample of patients in which items were eliminated if they showed low interpatient dispersal. Second, study of the placements given an item over the four cookbook recipes reveals little similarity (e.g., only two items recur in the top quartile of all four recipes; 60 per cent of the items occur in the top quartile of only one recipe). Third, several additional correlational findings combine to show that the cookbook was not succeeding merely by describing an "average patient" four times over. For example, the clinicians' Q description of their conception of the "average patient" gave very low validity for three of the four codes, and a "mean average patient" description constructed by pooling these clinicians' stereotypes was not much better (see Table 44–2). For Code 123' (interest-

ingly enough, the commonest code among therapy cases in this clinic) the pooled stereotype was actually more valid than rule-of-thumb Multiphasic readings. (This is Bayes' Theorem with a vengeance!) Nevertheless, I am happy to report that this "average patient" description was still inferior to the Multiphasic cookbook (significant at the .001 level).

In the little time remaining, let me ruminate about the implications of this study, supposing it should prove to be essentially generalizable to other populations and to other psychometric instruments. From a theoretical point of view, the trend is hardly surprising. It amounts to the obvious fact that the human brain is an inefficient recording and computing device. The cookbook method has an advantage over the rule-of-thumb method because it (*a*) samples more representatively, (*b*) records and stores information better, and (*c*) computes statistical weights which are closer to the optimal. We can perhaps learn more by putting the theoretical question negatively: when should we *expect* the cookbook to be inferior to the brain? The answer to this question presumably lies in the highly technical field of computing machine theory, which I am not competent to discuss. As I understand it, the use of these machines requires that certain rules of data combination be fed initially into the machine, followed by the insertion of suitably selected and coded information. Putting it crudely, the machine can "remember" and can "think routinely," but it cannot "spontaneously notice what is relevant" nor can

Table 44–2   Validities of Four Clinicians' Description of "Average Patient," of the Mean of These Stereotypes, and of the Cookbook Recipe (Outpatient Cases Only)

MMPI Curve Type	Validities of "Average Patient" Descriptions by 4 Clinicians	Validity of Mean of These 4 "Average Patient" Stereotypes	Validity of Cookbook Recipe
Code 123'	.63 to .69	.74	.88
Code 27'	−.03 to .20	.09	.69
Code 13'	.25 to .37	.32	.84
Code 87'	.25 to .35	.31	.68

it "think" in the more high-powered, creative sense (e.g., it cannot invent theories). To be sure, noticing what is relevant must involve the exemplification of some rule, perhaps of a very complex form. But it is a truism of behavior science that organisms can *exemplify* rules without *formulating* them. To take a noncontroversial example outside the clinical field, no one today knows how to state fully the rules of "similarity" or "stimulus equivalence" for patterned visual perception or verbal generalization; but of course we all exemplify daily these undiscovered rules. This suggests that as long as psychology cannot give a complete, explicit, quantitative account of the "dimensions of relevance" in behavior connections, the cookbook will not completely duplicate the clinician [11]. The clinician *here* acts as an inefficient computer, but that is better than a computer with certain major rules completely left out (because we can't build them in until we have learned how to formulate them). The use of the therapist's own unconscious in perceiving verbal and imaginal relations during dream interpretation is, I think, the clearest example of this. But I believe the exemplification of currently unformulable rules is a widespread phenomenon in most clinical inference. However, you will note that these considerations apply chiefly (if not wholly) to matters of *content*, in which a rich, highly varied, hard-to-classify content (such as free associations) is the input information. The problem of "stimulus equivalence" or "noticing the relevant" does not arise when the input data are in the form of preclassified responses, such as a Multiphasic profile or a Rorschach psychogram. I have elsewhere [10, pp. 110–111] suggested that even in the case of such prequantified patterns there arises the possibility of causal-theory–mediated idiographic extrapolations into regions of the profile space in which we lack adequate statistical experience; but I am now inclined to view that suggestion as a mistake. The underlying theory must itself involve some hypothesized function, however crudely quantified; otherwise, how is the alleged "extrapolation" possible? I can think of no reason why the estimation of the parameters in this underlying theoretical function should constitute an exception to the cookbook's superiority. If I am right in this, my "extrapolation" argument applies strictly only when a clinician literally *invents new theoretical relations or variables* in thinking about the individual patient. In spite of some clinicians' claims along this line, I must say I think it very rarely happens in daily clinical practice. Furthermore, even when it does happen, Bayes' Rule still applies. The *joint* probability of the theory's correctness, and of the attribute's presence (granting the theory but remembering nuisance variables) must be high enough to satisfy the inequalities I have presented, otherwise use of the theory will not pay off.

What are the pragmatic implications of the preceding analysis? Putting it bluntly, it suggests that for a rather wide range of clinical problems involving personality description from tests, the clinical interpreter is a costly middleman who might better be eliminated. An initial layout of research time could result in a cookbook whose recipes would encompass the great majority of psychometric configurations seen in daily work. I am fully aware that the prospect of a "clinical clerk" simply looking up Rorschach pattern number 73 J 10-5 or Multiphasic curve "Halbower Verzeichnis 626" seems very odd and even dangerous. I reassure myself by recalling that the number of phenotypic and genotypic attributes is, after all, finite; and that the number which are ordinarily found attributed or denied even in an extensive sample of psychological reports on patients is actually very limited. A best estimate of a Q-sort placement is surely more informative than a crude "Yes-or-No" decision of low objective confidence. I honestly cannot see, in the case of a *determinate trait domain* and a *specified clinical population*, that there is a serious intellectual problem underlying one's uneasiness. I invite you to consider the possibility that the emotional block we all experience in connection with the cookbook approach could be dissolved simply by trying it out until our daily successes finally get us accustomed to the idea.

Admittedly this would take some of the "fun" out of psychodiagnostic activity. But I suspect that most of the clinicians who put a high value on this kind of fun would have even more fun doing intensive psychotherapy. The great personnel needs today, and for the next generation or more, are for psychotherapists and researchers. (If you don't believe much in the efficacy of therapy, this is the more reason for research.) If all the thousands of clinical hours currently being expended in concocting clever and flowery personality sketches from test data could be devoted instead to scientific investigation (assuming we are still selecting and training clinicians to be scientists), it would probably mean a marked improvement in our net social contribution. If a reasonably good cookbook could help bring about this result, the achievement would repay tenfold the expensive and tedious effort required in its construction.

REFERENCES

1. CRONBACH, L. J., & MEEHL, P. E. Construct validity in psychological tests. *Psychol. Bull.*, 1955, **52**, 281–302.
2. DAILEY, C. A. The practical utility of the clinical report. *J. consult. Psychol.*, 1953, **17**, 297–302.
3. DAVENPORT, BEVERLY F. The semantic validity of TAT interpretations. *J. consult. Psychol.*, 1952, **16**, 171–175.
4. HALBOWER, C. C. A comparison of actu-arial versus clinical prediction to classes discriminated by MMPI. Unpublished doctor's dissertation, Univer. of Minn., 1955.
5. HATHAWAY, S. R. A coding system for MMPI profiles. *J. consult. Psychol.*, 1947, **11**, 334–337.
6. HOLSOPPLE, J. Q., & PHELAN, J. G. The skills of clinicians in analysis of projective tests. *J. clin. Psychol.*, 1954, **10**, 307–320.
7. KOSTLAN, A. A method for the empirical study of psychodiagnosis. *J. consult. Psychol.*, 1954, **18**, 83–88.
8. LITTLE, K. B., & SHNEIDMAN, E. S. The validity of MMPI interpretations. *J. consult. Psychol.*, 1954, **18**, 425–428.
9. LITTLE, K. B., & SHNEIDMAN, E. S. The validity of thematic projective technique interpretations. *J. Pers.*, 1955, **23**, 285–294.
10. MEEHL, P. E. *Clinical versus statistical prediction.* Minneapolis: Univer. of Minn. Press, 1954.
11. MEEHL, P. E. "Comment" on McArthur, C. Analyzing the clinical process. *J. counsel. Psychol.*, 1954, **1**, 203–208.
12. MEEHL, P. E., & ROSEN, A. Antecedent probability and the efficiency of psychometric signs, patterns, or cutting scores. *Psychol. Bull.*, 1955, **52**, 194–216.
13. PATERSON, D. G. Character reading at sight of Mr. X according to the system of Mr. P. T. Barnum. (Mimeographed, unpublished.)
14. ROSEN, A. Detection of suicidal patients: an example of some limitations in the prediction of infrequent events. *J. consult. Psychol.*, 1954, **18**, 397–403.
15. SKINNER, B. F. *The behavior of organisms.* New York: Appleton-Century-Crofts, 1938.

Response Styles and the
Assessment of Psychopathology

DOUGLAS N. JACKSON / SAMUEL MESSICK

The problem of discriminating powerfully between psychopathological syndromes with scores derived from responses to structured personality items is one of the more challenging unsolved tasks confronting the assessment specialist. A major impediment in such refined personality measurement is the existence of substantial sources of response bias pervading wide varieties of item content and often failing to elicit differential responses in various pathological groups. In an attempt to clarify the role of such response biases, the authors [44] have previ-

This article is reprinted from *Measurement in Personality and Cognition*, S. Messick and J. Ross (Eds.), 1962, with the permission of John Wiley and Sons. The research reported in the article is part of a series of studies on stylistic determinants in personality assessment supported by the National Institute of Mental Health, United States Public Health Service. Portions of this material also appear in Jackson, D. N., and Messick, S., Acquiescence and desirability as response determinants on the MMPI, *Educ. psychol. Measmt*, 1961, *21*, 771–790; and in Jackson, D. N., and Messick, S., Response styles on the MMPI: Comparison of clinical and normal samples, *J. abnorm. soc. Psychol.*, 1962, *65*, 285–299.

ously distinguished between the interpretation of behavior in terms of *content* and of *style*, and have suggested that stylistic response determinants, such as the tendency to respond desirably or to acquiesce to heterogeneous or neutral item content, might not only be considered as sources of systematic error, but as reflections of predispositions in the respondents which possibly represent important personality traits.

The principal focus of the present paper is upon the results of a series of investigations into the internal structure of the MMPI. In the discussion of these data, three points which we consider important in the assessment of psychopathology are emphasized: First, we attempt to clarify the distinctions between variance associated on the one hand with content and on the other with response style, and we describe a factor analytic method for deriving relatively precise estimates of the contributions of each of these components to total variance. Second, we evaluate and contrast content and stylistic response determinants on the

MMPI in three widely varying populations—prison inmates, hospitalized neuropsychiatric patients, and college students. Third, using these analyses as a point of departure, we draw some general inferences about the differential assessment of psychopathological conditions using structured questionnaires.

While the title of the present paper reveals accurately enough our emphasis on identifying stylistic determinants in structured personality inventories, it might have equally well been called, "The Quest for the Elusive Content." Actually, we are very much concerned with measuring content, but content—like a tarpon being hunted by a spear fisherman at 10 fathoms—usually appears somewhat closer, larger, and more easily captured than is actually the case. Our research has convinced us that questionnaire items which ignore response-style effects in the quest for content will leave the investigator with very little more than two or three scales from the tarpon that eluded him. While he might be able to convince his colleagues that tarpon really exist from the scales that he has found, they may remain unconvinced that tarpons can be reliably differentiated from sharks (that is, response sets), that they take on any particular form, that they are as large as claimed, or that the quest for them is worth the trouble, especially in shark-infested waters.

We do believe that the quest for content in structured personality questionnaires is well worth the trouble but that, to avoid adding to fish stories, one must learn to fish selectively for tarpon and for sharks—to differentiate clearly between content and stylistic determinants in the assessment of psychopathology and to appraise each separately. However, even sharks have economic value, and response style scores may tell us something of interest about the respondent; but to make such a determination it is all the more essential to differentiate clearly what is being assessed—content or style.

DISTINCTIONS BETWEEN COMPONENTS OF CONTENT AND STYLE

Wiggins [71], in a careful analysis of response consistencies in personality inventories like the MMPI, has suggested a further distinction between components of response variance—a distinction between *strategic, method,* and *stylistic* variance. By *strategic* variance, Wiggins refers to response variation which reflects a subject's similarity to a normative group in contrast with some criterion group. The nature of such variance depends upon the strategy of constructing scales to discriminate between criterion and normative populations and upon the nature of the criterion groups. By *method* variance [cf. 14], Wiggins refers to response consistencies attributable to constraints imposed by the available response options and to the idiosyncratic nature of particular item pools with respect to such characteristics as the proportion of true and false items and the variation in item popularity. By *stylistic* variance, Wiggins refers to expressive response consistencies, independent of specific item content, having relevance not only to the particular test format but to more general modes of commerce with the environment. Wiggins' analysis cuts across previous separations of response variance into content and stylistic components, and in the interest of clarity we should like to explicate further our distinction between content and style, with particular reference to personality questionnaire data.

In the present context, variance associated with *content* is considered to refer to response consistencies in certain defined assessment situations which reflect a particular set of broader behavioral tendencies, relatively enduring over time, having as their basis some unitary personality trait, need state, attitudinal or belief disposition, or psychopathological syndrome. The *item content* used to elicit such behavioral predispositions may be developed initially on theoretical or on *a priori* grounds, may be obvious or subtle, may be direct or indirect, and may be highly relevant or only slightly relevant to some particular prediction criterion. The initial defining property of content assessment is some form of *response consistency*, for if one cannot establish this primary requisite, then certain mathematical operations upon the response data, such as adding item endorsements to yield a total score, cannot with impunity be interpreted in terms of a particular latent dimension [cf. 58]. Of course, consistency is not the sole criterion for defining meaningful response content; it might be shown, for example, that certain traits which are trivial both theoretically and practically could be assessed reliably. Before the "meaning" of a test score can be understood, it is necessary to consider its linkages with theory [40] and to validate the test and the construct with any and all methods at the disposal of the investigator [25, 49], of which the differentiation of criterion samples from normative groups is but one. While agreeing with Wiggins [71] and others [26] that the empirical differentiation of pathological from normal samples is an important strategy in validational research, the value of experimental, physiological, cross-cultural, sociological, psychopharmacological, role-playing, judgmental, performance, behavior rating, clinical and biographical, anthropometric, and dream process studies, among others, should also be carefully considered as possible sources of evidence bearing upon construct validity.

The separation of *response style* from content can be made more clearly at the conceptual level than at the level of data for two important reasons: (a) a given response can be considered a function of each, in some proportion, but in any case confounded to a degree difficult to determine; (b) stylistic consistencies, such as the tendency to acquiesce, may reflect or be related in some degree to personality characteristics and need states. Thus, while the response style to endorse desirable personality items may not in itself be classi-

fiable simply as conformity, the fact that a relation exists between some aspects of conformity and a desirability response style [50] serves to illustrate that these styles may be related to, and sometimes moderate, content effects. Other examples of interactions between content and style may be found in the measurement of authoritarian attitudes, where it has been suggested that an all "true" item format [35] or an extremely-worded item style [44, 20, 18] may have greater empirical validity for appraising authoritarian behavior.

There is a further problem in defining response style, namely, that of differentiating trivial response biases, or method variance, from valid variance reflecting important behavioral predispositions. Wiggins [71] has approached this by defining method variance in distinction to stylistic variance. There is a serious difficulty in clearly separating these at the level of data, however, despite the importance of this distinction conceptually. If one confines an analysis to the internal structure of a single test, there is little basis for distinguishing response style from method variance. In any event, the interpretation of stylistic consistencies as method variance or bias on the one hand, or as valid indicators of personality traits on the other, depends as much upon the aims of the investigator and his preferred strategy of assessment as upon the potential validity coefficients obtained with diverse criteria for the particular response style in question. Whether interpreted as bias or as valid variance, accumulating evidence supports the view that where response style variance is pervasive and intimately associated in varying degrees with content, as it is in the MMPI, only the most careful analysis and separation of these components will allow inferences to be drawn regarding responses to items, particularly inferences regarding response content.

Subject to the above qualifications, variance associated with *response style* has reference to expressive consistencies in the behavior of respondents which are relatively enduring over time, with some degree of generality beyond a particular test performance to responses both in other tests and in non-test behavior, and usually reflected in assessment situations by consistencies in response to item characteristics other than specific content. These characteristics may include the following:

(a) Some aspect of the form or tone of item structure, such as difficulty level [36], positive or negative phrasing [cf. 8, 43, 17, 30], style of wording [44, 38, 13], ambiguity or specificity of meaning [8, 61, 66], and extreme generality vs. cautious qualification [18]; and

(b) Some general aspect of the connotations of the items, such as desirability [28], deviance [11, 65], controversiality [33, 37], communality [70, 71], subtlety [28, 37], or some perceived difference between communality and desirability, as revealed in the MMPI Lie scale or in scales derived empirically to detect malingering [19] or defensiveness [37].

Consistencies in response to formal item properties that are restricted in time to a single test session and recurrent consistencies observed only on a specific test form are referred to as *response sets* [21, 22].

RESPONSE STYLES ON THE MMPI

In an attempt to evaluate on the MMPI the respective contributions of consistent responses to item content on the one hand and of stylistic determinants on the other, three factor analytic studies were undertaken on three diverse samples—prison inmates, hospitalized neuropsychiatric patients, and college students. In these studies the two response styles of acquiescence and desirability were highlighted, and in order to appraise their relative effects new measures of both styles were constructed. Five

desirability (Dy) scales, with all of their items keyed true, were developed to obtain scores reflecting acquiescence at systematically varying levels of item desirability [44, 45]. Construction of the Dy scales was accomplished by dividing all MMPI items into five levels of judged desirability in terms of Heineman's [39] scale values and using a table of random numbers to select items within each level to comprise a "scale." Item overlap between keys for Dy and MMPI clinical scales was systematically limited by substituting additional randomly selected items for those initial Dy items found to be keyed also for clinical scales. The five scales developed in this manner were labeled Dy1 for the scale having the highest judged item desirability through Dy5 for the scale with the lowest judged item desirability; Dy3 was composed of items judged neutral in desirability. Each desirability scale contained 60 items except Dy1, which, because of the relative scarcity of extremely desirable items on the MMPI, contained only 50 [45].

By obtaining Dy scale reliabilities, intercorrelations, and relationships with MMPI clinical scales, it is possible to estimate the degree of response consistency due to the generalized stylistic components of acquiescence and desirability, as contrasted with variance attributable to responses to specific item content.

PRISON SAMPLE

The booklet form of the MMPI was administered under standard instructions to 201 male inmates of a state correctional institution [45]. Clinical and validity scales were scored in the usual way with one important exception: In order to appraise acquiescence variance systematically, separate scores were obtained for items keyed true and for items keyed false, thus producing two scores for each scale, the sum of which would generate the usual total scale score. This permitted an evaluation of the possibly differential influence of acquiescence on "true" and "false" items. In addition, Welsh's [69] "pure factor" scales, A and R, believed to reflect different combinations of desirability and acquiescence variance [44, 72], were also scored.

Intercorrelations were obtained among 30 MMPI variables (true and false parts of 11 clinical and validity scales, five Dy scales, and the K, A, and R scales), and the resulting matrix was factor analyzed by the method of principal components. Communalities were estimated by the highest

correlation in each column. An examination of the relative sizes of the 30 latent roots led to the retention of eight factors, which together accounted for 69.7 percent of the total variance. These factors were rotated analytically to a modified quartimax criterion of orthogonal simple structure [63].

The rotated factor loadings, together with the percentages of variance accounted for by each factor, are presented in Table 45–1. Two very large factors emerged, accounting

Table 45–1 Factor Loadings for the Prison Sample* (N = 201)

Variable	I	II	III	IV	V	VI	VII	VIII	h²
					Factors				
1. F_t	31	57	−02	11	48	01	−01	04	.67
2. F_f	−37	40	10	−07	−00	19	−23	33	.51
3. Hs_t	23	50	−46	−06	−10	−23	12	−02	.59
4. Hs_f	−06	66	−08	07	−06	−44	08	06	.66
5. D_t	50	51	−37	−12	02	09	−28	−12	.75
6. D_f	−61	35	04	−03	−13	−31	−25	06	.68
7. Hy_t	34	48	−55	00	02	−10	−02	−04	.66
8. Hy_f	−60	14	−13	−17	03	−51	01	14	.71
9. Pd_t	60	42	−22	−11	11	12	−13	20	.68
10. Pd_f	−51	03	08	−07	−06	−06	−10	45	.49
11. Mf_t	69	09	−07	−17	08	−26	−22	−10	.64
12. Mf_f	−46	17	−04	−50	−04	−12	01	12	.53
13. Pa_t	45	54	07	−07	42	−03	00	−01	.68
14. Pa_f	−61	−10	−11	−30	09	−30	−12	−03	.60
15. Pt_t	64	57	−25	−30	−05	−07	−05	−05	.91
16. Pt_f	04	59	−14	04	−29	−23	−14	11	.55
17. Sc_t	57	66	−11	−13	24	02	−05	01	.85
18. Sc_f	−10	52	07	01	−11	−03	−12	45	.52
19. Ma_t	79	21	−04	01	05	05	20	08	.73
20. Ma_f	−23	−22	−01	−02	06	−09	12	59	.47
21. Si_t	60	60	−01	−06	−16	14	−18	−27	.87
22. Si_f	−70	40	04	−11	−09	14	−07	−12	.71
23. K	−78	−37	00	05	17	−19	05	20	.85
24. Dy1	36	−79	−01	−01	08	03	00	01	.76
25. Dy2	55	−62	−08	−02	08	02	−04	−05	.71
26. Dy3	88	00	−00	05	−04	−07	00	−03	.78
27. Dy4	78	49	06	−05	−03	09	03	08	.86
28. Dy5	53	71	−09	−01	18	03	−04	−05	.82
29. A	71	56	−08	−28	−04	−05	−05	−09	.91
30. R	−82	21	04	−15	11	04	02	−02	.76
% Tot. Var.	31.4	21.8	3.0	2.3	2.5	3.4	1.5	3.8	69.7
% Com. Var.	45.0	31.3	4.3	3.3	3.6	4.9	2.1	5.4	

* Loadings above .25 are italicized for factors III–VIII.

for 45 and 31.3 percent of the common variance, respectively. The next six factors were extremely small in magnitude, together accounting for a portion of common variance less than one-fourth that explained by the first two factors. This finding is consistent with other factor analytic studies of MMPI scales, which have also usually yielded only two or three large common factors [32, 60].

The interpretation of these first two large dimensions is facilitated by examining a plot of their test vectors (Figure 45–1). Since the Dy3 scale was composed entirely

of "true" items of moderate desirability and heterogeneous content, it was considered to be a possible criterion measure of acquiescence. Hence the first axis was placed directly through the Dy3 vector by means of Saunders' [63] pattern quartimax procedure, the second axis being oriented orthogonal to the first in the plane of the two major dimensions. The first factor seemed clearly identifiable as acquiescence, since not only did Dy3 receive the highest loading on it, but all of the "true" scales had positive loadings and all but one of the "false" scales had negative loadings; the

Figure 45–1   *Prison sample.*

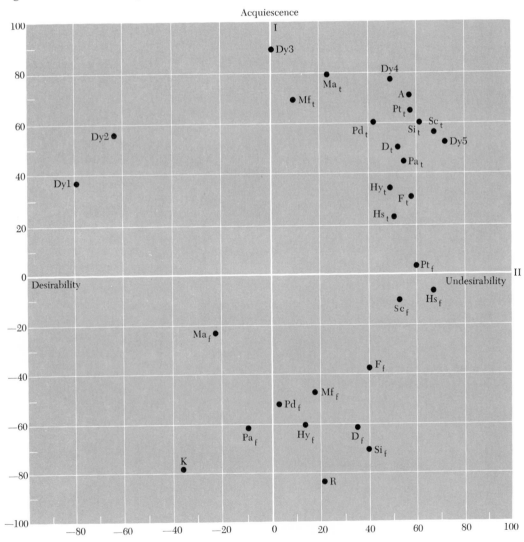

one exception, Pt_f, received an essentially zero coefficient. Thus, by differentiating true and false keys for MMPI scales, a complete separation of their loadings was obtained on the first factor. There were also marked tendencies for scales moderate in desirability, rather than those extremely desirable or undesirable, to show the highest positive and negative loadings on this factor.

The second factor displayed a marked separation in loadings for scales with high and low desirability values. This dimension was interpreted as a clear reflection at one extreme of the tendency to respond desirably and at the other extreme of the tendency to respond undesirably, as evidenced by a correlation between loadings on this second factor and the mean judged item desirability of each scale (with "false" items appropriately reflected) of .95.

Although the obtained pattern of test vectors on the first two factors is easily interpreted, it does not meet criteria for simple structure, nor was this to be expected. Rather, with scales varying on a continuum of average judged desirability and with an inseparable dependence in the same set of items of various levels of acquiescence-eliciting potential, we would expect the scale vectors to form a circle [64]. Such a circular array is evident in Figure 45–1, indicating a kind of reciprocity between acquiescence and desirability for a given scale—as desirability or undesirability of content increases from neutrality, the acquiescence component becomes smaller. The relative lack of vectors in the two left quadrants of Figure 45–1 is attributable in this battery to the poor representation of both "true" and "false" scales of highly desirable content. Inclusion of such scales would be expected to fill out the circle, with quadrants consisting of items keyed (a) desirable "true," (b) undesirable "true," (c) undesirable "false," and (d) desirable "false."

The remaining six factors taken together accounted for only 16.5 percent of the total variance and 23.6 percent of the common variance. Since they were individually quite small, explaining from 2.1 to 5.4 percent of the common variance each, interpretation was sometimes difficult. Interpretation was made particularly complicated by the fact that considerable item overlap exists between many of the scales with high loadings on these small factors. By eliminating from consideration factors probably attributable to item overlap, three dimensions (IV, VII, and VIII) remained which seemed to warrant psychological interpretations [see 45 for a discussion of item overlap factors and their appraisal].

Factor IV received moderate loadings for Mf_f, Pa_f, Pt_t, and A. From an examination of relevant item content of these scales, it would appear that high scorers would reject content suggestive of hyper-masculine "toughness" and cynicism, in denying, for example, that "most people are honest chiefly through fear of being caught" (common to Mf_f and Pa_f). They would also tend to admit more freely to diverse symptoms of anxiety. One might speculate that such persons would be deviant in a prison. It is notable that while Mf_f is highly loaded on this factor, Mf_t is not, which is consistent with their −.15 correlation but inconsistent with the MMPI practice of adding the two scales together. It also argues against a simple identification of Factor IV as femininity.

Factor VII, although quite small, provides a rare instance in which the true and false keys of a given scale, in this case D, appear on the same factor. Thus, there indeed appears to be some consistent responses to content in items characteristic of depressed persons when the major stylistic determinants are first partialled out by factor analysis. It is necessary, however, to take these stylistic determinants into consideration, since the original correlation between D_t and D_f was only −.11.

Factor VIII appeared to be a combination of correlated independent responses and item overlap. Although Ma_f and Pd_f on the one hand and Sc_f and F_f on the other have common items, there is little item dependence between these two sets of scales. All loadings, however, are in the false direction, and the item content associated with these scales would suggest that subjects scoring high on them might be reflecting tendencies to deny certain classes of deviant material. Clinically, high scores on the above (complete or total) scales are commonly associated with alcoholism [53], impulsivity, chronic trouble with the law, an amoral outlook, rebellion against established authority, a degree of social brashness, and employment instability—characteristics which might be represented in the aggregate with greater than average frequency within a prison inmate population, but which were also found in the following study to be of more general relevance.

HOSPITAL AND COLLEGE SAMPLES

Because the sample of prison inmates used in the above study might be deviant and might permit only limited generalization of the results, it was considered important to ascertain the relevance of the conclusions to other populations. The following investigation [46] seeks to replicate and amplify the previous study with both a wider sampling of populations and a broader array of MMPI scales.

Two different samples were employed, with separate analyses being performed for each. The first of these, the "hospital" sample, consisted of 194 patients—119 males and 75 females—from a state neuropsychiatric hospital. The second group, the "college" sample, was composed of 334 undergraduates—160 males and 174 females—all paid volunteers from introductory psychology classes at a state university.

As in the preceding analysis, separate scores were obtained for each subject on true- and false-keyed items of MMPI clinical and validity scales, along with scores on the five Dy scales. Separate "true" and "false" scores were also obtained for the following additional MMPI scales: J. A. Taylor's [67] Manifest Anxiety Scale

(MAS); Barron's [7] Ego Strength Scale (Es); Edwards' [28] Social Desirability Scale (SD); Hanley's [37] scale of test-taking defensiveness (Tt); the Cofer, Chance, and Judson [19] positive malingering scale (Mp); and Fulkerson's [34] acquiescence scale (Aq). Single scores were derived for Welsh's [69] MMPI pure factor measures, the predominantly true-keyed A scale and the all false R scale.

The two matrices of intercorrelations among these 40 MMPI variables (true and false parts of 15 MMPI scales, five Dy scales, and the L, K, A, R, and Aq scales) were factor analyzed separately for the hospital and college samples by the method of principal components. Communalities were estimated by the highest correlation in each column. An examination of the relative sizes of the 40 latent roots for each matrix led to the retention of nine factors in the hospital sample and 11 in the college sample, such a large number being deliberately chosen in an effort to clarify rotations [16].

The factors in each of the present groups were separately rotated analytically to an orthogonal patterned quartimax criterion [63], with acquiescence and desirability as the hypothesized large factors. An additional orthogonal rotation was applied to the first two factors in each sample to balance the loadings of Dy1 and Dy5 and of Dy2 and Dy4 on the first factor, as opposed to the alternative position obtained by making Factor I co-linear with Dy3. (There was little difference between these alternative alignments in the foregoing analysis of the prison data.) The rotated factor loadings for the hospital sample are presented in Table 45–2 and those for the college sample in Table 45–3.

Plots of test vectors on the first two large dimensions in each sample provide a clear basis for their interpretation (Figures 45–2 and 45–3). It should be noted that for each group there is again a complete separation of true- and false-keyed subscales on the first factor, so that in no case does a "true"

Table 45–2   Factor Loadings for the Hospital Sample* (N = 194)

Variable	Factors									h²
	I	II	III	IV	V	VI	VII	VIII	IX	
1. F_t	31	71	−26	−08	06	−04	21	09	27	.81
2. F_f	−29	64	−12	01	−16	−01	05	29	−20	.66
3. Hs_t	07	65	−07	04	65	01	00	−04	02	.85
4. Hs_f	−20	68	05	−06	47	26	05	10	−04	.81
5. D_t	18	75	00	47	25	12	−01	−05	−02	.90
6. D_f	−53	52	04	23	21	49	−05	04	−03	.70
7. Hy_t	13	69	−01	30	52	−01	−05	03	−03	.86
8. Hy_f	−61	04	04	11	43	32	−04	28	06	.76
9. Pd_t	44	68	−01	11	−08	03	−06	19	20	.77
10. Pd_f	−40	15	07	−05	−07	09	−18	46	06	.44
11. Pa_t	39	70	−02	08	04	−06	24	07	38	.85
12. Pa_f	−59	−23	03	17	13	18	−17	16	23	.60
13. Pt_t	27	81	00	41	18	04	−03	−08	06	.95
14. Pt_f	−16	70	−02	16	23	35	−02	07	−07	.73
15. Sc_t	30	84	−16	17	09	−09	09	06	19	.93
16. Sc_f	−16	73	−18	−09	02	07	09	26	02	.70
17. Ma_t	60	61	−06	−07	03	−17	01	12	13	.80
18. Ma_f	−34	−45	−03	−10	10	−04	15	57	01	.68
19. Si_t	33	79	02	24	−10	02	05	−32	−02	.93
20. Si_f	−69	29	02	08	−16	−02	−05	−31	00	.69
21. K	−55	−68	−07	−09	06	03	03	24	13	.87
22. Dy1	30	−84	−04	03	03	−03	01	−04	−03	.80
23. Dy2	60	−61	00	05	−02	02	05	04	07	.75
24. Dy3	79	39	06	00	04	05	−10	03	03	.80
25. Dy4	58	73	−09	07	−01	00	06	−04	−02	.89
26. Dy5	30	87	−08	20	03	−01	14	−02	10	.94
27. A	36	79	07	39	05	08	−02	−12	06	.95
28. R	−81	01	−10	05	09	16	10	−21	−05	.77
29. MAS_t	27	79	11	43	16	08	−05	−11	04	.94
30. MAS_f	−16	76	35	15	27	07	−14	00	02	.86
31. Es_t	63	−02	00	12	−19	−39	−20	20	−09	.69
32. Es_f	−45	−64	−02	−25	−28	−07	−17	12	−17	.85
33. SD_t	14	−76	−35	−11	−19	08	01	08	04	.78
34. SD_f	−28	−85	02	−30	−03	−03	−06	14	−06	.93
35. Tt_t	47	−18	−13	−06	00	−10	36	−07	−09	.43
36. Tt_f	−50	−56	−05	02	04	08	07	07	31	.69
37. Mp_t	59	−24	04	−26	−04	05	34	12	09	.62
38. Mp_f	−47	−56	04	−16	−05	−01	50	00	−01	.82
39. Aq	73	49	06	−17	−04	−05	−03	01	−06	.81
40. L	−39	−39	−02	05	−00	02	72	03	03	.83
% Tot. Var.	20.0	39.0	1.2	3.7	4.2	2.2	3.4	3.3	1.6	78.6
% Com. Var.	26.0	49.0	1.6	4.7	5.3	2.8	4.4	4.2	2.0	

* Loadings above .25 are italicized for factors III–IX.

Table 45–3   Factor Loadings for the College Sample* (N = 334)

Variable	I	II	III	IV	V	VI	VII	VIII	IX	X	XI	h²
								Factors				
1. F_t	35	57	−18	08	−09	−16	13	02	−17	24	00	.62
2. F_f	−26	44	02	*−45*	−11	−01	00	09	−03	−01	−12	.50
3. Hs_t	10	39	00	15	*27*	−06	−19	16	03	05	−38	.47
4. Hs_f	−11	67	−08	17	−04	20	−20	26	28	−01	−03	.72
5. D_t	17	69	−03	−09	*46*	18	04	−06	04	01	−13	.79
6. D_f	−61	28	−01	00	08	*33*	−04	22	09	−03	06	.62
7. Hy_t	14	58	−11	14	19	01	06	05	02	−01	*−45*	.63
8. Hy_f	−49	−11	−17	10	09	14	−13	55	20	−06	−03	.68
9. Pd_t	38	69	−14	−15	10	−18	06	19	−15	−05	−03	.77
10. Pd_f	−26	11	05	−02	−08	00	11	69	−02	−05	−01	.59
11. Pa_t	25	70	−12	10	22	−22	00	02	−07	−04	06	.68
12. Pa_f	−50	−28	*−46*	01	11	−01	−03	12	11	−05	−09	.59
13. Pt_t	31	79	−08	04	*42*	−04	−03	−08	04	−04	−03	.91
14. Pt_f	−07	63	−03	01	12	*31*	−04	13	04	−11	−03	.55
15. Sc_t	34	80	−15	−04	24	−13	−01	08	−11	−04	−13	.88
16. Sc_f	−12	60	−09	−19	−15	03	−12	11	−11	09	*−30*	.58
17. Ma_t	66	50	03	03	−09	−23	−07	04	−10	−06	−08	.78
18. Ma_f	−01	−37	03	−13	−03	−07	−04	55	−05	17	−02	.50
19. Si_t	21	76	12	−04	*33*	12	11	−36	02	09	06	.91
20. Si_f	−68	32	14	−04	03	−04	13	−27	−02	04	04	.67
21. K	−56	−65	−15	−04	−09	04	05	23	−03	04	−04	.82
22. Dy1	28	−79	07	01	11	−05	01	−04	−02	−05	06	.72
23. Dy2	50	−60	−12	−01	−02	−01	04	09	00	13	−08	.65
24. Dy3	79	31	−07	04	−01	12	09	−02	11	01	−08	.77
25. Dy4	51	76	02	−04	08	−10	−01	01	−03	−04	05	.86
26. Dy5	29	81	−05	02	22	−07	11	06	−04	13	−03	.84
27. A	32	80	00	−04	*43*	04	03	−06	07	01	02	.94
28. R	−80	01	−03	02	02	04	−07	−13	−04	01	19	.69
29. MAS_t	26	78	02	07	*43*	−03	−02	−04	17	−05	−04	.91
30. MAS_f	−19	71	02	11	14	02	−01	07	52	−08	−02	.85
31. Es_t	55	−09	05	−01	−04	−15	*32*	−04	09	−11	−23	.51
32. Es_f	−37	−60	10	−08	*−45*	07	10	04	−11	−06	00	.75
33. SD_t	39	−68	06	09	−10	−02	−04	−02	*−55*	−04	−01	.83
34. SD_f	−27	−82	−04	−12	*−32*	01	−12	12	−03	−04	08	.87
35. Tt_t	39	−24	−13	−02	−10	−05	*−31*	−13	−01	24	00	.41
36. Tt_f	−52	−53	*−33*	−01	16	02	01	12	03	00	−02	.70
37. Mp_t	57	−22	−22	05	−17	07	06	01	−11	*34*	−09	.59
38. Mp_f	−45	−52	08	07	−08	06	−07	−04	−09	*45*	−01	.70
39. Aq	74	40	08	−02	−13	−01	−12	−01	−07	−03	05	.76
40. L	−42	−32	03	−06	11	−06	−10	−01	05	*54*	01	.62
% Tot. Var.	18.0	33.0	1.6	1.1	4.3	1.4	1.2	4.2	2.3	2.2	1.6	70.9
% Com. Var.	26.0	46.0	2.3	1.6	6.1	2.0	1.7	6.0	3.2	3.1	2.3	

* Loadings above .25 are italicized for factors III–XI.

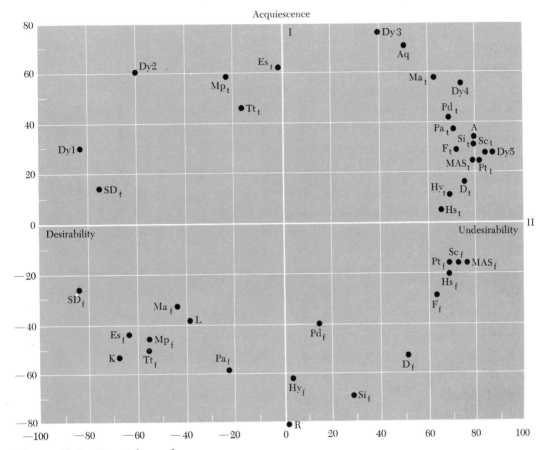

Figure 45–2   *Hospital sample.*

scale have a negative loading or a "false" scale a positive loading. Accordingly, this factor may be interpreted relatively unequivocally as acquiescence, a consistent tendency on the part of subjects to endorse or reject items. It should be noted that all of the Dy scales received positive loadings on this factor, a finding predictable from their all "true" keying, but that Dy3, a scale of items neutral in desirability, received the highest loading. As scales depart from neutrality in becoming either more desirable or more undesirable, their loadings on Factor I become more moderate.

In both the hospital and college samples, as in the prison sample previously discussed, the second factor is clearly identifiable in terms of individual differences in the consistent tendency to endorse desir-

able item content, as indicated by correlations above .90 in both samples between loadings on the second factor and independently obtained average desirability values for each scale [59]. For both samples the scales having the largest loadings on this factor included Dy1 in the desirable direction and Dy5 in the undesirable, both of which had been especially designed to be extreme in desirability but heterogeneous in content. Also obtaining high loadings in the desirable direction were the Edwards SD "true" and "false" subscales, which had been similarly selected for their extremeness in judged desirability [28]. Most of the MMPI clinical scales, reflecting as they do deviant and pathological content, received quite high loadings in the undesirable direction.

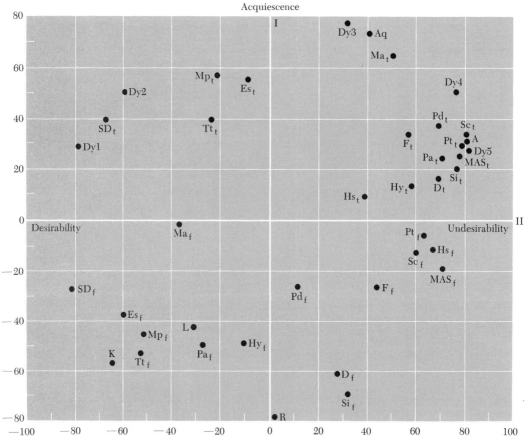

Figure 45–3   *College sample.*

A remarkable feature of these findings is the high degree of stability obtained across diverse samples. An inspection of Figures 45–2 and 45–3 reveals a strikingly similar pattern of factor loadings, even though one group was composed of neuropsychiatric patients and the other of superior young adults. The factor pattern again forms a circular array of vectors as noted previously in the prison study, only here the circle is more complete because of the addition of several scales keyed in the desirable direction, such as L, SD, Es, Tt, and Mp. While the means for the various clinical scales were quite different in the hospital and college groups, the underlying structure of response consistency was similar. One index of this similarity, the correlation between loadings on corresponding factors for the two samples, was in excess of .99 for the

desirability dimension and was .98 for the acquiescence factor. While the average *degree* of undesirable item endorsement was higher for the hospital group, the general consistencies in responding desirably or undesirably within each group were invariant.

In both samples the first two response style factors accounted for a major proportion of the common variance. In the hospital sample, the two factors together accounted for 75 percent of the common variance and 59 percent of the total variance, and in the college sample they accounted for 72 percent of the common and 51 percent of the total variance. The communalities were also quite high, particularly in the hospital sample. Thus, to a substantial degree correlations between MMPI scales, especially when subdivided into true and false subscales, could be reasonably well reproduced by knowledge of these two factors and without reference to any factors of content. These particular percentages, of course, reflect the specific method of scoring used—that of dividing standard MMPI scales into true- and false-keyed parts—a method which reveals the dominant role of acquiescence in influencing responses at the item level. When "true" and "false" subscales are added to yield a total score, of course, some of the acquiescence effect cancels out and the desirability factor should be even more pronounced [29]. However, imperfect balancing of "true" and "false" item means and variances on most MMPI scales still permits substantial generalized acquiescence effects [60].

In addition to the two large response style factors in each of the two analyses, seven factors in the hospital sample and nine in the college sample were retained for possible interpretation (Tables 45–2 and 45–3). The proportions of common and total variance accounted for by each of these factors is quite small, and an appreciable portion of this common variance is attributable to item overlap between scales, as distinguished from actual consistencies in responses to related content. The seven small factors in the hospital sample together accounted for just 25 percent of the common variance and 19.6 percent of the total variance; for the nine small factors in the college sample the percentages were 28.3 and 19.9, respectively.

Again eliminating from consideration factors probably attributable to item overlap, along with specific and inconsistent doublet factors, there remained four dimensions in the hospital sample (IV, V, VII, VIII) and three in the college sample (V, VIII, X) which seemed to warrant psychological interpretation.

Factor IV in the hospital sample and V in the college sample were among the largest of the small factors. The two dimensions are quite similar—each having high loadings on true-keyed neurotic and anxiety scales (D_t, MAS_t, A, Pt_t, $-SD_t$, $-Es_t$, Hy_t, Hs_t, Si_t).

There is considerable item overlap among these scales but the pervasiveness of this factor and its relative size suggests that it might be interpretable in terms of content. The content of these scales reflects heterogeneous neurotic symptoms, but the over-all impression suggests that "anxiety" may serve as a reasonably appropriate label. However, since all the scales load in the "true" direction, a more precise description would be "the tendency to endorse diverse anxiety items." A similar but broader tendency to accept a variety of psychiatric symptoms has frequently appeared as the first dimension in factor-analytic studies of the MMPI [60], although in the present study such a factor seems to emerge even after general acquiescence and desirability have been in effect partialled out by orthogonal axis placement. It may well be, as has been frequently suggested [5, 6, 44, 60, 69, 71], that acquiescence interacts with particular content areas in producing common patterns of responses; but such considerations should not overshadow the possible influence of item overlap in generating this particular factor.

Both Factor VII in the hospital sample and Factor X in the college sample are dominated by a high loading for the Lie scale and appear to reflect a type of naive test-taking defensiveness commonly associated with elevated Lie scale scores. The interpretation of this factor is aided considerably by the inclusion of the positive malingering scale (Mp), which was explicitly developed to assess faking. Persons scoring high on this factor would show a common tendency to respond deviantly in the desirable direction to items with a substantial disparity between their judged desirability and their modal probability of endorsement, like the item, "I read every editorial in the newspaper every day." Such items would also display large mean differences when answered under standard and faking instructions. This response tendency appears to be relatively independent of specific content areas and of the response styles of acquiescence and desirability represented in the first two factors [68]. Because responses to such scales may be interpretable in terms of both a tendency to respond consistently to certain formal properties of items and a mode of defense involving the maintenance of an excessively favorable self-concept [50], these scales might be considered to reflect stylistic aspects of responding. It should be noted that the K scale, frequently interpreted in terms of defensiveness [54], does not load the present factor, but is instead accounted for in terms of the first two dimensions of acquiescence and desirability.

Another dimension appearing in both the hospital and college analyses (Factor VIII in each case) was also represented in the prison sample. With the exception of Si, both parts of which load negatively, the high loadings are for false-keyed scales, with Ma$_f$ and Pd$_f$ prominently represented. Since these scales are usually associated clinically with impulsivity, alcoholism, rebelliousness, trouble with the law, employment instability, social brashness, and the like, we previously suspected this factor to be unique to the prison inmate population, but its appearance here suggests a broader relevance.

The hospital sample yielded an additional factor (V) not obtained in the other two groups. The highest loadings on this factor were received by both true and false parts of Hs and Hy. Since this factor provides an all too infrequent instance of "true" and "false" subscales loading in the same direction, a direct content interpretation seemed warranted and the label "somatic complaints" is suggested. The failure of this factor to appear clearly in the younger, healthier, and generally more highly educated college sample is probably due to a relative lack of variance for such subjects in reporting somatic preoccupations [41].

It is notable that none of the Dy scales were loaded substantially on any of the smaller factors in any of the samples. This finding suggests that the primary aim in developing these scales—that of maximizing

MMPI content heterogeneity while systematically varying desirability level—was achieved.

THE DIFFERENTIAL ASSESSMENT OF PSYCHOPATHOLOGY

The results from these studies of three diverse samples reveal a strikingly consistent pattern. In all three analyses, approximately three-fourths of the common variance and about one-half of the total variance was interpretable in terms of the response styles of acquiescence and desirability. Of the remaining very small factors, roughly half their variance was attributable to item overlap, and hence is of little or no psychological significance. While consistencies interpretable in terms of reliable responses to item content did indeed appear in all three samples, with moderate replication in the diverse groups, their aggregate contribution to the total response variance was not great in comparison with other sources of variance. To interpret scale scores presumably reflecting such content factors without taking into account the rather massive response style effects would be quite hazardous. Because of the marked influence of acquiescence and desirability on virtually all of these empirically derived scales from the MMPI, there is a decided tendency for the scales to share substantial common variance, particularly when "true" and "false" items are considered separately, causing considerable redundancy and further reducing any unique contribution of a given scale to the assessment of psychopathological behavior.

While our procedure of dividing standard scales into "true" and "false" subscales admittedly tended to highlight acquiescence in the response variance of the MMPI, it also revealed another important property of MMPI scales. Even after the general acquiescence factor was removed in the three samples, true and false keys for a given MMPI scale showed a marked tendency *not* to load on the same factors. In the prison sample only the D scale received consistent loadings for "true" and "false" parts on the same content factor. Just two of the scales, Si and Mp, yielded consistent loadings for "true" and "false" items in both the college and hospital samples; whereas Hs and Hy received consistent loadings on a factor found in the hospital sample only. This unfortunate property of most MMPI scales raises questions with respect to the logic of adding subscales which fail to share common variance, and does not add to the confidence with which characteristics can be unequivocally attributed to individuals on the basis of total scores obtained by adding true and false items for particular MMPI scales.

The present results therefore raise serious questions concerning the appropriateness and value of standard MMPI keys and scoring methods, and suggest that more efficient and more accurate procedures are possible. As has been pointed out elsewhere [23, 44], the original aim in MMPI construction of developing a method for predicting psychiatric diagnoses has generally not been fulfilled, a failure partially attributable to the heterogeneous and loosely defined Kraepelinian diagnostic criteria. Rather, MMPI scale scores have been increasingly used to draw inferences about traits or characteristics of respondents [69]. Unfortunately, this change in practice has been accomplished without a corresponding modification in scoring procedures and without adequate attention to the assumptions implicit in the use of total scores to locate respondents on some latent dimension. Notable among these assumptions is the requirement that scales be homogeneous, that an increasing score primarily reflect a greater degree of only one psychological trait or characteristic. It is evident that the MMPI scales described in the *Manual*—heterogeneous in content and in stylistic components—are unequal to this task. There is therefore an urgent need to evaluate fresh approaches to scale construction, with emphasis upon homogeneity as well as validity and with adequate consideration given to response sets in scoring and interpretation.

The consistent finding of systematic and very substantial response style effects on the MMPI thus raises important questions as to the conditions, if any, under which responses to structured items can be interpreted in terms of some particular content or criterion relevant to psychopathology. The response styles themselves, of course, may be related to psychopathology, and the search for identifiable personality correlates of these styles [44] should certainly continue, for there are already some promising initial results [9, 15, 18, 20, 27, 31, 42, 48, 47, 50, 52, 57]. However, with a "true-false" item format as in the MMPI, one rapidly approaches an upper limit on the amount of information elicited by items which permit massive response-style effects like generalized acquiescence and desirability bias. With dichotomous items yielding only "deviant-true" and "deviant-false" responses, one can identify respondents who vary predominantly on only two general stylistic dimensions [44, 65, 71]. If these two dimensions account for a very substantial proportion of the response variance, then the usefulness of the available information for differentiating among respondents with respect to particular psychopathological states or conditions must necessarily be limited. It is true that the presence or absence of various psychopathological conditions might well be reflected in differing weights for the two major response styles. This possibility is consistent with several attempts to differentiate among clinical groups psychometrically which have indeed uncovered only two canonical variates [62, 10, 51]. However, the empirical fact that various psychopathological states yield stylistic response patterns on the MMPI which are not distinctive provides a basis for understanding the general lack of discriminant validity associated with MMPI scale scores. To be sure, there are a few other potentially general response styles which might be elicited from MMPI items, such as the differential tendency to endorse deviantly items having high desirability but low communality values, like the Lie Scale [71], or to prefer items with absolutely or probabilistically phrased qualifiers [18]. However, it is doubtful that the number of such potential response-style variables is high on the MMPI, nor is their relevance to psychopathology known with certainty.

There is a question then as to whether or not the item format of the MMPI, providing such fertile ground as it does for powerful acquiescence and desirability effects, is the method of choice in the structured assessment of psychopathology. This question naturally devolves upon issues of validity per unit cost [24]. Berg [11, 12] has already suggested that it might be more economical to use a small number of items dealing with preferences for abstract drawings—provided one's purpose is to differentiate psychotics from normals [4, 2, 3]. However, in addition to convergent validity, there is a need for discriminant validity [14]. We submit that typically the clinician is at least as interested in differentiating a schizophrenic from a depressive as he is in distinguishing hospitalized patients from normals. While massive response sets apparently contribute to the differentiation of normals from mental patients and thus to convergent validity, in most cases such sets will prove to be a definite hindrance to unequivocal and refined differential diagnosis, and therefore militate against discriminant validity. Therefore, where interest is centered upon the differential assignment of characteristics relevant to personality or to psychopathology on the basis of test scores, experimental controls for response set biases are imperative. The particular form that such controls should take in the assessment of psychopathology is a question for further research [1, 55, 56, 58, 60].

REFERENCES

1. ADAMS, GEORGIA S. Techniques of minimizing or capitalizing upon response tendencies in structured self-report inventories. Paper read at Int. Congr. Psychol., Bonn, Germany, August, 1960.

2. ADAMS, H. E., & BERG, I. A. Affective tone of test option choice as a deviant response. *Psychol. Rep.*, 1961, 8, 79–85.

3. ADAMS, H. E., & BERG, I. A. Schizophrenia and deviant response sets produced by auditory and visual test content. *J. Psychol.*, 1961, 51, 393–398.

4. BARNES, E. H. The relationship of biased test responses to psychopathology. *J. abnorm. soc. Psychol.*, 1955, 51, 286–290.

5. BARNES, E. H. Response bias and the MMPI. *J. consult. Psychol.*, 1956, 20, 371–374.

6. BARNES, E. H. Factors, response bias, and the MMPI. *J. consult. Psychol.*, 1956, 20, 419–421.

7. BARRON, F. An ego-strength scale which predicts response to psychotherapy. *J. consult. Psychol.*, 1953, 17, 327–333.

8. BASS, B. M. Authoritarianism or acquiescence? *J. abnorm. soc. Psychol.*, 1955, 51, 616–623.

9. BASS, B. M. Development and evaluation of a scale for measuring social acquiescence. *J. abnorm. soc. Psychol.*, 1956, 53, 296–299.

10. BEECH, H. R., & MAXWELL, A. E. Differentiation of clinical groups using canonical variates. *J. consult. Psychol.*, 1958, 22, 113–121.

11. BERG, I. A. Response bias and personality: The deviation hypothesis. *J. Psychol.*, 1955, 40, 61–72.

12. BERG, I. A. The unimportance of test item content. In B. M. Bass and I. A. Berg (Eds.), *Objective approaches to personality assessment.* Princeton, N.J.: Van Nostrand, 1959. Pp. 83–99.

13. BUSS, A. H. The effect of item style on social desirability and frequency of endorsement. *J. consult. Psychol.*, 1959, 23, 510–513.

14. CAMPBELL, D. T. & FISKE, D. W. Convergent and discriminant validation by the multitrait-multimethod matrix. *Psychol. Bull.*, 1959, 56, 81–105.

15. CATTELL, R. B. *Personality and motivation structure and measurement.* Yonkerson-Hudson, N.Y.: World Book, 1957.

16. CATTELL, R. B. Extracting the correct number of factors in factor analysis. *Educ. psychol. Measmt*, 1958, 18, 791–838.

17. CHAPMAN, L. J., & BOCK, R. D. Components of variance due to acquiescence and content in the F scale measure of authoritarianism. *Psychol. Bull.*, 1958, 55, 328–333.

18. CLAYTON, MARTHA B., & JACKSON, D. N. Equivalence range, acquiescence, and overgeneralization. *Educ. psychol. Measmt*, 1961, 21, 371–382.

19. COFER, C. N., CHANCE, JUNE, & JUDSON, A. J. A study of malingering on the Minnesota Multiphasic Personality Inventory. *J. Psychol.*, 1949, 27, 491–499.

20. COUCH, A., & KENISTON, K. Yeasayers and naysayers: Agreeing response set as a personality variable. *J. abnorm. soc. Psychol.*, 1960, 60, 151–174.

21. CRONBACH, L. J. Response sets and test validity. *Educ. psychol. Measmt*, 1946, 6, 475–494.

22. CRONBACH, L. J. Further evidence on response sets and test design. *Educ. psychol. Measmt*, 1950, 10, 3–31.

23. CRONBACH, L. J. Review of "*Basic readings on the MMPI in psychology and medicine*" (G. S. Welsh & W. G. Dahlstrom, Eds.). *Psychometrika*, 1958, 23, 385–386.

24. CRONBACH, L. J., & GLESER, GOLDINE C. *Psychological tests and personnel decisions.* Urbana, Ill.: Univer. Illinois Press, 1957.

25. CRONBACH, L. J., & MEEHL, P. E. Construct validity in psychological tests. *Psychol. Bull.*, 1955, 52, 281–302.

26. DAHLSTROM, W. G., & WELSH, G. S. *An MMPI handbook: A guide to use in clinical practice and research.* Minneapolis: Univer. Minnesota Press, 1960.

27. DAMARIN, F. L., & MESSICK, S. Response styles as personality variables: Evidence from published multivariate research. Princeton, N.J.: Educational Testing Service Research Bulletin, 1965.

28. EDWARDS, A. L. *The social desirability variable in personality assessment and research.* New York: Dryden, 1957.

29. EDWARDS, A. L. Social desirability or acquiescence in the MMPI? A case study with the SD scale. *J. abnorm. soc. Psychol.*, 1961, 63, 351–359.

30. ELLIOTT, LOIS L. Effects of item construction and respondent aptitude on response acquiescence. *Educ. psychol. Measmt*, 1961, 21, 405–415.

31. FREDERIKSEN, N., & MESSICK, S. Response set as a measure of personality. *Educ. psychol. Measmt*, 1959, 19, 137–157.

32. FRENCH, J. W. *The description of personality measurements in terms of rotated factors.* Princeton, N.J.: Educational Testing Service, 1953.

33. FRICKE, B. G. Response set as a suppressor variable in the OAIS and MMPI. *J. consult. Psychol.*, 1956, 20, 161–169.

34. FULKERSON, S. C. An acquiescence key for the MMPI. Report No. 58–71. Randolph AF Base, Texas: USAF School of Aviation Medicine, July 1958.

35. GAGE, N. L., & CHATTERJEE, B. B. The psychological meaning of acquiescence set: Further evidence. *J. abnorm. soc. Psychol.*, 1960, 60, 280–283.

36. GAGE, N. L., LEAVITT, G. S., & STONE, G. C. The psychological meaning of acquiescence set for authoritarianism. *J. abnorm. soc. Psychol.*, 1957, 55, 98–103.

37. HANLEY, C. Deriving a measure of test-taking defensiveness. *J. consult. Psychol.*, 1957, 21, 391–397.

38. HANLEY, C. Responses to the wording of personality test items. *J. consult. Psychol.*, 1959, 23, 261–265.

39. HEINEMAN, C. E. A forced-choice form of the Taylor Anxiety Scale. Unpublished doctoral dissertation, State Univer. of Iowa, 1952.

40. HEMPEL, C. G. Fundamentals of concept formation in empirical science. In O. Neurath et al. (Eds.), *International encyclopedia of unified science.* Vol. 2, No. 7. Chicago: Univer. Chicago Press, 1955.

41. HOLLINGSHEAD, A. B., & REDLICH, F. C. *Social class and mental illness: A community study.* New York: Wiley, 1958.

42. JACKSON, D. N. Cognitive energy level, acquiescence, and authoritarianism. *J. soc. Psychol.*, 1959, 49, 65–69.

43. JACKSON, D. N. & MESSICK, S. A note on "ethnocentrism" and acquiescent response sets. *J. abnorm. soc. Psychol.*, 1957, 54, 132–134.

44. JACKSON, D. N., & MESSICK, S. Content and style in personality assessment. *Psychol. Bull.*, 1958, 55, 243–252.

45. JACKSON, D. N. & MESSICK, S. Acquiescence and desirability as response determinants on the MMPI. *Educ. psychol. Measmt*, 1961, 21, 771–790.

46. JACKSON, D. N., & MESSICK, S. Response styles on the MMPI: Comparison of clinical and normal samples. *J. abnorm. soc. Psychol.*, 1962, 65, 285–299.

47. JACKSON, D. N., MESSICK, S., & SOLLEY, C. M. How "rigid" is the "authoritarian"? *J. abnorm. soc. Psychol.*, 1957, 54, 137–140.

48. JACKSON, D. N., & PACINE, L. Response styles and academic achievement. *Educ. psychol. Measmt*, 1961, 21, 1015–1028.

49. LOEVINGER, JANE. Objective tests as instruments of psychological theory. *Psychol. Rep.*, 1957, 3, 635–694.

50. MARLOWE, D., & CROWNE, D. P. Social desirability and response to perceived situational demands. *J. consult. Psychol.*, 1961, 25, 109–115.

51. McCARTER, R. E. Emotional components of early recollections. ONR Technical Report and doctoral dissertation, Princeton Univer. Princeton, N.J.: Educational Testing Service, 1961.

52. McGEE, R. K. Response style as a personality variable: By what criterion? *Psychol. Bull.*, 1962, 59, 284–295.

53. MEEHL, P. E. Wanted—a good cookbook. *Amer. Psychologist*, 1956, 11, 263–272.

54. MEEHL, P. E., & HATHAWAY, S. R. The K factor as a suppressor variable in the MMPI. *J. appl. Psychol.*, 1946, 30, 525–564.

55. MESSICK, S. Dimensions of social desirability. *J. consult. Psychol.*, 1960, 24, 279–287.

56. MESSICK, S. Response style and content measures from personality inventories. *Educ. psychol. Measmt*, 1962, 22, 41–56.

57. MESSICK, S., & FREDERIKSEN, N. Ability, acquiescence, and "authoritarianism." *Psychol. Rep.*, 1958, 4, 687–697.

58. MESSICK, S., & JACKSON, D. N. The measurement of authoritarian attitudes. *Educ. psychol. Measmt*, 1958, 18, 241–253.

59. MESSICK, S., & JACKSON, D. N. Desirability scale values and dispersions for MMPI items. *Psychol. Rep.*, 1961, 8, 409–414.

60. MESSICK, S., & JACKSON, D. N. Acquiescence and the factorial interpretation of the MMPI. *Psychol. Bull.*, 1961, 58, 299–304.

61. NUNNALLY, J., & HUSEK, T. R. The phony language examination: An approach to the measurement of response bias. *Educ. psychol. Measmt*, 1958, 18, 275–282.

62. RAO, C. R., & SLATER, P. Multivariate analysis applied to differences between neurotic groups. *Brit. J. Psychol., Statist. Sect.*, 1949, 2, 17–29.

63. SAUNDERS, D. R. A computer program to find the best-fitting orthogonal factors for a given hypothesis. *Psychometrika*, 1960, 25, 199–205.

64. SCHAEFER, E. S. A circumplex model for maternal behavior. *J. abnorm. soc. Psychol.*, 1959, 59, 226–235.

65. SECHREST, L. B., & JACKSON, D. N. Deviant response tendencies: Their measurement and interpretation. University Park, Penna.: Pennsylvania State Univer. Research Bulletin No. 19, 1961.

66. STRICKER, L. Some item characteristics that evoke acquiescent and social desirability response sets on psychological scales. Princeton, N.J.: Educational Testing Service Research Bulletin, 1962.

67. TAYLOR, JANET A. A personality scale of manifest anxiety. *J. abnorm. soc. Psychol.*, 1953, 48, 285–290.

68. VOAS, R. B. Relationships among three types of response sets. Report No. 15. Pensacola, Fla.: Naval School of Aviation Medicine, 1958.

69. WELSH, G. S. Factor dimensions A and R. In G. S. Welsh & W. G. Dahlstrom (Eds.), *Basic readings on the MMPI in psychology and medicine*. Minneapolis: Univer. Minnesota Press, 1956. Pp. 264–281.

70. WIGGINS, J. S. Definitions of social desirability and acquiescence in personality inventories. In S. Messick & J. Ross (Eds.), *Measurement in personality and cognition*. New York: Wiley, 1962. Pp. 109–127.

71. WIGGINS, J. S. Strategic, method, and stylistic variance in the MMPI. *Psychol. Bull.*, 1962, 59, 224–242.

72. WIGGINS, J. S., & RUMRILL, C. Social desirability in the MMPI and Welsh's factor scales A and R. *J. consult. Psychol.*, 1959, 23, 100–106.

46~

Criteria for Judging the Adequacy of Interpretations

ROY SCHAFER

In thematic analysis, exemplification of themes may be carried out in a one-dimensional manner, that is, in terms of image-to-theme correlations. The ramifications of each image in depth and breadth thus might be explored. But, as the author has indicated elsewhere in discussions of the multiple determination of responses and the conceptual complexities of thematic analysis, thematic analysis of any image may be pursued on various levels and in various directions.

"An explosion," for example, suggests (1) intense hostility; (2) apprehension that defenses and controls will not contain this hostility; (3) an expectation that upon failure of containment, a violent and indiscriminate outburst will ensue; (4) an unconsciously carried definition of hostile impulses in primitive, destructive, anal-expulsive terms.

"The Liberty Bell with a crack in it," given by a 25-year-old patient belonging to an aristocratic Philadelphia family, ap-

This article is reprinted from *Psychoanalytic Interpretations in Rorschach Testing* by Roy Schafer, 1954, by permission of the author and Grune and Stratton, Inc.

pears to imply: (1) concern with independence, (2) which involves noteworthy rebelliousness, (3) and possibly death wishes (armed rebellion), (4) and which is probably directed against conservative, authoritarian, aristocratic parental images and traditions; (5) the image therefore suggests a generalized adolescent outlook and sense of crisis. Since this special concern with independence, rebellion and parental domination usually is a one-sided representation of intense ambivalence concerning these dimensions of experience, the theme therefore suggests that we also be on the alert for indications of strong dependent, submissive, conciliatory tendencies. As chronic adolescents frequently do, the patient may be vacillating between "surrender" tendencies and "revolt" tendencies. (6) Two aspects of the image may well pertain to the "surrender" side of the ambivalent rebellion: (a) "the crack" in the bell suggests a feeling in the patient that revolt has failed or will fail, or at least that it does not "ring true," and (b) the very symbol of rebellion, the Liberty Bell, like the Mayflower, has a genteel, conformist aspect, being sanctioned by generations of tradition, being a symbol of the "right kind of revolutionary spirit," and being linked to an extent with American aristocracy as well as to rebellion against hostile, absolute authority.

These examples indicate that exploring the subtleties of images and themes may lead us some distance from the raw responses. Our conclusions may be "fascinating," "deep" and "brilliantly explanatory," but they may have little or nothing to do with the specific patient. How are we to decide whether our explorations have led us home or astray, whether we have glittering gold in hand or just glitter? And how are we to distinguish between thoroughness and recklessness? We need criteria for judging what will be called the "adequacy" of interpretations. The following six criteria, to be considered in detail below, deserve particular attention: (1) there should be *sufficient evidence* for the interpretation; (2) the *depth* of the interpretation should be appropriate to the material available; (3) the *manifest form* of the interpreted tendency should be specified; (4) an estimate should be made of the *intensity* of the interpreted tendency; (5) a *hierarchic position* in the total personality picture should be assigned to the interpreted tendency; (6) both the *adaptive and pathological aspects* of the interpreted tendency should be specified. An interpretation need not meet all these criteria to be adequate or useful. It is the ideal interpretation that does meet them all. *But an interpretation should meet enough of these criteria to make sense psychologically and to represent a stand by the tester that is definite enough to be open to verification or refutation by carefully gathered clinical material.*

A. THERE SHOULD BE SUFFICIENT EVIDENCE FOR THE INTERPRETATION

What constitutes *sufficient* evidence is not easy to specify. With reference to the interpretations of the two preceding examples—the explosion and the cracked Liberty Bell—it might be objected that there is no justification for making so many inferences from single responses. Agreed. Fortunately, however, patients usually help us out by giving not one but a number of images, score patterns and attitude expressions that confirm, modify, offset or de-emphasize the interpretive leads provided by one response. Apropos of the cracked Liberty Bell example, records with rebellious, adolescent imagery often also contain prominent images of power, status and authority on the one hand and of passive submission on the other; they also often contain similarly authoritarian, rebellious and submissive test attitudes, and prominent emphasis on both *Space* responses (negativism, rebellion) and *Form-Color* responses (conformity, submission). In short, the case for any major interpretation must and ordinarily can be built on a number of pieces of evidence. One clue is never enough to establish a major trend.

This does not mean, however, that it is foolhardy to explore all possible implications of each response. The more such implications or hypotheses we detail as we go through the record, the more adequate our frame of reference for evaluating each new response and for achieving a final synthesis of interpretations. With respect to the explosion example, for instance, the charged imagery through the test may be mostly explosive (volcano, jet plane, fireworks, etc.) and may be compatible with all the implications of an explosion elaborated previously. But the charged imagery in the record may be mostly of a different sort; for example, although hostile on the whole, it may not be particularly explosive (blood, spear, trap, cannon, demon, etc.). In the latter instance the interpretive emphasis shifts from *explosive attack* in particular to *hostile attack* in general, the forms of expression of which may be quite varied, i.e., explosive, engulfing, piercing, and so on. In these two instances we see how different contexts may support different implications of a response, and we see thereby the value of initially spelling out as many reasonable implications of each response as possible.

Of course, when a response and its possible implications stand isolated from the bulk of the test material, they should be handled cautiously. There are instances, however, where only one or two responses express a certain trend but do so dramatically, as, for example, in the case of a sudden *M*—or *Confabulation*. These isolated but dramatic responses should as a rule be given careful interpretive attention.

Returning to the interpretation of the two examples that opened this chapter—the explosion and the cracked Liberty Bell—it might also be objected that there is no justification for assuming that the tester's associations to these images necessarily parallel those of the patient. Agreed again. The same counterargument holds, however, as has already been presented, namely, the final interpretation should ordinarily represent the *convergence* of several or many paths of associative elaboration. This principle of convergence is essentially no different from that which guides both dream analysis in psychoanalytic therapy and thematic analysis of Thematic Apperception test stories. Another counterargument, however, is that surprisingly many images conform reliably in their implications to popular stereotype and/or psychoanalytic experience in interpreting symbols and substitute-formations. These images are often not such unique or subtle creations as we might at first think. *More often it is the choice and patterning of these images that carry the patient's individual stamp.*

As a first general rule of evidence for thematic analysis, the following may therefore be stated: *the security with which we may formulate an interpretation is a function of the extent to which there is a convergence of the imagery themes, the formal scores, and the patient's test attitudes—considered singly, in relation to each other,* *and in sequence.*[1] The case studies to be presented later will illustrate the application of this rule.

Of course, other tests are indispensable in the search for secure interpretations that are at the same time specific and penetrating. Also, there are larger order convergences and complementary emphases to establish *among* tests. An entire volume would be needed to analyze and apply the principles and techniques of integrating Rorschach interpretations with interpretations based on other clinical test results; this cannot be undertaken here.

Genetic reconstructions based on Rorschach test responses deserve some attention in connection with the criterion of sufficient evidence. An example of what is meant by "genetic reconstruction" is the following: "Our experience with this card

---

[1] This type of total analysis of Rorschach results is not new. Rorschach's case study with Oberholzer attempted it [6]; Schachtel [8, 9], Schafer [10] and Beck [1] have applied it too. The latest statement on it has come from Phillips and Smith [5], who refer to it as "Type II sequence analysis" [pp. 243–256]. However, Phillips and Smith base their interpretations and integrations of scores, content and attitudes not on established theory and clinical observation, but on unreported data and on their own experience with "types" of patients. On this basis, they present far-reaching interpretations of almost every detail of every response; for example, they find profound significance for the total personality even in the incidental use of the first person pronoun [p. 244], in the "could be" preface to a response [p. 272], and in differences between beetle and bug [pp. 272–273; see also p. 120]. In these extreme respects, this approach gives little or no recognition to external reality, the ordinary requirements of verbal communication, and the existence of relatively autonomous, conflict-free thought; it implicitly dispenses with the ego and with regard for contexts of meaning, and it treats single response fragments as dynamically discrete, highly overdetermined, elaborate but transparent dreams or infantile fantasies. The authors cite genetic Rorschach data in support of some of their interpretations, but the gap between the data and the conclusions often seems great. The fact that some of the authors' inferences are plausible, convincing or even valid, does not, of course, justify their total approach. It only means that sharp observation or reasoning is combined with theoretical and methodological arbitrariness (see also Thiesen [13] and Schafer [12, footnotes on pp. 32–3, 118, and 130]).

(IV) suggests that the use of the choices, 'giant' and 'a big gorilla' is frequently indicative of a disturbed relationship with the father. It suggests in view of the previous projections, that the individual has a negative attitude toward a domineering, criticizing and overwhelming type of father-figure. *To speculate further, the need to prevent fear and annihilation has led to introjection of the ambivalently regarded father as a superego figure which now operates as a criticizing and devaluating force against his own drives and strivings to be an individual*" [italics mine; 3, pages 227–228]. While it is admittedly speculative, the last part of this interpretation infers complex genetic sequences from only one or a few isolated end results. The interpretation might well be valid in this instance, but psychologically it both presumes too much and is gratuitous.

The genetic reconstruction *presumes too much* because the person in question might very well have arrived at these response choices by quite a different genetic route. The father, for example, instead of being overwhelming in reality, may have actually been passive and ineffective on the whole. He may have become overwhelming only after considerable projection of hostility onto him by the child had occurred. He would then be a hostile father-figure, as inferred, but the superego structure of the individual in question would be quite different in this instance.

Other complicating considerations are these: (1) often, ambivalence felt toward both parents is split so that in the end one parent is all "good" and the other all "bad"; (2) often, a feeling is displaced from one parent to the other because it is less dangerous to feel that way about the latter parent; (3) often, in regression from problems in the relationship with one parent, problems in the relationship with the other parent are reactivated and possibly even dramatized to call attention away from the original, "trigger" problem. From a genetic point of view, how are we to know then whether the "overwhelming" Rorschach figure is necessarily the father, the true father or a fantasied father, only the father or hardly the father?

The genetic reconstruction cited is *gratuitous* because it is nothing more than a statement of a psychoanalytic proposition concerning the genesis of overwhelming father-figures. It is in no way derived from the Rorschach test responses. The Rorschach record can neither support nor refute the interpretation. The interpretation in effect does no more than remind the therapist to whom the report is submitted what Freud, Fenichel *et al.* have said about overwhelming father-figures.

Distinction between two types of genetic reconstruction is called for at this point. One type is that already discussed: it infers sequences of early relationships and details of the personalities involved from what the patient emphasizes at present. It thereby neglects the inevitable selectivity, distortion and other retrospective falsification in current representations of remote experience. How a patient spontaneously represents his past tells us how he needs to see that past *now*. At best this account is only fairly well correlated with the actual past. It is by no means identical with it. The present "autobiography" cannot therefore be taken at face value. Often it is only late in treatment before certain vital corrections are introduced into the patient's initial account of his past. The case history at the beginning and end of treatment may therefore read quite differently. A "horrible" mother may prove to have been an early Good Fairy, or a brother to whom one was "indifferent" may turn out to have been a key, positive or negative identification figure, even if from afar. For these reasons and those mentioned earlier, Rorschach images cannot be considered reliable indicators of the actual past. They reflect only the currently emphasized views of past relationships. Future research may establish that certain images or thematic categories may be safely taken to indicate actualities of early relationships and experiences, but the above considerations suggest that these findings will be at best in the nature of "trends," more of theoretical interest and orienting value than of immediate, individual clinical utility.

The other type of genetic reconstruction, and one which is sound, pertains to the evolution of character structure. These reconstructions are usually only implicit in test reports. When, for example, we say there is evidence of a compulsive character structure, we refer to certain personality characteristics which we assume could not exist in their present form and intensity unless they had been evolved through a long history of trial and error, choice and rejection, modification and extension of certain modes of defense and adaptation. By definition, a character structure is a life work and is enduring. It is not built overnight, and, once established, can be modified only slowly and with great difficulty. Similarly, if we say that repressive defense appears to occupy a basic position in another patient's strategy of adjustment, we imply a relatively stable, crystallized or structuralized personality feature which must have a long and central history. In no event, however, does the interpretation say how the patient got that way. The reconstruction therefore is formal and not etiological. This type of reconstruction is safer than the first type because it is general, and it is sounder because it is in line with all major current personality theories.

A third major and meaningful type of reconstruction may be mentioned, although it is not "genetic" in the usual sense of applying to the earlier years of life. This type of reconstruction concerns itself with the relatively recent past. It makes inferences concerning the patient's premorbid personality or about differences between his current state and one in the not too distant past. For example, it is often possible to discern diagnostic evidences of a recent psychotic break now "sealed over"; it is also often possible to estimate the premorbid I.Q. level when the I.Q. has been lowered by illness, or to speak of certain premorbid defenses that are now decom-

pensated or in vestigial form. Reconstructions such as these are like the implicit reconstructions and interpretations of character structure. Often they appear to be the only hypotheses that can reconcile apparent contradictions in the findings or can integrate seemingly scattered trends.

As a second rule of evidence for thematic analysis, the following may now be stated: *since at present there seems to be no evidence in Rorschach test records to support or refute genetic reconstructions concerning specific, important, early experiences and relationships, and since current representations of the remote past are historically unreliable even though revealing of current pathology, interpretation can and should pertain only to the present personality structure and dynamics of the patient or to changes in these in the relatively recent past.*

A last application of the criterion of *sufficient evidence* is that pertaining to the assignment of fixed symbolic meanings to the Rorschach blots themselves. Card VII, for example, has been held to represent the mother-figure, and all responses to this card to represent therefore conceptions of and attitudes toward the mother-figure [7]. Often, however, there appears to be no way of establishing from the record in hand whether and to what extent this symbolic, unconscious apperception of a mother-figure has occurred. Of course, if the responses to this card deal with "nasty old hags" (upper ⅓ or ⅔ or W), we have something to go on. But if the responses are remote from "mother" themes, if they include, for example, only clouds (W), a map (W), an animal head (middle ⅓), a butterfly (lower ⅓) and a vagina (lower middle), how are we to know that these responses are in reaction to or in any way involve a latent mother image?

It is of some theoretical and practical interest that the configurations, colors, shadings and popular content of certain cards and certain areas of certain cards commonly elicit psychodynamically meaningful and seemingly symbolic responses. The upper projection on Card VI, for example, is often seen as a penis and is also often reacted to with what seem to be symbolic variations on the penis theme (e.g., club, fist, rattlesnake, beacon, decanter). Similarly, the lower middle of Card VII is often seen as a vagina and is often reacted to with what seem to be symbolic variations on the vagina theme (e.g., church, haven, Madonna, gun emplacement, wound, chasm). A third example is responding to the area on Card III popularly seen as men with such variations as marionettes, devils, lambs, clipped French poodles or women. In these instances, there is warrant to assume that unconscious or preconscious apperception of sex organs or male human figures, as the case may be, has probably occurred. There is independent psychoanalytic evidence from the study of dreams, symptoms, parapraxes and free associations to support this assumption. Here, as in the case of the "nasty old hag" on Card VII, we have responses that seem to stand in some clear, if speculative, relation to the assumed latent meaning of the area in question. We are not flying blind.

When, however, it is assumed that the card or area in question *must* mean penis, vagina, man, etc., no matter what responses the patient gives to these areas, we are flying blind. We are, in fact, committing serious psychological errors. The errors lie in reasoning (1) as if no adaptive and defensive ego functions stand between the stimulus and the deep dynamics of the individual, (2) as if there are no relatively neutral images available to the patient in his efforts to cope with the stimuli, (3) as if there could be only one dynamic meaning in the card or area in question, (4) as if a statistical trend is the same as a perfect correlation, and (5) as if all we have learned about personality-rooted individual differences in perceptual thresholds and perceptual organizing principles were still unknown.

It is a different matter if one of the "symbolic" areas mentioned above is ob-

viously avoided or obviously disturbing in some other way. Unusual behavior with respect to a certain card or card-area ordinarily suggests that an anxiety-provoking response has been stimulated, even though this response may not be in consciousness. Hasty dismissal or ignoring of an area in a way that is out of keeping with the patient's usual test attitude is an instance of such disruption or "shock," even if none of the images offered seems to express anything significant. In other words, if test attitudes and behavior are included within the concept *response*, then we need not have a "symbolic" image before we may infer that a certain area with a common meaning has had a disturbing effect on the patient.

It is, however, a far cry from this position to that recently taken by Phillips and Smith [5]. They first disclaim attaching any fixed symbolic significances to the Rorschach cards. They claim only to be reporting research findings. Yet their reasoning makes it plain that they regard at least six of the cards as invariably conveying a basic theme to test subjects. Those subjects who show "shock" in reaction to these cards— "shock" being defined by such criteria as delayed reaction time, negative attitudes, and paucity or stereotypy of response—are said to be characterized by certain current dynamics and behavioral trends and by certain relatively specific past experiences and relationships which determine the present trends. For example:

> Shock on Card I is evidence for an unresolved and intense relationship with a mother or nurturing figure which appears to have permanent derivatives in the subject's current behavior. The mother may have been punitive and rejecting or dominating and overly concerned. In men, shock on Card I is associated with economic incompetence, a poor work record and psychosexual immaturity. Many of these men show generalized attitudes of resentment and hostility and a chip-on-the shoulder manner by surliness, arrogance, provocativeness and apparently insatiable demands. Men who show

this adjustment complex often express (or "act out") their dependency problems quite directly: assault, heavy drinking, temper tantrums, and stealing (which presumably reflects the theme "I'll take by force that which is not given") are common. Suicidal gestures occur in this group, but seem to be intended primarily as threats. In women, and less frequently in men, the most common behavior pattern associated with shock at I involves seclusiveness and suicidal threats or attempts which imply "Look what you've done to me." Usually these patients complain of feelings of loneliness and depression. Often they are characterized by excessive passivity and submission; by whining or nagging and consistent querulous demands; sometimes by listlessness, apathy, or even lethargy and apparent relinquishment of all self-assertion and initiative; sometimes by verbalizations which connote "I am only a child"; sometimes by jealousy of siblings, children and other competitors for nurturance.

It is not possible to assign the subject to one or another of these groups simply from the evidence of shock at Card I [5, page 201].

These remarks are distinguished by the absence of explicit rationale of the reported correlations, and by the presence of an *implicit* double rationale of fixed, symbolic card meanings on the one hand and the acceptability of far-reaching genetic reconstructions on the other. Card I emerges as the dependency-on-a-certain-kind-of-mother-figure card. Shock at Card I indicates intense, unresolved, infantile, behavior-dominating conflicts in this dynamic area. Whether the absence of such shock implies no great conflict and past traumata in this area is not discussed, but this implication would follow inevitably from the author's underlying mechanical conception of the response process. No evidence is offered and no argument elaborated that Card I in any way stimulates articulated or physiognomic images pertaining to mother, child, mother-and-child, "leaning" or "cling-

ing," or any other response or theme relevant to the reported correlation. Unless a plausible—if not convincing—rationale can be elaborated, and unless strong evidence for frequent or individually revealing, mediating imagery reactions (such as to the phallic configuration on Card VI) can be marshalled, this approach fosters mechanical interpretation by rote memory rather than flexible, psychological interpretation.[2]

There follows a third general rule of evidence for thematic analysis: *symbolic inferences should be based on actual responses, on clear-cut avoidance of responses, or on disruption of the response process ("shock") in reaction to cards or areas that commonly elicit emotionally charged images; symbolic inferences should not be based on fixed meanings assigned to certain cards and areas of cards, which meanings are assumed to hold for all patients and to explain ultimately all responses to the cards and areas in question.*[3]

To summarize briefly the answer to the question, "What constitutes sufficient evidence for an interpretation?", it may be said that at least several lines of inference should converge on the same interpretation, and that the starting points of these lines of inference should be actual images, scores, test attitudes, and behavior, and their interrelationships and sequences. For genetic reconstructions there can be no direct or reliable evidence in the test responses, and for fixed symbolic card-meanings there is at best suggestive and certainly not universal support in the test responses. Unless we see something of the process leading to the end result, we are safer and wiser to avoid genetic speculation and symbolic forcing.

---

[2] In view of the looseness with which the authors discuss some dynamic relationships (as that between dependency and assault), it begins to seem that theirs is the plight of the factor analyst desperately seeking a common denominator in highly diverse trends, and resorting to oversimplifications and overabstractions in this search.

[3] For discussion of a similar psychological error involved in the rationale of the Szondi test, see Schafer [11].

And, again, we are always safer and sounder if we base our final interpretations on the results of a battery of tests.

B. THE DEPTH OF THE INTERPRETATION SHOULD BE APPROPRIATE TO THE MATERIAL AVAILABLE

The term "deep" in psychoanalytic lingo has been used to refer to archaic, primitive, infantile, instinctual, usually rigidly repressed tendencies and conceptions. Sadistic impulses, castration fears, oral impregnation fantasies, death wishes against loved ones and the like may, in this sense, ordinarily be said to be "deep." What is not "deep," instinctual or archaic follows less the primary process (drive-dominated, magical, fluid, irrational) and more the secondary process (drive-regulating, realistic, orderly, logical). It is more a part of the ego than of the id. It includes such more or less rationalized, stabilized, conventionally conceptualized and reality-oriented derivatives of the archaic tendencies and conceptions as attitudes, overt style of interpersonal relationships and daydream content.

In the case, for example, of a Rorschach record with frequent references in it to food, mouths, teeth and devouring creatures, it seems legitimate, though not exhaustive, to apply the "deep" drive concept *oral* to these images. In the case of a record with frequent references in it to buttocks, feces, dirt, channels and explosions, it seems legitimate to apply the concept *anal* to these images. If the oral images deal mainly with food, open mouths, stomachs and infants, it seems legitimate to speak of themes of *passive, receptive orality,* while if the oral images deal mainly with teeth, jaws, webs, fangs and devouring creatures, it seems legitimate to speak of themes of *aggressive, demanding orality.* It must be remembered that unless we describe the manifest form of appearance of the trends in question, their relative intensity, how they are controlled, etc., these archaic,

instinctual concepts tell us little about the patient. In all of us, presumably, there are noteworthy amounts of orality, anality, and other instinctual trends.

Around the middle position on the continuum of depth, as defined above, there are such responses as Christmas tree, Santa Claus, hands raised in supplication, reclining or sleeping person, wishbone and lucky horseshoe. These responses bespeak a passive, receptive orientation without explicitly involving orality. It is likely that these images and this passive, receptive orientation derive from a basically oral emphasis, but we cannot say we have evidence for this inference in the test responses.

In contrast, records that contain relatively few responses, all of which are popular, near-popular or vague, and none of which is elaborated in detail or quality, allow chiefly or only interpretation of defenses and controls. These constricted records are at the opposite extreme of those that contain numerous references to infantile tendencies and conceptions. The defensive picture inferred from the constricted record may be one that is ordinarily associated with certain infantile trends—as in the case of defensive compulsiveness and anality. If, however, anality is not more or less directly implied in the test imagery or attitudes, the test interpretation proper should not push below the level of defense. The psychoanalytically-oriented therapist will know that marked compulsiveness, for example, is likely to represent to a large extent a defensive coping with tendencies that on their most primitive level are anally conceived and expressed. It is misleading to write test reports as if this anality is "seen" in the test record when actually only a common derivative of and defense against anality is seen.

As a rule, therefore, the depth to which interpretation may be carried should be determined by the material available in this and the other tests. From this point of view, as from the point of view of sufficiency of evidence elaborated in the preceding section, genetic reconstructions and fixed symbolic card meanings are arbitrary, presumptuous efforts to deepen interpretation *in spite of the patient.*

C. THE MANIFEST FORM OF THE INTERPRETED TENDENCY SHOULD BE SPECIFIED

This criterion of an adequate interpretation is far easier to mention than to meet. It is always difficult to be specific, let alone exhaustive, in regard to phenotypical expression. Often, we are able to infer the presence of a powerful trend but cannot say which of several possible manifest forms it tends to assume. For example, a strong homosexual trend may be indicated in the records of two male patients without there being additional evidence to indicate that one patient ends up heterosexually inhibited in behavior and the other ends up a Don Juan. Perhaps in part this is a matter of our still being insensitive to subtle cues in the records that could tell us which manifest form of expression to expect in certain cases. But undoubtedly the problem derives to a great extent from limitations of the Rorschach test as an instrument. Manifest behavior of any importance is, after all, invariably highly overdetermined; that is to say, it is a resultant of numerous interacting determinants. It cannot usually be explained by reference to one underlying trend. In the case of the two patients with strong homosexual trends, such other factors as specific identification figures, superego attitudes, social and cultural settings and values, type and strength of defenses, traumatic sexual experiences, and possibly constitutional predispositions would all have a great bearing on their ultimate overt pattern of sexual behavior. Some of these factors might also be indicated by the test results, but we would hardly be justified in assuming either that *all* relevant determinants are indicated or that we can always and with confidence so interrelate the indicated factors as to predict very specifically the final outcome in overt behavior. This is

one respect in which a battery of tests can be an enormous help. But considering the Rorschach test alone, we see now why it is much easier to insist that the manifest forms of interpreted tendencies be specified than it is to meet this demand.

As a rule, the deeper interpretations go, the more of this difficulty we meet. Interpreting defensive tendencies, for example, often allows (and includes) rather precise specification of manifest form, while interpreting drive tendencies often does not or cannot. For example, we may be rather specific about just how a compulsive person behaves compulsively, but we may be unable to say just how an anal instinctual emphasis is expressed in behavior.

It might be objected that if the manifest form of a trend cannot be specified, then the interpretation is not subject to tests of validity and is not therefore psychologically and scientifically meaningful. This objection is too hasty, however. For one thing, while one specific form of appearance of the trend might not be predictable, a limited variety of possible forms might be specified. To return to the example of the strong homosexual trend, certain forms of behavior are more likely to express this trend than others. We might predict, for instance, sexual inhibition or impotence or Don Juanism or eruption of homosexual feelings into consciousness or some meaningful combination of these. Yet, this buckshot predicting cannot be entirely satisfactory for it actually boils down to a prediction that some disturbance of heterosexual adjustment will be evident. If such disturbance is evident clinically, the fact of *a* disturbance does not directly validate the *homosexual* basis of the disturbance. Other pregenital problems, such as oral-dependency problems, could just as well "account for" the disturbance.

There is, however, another and more important rejoinder to the objection that no prediction of manifest form precludes scientifically necessary tests of validity. That is that the clinical material or other criterion might itself imply the same trend as the test material. The dreams, free associations, transference reactions and life history of the patient might all point *independently* in the direction of a strong homosexual trend. If two independent lines of inference—from test results and from clinical data—converge, then a test of validity has been carried out. Overt behavior has not been ignored but has been used as a stepping stone to this test of validity.

From all of these considerations it would seem unwarranted to insist that one criterion of an adequate interpretation is that it specify the manifest form of the interpreted trend. On the contrary. The difficulties in the way of reaching this ideal have been discussed first in order to demonstrate the complexity of the interpretive problem. There are in fact good reasons to support the inclusion of this criterion, particularly if we modify it so: "*Whenever possible,* the manifest form of the interpreted tendency should be specified."

For one thing, as has been mentioned already, interpretation of defensive operations usually allows specific description of overt behavior—for example, the meticulousness conscientiousness and pedantry associated with compulsive defenses, and the guardedness, suspiciousness and implicit arrogance associated with paranoid defenses. The same may be said of adaptive operations such as striving for rapport and for accurate reality testing.

For another thing, it is often possible to say something about the manifest form of a dynamic trend, particularly if the formal score patterns and test attitudes and behavior—*and the results of other tests*—are taken into account too. In the Rorschach test itself, the Don Juan type of overcompensation for homosexual tendencies might be expressed during the testing in an effortful, exaggerated poise and "manly," "clear thinking" efficiency, and in denial of anxiety through denial of shading in responses and through counterphobic imagery. The sexually inhibited patient with a strong homosexual trend might, in contrast, be timid, deferent and ingratiating during the testing,

and might give numerous anxious, phobic responses (using diffuse shading frequently and seeing fearful things in the blots).

These oversimplified examples indicate that interpretations which include emphasis on drive, defense and adaptation may more easily be brought into connection with overt behavior than one-dimensional interpretations. The drive, defense and adaptation interpretations require, however, scrutiny of all aspects of the Rorschach record and the consideration of these in the context of other clinical approaches to the patient.

As another example of anticipating manifest form, we may consider two records full of oral imagery, one of which is characterized by relatively arbitrary form, numerous color and shading responses that are weak in form, and demanding test attitudes, and the other of which is characterized by precise form, exaggerated emphasis on form as a determinant, and cold, impersonal test attitudes. In the former case we might expect rather open, ego-syntonic expression of oral, passive, dependent tendencies in interpersonal relationships, while in the latter case we might expect conspicuous efforts to stave off any feelings or relationships that smack of oral, passive, dependent tendencies. Both patients will be concerned with passivity in overt behavior, but one will be for it and the other against it. More about all of this will be discussed in *Section E* below on hierarchic location and integration of interpreted trends.

For the time being it may be said that: (a) because all important overt behavior is multiply determined in a complex fashion, the Rorschach test cannot always be expected to provide sufficient information to allow very specific prediction of the manifest forms of indicated trends; (b) interpretations simply of genotypic trends *are* subject to clinical validation because similar inferences concerning genotypic trends may be made independently from clinical data and the two sets of inferences subsequently compared; (c) defensive and adaptive manifestations are typically easier to specify than drive manifestations; (d) if on the one hand we pay close attention to scores, images and test attitudes, and on the other hand we think in terms of configurations of drives, defenses, and adaptive efforts, we will be in the best position to make fairly specific predictions of patterns of manifest behavior and we will have achieved fairly rich understanding of these patterns; (e) if we follow these principles and employ a battery of tests instead of the Rorschach test alone, we will be in the strongest position of all.

Yet, however strong our interpretive position, we must be careful not to overestimate or overstate our ability to understand and predict from test results. The patient's limits and resources with respect to adaptive, sublimatory activity and achievement are often difficult to estimate. They depend so much on situational supports and threats, and on significant events over which the patient may have little or no control. Also, these limits and resources are not easily definable inasmuch as one personality context or identity may foster a productive application of what might otherwise be a starkly pathological trend, while another might not. Of these matters we still know very little.[4] "Expert" dispositional recommendations on the basis of test results *alone* are therefore unsound and to be avoided.

D. THE INTENSITY OF THE INTERPRETED TREND SHOULD BE ESTIMATED

Because so many of the trends we infer from test results are very widespread if not universal, it is highly desirable to be able to estimate the strength of each trend we interpret. Otherwise our interpretations may become largely gratuitous. Borrowing a didactic device wittily employed by Holt with regard to the same problem in Thematic Apperception test interpretation [4, page 457], one might compose the follow-

[4] See pp. 572–573 for further discussion of this problem.

ing test report on a patient without ever having seen his Rorschach test results: "Although narcissism and hostility are indicated and there is at times a tendency to withdraw if frustrated, there are also longings for closeness to and dependence on others. Strong emotional stimulation tends to produce anxiety and to lower intellectual efficiency. Ambivalence toward parental figures is also suggested. [Etc.]" Because it applies to everyone, this report applies to no one. Its validity is perfect but perfectly spurious. The tester has not taken a stand on a single interpretation that would enable us to distinguish this patient from many or most others.

The tester's report would be useful and meaningful, though still not complete, if he had instead written the following: "This is an intensely narcissistic and hostile person who withdraws deeply in response to relatively slight frustration. Such longings for closeness to and dependence on others as are indicated appear to be overshadowed by the narcissism, hostility and withdrawal tendency. Extreme anxiety results if feelings are even moderately stimulated, and intellectual efficiency declines markedly. There are indications of ambivalence toward parental figures, but not sufficient basis in the test data to estimate the intensity of this ambivalence. In view of the preceding description of this patient, however, the ambivalence is likely to be extreme and conspicuous." *Intense, marked, extreme, slight, moderate* are at best only gross estimates, but the usual validating criteria—estimates based on clinical judgment—are no finer. Gross distinctions between patients are possible on this basis and so are gross checks of the validity of the interpretations. In effect, interpretations should cover a five-point rating scale: extreme (intense)—strong (marked, conspicuous)—moderate—weak (slight)—negligible.

As in the case of the three preceding criteria—sufficient evidence, appropriate depth, and specification of manifest form—this quantitative criterion of an adequate interpretation is not sufficient in itself to pinpoint a distinctive trend in the patient. It helps, of course. For example, if the manifest form of an infantile, instinctual trend such as oral aggressiveness cannot be specified, it is better at least to be able to say that the oral aggressiveness appears to be an extreme or strong trend. This gross quantitative specificity at least implicitly predicts that derivatives of this trend should not be difficult to discern clinically. Ideally, however, all six of the criteria being discussed should be met.

E. THE INTERPRETED TENDENCY SHOULD BE GIVEN A HIERARCHIC POSITION IN THE TOTAL PERSONALITY PICTURE

This criterion in some ways subsumes the previously discussed criteria of sufficient evidence, appropriate depth, specification of manifest form, and estimate of intensity. It requires that, insofar as possible, each trend interpreted be explicitly or implicitly related to other major trends. The trend in question may stand in relation to other trends as a defense, as that which is defended against, as an attitude that reflects a compromise between certain drives and defenses, as an overcompensation, as an emotional reaction (including anxiety and guilt), and the like. The point is to avoid chain-like interpretation in which each trend is simply juxtaposed to other trends, and no hierarchy of importance, generality, stimulus and response, push and restraint is established. A battery of tests is invaluable in organizing hierarchic test pictures; on the basis of the Rorschach test alone one cannot do a thorough job in this respect.

The two following brief examples of test reports should illustrate the difference between the chain and the hierarchy. (1) *Chain-like interpretation:* "The patient is very hostile. He also appears to be markedly anxious. He is compulsive but his efficiency is impaired." (2) *Hierarchic interpretation:* "Strong hostile impulses are indicated. The patient appears to try to

defend himself against these hostile impulses by heavy reliance on compulsive defenses. At the present time the compulsive defenses appear to be relatively weak or ineffective. The intense anxiety that is also indicated is likely to be largely in reaction to this impulse-defense instability." The latter interpretation is, of course, much bolder than the former, but it is not free improvisation. It applies certain clinically well-established dynamic patterns to the findings in order to synthesize them; it is not simply an *ad hoc,* meaningless dynamic integration of the interpretations. Such arbitrary *ad hoc* formulations are not uncommon in test reports. Words like *although, however* and *in addition* are used to give a semblance of integration to the interpretations; the end result is usually psychological nonsense. For example: "Although stereotyped in outlook, the patient is adaptive. In addition, however, he is very anxious."

Hierarchic integration is not, however, only a matter of applying well-established dynamic patterns to the test interpretations. *Such integration as is attempted should be based on sufficient evidence in the actual test responses themselves.* In the case of the hierarchic interpretation of hostility and compulsiveness presented above, we should have some supporting evidence, such as the following, in the record proper: (Card IX) "This is very messy: the colors run into each other and they don't go together anyway. I see a face here but the nose is too long (tiny edge detail). This looks like a pelvis (green; poor form). The whole thing could be an anatomical drawing (poor form; artificial color). Of course this part could look like the explosion of the atomic bomb (midline and lower red): I thought of that before but didn't mention it because the color is all wrong and the shape is too regular." In this sequence of responses we see first an anxious attempt to stave off a hostile image by resorting to unproductive compulsive criticism; then adaptively weak rare detail, poor form and artificial color; and finally the emergence of the hostile, explosive image—which by now, however, is under a rather sterile compulsive control. This sequence points toward just such an integration of interpretations as was offered above: hostility opposed by shaky compulsive defense with resulting anxiety.

Of course, assigning hierarchic position to interpretations presupposes a hierarchical personality theory. While it leaves much to be desired in this regard at the present time, Freudian psychoanalytic theory appears to be the theory best suited for this task. Such sets of concepts as drive-defense-adaptation, id-ego-superego (the "structural" concepts), unconscious-preconscious-conscious (the "topographic" concepts), and the interpersonally and culturally oriented attitudes-values-identity, all of which have a place in Freudian psychoanalytic theory, greatly facilitate hierarchic ordering of interpretations.

In these integrative efforts as nowhere else, what the tester brings to his work in the way of background and talent becomes centrally important. How ably he analyzes and synthesizes his clinical data will be determined by his general sophistication in the liberal arts and sciences, his study and understanding of the theoretical and clinical aspects of psychodynamics, the richness of his experiences with colleagues (in staff and individual conferences, etc.) as well as with patients, his self-awareness, sensitivity and perceptiveness, his tolerance for the error and ambiguity that so often and inescapably permeate clinical thought, and his wit, verbal facility and imaginativeness on the one hand balanced by his skeptical demand for solid evidence on the other.[5]

All these requirements for meaningful hierarchic interpretation also act as safe-

guards against persuasive, tightly integrated personality pictures that are, however, glibly elaborated and have little to do with the particular patient. This misleading glibness is a steady danger in ambitious test interpretation. A capacity on the part of the tester to say "I don't know," "I'm not sure," "I can't tie it together but . . ." can be, if not overworked, an invaluable asset.

To return to our interpretive criteria and problems, hierarchic integration of interpretations according to a more or less definite body of psychological assumptions and findings avoids another type of psychological nonsense besides the already mentioned *ad hoc* improvising, namely, juxtaposing dynamically contradictory interpretations. To say of a patient that he has "a strongly dependent, oral character" but that he has "basically healthy heterosexual drives" is an instance of this error by internal contradiction. To say in one paragraph of a report that the patient is "psychopathic" and in the next that he is "compulsive" is another such instance. Interpretations like these typically stem from a mechanical, chain-like handling of test signs and from the naive assumption that whatever "the test says," goes.

Actually, many seeming contradictions are reconcilable if appropriate integration of them is carried out. For example, the juxtaposed compulsive and psychopathic trends might be handled in at least two meaningful ways: (a) a psychopath may, for ingratiating purposes, assume a compulsive manner that, upon close examination, is found to be essentially empty and opportunistic; or (b) the patient may have been unable to integrate adequately a rebellious, impulsive, somewhat psychopathic trend and a submissive, conformist, compulsive trend, with the result that he may vacillate—like many an adolescent—between these two positions. Both of these patterns are frequently encountered and are dynamically meaningful. Seemingly contradictory trends in the test results may often express identical contradictory trends in the

---

[5] We are in this respect dealing with a problem of fundamental importance for the teaching of clinical psychology. We cannot, of course, turn out psychologists like automobiles on an assembly line, each identical in mode of operation, horsepower and miles-per-gallon. Even so, we still understand very little about how to teach in a systematic manner the fundamentals of this complex technique of hierarchically integrating clinical data. Our psychiatric and psychoanalytic colleagues are in no better a position.

personality of the patient. It is a help therefore, when it is at all appropriate, to think of the patient as being on a continuum between two contradictory poles with respect to each dominant trend indicated, and to try to ascertain his usual position on this continuum and the degree to which he shifts about on the continuum. Of the patient with prominent compulsive and psychopathic tendencies, we might say, for example, that his shifts of position on the *rebellion-submission continuum* appear to be frequent in occurrence and wide in amplitude.

Thus, giving each interpreted trend a hierarchic position in the total personality picture not only helps avoid psychological contradictions but may even capitalize on seeming contradictions and bring out basic patterns of conflict or contradiction within the patient. This hierarchic integration should be based on a personality theory and its body of findings and not on *ad hoc,* test-centered and sign-centered improvising.

F. THE ADAPTIVE AND PATHOLOGICAL ASPECTS OF THE INTERPRETED TENDENCIES SHOULD BE SPECIFIED

It is as vital to a good test report to assess the adaptive strengths of the patient as to assess his pathological tendencies. Very often, in fact, the same trend will have both adaptive and pathological aspects. Consider the defense of rigid reaction formation against hostility, for example. On the pathological side it involves, among other things, retarded development of an important aspect of the personality—appropriate, aggressive self-assertiveness. It also involves a basic lack of freedom in human relationships, and a saintly and sugary righteousness that justifiably alienates others. On the adaptive side, however, rigid reaction formation against hostility may involve noteworthy, even if superficial, tolerance, gentleness and helpfulness toward others. Or in the case of schizoid withdrawal into

fantasy life, we may have, on the pathological side, deep mistrust of human relationships and passive aggressiveness against others, and, on the adaptive side, a rich cultivation of artistic creativity. Of course, neither the pathological nor the adaptive aspects of these trends are fully accounted for by the trends themselves. The trends in question may, however, be focal points of one section of the personality analysis.

In other words, test interpretation should take account of the fact that people do not achieve complete sublimation of all infantile trends, complete security in all interpersonal relationships, complete resolution of all conflicts between drives or values or goals in life. It is only against this fundamentally neurotic ideal of health that compulsiveness, repression, dependence, aggressiveness, narcissism and the like may be thought of as invariably pathological. If real human beings are our measuring sticks, then compulsiveness, dependence, etc., must be viewed as trends that have their more or less constructive and limiting or destructive aspects. In some cases the constructive aspects may predominate, in others the limiting or destructive may predominate. But with respect to each patient we should try to establish in what ways and to what extent a certain trend helps and hinders his adjustment efforts.

We are at a point now where the concept "ego identity" may help us a great deal [2]. This concept promises to extend our understanding of the organizing functions of the ego by pointing up and clarifying how complex configurations of drives, defenses, capacities, attitudes and values may be organized around privately and usually unconsciously conceived social roles and expectations and self-images. The ego identity concept helps us see how the interaction of culture, bodily experience, and infantile as well as later relationships provides themes around which to organize experience and action. It shows how what may be a pathological trend in one identity configuration may become an asset in the next, because the latter gives it a new meaning and value. The ego identity concept also provides a key for understanding how formal aspects of functioning may express the content of major fantasies about the self—how, for example, in one instance meticulousness may represent a living out of the identity of an aristocrat (the clean, impeccable one) and in another instance the identity of a slave (the conscientious, subservient one).

Turning specifically to the Rorschach test, in one case the dominant approach to the inkblots may be artistic, while in the next it may be pseudo-masculine, anti-aesthetic and anti-intellectual. In each case the place of affect and hence the significance of color responses will be somewhat different. To the "artist," a shaded *Color-Form* response may stand for a positively valued, creative, integrative experience of affect, while to the pseudo-masculine patient it may stand for frightening, disorganizing, "feminine" affect. Also, at certain points of the response process, these dominant identity statements will be more prominent or better integrated than at others. The rise and fall of their prominence and integration will often mark areas of special adjustment difficulty or adaptive resources.

In addition, the emotional tone and/or intellectual evaluation with which the patient conveys his Rorschach images may be accepting in some instances and rejecting in others. This differential treatment of images may reflect major rejected as well as accepted identity solutions—what the patient dares not become as well as the role to which he must cling or in which he may take great pride. In one man's Rorschach test imagery, the passive, virginal little girl may come forward as the preferred, secretly maintained, "good" identity and may be associated with aesthetic sensitivity and cultural aspiration, while the sadistic, adult, heterosexual male figure may emerge as the rejected, "bad" identity and may be associated with the patient's inability to con-

solidate his accomplishments and use his assets productively. In another case, no identity may be treated favorably and negative images and themes of ruin, decay, and failure may predominate.[6]

Projective test interpretation oriented to ego identity problems requires taking into account the context of age, sex, educational and familial status, and cultural background. As these vary, the identity themes and problems vary. But in any case, identity solution or lack of solution appears to have a major bearing on the fate of various drives, defenses, abilities, etc.

It appears therefore that defining identity problems and solutions in test results may put us in a good position to recognize and weigh the adaptive aspects of major personality trends, pathological though these trends may seem in other respects. It is a major weak point in the interpretation of test results that we are often so much better at identifying pathological potentialities and weighing pathological trends than we are at identifying and weighing healthy, self-integrative "normal" trends.

G. SUMMARY

We have considered six general criteria for judging the adequacy of an interpretation. In summary it may be said that ideally an interpretation, if based on sufficient evidence, should push as far down to deep, archaic, infantile, instinctually-colored material as is appropriate and as far up to manifest, highly socialized forms of functioning as is appropriate. Equally important, the interpretation should include an estimate of the strength of the interpreted trend, should locate it hierarchically in the total personality picture, and should develop its adaptive as well as its pathological aspects. The more of these six criteria any actual interpretation meets, the more ade-

---

[6] The TAT stories should certainly be scrutinized for support and qualification of such interpretations.

quate and useful it will be. In every case, however, the interpretation should always be rooted in actual responses given by the patient. It should not derive simply from a textbook of psychoanalysis or from mechanical, symbolic interpretation of everything in sight. The interpretation should also always be oriented toward how people are actually put together and not toward *ad hoc*, test-centered improvising. When these conditions are more or less met, the interpretation ought to be open to at least a gross test of its validity—provided, of course, that the validating clinical material is sufficiently rich and meaningful to be used for validation purposes.

REFERENCES

1. BECK, S. J. *Rorschach's test. Vol. III. Advances in interpretation.* New York: Grune & Stratton, 1952.
2. ERIKSON, E. *Childhood and society.* New York: Norton, 1950.
3. HARROWER-ERICKSON, M. R., and STEINER, M. E. *Large scale Rorschach techniques.* Springfield, Ill.: C. C. Thomas, 1945.
4. HOLT, R. R. The case of Jay: interpretations and discussion. *J. proj. Tech.,* 1952, 16, 444–475.
5. PHILLIPS, L., and SMITH, J. G. *Rorschach interpretation: advance technique.* New York: Grune & Stratton, 1953.
6. RORSCHACH, H. *Psychodiagnostics.* Bern: Hans Huber; New York: Grune & Stratton, 1942.
7. ROSEN, E. Symbolic meanings in the Rorschach cards. *J. clin. Psychol.,* 1951, 7, 239–244.
8. SCHACHTEL, E. G. Subjective definitions of the Rorschach test situation and their effect on test performance. *Psychiatry,* 1945, 8, 419–448.
9. SCHACHTEL, E. G. Some notes on the use of the Rorschach test. In S. and E. Glueck, *Unraveling juvenile delinquency.* New York: Commonwealth Fund, 1950, 363–385.
10. SCHAFER, R. *The clinical application of psychological tests.* New York: International Universities Press, 1948.
11. SCHAFER, R. Review of *Introduction to the Szondi test* by S. Deri. *J. abnorm. soc. Psychol.,* 1950, 45, 184–188.
12. SCHAFER, R. *Psychoanalytic interpretation in Rorschach testing: theory and application.* New York: Grune & Stratton, 1954.
13. THIESEN, J. W. Assessment of current trends in psychodiagnosis. Unpublished paper read at 1953 meeting of American Psychological Association.

Chapter 47

Thematic Apperception Test: Interpretive Assumptions and Related Empirical Evidence

GARDNER LINDZEY

The chief purpose of this article is to state the assumptions customarily involved in interpreting the Thematic Apperception Test,[1] and to examine the logical considerations and some of the empirical evidence that can be used to verify or reject each of these assumptions.

Aside from certain historical ties to psychoanalysis, the theoretical and empirical continuity between projective testing

[1] These same assumptions are customarily employed in connection with other story-construction projective techniques, e.g., Make-A-Picture-Story Test, Four-Picture Test, Tri-Dimensional Apperception Test, etc.

This article is reprinted from the *Psychological Bulletin*, 1952, with the permission of the author and the American Psychological Association.

The paper is an outgrowth of a study of personality and the imaginative processes directed by Henry A. Murray and supported by grants from Rockefeller Foundation and the Laboratory of Social Relations, Harvard University. I am deeply grateful to a number of colleagues for their generosity in reading and criticizing this manuscript. My greatest single debt is to Henry A. Murray, whose constant stimulation and encouragement made this article possible.

and the remainder of psychology has been a subject of little interest. This is true in spite of an increasingly large amount of research and formulation in other areas of psychology that is directly pertinent to the activities involved in projective testing. In particular, the research of the "new-look" perceptionists represents an important and fertile link between projective testing and more traditional domains of psychology. The initial outline of such a continuity has been traced by Blake and Wilson [7] in a study of the influence of depressive tendencies upon selectivity in Rorschach response, Bruner [9] in a discussion of the Rorschach test, Lawrence [39] in an investigation of temporal factors in perception, Siipola [75] in an examination of the effect of color upon Rorschach response and Stein [76] in an ingenious study employing tachistoscopic exposure of Rorschach stimulus material. All of these studies illustrate the feasibility and fruitfulness of relating perception findings to material elicited by Rorschach-like techniques. One of the aims of the present paper is to stress the desirability of relating such theory and research to the findings of investigators who employ the Thematic Apperception Test.

One may legitimately object to my proposal to appraise empirically statements that I am treating as given, or axiomatic. However, it is not clear that all psychologists would concur in giving axiomatic status to these statements. As is true of so much of psychological formulation, the distinction here between analytic and empirical is not clearly delineated—what is one person's empirical generalization is another's axiom. Further, I believe most psychologists agree with MacCorquodale and Meehl [44] in subscribing to a methodological position that emphasizes the use of *only* analytic constructs that interact smoothly with available empirical knowledge. Consequently, examination of these assumptions in the light of empirical evidence seems justified on the one hand by the questionable axiomatic status of the assumptions and on the other by the general acceptance of psychologists that axioms should not violate observational data.

The assumptions to follow vary greatly in their generality. In fact, they are logically related only by virtue of their frequent use in the interpretation of material secured from one particular type of projective technique. They do not represent all of the assumptions employed in making such interpretations. I have attempted to include only those that are not sufficiently general to be common among all psychologists and yet, within the prescribed situation, are sufficiently common so that almost any individual engaged in this activity would employ them. For the latter reason, I am not concerned here with the assumptions involved in "formal" or "sign" analysis of story projective material where the meaning, or the thematic qualities, of the material is minimized, e.g., Balken and Masserman [3] and Wyatt [84]. Nor have I attempted to explore the assumptions involved in the more recent "sequence analysis" [1] of projective responses.

THE ASSUMPTIONS AND RELATED EVIDENCE

The assumptions are divided into three crude groups. First, the most general assumption, fundamental to all projective testing. Second, those assumptions that are concerned with procedures employed in determining the diagnostically significant portions of the fantasy productions. Third, those assumptions involved in relating the significant portions of the protocols to other forms of behavior.

Primary Assumption: In completing or structuring an incomplete or unstructured situation, the individual may reveal his own strivings, dispositions, and conflicts.[2]

Assumptions Involved in Determining Revealing Portions of Stories:

1. In the process of creating a story the story-teller ordinarily identifies with one person[3] in the drama, and the wishes, strivings, and conflicts of this imaginary person may reflect those of the story-teller.

   a. It is assumed further that the identification figure can be established through the application of a number of specific criteria; e.g., person appearing first in the story, person doing most of the behaving, person most similar to story-teller, etc.

   b. It is also assumed that additional figures in the stories such as father, mother, or brother often may be equated to the real-life counterparts of the story-teller and the behavior of the hero toward them used as indicative of the story-teller's reactions to these persons.

2. The story-teller's dispositions, strivings,

---

[2] The terms "strivings, dispositions, and conflicts" are meant to designate all the attributes or aspects of the person that the clinician is interested in or wishes to measure. One could readily add to this list such terms as: personality organization, primitive fixations, complexes, needs and press, or any others that seemed necessary to represent those aspects of the person that are being explored.

[3] Most investigators accept the possibility of multiple identifications. However, this necessitates the same assumption and only complicates somewhat the general problems of establishing interpretive rules.

and conflicts are sometimes represented indirectly or symbolically.

3. All of the stories that the subject creates are not of equal importance as diagnostic of his impulses and conflicts. Certain crucial stories may provide a very large amount of valid diagnostic material while others may supply little or none.

4. Themes or story-elements that appear to have arisen directly out of the stimulus material are less apt to be significant than those that do not appear to have been directly determined by the stimulus material.

5. Themes that are recurrent in a series of stories are particularly apt to mirror the impulses and conflicts of the story-teller.

Assumptions Involved in Deriving from Revealing Portions of Fantasy Material Inferences about Other Aspects of Behavior:

1. The stories may reflect not only the enduring dispositions and conflicts of the subject, but also conflicts and impulses that are momentarily aroused by some force in the immediate present.

   a. The further assumption is frequently made that both the enduring and temporary processes are reflected in stories in the same manner.

2. The stories may reflect events from the past of the subject that he has not himself actively experienced, but rather has witnessed or observed, e.g., street scene, story, motion picture.

   a. It is assumed further that, although the subject has not himself experienced these events, and is telling them as he observed them, the fact that he selects these events, rather than others, is in itself indicative of his own impulses and conflicts.

3. The stories may reflect group-membership or socio-cultural determinants in addition to individual or personal determinants.

4. The dispositions and conflicts that may be inferred from the story-teller's creations are not always reflected directly in overt behavior or consciousness.

I wish to emphasize that the research to be discussed in connection with the various assumptions can *not* serve as a validation of this kind of projective testing. At most, it can demonstrate that the very general assumptions lying behind this kind of activity are not in direct conflict with available empirical findings. This may increase the "plausibility" of projective interpretations, but the task of demonstrating the utility of specific rules of interpretation remains.

It is likewise important to realize that in this article I am omitting from consideration most of the pertinent empirical evidence resulting from clinical use of this technique. The omission of this idiographic research or observation is not the consequence of any feeling that such data are not of immense value. Rather, in an article emphasizing the relation of projective testing to the remainder of psychology, it seemed desirable to stress most heavily those kinds of research that came closest to meeting the experimenter's demand for empirical control and intersubjectivity of method. Thus, most of the evidence to be referred to has been secured with some attempt at maintaining adequate empirical controls.

DOES THE INDIVIDUAL REVEAL HIS OWN DISPOSITIONS AND CONFLICTS IN COMPLETING AN UNSTRUCTURED SITUATION?

This assumption is not limited to story-construction tests but lies at the heart of all projective testing. Fortunately, in view of its ubiquity, there is a host of very general experimental verification, some of it drawn from laboratory research.

One of the first investigators to point to the relationship between motivational factors and response in an unstructured situation was Sanford [71, 72]. He demonstrated in a series of experiments that the food responses of subjects varied as a function of the amount of food deprivation they had undergone. The responses were given in the act of telling stories to ambiguous pictures, making word associations, and in other situations where the stimulus was sufficiently unstructured to permit either food or non-food responses. This same general function was later demonstrated under somewhat different conditions by Levine, Chein, and Murphy [40] and McClelland and Atkinson [48]. The results of these three investigations do not agree in detail, but all were able to demonstrate some kind of variation in response to ambiguous stimulus situations as a function of food deprivation.

In an early study by Murray [55], it was shown that estimates of "maliciousness" of faces in photographs varied directly with an experimentally induced state of fear. After a fear-producing game children rated a series of photographed faces as significantly more malicious than they had rated the faces previous to the game. A recent study by Katz [34] has shown that the manner in which an individual completes an incompletely drawn face varies systematically with the kind of experience he has undergone previous to the activity. Thus, a group that had just failed on a test of reasoning ability differed significantly from a group that had just spent their time in a neutral activity. Presumably the manner in which the individual completed this unstructured situation was directly related to the motivational or emotional conditions aroused by the experimental treatment.

A series of investigations by Bruner and Postman [12] have demonstrated that when stimulus material is made ambiguous by very brief tachistoscopic exposure, the responses or "guesses" of the subjects vary systematically with motivational variables. These same investigators, as a result of their perception research, have come to occupy a much more extreme position than that implied by the above assumption. They suggest that:

> Most experimenters who have worked with need and attitude factors in perception have assumed, sometimes quite explicitly, that only in highly equivocal stimulus situations can such "nonsensory" factors operate. . . . But all stimulus situations are potentially equivocal and cease to be so only to the extent that selection, accentuation, and fixation have taken place. Perception occurring without the contribution of such adaptive factors is as unthinkable as perception without the mediation of receptive nerve tissue [11, p. 301]. . . . *Adaptive factors in perception are not limited to unstable stimulus situations* [11, p. 307].

In the light of this evidence, the assumption that motivational factors are revealed in completing unstructured situations seems clearly warranted.

DOES THE SUBJECT IDENTIFY WITH SOME FIGURE IN THE STORIES HE TELLS AND CAN THIS FIGURE BE ESTABLISHED RELIABLY?

There seem to be three modal positions that can be maintained in regard to identification in the story-telling process. First, we may make the assumption, indicated above, that there is *ordinarily* a single identification figure in each story. This assumption can be complicated greatly by a number of special conditions of the type already suggested by Murray [56]. Second, we may assume a continuum of identification with those figures in the stories that are very similar to the story-teller possessing a maximum of the subject's attributes and those that are very dissimilar possessing a minimum. This is the assumption made by Sears [74], who, working primarily with doll techniques and heavily influenced by the notion of "stimulus generalization," has suggested specifiable dimensions along which the degree of identification can be expected to vary. Thus, in doll play figures resembling the subject in age and sex will show more characteristics of the subject than those figures that are dissimilar in age and sex. Third, we might, with Henry [31], Piotrowski [58], and others, make no attempt to locate the hero but simply look on all characters in the constructed stories as representative of aspects of the story-teller.

This last alternative is perhaps the least happy, not only because a very large amount of diverse clinical experience militates against it, but also because it leads to certain drastic limitations upon the diagnostic use of the TAT. If we adopt this assumption, we are more or less forced to give up the attempt to appraise the subject's attitudes toward other persons. Thus, Piotrowski suggests that we eliminate the hero and assume "that every figure in the TAT stories expresses some aspect of the testee's personality" [58, p. 107], while somewhat later he suggests that many stories "reflect what the subject thinks and feels about persons represented by the TAT figures, i.e., about the old and the young, the male and the female" [58, p. 113]. Thus, with no rules for differentiating, we are told that all figures represent characteristics of the hero, but also that the characteristics of some figures represent the story-teller's attitudes toward other persons. If we assume that all figures are equally representative of the story-teller's characteristics, either we must give up attempts to appraise the subject's attitudes toward other persons through this instrument or else engage in some kind of dialectic in the effort to defend such attempts.

There is, as yet, no unequivocal answer to the question of which of the above assumptions is most useful. In order to show that the assumption of a single identification figure is warranted, it is necessary to demonstrate relationships between the behavior of the subject and the imaginary behavior of the hero that do not exist between the behavior of the subject and the behavior of non-hero figures. If this difference is not shown, one can always suggest that the sensitivity of the test to aspects of the subject is a result not of any specific identification process, but rather of a generalized reflection of motivational state of the sort that Murray [55], Bruner and Postman [12], and others have reported. Thus, even if *all* figures in the stories represented aspects of the story-teller, we might arbitrarily decide to use only a certain percentage of these figures as diagnostic of the story-teller's attributes, i.e., employ the hero and non-hero distinction, and we would still expect the test to show some sensitivity to variations in story-teller behavior even though we were wasting much of its power. Just as the subject's motivational states are reflected in free association, or in the presolution hypotheses of tachistoscopic response, so also the verbal flow accompanying the story-telling process may mirror motivational states without any intervening identification with particular actors in the stories.

The distinction between "heroes" or identification figures on the one hand and "non-heroes" on the other is greatly complicated by the fact that the story-teller's orientation or attitudes towards other persons is intimately related to his own psychic makeup. Thus, we might mistakenly employ an identification figure as representative of the story-teller's attitudes toward other people and actually secure considerable information about the individual's external orientation because of the similarity between "self" and "perceived other." Or, conversely, we might take a figure intended by the story-teller as an "other" object and find mirrored in it much of real pertinence to the story-teller's own personality structure.

What is needed to answer the above question is a clear demonstration of more intimate relations between "hero" behavior or attributes and the story-teller than can be shown between "non-hero" behavior and the story-teller. Results such as Bellak's [5] showing that the frequency of aggressive words rises when the individual is frustrated do not demonstrate that the identification figure is necessarily displaying more aggressive behavior. Nor are studies satisfactory that simply demonstate variations in "hero" activities or attributes that relate to behavior or attributes of the story-teller. Even if Bellak had shown that aggressive behavior on the part of heroes rose following frustration, this would still not provide the needed information. In this case it is quite possible that analysis of the behavior of the non-identification figures would reveal the same increase in aggressive behavior, indicating not identification, but simply an increase in verbal responses pertinent to the need or conflict in question.

Lindzey [43] has demonstrated that following a social frustration the incidence of aggressive acts in TAT stories carried out by heroes against others increased more than the incidence of aggressive acts carried out by "other" figures. If the incidence of the two kinds of acts is combined, the resulting shift is greater than the shift in either "self" or "other" figures alone. These findings are complicated by the fact that the frustration situation was of such a nature that both extrapunitive responses and a view of the environment as hostile and threatening would be expected to rise following the experimental treatment. Thus, the increase in aggressive responses on the part of non-hero figures might be considered a result of the increase in aggressive tendencies on the part of this story-teller *or* a reflection of the fact that the story-teller viewed the external world as a more hostile and threatening place. It is clear that what is needed is an experimental treatment where, given the subject's identification with a hero-figure, the predictions to be made for "hero" and "other" figures will either be opposed or widely different.

Accepting the desirability of locating identification figures, can these figures be specified precisely? Several studies [29, 79] in which relatively high inter-scorer reliability coefficients were secured imply that it *is* possible to obtain reliable agreement among different scorers in establishing the identification figure. Presumably, a positive correlation for need and press ratings could be secured only if the different raters were treating the same figures as hero. In addition, Mayman and Kutner [45] report complete agreement in 89 per cent of the cases between two raters who independently determined the identification figure for a series of 91 stories.

In general, then, the feasibility of the identification assumption cannot be clearly demonstrated at present, although empirical evidence suggests that identification figures can be established with reasonable reliability.

ARE IMPULSES AND CONFLICTS OF THE SUBJECT SOMETIMES REPRESENTED SYMBOLICALLY?

The clinical use of the concept of symbolism is intimately related to a number of psychological concepts employed by more rigorous and empirically oriented investigators. All behavior theorists have encountered the thorny problems posed by interchangeability or substitutability in behavior of stimuli and responses. These problems have led to the formulation of a number of psychological concepts including displacement, substitution, stimulus generalization, and vicarious mediation. Apparently most psychologists agree that when a response is interfered with either by internal or external barriers it will frequently become altered to another form or else be directed toward a new object. There is a large body of research, much of it carried out on animal subjects, demonstrating this relationship and exploring some of the conditions under which it operates [8, 15, 26, 32, 33, 39, 62, 63, 83]. Of the animal investigations, perhaps the most pertinent to our discussion is Miller's [54] demonstration that a learned aggressive response can be generalized or displaced from an original stimulus object (another rat) to a substitute stimulus (doll) when the first stimulus is made unavailable. This process can be considered a rough paradigm of symbolic representation.

A special question of considerable importance to the projective tester is whether symbolic transformations can, and customarily do, take place without awareness of the subject. Most of the clinical studies discussed below deal with symbolic representations which the subject was not aware of initially and which he could become aware of only under special conditions, e.g., interpretation or therapeutic change. This capacity of the organism to engage in symbolic representation without awareness of the process has been demonstrated under better controlled circumstances by other investigators. Diven [17] and Haggard [27] have both shown that a word may become a substitute stimulus for an electric shock and evoke a galvanic skin response that differentiates it from "non-shock" words, even where the subject is unaware of the connection between the word and the electric shock. In similar fashion, Mc-Cleary and Lazarus [46] showed that words to which a galvanic skin response had been conditioned through the use of electric shock could elicit the galvanic skin response even when exposed tachistoscopically at such rapid speeds as to prevent conscious recognition.

Certainly since Freud, the clinical interpretation of diagnostic material, whether projective or not, has depended heavily upon the assumption of symbolic transformations. There is some clinical-experimental and a host of clinical-observational evidence to indicate that symbolic transformations are quite customary in human behavior, particularly where unacceptable or antisocial impulses are involved.

In case histories conversion symptoms and compulsions frequently present themselves dramatically as evidence of the fact that a given conflict or forbidden impulse may secure expression in a manner only indirectly related to the original impulse. Thus, it is generally accepted that hand-washing compulsions often represent symbolically the desire of the individual to cleanse himself of the consequences of masturbation. Likewise, in doll therapy there is excellent evidence that the child is able to discharge against surrogate objects the same impulses and feelings that he has developed toward persons in the real world. The extent to which this relationship between symbol and real-life counterpart is unequivocally demonstrated varies with the individual case. However, in many instances the relationship is effectively demonstrated

as the symbolic behavior can be shown to vary directly with changes in the relationship between the subject and the referent of the symbol. Thus, the aggression directed against the father-doll may show a high inverse relationship to the extent to which the child is able to express such impulses against the original stimulus object—the father. Similarly, a symptom may disappear when the impulse or conflict that it is presumed to represent is dissolved by therapeutic procedure or through changes in the balance of environmental determinants. Levy [42] has described a number of clinical cases involving relatively convincing demonstration of symbolic representation of sibling rivalry, fear of castration, defecation, etc. Tomkins [80] reports the study of a single case under varying degrees of drunkenness. He found that in certain cases the hypothesized referent of the symbol was more and more directly represented as the amount of alcohol consumed increased.

Several investigators have attempted to combine the subject matter of clinical psychology with attempts at empirical control in the study of symbolic representation. An interesting study by Farber and Fisher [22] attempted to demonstrate the process of symbolic transformation by means of using hypnosis and asking subjects to create and interpret dreams. Although the study is not well controlled, if we accept the naïveté of the subjects, the evidence is impressive, for some of the subjects, that not only is symbolic representation an observed form of behavior, but also that the process of assigning symbols in large part corresponds with the rules established by Freud from his examination of dream protocols. Consistently, Krout [38] in a better-controlled investigation studied interpretations based upon the assumption that individuals responded to line drawings, representative of basic experiences or objects, *as if* they were the symbol referent. She found that these interpretations could be verified through the inspection of independently collected validation data. In other words, the subjects did appear to respond to the line drawings in a manner consistent with the nature of the object that the Freudian would view as lying behind this symbol. Franck [23] and Franck and Rosen [24] have reported two studies in which there is some evidence that the response of the individual to male and female symbols varies with his sex and relative maturity. Klein [35], employing the method of hypnotically inducing dreams, was able to show that the dreamer characteristically transformed or disguised external stimuli that were incorporated into the dream.

In general, then, controlled empirical evidence supplements clinical observation to imply the existence of tendencies for human subjects to represent dispositions and conflicts symbolically. The rules for determining the symbol-referent relations are as yet imperfectly understood, although there is evidence indicating the Freudian view of the symbolic process possesses some utility.

ARE THE STORIES THAT THE SUBJECT CREATES OF UNEQUAL IMPORTANCE AS DIAGNOSTIC OF HIS IMPULSES AND CONFLICTS?

It is possible to assume that any behavioral information, no matter how scanty, contains in it the necessary elements to permit a complete understanding of the individual in question. This derivative of strict Freudian determinism is still defended by some investigators. It implies a theoretical model that is able to incorporate all possible empirical relationships and predict these relationships so precisely that once a single value has been inserted into the closed theoretical system, every other construct in the system can be assigned a value. In view of the present state of psychological theory, this assumption seems an exceedingly unwise one. Nor does it appear to guide the actual behavior of most clinicians. The tendency to view different stories as possessing different degrees of psychological significance is rather clearly revealed

by the fact that not infrequently, even with twenty stories, the investigator will feel he has not sufficient material to make a diagnosis or come to any understanding of the dynamics of the individual in question. Apparently just as some sets of twenty stories are more difficult to interpret and are less revealing, so also some individual stories are less rewarding than others.

Although presumably implicitly present in the minds of most interpreters, the assumption is seldom mentioned and there has been little systematic attempt to state any criteria by means of which the more important stories are to be separated from the less important. Rapaport [61], who represents an exception to this generalization, has suggested that the more important stories may be distinguished in terms of certain "formal variables." He cites as illustration of these distinguishing characteristics: the consistency of the story with other stories of this individual, its consistency with stories told by other persons to this picture, the faithfulness with which the subject followed instructions in telling this story, and, finally, the extent to which the individual "has perceived and apperceived the picture adequately in all its parts."

Indirect evidence bearing on this question is provided by the common observation that stories derived from particular cards frequently have little information pertinent to given variables. Thus the individual interested in studying aggression may find that stories told to certain TAT cards will only rarely provide pertinent evidence. Not only do the stories told by the subject vary in significance but *for given purposes* the stories characteristically evoked by different cards vary in significance. Eron [20, 21] has shown that both incidence of themes and the emotional tone of stories differ significantly among the various TAT cards.

Although practical considerations and clinical experience indicate the necessity of an assumption of "crucial stories," there seems to be little empirical evidence that is directly pertinent.

ARE THEMES OR STORY ELEMENTS THAT
APPEAR TO ARISE DIRECTLY OUT OF THE
STIMULUS MATERIAL LESS SIGNIFICANT
THAN THOSE THAT ARE NOT DIRECTLY
DETERMINED BY THE STIMULUS
MATERIAL?

The extent to which this assumption is
embraced by projective testers is made
clear in the general emphasis upon the
importance of bizarre responses, sex reversals, etc. Rotter [69] gives it explicit
stress in his interpretive discussion of the
importance of "unusualness" of response
in the Thematic Apperception Test. In the
scoring of sentence completion responses,
Rotter [70] has reported finding special
diagnostic significance associated with
"twist" or "reversal" endings to incomplete
sentences. Weisskopf [81] has emphasized
the assumption heavily in her suggestion
that one method of estimating the diagnostic efficiency of projective stimulus material is through the use of a "transcendence
index." This index is derived from the descriptive comments of the subject in responding to the stimulus material that go
beyond "pure description."

The first difficulty we encounter in attempting to appraise this assumption is the
question of how to go about measuring the
degree to which a given response is determined by the stimulus material. This could
be determined by estimating the structural
similarities between the response and the
stimulus. Or, one might develop empirical
norms representing the common or usual
response elements for each stimulus. Rosenzweig [67, 68] has chosen the second
alternative in his attempt to establish "apperceptive norms." The function of these
norms, in large part, is to enable the interpreter to differentiate that which derives
naturally from the stimulus card from that
which is projective or personally determined. The norms reported by Eron [20]
could be used in similar fashion. Presumably most clinicians implicitly employ both
of these approaches. On the one hand they
note responses which are an obvious denial
of the observable elements in the stimulus

material, and on the other they build certain expectations in regard to what a "normal" story is to each stimulus and they
tend to place special interpretive emphasis
upon departures from these norms.

Some projective testers probably object
to this assumption on the grounds that
"any" response, no matter how normal or
directly derived from the stimulus material,
may have significance in projective protocols. They might point to this attribute as
one of the chief differentiae between mental testing (normative) and projective testing (idiosyncratic). It is certainly true that
the extent to which a response deviates
from the norm is much less a matter of
concern to the interpreter of projective
protocols than it is to the "mental tester."
However, the fact remains that if a particular response is given by one hundred per
cent of the persons taking the test, this
response cannot possess diagnostic significance unless it is combined with some
other response element that is less frequently encountered. In the latter case it is
clear that the second or less frequent response is determining the interpretation,
not the "normal" response. Nevertheless,
it must be remembered that even a response
given by a very high percentage of the
respondents may have broad significance as
in the case of a yes-no response to a specific
question. In the limiting case, a response
may be given by ninety-nine per cent of the
respondents and still be an important diagnostic sign, especially in those few cases
where it is not encountered.

Limited empirical justification for the
view that significance and "stimulus-bound-
edness" are negatively related is provided
in a study by McClelland, Burney, and
Roby [49]. They observed that *introduction*
by the story-teller of an affiliated person
into TAT stories where this person was not
present in the picture was related to an
experience the subjects had just undergone.
A count of affiliated persons without consideration of whether or not they were in
the picture did not reveal any relationship
with the experimental treatment.

Supporting this assumption, we have the observation that most perception researchers accept the generalization that the more ambiguous the material, the easier it is to observe the operation of directive or motivational factors. Thus, they suggest that in those cases where the response bears relatively little relation to the stimulus material we are especially apt to observe dynamic or motivational factors. Closely related also is Bruner's [10] and Postman's [59] suggestion that the perceptual process may be represented as involving a relationship between the predetermining tendencies of the individual on the one hand, and information or stimulus constraints presented by the environment on the other. They imply that the stronger the determining tendency, the less in the way of environmental supports are needed to produce a related percept and the more contradictory information will be needed to produce a percept in opposition to the predetermining tendency. The above assumption is quite similar to Bruner's and Postman's view, since it proposes that the stronger the stimulus constraints or supports, the less we know about the predetermining tendencies in the individual that have produced a response consistent with these constraints. However, if the stimulus material is not consistent with the report of the subject, presumably the predetermining tendency was sufficiently strong to produce an appropriate response, even though the stimulus did not call for it.

Thus, the assumption that stimulus-bound responses are less diagnostic than responses that do not depend so heavily upon stimulus constraints appears to fit well with available empirical data.

are heavy rational considerations favoring such a view. The presence of the same theme even when the stimulus situation has been thoroughly altered implies strongly that there are impelling forces within the individual creating these themes rather than their being the inevitable outcome of stimulus constraints. The same theme following a change in stimulus material suggests that the response is not tied directly to, or produced by, a single specific stimulus. Thus, we may infer that the response tendency possesses generality and is more likely to be related to motivational factors than the response linked to a single stimulus. Even if we accept the view that in all instances the stimulus is evoking the response in question, we know that one measure of the strength of a drive is the extent to which stimulus generalization or displacement will occur. Thus, if the individual can equate a large number of stimuli in order to make this response, we may infer that the instigation lying behind the response is quite strong.

In addition, if interpretations are favored that incorporate a large amount of material, those based upon recurrent themes have a natural advantage in that the interpretation of one theme is automatically applicable to all of the other themes in the series. Finally, the presence of recurrent themes permits the investigator to sample or test the conditions under which these themes make their appearance.

In general, then, this assumption seems to have been accepted consistently by most projective testers although there is little or no direct evidence demonstrating its utility. However, there are a number of rational considerations that support such an assumption.

ARE RECURRENT THEMES IN A SERIES OF STORIES PARTICULARLY LIKELY TO MIRROR THE IMPULSES AND CONFLICTS OF THE STORY-TELLER?

This is an assumption frequently stated but for which there is a minimum of pertinent empirical evidence. However, there

DO STORIES REFLECT NOT ONLY ENDURING DISPOSITIONS BUT ALSO MOMENTARY IMPULSES AND ARE THESE BOTH REFLECTED IN THE SAME MANNER?

Most investigators are primarily interested in the Thematic Apperception Test as a means of measuring enduring dispositions, although occasionally, especially in research, the measurement of situational or temporary instigations to behavior may be crucial.

There have been numerous studies showing the sensitivity of the instrument to temporary or situational determinants. Bellak [5] showed that the number of aggressive words in TAT stories increased when the story-teller was rebuked for the low quality of the stories he told. Sanford [71, 72] and Atkinson and McClelland [2] have shown that TAT protocols vary with food deprivation, and McClelland, Clark, Roby, and Atkinson [50] have shown story variation as a result of exposure to failure in a test situation. Rodnick and Klebanoff [66] have shown that TAT stories vary with relative success in a level of aspiration test. Lindzey [43] demonstrated that extrapunitive behavior on the part of the hero in TAT protocols increased significantly following failure in a social situation.

In similar fashion there are a number of studies that show the sensitivity of the stories to more enduring dispositions. It seems reasonable to accept individuals belonging to different psychiatric groups as differing in some enduring rather than situational attribute. Consequently, studies showing significant differences between groups separated on some diagnostic variable may be considered evidence of the test's sensitivity to enduring dispositions and conflicts. Balken and Masserman [3] observed significant differences in the TAT performance of patients categorized as conversion hysterics, anxiety hysterics, and obsessive compulsives. Renaud [64] was able with some difficulty to distinguish between psychoneurotics, traumatic brain disorder cases, and brain disease cases on the basis of TAT protocols. Cox and Sargent [16] found differentiating signs in the TAT performance of "stable" and "disturbed" school children. Working with mental hospital inmates Harrison [28] in approximately 77 per cent of the cases was able to identify accurately on the basis of TAT stories the psychiatric category in which the patient had been placed. He reports [29] similar results when "blind analysis" was employed, that is, when the tests were administered by a different person than the interpreter.

Further evidence of the sensitivity of the test to non-situationally determined motivation is supplied by studies such as Murray and Stein's [57] where a relatively high positive relationship was found between leadership ratings of ROTC candidates based on TAT performance and leadership ratings independently executed by officers of the men in question. Likewise, Henry's [31] study of the Navaho and Hopi suggests the ability of the test to discriminate these two groups, and further to supply psychological information concerning them that is consistent with information secured from extended observation or through the use of independent instruments. White [82] showed that there was a significant relationship between TAT response and the dispositions leading to hypnotizability. Harrison [28] in those cases where he was able to match descriptive statements based upon TAT responses with independent information derived from mental hospital case histories was correct in 82.5 per cent of the instances.

The question of whether temporary and enduring tendencies are reflected in stories in exactly the same fashion is important for two reasons. First, the clinician is primarily concerned with the more enduring tendencies and, therefore, it is desirable that he have some means of differentiating between these two classes of determinants. Second, some research, especially McClelland's [2, 50] has implied that through studying the effect of situational factors upon TAT performance it is possible to arrive at means of interpreting TAT stories to reveal the operation of more enduring tendencies. If the reflection of these two kinds of motivational factors should prove to be very similar or the same process this would be unfortunate for the clinician, who would then be faced with the difficulty or impossibility of knowing whether a given tendency was temporarily instigated or whether this was a more permanent characteristic of the individual in question. On the other hand, such similarity in process would encourage experimental treatments as feasible means of approaching the task of specifying more exactly the means of inferring enduring tendencies.

McClelland [47] has supplied some evidence that the enduring and temporary processes are reflected in the same manner. He has demonstrated that the differences in subjects' TAT responses following experimental induction of a motivational state (threatening test situation) is related to other measures of the individuals' behavior, e.g., academic performance. This implies that the response of the subject to the immediate situation is related to his more permanent patterns of response.

McClelland and Liberman [51] derived a system for scoring need achievement in TAT responses that was based upon the differences produced in TAT protocols following experimentally induced failure in a situation related to achievement. In addition, they demonstrated that achievement as measured by this scoring technique was related to performance in an anagrams test and also related to the speed with which certain kinds of achievement-related words could be recognized when exposed tachistoscopically. Thus, a measure of need achievement derived from a temporary instigation appeared to be related to other measures of achievement which were only distantly related to the initial instigating situation. While this evidence is not compelling, it does provide some support for the notion that temporary instigations affect TAT stories in a manner consistent with the way in which more enduring dispositions influence stories.

We appear to have excellent empirical evidence indicating that stories are responsive to both situational and enduring motivational factors. There is no conclusive evidence demonstrating the similarity or dissimilarity of the process whereby these two classes of determinants secure expression in the stories.

DO THE STORIES REFLECT EVENTS FROM THE PAST OF THE SUBJECT THAT HE HAS NOT HIMSELF ACTIVELY EXPERIENCED? ARE THESE EVENTS DIAGNOSTIC OF THE INDIVIDUAL'S DISPOSITIONS AND CONFLICTS?

Inquiry following the customary administration of the TAT has verified the hypothesis that individuals do incorporate material taken directly from scenes that they have witnessed or from movies or books they have been exposed to. Murray [56] has reported this. Further, any clinician who has worked at all extensively with the TAT has inevitably many cases in his own experience of stories drawn directly from the world of the novel or drama, frequently with accompanying remarks indicating explicitly that this was the case. This is directly consistent with Freud's [25] early dictum that each dream incorporates something from the events of the preceding day.

Given the influence of these non-participated events, the question then becomes one of whether motivational factors affect or are revealed in the recall of such experiences. The selective function of memory and the importance of motivational determinants in the memory process have been recognized for some time, certainly since the appearance of Bartlett's [4] treatise on memory. A number of studies have investigated, under reasonably well-controlled conditions, memory as a function of such motivational variables as political ideology, Edwards [19], Levine and Murphy [41]; value as measured by the *Study of Values*, McGinnies and Bowles [52]; sex membership, Clark [14]; mental set, Carmichael, Hogan and Walter [13]; attitude, Postman and Murphy [60]; punishment, McGranahan [53]. Although there are many other factors, e.g., primacy, recency, vividness, known to influence recall, it seems reasonably well established that motivational factors do serve as one important class of determinants of memory.

If we accept these studies as evidence of the extent to which memory is influenced by motivational factors, it seems reasonable that the individual, in the process of recalling past events or experiences, will reveal or expose important aspects of his own motivational state. Consequently, the assumption that the particular events remembered by the subject are diagnostic of his dispositions and conflicts appears to be supported by available empirical data.

DO STORIES REFLECT GROUP-MEMBERSHIP, CULTURAL OR SOCIAL DETERMINANTS AS WELL AS PERSONAL OR INDIVIDUAL DETERMINANTS?

This assumption simply implies consistent differences between the fantasy productions of individuals who belong to, or have been socialized in, different social groups. Thus, a certain amount of the variation in any TAT production can be accounted for by the fact that the individual has grown up in a given milieu or social role. The importance of the assumption derives from the fact that overlooking this kind of variation introduces a serious source of error in the interpretation of imaginative protocols from members of more than one social group.

Although little effort has been made to explore the variations in fantasy productions between many of the important groups of our own society, it is quite widely accepted or expected that these differences exist. Even such an important cleavage as that between male and female has been little explored so far as TAT behavior is concerned, while such variables as socioeconomic status, occupational role, and ethnic group-membership have also been of slight interest to most investigators. Rosenzweig and Fleming [68] have reported differences between a roughly equated group of men and women on a number of specific aspects of TAT response. An investigation by Riess, Schwartz, and Cottingham [65] designed as a critical appraisal of the Thompson [78] modification of the TAT led to the observation of certain relatively slight variations in story length as a

function of geographic residence and Negro-white group-membership.

Henry [31] in his investigation of Navaho and Hopi children found that inferences based upon his adaptation of the TAT related to independently secured information concerning the children and also that there were systematic differences between the Navaho and Hopi fantasy productions. In addition, he reports differences between Navaho subjects who were members of different subgroups in this society.

Although there is a paucity of empirical evidence demonstrating differences in fantasy production between various sociocultural groups, what evidence is available appears to support this assumption.

ARE IMPULSES AND CONFLICTS INFERRED FROM STORIES NOT ALWAYS REFLECTED DIRECTLY IN OVERT BEHAVIOR AND CONSCIOUSNESS?

Projective testers vary considerably in the manner in which they emphasize this assumption. Some see a very intimate relation between imaginative behavior and overt behavior. Thus, Piotrowski introduces nine rules designed to permit the translation of fantasied into overt with the following statement:

> The rules proposed in this article are a new attempt to solve the problem of the relationship between the TAT and overt behavior. Since the TAT is mainly an exercise in creative imagination, it should reflect the patient's ideas and drives regardless of whether or not they find a direct expression in overt behavior. Thus, parts of the TAT always reflect the overt behavior of the subject while other parts reflect ideas which are not as directly manifested in overt actions. If this be so, we need a rule by means of which we could differentiate these two parts of the TAT. The rules presented below have been formulated largely for the purpose of meeting that need [58, p. 105].

Others are more cautious in stating their views of the relation between story-behavior and overt behavior. Murray, in his introduction to the TAT, suggests:

> It may be stated, as a rough generalization, that the content of a set of TAT stories represents second level, covert . . . personality, not first level, overt or public . . . personality. There are plenty of ways of discovering the most typical trends; the TAT is one of the few methods available today for the disclosure of covert tendencies. The best understanding of the total structure of personality is obtained when the psychologist considers the characteristics of manifest behavior in conjunction with the TAT findings . . . [56, p. 16].

In similar vein, Korner states:

> . . . instead of deploring the fact that fantasy and reality behavior do not necessarily correspond, as we currently seem to be doing, we can use projective techniques as a shortcut to a person's fantasy and ideational life, which then can be compared and examined in the light of his present and past actual behavior patterns [37, p. 627].

Although the relationship between covert and overt is assessed differently by various investigators, all seem to agree that the relationship is not perfect—fantasy behavior does not exactly mirror overt behavior. This omnipresent assumption can serve one of two functions depending upon the orientation of the investigator. It *can* serve simply as a convenient means of avoiding the necessity of ever being wrong. Thus, whenever inferences based on story protocols fail to relate to appropriate independent measures or observations, the clinician may simply point to the above assumption and add that only the naïve would expect always to observe linear relationships between imaginal and overt or conscious behavior. On the other hand, the investigator can use this assumption as a signpost pointing to one of the most important and difficult empirical problems facing the projective tester. This problem is the determination of the conditions under which inferences based on projective material directly relate to overt behavior and the conditions for the reverse.

It is possible to defend the position that projective techniques should not be expected to provide statements concerning overt behavior. Such a view implies that the techniques will always be used only as an "imaginal supplement" to an otherwise adequate description of the individual. Thus, given a person who "behaves" in a particular way, examination of his fantasy productions may permit us to make consistent or to account for behavior that hitherto was unaccountable. Certainly this represents an important function of these techniques. Equally certain is the fact that this is not the only circumstance under which these instruments are used. They *are* used as means of inferring overt behavior tendencies and presumably with more adequate rules of transformation they would be so used much more widely.

Investigations by Sanford *et al.* [73] and Symonds [77], which unfortunately from the point of view of sampling were both based on adolescent populations, demonstrate clearly that in some cases instead of the impulses inferred from TAT records being reflected in behavior, their converse or opposite appear in behavior. This observation leads to the question of whether impulses that secure release in overt behavior may not need to be expressed in fantasy productions. However, the many positive relationships between imaginal impulses and overt behavior in these studies and others make it clear that it is not an either-or proposition and that the statement of the actual conditions under which the impulse is revealed or concealed must be complex.

Sanford *et al.* [73] studied the relationship in a group of school children between fantasy ratings derived from the TAT and overt behavior ratings provided by teachers who had observed the children. They found an average correlation of +.11 between the two sets of ratings indicating clearly that the fantasy ratings alone were not good predictors of overt behavior. However, there were striking differences between the different variables used in the extent to which fantasy and behavior corresponded.

For some needs there was a relatively high positive relationship, while for others there was a significant negative relationship between the overt and covert. In accounting for these findings, Sanford *et al.* suggested that those tendencies which were negatively sanctioned or prohibited would be high in fantasy and low in overt behavior, while those tendencies which were encouraged by society and for which the individual could secure complete overt expression would be high in behavior but low in fantasy. High ratings would be secured in both fantasy and overt behavior for those tendencies that society encouraged but did not permit complete freedom of expression in, e.g., achievement, dominance.

Murray [56] has suggested that tendencies not inhibited by cultural sanctions are apt to be highly correlated in their fantasy and overt expression. He reports a positive correlation of over .40 between fantasy and overt behavior for a group of college men on the following variables: abasement, creation, dominance, exposition, nurturance, passivity, rejection, and dejection. Negative correlations are reported between fantasy and overt for sex and no correlation between the two forms of expression for aggression and achievement. Korner [36] attempted to relate hostility as observed in a play situation with ratings of hostility in interpersonal relations with other children. She found no general relationship between the two sets of variables. Half of the children high on hostility in play situations were likewise high on hostility manifested in their dealings with other children. The remaining half who were high on hostility manifested in play situations were low on the second set of ratings. The investigator concluded that it was impossible to predict from the one situation to the other.

Symonds [77] related the fantasy themes of 40 adolescent boys and girls to adjustment ratings and teachers' ratings of behavioral characteristics. He concluded that the relationship between these two sets of variables was "insignificant and negligible."

Further evidence of the lack of a perfect relationship between fantasy and overt behavior is provided in those cases where an individual of known characteristics fails to reveal salient aspects of himself in his TAT constructions. Tomkins [80] reports the case of an individual who had a persistent spontaneous fantasy which included as an important theme a homosexual seduction. The TAT responses of this individual gave no sign of homosexual tendencies. In accounting for this and similar cases, Tomkins suggests that the important variables are the awareness of the subject of the impulse or tendency at question and the extent to which the tendency is condoned or accepted by society. If the impulse is known and unaccepted by society, the individual will prevent its appearance in the stories he tells. If he is unaware of the tendency, it will appear in his fantasy constructions even if it is negatively sanctioned by society. Bellak [6] reports several similar instances where TAT performance fails to reveal central aspects of the individual.

Relatively little has been done in the attempt to discover and formulate signs in the stories themselves that would provide evidence concerning the probability of overt expression. There is some evidence that, as Tomkins [79] proposes, the "psychological distance" maintained by the story-teller toward the impulse or disposition in question may be an important condition relating to the degree of overt translation.

Available empirical evidence clearly indicates that the assumed imperfect correlation between fantasied and overt behavior is warranted. However, at present, we are far from an adequate formulation of the signs or cues that might permit specification from fantasy protocols alone of the behavioral tendencies that will secure overt expression as opposed to those that will not.

RESEARCH IMPLICATIONS

Almost all of these asumptions point to further research that would be useful in clarifying their status. Perhaps more important than research aimed at further demonstrating the warranty of these same assumptions is research that attempts to provide a more exact statement of the conditions under which the assumptions are applicable and the way in which they can be related to empirical data. For example: what are the means by which the important story in a series can be determined? How can we determine whether or not a given fantasy impulse will receive overt expression? In what way do we determine whether or not a given response has been determined by the stimulus material? What are the circumstances under which symbolic transformations must be engaged in? How do we determine the empirical referent of a given symbol? Answers to these and a host of related questions are necessary before we can hope to provide the TAT user with an explicit, repeatable set of operations for inferring motivational states.

In addition to problems connected with the interpretive assumptions and the more specific questions implied in the above paragraph, there is also the matter of formulating explicitly a method of scoring TAT protocols that is practical, intersubjective, and able to embrace a reasonable number of the behavioral variables in common use. To a large extent standardization and specific interpretive rules must wait until some agreement has been reached by most TAT users as to the major aspects of TAT response that will be focused upon in analysis.

REFERENCES

1. Arnold, Magda B. A demonstration analysis of the TAT in a clinical setting. *J. abnorm. soc. Psychol.*, 1949, **44**, 97–111.
2. Atkinson, J. W., & McClelland, D. C. The projective expression of needs: II. The effect of different intensities of the hunger drive on thematic apperception. *J. exp. Psychol.*, 1948, **38**, 643–658.
3. Balken, Eva R., & Masserman, J. H. The language of fantasy: III. The language of the phantasies of patients with conversion hysteria, anxiety state, and obsessive-compulsive neuroses. *J. Psychol.*, 1940, **10**, 75–86.
4. Bartlett, F. C. *Remembering.* London: Cambridge Univ. Press, 1932.
5. Bellak, L. The concept of projection: an experimental investigation and study of the concept. *Psychiatry*, 1944, **7**, 353–370.
6. Bellak, L. Thematic apperception: failures and the defenses. *Trans. N.Y. Acad. Sci.*, 1950, **12**, 122–126.
7. Blake, R. R., & Wilson, G. P. Perceptual selectivity in Rorschach determinants as a function of depressive tendencies. *J. abnorm. soc. Psychol.*, 1950, **45**, 459–472.
8. Brown, J. S. The generalization of approach responses as a function of stimulus intensity and strength of motivation. *J. comp. Psychol.*, 1942, **33**, 209–226.
9. Bruner, J. S. Perceptual theory and the Rorschach Test. *J. Personality*, 1948, **17**, 157–168.
10. Bruner, J. S. Personality dynamics and the process of perceiving. In R. R. Blake & G. Ramsey (Eds.), *Perception: an approach to personality.* New York: Ronald Press, 1951. Pp. 121–147.
11. Bruner, J. S., & Postman, L. Tension and tension release as organizing factors in perception. *J. Personality*, 1947, **15**, 300–308.
12. Bruner, J. S., & Postman, L. An approach to social perception. In W. Dennis (Ed.), *Current trends in social psychology.* Pittsburgh, Pa.: Univ. Pittsburgh Press, 1948. Pp. 71–118.
13. Carmichael, L., Hogan, H. P., & Walter, A. An experimental study of the effect of language on the reproduction of visually perceived form. *J. exp. Psychol.*, 1932, **15**, 73–86.
14. Clark, K. B. Some factors influencing the remembering of prose materials. *Arch. Psychol., N.Y.*, 1940, No. 253.
15. Cofer, C. N., & Foley, J. P., Jr. Mediated generalizations and the interpretation of verbal behavior: I. Prolegomena. *Psychol. Rev.*, 1942, **49**, 513–540.
16. Cox, Beverly, & Sargent, Helen. TAT responses of emotionally disturbed and emotionally stable children: clinical judgment versus normative data. *Rorschach Res. Exch.*, 1950, **14**, 61–74.
17. Diven, K. Certain determinants in the conditioning of anxiety reactions. *J. Psychol.*, 1937, **3**, 291–308.

18. Douglas, Anna G. A tachistoscopic study of the order of emergence in the process of perception. *Psychol. Monogr.*, 1947, **61** (6), Whole No. 287.

19. Edwards, A. L. Political frames of reference as a factor influencing recognition. *J. abnorm. soc. Psychol.*, 1941, **36**, 34–50.

20. Eron, L. D. A normative study of the Thematic Apperception Test. *Psychol. Monogr.*, 1950, **64** (9), Whole No. 315.

21. Eron, L. D., Terry, Dorothy, & Callahan, R. The use of rating scales for emotional tone of TAT stories, *J. consult. Psychol.*, 1950, **14**, 473–478.

22. Farber, L. H., & Fisher, C. An experimental approach to dream psychology through the use of hypnosis. *Psychoanal. Quart.*, 1943, **12**, 202–216.

23. Franck, Kate. Preferences for sex symbols and their personality correlates. *Genet. Psychol. Monogr.*, 1946, **33**, 73–123.

24. Franck, Kate, & Rosen, E. A projective test of masculinity-femininity. *J. consult. Psychol.*, 1949, **13**, 247–256.

25. Freud, S. The interpretation of dreams. In A. A. Brill (Ed.), *The basic writings of Sigmund Freud.* New York: Modern Library, 1938. Pp. 181–552.

26. Grandine, Lois, & Harlow, H. F. Generalizations of the characteristics of a single learned stimulus by monkeys. *J. comp. physiol. Psychol.*, 1948, **41**, 327–338.

27. Haggard, E. A. Experimental studies in affective processes: I. Some effects of cognitive structure and active participation on certain autonomic reactions during and following experimentally induced stress. *J. exp. Psychol.*, 1943, **33**, 257–284.

28. Harrison, R. Studies in the use and validity of the Thematic Apperception Test with mentally disordered patients: II. A quantitative validity study. *Character & Pers.*, 1940, **9**, 122–133.

29. Harrison, R. Studies in the use and validity of the Thematic Apperception Test with mentally disordered patients: III. Validation by the method of "blind analysis." *Character & Pers.*, 1940, **9**, 134–138.

30. Harrison, R., & Rotter, J. B. A note on the reliability of the Thematic Apperception Test. *J. abnorm. soc. Psychol.*, 1945, **40**, 97–99.

31. Henry, W. E. The Thematic Apperception Technique in the study of culture-personality relations. *Genet. Psychol. Monogr.*, 1947, **35**, 3–315.

32. Hull, C. L. *Principles of behavior: an introduction to behavior theory.* New York: Appleton-Century, 1943.

33. Hull, C. L. The problem of primary stimulus generalization. *Psychol. Rev.*, 1947, **54**, 120–134.

34. Katz, I. Emotional expression in failure: A new hypothesis. *J. abnorm. soc. Psychol.*, 1950, **45**, 329–349.

35. Klein, D. B. The experimental production of dreams during hypnosis. *Univ. Texas Bull.*, 1930, No. 3009.

36. Korner, Anneliese F. *Some aspects of hostility in young children.* New York: Grune & Stratton, 1949.

37. Korner, Anneliese F. Theoretical considerations concerning the scope and limitations of projective techniques. *J. abnorm. soc. Psychol.*, 1950, **45**, 619–627.

38. Krout, Johanna. Symbol elaboration test: The reliability and validity of a new projective technique. *Psychol. Monogr.*, 1950, **64** (4), Whole No. 310.

39. Lashley, K. S., & Wade, Marjorie. The Pavlovian theory of generalization. *Psychol. Rev.*, 1946, **53**, 72–87.

40. Levine, R., Chein, I., & Murphy, G. The relation of the intensity of a need to the amount of perceptual distortion: a preliminary report. *J. Psychol.*, 1942, **13**, 283–293.

41. Levine, J. M., & Murphy, G. The learning and forgetting of controversial material. *J. abnorm. soc. Psychol.*, 1943, **38**, 507–517.

42. Levy, D. M. Projective techniques in clinical practice. *Amer. J. Orthopsychiat.*, 1949, **19**, 140–144.

43. Lindzey, G. An experimental examination of the scapegoat theory of prejudice. *J. abnorm. soc. Psychol.*, 1950, **45**, 296–309.

44. MacCorquodale, K., & Meehl, P. E. On a distinction between hypothetical constructs and intervening variables. *Psychol. Rev.*, 1948, **55**, 95–107.

45. Mayman, M., & Kutner, B. Reliability in analyzing Thematic Apperception Test stories. *J. abnorm. soc. Psychol.*, 1947, **42**, 365–368.

46. McCleary, R. A., & Lazarus, R. S. Autonomic discrimination without awareness:

an interim report. *J. Personality*, 1949, **18**, 171–179.

47. McClelland, D. C. Measuring motivation in phantasy: the achievement motive. In H. Guetzkow (Ed.), *Groups, leadership and men: Research in human relations.* Pittsburgh: Carnegie Press, 1951.

48. McClelland, D. C., & Atkinson, J. W. The projective expression of needs: I. The effect of different intensities of the hunger drive on perception. *J. Psychol.*, 1948, **25**, 205–222.

49. McClelland, D. C., Burney, R. C., & Roby, T. B. The effect of anxiety on imagination. Paper read at Eastern Psychological Assn., 1950.

50. McClelland, D. C., Clark, R. A., Roby, T. B., & Atkinson, J. W. The projective expression of needs: IV. The effect of need for achievement on thematic apperception. *J. exp. Psychol.*, 1949, **39**, 242–255.

51. McClelland, D. C., & Liberman, A. M. The effect of need for achievement on recognition of need-related words. *J. Personality*, 1949, **18**, 236–251.

52. McGinnies, E., & Bowles, W. Personal values as determinants of perceptual fixation. *J. Personality*, 1949, **18**, 224–235.

53. McGranahan, D. V. A critical and experimental study of repression. *J. abnorm. soc. Psychol.*, 1940, **35**, 212–225.

54. Miller, N. E. Theory and experiment relating psychoanalytic displacement to stimulus-response generalization. *J. abnorm. soc. Psychol.*, 1948, **43**, 155–178.

55. Murray, H. A. The effect of fear upon estimates of the maliciousness of other personalities. *J. soc. Psychol.*, 1933, **4**, 310–329.

56. Murray, H. A. *Thematic Apperception Test manual.* Cambridge: Harvard Univ. Press, 1943.

57. Murray, H. A., & Stein, M. I. Note on the selection of combat officers. *Psychosom. Med.*, 1943, **5**, 386–391.

58. Piotrowski, Z. A. A new evaluation of the Thematic Apperception Test. *Psychoanalyt. Rev.*, 1950, **37**, 101–127.

59. Postman, L. Toward a general theory of cognition. In J. Rohrer & M. Sherif (Eds.), *Social psychology at the crossroads.* New York: Harpers, 1951.

60. Postman, L., & Murphy, G. The factor

of attitude in associative memory. *J. exp. Psychol.*, 1943, **33**, 228–238.

61. Rapaport, D. The clinical application of the Thematic Apperception Test. *Bull. Menninger Clin.*, 1943, **7**, 106–113.

62. Razran, G. Stimulus generalization of conditioned responses. *Psychol. Bull.*, 1949, **46**, 337–365.

63. Razran, G. Attitudinal determinants of conditioning and of generalization of conditioning. *J. exp. Psychol.*, 1949, **39**, 820–829.

64. Renaud, H. Group differences in fantasies: head injuries, psychoneurotics, and brain diseases. *J. Psychol.*, 1946, **21**, 327–346.

65. Riess, B. F., Schwartz, E. K., & Cottingham, Alice. An experimental critique of assumptions underlying the Negro version of the TAT. *J. abnorm. soc. Psychol.*, 1950, **45**, 700–709.

66. Rodnick, E. H., & Klebanoff, S. G. Projective reactions to induced frustrations as a measure of social adjustment. *Psychol. Bull.*, 1942, **39**, 489. (Abstract)

67. Rosenzweig, S. Apperceptive norms for the Thematic Apperception Test: I. The problem of norms in projective methods. *J. Personality*, 1949, **17**, 475–482.

68. Rosenzweig, S., & Fleming, Edith. Apperceptive norms for the Thematic Apperception Test: II. An empirical investigation. *J. Personality*, 1949, **17**, 483–503.

69. Rotter, J. B. Thematic apperception tests: suggestions for administration and interpretation. *J. Personality*, 1946, **15**, 70–92.

70. Rotter, J. B., Rafferty, Janet E., & Schachtitz, Eva. Validation of the Rotter Incomplete Sentences Blank for college screening. *J. consult. Psychol.*, 1949, **13**, 348–355.

71. Sanford, R. N. The effects of abstinence from food upon imaginal processes: a preliminary experiment. *J. Psychol.*, 1936, **2**, 129–136.

72. Sanford, R. N. The effects of abstinence from food upon imaginal processes: a further experiment. *J. Psychol.*, 1937, **3**, 145–159.

73. Sanford, R. N., Adkins, Margaret M., Miller, R. B., *et al.* Physique, personality and scholarship: a cooperative study of school children. *Monogr. Soc. Res. Child Developm.*, 1943, **8**, No. 1.

74. Sears, R. R. Effects of frustration and anxiety on fantasy aggression. *Am. J. Orthopsychiat.*, 1951, **2**, 498–505.

75. Siipola, Elsa M. The influence of color on reactions to ink blots. *J. Personality*, 1950, **18**, 358–382.

76. Stein, M. I. Personality factors involved in the temporal development of Rorschach responses. *Rorschach Res. Exch.*, 1949, **13**, 355–414.

77. Symonds, P. M. *Adolescent fantasy: An investigation of the picture-story method of personality study*. New York: Columbia Univ. Press, 1949.

78. Thompson, C. E. The Thompson modification of the Thematic Apperception Test. *Rorschach Res. Exch.*, 1949, **13**, 469–478.

79. Tomkins, S. S. *The Thematic Appercep-tion Test*. New York: Grune & Stratton, 1947.

80. Tomkins, S. S. The present status of the Thematic Apperception Test, *Am. J. Orthopsychiat.*, 1949, **19**, 358–362.

81. Weisskopf, Edith A. A transcendence index as a proposed measure in the TAT. *J. Psychol.*, 1950, **29**, 379–390.

82. White, R. W. Prediction of hypnotic susceptibility from a knowledge of subjects' attitudes. *J. Psychol.*, 1937, **3**, 265–277.

83. Wickens, D. D. Stimulus identity as related to response specificity and response generalization. *J. exp. Psychol.*, 1948, **38**, 389–394.

84. Wyatt, F. Formal aspects of the Thematic Apperception Test. *Psychol. Bull.*, 1946, **39**, 491. (Abstract)

Chapter 48

What Can the Clinician Do Well?

PAUL E. MEEHL

In the preface to the book *Clinical versus Statistical Prediction*[1] which was, in part, responsible for this symposium, I wrote that students reacted to my lectures on prediction as to a projective technique. Many psychologists have responded to the book in the same way. I am therefore going to take this opportunity to repeat, with refinement and clarification, the statement of my essential position, reserving for another time at this Convention the presentation of empirical material from my current research.

First of all, I am puzzled by the extent to which both statisticians and clinicians perceive the book as an attack upon the clinician. On the contrary, my position was, and is, that the clinician performs certain unique, important, and unduplicable func-

[1] Meehl, P. E.: *Clinicial versus statistical prediction.* Minneapolis: Univer. Minnesota Press, 1954.

This article is published with the permission of the author. It was originally read at the symposium "Clinical Skills Revisited," September 4, 1959, American Psychological Association Convention, Cincinnati, Ohio.

tions, in some of which he has literally no competition. I think the book states this very clearly. (I hope it's true, since I occupy almost one-third of my time and earn a sizeable part of my income in clinical work!) But in current practice, clinicians spend a good deal of time and energy performing functions at which there is neither theoretical nor empirical reason for supposing them to be efficient. My position is not, therefore, one of being "for" or "against" the clinician, or proposing to eliminate him. I cannot understand, for example, how my friend Bill Hunt could possibly read me as viewing ". . . the exercise of clinical judgment as a necessary evil," as he states in the Bass and Berg volume, rather than, as for him, ". . . a fascinating phenomenon with a genuine predictive potential." Two full chapters of my book, and portions of two others, were devoted to analyzing (and defending!) the clinician's non-formalized judging and hypothesizing behavior, and I should have thought that my own fascination with the phenomenon was quite apparent.

However, I did want to influence clinical practice toward a more optimal utilization of skilled time, by removing the clinical judge from loci in the decision process where he functions ineffectively, thereby both (a) improving predictive accuracy and (b) freeing the clinician's time for other activities, whether cognitive or manipulative, in which he is efficient or unique.

Some feel that it was a disservice to formulate the problem in terms of opposition or competition, as clinical "versus" statistical prediction. Reading their discussions as sympathetically as my own bias permits, I remain persuaded that a pragmatically meaningful decision problem, involving a comparison between two distinguishable procedures, does exist. Discussions which have appeared during the last five years do necessitate some reformulations but, although I may be overly identified with my original position, I cannot regard them as fundamental. Given a set of data on a patient, and given the pragmatic necessity to make a certain decision, one may *either* combine these data, or selected portions thereof, in a formalized, mechanical, clerical fashion (of which the regression equation is only one example, perhaps not the most powerful); *or* he may invite a clinician, or a staff conference, to think and talk about these data and come to a decision. Now no one contends that the individual decisions resulting from these two methods of combining data will always coincide. This would be theoretically preposterous; and there is, of course, a massive body of experience to the contrary. In those numerous instances in which they *fail* to coincide, one must act in some way. If he acts in accordance with the decision provided by the clerical procedure, he has countermanded the judgment of the clinician or staff conference. If he acts in the other way, he has countermanded the statistical formula. *I have yet to see any cogent, or even plausible, criticism of this fundamental point, which was made clear by Sarbin 15 years ago.* It is thoroughly misleading to

speak of Sarbin or Meehl as fomenting a controversy, or as having set two procedures in "needless opposition" to each other. They *are in* daily opposition, manifest or covert; their opposition is an immediate logical consequence of a simple, undisputed fact: namely, that the human judge and the statistical clerk correlate less than 1.00 when required to make diagnoses, prognoses, or decisions from a given body of information. Nothing is gained by adopting a hysteroid, "sweetness-and-light" attitude, akin to Mr. Dooley's definition of democracy as a situation in which "everybody is equally better."

There has been an overemphasis upon the chapter in which I surveyed the then available empirical studies, some readers reacting with glee to the box score, and others stressing the fact that these studies are not ideal, as I also emphasized in summarizing them. Personally, I consider that chapter to be almost the least important part of the book. On the other hand, no detailed, rigorous analyses or criticisms of the *theoretical* and *methodological* considerations raised in the book have appeared. I am at a loss to know whether this is because everybody agrees with me, or because these considerations are mistakenly thought to be irrelevant. I am convinced that the *formal* arguments on the actuarial side are very powerful, and they ought not to be thus airily dismissed or by-passed.

Well, what can the clinician do well? However well or badly he does certain things, he alone can do them, and therefore it is administratively justifiable to occupy his time with them. He can, for instance, observe and interview the patient, functions which are not eliminable by any kind of statistics. He can *be* a person himself in relation to the patient, with all that this means for the helping process. He can construct hypotheses and carry out research to test them. Every hour saved out of those innumerable and interminable staff conferences and team meetings in which some clinicians seem to delight (you know, there are clinics where the average weekly hours of inter-staff contacts exceed those of staff-patient contacts!) can be devoted to seeing patients and doing research.

Among decisions which can, in principle, be arrived at either by a formalized or a judgmental method, I would now state the generalized clinical-statistical issue something like this: "Given a population of patients, with variable information on each; and a population of judges, with variable information on each; and a decision task imposed upon us pragmatically; *then,* at *which* points in the total decision-making process should we use *which judges;* and at which *other* points should a non-judgmental ('formal,' tabular, graphical, statistical, clerical, 'mechanical') operation be employed?"

It astounds me that, in spite of my having very carefully distinguished between *type of data* (i.e., psychometric or non-psychometric) and *method of combining data* (i.e., judgmental or formalized), numerous writers have continued to perpetuate the old confusion between these two; several have even quoted me as maintaining that tests are better predictors than non-test data! This is a remarkable projective distortion, especially since I am extremely skeptical myself as to the predictive power of the available tests in the personality field. I have held for some years that life-history and "mental status" variables are probably superior to existing tests, a superiority which I expect to become clear as actuarial methods of combining these non-psychometric data are more widely utilized.

In answering the general question for a given prediction problem, we must include the utilities of the several outcomes of right and wrong decisions, the cost (monetary and otherwise) of the alternative decision methods, and the distribution of hit-frequencies. "Equal hits" means "equal predictive success" only if hits are equally important whichever kind they are; and "equal predictive success," in turn, means "equal efficiency" only if one predictive method costs no more than the other.

The formulation is generalizable over all of the clinician's cognitive activity, whether predictive, postdictive, or diagnostic. Some have argued that the clinician doesn't "merely predict," but tries to influence the course of events, so that the problem posed is of little practical importance. This argument is philosophically naive. Selecting a certain line of action in order to influence the course of events is itself justified by implicative statements of the form, "If procedure X is carried out, the patient will respond in manner Y." And this, of course, is a prediction whether realized or counterfactual. A related error is made by those who have suggested that the clinician doesn't predict directly, but decides, upon the data he has, what additional data he needs before predicting. Not to act at a given moment in time, but to collect additional data of a specified kind is, of course, itself a decision; and is, like other decisions, rational or irrational, depending upon the probabilities and utilities involved.

In reporting a recent empirical study[2] I listed 6 factors or circumstances theoretically favoring clinical prediction. Although that list was not presented as exhaustive, I have not yet come across any examples, either factual or armchair, falling outside these six rubrics:

1. *Open-endedness:* It often happens that the predictive task is not presented in the form of a prespecified criterion dimension or exhaustive set of categories, but rather as an open-ended question where the very content of the prediction has to be produced by the predictor.

2. *Unanalyzed stimulus-equivalences:* Sometimes the scanning and classifying of the data, including the recognition of a certain fact or pattern as relevant, cannot proceed by explicit rules because the operative "rules" are laws of our mental life as yet unknown or incompletely known. Perceptual gestalts, psycho-

[2] Meehl, P. E.: "A comparison of clinicians with five statistical methods of identifying psychotic MMPI profiles." *J. counsel. Psychol.,* 1959, 6, 102–109.

logical similarities in physically dissimilar events, analogical and primary-process thinking, and similar inexplicit psychic processes are available to the predictor because he, being human, exemplifies laws which he may not be able to report because research has not yet elucidated them.

3. *Empty cells:* From time to time the prediction situation presents special cases in which a factor or configuration is highly relevant but has not occurred even in the course of very extended actuarial experience. In such cases the human judge must spontaneously notice the special circumstance and assign to it an estimated weight. In extreme instances such rare factors must be treated as "stop" items, being allowed to countermand an otherwise strong prediction reached by the formal (mathematical) procedure.

4. *Theory-mediation:* When a prediction can be made by the use of hypothetical mental constructs whose laws (usually very imperfectly known) are in such general form as to permit a variety of structural-dynamic arrangements *in concreto,* the predictive process is not straightforward because hypothesis-building is a creative, synthetic act for which automatic rules cannot be written. The fact$_1$ $\longrightarrow$ fact$_2$ sequence can always (in principle) be reduced to an actuarial generalization holding between members of the large (but finite) set of combinations and hence can be treated formally; whereas the fact$_1$ $\longrightarrow$ construct $\longrightarrow$ fact$_2$ sequence cannot always be thus formalized. The extreme case of this situation is the rare one in which the clinician actually invents new nomothetic *constructs* (as distinguished from thinking up new concrete exemplifications of familiar ones) in formulating a particular case. Freud's early analyses exemplify this case.

5. *Insufficient time:* In some predictive situations (e.g., interpretive psychotherapy) the pragmatic context requires that the prediction, to be of any use, must be reached in a very short time, even a matter of seconds, after the relevant data appear. A therapist cannot put his patient in cold storage while he, the therapist, runs off a P-technique factor analysis on a 28-variable correlation matrix derived from the patient's verbal productions during the preceding 30 minutes. Even if every office of the ten thousand skilled therapists in the U.S.A. were somehow provided with a high-calibre electronic computer, the time required for coding and feeding would make this science fiction fantasy an inadequate solution.

6. *Highly configurated functions:* Suppose that a configural relationship exists between a set of predictor variables and a criterion, but that the function is not derivable on rational grounds. We have to approximate this unknown optimal formula by empirical methods. Multivariable tests such as the Strong, MMPI, and Rorschach provide familiar instances of the problem. Clinicians skilled in the use of these devices find it helpful to have the several scores expressed graphically as a psychogram or profile, and this practice is not merely a matter of convenience in reading. Typically the clinician reports that his inferences from the profile are based partly upon discriminations he has learned to make among the various "patterns" which arise in an extended clinical experience. Usually these patterns are grouped into categories or types, but the clinician recognizes the existence of numerous intermediate forms so that the underlying function is presumably continuous. What seems to be happening is that an unknown configurated mathematical function is being approximately expressed via the graphical mode, utilizing the fact that differences and similarities of visual gestalten can be perceived without the percipient's knowing the underlying formula.

Each of these six presents its own special problems for research, and in most actual clinical judgments more than one is likely to be operative. Like Dr. Hoffman, I have chosen to investigate the sixth factor empirically, although I would readily agree that it is theoretically the least interesting. It has, however, the advantage of being somewhat easier to subject to quantitative analysis, and sizeable samples of such judgments are fairly easy to obtain.

Admittedly, a mere tally of the "box score" based upon heterogeneous studies comparing the efficiency of formal and judgmental methods of combining data is not as helpful, either for practical purposes or in giving us greater theoretical insight into the clinician's cognitive activity, as will be systematic studies of these six components as they appear at different stages of the total decision-making process. Where, in this chain of gathering facts and making inferences, is the skilled human judge indispensable? Where is he dispensable, but only with a loss in predictive accuracy? Where are his cerebrations inferior in their outcomes to the application of a formalized procedure, such as an actuarial table or mathematical equation? Many studies, in the several domains of predictive activity, will be needed to answer these questions.

However, since large amounts of time are being spent today making decisions by impressionistic, judgmental, and conversational methods (such as the staff conference), it is worthwhile to attempt a rough generalization as to the relative power of the two methods over diverse predictive domains. I cannot agree with those who consider that such a box score is either meaningless or unimportant. By the latest count, there are 35 studies which permit a comparison between the human judge and a clerical, formalized procedure for combining information. Many of these studies are not based upon clinical data of a high order, either in quantity or quality. However, I must emphasize that *many of the studies do involve amounts and quality of data quite comparable to what are routinely available in most clinical and counseling situations and which are being applied daily by clinicians in making their judgments.* The shortage of skilled professional personnel, which is certain to be with us (and in fact to get worse) during the lifetime of everyone in this room, makes it thoroughly unrealistic to argue that no significant comparison can be made unless it involves the kind of workup that a wealthy patient in a plush mental hospital receives at fancy prices. I would further point out that it is a quite unjustified assumption, commonly made by critics of the box score, that "naturally," if the quality and quantity of the clinical data, and the professional competence of the clinicians, were deliberately picked as being of a very high order, the clinician *would* show up markedly better than a souped-up, configural statistical prediction system *utilizing the same top-quality data.* This may or may not be true; some of us are still patiently watching the journals for the evidence.

Of the 35 studies known to me, 12 deal with predicting outcome in some kind of training or schooling; 8 with recidivism, delinquency, or parole violation; 3 with improvement of psychotics; 3 with psychiatric diagnosis, i.e., the attachment of a nosological label; 3 with the outcome of outpatient psychotherapy of neurotics; and 5 with personality description not covered by any of the preceding such as Q-sort characterization of a patient, aggression as inferred from the Rorschach, and the like. One study compares the two methods in organic medicine. If we define equal efficiency without regard for time and economics (a definition strongly biased against the statistical technique), we find 23 of the 35 studies showing a difference in favor of the statistical method, 12 studies showing approximate equality, and no study favoring the judgmental method. Of course from the social and economic viewpoint, this really means 35 studies on the actuarial side. The overall picture has, therefore, not changed since 1954, except that the proportion of "equal" outcomes has somewhat decreased.

I think that it is time for those who resist drawing any generalization from the published research, by fantasying what *would* happen if studies of a different sort *were* conducted, to do them. I claim that this crude, pragmatic box score *is* important, and that those who deny its importance do so because they just don't like the way it comes out. There are very few issues in clinical, personality, or social psychology (or, for that matter, even in such fields as animal learning) in which the research trends are as uniform as this one. Amazingly, this strong trend seems to exert almost no influence upon clinical practice, even, you may be surprised to learn, in Minnesota!

In the single study of medical diagnosis, it was found that a linear discriminant function combining the results of two biochemical tests did as well in differentiating types of jaundice as did internists who, in addition to these two tests, had available a large mass of other information, and averaged between 3 and 4 hours going over each patient's material! Some psycho-clinicians oppose the actuarial method on the ground that physicians have been practicing medicine for centuries without it. This argument completely mystifies me, since, with the exception of this one study, no comparison of the two methods in organic medicine has ever been made. The frequency of erroneous diagnoses in medicine is well known, and it is hard to imagine why anyone familiar with organic medicine would give such an argument any weight.

There are physicians who have begun to apply statistical techniques, the mathematics of decision theory, and electronic computers to medical diagnosis. Those psychologists who use the analogy with medicine counter-actuarially would be well advised to wait until we find out what happens there. It would be ironic indeed (but not in the least surprising to one acquainted with the sociology of our profession) if physicians in non-psychiatric medicine should learn the actuarial lesson from biometricians and engineers, while the psychiatrist continues to muddle through with inefficient combinations of unreliable judgments because he has not been properly instructed by his colleagues in clinical psychology, who might have been expected to take the lead in this development.

I understand (anecdotally) that there are two other domains, unrelated to either personality assessment or the healing arts, in which actuarial methods of data-combination seem to do at least as good a job as the traditional impressionistic methods: namely, meteorology, and the forecasting of security prices. From my limited experience I have the impression that in these fields also, there is a strong emotional resistance to substituting formalized techniques for human judgment. Personally, I look upon the "formal-versus-judgmental" issue as one of great generality, not confined to the clinical context. I do not see why clinical psychologists should persist in using inefficient means of combining data just because investment brokers, physicians, and weathermen do so. Meanwhile, I urge those who find the box score "35:0" distasteful to publish empirical studies filling in the score board with numbers more to their liking.

Chapter 49

A Blind Analysis of a Case of Multiple Personality Using the Semantic Differential

CHARLES E. OSGOOD / ZELLA LURIA

For more than a year the writers have been collecting semantic data from patients undergoing psychotherapy. This has been feasible through the cooperation of psychotherapists in various parts of the country. When the manuscript of "A Case of Multiple Personality" [3] arrived, the editor of the *Journal of Abnormal and Social Psychology,* without our knowledge, suggested to Thigpen and Cleckley that it would be interesting to have semantic data from each of the "personalities" in their patient. Thigpen and Cleckley accepted the suggestion and administered a form of the differential we have been using for this purpose to their patient in each of her three personalities. The editor also suggested that we might see how much these semantic data would allow us to infer about the patient without our having any knowledge of the

case history, protocol, or prognosis.[1] This appeared to be a useful and rather intriguing way to estimate the validity and sensitivity of this instrument. If we could infer descriptions of the three personalities which correspond with clinical observations, and if we could make reasonably accurate interpretations and predictions, we would be encouraged to continue our efforts to improve the semantic differential as a clinical tool.

THE SEMANTIC DIFFERENTIAL

The semantic differential is a combination of association and scaling procedures de-

[1] We wish to thank Dr. J. McV. Hunt, editor of the *Journal of Abnormal and Social Psychology,* for utilizing the opportunity presented by the work of Thigpen and Cleckley to arrange for the data in this study, for suggesting the blind analysis, and for his general encouragement. We are also very grateful to Drs. Thigpen and Cleckley for giving the semantic differential to their patient and for their interest in the instrument.

This article is reprinted from the *Journal of Abnormal and Social Psychology,* 1954, with the permission of the authors and the American Psychological Association.

signed to give an objective measure of the connotative meaning of concepts. The underlying logic [1] can be summarized as follows: The process of description or judgment can be conceived as the allocation of a concept to a set of experiential continua defined by pairs of polar terms. Thus the connotative meaning of a linguistically complex assertion, such as "My father has always been a rather submissive person," can be at least partially represented as

MY FATHER   active–:–:–:–:$\times$:–:–passive
MY FATHER   soft–:$\times$:–:–:–:–:–hard

The greater the strength of association, e.g., ". . . extremely submissive, a regular doormat," the more polarized, toward 1 or 7, the allocation [2]. Since many scales of judgment are highly intercorrelated (e.g., *good-bad, fair-unfair, honest-dishonest, kind-cruel,* and so forth all reflect mainly the single "evaluative" factor in judgments), a limited number of such continua can be used to define a semantic space within which the connotative meaning of any concept can be specified. This clearly indicates some variant of factor analysis as the basic methodology in developing such an instrument. Two such analyses have been completed, both providing evidence for three general factors, "evaluation," "potency," and "activity," and some unknown number of specific factors that are probably denotative in nature.

The form of semantic differential we have been using in studying psychotherapy is based on this factor analytic work. In the 10 scales used, it gives approximately equal weight to the first three factors isolated. These scales and their factor loadings are given in Table 49–1. The 15 concepts used in this form of the differential were selected after consultation with clinicians and pretesting for their differentiating power. Ideally, they should sample the major persons and problems involved in therapy-in-general; we are not entirely satisfied with the present set, however, and more work should be done here. The concepts used are also shown in Table 49–1. In the test form

Table 49–1   Concepts and Scales Used in This Analysis

Concepts		
LOVE	MENTAL	SELF-CON-
CHILD	SICKNESS	TROL
MY DOCTOR	MY MOTHER	HATRED
ME	PEACE OF	MY FATHER
MY JOB	MIND	CONFUSION
	FRAUD	SEX
	MY SPOUSE	

Scales and Their Factor Loadings			
Scales	Evalua-tion	Ac-tivity	Po-tency
Valuable-worthless	.79	.13	.04
Clean-dirty	.82	.03	−.05
Tasty-distasteful	.77	−.11	.05
Fast-slow	.01	.70	.00
Active-passive	.14	.59	.04
Hot-cold	−.04	.46	−.06
Large-small	.06	.34	.62
Strong-weak	.19	.20	.62
Deep-shallow	.27	.14	.46
Tense-relaxed	−.55	.37	−.12

itself, concepts are rotated against scales in such a way that each concept appears once with each scale, but with a maximum interval between successive appearances of both. The subject is instructed to do his checking rapidly, without struggling over particular items, to give his "immediate impressions." A 150-item form such as this usually takes less than 10 minutes to complete.

Reordering the raw data for a single subject on a single testing yields a matrix of N columns (here, 15 concepts) and i rows (here, 10 scales). The *meaning* of a particular concept to the subject, as defined by the operations of measurement here, is the profile of numbers in its column (or, more efficiently, the position in the n-dimensional space defined by the projection of these numbers onto the factors). *Difference in meaning* for two concepts is defined by the distance between their positions in this space, as computed by the generalized distance formula, $D = \sqrt{\Sigma d^2}$, in which d is the difference in allocation of the two con-

cepts on a single scale [2]. The more similar any two concepts are in connotative
meaning, the smaller will be the value of *D*.
Change in meaning (of the same concept at
different times during therapy, or in different "personalities") can be defined by the
same operation, except that *d* here refers to
the differences in allocation of the same
concept on the same scale at different testings. The mathematical properties of this
formula also allow us to represent the
semantic structure of an individual in a
concise form; computation of the distance,
D, of every concept from every other concept yields an *N/N* matrix (here, 15/15) of
distances which have the property of plotting within a space having dimensionality
equal to the number of factors. To the extent that the individual subject being studied uses the same three factors isolated in
our general factor work, his data will plot
accurately in three dimensions.

THE SEMANTIC DATA

At this point we should state exactly what
information we have about this case. We
know that we are dealing with a case of
triple personality, and these have been
labeled for us (presumably by the therapists who collected the semantic data) "Eve
White," "Eve Black," and "Jane." We suppose that the "White" and "Black" have
some connotative significance—certainly, as
will be seen, the quantitative semantic data
distinguish sharply between them. We also
know, of course, that the patient is a woman, presumably participating in some
kind of therapy; we do not know the stage
of therapy or whether or not she is hospitalized. We considered it also fair to ask
(from J. McV. Hunt) about the following
items of sociological status, because they
contribute to the meaningful interpretation
of certain concepts: Concept CHILD—does
this woman have a child? Yes, she does.
Concept SPOUSE—is this woman married?
Yes, she is. Concepts FATHER and MOTHER—
are her parents alive? The mother is, but

Hunt doesn't know about the father. Concept MY JOB—has this woman had a job
outside of homekeeping? Yes, she has. This
is the sum total of our external information
about the case.

The semantic differential was given to
this woman twice while "in" each of her
three personalities; a period of about 2
months intervened between the two testings.[2] The roman numerals I and II refer
to first and second testings respectively.
Since the form given at each testing was
actually a double form (each item repeated
once), we were able to estimate the reliability of these data. The immediate test-
retest reliability coefficients for each of the
testings are as follows: Eve White I, .82;
Eve White II, .90; Eve Black I, .65; Eve
Black II, .89; Jane I, .89; Jane II, .94. These
coefficients indicate (*a*) a general satisfactory level of reliability, (*b*) a consistent
trend in all three personalities toward
greater stability through time, and (*c*) that
Jane is the most consistent or stable personality over short intervals of time and
Eve Black is the least.

To obtain measures of semantic similarity
and structure, we computed the matrices of
D for each concept with every other concept, for each personality and testing. With
an ordinary desk calculator and a table of
square roots, these operations are very
simple and rapid. In order to conserve
space, the six matrices of *D* are not given
here. These "distances" are based on application of the formula given earlier across
all 10 scales. For convenience in plotting
the models which appear as Figures 49–1
to 49–6, the data for scales contributing to
each of the three factors were averaged and
new *D*'s computed. This, in effect, forces
those data into three dimensions and,
hence, into solid models that have no error.
The very slight amount of distortion, or loss
of information, resulting from this averaging process and restriction to three dimensions can be seen from the following cor-

[2] Raw data for Eve White, Eve Black, and Jane
are not included here, but may be found in the
original article.

relations between original (10 scale) and "factor" D matrices (3 average scales): Eve White I, .91; Eve White II, .93; Eve Black I, .96; Eve Black II, .98; Jane I, .86; Jane II, .92. In other words, nearly all of the variance in this woman's judgments can be accounted for in terms of three factors. Figures 49–1 to 49–6, then, provide quite accurate representations of the ways various concepts are related in each of the personalities; the smaller the distance between any two concepts the more similar in connotative meaning they are.

THE THREE PERSONALITIES AND THEIR CHANGES THROUGH TIME

The general assumption we are following is that "mental illness" is essentially a disordering of meanings or ways of perceiving from those characteristic of people judged "normal" in our society, and that the process of psychotherapy from the patient's point of view is essentially a reordering and changing of these meanings. Within the limitations of our type of measurement and our sampling of concepts, the locations and relations among concepts shown in Figures 49–1 to 49–6 can be thought of as pictures of how this woman perceives herself, the significant people about her, and certain modes of action—when functioning "in" her several personalities. We assume that this woman is receiving some kind of treatment through the period covered by our two samplings, I and II, and therefore look particularly for the types of changes in meaning that are taking place in the three personalities, as well as at the general nature of their organization. For purposes of ready comparison, all of the models are oriented in respect to the concept MY DOCTOR, which stays practically constant in meaning (*good, strong,* and *quite active*) through both time and personalities; spatially, in the figures, *good* is up and *bad* down, *active* to the left and *passive* to the right, and *strong* is away from the viewer while *weak* is near to or toward the viewer;

the solid ball represents the origin of the space, e.g., a hypothetical "meaningless" concept that would result from checking all 4's.

EVE WHITE

Semantic structures for Eve White I and II are shown in Figures 49–1 and 49–2. The most general characterization would be that *Eve White perceives "the world" in an essentially normal fashion, is well socialized, but has an unsatisfactory attitude toward herself.* Here the usual societal

FIGURE 49–1 *Eve White I.*

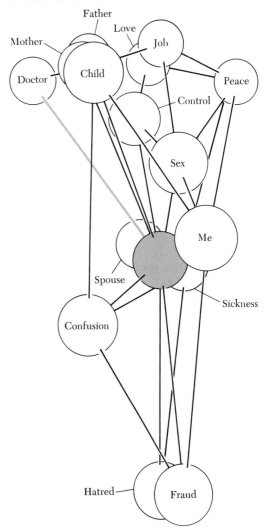

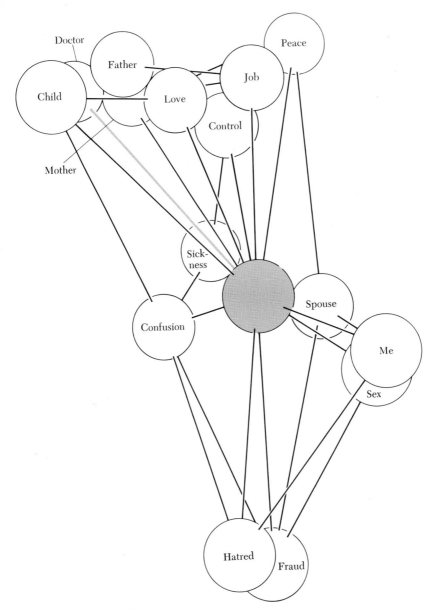

FIGURE 49–2   *Eve White* II.

"goods" are seen favorably—MY DOCTOR, MY FATHER, LOVE, SELF-CONTROL, PEACE OF MIND, and MY MOTHER are all *good* and *strong* whereas FRAUD, HATRED, and to some extent CONFUSION are *bad*. The chief evidence of disturbance in the personality is the fact that ME (the self concept) is considered a little *bad*, a little *passive,* and definitely *weak*. Substantiating evidence is the *weakness* of her CHILD, as she sees him

(or her), and the essential meaninglessness to her of MY SPOUSE and SEX. Note also the wide evaluative separation between LOVE and SEX. In the interval between testings I and II ME and SEX become more *bad* and *passive* and simultaneously become almost identical in meaning to her—and note that her conceptions of LOVE (a good, strong thing) and SEX (a bad, weak thing like herself) have moved still further apart.

EVE BLACK

Semantic structures for Eve Black I and II are shown in Figures 49–3 and 49–4. The most general characterization here would be that *Eve Black has achieved a violent kind of adjustment in which she perceives herself as literally perfect, but, to accomplish this break, her way of perceiving "the world" becomes completely disoriented from the norm.* The only exceptions to this dictum are MY DOCTOR and PEACE OF MIND, which maintain their *good* and *strong* characteristics, the latter, interestingly enough, also becoming *active* on II. But if Eve Black perceives herself as being *good*, then she also has to accept HATRED and FRAUD as positive values, since (we assume) she has strong hatreds and is socially fraudulent. So

we find a tight, but very un-normal, favorable cluster of ME, MY DOCTOR, PEACE OF MIND, HATRED, and FRAUD. What are positive values for most people—CHILD, MY SPOUSE, MY JOB, LOVE, and SEX—are completely rejected as *bad* and *passive*, and all of these except CHILD are also *weak* (this may be because CHILD was weak in Eve White and much of the change here is a simple "flip-flop" of meanings). Note that it is MOTHER in this personality that becomes relatively meaningless; FATHER, on the other hand, stays *good* but shifts completely from *strong* (in Eve White) to *weak*—possible implications of these familial identifications will be considered later. Note also that in this personality LOVE and SEX are closely identified, both as *bad, weak, passive* things.

FIGURE 49–3   *Eve Black* I.

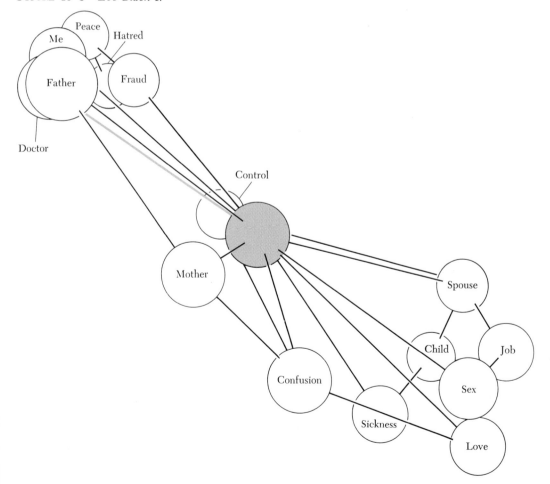

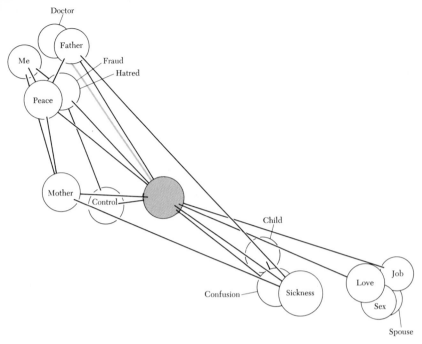

FIGURE 49–4 *Eve Black* II.

JANE

Semantic structures for Jane I and II are shown in Figures 49–5 and 49–6. The general characterization is that *Jane displays the most "healthy" meaning pattern, in which she accepts the usual evaluations of concepts by her society yet still maintains a satisfactory evaluation of herself.* MY FATHER, MY MOTHER, MY CHILD, and MY DOCTOR—most of the significant persons in her life—are seen as *good, strong,* and *active.* The major modes of behavior, PEACE OF MIND, LOVE, SELF-CONTROL, and MY JOB, are seen as equally *good* and *strong,* but *somewhat passive*—as if these ways of behaving and thinking were simply accepted without stress. The two socially agreed-upon evils, HATRED and FRAUD, are put in their proper places. The most significant characteristics of Jane's meaning system, however, are these: The self concept, ME, while still not *strong* (but not *weak,* either) is nearer the *good* and *active* directions of the semantic space; note also the close identification of ME and MENTAL SICKNESS, which here is *not* an unfavorable concept

to her. Her attitude toward her husband, MY SPOUSE, is for the first time meaningful (unlike Eve White) and tending toward the *good, strong, active* directions, like the other significant persons (unlike Eve Black). And LOVE and SEX (quite unlike Eve White) are both favorable and quite closely identified. The changes from testings I to II are simply such as to strengthen the "healthy" pattern evident in the first view. ME becomes considerably more *good* and *active;* MY SPOUSE for the first time becomes completely identified connotatively with MY DOCTOR and MY FATHER (and loses its tie with CONFUSION); and LOVE and SEX become intimately identified with each other and close in meaning to SELF-CONTROL and PEACE OF MIND.

The thumbnail semantic sketches of each personality just given make it intuitively evident that the semantic differential does draw sharp distinctions between the three personalities inhabiting one nervous system. It is possible to demonstrate these distinctions quantitatively by intercorrelating *D* matrices between personalities and

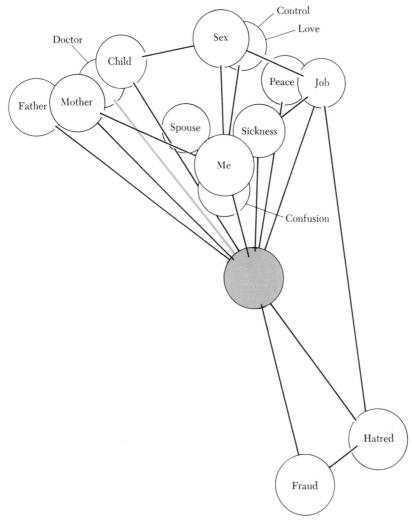

FIGURE 49–5   *Jane* I.

over time. If two of our models are generally similar in structure, such that large and small distances between concepts in one are reflected also in the other, then the *r* will be high. Table 49–2 gives these correlations. The first thing to note is that the correlation of each personality with itself (e.g., testings I and II) is regularly much higher than the correlation of that personality with any other personality (with the single exception of Eve White I and Jane I). This is quantitative justification for the statement that the semantic differential does differentiate between the several personalities of this woman. Whether it differentiates in a valid way is a matter that

can be judged only by relating our analysis to the detailed case history material available elsewhere [3].

Another important thing to note about these correlations is that Eve White and

Table 49–2   Correlations of *D*-Matrices between Personalities and over Time

	White I	White II	Black I	Black II	Jane I	Jane II
White I						
White II	.73					
Black I	−.06					
Black II		−.02	.86			
Jane I	.73		−.26			
Jane II		.53		−.08	.92	

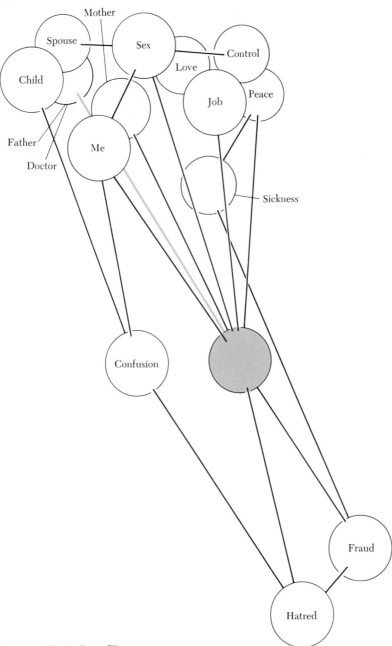

FIGURE 49–6 *Jane* II.

Jane (the two "socialized" personalities) are fairly highly correlated whereas the correlations of Eve Black with the other two are definitely low, even negative. In other words, Eve Black is clearly the most deviant and disordered personality. Finally, it should be noted that these three personalities differ somewhat in their stability, as indexed by the I/II correlations, Eve White being the least stable and Jane the most.

CHANGES IN MEANING OF SPECIFIC CONCEPTS

As noted earlier, the meaning of a specific concept is operationally defined as its profile against the differential (e.g., its position in semantic space). Change in meaning between testings I and II can be measured directly by the D between I and II profiles for the same concept. These D values are given under "Within Personalities, between Testings" in Table 49–3. Changes in meaning between personalities for the same concepts can be measured directly by the D between profiles for the same concept but as judged in two different personalities; these D values are given under "Between Personalities, within Testings" in Table 49–3.

SEMANTIC STABILITY THROUGH TIME

In general, although the differences are not great, Eve Black is the least stable personality through time and Jane the most stable (columns 2–4 in Table 49–3). The concept-by-concept data thus confirm the stability of Jane as shown in the structural data given above. For Eve White the most unstable or labile concepts are CHILD, MY MOTHER, FRAUD, HATRED, MY FATHER, CONFUSION, and SEX. For Eve Black the most labile concepts are LOVE, CHILD, MY JOB, MY MOTHER, MY SPOUSE, MY FATHER, and CONFUSION. For Jane the most unstable notions are ME, MY JOB, MY MOTHER, MY SPOUSE, HATRED, CONFUSION, and SEX. We note that the family constellation—mother, father, spouse, child—tend to be more susceptible to change through time within these personalities, but that the self concept stays relatively constant within personalities (e.g., the location of the self concept, in a sense, defines these three personalities). HATRED, SEX, and CONFUSION also seem to be points of stress.

SEMANTIC STABILITY BETWEEN PERSONALITIES

The data given in columns 5–10 in Table 49–3 make it clear that concept meanings in general shift more between Eve Black and the other two than between Jane and

Table 49–3   Changes in Meaning of Specific Concepts*

| Concept | Within Personalities, between Testings | | | Between Personalities, within Testings | | | | | |
| | D_{I-II} Eve White | D_{I-II} Eve Black | D_{I-II} Jane | D_{W-B} | | D_{W-J} | | D_{B-J} | |
				I	II	I	II	I	II
LOVE	.42	.67	.23	1.58	1.44	.35	.57	1.62	1.81
CHILD	.71	.96	.37	1.65	1.40	.68	.54	1.47	1.41
MY DOCTOR	.15	.05	.27	.23	.23	.28	.25	.30	.12
ME	.36	.32	.42	1.21	1.40	.60	.88	.83	.77
MY JOB	.27	.62	.42	1.30	1.43	.49	.43	1.19	1.54
MENTAL SICKNESS	.45	.45	.19	1.24	1.38	.40	.32	1.30	1.47
MY MOTHER	.54	.78	.46	.71	.78	.66	.23	1.02	.68
PEACE OF MIND	.40	.35	.41	.86	.66	.21	.28	.81	.61
FRAUD	.64	.12	.40	1.46	1.35	.73	.34	1.29	1.22
MY SPOUSE	.30	.62	.47	.67	.96	.61	.89	1.04	1.75
SELF-CONTROL	.32	.25	.24	.78	.80	.34	.39	.92	1.01
HATRED	.51	.19	.44	1.54	1.31	.51	.23	1.37	1.19
MY FATHER	.53	.71	.09	1.06	.60	.25	.43	1.06	.43
CONFUSION	.64	.67	.44	.86	.96	.71	.42	.98	.88
SEX	.62	.34	.47	1.10	.62	.63	1.20	1.45	1.76

* Numbers in italics indicate concepts that serve best to characterize differences between Eve White and Jane.

Eve White, this again substantiating the over-all correlations between total structures. The only concept that remains strictly constant in meaning through the personality changes in this woman is MY DOCTOR, although PEACE OF MIND and CONFUSION show greater stability than most others. It is interesting to note which concepts serve best to characterize the differences between Eve White and Jane (Eve Black shows gross differences on almost all concepts). These two "socialized" personalities differ from one another chiefly on ME, MY SPOUSE, and SEX, and these differences are increasing in magnitude through time. This clearly suggests this woman's sexual life as a core problem, Eve White being highly critical of all three concepts and Jane accepting them as positive values. It is also interesting to note in this connection that semantic differences between Eve White and Jane on CHILD, MY MOTHER, FRAUD, HATRED, and CONFUSION are decreasing through time.

INTERPRETATIONS OF THESE SEMANTIC DATA

The analyses of these personalities and their changes given so far have been descriptive rather than interpretive for the most part. In a sense, we have merely put into words what this woman herself, in her several personalities, has indicated by her check marks. The treatment of semantic differential data, from the patterns of check marks to construction of the models shown in Figures 49–1 to 49–6, is completely objective, and any investigator starting from the same data and following the rules would have to end up with the same pictures we have.

Making interpretations and predictions about this case on a "blind" basis is another matter entirely. In this section we go far beyond the objective data, and we are consequently much less confident about our statements. For one thing, neither of the writers is an experienced clinician—certainly not experienced with respect to the dynamics and characteristics of multiple personality. For another thing, we do not know at what stage in therapy our two testings were made, and interpretation would certainly vary greatly in terms of such information. It should also be pointed out that in the ordinary use of the semantic differential as a clinical tool (as compared with a blind analysis) many other sources of information would be available to support certain alternative interpretations and render others farcical. Let it be understood, then, that what follows is a flight into conjecture, in contrast with the preceding, factual reporting of semantic data.

INTERPRETIVE DESCRIPTIONS OF THE THREE PERSONALITIES

Eve White is the woman who is simultaneously most in contact with social reality and under the greatest emotional stress. She is aware of both the demands of society and her own inadequacies in meeting them. She sees herself as a passive weakling and is also consciously aware of the discord in her sexual life, drawing increasingly sharp distinctions between LOVE as an idealized notion and SEX as a crude reality. She maintains the greatest diversity among the meanings of various concepts. She is concerned and ambivalent about her CHILD, but apparently is *not* aware of her own ambivalent attitudes toward her MOTHER— and seems to become more resistant to this by testing II. Those psychoanalytically inclined may wish to identify Eve White with dominance of the *superego*: certainly, the superego seems to view the world through the eyes of Eve White, accepting the mores or values of others (particularly her mother) but continuously criticizing and punishing herself. If this case came to the psychotherapists with a voluntary, self-initiated plea for help, then it seems likely that Eve White was dominant at the time.

Eve Black is clearly the most out of contact with social reality and simultaneously the most self-assured. To rhapsodize, Eve

Black finds PEACE OF MIND through close identification with a God-like therapist (MY DOCTOR, probably a father symbol for her), accepting her HATRED and FRAUD as perfectly legitimate aspects of the God-like role. Naturally, she sees herself as a dominant, active wonder-woman and is in no way self-critical. She is probably unaware of her family situation. Those psychoanalytically inclined could say that the *id* looks out at the world through the eyes of Eve Black. Like a completely selfish infant, this personality is entirely oriented around the assumption of its own perfection. Actually, Eve Black seems to be more harmonious with the Adlerian than with the Freudian model, since personal perfection is apparently the demand acceded to rather than sexuality. If the case was committed to an institution, it seems likely that this personality was the reason for commitment.

Jane is the most puzzling of the three personalities, and our interpretation will have to depend upon assumptions about the stage of treatment (see below). Superficially, Jane is a very healthy personality: "all's well with the world, and day by day I'm getting better and better." Thus we find all the people in her life perceived as *good* and *strong* and *active* and all the socially approved modes of action perceived as *good* and *strong* and *passive*; SEX is LOVE-ly, her SPOUSE is becoming more like the noble DOCTOR all the time, and she is coming to perceive herself even, as a pleasant and reasonably active (if somewhat weak and submissive) person. But all this is a little too rosy, a little too pat. We note that Jane is becoming more and more "simple-minded"—all of her judgments tending to fall along a single factor of *good-strong* vs. *bad-weak*—which makes the Jane II model the most restricted and undiversified of all. Those psychoanalytically inclined may wish to view this personality as representing dominance of a self-deceptive *ego* which has woven a web of repression as to the state of reality; or, they may wish to view Jane as an essentially strong, healthy, and improving ego-dominated personality. In

any case, we doubt if Jane would have either come for therapy or have been institutionalized—as such.

POSSIBLE DYNAMISMS OPERATING IN THE CASE

Identification mechanisms. We say the patient "identifies" with some other person when her meaning of herself, ME, is semantically close to her meaning of the other person; e.g., if she sees her father as a kind, active, relaxed, etc. person and describes herself in the same terms, we infer identification. However, the pattern of identifications displayed by this patient seems unusual. Only in Eve Black, the obviously disoriented personality in terms of her values, is there clear differential identification—with her FATHER (and this may reflect the semantic tie-up between FATHER and MY DOCTOR). Jane shows some slight tendency toward closer identification with MOTHER, but it is not close. Eve White shows none with either parent. The fact that identification with FATHER (and MY DOCTOR) in Eve Black is accompanied by rejection of MOTHER to meaninglessness is suggestive of an underlying conflict in identifications. Note also, in this connection, that in Eve Black I the ascendancy of ME to the *good, strong, active* position is accompanied by making FATHER *weak*—as if she were taking over her father's role and putting her mother in her own previous place. And, interestingly enough, the concept SELF-CONTROL suffers the same fate as MOTHER. This picture of Eve Black is certainly suggestive of an *Electra complex* as the underlying dynamism. In "real" life, her MOTHER is or was the dominant, threatening figure—moralizing, demanding standards and SELF-CONTROL—and in Eve Black this woman escapes the pressure by rendering both MOTHER and SELF-CONTROL meaningless and simultaneously identifying with and taking her FATHER place (via the therapist). Suggestive evidence may be found: MOTHER is consistently *colder* than FATHER and usually more *tense* and *fast* (e.g., Factor 3). Identification of the self with the therapist in Eve Black is perfect, of course. The concept MY DOCTOR is the only personal concept to show perfect stability both between personalities and through time. The patient thus displays what might be called maximal *positive transference* in all three personalities; there is no sign of any negative transference at either testing, which may be indicative of the stage of therapy (e.g., early).

Significance of the patient's sexual life. Although Jane shows a rosy acceptance of normal sexual patterning—with LOVE and SEX linked and passively favorable, Eve White clearly displays awareness of a basic conflict in this area—SEX is early somewhat more distasteful than LOVE and becomes distinctly distasteful and dirty by testing II. In Eve White also we find ME and MY SPOUSE becoming linked with SEX in this unpleasant location. Eve Black, on the other hand, rejects both SEX and LOVE—but closely links them in her thinking. If we were to relate these facts with the Electra situation described above, the interpretation would be that her persisting conflict with her mother and attempts to identify with her father make it impossible for her to experience normal sexual satisfactions with her husband and to carry out the normal mother-wife-home role. Eve White is aware of this, in a sense, but Jane clearly is not. The concept MY JOB is interesting in this connection: its persistent linkages with LOVE, PEACE OF MIND, and SELF-CONTROL in the two "socialized" personalities, coupled with its linkage with SEX and MY SPOUSE in Eve Black, clearly suggests to us that this woman is interpreting MY JOB in the sense of "my job as a mother, wife, and home-builder" rather than in terms of her outside work (which we understand she has). In any case, there is clear evidence of involvement with her sex life as a major problem, and this may have been the presenting problem when she began therapy.

Repression and amnesia. Knowing that we are dealing with a case of multiple personality—usually characterized by complete dissociation between states—it is interesting to speculate on what meanings are repressed in the several personalities. It will be recalled that, operationally, meaninglessness of a concept is defined by its closeness to the origin (the solid balls in the models). This is probably to be interpreted as "connotative deadness" or "damping of affect" with respect to the concept involved. Within the matrix of our instrument, however, there is another way in which repression or amnesia may show up, and that is via a complete shift in meaning of the concept being judged (e.g., CHILD may shift from the personal reference of "my own youngster" to "children-in-general"). Looking back at the semantic data with these points in mind, we hazard the following guesses: Eve White probably has the best contact with reality and may not be amnesic at all (except for the other personalities); Eve Black may be amnesic for her mother and her own role as a mother and wife; Jane in Pollyanna fashion may be amnesic for her own problems, e.g., MENTAL SICKNESS and CONFUSION, and the indiscriminate way in which she lumps all socially favorable concepts at least suggests that she is judging CHILD, MOTHER, etc. in the abstract rather than as MY CHILD, MY MOTHER, and so forth.

INTERPRETATION I—ASSUMED EARLY STAGE OF THERAPY

The "original" personality, in the sense of being most characteristic of the woman her friends and relations knew, was Jane. The first testing of this personality shows a relatively weak ME that is associated with MENTAL SICKNESS; i.e., she was dimly aware of her own inadequacies but was striving to maintain a rigid acceptance of the real world and maintain an adequate home life. The people about her, with the exception of her husband, were seen as strong and active (perhaps threatening) in relation to herself, and her love life was regarded as a sort of deliberate, controlled duty. She was completely unaware of her (repressed) emotional ambivalence toward her mother, husband, and child. The things being hidden in this personality, and providing the force behind the eventual split, were (a) her Electra complex, (b) her repugnance for sexual relations with her husband, and (c) her ambivalent attitude toward herself. We suspect that she had a position in society that demanded "good front."

We must assume strong and about equal pressures toward solving the Electra complex, (a) by identifying with FATHER and asserting the self (id?), and (b) toward solving it by identifying with MOTHER and devaluing herself (superego?). This produces a two-way split away from the Jane pattern, one into Eve Black where selfish needs for superiority and playing the father role are achieved and another into Eve White where societal needs for submission and playing the mother role are achieved. This split, and the subsequent availability of the other roles, allows Jane to shift toward the "sweetness and light" view of the world, and this is clearly demonstrated by the changes between Jane I and Jane II. Eve White continues to become more simply and rigidly self-critical and Eve Black continues to become more simply and rigidly self-satisfied.

Assuming successful therapy is possible—which seems questionable—it will involve less and less time being spent in being Jane and Eve Black and a consequent shift into Eve White, where better contact and differentiation seems to be maintained. But here it will be necessary to bring Eve White to understand the reason for her depression, the role of her ambivalence toward her mother in her problem—which shows no signs of happening yet—and thence a gradual restructuring in which ME becomes more favorable, along with SPOUSE and SEX, and identifications with FATHER and MOTHER are reassigned. This will probably involve a period of negative transference, with MY DOCTOR and MOTHER becoming closely identified and being tem-

porarily shifted to *bad, strong,* and *active* directions of the semantic space. In other words, successful treatment will mean increasing time spent in, and a gradual restructuring of, Eve White to the point where it incorporates what is now Jane, but with a realignment of significant persons. On the other hand, if this woman is in a mental institution and remains there, it seems likely that Eve Black will become the dominant house she lives in. In either case, it is probable that Jane will appear less and less.

INTERPRETATION II—ASSUMED LATE STAGE OF THERAPY

If we assume that we are seeing the terminal stages of therapy with a case of this sort, then a quite different interpretation is necessary. The difference in interpretations hinges upon Jane, either as a deceptive and vanishing original personality (interpretation I) or as an increasingly healthy and augmenting personality (interpretation II). In the latter case we would assume that Eve White had been the "original" personality as people knew her—a socially acceptable wife and mother, but one laden with conflicts, anxieties, and self-criticism. The split in this case—into one personality in which the self-criticism completely disappears via irrationality (Eve Black) and another in which self-criticism vanishes via rationality (Jane)—seems less sensible, however. Jane seems unnecessary at this stage and really should have developed out of Eve White rather than being contemporaneous. If we assume there was a split in any case, Jane is clearly the most healthy personality, since LOVE and SEX are identified, the world is viewed in acceptable fashion, and the self concept is becoming more favorable all the time. The prediction here would be increasing time spent in Jane and less in the others. The stumbling blocks in the way of this interpretation are (a) the lack of any realignment of the system of parental identifications, and (b) the fact that Jane is becoming *less* diversified semantically (more "simple-minded") rather than the reverse. This second interpretation was actually the one we first adopted—because of the superficial "healthiness" of Jane—but consideration of all the evidence seems to favor the first interpretation. However, it should be noted that *if* this case is near the end of successful therapy, Jane is the only personality that combines both a normal view of the world and reasonable (increasing) acceptance of the self.

INTERPRETATION III—COMBINATION OF I AND II

It is possible to combine interpretations I and II by assuming that Jane is both the original personality which broke apart and the terminal personality which is being developed out of therapy. In this case, the early development of the case, probably in childhood, would be the same as that given under interpretation I—the conflicting parental identifications (id and superego determined respectively) were of about equal strength and finally became too intense to be contained within the self-deceptive personality organization of Jane. During the middle course of the case, when therapy was undertaken, we thus find all three personalities oscillating, temporary dominance of the mother and wife role being represented by Eve White, temporary dominance of the self-gratifying father role being represented by Eve Black, and temporary dominance of the face-saving, problem-solving ego being represented by Jane. Intentionally or unintentionally, the effect of therapy may be to strengthen the self-deceptive organization of Jane without resolving the underlying conflicts dramatized by Eve White and Eve Black. The oversimplified, Pollyanna-like way of perceiving herself as *good* along with all the other significant persons in her life yields a superficially happy person who views the world in an acceptable, if rigidly stereotyped, fashion. If the present combined interpretation approximates the actual situation, then we feel compelled to predict another breakdown at some later period in this person's life. In other words, the effect of therapy (whatever type it may have been) seems to have been further to strengthen the self-deceptive original organization of Jane, while making this personality even more rigid and insensitive to subtle differences in meaning and without resolving the underlying conflicts which created the original disturbance.

WHAT PRICE THERAPY?

It is impossible to tell from our semantic data whether the increasing simplification in structure characteristic of all three personalities is due to therapy itself or is happening despite therapy. However, a number of specialists in psychotherapy have from time to time expressed concern over the "hidden" effects of therapy even in so-called successful cases—particularly reduction in initiative, creativeness, and flexibility of the patient. Certainly in the present case we are witnessing an over-all reduction in differentiation of meanings. If overt behavior is in considerable part determined by meanings, as we believe it is, then we must expect Jane (if she is the terminal personality) to be now even less capable of behaving differentially to her mother, father, spouse, and child—they are all essentially undifferentiated "strong-active-goodness" to her. This would also be true, but to a lesser extent, of Eve White, although here we would assume an earlier stage of therapy and hence a possibility of secondary elaboration of semantic diversity under sensitive therapy.

Is rigidity of this sort a necessary price of therapy? In striving to achieve the goals of societal acceptability and individual happiness, does the therapist have to sacrifice the richness, individuality, and subtler adjustiveness of the patient? These are serious questions raised by the data of this single case—but not answered by them, of course. From the larger sample of cases we are presently working on, better answers may be forthcoming, but the cases are generally less severe. One other interesting phenomenon in the present cases should be mentioned: Despite the gross changes in meaning of concepts in the several personalities, and the over-all reduction in diversity, the semantic judgmental frame of reference remains constant. In other words, all three of the personalities in this woman utilize semantic scales in the same ways—the correlations between scales are the same for all three personalities and reduction in diversity in all of them is accomplished by a coalescence of *good, strong,* and *active* into a single evaluative dimension. Thus it would appear that the level of scale meanings is below that at which concepts vary, and common to all three personalities.

REFERENCES

1. Osgood, C. E. The nature and measurement of meaning. *Psychol. Bull.,* 1952, **49,** 192–237.
2. Osgood, C. E., & Suci, G. J. A measure of relation determined by both mean difference and profile information. *Psychol. Bull.,* 1952, **49,** 251–262.
3. Thigpen, C. H., & Cleckley, H. A. A case of multiple personality. *J. abnorm. soc. Psychol.,* 1954, **49,** 135–151.

Chapter 50

Objective Scoring of Projective Tests

WAYNE H. HOLTZMAN

Ever since L. K. Frank's first use of the term "projective method" in 1939 [15], there has been a rapid mushrooming of techniques for encouraging an individual to reveal aspects of his personality by the way in which he perceives, organizes, or relates to potentially affect-laden, ambiguous stimuli. Stemming largely from psychoanalytic theory, such projective techniques range all the way from free association in relatively unstructured situations to rather highly structured, formalized devices such as the Thematic Apperception Test. Before considering the problems of quantification and objective scoring, it might be instructive to examine closely the assumptions implicit in the projective method as contrasted to those underlying psychometric tests and measurement theory.

This article is reprinted from *Objective Approaches to Personality Assessment,* 1959, with the permission of the author and D. Van Nostrand Company, Inc.

PROJECTIVE COMPARED WITH PSYCHOMETRIC METHODS

Unlike the standardized aptitude test, the projective approach deals with the idiomatic expression of the individual as revealed in the context of his needs, fears, strivings, and ego-defensive behavior. As Frank has so aptly stated, "The essential feature of a projective technique is that it evokes from the subject what is, in various ways, expressive of his private world and personality process" [16, p. 47]. Given any projective technique where the subject is offered a wide latitude in which to reveal himself, the particular sample of responses obtained is assumed to reflect significant aspects of the subject's personality organization, if only the examiner can find the key to its interpretation.

Macfarlane and Tuddenham have pointed out that such an isomorphic assumption concerning the subject's test protocol and his personality leads to three corollaries that are rarely explicit: (a) belief that a protocol is a sufficiently extensive sampling of the subject's personality to warrant formulating judgments about it; (b) belief that the psychological determinants of each and every response are basic and general; and (c) belief that projective tests tap the durable essence of personality equally in different individuals [27, p. 34]. Many of the more wary, sophisticated projectivists would argue that none of these three assumptions *necessarily* follows from the basic assumption underlying the projective method—that even the best of projective test protocols is but a tiny fragment of the total personality, fraught with innumerable possibilities for misinterpretation. Nevertheless, in actual practice it is difficult to avoid falling into the dogmatic position of over-interpretation in an attempt to weave together a consistent picture of the personality dynamics presumably reflected by the clinical techniques employed. It can be argued that elaborate, clinical interpretations of personality from projective protocols often reveal more about the personality of the clinician than that of the subject.

In contrast to a projective technique, a psychometric test is based upon the fundamental assumption that an obtained score on the test reflects a hypothetical "true" score which is characteristic of the attribute in question for a given individual under specified testing conditions and at a given moment in time. Any deviation of the obtained score from the true score represents error of measurement which can be assessed provided one is willing to make certain assumptions about the nature of such errors. By defining the true score so that it includes all constant errors of measurement, the discrepancy between obtained and true score becomes a random error component. Since a random event by definition is uncorrelated with any other event, a general theory of measurement can be developed out of which components of error variance can be estimated, both with regard to the concept of reliability and the concept of validity [18].

Contrary to the opinion of some writers [37], such psychometric theory is not necessarily limited to a nomothetic universe where one is interested in group or interindividual differences. As Cattell [6] has been quick to point out, one can legitimately utilize psychometric theory for idiographic purposes by considering k different measures on m different occasions for a single person. Nor need psychometric theory be restricted to consideration of one response variable at a time—the oft heard criticism that a psychometric, statistical, or quantitative approach is too atomistic to provide more than a ridiculous caricature of the individual personality. While it is true that most contemporary uses of test scores deal with isolated traits, or at best with linear combinations of several traits, the advent of configural scoring methods [30], the possibilities of profile analysis [19], and other complex, multivariate procedures open new vistas for effective utilization of psychometric theory in the study of the individual personality.

Use of psychometric theory as a basis for assessment of personality commits one to a trait theory of personality. Postulating some sort of "true" score as a hypothetical construct to be inferred from observed scores is tantamount to saying that John Doe has X amount of the trait in question. It is not necessary, however, to think of John's possession of the trait as a "fixed" quantity. An individual's true score remains invariant only so long as the specific testing conditions remain constant and there is no real change in the individual with respect to the trait in question. A primary purpose of test standardization is to minimize constant sources of error that are ordinarily confounded with the inferred true score. Only errors of measurement that are random in nature can be adequately assessed and taken into account by the usual concepts of reliability and validity within contemporary psychometric theory.

Rosenzweig [37] has observed that assessment procedures can be ordered on a continuum depending upon the degree of structuring and control introduced by the assessor. At one extreme are the completely qualitative, unstructured methods of psychoanalysis, free association by a patient in the presence of an analyst. At the other extreme are highly structured paper-and-pencil tests which meet all the standards of psychometric theory. Projective techniques are seen as falling somewhere in between the particular position on the continuum depending upon the degree of standardization and control. In most instances, the projectivist has tried to preserve the qualitative, idiographic essence of the projective method while also searching for ways in which to categorize, quantify, and standardize the response variables underlying test behavior. He would like to have a technique for assessing personality which covers a wide band of the above continuum with a high degree of power throughout the range. Very few psychologists indeed have completely and consistently refrained from some form of abstraction later leading to quantification.

As soon as an individual decides to classify and enumerate any characteristics of a subject's responses to a projective technique, however crude and elementary the system, he has shifted from a purely projective point of view to a psychometric frame of reference. Such measurement may be quite nominal and only faintly resemble full-blown quantification. Nevertheless he has made the first and most significant step by classification of responses. For example, to classify a given response to an inkblot as a W assigns meaning to the response that transcends the idiosyncratic, private world of the subject. Unless one considers such symbols as W, D, and d, mere short-hand devices that have no real meaning beyond calling one's attention to certain aspects of the protocol, the symbols take on nominal characteristics of measurement. Those subjects who use the whole inkblot are seen as one class of individuals (W-tendency type), while those who use only a small part of the inkblot for their response are seen as another class (d-tendency type).

Such symbols of classification can be considered "signs" depicting specified characteristics abstracted from the raw protocol. More or less elaborate patterns of signs can be derived, either rationally or empirically, which point toward a syndrome or personality attribute to be inferred from the protocol. The pattern of signs may be complex and highly conditional so that predictive statements of the "if A and B but not C, then X" type can be formulated. Or the set of admissible signs may all contribute to some sort of "global" measure like the adjustment score derived from the Rorschach by Munroe's Inspection Technique [32]. Such clusters of signs may have some pragmatic value in predicting a criterion, but they have a disjunctive quality or arbitrariness which makes any theoretical interpretation exceedingly difficult. In most instances when a series of responses is classified, some types of response will appear more than once. Counting of such response frequencies is the first step in the construction of a quantitative scoring system. A Rorschach protocol with 10 movement responses would be thought of as indicating a greater tendency to see movement than a record with only two movement responses. Such a statement implies a crude kind of ordinal scale by which people can be ordered according to their degrees of M-tendency, provided the total number of responses is controlled.

As one becomes engrossed with the counting of symbols it is very easy to forget the nature of the projective material being classified. In his eagerness to make a given technique meet the demands of both psychometric and projective theory, the psychologist often compromises the two sets of conflicting standards to the point where the technique fails to accomplish either aim. There are some projective devices that should always be treated by qualitative methods of analysis since almost any attempt to abstract quantitative scores will fail to have any meaning. Other projective techniques may be altered sufficiently to yield scores meeting acceptable psychometric standards while at the same time preserving the projective nature of the task. It is too much to expect a technique designed originally as a purely projective method to lend itself to a meaningful kind of quantification without some revision, and in many projective techniques no amount of revision will produce adequate scores in the true psychometric sense.

Frank [16] has divided the projective techniques into five general kinds: constructive, interpretive, constitutive, cathartic, and refractive. The constructive methods consist of those techniques which require the subject to arrange materials into larger configurations or to produce drawings as in the Draw-A-Person Test. The interpretive methods are primarily verbal-associational techniques such as the Thematic Apperception Test. The best known example of a constitutive method is the Rorschach, in which the subject must organize relatively amorphous, unstructured inkblots into meaningful concepts. While most projective techniques may stimulate cathartic reactions, some, such as play therapy with dolls, are designed specifically for this purpose. The last of Frank's classes, the refractive method, is based upon the fact that any conventionalized mode of communication—handwriting, gestures, and other forms of expressive movement—may be used as an approach to the individuality of a person.

The above classification serves as a convenient basis for a more detailed discussion of scoring problems and quantifications in the analysis of projective techniques. Since cathartic methods cut across the other procedures, and since the analysis of expressive movement and individual style of communication can be considered as a special topic apart from more conventional projective methods, only the first three of Frank's classes will be discussed. Considerably more attention will be given to the Rorschach and related techniques than to the constructive or interpretive methods, partly because the Rorschach has been

studied longer and more exhaustively than any other projective test and partly because it provides an unusually good illustration of various problems of quantification encountered throughout the projective-psychometric continuum.

CONSTRUCTIVE METHODS

The way in which a child or adult arranges miniature life toys, draws a figure of a man or woman, or builds mosaics from colored pieces can reveal a great deal about his personality. Generally speaking, however, such creative productions are very difficult to analyze in any objective, quantitative fashion. Most clinicians only use qualitative procedures when dealing with constructive methods. Occasionally the characteristics of a construction may be classified to formalize its description, but inferences regarding personality, whether based upon symbolic interpretations or more direct expressions by the subject, remain at the clinical intuitive level. Of course, rating scales for recording clinical judgment can be employed with such materials, as with any other individual response or style of expression. But it is not difficult to see why quantification in the psychometric sense has failed to prove useful in the analyses of drawings or other creative products, even though the situation may be rather highly structured as in the Bender-Gestalt Test. Usually the construction has to be viewed as a whole or as only a very small number of separate units analogous to test items. The configuration, color, shading, and other characteristics of a drawing are complex, defying quantification in the usual sense. Nevertheless, in some special cases, fairly successful attempts have been made to score objectively certain limited aspects of such productions. Several of these will be briefly discussed.

Drawing a human figure has been employed rather extensively as a projective technique in recent years, largely due to the persistent studies of Karen Machover [28].

Working primarily from a psychoanalytic point of view in which the drawing is assumed to reflect the body image of self, Machover and others have developed systems of graphic analysis utilizing a sign approach to the scoring of drawings. For full use of the system, the subject must draw both a man and a woman so that comparisons of self-sex and opposite-sex figures can be made. A good example of this graphic sign method is the scale of figure drawing items which is presumed to measure field-dependency [50]. Sets of 40 items for men and 45 for women were constructed by Machover on the basis of a preliminary analysis. Criterion groups for the initial selection of items consisted of college students with high and low field dependence as measured by a battery of perceptual tests. A total score is obtained by summing the number of signs checked during the detailed analysis of the two figure drawings. Some of the signs are completely objective such as transparency, lack of ears, or hair shaded. Others, like consistency rating and rigidity rating, are subjective and require a clinical judge. For the most part, however, the list of signs is sufficiently objective to merit further study.

Graphic signs have been used with similar success by Pascal and Suttell in the objective scoring of drawings in the Bender-Gestalt Test [34]. The test consists of nine geometric forms that are copied by the subject. The number of scorable signs on each design varies from 10 to 13, with seven additional signs dealing with the total configuration of all nine drawings. Each sign is given a numerical weight varying from one to eight. The size of the weight was empirically determined in earlier studies differentiating normals from such groups as psychotics and organics.

A single score is obtained by summing the weights of positive signs; the higher the score the more pathological the record. Although much valuable information may have been sacrificed at the expense of obtaining a single quantitative index, the resulting score has sufficiently high relia-bility and validity in a variety of situations to prove highly useful as a screening procedure.

A third variation of semi-structured drawing which represents an attempt at objective quantification is the Drawing-Completion Test described by Kinget [23]. Eight squares are presented to the subject, each containing small, but suggestive, stimuli such as a dot, a wavy line, or a black square, around which the subject draws whatever he wishes. Kinget has attempted to develop a graphic system with a series of crudely quantitative variables, some based on content analysis and others dealing with style and expressive features of the drawings. A personality profile is constructed by recording signs and then adding them together in more abstract categories, somewhat like the first attempts to quantify the Rorschach. While the rationale behind the scoring system is highly speculative and smacks of armchair analysis without adequate empirical support, the method itself is interesting and sufficiently novel to deserve careful study.

Working with spontaneous finger paintings, a construction which has proved very difficult to quantify, Dorken [10] has developed a series of objectively defined rating scales for energy output, affective range, contact with reality, and clarity. Pictorial norms were used as points of reference to anchor the scales. The variable, Affective Range, illustrates the technique. "Spontaneous" colors, red and yellow, were each assigned scale values of three, blue and green were given values of two each, and the "somber" colors, black and brown, were each scored one. Combination colors were scored in relation to this primary scale. Test-retest reliability ranged from .13 to .84, depending upon the sample and time interval between administrations. By using a series of finger paintings, reasonably adequate summary scores on the four variables defined by Dorken should be possible.

It is significant to note that in each of the above examples of attempts to achieve objective scoring of projective techniques, the degree of quantification is pretty much limited to the complex sign approach in which numerous signs are scored, weighted, and summed to yield some sort of "global" but quantitative, measure which is purported to reflect important dimensions of personality. Ideally, the sign approach should begin with sufficient theoretical rationale to construct a coherent system. After careful operational definition of each sign, the objectivity of scoring should be determined by having at least two trained individuals independently score a large number of protocols. In some instances where several signs have similar rationales in their definition, their consistency should be examined empirically in a study to validate the construct which they theoretically represent [7]. In most cases, however, a straight empirical analysis without regard for the construct in question will be undertaken with the practical view in mind of establishing a weighting system that has maximum efficiency for predicting some criterion. In any case, the burden of proof concerning the reliability and objectivity of any proposed scoring system rests with the individual who proposes it.

INTERPRETIVE METHODS

Assessing personality from the way in which an individual reveals his fantasy life in telling a story or interpreting a scene goes back through centuries of mankind. However, the first notable attempt to develop a projective test for uncovering a person's needs, wishes, and related fantasies by having him tell stories was made by Morgan and Murray in 1935 [31]. In the past 20 years, Murray's Thematic Apperception Test (TAT) has become a standard projective technique, second only to the Rorschach in its widespread use both in the clinic and laboratory. Numerous other interpretive methods—Rosenzweig's Picture-Frustration Study [36], Bellak's Children's Apperception Test [22], and Shneidman's Make-A-Picture-Story Test [43], to mention but a few—stem

more or less directly from Murray's pioneering work and attest to the fruitfulness of the basic method.

Interpretive methods range all the way from one end of the projective-psychometric continuum to the other. Representative of the purely projective approach is the standard TAT analyzed entirely in a qualitative manner, focusing upon the content of stories and stylistic aspects of the story telling as illustrated by Stein [44]; such analysis draws heavily upon careful deduction and clinical intuition. Only one step removed from this intuitive approach is the more formal kind of qualitative analysis in which various characteristics of each story are classified according to theme expressed, kinds of affect, need categories, and the like. Such qualitative systems tend to vary considerably according to the predilection of the analyst. Representative of the diverse approaches to analysis of TAT protocols is Shneidman's [43] compilation of systems used by 15 different authorities working with the same TAT record.

Several investigators have developed sets of rating scales to be used with the TAT. One of the most extensive systems is Hartman's [21], consisting of five-point scales for 65 categories covering thematic elements, feeling qualities, topics of reference, and more formal characteristics, each of which can be scored for a given story. Total scores are obtained by summing ratings across stories. While such scales utilize the clinical skill of the interpreter, serious difficulties often arise when one is concerned with the objectivity of the scoring. When categories deal with the manifest aspects of a story, independent raters can generally agree at a satisfactory level to insure fair objectivity. But as soon as attention is focused upon covert aspects of the response or upon the personality of the story-teller rather than his production, agreement falls off sharply [46].

The reason for this greater subjectivity when dealing with the personality of the subject is apparent when one examines closely the nature of the factors influencing response to a TAT picture. Holt [22] discusses nine different determinants of the manifest response, ranging from situational context to personal style of the story-teller. The interpreter is faced with the very complex task of weighing the probable influence of each factor before he can arrive at an interpretation of the subject's personality. It is somewhat like having an equation with nine variables, several of which can be partially discounted while most remain unknown quantities. Several judges will weigh the unknowns quite differently, resulting in widely varying ratings.

This difference between *test-oriented systems* dealing with formal characteristics of the response and *personality-oriented systems* in which the interpreter makes direct inferences concerning the personality of the story-teller is fundamental. The more superficial or concrete the system, the more objective the scoring and the less relevant the derived variables to the personality of the subject. Young [51] developed a set of 23 well-defined traits, such as Anxiety, Dominance, and Need to be Loved, which could be used in rating the personality of the interpreter as well as the subject. Fifteen trained interpreters independently rated 12 TAT stories from seven different individuals: a total of 84 responses, on each of the 23 traits. Ratings on the same 23 traits were obtained for each of the 15 interpreters by a sociometric method. Even though the average agreement among interpreters was fairly high for such personality-oriented variables, differences in the interpreters' ratings proved significantly related to their own personalities, demonstrating the intrinsic subjectivity of such methods of analysis.

Several fairly objective variables dealing with story content seem sufficiently relevant to important aspects of the story-teller's personality to merit special attention. McClelland and his colleagues [26] have carefully developed the personality construct, Achievement Motive, and have demonstrated how it can be reliably scored in TAT stories. The scoring involves simple classifications of response elements by objective criteria that are then summed to yield an overall index of the individual's Need-Achievement score. A number of experimental studies are also cited indicating the validity of the personality construct.

A similar careful derivation of two test-oriented variables of relevance to the story-teller's personality was undertaken by Eron [12]. Using well-anchored rating scales, Eron and co-workers developed fairly objective measures of emotional tone and outcome that could be applied to single responses and summed to get an overall score. Both variables have satisfactory inter-scorer reliabilities, .86 for emotional tone and .75 for outcome. Eron is chiefly concerned with the development of norms for TAT themes that can be used to define the general characteristics of each card in terms of the ease with which certain themes are evoked. Such data for the TAT can be roughly thought of as analogous to difficulty level or other item-parameters in aptitude tests. A recent application of Eron's approach demonstrates how Guttman's scaling method can be employed using normative TAT data to construct a uni-dimensional scale for need-Sex [1].

A final example of an objective approach to the scoring of the TAT is one devised recently by Dana [9]. Three fundamental aspects of test behavior—approach to the situation, normality of response, and rarity of response—were used by Dana to define three variables amenable to objective scoring, Perceptual Organization, Perceptual Range, and Perceptual Personalization. Inter-scorer reliability in terms of percentage agreement between independent judges ranged from 76 to 94 for the three scoring categories in a study of 150 TAT stories. The unique aspect of Dana's approach is the fact that these three variables are sufficiently pertinent to a large variety of projective techniques to permit inter-test comparisons for sharpening the validity of the personality constructs involved.

Variations of the sentence completion method provide much more suitable data for psychometric development than the TAT. The technique consists of providing the subject with a list of incomplete sentences to which he responds with whatever completions come to mind. By wise selection of sentence stems, content fairly similar to the thematic apperception methods can be obtained. Of course the response is much more highly structured and discrete from one item to the next than is the case with the TAT. Herein lies the chief virtue of the method with respect to quantification.

Rotter and Willerman [38] developed one of the first sentence completion tests with high objectivity. Designed for large-scale screening purposes in the Army Air Force, their 40-item version yielded a single adjustment score having inter-scorer reliability of .89 and split-half reliability of .85. A refined version of this test designed for college students, the Rotter Incomplete Sentences Blank [39] has an objective scoring manual with reported interscorer reliability of .96 and split-half reliability of .84, unusually high for a projective technique.

Trites and his colleagues [47] developed a military version of the sentence completion method to a high degree of objectivity while at the same time dealing with a number of response-categories rather than just one. A scoring manual was written on the basis of 1038 test protocols which yielded inter-scorer agreement ranging from .80 to .96 for eight major variables, Conformity, Ego Esteem, Gregariousness, Sexuality Attitudes, Air Force–oriented Motivation, Hostility, Insecurity, and Unscorable Response. Although there is little direct evidence to support the validity of these variables with respect to the personality constructs implied, in a later factor analysis of inter-item correlations where the items had been scored dichotomously as indicating either a positive or negative attitude with reference to adjustment to flying, Trites [48] obtained four factors which were meaningfully linked to several of the original major variables.

It is instructive to note the characteristics of the sentence completion method which are responsible for achievement of satisfactory psychometric standards. Unlike the TAT, the number of discrete items can be very large, making possible an atomistic treatment of test elements without undue distortion of the technique. Where the TAT has at most 20 pictures, each with an infinite variety of complex responses possible, the sentence completion method has highly structured items for which the variety and extent of responses are relatively limited. The more circumscribed nature of the technique makes possible the development of an objective scoring manual for any variables that may be present in the response. That such psychometric treatment does not necessarily reduce the usefulness of a projective method is demonstrated by the repeatedly high validity obtained for the Rotter Incomplete Sentences Blank in assessing level of personal adjustment [39].

CONSTITUTIVE METHODS

The Rorschach test stands alone among projective techniques in the amount of attention, both clinical and experimental, which it has received during the past twenty years and illustrates problems encountered in scoring responses to constitutive methods. Quantitative analysis of responses to inkblots has ranged all the way from one extreme of the projective-psychometric continuum to the other. Some writers [25, 41] have pointed out how the Rorschach can be dealt with in a purely qualitative manner, emphasizing the dynamic and symbolic nature of the content and leaning heavily upon psychoanalytic theory and the intuitive skills of a clinician. Associations to inkblots are seen as only one step removed from completely free association in the psychoanalytic session. Others [20, 33] have shown how highly structured and completely objective multiple-choice methods can be applied to the study of individual differences in the perception of inkblots. And curiously enough, the same 10 inkblots are used throughout!

To what extent are these various degrees of structuring and quantification based upon sound principles of measurement theory? Does the Rorschach really span the entire projective-psychometric continuum with the high degree of power claimed by some of its proponents?

The most rudimentary form of quantification in the Rorschach is the assigning of symbols to certain kinds of responses which are then looked upon as signs pointing to various personality attributes or nosological classes. An excellent example of such a classification of qualitative signs is the analysis of verbalization described by Rapaport [35], who presents a very careful rationale for the scoring of such pathognomic verbalizations as confabulations, contaminations, confusion, absurd responses, and ideas of reference. Such signs are not additive except in the very crude sense that a number of positive signs in a single record tend to pile up in confirming the diagnosis.

The widely used "formal" scoring methods for the Rorschach represent attempts to measure the perceptual variables implicit in the response. The complex nature of the stimulus permits a wide latitude of location, of determinants, and conceptual content. Once decisions have been made as to what constitutes a discrete response, the number of such responses to a given inkblot or to all 10 Rorschach plates can be determined. Although there are some minor problems encountered in deciding when a verbalization is truly a response for purposes of scoring, one can safely assume that inter-scorer agreement as to number of responses (R) is quite high regardless of the judge's theoretical position. Similarly, the scoring of location, at least in its gross elements of whole, usual, large detail, or small and unusual detail, does not pose serious problems in the attaining of reasonable objectivity. Aside from specialized uses of content such as Elizur's anxiety score [11], the categorizing of concepts into human, animal, and other generic classes is quite straightforward also. The greatest difficulties in

achieving scoring objectivity arise in the realm of response-determinants.

Trying to determine those stimulus attributes which are responsible for eliciting a given response amounts to a kind of global psychophysics for which the general laws have yet to be worked out. Although logical in their conception, most scoring systems for determinants involve a number of highly arbitrary decisions, the wisdom of which is highly debatable. The subjectivity of the method, the influence of factors extraneous to the blots such as the examiner-subject interaction [40] and variation in style of inquiry [17] raise troublesome questions concerning the meaning of scores once achieved.

Presumably the inquiry phase of the Rorschach is designed to discover the characteristics of the inkblot which prompted the subject to give a response. The subject is asked by rather vague and indirect questions to introspect, to analyze the perceptual process and report to the examiner what about the blot suggests, for example, "a bloody finger," or "a pretty flower." A helpful subject who senses what the examiner is after may reply by saying, "It's shaped like a man's thumb and is colored red, suggesting blood." More than likely, however, the subject will say, "It just looks like it to me," leaving the examiner about where he started. And even if the subject does mention the color as playing a part in the concept, do we have any way of knowing whether the subject would have reported blood in the absence of color? How do we know it wasn't the combination of form and shading that suggested a bloody thumb? The unfortunate fact is that we simply don't know, although recent studies by Baughman [2] provide a better basis for guessing.

Zubin [52] has recognized this problem and has tried to overcome it by introducing a much more exhaustive inquiry than the usual brief, indirect questioning. In addition to asking many more questions per response, he has experimented with inquiry immediately following the response rather than waiting until all 10 inkblots have been administered. Sixty scales were constructed that could be applied in scoring a single response, provided the inquiry was sufficiently exhaustive. Five scales deal with location, six with the objective attributes of the stimulus, six with determinants or the relative importance of stimulus attributes in the formation of the percept, 14 with interpretation categories such as surface texture or strength of movement, three with organization activity, 15 with content, and 11 with other aspects of the single response such as reaction time and popularity. In addition, there are six scales dealing with variables present in the protocol as a whole. When one stops to think that Rorschach records frequently contain upward of 50 responses, the amount of energy invested in scoring 60 scales on each response is tremendous.

If a sufficient amount of information were available about the objective stimulus attributes and the correlates between these attributes and characteristics of the response, the amount of work required to utilize Zubin's system might be justified. However, the very nature of the complex stimulus confronting the subject in the form of an inkblot defies all but the crudest, global type of description as far as the specific stimulus attributes are concerned. With respect to the determinants or global psychophysics of the reported percept, even a highly trained introspectionist would be hard put to verbalize accurately the relative importance of various inkblots' characteristics in forming the percept. Since the greatest value for the Rorschach is claimed to be the study of psychopathology where the subject's ability to introspect accurately may be seriously impaired, there appears to be little real hope of obtaining the kind of information necessary to use many of the scales Zubin has proposed. Although Zubin's system may not really increase the objectivity of scoring for the Rorschach, since it is comprised largely of five-point scales for

recording clinical impression, his exhaustive approach immediately points out the fundamental weaknesses inherent in the standard methods of scoring.

In addition to the fact that objective scoring for most inkblot variables cannot be achieved without the use of arbitrary rules, the standard Rorschach is inherently poor as a psychometric device in some other important respects. Providing the subject with only ten inkblots and then permitting him to give as many or as few responses to each card as he wishes characteristically results in a set of unreliable scores with sharply skewed distributions, the majority of which fail to possess the properties of even rank-order measurements. One record with an R of 20 may be comprised of single responses to the first nine cards and 11 responses to Card X, while another may consist of two responses per card. Any of the usual scores with the possible exception of form level will have quite different meanings in the two contrasting protocols even though the total number of responses is constant. Add to this the difficulties arising when R varies from less than 10 to over 100, and it is easy to see why most quantitative studies involving the standard Rorschach yield confusing or negative results.

In a general review of statistical methods applied to Rorschach scores, Cronbach [8] has considered several ways in which the confounding effect of R upon most other variables can be reduced: (a) computing percentage ratios of each variable over R; (b) removing the linear effect of R by partial regression techniques; (c) reducing the effect of R by plotting the variable against R and drawing a freehand line fitting the medians of the columns (a crude form of curvilinear partial regression); or (d) dividing the total sample into a number of subgroups that are homogeneous with respect to R before proceeding with any quantitative analysis of other variables. The usual procedure of computing percentage ratios is highly unsatisfactory because of the crude metric qualities of most Rorschach variables and the lack of a linear relationship between R and other variables. In a study of 790 cases, Fiske and Baughman [14] demonstrated that the relationships between R and other scoring categories are usually complex and nonlinear. Consequently the usual linear regression methods for removing the confounding effect of R will generally fail. Given a standard free-response Rorschach, the only procedure which has any real promise for controlling R is to form subgroups according to R and analyze each one independently. But even this very inefficient procedure leaves unanswered the serious criticism that two records with identical number of responses may be quite different in meaning due to different patterning of responses across the 10 cards.

Recognizing the serious problems in the interpretation of scores when R is a variable, most clinicians make allowance for R in a crude intuitive way. Buhler [5] goes one step further by trying to structure the test administration so that three to five responses will be given to each blot. Blake and Wilson [4] avoid the problem in part by considering only the first response to each card. However, having only 10 responses from which to obtain scores, many of which occur rather rarely, creates a whole host of new problems in attempting to achieve satisfactory standards of measurement.

Standardization of testing conditions and development of procedures for administering the Rorschach to large groups at a time represent another attempt to achieve more objectivity. Munroe [32], Harrower [20], Sells [42], and others have demonstrated the feasibility of group procedures provided one is willing to sacrifice certain aspects of the more unstructured, personalized individual Rorschach. The usual procedure is to project each inkblot on a large screen for three minutes while the subject writes down his responses in a standard booklet. The number of responses is uncontrolled, the subject is usually given a very simple, direct inquiry concerning the role of shape,

color, movement, and texture, and location is indicated by drawing the outline of his percept on a miniature replica of the blot.

Most of the scoring difficulties inherent in the standard Rorschach are aggravated still further by use of such group methods. Where one at least has the opportunity for such things as the recording of verbalizations and individualized inquiry to help clear up scoring problems in the standard Rorschach, the group method deprives the examiner of all but the most superficial cues for scoring determinants, increasing further the arbitrary nature of the system.

If one uses standard paper-and-pencil aptitude tests as a model to be emulated, the most highly structured, psychometrically sound form of the Rorschach would appear to be a multiple-choice test with sufficiently standard instructions to permit its use with large groups of subjects. Under pressure of screening demands during wartime, Harrower and others [20] developed a multiple-choice version in which the subject chooses from a list of thirty concepts those three which look best to him for the particular blot in question. Fifteen of the 30 available concepts presumably indicate psychopathology while the remainder reflect normality. Harrower's own system of scoring is unusual and unnecessarily complicated. Normal answers are arbitrarily weighted "1" for any concept involving human movement, "2" for any that represent a popular response, "3" and "4" for those which involve color-form integration, and "5" for space responses. The set of abnormal answers is assigned weights varying from "6" to "9" in a similar arbitrary fashion. The total score obtained by summing the weights for the concepts chosen is confused in its meaning because of the arbitrary weighting system.

More recently, O'Reilly developed a simpler multiple-choice form with 12 choices per blot, four from psychotic records, four from neurotic records, and four from normals. The subject is asked to select the two concepts which best describe the inkblot. Answers are weighted on a three-point system with "1" for normal and "3" for psychotic. Almost complete separation of normals from psychotics was achieved in a cross-validation, although the neurotics had only slightly higher total scores than did the normals.

Another interesting, objective approach utilizing the multiple-choice format is the concept evaluation technique developed by McReynolds [29]. Using Beck's list of good and poor responses according to form level [3], McReynolds selected 25 good and 25 poor concepts spread throughout the 10 Rorschach plates. The subject is shown the location of the concept and asked to indicate whether or not the inkblot looks like the concept. Generally given after a standard Rorschach as part of the testing-the-limits phase, McReynolds' concept test yields an objective, scorable, reliable, and well-defined measure of the degree to which the subject can discriminate good from poor concepts. One of the main advantages of McReynolds' test is the fact that the number of discrete stimuli (intact areas of inkblots) has been increased from 10 to 50 by breaking up the standard 10 Rorschach plates into smaller components. This point is a highly significant departure from the usual ipsative method of allowing repeated response to the same stimulus and probably accounts for the satisfactory internal consistency (split-half reliability of .82) that McReynolds obtained.

As Harrower [20] has pointed out, the highly structured multiple-choice versions of the Rorschach are no longer equivalent to the standard individual Rorschach except for the inkblots themselves. One could go a step further and question whether or not tests that have completely fixed response alternatives can even be considered projective techniques. In all respects they appear to be objective tests of perception which may have implications for the measurement of important personality traits. The course of development from an unstructured projective technique to a completely structured objective test is complete.

A NEW SOLUTION

The fundamental question of how to develop psychometrically sound scoring procedures for responses to inkblots while also preserving the rich qualitative projective material of the Rorschach has been approached from a new point of view at The University of Texas.[1] The major modifications undertaken consist of greatly increasing the number of inkblots while limiting the number of responses per card to one, and extending the variety of stimulus colors, pattern, and shadings used in the original Rorschach materials. From an exploratory study it was concluded that a test containing 45 inkblots, to each of which only one response is given, would be feasible to construct and would probably tap essentially the same variables as the classical Rorschach method. Special efforts might have to be made, however, to develop materials which have high "pulling power" for responses using small details, space, and color and shading attributes to compensate for the tendency to give form-determined wholes as the first response to an inkblot.

Such a test would have several advantages over the standard Rorschach: (a) The number of responses per individual would be relatively constant. (b) Each response would be given to an independent stimulus, avoiding the weaknesses inherent in the Rorschach, where all responses are lumped together regardless of whether they are given to the same or different inkblots. (c) Making a fresh start in the production of stimulus materials, especially in view of recent experimental studies of color, movement, shading, and other factors in inkblot perception, would yield a richer variety of stimuli capable of eliciting much more information than the original 10 Rorschach plates. And finally, (d) a parallel form of

[1] Initial impetus for this research was given the writer by a Faculty Research Fellowship from the Social Science Research Council, Inc., of New York. More recently the research program has been supported by a grant-in-aid from the Hogg Foundation for Mental Health, The University of Texas.

the test could easily be constructed from item-analysis data in the experimental phases of test development, and adequate estimates of reliability could be obtained independently for each major variable.

The research to date has borne out all original expectations. Two matched alternate forms, A and B, of the Holtzman Inkblot Test have been developed, each containing 45 inkblots. Two additional blots are common to both forms of the test and appear as practice blots before the others. Instructions to the subject are similar to those used in the standard Rorschach with the exception that the subject is asked to give just the primary response to each card, and a brief, simple inquiry is made after each response where necessary to clarify the location or determinants. Administration of the test is easier than the Rorschach, and the subject generally finds giving only one response per card is a fairly simple task.

Six major variables are scored for each response, while a number of minor variables or qualitative signs are scored when deemed appropriate. The major variables were selected and defined according to the following criteria: (a) The variable had to be one which could be scored for any legitimate response. Variables which only rarely occurred were set aside for the moment. (b) The variable had to be sufficiently objective to permit high scoring agreement among trained individuals. (c) The variable had to show some *a priori* promise of being pertinent to the study of personality through perception. And (d) each variable must be logically independent of the others. Location, Form Appropriateness, Form Definiteness, Color, Shading, and Movement Energy Level were selected for intensive study and provided the basis for item-analyses in the final selection and matching of inkblots for Forms A and B.

Location as a variable was defined strictly in terms of the amount of blot used and the extent to which the natural gestalt of the blot was broken up by the

response. A three-point weighting system was adopted with "0" for wholes, "1" for large details, and "2" for small areas, making possible a theoretical range of scores from 0 to 90.

The scoring of color was based entirely upon the apparent primacy or importance of color, including black, gray, and white, as a response-determinant. When the subject named the color in his response, scoring was relatively simple. On rare occasions, when it was apparent that the response would have been highly improbable without the presence of color, credit for color was given even though never mentioned by the subject. A four-point system similar to the Rorschach was adopted with "0" for completely ignoring color and "3" for use of color as the sole determinant. Total scores for Color have a theoretical range from 0 to 135.

While subtle distinctions in the different uses of shading as a determinant are usually made in the Rorschach, no such differentiations are made in the Holtzman Inkblot Test. As with Color, the scoring of Shading was based solely upon the apparent primacy of shading as a determinant. Because pure shading responses are so rare, only a three-point scoring system was used, yielding a theoretical range from 0 to 90.

The scoring of movement is linked closely to content in most contemporary scoring systems for the Rorschach. Too frequently such practices lead to highly arbitrary convention as to whether or not movement is scored or how it is scored. In the Klopfer system [24], for example, "airplane" and "bat" present difficult problems. Can you be sure the airplane is flying? Even when an airplane does fly, there is no movement of its parts and no movement relative to any frame of reference unless landscape is added. Is "bat" to be scored FM for animal movement while "airplane" is scored Fm for inanimate movement when both concepts are really precision alternatives rather than uniquely different responses? The resulting picture is often highly confusing from a psychometric point of view. The essential character of the movement response is the energy level or dynamic quality of it, rather than the particular content. Leaning heavily upon Zubin [52], Sells [42], and Wilson [49], a five-point scale was adopted varying from "0" for no movement or potential for movement, through static, casual, and dynamic movement to a weight of "4" for violent movement such as whirling or exploding. Movement Energy Level ranges theoretically from "0" to 180.

Different authorities vary in the extent to which concept elaborations and specifications are confounded with the goodness of fit of the concept to the form of the inkblot. In the Holtzman Inkblot Test, Form Definiteness was defined independently of form level in the usual sense and refers solely to the definiteness or specificity of the form of the concept represented in the response, disregarding completely the characteristics of the inkblot. Working independently with a large number of concepts culled from inkblot responses, five psychologists placed them in rank order with the most form-definite concept at the top. The independent sets of ranked concepts were then merged to yield an overall rank order for the entire list. Cutting points were chosen so that five levels of Form Definiteness could be distinguished. The resulting set of examples served as a scoring manual, with a weight of "0" for the most indefinite concepts, such as anatomy drawing, squashed bug, or fire, and a weight of "4" for the most definite concepts, such as Indian chief, violin, or knight with a shield. Form Definiteness has a theoretical range from 0 to 180.

Form Appropriateness, the last of the six major variables, is by its very nature a subjective variable, requiring extensive preliminary work to make scoring reasonably objective. And yet, it is this very subjectivity which gives the variable great theoretical importance. Beck [3] recognized the likelihood that goodness of fit of the concept to the form of the inkblot would be closely related to degree of contact with reality and undertook a major study of form level that has proved to be one of the most valuable contributions to the Rorschach. Considerable effort was spent in arriving at acceptable standards for scoring Form Appropriateness. Different responses to each inkblot were listed separately for each location and rated independently by at least three judges. A seven-point scale was used with "0" representing extremely poor fit. Although there was good agreement of judges in most cases, a final judgment for each response was reached only after full discussion in conference. The resulting manual provides a guide to the scoring of Form Appropriateness on a three-point system with zero for unusually poor form and "2" for unusually good form. Form Appropriateness can range theoretically from 0 to 90.

The agreement among independent but well trained scorers for a sample of 46 records proved in general to be very high: product-moment correlations of .99 for Location, Form Definiteness, and Movement Energy Level, .97 for Shading, .95 for Color, and .91 for Form Appropriateness. Good estimates of reliability based upon internal consistency were obtained by using Gulliksen's matched random subtest method [18]. Correlations ranged from .80 for Form Appropriateness to .91 for Shading. All six variables proved to be reasonably normal and continuous in distribution. Studies are now underway to determine the correlations between Forms A and B with several time intervals and populations of subjects.

Once the standardization of the Holtzman Inkblot Test is complete, it should be possible to develop specialized multiple-choice versions of test for measuring variables of particular interest. Seymour Fisher and Sidney Cleveland have already had some success in developing a series of multiple-choice items to be used with 40 of Holtzman's inkblots which yields a measure of their Barrier Score [13]. The particular inkblots used were selected on the basis of earlier item-analysis data so that each blot would be accompanied by three fairly acceptable choices, one representing a barrier response (such as "a knight in armor"), one representing a penetration response (such as "x-ray"), and one which was neutral (such as "flower"). The subject was asked to check the one he liked most and place a different mark on the one he liked least, leaving the third choice blank. Both the Group Rorschach and the new multiple-choice test were given to 60 college students by Fisher and Cleveland. The correlation between the two sets of Barrier Scores was .64.[2] This fairly high correlation, coupled with the fact that the distribution of scores on the multiple-choice test was much greater than on the Rorschach and was more normally shaped, suggests that the multiple-choice Barrier Score would be superior to the measure reported earlier by Fisher and Cleveland [13].

Considerable ground has been covered in this analysis of the more common problems encountered in the objective scoring of projective techniques. The very nature of the projective hypothesis, that an individual will reveal something of his private self in the way in which he responds to ambiguous stimuli, has encouraged an almost unbelievably wide range of assessment techniques under the rubric of projective methods. In focussing upon quantitative methods of analysis and their objectivity as measured by reproducibility, a whole host of important problems concerning the meaning of projective responses has been deliberately side-stepped. Concepts of validity and their empirical determination, examiner-subject interactions, variability of response across different populations of subjects have been dealt with only tangentially if at all.

One cannot help but observe that few, if any, of these many projective devices can serve well two masters at the same time, particularly when their original purpose is exploitation of the projective hypothesis in the clinical diagnosis of personality. While

[2] Personal communication from Dr. Sidney E. Cleveland.

not necessarily incompatible, the assumptions and historical biases inherent in the projective approach on the one hand and those in the psychometric approach on the other are at opposite extremes of a continuum defined roughly in terms of the degree of structure and control of the subject's response that is imposed by the method. An unfortunate and bewildering array of inadequate quantification characterizes most projective techniques when there is pressure upon the projectivist to conform to the rigorous statistical standards of psychometric theory without concomitant pressure to revise the technique itself. A major challenge to psychologists interested in the objective assessment of personality is the development of psychometrically sound personality tests from available projective devices, a point made by Thurstone [45] 10 years ago which still stands today.

REFERENCES

1. AULD, F., JR., ERON, L. D., and LAFFAL, J. Application of Guttman's scaling method to the TAT. *Educ. psychol. Measmt*, 1955, 15, 422–435.
2. BAUGHMAN, E. E. A comparative analysis of Rorschach forms with altered stimulus characteristics. *J. proj. Tech.*, 1954, 18, 151–164.
3. BECK, S. J. *Rorschach's test: I. Basic processes.* New York: Grune & Stratton, 1944.
4. BLAKE, R. R., and WILSON, G. P., JR. Perceptual selectivity in Rorschach determinants as a function of depressive tendencies. *J. abnorm. soc. Psychol.*, 1950, 45, 459–472.
5. BUHLER, C., BUHLER, K., and LEFEVER, D. W. *Rorschach standardization studies.* Published privately by authors, 1948.
6. CATTELL, R. B. *Personality: A systematic theoretical and factual study.* New York: McGraw-Hill, 1950.
7. CRONBACH, L. J., and MEEHL, P. E. Construct validity in psychological tests. *Psychol. Bull.*, 1955, 52, 281–302.
8. CRONBACH, L. J. Statistical methods applied to Rorschach scores: A review. *Psychol. Bull.*, 1949, 46, 393–429.

9. DANA, R. H. An application of objective TAT scoring. *J. proj. Tech.*, 1956, 20, 159–163.

10. DORKEN, H., JR. The reliability and validity of spontaneous finger paintings. *J. proj. Tech.*, 1954, 18, 169–182.

11. ELIZUR, A. Content analysis of the Rorschach with regard to anxiety and hostility. *Rorschach Res. Exch.*, 1949, 13, 247–284.

12. ERON, L. D. Responses of women to the Thematic Apperception Test. *J. consult. Psychol.*, 1953, 17, 269–282.

13. FISHER, S., and CLEVELAND, S. D. *Body image and personality.* Princeton, N.J.: D. Van Nostrand, 1958.

14. FISKE, D. W., and BAUGHMAN, E. E. Relationships between Rorschach scoring categories and the total number of responses. *J. abnorm. soc. Psychol.*, 1953, 48, 25–32.

15. FRANK, L. K. Projective methods for the study of personality. *J. Psychol.*, 1939, 8, 389–413.

16. FRANK, L. K. *Projective methods.* Springfield, Ill.: C. C. Thomas, 1948.

17. GIBBY, R. G. Examiner influence on the Rorschach inquiry. *J. consult. Psychol.*, 1952, 16, 449–455.

18. GULLIKSEN, H. *Theory of mental tests.* New York: Wiley and Sons, 1950.

19. HAGGARD, E. A. *Intraclass correlation and analysis of variance.* New York: Dryden Press, 1958.

20. HARROWER, M. R. Group techniques for the Rorschach test. In Abt, L. E., and Bellak, L. (eds.) *Projective psychology.* New York: A. A. Knopf, 1950.

21. HARTMAN, A. A. An experimental examination of the Thematic Apperception Technique in clinical diagnosis. *Psychol. Monogr.*, 1949, 63, No. 303.

22. HOLT, R. R. The Thematic Apperception Test. In Anderson, H. H., and Anderson, G. L. (eds.) *An introduction to projective techniques.* New York: Prentice-Hall, 1951.

23. KINGET, G. M. *The Drawing-Completion Test.* New York: Grune & Stratton, 1952.

24. KLOPFER, B., and KELLEY, D. M. The Rorschach technique. Yonkers-on-Hudson, N.Y.: World Book Company, 1942.

25. LINDNER, R. M. The content analysis of the Rorschach protocol. In Abt, L. E., and Bellak, L. (eds.) *Projective psychology.* New York: A. A. Knopf, 1950.

26. McCLELLAND, D., ATKINSON, J. W., CLARK, R. A., and LOWELL, E. L. *The achievement motive.* New York: Appleton-Century-Crofts, 1953.

27. MACFARLANE, J. W., and TUDDENHAM, R. D. Problems in the validation of projective techniques. In Anderson, H. H., and Anderson, G. L. (eds.) *An introduction to projective techniques.* New York: Prentice-Hall, 1951.

28. MACHOVER, K. *Personality projection in the drawing of the human figure.* Springfield, Ill.: C. C. Thomas, 1948.

29. McREYNOLDS, P. Perception of Rorschach concepts as related to personality deviations, *J. abnorm. soc. Psychol.*, 1951, 46, 131–141.

30. MEEHL, P. E. Configural scoring. *J. consult. Psychol.*, 1950, 14, 165–171.

31. MORGAN, C. D., and MURRAY, H. A. A method for investigating phantasies: the Thematic Apperception Test. *Arch. Neurol. and Psychiat.*, 1935, 34, 289–306.

32. MUNROE, R. L. The inspection technique for the Rorschach protocol. In Abt, L. E., and Bellak, L. (eds.) *Projective psychology.* New York: A. A. Knopf, 1950.

33. O'REILLY, B. O. The objective Rorschach; a suggested modification of Rorschach technique. *J. clin. Psychol.*, 1956, 12, 27–31.

34. PASCAL, G. R., and SUTTELL, B. J. *The Bender-Gestalt Test.* New York: Grune & Stratton, 1950.

35. RAPAPORT, D., GILL, M., and SCHAFTER, R. *Diagnostic psychological testing. Vol. II.* Chicago: The Year Book Publishers, 1946.

36. ROSENZWEIG, S. The picture-association method and its application in a study of reactions to frustration. *J. Pers.*, 1945, 14, 3–23.

37. ROSENZWEIG, S. Idiodynamics in personality theory with special reference to projective methods. *Psychol. Rev.*, 1951, 58, 213–223.

38. ROTTER, J. B., and WILLERMAN, B. The Incomplete Sentence Test as a method of studying personality. *J. consult. Psychol.*, 1947, 11, 43–48.

39. ROTTER, J. B. Word association and sentence completion methods. In Anderson,

H. H., and Anderson, G. L. (eds.) *An introduction to projective techniques.* New York: Prentice-Hall, 1951.

40. SARASON, S. *The clinical interaction.* New York: Harper & Bros., 1954.

41. SCHAFER, R. *Psychoanalytic interpretation in Rorschach testing.* New York: Grune & Stratton, 1954.

42. SELLS, S. B., FRESE, F. J., JR., and LANCASTER, W. H. *Research on the psychiatric selection of flying personnel. II. Progress on development of SAM Group Ink-Blot Test.* Project No. 21-37-002, No. 2, Randolph Field, Texas: USAF School of Aviation Medicine, April, 1952.

43. SHNEIDMAN, E. S. *Thematic test analysis.* New York: Grune & Stratton, 1951.

44. STEIN, M. I. *The Thematic Apperception Test.* Cambridge, Mass.: Addison-Wesley, 1955.

45. THURSTONE, L. L. The Rorschach in psychological science. *J. abnorm. soc. Psychol.,* 1948, 43, 471–475.

46. TOMKINS, S. S. *The Thematic Apperception Test.* New York: Grune & Stratton, 1947.

47. TRITES, D. K., HOLTZMAN, W. H., TEMPLETON, R. C., and SELLS, S. B. *Psychiatric screening of flying personnel: Research on the SAM Sentence Completion Test.* Project No. 21-0202-0007, No. 3, Randolph Field, Texas: USAF School of Aviation Medicine, July, 1953.

48. TRITES, D. K. *Psychiatric screening flying personnel: Evaluation of assumptions underlying interpretation of sentence completion tests.* Report No. 55-33. Randolph Field, Texas: USAF School of Aviation Medicine, March, 1955.

49. WILSON, G. P. *Intellectual indicators in the Rorschach test.* Unpubl. doctoral dissertation, The University of Texas, Austin, Texas, 1952.

50. WITKIN, H. A., LEWIS, H. B., HERTZMAN, M., MACHOVER, K., MEISSNER, P. B., and WAPNER, S. *Personality through perception.* New York: Harper & Bros., 1954.

51. YOUNG, R. D., JR. *The effect of the interpreter's personality on the interpretation of TAT protocols.* Unpubl. doctoral dissertation, The University of Texas, Austin, Texas, 1953.

52. ZUBIN, J., and ERON, L. *Experimental abnormal psychology.* (Preliminary Edition) New York: New York State Psychiatric Institute, 1953.

Chapter 51

The Ideology of Research Strategies

SILVAN S. TOMKINS

The papers by Cattell on the psychometric approach to personality and by Holt on the clinical-experimental approach to personality [1] appear to have generated a discussion of one part illumination to two parts heat. As I listened to the enthusiastic recrimination between the rigorous, objective, psychometric multivariate experimentalists and the deep, sensitive clinicians I cannot escape the impression that we are host to an old familiar friend, the mote-beam mechanism. That we are united in our dissatisfaction with our present knowledge of the field of personality is abundantly clear. We differ only in our diagnosis of who shall be blamed, and how best each might atone and make restitution for his past sins and errors. It is not the first time that men have found it easier to tolerate their own failures when viewed, from a comfortable distance, in the behavior of others.

This article is reprinted from *Measurement in Personality and Cognition*, S. Messick and J. Ross (Eds.), 1962, with the permission of the author and John Wiley and Sons, Inc. It was given as a part of a conference on personality measurement sponsored by Educational Testing Service at Princeton, New Jersey, in October, 1960.

Our field is admittedly a difficult one, and our progress to date is somewhat less than the heart desires. Despite the revolutionary insights of Freud and the promise of factor analytic methods, there is an enduring, gnawing discontent which generates the flamboyant, inflated self-assertion of the clinician and factor analyst alike, and which also generates their mutually extrapunitive posture. To these somewhat jaded eyes and ears, the score is even, and lower than we would like it to be. It may well be that it will always so appear at the growing edge of our science or of any science. In knowledge as in virtue, there is no royal road. But it is just this suspicion which I think prompts the over-inflation, now of the value of free association in psychoanalytic space and, again, of the value of free rotation in factor analytic space. Neither method appears to me to have opened the royal road though both have opened exciting vistas. I will defend the pre-Freudian, pre-Thurstonean dogma that science begins and ends in an active brain enclosed in a body comfortably supported in an arm chair. In between these reflective moments are interposed a variety of fact findings, hypothesis testings, and statistical analyses designed to illuminate the cognition before and after. Which methods of fact finding, which methods of statistical analysis, appear to me to be of secondary importance so long as one has been bright enough, or persistent enough, or lucky enough, or all of these, to stumble onto something important. It seems highly improbable that any method will ever guarantee the discovery of truth. Nor should we forget that radical discovery is a rare event and that there are necessarily many more failures than successes. The whole spirit of the advocates of free association and of the protagonists of factor rotation belies to the investigator the fundamental recalcitrance of nature. The two methods have more in common than has been supposed. Each assumes that there are critical linkages between responses which will appear when the circumstances are made more favorable. Psychoanalysis assumes that the removal of the noise due to censorship and conscious control will lay bare these fundamental linkages, and factor analysis also assumes that co-variation of responses is the key to the underlying unities. Insofar as either of these methods does lay hold of co-variations, either in associations or other types of responses, we should be grateful for favors received. To suppose, however, that either method qua method has radically increased the probability either of discovery or of verification betrays an overweening optimism. It is as reasonable as the expectation that the invention of the correlation coefficient would surely produce laws, since one could now say how much co-variation there was between phenomena.

Personality appears to me to be organized as a language is organized, with elements of varying degrees of complexity— from letters, words, phrases, and sentences to styles—and with a set of rules of combination which enable the generation of both endless novelty and the very high order of redundancy which we call style. If we had to be blind about one or the other of these types of components, one should sacrifice the elements for the rules. Factor analysis appears to have made the opposite decision. It would tell what letters, or words, or phrases, or even styles were invariant and characteristic of a personality or of a number of personalities. I have not yet seen it generate the rules of combination which together with the elements constitute personality.

It is more than a matter of the linearity or non-linearity of relationships which the dynamic rules of combination generate. It is the sensitive variation of the dynamic relationships themselves which guarantee the complexity of the human being and at the same time complicate the problem for the theorist. If the human being is a computer, he has numerous programs and combinations of programs. So it frequently becomes more important to know whether the traits revealed by a factor analysis are themselves constant or labile, general or specific, or whether they vary in generality according to circumstance and if so why. I am supposing that a factor analysis of various measures of an operating automobile might reveal its components at the level of steering wheel, carburetor, brakes, and so on without yielding a model of the automobile as an integrated system. I would suppose that a factor analysis of a computer which never twice used the same program might be even less revealing. In short, it is my prejudice that factor analysis is as appropriate for the unravelling of a dynamic system as complex as man as a centrifuge might be, though the latter rotation would also yield some real and independent components of man's basic stuff.

It is no secret that my own orientation is closer to that of Holt than to Cattell. Holt's catholicism, his willingness to suspend judgment, his psychoanalytic orientation, his tolerance for variables which cannot yet be measured, his insistence on vigilance for the main chance, all of these recommend themselves to me, not as ends in themselves but as reasonable strategies of the logic of discovery.

This is probably because I was trained as

a philosopher and am still a philosopher, my own tragic destiny. When I could no longer tolerate the conceptual weightlessness of being orbited indefinitely in free-floating philosophic space, I descended, first to earth, and then into the underground, in Cambridge, Massachusetts, at the Harvard Psychological Clinic. Here, happily, for over a decade we observed, studied, and argued about human beings. The focus, as the title of Murray's first book [2] suggested, was *Explorations of Personality*. Difficult and unrewarding as any voyages of intended discovery can be, it never lacked excitement. Beyond the horizon was the truth about human nature, and if we failed to find the prize on one voyage we would surely capture it when we tried again. If this was a fool's paradise, it was at the least a paradise. After the war we were ultimately to be expelled from the Garden of Eden not for having tasted the fruit of the tree of knowledge, but for having been tempted by overweening pride and premature identification with God. The question changed from "Do I dare to eat an apple?" to "How can one be sure it really is an apple?" to "What do you mean by eating?", and finally to "Couldn't an automatic apple picker really do the thing more reliably?" My experience with philosophers had come full circle. I now found myself once again in the company of philosophers disguised as methodologists of psychology. Lest you think my dismay at this turn of events was entirely extrapunitive let me reassure you that there had been some return of the repressed in my own case too. I was busy showing that Mill's canons of inference could indeed be applied to the TAT [4], and then that this essential logic could be built into any projective test, and in particular into my own PAT [5], in such a way that a computer program could be written to do quite complex profile analyses which compared favorably with the analyses of the experienced clinician.

It would appear then, on the surface, that there is a very real consensus among the contributors to the present volume that reason, mathematics, logic, programming, and all the apparatus of objectivity are here to stay and that we are all on the side of the angels. There may nonetheless be a suspicion among you that Professor Holt and myself are only nouveau celestial and that we are conflicted and somewhat unreliable defenders of the power of reason and light, and consort from time to time with the Prince of Darkness. And in this suspicion you would be right. Why are we such reluctant angels? Basically, I think, because we cannot surrender our overweening pride and our secret hope that we are more than fallen angels and that some day we may no longer toil by the sweat of our logical and mathematical brows but eat of the fruit of the tree of knowledge and so be able to achieve the divine "aha" experience.

More seriously, I wish to defend the proposition that in any science the probability of information gain is directly proportional to the risk one is prepared to tolerate and that those who prefer verification over discovery and who prefer objectivity over subjectivity will necessarily enjoy limited gains in information.

All sciences range over a wide spectrum of complexity of affirmation and inference. Consider the differences between *tests* or *measures, laws,* and theoretical *systems.* Any measuring instrument or test, whether it be a ruler, a voltmeter, or a test for pregnancy, has essentially very modest aims. It purports to give a reliable answer to a very limited set of questions. Either the woman is pregnant or she is not; either the object measures one inch, two inches, three, four inches—up to 12 inches in the case of a ruler; either the object weighs one pound, two pounds—up to 30 pounds in the case of a baby scale; either the automobile is going 10, 20, or 100 miles an hour—such measures characteristically test simple variables and their power for any science is a derivative of the frequency of their use. Although a ruler or a scale will not *per se* generate laws or systems it will over and over again give some *limited* information about an *unlimited* number of test objects. It will tell that these 100,000 women are pregnant and those 100,000 are not. The instrument is usually designed for repeated use. Such a method, whether used in physics or psychology, is a highly specialized one, and a great price is paid for its undoubted virtues. That price is that it will never tell you more than that *some* aspect of a test object has *one* of a limited number of characteristics. There is a real question in my mind whether we possess one test in clinical psychology. We have characteristically wished to develop measuring instruments which permitted a bonus in the collection of information, frequently as an auxiliary type of further observation. The Rorschach and the TAT are clearly not tests in this sense, or at best they are sets of tests. My own very self-conscious attempt to devise such a simpleminded personality test has characteristically elicited the response that it doesn't give "enough" information to be very exciting—but neither does any test.

A law, in contrast to a test, is a much more pretentious affirmation. It says, at the very least, that if one aspect of a domain has one value, some other aspect of that domain also has a particular value. Such a law can ordinarily be expressed in a compressed form, mathematical or otherwise, so that the empirical determination of one variable specifies the value of another variable, with sufficient precision so that we need *not* in fact *test* the other variable. In contrast to a test, which is expected to keep on working until the end of time, a law lives on borrowed time. It is continually being subjected to experimental scrutiny to see whether it is a better law than one suspected, or what its boundary conditions are; as soon as exceptions to the law are found and a more general law formulated, the old law becomes a special case. In contrast to the test method, which is designed for continual repetition of the same procedure, no one ever repeats exactly the experiment by which a law is established, or at most it is replicated once or twice to make sure that what appeared to happen did in fact happen and is gen-

erally replicable. There would, however, be no point in repeating any of the classical experiments in any science except for pedagogical purposes. As soon as the finding has been established, the limits of the matter begin to be explored and variations of the conditions under which the law holds or breaks down are further probed.

Finally, a theoretical system is a still more pretentious set of affirmations. It may, as in the case of the Newtonian scheme, be based on a number of laws which together give a coherent account of a large domain or, as in the case of psychoanalytic theory, be based on a number of sub-theories.

As we go from tests, to laws, to theoretical systems, we increase the complexity of what is affirmed, and ordinarily also at the same time suffer certain paradoxical consequences. While the number of theoretical alternatives continues to increase as complexity increases, the resistance to change also increases. A new scale, or voltmeter, or ruler, is relatively easily introduced into a science. A new law is established with more difficulty and a theoretical system is surrendered only once in a while, because it explains too much and because it becomes increasingly difficult to construct an alternative which is better. The types of evidence, inference, and cognitive activity necessary to construct a test, a law, and a theoretical system are at the least of a quite different order of complexity.

The second distinction I would make in types of cognition and inference cuts across the foregoing distinction. I refer to the radical difference between discovery and proof. The cognitive process and types of inference which are necessary to demonstrate that a law is really a law seem to me quite distinct from those exciting, frustrating pursuits after will-o'-the-wisps, 99 percent of which prove to be blind alleys. The latter knowledge is born only in pain and error and there is no royal course through the vast uncharted sea of risk—and in the nature of the case there can be no royal road. This is not to say that the complexities of very high-order thinking may not be objectified. They can be and indeed are being objectified, in such attempts as the general problem solving program of Newell, Shaw, and Simon [3]. My argument is rather that such inference is as distinct from formal logical inference as a test is distinct from a theoretical system.

The spectrum of complexity which would be generalized by these two criteria, therefore, would range from the relatively simple demonstration, via the correlation coefficient, that a test did in fact test what it purported to test (that a scale, for example, gave honest weight under the average variation in temperature of the room in which it was used) to the attempt of a theorist to produce a theoretical system which would account for all the phenomena accounted for by the best present theoretical system, and then some. In the first attempt there are very few ways of failing, with reasonable intelligence and diligence, and in the latter attempt there are very few ways of succeeding, given the highest intelligence and the most passionate commitment to the enterprise.

If science is, as I think, a many-splendored thing, why do some of us choose to break our intellectual necks or to drown in a whirlpool of risk, and others of us insist on doing something in which both the probability of success is higher and in which the ease of demonstrating *that* we have succeeded is also guaranteed by reliance on the power of logic or mathematics?

I have for the past five years been studying this question in a variety of fields ranging from mathematics through philosophy, theories of education, jurisprudence, theology, and psychology. In every field there appear controversies which have been sustained over hundreds of years, evoking highly polarized and articulate positions and producing passionate commitment to one position and hostility to the other, and which appear to be supported by minimal empirical evidence. Further, it is the same argument which appears to be equally debated in mathematics, as in philosophy, jurisprudence, and psychology. The argument is whether a human being is the most real and valuable entity in nature, an end in himself—or whether that which is most real and valuable is some norm, some ideal essence quite independent of the human being. In philosophy it is, on the one hand, the extreme idealistic posture which holds that the world is created by man and, on the other hand, the extreme Platonic view that neither the world nor man is real or valuable, but that there exists an ideal set of essences, of which the world and man are imitations. In the humanistic view it is what the individual wants that defines what is good, true, and beautiful. In the normative view the individual must struggle to attain value and reality by conformity to the ideal norm. These two postures are generated, I believe, by socializations which stress either that the child is an end in himself, that he is loved for what he is, or which say that if he wishes to grow up to be a good human being he must conform to a norm administered by parents, whether he feels like it or not. Such initial self-evaluations then generate a resonance for one or another of the following types of ideologies in science. In mathematics one is impressed either by its *correctness* or its *freedom*. Thus Courant says of the "game" interpretation of mathematics, "If mathematics were only a game . . . no adult could be seriously interested in it . . . it would make of mathematics . . . a capricious . . . childish game." Poincaré on the same subject says, "Mathematics is a wonderful *game*. In it man achieves his highest reach . . . his greatest freedom . . . because in mathematics man is completely free to construct an infinite number of mathematical systems." The attitudes toward the word "game" appear to be diagnostic of a very general attitude toward childhood—toward *affect* and *ideation*—as ends in themselves which represent man's highest function, or else as childish impulses in the sense that they are capricious and to be outgrown. In art we see a recurrent polarity of classicism and romanticism, and in literary criticism a recurrent polarity of the image of the *lamp* versus the *mirror*. In theories of government there is a polarity between theories of the state as the major instrument through which men attain such limited freedom as is possible, versus theories of the state as of the people, for the people, and by the people.

In aesthetics there is a recurrent polarity between beauty as in the object, or in the mind of the beholder; in theories of education a recurrent polarity, now intensified, between education as the learning of information versus a stimulation of the potential of the individual. In theories of perception in psychology we see this polarity between those who would account for perception by an analysis of the stimulus, against those who regard the percept as a personal construct. Within the Rorschach we are confronted with the insistence on norms by Beck, and the more free-wheeling cognition of Klopfer.

Those who have insisted on the objec-

tive, whether in science or in art, have derogated man and insisted on certainty. Those who have insisted on the subjective have glorified man and stressed the value of both play and risk. It is our conviction that the humanistic ideology, in the long run, will yield both the greater and the surer payoff.

REFERENCES

1. MESSICK, S., & Ross, J. (Eds.) *Measurement in personality and cognition.* New York: John Wiley & Sons, 1962.
2. MURRAY, H. A. *Explorations in personality.* New York: Oxford Univer. Press, 1938.
3. NEWELL, A., SHAW, J. C., & SIMON, H. A. Elements of a theory of human problem solving. *Psychol. Rev.,* 1958, 65, 151–166.
4. TOMKINS, S. S. *Thematic Apperception Test.* New York: Grune, 1947.
5. TOMKINS, S. S., & MINER, J. B. *Tomkins-Horn Picture Arrangement Test.* New York: Springer, 1957.

Chapter 52 ~

Introduction from
A Factorial Study of Perception

LOUIS L. THURSTONE

Let us consider a personality as a dynamical system that will be described eventually by a limited number of parameters, each of which will be identified some day in terms of different aspects of the *physical* system that constitutes a person. Let us not get stalled here in disputes about systematic psychology, which is, on the whole, little more than the verbal elaboration of scientific ignorance. When the more important parameters of this dynamical system become known, we may find it necessary to discard some of the conventional psychological categories and distinctions that are more logical than scientific, such as the differentiation between cognition and conation and various descriptive categories in terms of social and overt end-products rather than in terms of the physical system that constitutes the person. We shall probably find that the fundamental parameters or factors are on the whole more primitive

This article is reprinted from *A Factorial Study of Perception* by L. L. Thurstone, 1944, with the permission of Mrs. Thelma G. Thurstone and the University of Chicago Press.

than our present logical classifications. Some of them will probably be quite specific and limited in range, while others may dominate and determine the style of a man's behavior and intellectual activities. The corresponding descriptive names for these parameters may or may not agree with the descriptive categories in terms of which people are now described in social discourse.

The usual procedure in studying personality in its intellectual as well as in its temperamental aspects has been to set up lists of performances or lists of questions that represent what we conceive to be socially important and useful categories and to look for individual differences and correlations with social criteria of various types of personal acceptability—to get along with people and to have mechanical aptitude are examples. In factorial studies we have departed from that pattern by setting up the performances so as to differentiate between factors even though some of the factors may not be of immediate practical importance. The differentiation between the two verbal factors V and W has been studied because of the possibility of identifying these factors more definitely and quite aside from their social or educational significance. As is so often the case, the result reveals the distinction to be of very considerable social and educational interest, even though that was not the primary objective in identifying the factors.

The present study is an attempt to proceed more directly to what might be conceived as the fundamental dynamical characteristics of a person without regard to the socially differentiable behavior that is determined by that system. Such an approach as is here represented is very much of a gamble, but it is not inconceivable that several exploratory studies may reveal fruitful leads. In selecting the measurements to be studied, we used several criteria. We should prefer measurements which cannot be easily influenced by the subject. The ideal test measurement is one that can be obtained from a passive subject who is not trying to race against time for a good score. Unfortunately, we have only a few such measurements. We have avoided those measurements that seemed likely to be restricted in significance, such as visual acuity, and we have preferred those measurements which might reflect some parameter of more central significance or association. It is a matter of personal opinion or guess at the present state of knowledge what such measurements might be. A few examples might be listed here. It seemed to us that the duration of negative movement after looking at the Exner spiral might be such a measurement. Others might be flicker-fusion rate, dark-adaptation time, the perceptual constancy effects, rate of alternation of ambiguous perspective, rate of reversals in retinal rivalry, and speed of closure under various conditions. All these effects might be of only local and ocular significance, but there is at least a possibility that individual differences here might be the outcropping of central parameters that might be significant in describing the dynamical system that constitutes the person.

A specific example and the possible psychological interpretation may help further to indicate the *type* of relations we are trying to find. In some experiments on individual differences in apparent-movement effects we varied the rate of the cycles from the slowest, which gives the appearance of intermittency, to the higher speeds, which produce good movement, and to the still higher rates, which produce the stationary state. The same observations were tried in descending order. It was observed here, as in the psychophysical method of limits, that the limen, or rate at which one state changes to the next state, was higher for ascent than for descent. This is typical of the limiting method, and it was not surprising to find it also in apparent movement. Individual differences were noted among the subjects in the laboratory, and one of them showed a considerable difference between the ascending and descending limens. That person is very deliberate in disposition and movement, and one wonders if the lag or displacement in the ascending and descending limens can be associated with analogous characteristics in the dynamics of personality. This hypothesis could be formally investigated to determine whether a characteristic in the psychophysical experiment is a reflection of a more general characteristic of the person as socially observed. If that should be the case, we should conclude that the factor or parameter determining a perceptual result is not confined to the ocular mechanisms involved but that it reflects more central characteristics.

It should be pointed out that we are deviating here from a current research pattern. If individual differences are found in some phase of perceptual dynamics which may be centrally determined, the habitual procedure would be to give the same subjects some personality schedule of questions and to compare the perceptual performance with some sort of personality score, but such a procedure might be misleading. It is probably better to list a few subjects whose perceptual performance has some conspicuous characteristic and to list also some subjects who do not have that characteristic or who are the opposite. Then we should ask how these subjects differ. If it should be found, for example, that the subjects who show considerable lag in the method of limits are noticeably more deliberate in movement and temperament than those who show little or no lag in the psychophysical experiments, then we should have a lead for further and more intensive study than if we merely had a correlation with a hodgepodge questionnaire of general social adjustment. A number of hypotheses of this general kind are involved in the perceptual tests of this exploratory study.

The fundamental hypothesis involved here is that the dynamics of perception, and of other restricted functions, are not isolated and that these several functions are so related that some characteristics of the person as a whole might be inferred from the dynamics of one of these functions. In these days when we insist so frequently on the interdependence of all aspects of personality, it would be difficult to maintain that any of these functions, such as perception, is isolated from the rest of the dynamical system that constitutes the person. The type of investigation we are here proposing consists in studying the dynamics of some function or of several functions and of identifying the differentiable parameters. The parameters will appear first as factors if we use the factorial methods, and later they will be known in terms of the physiological mechanisms involved. Observations should be made to determine possible associations between these parameters and the socially observable characteristics of people. By this general route we may be able eventually to arrive at a psychological understanding of personality with better foundations than by the logical categories which we are in the habit of imposing by the conventions of verbal description.

The present investigation of personality traits with the aid of perceptual material, and especially with the use of visual Gestalt effects, has for its principal purpose the presentation of ambiguous material to the subject with a definite and easily understandable judgment for him to make. The individual differences that we find in these effects are probably not of the peripheral kind involved in mere sensory acuity. The individual differences that are found depend on attitudes which the subject adopts spontaneously. He is rarely conscious of the existence of different attitudes that could be adopted voluntarily in these tasks. It is one hypothesis that the attitudes which the subject adopts spontaneously in making the perceptual judgments in these experiments reflect in some way the parameters that characterize him as a person.

53 ~

The Perception of the Upright

HERMAN A. WITKIN

All of us normally have a quick, automatic and correct sense of how we are located in space. We can tell without hesitation whether our bodies are upright or tilted, how much they are tilted and in what direction. This ready ability to orient ourselves to the vertical and horizontal axes of space has two bases. First, our bodies are acted upon by the force of gravity, the direction of which corresponds to the true upright. We apprehend the direction of gravity through the continuous postural adjustments we make to its pull. In addition to "feeling" our bodies, we see them against our surroundings. The "visual field," filled with prominent verticals and horizontals, provides our second basis for determining whether or not we are upright.

With equal ease and accuracy we can determine the positions of other objects. In hanging a picture on the wall, for example, we make it straight by comparison with our

own bodies, as well as with the axes of the surrounding walls, ceiling and floor.

Ordinarily the two standards available for determining the upright coincide in direction. It is therefore impossible to tell at any given moment whether an individual is establishing his position on the basis of how his body feels, how well it "fits" its surroundings, or both. Nor can we know whether, in hanging a picture, he is guided predominantly by the conspicuous lines of the surrounding room or by the position of his own body.

The question with which we began our studies was orthodox enough: What is the relative importance of the two standards used in the perception of the upright? More than 15 years ago our laboratory, then at Brooklyn College, began a study of this problem. Today, at the Downstate Medical Center of the State University of New York, we are investigating personality development in children. These areas of research seem very far apart, yet the present work grew out of the original studies. (Our collaborators at various stages in the development of the research have been S. E. Asch, H. B. Lewis, M. Hertzman, K. Machover, P. B. Meissner, S. Wapner, H. F. Faterson, R. B. Dyk, D. R. Goodenough and S. A. Karp.)

The transitions in our work reflect a general change that has been taking place in the psychologist's approach to perception, the process by which we form impressions about ourselves and our environment. Earlier studies had been focused primarily on characteristics of the stimulus and on sense-organ and neural functioning. Today many investigations are concerned in addition with the personality of the perceiver: his motivations, emotions and defenses. Research stimulated by this more comprehensive approach has disclosed significant connections between perception and personality. Such findings have had an important impact on our theoretical notions. Moreover, because perception can be studied under manageable laboratory conditions, proof of its close association with personality has opened up a promising experimental route to personality investigation.

In our first experiment we set out to "separate" the gravitational standard of the upright from the standard provided by the visual field, with the aim of evaluating the importance of each. Among the several situations we devised for this purpose, two proved especially productive. The apparatus for one consists of a small room that the experimenter can tilt to any degree to the left or right, and a chair for the subject that also can be tilted to the left or right. The structure and "interior decoration" of the room provide many clearly defined lines that accentuate its vertical and horizontal axes. With room and chair tilted by set amounts, the experimenter moves the chair at the subject's direction until the subject reports himself to be upright. The room—the limited world we have created for him—remains meanwhile in its initial tilted position. The conditions of the test thus separate the subject's two standards for judging the upright: the pull of gravity on his body and the direction of the tilted visual field are in disagreement. If, when he finally believes that he is "straight," the chair is close to the true upright, we may reasonably infer that he perceives body position primarily on the basis of sensations from within. On the other hand, if the chair is tipped far over toward the axes of the tilted room, he is determining body position mainly by reference to the visual field. His way of perceiving can thus be quantified, because he is required to carry out a meas-

FIGURE 53–1   *The tilting room–tilting chair test.*

urable action that reflects his perception. The measure is the number of degrees he is tilted when he reports himself straight.

The second test enabled us to study individuals' perception of the "straightness" of objects apart from their own bodies. The subject sits in complete darkness, facing a luminous rod in a luminous frame; the rod and frame can be moved independently of each other. He sees them first in tilted positions. Then, while the frame remains tilted, he directs the experimenter to move the rod until it appears upright. In some trials the subject sits erect, and in others his chair is tilted to one side.

Here again the visual field and the subject's bodily sensations are in disagreement, each indicating a different vertical. If he reports that the rod is straight when objectively it is tipped far toward the tilt of the frame, he is relying primarily on the visual field. If, on the other hand, he adjusts it close to the true upright, he is relying mainly on body position, and is relatively independent of the visual field. When the subject sits erect, it is of course easier for him to utilize body position as a standard of reference. The degree of tilt of the rod gives us a measure of the subject's way of perceiving.

These and other experiments at first suggested that the visual field tends to play the more important role. Very soon, however, a most striking and unexpected finding began to emerge from our studies. We found that people differed considerably in their manner of perceiving the upright. So great was the range of individual variation that it was impossible to derive any general conclusion about the perception of the upright that would hold true for all members of an experimental group.

In the search for an upright body position some people were always able to bring the chair close to vertical no matter how much the room was tilted. Obviously their orientation depended to a high degree on bodily sensations, and was influenced hardly at all by the position of the visual field. At the other extreme, some people had to be more or less aligned with the tilted room before they could perceive themselves as upright. Tilted as much as 35 degrees (in one extreme case 52 degrees), they answered "Yes" when asked: "Is this the way you sit when you eat your dinner?" The impression of uprightness, though mistaken, was immediate and automatic. However, when such people closed their eyes, they at once felt quite tilted. With their eyes still closed, they were able to bring themselves very close to the true upright. In this situation, providing the eyes are closed, anyone can adjust his body to the upright with little or no error. The marked differences among individuals manifested themselves only when the visual field had a chance to exert its influence.

Again, in establishing the position of the rod, some people were invariably able to bring the rod close to the true upright despite the extreme tilt of the frame. Other subjects saw the rod as straight only when it was aligned with the tilted frame and so was objectively far out of plumb.

We had set out to discover which of the two standards utilized in perception of the upright is the more important under various conditions, and we had found that our question was unanswerable. Instead we had encountered, under essentially identical conditions of stimulation, marked individual differences in spatial orientation. Such variation, it seemed clear, must stem basically from differences in characteristics of the perceivers, a possibility that had received little or no attention in traditional theories of perception. We decided to focus our subsequent investigations on a systematic study of the nature and origin of individual differences in perception.

Immediately we were confronted with the question: Does a person tend to determine the upright in the same way under various circumstances? We tested the same group of subjects in our series of orientation tests, and found them to be highly consistent in performance. Those who in the rod-and-frame test were able to adjust the rod close to the true upright by reference to body position were also able to make their bodies straight in the tilting-room–tilting-chair test. Others, consistently guided by the visual framework, tended to align the rod with the tilted frame and their own bodies with the tilted room. It is striking that the person perceives his own body and "neutral" external objects in a similar fashion.

Does a tendency toward one or the other of these ways of functioning characterize all of the individual's perception, and not his spatial orientation alone? To answer this question we tested the same group of subjects in a series of perceptual situations that in no way involve body position or orientation toward the upright, but do resemble the orientation tests in requiring the separation of an item from its surrounding field.

One of these is the "embedded-figures" test, in which the subject is asked to locate a simple figure "hidden" within a large complex figure (see Figure 53–2). People who tend to see the complex figure passively, in accordance with its dominant pattern, will of course have difficulty in locating the simple figure within it. We found that those who took a long time to discover the hidden figures were the same people who had tended to align their own bodies with the axes of the tilted room and to align the rod with the tilted frame.

The finding of significant relationships between performance in the orientation tests and performance in the embedded-figures test (and other non-orientation tests) helped us define more precisely the nature of the individual differences we had observed. With only the results of the orientation tests available, we had characterized perception in terms of primary reliance on either bodily sensations or the visual field. Now we had a broader basis of classification. In each case our experimental situations required the individual to separate some item—be it his own body, a rod or a simple geometric figure—from its background or context; to "break up" and deal analytically with a given situation; to maintain an active "set" against the influence of the surrounding field. We designated as "field-independent" those who showed a

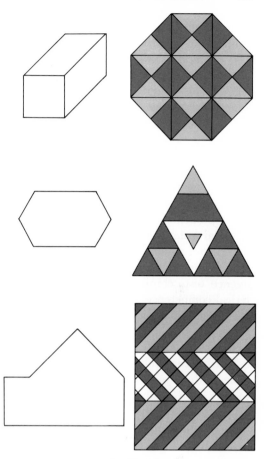

FIGURE 53–2 Embedded-figures experiment challenges the subject to find the patterns shown at left in the more complex patterns at right, and thereby tests his ability to perceive the visual field analytically. Facility at this task is correlated with ability to establish the upright independently of the visual field in the tilting-room and rod-and-frame experiments.

capacity to differentiate objects from their backgrounds. Conversely, the "field-dependent" subjects were those whose performance reflected relatively passive submission to the domination of the background, and inability to keep an item separate from its surroundings. In the general population perceptual performances reflecting the extent of field-dependence or field-independence are ranged in a continuum rather than constituting two distinct types. On the basis of this more comprehensive definition, we learned much more about characteristic styles of perceiving. We found a significant difference in perception between the sexes. Women as a group are likely to tip their bodies farther toward the axes of the tilted room, and the rod farther toward the axes of the tilted frame; and it takes them longer to discover the simple figures hidden in the complex designs of the embedded-figures test.

Investigations by ourselves and others have also shown that the way in which the individual perceives is an expression of a more general aspect of his functioning. Field-independent people, for example, excel at problems that require the isolation of essential components from a context and the recombination of these components in new relationships. Since our standard intelligence tests emphasize this kind of "analytical competence," field-independent children tend to achieve significantly higher I.Q.'s. We have been able to show that the higher I.Q.'s of such children result specifically from their relatively superior performance on those parts of intelligence tests that require such ability; they do not score significantly better than field-dependent children in questions concerned with vocabulary, information and comprehension. In the realm of social behavior various studies have shown that field-independent people are in general less dependent on others. They have greater ability to hold themselves apart from the pressures of their social environment, sometimes even to the point of isolation from other people. Ability to orient one's own body independently of the surrounding visual field, or to keep any object separate from its background, thus seems directly associated with capacity to function with relative autonomy of the social milieu in everyday life.

Our orientation tests had evidently tapped a source of important, deep-seated psychological differences among people. We determined next to investigate the origin and development of these differences. We began by studying changes in perception during growth. For this purpose we gave our battery of perceptual tests to separate groups of boys and girls of various ages between 8 and 20 years. At intervals

over a period of years we tested one group from the time they were 8 until they had reached 13, and another group from age 10 to age 17. These studies all led to the same conclusion: Children tend to be field-dependent early in their perceptual development and to become field-independent as they grow up (see Figure 53–3). The ability to determine the position of the body apart from the tilted room, to perceive the position of a rod independently of the tilted frame, to pick out a simple figure obscured by a complex context—all improve, on the whole, as the children become older. The change was particularly marked in the 8-to-13-year period. After this there was a tendency to level off, and even a slight tendency to regress.

Within these average trends the children showed marked differences at every age level. At the same time, all of the children we were able to follow over a seven-year period showed high stability of performance. They tended to maintain their same relative positions within the group as they grew older, even though averages for the group changed with age. These findings suggested that the child's perceptual style tends to be established early in life, and to remain relatively stable.

The field-dependent mode of perception is thus identified with earlier stages of growth and in this sense is more primitive. We were led by this finding to the general hypothesis that children who remain field-dependent, in comparison with most children their own age, may have made less progress in their general psychological development. Extensive personality studies confirmed this hypothesis.

Each child was evaluated by an interview and a series of projective tests (the Rorschach, Figure Drawing and Thematic Apperception tests, and a miniature-toy play situation). The psychologists knew nothing about how the children had performed in the perceptual situations. Guided by the general hypothesis of the study, however, they devised from these tests a series of "indicators" of relevant personality

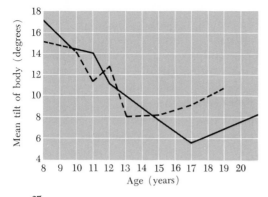

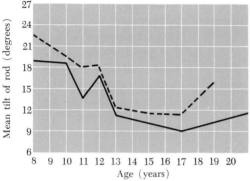

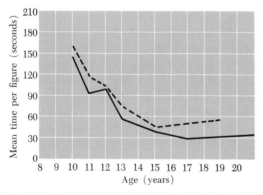

FIGURE 53–3   *Age curves for boys (solid line) and girls (broken line) in tilting-room (top), rod-and-frame (middle), and embedded-figures (bottom) experiments show progressive development in the direction of "field-independence" (that is, increasing capacity to overcome the influence of the surrounding field) as children grew older. Boys tend to be more "field-independent" than girls, and both sexes show a slight shift toward "field-dependence" in late teens.*

characteristics. The correlations found between these indicators and performance on the perception tests were checked by re-

peating the study with a new group of children.

In general these studies show that the organization of the personality of the field-independent child is more complex. He usually has a more definite sense of his role and status in the family. He tends to be more aware of his own needs and attributes and also of the needs and attributes of others. In terms of his age group he is usually able to function with greater independence in a variety of situations. The defenses and controls he has available to channel his impulses and direct his actions are generally better developed. More often than his field-dependent contemporaries he shows a desire and a capacity for active striving in dealing with his environment. His interests tend to be both wider and better developed.

It would be a mistake to infer that these traits necessarily imply better adaptation to life situations, or absence of pathology. Maladjusted children are found in both the field-independent and field-dependent groups. Personality disturbances in field-dependent children, however, tend to be of the kind that stem from relatively primitive, amorphous, chaotic personality structure. In field-independent children personality disturbance is more likely to take such forms as over-control, over-intellectualization and isolation from reality. Perceptual style does not by itself indicate whether a child will have a "healthy" personality; it may, however, suggest the form that pathological developments may take.

Searching deeper for the source of these basic differences among children, we asked ourselves: To what extent may constitutional characteristics of children contribute to the differences? To what extent are the differences determined by the life experiences of children, both in the family and in society, in the course of growing up? To answer these questions a broad program of research is clearly required. We considered the study of mother-child relationships to be a particularly good starting point. We based the undertaking on the hypothesis that children with a field-dependent style of perceiving are likely to have been hampered in their opportunity for psychological growth.

A group of 10-year-old boys whose perception, intelligence and personality we had already studied intensively were the subjects for this attempt. Each boy's mother was interviewed at home by an interviewer who did not know the child or the child's test results. The interviewer evaluated each mother's role in relation to her son in terms of whether it was predominantly "growth-constricting" or "growth-fostering." The method of evaluation may be better appreciated in the light of a few of the criteria by which a mother would be judged as growth-constricting: Because of fears and anxieties about her child, or especially strong ties to him, she markedly restricts the child's activities; her dominance and control are not in the direction of helping the child achieve increasing responsibility; her physical care of the child seems inappropriate to his age; she limits the child's curiosity and stresses conformity.

The classification of the mothers turned out to be significantly related to the children's perceptual performance. Boys with a field-dependent style of perceiving more commonly had mothers who were characterized as growth-constricting; field-independent boys more often had mothers characterized as growth-fostering.

Of course differences in early-life experiences do not tell the whole story. Constitutional differences among children may also be extremely important. Hence, parallel to our investigations of mother-child relationships, we have recently begun studies that may shed light on the possible connection between characteristics observed in infancy and the kinds of pervasive differences we found in later development.

The question of how we perceive the upright, with which we began, can now be seen as woven into the total fabric of an individual's adaptations and as related to the complex of experiences that have shaped this development. The finding of connections among areas of psychological functioning formerly considered quite unrelated suggests that even circumscribed perceptual processes need to be studied in the context of the individual's general psychological characteristics. The characteristics of the perceiver, however, do not constitute the sole determinants of perception. It would indeed be a mistake to conclude that each of us experiences a world of his own making. Our perceptions are basically anchored to "what is there," and they are significantly dependent on the particular kinds of sensory and neural equipment we possess. At the same time people have well-established, preferred ways of perceiving, attributable to variations in individual psychological organization and making for individual differences in perception under essentially the same conditions of stimulation. These preferred ways of perceiving are an integral, ever-present part of the individual's psychological make-up. Under some conditions, when the situation is vague and contains conflicting elements, they may play a large role in determining the perceptual outcome. Under other circumstances, as when the situation is clear and compelling, they may have no more than minimal expression.

The intimate linkage between perception and personality makes available a very useful approach to the experimental study of personality. Since the individual's responses in diverse situations all reflect a common core of personal attributes, his characteristic way of functioning can be identified by study of any one area of activity. Moreover, as we have seen in our work, perception lends itself to objective study under conditions that permit ready manipulation and control. This is not to suggest that such procedures should replace the methods devised by the clinical psychologist. With the further development and integration of both experimental and clinical methods, great forward strides are in prospect for the study of human psychology.

Chapter 54

Complexity-Simplicity
as a Personality Variable

FRANK BARRON

This is the fourth in a series of reports on the identification and measurement of a factor in perceptual preferences which seems to have considerable generality in human behavior. It may be described briefly as a bipolar factor which opposes a preference for perceiving and dealing with complexity to a preference for perceiving and dealing with simplicity, when both of these alternatives are phenomenally present and when a choice must be made between them. The kinds of phenomenal fields which have been the objects of the research to be reported here, and which seem to possess discriminable degrees of simplicity and complexity, are interpersonal relations and innerpersonal psychodynamics, politics and economics, religion, relations to authority, attitude towards sensual experience, social conformity and adherence to tradition, and originality and intellectual independence.

This article is reprinted from the *Journal of Abnormal and Social Psychology*, 1953, with the permission of the author and the American Psychological Association.

As we shall point out more fully later, a somewhat similar factor had previously been identified in the field of esthetic preferences by Eysenck, who attempted also to construct a measure of it [4, 5]. It was, however, rediscovered independently and more or less incidentally by Welsh, who published the first of the four reports referred to above [12]. A new measure of it was developed by Welsh and the present writer [3]. The latter explored some of its correlates in preferences for painting and in self-conception [2]. In the present paper we shall deal with further correlations of this dimension with variables in several areas of behavior. Before this further work is reported, however, a brief review of the findings which led up to it seems in order.

THE WELSH FIGURE PREFERENCE TEST

This series of investigations began with the construction by Welsh of a test consisting of several hundred line drawings in black ink on 3 × 5-in. white cards. He intended it as a nonverbal psychiatric diagnostic instrument, and sought originally to develop scales to measure such variables as Hysteria, Depression, Schizophrenia, Paranoia, and so on. The subject (S) was asked to indicate for each figure whether he liked it or did not like it, and thus to sort the drawings into two groups according to his preferences.

The effort to develop a diagnostic instrument is still in progress, but did not immediately meet with success. In seeking to understand the nature of the preferences being expressed, however, Welsh carried out a factor analysis of various scales defined on the basis of his own judgment as to the stimulus-character of the drawings: e.g., bilaterally symmetrical figures, three-dimensional figures, figures with many projections, figures with few projections, ruled-line drawings, free-hand drawings, angular figures, curved figures, and so on.

From this analysis, two factors emerged: an acceptance-rejection factor (expressing the general tendency of the subject either to like or to dislike the figures), and a second, bipolar factor, orthogonal to the first, whose poles, as determined by inspection of the figures, seemed to be simplicity (combined with a rather obvious, bilateral symmetry) and complexity (usually associated with a much less obvious kind of balance, which in previous reports has been referred to as "asymmetry").

This latter factor bears a close resemblance to that earlier identified by Eysenck, and named by him the K factor. Eysenck has demonstrated for a number of stimulus classes (colors, odors, paintings, polygons, poetry) the existence not only of a general factor of esthetic appreciation, but of a secondary, bipolar factor as well. The second factor presents the same polar opposition noted by Welsh, one pole being represented by preference for the simple polygon, the strong, obvious odor, the poem with the obvious rhyming scheme and the definite, unvarying, simple rhythm, and the simple, highly unified picture; at the other pole is preference for the more complex polygon,

the more subtle odors, the poem with a less obvious rhythm and a more variable and loose rhyming scheme, and the complex, more diversified picture.

THE BARRON-WELSH ART SCALE

A measure of this secondary, bipolar factor in the Figure Preference Test was constructed in much the same incidental manner as that in which the factor had been discovered. It had happened that several artists were included in the control sample which Welsh had used for comparison with psychiatric patients, and these artists all clustered together at the complex-asymmetrical pole of the factor. The present writer, in search for measures of artistic discrimination for inclusion in a battery of assessment procedures, recalled this finding, and was led to wonder whether the factor was not significantly related to ability to discriminate the good from the poor in artistic productions. In any case, the Figure Preference Test clearly consisted of stimulus material which might yield such a measure. The most straightforward way of checking on this seemed to be to give the entire 400-item test to a sample of artists and non-artists, and then to construct, by means of the item-analysis technique, a scale which would embody the differences between artists and nonartists in their preferences for the figures; and finally, of course, to cross validate the scale on new samples of artists and nonartists. This was accordingly done, and a highly reliable and valid scale resulted [3].

Inspection of the items in the scale quickly revealed that the secondary, bipolar factor which had emerged from the factor analysis was reproduced in the later empirically derived measure. The artists *liked* figures which were highly complex, asymmetrical, free-hand rather than ruled, and rather restless and moving in their general effect. (Several artists, in reacting to them, had described them as "organic.") The figures which were *liked* by people in general, however, were relatively simple, often bilaterally symmetrical, and regularly predictable, following some cardinal principle which could be educed at a glance. These figures were described by artists as "static," "dull," "uninteresting."

This convergence of the results of factor-analytic and external-criterion methodologies seems especially worth noting. Factor analysis not only revealed the psychological unity in perceptual preferences with which we are here dealing, but in addition provided the clue to an extremely important external correlate which could be used for straightforward empirical scale derivation. The scale is now properly designated as an Art Scale, but can be equally properly construed as a measure of the factor found by Eysenck and by Welsh. It has both psychological unity and external predictive power. Most of the remainder of this paper will be devoted to what Cattell refers to as "peripheral validation," which consists essentially of an extension of the investigation to correlates of the factor in areas of behavior which are, prima facie, remote from that in which the factor was discovered. First, however, we shall review briefly some previously reported findings concerning the relationship of these figure preferences to preferences in paintings and to self-descriptions.

ART PREFERENCES AND SELF-DESCRIPTION

The two test procedures which have already been analyzed and reported on [2] in relation to the Art Scale are the Gough Adjective Check-List [8] and a Painting Preference test assembled by the present writer. The former is a list of 279 common personally descriptive adjectives, from among which S is to select (by checking) those which he thinks describe himself; the latter consists of 105 postcard-size reproductions in color of paintings by a large number of European artists, which S is asked to sort into four groups according to the degree of his liking for the paintings.

The polarity noted in these three domains of figure preferences, art preferences, and adjective self-descriptions may best be summed up in this fashion:

I

In Figure Preferences
Preferring what is simple, regularly predictable, following some cardinal principle which can be educed at a glance.

In Art Preferences
Preferring themes involving religion, authority, aristocracy, and tradition.

In Adjective Self-checks
Contented, gentle, conservative, patient, peaceable, serious, individualistic, stable, worrying, timid, thrifty, dreamy, deliberate, moderate, modest, responsible, foresighted, conscientious.

II

In Figure Preferences
Preferring what is complex, irregular, whimsical.

In Art Preferences
Preferring what is radically experimental, sensational, sensual, esoteric, primitive, and naive.

In Adjective Self-checks
Gloomy, pessimistic, bitter, dissatisfied, emotional, pleasure-seeking, unstable, cool, irritable, aloof, sarcastic, spendthrift, distractible, demanding, indifferent, anxious, opinionated, temperamental, quick.

FURTHER RESULTS

The relationships cited in the preceding section were found in a sample of 40 male graduate students, from about a dozen departments of the University of California, who had taken part in weekend living-in assessments at the Institute of Personality Assessment and Research. These Ss had been carefully studied by means of a large number of objective tests and experimental procedures, and had also been interviewed concerning their personal history, their values and philosophical views, their professional aspirations, and so on. At the conclusion of the series of (four) assessments, they were all rated by the staff[1] on 40 variables which previous personality researches had indicated as being of general importance.

We are thus in a position to see how the simplicity-complexity dimension is manifested in many different areas of behavior, by correlating the Figure Preference measure with other variables. For the most part, we shall restrict ourselves to relationships obtaining in this one sample of 40 Ss. However, the scale was also given, together with some questionnaires, to a sample of over 100 male undergraduates in two Pennsylvania colleges, and the correlates of Complexity in that sample will be described. Data are also available from the assessment study of 80 other subjects (PhD candidates and medical school seniors) who took a revised form of the test.

For ease of reporting, we shall adopt the technique of drawing a composite picture of two ideal, modal persons, the simple and the complex, on the basis of the correlational results. The statistical support for the portrait will be cited as we go along.

Several cautions must be observed in interpreting such material, however. For one thing, since the picture is based entirely on group relationships, it will fail in some respects to do justice to unique patterning of the variables in individual cases. Like the average man, the composite simple or complex person would be hard to find.

In addition, one must be particularly cautious in evaluating the "goodness" and "badness" of the correlates of this dimension. As a previous report [2] pointed out, it is important to bear in mind that, in terms of the total constellation of factors making for personal effectiveness and pro-

fessional promise, simple persons and complex persons were equally represented among Ss who were rated as possessing that combination of attributes in high degree. This equal representation held also among the group of Ss with low ratings. One must conclude that both simplicity and complexity have their effective and ineffective aspects; they simply result in different sorts of merits and liabilities.

As we have indicated, in order to facilitate the reporting of the data, we shall adopt two conventions, one with regard to the scale and the other with regard to the designation of the Ss. The Barron-Welsh Art Scale will hereafter be referred to as a measure of the variable *Complexity*, since it is that feature of the scale which is of interest here, and since the scale is so scored that preferences like those of artists (hence, preference for the complex) earn S a high score, while preferences like those of people in general (i.e., preference for the simple) earn a low score. The designations *Complex person* and *Simple person* will be employed to indicate a modal high scorer and a modal low scorer, respectively, on this particular test.

THE CORRELATIONAL COMPOSITE

This description begins with personal tempo, which is usually a rather easily observed, surface attribute, complicated though its ramifications may be in the personal character. It is "surface" in the sense that it is what we are first presented with when we meet another person; we take in almost automatically such attributes as flow of speech, speed of response, rate and intensity of expressive movement, and expansiveness or constriction in interaction with the environment.

It will be recalled that on the Adjective Check-List our Complex Ss had described themselves as "quick" and "temperamental." The Simple Ss, on the other hand, had characterized themselves as "deliberate" and "dreamy." These self-descriptions would

[1] Staff members who participated in these assessments were D. W. MacKinnon, R. N. Sanford, Erik H. Erikson, R. S. Crutchfield, R. E. Harris, H. G. Gough, P. Dempsey, R. Taft, and the present writer. It need hardly be said that this entire research project is greatly indebted to the staff who contributed the ratings and carried out the assessment.

seem to be borne out by the staff's ratings of Ss on such variables as Personal Tempo, Verbal Fluency, and Constriction. The correlations with Complexity are, respectively, .50, .29, and −.42.[2] Thus, the Complex person is more intensely expressive, expansive, and fluent in speech than the Simple person. The Simple person, on the other hand, is seen as being more natural and likeable, and also as more straightforward and lacking in duplicity. (Complexity correlates −.44 with Naturalness, −.27 with Likeability, and .56 with Deceitfulness, as rated by the staff.) This picture of easy and uncomplicated simplicity is further supported by staff ratings of such factors as Good Judgment, Adjustment, and Abundance Values, all of which go with preference for the simple figures. (The r's with complexity are −.39, −.31, and −.34, respectively.)

"Adjustment" had here been defined as "getting along in the world as it is, adequate degree of social conformity, capacity to adapt to a wide range of conditions, ability to fit in." As we shall see later, this kind of adjustment is not an unmixed blessing; the "unadjusted" complex person, who does not fit in very well in the world as it is, sometimes perceives that world more accurately than does his better-adjusted fellow.

The negative correlation with Abundance Values, combined with the positive relationship of Complexity to Deceitfulness, merits some comment. Abundance Values was defined as "Sense of security and optimism regarding the future, absence of fears of deprivation, of being exploited, and of being cheated." Deceitfulness was identified with "duplicity, lack of frankness, guile, subterfuge." Again, one recalls the adjective self-descriptions of the Complex people: gloomy, pessimistic, bitter, dissatisfied, demanding, pleasure-seeking, spendthrift. There is certainly some suggestion here of early oral deprivation, of pessimism concerning the source of supply, which is

seen as untrustworthy and which must be coerced, or perhaps tricked, into yielding. It is as though the person had reason to believe that he would not "get what was coming" to him unless he made sure that he did, by whatever device might be available. It is this lack of infantile *trust* (as Erikson names it) that leads to adult duplicity and craftiness. One aspect of complexity then (and perhaps a penalty sometimes attaching to it) is, to render it in the common phrase, a sort of "two-facedness," an inability to be wholly oneself at all times. The more simple, natural, and likeable person finds it easier to be always himself.

This suggested relationship of Complexity with the derivatives of orality (i.e., character traits determined in part by a relatively long and intense oral stage of development in the child) receives some slight support from several other correlations. If it is true, as clinical evidence generally indicates, that oral fixation leads to feminine character traits in men, one would expect to find Complexity related to masculinity-femininity measures. This proves to be the case, the r with the Minnesota Multiphasic Personality Inventory Mf being .18, that with the Strong Interest inventory Mf (which is so scored that the feminine man earns a low score) −.39. Rated Effeminacy, defined as "Effeminate style and manner of behavior; softness," is also related to Complexity, the r being .29. Thus the Complex man has an attitude of acceptance towards his femininity, showing itself in soft, gentle, and effeminate behavior. In the light of this, it is not surprising to find both Sentience ("seeking and enjoying sensuous impressions, sensitive, esthetic") and Sensuality ("acceptance of and capacity for sensual gratification") being related positively to Complexity (r's of .25 and .26 respectively). This completes a picture of low but consistent correlations of Complexity with some of the derivatives of orality.

The preference for Complexity is clearly associated with originality, artistic expression, and excellence of esthetic judgment.

[2] All correlations reported in this paper are based on N's of 40, with the standard error therefore being .16.

Originality was one of the three criterion variables around which the assessment research program was organized, and every subject was rated by the faculty members of his department on the degree of Originality he had displayed in his work. The Complex person is seen as more original, both by the assessment staff and by the faculty of his department. The correlation with the criterion ratings on Originality is .30.

Complexity is also related to Basic Good Taste as measured by a test which presents various alternative arrangements of formal design elements and asks S to choose the most esthetically pleasing combination. This test, constructed by Sanford E. Gerard, is scored a priori in terms of known principles of composition. The correlation with Complexity is .44.

The Ss were also given a mosaic construction test devised by Turney, and known as the Turney Designs. In this test, the task is to construct a mosaic design in rectangular form from several hundred one-inch square solid-colored pieces of pasteboard (20 different colors being represented). The designs were then rated by members of the Art Department of the University, in terms of the artistic merit of the productions. The ratings thus obtained correlate .40 with Complexity.

To be purely speculative for the moment, one might wonder whether there is not some relationship between the more enduring and intense oral stage of development in our Complex Ss suggested by some of the data, and their evidently greater originality and sensitivity to the esthetic character of objects. Fowler [7] has shown that oral character traits are significantly associated with textural responses to shading on the Rorschach, and psychoanalytic writers, particularly Rank, have emphasized the relationship between femininity and artistic productiveness in men. Sanford (personal communication) has noted a tendency towards somewhat slower social development in the earlier years in original people, which would fit in nicely with the notion

that a person must, as it were, have more commerce with himself and his feeling states and less with the environment during childhood if he is later to have sufficient communication with his own depths to produce the original thought. In this view, originality evidenced in maturity is to some extent dependent upon the degree to which the person in early childhood was faced with a complicated relationship to the maternal source of supply, combined with his capacity to persist at and eventually to achieve some mastery of this earliest problem situation. The argument would be that this primitive experience of phenomenal complexity sets a pattern of response which results in slower maturation, more tentativeness about the final form of organization, a resistance to early crystallization of the personality, and finally, greater complexity in one's view both of the outer and of the inner worlds.

Perhaps such speculation is unwarranted, however, and in any case it is clear that a great many other factors are involved in determining originality. What can be said is that originality and artistic creativeness and discrimination are related to the preference for complexity, and that the latter bears some relationship to sentience and femininity in men.

The Complex person's greater flexibility in thought processes is shown by a correlation of $-.35$ with rated Rigidity, defined as "inflexibility of thought and manner; stubborn, pedantic, unbending, firm." A 22-item scale for Rigidity, developed by Gough and Sanford, yielded an r of $-.18$ with Complexity. The two scales (Rigidity and Complexity) were later found to be related significantly and negatively to one another in a sample of medical students (r of $-.36$).

That repressive overcontrol may sometimes be associated with the preference for simplicity has already been indicated by the correlation of $-.42$ of Complexity with Constriction, and by another correlation of .50 with Impulsiveness. It is shown also in the relation of the Complexity measure to psychiatric variables which are scaled on the Minnesota Multiphasic Personality Inventory. With Hysteria, for example, Complexity correlates −.30, while with Schizophrenia it correlates .37, and with Psychopathic Deviate .36. Thus Complexity goes along both with lack of control of impulse (the *Pd* scale) and with the failure of repression which characterizes the schizophrenic process. This is by no means to suggest that any of these graduate students showed schizophrenic tendencies of a pathological degree, but it is reasonable to suppose the *Sc* scale of the MMPI has built into it the correlates of the sort of free-floating symbolic activity and frank confrontation and expression of the unconscious which is often so startlingly present in schizophrenic patients. The *Hy* scale, on the other hand, picks up the tendency of S to repress aggressive and erotic impulses, or to render them innocuous by rationalization, reinterpretation, or gratification in a substitutive manner which will not cause conflict. At the risk of being oversimple, we might say that preference for the complex in the psychic life makes for a wider consciousness of impulse, while simplicity, when it is preferred, is maintained by a narrowing of that consciousness.

That the perceptual decision in favor of admitting complexity may make also for greater subjectively experienced anxiety is indicated by the correlation (.34) of Complexity with Overt Anxiety as measured by the Welsh Anxiety Index [11] on the MMPI. To tolerate complexity one must very often be able to tolerate anxiety as well, this finding would seem to say.

The negative correlation with *Hy*, and the positive correlation, of about the same magnitude, with *Sc* would seem to fit well with a finding of Eysenck's that his own measure of the Complexity-Simplicity dimension, the K test, correlates in this same direction with his Hysteria-Dysthymia factor.

Complexity is related negatively, although not significantly so, to Political-Economic Conservatism (−.22) and to Ethnocentrism

(−.27), as measured by Form 60 of the Levinson-Sanford scale [10]. These *r*'s are bound to be minimum estimates of the true relationship, since there was considerable restriction of range on both *PeC* and Ethnocentrism, the means being significantly lower than that of the general population. Some corroboration of this finding is furnished by attitudes expressed by Ss in the Pennsylvania sample, as we shall show later.

In addition to being less rather than more conservative, the person who prefers complexity is socially nonconformist. Staff ratings of Conformity correlate −.47 with Complexity, while the self-ratings of Ss on Conformity correlate −.53. Related to this is a correlation of −.29 between Complexity and Submissiveness, which was here defined as "deference, willingness to be led, compliance, over-ready acceptance of authority." In addition, Complexity correlates positively (.36) with the *F* scale of the MMPI. The *F* scale consists of items which are psychologically heterogeneous, the defining property of the scale being that all items in it have a low probability (about .1) of being answered in the scored direction. Thus, the higher the *F* score, the more likely it is that the subject holds a set of socially dissident and deviant opinions.

COMPLEXITY AND INDEPENDENCE OF JUDGMENT

There is one further bit of information, of a rather intriguing nature, which bears on this question of conformity. Asch [1] has devised an experimental social situation in which S is put under pressure to conform to a group opinion which is false. In this experiment, there are from eight to sixteen ostensible Ss, only one of whom, however, is naive; the rest are in the hire of the experimenter. The task is to judge which of three lines of variable length meets a standard line; or, put otherwise, to match the length of a given line with one of three lines which are themselves not equal to one another. The Ss, one by one, announce their judgments publicly. The naive S is so placed as to be one of the last to announce his judgment. On the critical trials, the hired majority gives a prearranged false answer. The experimental variable is called Yielding, which is defined as agreeing with group opinion when it is in error. Yielding scores, in the prototypical experiment, range from 0 to 12, zero yielding being known as Independence.

In this experiment, approximately 25 per cent of all Ss are Independent, while the 25 per cent at the other extreme of the distribution Yield from 8 to 12 times. These two quartiles were selected for intensive personality study, in which the present writer participated as a test consultant and analyst. Among the tests employed in this part of the research was the measure of Complexity whose correlates we have been describing.

Since the experiment and the personality study of Ss will be fully reported elsewhere, we shall note here only that the mean difference in Complexity scores between the Independents and Yielders was in the predicted direction, i.e., Independents were more Complex. In a sample of 40 Haverford College students, the difference was significant at the .001 level, while in a sample of 60 Temple University students it was significant at the .05 level. For both groups combined, the difference was significant at the .01 level.

We have referred earlier to the negative relation of Complexity to Adjustment, part of the definition of which involved "an adequate degree of social conformity," and "ability to fit in." It is indeed a delicate question as to what, in social conformity, is an adequate degree thereof; different people seem to make different requirements of others in this matter. It is almost implicit in the design of the Asch experiment that to abandon the evidence of one's own senses in favor of group opinion is carrying a good thing too far; while the popularity of many a modern nation within its own boundaries tends to become so categorical that even judicious dissent from this or that aspect of national policy may get labeled "disloyal,"

"deviationist" or, the shift in adaptation level in invective being what it is, something even worse.

In any event, it seems that these complex and independent Ss did not "fit in"; they faced up to the anxiety of being a minority of one, and continued to call the turn as they saw it. They accepted the fact that they held a different opinion from the rest of the group, and they were able to persist in their belief in their own opinion. Some, indeed, were not surprised at all at this, and seemed to take pleasure in being among the Opposition; others were made extremely anxious, to the point of panic; while there were other independent and complex Ss who, while somewhat perturbed, went their own way with unassertive but firm confidence in their own judgment. In this latter group, independence seemed more genuinely critical and differentiated; and it is this sort of independence which, when it is allied with complexity, should prove constructively unadjusted and actually productive of original work rather than simply a deviant attitude.

RESPONSES TO AN ATTITUDE QUESTIONNAIRE

In the same study, Asch and the present writer collaborated in the construction of a criterion-specific questionnaire, which consisted of 86 items which were especially selected, or written anew, to test particular hypotheses concerning personality differences between Independents and Yielders. Again, the results of this effort will be described in another publication; however, the results of an item analysis of the Independence questionnaire against the criterion of high or low score on Complexity may be given here. In this analysis, the Haverford and Temple groups were combined, and the questionnaire responses of the highest 27 per cent of scorers on the Complexity scale were compared with the lowest 27 per cent. Items which showed differences significant at the .05 level are given below.

ANSWERED TRUE BY HIGH SCORERS
ON COMPLEXITY

1. The unfinished and the imperfect often have greater appeal for me than the completed and the polished.
2. I could cut my moorings . . . quit my home, my parents, and my friends . . . without suffering great regrets.
3. Politically I am probably something of a radical.
4. I think I take primarily an esthetic view of experience.
5. I would enjoy the experience of living and working in a foreign country.
6. Many of my friends would probably be considered unconventional by other people.
7. Some of my friends think that my ideas are impractical, if not a bit wild.
8. I enjoy discarding the old and accepting the new.
9. When someone talks against certain groups or nationalities, I always speak up against such talk, even though it makes me unpopular.

ANSWERED TRUE BY LOW SCORERS
ON COMPLEXITY

1. I don't like modern art.
2. Disobedience to the government is never justified.
3. Perfect balance is the essence of all good composition.
4. Straightforward reasoning appeals to me more than metaphors and the search for analogies.
5. It is a pretty callous person who does not feel love and gratitude towards his parents.
6. Things seem simpler as you learn more about them.
7. I much prefer symmetry to asymmetry.
8. Kindness and generosity are the most important qualities for a wife to have.
9. When a person has a problem or worry, it is best for him not to think about it, but to keep busy with more cheerful things.

10. It is the duty of a citizen to support his country, right or wrong.
11. Barring emergencies, I have a pretty good idea what I'll be doing for the next ten years.
12. I prefer team games to games in which one individual competes against another.
13. An invention which takes jobs away from people should be suppressed until new work can be found for them.

Since these Ss were all undergraduate students in Pennsylvania colleges, and their average age was 19, it is of some interest to compare their characteristics with the correlates of Complexity noted in the sample of California PhD candidates. By grouping items, we may summarize the personality differences between the Complex and Simple persons in the Pennsylvania sample somewhat as follows:

The Complex person:
1. is artistic (4);
2. has unconventional friends, occasionally is visited by an impractical, not to say wild, idea, and would rather be creative and neurotic than normal and ordinary (6,7,10);
3. is politically somewhat radical, and can be militantly opposed to racial prejudice (3,9);
4. is aware of present imperfections, would welcome and has faith in future developments (1,2,5,8).

The Simple person:
1. doesn't like modern art (1);
2. particularly values kindness and generosity in a wife (as opposed to implied alternative values), and feels that the proper filial sentiments towards one's parents are love and gratitude (8,5);
3. feels that a citizen should support his country, right or wrong, and that disobedience to the government is never justified. Somewhat allied to this, he prefers a team effort to individual competition (2,10,12);

4. prefers symmetry to asymmetry, considers perfect balance the essence of good composition, and prefers straightforward reasoning to metaphors and the search for analogies (7,3,4);
5. has clear plans for the future, and considers that things seem simpler as you learn more about them (11,6);
6. believes that a person with a problem or worry should not think about it, and that inventions which take jobs away from people should be suppressed until new work can be found for them (9,13).

The general pattern is certainly similar to that shown by the correlations we have been reporting. In Pennsylvania as in California, preference for simplicity is associated with social conformity, respect for custom and ceremony, friendliness towards tradition, somewhat categorical moral judgment, an undeviating patriotism, and suppression of such troublesome new forces as inventions which would temporarily cause unemployment. This last item is almost prototypical of the simple person's orientation towards repression as a psychic mechanism. In the California sample, it was shown in the negative correlation of Complexity with Hysteria and the positive correlations with Psychopathic Deviate and Schizophrenia. Its derivatives appear in many other characteristic attitudes as well, such as acceptance or rejection of sensual experience, of conventional religion, of paintings of unclad ladies, and so on. For "invention," write "impulse," and it is not hard to see an analogy to the common clinical formulation of the function of repression in the hysterical character.

The correlates of preference for complexity in this undergraduate sample are, again, much like the correlates of the corresponding preference among the PhD candidates. Complexity goes along with artistic interests, unconventionality, political radicalism, strong cathection of creativity as a value (even at the expense of "normality," as the item puts it), and a liking for change.

It seems evident that, at its best, prefer-

ence for simplicity is associated with personal stability and balance, while at its worst it makes for categorical rejection of all that threatens disorder and disequilibrium. In its pathological aspect it produces stereotyped thinking, rigid and compulsive morality, and hatred of instinctual aggressive and erotic forces which might upset the precariously maintained balance.

There is a passage in Hugo's *Les Misérables* which is remarkably coincident with these observations. It occurs at that point in the narrative when Javert, the singleminded and merciless representative of the law, has turned his own world upside-down by allowing Jean Valjean, the outlaw whom he had so relentlessly pursued, and whom he finally had in his grasp, to escape. He says to himself, in this surprising moment, "There is something more then than duty." At this, ". . . he was startled; his balances were disturbed; one of the scales fell into the abyss, the other flew into the sky. . . ."

. . . To be obliged to acknowledge this: infallibility is not infallible, there may be an error in the dogma, all is not said when a code has spoken, society is not perfect, authority is complicate with vacillation, a cracking is possible in the immutable, judges are men, the law may be deceived, the tribunals may be mistaken . . . to see a flaw in the immense blue crystal of the firmament! . . .

Certainly it was strange, that the fireman of order, the engineer of authority, mounted upon the blind iron-horse of the rigid path, could be thrown off by a ray of light! that the incommutable, the direct, the correct, the geometrical, the passive, the perfect, could bend! . . .

Until now all that he had above him had been in his sight *a smooth, simple, limpid surface; nothing there unknown, nothing obscure; nothing which was not definite, coordinated, concatenated, precise, exact, circumscribed, limited, shut in, all foreseen;* authority was a plane; no fall in it, no dizziness before it. Javert had never seen the unknown except below. *The irregular, the unexpected, the disorderly opening of chaos,* the possible slipping into an abyss; that belonged to inferior regions, to the rebellious, the wicked, the miserable.[3]

This passage brings together many observations made intuitively by Hugo and arrived at in a more pedestrian manner in this research. A precise simplicity is seen to be related to authority, dogma, tradition, morality, constriction, and repression; the opposite of all these things is typified by the flaw in the crystal, by the irregular, by disorderly chaos; such qualities as are to be found in the inferior regions, where reside the rebellious, the wicked, and the miserable. The emphasis here is pathological, and the dichotomy absolute, but if we extend the range into normal behavior and admit the many shortcomings of the typology, there is considerable agreement between Hugo's [9] intuition and this set of correlations.

RESERVATIONS AND DISCREPANT FINDINGS

So far as the correlational results in the California sample are concerned, it is evident that they must be accepted with some caution, since there is considerable possibility that chance error alone would account for some of the significant correlations. In addition, some variables would be correlated with one another in this sample but not in the general population, and a correlation of Complexity with just one of a set of atypically related variables would contribute to misleading correlations of the others of that set with the Complexity variable.

However, the findings from the Temple and Haverford nonassessment samples would tend to increase our confidence that many of the correlations found in the California assessment group would stand up when subjected to further investigation. There is also another source of evidence, although it is open to some question. The correlates of a revised and significantly different form of the Complexity measure in

two other assessment samples (40 more PhD candidates, and 40 medical school seniors) are known. In general, they are very much the same as those reported in this paper; in some cases, the r's are higher ($-.39$ with PeC, e.g., and .45 and .39 with Originality). However, there are some discrepant findings which should be noted, even though the Complexity measures are not strictly comparable.

In the first place, the negative relations of Complexity to Naturalness, Likeability, and Adjustment become zero-order in both the medical and graduate student samples. In addition, the positive relationship with Deceitfulness disappears, being slightly negative in the second sample of graduate students and exactly zero in the medical sample.

Several relationships which were zero in the first California sample become significantly positive in both of the succeeding samples. Complexity shows correlations with Intellect of .42 and .41; with Breadth of Interest of .33 and .39; with Sense of Humor of .39 and .33; with Cathexis of Intellectual Activity of .42 and .29. (The correlations in the graduate school sample are given first, those in the medical sample second.)

Work is going forward on further investigation of these results. Within a year or so a sample of at least 200 Ss will have been assessed, which should yield fairly stable correlations. An effort is being made to develop other measures of the complexity-simplicity dimension, with some attention to capacity as well as preference for dealing with and resolving complex phenomenal fields. The scale is also being used in nonassessment settings, such as psychiatric clinics, and as stimulus material in memory experiments.

SUMMARY

This paper has described the correlates of a bipolar factor in perceptual preferences which opposes a preference for perceiving and dealing with complexity to a preference

---

[3] Italics mine.

for perceiving and dealing with simplicity, when both of these alternatives are phenomenally present and a choice is made between them. The correlates ramify through many areas of human behavior and attitudes, including innerpersonal psychodynamics, interpersonal relations, and more broadly social spheres of behavior, such as politics, religion, group interaction, and the like.

It was emphasized that these types have both their effective and ineffective aspects, so far as human functioning is concerned. At times there is considerable merit in the simple view, while on other occasions some ease may profitably be sacrificed for greater phenomenal richness.

A measure of this factor was described, and its correlates were reported. Calling the factor variable *Complexity*, we note this pattern of relationships to it:

1. It is related positively to personal tempo, verbal fluency, impulsiveness, and expansiveness.
2. It is related negatively in one sample to naturalness, likeability, lack of deceitfulness, adjustment, and abundance values, but in other samples a revised form of the measure shows no significant relationship to these variables, so that the finding must await further checking before being credited.
3. It is related positively to originality, good taste, and artistic expression, and its revised form in two other samples shows significant positive correlations with intellect, sense of humor, breadth of interest, and cathexis of intellectual activity (none of which were significantly related to it in the first sample).
4. It is related positively to sensuality, sentience, esthetic interest, effeminacy, and femininity in men.
5. It is related negatively to rigidity and constriction.
6. It is related negatively to control of impulse by repression, and positively

to expression of impulse and to breakdown of repression.
7. It is related negatively to political-economic conservatism, to subservience to authority, to ethnocentrism, and to social conformity.
8. It is related positively to independence of judgment.

REFERENCES

1. Asch, S. E. Effect of group pressure upon the modifications and distortion of judgments. In H. Guetzkow (Ed.), *Groups, Leadership and Men*. Pittsburgh, Pa.: The Carnegie Press, 1951.
2. Barron, F. Personality style and perceptual choice. *J. Pers.*, 1952, **20**, 385–401.
3. Barron, F., & Welsh, G. S. Artistic perception as a factor in personality style: Its measurement by a figure-preference test. *J. Psychol.*, 1952, **33**, 199–203.
4. Eysenck, H. J. The general factor in aesthetic judgments. *Brit. J. Psychol.*, 1941, **31**, 94–102.
5. Eysenck, H. J. "Type"-factors in aesthetic judgments. *Brit. J. Psychol.*, 1941, **31**, 262–270.
6. Eysenck, H. J. *Dimensions of personality*. London: Routledge, Kegan Paul, 1947.
7. Fowler, C. Personality correlates of the differential use of shading on the Rorschach test. Unpublished bachelor's thesis, Bennington College.
8. Gough, H. G. Predicting success in graduate training. A progress report. Berkeley: Univer. of California, Institute of Personality Assessment and Research, 1950. Hectographed.
9. Hugo, V. *Les Misérables*. New York: The Modern Library.
10. Levinson, D. J., & Sanford, R. N. A scale for the measurement of anti-Semitism. *J. Psychol.*, 1944, **17**, 339–370.
11. Welsh, G. S. An anxiety index and an internalization ratio for the MMPI. *J. consult. Psychol.*, 1952, **16**, 65–72.
12. Welsh, G. S. A projective figure-preference test for diagnosis of psychopathology: I. A preliminary investigation. Unpublished doctor's thesis, Univer. of Minnesota, 1949.

Chapter 55

The Generality of Cognitive Complexity
in the Perception of People and Inkblots

JAMES BIERI / EDWARD BLACKER

Theories of behavior that use perceptual or cognitive constructs have found it necessary to postulate some organizing or schematizing process which is held responsible for the active interpretation and representation of external events to the organism. The ego of Freudian theory is considered to mediate between the environment and the organism, while Lewin speaks of the ". . . functional firmness of the boundaries between individual and environment" in discussing the impact of the environment upon the individual [11, p. 107]. Tolman [14] discusses the conditions under which the "cognitive map" of the organism operates as an intervening variable in behavior. Bartlett [1] utilizes the concept of "schema" to refer to the organization of previous experience which affects behavior in a current situation. Piaget [12] discusses the developmental aspects of the assimilation and differentiation of the en-

This article is reprinted from the *Journal of Abnormal and Social Psychology*, 1956, with the permission of the authors and the American Psychological Association.

vironment. In a recent formulation, Kelly [9] has utilized the notion of a "personal construct system" to help explain the individual's behavior in actively perceiving and responding to the meaningful environment. All such formulations imply two things about the role of perception in behavior. First, perception is an active process involving a transformation of sensory data into a conceptual scheme consistent with the previous learning and experience of the individual. Secondly, the conceptual scheme is structured differently from one individual to another, and an understanding of these *structural* differences is of value in predicting the behavior of the individual. Thus, in Freudian theory the ego has certain reality-testing functions which are affected by its stage of development and its characteristic defenses. Lewin speaks of the degree of differentiation of the inner personal regions of the life space and Tolman discusses the effects of broad and narrow cognitive maps on behavior. If we assume that every individual has a cognitive system or scheme for construing his environment, there remains the problem of how we characterize the structure of this system so as to obtain meaningful predictions about behavior.

In an earlier paper [3], the position was taken that one way of approaching the problem of cognitive structure was to posit a dimension of complexity-simplicity. That is, an inference can be drawn about the relative complexity of an individual's cognitive system from the measured complexity of his perceptions of external events. Operationally, complexity is measured by the variability of responses given to a finite realm of stimuli. Essentially, we are asking, in how many different ways can a person perceive a certain set of events? The assumption is made that the more differentiated the system is relative to these events, i.e., the more alternative *perceptions* of an event are available, then the more alternative *behaviors* will be available in that situation.

An important question arises as to the generality of an individual's cognitive system from situation to situation. It seems evident that an individual with a developmental pattern of experiences varying from very intensive in some situations to little experience in others will have learned to approach these different situations with varying levels of cognitive complexity. However, it seems unwise to postulate a capricious specificity to the individual's cognitive behavior from situation to situation. Rather, it is assumed that relatively consistent, enduring modes of cognitive schematization will characterize the individual's behavior across situations. Genetically, we assume that as the individual's cognitive system develops in one realm of experience, it will tend to generalize to some extent to new realms of experience subsequently encountered by the individual. Vernon [15] has recently discussed the functions of "schemata" in different types of experimental perceptual situations. Vernon and others have criticized experimental studies of form qualities, constancy, and motivational factors as perhaps relying too much on transitory, artificial states rather than upon states and situations more readily encountered in everyday life.

In line with this criticism, and in view of the importance of the perception of people for personality theory, we would emphasize the primary importance of the individual's cognitive system as it is organized about the perception of people in his life space. Thus, among the first objects in the environment with which the infant has intimate contact are people. As most personality theories stress, the period of infancy and early childhood is one in which important, perhaps basic, perceptions and differentiations are developed relative to the future course of the individual's interpersonal experience. Might it not be then, that the structure of the cognitive system the child learns in relation to his perception of people is basic in determining the structure of the system relative to other stimuli and events in his life? Without being concerned now about the *causal* sequence involved, we can formulate the fundamental problem to be investigated in the present study: Can there be established a degree of generality between the complexity of the individual's cognitive system in the perception of people and in the perception of events that fall outside the immediate realm of interpersonal experience?

The measure of cognitive complexity in the perception of people that is used in this study has evolved from a series of attempts [3, 9] to express objectively the degree of differentiation an individual possesses in his perception of others. This measure will be described in detail in the section on method. The measure of complexity of cognitive behavior using nonhuman stimuli was derived from the behavior elicited on a modified Rorschach-test situation. Rorschach inkblots were used not only because of the importance and relevance of this instrument to clinical practice and research, but also because it affords two kinds of behavior which can be analyzed, namely, the *determinants* utilized in giving a response and the *content* of the response itself. In a manner to be discussed below, both the determinants given by an individual and the content given by an individual can be conceptualized as to their relative complexity. Again, it should be mentioned that the basic operation for measurement of cognitive complexity is essentially response variability to a prescribed realm of stimuli.

With these considerations in mind, we are now in a position to state the hypotheses to be tested:

I. Significant positive relationships exist between the complexity of subjects' perceptions of people and the complexity of their perceptions of inkblots relative to the determinants used.

II. Significant positive relationships exist between the complexity of subjects' perceptions of people and the complexity of their perceptions of inkblots relative to the content elicited.

METHOD

Subjects (Ss) in this study consisted of 40 male university undergraduates who were paid to serve in psychological experiments.

COMPLEXITY MEASURES

Perception of people.   The Repertory Test (Rep Test) devised by Kelly [9] for evoking "personal constructs" was used to obtain the perceptions of others. This technique consists of presenting S with the names of three persons known to him and asking S to sort the three in such a manner that two are perceived as alike or similar in some important personal way and different from the third in this respect. After S states the similarity of the two sorted together, he is asked the opposite of this perceived characteristic. Thus, S may sort two persons as similar to each other and different from the third because the two are "sincere," and the opposite of this *for* S might be "insincere." After the initial perception and its

opposite are obtained, S is presented with three more persons and asked to sort them in an analogous fashion. The names of the persons sorted have been placed on cards by S according to a standard list of "role titles" supplied by the experimenter (E). In the present study, the following role titles were used on the Rep Test:

a. Yourself

b. Your brother closest to you in age (or person most like a brother)

c. Your closest girl friend

d. The most successful person whom you know personally

e. Someone you know personally whom you admire

f. Someone you know personally whom you would like to help or for whom you feel sorry

These role titles were selected from a larger group of role descriptions used in previous research as offering maximum discrimination in terms of perceptions elicited. The six persons were sorted by S in all possible combinations of three such that no three names appeared together in a sort more than once. In all, 20 sorts were thus obtained, with a perception of similarity and its opposite being obtained on each sort. Essentially, then, S was confronted with a task in which he was asked to perceive a fixed number of stimuli in different combinations. The complexity of S's perceptions of others was measured in terms of the number of different perceptions (NDP) S gave in the 20 sorts. If, in giving a perceived similarity and difference on a sort, S gave the same verbal similarity *or* difference which he had given on a previous sort, it was scored as a repeated perception. It should be noted that a stringent criterion of response repetition was used, i.e., S had to use the *same* word or words in his perceived similarity or difference as used previously. Theoretically, S could receive a maximum complexity or NDP score of 20 or a minimum NDP score of one.

The NDP scoring was done by one of the authors. The reliability of this scoring was obtained by selecting ten protocols at random and having a judge score these records independently according to the criteria outlined above. The interscorer reliability coefficient for these ten cases was .92. In addition, an estimate of the stability of the NDP measure was obtained by repeating the sorting procedure with 19 Ss after an interval of two weeks. The test-retest reliability coefficient obtained was .82. The magnitude of this latter coefficient indicates an adequate degree of stability in this measure of the complexity of perceptions of others.

Perception of inkblots. Approximately two to three weeks after the Rep Test was administered, each S was given individually the modified Rorschach procedure so that every S would have a constant series of stimuli to perceive, a series that would be repeated so as to afford opportunity for variable interpretations to be evoked to the same stimuli. Thus, both the Rorschach situation and the Rep Test contain the crucial features necessary for our complexity measure.

The Rorschach modification used has been described in detail in another paper [4]. It consists of ten Rorschach large details (D), one from each of the ten cards. All other portions of the blot are blocked out by means of a template which exposes only the desired blot portion. Five of the blots are chromatic and five are achromatic. The particular blot details used were selected because of their judged ability to evoke a variety of responses, both in terms of content and in terms of determinants. Beck's notation [2] for the ten details thus selected, in order of administration, are: Card I, (D 4); Card II, (D 2); Card IV, (D 1); Card III, (D 2); Card V, (D 4); Card VIII, (D 2); Card VI, (D 4); Card IX, (D 1); Card VII, (D 9); Card X, (D 1).

The inkblots were presented to S using standard Rorschach instructions except for the following changes: (a) S was instructed to look at the *whole* blot portion in giving his response; (b) the blot was removed as soon as S gave one response; (c) if S started to rotate the card he was asked to keep it in the position in which it was handed to him. When S had given one response to each of the blots, he was told that he would be asked to go through them again, and this time he was to tell E *what else* each blot could be. Following this second series, the blots were again presented to S with the same instruction to tell E what else each could look like this time. After this third series, an inquiry was conducted in the usual manner, card by card. Thus, three responses were obtained from each blot, making a total of 30 responses given by each S.

All Rorschach records were scored according to the Klopfer scheme. Using ten randomly selected records interscorer reliability was found to average .85 for all scoring categories. The average agreement for the ten records was 83 per cent. Because of the relative infrequency of the various shading responses of the Klopfer type, all such responses were scored as *Sh*. Thus, seven determinant categories were scored, namely M, FM, Fm, F, Sh, FC, and CF. Because C responses occurred in only two records, they were treated as CF responses for our present purposes.

As mentioned previously, two general measures of complexity were derived from the Rorschach, i.e., determinant complexity and content complexity. Since no one basic measure of either determinant or content complexity has been developed, several measures of each were used. Determinant complexity was measured empirically in four ways by counting: (a) the total number of different determinants used by S in his 30 responses; (b) the total number of cards on which S repeated the same determinant at least two times; (c) the total number of cards on which S repeated the same determinant three times; (d) the total number of cards on which S gave three *different* determinants.

It is apparent that high scores on a and d and low scores on b and c reflect greater complexity. Content complexity was measured specifically in two ways by counting: (*a*) the total number of responses which were repeated by S on the same card; (*b*) the total number of cards on which a response was repeated. Low scores on both the *a* and *b* content measures reflect greater complexity. Interscorer reliability coefficients on both of these content-complexity measures, using ten randomly selected protocols, were .84 and .86 respectively. The distributions of scores of the NDP and Rorschach complexity measures are presented in Table 55–1.

RESULTS

The two experimental hypotheses were tested by correlating each S's NDP score (complexity of perceptions of people) with his complexity scores on the modified Rorschach. All complexity scores were found to be approximately normally distributed (Table 55–1). Using the Pearson product-moment coefficient, each of the six Rorschach complexity measures was correlated with the NDP measure. These findings are presented in Table 55–2.

It will be noted in Table 55–2 that Hy-

Table 55–1   Distributions of Scores of the NDP and Rorschach Complexity Measures (*N* = 40)

	Mean	Median	SD	Range
NDP	15.52	16.63	3.41	9–20
Determinant complexity				
a	5.97	5.99	0.76	4–7
b	7.65	7.70	1.60	4–10
c	2.38	2.10	1.91	0–7
d	2.30	2.32	1.55	0–6
Content complexity				
a	7.55	7.00	4.67	0–26*
b	3.25	3.50	2.52	0–9

* Includes one subject with extreme score of 26.

pothesis I is supported by significant correlations between the NDP measure and each of the four Rorschach determinant-complexity measures. Similarly, Hypothesis II is supported by the two significant correlations between the NDP measure and the Rorschach content-complexity measures. It is apparent that the various Rorschach measures of complexity are interrelated because of the way in which they were empirically derived. This would explain the relative homogeneity of the various correlations presented in Table 55–2. Inspection of Table 55–2 indicates the Rorschach content measures of complexity

Table 55–2   Intercorrelation of Rorschach Determinant and Content-Complexity Scores with Complexity Scores in the Perception of People (*N* = 40)

	NDP	Direction of Prediction	p*
Hypothesis I			
a. Number of determinants used	.27	positive	.05
b. Number of cards with two determinants repeated	−.40	negative	.005
c. Number of cards with three determinants repeated	−.39	negative	.01
d. Number of cards with three different determinants	.42	positive	.005
Hypothesis II			
a. Number of responses repeated	−.44	negative	.005
b. Number of cards on which a response was repeated	−.50	negative	.005

* One-tailed test.

and the Rorschach determinant-complexity measures correlate about equally with the NDP measure.

Complexity of response to two stimulus realms, i.e., people and inkblots, has been measured in this study by means of verbal behavior. Consideration of the verbal measures used might suggest that a variable such as verbal intelligence or fluency might account for much of the interrelatedness of behavior on these two perceptual tasks. In order to analyze this possibility, each S was given the vocabulary subscale of the Wechsler-Bellevue (Form I). These vocabulary scores were then correlated with the various Rorschach complexity measures and with the NDP measure. It was found that there were indeed significant correlations between four of the Rorschach complexity measures and the vocabulary scores. The absolute range of these relationships was from $r = .37$ to $r = .46$, the most pronounced correlations being found between the content-complexity measures and vocabulary. On the other hand, no correlation ($r = -.01$) was found between the NDP measure and vocabulary scores. Thus, we may assume that verbal facility, to the extent it is measured by vocabulary, is not responsible for the intercorrelations obtained in testing the experimental hypotheses. Indeed, when we partial out the effects of vocabulary on the relationships between the complexity measures, we find the correlations are increased, although not significantly. Parenthetically, the fact that the Rorschach measures correlated higher with the intelligence measure than did the NDP measure might be related to the fact that just as every S had to define the same words on the vocabulary test, every S perceived the same blot stimuli. On the Rep Test, however, each S perceived persons different from those perceived by other Ss.

Do any of the traditional Rorschach determinant categories bear any relationship to the Ss' ability to achieve complexity of response in their perceptions of people? In terms of standard Rorschach rationale, it might be expected that the M or human movement response would be related to complexity of the perception of people. In the first place, M is a perception in which a person is the content. Secondly, a common interpretation given the M response is that it involves more internalized, introversive, and possibly imaginative ways of approaching problems concerning the self and other. The results of correlating the various Rorschach determinants with the NDP measure are in line with this view. The correlation between M and NDP was .31 ($p = .05$, two-tailed test). Further, this was the only determinant which correlated with the NDP measure at a level significantly different from zero, the other correlations ranging from .04 to $-.06$. Thus, it would appear that the greater the tendency to perceive humans in inkblots the greater is the tendency to invoke more variable or complex perceptions of people on the sorting task.

DISCUSSION

The results of this study suggest that some degree of generality in the complexity of Ss' behavior can be demonstrated using two perceptual tasks involving personal and nonpersonal stimuli. It is assumed that this generality of behavior is referable to the complexity of the cognitive system of the individual. That is, the manner in which an individual structures and cognizes one realm of events bears some relationship to how he structures another realm of events. It must be emphasized, however, that this is not a chance sampling of events. In the present study, the underlying formulation has been that the individual's learning experiences in the realm of interpersonal relationships provide the basic core from which his cognitive system for construing the world is developed. The fact that there is some generality from the personal to the nonpersonal realms in the cognitive behavior of individuals suggests the trans-situational pervasiveness of some sort of cognitive or perceptual "attitudes" in human behavior, as other workers have posited [10]. Our results are also compatible with studies utilizing the Rorschach as a measure of perceptual rigidity [5, 6, 7, 8].

The theoretical problem remains of relating a concept such as the complexity of the cognitive system to the behavior of the individual. Clinically, we are often impressed by the manner in which patients may generalize behavior from one situation to another, perhaps "unrelated," situation. Reacting towards others "as if" they represented some earlier interpersonal relationships has been stressed by Sullivan in his concept of the "parataxic" mode of behavior. What is involved here is the way in which a patient conceptualizes other persons of importance to him, the way in which gradients of similarity and dissimilarity develop in perceiving others, and how subtle or crassly stereotyped the patient may be in these perceptions. These are among some of the behaviors which would seem to be related to such a formulation as the complexity of the individual's cognitive system. A beginning has been made in this direction by relating the cognitive-complexity variable to the predictive accuracy of the individual's behavior [3].

It is important that the methodological problems in obtaining an over-all measure of the degree of differentiation in one's perceptions of others be recognized. Although it has been demonstrated that an adequate degree of stability exists over time for the measure of cognitive complexity in the perception of people, certain basic problems are posed. For example, the sampling of the people involved in measuring the complexity of perceptions of others is crucial. They may be peers, family members, old, young, same sex, or opposite sex. Many people may be sampled, or only a few. It is apparent that generalization of findings such as those obtained in the present study should be limited by a consideration of these factors.

The use of the modified Rorschach blots in this study underscores a recognized but neglected area of investigation concerning Rorschach behavior, namely, the importance of variability of response both as to determinants and content. The fact that it was possible to demonstrate significant relationships between inkblot-response variability and degree of differentiation in perceiving others suggests the importance of such an approach to Rorschach performance. While perseverative and repetitive behavior on the Rorschach has received most clinical and research attention relative to certain diagnostic patterns, such as organicity and mental deficiency, the results of this study indicate that conceptualizing and analyzing response variability or complexity as a function of the general cognitive system of the *normal* individual may add an important dimension in incorporating Rorschach behavior into a systematic theoretical framework. In addition, the finding that content complexity is *at least* as related to complexity in perceiving people as is determinant complexity, is consistent with the increasing emphasis being placed upon content interpretation in Rorschach practice [13].

SUMMARY

The assumption is made that fundamental to an understanding of human behavior from a perceptual viewpoint is the underlying structure of the individual's cognitive system with which he actively interprets his social world. The structure of this system can be delineated as to its relative complexity-simplicity. It was reasoned that the generality of cognitive complexity, operationally defined by response variability, could be measured between a perceptual situation involving persons as stimuli and a perceptual task using inkblots as stimuli. Two experimental hypotheses were derived: I, Significant positive relationships exist between the complexity of Ss' perceptions of people and the complexity of their perceptions of inkblots relative to the *determinants* used and II, Significant positive relationships exist between the complexity of Ss' perceptions of people and their perceptions of inkblots relative to the *content* elicited. A measure of cognitive complexity of persons was derived from a concept-formation sorting task originally devised by Kelly [9]. The stability of this measure over time was demonstrated. A modified Rorschach inkblot task was used to measure cognitive complexity in the nonpersonal stimulus realm. The sample consisted of 40 undergraduate college males.

Significant relationships in the predicted direction were found for both experimental hypotheses, using several indices of complexity of response in the Rorschach situation for determinants and for content. Although intelligence correlated significantly with the inkblot measures of complexity, it appeared to play no role in producing the generality of cognitive complexity which was found. Of the various Rorschach determinant categories, only M correlated with the measure of complexity of perceptions of others at a level significantly different from zero. The theoretical and clinical significance of a variable such as cognitive complexity is discussed.

REFERENCES

1. BARTLETT, F. C. *Remembering*. Cambridge, England: Cambridge Univer. Press, 1932.
2. BECK, S. J. *Rorschach's test*. Vol. I: *Basic processes*. (2nd ed.) New York: Grune & Stratton, 1949.
3. BIERI, J. Cognitive complexity-simplicity and predictive behavior. *J. abnorm. soc. Psychol.*, 1955, **51**, 263–268.
4. BIERI, J., & BLACKER, E. External and internal stimulus factors in Rorschach performance. *J. consult. Psychol.*, 1956, **20**, 1–7.
5. COWEN, E. L., & THOMPSON, G. G. Problem solving rigidity and personality structure. *J. abnorm. soc. Psychol.*, 1951, **46**, 165–176.
6. ERICKSEN, C. W., & EINSTEIN, D. Perceptual rigidity and the Rorschach. *J. Pers.*, 1953, **21**, 386–391.
7. FISHER, S. Patterns of personality rigidity and some of their determinants. *Psychol. Monogr.*, 1950, **64**, No. 1 (Whole No. 307).
8. JOHNSON, L. C., & STERN, J. A. Rigidity on the Rorschach and response to intermittent photic stimulation. *J. consult. Psychol.*, 1955, **19**, 311–317.
9. KELLY, G. A. *The psychology of personal constructs*. Vol. I: *A theory of personality*. New York: Norton, 1955.
10. KLEIN, G. S. The personal world through perception. In R. R. Blake & G. V. Ramsey (Eds.), *Perception—an approach to personality*. New York: Ronald, 1951. Pp. 328–355.
11. LEWIN, K. *A dynamic theory of personality*. New York: McGraw-Hill, 1935.
12. PIAGET, J. *The construction of reality in the child*. New York: Basic Books, 1954.
13. SCHAFER, R. *Psychoanalytic interpretation in Rorschach testing*. New York: Grune & Stratton, 1954.
14. TOLMAN, E. C. Cognitive maps in rats and men. *Psychol. Rev.*, 1948, **55**, 189–208.
15. VERNON, M. D. The functions of schemata in perceiving. *Psychol. Rev.*, 1955, **62**, 180–192.

Chapter 56 ~

Stress Interview

DONALD W. MACKINNON

The following procedure was designed primarily to test the candidate's capacity to tolerate severe emotional and intellectual strain. The strain was created by rapid and merciless cross-questioning under disagreeable conditions with the aim of detecting flaws in a cover story which the candidate had been given only a few minutes to invent.

The method of conducting the test was as follows. At exactly 6:25 P.M. the whole group was assembled in the classroom and to them one of the members of the staff made the following statements:

> This evening we are going to conduct one of the most important tests of the whole program. What you are to do is simple, but it is necessary for the success of the procedure that you carry out every detail precisely. It is particularly essential that you be completely punctual in following the schedule set for you. Be-

This article is reprinted from *Assessment of Men,* Henry A. Murray (Ed.), 1948, with the permission of the author, the editor, Henry Murray, and Holt, Rinehart and Winston, Inc.

ginning at 6:30 you will go one by one into the small room labeled A-13. Each of you in your individual schedules will find the time of your own appointment recorded. In the room will be a clock and a set of directions on the table. You will remain there alone for exactly twelve minutes, reading and carrying out the directions. Are there any questions?

By the time these instructions had been given it was about 6:30 P.M., and at that hour the first candidate went to the little room, where, on entering, he found the clock on the table together with a paper on which the following was written:

INSTRUCTIONS FOR RESOURCEFULNESS TEST

Read these instructions carefully.

The examination you are to undergo is designed to test your resourcefulness, agility of mind, and ability to think quickly, effectively, and convincingly. This is an important test and it is important that you do well. *In twelve (12) minutes report to the basement room at the foot of the stairs.*

669

The test will measure your ability to establish and maintain a cover story for the situation outlined below. Your cover story must be told convincingly, intelligently, and clearly. The examiners will try to trip you up on your story, to lead you into inconsistencies, and in general to confuse you.

Several students in the past have failed in this test because they forgot or did not understand the directions and requirements. We are listing below the important "rules" of this examination. If you do not remember these rules you will fail.

1. YOUR COVER STORY MUST GIVE A PLAUSIBLE AND INNOCENT REASON FOR YOUR ACTIONS.

2. YOU MUST ANSWER EVERY QUESTION ASKED. ANSWERS LIKE, "I DON'T REMEMBER," "I DON'T KNOW," "I AM NOT PERMITTED TO DISCLOSE THAT INFORMATION," ETC. ARE NOT PERMISSIBLE AND WILL COUNT AGAINST YOU IN THE FINAL RATING.

3. YOU MUST AVOID BREAKING EITHER PERSONAL OR ORGANIZATIONAL SECURITY IN YOUR ANSWERS. NONE OF YOUR REPLIES SHOULD DISCLOSE YOUR FORMER OCCUPATION, PLACE OF RESIDENCE, ETC.

Here is the situation for which you are to construct a cover story:

A night watchman at 9:00 P.M. found you going through some papers in a file marked "SECRET" in a Government office in Washington. You are NOT an employee of the agency occupying the building in which this office is located. You had no identification papers whatsoever with you. The night watchman has brought you here for questioning.

In developing your cover story you may assume that you are clothed in any manner you wish.

At the expiration of the twelve minutes granted him to construct his story, the candidate immediately went downstairs to the basement room. A voice from within commanded him to enter, and on complying he found himself facing a spotlight strong enough to blind him for a moment. The room was otherwise dark. Behind the spotlight sat a scarcely discernible board of inquisitors, several members of the staff. The interrogator gruffly ordered the candidate to sit down. When he did so, he discovered that the chair in which he sat was so arranged that the full strength of the beam was focused directly on his face. The questioner then addressed him as follows:

If you had an innocent reason for being in the building where you were caught, we expect you to be able to give it to us without any hesitation. We warn you, however, that any statement you may make will be subjected to a searching examination, so you would do well to be very careful in what you tell us, and also very accurate. Our first question is, "Why were you in that building?"

In reply the candidate then began to tell his story as he had devised it. Perhaps he made use of the cover identity which he had been developing for himself ever since the security talk given on his arrival at S. Or perhaps he fabricated a whole new tale which he thought would explain more satisfactorily why he was discovered investigating a secret file. Whatever his story was, it was searchingly examined as soon as he had told it.

At first the questions were asked in a quiet, sympathetic, conciliatory manner, to invite confidence. Frequently this led the candidate to let down his guard and expand his story, adding unplanned details on the spur of the moment. After a few minutes, however, the examiner worked up to a crescendo in a dramatic fashion. Any error, slip of the tongue, forgetting, or even halting response was likely to be seized on by the examiner as a suspicious sign. When an inconsistency appeared, he raised his voice and lashed out at the candidate, often with sharp sarcasm. He might even roar, "You're a liar," or some such phrase, if a falsehood in the cover story became apparent. Sometimes, after such an outburst, the questioner might lapse back into his soothing tone and suggest that it was understandable that such a false statement might be made if the suspect wished to cover up in order to protect his family. Occasionally the candidate would bite at this bait, and agree, whereupon the examiner would burst out accusingly, yelling, "Now we have the truth—you admit that you lied."

At the beginning of the grilling the questions were put slowly and smoothly, but as the end neared they were hurled in rapid-fire, staccato fashion. The questioning was shifted quickly from one topic to another and then back again in a very confusing manner. Beginning with generalities, the questioner soon forced the accused to give particular, specific information. The accused was asked about exact dates, hours, addresses, telephone numbers, and proper names of people involved in his story. Later he was questioned on the wider field of his past life, his profession, his place of residence, and so forth. Many of these items he had not, of course, had time to work out in the twelve minutes immediately preceding the questioning, so he was forced to improvise answers on the spot.

Another stratagem, often employed by the interrogator in an effort to confuse the victim, was to repeat, after a lapse of a minute or two, details of his testimony incorrectly; for instance, rearranging the numerals in a telephone number or Army serial number, in order to see if the candidate recognized the change and also to fill his mind with a bewildering mass of figures. Sometimes, too, the questioner could make a suggestible candidate contradict himself by asking him a number of leading questions, to each of which he agreed, until the questioner could at last jump on an inconsistency. For example, by this technique, a candidate could often be made to agree that he had no dependents, that he was healthy, that he was a citizen, and that he was not in an essential industry or the Armed Services. If he were then asked, "What is your draft classification?" there was almost no reply he could make without involving himself in a contradiction. Or by a similar procedure it was sometimes possible to get a candidate to admit that he had arrived in Washington some days or weeks before with little money, and to lead him to deny any sources of income while he was in the city, and then suddenly to ask how he had supported himself while in Washington.

An effort was also made to keep the suspect tense by not allowing him to relax. He was made to sit upright in a hard chair. If he was smoking he was told to stop. If he crossed his legs, he was told to uncross them. If he lowered his head to avoid the light, he was commanded to look up. If he wore glasses, he was directed to take them off. All this served to keep him from attaining a comfortable position, so adding to his stress.

After ten minutes of such grilling the examiner broke off the questioning abruptly with a dissatisfied air, saying, "We now have abundant evidence that you have not been telling the truth. That is all." Then the board of staff members whispered together for a few seconds as if arriving at a verdict. Finally the examiner asked solemnly, "Your name is Buck, isn't it?" When the candidate assented, the interrogator announced, "It is our decision, Buck, that you have failed this test." There were then about five seconds of silence while the candidate's reaction was observed. Occasionally he would burst out at this pronouncement and protest, but more often he accepted it silently with some slight show of emotion. Then the examiner directed the candidate to go immediately up to a room on the third floor to see one of the members of the senior staff. Thereupon the subject left, to go to the Post-Stress Interview. After he had gone, and before the next subject was admitted, the staff observers rated the man who had just left the room on the personality variables of Emotional Stability and Security.

As usual, Emotional Stability was judged by the degree of control and poise exhibited by the subject, as well as by the extent to which he seemed to remain free of neurotic traits when placed under stress. Searching for evidences of tension, the staff members noted whether the candidate sat rigidly in his chair, whether he moved about restlessly, whether he smoked nervously, whether he played with objects in his hands or with his fingers or fingernails, whether he paid much attention to the bright light, and how he reacted to the sudden shouting of the examiner. The candidate was also watched for signs of autonomic disturbance, such as sweating, flushing, swallowing, or moistening of the lips. Other common signs of emotion were stuttering; blocking of speech, sometimes for many seconds; explosions of anger; weeping or lacrimation; and characteristic changes of facial expression, particularly when the candidate was told he had failed.

Positive indications of good Emotional Stability were judged to be an air of calm and dignity, little reaction to shouting or an insistence that it was not called for, quick responses, an aggressive effort to control the interview and prevent the questioner from talking down all opposition, and laughing or joking. Sometimes suspects would obviously appear to enter the spirit of the grilling and act a role, even on occasion pretending to appear frightened, as they would admit when the examination was over. Such behavior was, of course, a sign of emotional control rather than the contrary.

The rating of the candidate's ability to maintain Security was based on an estimate of his cautiousness, inconspicuousness, skills in misleading and bluffing, and resourcefulness. Also, taken into consideration was whether his story was plausible, ingenious, and original, as well as whether it followed the directions given him.

In conclusion, it should be pointed out that the Stress Interview was designed primarily to measure emotional stability under strain, which is a factor to be evaluated in selecting personnel or making a diagnosis of personality. The situation lent itself ad-mirably to our specific project of testing men who were being selected to do intelligence work, however, and this fact determined the specific characteristics of the procedure. Many of the candidates might some day have to live under cover, or their work might possibly involve them in a situation in which they would be either interrogator or suspect in a grilling of this sort.

Mild as this situation may seem from our description, it was nevertheless sufficiently stressful to arouse in some of our subjects crippling and incapacitating attacks of anxiety, and sometimes in just those candidates who by background and experience might have seemed most admirably qualified for undercover work. One refugee from Europe, who had had a brush with the Gestapo and had so skillfully come through the questioning to which they had subjected him that he was allowed to go free, became very much disturbed in the Stress Interview. In Post-Stress he asked to be released from S and from any commitments to the OSS. Attempts to quiet him were of no avail. The emotion stirred in him by Stress kept him awake that night; and the next morning his anxiety had reached the point where, in another situational test, he fainted. It was clear that it would be unwise to force him to finish the assessment program since he was completely unfit to operate in Europe under cover.

Another candidate, who as a boy had endured many hardships in Russia during World War I and during the Revolution, could not tolerate the emotions reactivated in him by the Stress Interview. Before his assessment was completed he, too, had to be returned to Washington and his home.

The mere instructions for the Stress Interview could serve as a most revealing projective test, as indeed they did strikingly on one occasion when a man, after reading the instructions, insisted that he could not go through with the test. A little later the director of S found the candidate in his bedroom, sitting on the edge of his cot, sobbing. Upon reading the instructions he had imagined that on reporting to the basement he would be beaten by the staff, and he was overcome with fear that under this provocation he might commit some extreme act of violence. As he talked with the director about some of his early experiences, a few of the factors responsible for his unusual reaction became clear, but the anxiety aroused by his fantasy continued to increase until, in his case, too, it seemed wisest to excuse him from the rest of the program.

POST-STRESS INTERVIEW

It is a maxim of secret agents and investigators that security breaks occur most frequently when a man is enjoying a moment of relaxation after a period of tension, for under such circumstances his inhibitory mechanisms are momentarily in abeyance, and he is off guard. It was our belief, therefore, that a candidate's ability to keep cover would not be adequately tested unless an effort were made to get him to reveal true facts about himself at a time of relaxation after tension. Consequently, immediately following his Stress Interview and the shock of hearing that he had failed, each candidate was told to report to a member of the staff on the third floor. There he was cordially greeted and made to feel at ease in the company of a sympathetic listener who, despite his innocent manner, would actually do his best to induce the candidate to break his cover. Though the chief purpose of this situation was to test the candidate's security, it served two other ends: it provided an opportunity to estimate the strength of the candidate's motivation for his proposed assignment, and his emotional stability. The Post-Stress Interview also allowed for catharsis of emotion and for reassurance of the candidate about his performance in Stress and Post-Stress.

The schedule was so arranged that there was no waiting between Stress and Post-Stress Interviews. Each candidate went immediately from the basement to the third floor, where he was greeted by an interviewer, who talked with him for ten minutes and then sent him on his way before the next man arrived.

The room in which the Post-Stress conversation took place was one of those on the third floor in which candidates knew that Personal History Interviews were held under X conditions. As a consequence, although all candidates had been specifically directed not to mention any facts about themselves except under specifically designated X conditions, they drifted easily, in this setting, into a discussion of past events. Afterward they often admitted, sometimes in an attempt to excuse their security breaks, that it was the room, as much as the manner of the staff member, that led them to fall naturally into a feeling of intimacy and a mood for confession in the Post-Stress Interview.

From the moment the candidate arrived upstairs, the interviewer did everything possible to encourage ease and relaxation after his stressful experience in the basement. He pointed to an easy chair and said hospitably, "Sit down and make yourself comfortable." He offered him a cigarette and himself lolled back informally in his chair. Then he asked in an offhand manner, "Well, how have things been going?" The question was phrased in this vague way in order to get the strategic advantage of having the candidate make the first reference to the Stress Interview. Two things were gained by this maneuver: first, it served to dissociate the Post-Stress and Stress situations, so helping to beguile the candidate into letting down the guard he had developed in the earlier test; and second, it enabled the interviewer to gauge, from the rapidity and vigor with which the candidate referred to the former test, the degree of his emotional involvement in it.

Almost always the candidate reported at once that things were going very badly, that he had just failed a very important test. The way in which a candidate said this—whether he interpreted it as failure in a single test or as failure in the whole assessment program—revealed much about his motivation for work in the OSS and his ability to tolerate failure and frustration. The emotion or lack of it with which he spoke, as well as his willingness or reluctance to discuss his experience, was noted. In any case, the interviewer, on being told of the failure, sympathized with the candidate, but not unduly.

The candidate was then asked how it had happened that he had failed. Some, by their replies, would indicate a subservient attitude to authority; others, an outspoken skepticism that they had failed; while still others revealed the kinds of alibis and rationalizations they were inclined to use to explain their failures. Whatever the reply, the interviewer pursued this topic further by asking the candidate how well he had felt he was doing while being grilled. Replies to this question frequently revealed not only a candidate's ability to make a dispassionate judgment at such a moment, but also how eager he had been to succeed in the Stress situation. From this, some indication of his motivation could be obtained.

Usually the interviewer sought next to investigate the kinds of errors which the candidate had made in Stress—this to trap the unsuspecting candidate into breaking cover. He might ask, "What details did they manage to trip you up on?" or "At what points did you find yourself treading on thin ice?" In reply, the candidate usually gave concrete examples of confusion or near confusion in his story, although occasionally one claimed, truthfully or not, that he knew of no flaws that were discovered in his story. What he replied was of little importance, for in either case the questioner's purpose had been achieved: the topic now concerned details of the cover story. Taking advantage of this transition, the interviewer said, employing some flattery if he believed it would be effective in the given case, "Of course, it's really impossible to think out all the aspects of a cover

story in twelve minutes. If it could be done, I'm sure you would have done it. Undoubtedly you used the device of employing experiences from your real life in constructing your fictional story, though of course so jumbled that no one could identify you." Almost invariably the candidate agreed that he had, whereupon the questioner asked in a matter-of-fact tone, "Just what events did you use from your real life and how did you alter them? I'm interested in the technique you used." At this point many a candidate broke cover.

The interviewer was always on the lookout for any slight evidence in the candidate's expression, actions, or manner of speech of his becoming suspicious that an effort was being made to break his cover. If no such signs appeared, the interviewer forged ahead in his efforts to get facts about the candidate's real life. If signs of uncertainty did appear, he immediately took steps to allay the candidate's suspicion by changing the topic. He wished to forestall any queries about X conditions at this time so that he could return to the attack later with more hope of success. If the subject actually began to ask whether X conditions prevailed, the interviewer interrupted the sentence if he could, or if this was not possible, he would give some vague answer such as, "Things are just as they were downstairs," and hurry on to another topic. A determined and alert candidate would, of course, not be trapped by this, but would insist upon a definite answer to his question. In such a case, the interviewer would admit that X conditions did not prevail.

The topic to which the interviewer turned the conversation whenever the candidate's suspicion forced him to change it was an explanation of the purpose of the interview. "The test downstairs is a fairly new test," he would say, "and we hope it is a good one. However, we need the comments of men who have experienced it and who know something about it, and therefore I have asked to have you sent up here.

I should greatly appreciate any criticisms you may have of it or any suggestions as to how it can be improved." This maneuver changed the line of the candidates' thought so radically that, in an effort to think of criticism, he often forgot about the perplexing problem of X conditions.

After the candidate had made some comments on the test, the examiner inquired, "Have we succeeded in creating a stressful situation downstairs? How did you feel during it? Did the grilling upset you?" In his replies to these queries the candidate revealed much about his emotional stability, and this topic was pursued as long as it appeared to be fruitful.

Then came another transition, again for the purpose of going to a field in which it was easy to lure the unsuspecting into breaking cover, "Have you ever been in such a situation before?" the interviewer would ask. "For instance, were you ever cross-examined, as in court, or interviewed for a job? Perhaps you have done some such interviewing yourself?" Treading gingerly, the questioner might try in this way to get information about the candidate's vocation. If this failed the examiner might ask, "Well, in college weren't you ever grilled like this in a fraternity initiation?" and, caught off his guard, the candidate might reply that he never went to college or, conversely, state the name of his college or even of his fraternity.

Another fruitful issue to raise at this juncture was that of childhood events. The interviewer might say, "As a psychologist I've been wondering whether there weren't times in your childhood somewhat similar to this—times when you concealed petty things from your parents by telling fibs when they questioned you." Most students would agree that there had been such episodes, whereupon the interviewer would ask, "Did your family make a great point of complete truthfulness and honesty? Perhaps you are like some candidates we have had at S who have found it difficult to make up a cover story because their early

training in honesty made it hard for them to tell lies." Often this approach led quite naturally into a discussion of the candidate's childhood, his parents, and often his religion.

If a further line of attack on the candidate's cover was desired, an effort could be made to get him to reveal the branch of the OSS for which he worked. One way to do this was to ask, "Do you think this really is a good test?" After the candidate had replied, the interviewer might ask, "Do you think it is a good test for members of your branch? By the way, which branch do you belong to?"

Usually when these questions had been answered, the allotted time for Post-Stress was nearly over, so the interviewer asked if X conditions had existed during the conversation. Candidates responded to this in different ways, which gave excellent insight into their security consciousness as well as into their intellectual resourcefulness and emotional stability. Some looked stunned and guilty, admitting immediately that they had been caught. Frequently they were ashamed and distressed to realize that by breaking cover they had failed another test. Others bluffed at this point, or perhaps said correctly that all the facts they had related about their "real life" were false. (This could be confirmed from the Personal History Forms they had filled out the first night; indeed, all "facts" told by candidates in Post-Stress had to be checked in this way, for a really clever candidate might "confess" to have broken cover in Post-Stress only to have a check of his story reveal that all that he had said was a cover which he had kept intact. Sometimes, it must be confessed, we did not know who was deceiving whom in the Post-Stress Interview.) Still others insisted that they had assumed all along that they were under X conditions, and gave a variety of reasons and rationalizations for making this assumption.

The interviewer then told them, if they had broken cover, that they had erred in doing so and instructed them to be more careful in the future, a lesson which most candidates thought had been well learned and which they took in good spirit. Those, on the other hand, who had gone through the Post-Stress Interview without breaking cover were complimented and told to continue the good work.

From this point on in the interview everything was done to help the candidate regain his equanimity and to prevent his becoming embittered toward the assessment program by the evening's events. First he was asked how he had felt when he had been told downstairs that he had failed. Then he was questioned about how much he had wished to succeed in the test. After that he was told that it was very likely that he had not failed, and that as a matter of fact he probably had done very well. It was explained to him that all the candidates were told at the end of the Stress-Interview that they had failed, even if in reality their performances had been good. It was explained that such an announcement had been made to test their emotional reactions. Then the candidate was reassured and asked to pardon the staff for appearing to have been so inconsiderate. He was told that it was thought essential to see how well he could withstand such strain, and he was complimented on his control under these difficult circumstances. Finally, he was requested not to tell the other candidates what had occurred until all had been through both sessions. With this the interview was concluded. After the candidate had left the room, the Post-Stress interviewer rated him on the six-point scale on Security, Emotional Stability, and Motivation for his Assignment in OSS.

Chapter 57

The Leaderless Group Discussion

BERNARD M. BASS

The history, applicability, reliability, and validity of the leaderless group discussion as a means of assessing variations among persons in the tendency to exhibit successful leadership behavior has been appraised in a wide variety of research studies. While the procedure was originated as a psychological technique in Germany over thirty years ago, it is only in the last decade that systematic reliability and validity studies have appeared.

High interrater agreement and high test-retest reliabilities have been reported consistently, especially where descriptive behavior check lists have been used as the rating technique.

Group size, length of testing time, type of problem presented, directions, seating arrangement, number of raters, and rating procedure influence to a greater or lesser extent performance in the leaderless group discussion (LGD) as well as the reliability and validity of LGD ratings. Studies of the

This article first appeared in the *Psychological Bulletin*, 1954, and is reprinted with the permission of the author and the American Psychological Association. Only the summary is reprinted here.

effects of many of these have appeared since 1950.

According to both deductive and inductive evidence, a valid assessment of the tendency to display successful leadership should correlate with: (*a*) status as measured by rank, when the assessment is based on performance among associates of different rank; (*b*) esteem in real life as estimated by merit ratings; (*c*) successful leadership performance in other quasi-real and real-life situations; (*d*) personal characteristics as measured by psychological tests, such as capacity, proficiency, responsibility, and participation. On the whole, ratings based on performance in the LGD tend to do this. Therefore, it is inferred that they have some validity as assessments of the tendency to display successful leadership, i.e., leadership potential.

Other evidence suggests that the successful leadership behavior observed in the LGD concerns primarily initiation of structure rather than consideration of the welfare of others.

The preceding analysis, coupled with recommendations made by others working

677

in the field of situational tests, such as Weislogel [5], leads us to the following hypotheses:

1. To maximize the reliability and validity of the LGD and other situational tests, scoring techniques should *minimize* reliance on the ability of observers to infer differences in personality traits and future tendencies among examinees. Observers should merely report or evaluate the immediate behavior they observe. For example, in an unpublished study, the author found that two Army colonels' estimates of the potential as Army officers of ROTC examinees were less valid as predictors of the merit ratings of the examinees than were the colonels' check list descriptions of who initiated structure during the LGD. Similar results were noted in a study of fraternity members reported by the author and White [1].

   When the observer makes an inference about the future behavior of an examinee from the observations of the examinee during the LGD, several potential errors are likely. The observer may err in deciding on which dimensions to make inferences; he may err in collating his observations with the future behavior to be predicted; and finally, the dimensions on which the inferences are made may be private ones which cannot be shared with other observers. The errors may be constant, variable, or both. Lack of knowledge and control over such errors disappears when raters are merely asked to describe what they observed and these descriptions are used as predictors.

   Further reduction of uncontrolled raters' errors may be made in the following ways:

   a. Objective criteria for describing specific behaviors can be used [5]. In the LGD, the actual number of times a participant suggests a new approach to a problem can be noted instead of rating "to what extent did the participant suggest new approaches to problems."

   b. Forced-choice check lists can be used instead of present check lists. Otis' [3] recent successful application of the forced-choice technique to interviewer ratings indicates promise for applying the same procedure to the LGD.

2. To maximize validity, problems that are equally ambiguous to all participants, and that require the initiation of structure for their solution, should be used. Where interest is in forecasting leader behavior in real life, the structure to be set up should approximate the real-life setting as much as possible.

3. Since the LGD correlates fairly highly with most other intellectual or verbal situational tests, the use of many situational tests in a battery to forecast leadership potential is of doubtful utility. Thus, leadership ratings based on a one-hour LGD correlated above 60 with leadership assessments based on the three days of OSS situational testing [2]. A similar correlation between the LGD and an entire battery of situational tests was found by Vernon [4]. However, a significant proportion of the variance in over-all potential as a successful leader, unaccounted for by LGD, may be predicted by a fairly pure active or mechanical, initially leaderless, situational test which minimizes variance due to verbal ability.

4. Compared to paper-and-pencil techniques, the LGD is expensive; compared to the individual interview, in many locales, it may prove economical. The LGD appears feasible administratively, especially in military programs screening OCS or advanced ROTC applicants, in civil service examinations, in screening college seniors who are to be assessed at their colleges for management trainee positions, and anywhere else where "boards" have been used traditionally, such as in the selection of public school teachers.

5. While the LGD appears to have some validity as a predictor of the tendency to be a successful leader in a number of situations, especially in comparison to other assessment techniques, tailor-made batteries of paper-and-pencil tests will undoubtedly yield higher validities in designated situations. However, it may be that just as the brief intelligence test is applicable for predicting trainability

for many skilled occupations, so the LGD will provide a general technique for partially assessing potential success as a leader in a relatively wide range of situations.

6. A number of situations in which the LGD is less likely to be successful may include the following:

a. The LGD is less likely to be valid for measuring or forecasting esteem or leadership potential when examinees can be tested only among others of different rank. In such a case, status—and not esteem or personality—will determine who succeeds in the LGD.

b. The LGD is less likely to be useful where factors peculiar to the situation block initiation of structure where no structure exists. Conceivably, in certain military settings for example, the examinees may be imbued with the dictum "never volunteer for anything." However, exactly how this would affect LGD validities is unknown.

c. Another unknown is the effect of the average verbal aptitude and educational status of the participants on the validity and utility of the LGD. It is expected that where this mean falls below a certain minimum, LGD forecasting efficiency may suffer.[1]

d. Since achievement and intelligence

---

[1] Subsequent to the preparation of this manuscript, the author found no systematic correlation between mean ACE scores and the validity (as estimated by correlation with real-life esteem) of 64 leaderless group discussions among college students.

---

appear to correlate with LGD performance as well as with success as a leader in real life, any restriction in the range of intelligence or achievement of LGD participants would be likely to reduce the forecasting efficiency of the LGD. Conversely, the greater the variance in intelligence and achievement of participants, the more likely is the LGD to accurately assess leadership potential.

e. Finally, the less the leadership situation for which we are selecting leaders requires verbal communication or verbal problem solving, the less likely is the LGD to be useful as a measure or predictor of the tendency to exhibit successful leadership.

REFERENCES

1. Bass, B. M., & White, O. Situational tests: III. Observers' ratings of leaderless group discussion participants as indicators of external leadership status. *Educ. psychol. Measmt*, 1951, 11, 355–361.

2. OSS Assessment Staff. *Assessment of men*. New York: Rinehart, 1948.

3. Otis, J. L. The effectiveness of the selection interview in appraising personality of salesmen. *Amer. Psychologist*, 1953, 8, 468. (Abstract)

4. Vernon, P. E. The validation of civil service selection board procedures. *Occup. Psychol.*, 1950, 24, 75–95.

5. Weislogel, R. L. The development of situational performance tests for various types of military personnel. *Amer. Psychologist*, 1953, 8, 464. (Abstract)

Chapter 58 ~

Satisfactions and Interests

EDWARD K. STRONG

During the last 37 years I have learned some things about interests, but I confess I have taken satisfaction for granted—which I think is pretty much what most psychologists have done. The term is employed in everyday language and defined in the dictionary. It plays an important role in all theories of motivation. For over three decades surveys of job satisfaction of employees have been conducted costing thousands of dollars. Nevertheless I am very doubtful if any ten experts would agree on a specific definition of the term.

Years ago I contended that there was ". . . no better criterion of a vocational interest test than that of satisfaction enduring over a period of years" [10, p. 385]. I have actually never used satisfaction as a criterion on the ground that there seemed to be no good way to measure it. Such correlations as have been reported between interest scores and satisfaction have been for the most part too low to be of practical significance.

This article is reprinted from the *American Psychologist,* 1959, with the permission of the author and the American Psychological Association. It is based on the fifth Walter Van Dyke Bingham Memorial Lecture, given at the University of Minnesota on April 10, 1958.

JOB SATISFACTION AND JOB SUCCESS

Most people have assumed that job satisfaction or morale contributes to production. It came as a shock to me, as it must have come to many others, to read Brayfield and Crockett's [1] review of the literature and to learn that there is little or no evidence to support the assumption. In a still more recent review, Herzberg, Mausner, Peterson, and Capwell [2] report some relationship between morale and production, but in most of the investigations where there were positive relations they were low correlations. Reading these two reviews and that of Viteles [11] and many of the articles on which these reviews are based leaves one bewildered. Definitions of the key terms are conspicuous by their absence and must differ greatly, judging by the context. Many statements by one writer are contradicted by another.

What is satisfaction? Some say it is a kind of feeling as simple as pleasantness; others contend it is a complex of feeling, emotion, and sensation. If the latter, do the proportions of these three ingredients vary each time? Contrast the satisfaction of eating dinner and resting afterwards with a full stomach with the satisfaction of finding a house to rent after hunting many weary days. The mother tells her daughter as she leaves the home to have a good time and asks when the girl returns: "Did you have a good time?" Is having a good time what is meant by satisfaction?

Employee surveys are called attitude or job satisfaction or morale surveys. The terms are sometimes used synonymously and sometimes not. In the absence of generally accepted definitions it is suggested that job satisfaction be employed when the worker is thought of as an individual and that morale be used when the worker is thought of as a member of a group. Perry defines morale as ". . . a state of mind which characterizes groups of men when they are engaged in some action. . . . The essence of it is that the group holds together and holds to its objective, despite events that are calculated to divide and dishearten" [7]. An employee is an individual and a member of one or more groups. It is appropriate to consider both his job satisfaction and his morale. But seemingly there should be some difference in the inventories designed to measure these two attitudes towards one's job. Inventories regarding morale should contain items relative to the man's involvement with his company, his union, and the members of his department. Are the low correlations between production and job satisfaction caused in part at least by inadequate measurement of job satisfaction? Consider briefly how job satisfaction has been measured.

Employee surveys since the pioneer days of Houser have typically consisted of two parts: the first part asking a few questions as to the man's overall satisfaction with his job; the second asking whether he liked or was satisfied with all manner of factors, such as income, supervision, cafeteria, pension system, and so on. A summary of the responses in the first part was supposed to measure the employee's overall satisfaction. Responses to the items in the second part that pertained to each job factor were summarized in order to show how satisfied or dissatisfied employees were regarding the various factors. The purpose of such surveys has been to aid management to improve production by determining the causes of dissatisfaction and by identifying the departments with low morale. Much of the literature is devoted to the causes or job factors presumably associated with dissatisfaction, their relative importance, and what can be done to improve conditions. Surveys have been worth-while to the extent that management has made intelligent use of the results—which has not always been done.

One reason why job satisfaction inventories do not correlate with production is that the items do not furnish good measures of the specific job factors. In one investigation, for example, four questions were used to measure each of four factors; the intercorrelations among the four items ranged from .39 to .52. A summary of the responses of four such questions can only roughly approximate what they purport to measure.

Even if we had good measures of job factors, which we do not have, some of the factors would not correlate particularly with production. Seemingly, health should be directly related to production. But some employees who suffer from poor health plug along regardless, and other employees absent themselves whenever they have the sniffles. Consider one very simple example of physical condition, that of toothache. If we rate production on a scale of -3 to $+3$ (where -3 represents absence from work and zero production, and $+3$ represents maximum production) and similarly rate satisfaction-dissatisfaction from toothache (where -3 represents such severe pain the man is absent at his dentist, the rating of -2 represents a decrease of 2 from normal rating in production, and the rating of -1 represents a decrease of 1 from normal production), then we will have a correlation of .42 when 35% of employees have ratings of -3, -2, and -1 in dissatisfaction from toothache. If the percentage of employees so affected drops to 15%, the correlation is .26; if the percentage is further decreased to 10%, the correlation is .20. It is unlikely that the percentage of employees seriously affected by toothache is ever as high as 10%, so that the correlation would be appreciably below .20 although the data were arranged so that there was high correlation between suffering from toothache and decrease in production.

In order to obtain a significant correlation between satisfaction-dissatisfaction and production, we must have a situation where dissatisfaction produces decrease, and satisfaction produces increase, in production; and, furthermore, where a fair percentage of employees rate the factor high or low. It is doubtful if most job factors are so related to production.

Consider a second condition, that of being in love. Here we might obtain very high or very low overall satisfaction-dissatisfaction responses depending upon the current behavior of the loved one. It seems probable that those suffering from this malady, whether satisfied or not, would exhibit decrease in production since the employee's attention would be distracted by daydreaming about last night and what will happen on the next date.

The factor of age has a curvilinear relationship with production. The youngest and oldest employees are more satisfied than those about 30 years of age. The factor of age will reduce the correlation when it is mixed in with other factors.

Those of you who are interested should consider how satisfaction-dissatisfaction relative to each aspect of a job could be related to success on the job and also estimate what percentage of employees would be particularly satisfied or dissatisfied on any one day.

A still more serious difficulty arises when responses to all the items on an inventory are summarized on the assumption that, if job satisfaction is to be measured, all aspects of the job should be taken into account. Here, inadequate measures of each factor are combined without much consideration as to the relationships between the factors—a procedure which makes our statisticians fairly froth at the mouth. A way must be found to consider only those who are really satisfied or dissatisfied with each job factor and to disregard those who don't really care about the factor. In the case of toothache there may be perfect correlation with production among the very few suffering with toothache and zero correlation among the great majority. Data based on all of them will not correlate as high as .10. How can you expect to learn how production is related to satisfaction with the job and with expectation of advancement when people with such attitudes are combined with girls who expect to marry and quit work? We need to develop adequate measures of each factor and determine the relationship to an adequate criterion before attempting a summary of all factors.

One way to discover what a test should measure is to note the nature of its items. Four types of questions are found in survey questionnaires: questions asking for facts, opinions, likings, and satisfactions. The proportions of these types vary greatly among survey inventories.

The evidence is clear that facts and opinions about working conditions are colored by feeling—as is every aspect of behavior. It is therefore appropriate to use fact and opinion questions to indicate feeling. Responses should, however, differ according as one is asked: Does your supervisor treat all alike? Do you like your supervisor? Are you satisfied to work under your supervisor? Most inventories ask many interest questions: "Do you like or dislike this and that?" Considering that the inventory is to measure job satisfaction or morale, it is surprising that there are not more items which ask: "Are you satisfied or not with this and that?" Relatively few items inquire as to the man's involvement with his fellows and the company.

The correlations between job satisfaction and production are low not only because measures of job satisfaction are inadequate but because measures of success on the job are also inadequate. It is well recognized that production is not a complete measure of success on the job. There is possibly no more difficult problem in industrial psychology than the determination of adequate criteria of success. Furthermore, in a surprisingly high proportion of jobs there is no way to measure amount of production, and in many cases where it can be measured, as on an assembly line, the measure is far more a measure of flow of work, determined by management, than it is a reflection of the man's ability and willingness to do the work. It is not surprising that psychologists resort so often to ratings of supervisors as their criterion of success. Psychologists have so far contributed relatively little to this task. I have great faith in the ability of psychologists to develop an adequate test of any specifically defined activity; but, if the activity is not definitely defined, the first step should be to define the activity, not to attempt to devise tests that correlate .20, maybe .30, with something that it is hoped represents the activity. It would seem at the present time that both psychologists and management should concentrate on what is meant by success on a given job. When that is accomplished, management ought to be able to measure success on the job, and psychologists should aid in the analyses and devise tests which will predict in advance who will be successful and, I hope, also who will be interested and reasonably satisfied.

What shall be done with job surveys? Three alternatives are evident. First, continue the surveys for their practical value to business management but discontinue trying to prove that morale increases production appreciably. Second, accept the necessity of morale for its own sake. Modern personnel practice stresses that men must be selected so as to be both useful and happy. Maybe we should assume that good morale means general contentment, happiness, satisfaction on the part of all, top management as well as employees. No instructor, supervisor, or army officer wants the people under him to be complaining and criticizing everything that has to be

done. Third, develop adequate measures of morale and success on the job. If there were adequate measures, might there not be much higher correlations between them?

Unquestionably much has been learned from job satisfaction surveys of practical use to business and of theoretical value to psychology. It is doubtful, however, if additional surveys will add much more of theoretical value. It now seems highly desirable to isolate and define the basic components and find some way to measure each of them. These are problems for psychologists to tackle. They are not easy or we would know more about them than we do today.

OPINION, ATTITUDE, INTEREST, AND SATISFACTION

Consider now four basic concepts: opinion, attitude, interest, and satisfaction. First, what is *opinion*, often referred to as attitude? An opinion is a mental reaction to the relationship between this and that. Many items in an employee survey are opinion items, such as: "Do you work better on a clear or rainy day?" Responses to the questions are either "Yes" or "No" based on facts, more or less, but primarily indicating belief or disbelief. Belief is a feeling comparable to pleasantness, liking, and satisfaction. Opinions concerning religion and membership in the Republican or Democratic party are about as stable as anything we have in life. But many judgments are based on conversation, hearsay, not personal experience, and change about as readily as styles. The hullabaloo following the appearance of Sputnik is a striking example of a whole country losing faith in what they had previously believed. Because opinion items are not as stable as interest items, it is doubtful that they can be as useful as interest items in predicting future behavior. Research is needed to answer this and many other related problems well set forth by Sherif and Cantril [8] and by McNemar [3].

A second term is *attitude*. This term has

a great vogue today. But what does it signify? Nelson [5] lists 23 rather distinct characterizations of the term. Sherif and Cantril tell us the term is in a very confused state, and McNemar reminds us that "no one has ever seen an attitude." Seemingly its best usefulness is its ambiguity. When a psychologist does not want to disclose his real purpose, as is typically the case with employee surveys, he may call his inventory a job attitude survey.

Several have given definitions of attitude. Peak's definition of attitude is useful here. She defines attitude [6] as ". . . a hypothetical construct which involves organization around a conceptual or perceptual nucleus *and* which has affective properties." Concepts and percepts are acquired reactions to a combination of sensations. They are mental activities, and most of them initiate overt activities. It is not merely that sensations are organized into a concept so that no two persons have exactly the same concept but that such concepts are *used* in some manner that is important. What happens when I say the word "baseball"? Do you see the word, or think of keeping score, as you used to do in high school, or do you think of watching a game, or of playing the game, of playing short stop, or knocking out a home run? If the concept is emphasized, then according to Peak we have an attitude; if the activity is emphasized, we have a habit, a skill, or an interest. Psychologists are prone to call activities by many names depending upon the aspect that is emphasized. Thus the activity of skating is called a habit or a skill when its motor coordination acquired by repetition is emphasized; it is called an interest when its feeling quality is emphasized.

Five characteristics of *interests* may be mentioned. First, they are acquired in the sense that feeling becomes associated with the activity. We are not referring to the learning of an activity itself, such as writing one's name, which usually requires many repetitions. We are referring to the associating of feeling with an activity. Such association results from one or only a few experiences—once stung by a bee, one dislikes bees the rest of his life. About all that can be said about the associating process is that, when an activity is useful, aids in reaching some goal, pleasant feeling is attached to it; when the activity is not useful, brings some disagreeable consequence, unpleasant feeling is attached.

Second, interests are persistent. Sometimes disliking is replaced by liking and vice versa; many start out disliking olives and acquire a taste, a pleasant feeling, for them. But, all in all, interests are surprisingly permanent.

A third characteristic of interests is intensity. One can not only immediately indicate whether he likes or dislikes an activity, but one can also immediately indicate his relative preferences for different activities.

The fourth and fifth characteristics are acceptance-rejection and readiness to act. For example, the waitress says: "Will you have some garlic bread?" My wife's response is, "Yes, please"; my own response is, "No, thanks." She likes garlic and goes toward it; I dislike garlic and reject it. Such acceptance-rejection implies action, direction, choice. Such preferences typify readiness to act in the sense that a habit or memory is a readiness to act. The query of the waitress is a stimulus, and the already acquired interest, habit, memory, whatever one wants to call it, functions. The associated value, or feeling quality, determines whether the activity will be accepted or rejected, whether the organism will go toward or away from, whether it will continue the status quo or discontinue it. It must also be noted that many activities develop in time so as to bring sufficient pleasure to be employed for their own sake. So we smoke, chew gum, play bridge, or golf for the fun of it.

It is not surprising that interest tests predict the direction in which a person will go, for each item is indicative of preference, choice, direction to go. Interest tests are diagnostic because no two persons have acquired the same list of activities nor are the activities classified in the same manner as liked or disliked. Moreover, people engaged in an occupation have to a marked degree similar interests, and so people in one occupation can be differentiated from the members of other occupations.

How shall *satisfaction* be defined? Here again there are many definitions of satisfaction, but most of them emphasize three aspects: first, arrival at a goal, Webster says "fulfillment of a need or desire"; second, pleasant feeling or contentment; and third, a relatively quiescent condition. A sleepy cat purring on a rug, or contented cows, come to mind. But satisfaction occurs not merely when the goal is reached but also long before. These two satisfactions may be referred to as actual and anticipated satisfaction. Anticipation of one's date next Friday night is often much more exciting than the actuality.

Dissatisfaction is the opposite of satisfaction as far as feeling goes, but the overt activities accompanying satisfaction and dissatisfaction are quite different. In the case of actual satisfaction, the series of activities has been completed or nearly so, tension is released, and quiescence follows. In the case of anticipated satisfaction, activities may continue for years, as in the case of the boy planning to be a physician. Here is long range planning, continuing effort. Dissatisfaction arises because the individual is prevented from reaching his goal. He must find some way to circumvent the obstacle, or he must forego his desire. Any interference with one's purpose is frustrating with release of energy and anger. Such explosive behavior is very different from the quiescence of reaching a goal or the long term planning associated with anticipated satisfaction. Expressed in another way, anticipated satisfaction accompanies progress toward a goal, while dissatisfaction arises when progress is prevented.

I have had a lot of fun asking my colleagues what is the difference between interests and satisfactions. They start out quite sure they know and often end up quite confused. One distinction is that interests are associated with activities, and satisfactions are not. It is true that there are certain activities regularly employed to satisfy bodily needs, but the striking characteristic in securing satisfaction is that one uses whatever activities are available and may use a different combination of activities each time a goal is sought. Aside from the final, consummatory activity, satisfaction cannot be identified in terms of activities, as can interests.

Can interests and satisfactions be differentiated in terms of feeling? Interests are liked or disliked; there seems to be no qualitative difference in the liking of different activities. Satisfactions of bodily needs differ in quality. But possibly this is so because of the presence of different sensations. If the sensations were eliminated, would the remaining satisfactions be similar in such cases? What about goals other than bodily needs? Are there qualitative differences in the satisfactions of earning an A grade, in winning the high jump, in finding a house to rent, and so on? On the negative side, disliked activities tend to be ignored. But if one is forced to employ a disliked activity, as fixing a flat tire, the reaction is more typically dissatisfaction than disliking; then one grumbles, complains, swears, and even exhibits all the symptoms of anger.

Finally how can satisfaction-dissatisfaction be measured? We have already mentioned how job satisfaction is measured and that improvements are greatly needed before adequate measurements can be obtained as to how much satisfaction-dissatisfaction is associated with each job factor. Before considering a different procedure, let us eliminate measurement of satisfaction-dissatisfaction of past events on the grounds that they cannot be measured with any accuracy; and even if they could, they would be of little value.

A man who liked to fish and to golf but no longer does so because of old age continues to say he likes such activities. It is possible that, if he were asked to arrange a long list of activities in order of preference, he would not rank fishing and golf as high as he would have done 20 years earlier. Nevertheless he still likes them. The question is: Can one feel satisfaction for past events in similar fashion? I once hiked through heavy brush in hot weather for over 24 hours without food or water. It must have been very rugged, but I cannot now conjure up the thirst and fatigue I must have experienced. I can only recall the incident and enjoy talking about it as I am doing now. My old friend Hollingworth would have exclaimed: "That exemplifies the oblivescence of the disagreeable." My present feeling of pleasure at having done it is very different from how I must have felt at the time. Consider another incident. A violent argument arises in the machine shop as to how a job is to be done. The man who wins feels satisfied, the other dissatisfied. Now, if as so often happens the incident is forgotten the next day and there is no bad feeling on either side, then there is no existing satisfaction or dissatisfaction. And if so, is there any value today in trying to measure the feelings of yesterday? But if the loser in the argument continues to be sore, then such existing dissatisfaction may have a bearing on his overall satisfaction-dissatisfaction.

What about satisfaction-dissatisfaction concerning a goal not yet attained. Here three components are evident: the goal, the dissatisfaction of today, and the anticipated satisfaction of tomorrow. The difference between the last two is, however, more significant than either, or both, considered separately.

In attempting to explain persistence of motivation Peak suggests that it is the ". . . discrepancy rather than the affect which is the important source of continuing action." It is the difference between ". . . Harry's feeling about his present job . . . and his feeling for the ideal job that he imagines" that is the source of persistent efforts to achieve the ideal. This agrees with what I have long taught: that motivation, or ". . . intensifying the want of a prospect in selling, involves, first, making him realize how unpleasant his present situation is, and

second, making him anticipate as much as possible the enjoyment he will have when he reaches his desired goal" [9]. Morse [4] has this same conception in mind when she says that "satisfaction depends basically upon what an individual wants from the world and what he gets." We would suggest substituting what "he expects to get" for "what he gets."

MEASUREMENT OF MOTIVATION

What we are proposing is the measurement of motivation rather than satisfaction of a given moment. Motivation is a more dynamic aspect of behavior than satisfaction and should prove more useful in predicting future behavior. It is worth-while to know how an employee feels towards this or that right now, today. But it is more important to know whether he is going to continue in his present type of work, to continue with the company, or to do something else. Job surveys have asked: "How satisfied are you with this and that?" In contrast we ask: "What do you want?" "What do you expect to get?" and "What do you think are the chances you will get what you want?" The difference between aspiration and expectation affords a basis of estimating degree of dissatisfaction; but likelihood that the expectation will be achieved must also be taken into account. The greater the expectation, the greater is the anticipated satisfaction.

It should be noted in passing that measurement of motivation is similar to measurement of interests in that neither predicts how far or how fast one will go, for success is primarily a matter of ability, but both indicate direction, which of many activities will be engaged in.

Specific goals must be considered as well as present dissatisfaction and anticipated satisfaction. It is futile to compare the feelings of a girl who is working hard to make good and become office manager with those of a girl who is planning to quit work, marry, and have a home of her own, even though at the moment they are both dissatisfied with their progress toward their different goals.

Goals are phantasies, wishes, daydreams, aspirations, plans. Goals are often called needs. Some of them are needs but most have evolved as the result of social pressures, often expressed as "Keeping up with the Joneses." Many of these seem imperative, but does one have to keep up with the Joneses in every respect?

Have we any idea of how many different goals the men and women in this country possess, if all were expressed in standard terminology? Does a given man possess during his lifetime all possible goals or only a few? If the latter, why has he these particular goals? Again, how many goals does a man have at a given time? It is also important to know whether each goal is accompanied by its own satisfaction-dissatisfaction quality or do all these qualities more or less fuse together? In other words, does unhappiness because of one's wife affect one's attitude toward one's job, and vice versa? Does the dissatisfaction at being fired from one's job and the satisfaction from one's girl's promise to marry him alternate so that he fluctuates from dissatisfaction to satisfaction; or do the two fuse, and if so is the fusion a mere average or a weighted average in terms of their relative significance?

Goals differ also in complexity. There are simple goals such as getting to class on time and complex goals such as planning, while still in high school, to graduate from college. Such long-distant goals necessitate careful planning in terms of many subgoals, as selecting the courses necessary to enter college, getting good enough grades, selection of a college, etc.

It is necessary to determine not only a man's goals but the chance, the likelihood, of his attaining his goal. Likelihood is dependent here not upon the actual facts but upon the man's opinion or belief. A former student resigned because he saw no future in being moved from one job to another, not knowing that he was being groomed for an important position. The greater the chance, the greater is the anticipating satisfaction; the less the chance, the greater is the dissatisfaction. When there is no chance, the man may quit (a friend of mine committed suicide), or nurse a grudge, or abandon his goal (often not easy to do), or find a substitute goal. Likelihood may be expressed in terms of money as in buying an auto or home; or it may be expressed in terms of effort, that is, practice or study; or in terms of willingness to forego other goals, often called pleasures.

With many goals there is a cycle from dissatisfaction to satisfaction, repeated over and over. A simple example is eating. Three times a day we want to eat, are satisfied, and quit thinking about eating for a short while. Another example pertains to salary. Start with dissatisfaction, then anticipated satisfaction when the grapevine reports there will be raises, then satisfaction when the increase is received, then little thought of the subject gradually changing to dissatisfaction. Answers to the static question, "Are you satisfied with your salary?" depends upon where the man is in such a cycle. The more dynamic questions of: "What salary do you want a year hence, five years hence?" and "What do you think the chances are of obtaining such salaries?" should provide a more forward looking picture of the man's reaction to his salary. Whether men can look five years ahead or not is something to be determined. A few years ago I tried out such questions with college seniors; the great majority could not or would not give anything like definite answers.

Satisfaction in the long run necessitates improvement, progress. A golfer who had never had a better score than 85 would be elated with 84. But if he had 84 every time for several weeks, he would become steadily more dissatisfied; only an 83 or better would give him satisfaction. Many investigators have pointed out that men about 30 years old are more dissatisfied than younger and older men. Is this not due to the fact that such 30-year-old men have come to realize that future progress is limited, that they are not going to realize their aspirations? Some remain disgruntled, but many seek satisfaction in other activities.

The term "level of aspiration" has considerable vogue today. Presumably it represents fairly well formulated to clear-cut formulation of one's goals. Why does one young man aspire to be a lawyer and his brother follow in the footsteps of his father, a coal miner? We always come back to the old, old problem: did the two go in different directions because of environmental educational pressures or because their genes were different? I have a hunch that many adult goals have evolved out of phantasies and daydreams. A 10-year-old girl dreamed of accompanying Allan Quartermain on wild adventures in Africa; later on she has always said "Yes" to her husband's harum-scarum expeditions. Is there any connection? Why did she indulge in exploration and physical danger instead of being a movie actress, a princess, or a Cinderella? How can one ascertain what daydreams a person has, considering that daydreams are usually viewed as too personal, too self-revealing, to be divulged to anyone? No psychologist will achieve fame by predicting future behavior on the basis of well formulated plans; the really tough task is to predict behavior in terms of the antecedents of such plans.

I hope it has occurred to you that there are two great problems: What can this person do, what are his abilities, what can he accomplish if his abilities are properly trained; and, second, what does he want to do, which way does he want to go in life? His satisfaction, happiness, contentment is dependent upon the direction he is permitted to go. Happiness and success are interrelated, but all counseling services both educational and industrial must seek reasonable success for their counselees and also happiness now and in the future. Such counseling is dependent upon a determination of capacities on the one hand and goals on the other hand. We have made far more progress in measuring capacities than in ascertaining men's goals.

I have asked many questions for which I don't know the answers. There are hundreds of difficulties in all this—I am tempted to say a million difficulties. A good research man ought not to be dismayed; rather he should glory in the complexities—a tough job is far more fun than an easy one.

REFERENCES

1. BRAYFIELD, A. H., & CROCKETT, W. H. Employee attitudes and employee performance. *Psychol. Bull.*, 1955, **52**, 396–424.
2. HERZBERG, F., MAUSNER, B., PETERSON, R. O., & CAPWELL, D. F. *Job attitudes: Review of research and opinion.* Pittsburgh: Psychological Services of Pittsburgh, 1957.
3. MCNEMAR, Q. Opinion-attitude methodology. *Psychol. Bull.*, 1946, **43**, 289–374.
4. MORSE, N. C. *Satisfaction in the white-collar jobs.* Ann Arbor: Institute for Social Research, 1953.
5. NELSON, E. Attitudes: I. Their nature and development. *J. gen. Psychol.*, 1939, **21**, 367–399.
6. PEAK, H. Attitude and motivation. In *Nebraska symposium on motivation*, 1955.
7. PERRY, R. B. National morale. *Educ. Rec.*, 1942, **23**, Supple. No. 15.
8. SHERIF, M., & CANTRIL, H. The psychology of attitudes. Part I. *Psychol. Rev.*, 1945, **52**, 295–319.
9. STRONG, E. K., JR. *Psychological aspects of business.* New York: McGraw-Hill, 1938.
10. STRONG, E. K., JR. *Vocational interests of men and women.* Stanford: Stanford Univer. Press, 1943.
11. VITELES, M. S. *Motivation and morale in industry.* New York: Norton, 1953.

Chapter 59

The Strong Vocational
Interest Blank in Individual Cases

JOHN G. DARLEY / THEDA HAGENAH

As the counselor studies his available data on the abilities, achievement, interests, personality, and background of the student he is about to interview, he formulates several hypotheses or "hunches" about the particular problems involved in the case; he may also see in the data several alternative courses of action that the student might follow in order to reach a satisfactory educational or vocational or personal goal. We assume, in the discussion that follows, the presence of test material at some point in the counseling process; we are not here dealing with the problem of alternative forms of therapy, which has loomed unnecessarily large in the literature of counseling in recent years. We assume further that the best possible use must be made of the test results if the student is to be aided in reaching appropriate decisions about his

own future. While the power of decision resides with the student, the professional responsibility for adequate interpretation of the data lies with the counselor, regardless of the particular doctrines that may be most attractive to him.

The formulation of hypotheses before the interview and the actual conduct of the counseling interview are separate processes. We shall not attempt a detailed treatment of interviewing; it is sufficient for our present purposes to point out that sometime during the interview series it will be necessary for the counselor to interpret the interest measurement, in relation to the claimed occupational choices of the student.

Let us assume the following situation. The student lists as his claimed choices business, engineering, and "executive work"; his primary pattern of interests on the Strong Vocational Interest Blank falls in the social service or welfare group of keys, with A and B+ scores on the majority of keys in this family. He has no dominant pattern of interests in the scientific group of keys, and only a secondary pattern in the business detail group. At some point in the counseling interview series, the counselor can make this bald statement: "You have the same kind of interests as successful personnel managers or Y.M.C.A. secretaries or school superintendents." With minor modifications, this is probably the standard approach to interpretation. It is also the least effective approach and the one most likely to lead the student and counselor into ever deeper morasses of interpretive difficulties. The reasons for our conclusion on this point are derived from material previously presented, as well as from considerable experience in interest measurement interpretation. We list these reasons below:

1. The student's spoken or unspoken response is usually "How can you say that; I've never had any experience in jobs like those?" At this point the counselor must backtrack and introduce a rather incoherent explanation of the origin and standardization of the Strong Vocational Interest Blank, to his own and the student's confusion.

2. If the student accepts the counselor's statement without raising the experience issue in some form, the chances are he will reinterpret the statement then or later to mean that he has the *ability* to be a successful worker in any one of the three named occupations; these by understandable motivational transformation become the fields of work in which someone guaranteed he would succeed.

3. Such categorical interpretive statements run still another risk: they flout countless stereotypes, prejudices, specific dislikes, or occupational misconceptions evoked by occupational labels, either in the student or in his parents. Very few people know what a personnel manager does, and there are substantial and not always complimentary stereotypes about school

superintendents or Y.M.C.A. workers. The further fact that these labels are directly at variance with the student's claimed choices also operates to set up resistance, even though his claimed choices may have error factors in them.

4. Such statements run the risk of moving the discussion too early in counseling to the temporarily irrelevant factors of opportunities, salaries, prestige values, and training requirements, at the expense of the more important purpose of exploring the motivations, value systems, and insights from available past experiences of the student. The counselor is forced to waste precious time giving information, if he has any, on these irrelevant factors at this stage of counseling, before establishing an understanding of the meaning of interest types or families as motivational phenomena.

5. Such statements also fail to take account of the vital factors of levels of ability and past achievement which tend to be the best predictors of level of future academic achievement. They also fail to take account of any educational disabilities or other barriers to achievement, and they may neglect evidence of congruence or lack of congruence in other parts of the case data. We have pointed out that interest patterns are *relatively* independent of ability levels and academic achievement levels; thus, any form of test interpretation that does not recognize both types of behavior will be misleading. It does no good to identify a particular set of interests if the individual lacks the ability to implement them in required training programs. This error in interest interpretation is particularly tragic where the occupations being discussed are those for which society demands college training before entry and certification. It is likewise inexcusable in those cases where the occupation may

be entered either with or without specific advanced training, as in the case of general business interests. But at least in these latter cases the counselor can cover his error by explaining that success or satisfaction may be possible in the occupation even though success may not, because of inadequate ability, be possible in a curriculum which bears some resemblance to the occupational title but which is not yet an essential prerequisite for job entry.

6. Such statements also fail to take into account the problem regarding the present-day representativeness of norm groups on the Strong Vocational Interest Blank, or the possible occupational specialties, as seen in the research on new scoring keys for the fields of medicine and psychology.

7. Such statements omit consideration of possible changes of measured interests. Although we have interpreted the weight of the evidence as supporting the idea of stability of interests, we have recognized that changes in both general patterns and specific scores may occur. Furthermore, if the student involved is in the early high school years, there is a somewhat greater probability of change on retesting and a somewhat greater error factor, therefore, in the discussion of scores on specific keys.

8. Such statements are also insensitive either to the possibility of the faking of interest scores or to the possibility of cultural determinants, as exemplified in the work of McArthur [2], in both claimed and measured interests.

The direct report of specific interest scores, which for the foregoing reasons we consider ineffective in counseling, may be contrasted with what we believe to be an effective alternative. Suppose, in this hypothetical case, no reference is made to interest measurement until relatively late in the counseling process. Suppose, further,

that the counselor permits the student to work through and verbalize the reasons for his three claimed choices. It may be that the student has done only superficial thinking about jobs, and this fact itself is important to know. But the counselor may also discover the specific factors leading to the choices: information (or misinformation) regarding salary scales and "overcrowded" or "undercrowded" fields and job duties; satisfactions expected from work; self-estimates of strengths and weaknesses; evidences of family pressure or tradition dictating certain choices; self-estimates of the aspirations and motives that are operative in the choices; and evidence about life experiences to this date that have shaped the choices.

Suppose, finally, that the counselor is familiar with the interest types or interest families growing out of factor analysis studies, and that he also knows something of the literature we have reviewed regarding the relations between interests and personality.

Given these suppositions, the counselor should then be able to elicit from the student, by appropriate questioning, an evaluation of the kinds of activities and experiences which indicate or contra-indicate either the claimed or measured interests. Specifically, in the example we have cited, unhappy experiences or clearly poor performance in mathematics would contra-indicate the claimed choice of engineering. Participation in Hi-Y work and summer camp jobs might be found supportive of the measured social service patterns. A discussion of "executive work" as a pervasive problem of dealing with people might take it out of the claimed realm of business interests alone.

Notice that the counselor has not yet presented any interpretation of the interest scores; he has used them in guiding the discussion on a level meaningful to the student and in such a way as to clarify the student's thinking about the world of work and his relation to it. At or near this point in the counseling process, the counselor can then make a more direct interpretation, somewhat as follows: "We can read the interest test you took to say that your basic interests seem to be those involved in helping people or in working with them in order to make their lot easier, rather than being engaged in impersonal, scientific activities, or in making a big fortune in business activities." In the discussion of this interpretation in terms of how the student has evaluated his experiences to date, the counselor may refer to specific occupational labels as *representatives* of the basic interest type or family. Thus he would say: "Basic interests like yours might find satisfaction in the job of personnel manager, for example." Here would follow a description of the job duties, responsibilities, and training requirements of the occupational title. The counselor could go on to say: "These same interests could bring you satisfaction in the type of work that a Y.M.C.A. secretary does. So far as training is concerned, these two jobs—personnel manager or Y.M.C.A. secretary—require somewhat different types of abilities and aptitudes, as we can see in looking at the two training programs. Therefore it becomes important next to get some estimate of your abilities and past achievement in related subjects, to see how they might line up with the two training programs."

In this form of interpretation, the primary interest pattern is introduced first as a unitary, general idea and discussed first in terms of the individual's knowledge of himself and his past experience. Then, the specific occupational titles included within the primary pattern may be introduced and discussed as examples or illustrations of the family of interests. In this manner, some allowance can be properly made for differences in ability and achievement among individuals, as these factors relate to training demands.

The advantages of this interpretive procedure would seem to be fairly clear. It reduces to a minimum the evocation of resistance growing out of stereotypes or prejudices which the student and his family may have about job labels. It permits the student and the counselor to discuss the various *levels* of ability or achievement required for a wide range of jobs *within* a particular family of interests. It gives the student a clearer understanding of the place of interests in his planning, since the counselor can refer to the student's responses to his earlier questions and show how they relate to an interest type theory. It permits interests to be seen in proper perspective as the *societal* translation of *individual* motives and personality needs. It permits somewhat greater generalization of the available data, because occupations claimed by the student can be related to the various interest families, and in those cases where no specific occupational key exists on the interest inventory to match the student's claimed choice, the claimed choice can be related to the most similar occupations for which scoring keys do exist. It permits the student to deal somewhat more impersonally with his own motivational drives, divorced from the fixations that so often accompany a specific occupational title.

Counselors who work with high school and college students must keep in mind one other aspect of the use of interest measurement: there is a basic difficulty in using an *occupationally standardized* test for purposes of *educational or curricular* differentiation. This difficulty grows out of the fact that there is no one-to-one correspondence between curricular and job requirements; indeed in some fields there is no adequate similarity or overlap between the two sets of requirements. We have earlier presented evidence that there is little relation between measured interests and achievement in college. Popular examples of this come to mind for all counselors: the student who looks upon law school as "good basic training for business" or the student's father who is sure that the engineering curriculum will teach his son "how to think straight" are familiar examples. Many college women show primary patterns in the interest family that includes secretarial and office workers. Yet, when faced with the theoretical and technical economics and accounting of the existing school of commerce or business administration, they develop a real enthusiasm for a liberal arts major. The measured interest pattern may be a perfectly true picture of their most likely job adjustment before marriage, and the liberal arts major plus six months in a commercial business college may be an excellent solution to their total educational needs.

Thus the counselor need not try to force a one-to-one correspondence between curricular choices and occupational choices. Given certain levels of ability and motivation, the student will succeed in college in a great variety of possible curriculums, more or less synonymous with his measured interests. There should be no urge, on the counselor's part at least, to predict curricular failure if the educational plans of the student are not isomorphic with his measured interests. A substantial number of freshmen entering an engineering school have technical or skilled trades interests, albeit they have substantial ability based on average entrance test performance and high school grades. Who can say that undertaking engineering training is unwise or irrelevant for their ultimate occupational adjustment?

We place considerable emphasis, in general counseling work, on the *pattern* interpretation of the Strong Vocational Interest Blank, as distinct from the interpretation of specific letter grade scores on particular occupational keys. This has been an intentional emphasis. It appears to us to be more effective, in the great majority of cases, to work through the pattern analysis procedures and eventually to arrive at specific occupational letter grades, as counseling progresses, than to begin by emphasizing letter grades. Admittedly more than one counseling interview is assumed in this kind of case work. The process of counseling should permit the student to seek out relevant occupational information, to undergo tryout experiences, to contrast his own strong and weak points in ability, and to come to terms with his own value systems and personality needs and motivations. As will be seen in most of the illustrative cases that follow, quite a few interviews may be involved.

It is well to point out, however, that in those cases where the specific claimed choices are substantiated by specific measured interests, there is every reason to use the occupational scores directly, *provided* that due attention has been paid to relevant ability, achievement, and personality factors and provided that these latter factors are also consonant with the training and entry requirements in the field of the claimed and measured interests. Such cases may be more infrequent than one might wish for in a world of high academic mortality.

WALTER W. HATCH: CONGRUENCE BETWEEN CLAIMED AND MEASURED INTERESTS

Each year, the Student Counseling Bureau accepts approximately 200 adult clients, partly as a public service and partly as a means of extending its case work experience over a wider range of problems. The first two cases we have chosen are drawn from this group of clients, to illustrate congruence and conflict between claimed and measured interests.

Walter Hatch came to the Bureau about a month after he had resigned his position as general sales manager of a metal products company. His reason for coming was to find out more about himself, before he went through company testing and screening programs for several sales managership positions he was considering.

Mr. Hatch was a tall, handsome man, thirty-six years old, who appeared well poised and effective in the preliminary interview. At the time of high school graduation, he had been in the lowest quarter of his graduating class both in high school achievement and in college entrance test performance. He had attended a small college in this area for two years before leaving to enter the sales field. At the time of his contacts with the Bureau, he was married and had two young children.

With the exception of a year in the Navy, he had been continuously employed since 1939 as merchandise or sales manager for three different companies making metal products; these positions had lasted, respectively, for eight years, four years, and one year, and his salary in his last position was three times the salary he had made when he started work. He had left his most recent job because of a company reorganization and change in policy. The entire work record was a successful one in the business contact field. One of the positions he was currently considering involved a salary of $25,000 per year.

The counselor arranged for Mr. Hatch to take three tests before the next interview: the Wechsler-Bellevue, the Strong Vocational Interest Blank, and the Minnesota Multiphasic. Figure 59–1[1] portrays the results of the Strong. The Wechsler yielded a full scale I.Q. of 117, with no discrepancy between the performance and verbal subscales. The Multiphasic showed no scores of clinical significance.

In Figure 59–1 it is quite clear that Mr. Hatch rejects the interests of men in the first three major families of occupations, and tends to fall in the chance score ranges of the social service and business detail group. He shows a clear primary pattern in the business contact group and a secondary pattern in the verbal-linguistic group. The extremely high occupational level score is also noticeable on the non-occupational keys.

The second interview with Mr. Hatch was devoted primarily to a discussion of the test results, in terms of his self-appraisal and the new jobs he was considering. He reported that he had consistently enjoyed the work he had done in the sales field and that he had very high ambitions for himself. He phrased his level of ambition in terms of a salary of $50,000 a year. At this income level, he would have both economic security and freedom to do what he chose. His only dissatisfaction was that he was not moving as rapidly as he would like toward this goal. His interest test was interpreted as indicating congruence between claimed and measured interests, and as supporting his claimed satisfaction with business contact jobs; he was well satisfied with this analysis. He interpreted his general level of performance on the Wechsler as indicating that, somewhat to his relief, he was "no dummy."

One is struck by the high degree of congruence between claimed and measured interests, and between measured interests and work history. It would be fairly safe to predict that Mr. Hatch would continue in the business contact field as both a successful and a satisfied worker. Since he had moved from a 1939 annual income of approximately $5000 to a 1952 income of approximately $15,000, and was at the time of counseling a candidate for an annual income of $25,000, he may even reach his ultimate goal of $50,000 a year without too much trouble, thus removing the mild dissatisfaction under which he labors!

EDWIN B. ADCOCK: CONFLICT BETWEEN CLAIMED AND MEASURED INTERESTS

At the time Mr. Adcock came to the Bureau, in 1954, he too was working in the business contact field, as a life insurance salesman. There his resemblance to Mr. Hatch ends. After eight interviews and a retesting on the Strong Vocational Interest Blank, we are still quite dubious about what the future holds for Mr. Adcock, who is presently employed in a sales management position.

Edwin Adcock came to the Bureau at the suggestion of one of the ministers of his church. For approximately three years he had been selling life insurance, but he was not satisfied with this work and was

---

[1] In Figure 59–1, as in all subsequent figures showing the Strong Vocational Interest Blank profiles, we are indebted to Elmer J. Hankes, of TESTSCOR, Minneapolis, for providing the modification of his scoring profile for the Strong Vocational Interest Blanks. The art work and the profiling for the relevant figures throughout this chapter were originally done by his staff.

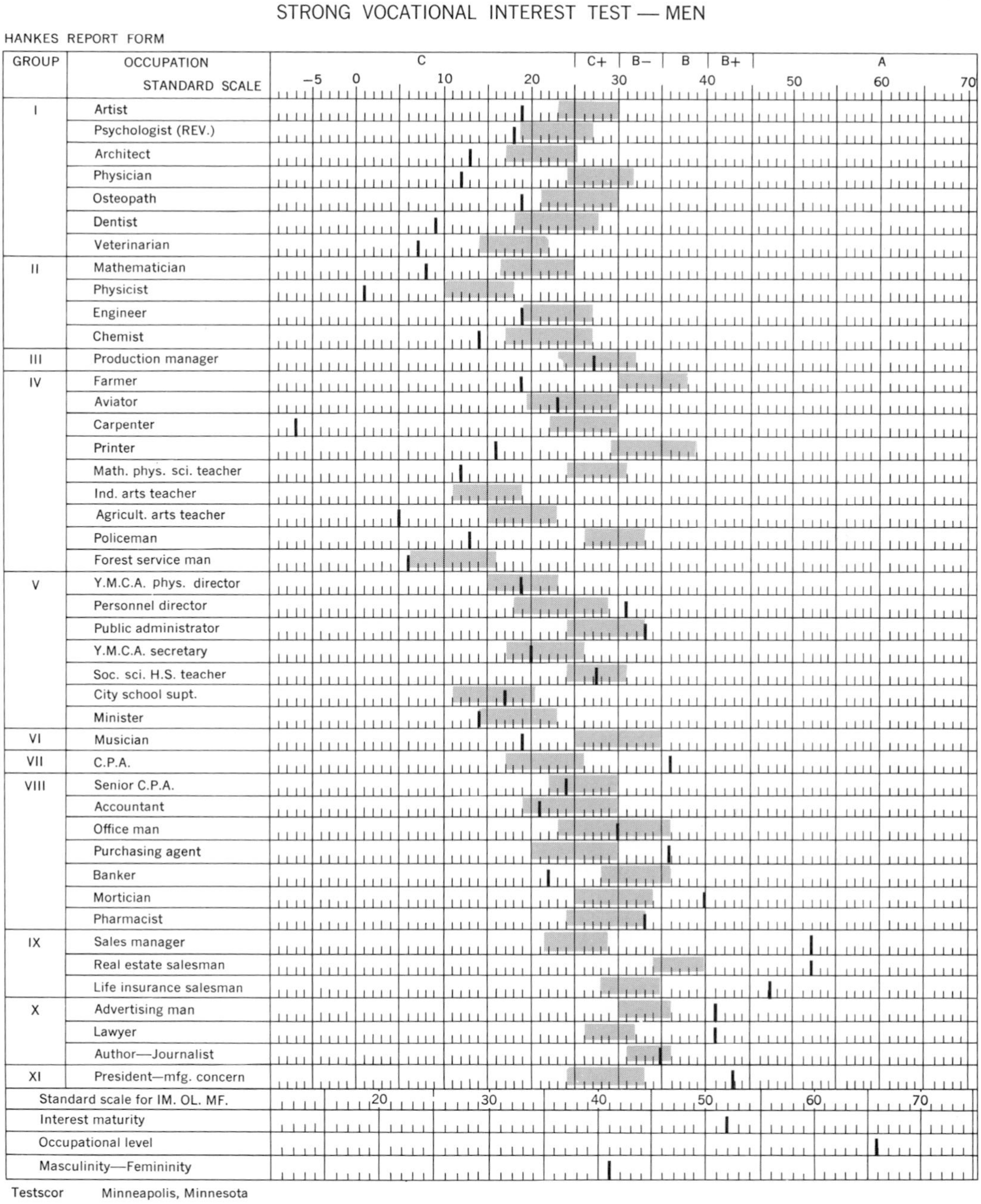

STRONG VOCATIONAL INTEREST TEST — MEN

HANKES REPORT FORM

GROUP	OCCUPATION / STANDARD SCALE	C		C+	B−	B	B+	A	
		−5 0 10 20		30		40		50 60	70
I	Artist								
	Psychologist (REV.)								
	Architect								
	Physician								
	Osteopath								
	Dentist								
	Veterinarian								
II	Mathematician								
	Physicist								
	Engineer								
	Chemist								
III	Production manager								
IV	Farmer								
	Aviator								
	Carpenter								
	Printer								
	Math. phys. sci. teacher								
	Ind. arts teacher								
	Agricult. arts teacher								
	Policeman								
	Forest service man								
V	Y.M.C.A. phys. director								
	Personnel director								
	Public administrator								
	Y.M.C.A. secretary								
	Soc. sci. H.S. teacher								
	City school supt.								
	Minister								
VI	Musician								
VII	C.P.A.								
VIII	Senior C.P.A.								
	Accountant								
	Office man								
	Purchasing agent								
	Banker								
	Mortician								
	Pharmacist								
IX	Sales manager								
	Real estate salesman								
	Life insurance salesman								
X	Advertising man								
	Lawyer								
	Author—Journalist								
XI	President—mfg. concern								
	Standard scale for IM. OL. MF.	20 30		40		50		60	70
	Interest maturity								
	Occupational level								
	Masculinity—Femininity								

Testscor   Minneapolis, Minnesota

FIGURE 59–1 *Profile for Walter W. Hatch.*

contemplating a change in jobs. At the time of the preliminary interview, he was a nice-looking, well-groomed man, at ease, but quick to admit that he wasn't getting along well and was having trouble "getting going" in life insurance sales. He was thirty-two years old, married, and the father of two young children.

He had graduated from a small eastern college, majoring in geology and engineering. Both his parents were college graduates, and an older brother was also a college graduate and a practicing chemical engineer. After three years in military service, he had gone to work as a civil engineer for a mining company in Minnesota, at a salary of $225 per month. He stayed on this job for one year, during which time he was married. After leaving the engineering job, he moved back east and started as a salesman with a food products company. He had felt that he could make more money in selling, although he started the sales job at the same salary as his engineering job—$225 per month. Because the salary did not increase, he left this job after one year, moved to the Middle West again, and started as a commission salesman for a manufacturer of luxury items. This job lasted about three years, until he was discharged. It was then that he started selling insurance on commission, but he was not enthusiastic about the work, and did not feel that he was getting any place. Just before coming to the Bureau, he had been offered a job as sales engineer for a local manufacturing firm, at an increased income, but the job would require that he move east again, and he was reluctant to accept it. The offer had started him thinking about his future, however, and it was part of the motivation that brought him to the Bureau.

Figure 59–2 shows the first Strong Vocational Interest Blank taken by Mr. Adcock, in January. At the same time, he took a scholastic ability test, the Allport-Vernon Scale of Values, and the Minnesota Multiphasic. The ability measure placed him in the top 10 per cent of a local college norm population and can generally be interpreted as showing a superior level of ability. There were no clinically significant scores on the Multiphasic. The Allport-Vernon scores appear in the accompanying tabulation, translated into local percentile norms.

	Raw Score	Local Percentiles
Theoretical	32	62
Economic	34	63
Aesthetic	26	64
Social	26	27
Political	27	26
Religious	35	64

It is evident in Figure 59–2 that at age thirty-two Mr. Adcock has no clear primary pattern on the Strong, but he does have at least an A on the engineering key and a B+ score on the chemist's key. There is also a weak secondary pattern in the biological science group. Yet in the business contact group of occupations and specifically on the life insurance key itself, there is a fairly clear pattern of rejected interests. The occupational level scale is high, indicative of some prestige drive, but the Allport-Vernon results do not show clearly defined value systems, except for a tendency to reject both the "political" values which one expects of those with pragmatic and money-making interests, and the "social" values which are based on some concern for the well-being of others.

Four interviews, in fairly rapid succession, followed after these tests were completed. In these interviews, Mr. Adcock repeatedly volunteered the information that the engineering job he had first held had been the most enjoyable and meaningful to him. The fact that his earning power had not markedly increased after entering sales work did not, however, emerge in his thinking too clearly, even though desire for a higher salary was his reason for leaving the engineering field originally. His present income he reported as approximately $3900 per year. It was during this part of counseling that he and the counselor reviewed duties and opportunities in sales engineering jobs, straight engineering work, sales work, and work that would essentially keep him in office management rather than sales activities. There was also some discussion of parental standards and some hint that he had failed to live up to these standards in his own career. Finally, after the fourth interview, he decided that he must start looking for some other job, and that he must leave the field of insurance selling.

After two months he returned to the counselor with a definite offer of another sales engineer's job with a local manufacturing concern. He had almost decided to take this position, but the possibility of

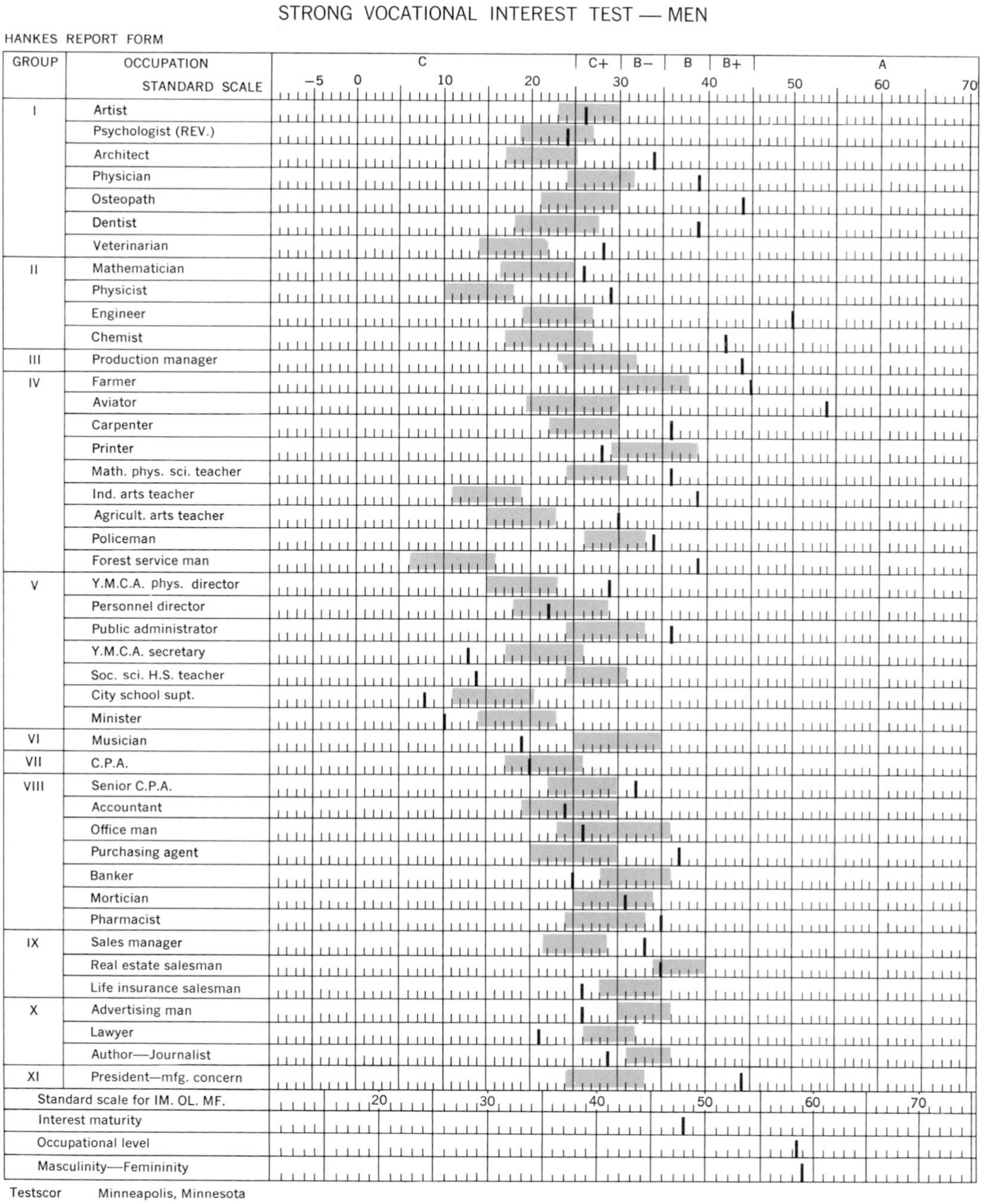

STRONG VOCATIONAL INTEREST TEST — MEN

HANKES REPORT FORM

GROUP	OCCUPATION / STANDARD SCALE	C	C+	B−	B	B+	A
		−5 0 10 20	30		40		50 60 70
I	Artist						
	Psychologist (REV.)						
	Architect						
	Physician						
	Osteopath						
	Dentist						
	Veterinarian						
II	Mathematician						
	Physicist						
	Engineer						
	Chemist						
III	Production manager						
IV	Farmer						
	Aviator						
	Carpenter						
	Printer						
	Math. phys. sci. teacher						
	Ind. arts teacher						
	Agricult. arts teacher						
	Policeman						
	Forest service man						
V	Y.M.C.A. phys. director						
	Personnel director						
	Public administrator						
	Y.M.C.A. secretary						
	Soc. sci. H.S. teacher						
	City school supt.						
	Minister						
VI	Musician						
VII	C.P.A.						
VIII	Senior C.P.A.						
	Accountant						
	Office man						
	Purchasing agent						
	Banker						
	Mortician						
	Pharmacist						
IX	Sales manager						
	Real estate salesman						
	Life insurance salesman						
X	Advertising man						
	Lawyer						
	Author—Journalist						
XI	President—mfg. concern						
	Standard scale for IM. OL. MF.	20 30	40		50		60 70
	Interest maturity						
	Occupational level						
	Masculinity—Femininity						

Testscor   Minneapolis, Minnesota

FIGURE 59–2   *Profile for Edwin B. Adcock at the initial session.*

change had so concerned him that he couldn't take the final step. The counselor again reviewed with him the available test evidence and the problems of decision-making that he faced. Three months later he returned, saying that he had turned down the sales engineering job, but was now worrying about a branch manager's job in the insurance company with which he was still employed. This paid $5000 per year, and had a good many tensions built into it. At this point, he arranged to repeat the Strong Vocational Interest Blank, with the results shown in Figure 59–3. There is no major *functional* change in the retest; the similarity to the interests of engineers

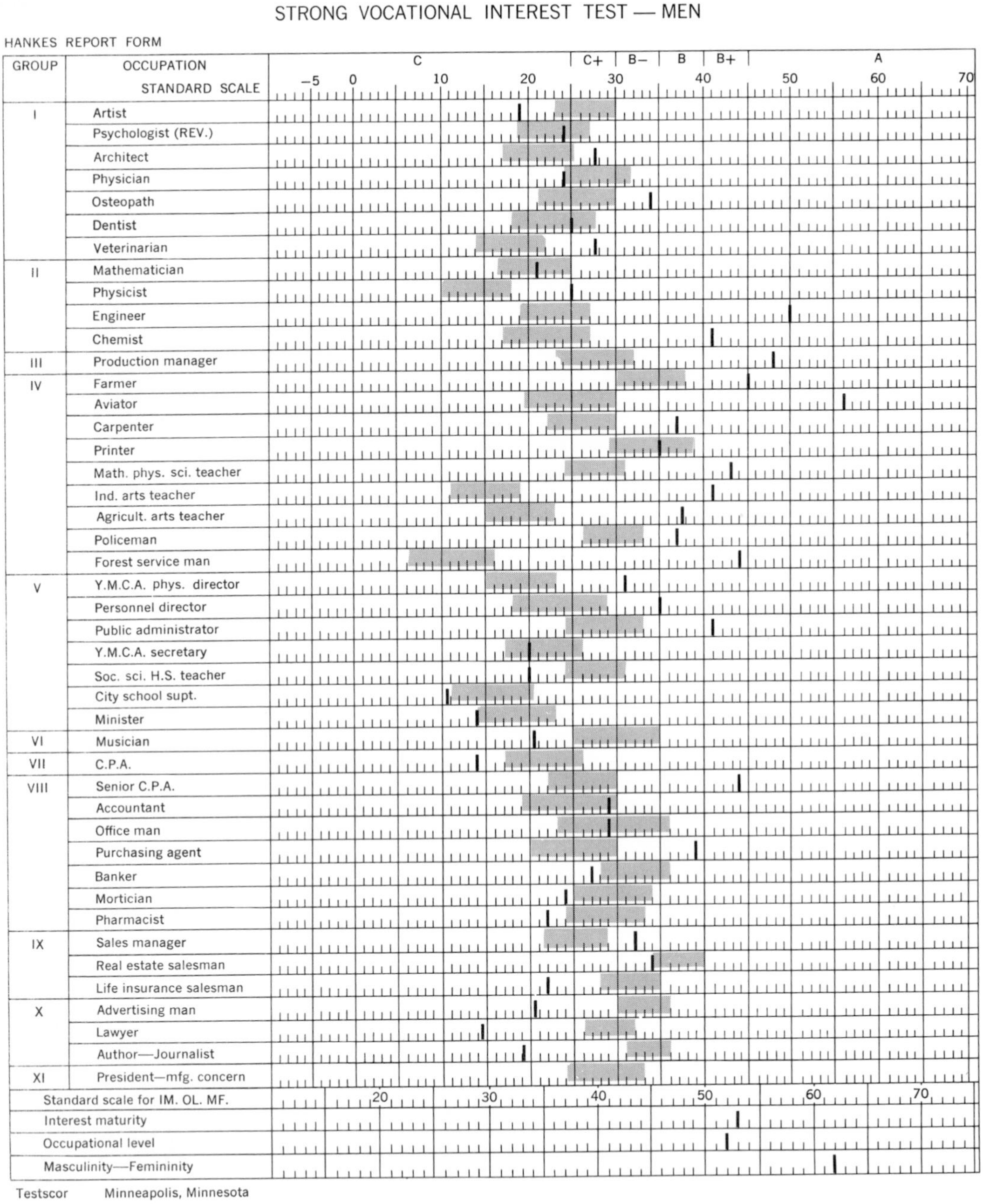

STRONG VOCATIONAL INTEREST TEST — MEN

HANKES REPORT FORM

GROUP	OCCUPATION				C			C+	B−		B	B+			A		
	STANDARD SCALE	−5	0		10		20		30			40		50		60	70
I	Artist																
	Psychologist (REV.)																
	Architect																
	Physician																
	Osteopath																
	Dentist																
	Veterinarian																
II	Mathematician																
	Physicist																
	Engineer																
	Chemist																
III	Production manager																
IV	Farmer																
	Aviator																
	Carpenter																
	Printer																
	Math. phys. sci. teacher																
	Ind. arts teacher																
	Agricult. arts teacher																
	Policeman																
	Forest service man																
V	Y.M.C.A. phys. director																
	Personnel director																
	Public administrator																
	Y.M.C.A. secretary																
	Soc. sci. H.S. teacher																
	City school supt.																
	Minister																
VI	Musician																
VII	C.P.A.																
VIII	Senior C.P.A.																
	Accountant																
	Office man																
	Purchasing agent																
	Banker																
	Mortician																
	Pharmacist																
IX	Sales manager																
	Real estate salesman																
	Life insurance salesman																
X	Advertising man																
	Lawyer																
	Author—Journalist																
XI	President—mfg. concern																
	Standard scale for IM. OL. MF.			20		30		40		50			60		70		
	Interest maturity																
	Occupational level																
	Masculinity—Femininity																

Testscor   Minneapolis, Minnesota

FIGURE 59–3   *Profile for Edwin B. Adcock at subsequent retesting.*

persists; the rejection of sales interests persists; the occupational level score decreases somewhat.

Upon returning for a review of the retest, Mr. Adcock informed the counselor that he had accepted the branch manager's position with the insurance company and was getting ready to move his family to another city to start work there.

After a sales career of almost seven years, he has managed only to shift out of the direct contact phase of selling and into a branch office management position in a sales organization. It is likely that this new employment will make fewer demands upon him, but it is not likely that it will be a fully satisfying occupational adjustment. Mr. Adcock had originally chosen a field of work for which he was well suited by ability and by interests, but in pursuit of a higher income had moved into work that was never satisfying and that never eventuated in the income he had expected. In one sense, his case illustrates cultural trapping; he can return to the field of engineering only with the greatest difficulty, since he has lagged so far behind current developments by the absence of seven years; he can escape the field of selling only with the greatest difficulty, since his work history is so extensive in this field, even though it has not been personally satisfying to him and even though his success in it, as judged by external criteria, has been modest at best.

Even if one takes the position that Mr. Adcock himself lacked certain motivations and capacities for resolving his own fate—and some of the clinical data would indicate that his was not a strong personality—the fact remains that the compromise he has chosen is not one to lead to a successful and satisfying career for him, and that the compromise tends to be dictated by the realities of the labor market itself. He is well past the point of no return.

BRIAN DONET: NO PRIMARY INTEREST PATTERNS

The individual with multiple primary interest patterns, and the abilities to back them up, provides an interesting and hopeful puzzle for counselors. At the other extreme is the individual with no primary interest patterns. Such a record appears in the case of Brian Donet.

He first came to the Bureau in his sophomore year at the university; he was thinking of dropping out of school and was uncertain about what vocational plan he should follow.

At the end of his junior year Brian had left the private high school in which he was enrolled to enter aviation training. Two years later he was discharged from military service as a second lieutenant, bombardier. On the basis of his performance on the tests of General Educational Development, he was granted the equivalent of a high school diploma, and had started the predentistry sequence at the university. His work was satisfactory in this field, and he was within one quarter of entering the professional school, when he changed his mind and started to take prebusiness courses. His grades were unsatisfactory in this work, and he was about to be dropped from school. It was at this point that he came to the Bureau.

His father was a successful professional man in the community; both parents had had college educations; an older sister was a college graduate and a younger brother was doing extremely satisfactory work in an eastern college. Brian's own vocational choices were as follows: personnel management; medicine; wild life conservation work; store manager; aviation.

Figure 59–4 shows some of the test material that was collected during the case work with Brian. The entries in the date column indicate when the various tests were administered.

On the various ability measures, it would appear that this student was at least an average scholastic risk, perhaps slightly above average for the work in the liberal arts college. Yet in his high school grades (not reported here), in the sophomore culture test, and in his college grades he had tended to fall below the level of achievement that would have been predicted for him on the basis of ability tests alone. The results of the Multiphasic (not shown here) were essentially negative, but the results of the Minnesota Personality Scale showed a fairly clear deviation on the measure of social adjustment.

Figure 59–5 portrays the results of the Strong Vocational Interest Blank given at

NAME ___Donet, Brian___ COLLEGE ___SLA___ CLASS ___Soph.___ SEX ___M___ AGE ___22___

DATE	NAME OF TEST	PERCENTILE	NORM GROUP	10 20 30 40 50 60 70 80 90
1-46	A.C.E.	64	U. Fr.	
1-46	Coop. English	55	SLA-G.C. Fr.	
1-46	Minn. Personality Inv.			
	Morale	94		
	Social Adj.	17		
	Family	74		
	Emotionality	86		
	Econ. Conserv.	98		
10-47	Coop. Culture			
	Cont. Soc. Prob.	13	SLA Soph.	
	Hist. & Soc. Stud.	26		
	Literature	1		
	Science	78		
	Fine Arts	21		
	Mathematics	40		
4-48	Ohio Psych.	81	SCB Fr.	
8-54	Ohio Psych.	87	SLA Fr.	
9-54	Allport-Vernon			
	Theoretical	70	SCB Men	
	Economic	99		
	Aesthetic	12		
	Social	27		
	Political	78		
	Religious	17		

FIGURE 59-4 *Test material for Brian Donet.*

this time. There is clearly no primary interest pattern on this profile; there is no secondary interest pattern; and there is no clear rejection pattern. Most of the scores fall at or near the chance range.

In two interviews subsequent to the testing, the picture of indecision and cultural pressure and lack of interests emerged more clearly. Brian had talked vaguely to many friends and adults about "going into business"; he reported that no clear course of action had appealed to him on the basis of these talks. He discussed with the counselor the desirability of canceling out of school before he was officially dropped. He compared his dubious performance with the superior records of both his sister and

brother. He explained that his family resources were such that he would always be well taken care of, and that there was no great reason for him to worry about choosing a career. In this respect his history is similar to some of the findings in McArthur's studies at Harvard [2, 3]. Since a college education is "a good thing," he decided to transfer to a smaller school, just to get a degree. On this note the interviews ended.

Unfortunately, it developed that none of the small colleges in this area would accept Brian on transfer, in view of his total grade record. Brian dropped out of school and got his first job at age twenty-three, during that summer, with a retail credit organiza-

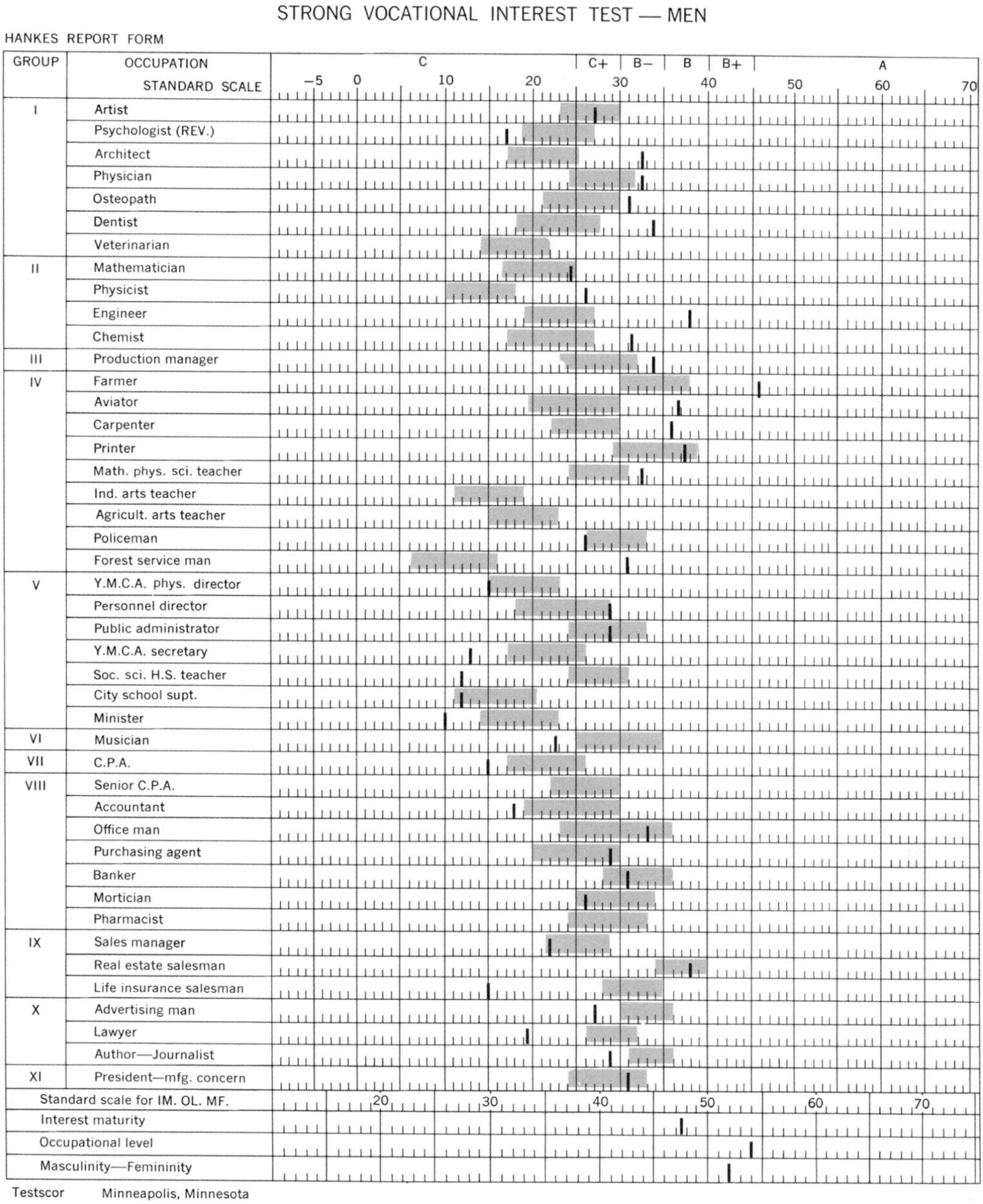

STRONG VOCATIONAL INTEREST TEST — MEN

HANKES REPORT FORM

GROUP	OCCUPATION / STANDARD SCALE	C	C+	B−	B	B+	A

FIGURE 59–5   *Profile for Brian Donet.*

tion. At the opening of school in the fall term, he was readmitted to the university on strict probation; we kept a continuous check on his grades, and he managed to graduate with a baccalaureate degree, on schedule, two years later. He had majored in geography; his plan was to find employment with an import-export organization.

Four years later, Brian returned to the Bureau, and we were able to bring his work history up to date. After graduation, he had started work as a clerk in an automobile branch factory; he remained in that position for about three years, and was then promoted to an assistant managership in the sales division, a consumer survey unit, at a salary of $6000 per year. This was not working out well for him, and he was thinking of leaving the company. His alternative vocational plans included the following: returning to complete training in dentistry; entering the field of hotel management; taking more training in the field of hospital management; just changing jobs and taking anything he could find.

Figure 59–6 shows the Strong Vocational Interest Blank completed at the time of this contact with Brian. On Figure 59–4 we have also reported the scores of two other tests given at about this same time—the Allport-Vernon and the Ohio Psychological Examination. On the ability measure, it is again clear that this is an individual of better than average scholastic ability; this

FIGURE 59–6   *Profile for Brian Donet six years later.*

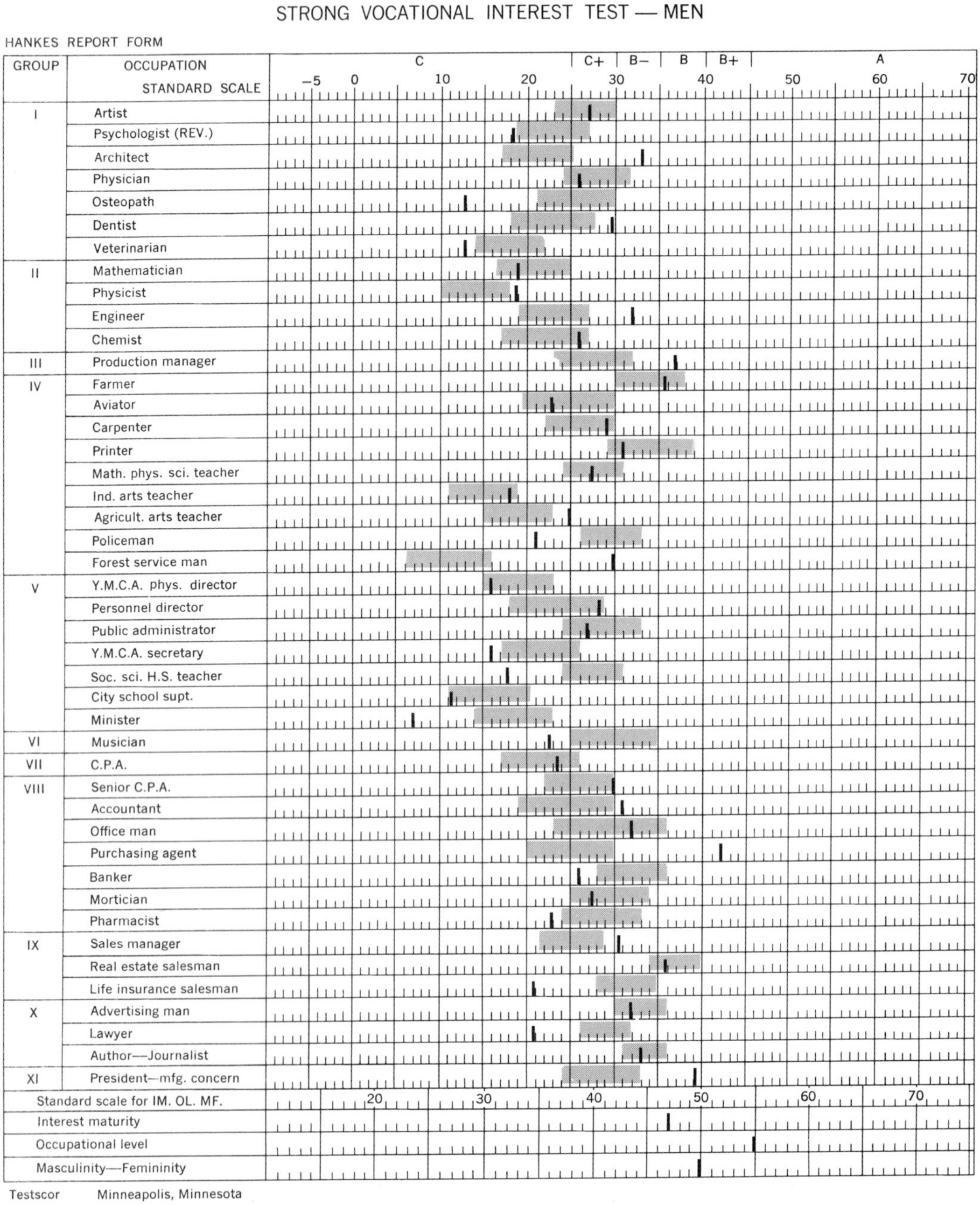

STRONG VOCATIONAL INTEREST TEST — MEN

factor places no limitation on vocational planning. But the Strong profile remains as flat and indeterminate as the one taken six years earlier; there are no patterns. The interpretation of the Allport-Vernon scores should be related to the way of life he has known—high values on prestige and status and on "practical affairs." Thus, at age thirty, Brian remained much as he had been throughout the six years of our contacts with him: a man of substantial ability, but with no driving vocational interests to give shape and meaning to his life. That this is not alone a matter of family status is indicated in the superior record of his younger brother, whose career was more focused and more outstanding in terms of vocational interests. As Brian left the Bureau, he was still undecided, still drifting, and still unmotivated. There is little likelihood that interests will ever emerge in his case.

NORTON BROWN: FAMILY TRADITIONS AND INTEREST PATTERNS

Counselors are quite aware of the many subtle or direct pressures that families can exert on the vocational planning of students. The case of Norton Brown illustrates this form of pressure in a mild way. Norton came to the Bureau during the Christmas holidays of his senior year in high school. He wanted help in working out his educational and vocational plans. The arrangements for this had been made by his parents. He listed his vocational choices as follows: scientific or medical research; forestry sciences; physician; engineer; nursery or greenhouse work.

Both parents and two uncles were in medical practice in a clinic in one of the small communities of Minnesota; their practice was eminently successful and Norton could plan on entering the field of medicine without any trouble if he completed the professional school work. It was fairly evident that his family hoped he would do this, but his own occupational plans did not give a high priority to medicine; in fact they were generally at a somewhat lower status level than the family's own socioeconomic level. Figure 59–7 shows the results of various tests given in this case during 1948–1949. It is quite obvious that Norton not only had superior scholastic ability, but had also achieved in line with this ability. He was in the top 2 per cent of his graduating class in high school; his performance on standard achievement tests in English, mathematics, and social sciences was near the top of the respective norm groups.

Figure 59–8 contains the results of the Strong Vocational Interest Blank given late in 1948. The relatively low occupational level score and the high masculinity-femininity score are both interesting in the nonoccupational set of keys. There is no clear primary pattern, but there is something of a pattern in the technical group of keys,

FIGURE 59–7   *Test material for Norton Brown at the initial session.*

NAME ____Brown, Norton____ COLLEGE _Pre-College_ CLASS _Pre-College_ SEX _M_ AGE __17__

DATE	NAME OF TEST	PERCENTILE	NORM GROUP	10 20 30 40 50 60 70
	High School Rating	98		
11-48	Ohio Psych.	99	SCB Fr.	
11-48	Coop. English	96	SLA-G.C. Fr.	
11-48	Coop. Social Studies	100	SLA Fr.	
11-48	Coop. Gen. Math	96	SLA Fr.	
2-49	A.C.E.		U. Fr.	
2-49	Coop. English	99	SLA-G.C. Fr.	
8-49	Ohio Psych.	100	SLA Fr.	

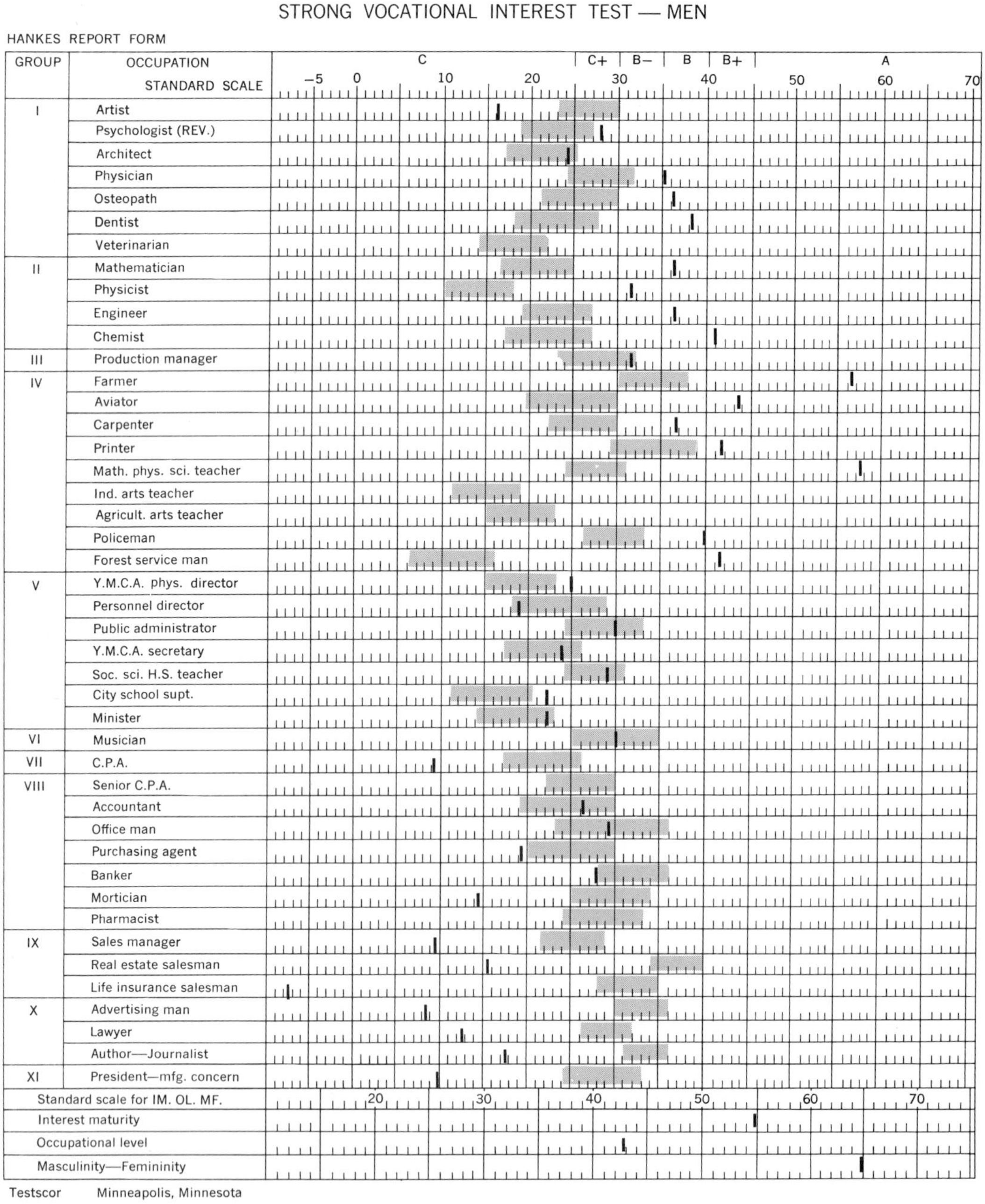

STRONG VOCATIONAL INTEREST TEST — MEN

HANKES REPORT FORM

GROUP	OCCUPATION / STANDARD SCALE	C	C+	B−	B	B+	A
I	Artist						
	Psychologist (REV.)						
	Architect						
	Physician						
	Osteopath						
	Dentist						
	Veterinarian						
II	Mathematician						
	Physicist						
	Engineer						
	Chemist						
III	Production manager						
IV	Farmer						
	Aviator						
	Carpenter						
	Printer						
	Math. phys. sci. teacher						
	Ind. arts teacher						
	Agricult. arts teacher						
	Policeman						
	Forest service man						
V	Y.M.C.A. phys. director						
	Personnel director						
	Public administrator						
	Y.M.C.A. secretary						
	Soc. sci. H.S. teacher						
	City school supt.						
	Minister						
VI	Musician						
VII	C.P.A.						
VIII	Senior C.P.A.						
	Accountant						
	Office man						
	Purchasing agent						
	Banker						
	Mortician						
	Pharmacist						
IX	Sales manager						
	Real estate salesman						
	Life insurance salesman						
X	Advertising man						
	Lawyer						
	Author—Journalist						
XI	President—mfg. concern						
	Standard scale for IM. OL. MF.						
	Interest maturity						
	Occupational level						
	Masculinity—Femininity						

Scale values: −5 0 10 20 30 40 50 60 70

Standard scale for IM. OL. MF.: 20 30 40 50 60 70

Testscor   Minneapolis, Minnesota

FIGURE 59–8   *Profile for Norton Brown at the second testing.*

with a secondary pattern in the physical science group. The interests in the biological science fields are not even at the secondary level, and the complete rejection of the interests of the business contact or verbal-linguistic families is clearly marked.

At this point, there was a certain congruence in Norton's case between some of his claimed interests, his low occupational level score, and his measured interests in the technical family of occupations. To offset this congruence, however, was his extremely high ability level and his family's general socioeconomic level. In the counseling interview that was given over to the interpretation of the various test results, it was obvious that Norton was aware of these two sets of forces operating in his planning; he simply could not find much driving enthusiasm for medicine, even though he recognized that this choice would be the easiest for him to make. On the other hand he was not then quite mature enough or clear enough on his own alternative motivations to break with the family tradition. In planning the work of the freshman year, it was possible to arrange his schedule so that a final decision could be postponed until he had tried out college courses in several of the sciences, and this was done with the counselor's help.

In the orientation program for new freshmen, Norton was again given the Strong Vocational Interest Blank as part of a college testing program in the summer of 1948, just before he entered the university. These results are shown in Figure 59–9. The technical interests are about as they were, but now there is a fairly strong primary pattern in the physical science family of occupations. The rest of the profile is quite comparable to the results obtained seven or eight months earlier.

Norton dropped in at the Bureau in the spring of his sophomore year just to let us know how he was getting along. At that time he was following through on a major in the field of physics and a minor in mathematics; he had given up the idea of medicine; and he was planning on graduate study either at Minnesota or an eastern college. He was a much more mature, self-confident individual than when we had first seen him. He had made almost a straight A average in all his course work, and the university had provided him with a degree of growth in independence that was startling. He was considering the possibility of work in the field of biophysics, but there was no particular conflict involved in his thinking about vocations now, and he was in a position to make informed and rational choices.

We followed his records later to discover that he had graduated from the university with honors in physics and that he was arranging to go on for the doctoral degree in this field, so that he could ultimately have a career in research and teaching.

There are much more severe and crippling family conflicts over vocational choices than we found in Norton's case. Fortunately, the pressures from his family for the traditional choice of medicine were never great, even though Norton himself felt somewhat under duress to carry on the family tradition. He was able to work through this problem and go on to a choice that served more of his needs, and this was accomplished partly through the insight he gained from the interest blank.

HAROLD NORTON: DISCREPANCY BETWEEN INTERESTS AND ABILITIES

Counselors are all too familiar with the cases of students whose claimed interests exceed their ability levels. The records in Harold Norton's case illustrate this problem. Quite often there is no satisfactory *counseling* solution, and the individual moves through a series of mild or drastic failure experiences before reaching a level of choice consonant with his total capacities.

Harold graduated from high school in one of the smaller cities of the state. His high school grade average placed him just outside the lowest third of the senior class, and his scores on the state-wide entrance testing program placed him in the lowest 10 or 12 per cent of a state-wide sample of entering college freshmen. Because of this evidence, he was assigned to the General College when he applied for admission to the university, even though he had hoped to enter the Institute of Technology. In the fall of his freshman year, he took the test battery used by the General College for counseling purposes. These various scores appear on Figure 59–10; the September 1950 test results corroborate the test results from the earlier March state-wide testing.

The Strong Vocational Interest Blank, also taken in September 1950, appears in

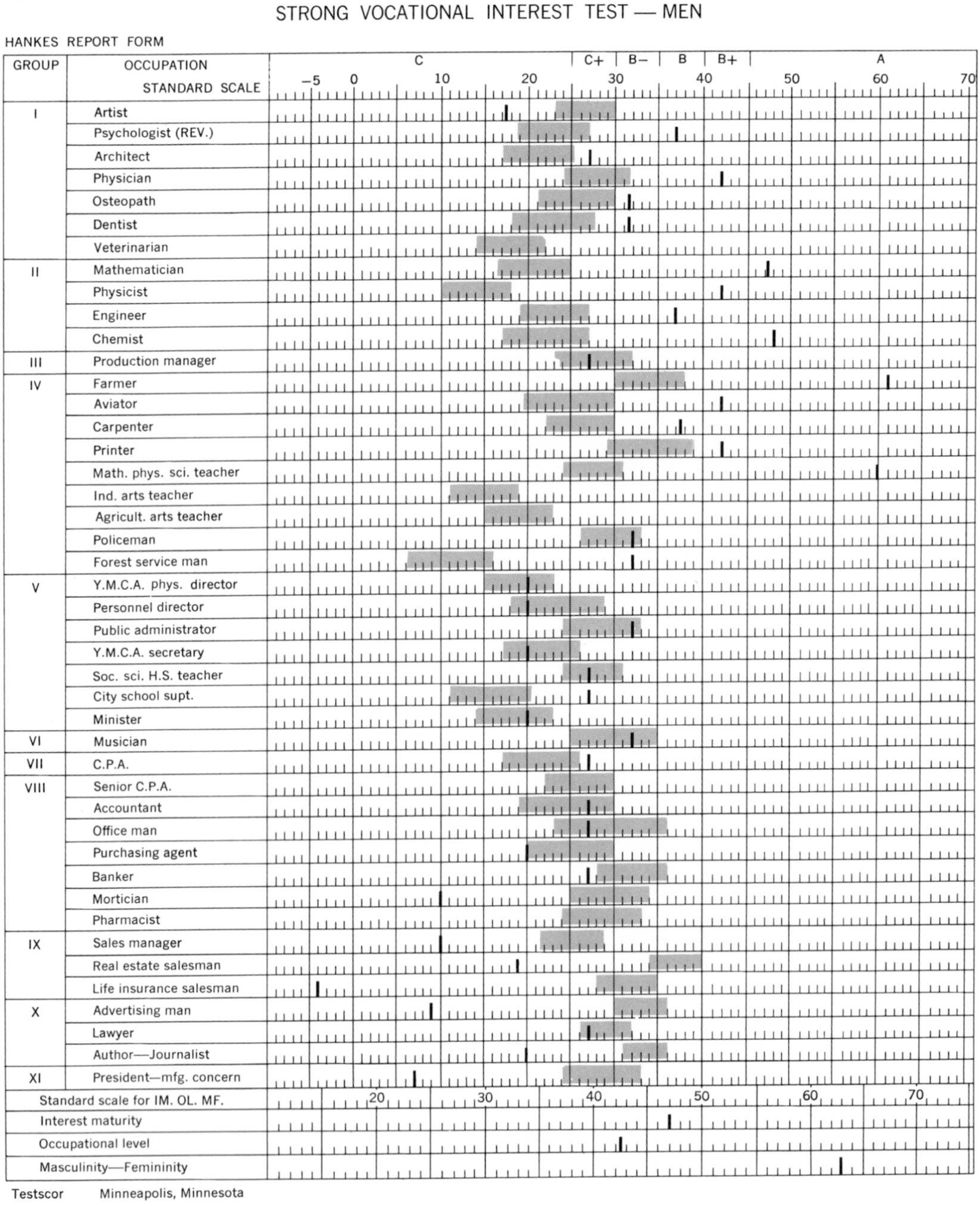

STRONG VOCATIONAL INTEREST TEST — MEN

HANKES REPORT FORM

GROUP	OCCUPATION STANDARD SCALE	C -5 0 10 20	C+	B−	B	B+	A 30 40 50 60 70
I	Artist						
	Psychologist (REV.)						
	Architect						
	Physician						
	Osteopath						
	Dentist						
	Veterinarian						
II	Mathematician						
	Physicist						
	Engineer						
	Chemist						
III	Production manager						
IV	Farmer						
	Aviator						
	Carpenter						
	Printer						
	Math. phys. sci. teacher						
	Ind. arts teacher						
	Agricult. arts teacher						
	Policeman						
	Forest service man						
V	Y.M.C.A. phys. director						
	Personnel director						
	Public administrator						
	Y.M.C.A. secretary						
	Soc. sci. H.S. teacher						
	City school supt.						
	Minister						
VI	Musician						
VII	C.P.A.						
VIII	Senior C.P.A.						
	Accountant						
	Office man						
	Purchasing agent						
	Banker						
	Mortician						
	Pharmacist						
IX	Sales manager						
	Real estate salesman						
	Life insurance salesman						
X	Advertising man						
	Lawyer						
	Author—Journalist						
XI	President—mfg. concern						
	Standard scale for IM. OL. MF.	20 30 40 50 60 70					
	Interest maturity						
	Occupational level						
	Masculinity—Femininity						

Testscor   Minneapolis, Minnesota

FIGURE 59–9 *Profile for Norton Brown.*

Figure 59–11. The A score for the occupation of engineer and the B+ score for the occupation of chemist do not constitute a real primary pattern, but they represent some of the high points on the profile. There are similar high points among the technical group of occupations, but again not quite to the level of a primary pattern. The biological family of occupations shows a few B+ and B scores, but not to the full level of a secondary pattern. Harold's claimed vocational choices were as follows: mechanical testing and designing; inventing; and auto racing. He listed occupations

NAME _____ Norton, Harold _____ COLLEGE _General_ CLASS ___Fr.___ SEX ___M___ AGE ___18___

DATE	NAME OF TEST	PERCENTILE	NORM GROUP	10 20 30 40 50 60 70 80 90
	High School Rating	34		
3-50	A.C.E.	11	U. Fr.	
3-50	Coop. English	7	SLA-G.C. Fr.	
9-50	Ohio Psych.	9	SCB	
1-51	Coop. Reading Comp.	10	Ent. Fr.	
1-51	Wechsler-Bellevue	101 I.Q.		

FIGURE 59–10   *Test material for Harold Norton.*

involving mechanical or technical skills as the family of occupations in which he was most interested.

During his first year in the university, he sought help from the Bureau's reading and study skills program, in an effort to make it possible for him to get better grades. The tests appearing in Figure 59–10 and dated "1-51" cover the evidence obtained at this time. It is quite clear that his ability level on the Wechsler-Bellevue is not up to full professional college work and it is also clear that his reading comprehension skills are quite low in comparison with entering college freshmen. There was little that could be done for him in the improvement of study or reading skills, and certainly we could not bring him to a level that would greatly improve his chances of academic success in a four-year engineering course.

We next saw Harold in the fall of his third year in the university. He had completed a full first year, with about a C average, in the General College; he had then transferred to one of the two-year technical aide curriculums in the Institute of Technology and made slightly better than a C average in the draftsman's course. He had then managed to transfer to the four-year engineering sequence, in which he was registered at the time of our new contact. He repeated the Strong Vocational Interest Blank, with the results shown in Figure 59–12. Now the results are somewhat clearer: the full primary pattern in the technical field of occupations has emerged, with the expected low occupational level

score among the three non-occupational keys; the physical science pattern has disappeared; and there is a fairly strong secondary pattern in the business detail area.

It was obvious from the grades in the engineering courses that Harold was not long for the Institute of Technology; however, he had been trying to stay in school in order to complete the last two advanced years of the Air Force ROTC program, which would eventuate in a reserve commission if he managed to graduate. On the assumption that he might experience difficulty in graduating, he had applied for admission to the aviation cadet training program.

At the end of the fall quarter of his third year in the university, and his first year in a full four-year professional course, his grades were so low as to warrant the cancellation of his registration. Upon follow-up, we learned that he had been admitted to the aviation cadet training program of the Air Force.

No one can say with any certainty that his years in the university had been wasted; yet it is obvious that so long as he phrased his claimed vocational interests in terms of the competitive demands of a professional engineering curriculum, the odds for success were heavily against him by virtue of his limited academic abilities and poor background of educational skills. The results of the interest inventory more nearly foreshadowed the kind of ultimate job adjustment Harold would make. Had he completed the two-year drafting course, he

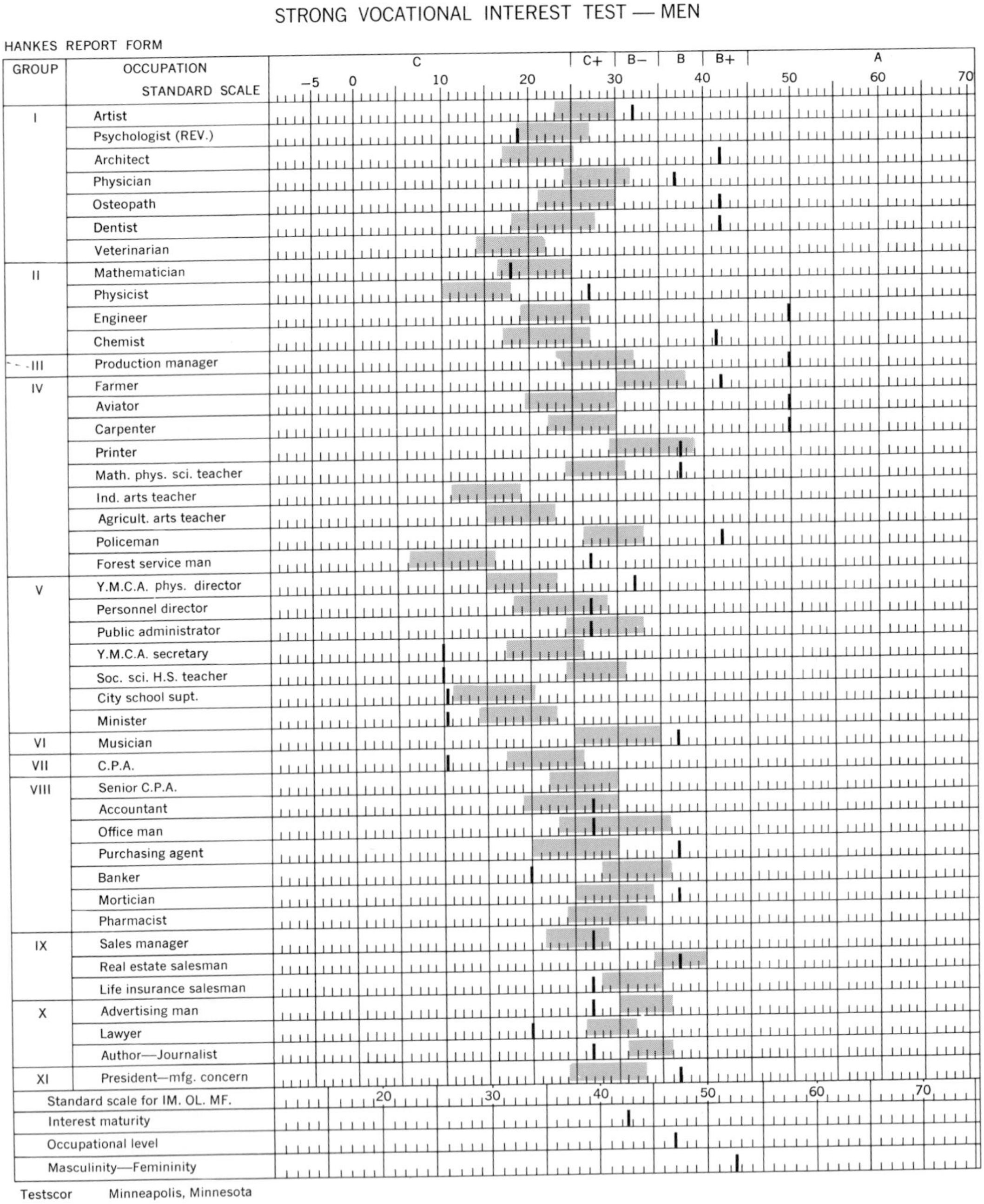

STRONG VOCATIONAL INTEREST TEST — MEN

HANKES REPORT FORM

GROUP	OCCUPATION STANDARD SCALE	C	C+	B−	B	B+	A
I	Artist						
	Psychologist (REV.)						
	Architect						
	Physician						
	Osteopath						
	Dentist						
	Veterinarian						
II	Mathematician						
	Physicist						
	Engineer						
	Chemist						
III	Production manager						
IV	Farmer						
	Aviator						
	Carpenter						
	Printer						
	Math. phys. sci. teacher						
	Ind. arts teacher						
	Agricult. arts teacher						
	Policeman						
	Forest service man						
V	Y.M.C.A. phys. director						
	Personnel director						
	Public administrator						
	Y.M.C.A. secretary						
	Soc. sci. H.S. teacher						
	City school supt.						
	Minister						
VI	Musician						
VII	C.P.A.						
VIII	Senior C.P.A.						
	Accountant						
	Office man						
	Purchasing agent						
	Banker						
	Mortician						
	Pharmacist						
IX	Sales manager						
	Real estate salesman						
	Life insurance salesman						
X	Advertising man						
	Lawyer						
	Author—Journalist						
XI	President—mfg. concern						
	Standard scale for IM. OL. MF.						
	Interest maturity						
	Occupational level						
	Masculinity—Femininity						

Testscor   Minneapolis, Minnesota

FIGURE 59–11   *Profile for Harold Norton at the initial testing.*

might have been farther ahead in getting the technical training that would meet his needs. There was little we could do for him, except to be there when he wanted to see us, and support him while he gradually faced up to the limits imposed by his ability level.

No single work can do full justice to the research materials that have accumulated over more than twenty-five years in this field of measurement. Nor has it been possible to impose an all-inclusive theory on the data. We have tried primarily to array the available information in such a way as

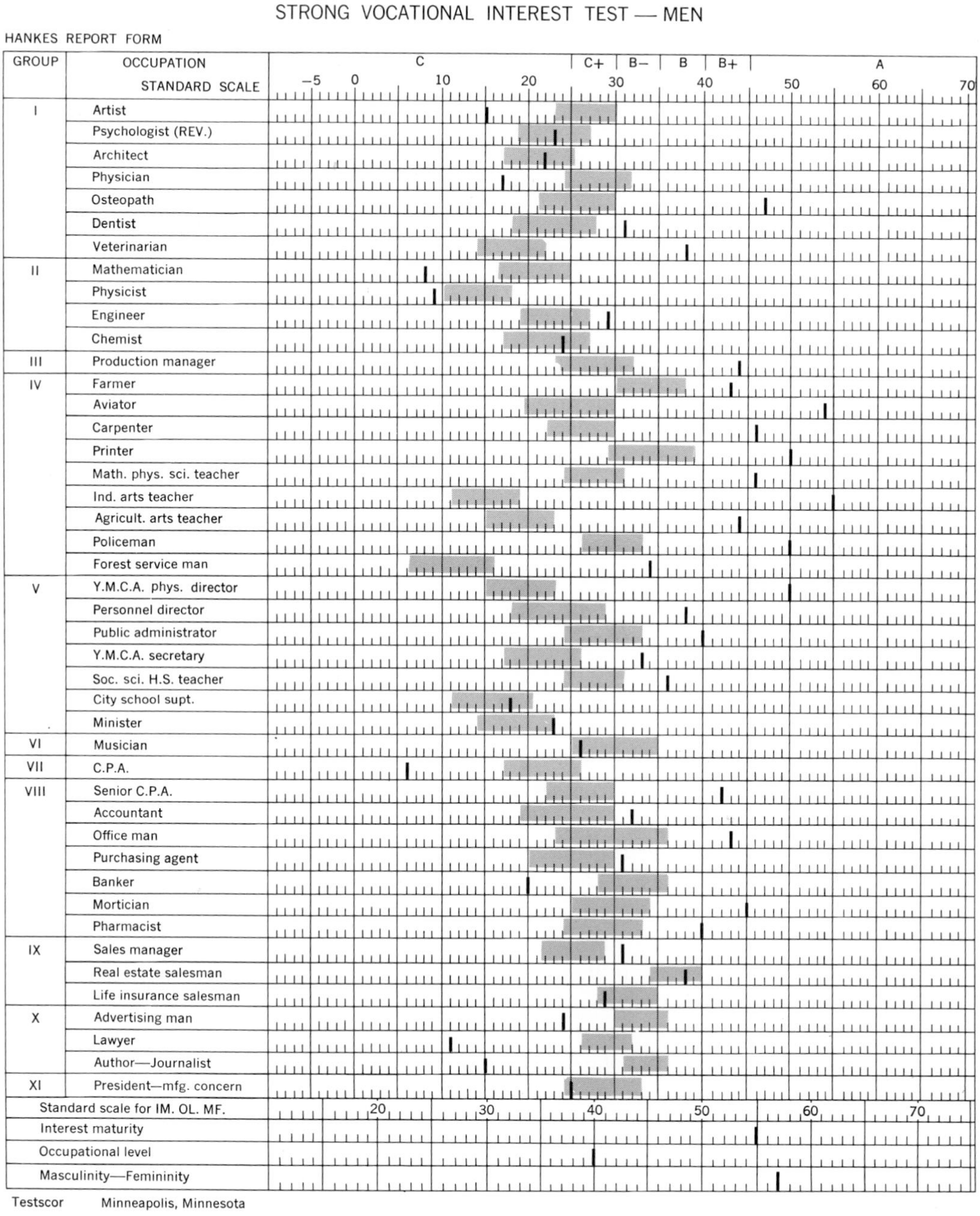

STRONG VOCATIONAL INTEREST TEST — MEN

HANKES REPORT FORM

GROUP	OCCUPATION / STANDARD SCALE	C (−5 0 10 20)	C+	B−	B	B+	A (50 60 70)
I	Artist						
	Psychologist (REV.)						
	Architect						
	Physician						
	Osteopath						
	Dentist						
	Veterinarian						
II	Mathematician						
	Physicist						
	Engineer						
	Chemist						
III	Production manager						
IV	Farmer						
	Aviator						
	Carpenter						
	Printer						
	Math. phys. sci. teacher						
	Ind. arts teacher						
	Agricult. arts teacher						
	Policeman						
	Forest service man						
V	Y.M.C.A. phys. director						
	Personnel director						
	Public administrator						
	Y.M.C.A. secretary						
	Soc. sci. H.S. teacher						
	City school supt.						
	Minister						
VI	Musician						
VII	C.P.A.						
VIII	Senior C.P.A.						
	Accountant						
	Office man						
	Purchasing agent						
	Banker						
	Mortician						
	Pharmacist						
IX	Sales manager						
	Real estate salesman						
	Life insurance salesman						
X	Advertising man						
	Lawyer						
	Author—Journalist						
XI	President—mfg. concern						
	Standard scale for IM. OL. MF.	20 30 40			50 60 70		
	Interest maturity						
	Occupational level						
	Masculinity—Femininity						

Testscor   Minneapolis, Minnesota

FIGURE 59–12   *Profile for Harold Norton at the second testing.*

to provide a comprehensive description of the field of vocational interest measurement and to establish a basic summary from which further research and theory may proceed more effectively. We have tried also to show the importance of interest measurement in the total counseling proc-ess, so far as it mirrors an important aspect of the individual's behavior and predicts his future adjustment.

It seems to us that measured vocational interests reflect the culmination of the developmental and socializing process in our society—a society in which the individual's prestige, status, satisfaction, and contribution are closely tied to occupational labels and occupational tasks. The behavior measured by vocational interest inventories is well determined before job entry and job experience. Individuals, to the extent that they can control their lives, seek out occupations permitting free play for their personality patterns, perceptual habits, and value systems. This search is often confused and halting because the vocabulary of the world of work does not easily translate into the vocabulary descriptive of individual personality and motivation.

The evidence points to the relatively early development of interest patterns—by age fifteen or sixteen—and the comparative stability of patterns thereafter. For a society desperately needing talent, the evidence also indicates clearer differentiation of interests among the more able and more mature young people in our high schools and colleges.

The major impact of the many research studies we have discussed lies in the implicit recognition that interest measurement is truly within the domain of personality and motivation. The role of learning in the formation of interests remains unclear and in need of further study. The idea of a continuum of satisfactions, from intrinsic to extrinsic, helps to clarify the problem of a lower limit of interest differentiation, as it must relate to motivational theory. The longitudinal research, most notably the studies of Tyler, stresses role development and differentiation as a factor fundamental to the development of vocational interests. These interpretations, however, by no means exhaust or exclude alternative concepts of interest development as part of personality theory.

We are handicapped by virtue of the fact that psychology has no single, dominant theory of personality or motivation. When and if one emerges, we may safely assume that it will have to encompass the findings of interest measurement. For the present we can say only that occupational interests are part and parcel of the individual's total striving for adjustment, and grow out of needs arising in his personality development.

At the level of straight empiric findings, including individual case work, the Strong Vocational Interest Blank taps behavior that is meaningful, stable, predictive, and dynamic. We believe that the next quarter century will see accelerated understanding and research in this area of assessment.

REFERENCES

1. DARLEY, J. G., and HAGENAH, THEDA. *Vocational interest measurement: theory and practice*. Minneapolis: The University of Minnesota Press, 1955.
2. McARTHUR, C. Long-term validity of the Strong interest test in two subcultures. *J. appl. Psychol.*, 1954, 38, 346–353.
3. McARTHUR, C., and STEVENS, LUCIA B. The validation of expressed interests as compared with inventoried interests: a fourteen-year follow-up. *J. appl. Psychol.*, 1955, 39, 184–189.

Chapter 60

Expected Developments in Interest and Personality Inventories

G. FREDERIC KUDER

I approach this subject with considerable hesitation. I have an uneasy feeling there are some who believe that the best possible progress, so far as self-inventories are concerned, would be simply to eliminate them. Perhaps, indeed, that will be their ultimate fate, and perhaps I should now take my seat and release the next nine and one-half minutes for the discussion of more durable measures. However, these questionnaires seem to be rather robust at the moment. Perhaps, therefore, you will not take it amiss if I spend a few moments on what may happen to them in the fairly *near* future.

SPECIFICATIONS FOR COLLECTIONS OF ITEMS

In the next few years I expect considerable progress in formulating specifications for

This article is reprinted from *Educational and Psychological Measurement*, 1954, with the permission of the author and the copyright holder.

collections of items designed to be scored for a number of criteria. We cannot expect the set of items assembled on the first or second attempt to be particularly well balanced or to be the most efficient possible for the time required. A series of analyses and revisions is almost inevitable. But a few guiding principles should shorten the process of developing a good instrument, and we are now in a position, I believe, where we can, on the basis of theory and experience, set down various specifications for such a collection of items. One of the requirements might well be that the items should be fairly evenly distributed throughout factor space in the general domain appropriate to the criteria. A similar requirement might be that the collection should be assembled in such a way that it will be possible to develop, without distortion, a fairly reliable measure in any direction within the factor space represented.

In setting up specifications for our hypothetical collection of items we would also do well to remember that it is often more important to get representation of a fairly large number of different and pertinent areas than it is to obtain large samples of a very few areas. Here is an instance in which cultural lag is particularly noticeable in the measurement field. We have known for years, for example, that given two tests of equal validity but with only half enough time available for administering both tests, it is almost always better, from the standpoint of validity, to cut both tests in half than to use only one of the tests. This principle, when generalized, means that it is better to put the emphasis on trying out, systematically, items in as many promising and relatively independent areas as possible. This approach can be carried to the absurd extreme, but I do not think our errors have generally been in that direction.

The approach mentioned almost necessarily involves some sacrifice in reliability of measurement in each specific area, but in many cases any resulting loss in validity will be more than compensated for by the more complete coverage of factors related to a selected criterion. If we can have both high reliability and good coverage, so much the better, but practical considerations are likely to force some compromise between the two. There is, no doubt, a happy medium which is best for the limitations imposed by each specific situation, and I expect to see considerable theoretical and empirical work done on this problem.

THE DETECTION AND PREVENTION OF FAKING

The detection of faking is a subject which is of particular importance in this field of interest and personality. It would seem to be self-evident that there is no way of *compelling* any one to answer questions carefully and sincerely. Many years ago Strong and Steinmetz demonstrated in independent studies that scores on the *Strong Vocational Interest Blank* can be shifted markedly in the desired direction. The evidence from these and subsequent studies by others leaves little room for doubt that interest and personality inventories *can* be faked. Whether a subject *chooses* to prevaricate is another matter which apparently depends pretty much upon the situation and the disposition of the subject. It appears that sincere answers often are actually obtained even when it would seem to be to the advantage of the subject to dissimulate.

Whether a person has chosen to fake may be an academic question in many cases. But there are many situations in which there is strong motivation for distorting answers, and methods for determining whether faking has occurred become important. The MMPI is the outstanding example today of a test for which evidence on this point is available. I expect to see rather intensive research on this problem, and suspect some interesting devices will be built into new tests.

Methods for discouraging and preventing faking are also likely to be worked out. In this connection, I look for a trend in occupational inventories away from items with obvious vocational significance. One of the first interest inventories developed consisted entirely of titles of occupations. Such items are, of course, the most obvious kind possible. We know, by now, that some questions can be found which are related to job satisfaction and which are not obvious to the subject. In the course of time, we may be able to build inventories composed entirely of such items. This trend will probably be a slow one, for we discover the less obvious items only by the tedious process of trial and error.

THE USE OF INVENTORIES AS PROJECTIVE DEVICES

Another promising trend is the one involving having items answered under hypothetical conditions. If these conditions are made vague enough, this procedure amounts to using inventories as projective devices. If we ask a subject to answer a blank so as to make the best impression on anyone who might see the answers, the subject can interpret "anyone" in any way he sees fit, and, we hope, in a way characteristic of his own general attitudes. Items administered in this form can, of course, be analyzed with respect to various criteria, and the pattern they make with the same items administered under standard conditions can also be analyzed with respect to the criteria. One nice advantage of the hypothetical approach is that the items are probably much more difficult to fake. It is possible that the conventional form of administration may sometimes be dispensed with altogether, as in the case of certain empathy tests.

It has been my experience that quite often the scores from tests given under the hypothetical conditions have little or no relation to scores obtained under standard conditions. For example, I find that a scale concerned with a preference for being active in groups correlates almost exactly zero with itself when taken first in the standard way and then so as to make the best possible impression. This is true also of a scale concerned with a preference for familiar and stable situations. And yet these scales are actually somewhat more *reliable* when given according to the best impression directions than when taken in the standard fashion. Differences between the scores are, therefore, highly reliable, and give promise for study as predictor variables.

PATTERN INTERPRETATION

The importance of the reliability of the differences between scores is a point which has often been overlooked. Whenever profiles are used, there is implicit in the situation an evaluation of differences between scores. I expect more and more emphasis to be given to the importance of the reliability of these differences. We know that the differences between scores on two highly correlated tests are themselves quite unreliable. Yet how often are differences between such tests treated as though they were highly significant! On the other hand, if tests are uncorrelated, the reliability of differences in scores is just as reliable as the original tests. If profiles are to mean anything, the differences between the variables in them must be reliable. This requires inevitably that the measures used must be selected and developed so as to overlap relatively little. For profile analysis we need reliable and independent measures, and I expect more emphasis on this objective in the future. It is a happy coincidence that such sets of measures simplify greatly the job of developing prediction equations.

There will, of course, be continued attention and progress in the interpretation of sets of test scores. These techniques will vary from the extremely simple ones which require little work and time to those that are costly in terms of time and money, but which are designed to squeeze a maximum of information out of the available data. It will be recognized, of course, that the technique appropriate for any situation will depend upon a number of considerations. I hope that some principles as to which technique is likely to be most fruitful within the limitations of a specific situation will be developed for the guidance of test technicians and counselors.

Now that the use of larger and larger numbers of cases apparently is becoming feasible, I expect to see more projects using the method of studying people with identical patterns, following certain Weather Bureau techniques used for weather predictions. This approach, of course, has the notable advantage that it does not assume linear relations among the variables involved. There will also no doubt be more and more attention given to patterns of responses to individual items and to patterns of responses to small groups of items. Apropos of this I want to mention two excellent contributions to the pattern problem, one by Gaier and Lee [2] and one by Cronbach and Gleser [1].

ITEM ANALYSIS

Quite a bit of attention has been given in recent years to the development of techniques of item analysis which take account of item overlapping when combining selected items for the prediction of a criterion, without actually computing the item intercorrelations, a job which is usually not feasible. There is room for much more progress along this line, however. I think there will be considerable application of an approach which I shall call the criterion vector method of test construction. This method involves building up a test by selecting items so that the composite will have as nearly as possible the same order of correlations with the tests in the experimental battery as the criterion has with them. If all true variance in the items is accounted for by the tests in the battery, this approach is as effective as considering item intercorrelations, but it involves getting only the correlations of each item with all the tests rather than with all other items and is, therefore, a practical procedure even when the number of items is large.

Of course all this work to allow for item overlapping becomes unnecessary if a composite of items is well designed. If the items are evenly distributed in factor space, as suggested earlier, the centroid of the items with significant validities should come close to coinciding with the criterion vector. In this case, all that is necessary in the construction of a scale is to obtain the correlations of the items with the criterion. The overlapping of items is automatically allowed for. However, the development of such composites will be a time-consuming task. We can expect that the objective of a perfectly uniform distribution of items in factor space will be only approximately achieved. In the meantime, there will continue to be a need for other techniques which allow for item overlapping.

In the face of the trend toward short-cut methods of allowing for item overlapping, we may note that machines have been developed which make it easier to obtain large tables of item intercorrelations, and I expect to see larger and larger tables of this sort. One investigator has recently obtained the 44,850 intercorrelations of 300 items. I hesitate to guess how large a job some courageous soul will tackle within the next ten years. I note with some incredulity that one writer has mentioned at least the possibility of getting the 499,500 intercorrelations from a thousand items.

FACTOR ANALYSIS

There will, no doubt, be more factor analyses. In the future, however, I expect more success in building tests which come close to matching the factors identified by the analyses. The identification of factors does not automatically endow an investigator with good measures of those factors, but this fact has not always been recognized. One does not have to look far in the personality field to find batteries of measures which overlap markedly although designed to measure factors found in the original analysis to be theoretically independent. I think that by now we have more insight into the problem and principles involved, and recognize that the job is not quite as simple as it may have at first appeared. We know that it is not enough merely to attempt to build a measure of a factor by the method of internal consistency. As items are selected for a factor, the correlations of the growing composite with the other factors must be carefully controlled. The criterion vector method of test construction, mentioned previously, is appropriate to this situation when the factor for which the scale is being constructed is taken as the criterion. In the future, we should be more successful in building tests to fit the factors.

This paper could go on and on, but fortunately for you there is a time limit. Some items should at least be mentioned. I expect to see more use of suppressor variables in the future. We are likely to see more attempts to develop alternatives for preference items which have equal appeal or apparent equal social approval, although I am inclined to regard this objective as a will-o'-the-wisp, for reasons I wish there were time to mention. I think the empirical search for promising theoretical variables will continue to be fruitful in this field. There will no doubt be growing interest in tests of empathy. I expect to see increased attention given to the satisfaction a person gets from a course or a job as a criterion.

All in all, we can look forward to quite a number of interesting developments.

REFERENCES

1. CRONBACH, L. J., & GLESER, G. C. Assessing similarity between profiles. *Psychol. Bull.*, 1953, 50, 456–473.
2. GAIER, E. L., & LEE, MARILYN C. Pattern analysis: the configural approach to predictive measurement. *Psychol. Bull.*, 1953, 50, 140–148.

Part *7* ~

ASSESSMENT OF
ATTITUDES

Until the late 1920s, there had been only a few isolated attempts at measurement in the general area of social psychology. Bogardus, for example, derived a social distance scale for the degree of acceptability of various national groups by asking subjects whether members of a particular nationality should be admitted to this country as visitors only or whether they would also be acceptable as citizens, as equals in employment, as neighbors, as personal friends, or as relatives by marriage.[1] Another instance was a study by Allport and Hartman, who attempted to set up for each of a number of political issues a series of attitude statements representing gradations of opinion from one extreme of favorableness to the other.[2] Students were then asked to check the one statement on each issue that best represented their own opinion. For a given issue, frequency counts of the endorsements of each statement were arrayed in a column diagram, with the units on the base line representing the rank order of the statements. Since the

[1] Bogardus, E. S. Measuring social distance. *J. Appl. Sociol.*, 1925, **9**, 299–308.
[2] Allport, F. H., and Hartman, D. A. Measurement and motivation of atypical opinion in a certain group. *Amer. polit. Sci. Rev.*, 1925, **19**, 735–760.

interval separating any two statements on the base line was completely arbitrary, however, these frequency diagrams could not be interpreted as distributions of the favorableness of attitude nor could measures of central tendency or variability of attitude in a group be meaningfully assayed.

This latter study captured the interest of Louis L. Thurstone, who was at the time engaged in developing the law of comparative judgment and new methods of psychophysical analysis.[3] Although the law of comparative judgment had arisen in the context of psychophysics, it was in no way dependent upon the measurement of any physical properties and it provided a unit of measurement, the discriminal dispersion, that was frankly subjective. This new subjective measurement could be applied to derive psychological scales for stimulus properties having no measurable physical counterparts—even those evoking social and aesthetic reactions—as long as consistent comparative judgments could be made with respect to the attribute in question. Thurstone, eager to extend these methods to the study of "interesting stimuli," applied the new psychophysical principles to some of the attitude statements used by Allport and Hartman, thereby deriving a rational base line for the distribution of opinion such that equal intervals on the scale represented "equally often-noticed shifts in opinion or equal-appearing opinion differences."[4]

Thurstone recognized the importance of his new subjective metric for the general problem of measuring social attitudes and published in 1928 an influential paper with the forthright title "Attitudes Can Be Measured," outlining the basic rationale of his approach.[5] Essentially, he proposed that a group of judges be asked to evaluate the degree of favorableness or unfavorableness of selected statements toward some attitudinal object, using such judgment methods as paired comparisons, rank order, equal-appearing intervals, or successive intervals. In the method of paired comparisons, for example, judges were presented with all possible pairs of the selected statements and were asked to indicate which statement in each pair appeared more favorable; in the method of equal-appearing intervals, subjects were instructed to sort the statements into a set of ordered categories, usually nine or eleven, in such a way that the categories appeared to represent equally spaced gradations of opinion. Scale values representing the relative favorableness of each statement toward the issue in question were then derived by applying the law of comparative judgment (or some closely related mathematical model).[6] Statements were selected for the final scale to

[3] Thurstone, L. L. *The measurement of values.* Chicago: Univer. of Chicago Press, 1959.

[4] Thurstone, L. L. The measurement of opinion. *J. abnorm. soc. Psychol.,* 1928, **22**, 415–430.

[5] Thurstone, L. L. Attitudes can be measured. *Amer. J. Sociol.,* 1928, 33, 529–554.

[6] Detailed descriptions of these judgment scaling methods (and of other scaling techniques mentioned in these comments) may be obtained in Edwards, A. L. *Techniques of attitude scale construction.* New York: Appleton-Century-Crofts, 1957; Green, B. F. Attitude measurement. In G. Lindzey (Ed.), *Handbook of Social Psychology,* Cambridge, Massachusetts: Addison-Wesley, 1954; and Torgerson, W. S. *Theory and methods of scaling.* New York: Wiley, 1958.

produce an evenly graduated series of scale values for the entire range of opinion. These statements were subsequently administered to appropriate groups of respondents, who were asked to indicate their agreement or disagreement with each item; the favorableness of each respondent's attitude was estimated by the average scale value of the items he endorsed. Under the impetus of these developments, there was a burgeoning of research on social attitudes: for many years thereafter these judgment methods were widely applied to construct attitude scales about all sorts of issues for administration to all sorts of groups.[7]

In 1932, Rensis Likert proposed a quite different approach to attitude measurement—the application of item-analysis techniques from the mental testing field directly to the subjects' responses of agreement and disagreement; no prior judgments of the favorableness of the statements were required.[8] In this procedure, which is called the method of summated ratings, subjects usually indicated the degree of their agreement or disagreement with each item by selecting one of five response alternatives—e.g., strongly disagree, disagree, undecided, agree, and strongly agree. These response categories were typically assigned simple scoring weights of one to five, and a respondent's scale score was taken as the sum of his scores on the separate items. Statements were selected for the final attitude measure in terms of their discriminatory power in significantly differentiating between subjects scoring in the upper and lower quartiles of the total scale (or in terms of the magnitude of correlation between the item response and the total score).

Other response methods of attitude scaling were subsequently introduced, notably scalogram analysis by Louis Guttman and latent structure analysis by Paul Lazarsfeld. Scalogram analysis is a technique for ordering items and individuals so that a respondent agreeing with a particular item will also agree with all items lower in rank order.[9] If

---

[7] Generalizations of these judgment models have also been proposed for the multidimensional scaling of stimuli varying on several relevant dimensions simultaneously. Instead of judging the degree of favorableness or unfavorableness of single statements with respect to some specified attitudinal variable, subjects are asked to judge the degree of similarity or difference of pairs of statements with respect to their overall attitudinal implications. Scale values are then derived to represent the relative differences (or "psychological distance") among the statements. These distance values are subsequently analyzed by procedures closely related to factor analysis to ascertain the number of dimensions implied by the judged stimulus differences and to determine scale values for the statements on each dimension uncovered. Multidimensional scaling methods have thus far been applied to attitude statements, however, in only a few instances (Abelson, R. P. A technique and a model for multidimensional attitude scaling. *Publ. Opin. Quart.*, 1954–1955, **18**, 405–418; Messick, S. The perception of social attitudes. *J. abnorm. soc. Psychol.*, 1956, **52**, 57–66.)

[8] Likert, R. A technique for the measurement of attitudes. *Arch. Psychol.*, 1932, No. 140; Murphy, G., & Likert, R. *Public opinion and the individual.* New York: Harper, 1937.

[9] Guttman, L. A basis for scaling qualitative data. *Amer. Sociol. Rev.*, 1944, **9**, 139–150; Guttman, L. The problem of attitude and opinion measurement. In S. A. Stouffer et al., *Measurement and prediction.* Princeton, New Jersey: Princeton Univer. Press, 1950; Guttman, L. The basis for scalogram analysis. In S. A. Stouffer et al., *Measurement and prediction*, Princeton, New Jersey: Princeton Univer. Press, 1950.

there were no exceptions to this pattern, it would be possible to reproduce from a person's total score alone his separate responses to each of the statements. Such a set of items, called a perfect Guttman scale, is said to be unidimensional. However, since perfect patterns of responses rarely occur, one must evaluate the extent to which a unidimensional scale has been achieved in practice by means of some coefficient of reproducibility that indexes the proportion of item responses correctly reproduced; such coefficients are discussed in detail in Chapter 16.

Lazarsfeld's latent structure analysis provides a general mathematical model relating the probability of item endorsement (and of joint item endorsement) to position on an underlying latent variable, such as attitude. Depending upon the assumptions made about the distribution of the attitude variable and about the form of the function relating probability of endorsement to the latent variable, it is possible to show that many other measurement methods—such as summated ratings, Guttman scaling, test theory, and factor analysis—are special cases of latent structure analysis.[10] The latent structure model has thus been of enormous heuristic value, but unique scaling methods derived from it have rarely been applied in substantive attitude research.

Measures of attitude developed by any of these methods should be evaluated, as Green emphasizes in the first article in Part 7, in terms of the same standards as any other psychological measure—namely, in terms of the consistency and reliability of response and the convergent and discriminant validity exhibited by its pattern of correlates. This latter requirement of construct validity is necessary to support the inference that the observed consistency in response to social objects is due to (and signifies the operation of) an underlying social attitude. But to pursue this process of construct validation one of course needs more than a provisional measure of the attitude and an array of correlations with other variables. Some conception of the nature of the attitude is required to serve as an initial framework for evaluating the consistency and appropriateness of the obtained correlates. Verbally expressed opinions about a particular social object, for example, might be found in some cases to be poorly correlated with observed actions taken toward the object. The implications of such a finding for the construct validity of the opinion measure, however, would depend upon whether one viewed attitude as a feeling of positive or negative affect toward the object, as Thurstone did, or as a primary action tendency determining specific behaviors.[11]

[10] Lazarsfeld, P. F. The logic and mathematical foundation of latent structure analysis. In S. A. Stouffer et al., *Measurement and prediction*. Princeton, New Jersey: Princeton Univer. Press, 1950; Green, B. F. Attitude measurement. In G. Lindzey (Ed.), *Handbook of Social Psychology*. Cambridge, Massachusetts: Addison-Wesley, 1954; Green, B. F. Latent structure analysis and its relation to factor analysis. *J. Amer. Statist. Ass.*, 1952, **47**, 71–76; Lazarsfeld, P. F. Latent structure analysis and test theory. In H. Gulliksen & S. Messick (Eds.), *Psychological scaling*. New York: Wiley, 1960.

[11] Thurstone, L. L. Comment on Nettler and Golding's paper "The Measurement of Attitudes toward the Japanese in America." *Amer. J. Sociol.*, 1946, **52**, 39–40; see also LaPiere, R. T. Attitudes vs. actions. *Social Forces*, 1934, **14**, 230–237.

The notion of attitude was elevated to a central position in social psychology by Thomas and Znaniecki in their heroic study of *The Polish Peasant in Europe and America*. In their view, attitude is "a process of individual consciousness which determines real or possible activity of the individual in the social world." An attitude is thus a "tendency to act," and as such, it is directed—an attitude is "always fundamentally an attitude toward something."[12] This general conception has been endorsed in several formulations, including Allport's famous dictum: "An attitude is a mental and neural state of readiness, organized through experience, exerting a directive or dynamic influence upon the individual's response to all objects and situations with which it is related."[13]

In Chapter 61, Bert F. Green reviews several definitions of attitude and concludes that the critical feature is response covariation: "An individual's social attitude is an enduring syndrome of response consistency with regard to a set of social objects." But a syndrome of response consistency in some form is basic to all psychological measurement—it does not distinguish measures of social attitude. The latter must be further differentiated in terms of the content of the social objects to which the attitude is directed and the mode of response in which the consistency is expressed. Green distinguishes three types of attitudes as a function of response mode: elicited verbal attitudes, which are inferred from consistent reactions to questions; spontaneous verbal attitudes, which are inferred from remarks volunteered in informal settings; and action attitudes, which are inferred from observed behaviors. This distinction stems from a realization that it may not be warranted to generalize the operation of an attitude beyond the particular universe of response from which it was derived—that what a man says consistently in public or in response to direct inquiry may not agree with his actions in the face of social, economic, and political pressures or with his feelings expressed privately to a friend. Furthermore, he may have some beliefs that he will not discuss at all and some that he will not admit even to himself. Thus, many of the same processes of self-deception and willful distortion that plague personality measurement also operate to invalidate attitude measurement. Attitude researchers have responded to this challenge, however, in much the same way as their counterparts in the personality area—by attempting to circumvent these facades through the use of indirect, disguised techniques. These disguised procedures include variations of projective methods, such as the Thematic Apperception Test and the sentence completion technique, as well as purportedly objective tasks in which attitudes toward the selected social content tend to introduce systematic biases in the performance, such as tests of information, critical thinking, perception, and memory. These indirect tech-

---

[12] Thomas, W. I., & Znaniecki, F. *The Polish peasant in Europe and America.* 5 Volumes. Boston: Badger, 1918–1920. See also Blumer, H. An appraisal of Thomas and Znaniecki's *The Polish Peasant in Europe and America. Critiques of Research in the Social Sciences: I.* New York: Social Science Research Council, 1939.

[13] Allport, G. W. Attitudes. In C. M. Murchison (Ed.), *Handbook of Social Psychology.* Worcester, Massachusetts: Clark University Press, 1935.

niques are briefly discussed by Green in Chapter 61; more comprehensive reviews have been provided by Campbell and by Weschler and Bernberg.[14]

In Chapter 62, Adorno, Frenkel-Brunswik, Levinson, and Sanford outline the methodology used in their monumental study, *The Authoritarian Personality*.[15] Their approach, which combines the use of factual questions and opinion-attitude scales with projective "open-ended" questions, clinical interviews, and the Thematic Apperception Test, reflects a conviction that multiple methods employing indirection and disguise are required for a valid characterization of antidemocratic attitudes—such as ethnocentrism—which are contrary to the general sociocultural milieu of the respondent. The authors noted that such social attitudes, whether profascist or prodemocratic, rarely occur as isolated beliefs, but are typically part of an organized framework of attitudes and values called an ideology that provides a characteristic way of thinking about man and society. These ideologies in turn are grounded in the psychological needs of the individual. It thus appeared necessary for a proper understanding of antidemocratic attitudes not only to assess them at the level of expressed opinion, but also to ferret out their ideological and personality underpinnings. An important feature of this work was the attempt to develop an attitude scale, the California F scale, that would indirectly tap implicit antidemocratic trends in the personality. This was done by constructing items to serve as rationalizations for the irrational wishes and fears that tend to dispose individuals toward an authoritarian stance.

This attempt to make the items of the California F scale indirect by casting them in the form of rationalizations, however, resulted in a set of sweepingly-worded, plausible-sounding generalities that were particularly conducive to uncritical acceptance (or to routine rejection) on the basis of the item form rather than the particular item content. As Messick and Jackson point out in Chapter 63, such a tendency toward uncritical acceptance, which is called an acquiescent response set, is especially troublesome on the California F scale, since all of its items are worded in the same direction—agreement indicating authoritarian tendencies. The operation of the response set is thus perfectly confounded with the content determinants of response, and it is impossible to appraise their relative contributions to scale scores or to observed correlations without introducing items worded in the opposite direction (or utilizing some experimental method for controlling the response set, such as a forced-choice item format). Messick and Jackson briefly review some of the F scale studies that incorporated such reversed wordings to demonstrate the confounding influence of acquiescent response set.

In Chapter 64, Nathan Kogan modifies the standard Likert attitude-scaling procedure to take into account the possible influence of ac-

[14] Campbell, D. T. The indirect assessment of social attitudes. *Psychol. Bull.*, 1950, **47**, 15–38; Weschler, I. R., & Bernberg, R. E. Indirect methods of attitude measurement. *Int. J. Opin. Attitude Res.*, 1950, **4**, 209–218.

[15] Adorno, T. W., Frenkel-Brunswik, Else, Levinson, D. J., Sanford, R. N. *The Authoritarian Personality*. New York: Harper, 1950.

quiescence in the process of scale construction. In developing a scale of attitudes toward old people (OP), Kogan constructed both positive and negative versions of every item and derived, using the usual item-analysis statistics, separate subscales for both favorable (OP+) and unfavorable (OP−) attitudes. By comparing the substantial correlation obtained between these positive and negative subscales with their respective reliabilities, he was able to demonstrate that the contribution of acquiescence in this instance was relatively small. At the same time, however, the positive and negative OP subscales were found to display differential correlations with other measures as a function of their direction of wording, thereby indicating that many of the correlations between distinct content scales were partly, and sometimes substantially, due to response set. This finding neatly exemplifies the importance of keeping positive and negative items separate in the evaluation of correlates.

In the final Chapter of Part 7, Brayfield and Crockett review several studies relating employee attitudes to employee performance and find evidence for little or no association, except between measures of dissatisfaction and withdrawal from the job. These findings offer one more warning that specific behaviors are multiply determined and must be considered in situational, socioeconomic, and political terms, as well as in terms of individual attitudes. The authors intend this review of negative findings primarily as a call for greater attention to situational and interpersonal demands in developing hypotheses about the role of employee attitudes and morale in job performance. It is not too surprising that dissatisfied workers should be absent more often and change jobs at a higher rate than satisfied workers, but is the motivational basis for a direct relation between positive satisfaction and job performance equally plausible? Increased personal productivity may serve few of the employee's goals either inside or outside the company, and it may even hamper relations with his fellow workers and the union. Even when increased productivity does represent an appropriate path to a goal, such as promotion, failure to achieve this goal by a particular time may cause dissatisfaction, resulting in a high producer being possibly less satisfied than a low producer. If such motivational dynamics are taken into account to determine the meaning of productivity for the individual, it may be possible to develop differential expectations for the relation between employee attitudes and job performance as a function of specific conditions. Failure to do this would tend to result in average correlations that are not only low but meaningless.

Chapter 61

Attitude Measurement

BERT F. GREEN

THE CONCEPT OF ATTITUDE

To be able to understand how attitudes can be measured, we first need to examine the concept of attitude. Like many psychological variables, attitude is a hypothetical or latent variable, rather than an immediately observable variable. The concept of attitude does not refer to any one specific act or response of an individual, but is an abstraction from a large number of related acts or responses. For example, when we state that individual *A* has a less favorable attitude toward labor organizations than individual *B*, we mean that *A*'s many different statements and actions concerning labor organizations are consistently less favorable to labor than are *B*'s comparable words and deeds. We are justified in using a comprehensive concept like attitude when the many related responses are consistent. That is, if people who disapprove of the closed shop are also likely to want to outlaw strikes, and to oppose minimum wage

This article was reprinted from the *Handbook of Social Psychology*, 1954, with permission of the author and Addison-Wesley Publishing Company, Inc.

laws, then it seems reasonable to speak of an antilabor attitude.

In general terms, a latent variable is used to describe the consistency or covariation of a number of different responses to stimuli of the same general class. The variable is viewed as mediating the stimuli and the responses. The responses are said to covary because they are all mediated by the same hypothetical variable. The latent variable is useful because it unifies a set of data, namely, the observed responses. Hypothetical variables of this kind have been called *traits, intervening variables* [31], *latent variables* [27], *genotypes* [9], and *factors* [45]. The observable data have been called *manifest variables, phenotypes,* and *indicants* [43].

Many definitions of social attitudes have been proposed. These definitions seem to have a common theme that suggests the manner in which attitude may be viewed as a latent variable. This theme is the concept of attitude as a consistency among responses to a specified set of stimuli, or social objects.

Consider a few examples. Krech and Crutchfield [25, p. 152] view attitude as

". . . an enduring organization of motivational, emotional, perceptual, and cognitive processes with respect to some aspect of the individual's world." An enduring organization of psychological processes seems to imply a consistency of response patterns. For Doob [11] an attitude refers to an implicit response that is both anticipatory and mediating in reference to patterns of overt responses, that is evoked by a variety of stimulus patterns, and that is considered socially significant in the individual's society. Overt responses are consistent in that they are mediated by the implicit response. Allport [2, p. 810], after reviewing many early definitions of attitude, concluded that "an attitude is a mental and neural state of readiness exerting a directive influence upon the individual's response to all objects and situations with which it is related." Fuson [14] defines an attitude as the probability of occurrence of a defined behavior in a defined situation. Campbell [7] suggests that a social attitude is evidenced by consistency in response to social situations.

It is apparent from these examples that the concept of attitude implies a consistency or predictability of responses. An attitude governs, or mediates, or predicts, or is evidenced by a variety of responses to some specified set of social objects or situations. Campbell [7, p. 31] has summarized this view neatly in presenting an operational definition of attitude: *"An individual's social attitude is an [enduring] syndrome of response consistency with regard to [a set of] social objects."*

This definition does not divest attitudes of their affective and cognitive properties, which may be properties of, or correlates of, the responses that comprise the attitude. However, attention is focused on the characteristic of attitude that is basic to all attitude measurement: response covariation. In each measurement method, covariation among responses is related to the variation of an underlying variable. The latent attitude is defined by the correlations among responses.

The set of social objects that forms the reference class of an attitude distinguishes attitude from other psychological variables such as habit, temperament, drive, or intelligence. It is of secondary importance whether we call the variable an attitude, or a trait, or a habit. The operational definition will always be in terms of the referent class of stimuli.

The content of an attitude is determined by the responses which constitute it. The set of behaviors comprising an attitude will be called an *attitude universe*—Guttman [20] developed the idea of a universe in connection with his scaling method; his approach seems applicable to the general measurement problem. The elements of this universe are manifest variables—the responses to specific situations. A sample of these elements is used to measure the attitude; from this sample of behavior an inference can be made about the entire universe. For example, if a sample of elements is homogeneous, it is reasonable to infer that the universe also is homogeneous. Furthermore, the scores of individuals on this scale may be taken as representative of their behavior as described by the universe of elements. On the other hand, homogeneous subsets of elements may be found within the original universe, implying that several dimensions are represented in the original attitude universe.

Conceptually, then, attitude measurement involves sampling a behavior universe, and measuring the universe by means of the sample. This means that the sample of elements should be representative. If only a small subset of the total attitude universe is sampled, then inference beyond this subset is not legitimate. Of course, in practice we seldom have the universe, but only the sample. We may characterize the elements of the hypothetical universe by means of the sample; however, it is very important not to overgeneralize. From a sample of verbal responses to questions about opinions, one should not make inferences about behavior other than verbal responses to similar verbal questions. It may be that responses to these verbal questions are correlated with responses in nonverbal situations, but this must be determined experimentally.

The concepts of attitude universe and subuniverse are certainly not precise, but they are helpful in formulating the measurement problem, and will be particularly useful in discussing validity.

As we have defined it, an attitude is a latent variable, since its meaning is derived from the covariation of responses in some attitude universe. To obtain a more precise definition of an attitude, we need a mathematical model that relates the responses, or observed variables, to the latent variable. Each psychological scaling method either states or implies such a model. The problem of measuring an attitude is one of selecting a scaling model by which the response data can be related to the attitude variable.

PROPERTIES OF SCALES

Different scaling methods have different properties. To select a scaling method wisely, it is important to understand the various properties of scales of measurement.

The quantification of psychological attributes has been the subject of much debate. Some scientists, including Ferguson, Myers, Bartlett, *et al.* [12], Bergmann and Spence [4], and Johnson [23], have argued that much psychological measurement is not true measurement, since it does not conform to the methods and definitions used in physical measurement. They point out that most physical scales have the property of additivity, and that this property may be demonstrated experimentally. An operational definition of the sum of two lengths may be achieved by laying two sticks end to end; in the case of weight, two weights and a balance are needed. By what psychological experiment, it is asked, may two pitches be added, or two attitudes?

One answer has been given by Gulliksen [15]. He showed that a logical extension of the concept of additivity will allow scales devised by the method of paired compari-

sons to be classed as additive. In this case the difference between two scale values is defined operationally. The experiment consists in determining the proportion of trials on which stimulus *i* is judged to be greater than stimulus *j* with respect to the attribute in question. A transformation based on the normal distribution relates this observed proportion to the difference between the scale values of the two stimuli. If the differences between the scale values of all pairs of stimuli are mutually consistent, e.g., $(S_i - S_j) + (S_j - S_k) = (S_i - S_k)$, then the additive property of the scale is established.

The argument about the properties of a scale of measurement has led to a broader conception of the nature of measurement. Stevens [43], Lorge [29], and others have pointed out that in its broadest sense, *measurement is the assignment of numerals to objects, events, or persons, according to rules.* With the rules properly defined, the numerals may be used to represent relations among the objects, and to compare these objects with other sets of objects similarly measured. The result of a measurement is a *scale*. A scale comprises the set of numerals given to the objects by using a certain rule of assignment. The objects are then said to be scaled.

Objects may be measured according to many different rules, each of which leads to a scale with special properties. Stevens [43] distinguishes among *nominal, ordinal, interval,* and *ratio* scales. In a nominal scale, objects are placed in several mutually exclusive categories, but there is no necessary relation among the categories. The number assigned to the objects in a category serves as a label, but has no quantitative meaning. Any other set of labels would be adequate if each original label is replaced by a different label in the new set (i.e., a one-to-one transformation). When objects can be arranged in a rank order with respect to some variable, they are said to form an ordinal scale. Numbers may be assigned to the objects if the numbers are in the same rank order as the objects. (Any monotonic transformation is permissible.) We might obtain an ordinal scale of the hardness of the several solid substances by determining which substances scratch which other substances. When the intervals between objects on a scale can be measured, then an interval scale exists. An interval scale of hardness would require some experimental method to determine *how much* harder substance A was than substance B. We could then assign a number to each substance so that the difference between the two values indicated the extent of the difference in hardness. Another set of numbers could be substituted for the original set only if there were a linear relationship $(y = ax + b)$ between the two sets of numbers. A ratio scale results when there is some way of showing how many *times* greater one object is than another. Numbers are assigned to the objects so that the numbers have the same ratio as the experimentally determined ratios of the objects. A ratio scale implies a fixed zero point, so that the only admissible transformation is multiplication by a constant $(y = ax)$. Weight forms a ratio scale because we can show that four pounds is four times as heavy as one pound, and similarly for all pairs of weights.

This classification is not complete, although it includes the main properties of scales. Coombs [8, 9] has suggested several scales that fall between nominal and ordinal scales. For example, we could have an ordered set of categories, with objects within a category being unordered. A partially ordered set of objects would result if some objects could not be ordered with respect to some other objects. Coombs has also suggested an "ordered metric," in which the objects are ordered, and the intervals between objects on the scale are also ordered.

Ordinal, interval, and ratio scales are defined with respect to a single dimension along which the objects are placed. These definitions can be extended to include multidimensional scales. It is an experimental question whether the relations among the objects are consistent with a one-dimensional continuum. For example, we might find an inconsistent set of differences, such as $A - B = 4$, $B - C = 3$, $A - C = 5$. Here, if the result is not to be called "error," the quantities must be referred to a two-dimensional scale. A, B, and C could be represented as points on a plane, with the obtained differences taken as the distances between the points, whereupon A, B, and C would be the vertices of a right triangle. For example, in a scale of colors, A and B might differ only in saturation, and B and C might differ only in hue, while A and C might differ in both saturation and hue. In this case, A and C would appear to be more dissimilar than A and B, or B and C. Although multidimensional scaling will not be treated here—see Torgerson [47] and Bennett [3]—the general concept is basic to the various definitions of unidimensionality that will be met later.

DEFINITIONS

The terms *measurement, scale, attitude,* and *attitude universe* have been defined above. In this section we give definitions for other terms which we shall use in special senses.

Attitude measurement consists in assessing an individual's responses to a set of social objects or situations. This is done by observing a sample of behavior from an attitude universe. Each behavioral element in the attitude universe is the response to a particular situation or object. The particular situation or object that evokes the response, together with a specified set of response categories, is called an *item*. An item is a manifest variable. The statement, "The government should own the coal mines," together with two response categories, "agree" and "disagree," forms an item. The same statement, with five response categories, "strongly agree," "agree," "neutral," "disagree," "strongly disagree," is a different item. In the statistical analysis, the response categories to the latter may be combined to produce a dichotomous variable, but from the respondent's point of view, the two items require slightly different kinds of responses.

A number assigned to an individual's item response is an *item score*. In the first example, "agree" might be scored 1, and "disagree," 0. The proportion of people who give a certain response to an item determines the *popularity* of that response. The popularities of the various responses to an item are the *item marginals*. For dichotomous items, it will be convenient to specify arbitrarily one of the response alternatives as the positive response. It will be sufficient to consider only the popularity of the positive response, and thus a single marginal for each item. The popularity of a positive response to item i will be symbolized by p_i. We shall also use p_{ij} for the proportion of people responding positively to both items i and j, p_{ijk} for the proportion responding positively to all three items i, j, and k, etc.

Any collection of items will be called a *questionnaire*. Other terms, such as test, inventory, and scale, have been used in the literature. The term *questionnaire* is free from some of the connotations of the other terms. A questionnaire may contain items from different attitude universes, although usually only a single universe is represented. The distinction will be clear from the context.

An individual whose attitude is being measured will be called a *respondent*. A number, derived from his item responses, that represents his position on the latent variable is called a *scale score*, or simply a score. The scores form the *attitude scale*. The scale implies a system for obtaining a score from an individual's item responses. The term *scale* will occasionally be used to refer to this scoring system.

THE EVALUATION OF SCALES

To evaluate a scale, statistical evidence is needed concerning the properties of the scale. The *reliability* of the scale is of pri-

mary importance. A statement should also be provided about the *attitude universe* represented by the scale—that is, what items might have been used. Evidence of correlational *validity* is of paramount interest, since the utility of the scale will depend on its relationship with other variables and its ability to predict other behavior.

Facts such as these are necessary to specify what is meant by the label that is attached to the scale, and to ensure against false interpretations of that label. Putting a name on a scale creates a serious social obligation that cannot be fulfilled without experimental evidence concerning the properties of the scale.

RELIABILITY

The reliability of the scale is an index of the extent to which repeated measurements yield similar results. We shall not discuss the reliability of group statistics such as means and proportions, where discrepancies are due to sampling different individuals. Rather, our primary concern is with the reliability of an individual's score. If chance fluctuations cause relatively large shifts in an individual's score, then any particular determination of the score is practically meaningless. We would not expect such scores to correlate highly with other variables. Since attitude scales are developed as research tools for studying the relation of attitudes to other variables, high reliability is an indispensable property of a scale.

Reliability has two aspects, which Cronbach [10] has called *stability* and *equivalence*. These are new names for test-retest reliability and parallel-form reliability, respectively.

If the same questionnaire is administered to the same group of respondents on two separate occasions, there will be some shifts in the scores of individuals. The correlation between these scores is the test-retest reliability or the coefficient of stability. Memory and familiarity with the scale will tend to increase stability; extending the time interval between administrations will tend to decrease stability.

Low stabilities of attitude scales have been defended on the grounds that attitudes are dynamic and should be expected to change. This may be true, but it is difficult to see how an attitude scale can be a useful predictive instrument if the scores are not stable. Furthermore, there is a considerable difference between consistent shifts in response syndromes and sporadic changes in specific response tendencies. In studies of attitude change we are concerned with consistent shifts of response syndromes. In this case, low stability of the score is expected. But it is important to know the reliability of the *change*. This can be discovered by means of equivalent scales.

If our purpose is to measure an attitude universe by means of a sample of items, then we must determine what score differences could be expected if a different sample of items were chosen. Scales based on equivalent samples of items from the same universe should yield very similar scores. The correlation between such "parallel" scales is called the coefficient of equivalence, or the parallel-form reliability. It measures the extent to which the scale is specific to the particular items used. We are not justified in generalizing beyond the specific items in the scale unless equivalence is demonstrated. The concept of an attitude universe implies that there are many items which might have been used in the questionnaire. If, in fact, an equivalent set of items cannot be produced, the notion of an attitude universe becomes meaningless. Of course, in some situations we are interested in a scale for a specific set of items, but more often we would like to generalize to a larger class of possible items.

Two scales derived from different samples of items from the same universe should be highly correlated. However, we would also like the two scales to have similar scale-score distributions, similar patterns of inter-item correlations, and similar reliabilities. Such equivalent, or parallel, scales are best constructed from matched or paired samples of items. If possible, items with similar response distributions should be paired, i.e., items with equal marginals. Paired items should also have a similar degree of relationship with the total scale. Parallel scales constructed in this way, if they have high coefficients of equivalence, can be used interchangeably.

There are several methods for estimating the coefficient of equivalence from a single set of items. These methods depend on the strength of the interrelationships among the items, that is, on the *homogeneity* of the scale. The most familiar of these methods is the split-half technique. In this technique, the items are divided into two subsets, either matched or random (odd-even), and a scale is developed for each subset. The correlation between these scales may be used with the Spearman-Brown formula to estimate the equivalence of the original scale. (Technically, the Spearman-Brown formula is applicable only when the scale score is a weighted or unweighted sum of the item scores.) Guttman [18, 19] has shown that his coefficient of reproducibility is in some cases a lower bound of equivalence. The Kuder-Richardson formulas, especially formula' (20) which Cronbach [10] has called coefficient α, have been widely used as estimates of equivalence. Loevinger's [28] coefficient of homogeneity is a direct index of the homogeneity of the items; it does not estimate the reliability of the scale. A discussion of some of these methods, as well as a thorough treatment of reliability, may be found in Gulliksen [17].

UNIDIMENSIONALITY AND HOMOGENEITY

A unidimensional scale measures a single variable. In general, the property of unidimensionality means that people with the same score have about the same attitude. If the scale is actually a reflection of more than one attitude, so that it acts as the combination of two or more scales, then the same score can represent very different attitude patterns. For example, a scale of ethnocentrism composed of five items concerning attitudes toward Negroes, five items concerning attitudes toward Italians, and five items concerning attitudes toward the British would probably not be homogeneous. A median score might indicate median attitudes toward all three groups, or a strong anti-Negro attitude combined with a median attitude toward Italians and a strong pro-British attitude, or any other similar combination. Of course, if the three attitudes are highly correlated, then such a scale could be considered homogeneous and unidimensional, since ambiguous interpretations of scores would be improbable.

Operationally, unidimensionality and homogeneity have essentially the same meaning. Both are defined in terms of the degree of covariation among the items. In general, if the items on a scale are highly interdependent, then the items are homogeneous and the scale is unidimensional. More specific considerations must be discussed in connection with particular scaling methods, since each method contains its own definition of unidimensionality.

A homogeneous scale is, in general, a reliable scale. In the previous section we noted that several methods of estimating the coefficient of equivalence are based on homogeneity. In these methods it is assumed that the degree of relationship or covariation among the items in a scale is representative of the degree of covariation to be expected between these items and an equivalent set of items. However, it is possible for two highly correlated parallel scales not to be homogeneous. The scale described in the preceding paragraph could be highly reliable yet not homogeneous. Thus, if equivalence is measured by correlating two equivalent scales, additional evidence of homogeneity is needed.

VALIDITY

If a scale is reliable and homogeneous, it measures some variable. The problem of validity is to discover what it measures.

If the scale lives up to our definition of attitude, then it measures an attitude universe. The first problem in validation is to delimit and define this attitude universe.

It is helpful to distinguish at least three kinds of attitude universes. Most attitude questionnaires consist of items in which the respondent is asked to give some verbal response. This verbal response is quite often a statement of the respondent's opinion, or some other form of self-description. These attitude universes may be called *elicited verbal attitudes*. The opinions expressed by individuals in normal conversation with friends may be classed as elements of *spontaneous verbal attitudes*. A third class of behavior is verbal or nonverbal behavior directed toward an object in the referent class. We may call the corresponding universe an *action attitude*. For example, a restaurant manager might tell a survey interviewer that he would not serve Negroes, he might assure his friends that he won't serve Negroes, and he might refuse service to a Negro in his restaurant. It might also happen that the three responses are not so consistent.

Responses in any of these areas may be scaled. Although most of our attitude scales measure elicited verbal attitudes, other scales are equally possible. With clever observational techniques, scales could be developed for spontaneous verbal attitudes and for action attitudes.

These classes of attitude are not exhaustive. The indirect techniques lead to further attitude universes. Also, subclasses can be made within the three stated classes. Action attitudes are particularly diverse, but little measurement has been done in that area, so that breakdowns are as yet unnecessary.

A description of the attitude universe is necessary in order to determine whether the scale measures this universe. Essentially, this means characterizing the items which might have been used in the questionnaire. Many investigators would say that, as a representation of an attitude universe, the scale is valid by definition, or has face validity. Gulliksen [16] has used the term *intrinsic* validity for this situation, and has suggested some experimental methods for determining whether a scale is intrinsically valid. One method is to study the judgments of a group of experts. A large set of items could be assembled which the experimenter believes to be in the same attitude universe as the items on the scale. Experts could rate these items as well as the items on the scale for relevance to the attitude being considered. Alternatively, several experts could each submit a questionnaire that is believed to be a measure of the attitude universe. These questionnaires could be administered and their intercorrelations investigated by factor analysis to see if a single common factor is exhibited by the several scales. Such techniques promise to give at least a partial solution to the plaguing problem of attitude scale validity.

The second major method of determining what a scale measures is to find the variable with which it correlates. By definition, an attitude scale for one universe cannot *measure* a second universe. However, if it correlates highly with the second universe, then it may legitimately be used as a substitute for such a measure. In particular, an elicited verbal attitude scale can never be a measure of an action attitude, but it may be taken as an indicant of the action attitude if a reasonably high correlation exists between the two. Since this is often the aim of elicited verbal attitude scales, correlation with an action attitude is called its validity for the action attitude or just its validity.

Unfortunately, it is difficult to determine whether such a correlation exists. The validity of elicited verbal attitudes has often been appraised by selecting two groups of people who are judged to have different action attitudes, and then demonstrating that their elicited verbal attitudes differ in the expected direction. A major difficulty of this *known group* validation is that the magnitude of the relationship cannot be easily evaluated. Furthermore, the groups are seldom very well "known." The ideal method of determining correlational validity would be to develop an action attitude scale, which might consist of a set of standardized social situations, or a behavior checklist which would require extensive observation of each individual.

Many investigations have found that specific acts or action attitudes often cannot be predicted very accurately from elicited verbal attitudes. The classic demonstration of the lack of correspondence of verbal and nonverbal behavior is that of LaPiere [26]. He accompanied a Chinese couple on some of their travels, and later queried the managers of the restaurants, hotels, and auto camps that they had visited. Over 90% said they would not accept Chinese guests, whereas all of them had done so.

Emphasis on the validity of verbal attitude scales for predicting action attitudes often obscures the fundamental issue in attitude research. We are interested in the relation of attitudes to other variables, such as socioeconomic status, education, exposure to propaganda, or other attitudes. If we wish to study the relation of elicited verbal attitudes to such variables, then we need a scale that measures elicited verbal attitude. If we want to investigate the correlates of spontaneous verbal attitudes, or action attitudes, then we need scales that measure these attitudes directly. It is only when we attempt to use a scale based on elicited verbal attitude as an indicant of action attitude that this question of validity is paramount.

ITEMS AND QUESTIONNAIRES

Items are the elements from which attitude scales are constructed. The usefulness of a scale, as well as the definition of the attitude that it measures, depends ultimately on the items of which it is composed. Ingenuity and insight are at a premium in designing items that will yield valid and useful scales.

There are many types and forms of items that may be used to assess an attitude.

Item *type* refers to the content of the item, while item *form* refers to the manner in which the item is related to the latent continuum. The scaling methods are largely indifferent to the type of item used, although certain requirements are made concerning the form of the item. The scaling methods usually include procedures for detecting and eliminating items which do not meet these formal requirements.

ITEM TYPES

A great many types of items have been used in attitude research. Although the scaling methods are usually used with opinion statements, this is not necessarily the case. Almost any item can be used if it has a specified set of possible responses. Although we shall not attempt a survey of all possible item types, we shall give a few examples to illustrate the range of item types that can be encompassed by the scaling techniques.

The most widely used item type is the opinion statement. The respondent may be asked whether he agrees with the statement, or he may be required to indicate his opinion on a five-point scale from "strongly agree" to "strongly disagree." Occasionally the respondent is asked which of several explicitly presented opinions on the issue is most nearly like his own opinion. Open-ended questions may be used. Here the respondent expresses his own opinion, and the response is later placed in one of a fixed number of categories. Thurstone and Chave [46] suggested that opinion statements could be obtained for objective questionnaires by collecting the responses to open-ended opinion questions.

The responses to opinion statements are notoriously sensitive to changes in the wording of the statement. This is a more serious problem in single-question opinion polling than in attitude scaling, where the use of several statements can partially offset the effect. However, this does not constitute a license for sloppy wording in attitude items. In a readable book, *The Art of Asking Questions,* Payne [37] discusses the many pitfalls to be avoided in preparing opinion statements or questions. Payne [36, 37] also discusses the problem of meaning. People are often willing to state opinions about issues that are meaningless to them. It is important that the opinion statement be relevant to the respondent as well as to the attitude. [This issue is treated in greater detail in 30.]

The use of opinion statements is tantamount to asking the respondent for a structured description of his verbal attitude. In contrast, Rosander [39] asked for a description of the respondent's action attitude. He posed several hypothetical situations and described a particular action; the respondent indicated whether he would have taken that action. One item from a scale of attitudes toward Negroes is: "You are reading in a public library. A Negro enters and sits down beside you. You leave the library at once." Pace [35] used similar items for general social-economic-political attitudes. F. H. Allport and Hanchett [1] used this type of item to study war-producing behavior. Validities found with these action-oriented items indicate that they are very promising.

A similar idea was used by Horowitz and Horowitz [22] in studying the development of attitude toward the Negro in young children. In their "Faces" test the child was shown a set of pictures of white and colored children and was asked to point out the one he wanted to play with, to eat with, etc. The child could also be asked to rank the faces in order of preference. Mussen [32] reports a validity of .52 for this test, using a criterion of sociometric choice at an interracial summer camp.

The methods for the selection of OSS personnel developed during the war by the OSS assessment staff [34] could be adapted for use in action attitude research. Essentially the technique would involve establishing a series of standardized social situations relevant to the attitude in question, and studying the behavior of the individual in these situations. One could presumably establish an objective scale based on the responses in a number of these standard social situations. Kelley and Fiske [24] used these methods to study the selection of students in clinical psychology.

Action attitudes can be measured by behavior rating scales. The items could be the determination of presence or absence of a certain action in a particular social situation. Such scales would be similar to a scale based on standard social situations. In this case, however, the scales would depend on raters who knew the individual well. The rater could be the individual himself or some close acquaintance. Great care must be taken to make the rater's job objective, so that reliable results can be expected.

When the purpose of the attitude questionnaire is disguised, the measurement has been called *indirect*. Campbell [7] and Weschler and Bernberg [48] have provided comprehensive reviews of these indirect methods. At least two major categories of indirect items can be distinguished: items of the projective type and items based on the selective distortion of psychological processes.

Several investigators have used items similar to those on the Thematic Apperception Test. Proshansky [38] used ambiguous pictures of labor situations to measure attitude toward labor. The measurement was a rating made on the basis of the respondent's written interpretations of the pictures. Fromme [13] used political cartoons with four alternative captions. The respondent selected the best caption for each cartoon, and gave reasons for his selections. Although Fromme's analysis was qualitative, an objective scale could be developed easily. Sanford [40] studied worry by using items similar to those on the Rosenzweig Picture Frustration Test. For example, in a cartoon depicting two men, one is asking the other what he is worried about. The respondent is required to supply the second man's response.

Several indirect methods are based on the premise that attitudes interfere with psychological processes such as learning, perception, and remembering. The selective distortion of these processes is a prominent phenomenon in social psychology. Consistency among such distortions is closer to some traditional conceptions of attitude than is consistency among opinions.

Several investigators have used items based on the distortion of actual or assumed facts. Smith [42] used statements labeled as facts; the respondent indicated whether he believed the statement to be true. Newcomb [33] found that errors on an information test were related to the respondent's attitude. In Hammond's [21] "error choice" technique, a factual question is asked, with two response alternatives available, each equally far from the truth, but in different directions. For example, "The number of man-days lost because of strikes from January to June was (1) 34.5 million, (2) 98.6 million." Bernberg [5] devised a scale of industrial morale based on this method of "error choice."

The selective distortion of logical reasoning has been used by Thistlethwaite [44] as a basis for attitude items. He paired neutral and "loaded" items of the same (valid or invalid) syllogism. The subject is asked to indicate for each item whether the conclusion is justified by the premise. An example of a "loaded" (invalid) syllogism is: "Given: If production is important, then peaceful industrial relations are desirable. If production is important, then it is a mistake to have Negroes for foremen and leaders over whites. Therefore: If peaceful industrial relations are desirable, then it is a mistake to have Negroes for foremen and leaders over whites."

Indirect attitude items may also be based on distortion of perception and memory. Horowitz and Horowitz [22] invented an *Aussage Test*, which might also be titled "The 'Have you stopped beating your wife' Test." A complicated picture is presented for two or three seconds, after which the respondent is asked misleading questions such as "What is the colored man in the corner doing?" Stereotyped responses are often obtained concerning the nonexistent colored man.

That the relation between these indirect items and scales based on opinion statements may be complex is shown by Bray's [6] study of prejudice. He used Sherif's [41] autokinetic situation with confederates who were Negroes or who were introduced to the subjects as Jews. The amount of conformity of subjects' reports to confederates' reports could not be directly predicted by scores on attitude scales composed of opinion statements. Rather, the interaction of the attitude scores and personality variables such as irritability, social ascendancy, and self-confidence were of major importance in determining the conformity of reports.

REFERENCES

1. ALLPORT, F. H., & HANCHETT, GERTRUDE A. The war-producing behavior of citizens: A scale of measurement with preliminary results in imagined situations. *J. Soc. Psychol.,* 1940, 11, 447–490.
2. ALLPORT, G. W. Attitudes. In C. Murchison (Ed.), *A handbook of social psychology.* Worcester: Clark Univer. Press, 1935. Pp. 798–844.
3. BENNETT, J. F. A method for determining the dimensionality of a set of rank orders. Unpublished doctoral dissertation, Univer. of Michigan, 1951.
4. BERGMANN, G., & SPENCE, K. W. The logic of psychological measurement. *Psychol. Rev.,* 1944, 51, 1–24.
5. BERNBERG, R. E. The direction of perception technique of attitude measurement. *Int. J. Opin. & Attitude Res.,* 1951, 5, 397–407.
6. BRAY, D. W. The prediction of behavior from two attitude scales. *J. abnorm. soc. Psychol.,* 1950, 45, 64–84.
7. CAMPBELL, D. T. The indirect assessment of social attitudes. *Psychol. Bull.,* 1950, 47, 15–38.
8. COOMBS, C. H. Psychological scaling without a unit of measurement. *Psychol. Rev.,* 1950, 57, 145–158.
9. COOMBS, C. H. A theory of psychological scaling. *Engineering Research Institute, Bulletin No. 34.* Ann Arbor, Mich.: Univer. of Michigan Press, 1952.
10. CRONBACH, L. J. Coefficient alpha and the internal structure of tests. *Psychometrika,* 1951, 16, 297–334.
11. DOOB, L. W. *Public opinion and propaganda.* New York: Henry Holt, 1948.
12. FERGUSON, A., MYERS, C. S., BARTLETT, R. J., et al. Quantitative estimation of sensory events. *Final Report, Adv. of Sci.,* 1940, 2, 331–349.
13. FROMME, A. On the use of certain qualitative methods of attitude research: A study of opinions on the methods of preventing war. *J. soc. Psychol.,* 1941, 13, 429–459.
14. FUSON, W. M. Attitudes: A note on the concept and its research context. *Amer. sociol. Rev.,* 1942, 7, 856–857.
15. GULLIKSEN, H. Paired comparisons and the logic of measurement. *Psychol. Rev.,* 1946, 53, 199–213.
16. GULLIKSEN, H. Intrinsic validity. *Amer. Psychologist,* 1950, 5, 511–517.
17. GULLIKSEN, H. *Theory of mental tests.* New York: Wiley, 1950.
18. GUTTMAN, L. A basis for analyzing test-retest reliability. *Psychometrika,* 1945, 10, 255–282.
19. GUTTMAN, L. The test-retest reliability of qualitative data. *Psychometrika,* 1946, 11, 81–95.
20. GUTTMAN, L. The problem of attitude and opinion measurement. In S. A. Stouffer et al. (Eds.), *Measurement and prediction.* Princeton, N.J.: Princeton Univer. Press, 1950. Pp. 46–59.
21. HAMMOND, K. R. Measuring attitude by error-choice: An indirect method. *J. abnorm. soc. Psychol.,* 1948, 43, 38–48.
22. HOROWITZ, R. E., & HOROWITZ, E. L. The development of social attitudes in children. *Sociometry,* 1938, 1, 301–338.
23. JOHNSON, H. M. Pseudomathematics in the mental and social sciences. *Amer. J. Psychol.,* 1936, 48, 342–351.
24. KELLEY, E. L., & FISKE, D. W. *The prediction of performance in clinical psychology.* Ann Arbor, Mich.: Univer. of Michigan Press, 1951.
25. KRECH, D., & CRUTCHFIELD, R. S. *Theory*

and problems of social psychology. New York: McGraw-Hill, 1948.

26. LaPiere, R. T. Attitudes vs. actions. *Soc. Forces,* 1934, 14, 230–237.

27. Lazarsfeld, P. F. The logic and mathematical foundation of latent structure analysis. In S. A. Stouffer et al. (Eds.), *Measurement and prediction.* Princeton, N.J.: Princeton Univer. Press, 1950. Pp. 362–412.

28. Loevinger, Jane. A systematic approach to the construction and evaluation of tests of ability. *Psychol. Monogr.,* 1947, 61, No. 4.

29. Lorge, I. The fundamental nature of measurement. In E. F. Lindquist (Ed.), *Educational measurement.* Washington, D.C.: American Council on Education, 1951, Pp. 533–559.

30. Maccoby, Eleanor E., & Maccoby, N. The interview: A tool of social science. In G. Lindzey (Ed.), *Handbook of social psychology.* Reading, Mass.: Addison-Wesley, 1954. Pp. 449–487.

31. MacCorquodale, K., & Meehl, P. E. On a distinction between hypothetical constructs and intervening variables. *Psychol. Rev.,* 1948, 55, 95–107.

32. Mussen, P. H. The reliability and validity of the Horowitz Faces test. *J. abnorm. soc. Psychol.,* 1950, 45, 504–506.

33. Newcomb, T. M. The influence of attitude climate upon some determinants of information. *J. abnorm. soc. Psychol.,* 1946, 41, 291–302.

34. OSS Assessment Staff. *The assessment of men.* New York: Rinehart, 1948.

35. Pace, C. R. A situations test to measure social-political-economic attitudes. *J. soc. Psychol.,* 1939, 10, 331–344.

36. Payne, S. L. Thoughts about meaningless questions. *Publ. Opin. Quart.,* 1950, 14, 687–696.

37. Payne, S. L. *The art of asking questions.* Princeton, N.J.: Princeton Univer. Press, 1951.

38. Proshansky, H. A projective method for the study of attitude. *J. abnorm. soc. Psychol.,* 1943, 38, 383–395.

39. Rosander, A. C. An attitude scale based upon behavior situations. *J. soc. Psychol.,* 1937, 8, 3–15.

40. Sanford, F. H. The use of a projective device in attitude surveying. *Publ. Opin. Quart.,* 1950, 14, 697–709.

41. Sherif, M. An experimental approach to the study of attitudes. *Sociometry,* 1937, 1, 90–98.

42. Smith, G. H. Beliefs in statements labelled fact and rumor. *J. abnorm. soc. Psychol.,* 1947, 42, 80–90.

43. Stevens, S. S. Mathematics, measurement, and psychophysics. In S. S. Stevens (Ed.), *Handbook of experimental psychology.* New York: Wiley, 1951. Pp. 1–49.

44. Thistlethwaite, D. Attitude and structure as factors in the distortion of reasoning. *J. abnorm. soc. Psychol.,* 1950, 45, 442–458.

45. Thurstone, L. L. *Multiple factor analysis.* Chicago: Univer. of Chicago Press, 1947.

46. Thurstone, L. L., & Chave, E. J. *The measurement of attitude.* Chicago: Univer. of Chicago Press, 1929.

47. Torgerson, W. S. Multidimensional scaling: I. Theory and method. *Psychometrika,* 1952, 17, 401–419.

48. Weschler, I. R., & Bernberg, R. E. Indirect methods of attitude measurement. *Int. J. Opin. & Attitude Res.,* 1950, 4, 209–218.

Chapter *62* ~

The Authoritarian Personality—Methodology

R. N. SANFORD / T. W. ADORNO
ELSE FRENKEL-BRUNSWIK / D. J. LEVINSON

To attack the problems conceptualized regarding the role and functions of ethnic prejudice within personality required methods for describing and measuring ideological trends and methods for exposing personality, the contemporary situation, and the social background. A particular methodological challenge was imposed by the conception of *levels* in the person; this made it necessary to devise techniques for surveying opinions, attitudes, and values that were on the surface, for revealing ideological trends that were more or less inhibited and reached the surface only in indirect manifestations, and for bringing to light personality forces that lay in the subject's unconscious. And since the major concern was with *patterns* of dynamically related factors—something that requires study of the total individual—it seemed that the proper approach was through intensive clinical studies. The significance and practical importance of such studies could not be gauged, however, until there was knowledge of how far it was possible to generalize from them. Thus it was necessary to perform group studies as well as individual studies, and to find ways and means for integrating the two.

Individuals were studied by means of interviews and special clinical techniques for revealing underlying wishes, fears, and defenses; groups were studied by means of questionnaires. It was not expected that the clinical studies would be as complete or profound as some which have already been performed, primarily by psychoanalysts, nor that the questionnaires would be more accurate than any now employed by social psychologists. It was hoped, however—indeed it was necessary to our purpose—that the clinical material could be conceptualized in such a way as to permit its being quantified and carried over into group studies, and that the questionnaires could be brought to bear upon areas of response ordinarily left to clinical study. The attempt was made, in other words, to bring methods of traditional social psychology

737

into the service of theories and concepts from the newer dynamic theory of personality and in so doing to make "depth psychological" phenomena more amenable to mass-statistical treatment, and to make quantitative surveys of attitudes and opinions more meaningful psychologically.

In the attempt to integrate clinical and group studies, the two were carried on in close conjunction. When the individual was in the focus of attention, the aim was to describe in detail his pattern of opinions, attitudes, and values and to understand the dynamic factors underlying it, and on this basis to design significant questions for use with groups of subjects. When the group was in the focus of attention, the aim was to discover what opinions, attitudes, and values commonly go together and what patterns of factors in the life histories and in the contemporary situations of the subjects were commonly associated with each ideological constellation; this afforded a basis on which to select individuals for more intensive study: commanding first attention were those who exemplified the common patterns and in whom it could be supposed that the correlated factors were dynamically related.

In order to study potentially antidemocratic individuals it was necessary first to identify them. Hence a start was made by constructing a questionnaire and having it filled out anonymously by a large group of people. This questionnaire contained, in addition to numerous questions of fact about the subject's past and present life, a variety of antidemocratic statements with which the subjects were invited to agree or disagree. A number of individuals who showed the greatest amount of agreement with these statements—and, by way of contrast, some who showed the most disagreement or, in some instances, were most neutral—were then studied by means of interviews and other clinical techniques. On the basis of these individual studies the questionnaire was revised, and the whole procedure repeated.

The interview was used in part as a check upon the *validity* of the questionnaire, that is to say, it provided a basis for judging whether people who obtained the highest antidemocratic scores on the questionnaire were usually those who, in a confidential relationship with another person, expressed antidemocratic sentiments with the most intensity. What was more important, however, the clinical studies gave access to the deeper personality factors behind antidemocratic ideology and suggested the means for their investigation on a mass scale. With increasing knowledge of the underlying trends of which prejudice was an expression, there was increasing familiarity with various other signs or manifestations by which these trends could be recognized. The task then was to translate these manifestations into questionnaire items for use in the next group study. Progress lay in finding more and more reliable indications of the central personality forces and in showing with increasing clarity the relations of these forces to antidemocratic ideological expression.

THE TECHNIQUES

The questionnaires and clinical techniques employed in the study may be described briefly as follows:

THE QUESTIONNAIRE METHOD

The questionnaires were always presented in mimeographed form and filled out anonymously by subjects in groups. Each questionnaire included (1) factual questions, (2) opinion-attitude scales, and (3) "projective" (open answer) questions.

1. The *factual questions* had to do mainly with past and present group memberships: church preference and attendance, political party, vocation, income, and so on. It was assumed that the answers could be taken at their face value. In selecting the questions, we were guided at the start by hypotheses concerning the socio-

logical correlates of ideology; as the study progressed we depended more and more upon experience with interviewees.

2. *Opinion-attitude* scales were used from the start in order to obtain quantitative estimates of certain surface ideological trends: anti-Semitism, ethnocentrism, politico-economic conservatism. Later, a scale was developed for the measurement of antidemocratic tendencies in the personality itself.

Each scale was a collection of statements, with each of which the subject was asked to express the degree of his agreement or disagreement. Each statement concerned some relatively specific opinion, attitude, or value, and the basis for grouping them within a particular scale was the conception that taken together they expressed a single general trend.

The general trends to which the scales pertained were conceived very broadly, as complex systems of thought about wide areas of social living. To define these trends empirically it was necessary to obtain responses to many specific issues—enough to "cover" the area mapped out conceptually—and to show that each of them bore some relation to the whole.

This approach stands in contrast to the public opinion poll: whereas the poll is interested primarily in the distribution of opinion with respect to a particular issue, the present interest was to inquire, concerning a particular opinion, with what other opinions and attitudes it was related. The plan was to determine the existence of broad ideological trends, to develop instruments for their measurement, and then to inquire about their distribution within larger populations.

The approach to an ideological area was to appraise its grosser features first and its finer or more specific features later. The aim was to gain a view of the "over-all picture" into which smaller features might later be fitted, rather than to obtain highly precise measures of small details in the hope that these might eventually add up to something significant. Although this emphasis upon breadth and inclusiveness prevented the attainment of the highest degree of precision in measurement, it was nevertheless possible to develop each scale to a point where it met the currently accepted statistical standards.

Since each scale had to cover a broad area, without growing so long as to try the patience of the subjects, it was necessary to achieve a high degree of efficiency. The task was to formulate items which would cover as much as possible of the many-sided phenomenon in question. Since each of the trends to be measured was conceived as having numerous components or aspects, there could be no duplication of items; instead it was required that each item express a different feature—and where possible, several features—of the total system. The degree to which items within a scale will "hang together" statistically, and thus give evidence that a single, unified trait is being measured, depends primarily upon the surface similarity of the items—the degree to which they all say the same thing. The present items, obviously, could not be expected to cohere in this fashion; all that could be required statistically of them was that they correlate to a reasonable degree with the total scale. Conceivably, a single component of one of the present systems could be regarded as itself a relatively general trend, the precise measurement of which would require the use of numerous more specific items. As indicated above, however, such concern with highly specific, statistically "pure" factors was put aside, in favor of an attempt to gain a dependable estimate of an over-all system, one which could then be related to other over-all systems in an approach to the totality of major trends within the individual.

One might inquire why, if we wish to know the intensity of some ideological pattern—such as anti-Semitism—within the individual, we do not ask him directly, after defining what we mean. The answer, in part, is that the phenomenon to be measured is so complex that a single response would not go very far toward revealing the important differences among individuals. Moreover, anti-Semitism, ethnocentrism, and politico-economic reactionism or radicalism are topics about which many people are not prepared to speak with complete frankness. Thus, even at this surface ideological level it was necessary to employ a certain amount of indirectness. Subjects were never told what was the particular concern of the questionnaire, but only that they were taking part in a "survey of opinions about various issues of the day." To support this view of the proceedings, items belonging to a particular scale were interspersed with items from other scales in the questionnaire. It was not possible, of course, to avoid statements prejudicial to minority groups, but care was taken in each case to allow the subject "a way out," that is to say, to make it possible for him to agree with such a statement while maintaining the belief that he was not "prejudiced" or "undemocratic."

Whereas the scales for measuring surface ideological trends conform, in general, with common practice in sociopsychological research, the scale for measuring potentially antidemocratic trends in the personality represents a new departure. The procedure was to bring together in a scale items which, by hypothesis and by clinical experience, could be regarded as "giveaways" of trends which lay relatively deep within the personality, and which constituted a *disposition* to express spontaneously (on a suitable occasion), or to be influenced by, fascist ideas.

The statements in this scale were not different in form from those which made up the surface ideology scales; they were direct expressions of opinion, of attitudes, or of value with respect to various areas of social living—but areas not usually touched upon in systematic presentations of a politico-socioeconomic point of view. Always interspersed with statements from other scales, they conveyed little or nothing to the subject as to the nature of the real question being pursued. They were, in the main, statements so designed as to serve as rationalizations for irrational tendencies. Two statements included in this scale were the following: (a) "Nowadays with so many different kinds of people moving around so much and mixing together so freely, one has to be especially careful to protect himself against infection and disease" and (b) "Homosexuality is an especially rotten form of delinquency and ought to be severely punished." That people who agree with one of these statements show a tendency to agree with the other, and that people who agree with these two statements tend to agree with open antidemocratic statements, e.g., that members of some minority group are basically inferior, is hardly to be explained on the basis of any obvious logical relation among the statements. It seems necessary, rather, to conceive of some underlying central trend which expresses itself in these different ways. Different people might, of course, give the same response to a statement such as the above for different reasons; since it was necessary to give the statements at least a veneer of rationality, it was natural to expect that the responses of some people would be determined almost entirely by the rational aspect rather than by some underlying emotional disposition. For this reason it was necessary to include a large number of scale items and to be guided by the general trend of response rather than by the response to a single statement; for a person to be considered potentially antidemocratic in his underlying dynamic structure, he had to agree with a majority of these scale items.

The development of the present scale proceeded in two ways: first, by finding or formulating items which, though they had no manifest connection with open antidemocratic expressions, were nevertheless highly correlated with them; and second, by demonstrating that these "indirect" items were actually expressions of antidemocratic potential within the personality as known from intensive clinical study.

3. *Projective questions*, like most other projective techniques, present the subject

with ambiguous and emotionally toned stimulus material. This material is designed to allow a maximum of variation in response from one subject to another and to provide channels through which relatively deep personality processes may be expressed. The questions are not ambiguous in their formal structure, but in the sense that the answers are at the level of emotional expression rather than at the level of fact and the subject is not aware of their implications. The responses always have to be interpreted, and their significance is known when their meaningful relations to other psychological facts about the subject have been demonstrated. One projective question was, "What would you do if you had only six months to live, and could do anything you wanted?" An answer to this question was not regarded as a statement of what the subject would probably do in actuality, but rather an expression having to do with his values, conflicts, and the like. We asked ourselves if this expression was not in keeping with those elicited by other projective questions and by statements in the personality scale.

Numerous projective questions were tried in the early stages of the study, and from among them eight were selected for use with most of the larger groups of subjects: they were the questions which taken together gave the broadest view of the subject's personality trends and correlated most highly with surface ideological patterns.

CLINICAL TECHNIQUES

1. *The interview* was divided roughly into an ideological section and a clinical-genetic section. In the first section the aim was to induce the subject to talk as spontaneously and as freely as possible about various broad ideological topics: politics, religion, minority groups, income, and vocation. Whereas in the questionnaire the subject was limited to the topics there presented and could express himself only by means of the rating scheme offered, here it was important to know what topics he would bring up of his own accord and with what intensity of feeling he would spontaneously express himself. As indicated above, this material afforded a means for insuring that the questionnaire, in its revised forms, more or less faithfully represented "what people were saying"— the topics that were on their minds and the forms of expression that came spontaneously to them—and provided a valid index of antidemocratic trends. The interview covered, of course, a much wider variety of topics, and permitted the expression of more elaborated and differentiated opinions, attitudes, and values, than did the questionnaire. Whereas the attempt was made to distill from the interview material what seemed to be of the most general significance and to arrange it for inclusion in the questionnaire, there was material left over to be exploited by means of individual case studies, qualitative analyses, and crudely quantitative studies of the interview material by itself.

The clinical-genetic section of the interview sought to obtain, first, more factual material about the subject's contemporary situation and about his past than could be got from the questionnaire; second, the freest possible expressions of personal feelings, of beliefs, wishes, and fears concerning himself and his situation and concerning such topics as parents, siblings, friends, and sexual relationships; and third, the subject's conceptions of his childhood environment and of his childhood self.

The interview was conducted in such a way that the material gained from it would permit inferences about the deeper layers of the subject's personality. The technique of the interview will be described in detail later. Suffice it to say here that it followed the general pattern of a psychiatric interview that is inspired by a dynamic theory of personality. The interviewer was aided by a comprehensive interview schedule which underwent several revisions during the course of the study, as experience taught what were the most significant underlying questions and what were the most efficient means for evoking material bearing upon them.

The interview material was used for estimation of certain common variables lying within the theoretical framework of the study but not accessible to the other techniques. Interview material also provided the main basis for individual case studies, bearing upon the interrelationships among all the significant factors operating within the antidemocratic individual.

2. The *Thematic Apperception Test* is a well-known projective technique in which the subject is presented with a series of dramatic pictures and asked to tell a story about each of them. The material he produces can, when interpreted, reveal a great deal about his underlying wishes, conflicts, and mechanisms of defense. The technique was modified slightly to suit the present purposes. The material was analyzed quantitatively in terms of psychological variables which are found widely in the population and which were readily brought into relation with other variables of the study. As a part of the case study of an individual an analysis in terms of more unique personality variables was made, the material here being considered in close conjunction with findings from the interview.

Though designed to approach different aspects of the person, the several techniques actually were closely related conceptually one to another. All of them permitted quantification and interpretation in terms of variables which fall within a unified theoretical system. Sometimes two techniques yielded measures of the same variables, and sometimes different techniques were focused upon different variables. In the former case the one technique gave some indication of the validity of the other; in the latter case the adequacy of a technique could be gauged by its ability to produce measures that were meaningfully related to all the others. Whereas a certain amount of repetition was necessary to insure validation, the main aim was to fill out a broad framework and achieve a maximum of scope.

The theoretical approach required in each case either that a new technique be designed from the ground up or that an existing one be modified to suit the particular purpose. At the start, there was a theoretical conception of what was to be measured and certain sources which could be drawn upon in devising the original questionnaire form and the preliminary interview schedule. Each technique then evolved as the study progressed. Since each was designed specifically for this study, they could be changed at will as understanding increased, and since an important purpose of the study was the development and testing of effective instruments for diagnosing potential fascism, there was no compulsion to repeat without modification a procedure just in order to accumulate comparable data. So closely interrelated were the techniques that what was learned from any one of them could be applied to the improvement of any other. Just as the clinical techniques provided a basis for enriching the several parts of the questionnaire, so did the accumulating quantitative results indicate what ought to be concentrated upon in the interview; and just as the analysis of scale data suggested the existence of underlying variables which might be approached by means of projective techniques, so did the responses on projective techniques suggest items for inclusion in the scales.

The evolution of techniques was expressed both in expansion and in contraction. Expansion was exemplified in the attempt to bring more and more aspects of antidemocratic ideology into the developing picture and in the attempt to explore enough aspects of the potentially antidemocratic personality so that there was some grasp of the totality. Contraction took place continuously in the quantitative procedures as increasing theoretical clarity permitted a boiling down so that the same crucial relationships could be demonstrated with briefer techniques.

Chapter 63

The Measurement of Authoritarian Attitudes

SAMUEL MESSICK / DOUGLAS N. JACKSON

The publication of *The Authoritarian Personality* [1] has led to the widespread use of the F scale as an attitudinal indicant of a personality syndrome. The use of this scale has been justified by its presumed validity—by the demonstration that high scorers differ significantly from low scorers on a wide variety of characteristics consistent with the theoretical orientation from which the scale was derived. For instance, the F scale has been shown to correlate with measures of ethnocentrism [1], rigidity [4], dogmatism [33], xenophobia [5], and suggestibility [15]. Constructs such as misanthropy [35] and intolerance for ambiguity [3] have been related to the ethnocentrism scale and by implication to the highly related F scale.

ACQUIESCENT RESPONSE SET AND THE CALIFORNIA F SCALE

Some recent evidence suggests that consistent responses to the particular form of

This article is reprinted from *Educational and Psychological Measurement*, 1958, with the permission of the copyright holder, G. Frederic Kuder.

the attitude statements used rather than to their content may be a significant factor in the above correlations. Items from both the California E scale and F scale are so worded that agreement with them indicates "ethnocentric" or "authoritarian" attitudes, while disagreement presumably indicates unprejudiced and equalitarian sentiments. These items are *positively stated* in the sense that agreements are scored in the direction of the scale label, e.g., in the authoritarian direction; they are *negative* in the sense that agreement indicates socially undesirable attitudes, such as prejudice, intolerance, and predisposition to fascism.

The recent investigations of Bass [2, 28], Jackson [17], Jackson and Messick [18], and others [19, 22] have emphasized the hazards of such a unidirectional item form in using the F scale as a measure of attitude. These studies assessed the relationships between F scale items in their original positively-stated form and F scale items rewritten in various "reversed" forms, so that disagreement rather than agreement could be considered an indication of authoritarian attitudes. In one of these reversed F scales [17, 18] for example,

743

"Obedience and respect for authority are the most important virtues children should learn" was modified to read "A love of freedom and complete independence are the most important virtues children should learn," and "No weakness and difficulty can hold us back if we have enough will power" was changed to "All the will power in the world will not help us when weaknesses and difficulties stand in our way," etc. In constructing this reversed F scale, an attempt was made to rewrite each item so that the content would appear to reflect a viewpoint opposed to the original while retaining a similar style of expression. The correlations between agreement to original items and to various reversed forms were *not* found to be high and negative as would be expected from consistent responses to item content [2, 22] and were sometimes found to be significantly positive [18, 19].

These findings, along with other evidence [7, 34] obtained with the F scale, indicate the presence of what Cronbach [8] has called an acquiescent response set, and they have implications for interpreting the reported high correlations between the F scale and other measures. For example, there is a possibility that the observed covariation of responses to the F scale and the E scale may be in part attributable to a consistent generalized tendency to agree or acquiesce to items in print, rather than being solely a function of consistent ideological beliefs. If this generalized tendency to agree with items independent of their content were adequately controlled, many relationships previously obtained with the F scale might be different. For example, Jackson and Messick [18] have recently obtained a positive correlation of .23 between agreement to reversed F scale items and Gough's intolerance scale [13] and a correlation of .03 between the E scale and the reversed F scale. On the basis of consistent responses to item content alone, both of these correlations should have been significantly negative. Jackson, Messick, and Solley [19] have shown that it was possible to obtain a "rigid" performance on Einstellung

water-jar problems both from subjects who agreed with original F scale items, as previously observed by Brown [4], and from subjects who agreed with reversed F scale items. This result was interpreted as an indication that each of the measures reflected conformity and overgeneralization rather than that individuals who hold a particular belief should necessarily be labeled "rigid."

These studies emphasize the importance of acquiescence in relationships between the *F scale* and other measures, but more research is necessary before the findings are generalized to the E scale and its correlates. The conclusion, for example, that the correlation reported by Rokeach [32] between ethnocentrism and Einstellung rigidity is primarily attributable to acquiescence or response set may not be warranted by evidence obtained with the F scale. It is particularly difficult to reverse the direction of ethnocentrism items in a meaningful way and at the same time retain similar styles of expression, and, as Prentice [31] suggests, the use of positive or negative items or a mixture of both may be immaterial in the measurement of ethnic prejudice.

PROBLEMS OF INTERPRETATION AND EXPERIMENTAL CONTROL

It should be noted that an acquiescent response set probably operates to increase the reliability of the F scale and that it can also increase the scale's empirical validity, depending upon the correlation of the response set with the criterion. Thus, as Cronbach [9] has pointed out, a response set might not only be an internally consistent but momentary response tendency that operates through one testing and shifts with time, it may also have a stable and valid component which reflects a consistent individual style or personality trait. However, further research is necessary to investigate the specific nature of response acquiescence, its possible stability as a trait, and its unity of function. It would be important to know whether acquiescent response set acts as a unitary general tendency or whether there are different kinds of acquiescence. At a conceptual level at least, it would seem possible to distinguish between a tendency to agree with any statement and a tendency to agree with sweeping generalizations. Similarly, there may be complementary response sets such as "negativism" or "criticalness," which might represent tendencies to disagree with diverse items. Whether or not such tendencies can be differentiated experimentally, of course, is a different matter. But the ease with which such examples can be suggested without contradictory evidence illustrates the need for research in this area.

Leavitt, Hax, and Roche [22] have indicated that the acquiescent response set in the F scale operates in the appropriate direction to increase the discriminatory power of the scale. Indeed, acquiescent tendencies are consistent with the personality theory underlying the F scale since the term "authoritarian submission" was one of those used to describe the authoritarian syndrome. However, the increase in discriminatory power comes from a confounding of two response determinants, the form of an item and its content, thus making it difficult to interpret an individual's total score on the F scale or to ascribe to him any characteristics on the basis of item content. Thus, although an acquiescent response set may increase the empirical validity of the F scale, it tends to reduce the logical validity reflected by the content of the items.

If an individual's responses to F scale items are determined partly by belief and partly by response acquiescence, it is particularly difficult to know what meaning to ascribe to a total score that is the sum of individual item scores. Is a high scorer on the F scale someone who agrees with the content of the items? Does he really believe both that "familiarity breeds contempt" and that "we are bound to admire and respect a person if we get to know him well?" Or is he merely acquiescent and submissive, exhibiting a tendency to agree instead of affirming an ideology or belief? Of course, the score may also indicate an interaction of the two—but in what proportions? Does the particular combination of acquiescence and belief elicited by the F scale differ from person to person? It would seem necessary that these questions be answered if responses to the F scale in its present form are to be interpreted consistently.

One possible solution to these problems would be the development of independent measures of authoritarian belief and of acquiescence. For instance, if it were decided to measure acquiescence as a trait or a personal style, then it would seem desirable to have the index as unconfounded as possible from content variables. One approach might be to use statements that are so heterogeneous and multidimensional that any consistencies found in agreements to these statements could not be considered due to latent attitudes of specific content. If it were decided to measure only authoritarian belief, it would seem desirable to use sets of relatively homogeneous items and to control for acquiescent response set experimentally. If it were decided to use an interaction between acquiescence and content as an indicant of the authoritarian personality, then it would also be desirable to measure both effects independently in order to evaluate such an interaction.

There are several possible procedures for controlling acquiescent response set, such as the use of forced-choice, paired-comparison, or multiple-choice item forms. If attitude content is to be appraised with minimum confusion, attempts should also be made to reduce ambiguity [8], to eliminate inane and cliché-like wordings, and to utilize topics that are important and meaningful to the respondents. The accepted test practice [25] of phrasing half the items positively and half negatively may also be appropriate in some cases. However, this half positive, half negative method of control is difficult to use with some items, since the reversed wordings are often complicated, trivial, or artificial sounding. Original and reversed items were used in the research mentioned above mainly to demonstrate the presence of acquiescence; their use should not necessarily be interpreted as a general endorsement of the technique as a control for response set.

It should also be pointed out that controlling for acquiescence is an experimental problem, not a measurement one, in the sense that scaling models themselves have no provisions for response sets. The models do place some requirements on item form in terms of appropriate trace lines or operating characteristics [14], but practically no restrictions are placed upon the direction of item content. In fact, response sets can even make it easier to obtain a unidimensional scale. Just as acquiescence can increase the reliability and empirical validity of a set of items, so it can also increase their homogeneity or reproducibility. However, it might be possible, although probably not necessary, to eliminate this hazard formally by incorporating some restrictions into the models themselves; it is usually eliminated informally in terms of accepted test practices and recommendations.

There is another experimental problem in addition to response set which may be important to consider in future attempts to measure authoritarian belief or other social attitudes. This is the problem of the social desirability of the statements in the scale. Allen Edwards [11] recently scaled a set of items by the method of successive intervals with respect to an attribute of social desirability. He then plotted the social desirability scale values against the proportion of agreements to these statements obtained from a different sample, and he found a correlation of .87. Of course, the argument is somewhat circular, but the high positive correlation between the tendency to agree with an item and that item's judged social desirability cannot be ignored. This fact has led Edwards in his recent development of a personality inventory [12] to use an item form with forced choices between two statements that are equated in social desirability—a form that also usually controls for acquiescent response set.

DIMENSIONALITY IN THE MEASUREMENT OF AUTHORITARIANISM

The problem of assessing beliefs by eliciting and interpreting agreements with statements is a general problem of attitude measurement—a problem which the recent advances in measurement theory [14, 16, 21] attempt to solve by providing models that relate latent variables of attitude to the manifest data of item responses. Many problems of interpretation and measurement remain after experimental difficulties like response sets are controlled. In fact, the same kind of difficulty involved in interpreting a total score which reflects both content and acquiescence also occurs in interpreting total scores which reflect more than one content dimension. This is an important consideration since there is evidence that the F scale does not represent a single unidimensional continuum but rather a complex of several traits [6, 29], and, indeed, authoritarianism was originally conceived in terms of a system of presumably interrelated components such as aggression, conventionalism, and stereotypy [1]. However, within such a framework there are certain difficulties involved in interpreting a total score. Two individuals can have identical scores—one because of agreements to aggression items, for example, and the other because of agreements to conventionalism items. Are the same characteristics to be ascribed to these people on the basis of identical total scores?

Thus, the use of a single total score, such as the one obtained for the F scale via the method of summated ratings [23], is difficult to interpret with heterogeneous items. Green [14] has pointed out that the Likert scoring procedure implies a mathematical model involving a single common factor. Such a model assumes that intercorrelations among the items are due to a single underlying factor to which the items are all mutually related and that apart from the effect of this dimension, the items are independent. The ease of interpretation of a total score for authoritarianism, then, depends upon the extent to which the F scale reflects such unidimensional properties.

If the postulated traits composing the authoritarian cluster are all mutually interrelated, then certain general characteristics can be ascribed to respondents on the basis of F scale scores, in the same way that total mental age scores are interpreted on intelligence tests. However, as the authors of *The Authoritarian Personality* [1] point out, the average correlation between each F scale item and the total score, even considering the consistency contributed by response set, is only about half that of the multi-factor Stanford-Binet. Also, oblique rotations were not indicated for obtaining simple structure in a factorial exploration of authoritarianism by O'Neil and Levinson [29]. The F scale items were found to have high loadings on either one or the other of two orthogonal factors, thus arguing against the use of a total score as a meaningful index of general authoritarianism.

However, evidence concerning interrelationships among F scale items is far from definitive, and the point being made here is not only that total scores are equivocal because of a failure to demonstrate correlated subsystems. The total score would be equivocal even then, since more than one number is usually required to place a point in a multidimensional space, even if the dimensions are correlated. The notion to be emphasized here is that the use of a single total score is an unfortunately simplified reflection of a dynamic theory that postulates a complex of traits. In practice, authoritarians are considered to be merely high-scorers on the F scale, and variations in more than one dimension, which might be consistent with the underlying theory, are not permitted to occur. Thus a single unidimensional scale of authoritarianism, apart from being extremely difficult if not impossible to obtain, is probably not even desirable theoretically.

An alternative strategy for measuring the complex of traits composing authoritarianism would be to isolate the relevant dimensions of the cluster and attempt to measure each one separately with homogeneous scales [6]. Factor analysis would be helpful in this approach, provided care was taken to avoid reflecting differences in item popularities in the particular measure of item intercorrelation used. Thurstone's judgment scaling methods of paired comparisons [36] and successive intervals [10], along with the recent multidimensional extensions of these techniques [27], might also prove helpful in item selection.

According to Loevinger [25], the possibility of constructing statistically homogeneous scales was considered and rejected by the authors of *The Authoritarian Personality* on the grounds that item intercorrelations in this area are inevitably low. But Loevinger's point [25] is well taken that "it is exactly because the correlations . . . are intrinsically low that the shrewdest statistical means are needed to detect the difference between manifestations of a common trait, manifestations of different but correlated traits, and chance correlations." The use of heterogeneous items in the Likert technique has also been defended on the grounds that statements can be included which need not be related in an overt and logical manner to the attitude measured [20] and that richness and clinical usefulness is thereby obtained [26]. Indeed, heterogeneity may be advantageous if interpretations are made of individual responses to individual items, unreliable though they may be. Heterogeneity may also add to adequacy of coverage and predictive efficiency. But when item responses are added up to yield a total score, the psychological interpretation of that score would seem to depend upon the extent to which the scale possesses the mathematical properties implied by adding the numbers.

The experimenter's purposes, then, and the nature of the problem under investigation should be considered in selecting scaling devices and measurement approaches. There are many advantages in using sets of statistically homogeneous scales for the measurement of a particular area in that the dimensionality of the domain is considered in selecting the variables and item interrelationships are used to construct the scales. However, care must be taken to insure that all the relevant dimensions are included, and in the personality area these variables are not always to be interpreted in terms of common item content. Some important consistencies might exist in stylistic responses to items heterogeneous in content, consistencies which may be overwhelmed in scales emphasizing unidimensional content. Thus, two people agreeing with different heterogeneous statements may in fact be comparable in some tendency to act in a given direction—in a tendency to acquiesce, for example. It is thus not certain that independent measures of the same unidimensional processes in different people provide the best possible means for *predicting* stylistic behavior [30], but such unidimensional measures are of considerable help in attributing characteristics to individuals on the basis of their responses to item content.

OVERVIEW

An acquiescent response set elicited by F scale items has a systematic, cumulative effect upon scores. This acquiescent component in correlations between the F scale and other variables makes interpretation difficult and previous one-to-one correspondences questionable. It is true that response acquiescence may be important in its own right as a personality trait or individual style rather than being merely a momentary response set elicited by a particular testing situation. But, in any event, its appearance in the California F scale is completely confounded with content variables, making it impossible to tell whether a particular item response is reflecting acquiescence or belief.

This problem of interpretation suggests the need for a revision of the F scale as a measure of attitudes, a revision which could be attempted in several ways. One approach would begin with the theory described in *The Authoritarian Personality* as a source of ideas for constructing items. Since this theory considers authoritarianism

to be a complex system of interrelated components, it would seem reasonable to isolate some dimensions of this system statistically. Then homogeneous scales could be constructed to measure each of the isolated traits separately. Effects such as acquiescence or social desirability should be eliminated by experimental controls or perhaps isolated and measured independently as relevant variables. Since there are several methods for controlling acquiescent response set (such as using multiple-choice items, forced-choice paired comparisons, or phrasing half the items positively and half negatively), the efficiency of the controls themselves and their possible effects upon content interpretation must also be studied and evaluated. If the personality theory is supported by an empirical isolation of interrelated factors, then this approach would yield a set of scales to measure various aspects of the authoritarian syndrome and would permit a re-evaluation of previously established correlates of authoritarian ideology.

REFERENCES

1. ADORNO, T. W., FRENKEL-BRUNSWIK, ELSE, LEVINSON, D. J., & SANFORD, R. N. *The authoritarian personality.* New York: Harper & Brothers, 1950.
2. BASS, B. M. Authoritarianism or acquiescence? *J. abnorm. soc. Psychol.,* 1955, 51, 611–623.
3. BLOCK, J., & BLOCK, JEANNE. An investigation of the relationship between intolerance of ambiguity and ethnocentrism. *J. Pers.,* 1951, 19, 303–311.
4. BROWN, R. W. A determinant of the relationship between rigidity and authoritarianism. *J. abnorm. soc. Psychol.,* 1953, 48, 469–476.
5. CAMPBELL, D. T., & McCANDLESS, B. R. Ethnocentrism, xenophobia, and personality. *Human Relat.,* 1951, 4, 185–192.
6. CHRISTIE, R. Authoritarianism re-examined. In R. Christie & M. Jahoda (Eds.), *Studies in the scope and method of "The Authoritarian Personality."* Glencoe, Ill.: Free Press, 1954.
7. COHN, T. S. The relation of the F scale to a response set to answer positively. *Amer. Psychologist,* 1953, 8, 335.

8. CRONBACH, L. J. Response sets and test validity. *Educ. psychol. Measmt*, 1946, 6, 475–494.

9. CRONBACH, L. J. Further evidence on response sets and test design. *Educ. psychol. Measmt*, 1950, 10, 3–31.

10. EDWARDS, A. L. The scaling of stimuli by the method of successive intervals. *J. appl. Psychol.*, 1952, 36, 118–122.

11. EDWARDS, A. L. The relationship between the judged desirability of a trait and the probability that the trait will be endorsed. *J. appl. Psychol.*, 1953, 37, 90–93.

12. EDWARDS, A. L. *Edwards personal preference schedule.* New York: Psychological Corporation, 1953.

13. GOUGH, H. G. Studies of social intolerance: I–IV. *J. soc. Psychol.*, 1951, 33, 237–271.

14. GREEN, B. F. Attitude measurement. In G. Lindzey (Ed.), Vol. 1. *Handbook of social psychology.* Cambridge, Mass.: Addison-Wesley, 1954.

15. GUBA, E. G., & GETZELS, J. W. The construction of an other-directedness instrument, with some preliminary data on validity. *Amer. Psychologist*, 1954, 9, 385.

16. GUTTMAN, L. The basis for scalogram analysis. In S. Stouffer, et al. *Measurement and prediction.* Princeton: Princeton Univer. Press, 1950.

17. JACKSON, D. N. Stability in resistance to field forces. Unpublished Ph.D. Thesis, Purdue University, 1955.

18. JACKSON, D. N., & MESSICK, S. J. A note on ethnocentrism and acquiescent response sets. *J. abnorm. soc. Psychol.*, 1957, 54, 132–134.

19. JACKSON, D. N., MESSICK, S. J., & SOLLEY, C. M. How "rigid" is the "authoritarian"? *J. abnorm. soc. Psychol.*, 1957, 54, 137–140.

20. JAHODA, MARIE. Introduction. In R. Christie & M. Jahoda (Eds.), *Studies in the scope and method of "The Authoritarian Personality."* Glencoe, Ill.: Free Press, 1954.

21. LAZARSFELD, P. F. The logical and mathematical foundation of latent structure analysis. In S. Stouffer, et al. *Measurement and prediction.* Princeton: Princeton Univer. Press, 1950.

22. LEAVITT, H. J., HAX, H., & ROCHE, J. H. "Authoritarianism" and agreement with things authoritative. *J. Psychol.*, 1955, 40, 215–221.

23. LIKERT, R. A technique for the measurement of attitudes. *Arch. Psychol.*, 1932, No. 140.

24. LOEVINGER, JANE. The technic of homogeneous tests compared with some aspects of "scale analysis" and factor analysis. *Psychol. Bull.*, 1948, 45, 507–529.

25. LOEVINGER, JANE. Some principles of personality measurement. *Educ. psychol. Measmt*, 1955, 15, 3–17.

26. McKINLEY, J. C., & HATHAWAY, S. R. The Minnesota Multiphasic Personality Inventory v. hysteria, hypomania, and psychopathic deviate. *J. appl. Psychol.*, 1944, 28, 153–174.

27. MESSICK, S. J. Some recent theoretical developments in multidimensional scaling. *Educ. psychol. Measmt*, 1956, 16, 82–100.

28. MESSICK, S. J., & JACKSON, D. N. Authoritarianism and acquiescence in Bass's data. *J. abnorm. soc. Psychol.*, 1957, 54, 424–426.

29. O'NEIL, W. M., & LEVINSON, D. J. A factorial exploration of authoritarianism and some of its ideological concomitants. *J. Pers.*, 1954, 22, 449–463.

30. PEAK, HELEN. Problems of objective observation. In L. Festinger & D. Katz (Eds.), *Research methods in the behavioral sciences.* New York: Dryden, 1953.

31. PRENTICE, N. M. The comparability of positive and negative items in scales of ethnic prejudice. *J. abnorm. soc. Psychol.*, 1956, 52, 420–421.

32. ROKEACH, M. Generalized mental rigidity as a factor in ethnocentrism. *J. abnorm. soc. Psychol.*, 1948, 43, 259–278.

33. ROKEACH, M. The nature and meaning of dogmatism. *Psychol. Rev.*, 1954, 61, 194–204.

34. SHELLEY, H. P. Response set and the California attitude scales. *Educ. psychol. Measmt*, 1956, 16, 63–67.

35. SULLIVAN, P. L., & ADELMAN, J. Ethnocentrism and misanthropy. *J. abnorm. soc. Psychol.*, 1954, 49, 246–250.

36. THURSTONE, L. L. Psychophysical analysis. *Amer. J. Psychol.*, 1927, 38, 368–389.

Chapter 64

Attitudes toward Old People

NATHAN KOGAN

In recent years there has been considerable discussion regarding the "minority group" status of old people in American society. Barron [5], for example, has stressed some of the similarities between the position of the aged and of ethnic, racial, and religious minorities on the American scene. In particular, Barron refers to the stereotyping of the aged by other age groups and the discrimination against older people in employment and other areas of life.

More recently, Drake [10] has pointed to some of the major differences between the status of old people and that of the traditional minorities in the United States. These differences stem from the fact that the aged do not constitute an independently functioning subgroup with a unique

.This article is reprinted from the *Journal of Abnormal and Social Psychology*, 1961, with the permission of the author and the American Psychological Association.

This study was supported by the National Institute of Mental Health, United States Public Health Service, under Research Grant M-1867, and was conducted under the auspices of the Age Center of New England, Inc.

history, language, and culture. With these considerations in mind, Drake suggests that old people be designated a "quasi-minority."

Proceeding upon the assumption that old people in American society are devalued, Linden [15, 16] has outlined various cultural influences considered responsible for such devaluation. Illustrative of these influences, according to Linden, are the diminishing acceptance of family responsibilities toward one's elders, the decline in respect toward the aged as a consequence of loss of their position of authority, and the exaggerated premium placed on the physical and psychological attributes of youth.

Empirical support for a minority or quasi-minority view of old people is offered in a paper by Tuckman and Lorge [23]. They examined the incidence of yes and no responses to a set of statements reflecting stereotypes and misconceptions about the aged in such general areas as physical change, family relationships, personality traits, etc. While this work is of interest as an initial empirical venture in the field, Tuckman and Lorge make no use of attitude scaling procedures and pay little attention to psychological correlates of attitudes toward old people.[1]

The present research is directly concerned with the development of a Likert scale to facilitate the study of attitudes toward old people with respect to both norms and individual differences. The search for correlates of these attitudes proceeded along several directions. First, with a minority group model in mind, we asked whether attitudes toward old people would be related to authoritarianism, anomie, and ethnic prejudice. Second, we considered Barker's [3] discussion of the minority group aspects of physical disability in our society, and, accordingly, inquired whether attitudes toward old people would be associated with attitudes toward people distinguished by various physical disabilities. Third, since mental deterioration is often alleged to be an important attribute of old age, the relationship between attitudes toward the mentally ill and toward old age was examined. Finally, we hypothesized that there would be significant relationships between attitudes toward old people and such personality dimensions as autonomy, achievement, nurturance, self-esteem, and misanthropy; subjects more favorably disposed toward old people were expected to exhibit stronger tendencies toward self-esteem and nurturance, while subjects more unfavorably disposed were expected to have stronger needs with respect to misanthropy, autonomy, and achievement.

METHOD

SUBJECTS

Students enrolled in introductory classes in psychology served as subjects. Two male samples ($N = 128$ and 186) were obtained

---

[1] A complete bibliography of this work through 1955 is available in Shock [21]. In a more recent paper, Tuckman and Lorge [24] concern themselves with personal psychological and physiological symptoms and their projection onto old people as stereotypes.

from Northeastern University. One sample ($N = 168$, 87 males and 81 females) was obtained from Boston University.

MEASURING INSTRUMENTS

A set of 17 items expressing negative sentiments about old people was constructed. A second set of 17 items was then devised the content of which was the reverse of the first set. There were, thus, 17 matched positive-negative pairs. These are shown in Table 64–1.

Some of the items were adapted from available ethnic minority items by the simple substitution of the "old people" referent. Other statements derive from the author's and others' intuitions regarding stereotypes and feelings about old people in our society. Some a priori clustering of the items is possible on the basis of their manifest content. Thus, Item Pairs 1, 5, and 12 are all concerned with the residential aspects of old people's lives with special reference to segregation, maintenance of home, and character of neighborhood, respectively. Item Pairs 2 and 8 reflect the degree to which vague feelings of discomfort and tension are experienced in the company of old people. The extent to which old people vary among one another is tapped by Item Pairs 11 and 13. The nature of interpersonal relations across age generations—conflicted or benign—is implied in Item Pairs 9, 10, and 16. The theme of dependence is represented by Item Pairs 4 and 17. Item Pairs 3 and 6 refer to the cognitive style and capacity of old people. Qualities of old people with respect to personal appearance and personality are cited in Item Pairs 14 and 15. Finally, Item Pair 7 does not readily cluster with any of the other items.

These items were interspersed among items from other attitude scales, thereby partially disguising the presence of logical opposites among the "old people" statements and providing the necessary data for the study of correlates. Most of these additional items were taken from the California

Table 64-1 Means, Standard Deviations, Item-Sum Correlations (r_{IS}), and Matched Item Pair Correlations (r_{NP}) for "Old People" (OP) Items*

Item	BU Sample (N = 168)				NU-I Sample (N = 128)				NU-II Sample (N = 186)			
	M$	SD	r_{IS}	r_{NP}	M	SD	r_{IS}	r_{NP}	M	SD	r_{IS}	r_{NP}
1 N† It would probably be better if most old people lived in residential units with people of their own age.	3.01	1.54	.40		3.25	1.78	.47		3.34	1.75	.49	
1 P† It would probably be better if most old people lived in residential units that also housed younger people.	3.52	1.55	.34	.26	3.53	1.61	.36	.42	3.73	1.67	.32	.32
2 N There is something different about most old people: it's hard to figure out what makes them tick.	2.90	1.40	.57		3.06	1.47	.48		3.01	1.35	.54	
2 P Most old people are really no different from anybody else: they're as easy to understand as younger people.	3.90	1.63	.61	.27	3.72	1.71	.63	.18	3.69	1.56	.57	.33
3 N Most old people get set in their ways and are unable to change.	4.89	1.46	.41		5.18	1.45	.39		5.07	1.49	.49	
3 P Most old people are capable of new adjustments when the situation demands it.	3.96	1.62	.54	.35	3.86	1.77	.33	.17	4.15	1.71	.55	.25
4 N Most old people would prefer to quit work as soon as pensions or their children can support them.	2.08	1.11	.32		2.15	1.17	.10		2.28	1.31	.30	
4 P Most old people would prefer to continue working just as long as they possibly can rather than be dependent on anybody.	2.38	1.13	.28	.38	1.99	.73	.18	.31	2.24	1.07	.32	.35
5 N Most old people tend to let their homes become shabby and unattractive.	2.22	1.15	.47		2.28	1.12	.38		2.43	1.29	.41	
5 P Most old people can generally be counted on to maintain a clean, attractive home.	2.95	1.31	.55	.42	2.69	1.20	.49	.21	2.63	1.18	.59	.32
6 N It is foolish to claim that wisdom comes with old age.	4.05	1.98	.19		3.73	2.00	.10					
6 P People grow wiser with the coming of old age.	3.71	1.49	.26	.40	4.06	1.74	.13	.41				

	Statement											
7 N	Old people have too much power in business and politics.	2.77	1.29	.49		3.36	1.67	.41		3.40	1.72	.40	
7 P‡	Old people should have more power in business and politics.	5.15	1.03	.34	.12	5.22	1.19	.36	.13	5.49	1.09	.09	.24
8 N	Most old people make one feel ill at ease.	2.82	1.30	.51		3.01	1.32	.50		3.03	1.37	.56	
8 P	Most old people are very relaxing to be with.	3.95	1.47	.67	.30	3.65	1.51	.67	.34	3.70	1.49	.62	.44
9 N	Most old people bore others by their insistence on talking about the "good old days."	3.64	1.48	.58		3.55	1.56	.53		3.53	1.60	.61	
9 P‡	One of the most interesting and entertaining qualities of most old people is their accounts of their past experiences.	2.79	1.37	.27	.16	2.54*	1.30	.23	.17	2.65	1.29	.32	.26
10 N	Most old people spend too much time prying into the affairs of others and giving unsought advice.	3.63	1.54	.65		3.41	1.59	.70		3.95	1.57	.67	
10 P‡	Most old people tend to keep to themselves and give advice only when asked.	4.84	1.38	.47	.25	4.74	1.54	.29	.23	4.67	1.51	.41	.26
11 N	If old people expect to be liked, their first step is to try to get rid of their irritating faults.	3.82	1.56	.44		3.87	1.69	.48		4.17	1.56	.43	
11 P	When you think about it, old people have the same faults as anybody else.	2.60	1.31	.41	.07	2.51	1.25	.49	.14	2.67	1.36	.55	.13
12 N	In order to maintain a nice residential neighborhood, it would be best if too many old people did not live in it.	2.37	1.41	.48		2.69	1.65	.25		2.58	1.63	.49	
12 P	You can count on finding a nice residential neighborhood when there is a sizeable number of old people living in it.	3.62	1.42	.36	.25	3.46	1.48	.34	.31	3.90	1.51	.34	.06
13 N	There are a few exceptions, but in general most old people are pretty much alike.	2.60	1.56	.37		2.74	1.63	.42		3.15	1.80	.44	
13 P	It is evident that most old people are very different from one another.	3.63	1.56	.42	.41	3.65	1.74	.38	.41	4.05	1.68	.33	.33

Note: All footnotes for Table 64–1 are on p. 754.

Table 64-1   Means, Standard Deviations, Item-Sum Correlations (r_{IS}), and Matched Item Pair Correlations (r_{NP}) for "Old People" (OP) Items* (Continued)

Item	BU Sample (N = 168)				NU-I Sample (N = 128)				NU-II Sample (N = 186)			
	M§	SD	r_{IS}	r_{NP}	M	SD	r_{IS}	r_{NP}	M	SD	r_{IS}	r_{NP}
14 N Most old people should be more concerned with their personal appearance; they're too untidy.	3.01	1.36	.44		2.99	1.44	.54		3.08	1.39	.49	
14 P Most old people seem to be quite clean and neat in their personal appearance.	3.54	1.60	.57	.48	3.27	1.48	.56	.44	3.32	1.49	.59	.61
15 N Most old people are irritable, grouchy, and unpleasant.	2.34	.94	.54		2.47	1.22	.46		2.69	1.45	.55	
15 P Most old people are cheerful, agreeable, and good humored.	3.62	1.40	.66	.27	3.35	1.36	.64	.25	3.47	1.51	.61	.40
16 N Most old people are constantly complaining about the behavior of the younger generation.	4.89	1.62	.50		5.18	1.67	.52		5.49	1.46	.54	
16 P One seldom hears old people complaining about the behavior of the younger generation.	5.47	1.13	.49	.41	5.59	1.19	.33	.50	5.75	1.08	.25	.34
17 N Most old people make excessive demands for love and reassurance.	3.96	1.63	.46		3.96	1.68	.50		3.92	1.54	.52	
17 P Most old people need no more love and reassurance than anyone else.	4.54	1.55	.39	.19	4.41	1.79	.27	.27	4.46	1.53	.43	.11
Total negative scale (OP−)	54.87 3.23¶	11.04			56.84 3.35	11.00			54.17 3.40	12.28		
Total positive scale (OP+)	64.14 3.77	10.90			62.13 3.65	9.70			60.42 3.77	10.47		

* The magnitude of r's required for statistical significance is as follows: for N = 168, .15 at the .05 level and .20 at the .01 level; for N = 128, .17 at the .05 level and .23 at the .01 level; for N = 186, .14 at the .05 level and .19 at the .01 level.

† Items are listed in pairs, N representing the negatively worded form and P the positively worded form.

‡ Revised form of the item used with NU-II sample. The revised items read as follows:
7 P Old people have too little power in business and politics.
9 P One of the more interesting qualities of most old people is their accounts of their past experiences.
10 P Most old people respect others' privacy and give advice only when asked.

§ Negative and positive means were made comparable by subtracting the positive means from 8.00. By this step, higher mean values reflect more unfavorable attitudes for both positive and negative items.

¶ Per item means.

F and anti-Negro scales [1], Srole's [22] Antiminority and Anomie scales, Gilbert and Levinson's [12] scale of attitudes toward mental illness and the attitude-to-blindness scale of Cowen, Underberg, and Verrillo [9]. In addition, items measuring attitudes toward totally deaf and crippled persons were constructed, and, in some cases, adapted from the attitude-to-blindness scale cited above. In the case of the items taken from the F Scale and the Gilbert and Levinson mental illness scale, a set of matched items of opposite sign was added to the final battery. Six response categories were provided for all of the items: "strongly disagree," "disagree," "slightly disagree," "slightly agree," "agree," and "strongly agree." These categories were scored 1, 2, 3, 5, 6, and 7, respectively, with a score of 4 assigned in the rare case of failure to respond to an item.

All three samples received the F Scale items, two samples received the Anomie scale, and one sample received all of the remaining scales. Two of the three samples, in addition, were given a set of 30 true-false personality items taken largely from Murray's *Explorations in Personality* [17] volume, and the Brodbeck and Perlmutter [6] self-dislike scale.

RESULTS

OLD PEOPLE SCALES

Table 64–1 presents the basic data for "old people" items and scales (hereafter referred to as OP items and scales). Consider first the scale means shown at the bottom of Table 64–1. A high degree of consistency among the sample means is evident. In all three samples, for example, the negatively worded statements elicit more favorable sentiments. In other words, subjects disagree more with statements commenting adversely on old people than they agree with statements praising old people. A test for the statistical significance of these overall mean differences yields t's significant beyond the .01 level for each of

the samples. Note further that the per item means are uniformly smaller than 4.00— the hypothetical indifference point. These college subjects, then, tend, in general, to be more favorable than unfavorable in their attitudes toward old people as manifested by responses to the OP items of the present battery.

For the BU sample, it was possible to examine sex differences in OP scale means. For both the positive and negative OP scales, no significant differences obtained. This does not imply, of course, that there are no sex differences for specific OP items.

Reliability coefficients and interscale correlations are listed in Table 64–2. The former (in the diagonals of the table) range from .66 to .85. There is a trend toward greater reliability for the OP— as opposed to the OP+ scale. The magnitude of the OP— reliability coefficient for the NU-II sample suggests that few additional item modifications are required. The OP+ scale, on the other hand, falls somewhat short of an acceptable reliability level, despite item revisions for the NU-II sample.

Consider next the interscale correlations in Table 64–2. In the construction of matched pairs, we attempted to build genuine logical opposites in terms of connotative meaning rather than retain virtually identical wording in both members of the item pair. This procedure was followed in order to disguise the presence of logical opposites among the items. We wanted to discourage consistency of response based on sheer recognition of almost identically worded opposites.

There is, however, a price paid for such

Table 64–2   Odd-Even Reliability Coefficients (Spearman-Brown) and Interscale Correlations for the OP Scales

Scale	BU Sample (N = 168)		NU-I Sample (N = 128)		NU-II Sample (N = 186)	
	OP−	OP+	OP−	OP+	OP−	OP+
OP−	.76	.51	.73	.52	.83	.46
OP+		.77		.66		.73

freedom in item wording when subjects endorse or reject two items of presumably opposite meaning. One might account for such findings in terms of response set, ambivalent feelings regarding the object of the attitude, or poorly constructed opposites; or, more likely, a combination of all of these might be involved. This problem has been cogently discussed in the case of F Scale items by Christie, Havel, and Seidenberg [8].

In the present case, product-moment coefficients between positively and negatively worded scales are uniformly positive. As Table 64–2 shows, r's between OP+ and OP− range from .46 to .52 in the three samples, all significant beyond the .01 level. Given correlations that can theoretically range from +1.00 (perfect logical consistency) to −1.00 (perfect logical inconsistency), content must necessarily be a more powerful influence than response set for the OP items of the present battery.

OLD PEOPLE ITEMS

Substantial variations in mean levels across OP items may be noted. It is especially noteworthy that the Item Pair 16 with the highest means—i.e., most unfavorable toward old people—concerns old people's feelings about the younger generation. No single item pair seems to stand out at the favorable end of the attitude continuum. Rather, there are a number of cases where one or both members of an item pair yield means less than 3.00.

Individual items range widely in the extent of their correlation (r_{IS}) with positive and negative sum scores. It will be noted that Item Pair 6 yields very low r_{IS} values for both the BU and NU-I samples and was, accordingly, not used with the NU-II sample. Apparently, the association between wisdom and old age tapped by Item Pair 6 is off the favorability-unfavorability continuum represented by the other "old people" items. Perhaps, the aphoristic quality of that item pair militates against adequate discriminability.

Item Pair 4 also yields rather low item-sum correlation coefficients. Modification of this item pair is recommended in future work with the OP scales. A suggested modification would eliminate the combination of support by children and by pension in Item 4N. There is an obvious value distinction between support by one's children and support by a pension plan to which one has financially contributed.

An additional consideration in the revision of items is the size of r_{NP}—the correlation between the matched positive and negative items. There is considerable variation among specific OP item pairs in the extent to which the subjects respond to the positive and negative member of the pair in a consistent fashion. Again we may note that such variation could well reflect success in constructing logically opposite item pairs. So, for example, Item Pair 7 does not meet specifications of logical oppositeness, for the negative member of the pair is a descriptive statement while the positive member is a statement advocating change. It is hardly surprising under these circumstances that r_{NP} values in the BU and NU-I samples are nonsignificant. However, when Item 7P was revised for the NU-II sample (cf. Footnote §, Table 64–1), the r_{NP} value increased, but at the unfortunate price of a sharp drop in the item-sum correlation (r_{IS}). Clearly, further modifications would seem to be in order for Item Pair 7.

Revision of Item 9P was also deemed advisable in view of fairly low r_{NP} (as well as low r_{IS}) values. We suspected that the reference to "entertaining qualities" in the item could be interpreted by subjects in a satirical vein and, accordingly, dropped the presumably offending words in the revised version used with the NU-II sample. A slight increase in r_{IS} and a substantial increase in r_{NP} resulted. It should be noted, however, that r_{IS} for Item 9P is considerably smaller than the corresponding value for its matched negative.

Finally, Item 10P was revised in an effort to make that item more positive in its connotation. In its original form, the item suggests that old people are inclined to avoid interpersonal relations with others. While the revised wording no longer carries this connotation, no appreciable increase in r_{IS} and r_{NP} was observed in the NU-II sample.

In sum, it should be emphasized that the variability in r_{NP} coefficients for specific item pairs is entirely within the positive band of the correlational spectrum. Further, of the 50 r_{NP} values reported in Table 64–1, 43 are statistically significant at the .05 level or better in the positive, i.e., logically consistent, direction. These results further emphasize that the OP items tap something more than stylistic response tendencies.

RELATIONS WITH AUTHORITARIANISM

We turn next to the various correlates of attitudes toward old people. It is in the examination of correlates that the advantage of using both positively and negatively worded items is especially evident. Several statistically significant relationships obtained between attitudes toward old people and other attitudinal variables based on items worded in the same direction might well be spurious relationships attributable largely to response set tendencies. This phenomenon is best illustrated by the results shown in Table 64–3.

In each of the samples, statistically significant correlations ranging from .21 to .28 are obtained between F Scale scores for items worded in the authoritarian direction and scores based on negatively worded OP items. It should be noted that these results are consistent for both a conventional type of F Scale (administered to the BU and NU-I samples) and a "pure" factorially derived scale of "acceptance of authority" (administered to the NU-II sample). The correlations suggest that more authoritarian persons are more *unfavorably* disposed toward old people. When, however, these authoritarianism scores are related to scores based on positively worded "old people" items, the correlation coefficients are in the negative direction, i.e., more authoritarian individuals are more *favorably* disposed to-

Table 64–3 Intercorrelations (Product-Moment r's) of "Old People" Scales with Authoritarianism and Anomie Scales

Scale	Sample	"Old People" Scales OP+	OP−
Authoritarianism original (F+)	BU	−.12	.28†
	NU-I	−.16	.21‡
	NU-II	−.29†	.21†
Authoritarianism opposites (F−)°	BU	.04	.10
	NU-I	.06	.08
	NU-II	−.06	−.22†
Anomie (A)	NU-I	.17‡	.39†
	NU-II	.20†	.45†

° Scored in the content direction consistent with F+, i.e., higher scores reflect more authoritarianism.
† Significant at the .01 level.
‡ Significant at the .05 level.

ward old people. In the latter case, however, only the r for the NU-II sample is significant.

For items worded in the nonauthoritarian direction, the r's tend toward low nonsignificant values. The significant negative correlation between F− and OP− for the NU-II sample is in the opposite direction and of approximately the same magnitude as the r between F+ and OP− for that sample. There seems little doubt, then, that response set effects partially account for relations between F and OP. Even if F+ items constitute a more valid measure of authoritarianism than do F− items [11], the fact remains that F+ correlates in opposite directions with positively and negatively worded OP items. It seems doubtful that the slightly lower reliability of the positive OP scale could account for the extent of this inconsistency.

Correlations between F+ and F− were .42, .27, and .26 for the BU, NU-I, and NU-II samples, respectively. While these r's— all significant beyond the .01 level in the content direction—suggest a reasonable degree of success in the selection of reversed F items, reliabilities for F− (.27, .10, .46) are considerably lower than for

F+ (.62, .73, .60) in the BU, NU-I, and NU-II samples, respectively.

RELATIONS WITH ANOMIE

Consider next the Anomie (A) scale. As defined operationally by Srole's [22] items, the anomie variable measures such characteristics as the subjects' pessimism about the future, helplessness in the face of powerful social forces, and inability to find meaning or purpose in life. Here we did not attempt the construction of items of opposite sign. The influence of response set effects may be gauged, however, in terms of the direction and magnitude of the correlations between A and the two OP scales. As Table 64–3 shows, the r's are considerably higher with the negatively worded OP scale than with the positively worded version in the two samples tested. However, while the r's drop in the latter case, they remain statistically significant in a logically consistent direction. In sum, subjects unfavorably disposed toward old people are more disposed toward anomie.

Is anomie also related to attitudes toward the other minority groups represented in the present study? Correlations between anomie, on the one hand, and scales for attitudes toward ethnic and physically disabled minorities, on the other, range from .28 to .44 in the NU-II sample, all significant beyond the .01 level. Unfortunately, these r's are based on items worded in but one direction, and, hence, are susceptible to the usual effects of response set. Indeed, when anomie is correlated against the two "mental illness" scales, the r of .40 between A and MI– is highly significant, while r between MI+ and A is a mere .04.

RELATIONS WITH ANTIMINORITY ATTITUDES

Correlations between the OP and the various antiminority scales are listed in Table 64–4. Since these results are based

on a single sample, conclusions drawn from them must necessarily be considered tentative. This is particularly the case for the various scales in Table 64–4 original to the present investigation. Here, we simply are dealing with sum scores for items grouped together on the basis of manifest content. The reliabilities of these newly constructed "scales" are surprisingly high, however, given the small number of items they contain. Thus, the Spearman-Brown coefficients for the five-item "deafness" and "cripple" scales range from .51 to .60.

Inspection of Table 64–4 reveals that the large majority of r's are significant beyond the .01 level. For the "mental illness" scales, highly significant positive correlations are found between items worded in the same direction on the two scales, but r's drop to nonsignificant levels when obtained between scales worded in opposite directions. Table 64–4 further shows that Srole's Antiminority scale, the California anti-Negro scale, and the scales comprising the various physical disability groupings are all significantly related to the OP scales when response set effects are held constant.

Table 64–4   Intercorrelations (Product-Moment r's) of "Old People" Scales with Antiminority and Disability Scales (NU-II Sample)*

Scale	OP+	OP–
Mental illness positive (MI+)†	.33	.08
Mental illness negative (MI–)	.11	.46
Anti-Negro (AN)	.21	.46
Antiminority (AM)	.25	.43
Blindness (B)	.28	.52
Deafness (Dx)‡	.21	.48
Deafness (Dy)§	.33	.50
Cripple (Cx)‡	.23	.53
Cripple (Cy)§	.21	.42

* For $N = 186$, r's of .14 and .19 are significant at the .05 and .01 levels, respectively.
† Scored in the content direction consistent with MI–, i.e., higher scores reflect more negative attitudes toward the mentally ill.
‡ Adapted from Cowen et al. [9] blindness items by appropriate substitution of disability group.
§ Items constructed by the author.

While such effects may exert an influence, suggested by the larger *r*'s in the OP negative as opposed to the OP positive column, item content would seem to be of major importance in the present case. In sum, subjects negatively disposed toward old people tend to hold unfavorable attitudes toward ethnic, physical disability, and (possibly) mental illness minorities.

NORMATIVE DATA FOR CORRELATES OF THE OP SCALES[2]

The F+ scale means and *SD*s for the BU and NU-I samples are very similar in magnitude to norms listed in *The Authoritarian Personality* for college student samples. The five-item F Scale used with the NU-II sample seems to elicit stronger authoritarian sentiments. It will be recalled that these items dealt exclusively with "acceptance of authority," and were very possibly less extreme in connotation than many of the F Scale items used with the first two samples.

Anomie scores in the present samples are of lower magnitude than authoritarianism scores. Unfortunately, norms for college subjects are not available for the Anomie scale. The various antiminority scales yield consistently low means. In general, subjects are more likely to hold favorable than unfavorable sentiments about the various "minorities" sampled by the items of the present study. It should be noted, in addition, that the means and *SD*s obtained for the AN and B scales correspond quite closely to those reported by Adorno et al. [1] and Cowen et al. [9], respectively. All of the "minority" scale per item means are

lower than the per item means for the negative OP scale shown in Table 64–1. Comparison with the positive OP scale is not warranted in view of the uniformly negative direction of the antiminority items.

For the particular items employed in the present study, then, subjects more readily express negative sentiments toward old people than toward members of ethnic, mentally ill, and physically disabled groups. This finding must, of course, be considered highly tentative since items across minority clusters vary in content and wording over and above the difference in minority group referent. Further work along these lines might well take the form of developing a pool of items whose content would be applicable to a wide array of minorities.

PERSONALITY CORRELATES OF THE OP SCALES

It will be recalled that certain explicit predictions were made regarding a number of personality dimensions. A factor analysis of the 30-item true-false personality inventory was carried out, combining the BU and NU-I samples and including sex of the subject as a variable. Seven factors were extracted by the Principal Axes method and these were then rotated to a quartimax solution [18].[3] The first three factors are relatively clear. Factor I has highest loadings on those items involving nurturant concern for others. Factor II yields highest loadings on items expressing feelings of self-doubt in relations with other people. Factor III appears to tap rejective misanthropic sentiments. The remaining factors account for relatively small portions of the overall variance. Sex of the subject yields the highest loading on Factor IV. Loadings of the other items on this factor are quite low. Factor V involves sentiments of yielding to or resisting others' judgments or wishes. Factor VI shows highest loadings

[2] A one-page table giving the means, standard deviations, and reliability coefficients for correlates of the OP scales has been deposited with the American Documentation Institute. Order Document No. 6691 from ADI Auxiliary Publications Project, Photoduplication Service, Library of Congress; Washington 25, D.C., remitting in advance $1.25 for microfilm or $1.25 for photocopies. Make checks payable to: Chief, Photoduplication Service, Library of Congress.

[3] A three-page table listing factor loadings (quartimax) for the personality inventory items has been deposited with ADI (see Footnote 2).

on items expressing doubt about personal achievement. Factor VII accounts for a minute portion of the variance, and, hence, was not considered further.

Factor scores for individuals were derived from the factor loadings and correlated with OP scale scores (Table 64–5). In general the results are in the predicted direction. Factor I—essentially a nurturance factor—is significantly correlated with OP scale scores. The more favorably subjects are disposed toward old people, the greater their score on Factor I in the nurturant direction. Rejective, misanthropic sentiments tapped by Factor III correlate significantly in the predicted direction for only the positive OP scale, suggesting that the observed relation is partially attributable to response set effects. It should be noted that the factors containing the autonomy and achievement items did not correlate with attitudes toward old people, though this may be a reflection of the small number of items representing those dimensions in the inventory. Finally, there seems to be no simple relation between self-esteem tendencies and feelings about old people.

DISCUSSION AND CONCLUSIONS

That attitudes toward old people are scalable is strongly indicated by the present data. The use of items worded in opposite directions has permitted us to examine the extent to which response set effects permeate the various scales. Correlations between the matched positive and negative "old people" scales are in the content direction, but of moderate size. Compared to

Table 64–5 Correlations (Product-Moment r's) between OP Scales and Factor Scores Derived from Personality Inventory ($N = 296$)

Scale	I°	II	III†	IV	V	VI
OP+	.14‡	.06	.18§	−.07	.03	−.09
OP−	.21§	−.04	.07	.03	.10	.05

° High scores are in the nonnurturant direction.
† High scores are in the misanthropic direction.
‡ Significant at the .05 level.
§ Significant at the .01 level.

the present attitude domain, undergraduate subjects seem to show greater logical consistency in responding to ethnic minority items [19], but greater inconsistency in regard to authoritarianism [8].

Consider next the relationships observed between attitudes toward old people and other attitudinal variables. Of particular interest is the fact that attitudes toward old people are related to feelings of anomie and apparently unrelated to authoritarian tendencies. This result is in marked contrast to the finding that prejudice toward ethnic minorities is associated with both authoritarianism and anomie [20, 22]. Hence, while "old people" may constitute a minority, such status does not necessarily render them equivalent to ethnic minorities in their relationship to authoritarianism. This is hardly surprising when one considers the unique features of old people as attitude objects. Old people cannot be categorized in strictly outgroup terms, for most individuals will have old people as members of their families. In addition, old people constitute a minority to which most persons will eventually belong. Given these conditions, one might expect a slight positive association between authoritarianism and favorable attitudes toward old people. Note, however, that old people do not occupy an authoritative position in our society, and, indeed, are often weak, exposed, and highly vulnerable. Given the alleged connection between authoritarianism and contempt for weakness, it would follow that the more authoritarian individuals should be more negatively disposed toward old people. Since no consistent significant relationship was found between the two variables in question, countervailing forces of the kind described may be responsible.

How can we account for the significant relationship between feelings of anomie and attitudes toward old people? Certainly, agreement with anomie items implies that the subject has a precarious and threat-oriented view of life. Old age, in the eyes of such subjects, might well represent that period of life when their pessimistic predictions have been confirmed, i.e., old people have no future, are helpless, and awaiting death without life's meaning made clear; and, indeed, the views of these subjects have some basis in reality for many old people in American society. It seems reasonable, then, that feelings of anomie and negative attitudes toward old people would be related, for the more anomic subjects would be likely to perceive the aged as symbolic of that period of life when an individual is least able to cope with a hazardous environment.

It will be recalled that the relation between attitudes toward old people and toward mentally ill persons was not entirely free of response set effects. The consistent significant relationships found between attitudes toward old people and toward physically disabled groups, however, suggest that subjects are more likely to associate aging with a state of physical disability as opposed to one of mental illness. It should be noted, however, that the Gilbert and Levinson mental illness scale does not contain any items referring specifically to the mental deterioration associated with senility. Subjects may well consider the latter to have a physical locus, and, hence, to be distinguishable from mental illness conceived more generally. Finally, subjects who are prejudiced against ethnic minorities tend to be negatively disposed toward old people, though, as we have seen, the two sets of attitudes do not seem to have a common base in authoritarian tendencies.

In sum, the present data suggest that there is a general trend for subjects to be positively or negatively disposed toward a wide variety of groups deviating in some respect from a hypothetical norm of similarity to self. Hence, for negatively disposed subjects, members of ethnic minorities, physically disabled persons, old people, and possibly mentally ill people are groups to be avoided or rejected. While parts of this broad attitude complex seem to relate directly to a concept of the authoritarian personality, other parts do not. There is some indication in the present data that

Srole's concept of anomie may be most relevant to the formation of a wide range of attitudes, though a definitive statement along these lines must necessarily await the development and application of reversed scales for the many variables in question.

Much of the discussion thus far has been couched in terms of the negative end of the attitude continuum. The observed relation between positive attitudes toward old people and nurturant personality dispositions helps to clarify the opposite end of the attitude dimension under consideration. If persons with strong nurturance needs are attracted to those in need of succorance, old people may be highly appropriate objects in this regard. For there is considerable evidence that dependency is one of the more salient qualities attributed to old people by the younger generation [13]. While such dependency would arouse positive sentiments in nurturant persons, the dependent state of the older person is likely to arouse ambivalence or conscious hostility in those less inclined in the nurturant direction. Unfortunately, we do not know whether nurturant needs play a part in positive orientations toward other kinds of minorities. It is conceivable, however, that the extent of the relationship would be a function of the prominence of dependency as a characteristic of the minority group in question.

SUMMARY

The present paper reports on the development of a Likert scale for assessing attitudes toward old people and discusses empirical relations found between such attitudes and other attitudinal and personality variables. Three samples of college undergraduates served as subjects.

"Old people" items were constructed in the form of positive-negative pairs, yielding two "old people" (OP) scales: a scale containing items making unfavorable reference to old people and a scale containing matched favorably worded items. Item and scale means and standard deviations are reported, as are item-sum correlations and scale reliabilities. The use of matched positive-negative item pairs permitted a test of the extent to which response set effects permeate the scales. Correlations between positive and negative scales were significant in the direction of logical consistency of response. In addition, all correlations between the positive and negative members of specific item pairs were in the logically consistent direction, the large majority significantly so.

A number of significant relationships observed between attitudes toward old people and other attitudinal and personality variables proved to be partially attributable to response set effects. We were forced to conclude on this basis that no clear consistent relation obtained between authoritarianism as measured by the F Scale and attitudes toward old people. On the other hand, unfavorable attitudes toward old people were associated with feelings of anomie, and with negative dispositions toward ethnic minorities and a variety of physically disabled groups. A nurturance factor derived from a brief personality inventory given to the subjects was significantly correlated with OP scale scores, the more nurturant subjects being more positively disposed toward old people. Theoretical interpretations of observed associations between the OP scales and other measures are advanced in the body of the paper.

REFERENCES

1. ADORNO, T. W., FRENKEL-BRUNSWIK, ELSE, LEVINSON, D. J., & SANFORD, R. N. The authoritarian personality. New York: Harper, 1950.
2. BALES, R. F., & COUCH, A. A factor analysis of values. Unpublished manuscript, Laboratory of Social Relations, Harvard University, 1956.
3. BARKER, R. G. The social psychology of physical disability. J. soc. Issues, 1948, 4, 28–38.
4. BARKER, R. G., WRIGHT, BEATRICE A., MEYERSON, L., & GONICK, MOLLIE R. Adjustment to physical handicap and illness: A survey of the social psychology of physique and disability. (Bulletin 55, revised) New York: Social Science Research Council, 1953.
5. BARRON, M. L. Minority group characteristics of the aged in American society. J. Geront., 1953, 8, 477–482.
6. BRODBECK, A. J., & PERLMUTTER, H. V. Self-dislike as a determinant of marked ingroup-outgroup preferences. J. Psychol., 1954, 38, 271–280.
7. CHAPMAN, L. J., & CAMPBELL, D. T. Response set in the F Scale. J. abnorm. soc. Psychol., 1957, 54, 129–132.
8. CHRISTIE, R., HAVEL, JOAN, & SEIDENBERG, B. Is the F Scale irreversible? J. abnorm. soc. Psychol., 1958, 56, 143–159.
9. COWEN, E. L., UNDERBERG, RITA P., & VERRILLO, R. T. The development and testing of an attitude to blindness scale. J. soc. Psychol., 1958, 48, 297–304.
10. DRAKE, J. T. The aged in American society. New York: Ronald, 1958.
11. GAGE, N. L., LEAVITT, G. S., & STONE, G. C. The psychological meaning of acquiescence set for authoritarianism. J. abnorm. soc. Psychol., 1957, 55, 98–103.
12. GILBERT, DORIS C., & LEVINSON, D. J. Ideology, personality, and institutional policy in the mental hospital. J. abnorm. soc. Psychol., 1956, 53, 263–271.
13. GOLDE, PEGGY, & KOGAN, N. A sentence completion procedure for assessing attitudes toward old people. J. Geront., 1959, 14, 355–363.
14. JACKSON, D. N., & MESSICK, S. J. A note on "ethnocentrism" and acquiescent response sets. J. abnorm. soc. Psychol., 1957, 54, 132–134.
15. LINDEN, M. E. Effects of social attitudes on the mental health of the aging. Geriatrics, 1957, 12, 109–114.
16. LINDEN, M. E. Relationship between social attitudes toward aging and the delinquencies of youth. Amer. J. Psychiat., 1957, 114, 444–448.
17. MURRAY, H. A. Explorations in personality. New York: Oxford, 1938.
18. NEUHAUS, J. O., & WRIGLEY, C. The

quartimax method: An analytical approach to orthogonal simple structure. *Brit. J. statist. Psychol.*, 1954, **7**, 81–91.

19. PRENTICE, N. M. The comparability of positive and negative items in scales of ethnic prejudice. *J. abnorm. soc. Psychol.*, 1956, **52**, 420–421.

20. ROBERTS, A. H., & ROKEACH, M. Anomie, authoritarianism, and prejudice: A replication. *Amer. J. Sociol.*, 1956, **61**, 355–358.

21. SHOCK, N. W. *A classified bibliography of gerontology and geriatrics.* (Supplement I, 1949–1955) Stanford, Calif.: Stanford Univer. Press, 1957.

22. SROLE, L. Social integration and certain corollaries: An exploratory study. *Amer. sociol. Rev.*, 1956, **21**, 709–716.

23. TUCKMAN, J., & LORGE, I. Attitudes toward old people. *J. soc. Psychol.*, 1953, **37**, 249–260.

24. TUCKMAN, J., & LORGE, I. The projection of personal symptom into stereotype about aging. *J. Geront.*, 1958, **13**, 70–73.

25. ZOLA, I. K., & SCARR, H. A. Attitude dimensions in older people. Progress Report, October 1958. NIMH Project M-1402. (Available from the Age Center of New England, Inc., 160 Commonwealth Ave., Boston 16, Mass.)

Chapter 65

Employee Attitudes
and Employee Performance

ARTHUR H. BRAYFIELD / WALTER H. CROCKETT

The systematic investigation of employee attitudes is a relatively recent development in American business and industry. Although Houser and his associates [26] pioneered in this field in the early 1920's there was little active interest until early in World War II when employee attitude surveys began to flourish [49, p. 7]. Currently there is an abundant and growing literature on the use of this personnel tool [56].

Only infrequently, however, are discussions of the correlates of employee attitudes found and these are almost never substantiated by empirical evidence. Where we have located relevant discussions in the personnel and psychological literature a common assumption predominates—employee attitudes bear a significant relationship to employee performance. These are sample quotations: ". . . morale is not an abstraction. Rather it is concrete in the

This article is reprinted in abbreviated form from *Psychological Bulletin*, 1955, with the permission of the authors and the American Psychological Association.

764

sense that it directly affects the quality and quantity of an individual's output." "Numerous investigations have established the certainty that productive efficiency fluctuates with variations in interest and morale." ". . . employee morale . . . reduces turnover. It makes labor trouble and strikes less likely. It cuts down absenteeism and tardiness; lifts production."

It is of some practical and theoretical interest to establish the relationships which exist between employee attitudes and employee performance. The purpose of this review is to examine and summarize the empirical literature which bears upon these relationships and to engage in some discussion of the methodological and theoretical considerations involved in such investigations.

Examination of the literature reveals that it is (a) recent, and (b) frequently peripheral in the sense that relevant data were collected and analyzed incidental to some other objective.

We have established certain conditions

for the inclusion of materials in this review. First, the indices of employee attitudes must permit classification of respondents along some attitude continuum. Second, the indices of employee attitudes must have been obtained directly from the employees themselves. Although we are willing to include ratings of job performance by supervisors and others, if no other criteria of performance are available, we are not willing to accept estimates of *attitudes* by someone other than the individuals themselves. Performances, we would contend, are less easily disguised by the individual and less readily distorted by the observer than are attitudes. Third, the investigations must have been conducted in industrial or occupational settings. Within the limitations of interlibrary loan service our coverage is complete through July, 1954. We have made no effort to unearth unpublished studies although we report several, including three studies by one of us.

The following scheme was adopted as a convenient and meaningful way of categorizing the literature.

1. Daniel Katz and Robert Kahn [33, p. 657] have suggested that "in social structures it is important to distinguish between: (1) the motivation to stay within the system, to remain a part of the group and (2) the motivation to act in a differential manner within that system." We have thus distinguished between those studies which involve performance on the job and those which involve withdrawal from the job (absences, accidents, turnover).

2. Within the above breakdown we have made a further differentiation based upon research design. One major design relates the attitudes of individuals to their performances as individuals. A second design relates the attitudes of the members of groups to their performances as groups.

3. A still further classification differen-

tiates between studies in which a single index of attitudes either as a single item or as a summation of items was used and those few in which multiple indices were used.

We have not attempted to define such terms as job satisfaction or morale. Instead, we have found it necessary to assume that the measuring operations define the variables involved. Definitions are conspicuous by their absence in most current work in this area.

Where reliability data are reported for the attitude and performance measures, we have included them in our summaries. We also have attempted to specify whether or not the attitude data were collected under conditions which preserved the anonymity of the subjects. Throughout the first section of the paper we have tried to hold comments on methodology to a minimum, postponing detailed methodological considerations until the substantive material has been covered.

Before summarizing and discussing the literature it may be appropriate to describe the investigation which, as far as we can determine, initiated research in this area of industrial psychology. The classic study relating attitudes and performance in an industrial setting was conducted by Kornhauser and Sharp [39] in 1930 in Neenah, Wisconsin, in the mill operated by the Kimberly-Clark Corporation. Between 200 and 300 young girls engaged in routine repetitive jobs at machines were studied. Both questionnaires and interviews were used. The questionnaires were patterned after those developed by Houser and covered a range of specific attitudes—toward supervisors, repetitiveness and speed of work, personnel policies, wages, and the like. Scores were computed for groups of items and item responses were analyzed. Intercorrelations among different item groups ran about .4 to .5. Reliabilities were thought to be somewhat higher.

The finding on relationship of attitudes

to performance is summed up in the statement that "Efficiency ratings of employees showed no relationship to their attitudes." No description is given of the rating system. Further, the authors say, "In one group of 20 girls for whom we had comparable output records, three of the four with the most unfavorable attitudes were first, second, and fourth in production and the two most favorable were near the bottom in production."

With respect to the criterion of withdrawal from the job, Kornhauser and Sharp reported that "Unfavorableness of job attitudes is slightly correlated with lost time because of sickness."

Relations between attitudes and intelligence, age, schooling, marital status, home life, emotional adjustment, and supervision also were studied. This early report should be read by anyone seriously interested in this area of investigation.

PERFORMANCE ON THE JOB

INDIVIDUAL ANALYSIS

Three unpublished studies have used the Brayfield-Rothe Job Satisfaction Blank [4] as an index of job satisfaction. In 1943 Brayfield [3] started work on the development of a scale intended to give what might be called a global measure of job satisfaction. It was predicated on attitude theory and applied the Thurstone scaling technique. After some preliminary work Likert's scoring technique was applied to 18 Thurstone-scaled items to produce an index which had a range of scores from 18 through 90 with a neutral or indifferent point at 54. The resulting scale gave a corrected split-half reliability coefficient of .87 when used with 231 women office employees. It differentiated between adults enrolled in a night class in personnel psychology who were employed in personnel jobs and similar students who were employed in non-personnel jobs. For the same group, a correlation of .91 was obtained between the Brayfield-Rothe and the Hoppock Job Satisfaction Blank.

In 1944, in connection with a larger study Brayfield [3] collected data on 231 women office employees working for the same firm but employed in 22 different offices throughout the country. The scale was administered to small groups of individuals as part of a test battery. All materials were signed. At the same time supervisor's ratings on a graphic rating scale were obtained for all employees in the sample. A total score was computed from three items covering quantity, quality, and over-all worth to the company. About two-thirds of the employees were rated by two supervisors and the ratings were averaged. Reliabilities of ratings are unknown although in one office it was possible to compare two supervisors who had rated the same 23 women. The intercorrelation was in the low seventies.

When job satisfaction scores for these women clerical workers were compared with their performance ratings, a correlation of .138, significant at the 5% level, was found. To control for the influence of job level, the 231 women were classified into six groups as follows: Stenographers (50); General Clerical (40); Typists (38); High Level Machine Clerical (36); Low Level Machine Clerical (34); Entry (33). The correlations for the first five groups ranged from −.06 to +.13. None were significant. The correlation for the group of 33 inexperienced and untrained girls (Entry) was .387, significant at the 5% level. An additional group of 35 women telephone order clerks provided a correlation of .26 which was not significant.

In 1950, Brayfield and Mangelsdorf obtained data on 55 second-, third-, and fourth-year plumber apprentices employed in a number of firms in Oakland, California. All were enrolled four hours per week in a public vocational school. The subjects completed the Brayfield-Rothe job satisfaction scale during classes as part of a testing program in which all the materials were identified by name of respondent. The corrected split-half reliability coefficient was .83. Performance ratings were obtained for each plumber from his foreman or employer. The rating form consisted of 25 scaled items in check list form developed by Goertzel [19, p. 117], who attempted to provide a generalized scale that could be used for assessment of workers on any type of job. For various groups of workers Goertzel found a correlation of approximately .80 between ratings on two forms of 25 items each. The correlation between job satisfaction scores and ratings was .203, which is not significant.

In 1953, Brayfield and Marsh studied the measured characteristics of 50 farmers enrolled four hours per week in a veterans' on-job training program. The median age of the subjects was in the early thirties. They had lived on farms most of their lives; all were managing their own farms. Among other materials they completed the Brayfield-Rothe job satisfaction scale. All materials were signed. The corrected split-half reliability coefficient was .60; if the three subjects with the most inconsistent responses had been eliminated, the reliability coefficient would have become .77.

The subjects' performance as farmers was rated by their instructors who ranked them in order of effectiveness. Sixteen farmers were ranked by one instructor, 14 by a second, and the remaining 20 by another. Ranks were transmuted into "scores" [18] and cast into a single distribution. Rerankings after several months, when similarly treated, correlated .86 with the original rankings. Instructors were not aware that they would be asked to re-rank their students.

For the 50 farmers the correlation between job satisfaction scores and performance ratings was .115, which is not significant. If the three "erratic" subjects had been eliminated, the correlation would have become .133.

The same job satisfaction scale was used in 1953 in an unpublished study by Roger Bellows and associates of 109 Air Force control tower operators.[1] The correlation with individual proficiency ratings was .005.

Gadel and Kriedt [17] report a study employing a design similar to that used in the investigations just described. One hundred and ninety-three male IBM operators working in the machine rooms of numerous divisions of the Prudential Insurance Company home office completed and signed a 10-item job satisfaction questionnaire ". . . designed to cover a variety of attitudes related to work duties." The performance criterion consisted of rank-order ratings on over-all job performance made by the immediate supervisor. Ratings were converted to standard scores and correlations were computed for each of the groups. The resulting correlations were averaged using the Fisher z transformation. The relationship between job satisfaction and performance was found to be .08.

The Life Insurance Agency Management Association has engaged in job satisfaction studies since the early 1940's. A report of their work which falls into the research classification under consideration was published by Habbe [23] in 1947. Job satisfaction questionnaires were mailed out to 9,353 insurance agents. Seventy-five per cent were returned of which more than 90% were usable. Signatures were not requested although quite a few agents did identify themselves. The blank contained questions asking about single phases of the job to be answered by one of five alternatives indicating satisfaction or dissatisfaction. A single question asked "How do you feel about your job as a life underwriter?" The performance rating was in the form of a self-report since each agent was asked to check whether his previous year's production was "under $200,000" of insurance or "$200,000 or over." Agents producing under $200,000 scored 4.15 on what evidently was the single general satisfaction item as compared to 4.11 for the high producers. The "Extremely Satisfied" score is 5.00. The re-

---

[1] R. M. Bellows. Personal communication, June 30, 1954.

lationship is insignificant or slightly in favor of the lower producers. It should be noted that this performance criterion is a self-report and that the break at the $200,000 point might not be the best point for analyzing the relationship.

Baxter and his associates [1] have recently reported a training evaluation study concerned with new debit insurance agents (service and sell weekly and monthly premium, ordinary, and group insurance for families within a specific geographical territory). Included in the data collected were responses to a comprehensive job satisfaction attitude questionnaire with items varying in number from 32 to 43 depending upon when it was administered. Respondents apparently were identified. Supervisor ratings on a 5-point, 9-item graphic rating scale were collected. Sales volume figures were obtained for each agent for his first year on the job. Although the correlations between the job satisfaction index and the performance criteria were not reported, the investigators have made them available.[2] For 223 agents the correlation between satisfaction and supervisor's rating is .23, significant at the 1% level. The correlation between satisfaction and sales volume is .26, also significant at the 1% level. This is the only study in this classification which uses an objective performance criterion. The incentive situation is also more clear-cut here except perhaps for the farmers. Although this correlation is significant, it is quite low.

One of the most carefully done studies which we have inspected is Mossin's [48] investigation of the selling performance and what he termed contentment of 94 teen-age female retail sales clerks in a large New York department store. His performance criteria of 12 items were based on the ratings of four experienced and specially trained shoppers. Ratings on five items formed a composite labeled "Selling Attitudes." Ratings on three other items were

combined as an index of "Selling Skills." The intercorrelation was .76. In addition, the entire 12 items formed a composite which correlated beyond .9 with each of the other criteria. Several detailed analyses of the reliability of the criteria were made including intercorrelations among the four shoppers. A minimum estimate of the reliability of the criteria would be that they exceeded .7 and might actually have been somewhat higher.

Mossin used two job satisfaction measures. One was an over-all composite rating secured by combining the scores on 6 attitude items inquiring about "affective dispositions" toward departmental assignment, merchandise assignment, relations with customers, relations with fellow salesgirls, relations with supervisors, and working conditions, along with one item regarding intention to remain in retail selling plus one item requiring a self-appraisal of sales ability. The second index was a single multiple-response item asking "How you REALLY feel toward your job." Responses on these two indices of job satisfaction were obtained during an individual data collection session with the investigator. Therefore, the respondents were identified. The correlation between the two satisfaction criteria was .53.

The composite job satisfaction score correlated −.07 with the Attitudes criterion and −.03 with the Skill criterion. The single-item job satisfaction index correlated .15 and .06, respectively. None of these is significant. No results were reported for the 12-item composite performance criterion although it may be inferred that they would be of approximately the same magnitude since it was highly correlated with the other two criteria. This is a carefully executed investigation and should be consulted by anyone working in this general area.

The final major investigation in this series, by Bernberg [2], is the only one to use differentiated attitude measures. He included a measure of group morale as identified by 34 "indirect method" items, a

[2] B. Baxter. Personal communication, February 17, 1954.

12-item scale presumed to measure an employee's acceptance of the formal organization (e.g., "I think this company treats its employees worse than any other company does"), a 0–100 thermometer scale with seven verbal referent points based on the single statement, "On the whole, I believe that the supervisor in my group is a man who knows his job and is a leader," and a similar thermometer scale for the self-rating statement, "On the whole, I believe that my group has a high degree of morale. By that, I mean the men work willingly and cheerfully as a well organized team." The intercorrelations among the four indices as computed for 890 hourly paid workers in a large aircraft manufacturing plant ranged from .47 to .77 with the median at .5. Split-half reliabilities for the two multi-item scales were approximately .8.

Questionnaires embodying these measures were sent home with more than 1,000 employees of an aircraft plant. No returns were accepted after 48 hours, by which time 88% were back. Presumably the respondents were identified. The performance criterion was the average weighted score of a graphic rating scale with the five dimensions of adaptability, dependability, job knowledge, quality, quantity. The split-half reliability was .8.

The correlations between the four attitude measures and the performance criterion ranged from .02 to .05.

Four miscellaneous studies warrant brief mention only. An English doctoral dissertation [40] is reported to include the finding that it was clearly determined that "there is almost no relationship between proficiency and satisfaction among [British] post office counter clerks."[3] Kerr [38] reports a master's study finding of a correlation of −.76 between a 10-item job satisfaction measure and employer reports on the frequency of what he termed grievance, advice, and catharsis conferences with employees in two very small Indiana plants.

The study is relevant mainly as suggesting a possible performance criterion for investigation. Chase [7] has a very inadequately described study which purports to find a small positive relationship between superintendent's ratings and teacher's satisfaction. Brody's [5] master's thesis at New York University describes an investigation in which the relationship between Hoppock Job Satisfaction Blank scores and production under a piece work incentive plan correlated .68 for 40 employees. This is an extraordinary finding. However, examination of the raw data in the Appendix casts serious doubt on the meaningfulness of the correlation. Two groups working under different incentive conditions are lumped together. For the 22 cases which might actually be legitimate subjects, the Hoppock scores do not conform to any known appropriate scoring system for that particular Blank. The production data are bimodal.

At this point we can summarize the findings for this research design. The prototype study used a single over-all index of employee attitudes variously titled job satisfaction or morale. Respondents were identified. A distribution of individual scores was related to some index of individual performance on the job. Customarily, a single occupational group was studied. When 14 homogeneous occupational groups and one large sample of assorted hourly factory workers were studied, statistically significant low positive relationships between job satisfaction and job performance were found in two of the 15 comparisons. These results, pointing to an absence of relationships, are in line with the findings of the pioneering Kornhauser and Sharp investigation.

GROUP ANALYSIS

The essentials of this design are as follows. Employee attitudes are determined individually, but the average for the group or the percentage responding in a certain manner is related to some estimate of performance or productivity for the group as a

[3] Reported by Heron, A. Industrial psychology. *Ann. Rev. Psychol.*, 1954, 5, 203–228.

whole. This arrangement requires at least two groups. Characteristically, comparisons are by departments within a firm rather than by occupation.

The antecedents of this approach are to be found in a study by Rensis Likert which was reported in a privately circulated document in 1941. We have not examined the report. According to a reference to it in one of Katz's [30] papers, the morale of insurance agents in 10 agencies rated superior in operational efficiency by the home offices of nine companies was compared to that of agents in 20 agencies rated below average. We infer that some form of attitude questionnaire was used since Likert conducted the study, although interviews may have been involved. Katz says that "Morale was found to be significantly related to the criterion." This study is mainly of historical interest.

Three studies employing this design or a modification of it utilized a single index of employee attitudes. Katz and Hyman [32] report a study which they supervised during World War II under the general direction of Likert. Their concern was with employee morale in shipyards and its relation to productivity, among other considerations. Two summary measures of morale were used, both of which were obtained from personal interview protocols. One was a yes-no answer to the question: "Have you ever felt like quitting the yards?" The rank order of the percentage who had felt like quitting was compared with an index of productivity (time to turn out a ship) for the five shipyards being studied. The two rank orders agreed fairly well. The second measure of employee attitudes was furnished by the responses to 7 items regarding specific aspects of the working situation and environment. The relationship to productivity was somewhat less marked than the first comparison although the authors comment that "In general the yards with high productivity were the yards with high worker morale." It should be remarked that, although the productivity differences were very great among the yards,

the morale differences were really quite small; the morale scores for the five yards were 9.3, 9.4, 10.0, 10.0, 10.9.

Giese and Ruter [20] employed this design in a study of employees of a small national mail order company. It is one of the few studies which had as its primary purpose the determination of the relationship in which we are interested. In fact, the aim of the study was to devise a method for predicting the morale of departments from objective data. The only description of the attitude measure is "A morale questionnaire was scored so that a quantitative score was available." There is no statement regarding the anonymity of the subjects. Three objective measures of efficiency were available. For each of 25 departments there were available three average measures of efficiency and one average morale score. When correlations based on group averages were computed they were found to range between .15 and .27. None of these is significant (our determination).

The Triple Audit studies [62] of the Industrial Relations Center at the University of Minnesota fall into this research design category. Here the firm was the basic unit of comparison. Since the number of firms studied was small, only seven, the authors advise that it is impossible to draw any conclusions about the relationships obtained.

The next series of studies reviewed here used the same design but differ from the three just mentioned in that they make some differentiation among employee attitudes. That is, they make some attempt to specify component parts.

The early work of Likert and Katz has been continued by them at the University of Michigan since the war. The prototype study was undertaken in 1947 in the Prudential Insurance Company, and findings were reported in some detail in 1950 [34]. Although the objectives were broad, an important portion of the study was devoted to exploring the relationships between employee attitudes and productivity.

One and one-half hour free answer interviews covering 53 questions were held with 419 nonsupervisory clerical workers in 24 different sections. Responses were coded. The sections were arranged in parallel pairs in order to hold constant as many factors as possible. One set of 12 sections was designated as high productivity on the basis of production records while the parallel set was composed of low productivity sections. The authors note that productivity differences between the pairs were not great, rarely more than 10 per cent. Each of the high-low productivity pairs consisted of two sections handling the same type of work with the same type of people at the same job levels and were very similar on a number of factors.

A unique feature was the construction of four indices of attitudinal variables. The differentiations were made on a theoretical basis with some empirical confirmation for the relationship among the items used in each index. Four variables were specified: (a) pride in work group; (b) intrinsic job satisfaction; (c) company involvement; and (d) financial and job status satisfaction. Pride in work group was the most independent of the four; the remaining three intercorrelated around .4.

When these morale indices were related to productivity, only pride in work group showed a distinct relationship. Productivity groups were also differentiated by three specific attitude items not included in the morale indices.

A second study of similar design investigated these relationships among section hand employees of the Chesapeake & Ohio Railroad [35]. Somewhat different morale items with more emphasis upon individual items were used in intensive interviews. Productivity criteria consisted of over-all quality and quantity ratings by supervisors. There was some slight support for the previous finding of a relationship between pride in work group and productivity. The authors emphasize the lack of relationships found between employee attitudes and productivity.

Both Michigan studies, but particularly the insurance company one, may be studied with profit. The investigators are self-critical and also provide hypotheses for further investigation. The investigations are excellent examples of both the virtues and the shortcomings of survey techniques. Both illustrate attempts to measure a large number of variables with less precision perhaps than is ultimately desirable. These well-publicized studies are important in our present context because they have called into question a common assumption about an important relationship, have perhaps stimulated research elsewhere, and have produced a great amount of theorizing about motivation in industry.

Three recent investigations are patterned somewhat after the Michigan inquiries. Two studies by Comrey and associates [9, 10] are considerably less well reported. The findings, among Forest Service and Employment Service personnel, lend some slight support to the Michigan report of a relationship between attitudes toward the group and performance. Weschler [60] found a slightly negative relationship between a single-item index of job satisfaction and production among employees in two comparable groups of a Naval research laboratory. He obtained a similar result for a single-item index of work group morale.

A recent study by Lawshe and Nagle [41] warrants extended comment. Two hundred and eight non-supervisory office employees in 14 work groups at a plant of the International Harvester Company completed a 22-item questionnaire which was described by the authors as an attitude toward supervisor measure. The corrected split-half reliability was .92. There is no report regarding the anonymity of the respondents. The scores were related to group productivity.

A paired comparison rating of productivity by six plant executives was used. Each executive compared from 8 to 14 work groups under instructions to indicate ". . . the department in each pair which is, in your opinion, doing its job better." Ratings were converted to standard scores and averaged. The reliability of the means of all six raters was estimated to be .88. The authors are careful to point out that "one does not know for sure what the raters really had in mind when they rated." They suggest that "how little trouble the work group caused, whether or not it had the answers when called upon, whether or not it could cope with rush situations, and similar considerations are believed to have been the prime factors in the executives' ratings."

The average rating of each work group was correlated with average attitude toward the supervisor score in the work group. The resulting Pearson coefficient was .86, significant at the 1% level for $N = 14$. This is, of course, a remarkable result. A whole superstructure of industrial psychology could well be erected on this finding; stranger things have happened. However, the authors sound a note of caution: "On the basis of this study it can be concluded only that the behavior of the supervisor, as perceived by the employees, is highly related to the productivity of the group as perceived by higher management."

It occurs to us that it may be a misnomer to call the questionnaire an attitude questionnaire. It might well be considered to be a supervisor behavior- or performance-rating device. For example, the questions included such things as, does he: give you straight answers, avoid you when he knows you want to see him about a problem, criticize you for happenings over which you have no control, delay in taking care of your complaints, keep you informed, give you recognition, show interest in your ideas, follow through on his promises, explain to you the "why" of an error to prevent recurrence, give you sufficient explanation of why a work change is necessary. There is supporting evidence for a finding that supervisory performance is related to productivity [34]. It might be suggested further that the obtained correlation really expresses the relationship between supervisor performance ratings by employees and supervisor performance ratings by the executives since the performance of a work group may be judged in part at least on the basis of the observation of the supervisor and certainly on his reports. We suggest that the finding is relevant to current work on supervisor performance and productivity, but we are skeptical of its direct relationship to the area of research being examined in this review despite the title.

The results from the study design which we have described in this section are substantially in agreement with the previous findings of minimal or no relationship between employee attitudes and performance. They do supply the hint that morale, as a group phenomenon, may bear a positive relationship to performance on the job.

WITHDRAWAL FROM THE JOB

As indicated earlier we have differentiated between performance on the job and withdrawal from the job. In this section we briefly summarize the trend of the evidence when employee attitudes are related to some form of withdrawal from the job. Withdrawal is indicated by absence and tardiness, by accidents (under one assumption), and by turnover or employment stability.

ABSENCES

Individual analysis. The individual analysis design has been used in four studies. In another of the Triple Audit studies, Yoder and associates [62] employed a 66-item employee attitude questionnaire which yielded a total score as an index of general attitude. Respondents apparently were unidentified. Absence and tardiness data were *furnished by the respondents* on the questionnaire face sheet. Five groups of employees were studied including office workers, department store personnel, and manufacturing employees. No statistically significant relationships were found between the attitude index and absences. One significant relationship was found for tardiness. Four others were insignificant.

In a study of worker attitudes toward merit rating, Van Zelst and Kerr [55] include data relevant to our topic. Three hundred and forty employees selected by their employers in 14 firms out of the 50 invited to participate furnished a *self-report* of their absences and tardinesses. Two Hoppock-type job satisfaction items were combined to give a single index. Respondents apparently were anonymous. Job satisfaction correlated .31 with a favorable absentee record and .26 with a favorable tardiness record. These are significant at the 1% level.

Bernberg [2] used four different measures of absence and tardiness which had split-half reliabilities in the seventies. These data were taken from the company records. The intercorrelations with the four measures of employee attitudes of the 890 aircraft plant workers ranged from −.05 to +.07.

Group analysis. The group analysis design also has been used in four studies. Giese and Ruter [20] found an insignificant relation between tardiness and a single morale score when the group averages of employees in 25 departments of a mail order house were correlated. However, the correlation of −.47 between the morale index and absences is significant at the 5% level (our determination).

Kerr and associates [38] obtained mean scores on his 10-item Tear Ballot job satisfaction blank for the employees in 30 departments of a Chicago plant presumably under conditions of anonymity. They used six measures of absenteeism. This is a major contribution of the study since there are numerous problems in indexing absenteeism. The importance of such an analytical approach is evident when it is observed that job satisfaction correlated .51 with total absenteeism rate but correlated −.44 with unexcused absenteeism. One other relationship was statistically significant.

In their wartime morale studies, Katz and Hyman [31] used six specific attitude items. These morale indices were positively related to absenteeism. The magnitude of the relationship is typified by responses to this item: 44% of the workers disliking their jobs were categorized as absentees as compared with 36% who liked their jobs.

Perhaps the most extensive investigation has been made by Metzner and Mann [46] of the Michigan Survey Research Center. The data were collected in the Detroit Edison Company according to a design similar to the Prudential and Chesapeake & Ohio studies. Anonymous questionnaires provided the attitudinal data. White-collar and blue-collar men and white-collar women were the subjects. The most striking finding was that there was no relationship between absences and attitudes toward any aspect of the work situation for white-collar women. Among white-collar men, 10 out of 15 attitudinal measures showed significant relationships at the 10% level. Eight of these were significant at the 5% or 1% levels. However, when job level or grade was controlled to some extent by grouping into high- and low-skill levels, there was practically no relationship between attitudes and absences for the high-skill level jobs for the seven items it was possible to study. A fairly consistent relationship remained for the low-skill level jobs. Among the 18 items used with the 251 blue-collar men, nine were significant at the 10% level or better, six being at the 5% level or better. Incidentally, these are all percentage differences among various absence categories and the adjacent category differences are not particularly impressive although the differences between the extreme categories are appreciable.

ACCIDENTS

Hill and Trist [25], English investigators, have recently suggested that "Accidents [may] be considered as a means of withdrawal from the work situation through which the individual may take up the role of absentee in a way acceptable both to himself and to his employing organization." Accidents are considered to involve the ". . . quality of the relationship obtaining between employees and their place of work." In an empirical test of this hypothesis they found accident rates to be positively associated with other forms of absences and to be most strongly associated with the least sanctioned forms of absence. Their study does not, of course, bear directly on our immediate concern. We include it to indicate a possible linkage with absence data.

Group analysis. We have found two studies on the relationship between employee attitudes and accidents. Stagner and associates [53] used a group analysis design to study the job satisfaction of railroad employees. A total of 715 employees in 10 divisional groups, 2 accounting offices, and 12 shops were included. Fifteen specific items of an apparently anonymously administered questionnaire were given arbitrary weights based on the percentage of employees checking and were summed to give a single job satisfaction index. Mean satisfaction scores by groups were correlated with group accident rates. The obtained correlations are negative and small. Surprisingly, the authors conclude that "We thus feel considerable confidence in the conclusion that working in a group with a high accident rate will tend to make the individual worker anxious, and reduce his satisfaction with his job." However, the correlations are not statistically significant (our determination), and the causal sequence indicated in the quote is speculation.

The Triple Audit [62] studies also considered accidents. Although the authors have entered a general disclaimer as to the significance of their group design findings, the accident finding is intriguing. Employees in the three firms with fewer than average accidents had a mean attitude score of 133 while the employees in the three firms with more than average accidents had a mean score of 143. From these limited data it appears that there is a tendency for the firms with higher accident rates to have more favorable attitude scores. The data are interesting but should not be given disproportionate emphasis.

EMPLOYMENT STABILITY

Individual analysis. Employment stability remains to be studied. In a study comparing indirect and direct methods of appraising employee attitudes, Weitz and Nuckols [59] provide relevant although peripheral data. This is an individual analysis design. Two attitude questionnaires, one composed of 18 indirect items and one consisting of 10 direct questions, were mailed to more than 1,200 insurance agents representing one company in the southern states. Forty-seven per cent submitted answers. The respondents were identified. Total scores for each of the questionnaires were then related to survival during a one-year period. The direct method correlated .20, significant at the 1% level; the indirect method correlated insignificantly with survival. There was some sample bias resulting from the fact that a disproportionately small number of men, who subsequently terminated, responded.

Kerr [37] correlated total Tear Ballot job satisfaction scores obtained individually but without identification from 98 miscellaneous wage earners with an index of *self-reported* past job tenure (number of years on labor market divided by number of employers). The result for an unweighted total satisfaction score was .25, significant at the 5% level. Thus there seems to be a slight positive relationship between attitude toward present employment and past employment stability among the members of a heterogeneous group making self-reports on their employment records.

Van Zelst and Kerr [55] correlated total score on two Hoppock-type items with *employee reports* of previous job tenure. The obtained correlation was .09.

Friesen [16] recently has attempted to measure employee attitudes using an incomplete sentences technique. He developed four scales comprising a total of 81 items. These he labeled Working Situation, Work, Self, Leisure. He studied women office workers from one company with N's ranging from 38 to 70. The blanks were signed. Split-half reliability coefficients for the four scales ranged from .68 to .82. Intercorrelations among the scales ranged from .26 to .72 with Working Situation and Work being the two most highly correlated. Friesen attempted to validate the scales by obtaining modified "Guess Who" ratings from seven to nine fellow employees for each member of his sample. These ratings had uncorrected reliability coefficients ranging from .57 to .78. Their obtained correlations with the attitude scales were moderately high, being .59, .67, .45, and .52, respectively. When the four attitude scales were related to a criterion of employment stability (two or more years with each employer versus less than two years with each employer) the biserial correlations were .43, .53, .37, and .22, respectively. All were significant at the 4% level or better. This is a *retrospective* measure of employment stability.

Two attitude items, chance to make decisions on the job, and a feeling they were making or had made an important contribution to the success of the company, were significantly related to turnover in a study by Wickert [61]. This study has the limitation that the employees who had left the company were interviewed after their departure.

Group analysis. The group analysis design has been used in three studies previously described. In the Giese and Ruter [20] investigation, morale scores correlated $-.42$ with a per cent turnover criterion for 25 departments. This is significant at the 5% level (our determination). Kerr [38] found the relationship between total Tear Ballot score and turnover in 30 departments to be $-.13$, which is not significant. The

Triple Audit studies [62] found average monthly turnover to be unrelated to attitudes in seven companies.

With respect to withdrawal from the job, then, there is some evidence, mainly from the group design studies, of a significant but complex relationship between employee attitudes and absences. The investigations reviewed here also lend some support to the assumption that employee attitudes and employment stability are positively related. The data on accidents and attitudes are extremely limited, but they do not support any significant relationships.

In summary, it appears that there is little evidence in the available literature that employee attitudes of the type usually measured in morale surveys bear any simple—or, for that matter, appreciable—relationship to performance on the job. The data are suggestive mainly of a relationship between attitudes and two forms of withdrawal from the job. This tentative conclusion, contrary as it is to rather widely held beliefs, warrants an attempt to identify and evaluate some of the factors which may account for these results.

We shall first discuss theoretical issues and conclude with some possible implications for future research.

THEORETICAL CONSIDERATIONS

MORALE AS AN EXPLANATORY CONCEPT IN INDUSTRIAL PSYCHOLOGY

One principal generalization suffices to set up an expectation that morale should be related to absenteeism and turnover, namely, that organisms tend to avoid those situations which are punishing and to seek out situations that are rewarding. To the extent that worker dissatisfaction indicates that the individual is in a punishing situation, we should expect dissatisfied workers to be absent more often and to quit the job at a higher rate than individuals who are satisfied with their work. Since the general proposition about the effects of reward has received a great amount of verification in psychology, it is not strange that it has been carried to the analysis of absenteeism and turnover.

A plausible connection between satisfaction and performance on the job is less obvious. Let us consider specifically the possible relationship between satisfaction and productivity. Under conditions of marked dissatisfaction it is likely that low productivity may serve as a form of aggression which reflects worker hostility toward management. But the hypothesis that production should increase monotonically with increases in satisfaction apparently rests on the assumption that the worker will demonstrate his gratitude by increased output, or that the increased satisfaction frees certain creative energies in the worker, or that the satisfied employee accepts management's goals, which include high production.

In any event, it is commonly hypothesized that, whatever the causes, increased satisfaction makes workers more motivated to produce. Given this condition, it should follow that increased productivity can be attained by increasing worker satisfaction. We are going to advance the proposition that the motivational structure of industrial workers is not so simple as is implied in this formula. We feel that research workers have erred by overlooking individual differences in motivations and perceptions because of their concern with discovering important and applicable generalizations. Most of what follows is an effort to point out areas in which differences between workmen may make a difference in their adjustment to the situation.

At the outset let us make it clear that we expect the relation between satisfaction and job performance to be one of concomitant variation, rather than cause and effect. It makes sense to us to assume that individuals are motivated to achieve certain environmental goals and that the achievement of these goals results in satisfaction. Productivity is seldom a goal in itself but is more commonly a means to goal attainment. Therefore, as G. M. Mahoney [personal communication] has suggested, we might expect high satisfaction and high productivity to occur together when productivity is perceived as a path to certain important goals and when these goals are achieved. Under other conditions, satisfaction and productivity might be unrelated or even negatively related.

In the light of this consideration, we shall center our discussion on an analysis of industrial motivation as it relates specifically to employee satisfaction and to productivity.

For the sake of convenience we may distinguish between threats and rewards as incentives to productivity. Goode and Fowler [21] have described a factory in which morale and productivity were negatively related but productivity was kept high by the continuance of threats to workers. Here the essential workers—people with considerable skill—were marginal to the labor force because of their sex or because of physical handicaps. Since the plant was not unionized, it was possible for management to demand high productivity from these workers on threat of discharge. This meant that the workers, although most dissatisfied with their jobs, produced at a very high rate because of the difficulty they would face in finding another position should they be discharged.

There is little doubt that threat was widely used as a motivating device in our own society in the past and is presently used in more authoritarian societies. However, it is doubtful if any great amount of at least explicit threat is currently used by industries in this country in efforts to increase productivity or reduce absenteeism. First of all, considerable change has occurred in management philosophy over the past fifty years, and such tactics are repugnant to many industrial concerns. Secondly, the growth of unions has virtually outlawed such tendencies except in small, semimarginal industries which are not unionized.

Threats of discharge, then, probably do not operate as incentives unless the worker falls considerably below the mean in quantity and/or quality of output. For a number of reasons management has settled upon rewards for motivating workers to produce, including such tangible incentives as increased pay and promotion, as well as verbal and other symbolic recognition. Let us examine whether this system of rewards actually provides motivation for increased productivity by the worker.

It is a commonplace observation that motivation is not a simple concept. It is a problem which may be attacked at a number of different levels and from many theoretical points of view. Whatever their theoretical predilection, however, psychologists generally are agreed that human motivation is seldom directed only toward goals of physical well-being. Once a certain minimum level of living has been achieved, human behavior is directed largely toward some social goal or goals. Thus, in our own society, goals such as achievement, acceptance by others, dominance over others, and so on, probably are of as great concern to the average workman as the goals of finding sufficient food and shelter to keep body and psyche together.

We assume that social motives are of considerable importance in industry. We assume, further, that the goals an individual pursues will vary, depending upon the social systems within which he is behaving from time to time. Most industrial workers probably operate in a number of social systems. Katz and Kahn [33] suggest four such systems: first, the system of relations outside the plant; and, within the plant, the systems of relationship with fellow workers on the job, with members of the union, and with others in the company structure. We may ask whether job performance, and particularly productivity, is a path to goal achievement within these various sets of social relations.

Outside the plant. It is often argued that any worker who is motivated to increase his status in the outside community should be motivated toward higher productivity within the plant. Productivity frequently leads directly to more money on the job, or involves movement to jobs with higher prestige or with authority over others. If productivity does result in such in-plant mobility, increased output may enable the individual to achieve a higher level of living, to increase his general status in the community, and to attempt such social mobility as he may desire. In this way productivity may serve as a path to the achievement of goals outside the plant.

The operation of this chain of relationships, however, depends not only upon the rewards given the high producer, but also upon the original motivation of the workman to increase his status position in the outside community. The amount of status motivation among production-line employees is open to question. Certainly the findings of Warner [57], Davis and Gardner [12], and others [6, 11, 13] indicate that there are systematic differences in the goals which are pursued in the different segments of our society. It is not impossible that a very large proportion of America's work force is only minimally motivated toward individual social achievement. The assumption that such a motivation does exist may reflect in considerable part a projection of certain middle-class aspirations onto working-class employees.

Furthermore, it is not unlikely that the reference group against which an individual workman evaluates his success may be only a segment of the community, rather than the community as a whole. An individual whose accomplishments are modest at best when compared with the range of possible accomplishments in the community may have a feeling of great accomplishment when he compares his achievements with those of others in his environment. If this is true, and if he desires to continue to operate within this segment of society, any further increase in rewards within the plant might lead to his exclusion from personally important groups outside the plant rather than to increased prestige in such groups.

Finally, there are many goals outside the industrial plant which may be socially rewarding to the individual and which require only minimal financial and occupational rewards inside the plant. Active participation in veterans' organizations, in churches, in recreational programs and similar activities may be and frequently are carried out by individuals at all positions in the industrial hierarchy. As a matter of fact, to the extent that the individual receives extensive social rewards from such activities, he may have only slight interest in his work on the job, and he may continue to remain in industry only to maintain some minimum economic position while carrying out his outside functions. For such an individual, high productivity may lead to *no* important goals.

Relations with other workers in the plant. The studies by Elton Mayo and his associates [43, 50, 51] introduced the work group into the analysis of industry, and a wealth of subsequent investigations have confirmed the importance of on-the-job groups. Throughout these studies has run the observation that members of the work group develop group standards of productivity and attempt to force these standards upon those workmen who deviate. Thus, in the Bank Wiring Room [51] it was the socially maladjusted individual, the deviant from the work group, who maintained a level of production above that of the group even though his native ability was considerably below that of many of the others.

Mathewson's [42] classic study of restriction of output among unorganized workers was an early demonstration of the operation of group norms.

Schachter and associates [52] have conducted an experiment which indicates that in cohesive groups an individual's productivity may be either raised or lowered, depending upon the kind of communications directed toward him by congenial co-workers. In an actual factory setting, Coch and French [8] presented existent groups with evidence that a change in job methods and in productivity was necessary if the factory was to remain in a favorable position relative to other, competing factories. These groups, through group discussion, arrived at a decision as to the proper job set up, and modified the group judgment of "fair" output markedly upward.

There is evidence, then, that the level of performance on the job frequently depends upon a group norm, and that performance level may be changed by changing the group norm in a direction desired by management. This change in the norm probably results from a conviction among the workers that higher production is in their own interest as well as management's, i.e., that their interests and management's interests coincide. This raises the perplexing question of whether, with regard to productivity, the interests of management and labor do, in fact, coincide.

Management, presumably, is interested in higher production as a way of reducing the ratio of cost to output, and thereby bettering management's financial and competitive position. In an expanding market, the argument goes, this makes possible the expansion of the company, increased wages, a larger labor force, and general prosperity not only for the corporation but for the employees as well.

The case may not be so attractive to the workers, especially when the market is not expanding and demand for the product is constant, nearly constant, or declining. In this event, higher productivity per worker means that fewer people are required for the same level of output, or that fewer hours are worked by the same number of workers. In either case, many workers may lose, rather than gain, by the increase in productivity. It may be argued that in normal times such individuals usually find fairly rapid employment in some other segment of the economy. However true this may be, from the viewpoint of the individual workman this involves a considerable disruption in working habits and in his social life in general, and is to be avoided wherever possible. Viewed in this light the interests of management and labor are inimical.

As psychologists we steer clear of such arguments. But we should be sensitive to the fact that the question is a debatable one, that a final decision will probably rest upon values rather than data, that each side is capable of convincing arguments, and that the perception of a certain inevitable conflict of interests between the two groups is honestly and intelligently held by many people. We should also recognize that any reduction in work force after a joint labor-management effort to increase productivity will likely be interpreted as resulting from the increased productivity, and may lead to a future avoidance not only of high productivity levels but also of labor-management cooperation.

At any rate, we often find that individual workers interpret higher productivity as counter to the interests of the employees. To the extent that this perception constitutes a group norm, such motives as are rewarded through the individual's social relationships with other workmen may be blocked by increased productivity. In such cases, productivity may serve as a path to certain goals, but as a block to social acceptance.

The union structure. One system of relationships of considerable importance in many industrial concerns is the union. In many companies much of what was said in the preceding section may be extended to refer also to the relations of the worker in the system of social relations within the union.

In some plants high productivity is not a deterrent to active union participation. Nevertheless, it probably is true that productivity is seldom a prerequisite for advancement within the union hierarchy. If the individual is oriented toward the union structure, it is unlikely that high productivity will serve as a path to such goals, whatever its effect on other goals he may pursue.

The company structure. We have indicated above that many of the worker's social motives outside the plant, as well as his desires for in-plant associations with fellow workmen and within the union, may be only slightly affected by increases in productivity and sometimes may be blocked by increased productivity. The apparent range of goals that a worker may have is so wide that productivity may be a path to only a few of them.

However, workers are often motivated toward goals within the plant such as turning out a quality product, higher wages, and promotion. Let us examine the relationship between satisfaction and productivity for workers who are motivated toward these in-plant goals.

At the start it is evident that productivity and quality are sometimes mutually exclusive. If the individual must concentrate on maintaining high quality work, speed of production probably plays a secondary role. Conversely, if he must emphasize speed, quality often must be reduced to some degree. The speed-quality dilemma is sometimes resolved by making the individual work units so routine and concerned with such minute changes in the material that increased speed will not affect the quality of the product. However, if a worker is more highly motivated when he is performing some meaningful job, the above procedure may be resolving one dilemma by raising another. At any rate, the artisan, motivated toward the goal of quality, may be highly satisfied with his job while turning out a very limited number of finished pieces per unit of time. If he is forced to increase productivity and lower in some measure the quality, we might expect his satisfaction to decrease. For such a person satisfaction and productivity would be negatively related.

Consider now the individual who is motivated toward higher wages and promotion.

While these rewards may not be exclusively dependent upon job performance, at the same time productivity and other aspects of performance often are weighted heavily at promotion time in most companies. In other words, productivity and other aspects of job performance constitute a path to the goal of promotion and wage increases.

Now it is likely that people with aspirations to change position in the company structure will often be quite dissatisfied with their present position in the company. Aspiration to move within a system implies not only a desire for some different position in the future, but some degree of dissatisfaction with the position one is presently occupying. The amount of dissatisfaction probably depends upon the length of time the individual has occupied this position. Thus, although productivity may be a path to the goal, failure to achieve the goal to date may result in dissatisfaction and the high producer may be less satisfied than the low producer.

Evidence sustaining this point of view is to be found in Katz and associates' [34] report of a large insurance company in which the best, most productive workers were also considerably more critical of company policy than were less productive workers. S. Lieberman reports a similar finding in a large appliance factory.[4] A year after all workers in the factory had filled out a questionnaire, Lieberman compared the earlier responses of those who had been promoted to foreman with a matched group of workers who were not promoted. Those promoted had been significantly less satisfied with company practices at the earlier time than had the control group.

Once again the question arises as to what is meant by satisfaction. It may be that extremely high satisfaction is indicative of a certain amount of complacency, a satisfaction with the job as it is, which may be only slightly related to job performance, if it is related at all. On the other hand, individuals who are highly motivated may perceive productivity as a path to their goals, but may also be more realistically critical of whatever deficiencies exist within the organization. They may feel, in addition, that their output is not being rewarded as rapidly as it deserves.

IMPLICATIONS FOR FUTURE RESEARCH

We have arrived at two conclusions: first, that satisfaction with one's position in a network of relationships need not imply strong motivation to outstanding performance within that system, and, second, that productivity may be only peripherally related to many of the goals toward which the industrial worker is striving. We do not mean to imply that researchers should have known all along that their results would be positive only infrequently and in particular circumstances. We have been operating on the basis of hindsight and have attempted to spell out some of the factors which may have accounted for the failure of industrial investigators to find positive relationships in their data.

However, certain implications seem logical from the foregoing sections of this report. Foremost among these implications is the conclusion that it is time to question the strategic and ethical merits of selling to industrial concerns an assumed relationship between employee attitudes and employee performance. In the absence of more convincing evidence than is now at hand with regard to the beneficial effects on job performance of high morale, we are led to the conclusion that we might better forego publicizing these alleged effects.

The emphasis on predicting job performance, and particularly productivity, rests upon the acceptance of certain values. That is, the many studies that have used productivity as the criterion to be predicted have been performed because productivity has direct economic value to industry, and, presumably, to society at large. But the fact that it has economic value does not mean that job performance is the only, or even

---

[4] S. Lieberman. Personal communication, July 15, 1954.

the most important, aspect of organizational behavior. From the viewpoint of studying, analyzing, and understanding the industrial setting and individual reactions thereto, productivity and other aspects of job performance may be only one of several important factors. It would seem worthwhile to study the causes, correlates, and consequence of satisfaction, per se. It seems possible, for example, that conditions conducive to job satisfaction will have an effect on the quality of the workman drawn into the industry, the quality of job performance, and the harmony of labor-management relations. Such potential correlates, among others, merit exploration.

Another potentially fruitful approach involves studying the differential effect of particular kinds of management practices upon the attitudes and performances of workers with different motives, aspirations, and expectations. The appropriate questions may concern how, for particular workers, productivity comes to be perceived as instrumental to the achievement of some goals but not others, while for other workers a different perception develops.

The experimental approach has largely been neglected in this area of industrial research, yet the control of variables that it provides seems essential to the development and refinement of our knowledge in the area. Certainly, where experimentation has been used, as by Schachter and associates [52] and by Coch and French [8], the results have been both enlightening for the understanding of present problems and encouraging for its future application. As our concepts become increasingly precise, we may expect an increased use of experimentation both within the industrial setting and in the laboratory.

Perhaps the most significant conclusion to be drawn from this survey of the literature is that the industrial situation is a complex one. We have suggested that an analysis of the situation involves analysis not only of the individual's relation to the social system of the factory, the work group, and the union, but the community at large as well. It is important to know what motives exist among industrial workers, how they are reflected in the behavior of the workers, and how the motives develop and are modified within the framework of patterned social relationships in the plant and in the larger community.

We seem to have arrived at the position where the social scientist in the industrial setting must concern himself with a full-scale analysis of that situation. Pursuit of this goal should provide us with considerable intrinsic job satisfaction.

REFERENCES

1. Baxter, B., Taaffe, A. A., & Hughes, J. F. A training evaluation study. *Personnel Psychol.*, 1953, **6**, 403–417.

2. Bernberg, R. E. Socio-psychological factors in industrial morale: I. The prediction of specific indicators. *J. soc. Psychol.*, 1952, **36**, 73–82.

3. Brayfield, A. H. *The interrelation of measures of ability, aptitude, interests, and job satisfaction among clerical employees.* Unpublished doctor's dissertation, Univer. of Minnesota, 1946.

4. Brayfield, A. H., & Rothe, H. F. An index of job satisfaction. *J. appl. Psychol.*, 1951, **35**, 307–311.

5. Brody, Mildred. *The relationship between efficiency and job satisfaction.* Unpublished master's thesis, New York Univer., 1945.

6. Centers, R. *The psychology of social classes.* Princeton: Princeton Univer. Press, 1949.

7. Chase, F. S. Factors for satisfaction in teaching. *Phi Delta Kappan*, 1951, **33**, 127–132.

8. Coch, L., & French, J. R., Jr. Overcoming resistance to change. *Hum. Relat.*, 1948, **1**, 512–532.

9. Comrey, A. L., Pfiffner, J. M., & Beem, Helen P. Factors influencing organizational effectiveness. I. The U.S. Forest Survey. *Personnel Psychol.*, 1952, **5**, 307–328.

10. Comrey, A. L., Pfiffner, J. M., & Beem, Helen P. Factors influencing organizational effectiveness. II. The Department of

Employment Survey. *Personnel Psychol.,* 1953, **6,** 65–79.

11. DAVIS, A. *Social class influences upon learning.* Cambridge: Harvard Univer. Press, 1948.

12. DAVIS, A., GARDNER, B. B., & GARDNER, MARY R. *Deep south: A social and anthropological study of caste and class.* Chicago: Univer. of Chicago Press, 1941.

13. ERICSON, MARTHA C. Social status and child rearing practices. In T. M. Newcomb & E. L. Hartley (Eds.), *Readings in social psychology.* New York: Holt, 1947. Pp. 494–501.

14. EVANS, C. E. Item structure variation as a methodological problem in an employee survey. *Amer. Psychologist,* 1949, **4,** 280. (Abstract)

15. FESTINGER, L., & KATZ, D. (Eds.) *Research methods in the behavioral sciences.* New York: Dryden Press, 1953.

16. FRIESEN, E. P. The incomplete sentences technique as a measure of employee attitudes. *Personnel Psychol.,* 1952, **5,** 329–345.

17. GADEL, MARGUERITE S., & KRIEDT, P. H. Relationships of aptitude, interest, performance, and job satisfaction of IBM operators. *Personnel Psychol.,* 1952, **5,** 207–212.

18. GARRETT, H. E. *Statistics in psychology and education.* New York: Longmans, Green, 1947.

19. GHISELLI, E. E., & BROWN, C. W. *Personnel and industrial psychology.* New York: McGraw-Hill, 1948.

20. GIESE, W. J., & RUTER, H. W. An objective analysis of morale. *J. appl. Psychol.,* 1949, **33,** 421–427.

21. GOODE, W. J., & FOWLER, I. Incentive factors in a low morale plant. *Amer. sociol. Rev.,* 1949, **14,** 618–624.

22. GUILFORD, J. P. *Psychometric methods.* New York: McGraw-Hill, 1954.

23. HABBE, S. Job attitudes of life insurance agents. *J. appl. Psychol.,* 1947, **31,** 111–128.

24. HAMEL, L., & REIF, H. G. Should attitude questionnaires be signed? *Personnel Psychol.,* 1952, **5,** 87–91.

25. HILL, J. M. M., & TRIST, E. L. A consideration of industrial accidents as a means of withdrawal from the work situation. *Hum. Relat.,* 1953, **6,** 357–380.

26. HOUSER, J. D. *What the employer thinks.* Cambridge: Harvard Univer. Press, 1927.

27. HYMAN, H. H. *Interviewing in social research.* Chicago: Univer. of Chicago Press, 1954.

28. JAHODA, MARIE, DEUTSCH, M., & COOK, S. W. (Eds.) *Research methods in social relations.* New York: Dryden Press, 1951.

29. KAHN, R. L. *A comparison of two methods of collecting data for social research: The fixed-alternative questionnaire and the open-ended interview.* Unpublished doctor's dissertation, Univer. of Michigan, 1952.

30. KATZ, D. Morale and motivation in industry. In W. Dennis (Ed.), *Current trends in industrial psychology.* Pittsburgh: Univer. of Pittsburgh Press, 1949. Pp. 145–171.

31. KATZ, D., & HYMAN, H. Industrial morale and public opinion methods. *Int. J. Opin. Attit. Res.,* 1947, **1,** 13–30.

32. KATZ, D., & HYMAN, H. Morale in war industry. In T. M. Newcomb & E. L. Hartley (Eds.), *Readings in social psychology.* New York: Holt, 1947. Pp. 437–447.

33. KATZ, D., & KAHN, R. L. Some recent findings in human relations research in industry. In G. E. Swanson, T. M. Newcomb & E. L. Hartley (Eds.), *Readings in social psychology.* New York: Holt, 1952, Pp. 650–665.

34. KATZ, D., MACCOBY, N., & MORSE, NANCY. *Productivity, supervision and morale in an office situation.* Univer. of Michigan: Survey Research Center, 1950.

35. KATZ, D., MACCOBY, N., GURIN, G., & FLOOR, L. G. *Productivity, supervision and morale among railroad workers.* Univer. of Michigan: Survey Research Center, 1951.

36. KENDALL, PATRICIA L., & LAZARSFELD, P. F. Problems in survey analysis. In R. K. Merton & P. F. Lazarsfeld (Eds.), *Continuities in social research.* Glencoe, Ill.: Free Press. 1950.

37. KERR, W. A. On the validity and reliability of the job satisfaction Tear Ballot. *J. appl. Psychol.,* 1948, **32,** 275–281.

38. KERR, W. A. Summary of validity studies of the Tear Ballot. *Personnel Psychol.,* 1952, **5,** 105–113.

39. KORNHAUSER, A., & SHARP, A. Employee

attitudes: suggestions from a study in a factory. *Personnel J.*, 1932, **10**, 393–401.

40. KRISTY, N. F. *Criteria of occupational success among post office counter clerks.* Unpublished doctor's thesis, Univer. of London, 1952.

41. LAWSHE, C. H., & NAGLE, B. F. Productivity and attitude toward supervisor. *J. appl. Psychol.*, 1953, **37**, 159–162.

42. MATHEWSON, S. B. *Restriction of output among unorganized workers.* New York: Viking Press, 1931.

43. MAYO, E. *The social problems of an industrial civilization.* Cambridge: Graduate School of Business Administration, Harvard Univer., 1945.

44. McNEMAR, Q. Opinion-attitude methodology. *Psychol. Bull.*, 1946, **43**, 289–374.

45. METZNER, HELEN, & MANN, F. A limited comparison of two methods of data collection: the fixed alternative questionnaire and the open-ended interview. *Amer. sociol. Rev.*, 1952, **17**, 486–491.

46. METZNER, HELEN, & MANN, F. Employee attitudes and absences. *Personnel Psychol.*, 1953, **6**, 467–485.

47. MORSE, NANCY C. *Satisfactions in the white-collar job.* Univer. of Michigan, Survey Research Center, 1953.

48. MOSSIN, A. C. *Selling performance and contentment in relation to school background.* New York: Bureau of Publications, Teachers Coll., Columbia Univer., 1949.

49. RAUBE, S. A. *Experience with employee attitude surveys* (Studies in Personnel Policy, No. 115). New York: National Industrial Conference Board, 1951.

50. ROETHLISBERGER, F. J. *Management and morale.* Cambridge: Harvard Univer. Press, 1943.

51. ROETHLISBERGER, F. J., & DICKSON, W. J. *Management and the worker.* Cambridge: Harvard Univer. Press, 1939.

52. SCHACHTER, S., ELLERTSON, N., McBRIDE, D., & GREGORY, D. An experimental study of cohesiveness and productivity. *Hum. Relat.*, 1951, **4**, 229–238.

53. STAGNER, R., FLEBBE, D. R., & WOOD, E. F. Working on the railroad: a study of job satisfaction. *Personnel Psychol.*, 1952, **5**, 293–306.

54. THORNDIKE, R. L. *Personnel selection.* New York: Wiley, 1949.

55. VAN ZELST, R. H., & KERR, W. A. Workers' attitudes toward merit rating. *Personnel Psychol.*, 1953, **6**, 159–172.

56. VITELES, M. S. *Motivation and morale in industry.* New York: Norton, 1953.

57. WARNER, W. L., & LUNT, P. S. *The social life of a modern community.* New Haven: Yale Univer. Press, 1941.

58. WEDELL, C., & SMITH, K. U. Consistency of interview methods in appraisal of attitudes. *J. appl. Psychol.*, 1951, **35**, 392–396.

59. WEITZ, J., & NUCKOLS, R. C. The validity of direct and indirect questions in measuring job satisfaction. *Personnel Psychol.*, 1953, **5**, 487–494.

60. WESCHLER, I. R., KAHANE, M., & TANNENBAUM, R. Job satisfaction, productivity and morale: a case study. *Occupational Psychol.*, 1952, **26**, 1–14.

61. WICKERT, F. R. Turnover, and employees' feelings of ego-involvement in the day-to-day operations of a company. *Personnel Psychol.*, 1951, **4**, 185–197.

62. YODER, D., HENEMAN, H., JR., & CHEIT, E. F. *Triple audit of industrial relations.* Minneapolis: Univer. of Minnesota Press, 1951.

THE TECHNIQUE
OF ASSESSMENT

Developments in the logic and methodology of psychological assessment have been impressive in recent years, but their application presupposes that certain elementary conditions of test administration and scoring have been fulfilled. Similarly, the adequate interpretation of test results requires that scores be expressed in terms permitting comparison with reference samples from specifiable and appropriate populations.

Harold G. Seashore in the first chapter of Part 8 provides a clear, concise description of methods for expressing test results. In weighing the advantages of each method, Seashore emphasizes the practical importance of determining an assessee's position in a particular population in a way that fosters ease and clarity of interpretation.

In Chapter 67, Irving Lorge and Robert L. Thorndike describe procedures for establishing norms for the Lorge-Thorndike Intelligence Tests. The care with which this normative study was planned and executed, as well as the attention given to the techniques of stratified sampling, make it a model of its type. In addition, the procedures are described in sufficient detail to permit the prospective user to evaluate the representativeness of the sample in terms of known demographic characteristics, as well as its appropriateness for his own particular purposes.

It is an obvious fact that improperly administered or carelessly scored tests will lead to erroneous estimates of abilities or traits. Clearly, published norms can be applied with confidence only when there is adherence to standardized instructions, time limits, and conditions of administration. Similarly, care should be exercised in the mechanics and arithmetic of scoring and compiling test results. The application of quality control to test scoring would appear to be such an elementary consideration that we would not mention it here were it not for the fact that research has uncovered some rather shocking levels of error on the part of test users. Phillips and Weathers, in Chapter 68, provide an analysis of the kind and frequency of errors made in scoring standardized tests. Unfortunately, this range of errors is probably not atypical of practice in many quarters.

The three selections included here discuss several important ways in which more accurate test scores and interpretations may be obtained. They were of course meant to be illustrative rather than exhaustive, and the reader is referred to any one of several excellent texts in the testing and measurement field for extensive coverage of the elements of test administration, norms, and interpretation.

66 ~

Methods of Expressing Test Scores

HAROLD G. SEASHORE

An individual's test score acquires meaning when it can be compared with the scores of well-identified groups of people. Manuals for tests provide tables of norms to make it easy to compare individuals and groups. Several systems for deriving more meaningful "standard scores" from raw scores have been widely adopted. All of them reveal the relative status of individuals within a group.

The fundamental equivalence of the most popular standard score systems is illustrated in Figure 66–1. We hope the chart and the accompanying description will be useful to counselors, personnel officers, clinical diagnosticians and others in helping them to show the uninitiated the essential simplicity of standard score systems, percentile equivalents, and their relation to the ideal normal distribution.

Sooner or later, every textbook discussion of test scores introduces the bell-shaped normal curve. The student of testing soon learns that many of the methods of deriving meaningful scores are anchored to the dimensions and characteristics of this curve. And he learns by observation of actual test score distributions that the ideal mathematical curve is a reasonably good approximation of many practical cases. He learns to use the standardized properties of the ideal curve as a model.

Let us look first at the curve itself. Notice that there are no raw scores printed along the baseline. The graph is generalized; it describes an idealized distribution of scores of any group on any test. We are free to use any numerical scale we like. For any particular set of scores, we can be arbitrary and call the average score zero. In technical terms we "equate" the mean raw score to zero. Similarly we can choose any convenient number, say 1.00, to represent the scale distance of one standard deviation.[1] Thus, if a distribution of scores on a particular test has a mean of 36 and a standard deviation of 4, the zero point on the baseline of our curve would be equivalent to an orig-

This article is reproduced from *Test Service Bulletin*, No. 45, 1955, with the permission of the author and The Psychological Corporation.

[1] The mathematical symbol for the standard deviation is the lower case Greek letter sigma or σ. These terms are used interchangeably in this article.

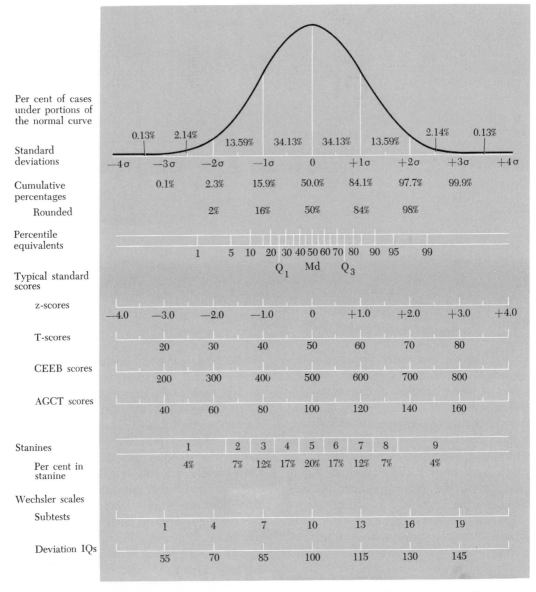

Per cent of cases under portions of the normal curve

Standard deviations

0.13%   2.14%   13.59%   34.13%   34.13%   13.59%   2.14%   0.13%

−4σ   −3σ   −2σ   −1σ   0   +1σ   +2σ   +3σ   +4σ

Cumulative percentages

0.1%   2.3%   15.9%   50.0%   84.1%   97.7%   99.9%

Rounded

2%   16%   50%   84%   98%

Percentile equivalents

1   5   10   20 30 40 50 60 70 80   90 95   99

Q_1 Md Q_3

Typical standard scores

z-scores

−4.0   −3.0   −2.0   −1.0   0   +1.0   +2.0   +3.0   +4.0

T-scores

20   30   40   50   60   70   80

CEEB scores

200   300   400   500   600   700   800

AGCT scores

40   60   80   100   120   140   160

Stanines

1   2   3   4   5   6   7   8   9

Per cent in stanine

4%   7%   12% 17% 20% 17% 12%   7%   4%

Wechsler scales

Subtests

1   4   7   10   13   16   19

Deviation IQs

55   70   85   100   115   130   145

inal score of 36; one unit to the right, $+1\sigma$, would be equivalent to 40, $(36 + 4)$; and one unit to the left, -1σ, would be equivalent to 32, $(36 - 4)$.

The total area under the curve represents the total number of scores in the distribution. Vertical lines have been drawn through the score scale (the baseline) at zero and at 1, 2, 3, and 4 sigma units to the right and left. These lines mark off subareas of the total area under the curve. The numbers printed in these subareas are per cents—*percentages of the total number of*

people. Thus, 34.13 per cent of all cases in a normal distribution have scores falling between 0 and -1σ. For practical purposes we rarely need to deal with standard deviation units below -3 or above $+3$; the percentage of cases with scores beyond $\pm 3\sigma$ is negligible.

The fact that 68.26 per cent fall between $\pm 1\sigma$ gives rise to the common statement that in a normal distribution roughly two-thirds of all cases lie between plus and minus one sigma. This is a rule of thumb every test user should keep in mind. It is very near to the theoretical value and is a useful approximation.

Below the row of deviations expressed in sigma units is a row of per cents; these show *cumulatively* the percentage of people which is included *to the left* of each of the sigma points. Thus, starting from the left, when we reach the line erected above -2σ, we have included the lowest 2.3 per cent of cases. These percentages have been rounded in the next row.

Note some other relationships: the area between the $\pm 1\sigma$ points includes the scores which lie above the 16th percentile (-1σ) and below the 84th percentile $(+1\sigma)$—two major reference points all test users should know. When we find that an individual has a score 1σ above the mean, we conclude that his score ranks at the 84th percentile in the group of persons on whom the test was normed. (*This conclusion is good provided we also add this clause, at least subvocally: if this particular group reasonably approximates the ideal normal model.*)

The simplest facts to memorize about the normal distribution and the relation of the *percentile* system to deviations from the average in sigma units are seen in the chart. They are

Deviation from the mean	-2σ	-1σ	0	$+1\sigma$	$+2\sigma$
Percentile equivalent	2	16	50	84	98

To avoid cluttering, the graph reference lines have not been drawn, but we could mark off ten per cent sections of area under the normal curve by drawing lines vertically from the indicated decile points (10, 20, . . ., 80, 90) up through the graph. The reader might do this lightly with a colored pencil.

We can readily see that ten per cent of the area (people) at the middle of the distribution embraces a smaller *distance* on the baseline of the curve than ten per cent of the area (people) at the ends of the range of scores, for the simple reason that the curve is much higher at the middle. A person who is at the 95th percentile is farther away from a person at the 85th percentile in units of *test score* than a person at the 55th percentile is from one at the 45th percentile.

The remainder of the chart, that is, the several scoring scales drawn parallel to the baseline, illustrates variations of the *deviation score* principle. As a class these are called *standard scores*.

First, there are the *z-scores*. These are the same *numbers* as shown on the baseline of the graph; the only difference is that the expression, σ, has been omitted. These scores run, in practical terms, from -3.0 to $+3.0$. One can compute them to more decimal places if one wishes, although computing to a single decimal place is usually sufficient. One can compute z-scores by equating the mean to 0.00 and the standard deviation to 1.00 for a distribution of any shape, but the relationships shown in this figure between the z-score equivalents of raw scores and percentile equivalents of raw scores are correct only for normal distributions. The interpretation of standard score systems derives from the idea of using the normal curve as a model.

As can be seen, T-scores are directly related to z-scores. The mean of the raw scores is equated to 50, and the standard deviation of the raw scores is equated to 10. Thus a z-score of $+1.5$ means the same as a T-score of 65. T-scores are usually expressed in whole numbers from about 20 to 80. The T-score plan eliminates negative numbers and thus facilitates many computations.[2]

The College Entrance Examination Board uses a plan in which both decimals and negative numbers are avoided by setting the arbitrary mean at 500 points and the arbitrary sigma at another convenient unit, namely, 100 points. The experienced tester or counselor who hears of a College Board SAT-V score of 550 at once thinks, "Half a

---

[2] T-scores and percentiles both have 50 as the main reference point, an occasional source of confusion to those who do not insist on careful labelling of data and of scores of individuals in their records.

sigma (50 points) above average (500 points) on the CEEB basic norms." And when he hears of a score of 725 on SAT-M, he can interpret, "Plus 2¼σ. Therefore, better than the 98th percentile."

During World War II the Navy used the T-score plan of reporting test status. The Army used still another system with a mean of 100 and a standard deviation of 20 points.

Another derivative of the general standard score system is the *stanine* plan, developed by psychologists in the Air Force during the war. The plan divides the norm population into nine groups, hence, "standard nines." Except for stanine 9, the top, and stanine 1, the bottom, these groups are spaced in half-sigma units. Thus, stanine 5 is defined as including the people who are within $\pm 0.25\sigma$ of the mean. Stanine 6 is the group defined by the half-sigma distance on the baseline between $+0.25\sigma$ and $+0.75\sigma$. Stanines 1 and 9 include all persons who are below -1.75σ and above $+1.75\sigma$, respectively. The result is a distribution in which the mean is 5.0 and the standard deviation is 2.0.

Just below the line showing the demarcation of the nine groups in the stanine system there is a row of percentages which indicates the per cent of the total population in each of the stanines. Thus 7 per cent of the population will be in stanine 2, and 20 per cent in the middle group, stanine 5.

Interpretation of the Wechsler scales (W-B I, W-B II, WISC, and WAIS) depends on a knowledge of standard scores. A subject's raw score *on each of the subtests* in these scales is converted, by appropriate norms tables, to a standard score, based on a mean of 10 and a standard deviation of 3. The sums of standard scores on the Verbal Scale, the Performance Scale, and the Full Scale are then converted into IQs. These IQs are based on a standard score mean of 100, the conventional number for representing the IQ of the average person in a given age group. The standard deviation of the IQs is set at 15 points. In practical terms, then, roughly two-thirds of

the IQs are between 85 and 115, that is, $\pm 1\sigma$.[3] IQs of the type used in the Wechsler scales have come to be known as *deviation IQs*, as contrasted with the IQs developed from scales in which a derived mental age is divided by chronological age.

Users of the Wechsler scales should establish clearly in their minds the relationship of subtest scaled scores and the deviation IQs to the other standard score systems, to the ordinary percentile rank interpretation, and to the deviation units on the baseline of the normal curve. For example, every Wechsler examiner should recognize that an IQ of 130 is a score equivalent to a deviation of $+2\sigma$, and that this IQ score delimits approximately the upper two per cent of the population. If a clinician wants to evaluate a Wechsler IQ of 85 along with percentile ranks on several other tests given in school, he can mentally convert the IQ of 85 to a percentile rank of about 16, this being the percentile equal to a deviation from the mean of -1σ. Of course he should also consider the appropriateness and comparability of norms.

Efficiency in interpreting test scores in counseling, in clinical diagnosis, and in personnel selection depends, in part, on facility in thinking in terms of the major interrelated plans by which meaningful scores are derived from raw scores. It is hoped that this graphic presentation will be helpful to all who in their daily work must help others understand the information conveyed by numerical test scores.

---

[3] Every once in a while we receive a letter from someone who suggests that the Wechsler scales ought to generate a wider range of IQs. The reply is very simple. If we want a wider range of IQs all we have to do is to choose a *larger arbitrary* standard deviation, say, 20 or 25. Under the present system, $\pm 3\sigma$ gives IQs of 55 to 145, with a few rare cases below and a few rare cases above. If we used 20 as the standard deviation we would *arbitrarily* increase the $\pm 3\sigma$ range of IQs from 55–145 to 40–160. This *is* a wider range of numbers! But, test users should never forget that adaptations of this kind do not change the responses of the people who took the test, do not change the order of the persons in relation to each other, and do not change the psychological meaning attached to an IQ.

Chapter 67

Procedures for Establishing Norms

IRVING LORGE / ROBERT L. THORNDIKE

Setting up norms for an intelligence test requires ideally that the test be administered to samples of individuals of given ages who are fully representative of a specified total population. The population which test-makers usually hope to approximate is the population of individuals in that age group in the complete United States population. Any operation of norming is at best an approximation to this ideal, but various types of information make it possible to improve this approximation.

NORMING POPULATION

More than 136,000 children in 44 communities in 22 states were used to standardize the Lorge-Thorndike Intelligence Tests. [For a listing of the communities which cooperated in preliminary tryouts, special testing projects, and norming, see 1, page 16.]

This article was reprinted from *Technical Manual, Lorge-Thorndike Intelligence Tests,* 1957, with permission of the authors and the Houghton-Mifflin Publishing Company.

An adequate norming population cannot be established merely by testing great numbers. If the sample is biased, increasing its size will only serve to stabilize its bias. Special steps must be taken to eliminate bias from the sample used in establishing test norms.

ELIMINATING BIAS

The basic procedure for ruling out bias in the norms for the Lorge-Thorndike Tests was to select a stratified sample of communities on which to base the norms. Communities were stratified on a composite of factors which have been found to be related to the measured intelligence of children in the community [2]. Each community which volunteered to serve in the normative testing was evaluated with respect to the factors of (1) percent of adult illiteracy, (2) number of professional workers per thousand in the population, (3) percent of home ownership, and (4) median home rental value. On the basis of a composite of these factors, each community was

791

classed as: Very High, High, Average, Low, or Very Low. All the pupils present in each grade in the community were to be tested. With a few exceptions, each community carried out testing in all grades from the kindergarten or first grade through high school. This procedure eliminated any accidental bias that could occur in intracommunity sampling. Score distributions for each *age* group were prepared separately for each of the five levels of communities. These distributions were then combined, each distribution being weighted according to the estimated proportion of the total population living in such communities. The composite score distribution was used as a basis for the final conversion into I.Q. equivalents.

The computational steps in arriving at the basic deviation I.Q. equivalents may be outlined as follows:

1. Raw score distributions were prepared for each grade group for a selection of near-average communities.
2. Raw scores for all grades which had taken the same level of the test were converted into a single standard score scale.
3. In certain marginal grades, two successive levels of the test were given to the same pupils (i.e., in grade 7, certain groups were given Level 3, Form A followed by Level 4, Form B, or vice versa).
4. Using an equi-percentile procedure, equivalent values were determined for the score scales of successive levels of the test.
5. A single standard score scale was set up for all levels of the test.
6. Standard score distributions were prepared for each age group for each level of community.
7. A weighted composite distribution for the different community types was assembled.
8. Assuming a population mean of 100 and a standard deviation of 16, devia-

tion I.Q. equivalents were determined for each age group.
9. The deviation I.Q. equivalents were established for each raw score value for appropriate levels of the test, based on the analysis of from ten to twenty thousand test scores for each of the levels, forms, and batteries.

TYPES OF NORMS

Four types of norms have been developed: (1) intelligence quotient equivalent, (2) grade percentile, (3) grade equivalent, and (4) age equivalent.

The intelligence quotients will probably be the most generally useful. However, some users may wish to express a child's performance in terms of an age or grade equivalent. Results expressed in this way may be easier to compare with achievement test data. In some cases, it may be desirable to compare a pupil with his grade group; therefore, grade percentiles are provided.

With reference to age- and grade-equivalent norms, a question may arise about their comparability, i.e., does one year of growth expressed in terms of grade equivalents parallel one year of growth expressed in age equivalents? In general, each year of change in grade corresponds to a year of change in age. However, this is not quite true at the extremes of the age and grade range. Here, presumably, some degree of selection of those pupils who have entered early or who have remained in school late has served to disturb the relationship. One would expect the standard deviation to be slightly larger in an age group than in a grade group, because there is still enough acceleration and retardation to make a grade group somewhat more homogeneous than an age group.

Table 67–1 presents the median I.Q.'s for each age group of the pupils in the standardization population, which has been divided according to socio-economic level of community. The pattern of the median I.Q.'s shown in these data is very consistent.

The data confirm the importance of sampling all socio-economic strata in a norming population. They also point up the fact that the *Nonverbal* I.Q.'s from the Lorge-Thorndike Tests exhibit the same pattern as the *Verbal* I.Q.'s.

Table 67–1   Median I.Q.'s on Lorge-Thorndike Intelligence Tests for Communities at Specified Socio-economic Levels

Age	Nonverbal (Primary: Ages 6, 7, and 8)					Verbal				
	High High	High	Average	Low	Low Low	High High	High	Average	Low	Low Low
6–0	106.2	104.1	103.5	99.0	96.7					
7–0	107.2	104.0	101.3	96.3	89.5					
8–0	107.4	104.1	101.5	97.4	87.7					
9–0	106.6	102.8	101.3	98.1	87.8	107.4	103.3	101.7	96.7	89.8
10–0	105.5	103.4	101.9	97.9	88.4	106.8	103.5	101.5	96.4	90.5
11–0	106.9	103.7	102.1	97.1	86.9	107.3	103.3	101.9	97.0	90.4
12–0	106.3	103.2	102.3	96.8	86.4	108.0	103.0	101.5	96.2	89.9
13–0	105.0	103.7	102.0	96.3	86.4	107.2	103.6	101.1	95.4	90.0
14–0	103.9	104.1	101.9	95.9	85.8	106.1	104.2	101.6	94.8	88.2
15–0	104.7	104.9	102.2	95.3	86.9	104.3	102.4	101.3	93.8	87.1
16–0	102.8	104.1	102.4	97.1	88.8	103.6	102.7	101.5	93.6	87.3
17–0	102.9	104.1	101.2	97.1	89.3	104.7	103.5	101.1	93.8	87.7
Md	105.8	104.0	102.0	97.1	87.8	106.8	103.3	101.5	95.4	89.8

REFERENCES

1. *Technical Manual, Lorge-Thorndike Intelligence Tests.* Boston: Houghton-Mifflin, 1957.

2. THORNDIKE, R. L. Community variables as predictors of intelligence and academic achievement. *J. educ. Psychol.*, 1951, 42, 321–338.

Chapter 68

Analysis of Errors Made in Scoring Standardized Tests

BEEMAN N. PHILLIPS / GARRETT WEATHERS

From the beginning of the testing movement there has been great concern over the validity and reliability of tests, and tremendous efforts have been made to develop tests which are as valid and as reliable as possible. However, such efforts are largely negated if tests are not accurately scored, for it is a truism that a test can be no better than the person who scores it. A test may be constructed and standardized to have high validity and reliability, as indicated in the manual; but if it is not correctly scored it is of questionable value and may result in great harm to the examinees. For this reason, it is important to know how accurately standardized tests are scored by individuals, and the problem takes on added significance when it is realized that the majority of standardized tests are hand scored.

Since a large proportion of standardized

This article is reprinted from *Educational and Psychological Measurement*, 1958, with the permission of the authors and the copyright holder, G. Frederic Kuder.

tests are used in the public school, a study was made of tests scored by teachers in a large city school system. The tests scored by these teachers were analyzed in an effort to determine: (a) the number and type of errors made, (b) the errors of different teachers, and (c) the effects of these errors on test results.

METHODS

Twenty-seven third grade and twenty-four fifth grade teachers were used in this study. These teachers were randomly selected and represented about one fourth of the teachers in the system in these two grades.

A total of 5017 subject tests of the Stanford Achievement Test, Elementary and Intermediate, were scored by these teachers. All tests were later rescored by members of the research and testing department. Scoring errors were analyzed by teachers and classified as errors due to: (a) counting, (b) failure to use key correctly, (c) failure to follow specific instructions given for each subject test, (d) incorrect use of table—used wrong table, used raw score instead of converted score, or transposed numbers, (e) computation—failure to compute correctly. Each incorrectly scored test also was checked to determine the effect of the error on the grade equivalent assigned.

RESULTS

Of the 5017 subject tests scored by these teachers there were 1404 or 28 per cent with errors. In Table 68–1 these errors are classified according to type.

Examination of Table 68–1 indicates that the most common error involved counting. It accounted for almost half of the errors found. The failure to use specific instructions was the next most frequently occurring type of error. Not using the key properly and using the wrong table accounted for most of the remaining errors.

The number of errors committed by different teachers is shown in Table 68–2. Since teachers scored different numbers of tests, it was necessary to express their errors in terms of a constant—the number of errors per 100 tests scored.

Table 68–2 reveals that there were some teachers who made practically no errors. At the same time, there were others who made errors on more than half of the tests they scored. No information was obtained on what caused such tremendous variation among teachers.

In examining individual teacher errors, a great deal of variation also was found in the type of error committed. In ten cases, counting inaccuracies accounted for most of the errors committed. In eight other cases, failing to follow instructions, using the wrong table, or improperly using the key accounted for most of the errors. In the remainder, there was no strong predominance of one type of error over others.

The effects of these errors on the grade equivalents assigned pupils on the subject tests are shown in Table 68–3. It shows the changes in grade equivalents resulting from the errors which were made, including the smallest change, the median change, and the largest change.

In examining Table 68–3 it is evident that the large majority of errors caused a change of less than one-half of a grade equivalent. About half of the grade equivalents were lowered by from 0.1 to 3.5 grade equivalents, or a median of .29 grade equivalents. Those which were raised were raised by from 0.1 to 3.8 grade equivalents, and for these cases the median increase was .31 grade equivalents.

CONCLUSIONS

The purpose of this study was to ascertain how many errors teachers make in scoring standardized tests, the nature of these errors, and their effects on test results. It was found that 28 per cent of the tests had

Table 68–1   Scoring Errors Classified According to Type

Type of Error	Frequency	Per Cent of Total
Counting	630	44.8
Instructions	366	26.1
Use of key	209	14.9
Use of tables	189	13.5
Computation	10	0.7
Total	1404	100.0

Table 68–2   Teachers Classified According to Number of Errors Made

Errors per 100 Subject Tests Scored	Number of Teachers	Per Cent of Total
Less than 10	9	17.6
10–19	14	27.5
20–29	13	25.5
30–39	10	19.6
40–49	2	3.9
50–59	3	5.9
Total	51	100.0

Table 68–3   Effects of Errors on Grade Equivalents Assigned to Subject Tests

Effect of Error	Difference between Corrected and Uncorrected Grade Equivalent							Change in Grade Equivalent			Total Number of Errors
	.1–.5	.6–1.0	1.1–1.5	1.6–2.0	2.1–2.5	2.6–3.0	3.1 plus	Smallest Change	Median Change	Largest Change	
Raised grade equivalent	508	66	36	9	8	6	6	.1	.31	3.8	639
Lowered grade equivalent	562	81	28	7	6	5	4	.1	.29	3.5	693
Total	1070	147	64	16	14	11	10				1332°

° There were 72 errors which did not change the grade equivalent.

some kind of error, although teachers varied greatly in the number of errors committed. As a result, some of the assigned grade equivalents were actually as much as 3.8 too high or 3.5 too low, the median error being .30 grade equivalents. Although the big majority of these errors fell within the limits of the standard errors on the tests, the potential effect of the large errors on the pupils involved must be considered. A great deal of emphasis is put on test results, and greater care is needed to avoid the injustices which might result from the use of such erroneous test data.

The results of this study also suggest that many of the scoring errors of teachers could be eliminated by greater familiarity with the test manuals and test scoring procedures. This would eliminate many of the errors due to using the wrong table or misusing the key, although it is doubtful that it would have much effect on counting errors.

The great variation in the number of errors committed by different teachers indicates that some teachers are "error-prone." This suggests the need for studies of the characteristics of teachers who make numerous errors, and this in turn may open the way for devising steps and procedures to decrease the number of errors.

An alternative would be to have all standardized tests machine-scored, and in many school systems this is a common practice whenever possible. However, this would not solve the problem in the lower grades where most standardized tests cannot be machine scored. Here the only solution appears to be what has already been suggested; i.e., working with teachers and devising various techniques and procedures for insuring greater scoring accuracy.

Part 9

THE ETHICS OF
ASSESSMENT

Psychologists and educators have long been concerned about the ethical basis for the practice of psychological assessment. This concern is exemplified in the "Ethical Standards of Psychologists," reprinted in Chapter 69, wherein tenets of acceptable practice are set forth on several points directly related to assessment, such as confidentiality of records, invasion of privacy, client welfare, test interpretation, test publication, and research precautions. Since this concern about ethical standards probably stemmed originally from a desire to curb incompetent and unethical practitioners, one might have expected it to fade away as an issue once a set of practical guidelines for professional conduct had been duly sanctioned. Attention would then very likely shift instead to the establishment of workable control mechanisms for enforcing the accepted standards. Yet, concern over the ethical basis of assessment persists—primarily because it has not been possible to formulate a coherent set of principles that would govern consistently all the legitimate uses and purposes of testing. This impasse has arisen because the social values that should have determined principles of conduct in these areas are unfortunately sometimes in conflict. As a result, we are frequently faced with competing norms of behavior that cannot be resolved on the basis of universal principle, but must be adjudicated on the basis of current policy.[1]

The core of this conflict in values is summarized in the first two sentences of Chapter 69: "The psychologist believes in the dignity and worth of the individual human being. He is committed to increasing man's understanding of himself and others." There are times, however, when these two basic commitments clash, when the attempt to increase man's understanding of himself and others as a means of advancing individual and general welfare may also necessitate an infringement upon individual freedom of choice. Such situations arise in several areas of assessment practice. In the clinic, for example, a certain line of inquiry may represent an embarrassing invasion of privacy for a particular patient; but at the same time, the information disclosed may be valuable for his future treatment. When does one consideration warrant offsetting the other? In the conduct of research, the psychologist is obligated to protect the subject from exposure to emotional stress. He should also respect the subject's inherent right to decide for himself, on the basis of his own evaluation of the potential consequences, whether or not he wishes to participate in the proposed experiment. But the psychologist also has an obligation to science to avoid the kinds of biases that might result if enough specific information were given in advance to make meaningfully informed prior consent possible. When does the significance of the research problem justify withholding information or even misleading the subject in order to study his behavior?

In the case of academic or industrial selection, the psychologist again has multiple loyalties. He is concerned on the one hand that the institution base its selection decisions on optimally valid and economical testing procedures and on the other hand that the assessment experience itself not be unduly distressing to the applicant. Since the individual does not have to apply for a particular job or for admission to a particular college if he doesn't want to, the institution usually enjoys considerable scope in the kinds of personal information it can require of a candidate. But how much inquisition into personal affairs is justifiable in the name of validity or economy? And validity for what? Does the applied psychologist's professional responsibility end with the successful prediction of any set of specific criteria defined by the particular institution? Or does it extend to an appraisal of what those institutional criteria ought to be in terms of the purposes and values of society? And what if the methods used to achieve the immediate goals of the institution turn out to be detrimental to the ultimate goals of the larger group? In Chapter 70, Dael Wolfle discusses just such a predicament: After arguing persuasively for the

---

[1] For a further discussion of value conflicts in assessment practice and their implications for regulation and policy making in the testing field, see Messick, S. Personality measurement and the ethics of assessment. *Amer. Psychologist*, 1965, **20**, 136–142.

general value of maximizing the diversity of talent both within and among individuals, Wolfle points out that several methods of academic selection—such as the use of general aptitude scores, average grades, and rank in class—tend to have the contrary effect of reducing variability among group members. It would thus seem important to see if academic selection decisions could be based equally well, even if less economically, upon multiple tests of specific abilities and traits, so that the diversity of specialized talents might be highlighted and capitalized upon.

With these kinds of conflicts in values underlying many applications of assessment, it is not surprising that criticisms of psychological testing should erupt in some quarters. In Chapter 71, for example, William H. Whyte, Jr., advises aspiring business executives to cheat on personality tests and offers some valuable pointers on how to proceed. Whyte recommends this recourse to subterfuge as an antidote against the increasing use by personnel psychologists of various personality tests that in his view bear little relation to job performance. He is particularly indignant about tests dealing with neurotic tendencies and psychopathology: "The Organization has no business at all to throw these questions at you, but its curiosity is powerful." It is clear from the overall tone of his presentation that to his mind the organization has no business throwing *any* personal or socially sensitive questions at you, so that deceptive countermeasures seem warranted in self-defense. Yet this remedy completely ignores one side of the issue: Any right of the company to utilize in its employment decisions relevant information about temperament, practical judgment, attitudes, or values has been dismissed by implication. Personnel testing has been reduced to a battle of wits between examiner and examinee. Surely the interests of both would be better served if concerted efforts were made to improve the conditions of testing. For example, at the beginning of the testing session the examinee could be explicitly reminded of his rights to privacy, thereby making it clear at the outset that the examiner does not treat such boundaries lightly—that private matters will not be intruded upon for trivial or irrelevant reasons. The examinee should also be informed about the purposes and uses to which his scores will be put and about the degree of confidentiality of the records. Such assurances should help to allay any impression that the assessment program is merely an instrument of the company's "powerful curiosity" and should highlight the potential importance of the requested information for making appropriate personnel decisions.

In recent years, however, animosity toward testing has deepened, and the new criticisms are not limited to the accuracy of tests or their relevance to decision criteria. Concern is also voiced about the social consequences of their use. It is charged, for example, that the emphasis tests place upon a common standard of performance represses individuality, that the rigid interpretation of test scores in terms of permanent status undermines self-esteem and limits motivation for improvement, that the use of tests in selection is antidemocratic and a subversion of equalitarian values, and that the availability of test records provides a potential basis for state control.[2] These negative attitudes toward testing are frequently symptomatic of broader ideological commitments with enough force to precipitate drastic opposition to testing applications, as witness the test burning incident described by Gwynn Nettler in Chapter 72. Nettler concludes from this ordeal that concerted action is necessary to make matters better, such as massive efforts at public education on the value of tests and the motives of testers, coupled with specialized explanations to potential research populations about the purposes, methods, and benefits of large-scale testing programs.[3] But unfortunately it is not just a question of improving the public relations of a blameless, misunderstood profession: There is also a pressing need for the improved regulation of testing practice, as Stagner illustrates in Chapter 73 with his description of the huckstering tactics used by high-pressure test salesmen to foist worthless assessment programs on gullible personnel managers.

It seems clear, then, that not only should tests be evaluated in terms of their measurement properties, but testing applications should be evaluated in terms of their social consequences. In Chapter 74, Samuel Messick discusses these dual requirements in the context of college selection, but his main points hold for any assessment application. Two questions should be asked whenever a test is proposed for a particular use: (1) Is the test any good as a measure of the characteristic it purports to assess? (2) Should the test be used for this purpose? The first question is a scientific one and may be answered by appraising the test's psychometric properties, including its construct validity. The second question is an ethical one, and its answer requires an evaluation of the potential consequences of the testing in terms of social values. We should be careful not to delude ourselves that answers to the first question are also sufficient answers to the second—except, of course, when a test's poor psychometric properties preclude its use. In the arena of assessment practice, public responsibility is demanded. And the justification of test use by an appeal to empirical validity is not enough.

[2] For an examination of the nature and sources of negative attitudes toward testing, see Brim, O. G. American attitudes toward intelligence tests. *Amer. Psychologist*, 1965, **20**, 125–130; and Ebel, R. L. The social consequences of educational testing. In Anne Anastasi (Ed.), *Testing problems in perspective*. Washington, D.C.: American Council on Education, 1966.

[3] For an example of extensive preliminary groundwork and public education in connection with a research program that nonetheless was almost aborted by the emergence of a vocal opposition, see Eron, L. D., & Walder, L. O. Test burning: II. *Amer. Psychologist*, 1961, **16**, 237–244.

Chapter 69

Ethical Standards of Psychologists

AMERICAN PSYCHOLOGICAL ASSOCIATION

The psychologist believes in the dignity and worth of the individual human being. He is committed to increasing man's understanding of himself and others. While pursuing this endeavor, he protects the welfare of any person who may seek his service or of any subject, human or animal, that may be the object of his study. He does not use his professional position or relationships, nor does he knowingly permit his own services to be used by others, for purposes inconsistent with these values. While demanding for himself freedom of inquiry and communication, he accepts the responsibility this freedom confers: for competence where he claims it, for objectivity in the report of his findings, and for consideration of the best interests of his colleagues and of society.

This article is reprinted from the *American Psychologist,* 1963, with the permission of the American Psychological Association.

SPECIFIC PRINCIPLES

PRINCIPLE 1. RESPONSIBILITY

The psychologist,[1] committed to increasing man's understanding of man, places high value on objectivity and integrity, and maintains the highest standards in the services he offers.

a. As a scientist, the psychologist believes that society will be best served when he investigates where his judgment indicates investigation is needed; he plans his research in such a way as to minimize the possibility that his findings will be misleading; and he publishes full reports of his work, never discarding without explanation data which may modify the interpretation of results.

[1] A student of psychology who assumes the role of psychologist shall be considered a psychologist for the purpose of this code of ethics.

b. As a teacher, the psychologist recognizes his primary obligation to help others acquire knowledge and skill, and to maintain high standards of scholarship.

c. As a practitioner, the psychologist knows that he bears a heavy social responsibility because his work may touch intimately the lives of others.

PRINCIPLE 2. COMPETENCE

The maintenance of high standards of professional competence is a responsibility shared by all psychologists, in the interest of the public and of the profession as a whole.

a. Psychologists discourage the practice of psychology by unqualified persons and assist the public in identifying psychologists competent to give dependable professional service. When a psychologist or a person identifying himself as a psychologist violates ethical standards, psychologists who know firsthand of such activities attempt to rectify the situation. When such a situation cannot be dealt with informally, it is called to the attention of the appropriate local, state, or national committee on professional ethics, standards, and practices.

b. The psychologist recognizes the boundaries of his competence and the limitations of his techniques and does not offer services or use techniques that fail to meet professional standards established in particular fields. The psychologist who engages in practice assists his client in obtaining professional help for all important aspects of his problem that fall outside the boundaries of his own competence. This principle requires, for example, that provision be made for the diagnosis and treatment of relevant medical problems and for referral to or consultation with other specialists.

c. The psychologist in clinical work recognizes that his effectiveness depends in good part upon his ability to maintain sound interpersonal relations, that temporary or more enduring aberrations in his own personality may interfere with this ability or distort his appraisals of others. There he refrains from undertaking any activity in which his personal problems are likely to result in inferior professional services or harm to a client; or, if he is already engaged in such an activity when he becomes aware of his personal problems, he seeks competent professional assistance to determine whether he should continue or terminate his services to his client.

PRINCIPLE 3. MORAL AND LEGAL STANDARDS

The psychologist in the practice of his profession shows sensible regard for the social codes and moral expectations of the community in which he works, recognizing that violations of accepted moral and legal standards on his part may involve his clients, students, or colleagues in damaging personal conflicts, and impugn his own name and the reputation of his profession.

PRINCIPLE 4. MISREPRESENTATION

The psychologist avoids misrepresentation of his own professional qualifications, affiliations, and purposes, and those of the institutions and organizations with which he is associated.

a. A psychologist does not claim either directly or by implication professional qualifications that differ from his actual qualifications, nor does he misrepresent his affiliation with any institution, organization, or individual, nor lead others to assume he has affiliations that he does not have. The psychologist is responsible for correcting others who misrepresent his professional qualifications or affiliations.

b. The psychologist does not misrepresent an institution or organization with which he is affiliated by ascribing to it characteristics that it does not have.

c. A psychologist does not use his affiliation with the American Psychological Association or its Divisions for purposes that are not consonant with the stated purposes of the Association.

d. A psychologist does not associate himself with or permit his name to be used in connection with any services or products in such a way as to misrepresent them, the degree of his responsibility for them, or the nature of his affiliation.

PRINCIPLE 5. PUBLIC STATEMENTS

Modesty, scientific caution, and due regard for the limits of present knowledge characterize all statements of psychologists who supply information to the public, either directly or indirectly.

a. Psychologists who interpret the science of psychology or the services of psychologists to clients or to the general public have an obligation to report fairly and accurately. Exaggeration, sensationalism, superficiality, and other kinds of misrepresentation are avoided.

b. When information about psychological procedures and techniques is given, care is taken to indicate that they should be used only by persons adequately trained in their use.

c. A psychologist who engages in radio or television activities does not participate in commercial announcements recommending purchase or use of a product.

PRINCIPLE 6. CONFIDENTIALITY

Safeguarding information about an individual that has been obtained by the psychologist in the course of his teaching, practice, or investigation is a primary obligation of the psychologist. Such information is not communicated to others unless certain important conditions are met.

a. Information received in confidence is revealed only after most careful deliberation and when there is clear and imminent danger to an individual or to society, and then only to appropriate professional workers or public authorities.

b. Information obtained in clinical or consulting relationships, or evaluative data concerning children, students, employees, and others are discussed only for professional purposes and only with persons clearly concerned with the case. Written and oral reports should present only data germane to the purposes of the evaluation; every effort should be made to avoid undue invasion of privacy.

c. Clinical and other case materials are used in classroom teaching and writing only when the identity of the persons involved is adequately disguised.

d. The confidentiality of professional communications about individuals is maintained. Only when the originator and other persons involved give their express permission is a confidential professional communication shown to the individual concerned. The psychologist is responsible for informing the client of the limits of the confidentiality.

e. Only after explicit permission has been granted is the identity of research subjects published. When data have been published without permission for identification, the psychologist assumes responsibility for adequately disguising their sources.

f. The psychologist makes provision for the maintenance of confidentiality in the preservation and ultimate disposition of confidential records.

PRINCIPLE 7. CLIENT WELFARE

The psychologist respects the integrity and protects the welfare of the person or group with whom he is working.

a. The psychologist in industry, education, and other situations in which conflicts of interest may arise among various parties, as between management and labor, or between the client and employer of the psychologist, defines for himself the nature and direction of his loyalties and responsibilities and keeps all parties concerned informed of these commitments.

b. When there is a conflict among professional workers, the psychologist is concerned primarily with the welfare of any client involved and only secondarily with the interest of his own professional group.

c. The psychologist attempts to terminate a clinical or consulting relationship when it is reasonably clear to the psychologist that the client is not benefiting from it.

d. The psychologist who asks that an individual reveal personal information in the course of interviewing, testing, or evaluation, or who allows such information to be divulged to him, does so only after making certain that the responsible person is fully aware of the purposes of the interview, testing, or evaluation and of the ways in which the information may be used.

e. In cases involving referral, the responsibility of the psychologist for the welfare of the client continues until this responsibility is assumed by the professional person to whom the client is referred or until the relationship with the psychologist making the referral has been terminated by mutual agreement. In situations where referral, consultation, or other changes in the conditions of the treatment are indicated and the client refuses referral, the psychologist carefully weighs the

possible harm to the client, to himself, and to his profession that might ensue from continuing the relationship.

f. The psychologist who requires the taking of psychological tests for didactic, classification, or research purposes protects the examinees by insuring that the tests and test results are used in a professional manner.

g. When potentially disturbing subject matter is presented to students, it is discussed objectively, and efforts are made to handle constructively any difficulties that arise.

h. Care must be taken to insure an appropriate setting for clinical work to protect both client and psychologist from actual or imputed harm and the profession from censure.

PRINCIPLE 8. CLIENT RELATIONSHIP

The psychologist informs his prospective client of the important aspects of the potential relationship that might affect the client's decision to enter the relationship.

a. Aspects of the relationship likely to affect the client's decision include the recording of an interview, the use of interview material for training purposes, and observation of an interview by other persons.

b. When the client is not competent to evaluate the situation (as in the case of a child), the person responsible for the client is informed of the circumstances which may influence the relationship.

c. The psychologist does not normally enter into a professional relationship with members of his own family, intimate friends, close associates, or others whose welfare might be jeopardized by such a dual relationship.

PRINCIPLE 9. IMPERSONAL SERVICES

Psychological services for the purpose of diagnosis, treatment, or personalized advice are provided only in the context of a professional relationship, and are not given by means of public lectures or demonstrations, newspaper or magazine articles, radio or television programs, mail, or similar media.

   a. The preparation of personnel reports and recommendations based on test data secured solely by mail is unethical unless such appraisals are an integral part of a continuing client relationship with a company, as a result of which the consulting psychologist has intimate knowledge of the client's personnel situation and can be assured thereby that his written appraisals will be adequate to the purpose and will be properly interpreted by the client. These reports must not be embellished with such detailed analyses of the subject's personality traits as would be appropriate only after intensive interviews with the subject. The reports must not make specific recommendations as to employment or placement of the subject which go beyond the psychologist's knowledge of the job requirements of the company. The reports must not purport to eliminate the company's need to carry on such other regular employment or personnel practices as appraisal of the work history, checking of references, past performance in the company.

PRINCIPLE 10. ANNOUNCEMENT OF SERVICES

A psychologist adheres to professional rather than commercial standards in making known his availability for professional services.

   a. A psychologist does not directly solicit clients for individual diagnosis or therapy.

   b. Individual listings in telephone directories are limited to name, highest relevant degree, certification status, address, and telephone number. They

may also include identification in a few words of the psychologist's major areas of practice; for example, child therapy, personnel selection, industrial psychology. Agency listings are equally modest.

   c. Announcements of individual private practice are limited to a simple statement of the name, highest relevant degree, certification or diplomate status, address, telephone number, office hours, and a brief explanation of the types of services rendered. Announcements of agencies may list names of staff members with their qualifications. They conform in other particulars with the same standards as individual announcements, making certain that the true nature of the organization is apparent.

   d. A psychologist or agency announcing nonclinical professional services may use brochures that are descriptive of services rendered but not evaluative. They may be sent to professional persons, schools, business firms, government agencies, and other similar organizations.

   e. The use in a brochure of "testimonials from satisfied users" is unacceptable. The offer of a free trial of services is unacceptable if it operates to misrepresent in any way the nature or the efficacy of the services rendered by the psychologist. Claims that a psychologist has unique skills or unique devices not available to others in the profession are made only if the special efficacy of these unique skills or devices has been demonstrated by scientifically acceptable evidence.

   f. The psychologist must not encourage (nor, within his power, even allow) a client to have exaggerated ideas as to the efficacy of services rendered. Claims made to clients about the efficacy of his services must not go beyond those which the psychologist would be willing to subject to professional scrutiny through publishing his results and his claims in a professional journal.

PRINCIPLE 11. INTERPROFESSIONAL RELATIONS

A psychologist acts with integrity in regard to colleagues in psychology and in other professions.

a. A psychologist does not normally offer professional services to a person receiving psychological assistance from another professional worker except by agreement with the other worker or after the termination of the client's relationship with the other professional worker.

b. The welfare of clients and colleagues requires that psychologists in joint practice or corporate activities make an orderly and explicit arrangement regarding the conditions of their association and its possible termination. Psychologists who serve as employers of other psychologists have an obligation to make similar appropriate arrangements.

PRINCIPLE 12. REMUNERATION

Financial arrangements in professional practice are in accord with professional standards that safeguard the best interest of the client and the profession.

a. In establishing rates for professional services, the psychologist considers carefully both the ability of the client to meet the financial burden and the charges made by other professional persons engaged in comparable work. He is willing to contribute a portion of his services to work for which he receives little or no financial return.

b. No commission or rebate or any other form of remuneration is given or received for referral of clients for professional services.

c. The psychologist in clinical or counseling practice does not use his relationships with clients to promote, for personal gain or the profit of an agency, commercial enterprises of any kind.

d. A psychologist does not accept a private fee or any other form of remuneration for professional work with a person who is entitled to his services through an institution or agency. The policies of a particular agency may make explicit provision for private work with its clients by members of its staff, and in such instances the client must be fully apprised of all policies affecting him.

PRINCIPLE 13. TEST SECURITY

Psychological tests and other assessment devices, the value of which depends in part on the naivete of the subject, are not reproduced or described in popular publications in ways that might invalidate the techniques. Access to such devices is limited to persons with professional interests who will safeguard their use.

a. Sample items made up to resemble those of tests being discussed may be reproduced in popular articles and elsewhere, but scorable tests and actual test items are not reproduced except in professional publications.

b. The psychologist is responsible for the control of psychological tests and other devices and procedures used for instruction when their value might be damaged by revealing to the general public their specific contents or underlying principles.

PRINCIPLE 14. TEST INTERPRETATION

Test scores, like test materials, are released only to persons who are qualified to interpret and use them properly.

a. Materials for reporting test scores to parents, or which are designed for self-appraisal purposes in schools, social agencies, or industry are closely supervised by qualified psychologists or counselors with provisions for referring and counseling individuals when needed.

b. Test results or other assessment data used for evaluation or classification are communicated to employers, relatives, or other appropriate persons in such a manner as to guard against misinterpretation or misuse. In the usual case, an interpretation of the test result rather than the score is communicated.

c. When test results are communicated directly to parents and students, they are accompanied by adequate interpretive aids or advice.

PRINCIPLE 15. TEST PUBLICATION

Psychological tests are offered for commercial publication only to publishers who present their tests in a professional way and distribute them only to qualified users.

a. A test manual, technical handbook, or other suitable report on the test is provided which describes the method of constructing and standardizing the test, and summarizes the validation research.

b. The populations for which the test has been developed and the purposes for which it is recommended are stated in the manual. Limitations upon the test's dependability, and aspects of its validity on which research is lacking or incomplete, are clearly stated. In particular, the manual contains a warning regarding interpretations likely to be made which have not yet been substantiated by research.

c. The catalog and manual indicate the training or professional qualifications required for sound interpretation of the test.

d. The test manual and supporting documents take into account the principles enunciated in the *Technical Recom-*

mendations for Psychological Tests and Diagnostic Techniques.

e. Test advertisements are factual and descriptive rather than emotional and persuasive.

PRINCIPLE 16. RESEARCH PRECAUTIONS

The psychologist assumes obligations for the welfare of his research subjects, both animal and human.

a. Only when a problem is of scientific significance and it is not practicable to investigate it in any other way is the psychologist justified in exposing research subjects, whether children or adults, to physical or emotional stress as part of an investigation.

b. When a reasonable possibility of injurious aftereffects exists, research is conducted only when the subjects or their responsible agents are fully informed of this possibility and agree to participate nevertheless.

c. The psychologist seriously considers the possibility of harmful aftereffects and avoids them, or removes them as soon as permitted by the design of the experiment.

d. A psychologist using animals in research adheres to the provisions of the Rules Regarding Animals, drawn up by the Committee on Precautions and Standards in Animal Experimentation and adopted by the American Psychological Association.

PRINCIPLE 17. PUBLICATION CREDIT

Credit is assigned to those who have contributed to a publication, in proportion to their contribution, and only to these.

a. Major contributions of a professional character, made by several persons to a common project, are recognized by joint authorship. The experimenter or author who has made the principal contribution to a publication is identified as the first listed.

b. Minor contributions of a professional character, extensive clerical or similar nonprofessional assistance, and other minor contributions are acknowledged in footnotes or in an introductory statement.

c. Acknowledgment through specific citations is made for unpublished as well as published material that has directly influenced the research or writing.

d. A psychologist who compiles and edits for publication the contributions of others publishes the symposium or report under the title of the committee or symposium, with his own name appearing as chairman or editor among those of the other contributors or committee members.

PRINCIPLE 18. RESPONSIBILITY TOWARD ORGANIZATION

A psychologist respects the rights and reputation of the institution or organization with which he is associated.

a. Materials prepared by a psychologist as a part of his regular work under specific direction of his organization are the property of that organization. Such materials are released for use or publication by a psychologist in accordance with policies of authorization, assignment of credit, and related matters which have been established by his organization.

b. Other material resulting incidentally from activity supported by any agency, and for which the psychologist rightly assumes individual responsibility, is published with disclaimer for any responsibility on the part of the supporting agency.

PRINCIPLE 19. PROMOTIONAL ACTIVITIES

The psychologist associated with the development or promotion of psychological devices, books, or other products offered for commercial sale is responsible for ensuring that such devices, books, or products are presented in a professional and factual way.

a. Claims regarding performance, benefits, or results are supported by scientifically acceptable evidence.

b. The psychologist does not use professional journals for the commercial exploitation of psychological products, and the psychologist-editor guards against such misuse.

c. The psychologist with a financial interest in the sale or use of a psychological product is sensitive to possible conflict of interest in his promotion of such products and avoids compromise of his professional responsibilities and objectives.

Chapter 70

Diversity of Talent

DAEL WOLFLE

A problem of continuing concern is the extent to which we are properly developing and utilizing the nation's intellectual resources. For both realistic and practical reasons it is desirable that we make better provisions than we have in the past for the full development of human talent. The more fundamental reason is that one of the basic ideals of a free society is the provision of opportunity for each person to develop to his full capacity. This ideal has been expressed in many ways, yet from time to time we need to remind ourselves that it lies at the very cornerstone of our form of society. *The Pursuit of Excellence*, the Rockefeller report on education, of which John Gardner [5] was the principal author, phrased it this way:

> The greatness of a nation may be manifested in many ways—in its purposes, its courage, its moral responsibility, its cultural and scientific eminence, the tenor of its daily life. But ultimately the source of its greatness is in the individuals who constitute the living substance of the nation. . . .

This article is reprinted from the *American Psychologist*, 1960, with the permission of the author and the American Psychological Association.

Our devotion to a free society can only be understood in terms of these values. It is the only form of society that puts at the very top of its agenda the opportunity of the individual to develop his potentialities. It is the declared enemy of every condition that stunts the intellectual, moral, and spiritual growth of the individual. No society has ever fully succeeded in living up to the stern ideals that a free people set themselves. But only a free society can even address itself to that demanding task.[1]

The idealistic reason for fostering the full development of talent is expressed in the quotation just read. There is also an urgent practical reason: the nation has an increasing need for many kinds of highly developed talent. Earlier in our history, the most critical need was for land for an expanding agriculture and then later for financial capital for an expanding industry. But now the critical need is for men and women with ideas and highly developed talents, men and women who can teach, who can roll back the boundaries of ignorance, who can

[1] From *The Pursuit of Excellence: Education and the Future of America.* Copyright © 1958 by Rockefeller Brothers Fund, Inc. Reprinted by permission of Doubleday & Company, Inc.

manage complex organizations, who can perform the diverse and demanding tasks upon which the further development of a free, industrial society depends.

World War II marks the time at which there began to be clear recognition that the need for resources of land and capital had been surpassed by the need for resources of human talent. Prior to World War II we lived through the worst depression in our history. It was not people that we needed, but rather work for the people we had. In the years before the depression, most of the labor force was engaged in farming and in those trades and vocations that make relatively little demand upon man's higher intellectual capacities. It was in World War II that we were pinched for men and brains. It was then that we also began to recognize that invention could be deliberately planned. The scientific and engineering achievements of the war period provided dramatic evidence that some major problems could be solved and some major new inventions produced when imaginative and talented men set their minds to the task. With this wartime demonstration as a model, it seemed likely that organized research could be fruitfully applied on a large scale to industrial problems. There followed a great growth in industrial research, in industrial production, and in interest in the nation's supply of intellectual resources.

My personal involvement in the study of the nation's intellectual resources began in 1950 when I became Director of the Commission on Human Resources and Advanced Training. This commission was established by the American Council of Learned Societies, the American Council on Education, the National Academy of Sciences, and the Social Science Research Council. When the commission's report was published [12], it brought together a considerable range of information concerning the supply of talented persons in the United States, the demand for their talents, and the potential supply from which we might draw in the future. Since 1954, public interest in the problem of making fuller use of our intellectual resources has been increased by other studies, by the technological achievements of the USSR, and by a growing recognition of our obligation to help less fortunate nations climb to a higher level of industrial, educational, and personal well-being.

One of the studies of the Commission on Human Resources and Advanced Training dealt with the extent to which the United States succeeds in educating those young persons who have the intellectual capacity for higher education. Our statistics on this point have been widely used. But the figures we published in 1954 are now out of date and should be replaced. I am glad, therefore, to have the permission of Donald S. Bridgman to quote more recent figures which he has compiled and which will soon be published by the National Science Foundation.

Bridgman was one of my colleagues on the Commission on Human Resources and Advanced Training. He has continued to be interested in how many bright students we are getting, or failing to get, into college. He has considered—as have others—that students in the top 30% of the ability distribution are qualified for college work. Of young men in this ability range, Bridgman's figures show that approximately 45% now graduate from college. Of the 55% who do not, approximately one-fifth fail to finish high school, two-fifths finish high school but do not enter college, and two-fifths enter college but do not finish. Thus we are getting into college about two-thirds of the upper 30% of boys, and about two-thirds of those who enter stay to graduate.

The figures for girls show fewer completing college and more dropping out at earlier stages. Of 100 girls in the top 30% in ability, approximately 30 graduate from college. Of the 70 who do not, about 10 fail to finish high school, 40 finish high school but do not enter college, and 20 enter college but do not graduate.

Of the top 30% in general intellectual ability, for the two sexes combined, nearly 60% enter college, and close to 40% earn bachelor's or higher degrees. If we examine a smaller and more highly selected group, say the top 10% or the top 5% on the intelligence distribution, the retention rates are appreciably higher.

How should we judge these figures? If we compare them with figures from other countries, we have a right to be proud of our record. If we compare them with our own performance in earlier years, we can take pride in the improvement. But if we examine them in terms of our growing need for persons with high ability and advanced education, the current figures give us reason for concern. We should seek to increase the percentage of able young men and women who receive a higher education, but even as we seek that increase we can already foresee the limits on future improvement under our present methods of selection and education. As we look to the future, we must consider how to make better use of our resources of talent.

THE ENCOURAGEMENT OF TALENT

The obvious first response to this problem is that we should be more active in the encouragement of talented young persons. Thus Charles H. Brower [3], President of the advertising firm, Batton, Barton, Durstine, and Osborne, said recently to the Advertising Federation of America:

> I ask only that we look for talent and excellence as avidly as we look for . . . many of our less valuable natural resources. . . .
>
> Our educators, our ministers, our editors, our businessmen, our unions, and our organizations . . . should join in a mammoth talent hunt to uncover [the] treasure of brains which . . . is hiding in unlikely places all over America.

In actuality, a talent hunt has long characterized both the American culture and a number of other cultures. Part of this hunt has been systematically organized; much of it has been informal, unorganized, and on an individual basis.

Walter Bingham once told me that he approached the end of high school with no thought of entering college. One day one of his teachers took him aside and planted the idea that led him to enroll at Kansas University the following fall. I wonder how often a similar scene has occurred in the early lives of men and women who later entered the professional or learned fields. George Beadle, who was awarded the 1958 Nobel Prize in Physiology and Medicine, tells an almost identical story: a Nebraska farm boyhood, a father uninterested in higher education, and an inspiring teacher who urged the future Nobel laureate to enter the University of Nebraska. There must be many other eminent men and women who could tell similar stories: bright, industrious students with potentialities far exceeding the range of vision acquired from home and community, whose sights were lifted by a teacher or an older friend who took the trouble to encourage talent. I am glad that Bingham told me how he was encouraged to go to college, for perhaps that experience helps to explain his abiding interest in the identification and encouragement of talented youngsters.

The incident also illustrates the principle to which I wish to give first attention. The principle is this: talent requires encouragement. Certainly there are exceptions, or at least apparent exceptions: each of us could name greatly gifted men who rose from poor surroundings, overcoming great obstacles, seemingly driven by a force that no hardships and no obstacles could impede. There may be exceptions, but it is neither safe nor realistic to assume that high ability is always accompanied by high motivation, that human talent will override obstacles to find its own way to fruition. Nor is it safe to assume that the necessary inspiration or encouragement will always be provided by the family.

In an illuminating study of the role of personal encouragement in the lives of bright students, Swanson [11] interviewed men who, some twenty years earlier, had been superior high school seniors. Some of these men had gone to college; others had quit at the end of high school. Swanson tried to find out what influences had determined which of these men had gone to college and which had not. One of the clearest differences was the simple fact that someone—a teacher, a minister, a relative, or a friend—had encouraged some of the men to go to college, while others could not recall that anyone had ever suggested that they should continue formal education beyond high school. Certainly other factors than this one were involved; much besides a few conversations on the topic determines how long a student stays in school. But it is significant that the men who went to college were usually actively encouraged to do so, sometimes encouraged by several people, while those who did not enter college could not recall this kind of personal encouragement.

Walter Bingham might or might not have attended college had his teacher not encouraged him. I think perhaps he might, for another story of his youth shows a character already marked by determination and self-confidence. He made straight A's his first year in college, a good record for a 16-year-old boy who was the youngest student on the campus. But he established no firm friendships and did not want to return to Kansas University. Where should he go? He applied to two colleges, he told me. One promptly accepted him; the other did not reply. When summer came to an end and it was again time to go off to college, in which direction should he head: to the college that had accepted him or to the one that had ignored him? The safe and cautious solution would have been to go to the college that had accepted him, but young Walter was more venturesome. He concluded that the college that was eager to have him must not have many good students and that the college that did not seem to care whether he came or not must therefore be the better institution. So, off he went to Beloit, the college that had not acknowledged his application, but that did accept him on arrival and that turned his

interest toward psychology. I suspect that a 17-year-old boy who possessed the self-assurance evident in this decision might well have gone to college anyway, whether or not a particular teacher had urged him. But we cannot be sure. Perhaps we are able to honor Bingham because we are in reality also honoring the high school teacher who recognized his talent and encouraged him to develop it.

Anecdotes are useful if they illustrate a significant principle, but it is time to return to the principle: talent requires encouragement if it is to reach its full development. The encouragement may come from parents or other interested individuals, or encouragement may be built into the customs and traditions that characterize a particular social group. Scotland has produced an unusually large number of notable men. This high intellectual productivity has been explained as resulting from widespread interest among the Scots in seeking out and encouraging talent. Whether this explanation would withstand critical analysis, I do not know, but that there are major differences in intellectual productivity among different social and ethnic groups is completely clear.

SOCIAL FACTORS IN TALENT DEVELOPMENT

About ten years ago the Social Science Research Council's Committee on the Identification of Talent began an investigation of some of these differences. The committee received a substantial grant from the John and Mary R. Markle Foundation and decided that this grant should not be used in attempts to improve aptitude tests or other existing methods of identifying talent, but should rather be used to investigate some of the social conditions that help to determine how talent manifests itself and how it is stunted or made to blossom. One of the studies that we supported was by Fred Strodtbeck [10]. Strodtbeck started by selecting a number of bright, teen-age boys. Half were Jewish, half Italian. He then set out to analyze the Italian-Jewish cultural differences and to determine how these differences influence the aspirations and education of growing boys. This he did by studying the values that characterized the thinking of the families of each of his subjects, and the patterns of social interaction among the father, the mother, and the bright son. He found that in a number of quite detailed respects Jews have values more likely to promote high achievement than do Italians and that there is greater agreement among Jewish family members on these values.

I do not want to go into detail concerning Strodtbeck's study, but I cite it as an example of the possibility of investigating the social factors that influence the extent to which potentially high ability will actually be developed. I might have cited other studies, such as the Quincy (Illinois) Youth Development Project of Robert F. De Haan and Robert J. Havighurst, or the different approach of Anne Roe, or the still different work of Samuel Stouffer. Instead of extending this list, let me merely call attention to the importance of learning more than we now know about the social conditions that influence the development and utilization of talent. We need better information concerning the family as a social system, the school as a social system, and the ways in which these social systems encourage talent or hinder its development.

POLICY FOR TALENT DEVELOPMENT

The encouragement of talent is clearly desirable, and so is the better understanding of the social conditions that aid or hinder its development, both because the individual with talent is thus more likely to reach closer to his full potential and because the nation is more likely to gain the advantage of his high ability. But it is not sufficient simply to say that we should encourage talent wherever we find it. There is an additional, and psychologically more interesting, question to take up.

This psychologically more interesting question has to do with the development of an underlying policy or strategy of talent development. If one of us were suddenly assigned responsibility for developing a national policy of talent development, I wonder what he would do. No single one of us is likely to be given this responsibility, but collectively it is shared by many persons, whether they realize it or not. Every person who constructs or interprets a test or other measure for the selection of scholarship or fellowship winners, every college admissions officer, every guidance counselor, every educational philosopher or administrator, and every teacher daily makes decisions that in fact do help to determine how the nation's intellectual resources are developed and utilized. Their actions constitute our unanalyzed, but nonetheless determining, present policy.

We have, in the past, concerned ourselves chiefly with the techniques of identifying talented persons and furthering their education. So long as our work is controlled primarily by technique, the major directions will be determined by the techniques themselves, the criteria that we find most reliable, and relevant statistical and experimental considerations. These factors should continue to concern us. But by themselves they are not enough. It is time to give consideration to questions of social value, purpose, or ultimate objective. I suggest that it is time for those of us who are professionally most concerned to consider the policy issues and to try to develop a strategy that will maximize the achievement and social value of the persons whose talents we seek to identify and develop.

Two aspects of such a policy are obvious. First is the desirability of encouraging the full development of all forms of socially useful talent. Of this point I have already spoken. Second is the need for a better understanding of the social and cultural factors that stimulate or retard the development of talent. Of the need for research I have also spoken.

After these two points, what comes next?

In addition to identifying talented young-sters and helping them to secure an edu-cation commensurate with their abilities, in addition to conducting research, we must also consider how the talent we are devel-oping can be so distributed as to result in the greatest accomplishment. The recom-mendation that I will make on this point is likely to be controversial. In order to point up the issue clearly, I will start with what may seem to be an extreme point of view.

THE VALUE OF DIVERSITY

In the selection and education of persons of ability, it is advantageous to a society to seek the greatest achievable diversity of talent: diversity within an individual, among the members of an occupational group, and among the individuals who constitute a society.

In speaking of diversity among individ-uals, I am using words in their ordinary meaning; but when I speak of diversity within an individual, the expression sounds strange. There is no customary term for the idea I am trying to express, for the ad-jectives with good connotations mean the opposite of what I am trying to say. I am not talking about the well-rounded individ-ual, or the broad scholar, or the man of many talents. These are qualities we ordi-narily respect; but I wish to make a case for the opposite, for the man who has developed some of his talents so highly that he cannot be well-rounded, for the one who may be called uneven or one-sided but in whom at least one side has been developed to the level of real superiority. For the sake of symmetry with the concept of diversity among individuals, I have called this kind of development diversity within an indi-vidual. If the expression still seems strange, its meaning will become clearer as we go along.

One further explanation is essential. I do not wish to maximize variance or diversity by having some persons very bright and others very dull. Obviously we want each person to reach the highest level of which he is capable. But even if we were doing as well as we know how to do in the identi-fication and education of talented persons, the problem of optimal deployment of their various talents would still be a question of undiminished psychological and social in-terest. Even under these circumstances, a strong case can be made for the proposition that the value of a nation's intellectual re-sources—or the total achievement—would be maximized by maximizing the variety of abilities within and among individuals. This is not a new idea; but the point needs repe-tition and also needs analysis, for even though we agree upon the value of diver-sity, strong forces are constantly at work in the opposite direction. These forces tend to make us more, rather than less, alike and tend to prevent the uneven development of a talented individual.

Many of the methods that have been developed for dealing with people in groups have the effect of reducing the vari-ability among the group members. Ex-amples are the use of uniform lesson assign-ments and the use of general aptitude measures and the average grade or the rank in class as devices for selecting students for the next higher educational level. Ad-vertising procedures, trade union policies, wage scales, and a variety of other forces also work in the direction of uniformity rather than diversity. These tendencies are supported by popular attitudes that place a premium on uniformity and conformity rather than upon diversity and individ-uality. Lyle Spencer quotes the mother of three bright children as saying: "I'm not interested in geniuses, all I want to do is to raise my kids to be normal, well-adjusted adults." Many parents would agree; they want their children to be like other chil-dren, and not to be different. Teachers, too, sometimes express this attitude. De Haan and Havighurst [4] quote a teacher as say-ing: "When I am finished with my class in June, the slow children are a little faster, and the fast have slowed down a bit."

Years ago, Truman Kelley protested this

attitude and leveled his guns against school teachers and officials who exhibit it. He called them pedagogical plainsmen and accused them of preferring intellectual plains to intellectual hills and valleys. They were, he wrote, so obsessed with averages and norms that they devoted themselves to ". . . the weary process of shovelling to fill valleys and steady erosion to remove mountains of human capacity."

Had Harold Benjamin not already preempted the title, I might have called this address "The Cultivation of Idiosyncrasy," for the major point of my argument is that the cultivation of diversity is desirable both for the individual young persons whose futures lie in our hands and for the society in which they will live and work. I cannot use Benjamin's title, but I can quote a few of his paragraphs [1]. The wit and humor with which he approached serious problems has illuminated many an educational discussion, and the fable he used in opening the Inglis lecture at Harvard in 1949 illustrates the point I want to make. The fable is the story of the school in the woods.

All the animals had to take all the subjects. Swimming, running, jumping, climbing, and flying made up the required curriculum. . . .

Some animals, of course, were better students than others. The squirrel, for example, got straight A's from the first in running, jumping, and climbing. He got a good passing grade, moreover, in swimming. It looked as though he would make Phi Beta Kappa in his junior year, but he had trouble with flying. Not that he was unable to fly. He could fly. He climbed to the top of tree after tree and sailed through the air to neighboring trees with ease. As he modestly observed, he was a flying squirrel by race. The teacher of flying pointed out, however, that the squirrel was always losing altitude in his gliding and insisted that he should take off in the approved fashion from the ground. Indeed, the teacher decided that the taking-off-from-the-ground unit had to be mastered first, as was logical, and so he drilled the

squirrel day after day on the take-off. . . .

The squirrel tried hard. He tried so hard he got severe Charley horses in both hind legs, and thus crippled he became incapable even of running, jumping, or climbing. He left school a failure, and died soon thereafter of starvation, being unable to gather and store nuts.

Benjamin continued the fable to relate the difficulties of the snake, the eagle, and the gopher. I shall quote only the story of the eagle.

The eagle was a truly brilliant student. His flying was superb, his running and jumping were of the best, and he even passed the swimming test, although the teacher tried to keep him from using his wings too much. By employing his talons and beak, moreover, he could climb after a fashion and no doubt he would have been able to pass that course, too, except that he always flew to the top of the problem tree or cliff when the teacher's back was turned and sat there lazily in the sun, preening his feathers and staring arrogantly down at his fellow students climbing up the hard way. The teachers reasoned with him to no avail. He would not study climbing seriously. At first he turned aside the faculty's importunities with relatively mild wisecracks and innuendoes, but as the teachers put more pressure upon him he reacted with more and more feeling . . . [and finally quit school altogether].

I wonder how many human students have been similarly frustrated and had their talents stunted by being required to climb slowly step by step, instead of being encouraged to soar rapidly to the heights of which they were capable.

I have said that it is socially valuable to maximize diversity. Now let me try to prove the point. I should like to be able to give a rigorous proof; for, if the assertion is correct, there flow from it a number of implications for the professional work of psychologists, guidance counselors, teachers, and all who deal professionally with the identification, education, and utilization of talented persons. The proof cannot be rigorous, for we do not have adequate measures of amount of talent, of achievement, or of the social value of achievement. But it is possible to analyze these variables and to examine their interrelationships. The exercise leads convincingly to the conclusion that maximum diversity results in maximum social value.

Let us start the analysis with two points on which there is general agreement. The first is that individuals vary in the total amount of talent or ability they possess. This simple statement overlooks the whole nature-nurture problem, the effects of education, and all of the difficulties of measuring talent. Moreover, it oversimplifies the whole matter by treating ability as a trait that an individual possesses rather than as an attribute of the behavior he exhibits. Nevertheless, to say that different individuals possess different total amounts of ability is a convenient way of stating an idea that is generally accepted.

The second point is that ability is not a unitary trait but expresses itself in various forms or special abilities. We may side with L. L. Thurstone in believing that a relatively small number of more or less independent primary abilities provide a satisfactory description of human ability, or we may side with Godfrey Thompson in postulating a large number of highly specialized abilities. For our purpose, it makes little difference which of these positions one prefers. All that is essential is that we agree that ability is a many-sided affair and that an individual may be better in one kind of ability than he is in another.

Now let us suppose that an individual could distribute his ability over various kinds of performances in any way he preferred. Within limits, this is a reasonable proposition, for each individual does exercise some control. If a student neglects the academic subjects in order to practice on the piano, he will become a better pianist, and a poorer scholar. Alternatively, he can concentrate on something else and neglect the piano entirely. Students constantly

make educational decisions, allocate study time, choose schools, select reading matter, or neglect their studies. All such decisions influence the extent to which one or another ability will be developed.

Now let us move from this realistic situation to its unrealistic limit, and to simplify the task let us arbitrarily assign some numbers to the situation. Suppose that a given individual has 1,000 units of ability—another individual might have more or fewer—and let us suppose that he can distribute these 1,000 units in any way he chooses over 20 different kinds of ability. If he wishes to be a completely well-rounded individual, he would assign 50 units to each of the 20 abilities. Or, he might select the 10 kinds of ability that he thinks most important and assign 100 units to each, neglecting completely the other 10 kinds of ability because they seem to him to be unimportant. Or, at the extreme, as a kind of talent gambler, he might stake his whole 1,000 units on one kind of ability and neglect the other 19 completely. Which of these ways of distributing his total talent fund would be best for the individual?

A parallel question can be asked from the point of view of society. Suppose that society rather than the individual decides how the 1,000 units will be distributed. Which would best serve society: to assign 50 units to each of 20 different kinds of ability, 100 units to each of 10 kinds, or the whole 1,000 units to a single ability?

We cannot answer these questions without considering the values involved. In real life, these values are often conflicting. The eminent young mathematician has to help care for the children, occasionally to repair the lawn mower, and take his turn in helping to run the affairs of the local Boy Scout troop. As a mathematician, he might like to concentrate all of his units of ability on mathematics. But as a human being with other interests, he has to save some of those units for other and quite nonmathematical kinds of ability and achievement. In real life, many conflicting value considerations are involved, but let us neglect them for the time being and concentrate on the problem of maximizing the social value of human talents.

The value that society places upon different levels of accomplishment does not vary directly with the amount of achievement or its underlying ability, but increases more rapidly than does the amount. A graph relating amount of talent and its social value would be a curve rather than a straight line—doubling the amount of ability more than doubles its value; doubling again the amount again more than doubles the value. The relationship can be illustrated with some arbitrary numbers: if one unit of ability is worth one dollar to society, 50 units are worth more than $50; perhaps 50 units are worth $100. Similarly for larger amounts, 100 units may be worth $500, and 1,000 units may be so valuable as to be priceless. These particular numbers are arbitrary, but that the relationship is non-linear is clear. The salaries paid to chemists or engineers or members of other professions are not symmetrically distributed about a mean. The distributions are skewed, with a longer tail above the mean than below it. Moreover, there is general recognition that the salaries paid to the ablest people fall far short of being commensurate with their ability. On the ordinary scale of salaries for writers, physicists, and public servants, we make no effort to pay appropriate salaries to a Shakespeare, an Einstein, or a Winston Churchill.

We use other means to compensate outstanding persons whose salaries are not commensurate with their ability. We award Gold Medals to Olympic winners, Nobel Prizes to great scientists, Pulitzer Prizes to outstanding authors and editors, and we have other honors with which we recognize excellence in other fields. Partly by the amounts of money paid for different levels of ability and partly in other forms of compensation, society demonstrates that the value it places on talent increases more rapidly than does the amount of talent.

Now we can return to the question of the most valuable way of distributing talents.

From the standpoint of society, the best way to distribute talent is to take maximum advantage of differences in aptitude, interest, and motivation by having each individual concentrate on the thing he can do best. Instead of having the 1,000-unit man distribute his ability 50 units on each of 20 kinds of ability or 100 units on each of 10, have him concentrate the whole 1,000 units on a single ability. In Harold Benjamin's fable, have the eagle be the best flyer in the world and forget about his ability to swim or climb, have the squirrel be the best climber in the world and stop worrying about his inability to fly. In human affairs, follow the same principle. Have one man be the best he can possibly become in one line and another the best he can possibly become in another line. Thus we would have the best physicist, the best poet, the best mathematician, and the best dramatist possible. The total value of the talents so distributed would be incomparably greater than would be the value of the same number of units of talent spread more uniformly over the different men and the different abilities involved.

Recommending that each person be helped to achieve the highest level he can reach in the area in which he has the greatest talent and interest is not the same as recommending that every scholar be a narrow specialist. Some, however, should be specialists, and some should specialize in relatively narrow fields. Physics is generally recognized as the most highly developed science. Further advances are most likely to be made by physicists who concentrate on a particular area of physics. Thus we want highly specialized physicists. But we also want physicists of wider interest and knowledge: persons who can bridge the gaps between physics and biology or physics and other sciences, persons who are interested in the practical applications of physical principles, and persons who are interested in attempting to translate physics into terms that the rest of us can try to understand. This diversity among physicists is essential if physics itself is to advance and if other fields of intellectual and practical endeavor are to benefit maximally from those advances.

From the standpoint of social value, maximum diversity would be the ideal; but like many another ideal, it is unattainable. In real life we must recognize that the best mathematician in the world must do something besides mathematics and that the best poet cannot spend all his energy on poetry. But the fact that the extreme case is unrealistic does not destroy the principle. The principle is this, and I state it now in realistic rather than imaginary terms: to the extent that we can control the distribution of talent, it is socially desirable to maximize the diversity, both within and among individuals.

This is the ideal. Before we consider methods of reaching toward that ideal, it is worthwhile briefly to look at its opposite, for then we will have set the boundaries within which we can maneuver in our educational and guidance practices.

In *Brave New World*, Aldous Huxley [7] described a society in which most individuals were born as members of batches. Born, you will remember, is not the right word; old-fashioned human birth had been replaced by a kind of controlled embryology in which any desired number of identical individuals could be developed from a single fertilized egg. The eggs were developed in vitro, and at the proper time babies, instead of being born, were decanted. Through controlled nutrition, and through proper training and education, the members of a batch could be made to have any desired level of ability, and all the members of a batch were as alike as identical twins that had been reared together. We can dismiss *Brave New World* as satirical exaggeration; but we cannot dismiss the kind of society that Huxley was satirizing, for there are forces in society that tend in the direction of homogeneity, and there are cultural values that make homogeneity seem desirable.

Between the unreality of *Brave New World* and the unreality of maximum diversity there is a wide range. Within this range we have considerable room to choose the kind of society we want ours to be. Ultimately the essential choices will be made by the nation as a whole, through the processes of democratic action. But in a more immediate sense, and on the important aspect of talent distribution, choices must be made by those persons who are professionally engaged in the development and handling of talent.

As to how far we should go in the direction of diversity, I have only two suggestions, and both must be stated in general terms. One is that we should go as far as we can. The other is that the greater the ability with which we are dealing, the greater is the amount of idiosyncrasy we can tolerate. The brief and brilliant career of the Indian mathematician Ramanujan [9] illustrates both principles. The name may be strange, for Ramanujan was a mathematicians' mathematician and was little known outside of mathematical circles. Yet he has been described as ". . . quite the most extraordinary mathematician of our time." At the age of 15, he was loaned a copy of Carr's *Synopsis of Pure Mathematics*. This was all he had, and all he needed, to start him off on a strange, unorthodox, and inspired career of mathematical innovation. Working completely alone, he rediscovered much that had been developed by earlier mathematicians; he followed some false leads and made some mistakes; but in some fields of mathematics his power and originality went beyond any other mathematician in the world.

On the basis of his obvious brilliance, he was given a scholarship; but he lost it at the end of the first term because he failed his examination in English. He never did earn a university degree; but at the age of 25, after working for some years as a clerk, he was given a fellowship at Cambridge where he went to work with G. H. Hardy. Hardy faced the problem of deciding how much he should let Ramanujan go his own way, and how much he should try to correct his mistakes and make him into a more orthodox mathematician. Hardy expressed his dilemma in these words:

It was impossible to ask such a man to submit to systematic instruction, to try to learn mathematics from the beginning once more. I was afraid too that, if I insisted unduly on matters which Ramanujan found irksome, I might destroy his confidence or break the spell of his inspiration. On the other hand there were things of which it was impossible that he should remain in ignorance. . . . It was impossible to let him go through life supposing that all the zeros of the Zeta-function were real.

The moral of the story is that, if we are dealing with a Ramanujan, we can put up with a great deal of eccentricity; if we are dealing with a lesser mind, we can insist on more conformity. Even with a Ramanujan there is a limit, but let us in all cases push that limit as far out as we can.

IMPLICATIONS

Let me now briefly suggest some of the implications of the principle that it is socially valuable to increase the diversity of talent. Each of these implications relates to practices that are under our professional control.

The first implication is that it is desirable to make wider use of tests of special ability or aptitude to supplement our tests of general ability. De Haan and Havighurst [4] found, in a survey of 40 school systems, that nearly all used tests of general intellectual ability as a means of appraising the potential of their students, but only three used tests of special aptitudes. Failure to use special tests increases the danger of overlooking students with unusually high potential in art, music, creative writing, and other abilities that are not well measured by the usual tests of general intellectual aptitude.

A second implication is that it is desirable to increase the use of separate scores for separate types of ability and to decrease the use of single scores that represent the sum or combination of several part scores. When students are being selected for awards or for admission to the next higher educational level, global measures are the easiest ones to use. Moreover, global measures are the ones that are likely to give the highest validity coefficients. Most of our usual measures of success are factorially complex and can be better predicted by factorially complex tests than by factorially simpler ones.

We pay a price, however, for the ease of use and for the higher validity of general measures of aptitude. The price we pay for using general measures is that we reduce the apparent size of the pool of talent on which we can draw. Relying solely on tests of general intellectual aptitude reduces the size of the talent pool because various kinds of ability, although usually positively correlated with one another, are by no means perfectly correlated. In the Quincy youth development study, selection of the top 10% of the children in general intellectual ability, the top 10% in leadership, and the top 2% in drawing ability included 16% of the total population. The authors estimate that, had they also included the top 10% each in music, dramatic ability, creative writing, and mechanical ability, they would have brought into their talent development program 20–25% of the total child population [4].

In Kenneth Little's study [8] of Wisconsin high school graduates, he used the usual measures of high school grades and general intelligence. But he went beyond these measures by asking the teachers to identify those of their students who were specially gifted in any field. About 20% of the students so identified had not ranked in the upper quarter of their graduating class in either general scholastic achievement or general mental ability. Included were students whom the teachers identified as being specially gifted in art, music, science, and other fields. Clearly the use of tests of special aptitude and the use of individual grades and scores rather than averages identifies a larger number of talented young persons and thus lays the basis for the development of a larger and more diversified talent pool.

An opportunity to use the more detailed information made available by separate scores is found in the award of scholarships and fellowships. The person who is high on every score and thus high on the sum or average of his scores should, of course, be encouraged to continue his education, and such students clearly merit awards, scholarships, and fellowships. But when we drop down a step or two below the generally superior level, we still tend to base awards on the average score instead of looking for evidence of exceptionally high merit in individual fields or abilities. I would suggest that in awarding scholarships when we reach this slightly lower general level, we make some of the awards to students who have earned very high marks on individual tests or measures of ability. We will probably experience some lowering of validity coefficients, we may make awards to a few unproductive eccentrics; but we will enhance our chances of picking up a few persons so highly gifted and so intensely interested along one line that they have neglected, or rebelliously disdained, to keep pace with their fellows in other lines.

A third implication is that the patterning of abilities should be avoided in the selection or guidance of persons entering or contemplating entering a particular occupation. You may recall the long history of unsuccessful efforts to find the optimal pattern of abilities and personality traits that characterize the successful members of an occupational group. No one has stated the hope for such patterns better than Clark Hull [6], who, thirty years ago, pointed out that vocational guidance would be easy if we had measures of the various kinds of ability and if we had carried out the analyses necessary to determine the weight with which each type of ability enters into the determination of success in each of a variety of occupations. Under the system

that Hull anticipated, an applicant for vocational guidance would be given a battery of tests that measured all of the major types of ability. His scores on these tests would be fed into a computer which already contained in its storage unit the regression weights of each ability on each of a variety of occupations. The sum of the products of the ability scores and the corresponding regression weights for a given occupation would then be automatically computed and would represent the applicant's predicted standard score for success in that occupation. With a modern computer, it would be possible to determine very quickly the predicted standard scores for success in each of a large number of occupations.

In the days since Hull wrote this description, the necessary computers have reached a high stage of development; tests of different kinds of ability have been improved, although not nearly so much as the computers. But we have also learned enough about ability, vocations, and the factors that make for success to have concluded that the kind of differential prediction that Hull described is not feasible. A major reason is that relatively diverse patterns of ability are consistent with success in a single vocation. Any professional field includes opportunities for such a variety of persons—persons differing in abilities and differing in personality traits—that there is no simple or single pattern that is either essential or sufficient. Consider engineering, or medicine, or psychology, or any other field of work that demands intellectual ability. Each title covers a wide variety of tasks; each field includes opportunities for a wide variety of persons.

The search for a pattern characteristic of each profession has failed. As I have considered this failure, I have become convinced that we were on the wrong track in looking for distinctive patterns. For law, medicine, engineering, psychology, and other fields are enriched by having within their ranks a wide range of patterns of ability.

CONCLUSION

It would be possible to present other implications of the values of diversity, implications for the guidance and for the education of talented students. A general discussion of these fields would take far too long, and I will refrain, for now it is time to conclude. The needs of the nation for highly developed talent are growing and will continue to grow. This is an inevitable feature of the kind of complex, industrialized, specialized society in which we live. If we are to make full use of our intellectual resources, the first requisite is that we employ all the means at our command to encourage the development of talent. The second requisite is that we learn more about the social factors that aid or impede the development of talent.

I expect that these two points are non-controversial. I am not so sure about the third point that I have advanced. Some of you may disagree with part or all of what I have said about the strategy of optimal distribution or deployment of talent. I readily grant the privilege of disagreement, for you have given me the opportunity to argue that we should go beyond personal action and beyond scientific research to consider the question of how our professional activities concerned with talent can be supported and unified by an underlying policy of talent development—a policy that seeks to maximize achievement and thus to maximize the value to society of our resources of talent.

What I have attempted to do is to state the first principles of a strategy of talent development, a strategy that provides a unifying rationale for our efforts to improve the construction and interpretation of tests, and the counseling, guidance, and education of talented young minds. The strategy is one of increasing the diversity of talent, in an individual, within an occupation, and in society. There will always be counter-pressures that must be respected; but to the extent that we succeed in increasing the diversity of talent, we will have increased its value to society.

REFERENCES

1. BENJAMIN, H. *The cultivation of idiosyncrasy.* Cambridge, Mass.: Harvard Univer. Press, 1955.
2. BRIDGMAN, D. S. *Losses of intellectual talent from the educational system prior to graduation from college.* Washington, D.C.: NSF, in press.
3. BROWER, C. H. The year of the rat. Address to Advertising Federation of America, Boston, February 9, 1960.
4. DE HAAN, R. F., & HAVIGHURST, R. J. *Educating gifted children.* Chicago: Univer. Chicago Press, 1957.
5. GARDNER, J. W., et al. *The pursuit of excellence: Education and the future of America.* (The "Rockefeller" report on education) Garden City, N.Y.: Doubleday, 1958.
6. HULL, C. L. *Aptitude testing.* Yonkers-on-Hudson, N.Y.: World Book, 1928.
7. HUXLEY, A. *Brave new world.* Garden City, N.Y.: Doubleday, Doran, 1932.
8. LITTLE, J. K. A state-wide inquiry into decisions of youth about education beyond high school. Univer. of Wisconsin, 1958.
9. NEWMAN, J. R. Srinivasa Ramanujan. In *Lives in science.* New York: Simon & Schuster, 1957. Pp. 257–269.
10. STRODTBECK, F. L. Family interaction, values, and achievement. In D. C. McClelland, et al., *Talent and society.* Princeton, N.J.: Van Nostrand, 1958. Pp. 135–194.
11. SWANSON, E. O. Is college education worthwhile? *J. counsel. Psychol.*, 1955, **2,** 176–181.
12. WOLFLE, D. *America's resources of specialized talent.* New York: Harper, 1954.

Chapter 71

How to Cheat on Personality Tests

WILLIAM H. WHYTE, JR.

The important thing to recognize is that you don't win a good score: you avoid a bad one. What a bad score would be depends upon the particular profile the company in question intends to measure you against, and this varies according to companies and according to the type of work. Your score is usually rendered in terms of your percentile rating—that is, how you answer questions in relation to how other people have answered them. Sometimes it is perfectly all right for you to score in the 80th or 90th percentile; if you are being tested, for example, to see if you would make a good chemist, a score indicating that you are likely to be more reflective than ninety out of a hundred adults might not harm you and might even do you some good.

By and large, however, your safety lies in getting a score somewhere between the 40th and 60th percentiles, which is to say, you should try to answer as if you were like

everybody else is supposed to be. This is not always too easy to figure out, of course, and this is one of the reasons why I will go into some detail in the following paragraphs on the principal types of questions. When in doubt, however, there are two general rules you can follow: (1) When asked for word associations or comments about the world, give the most conventional, run-of-the-mill, pedestrian answer possible. (2) To settle on the most beneficial answer to any question, repeat to yourself:

a. I loved my father and my mother, but my father a little bit more.
b. I like things pretty well the way they are.
c. I never worry much about anything.
d. I don't care for books or music much.
e. I love my wife and children.
f. I don't let them get in the way of company work.

Now to specifics. The following questions are examples of the ordinary, garden variety of self-report question:

This article is reprinted from *The Organization Man,* 1956, with the permission of Simon and Schuster, Inc.

Have you enjoyed reading books as much as having company in?

Are you sometimes afraid of failure?

Do you sometimes feel self-conscious?

Does it annoy you to be interrupted in the middle of your work?

Do you prefer serious motion pictures about famous historical personalities to musical comedies?

Generally speaking, they are designed to reveal your degree of introversion or extroversion, your stability, and such. While it is true that in these "inventory" types of tests there is not a right or wrong answer to any *one* question, cumulatively you can get yourself into a lot of trouble if you are not wary. You can easily see what is being asked for in questions such as the first or third.

Stay in character.   The trick is to mediate yourself a score as near the norm as possible without departing too far from your own true self. It won't necessarily hurt you, for example, to say that you have enjoyed reading books as much as having company in. It will hurt you, however, to answer every such question in that vein if you are, in fact, the kind that does enjoy books and a measure of solitude. Strive for the happy mean; on one hand, recognize that a display of too much introversion, a desire for reflection, or sensitivity is to be avoided. On the other hand, don't overcompensate. If you try too hard to deny these qualities in yourself, you'll end so far on the other end of the scale as to be rated excessively insensitive or extroverted. If you are somewhat introverted, then, don't strive to get yourself in the 70th or 80th percentile for extroversion, but merely try to get up into the 40th percentile.

Since you will probably be taking not one, but a battery of tests, you must be consistent. The tester will be comparing your extroversion score on one test with, say, your sociability score on another, and if these don't correlate the way the tables say they should, suspicion will be aroused. Even

when you are taking only one test, consistency is important. Many contain built-in L ("lie") scores, and woe betide you if you answer some questions as if you were a life of the party type and others as if you were an excellent follower. Another pitfall to avoid is giving yourself the benefit of the doubt on all questions in which one answer is clearly preferable to another, viz.: "Do you frequently daydream?" In some tests ways have been worked out to penalize you for this. (By the same token, occasionally you are given credit for excessive frankness. But you'd better not count on it.)

Be emphatic to the values of the test maker.   A question might ask: "Do you prefer serious motion pictures about famous historical personalities to musical comedies?" If you answer this question honestly you are quite likely to get a good score for the wrong reasons. If you vote for the musical comedies, you are given a credit for extroversion. It might be, of course, that you are a very thoughtful person who dislikes the kind of pretentious, self-consciously arty "prestige" pictures which Hollywood does badly, and rather enjoy the musical comedies which it does well. The point illustrated here is that, before answering such questions, you must ask yourself which of the alternatives the testmaker, not yourself, would regard as the more artistic.

Choose your neurosis.   Be very much on your guard when you come across questions such as the following, where you are asked to indicate whether you agree, disagree or are uncertain.

a. I am going to Hell.
b. I often get pink spots all over.
c. The sex act is repulsive.
d. I like strong-minded women.
e. Strange voices speak to me.
f. My father is a tyrant.

Such questions were originally a by-product of efforts to screen mentally disturbed people; they measure degrees of neurotic tendency and were meant mainly for use in mental institutions and psychiatric clinics. The Organization has no business at all to throw these questions at you, but its curiosity is powerful and some companies have been adopting these tests as standard. Should you find yourself being asked about spiders, Oedipus complexes, and such, you must, even more than in the previous type of test, remain consistent and as much in character as possible—these tests almost always have lie scores built into them. A few mild neuroses conceded here and there won't give you too bad a score, and in conceding neuroses you should know that more often than not you have the best margin for error if you err on the side of being "hypermanic"—that is, too energetic and active.

Don't be too dominant. A question which asks you what you would do if somebody barged in ahead of you in a store, is fairly typical of the kind of questions designed to find out how passive or dominant you may be. As always, the middle course is best. Resist the temptation to show yourself as trying to control each situation. You might think companies would prefer that characteristic to passivity, but they often regard it as a sign that you wouldn't be a permissive kind of leader. To err slightly on the side of acquiescence will rarely give you a bad score.

Incline to conservatism. Questions such as the following, which ask you to comment on a variety of propositions, yield a measure of how conservative or radical your views are.

   a. Prostitution should be state supervised.
   b. Modern art should not be allowed in churches.
   c. It is worse for a woman to have extramarital relations than for a man.
   d. Foreigners are dirtier than Americans.
   e. "The Star-Spangled Banner" is difficult to sing properly.

To go to either extreme earns you a bad score, but in most situations you should resolve any doubts you have on a particular question by deciding in favor of the accepted.

Similarly with word associations. In the following questions, each word in small capitals is followed by four words, ranging from the conventional to the somewhat unusual. You are asked to underline the word you think goes best with the word in small capitals.

   a. UMBRELLA (rain, prepared, cumbersome, appeasement)
   b. RED (hot, color, stain, blood)
   c. GRASS (green, mow, lawn, court)
   d. NIGHT (dark, sleep, moon, morbid)
   e. NAKED (nude, body, art, evil)
   f. AUTUMN (fall, leaves, season, sad)

The trouble here is that if you are not a totally conventional person you may be somewhat puzzled as to what the conventional response is. Here is one tip: before examining any one question closely and reading it from left to right, read vertically through the whole list of questions and you may well see a definite pattern. In making up tests, testers are thinking of ease in scoring, and on some test forms the most conventional responses will be found in one column, the next most conventional in the next, and so on. All you have to do then is go down the list and pick, alternately, the most conventional, and the second most conventional. Instead of a high score for emotionalism, which you might easily get were you to proceed on your own, you earn a stability score that will indicate "normal ways of thinking."

Don't split hairs. When you come to hypothetical situations designed to test your judgment, you have come to the toughest of all questions. In this kind there are correct answers, and the testers make no bones about it. Restricted as the choice is, however, determining which are the correct ones is extremely difficult, and the more intelligent you are the more difficult. One tester, indeed, states that the measurement of practical judgment is "unique and statistically independent of such factors as intelligence, and academic and social background." He has a point.

What would you do if you saw a woman holding a baby at the window of a burning house:

    a. Call the fire department.
    b. Rush into the house.
    c. Fetch a ladder.
    d. Try and catch the baby.

It is impossible to decide which is the best course of action unless you know how big the fire is, whether she is on the first floor or the second, whether there is a ladder handy, how near by the fire department is, plus a number of other considerations.

On this type of question, let me confess that I can be of very little help to the reader. I have made a very thorough study of these tests, have administered them to many people of unquestioned judgment, and invariably the results have been baffling. But there does seem to be one moral: don't think too much. The searching mind is severely handicapped by such forced choices and may easily miss what is meant to be the obviously right answer. Suppress this quality in yourself by answering these questions as quickly as you possibly can, with practically no pause for reflection.

The judgment questions illustrated by the following, are much easier to answer.

    a. Which do you think is the best answer for the executive to make in the following situation:
    Worker: "Why did Jones get the promotion and I didn't?"
    Executive:
        1. "You deserved it but Jones has seniority."
        2. "You've got to work harder."
        3. "Jones's uncle owns the plant."
        4. "Let's figure out how you can improve."
    b. A worker's home life is not the concern of the company.   Agree . . . Disagree . . .

    c. Good supervisors are born, not made. Agree . . . Disagree . . .
    d. It should be company policy to encourage off-hours participation by employees in company-sponsored social gatherings, clubs, and teams. Agree . . . Disagree . . .

The right answers here are, simply, those which represent sound personnel policy, and this is not hard to figure out. Again, don't quibble. It is true enough that it is virtually impossible to tell the worker why he didn't get promoted unless you know whether he was a good worker, or a poor one, or whether Jones's uncle did in fact own the plant (in which case, candor could be eminently sensible). The mealymouthed answer 4—"Let's figure out how you can improve"—is the "right" answer. Similarly with questions about the worker's home life. It isn't the concern of the company, but it is modern personnel dogma that it should be, and therefore "agree" is the right answer. So with the question about whether good supervisors are born or made. To say that a good supervisor is born deprecates the whole apparatus of modern organization training, and that kind of attitude won't get you anywhere.

Know your company. Questions such as the following are characteristic of the kind of test that attempts to measure the relative emphasis you attach to certain values—such as aesthetic, economic, religious, social.

    a. When you look at a great skyscraper, do you think of:
        1. our tremendous industrial growth
        2. the simplicity and beauty of the structural design
    b. Who helped mankind most?
        1. Shakespeare
        2. Sir Isaac Newton

The profile of you it produces is matched against the profile that the company thinks is desirable. To be considered as a potential executive, you will probably do best when

826   THE ETHICS OF ASSESSMENT

you emphasize economic motivation the most; aesthetic and religious, the least. In the first question, accordingly, you should say the skyscraper makes you think of industrial growth. Theoretical motivation is also a good thing; if you were trying out for the research department, for example, you might wish to say that you think Sir Isaac Newton helped mankind more than Shakespeare and thereby increase your rating for theoretical learnings. Were you trying out for a public relations job, however, you might wish to vote for Shakespeare, for a somewhat higher aesthetic score would not be amiss in this case.

There are many more kinds of tests and there is no telling what surprises the testers will come up with in the future. But the principles will probably change little, and by obeying a few simple precepts and getting yourself in the right frame of mind, you have the wherewithal to adapt to any new testing situation. In all of us there is a streak of normalcy.

Chapter 72

Test Burning in Texas

GWYNN NETTLER

By a 5–1 vote the governing board of the Houston Independent School District, one of the largest in the nation, in June 1959 ordered burned the answer sheets to six socio-psychometrics administered to some 5,000 ninth graders. Four of these instruments were taken from a pilot study of the National Talent Project to be administered by the University of Pittsburgh and the American Institute for Research in 1960; the remaining instruments were added by local psychologists interested in forecasting the realization of talent and in the assessment of psychological health.

The board also instructed the assistant superintendent in charge of special services, whose office had served as repository for tests administered in other school systems within the county, to return several thousand additional answer sheets to a dozen participating districts that they might reconsider submission of these results.

This article is reprinted from the *American Psychologist*, 1959, with the permission of the author and the American Psychological Association.

The action of the Houston trustees destroyed the labors of responsible school personnel and social scientists. It countermanded the administrative decision of its own school executives to participate in such a study and challenged the thoughtfulness of all the other school officials who, at a March meeting of the County Superintendent's Association, had agreed to take part in this project guided by its own members and subsidized by the Hogg Foundation for Mental Health of the University of Texas. The board's public action, and the response of the metropolitan press, exposed a prevailing misunderstanding of the nature of a psychometric and suspicion of the good sense of psychologists.

The instruments that had been used included a Vocabulary-Information Profile Test, an Interest Blank, a High School Personality Test, a Student Information Blank that included self-evaluating items on health, a sociometric rating device, and the Youth Attitude Scales. These last measures, which contained most of the troublesome items, concern students' perceptions of

827

themselves and their relations with their families, teachers, and peers. These scales are not part of the National Talent Project but were adapted from questionnaires used in the 1956 Texas Cooperative Youth Study that had been administered to more than 13,000 children in 169 schools throughout the state without parental objection.[1]

The Houston test burning came as a result of a few telephone calls (no one knows how many) from parents complaining, at the outset, to two of the seven trustees concerning the content and purpose of the tests. The metropolitan press was alerted and published stories in advance of the school board meeting promising a ruckus (board meetings are televised) under such headlines as Parents Protest Test Questions, Parents Still Boiling over Those "Talent Hunt" Questions, and Dr. McFarland [the superintendent] Faces Tough Monday Night.

According to newspaper accounts parents were objecting to having their children respond to such items as:

I enjoy soaking in the bathtub.
A girl who gets into trouble on a date has no one to blame but herself.
If you don't drink in our gang, they make you feel like a sissy.
Sometimes I tell dirty jokes when I would rather not.
Dad always seems too busy to pal around with me.

Houston school board members, with one exception, seconded the allegation of some parents that these and similar questions (a) could serve no useful function in a talent search or in the guidance of children ("If you can show me one iota of value to these tests," one trustee is quoted as saying, "I'll quit the board") and that (b) such

questions might undermine a child's moral character. One board member saw the tests as an additional symptom of the encroachment of "outside agencies" upon local school systems.

News items and exchanges in the letters-to-the-editor columns continued for at least two weeks after the Houston board's decision. Within 24 hours of the televised meeting one citizen prepared an application for a court order restraining officials from burning test results only to learn that the answer sheets had been destroyed earlier in the day.

The clamor spread to the suburban Spring Branch school district where the superintendent was called upon for an explanation in a meeting at which it was announced, incidentally, that the DAR was interested in the possible subversive uses of psychological instruments and that it had prepared a list of proscribed tests. A spokesman for the antitest group also suggested that answers to some of the questions—as, for example, those on family income, family size, and home ownership—would be of value to communists. The Spring Branch board decided that, rather than destroy the answer sheets of all students for all tests, parents who objected to the inclusion of their child's responses would be given the opportunity to request deletion. As of this writing, some six weeks after this decision, 11 parents of a possible 750 have made this request.

Social scientists and interested citizens, concerned that the Houston board action not go unprotested, conferred informally to discuss measures that might effectively indicate to the community the questionable wisdom of the board's decision (Once the tests had been administered, why destroy the *results?* And why without a hearing? And why the results of *all* tests of *all* students?). As a result of these telephonic and luncheon conclaves, it was apparent that no organized civic or professional body felt justified in making further remonstrance and that, pragmatically, any continued debate with the school board and its sup-

---

[1] Preliminary findings of the Texas Cooperative Youth Study are reported by Bernice M. Moore and Wayne H. Holtzman, "What Texas Knows About Youth," in the *National Parent-Teacher,* September, 1958, pages 22–24. A detailed report was published in 1960 by the University of Texas Press.

porters aired in the press would probably result in victory for the board with possible harmful consequences for other phases of school testing programs.

Each man will read his own lessons from the events outlined above; I should like to suggest these:

1. In general, the public relations of psychometricians is in a sad state and in need of repairs.

   a. There are national bodies interested in attacking psychology and psychologists as potential instruments of state control, *ergo,* of communism.

   b. We have not been able to explain the role of tests in personnel selection procedures to a wide audience.

   c. The press, with few exceptions, is a dubious factor in the fair reporting of our case if only because the rationale of testing is difficult to explain to editors and reporters.

2. It seems advisable that future large-scale testing programs be preceded by a public "warm up" explaining to as broad a segment of the public as possible the purposes and methods of such research. For example, effort spent in the education of PTAs and boards of education in advance of

such surveys may prevent such loss as Houston has suffered.

3. Psychologists are behaving "ethnocentrically" in assuming that their ethic is shared by the people they study. The statement of "Ethical Standards of Psychologists" carried in the June issue of the *American Psychologist* holds:

As a scientist, the psychologist believes that society will be best served when he investigates where his judgment indicates investigation is needed . . . [page 279].

The psychologist in the practice of his profession shows sensible regard for the social codes and moral expectations of the community in which he works . . . [page 279].

When the student of behavior works in a xenophobic and individualistic community, he cannot assume that his scientifically honorable intentions will be considered morally justifiable by those whom he seeks to help. Even though the scientist says, in effect, "I am studying you, and asking you these questions, for your own good," his subject may respond, "It is part of my 'good' that you desist from your intrusion of my privacy."

As with all such conflicts in ethics (in ultimate values), facts are irrelevant—and consequences too.

Chapter 73

The Gullibility
of Personnel Managers

ROSS STAGNER

Psychological services are being offered for sale in all parts of the United States. Some of these are bona fide services by competent, well-trained people. Others are marketing nothing but glittering generalities having no practical value.

In the field of engineering, chemistry, power sources, and raw materials supply, the average businessman has learned to think realistically and to demand quantitative evidence concerning the value of an item before buying it. In the novel field of psychological measurement, on the other hand, many executives are still amazingly gullible. They often purchase expensive "employee selection" programs with no scientific evidence that the service offered has any value whatever.

A common device of the high-pressure salesman who is dispensing a fake line of psychological "tests" runs something like this: "Statistics can be used to prove any-

thing. Let me give you a real demonstration. You take this personality test yourself, and I'll give you the report based on your scores. If you don't agree that it is amazingly accurate, I won't even try to sell it to you." The gullible personnel manager takes the test, reads the report, is amazed by its accuracy, and spends a lot of his company's money for a device not worth the paper and printing.

Does this sound too extreme? Do you think the personnel manager is the best possible judge of a report on his own personality? Do you think this is the only sound basis for deciding about the validity of a test? Skeptics will be interested in the following report of a simple experiment conducted with a conference of personnel managers at the University of Illinois.

METHOD

The procedure involved giving the personnel managers a published personality inven-

This article is reprinted from *Personnel Psychology,* 1958, with the permission of the author and Personnel Psychology, Inc.

tory and collecting the blanks for scoring, assuring them that the reports would be returned within a few hours. The test was actually scored, according to the published key. However, *two* reports were prepared, one using a mimeographed profile sheet which showed each man exactly how he scored as compared with norm groups; this gave him a quantitative result which could be used practically. The other report was a "fake" personality analysis published by Forer [2] with slight modifications to make it more plausible. The thirteen items shown in Table 73–1, which were collected by Forer from dream books and astrology charts, were interspersed with rather critical comments about the personality being tested. The person's name was written in red pencil at the top of the sheet, and the thirteen items listed were circled in red; thus, every man received an identical "personality analysis."

At the second meeting of the group, the fake report was distributed first. Everyone was asked to read only his own personality analysis, which was given by the items marked in red. Thus it appeared that each individual was getting a report designed for himself alone. (No such direct assertion was made by the speaker, but the illusion was effectively communicated.)

Each man was then asked to read over the items marked for him and decide how accurate he thought the description was.

Table 73–1   Evaluations of Items by 68 Personnel Managers When Presented as a "Personality Analysis"

Item	Judgment as to Accuracy of Item Per Cent† Choosing				
	a*	b	c	d	e
1. You have a great need for other people to like and admire you	39	46	13	1	1
4. You have a tendency to be critical of yourself	46	36	15	3	0
5. You have a great deal of unused capacity which you have not turned to your advantage	37	36	18	4	1
7. While you have some personality weaknesses, you are generally able to compensate for them	34	55	9	0	0
9. Your sexual adjustment has presented problems for you	15	16	16	33	19
10. Disciplined and self-controlled outside, you tend to be worrisome and insecure inside	40	21	22	10	4
12. At times you have serious doubts as to whether you have made the right decision or done the right thing	27	31	19	18	4
15. You prefer a certain amount of change and variety and become dissatisfied when hemmed in by restrictions and limitations	63	28	7	1	1
16. You pride yourself as an independent thinker and do not accept others' statements without satisfactory proof	49	31	12	4	4
18. You have found it unwise to be too frank in revealing yourself to others	31	37	22	6	4
20. At times you are extroverted, affable, sociable, while at other times you are introverted, wary, reserved	43	25	18	9	5
21. Some of your aspirations tend to be pretty unrealistic	12	16	22	43	7
23. Security is one of your major goals in life	40	31	15	9	5

* Definitions of scale steps as follows: a. amazingly accurate.   b. rather good.   c. about half and half. d. more wrong than right.   e. almost entirely wrong.
    † Not all percentages add to 100% because of omissions by an occasional subject.

He was provided with a 5-step scale, as follows: amazingly accurate; rather good; about half and half; more wrong than right; almost entirely wrong. He was asked to check this scale both for over-all impression and for each of the items marked in red.

After the "validity analysis" had been collected, the participants were asked to compare their personality reports. Upon discovering that all were identical, they set up a terrific noise, apparently compounded of resentment at being duped and amusement at themselves for being tricked.

After brief discussion, the genuine profile sheets were distributed and the difference between glittering generalities and a quantitative set of scores emphasized. The importance of statistical data on reliability and validity was also discussed at this point.

RESULTS

Perhaps the most important results were to be found in the insights reported by the participants, who quickly grasped the significance of the demonstration. However, numerical findings will be of some interest.

In terms of over-all evaluation of the "fake analysis," 50% of a group of 68 personnel managers marked the description as amazingly accurate. Other judgments divided between "rather good" (40%) and "about half and half" (10%).

For comparison, we may cite results of two other groups. In a group of college students, 25% considered this same "personality analysis" to be "amazingly accurate" and another 37% judged it "rather good." In a class of industrial supervisors studying "human relations," the same personality analysis was considered "amazingly accurate" by 37%, with 44% rating it "rather good." Thus 62% of the students and 81% of the supervisors, as compared with 90% of the personnel men, chose the first two steps on the validity scale defined in Table 73–1. The two industrial groups are not significantly different; the greater

skepticism of the students may have been due to their greater familiarity with test forms, and perhaps to some skepticism about the intent of the instructor.

The results for a group of 68 personnel managers on the eleven specific items are given in Table 73–1. It is clear from this table that any report using sentences such as those making up items 15, 16, 4, 20, 23, and 10 will be popular with the recipient. Even items 1, 5, 7, and 18 will get a good reception. Only items 9, 12, and 21 failed to get an enthusiastic approval from at least 30% of the population.

Similar results were obtained from the group of supervisors, as well as from several classes of college students. It thus appears that the present finding need not be limited to personnel managers alone, although they merit special consideration because of their role in deciding upon employee selection devices.

DISCUSSION

Industrial psychologists have some valuable wares to sell. But quacks and charlatans are always quick to move in on a new field and replace solid utility with glittering generalizations. The astonishing aspect of this demonstration to a professional psychologist is the credulity of the industrialist.

The sweeping character of the statements utilized in the fake personality analysis should be readily recognized. These propositions are so general that they can apply to anyone; as we note, 30% to 50% of a group of practicing personnel men accept most of them as "amazingly accurate" in an imputed self-description. Thus the shrewd salesman can easily dupe the personnel man, by appealing to his belief that his own judgment is better than statistics. (Dozens of such demonstrations will be required to shake this belief in some industrialists' minds.) Seeing that the "test" elicits such remarkable insights into his own personality, the personnel manager concludes that it will do equally well with the applicants he wishes to analyze. It will, of course, do exactly as well; that is, it will spew out glittering generalizations which apply to everyone and are distinctive for no one. It will have no differential value for selection, placement, training or any other personnel function.

It should be noted that these fake "personality reports" need not be phrased identically. The salesman need not use all 13 of the items given in Table 73–1 for a given person, nor is he limited to these; there are many others, equally acceptable, some more flattering (these go to the higher executives). Thus the salesman can "test" several men in one organization without running out of nice generalizations. By judicious combinations of such items he can continue for quite a while without saying anything.

The present findings are not unique. Forer [2] found that typical college students were easily taken in by his items. Sundberg [3] reports that few people choose their own personality diagnosis, based on the Minnesota Multiphasic Personality Inventory, when it is matched with a set of vague generalizations like these. Dunnette [1] comments, "It is an unfortunate fact that many otherwise hard-headed businessmen are today behaving in a rather gullible fashion" in regard to tests, and he credits Dr. Paul E. Meehl with coining the phrase, "the Barnum effect," to refer to the deceptive effect of these glittering generalities incorporated in testing reports.

These observations will not, it is hoped, decrease the interest of personnel men in professionally sound, scientifically evaluated personality measures. While most psychologists are cautious in recommending such devices, it seems certain that they can be utilized in certain industrial situations. Especial importance should be attached to the presence of quantitative data on reliability, on group norms, and on validation. Curiously enough, it seems that the third of these is least important. Validation needs to be repeated inside the establishment, with reference to criteria of performance appropriate to the position under study. But a test which does not elicit reliable individual differences, and a satisfactory spread of scores when applied to populations comparable to that in the establishment, cannot function as a personnel device. At best it may make the employees think management is interested in them; at worst, it may result in erroneous placements, waste and personnel disturbance.

The old Roman saying runs, *Caveat emptor*—let the buyer beware. This holds for personnel testing devices, especially as regards "personality tests." The personnel manager should avoid being seduced by the flattering report on his own fine qualities into purchasing a test which is worthless when evaluated scientifically.

REFERENCES

1. DUNNETTE, M. D. Use of the sugar pill by industrial psychologists. *Amer. Psychologist*, 1957, 12, 223–225.
2. FORER, B. R. The fallacy of personal validations: a classroom demonstration of gullibility. *J. abnorm. soc. Psychol.*, 1949, 44, 118–123.
3. SUNDBERG, N. D. The acceptability of "fake" versus "bona fide" personality test interpretations. *J. abnorm. soc. Psychol.*, 1955, 50, 145–147.

Chapter *74~*

Personality Measurement and College Performance

SAMUEL MESSICK

In this paper I will discuss personality measurement primarily in terms of its potential contributions to the prediction of college performance. In this context, two major questions arise: (1) Are personality tests any good as measures of the purported personality characteristics? (2) What should these tests be used for? The first question is a scientific one and may be answered by an evaluation of available personality instruments against scientific standards of psychometric adequacy. The second question is at least in part an ethical one and may be answered by a justification of proposed uses for a test in terms of ethical

This paper was reprinted from the *Proceedings of the 1963 Invitational Conference on Testing Problems,* 1964, with permission of the author and the publisher, Educational Testing Service. A preliminary version of some portions of this paper was prepared for the Committee of Examiners in Aptitude Testing of the College Entrance Examination Board. The author wishes to thank Dr. Salvatore Maddi for his many suggestions about the nature of the problems and the organization of the material. Grateful acknowledgment is also due Sydell Carlton, Norman Frederiksen, John French, Nathan Kogan, and Lawrence Stricker for their helpful comments on the manuscript.

standards and social or educational values. I will first discuss the scientific standards for appraising personality measures and will then consider how well these standards are typically met by instruments developed by each of three major approaches to personality measurement. The final section of the paper will discuss some of the ethical problems raised when personality measures are used for practical decisions.

The major measurement requirements in personality, as in psychology generally, involve (1) the demonstration, through substantial consistency of response to a set of items, that *something* is being measured; and (2) the accumulation of evidence about the nature and meaning of this "something," in terms of the network of the measure's relations with theoretically relevant variables and its lack of relation with theoretically unrelated variables [1, 9, 10, 18, 22, 48]. In psychometric terms, these two critical properties for the evaluation of a purported personality measure are the measure's *reliability* and its *construct validity.*

An investigation of the measure's relations with other well-known variables may also provide a basis for determining whether the thing measured represents a relatively separate dimension with important specific properties or whether its major variance is predictable from a combination of other, possibly more basic, characteristics. Such information bears upon the status of the construct as a separate variable and upon the structure of its relations with other variables.

Whether the measure reflects a separate trait or a combination of characteristics or, indeed, whether the proposed construct is a valid integration of observed response consistencies or merely a gratuitous label, there is still another important property of the measure that can be independently evaluated—namely, its usefulness in predicting concurrent and future non-test behaviors as a possible basis for decision making and social action. For such purposes, which primarily include classification and selection situations, it is necessary that the measure display *predictive validity* in the form of substantial correlations with the criterion measures chosen to reflect relevant performances in the non-test domain. Although some psychologists would argue that such predictive validity is all that's necessary to warrant the use of a measure in making practical decisions, it will be maintained here that predictive validity is not sufficient and that it may be unwise to ignore construct validity even in practical prediction problems [27, 28, 36]. This point will be discussed more fully later.

Just as a test has as many empirical validities as there are criterion measures to which it has been related, so too may a test display different proportions of reliable variance or reflect different construct interpretations, primarily because the motivations and defenses of the subjects are implicated in different ways under different testing conditions. Thus, instead of talking about the reliability and construct validity (or even the empirical validity) of the *test* per se, it might be better to talk about the reliability and construct validity of the *responses* to the test, as summarized in a particular score, thereby emphasizing that these test properties are relative to the processes used by the subjects in responding [46]. These processes, in turn, may differ under different circumstances, particularly those affecting the conceptions and intentions of the subjects. Thus, the same test, for example, might measure one set of things if administered in the context of diagnostic guidance in a clinical setting, a radically different set of things if administered in the context of anonymous inquiry in a research laboratory, and yet another set if administered as a personal evaluation for industrial or academic selection. Furthermore, these different testing settings impose different ethical constraints upon the manner and conditions of eliciting personal, and what the subject may consider private, information [17, 64].

This point that personality tests, and even personality testers, may operate differently under different circumstances was one of the main reasons I initially chose to limit the present discussion to a particular context—namely, personality measurement in relation to college performance. Various contexts differ somewhat in the types of problems posed for personality measurement, but the timely context of assessment for college contains nearly all the problems at once. Of major concern in considering this context, however, is the inherently evaluative atmosphere of the testing settings. This means that we must take into account not only the ubiquitous response distortions due to defense mechanisms of self-deception and personal biases in self-regard [cf. 29], but also the distortions in performance and self-report that are at least partially deliberate attempts at faking and impression management [cf. 33].

The extent to which attempts are made to handle the problems of both deliberate misrepresentation and unintentional distortion becomes an important criterion for evaluating personality instruments, particularly for use in evaluative settings. Many personality measures have been developed in research contexts where deliberate misrepresentation may have been minimal; little is known of their psychometric properties under conditions of real or presumed personal evaluation. Some personality tests include specific devices for detecting faking, such as validity or malingering keys, which would enable students with excessive "lie" responses to be spotted and would also permit the use of the control scores as suppressor variables in correcting other scales [50]. Other personality instruments rely on test formats that attempt to make faking difficult, such as the use of forced-choice techniques on questionnaires or of objective performance measures where the direction of faking is not obvious. Still other procedures use indirect items and disguised façades to circumvent the subject's defensive posture [7, 8, 47].

PSYCHOMETRIC PROBLEMS IN SOME TYPICAL APPROACHES TO PERSONALITY MEASUREMENT

We have considered several psychometric criteria for evaluating personality measures: reliability, empirical validity in predicting criteria or non-test behaviors, the structure of relations with other known variables, the adequacy of controls for faking and distortion, and—more basic because it subsumes aspects of the preceding properties—construct validity. We will now inquire how well these standards are typically met by instruments developed by three major approaches to personality measurement—self-report questionnaires, behavior ratings, and objective performance tests.

SELF-REPORT INVENTORIES

Before various types of self-report questionnaires are discussed, the general problem of stylistic consistencies or response sets on such instruments should be broached [15, 40]. A major portion of the response variance on many personality inventories,

particularly those with "True-False" or "Agree-Disagree" item formats, has been shown to reflect consistent stylistic tendencies that have a cumulative effect on presumed content scores [23, 24, 41, 42]. The major response styles emphasized thus far are the tendency to agree or acquiesce [14, 54], the tendency to respond desirably [23, 51], the tendency to respond deviantly [5, 62], and, to a lesser extent, the tendency to respond extremely in self-rating [59]. These response styles have been conceptualized and studied as personality variables in their own right [40], but their massive influence on some personality inventories can seriously interfere with the measurement of other content traits [43]. The problem becomes one of measuring response styles as potentially useful personality variables and at the same time controlling their influence on content scores [52, 78]. The extent to which controls for response styles have been effective in reducing overwhelming stylistic variance becomes an important criterion in evaluating the measurement characteristics of self-report instruments.

We will consider three kinds of self-report or questionnaire measures of personality: (1) a type that I will call a *factorial inventory,* in which factor analysis or some other criterion of internal consistency is used to select items reflecting homogeneous dimensions [11, 12]; (2) *empirically derived inventories,* in which significant differentiation among criterion groups is the basis of item selection; and (3) *rational inventories,* in which items are chosen on logical grounds to reflect theoretical properties of specified dimensions.

Factorial inventory scales are developed through the use of factor analysis or other methods of homogeneous keying [38, 49, 74] to isolate dimensions of consistency in response to self-descriptive items. The pool of items collected for analysis usually consists of a conglomeration of characteristics possibly relevant to some domain and sometimes includes items specifically written to represent the variables under study.

The most widely known of the current factored inventories are the Cattell 16 Personality Factor Questionnaire and the Guilford-Zimmerman Temperament Survey. Becker's [3] recent empirical comparison of the Cattell questionnaire with an earlier form of the Guilford scales has revealed an equivalence between four factors from the two inventories and substantial similarity for two other factors. Although considerable factor analytic evidence at the item level generally supports the nature of the scales [11, 35], when two subscale scores were used to represent each factor supposedly measured by these inventories, Becker [3] found only eight distinguishable factors within the 16 P. F. and only five within 13 Guilford scales.

These factorial inventories were developed primarily in research settings, so that attention must be given to possible defensive distortions induced by their use in evaluative situations. Although procedures for detecting faking have been suggested, their systematic use has not been emphasized, nor has their effectiveness been clearly demonstrated. Further, empirical controls for response styles have usually not been included, although their operation has recently been noted on some of the factor scales [3, 4].

In the construction of *empirically derived inventory* scales, items are selected that significantly discriminate among criterion groups. The most widely known examples are scales from the Minnesota Multiphasic Personality Inventory (MMPI) and from the California Psychological Inventory (CPI). The justification of these scales is in terms of their empirical validity and their usefulness in classifying subjects as similar or dissimilar to criterion groups. Scale homogeneity, reliability, and construct validity are seldom emphasized. The difficulty arises when these scales are used not to predict criterion categories but rather to make inferences about the personality of the respondent. This latter use has become the typical one [73], but such application cannot be justified by empirical validity alone—homogeneity and construct validity become crucial under such circumstances [16, 40, 43].

Because of their widespread use in clinical settings, considerable attention has been given to the problem of faking, particularly on the MMPI. Several scales are available for detecting lying and malingering (L, Mp, Sd, etc.), along with a validity scale (F) for uncovering excessive deviant responses [19]. A measure of "defensiveness" (K) is also used both as a means of detecting this tendency and as a suppressor variable for controlling test-taking attitudes [50]. Several studies of the effectiveness of these scales have indicated a somewhat variable, and usually only moderate, level of success [73, 77].

A major problem on the MMPI and CPI is the predominant role of the response styles of acquiescence and desirability, which in the former instrument define the first two major factors and together account for roughly half the total variance [24, 39, 41, 42]. Presumably, these response styles are correlated with the criterion distinction utilized in the empirical scale construction [72], but their massive influence on these inventories drastically interferes with the attempted measurement of other content traits and limits their possible discriminant validity [43].

Rational inventories comprise items that have been written on theoretical or logical grounds to reflect specified traits. That such scales measure something is demonstrated subsequently by high internal consistency coefficients; that they measure distinguishable characteristics is shown by relatively low scale intercorrelations. Factor analysis is also sometimes used subsequently to investigate scale interrelations [65]. On some of these inventories, such as Stern's Activities Index, little attention has been given initially to the role of response styles, while on others, such as Edwards Personal Preference Schedule (EPPS), the major attraction has been the attempt to limit stylistic variance.

The EPPS employs a forced-choice item

format: statements are presented to the subject in pairs, the members of each pair having been previously selected to be as equal as possible in average judged desirability. The respondent is required to select from each pair the statement that better describes his personality. Such forced-choice items do not offer an opportunity for the response style of acquiescence to operate. Further, since the paired statements are also approximately matched in desirability, a consistent tendency to respond desirably should in principle have relatively little effect upon item choices [13, 23, 25]. Even though desirability variance is not eliminated thereby, primarily because of the existence of consistent personal viewpoints about desirability that cannot be simultaneously equated [6, 37, 45, 51, 61], the forced-choice approach offers considerable promise for reducing the overwhelming influence of response styles on questionnaires [58]. Unfortunately, the EPPS can still not be recommended for other than research purposes because insufficient evidence exists concerning its empirical and construct validity [66].

The different approaches to scale construction that distinguish factorial, empirically derived, and rational inventories might well be combined into a single measurement enterprise, wherein scale homogeneity, construct validity, and the theoretical basis of item content, as well as empirical differentiation, would be successively refined in an iterative cycle [48, 58]. In this way the differences among the approaches, depending as they would upon the particular point in the cycle that one chose to start with, would become trivial, and scales would be systematically developed in terms of joint criteria of homogeneity, theoretical relevance, construct validity, and empirical utility.

BEHAVIOR RATINGS

Behavior ratings represent a second major approach to personality measurement. Direct ratings of behavior, both of

job performance and of personality characteristics, have been frequently employed in educational and industrial evaluation [75]. Personality ratings, however, have seldom been formally or systematically used in the typical selection situation for many reasons, one of them being the difficulty of obtaining reliable or comparable ratings for candidates coming from different sources. However, if teacher- and peer-ratings of personality made in college, for example, were to prove valid in predicting behavioral criteria of college success [cf. 69] and if these ratings could, in turn, be predicted by other measures (such as self-report inventories), then the predicted ratings might be useful in pre-college decisions. Behavior ratings that correlate with college success could thus serve as intermediate criteria for validating self-report measures of the same dimensions.

Cattell [11] has isolated approximately 15 dimensions from behavior ratings, reflecting such qualities as ego strength, excitability, dominance, and surgency. Tupes and Christal [70], on the other hand, in analyzing the same rating scales and in a few cases the same data, provided evidence for only five strong and recurrent factors, which were labeled extroversion, agreeableness, conscientiousness, emotional stability, and culture [see also 57]. Cattell [11] has also claimed a congruence between most of his behavior rating factors and their questionnaire counterparts, which suggests that questionnaire scales can indeed predict rating dimensions. Cattell's claim of a one-to-one matching of behavior rating and questionnaire factors has been challenged by Becker [2], however, who concluded that available evidence did not support the alleged relation.

Norman [58], on the other hand, has clearly demonstrated that questionnaire scales can be developed that will correlate substantially with behavior rating factors. In his particular study, he attempted to predict the five rating factors obtained by Tupes and Christal [70, 71] from peer nominations. Since these ratings had previously exhibited substantial validity in predicting officer effectiveness criteria at the USAF officer candidate school [69], the subsequent prediction of these ratings by questionnaire scales has direct implications for selection.

Incidentally, Norman's [58] scale construction procedure involved an extremely promising technique for handling faking in evaluative settings. Items in a forced-choice format equated for "admission-to-OCS desirability" were administered under normal and faking instructions. In the construction of the scales, the items were balanced between those showing a mean shift under faking instructions in the direction of the keyed response and those showing a mean shift away from the keyed response. Mean scores for the resulting scales were thus equated under normal and faking conditions, and, in addition, powerful detection scales were developed to isolate extreme dissemblers.

OBJECTIVE PERFORMANCES TESTS

The third major approach to personality measurement considered here is the objective performance test. According to Campbell [8], an objective measure of personality, like an objective measure of ability or achievement, is a test in which the examinee believes that he should respond accurately because correct answers exist as a basis for evaluating his performance. Cattell [11], on the other hand, considers a test objective if the subject is unaware of the manner in which his behavior affects the scoring and interpretation, a property that Campbell [8] prefers to use in the definition of indirect measurement.

Cattell's [11] analyses of objective performance measures of personality have uncovered approximately 18 dimensions, with such labels as harric assertiveness, inhibition, anxiety, and critical practicality. Thurstone [68] and Guilford [e.g., 34] have also developed measures of several perceptual and cognitive dimensions that represent objective tests of personality. Meas-

ures of speed and flexibility of closure [68], for example, and of ideational fluency appear more congenial in a personality framework than in the traditional ability formulation [cf. 11, 34, 80]. Some of Guilford's [34] work on divergent thinking also deals with stylistic restrictions in the generation and manipulation of ideas, which appear as much like personality consistencies as measures of "maximum performance" abilities [17].

In many cases, the objective nature of these tests makes it difficult to decide how to fake, since some look very much like ability tests and appear to have clear adaptive requirements that subjects should strive to achieve. Test properties, however, have been studied primarily in research contexts, where deliberate faking may have been minimal. Certain characteristics may change under other conditions. Available objective tests also tend to be unreliable, primarily because they have been deliberately kept short for use in large test batteries. Because of practice and order effects on some of the procedures, however, there is no guarantee that high reliabilities can be obtained simply by lengthening the tests.

Considerable attention has been given in recent years to certain stylistic dimensions in the performance of cognitive tasks [30, 31, 79, 80]. These personality dimensions have been conceptualized as cognitive styles, which represent a person's typical modes of perceiving, remembering, thinking, and problem-solving. Approaches to the measurement of these variables have routinely included objective procedures. Some examples of these dimensions are (1) *field-dependence-independence*—" . . . an analytical, in contrast to a global, way of perceiving [which] entails a tendency to experience items as discrete from their backgrounds and reflects ability to overcome the influence of an embedding context" [80; see also 44, 53]; (2) *leveling-sharpening*—a dimension where subjects at the leveling extreme tend to assimilate new material to an established framework, whereas sharpeners, at the other extreme, tend to contrast new material with the old and to maintain distinctions [30]; and (3) *category-width preferences*—a dimension of individual consistencies in modes of categorizing perceived similarities and differences, reflected in consistent preferences for broad or narrow categories in conceptualizing [30, 32, 55, 60, 63].

Both the cognitive nature and the stylistic nature of these variables make them appear particularly relevant to the kinds of cognitive tasks performed in academic settings. Certain types of subject matter and certain problems or problem formulations might favor broad categorizers over narrow categorizers, for example, or levelers over sharpeners, and vice versa. This "vice versa" is extremely important: since it is unlikely that one end of such stylistic dimensions would prove uniformly more adaptive than the other, the relativity of their value should be recognized. (Incidentally, the possibility of such relativity of value might well be extended to other personality variables where the desirability of one end of the trait has usually been prejudged. What conceptions would change, for example, if "flexibility vs. rigidity" had been called "confusion vs. control"?)

It is quite possible that we have already unwittingly included such stylistic variance in some measures of intellectual aptitude, such as the SAT, but if this is the case, the nature and direction of its operation should be specified and controlled. It is possible, for example, that the five-alternative multiple-choice form of quantitative aptitude items might favor subjects who prefer broad categories on category-width measures. Quick, rough approximations to the quantitative items might appropriately be judged by these subjects to be "close enough" to a given alternative, whereas "narrow range" subjects may require more time-consuming exact solutions before answering. Significant correlations between category preferences and quantitative aptitude tests have indeed been obtained and have been found to vary widely as a function of the spacing of alternatives on multiple-choice forms of the quantitative aptitude tests [56].

THE ETHICS OF SELECTION

In considering personality measures of potential utility in the evaluative context of college performance, I have tried to give the impression that many measures are available but none is adequate when systematically evaluated against psychometric standards. In addition, I have tried to give some indication of the rapidly advancing technology that is evolving in personality measurement to support research efforts. In the relatively near future, this technology may produce personality measures that are acceptable by measurement and prediction standards, so that the question may soon arise in earnest as to the scope of their practical application. We have considered some of the scientific standards for deciding their appropriateness, but what about the ethical ones?

The choice of any particular personality measure for use, say, in college admission involves an implicit value judgment, which, at the least, should be made explicit in an educational policy that attempts to justify its use. One compelling justification for using personality measures in college selection would be to screen out extreme deviants. Colleges would be well advised, for example, to consider rejecting assaultive or suicidal psychotics, and some schools might wish to eliminate overt homosexuals. The use of personality measures for differentiating among normal subjects might also be justified in terms of empirical validity. After all, as long as there are many more candidates for admission than can be accepted, it seems better to make selections on the basis of valid measures than on the basis of chance. But is empirical validity enough? Validity for what? Certainly the role of the criterion in such an argument must be clearly specified.

The relevant domain of criterion performances should be outlined and attempts should be made to develop appropriate criterion measures. Since different criterion domains can be defined for different aspects of college success, selection might be oriented toward several of them simultaneously or toward only a few. Consider some of the possibilities: In *selection for academic performance*, criterion measures might include global grade-point averages, separate grades for different subject-matter fields, or standardized curriculum achievement examinations. In *selection for college environment*, criterion measures could be set up in terms of desired contributions to extracurricular college life (such as football playing and newspaper editing) or in terms of balancing geographic, social class, sex, and, perhaps, temperament distributions in the student body. If the demands and pressures of the college environment and social structure have been studied, criterion standards might also be specified for selecting students with congenial needs that will fit well with (and hopefully have a higher probability of being satisfied by) the college environment [cf. 65]. We could also talk in terms of *selection for ultimate career satisfaction* and *selection for desirable personal characteristics* [cf. 20]—or for desirable attitudes.

In each of these cases, it should be emphasized that potential predictor measures are not evaluated in terms of their empirical validity for *criterion behaviors* but rather in terms of their prediction of *criterion measures*, which, in turn, are presumed to reflect the criterion behaviors of interest. And these criterion measures should be evaluated against the same psychometric standards as any other measures. Not only should they be reliable, but also the nature of the attributes measured should be elucidated in a construct validity framework [21]. Since each of these criterion measures may also contain some specific variance that is not particularly related to the criterion behaviors, one should also be concerned that an obtained validity coefficient reflects a correlation with relevant domain characteristics and not with irrelevant variance incidentally reflected in the putative criterion measure. Thus, the question of the *intrinsic validity* of the predictor and of the criterion measures should be broached, even if in practice many of the answers may seem presumptive ones [36]. In the last analysis, ultimate criteria are determined on rational grounds in any event [67]. Should a reading comprehension test predict grades in gunner's mate school [27]? Should a college that found docile, submissive students receiving higher grades in freshman courses select on this basis, or should they consider revising their grading system? Such decisions might become more difficult if the personality characteristics involved had more socially desirable labels.

Just as we have been concerned about predicting grades not as they are but as they should be [26, 28], so too should we be concerned not only with predicting personality characteristics that are presently considered desirable for college students but also with deciding which characteristics, if any, should be considered desirable. It is possible, for example, that certain prepotent values, such as the desire for diversity, would override decisions to select students in terms of particular personal qualities. The very initiation of selection on any given personality variables might lead to conformity pressures toward the stereotype implied by the selected characteristics. Apart from the effects of the selection itself, such pressures to simulate desired personal qualities would probably decrease diversity in the college environment and in the personalities of the students. Wolfle [81] and others have emphasized the value of diversity and even the value of uneven acquisition of skills within individuals as important contributors to the optimal development of talent. Restrictions upon diversity, however subtle, should therefore be undertaken cautiously.

I'd like to close metaphorically with a story of the lineage of King Arthur. At the end of the second book of *The Once and*

Future King, T. H. White [76] points out that Arthur's half-sister bore him a son, Modred, who was his ultimate downfall, that on the eve of the conception Arthur was a very young man drunk with the spoils of recent victory, that his half-sister was much older than he and active in the seduction, and that Arthur did not know that the woman was his sister. But it seems that "in tragedy, innocence is not enough." And in the use of personality measures in college admission, empirical validity is not enough.

REFERENCES

1. BECHTOLDT, H. P. Construct validity: A critique. *American Psychologist*, 1959, 14, 619–629.
2. BECKER, W. C. The matching of behavior rating and questionnaire personality factors. *Psychological Bulletin*, 1960, 57, 201–212.
3. BECKER, W. C. A comparison of the factor structure and other properties of the 16 P.F. and the Guilford-Martin Personality Inventories. *Educational and Psychological Measurement*, 1961, 21, 393–404.
4. BENDIG, A. W. "Social desirability" and "anxiety" variables in the IPAT Anxiety Scale. *Journal of Consulting Psychology*, 1959, 23, 377.
5. BERG, I. A. Response bias and personality: The deviation hypothesis. *Journal of Psychology*, 1955, 40, 60–71.
6. BORISLOW, B. The Edwards Personal Preference Schedule (EPPS) and fakability. *Journal of Applied Psychology*, 1958, 42, 22–27.
7. CAMPBELL, D. T. The indirect assessment of social attitudes. *Psychological Bulletin*, 1950, 47, 15–38.
8. CAMPBELL, D. T. A typology of tests, projective and otherwise. *Journal of Consulting Psychology*, 1957, 21, 207–210.
9. CAMPBELL, D. T. Recommendations for APA test standards regarding construct, trait, or discriminant validity. *American Psychologist*, 1960, 15, 546–553.
10. CAMPBELL, D. T., & FISKE, D. W. Convergent and discriminant validation by the multitrait-multimethod matrix. *Psychological Bulletin*, 1959, 56, 81–105.
11. CATTELL, R. B. *Personality and motivation structure and measurement*. Yonkers-on-Hudson, N.Y.: World Book Co., 1957.
12. COMREY, A. Factored homogeneous item dimensions: A strategy for personality research. In S. Messick & J. Ross (Eds.), *Measurement in personality and cognition*. New York: Wiley, 1962.
13. CORAH, N. L., FELDMAN, M. J., COHEN, I. S., GRUEN, W., MEADOW, A., & RINGWALL, E. A. Social desirability as a variable in the Edwards Personal Preference Schedule. *Journal of Consulting Psychology*, 1958, 22, 70–72.
14. COUCH, A., & KENISTON, K. Yeasayers and naysayers: Agreeing response set as a personality variable. *Journal of Abnormal and Social Psychology*, 1960, 60, 151–174.
15. CRONBACH, L. J. Further evidence on response sets and test design. *Educational and Psychological Measurement*, 1950, 10, 3–31.
16. CRONBACH, L. J. Review of *Basic readings on the MMPI in psychology and medicine* (G. S. Welsh & W. G. Dahlstrom, Eds.), *Psychometrika*, 1958, 23, 385–386.
17. CRONBACH, L. J. *Essentials of psychological testing*. New York: Harper, 1960.
18. CRONBACH, L. J., & MEEHL, P. E. Construct validity in psychological tests. *Psychological Bulletin*, 1955, 52, 281–302.
19. DAHLSTROM, W. G., & WELSH, G. S. *An MMPI handbook*. Minneapolis: Univer. of Minnesota Press, 1960.
20. DAVIS, J. A. Desirable characteristics of college students: The criterion problem. Paper read at the APA symposium on "New Concepts and Devices in Measurement," 1963.
21. DUNNETTE, M. D. A note on *the* criterion. *Journal of Applied Psychology*, 1963, 47, 251–254.
22. EBEL, R. L. Must all tests be valid? *American Psychologist*, 1961, 16, 640–647.
23. EDWARDS, A. L. *The social desirability variable in personality assessment and research*. New York: Dryden, 1957.
24. EDWARDS, A. L., DIERS, C. J., & WALKER,

J. N. Response sets and factor loadings on 61 personality scales. *Journal of Applied Psychology*, 1962, 46, 220–225.

25. EDWARDS, A. L., WRIGHT, C. E., & LUNNEBORG, C. E. A note on "social desirability" as a variable in the Edwards Personal Preference Schedule. *Journal of Consulting Psychology*, 1959, 23, 558.

26. FISHMAN, J. A. Unsolved criterion problems in the selection of college students. *Harvard Educational Review*, 1958, 28, 340–349.

27. FREDERIKSEN, N. Statistical study of the achievement testing program in gunner's mates schools. (Navpers 18079), 1948.

28. FREDERIKSEN, N. The evaluation of personal and social qualities. In *College admissions*. New York: College Entrance Examination Board, 1954.

29. FRENKEL-BRUNSWIK, ELSE. Mechanisms of self deception. *Journal of Social Psychology*, 1939, 10, 409–420.

30. GARDNER, R. W., HOLZMAN, P. S., KLEIN, G. S., LINTON, H. B., & SPENCE, D. P. Cognitive control. *Psychological Issues*, 1959, 1, Monograph 4.

31. GARDNER, R. W., JACKSON, D. N., & MESSICK, S. Personality organization in cognitive controls and intellectual abilities. *Psychological Issues*, 1960, 2, Monograph 8.

32. GARDNER, R. W., & SCHOEN, R. A. Differentiation and abstraction in concept formation. *Psychological Monographs*, 1962, 76, No. 41 (Whole No. 560).

33. GOFFMAN, E. *The presentation of self in everyday life*. New York: Doubleday Anchor Books, 1959.

34. GUILFORD, J. P. *Personality*. New York: McGraw-Hill, 1959.

35. GUILFORD, J. P., & ZIMMERMAN, W. S. Fourteen dimensions of temperament. *Psychological Monographs*, 1956, 70 (Whole No. 417).

36. GULLIKSEN, H. Intrinsic validity. *American Psychologist*, 1950, 5, 511–517.

37. HEILBRUN, A. B., & GOODSTEIN, L. D. Relationships between personal and social desirability sets and performance on the Edwards Personal Preference Schedule. *Journal of Applied Psychology*, 1959, 43, 302–305.

38. HENRYSSON, S. The relation between factor loadings and biserial correlations in item analysis. *Psychometrika*, 1962, 27, 419–424.

39. JACKSON, D. N. Stylistic response determinants in the California Psychological Inventory. *Educational and Psychological Measurement*, 1960, 20, 339–346.

40. JACKSON, D. N., & MESSICK, S. Content and style in personality assessment. *Psychological Bulletin*, 1958, 55, 243–252.

41. JACKSON, D. N., & MESSICK, S. Acquiescence and desirability as response determinants on the MMPI. *Educational and Psychological Measurement*, 1961, 21, 771–790.

42. JACKSON, D. N., & MESSICK, S. Response styles on the MMPI: Comparison of clinical and normal samples. *Journal of Abnormal and Social Psychology*, 1962, 65, 285–299.

43. JACKSON, D. N., & MESSICK, S. Response styles and the assessment of psychopathology. In S. Messick & J. Ross (Eds.), *Measurement in personality and cognition*. New York: Wiley, 1962.

44. KAGAN, J., MOSS, H. A., & SIGEL, I. E. The psychological significance of styles of conceptualization. In J. C. Wright & J. Kagan (Eds.), Basic cognitive processes in children. *Monographs of the Society for Research in Child Development*, 1963, 28, No. 2, 73–112.

45. LAPOINTE, R. E., & AUCLAIR, G. A. The use of social desirability in forced-choice methodology. *American Psychologist*, 1961, 16, 446 (Abstract).

46. LENNON, R. Assumptions underlying the use of content validity. *Educational and Psychological Measurement*, 1956, 16, 294–304.

47. LOEVINGER, JANE. Some principles of personality measurement. *Educational and Psychological Measurement*, 1955, 15, 3–17.

48. LOEVINGER, JANE. Objective tests as instruments of psychological theory. *Psychological Reports*, 1957, 3, 635–694.

49. LOEVINGER, JANE, GLESER, GOLDINE, & DuBOIS, P. H. Maximizing the discriminating power of a multiple-score test. *Psychometrika*, 1953, 18, 309–317.

50. MEEHL, P. E., & HATHAWAY, S. R. The K factor as a suppressor variable in the MMPI. *Journal of Applied Psychology*, 1946, 30, 525–564.

51. MESSICK, S. Dimensions of social desirability. *Journal of Consulting Psychology,* 1960, 24, 279–287.

52. MESSICK, S. Response style and content measures from personality inventories. *Educational and Psychological Measurement,* 1962, 22, 41–56.

53. MESSICK, S., & FRITZKY, F. J. Dimensions of analytic attitude in cognition and personality. *Journal of Personality,* 1963, 31, 346–370.

54. MESSICK, S., & JACKSON, D. N. Acquiescence and the factorial interpretation of the MMPI. *Psychological Bulletin,* 1961, 58, 299–304.

55. MESSICK, S., & KOGAN, N. Differentiation and compartmentalization in object-sorting measures of categorizing style. *Perceptual and Motor Skills,* 1963, 16, 47–51.

56. MESSICK, S., & KOGAN, N. Category width and quantitative aptitude. Princeton, N.J.: Educational Testing Service, Research Bulletin 64–20, 1964.

57. NORMAN, W. T. Toward an adequate taxonomy of personality attributes: Replicated factor structure in peer nomination personality ratings. *Journal of Abnormal and Social Psychology,* 1963, 66, 574–583.

58. NORMAN, W. T. Personality measurement, faking, and detection: An assessment method for use in personnel selection. *Journal of Applied Psychology,* 1963, 47, 225–241.

59. PEABODY, D. Two components in bipolar scales: Direction and extremeness. *Psychological Review,* 1962, 69, 65–73.

60. PETTIGREW, T. F. The measurement and correlates of category width as a cognitive variable. *Journal of Personality,* 1958, 26, 532–544.

61. ROSEN, E. Self-appraisal, personal desirability, and perceived social desirability of personality traits. *Journal of Abnormal and Social Psychology,* 1956, 52, 151–158.

62. SECHREST, L. B., & JACKSON, D. N. Deviant response tendencies: Their measurement and interpretation. *Educational and Psychological Measurement,* 1963, 23, 35–53.

63. SLOANE, H. N., GORLOW, L., & JACKSON, D. N. Cognitive styles in equivalence range. *Perceptual and Motor Skills,* 1963, 16, 389–404.

64. Standards of ethical behavior for psychologists. *American Psychologist,* 1963, 18, No. 1, 56–60.

65. STERN, G. G. The measurement of psychological characteristics of students and learning environments. In S. Messick & J. Ross (Eds.), *Measurement in personality and cognition.* New York: Wiley, 1962.

66. STRICKER, L. J. A review of the Edwards Personal Preference Schedule. In O. K. Buros (Ed.), *The Sixth Mental Measurements Yearbook.* Highland Park, N.J.: Gryphon Press, 1965.

67. THORNDIKE, R. L. *Personnel selection.* New York: Wiley, 1949.

68. THURSTONE, L. L. *A factorial study of perception.* Chicago: Univer. Chicago Press, Psychometric Monograph No. 4, 1944.

69. TUPES, E. C. Relationships between behavior trait ratings by peers and later officer performance of USAF Officer Candidate School graduates. USAF PTRC tech. Note, 1957, No. 57–125.

70. TUPES, E. C., & CHRISTAL, R. E. Stability of personality trait rating factors obtained under diverse conditions. USAF WADC tech. Note, 1958, No. 58–61.

71. TUPES, E. C., & CHRISTAL, R. E. Recurrent personality factors based on trait ratings. USAF ASD tech. Rep., 1961, No. 61–97.

72. WAHLER, H. J. Response styles in clinical and nonclinical groups. *Journal of Consulting Psychology,* 1961, 25, 533–539.

73. WELSH, G. S., & DAHLSTROM, W. G. (Eds.). *Basic readings on the MMPI in psychology and medicine.* Minneapolis: University of Minnesota Press, 1956.

74. WHERRY, R. J., & WINER, B. J. A method for factoring large numbers of items. *Psychometrika,* 1953, 18, 161–179.

75. WHISLER, T. L., & HARPER, SHIRLEY F. (Eds.). *Performance appraisal.* New York: Holt, Rinehart, & Winston, 1962.

76. WHITE, T. H. *The once and future king.* New York: Putnam, 1958.

77. WIGGINS, J. S. Interrelations among MMPI measures of dissimulation under

standard and social desirability instructions. *Journal of Consulting Psychology,* 1959, 23, 419–427.

78. WIGGINS, J. S. Strategic, method, and stylistic variance in the MMPI. *Psychological Bulletin,* 1962, 59, 224–242.

79. WITKIN, H. A., LEWIS, H. B., HERTZMAN, M., MACHOVER, K., MEISSNER, P. B., &

WAPNER, S. *Personality through perception.* New York: Harper, 1954.

80. WITKIN, H. A., DYK, R. B., FATERSON, H. F., GOODENOUGH, D. R., & KARP, S. A. *Psychological differentiation.* New York: Wiley, 1962.

81. WOLFLE, D. Diversity of talent. *American Psychologist,* 1960, 15, 535–545.

Name Index

Aaronson, B. S., 527, 528
Abelson, R. P., 4, 20, 362, 367, 719
Abt, L. E., 121, 631
Adams, C. R., 342, 343
Adams, G. S., 556
Adams, H. E., 267, 277, 556
Adams, J. K., 290, 299
Adelman, J., 743, 749
Adelson, M., 303, 304
Adkins, D. C., 111, 119
Adkins, M. M., 588, 589, 592
Adler, A., 611
Adorno, T. W., 87, 115, 119, 192, 194, 722, 737, 743, 746–748, 755, 759, 762
Alexander, H. W., 238, 240
Allport, F. H., 717, 718, 733, 735
Allport, G. W., 497, 503, 696, 702, 703, 721, 726, 735
Ames, A., Jr., 129
Anastasi, A., 61, 62, 75, 138, 145, 319, 325, 411, 800
Anderson, G. L., 192, 194, 631, 632
Anderson, H. H., 192, 194, 631, 632
Anderson, S. B., 370, 371
Anderson, T. W., 110, 119
Arnold, M. B., 576, 590
Asch, S. E., 643, 655, 656, 660
Ash, P., 524, 528
Atkinson, J. W., 578, 585, 590, 592, 622, 631
Attlee, C., 426
Auclair, G. A., 838, 843
Auld, F., Jr., 622, 630
Ayer, A. J., 126, 131

Babcock, M. E., 458, 468
Baker, H. J., 461, 467
Baker, R. W., 26, 39
Bales, R. F., 762
Balken, E. R., 576, 585, 590
Barker, R. G., 751, 762
Barnes, E. H., 267, 270, 271, 277, 553, 556
Barron, F., 192, 194, 496, 503, 512, 548, 556, 649–652, 656, 660
Barron, M. L., 750, 762
Bartlett, F. C., 25, 38, 468, 586, 590, 661, 668
Bartlett, R. J., 727, 735
Bartley, S. H., 42, 157
Bass, B. M., 277, 514, 544, 555, 556, 594, 677–679, 743, 744, 748
Baughman, E. E., 624, 626, 630, 631
Baxter, B., 768, 781
Bayes, T. R., 397, 404–406, 410, 411, 532, 538, 539
Bayley, N., 111, 119, 471
Beach, F. A., 23, 24, 38
Beadle, G., 811
Beall, G., 526, 528
Bechtoldt, H. P., 42, 58, 75, 133, 138, 139, 142–145, 147, 152, 154, 155, 368, 371, 834, 842
Beck, L. W., 65, 75, 134, 145
Beck, S. J., 561, 574, 627, 629, 630, 638, 664, 668
Becker, W. C., 837, 838, 842
Beech, H. R., 555, 556
Beem, H. P., 771, 781
Bellak, L., 579, 585, 589, 590, 621, 631
Bellows, R., 767
Bender, L., 60, 619, 620

Subject Index

California Psychological Inventory (CPI), 495, 498, 837
  Fe (femininity) scale, 495
Camouflaged Words Test, 429
Cards Test, Thurstone's, 425
Carlson's visual-memory factor, 339
Carnegie Mental Abilities Tests, 461, 463–465
  Analogies Test, 461, 464–465
  Disarranged Sentences, 461, 463, 465
  Number Series II Test, 461, 464–465
Cartesian products of sets, 444–445
Category-width preferences, 840
Cattell's condensed personality sphere set, 375
Cattell's covariation chart, 300–303
Cattell's N-technique, 64
Cattell's peripheral validation, 651
Cattell's 16 Personality Factor Questionnaire, 837
CAVD (intelligence test), Thorndike's, 416
Centroids, computation of, 297
Chance variance, 226, 228, 230
Change, measurement of, 164
Character structure, 563
Children's Apperception Test, Bellak's, 621
Class models, 101–102, 105
Classical validity, 79–82, 142–143
Classification, 47–48
Cleckley's semantic dementia, 519
Clerical aptitude, 341
Clinical effectiveness factor, 352
Clinical inference, 508–510
Clinical prediction, advantages of, 596–597
Coefficient of reproducibility, Guttman's, 100, 730
Coefficient alpha, Cronbach's, 254, 256, 730
Cofer, Chance, and Judson's positive malingering (Mp) scale, 548, 553
Cognitive abilities, 422–426, 430
Cognitive complexity, 512–513, 661–664, 667–668
Cognitive consistencies, 420
Cognitive map, Tolman's, 661
Cognitive structure, 662
Cognitive styles, 481–488, 839
College Board Scholastic Aptitude Test, 357, 789–790, 840
College objectives, 354–357
Common-factor analysis, 438, 440
Common-factor scores, 446
Common factors, 310–316, 339–445
  for mental abilities, 441–442
Common variance, 311, 546–547, 552–555
Communality concept, 441
Comparative judgment, law of, 9, 718
Comparative psychology, 23–24
Completion Test, Thurstone's, 462–464
Complexity, 512–513, 649–668
  cognitive, 512–513, 661–668
  content, 664–665, 667–668
  preference for, 649–660
Complexity-simplicity, 512, 662, 667
Complexity variables, 652–660

Component structure analysis, 106
Components of construct validity, 92–109
  external, 107–109
  structural, 97–107
  substantive, 92–97, 107
Compulsive rigidity, 60
Compulsiveness, 364–367
Concept Mastery Test, Terman's, 471, 495
Concepts, 135–138, 141–144, 158
Concomitant variation, Mill's method of, 297
Concurrent validity (see Validity, concurrent)
Configural scoring, 104–105
Congruent validity, 57
Constant error, 221
Construct validity (see Validity, construct)
Constructs, 29–30, 36, 59–75, 83, 86, 97, 127–129, 136–144, 166, 321, 597
  data-oriented, 166
  nomothetic, 597
  theoretical, 166
Content versus style, 541–544
Content complexity, 664–665, 667–668
  in Rorschach test, 664–665, 667–668
Content factor, 553–554
Content validity (see Validity, content)
Content variance, 541–542
Convergent-production abilities, 428–430
Convergent-thinking factor, 422, 428–430, 488–490
Convergent validity (see Validity, convergent)
Coombs' ordered metric, 728
Coombs' theory of psychological scaling, 86
Cooperative General Science Test (CGST), 370
Cooperative Vocabulary Test, 372–373
Cornell technique of scale analysis, 99
Correction for guessing, 204–205
Correlation, 27, 183, 206–207, 212–213, 231–232, 252, 260–263, 266, 286, 311–314, 369–370
  biserial, 206–207, 252
  Flanagan, 252
  between means, 314
  multiple, 286
  odd-even, 183
  part-test, 231–232
  partial, 27, 212–213, 260–263, 266, 369–370
  point biserial, 206–207, 252
Correlational psychology, 2, 22–33, 36–37
Coulomb's inverse-square law of electrical attraction, 280
Counseling interview, 689–700, 704, 706–710
Courant's game interpretation of mathematics, 637
Covariance, 236–237, 261, 362
  analysis of, 362
  between-test, 236
  within-test, 236
Covariation, 300–302, 319
Covariation chart, 115–116, 300–303
  Cattell's, 300–303